Rechtsvergleichung und Rechtsvereinheitlichung

herausgegeben von der
Gesellschaft für Rechtsvergleichung e. V.

110

ARTIBUS INGENUIS J·C·B·M· 1·8·0·1

German National Reports on the 22nd International Congress of Comparative Law

edited by

Stefan Grundmann and
Caroline Sophie Rapatz

Mohr Siebeck

Stefan Grundmann, born 1959; Professor of Civil Law, European and International Private and Business Law, Comparative Law and Legal Theory at the Humboldt-Universität Berlin.
orcid.org/0000-0003-2703-705X

Caroline Sophie Rapatz, born 1983; Professor of Civil Law, European and International Private and Procedural Law, Comparative Law at the Christian-Albrechts-University of Kiel.
orcid.org/0000-0002-6684-6987

ISBN 978-3-16-200758-2 / eISBN 978-3-16-200759-9
DOI 10.1628/978-3-16-200759-9

ISSN 1861-5449 / eISSN 2569-426X (Rechtsvergleichung und Rechtsvereinheitlichung)

The Deutsche Nationalbibliothek lists this publication in the Deutsche Nationalbibliographie; detailed bibliographic data are available on the Internet at *https://dnb.dnb.de.*

Typesetting: SatzWeise, Bad Wünnenberg. Printed on non-aging paper.

Mohr Siebeck GmbH & Co. KG, Wilhelmstraße 18, 72074 Tübingen, Germany
www.mohrsiebeck.com, info@mohrsiebeck.com

Preface by the Editors

The 22nd General Congress of Comparative Law will be held from September 29th to October 2nd, 2026. As the internationally leading forum for the discussion of themes, issues and methods of comparative law, every four years the Congress brings together academics from all legal disciplines and all regions of the globe. It is a special honour and pleasure for the German Association for Comparative Law that this year, the Congress will convene in Germany, hosted by Prof. Dr. Dr. Stefan Grundmann at the Humboldt-Universität zu Berlin.

The 22nd General Congress covers nearly thirty thematic sessions, reflecting the broad scope of current comparative law scholarship. Their subjects encompass all legal disciplines, ranging from legal history and legal theory via a plethora of specialized areas of law to legal education and methodology and legal pluralism. The topics chosen by the Academy range from classical questions of constitutional, administrative, criminal, civil and commercial law – often viewed through a new lens – to forward-looking, cross-cutting issues like "Imitation as a tool of legal change" or "The Decolonial turn in comparative law".

For each of the sessions organized by the Academy in Berlin, National Reports from different jurisdictions provide the main source material for the General Reporters appointed by the Academy. For each of these nearly thirty panels, the German Association for Comparative Law has named a National Reporter to contribute the perspective of German law to the issue at hand. Their reflections will become an integral part of the considerations and discussions at the Congress.

This volume presents a collection of the large majority of the German National Reports to the Berlin Congress. The order of the reports reflects the systematic order in which the topics are proposed by the International Academy of Comparative Law. Typically, National Reports are provided on the basis of questionnaires developed by the General Reporters; the internal structure of many of the reports in this book reflects this practice, as well as the plurality and variety of approaches chosen by General Reporters for different subject areas.

Following the Congress, many of the General Reporters will bring together their General Report as well as selected National Reports for publication in a thematic volume. In addition, a collection of all General Reports will be published by the Academy. We hereby make reference to these other Congress publications, and warmly invite the reader to explore these volumes. The German Association for Comparative Law is grateful to the Academy for their permission to publish an advance collection of the German national reports – continuing a tradition established also by various other national sub-organisations to the Academy.

On behalf of the German Association of Comparative Law, the editors express their sincere thanks to Ms. Judith Zölke for her invaluable assistance in the collection and administration of the German National Reports, as well as to the team of student and graduate assistants at the Institute for European and International Private and Procedural Law at Christian-Albrechts-Universität zu Kiel, led by Mr Fynn Baas, for their support in preparing the manuscripts for publication. We are also deeply grateful to the team at our publisher Mohr Siebeck, especially Dr. Julia Caroline Scherpe-Blessing and Ms. Silja Verena Meister, without whose cooperation it would not have been possible for this volume to be published in time.

Berlin / Kiel, March 2026 Stefan Grundmann and Caroline S. Rapatz

Table of Contents

Teaching Comparative Law Subjects in Germany[1]

Mareike Schmidt

I. Introduction

The first systematic survey of comparative law teaching in Germany was carried out in 1951 by Bernhard C. H. Aubin and Konrad Zweigert on behalf of the German Society of Comparative Law.[2] Their questionnaire, sent to the 16 West German law schools, was answered by 14 and confirmed the impression that comparative law received neither the attention nor the teaching it deserved in the post war university system.[3] This country report is different in its scope. On the one hand, it is much more modest in that the primary emphasis here is on presenting the status quo of the teaching of comparative law in Germany rather than on its evaluation.[4] On the other hand, it aims to report on the teaching of comparative law in the currently existing 46 German law schools. Unless stated otherwise, the report focuses on the traditional German law programmes leading to the first state examination. Degree programmes that do not qualify for regulated legal professions, in particular stand-alone bachelor's or master's programmes outside the state examination track, as well as the legal clerkship (*Referendariat*) are excluded. Where relevant, master's and doctoral programmes are mentioned, but the information is necessarily less systematic.

Regarding the content, this report follows the questionnaire provided by the general reporter, Barbara Pozzo. The focus is thus on the role of courses on comparative law, which is here understood as the systematic comparison of two or more legal systems, legal families, or legal solutions across jurisdictions.[5] The teaching of foreign law without a substantial comparative perspective has there-

[1] The author is grateful to Hannah Baumgarten and Carolin Joos for their invaluable research assistance and further acknowledges the use of AI-based language support in the drafting of this report. All substantive content and evaluations remain the author's sole responsibility.

[2] Published as *Aubin/Zweigert*, Rechtsvergleichung im deutschen Hochschulunterricht, 1952.

[3] *Aubin/Zweigert* (ibid.), 9 et seqq.

[4] For a comprehensive discussion of comparative law as a pedagogical challenge in the German context, see Brockmann/Pilniok/Schmidt (eds.), Rechtsvergleichung als didaktische Herausforderung, 2020.

[5] In line with prevailing approaches in contemporary legal education in Germany, the focus of this report lies on comparisons between contemporary state legal systems, thus generally excluding courses dealing primarily with historical legal orders or with the legal norms of non-state communities.

fore not been included systematically, although the distinction can be blurred in practice.

The report is primarily based on publicly available sources, including course catalogues and descriptions for the academic year 2024/2025, examination regulations and other legal requirements, as well as other information from university websites. It must be noted that these data are limited with respect to the information they provide regarding actual teaching practices. The report thus aims to identify typical patterns, tendencies, and institutional frameworks of comparative law teaching in Germany rather than to provide an exhaustive or statistically representative account.

The structure of the report in principle follows that of the questionnaire, with minor adjustments based on the distinctive characteristics of German legal education.

II. The Background

Describe briefly the historical background of the legal system of your country. Do you think that comparative law could help explain better the historical origin of your legal system?

The modern German legal system was to a considerable extent formed in the large codifications undertaken at the end of the 19th century, such as the Penal Code, the Code of Civil Procedure, the Commercial Code, and the Civil Code, which all entered into force in the German Empire between 1872 and 1900. Previously, the legal system was fragmented, partially formed by local laws, partially originating from Roman law. Comparative legal work had a significant impact on the drafting of the codifications, looking at both the existing local laws as well as codes from other states.[6]

With regard to the role of comparative law in understanding the German legal system, one can thus say that certainly a deep understanding of the origins of the major German codifications benefits significantly from comparative legal insights. However, for the teaching of the central fields of German law, comparative law's role is generally not so much seen in its influence on the historic origins of the codifications. Historically, the more interesting connection of German law and comparative law tends to be seen in the influence of major German codifications on other countries' domestic laws, such as the role of the German Civil Code as model for other countries like Brazil, Greece, Japan, and Switzerland. Comparative law's role is generally deemed to be more important with regard to (more or less) contemporary issues in German law, in particular when it comes to

[6] Cf. *Dölle*, in: von Caemmerer/Friesenhahn (eds.), Hundert Jahre deutsches Rechtsleben, vol. 2, 1960, 19, 23 et seqq.

the influence of supranational, i.e. European Union, or international law and (other) projects of unification and harmonisation of law.

Aubin and Zweigert, in their study on the teaching of comparative law in Germany after World War II, forcefully argued that the true pedagogical value of comparative law specifically lies beyond the teaching of domestic law.[7] They propose to rather see comparative law as a fundamental science ('*Grundlagenwissenschaft*') and to re-establish it as a central factor in legal education.[8] Their idea that comparative law can contribute to the 'necessary intellectualisation and humanisation of legal education in Germany'[9] may still be shared by many professors teaching comparative law in Germany today.[10]

Describe the curriculum to become a lawyer in your country: E.g. after university, is it necessary to accomplish a practice? Is a state exam/bar exam necessary to become a lawyer?

Access to all legal professions (judges, lawyers, notaries, prosecutors) in Germany is contingent on the passing of two consecutive state examinations. The first one is on average taken after 4.5 years of studies at a university's law school, the second forms the end of a two-year clerkship. This structure is laid down in the German Judiciary Act (*Deutsches Richtergesetz*) and, within that framework, the respective laws and regulations of the 16 *Länder* (states).

In the field of law, the university curriculum does not adhere to the bachelor/master system that is otherwise widely implemented in Germany.[11] The German Judiciary Act stipulates that students must successfully complete the study of the compulsory subjects, in addition to a so-called area of specialisation (*Schwerpunktbereich*) comprising elective subjects, as well as a foreign language requirement and three months of internships during the semester breaks. The compulsory subjects include 'the core areas of civil law, criminal law, public law and the law of procedure, including their links to European law'.[12] Since 2021, the programme has further incorporated a compulsory module addressing the injustices perpetrated by the National Socialist regime and the Communist dictatorship in Germany. The final compulsory element is a so-called foundational component, defined as 'the methodology of legal science and the philosophical, historical and

---

[7] *Aubin/Zweigert* (fn. 2), 23 et seqq.

[8] *Aubin/Zweigert* (fn. 2), 28 et seq.

[9] *Aubin/Zweigert* (fn. 2), 29 ('*zur notwendigen Vergeistigung und Humanisierung der Rechtsausbildung in Deutschland*').

[10] In particular, it will resonate with those who consider comparative law to be a 'foundational subject' in legal education, cf. on this issue question sub II., p. 4 below (at fn. 14). *Kötz*, in: Brockmann/Pilniok/Schmidt (eds.), Rechtsvergleichung als didaktische Herausforderung, 2020, 19, 22, even highlights comparative law's particular importance as '*door opener* for the other foundational subjects' (emphasis in the original).

[11] Recently, however, law schools have started introducing a bachelor's degree which students who have successfully followed the course of law studies can obtain prior to taking the (state part of) the first state examination.

[12] Section 5a(2) sent. 3 German Judiciary Act.

social foundations'.[13] Comparative law is widely regarded as a foundational subject in this context despite the absence of any explicit reference to it in the German Judiciary Act.[14] With regard to the areas of specialisation, the universities are at liberty to decide on their content.[15] Consequently, these vary considerably between universities. Since 2003, the administration of examinations in the areas of specialisation has been the responsibility of the universities, constituting 30 per cent of the grade of the first state examination.

Exams, both during university studies as well as in the first state examination are mostly written exams primarily focusing on doctrinal methods and a particular form of discussing case hypotheticals in the so-called *Gutachtentechnik*.[16] To a much lesser degree, there are also oral exams as well as term papers.

The first state examination is followed by a legal clerkship (*Referendariat*). This consists of two years of practical training, where candidates work for three to nine months in different legal professions in all major fields of law. Mandatory placements include courts, administrative authorities, and law firms. Candidates are free to complete part of their clerkship abroad.[17] The clerkship ends with the second state examination, which also consists of written and oral exams. With successful completion, the former candidate is considered a *Volljurist* (fully qualified jurist) and allowed to practice as a lawyer as well as to apply for positions in the judiciary.

Is comparative law an exam subject in competitions to enter legal professions?

While the two German state examinations in law are not competitions in a narrow sense, they do form the central hurdle for entering the legal professions in Germany.[18] Comparative law is not a compulsory subject for either of these examinations. Even the foundational subjects in general are not part of any written

---

13 Section 5a(2) sent. 3 German Judiciary Act.

14 While most comparative law scholars seem to take it for granted that comparative law forms a foundational subject (e. g. *Kötz* [fn. 10], 21; in the same vein: *Wissenschaftsrat [German Science and Humanities Council]*, Prospects of legal scholarship in Germany, 2012, 35, www.wissenschaftsrat.de/download/archiv/2558-12_engl.html [13.02.2026]), there is some disagreement in this regard, cf. *Funke*, in: Krüper (ed.), Rechtswissenschaft lehren, 2022, § 15 n. 43 et seq. (with further references). With regard to legal provisions on legal education, in Baden-Württemberg, comparative law is explicitly named as a foundational subject in Section 3(1) sent. 2 of the Ministry of Justice's Ordinance on Legal Education and Exams as of 2019; at university level, around one fourth of Germany's law schools expressly consider comparative law a foundational subject based on their study regulations and guidelines; examples outside Baden-Württemberg include the Universities of Bochum and Bremen as well as Saarland University.

15 The German Judiciary Act only stipulates that they 'serve to supplement university studies, to deepen knowledge of the compulsory subjects to which they relate and to impart the interdisciplinary and international bearing of the law', cf. Section 5a(2) sent. 4 German Judiciary Act.

16 This is a form of structured legal analysis somewhat similar to the US-American 'IRAC' (Issue-Rule-Application-Conclusion) style.

17 Section 5b(3) sent. 1 German Judiciary Act.

18 Cf. question sub II, pp. 3 et seq. above.

exams in these examinations; they will only occasionally be examined orally, depending upon the focus of the individual examiners.[19] It will thus be the absolute exception for comparative law to be tested in the state parts of the state examinations. It may nonetheless contribute to the grade of the first state examination where a student selects a specialisation that includes comparative law as a compulsory element.[20]

III. Where Is Comparative Law Taught?

Is comparative law taught in law school? At which level (undergraduate level, postgraduate level, PhD level)?

Comparative law is taught at virtually all German law schools. Only for four out of 46 law schools this could not be positively ascertained.[21] Courses in comparative law will usually comprise two hours per week per semester. They are offered at different stages of legal education, most notably as one of the foundational subjects[22] and thus frequently in the first semesters of studies,[23] or within the areas of specialisation, meaning towards the end of law school. In quantitative terms, measured by the number of courses offered, the areas of specialisation are central to the teaching of comparative law: According to the data gathered, almost two thirds of the comparative law courses form part of areas of specialisation. The number of foundational subject courses on comparative law is far smaller; it should be kept in mind, however, that these courses are typically taught as large lectures and therefore tend to have a substantially higher number of participants than courses in the areas of specialisation.

Another option is for comparative law classes, typically then taught in English, to be considered as either the mandatory foreign language qualification every law student has to obtain (one semester course of two hours per week during their

---

[19] According to experts, the foundational subjects 'play almost no role' in the state part of the first state examination, cf. *Wissenschaftsrat* (fn. 14), 64.

[20] On the role of areas of specialisations cf. question sub II., pp. 3 et seq. above (in general) and questions sub II., pp. 5 et seq. and sub II., pp. 6 et seq. below (on its role regarding the teaching of comparative law).

[21] No relevant information was found for the Universities of Lüneburg and Marburg, EBS Universität and BSP Business and Law School; however, the first three institutions have several professorships whose titles include the term 'comparative law,' thus making it likely that comparative law will nevertheless be taught there at least occasionally.

[22] On the question whether comparative law is seen as a foundational subject or not cf. fn. 14 above.

[23] Many law schools require foundational subjects in the early semesters, sometimes as a prerequisite for further studies (e. g. Bochum, Leipzig, Münster), while others also mandate such courses at a later stage (e. g. Hamburg, Bonn, Heidelberg). Saarland University recommends comparative law in the fifth semester.

course of studies)[24] or as part of a more intensive foreign law and language certificate.[25]

In addition, comparative law is offered in some master's programmes, particularly those with an international or comparative orientation.[26] At doctoral level, comparative law is pursued mainly through individual supervision rather than through structured coursework.[27]

Is comparative law taught in any other course or school? Which one? (E.g. political science, anthropology, cultural mediation?)

At the law schools, comparative law courses are predominantly addressed to law students, though in some cases they are open to students from other disciplines, such as political science, history, social sciences in general, or theology. There is no indication that comparative law is taught as an autonomous subject outside law schools, nor that it is systematically addressed to non-law students.

Is comparative law a compulsory subject at any of these courses?

As a general matter, comparative law is not a compulsory subject in German legal education and is typically taught as an elective. Students may thus complete their legal studies without attending any comparative law course, despite the fact that the legal training acts or regulations of certain *Länder* (states) place particular emphasis on the international context.[28]

Within certain areas of specialisation, comparative law courses may, however, be defined as mandatory components. In quantitative terms, about half of the law schools offer an area of specialisation where comparative law forms part of the core subjects that are assessed in the final exam of the respective area of specialisation. Generally, these are more likely to be focused on private law,[29] slightly less

---

[24] Where comparative law can count towards the foreign language requirement (e.g. at Halle-Wittenberg), students may usually take it at any stage of their studies.

[25] At least one third of universities offer programmes introducing law students to foreign legal systems and terminology. These programmes generally encompass a total of 16 hours of courses per week over the course of four semesters. They frequently incorporate introductions to the respective foreign legal systems, albeit without necessarily adopting a comparative approach.

[26] Some master's programmes are inherently comparative in their approach (e.g. 'Comparative and Global Law', recently started at the University of Münster) others expressly focus on a specific foreign legal system and typically also include comparative law aspects (e.g. 'Chinese Law and Comparative Law' at the University of Göttingen in cooperation with the University of Nanjing).

[27] For more information on comparative law at the level of doctoral studies, see question sub VII., pp. 15 et seq. below.

[28] Cf., e.g. in Rheinland-Pfalz and Hamburg.

[29] Relevant areas of specialisations often focus on comparative law and private international law or on international, European, and/or foreign law of civil procedure and can be found at a fairly large number of law schools (e.g. in Bonn, Erlangen-Nürnberg, Hamburg, and München).

on public law,[30] and rather rarely on criminal law.[31] Exceptionally, specific comparative law areas of specialisation are offered, in which comparative law consequently also forms a compulsory component.[32]

Beyond the regular course of studies leading up to the first state examination, comparative law may occasionally be compulsory, for example in individual master's programmes;[33] however, no general pattern can be identified on the basis of the available data.

IV. The Class of Comparative Law

How is a class where comparative law is taught generally composed?

As there is a wide range of different formats in which comparative law is taught, no general answer to this question can be given. Within the regular formats (i.e. excluding study abroad programmes, excursions, etc.), the range extends from small seminar formats where one professor might teach a rather small number of students (usually 5 to 15 or 20, possibly up to around 30) to large lecture formats with possibly hundreds of students in the lecture hall. Depending on the location of the course in the curriculum, participants will be at different stages of their studies. Most of the courses primarily target German law students preparing for the first state examination. However, particularly when taught in English, comparative law courses also tend to attract a considerable number of exchange students and are in some cases specifically intended for this group.

How many foreign students attend the law school in your country?

The Federal Statistical Office of Germany provides annual data on the number of students enrolled in law.[34] According to the latest available figures for the winter term 2024/2025, a total of 115,272 students were enrolled, of whom 9,269 were foreign nationals. This corresponds to approximately 8 % of all law students. Over the past decade, the proportion of foreign students in law has fluctuated between roughly 8 % and 9 %. A noticeable decline occurred in the winter term 2020/2021,

[30] Examples with a public law focus include areas of specialisations such as 'State and Administration in Transition' at Humboldt-University Berlin and 'International, Transnational, and European Law' in Martin-Luther-Universität Halle-Wittenberg.

[31] The only example found is the area of specialisation in criminology at the University of Würzburg.

[32] E.g. at the Universities of Greifswald and Würzburg.

[33] Cf. programmes mentioned in fn. 26 above as well as the programme on 'German Law and European Comparative Law' at Saarland University.

[34] All figures are based on data available at https://www-genesis.destatis.de/datenbank/online/url/1eec1601 (13.02.2026). They refer to students enrolled in law (*Rechtswissenschaften*) in general and do not differentiate between specific degree structures or examination tracks.

which is likely attributable to the Covid-19 pandemic. Since then, the numbers have remained at a slightly lower but relatively stable level.

How many foreign professors teach comparative law or foreign law at law schools?

There are no aggregate data available that would allow for a reliable quantification of foreign professors teaching comparative or foreign law at German law schools. Overall, it remains rather uncommon for scholars who have obtained their full legal education outside Germany to hold full professorships at German law schools,[35] although notable exceptions do exist.[36] As a rare point of reference, the German Science and Humanities Council (*Wissenschaftsrat*) reported in 2010 that 26 foreign law professors were employed full-time at German higher education institutions, corresponding to approximately 2.8 per cent of all law professors at the time.[37] Not all of these professors, however, can be assumed to teach comparative or foreign law.[38]

Below the level of full German professorships, foreign scholars are more frequently involved in teaching at German law schools. They typically contribute in the form of temporary teaching assignments, for example by offering introductions to their home jurisdictions, participating in international or comparative courses, or supporting moot courts and similar formats. In addition, in law schools that offer programmes focused on specific foreign jurisdictions, foreign scholars are regularly involved in teaching as part of these institutionalised programmes, often in cooperation with partner universities abroad.[39]

Are there programs of visiting professors from abroad to teach comparative law? Do you have programs to encourage professors to teach abroad?

Germany does not have a centralized or dedicated national (or state) program specifically aimed at sending or hosting visiting professors to teach comparative law. However, several international mobility initiatives facilitate academic exchanges, including in law, that in the legal field are likely to include teaching of comparative law or on foreign legal systems.

---

35 In most cases, such persons will not have passed both German state examinations, a formal qualification that still plays a decisive role in appointments to full professorships.

36 E.g. Prof. Dr. Yuanshi Bu, LL.M. (Harvard), Chair of International Economic Law with a Focus on East Asia, University of Freiburg; Prof. Dr. James Fowkes, LL.M. (Yale), Professor of Foreign and International Law, University of Münster; Prof. (NTU) Dr. Georg Gesk, Chair for Chinese Law, University of Osnabrück; Prof. Dr. Thoko Kaime, Chair of African Legal Studies, University of Bayreuth; Prof. Dr. Eva van der Zee, Assistant Professor for International Law with a Focus on Behavioral Law & Economics, University of Hamburg.

37 *Wissenschaftsrat* (fn. 14), 91.

38 Professor van der Zee (cf. fn. 36), for instance, does not teach Dutch or comparative law, but various subjects in the field of law and economics and public international law.

39 See, e.g. the master's programme 'Chinese Law and Comparative Law' offered by the Universities of Göttingen and Nanjing.

The most significant of these frameworks is the Erasmus+ program, supported by the European Union.[40] It enables higher education staff from participating countries[41] to teach abroad for stays between 2 and 60 days.[42] Within this framework, Erasmus+ enables substantial inbound and outbound academic mobility with roughly 8,000 to 9,000 academics moving in either direction in 2024 alone.[43]

Alongside Erasmus+, the German Academic Exchange Service (DAAD) operates several programmes encouraging German academics to teach abroad.[44] These include the Johann Gottfried Herder Programme for retired professors undertaking semester-long teaching assignments, as well as DAAD-funded lecturer positions typically held by post-doctoral scholars. At present, there are six such positions in law: one in Hungary, two in France, and three in the United Kingdom.[45] Further DAAD programmes support longer-term (two to five years) or shorter-term (several weeks to six months) teaching stays at foreign universities.

In addition, there are country-specific programmes such as the Swiss-European Mobility Programme[46] and the Fulbright Scholar Grant. The latter funds U.S. academics to teach or conduct research in Germany, and explicitly encourages the inclusion of lecturing components, in order to benefit German students and faculty.[47]

At the institutional level, individual universities complement these national and European schemes with their own initiatives. These include, for example, fellowship programmes for visiting scholars with a teaching component,[48] joint international courses,[49] or participation in international university net-

[40] Cf. www.erasmus-plus.ec.europa.eu (13.02.2026).

[41] These include all 27 EU member states, plus Iceland, Liechtenstein, North Macedonia, Norway, Serbia, and Turkey; in addition, a vast number of states are accepted as partners to the program with limited participation.

[42] Regarding outbound mobility, some German universities tend to encourage shorter stays of a maximum of one or two weeks (e.g. Hamburg, Potsdam, Heidelberg), while others do not impose such restrictions (e.g. Würzburg, Berlin [FU], Halle-Wittenberg).

[43] European Commission: Directorate-General for Education, Youth, Sport and Culture, Erasmus+ annual report 2024 – Statistical annex, Publications Office of the European Union, 2025, 32 et seqq., https://data.europa.eu/doi/10.2766/6002858 (13.02.2026); discipline-specific data for law are not available.

[44] Cf. www.daad.de/de/im-ausland-studieren-forschen-lehren/lehren-im-ausland/ (13.02.2026).

[45] Cf. www.daad.de/de/im-ausland-studieren-forschen-lehren/lehren-im-ausland/daad-lektorenprogramm/karte/?profiles=12 (13.02.2026).

[46] Programme similar to Erasmus+; cf. https://movetia.ch/en/funding-opportunities/stays-abroad-for-staff-in-higher-education (13.02.2026).

[47] Fulbright Germany frames this as being '[i]n the interest of German students and teachers, who benefit greatly from U.S. lecturing methods', https://fulbright.de/en/grants/program/fulbright-scholar-grant-including-inter-country-travel-grant (13.02.2026).

[48] E.g. the Magdalene Schoch Fellowship Program at the University of Hamburg's Faculty of Law.

[49] E.g. the German-language law program focused on private law recently initiated by the University of Passau in cooperation with Károli Gáspár University of the Reformed Church in

works.[50] Taken together, such initiatives further contribute to the presence of visiting professors and to opportunities for German academics to teach abroad.

V. The Content of the Course of Comparative Law

As already outlined above, comparative law in Germany is taught in a wide variety of formats and institutional contexts, reflecting the high degree of academic freedom traditionally granted to university professors. This freedom extends to the content, structure, and teaching methods of individual courses. Since comparative law does not form part of the state examination,[51] it is subject to even fewer structural constraints than courses in the compulsory curriculum. Accordingly, any general observations on the content of comparative law courses can only describe typical patterns rather than fixed models. The answers to the questions in this section therefore focus on general courses in comparative law, including those that concentrate on one of the major branches of law, namely private, public, or criminal law.

How is a course of comparative law structured? E.g. does it include a methodological part? Does it include an introduction to the legal systems of the world? Which legal systems are generally taken into consideration? Are cases discussed in comparative law perspective? Does the course include a comparative law analysis in specific fields? (E.g. contract law, family law, tort law?) Are there separate courses for private and public comparative law?

Comparative law in Germany is frequently taught along the *traditional disciplinary lines* of private law, public law, and – significantly less frequently – criminal law. Many courses are expressly designated as 'comparative private law', 'comparative public law' or 'comparative criminal law'. Even where courses bear the general title 'comparative law', in practice they will regularly focus on only one of these branches, often private law. Courses that explicitly combine comparative perspectives across two or all three major branches of law are rather rare.

Within this disciplinary framework, courses may concentrate on *specific fields of law*. In public law, a particularly strong emphasis can be observed on comparative constitutional law. In private law, comparative analyses of contract law are common; in some cases, these are complemented by tort law, consumer law, or unjust enrichment. More specialized courses depend largely on the expertise and research focus of individual professors and may address fields such as comparative competition law, civil procedure, or family law.

Hungary and funded by the DAAD; see also the cooperation between the Universities of Göttingen and Nanjing (fn. 39).

[50] E.g. the THEMIS Network, a collaboration of 11 universities across Europe, New Zealand, Taiwan, and Hong Kong, for a 'Joint Certificate in International and Business Law', of which the Freie Universität Berlin forms part.

[51] Cf. question sub II., pp. 4 et seq. above.

Seminars in comparative law are especially likely to focus on narrowly defined subjects, such as specific property law institutions or institutional questions like the separation of powers in comparative perspective. At the same time, there are indications that even general introductory lectures in comparative law may include *comparative analyses of selected doctrinal fields*, for example in contract law, tort law, or property law.

Against this background of disciplinarily differentiated and often substantively focused courses, it is nevertheless possible to identify a *typical internal structure* of comparative law classes: They will usually start out with foundational aspects of comparative law, i.e. the aims, methods, and functions of comparative law. This part may also include an historical overview of the development of comparative law. The course will then move on to provide an overview of different legal families or traditions. A third major part usually rounds off the course by comparing specific institutions of the legal field discussed. The typical move, then, is from general to specific, and from macro to micro comparisons. This structure corresponds to the one adopted by Zweigert and Kötz in their textbook[52] and appears to be followed most closely in private law courses, whereas greater structural variation can be observed in public and criminal law.

Within this general structure, different teaching techniques are employed.[53] The use of *cases* as a teaching technique is a common feature in the teaching of comparative law. This is evidenced both by a substantive number of course descriptions explicitly referring to the discussion of cases and by the publication of text or study books including this genre.[54] At the same time, cases do not appear to function as a defining structural element of comparative law courses in Germany.

Another recurring aspect of comparative law teaching concerns the selection of the *legal systems* included. Comparative law courses generally include common law legal systems, either in general or with specific references mostly to UK and US. Many of them also include France. Frequently, a general reference is made to European legal systems in general, or selected European jurisdictions in particular. Some courses pay specific attention to the role of comparative law in legal unification and harmonisation projects. Beyond this, legal systems expressly mentioned more than once in the publicly available descriptions of general comparative law courses include China, Italy, and Switzerland. Some courses will include other legal systems, most notably 'Africa' in general or selected African jurisdictions. It is notable that the more specific the courses are in terms of their

---

52 *Zweigert/Kötz*, Einführung in die Rechtsvergleichung, 3rd ed. 1996; for more details see question sub V., p. 12 below.

53 For more detailed discussion of teaching methods see questions sub VI., p. 14 below.

54 *Mäsch/Arnold*, Übungen in Internationalem Privatrecht und Rechtsvergleichung, 6th ed. 2022; *Koch/Magnus/Winkler v. Mohrenfels*, IPR und Rechtsvergleichung, 4th ed. 2010; additionally, sample examinations in case format are sometimes also published in journals for law students, e.g. *Kleinschmidt*, JuS 2009, 536 et seqq.

subject matter, the greater the variance in terms of the legal systems covered. In courses with a narrow thematic focus, references can be found, inter alia, to Islamic law, Iberian and Latin American jurisdictions, Japan or Asia more generally, as well as to Scandinavian jurisdictions and a range of other legal systems.

Is there any handbook that is used with a certain preference in the teaching of comparative law?

While publicly available information on textbook recommendations for comparative law is scarce, the limited number of explicit literature references, complemented by informal information from colleagues, nevertheless allows for a clear answer: Despite its latest edition having been published in 1996 and its strong focus on private law, the textbook by Konrad Zweigert and Hein Kötz[55] remains the most frequently recommended reading in comparative law classes. Other works are recommended less frequently, yet remain relevant either because of their greater thematic specialisation or because they offer a more recent treatment of the subject. These include general German or English-language textbooks,[56] textbooks on specific fields,[57] comprehensive reference works,[58] as well as more source- or case-oriented materials.[59]

Is the final exam oral or written? Do students have the possibility of writing a paper?

The form of assessment is dependent on the respective course, and therefore no general answer can be given. It should be noted that not all comparative law courses necessarily conclude with an examination. The extant data would appear to suggest that, in those cases where such examinations are conducted, the proportions of written and oral examinations are approximately equal. In certain courses, the assessment is conducted through the submission of a final paper (*Hausarbeit*).[60] In instances where comparative law classes are offered as part of the areas of specialisation, students are usually also given the option of writing their *Schwerpunktarbeit*, i. e. the final paper concluding the area of specialisation, in this context.[61] Occasionally, students may be permitted to select from a range of assessment types.

---

55 *Zweigert/Kötz* (fn. 52).

56 Such as *Kischel*, Rechtsvergleichung, 2015; *Siems*, Comparative Law, 3rd ed. 2022; *Prinz von Sachsen Gessaphe*, Rechtsvergleichung, 2025.

57 E. g. *Heringa*, Constitutions Compared, 7th ed. 2023.

58 E. g. Reimann/Zimmermann (eds.), The Oxford Handbook of Comparative Law, 2nd ed. 2019.

59 Such as *Schwenzer/Müller-Chen*, Rechtsvergleichung: Fälle und Materialien, 1996; *Mäsch/Arnold* (fn. 54).

60 Critical with respect to the limitations of the typical written exams and stressing the advantages of term papers: *Brockmann/Schmidt*, in: Brockmann/Pilniok/Schmidt (eds.), Rechtsvergleichung als didaktische Herausforderung, 2020, 1, 11 et seqq.

61 Cf. also question sub VII., p. 15 below.

Do comparative law courses imply an interdisciplinary approach? (E. g. law and literature, law and economics…) Is legal linguistics/legal translation taken into consideration in the teaching of comparative law? Are legal anthropology aspects taken into consideration?

In Germany, comparative law is predominantly taught as a distinct legal discipline, emphasising the structures of legal systems and doctrinal analysis. *Interdisciplinary approaches* accordingly remain the exception rather than the rule. This is particularly true for general introductory lectures in comparative law, whereas thematically focused courses or seminars may more readily incorporate perspectives from other disciplines.[62]

Legal linguistics and *professional legal translation* are not regularly or systematically integrated into the teaching of comparative law in Germany. Where questions of legal terminology or the difficulties of translating legal concepts across languages arise in comparative law courses, they typically do so only incidentally and without forming part of a structured engagement with legal linguistics or translation studies. In the publicly accessible course materials, explicit reference to translation-related issues could be found only in a course offered at the FernUniversität in Hagen. More generally, legal linguistics and professional legal translation tend to be addressed within programmes in linguistics or translation studies rather than in law curricula.

Likewise, judging from the accessible course descriptions, *legal anthropology* does not appear to be regularly included in comparative law classes. This observation is consistent with the traditionally rather marginal role of legal anthropology in German law schools[63] and with the standard comparative law textbooks, which typically address legal anthropology only in terms of conceptual delimitation rather than as an integrated component of comparative analysis. One notable exception identified in the accessible materials is the comparative law course at Martin-Luther-Universität Halle-Wittenberg. This course is jointly taught by three members of the law school, specialising respectively in private law, public law, and legal anthropology. Reflecting this composition of the teaching staff, the course includes a substantive amount of legal anthropological aspects. It is no coincidence that Halle University stands out in this regard, as Halle is also home to the Max Planck Institute for Social Anthropology, whose department for Law & Anthropology cooperates closely with the local law school.

[62] The class 'Colonial Legacies in Public Law' taught by Philipp Dann at Humboldt University Berlin may serve as an example for such an interdisciplinary approach; according to its course description, it combines comparative constitutional law with perspectives drawn from history and political theory, in particular post- and decolonial theories.

[63] To the best of the author's knowledge, no German law school currently has a chair for legal anthropology. In general, scholars working in the field of legal anthropology or law and anthropology at German universities are more likely to be found as part of the institutes for social and cultural anthropology.

VI. Teaching Methodologies

In the teaching of comparative law, is account taken of new technologies? Are new teaching methods such as the 'flipped classroom' being considered? Do legal clinics and moot courts find a place in the teaching of comparative law?

The use of new, i.e. primarily *digital technologies* in legal education has been discussed and experimented with in Germany under the heading of 'e-learning' for more than twenty years.[64] The term covers the use of learning management systems, blended and online teaching (synchronous or asynchronous), the integration of videos, podcasts, or classroom response systems – and thus also *flipped classroom* formats –, as well as e-assessments and other digital formats. Given the wide range of approaches and the lack of empirical data, it is not possible to provide specific information on their use in comparative law teaching.

As a rough approximation, learning management systems may be considered standard in German higher education, although often limited to the provision of course information and materials. The Covid-19 pandemic triggered extensive emergency remote teaching and likely increased the use of recorded lectures and video-based formats. The familiarity with teaching via video-conferencing tools nowadays offers opportunities for comparative teaching formats by way of international cooperation.[65] Beyond this, there is no clear evidence of systematic use of specific innovations with respect to *teaching methods* in comparative law. Individual instructors may experiment with formats such as the 'flipped classroom', and non-core subjects like comparative law may offer greater freedom in this regard. Overall, however, there are no identifiable overarching initiatives in this regard in law schools in general, let alone for comparative law classes in particular.

Experiential learning formats like *legal clinics* and *moot courts* do not play a systematic role in comparative law teaching. Only isolated examples could be identified, including a comparative law–oriented moot court offered by the Fern-Universität in Hagen as part of a transnational distance-learning project as well as the competition 'Comparative Law in Action' organised by IE University in Madrid. Participation from German institutions appears largely confined to specialised master's programmes rather than the regular state examination curriculum.

[64] For early discussion see *Hilgendorf*, JZ 2005, 365 et seqq.; *Eirich*, Jura 2005, 277 et seqq.; for a recent overview on the role of new media in legal education in Germany see the special issue on media didactics: ZDRW, 2023, 87 et seqq.

[65] E.g. – albeit not a classical comparative law class – the 'Global Law Classroom' programme, offered, inter alia, at the University of Hannover; cf. www.fd.ulisboa.pt/wp-content/uploads/2025/08/Welcome-to-the-Global-Law-Classroom-2025.pdf (13.02.2026).

VII. The Place of Comparative Law in the Law School

Are students allowed to conclude their law curriculum with a master's thesis in comparative law?

Students enrolled in law courses that culminate in the first state examination will generally have to write a term paper in their area of specialisation. This is the closest equivalent to a master's thesis within the German legal education system. Some law schools have (more or less) recently introduced a bachelor's course which allows students to follow the regular law school curriculum and be awarded a bachelor's degree without taking the state examination. In these cases, the term paper in the area of specialisation is considered a bachelor's thesis. Depending on the area of specialisation, this paper may be written in comparative law.

Are there specific PhD programs in comparative law?

As far as can be seen, there are no PhD programmes in Germany specifically dedicated to comparative law.[66] Generally speaking, doctoral degrees in law in Germany are still predominantly obtained outside structured doctoral programmes, even though such programmes have become more numerous in the past decade. This structural feature does not, however, imply a marginal role of comparative law at doctoral level. On the contrary, a substantial number of comparative law dissertations are written outside structured programmes under individual supervision. This is reflected, for instance, in the publication series of the German Society for Comparative Law (*Gesellschaft für Rechtsvergleichung e.V.*), which includes numerous doctoral theses. Empirical research further indicates a marked discrepancy between the comparatively high number of doctoral projects in comparative law and the relatively limited presence of comparative law in teaching.[67]

Within the small number of structured doctoral programmes related to comparative law, two types can be distinguished: The first type has an explicit comparative legal focus, meaning that it only includes candidates whose dissertations follow a comparative methodology. Evidence of two such programmes was found, one on 'Unity and Difference in the European Legal Area'[68], the other on

[66] The German-French Doctoral College for Comparative Public Law (*Deutsch-Französisches Doktorandenkolleg zur Rechtsvergleichung im öffentlichen Recht*) might form an exception in this regard; however, it is not formally a structured PhD program, but rather a tri-national network built to strengthen supervision of comparative legal dissertation projects; cf. www.jus-publicum.eu/projektbeschreibung (13.02.2026).

[67] *Hobe/Marauhn*, Internationalrechtliche Lehre in Deutschland, Österreich und der Schweiz – eine Bestandsaufnahme, 15.06.2016, www.dgfir.de/_files/ugd/6d67ab_6d6de3ee66024ef0befe1937c45d9bc8.pdf (13.02.2026).

[68] Affiliated with the European Law School based at the Faculty of Law of Humboldt University Berlin, cf. www.european-law-school.eu/de/pr/epeder (13.02.2026).

'Successful Dispute Resolution in International Law'[69]; however, none of them seems to be operational any more. Within the second type of programmes, a comparative law approach is not a prerequisite for joining, but comparative legal projects are expressly welcomed. The doctoral programmes at the University of Göttingen in Public International Law or the Albrecht Mendelssohn Bartholdy Graduate School of Law at the University of Hamburg can serve as examples of this type. In addition, programmes that do not fall under either of these types may still provide comparative-law courses.

Beyond doctoral programmes at law schools, comparative law at doctoral level is also institutionally embedded in Germany through specialised research institutions that regularly supervise and host doctoral projects in comparative law. In particular, the eight Max Planck Institutes engaged in legal research, most notably the ones in Hamburg and Heidelberg, provide an important framework in this regard, without themselves constituting PhD programmes in the formal sense.[70]

Is it considered successful from a professional point of view to have a master's thesis/PhD thesis in comparative law?

Regarding positions in legal practice, comparative law qualifications tend to be seen as an asset primarily when it comes to the ability to act in the international sphere.[71] In particular, international law firms or other employers with international contacts, such as multi-national enterprises, will usually welcome graduates with comparative law qualifications because they expect them to be particularly well qualified regarding cross-jurisdictional communication and understanding.[72] Of particular value is an understanding of the functioning of either a specific, relevant jurisdiction other than the domestic one, or of other jurisdictions in general, in order to assess and understand potential differences and challenges arising from diversity of legal cultures or mentalities, including the strength of a specific (type of) argument when it is presented in an international context.[73] In this regard, a master's degree (LL.M.) from a foreign country may

---

69 A cooperation of the Faculty of Law of University of Heidelberg and the law-oriented Max Planck Institutes in Heidelberg and (formerly) Luxemburg, cf. www.ipr.uni-heidelberg.de/graduiertenkolleg/ (13.02.2026).

70 The Max Planck Law network has recently taken steps towards offering a lean form of structured course components for PhD candidates; cf. https://law.mpg.de/curriculum/ (13.02.2026).

71 Convincingly arguing for their relevance with regard to the practice of domestic courts and making suggestions for their inclusion in legal education in general, cf. *Martini*, in: Brockmann/Pilniok/Schmidt (eds.), Rechtsvergleichung als didaktische Herausforderung, 2020, 47 et seqq.

72 *Hachem*, in: Brockmann/Pilniok/Schmidt (eds.), Rechtsvergleichung als didaktische Herausforderung, 2020, 75, 78 et seqq.; *Hachem* (ibid., 76 et seqq.) also stresses that comparative legal training helps to maintain innovative strength of legal practice.

73 *Hachem* (fn. 72), 75, 79 et seq.

well serve the purpose without the program being specifically comparative in nature, such as in the M.C.L. programmes.

At academic level, does your legal system recognise the possibility of having a career in comparative law as a separate and autonomous field?

The classical path to a professorship in law usually requires that one has a recognised specialisation (typically evidenced by the so-called *venia legendi*) in either private, public, or criminal law. While comparative law can form part of a *venia legendi*, it is rarely – if ever – awarded exclusively. This corresponds with the typical professorship positions offered by German universities and the denominations of professorships at German law schools: Regularly, these will be for private, public, or criminal law plus additional, more specific fields of law, and/or foundational subjects, one of which may be comparative law.[74] As such an additional qualification, comparative law will frequently be seen as a plus; it will hardly ever, however, suffice as a separate and autonomous field. This is, of course, closely connected to what has been set out above regarding the compulsory subjects for the first state examination:[75] As every law school has to make sure they offer all compulsory courses, (at least) smaller law schools will generally not be able to afford the luxury of a colleague who only teaches comparative law and thus does not teach in the compulsory courses.

How many professors of comparative law are there in your country?

Any answer to this question necessarily depends on how the notion of a 'professor of comparative law' is defined. One possible criterion would be whether comparative law is explicitly included in the title of a professorship. However, this does not necessarily correlate with the extent to which the respective professor actually teaches comparative law. Moreover, comprehensive and reliable data that would allow for a systematic assessment across German law schools are not publicly available.[76] Against this background, only a highly cautious approximation can be proposed. It appears that most German law schools have between one and five full-time tenured professors whose chair title explicitly includes comparative law, resulting in a total number ranging from 46 to 230. This estimate is necessarily approximate and should be regarded as a provisional indication rather than a definitive conclusion.

---

[74] On comparative law as a foundational subject see fn. 14 and accompanying text above.

[75] Cf. question sub II., pp. 3 et seq. above.

[76] The only data available define a wide range: the non-comprehensive course list compiled for this report identifies 48 full professors who actually teach comparative law, whereas the German Society for Comparative Law lists approximately 580 professors among its members.

Which is the role of comparative law in your law schools altogether?

The analysis has demonstrated that students interested in studying comparative law will have the opportunity to do so at virtually all German law schools, primarily as a foundational subject or in the areas of specialisation. However, no student will be compelled to undertake such a specialisation. The teaching of comparative law is not structurally secured in legal education, but ultimately depends on individual preferences of the instructors, with some incentives existing to include comparative legal perspectives in the academic careers. With regard to the content, one cannot speak of a canonisation, as there is a significant variance amongst courses. However, at least in private law, the textbook by Zweigert and Kötz[77] still has a formative impact. Furthermore, with regard to the legal systems taken into consideration, the focus remains predominantly traditional and 'Western' with a notable absence of adequate inclusion of the Global South, although there are notable exceptions to this. The concept of 'decolonial comparative law', as it is prominently advocated and practised at the Max Planck Institute for Comparative and International Private Law in Hamburg,[78] is thus still a primarily scholarly endeavour. There are hardly any indications that it has reached legal education yet.

It is perhaps unsurprising that the teaching of comparative law is in general alignment with the prevailing focus of German legal education (and, to a large extent, also scholarship), in two respects: Firstly, the primary focus is disciplinary rather than systematically incorporating knowledge from other disciplines. Secondly, there is lesser emphasis on overarching methodical and conceptual questions, with a greater emphasis placed on concrete features of selected legal systems and concrete comparisons regarding specific questions.

In summary, returning to the *enquête* by Aubin and Zweigert, it becomes apparent that, even 75 years later, comparative law has not assumed the central role in the curriculum that the authors had hoped for.[79] Nevertheless, while their observation that the design of comparative law courses is shaped by 'local and personal coincidences'[80] may still hold true, this influence now appears confined largely to pedagogical details rather than to the subject's overall curricular standing.

---

77 *Zweigert/Kötz* (fn. 52).

78 Cf. *Salaymeh/Michaels*, RabelsZ 86 (2022), 166 et seqq.

79 They advocated for comparative law classes totalling 16 semester hours per week, spread over three to four semesters, cf. *Aubin/Zweigert* (fn. 2), 31 et seqq., 40.

80 *Aubin/Zweigert* (fn. 2), 22 ('örtliche und persönliche Zufälligkeiten').

Mistrust in the Trust, but Overconfidence in *fiducia*?

The Uneasy Relationship of German Law to Trust-Like Legal Instruments[1]

Caroline Sophie Rapatz

I. Introduction

Common law trusts[2] are as fascinating as they are elusive. Shaped mainly by jurisprudence and ultimately rooted in equity, they are difficult to grasp for civil law-trained lawyers as a technical-constructive concept. Their multi-faceted and flexible character allows for a plethora of applications, ranging from estate planning to asset protection, but outside of the common law sphere it contributes to their reputation as enigmatic entities. Civil law jurisdictions are habitually reluctant to accept, adapt, or accommodate common law trusts. In recent decades, however, more and more legal systems are following the siren's call of the scintillating common law-style trusts.[3] While the first wave of the "rush to trusts" remained largely confined to common law jurisdictions, its second wave triggered the establishment of legal instruments more or less strongly inspired by, and similar to, English-model trusts in various civil law systems.[4] Many jurisdictions in continental Europe are gradually opening up to the idea of trusts.

Germany is clearly not one of them. German law does not contain a general legal institution that corresponds to trusts, either conceptually or functionally. There have been no legal transplants[5], no constructions modelled on the English prototype, not even imitations drawing partial inspiration from the common law tradition or its more recent civilian spin-offs. German legal rules do not make reference to trusts, and German literature remains reluctant to draw parallels. So

---

[1] The author thanks Lennart Matzen for his excellent support in answering the Questionnaires and providing research assistance for this National Report.

[2] On the term "trust" or "trusts", see *Lupoi*, draft General Report "Trusts in non common law countries", as electronically communicated by the General Reporter to the National Reporters (2026), 1 et seqq.

[3] See, e.g. *Lupoi*, Pravovedenie 67 (2023), 21 et seqq.

[4] See, with further references, *Lupoi*, Pravovedenie 67 (2023), 21, 27 et seqq. – Sceptically *von Bar*, EuZW 2018, 925 et seqq.

[5] On transplants, see *Graziadei*, in: Reimann/Zimmermann (eds.), The Oxford Handbook of Comparative Law, 2nd ed. 2019, 442 et seqq.

far, no serious initiatives to introduce such a trusts-based instrument to the German legal system have been attempted.

The question whether German law contains functional equivalents to trusts cannot, however, be answered as easily. The response depends largely on how "trusts" and "functional equivalent" are defined. Notoriously, there is no universal, reliable delineation of the nature or constituent elements of trusts in the English law tradition.[6] The more general definition in Art. 2 of the 1985 Hague Trust Convention[7] amounts to a programmatic compromise rather than a workable formula allowing for a dependable classification of legal instruments. Without clear guidelines of what must be considered the indispensable elements of trusts, it is extremely difficult to classify legal instruments and institutions as (at least to some extent) similar to them. This insecurity is highlighted by the German response to the European Commission's request for Member States to notify "trusts and similar legal arrangements" according to Art. 31(10) of the Money Laundering Directive[8]: the initial reply of "nothing"[9] was modified to two notifications[10] within less than two years, without any intervening change in German law.

In addition, whether, and if so, which institutions of German law can be considered functionally equivalent to trusts depends on how close a resemblance one requires for such a classification. This may, of course, be context-dependent: the above-mentioned notification to the Commission, for instance, only envisaged the directive's scope of money laundering and terrorist financing prevention, and consequently is limited to those scenarios. If, from a more general perspective, one demands structural or conceptual similarities, and/or a correspondence in core elements (whatever they may be), in order to affirm equivalence, then German law has nothing to offer. Based on such a narrow understanding, this National Report would be sadly short.

However, "functional equivalent to trusts" or "substitute for trusts" can – and should – be understood more broadly. In keeping with the classic functional method of comparative law,[11] legal institutions can be considered functionally

---

[6] *Lupoi*, Pravovedenie 67 (2023), 21, 24; on the difficulty of defining the constituent elements of "trusts" vis-à-vis "trust-like institutions" *Gretton*, in: Smith (ed.), The Worlds of the Trust, 2013, 524, 541 et seqq.

[7] Convention of 1 July 1985 on the Law Applicable to Trusts and on their Recognition, available at https://www.hcch.net/en/instruments/conventions/full-text/?cid=59 (last accessed 12.03.2026) – *Lupoi*, Pravovedenie 67 (2023), 21, 24; *Harris*, The Hague Trust Convention, 2002, 111 et seqq.

[8] Directive (EU) 2015/849 of the European Parliament and of the Council of 20 May 2015 on the prevention of the use of the financial system for the purposes of money laundering or terrorist financing, OJ 2015/L 141/73; now amended and repealed by Directive (EU) 2024/1640, OJ 2024/L 1640/1.

[9] OJ 2019/C 360/05, 28.

[10] OJ 2020/C 136/05, 7.

[11] See *Zweigert/Kötz*, Einführung in die Rechtsvergleichung, 3rd ed. 1996, 33 et seqq. and *Michaels*, in: Reimann/Zimmermann (eds.), The Oxford Handbook of Comparative Law, 2nd ed. 2019, 345 et seqq.

equivalent if they offer a solution to the same problem. Based on such an understanding, legal institutions may be categorized as "trust-like" if they fulfil, at least to some extent or in some contexts, the same role as trusts, pursuing similar aims or providing solutions to problems which are typically addressed by trusts. As German law contains a surprisingly high number of such legal institutions (often context-specific), this National Report is based on this broad notion of functional equivalence.

Departing from the scenario outlined in Questionnaire 1, the notoriously reluctant stance of German law vis-à-vis trusts is sketched, and the conceptually and technically different approaches of German law to achieve "trust-like" results outlined (II.). Based on the responses to Questionnaire 2, the alternative approach of German law, the *fiducia* as a general concept underlying many private law instruments, is presented (III.). The results will facilitate brief conclusions (IV.).

II. Rejecting Trusts – Constructing Alternatives

Trusts of common law origin do not enjoy a good reputation in the German legal sphere, nor is their "import" to Germany facilitated.[12] If the trustee of an English trust purchases an immovable in Germany, acting within his powers as trustee, he can only do so in his own name, but not in the name of the trust. As German law does not consider common law trusts to have legal personality or legal capacity, they cannot acquire *in rem* rights under German property law rules, especially not in immovables.[13] Legal ownership has to be acquired by the trustee, who will be registered in the land register (*Grundbuch*) and considered the full owner in all relationships with third parties (external relationships); the restrictions he is subject to as trustee vis-à-vis the other trust parties (internal relationships) have effect only on the obligatory, but not on the *in rem* level (see also III.1). A mention of the trust and/or the position as trustee, whenever possible, is advisable (e. g. for transparency or tax reasons) – but from a property law point of view, it is neither necessary nor is any legal effect attributed to it, and an additional mention of the position as trustee is not permitted in the *Grundbuch*.[14] This becomes especially evident in the scenario of a succession in the role of trustee: If the succeeding trustee wishes to sell the German immovable purchased by the previous trustee, he cannot simply do so. Ownership acquired by the previous trustee is not automatically transferred to the succeeding trustee upon taking over the position as

---

[12] For a succinct overview of the treatment of common law (especially US American) trusts in Germany, see *Schuhmacher/Akbaba*, BKR 2018, 319, 320 et seqq.

[13] See Federal Court of Justice (*Bundesgerichtshof* – hereinafter: BGH) 13.06.1984 – IVa ZR 196/82, IPRax 1985, 221, 223; *Süß*, in: Herrler (ed.), Gesellschaftsrecht in der Notar- und Gestaltungspraxis, 2nd ed. 2021, § 23 n. 227 with further references.

[14] Cf. for entries as fiduciary Higher Regional Court Cologne (*Oberlandesgericht Köln*) 11.12.2023 – 2 Wx 203/23, BeckRS 2023, 42248.

trustee, as it is linked to the individual person and not the role of trustee. As non-owner, the succeeding trustee can validly conclude the sales contract (law of obligations), but he cannot fulfil the contractual duty of transferring ownership (property law), as this can only be effectuated by the legal owner. There are two possible ways to complete the sale envisaged by the succeeding trustee. Either the previous trustee has to transfer ownership to the succeeding trustee, who can then, as new owner, transfer ownership to the buyer himself. Alternatively, ownership could be transferred to the buyer directly by the previous trustee, acting as directed by the succeeding trustee; while this is a practical solution if all parties are cooperating, it carries various risks like the previous trustee's non-collaboration or death.

These scenarios highlight the unbroken traditional German stance of scepticism vis-à-vis trusts. It is also reflected in the uneasy relationship of German conflict-of-laws with them;[15] Germany has neither signed nor ratified the 1985 Hague Trust Convention. The manifold legal policy reasons for this extremely reluctant attitude contain elements of a general "fear of the unknown" and a specific suspicion of positivists towards the uncontoured instruments and remedies developed by English case law. From the vast range of possible uses and designs for trusts, the spectacular ones with "bad press" tend to eclipse the more commonplace, legitimate ones – trusts are frequently considered as vehicles for money laundering, tax evasion, the protection (or squirrelling away) of assets from creditors or similar unpalatable goals.[16] Concerns about these real or perceived dangers and the (possible) abuse of trusts to circumvent and undermine legal rules and sociopolitical aims[17] – e.g. the compulsory share of German succession law (§§ 2303 et seqq. German Civil Code – *Bürgerliches Gesetzbuch*, hereinafter: BGB)[18] – overshadow any discussion of trusts.

In addition, German law faces the problem that the mechanisms of common law trusts are difficult to reconcile with or integrate into civil law structures.[19] At the core of this problem lies the role and conceptual framework of ownership. A differentiation between "legal ownership" and "equitable ownership" cannot be reproduced in a legal system without a law-equity dichotomy – all misconceptions about supposed "divided" ownership aside.[20] Instead, the traditional civil law understanding of ownership posits it as an absolute, all-encompassing right

---

[15] *Mansel*, in: J. von Staudingers Kommentar zum Bürgerlichen Gesetzbuch: Art. 43–46 EGBGB (Internationales Sachenrecht), 2015, Art. 43 EGBGB n. 550 et seqq. with further references.

[16] See *Lupoi*, Pravovedenie 67 (2023), 21, 27 et seqq. on asset protection as a central attractivity factor.

[17] E.g. *Bennett/Hofri-Winogradow*, Oxford Journal of Legal Studies 41 (2021), 692 et seqq.

[18] On the public policy character attributed to the compulsory share, see BGH 29.6.2022 – IV ZR 110/21, BGHZ 234, 166.

[19] See, e.g., *von Bar*, EuZW 2018, 925 et seqq.

[20] *Lupoi*, Pravovedenie 67 (2023), 21, 39; Staudinger/*Mansel* (fn. 15), Art. 43 EGBGB n. 535 et seqq.

(cf. § 903 BGB) which can be encumbered, but not divided into different facets.[21] The compatibility of the common law trusts construction with this property law foundation is limited.[22]

Closely related is the reluctance of civil law systems to accept that assets with the same ownership may still be considered to belong to different classes of patrimony, with limitations on the power of disposal and creditors able to attach only the assets in the class affected to them.[23] The traditional continental approach allows for only one patrimony per person (and one person per patrimony), without a segregation of assets.[24] While this stance has been somewhat relaxed in recent years in various jurisdictions,[25] German law remains reluctant. Generally, if liability is to be limited to certain assets or a certain portion of patrimony, a new patrimony with a new (legal) person as owner has to be created – beyond the (temporary) separate classes of patrimony (*Sondervermögen*) provided for by law for specific contexts (e. g. succession law[26], see III.4), no segregation of patrimony is permitted.[27] In classic civil law legal structures, segregating assets into an isolated patrimony class thus suggests creating a new legal entity as the holder of this separate patrimony.[28] In the context of trusts equivalents, the prime example of this is the foundation with legal personality (*rechtsfähige Stiftung*, §§ 80 et seqq. BGB). While this instrument may be employed to pursue goals that would typically be achieved through trusts in common law jurisdictions, and is understood as a fiduciary instrument, its core characteristic of legal personality constitutes a fundamental discrepancy to the trusts approach,[29] and the strict prerequisite of administrative oversight attests to very different origin and conceptual design. It will thus not be further explored in this National Report.

Very frequently, German law uses another, structurally different approach to create trust-substitute instruments: It accepts a general mechanism of *fiducia* rooted in the *fiducia* of Roman law. This *fiducia* concept, designated *Treuhandverhältnis* (frequently abbreviated to *Treuhand*), manifests itself in many legal institutions, situations and relations. Despite their broad variety and differences in design, their central common characteristic is that the principal (*Treugeber*) transfers rights or powers to the fiduciary (*Treuhänder*) who thus obtains legal powers to act in external relations with third parties, while bound to safeguard

[21] *Lakkis*, in: Gsell/Krüger/Lorenz/Reymann (eds.), BeckOGK BGB, 01.09.2025, § 903 BGB n. 49.

[22] For a nuanced analysis, see *Matthews*, in: Smith (ed.), The Worlds of the Trust, 2013, 313 et seqq.

[23] *Lupoi*, Pravovedenie 67 (2023), 21, 35.

[24] *Lupoi*, Pravovedenie 67 (2023), 21, 34 et seqq.; BeckOGK/*Lakkis* (fn. 21), § 903 BGB n. 53.

[25] E. g. in France with the introduction of the "*entrepreneur individuel à responsabilité limité*", introduced by loi nº 2010–658 of 15 June 2010. – See *Lupoi*, Pravovedenie 67 (2023), 21, 34.

[26] E. g. a community of heirs before the partitioning of the estate.

[27] *Mössner*, in: Gsell/Krüger/Lorenz/Reymann (eds.), BeckOGK BGB, 01.03.2025, § 90 n. 142.

[28] See *Lupoi*, Pravovedenie 67 (2023), 21, 35 for the tendency of non-common lawyers to interpret trusts as legal persons or entities.

[29] *Lupoi*, Pravovedenie 67 (2023), 21, 35.

the interests of the principal in their internal relations.[30] The result is a situation where the power to act exceeds the permission to do so – the fiduciary can validly and bindingly do more than he is allowed to.[31]

This approach is facilitated by the sharp distinction German law draws between the law of obligations (*Schuldrecht*) and property law (*Sachenrecht*) due to the principle of separation and abstraction (*Trennungs- und Abstraktionsprinzip*). It allows for constructions that effect a full and unconditional transfer of the *in rem* right, resulting in an absolute position on the property law level, but restrict it by contractual limitations on the obligatory level. A poignant example of this is the wide-spread acceptance of fiduciary security rights in German law; another area of application is the possibility to maintain a fiduciary account (*Treuhandkonto*). Contractual limitations to the fiduciary's powers may be expressly agreed upon, be inferred from the circumstances or context, or result from the nature of the contractual relationship.[32] The advantage of this model is the flexibility it offers, as contracts may be adapted to suit the parties' individual needs. Its downside is that contractual constraints unfold their consequences only *inter partes*, while the *in rem* right is effective *erga omnes* – the fiduciary truly "holds" assets or legal powers "in confidence".

This construction arrives at a divergence between (property law) "owning" and (contract law) "belonging" which to some extent mirrors the dichotomy between ownership under common law and belonging in equity at the core of English trusts.[33] The major difference vis-à-vis trusts is the contractual nature of *fiducia* instruments, which fundamentally differs from the non-contractual nature of equity-based trusts.[34] One can, however, argue that this approach converges with the view of a trust as a relationship developed in some jurisdictions, e. g. Louisiana.[35] Another distinction is the minor part the beneficiary plays in the *fiducia*: The *Treuhandverhältnis* is centred around the relationship between the principal and the fiduciary – it largely ignores the position of the beneficiary, whose separate existence is not even necessarily required.[36]

---

30 BGH 10.12.2003 – IV ZR 249/02, BGHZ 157, 178; BGH 9.12.1993 – IX ZR 100/93, BGHZ 124, 298, 303; BGH 5.11.1953 – IV ZR 95/53, BGHZ 11, 37, 43.

31 *Schubert*, in: Säcker/Rixecker/Oetker/Limperg/Schubert (eds.), Münchener Kommentar zum BGB, vol. 1, 10th ed. 2025, § 164 BGB n. 58. – In German, this is typically summarized as "*rechtlich mehr können als dürfen*", see e. g. *Coing*, Die Treuhand kraft privaten Rechtsgeschäfts, 1973, 100 et seqq.

32 For example, it is inferred from the security purpose of a land charge that it can only be enforced as far as is necessary for the payment of the secured debt (see, e. g., *Lieder*, in: Säcker/Rixecker/Oetker/Limperg/Schubert (eds.), Münchener Kommentar zum BGB, vol. 8, 10th ed. 2026, § 1191 BGB n. 96), and that it has to be transferred back to the security provider once its finality has been achieved (BGH 27.11.1997 – GSZ 1 u. 2/97, BGHZ 137, 212).

33 See *Lupoi*, draft General Report (fn. 2), 19 et seqq.

34 *Lupoi*, draft General Report (fn. 2), 17 et seqq.

35 Louisiana Laws Revised Statutes, § 9:1731 (2025), available at https://law.justia.com/codes/louisiana/revised-statutes/title-9/rs-9-1731/ (last accessed 12.03.2026).

36 Poignantly *von Bar*, EuZW 2018, 925, 932: "Das Zivilrecht denkt aus der Perspektive des Treugebers, das englische Recht aus der Sicht des Begünstigten."

III. The *fiducia*: A General Concept

Surprisingly, although many legal constructions are based on the general principle of a *fiducia*,[37] this core mechanism is neither defined nor regulated by positive law[38] – in fact, the BGB does not contain the word "*Treuhand*". Consequently, notions of "fiduciary obligation" or references to the English law of trusts are completely absent from primary legal sources. The legal institution is presumed to exist, but no regulatory framework is provided for it. In some contexts, rules have been established for specific issues; other than that, recourse may be taken to the rules for mandates (§§ 662 et seqq. BGB).[39]

Under German law, a *fiducia* results from a legal relationship. Consequently, it does not have legal personality, and neither itself nor the assets managed through it constitute a separate legal entity. *Treuhandverhältnis* is not a legal institution *per se*; rather, it describes the "fiduciary character" of legal relationships arising in various situations and contexts. The core characteristic of power to act exceeding permission to do so (see II.) leads to a large number, and divergent kinds, of legal instruments, transactions and relationships being considered fiduciary in nature. The lack of a clear definition or positive law framework exacerbates the difficulties of unambiguous classification.

This is reflected in the frequently inconsistent terminology employed to refer to such legal situations and relationships: While the shortened term "*Treuhand*" is frequently employed only for contractually established types of *fiducia*, "*Treuhandverhältnis*" (fiduciary relationship) may be more generally understood to refer to all legal relationships containing at least some elements of a *fiducia*. In addition, it is not uncommon for reference to *fiducia* being made not with regard to the legal relationship as such, but rather focusing on the duties resulting from it, namely the "fiduciary obligation" (*fiduziarische Bindung*) of the party assuming the role of fiduciary.[40] Generally, it should be noted that the term "*Treuhand*" is an abstract term for a general (albeit rather vague) category rather than a specific designation for a clear-cut legal institution.

To restrict the *Treuhand* notion, occasionally additional criteria are suggested – notably, considering only transfers of (full) rights a *Treuhand* (so-called *fiduziarische Treuhand*), but not transfers of (partial) legal powers. While courts traditionally considered the direct transfer of assets from the principal to the fiduciary

---

[37] See fundamentally *Coing* (fn. 31) and *Henssler*, AcP 196 (1996), 37 et seqq.

[38] MüKo/*Schubert* (fn. 31), § 164 BGB n. 58.

[39] These rules are applied directly if the legal relationship is gratuitous; for non-gratuitous legal relationships, § 675 BGB on the management of the affairs of another refers to the rules on mandate. – See, e.g. *Fleischer*, in: Drescher/Fleischer/Schmidt (eds.), Münchener Kommentar zum HGB, vol. 2, 6th ed. 2026, § 105 HGB n. 497.

[40] E.g., in the context of security rights with regard to the duties of the creditor/secured party.

a prerequisite,[41] exceptions were admitted[42] and the Federal Court of Justice leaving the issue open in 2003[43] points to a more generous understanding in the 21st century.

1. Concept, Purposes and Types of Treuhand

Depending on the finality of a *Treuhand*, a distinction has to be drawn between *fiduciae* for administrative purposes (*Verwaltungstreuhand*) and for security purposes (*Sicherungstreuhand*).[44] An administrative *fiducia* results when assets are transferred from the patrimony of the principal to the fiduciary, who administers them according to the agreed purpose in the principal's interest. A classic example is the fiduciary account (*Treuhandkonto*), other applications are representation agreements with collecting societies, property and film funds, or liquidation. The administrative *fiducia* is an altruistic *fiducia* (*uneigennützige Treuhand*): The fiduciary serves primarily – or only – the interest of another, typically the principal. On the contrary, the security *fiducia* is considered a *fiducia* for the own benefit of the fiduciary (*eigennützige Treuhand*), as the fiduciary acts also – often even primarily – in his own interest. It comes to bear in the most popular security rights, the transfer of ownership for security purposes (*Sicherungsübereignung*) and the security land charge (*Sicherungsgrundschuld*).

According to the content, three types of *Treuhand* can be distinguished. A *fiducia* based on transfer of title (*Vollrechtstreuhand*) results when full *in rem* rights over the assets are transferred to the fiduciary: As rightholder (e. g. owner), he has unlimited power to act in his own name in the external relations with third parties, while in the internal relations with the principal, he is restricted by the fiduciary agreement.[45] On the contrary, with a *fiducia* based on authorization (*Ermächtigungstreuhand*), the principal remains the rightholder regarding the assets, while the fiduciary is authorized to dispose of them (§ 185(1) BGB), acting as an indirect agent.[46] While the *Vollrechtstreuhand*, effecting the transfer of *in rem* rights, is called a "true *fiducia*" (*echte Treuhand*), the *Ermächtigungstreuhand*, limiting the transfer to powers of disposition, is frequently termed a "pseudo *fiducia*" (*unechte/uneigentliche Treuhand*). Neither of the two forms corresponds to the "split ownership" of common law trusts; one can, however, argue that with the *fiducia* based on transfer of title, the benefits traditionally associated with ownership, namely legal and economic allocation, and with the *fiducia* based on

---

[41] BGH 30.10.1959 – IV ZR 69/59, BeckRS 1959, 31390530, in keeping with the position established by the *Reichsgericht*.

[42] E. g. BGH 5.11.1953 – IV ZR 95/53, BGHZ 11, 37, 40.

[43] BGH 24.06.2003 – IX ZR 75/01, BGHZ 155, 227, 231.

[44] See *Coing* (fn. 31), 89; MüKo/*Schubert* (fn. 31), § 164 BGB n. 59 with further references.

[45] MüKo/*Schubert* (fn. 31), § 164 BGB n. 60.

[46] MüKo/*Schubert* (fn. 31), § 164 BGB n. 61; *Coing* (fn. 31), 96 et seqq.

authorization, the powers traditionally associated with ownership, namely rightholdership and power to dispose, are divided between different persons. A third type of *Treuhand* is proposed for scenarios where the principal remains rightholder and the fiduciary acts as agent (§§ 164 et seqq. BGB) with particularly strong restrictions vis-à-vis the principal to safeguard his interests; however, as this construction produces effects only in their internal relationship, it is more aptly classified as a particular variety of agency rather than a type of *Treuhand.*[47]

2. *Manifestations of* Treuhand

There is a plethora of *Treuhand*-based constellations in German law, resulting from very different contexts. In the confines of this National Report, a selection of the most striking examples must suffice:

A *Treuhandverhältnis* frequently arises in the context of (gratuitous) mandate (§§ 662 et seqq. BGB) or (non-gratuitous) management of the affairs of another (§§ 675 et seqq. BGB), e. g. with regard to the mandatary's duty to surrender assets received for or obtained through the performance of the mandate (§ 667 BGB). This illustrates the close relationship, and blurry boundaries, between *fiducia* and agency.[48]

Fiduciary security rights, based on a transfer rather than an encumbrance of the collateral asset, are extremely widespread in Germany. For movables, the non-possessory transfer of ownership for security purposes is ubiquitously used instead of the possessory pledge; for immovables, the security land charge is by far more popular than the hypothec. Aside from considerations of non-publicity, the major perceived advantage is the non-accessory nature of these security rights, as their purely contractual creation allows for great flexibility.[49]

Fiduciary bank accounts, with the account holder acting as fiduciary, can take either the form of a *Vollrechtstreuhand* or an *Ermächtigungstreuhand.* A common example are the rent security deposit accounts prescribed by law (§ 551(3) BGB).[50] For attorneys and notaries, a special form of fiduciary account (so-called *Anderkonto*) has been developed.[51]

In company law, when a fiduciary holds a share but is bound by a fiduciary agreement in his exercise of the shareholder's rights, the result amounts to an

---

[47] MüKo/*Schubert* (fn. 31), § 164 BGB n. 62.

[48] See *Lupoi,* Pravovedenie 67 (2023), 21, 41 on the *contrat fiduciare* of Luxembourg law in this respect.

[49] See, especially on the role of the security agreement, *Oechsler*, in: Säcker/Rixecker/Oetker/Limperg/Schubert (eds.), Münchener Kommentar zum BGB, vol. 8, 10th ed. 2026, Anh. §§ 929–936 BGB n. 25 et seqq. and *Bülow*, Recht der Kreditsicherheiten, 10th ed. 2021, n. 1247 et seqq.

[50] For a comprehensive overview, see *Hadding/Häuser*, in: Ellenberger/Bunte (eds.), Bankrechts-Handbuch, 6th ed. 2022, § 21 n. 1 et seqq.

[51] For specifics, see *Hadding/Häuser*, in: Ellenberger/Bunte (eds.), Bankrechts-Handbuch, 6th ed. 2022, § 22 n. 1 et seqq.

indirect shareholding.[52] This construction is used to serve very different purposes, ranging from simplification through a concentration of shares (e.g. in a family company) via the concealment of the identity of the economic holder of the shares to fund models as the most important field of use.[53]

Various instruments of succession law are based on the idea of *fiducia*, and create fiduciary relationships. As the (family) *fideicommissum* (*(Familien-)Fideikommiss*) was abolished in Germany,[54] there is no *heres fiduciarius* in modern German law. However, when provisional and reversionary heirs (*Vor- und Nacherben*, §§ 2100 et seqq. BGB) are appointed, the provisional heir becomes owner of the estate assets, but the estate remains separate from his personal patrimony and he is bound to manage it in the interest of the reversionary heir, with limits to his powers of disposition (§§ 2113 et seqq. BGB) – effectively acting as fiduciary. A fiduciary relationship in many respects similar to those achievable by common law (succession) trusts may also result from the appointment of an executor (*Testamentsvollstrecker*, §§ 2197 et seqq. BGB). The facets of the legal position of ownership are split between the heir (owner/rightholder) and the executor (power of disposal): The heir, as owner, may not dispose of estate assets subject to executorship (§ 2211 BGB), while the executor is bound by fiduciary duties towards the heir in his administration of the estate (e.g. § 2216 BGB). Notably, both reversionary heirship and administrative execution are central elements in estate planning aimed at providing for family members with special needs (*Behinderten-/Bedürftigentestament*)[55] – goals typically achieved by trusts in other jurisdictions.[56]

Applying the principles of the *fiducia*, practitioners have developed a foundation-*fiducia* hybrid: The foundation without legal personality (*nichtrechtsfähige Stiftung*), also called dependent foundation (*unselbständige Stiftung*) or fiduciary foundation (*Treuhandstiftung*).[57] It results when assets are transferred to a natural

[52] MüKo/*Fleischer* (fn. 39), § 105 HGB n. 487; for an overview with further references, see et seqq. as well as *Lieder*, in: Oetker (ed.), Handelsgesetzbuch, 8th ed. 2024, § 105 HGB n. 77 et seqq.

[53] MüKo/*Fleischer* (fn. 39), § 105 HGB n. 495; *Henssler*, AcP 196 (1996), 37, 79 et seqq.

[54] §§ 1(1), 30(1) Gesetz über das Erlöschen der Familienfideikommisse und sonstiger gebundener Vermögen, 06.07.1938, Reichsgesetzblatt 1938 I 825. Its aim of dynastically binding and keeping a family fortune over generations rather resembled the "dynasty trusts" permitted by many United States jurisdictions.

[55] See on recent developments e.g. *Schönenberg-Wessel*, NJW 2023, 2625 et seqq. – Such testamentary designs are not considered against public policy or *contra bonos mores*, see e.g. BGH 19.01.2011 – IV ZR 7/10, BGHZ 188, 96; BGH 20.10.1993 – IV ZR 231/92, BGHZ 123, 368; BGH 21.03.1990 – IV ZR 169/89, BGHZ 111, 36.

[56] See, e.g., legge n. 112 Disposizioni in materia di assistenza in favore delle persone con disabilità grave prive del sostegno familiare, 22.06.2016, GU n. 146, providing for the acceptance of foreign trusts to such ends in otherwise trust-sceptical Italy.

[57] See *Coing* (fn. 31), 57 et seqq.; *Weitemeyer*, in: Säcker/Rixecker/Oetker/Limperg/Schubert (eds.), Münchener Kommentar zum BGB, vol. 1, 10th ed. 2025, § 80 BGB n. 199 et seqq.; *Hushahn*, in: Heckschen/Herrler/Münch(eds.), Beck'sches Notar-Handbuch, 8th ed. 2024, § 19 n. 147 et seqq.; a comprehensive overview is offered by *Wallenhorst/Wallenhorst*, Die Treuhandstiftung, 2023.

or legal person with the stipulation that they are to be administered as a class of patrimony economically separate from the transferee's other patrimony, and used for the promotion of a certain purpose.[58] Although such foundations are more widespread in practice than foundations with legal personality, there are no provisions regulating them; §§ 80 et seqq. BGB are not applicable.[59] They are instead governed and limited by the rules of the law of obligations or succession law, depending on their design: The parties may choose whether to configure the foundation by a (fiduciary) mandate/contract for the management of the affairs of another (§ 662, § 675 BGB) or by a donation under a condition (§ 525 BGB),[60] or effect it through a disposition *mortis causa* establishing a testamentary burden (§ 1940, §§ 2192 et seqq. BGB). Depending on their purpose, their context and their individual design, foundations without legal personality may be employed for situations and objectives which are typically the domain of trusts.[61] In many regards, this type of foundation can be considered as a *fiducia* rather than a foundation.

Consequently, a *Treuhandverhältnis* may be employed to serve a multitude of different purposes, solely or in combination. The general concept is not restricted to specific activities, although its individual manifestations are limited to their respective contexts. Through a *Treuhandverhältnis*, gifts can be achieved as well as business purposes, and it may be aimed at specific activities of public interest. The flexibility of purposes and applications of such *fiduciae* is extremely enhanced by the fact that there is no need for a separate, designated (identified or identifiable) beneficiary to whom advantages are provided – as evidenced especially in the *fiducia* for the own benefit of the fiduciary.

3. Creation

German law contains no explicit rules or prerequisites for the creation of a *fiducia*. Typically, fiduciary relationships result from a contract: A contractual agreement may aim at the establishment of a *fiducia* as its main purpose, or contain more or less complete rules governing the fiduciary relationship resulting from it (e.g. security agreement, contract for the management of the affairs of another). The fiduciary contract determines the fiduciary and the assets given in *fiducia*, the purpose of the *fiducia*, and the competences of the fiduciary as well as their limitations.[62] While no recourse can be taken to positive law, contractual gaps

---

[58] BGH 12.03.2009 – III ZR 142/08, BGHZ 180, 144, n. 14.

[59] MüKo/*Weitemeyer* (fn. 57), § 80 BGB n. 199.

[60] BGH 12.03.2009 – III ZR 142/08, BGHZ 180, 144, n. 15; MüKo/*Weitemeyer* (fn. 57), § 80 BGB n. 209 et seqq.

[61] The German notification for the Money Laundering Directive designated foundations without legal personality for the founder's own benefit and legal creations structurally and functionally resembling such foundations as legal arrangements similar to trusts, OJ 2020/C 136/05, 7.

[62] *Coing* (fn. 31), 109 et seqq. – For an in-depth analysis of fiduciary contracts, see *Grundmann*, Der Treuhandvertrag, 1997.

may be filled with the help of implicit agreements inferred from the circumstances (especially for frequent, well-established kinds of *fiducia*, e.g. fiduciary security rights[63]) and supplementary interpretation.

Fiduciary contracts for the creation of a *Vollrechtstreuhand* typically contain two elements, in keeping with the distinction between the obligatory and property levels: The *in rem* transfer of rights or powers to the fiduciary, and the obligatory fiduciary agreement restricting his use of them. A prime example for this is the security agreement for fiduciary security rights.[64] A *fiducia* may also result from a will, most notably in cases of provisional and reversionary heirs, executors, or fiduciary duties resulting from testamentary burdens (§ 1940 BGB). However, a unilateral declaration of the principal to serve as fiduciary cannot result in the creation of a *Treuhandverhältnis* under German law: It necessarily presupposes two parties, with the fiduciary distinct from the principal.

There is no public register for the registration of *Treuhandverhältnisse* as such.[65] The majority of them remain obscured from public view, which is frequently considered a benefit.

4. Parties and Roles

In principle, any natural or legal person can act as the principal of a *Treuhandverhältnis*, and any natural or legal person can serve as the fiduciary. Constraints may result from the context, or the rules for specific manifestations – e.g. only a person with full legal capacity can be appointed as executor (§ 2201 BGB).

Similarly, there are no restrictions on who may take on the role of beneficiary – generally, any natural or legal person or any other purpose may be designated, with possible context-specific constraints. Notably, under German law, a separate beneficiary is not a necessary prerequisite for a *fiducia*. The principal himself may be a beneficiary, or the sole beneficiary – this is frequently the case in practice, e.g. with mandates.[66]

Likewise, a protector is not envisaged in the German *fiducia* model, and such a role would be rather uncommon in most circumstances. Nevertheless, due to contractual freedom and flexibility of design, such an oversight position could be established and its powers specified by contract. A certain (mutual) control over executors, for instance, is often effectuated by the appointment of more than one executor.

---

[63] See fn. 32.

[64] MüKo/*Schubert* (fn. 31), § 164 BGB n. 58.

[65] Depending on the situation, the fiduciary's position as such may be noted in public registers, e.g. reversionary heirs and executors are to be noted in the land register (§§ 51, 52 Land Register Act – *Grundbuchordnung*). A registration in the transparency register may be required under anti-money laundering regulations.

[66] *Coing* (fn. 31), 88.

As the details of the *Treuhandverhältnis* are left to the contractual agreement of the parties, they can shape their powers and duties to a large extent; restrictions may result from the constraints of individual areas of application, or context-specific rules.

The principal can, in principle, reserve certain powers to himself, instruct the fiduciary, and sue the fiduciary in case of a breach of duties. A frequent example of the latter is a claim for damages for breach of contract (§§ 280 et seqq. BGB) if the holder of a fiduciary security right acts in breach of the security agreement, e. g. by transferring ownership of the assets to a third party before the debtor's default. The principal may also hold the power to remove the fiduciary, or to change the beneficiaries (if there are such).

The fiduciary's role and competences depend to a large extent on the type of *Treuhandverhältnis*, as well as the contractual specifications. Typical duties include the management of the assets in the interest of the principal, or the surrender of the assets when the *fiducia* is terminated. If there are distinct beneficiaries, the fiduciary can typically neither select the beneficiaries within a class nor decide what to give to them, but he may be given contractual or testamentary permission to do so, e. g. an executor authorized to distribute assets between heirs at his reasonable discretion.

If the *Treuhandverhältnis* envisages third-party beneficiaries, it typically includes rules safeguarding their interests and protecting them from mistakes by the fiduciary in the management of the assets. These may be contained either in the legal framework for specific types of *Treuhand* (e. g. in the succession context) and/or take the form of individual contractual obligations. In addition, beneficiaries may take recourse to general liability rules. Beneficiaries are not generally entitled to see the accounts of the *fiducia*, but such a right may be explicitly provided for (e. g. executor, § 2218 BGB; provisional heir, § 2230(2) BGB) or may be contractually stipulated; for a principal-beneficiary, a right to information and account-rendering results from § 666 BGB on mandates. The right to sue the fiduciary claiming maladministration or breach of *fiducia* arises from the underlying contract; consequently, a principal-beneficiary always has this right, and non-principal-beneficiaries may assert it if the contract entails a (protective) effect in favour of them as a third party (*Vertrag mit Schutzwirkung zugunsten Dritter*).

5. Assets, Creditors and Tax

With a *Vollrechtstreuhand*, the fiduciary acquires full ownership of the assets. On the property law level, his powers are unrestricted and he can validly effect disposals *in rem*; the contractual fiduciary duties regarding the assets (e. g. management, return) have only obligatory effect. As a result, the fiduciary is able e. g. to validly transfer ownership to a third party even if bound not to do so by the fiduciary agreement, the only remedy available being damages for breach of contract.[67] The assets do, however, not belong to or form a patrimony of their own, nor are they segregated from the fiduciary's other assets within his patrimony. If the fiduciary acquires assets in the scope of the *Treuhandverhältnis*, these assets typically become subject to the *fiducia*; while there is no general statutory provision for such a subrogation, special rules prescribe it for certain types of *fiducia* (e.g. § 2111 BGB), and in most other cases it will result from the contractual agreement or § 667 BGB.

There are no specific remedies for creditors of the principal against his transferring assets to a fiduciary. Depending on the circumstances, general remedies may be available, e.g. insolvency avoidance proceedings (§§ 129 et seqq. Insolvency Code [*Insolvenzordnung*] and Avoidance Code [*Anfechtungsgesetz*]) for asset transfers during the "suspect period", or claims for damages (e.g. contractual claims, §§ 280 et seqq. BGB).

Even though the fiduciary acquires ownership of the assets, they will not be liable for his own debts. Protection against creditors is effected procedurally: The principal can initiate third-party proceedings to oppose compulsory enforcement regarding the assets (§ 771 Code of Civil Procedure – *Zivilprozessordnung*), as they are considered to belong to him in terms of economic and liability allocation.[68] In insolvency, the principal has a right to separation of the assets according to § 47 Insolvency Code (*Insolvenzordnung*).[69] Conversely, the fiduciary's personal assets may be attached by his creditors for the debts incurred by him personally. If the obligations contracted by the fiduciary for the *fiducia* cannot be met by its assets, the fiduciary may be personally liable, depending on the type of *Treuhand*.[70] If there is an improper transfer of assets by the fiduciary to third parties, the beneficiaries generally do not have the right to sue these third parties (unless tort or unjust enrichment rules exceptionally provide such an option[71]).

On the contrary, with an *Ermächtigungstreuhand*, ownership of the assets remains with the principal and only all or specific powers of disposition are transferred to the fiduciary. As a consequence, the allocation of and access to assets is not affected by the *fiducia* but depends on the principal. Such kinds of *Treuhand* are not only fundamentally different from trusts,[72] but also quite far removed from the *fiducia* (hence "pseudo *fiducia*").

---

[67] *Henssler*, AcP 196 (1996), 37, 47 et seqq. – It is impossible to exclude the power to dispose with *in rem* effect, BGH 5.11.1953 – IV ZR 95/53, BGHZ 11, 37, 43; BGH 04.04.1968 – II ZR 26/67, NJW 1968, 1471; for a dogmatic attempt in this regard, see *Gruber*, AcP 202 (2002), 435 et seqq.

[68] BGH 5.11.1953 – IV ZR 95/53, BGHZ 11, 37, 43; BGH 08.02.1996 – IX ZR 151/95, NJW 1996, 1543; *Preuß*, in: Vorwerk/Wolf (eds.), BeckOK ZPO, 59th ed., 01.12.2025, § 771 ZPO n. 14; *Hadding/Häuser* (fn. 50), § 21 n. 62 et seqq.

[69] *Brinkmann*, in: Hirte/Vallender (eds.), Uhlenbruck Insolvenzordnung, 16th ed. 2025, § 47 InsO n. 79 et seqq. with further references.

[70] *Henssler*, AcP 196 (1996), 37, 72 et seqq.

[71] This could be the case, e.g., under § 816 BGB, as an exception from the general principle of the priority of performance-based claims (*Vorrang der Leistungskondiktion*).

[72] *Lupoi*, draft General Report (fn. 2), 20.

Hybrid scenarios result under the specific rules of succession law. In cases of reversionary heirship, the provisional heir acquires full ownership of the estate assets, but as his legal position is limited in time, they are not integrated into his personal patrimony; rather, they remain a legally segregated class of patrimony.[73] In cases of the appointment of an executor, the heir becomes owner of the estate assets, but as far as they are administered by the executor, they constitute a patrimony class separate from the heir's personal patrimony,[74] with the consequence that they are not at the disposal of the heir's creditors (§ 2214 BGB).

Being neither a legal person nor entity, a *fiducia* is not a taxpayer as such. For fiduciary relationships, an exception is made from the general fiscal rule that assets are attributed to their owner (§ 39(1) Fiscal Code – *Abgabenordnung*): Assets are attributed to the beneficiary, or the security provider in case of ownership transfers for security purposes (§ 39(2) no. 1 Fiscal Code).[75] In fiduciary security rights scenarios, it is thus the principal who is subject to income tax, and in other scenarios the beneficiary (frequently identical with the principal). There is no tax on the transfer of assets from the principal to the fiduciary, as from the tax perspective, the principal continues to be considered the owner. For the transfer of assets from the fiduciary to the beneficiaries, no tax is envisaged *per se*, but gift tax or income tax may apply depending on the circumstances.

6. *Death and Termination*

The consequences of the fiduciary's death for the assets, or the power of asset management, depend on the type of *Treuhandverhältnis* and the individual contractual stipulation. Under general principles, the fiduciary's heir(s) fully enter into his legal position as universal successors (§ 1922 BGB). As they succeed to all rights and obligations, they acquire assets and management power, and are constrained by the fiduciary agreement. However, there are many exceptions from this general principle. In the frequent case that the *Treuhandverhältnis* is based on a mandate, the default rule of the extinction of a mandate on the death of the mandatary (§ 673 BGB) entails the end of the *fiducia* – while ownership of the assets automatically passes from the fiduciary to his heirs, they do not have management power, and are bound to reverse the assets. On the death of an executor, his office expires (§ 2225 BGB); a new executor may need to be appointed. On the death of a provisional heir, reversionary succession occurs (§ 2139 BGB): The inheritance devolves to the reversionary heir, the *fiducia* ceases.

---

[73] *Küpper*, in: Gsell/Krüger/Lorenz/Reymann (eds.), BeckOGK BGB, 01.01.2026, § 2100 BGB n. 6 et seqq.

[74] *Lange*, in: Hau/Poseck (eds.), BeckOK BGB, 77th ed., 01.02.2026, § 2197 BGB n. 2.

[75] See *Koenig*, in: Koenig (ed.), Abgabenordnung, 6th ed. 2026, § 39 AO n. 53 et seqq. with further references.

7. Breach and Litigation

Courts cannot decide of their own volition to rescind a *Treuhandverhältnis* as a consequence of a serious breach by the fiduciary. Under the principle of party disposition (*Dispositionsgrundsatz*), it is for the parties to determine the subject matter of proceedings (§ 253(2) no. 2 ZPO). Litigation has to be initiated by the principal or a beneficiary against the fiduciary; depending on the claim it is based on (e. g. breach of contract, §§ 280 et seqq. BGB; rescission, §§ 323 et seqq. BGB), this may entail the end of the *fiducia*. However, this remains a matter between the parties, and there is no rescission by the court.

Litigation on matters of a *Treuhandverhältnis* falls within the competence of ordinary courts. There are no specialised courts devoted to *fiducia* litigation. Arbitration is allowed in such matters, according to general rules and principles of German civil procedure.

IV. Conclusion

German law does not accept common law trusts, nor does it contain legal institutions that could be considered trust equivalents in a narrow sense. However, the brief overview of this National Report has illustrated that the German legal system does provide for instruments that may be considered functional equivalents, as they may be utilized as substitute solutions in situations where common law jurisdictions typically employ trusts: The general concept of *fiducia* provides for a versatile basis for creating trust substitute instruments in a wide range of scenarios. The resulting stance of on the one hand refusing to recognize trusts as legal institutions, and on the other hand (over)generously accepting the legal concept of *fiducia* in a multitude of situations and without any positive law basis or restriction, appears increasingly contrary. One may wonder whether this dichotomy between deep-rooted mistrust in trusts and practice-driven overconfidence in *fiducia* should continue to be upheld – especially as with the creation of fiduciary foundations, practitioners have established a legal institution that is rather closely aligned with trusts.

In terms of structure and content, the approach of German law differs fundamentally from that of trusts in various regards. Its solutions largely build on the distinction between obligatory duties and property rights fundamental to German private law. While the absolute nature of asset ownership remains untouched, it is fenced in by contractual limitations and duties left to a large extent to the parties' discretion. This openness to contractual design and the leeway given to private autonomy raise the question whether "imported" common law trusts could (and should) be accepted in Germany, at least to a certain extent, for example by treating them as fiduciary foundations.

Likewise, the popularity of fiduciary legal constructs suggests that it might be worthwhile formally introducing a trust-substitute instrument into the German legal system. The concept of segregated assets or fragmented patrimonies seems like a promising approach, as such a notion already exists for some *fiducia* forms, and its compatibility with the civil law has been successfully tested in other jurisdictions. Restricting such an instrument to specific situations, and establishing its rules and limits, might counter the (perceived) dangers of attempts at abuse and provide clarity with regard to asset liability. Such a legislative initiative would certainly serve to integrate German law in the current more trust-friendly lines of development that can be discerned within the civil law world. But of course, it remains open to debate whether actual needs would justify such an effort – and to what extent such a legal institution could be considered a trust, or trust-like.

Freedom and Security

Gregor Kirchhof[1]

I. The Starting and Calibration Points of German Public Powers

The starting point for the German Basic Law (*Grundgesetz* – GG) and for German statehood is man. The people adopted the Basic Law "conscious of their responsibility before God and man" (Preamble). In accordance with the first Article of the Constitution (Art. 1 para. 1 of the Basic Law), human dignity is inviolable. Art. 1 para. 2 of the Basic Law goes on to pledge the Basic Law to inviolable and inalienable human rights as the basis of every human community, of peace and of justice in the world. This is where a general claim to legitimacy is formulated with remarkable audacity. There are no legitimate public powers without human rights, and hence without freedom. Fundamental rights are the starting and calibration points of public powers in Germany.

Striving to guarantee security is equally a matter of course for the German State. *Thomas Hobbes*[2] expressed this primal mandate, which constitutes and legitimises the State, early on. The Basic Law is part of this tradition, even if it does not explicitly regulate security concerns. The State's security mandate is stipulated in responsibility for man and for peace, as well as in other articles[3]. In the words of the Federal Constitutional Court,[4] the "security of the State as a constituted power for peace and order, and the security that it is to guarantee, whilst respecting the dignity and intrinsic value of the individual", is a matter of course for the State.

The Federal Constitutional Court furthermore makes clear here the necessary balance which characterises the Basic Law, and which is vital to the relationship between freedom and security. Unlike with *Thomas Hobbes*, and particularly similar to *John Locke*[5] and *Immanuel Kant*[6], security is not placed above freedom,

---

[1] I would very much like to thank my Chair, and in particular *Annalena Lederer*, *Laura Mähle* and *Pascal Klein*, for their valuable support.

[2] *Thomas Hobbes*, Leviathan [1651], Part II, Chapters 17 and 26.

[3] Preamble and Art. 1 para. 2 of the Basic Law above; see also Art. 13 paras. 4 and 7, Art. 24 para. 2, Art. 35 para. 2, Art. 73 para. 1 No. 10, Art. 87a and Art. 115a et seqq. of the Basic Law.

[4] Decisions of the Federal Constitutional Court (BVerfGE) 115, 320 (346); 49, 24 (56 et seqq.); own translation.

[5] *John Locke*, Two Treatises of Government. The Second Treatise [1690], Chapters 8 and 11.

[6] *Immanuel Kant*, Grundlegung zur Metaphysik der Sitten [1785], 2005, 421; see also same author, Metaphysik der Sitten [1797], 1954, 214.

and freedom is also not placed above security. In fact, man is prioritised, with the dual concerns of freedom and security. Man lives in a community. This therefore naturally calls for consideration to the interests of others. "Act only on that maxim through which you can at the same time will that it should become a universal law", according to the famous words of *Immanuel Kant*."[7] The Basic Law stipulates the requisite balance between the freedoms inter se, and the balance with security that this necessitates. It is a central mandate for state power.

II. Guaranteeing Security in a Practical Concordance

1. Rooted in Freedom – An Open Definition of Security

The concern of guaranteeing security is a matter of course for the German State and the Basic Law[8]. Germany seeks to carry out this mandate externally in international cooperation, especially as a member of the European Union, NATO and the United Nations. Internally, it gains substance from non-constitutional law, and here in particular from police and security law. But the law does not contain an unambiguous, all-embracing definition of security. Security is quite deliberately openly defined, and lent concrete form in the context of the respective case.

This open concept is logical for five reasons. Firstly, security is endangered by a wide variety of risks and threats, ranging from administrative offences through criminal acts and cyberattacks to war. This means – secondly – that the legal assets affected are divergent, and – thirdly – that the concerns being pursued vary widely if internal, external or IT and cybersecurity need to be guaranteed. Fourthly, the freedom-based starting point of the Basic Law[9] requires an open security concept. The guaranteed fundamental rights act towards the State as a defensive right, limiting state powers. In order to guarantee security, public authorities frequently need to encroach on fundamental rights if identity is established, remand detention ordered, a computer searched, or soldiers protect the country. These measures are only constitutional if security concerns constitutionally justify the encroachments on the freedom rights[10]. The Constitution does not however call for an all-embracing legal definition of security, but for a weighing in individual cases. The interests in question are to be balanced out in the concrete case, or in the striking words of *Konrad Hess*, placed in a practical concordance[11].

---

[7] *Immanuel Kant*, Groundwork of the Metaphysics of Morals. translated by H. J. Paton, 1964, 88.

[8] At I above.

[9] At I above.

[10] At III below.

[11] *Konrad Hesse*, Grundzüge des Verfassungsrechts der Bundesrepublik Deutschland, 20th ed. 1995, paras. 317 et seqq.

Security concerns may precede freedom or other legal interests, but also follow them. On the basis of the weighing that is always needed, German law understands security as a condition in which people or digital goods and legal interests are not at risk. This definition may, fifthly, not be misunderstood as an ideal condition of complete internal and external peace. The freedom-based state based on the rule of law does not seek absolute freedom or justice, and deliberately refrains from establishing complete security, even were this to be possible. Security may also not be misunderstood as a comprehensive entitlement, detached from the respective context. This does not limit the significance of security. Quite the contrary, the open definition is a prerequisite for freedom, which in turn is not possible without security[12].

2. *A Fundamental Right to Security?*

Fundamental rights are to be respected as defensive rights. The State is furthermore obliged to protect the fundamental right guarantees[13]. There are some who derive from the protective dimension of fundamental rights a fundamental right to security. In fact, security is to be constitutionally guaranteed[14]. This also follows from the protective dimension of fundamental rights, in particular from the protection of life, physical integrity (Art. 2 para. 2 of the Basic Law), and property (Art. 14 of the Basic Law). The Basic Law, however, deliberately does not provide for a distinct fundamental right to security. The elementary state mandate of security, and the protection of fundamental rights should not be misunderstood such that security always enjoys priority over freedom. The practical concordance would fail if one concern were to take on a higher rank from the outset, and independently of the concrete case. Any state requirement on citizens, potentially derivable from the fundamental right to security, to always conduct themselves in a manner in compliance with security, is also not compatible with the freedom concerns of the Basic Law and the necessary balance of freedom and security.

3. *External, Internal and Cybersecurity*

There is a need for a precise legal definition of security, given the risks, threats and legal interests concerned. This involves distinguishing between three fundamental, partly interconnected categories, namely external, internal and IT or cybersecurity[15].

External security focusses on defending against risks for the State originating outside national territory. These risks are frequently caused by other states, and

---

12 *Wilhelm von Humboldt*, Ideen zu einem Versuch, die Grenzen der Wirksamkeit des Staates zu bestimmen, 1792, 20; see also at IV below.

13 At III. 2 below.

14 At 1. and I above.

15 At 1 above.

Russia's war of aggression against Ukraine has served as their prime example in recent times. Added to this are further threats to external security caused by international organised crime and terrorism, or collapsed states. Especially in these cases, the lines between external and internal security, however, become blurred. This also makes it clear that security cannot be exhaustively defined. The Constitution imposes the condition of the protection of external security in the provisions on the Armed Forces (Art. 87a of the Basic Law) and of a state of defence (Art. 115a et seqq. of the Basic Law)[16]. It also receives concrete form via non-constitutional law, in particular the Parliamentary Participation Act (*Parlamentsbeteiligungsgesetz*), the Soldiers Act (*Soldatengesetz*), the Federal Intelligence Service Act (*Gesetz über den Bundesnachrichtendienst*), and the Article 10 Act.

Internal security focusses on risks and threats arising on national territory. The State uses its monopoly of power and coercive means here as a last resort within defined rules. The classical example is combatting crime in the country. Internal security is however not restricted to this struggle nor to police and security law. A change has already taken place in policing. According to its original mandate, it is to avert existing risks. It has however been doing more to prevent risks for several years. All in all, internal security encompasses the integrity of the legal order, the integrity of the legal interests of the individual, as well as the continued existence and functioning of the State and its institutions. It is consequently protected by a variety of state institutions, by the police and the public prosecution office, the administration, the executive, parliaments and courts, also political parties, associations and non-governmental organisations, as well as other forces of a free society. The democratic state based on the rule of law defends itself.

IT or cybersecurity has also developed the definition of security as a reaction to new threat scenarios. It includes protection against cyberattacks, particularly against cyber-espionage, cyber-surveillance or cyber-sabotage. Suitable provisions can be found in the Article 10 Act, amongst other places, as well as in the laws on IT security.

4. Risks for Security – Different Definitions of Risks

Security is threatened by risks. The open definition of security is therefore especially detailed by legal definitions of "risk". Particularly the legal boundaries imposed on state security measures are tried and tested in police and security law. As a matter of principle, a risk is understood here as the possibility that a legal interest may be harmed. The Basic Law allots primary legislative competence for police law and the law on risk aversion not to the Federation, but to the Federal *Länder*. The police and security laws of the *Länder* make a fundamental distinc-

[16] At 1 above.

tion between the abstract and the concrete risk. The concrete risk is very largely defined in parallel in most laws. It applies if "there is an adequate probability in individual cases that damage will occur to public security or order in the foreseeable future"[17]. This is contrasted with abstract risks occurring only with a sufficient probability according to general experience or the knowledge of expert agencies[18].

Using the probability that the risk will occur, the grievousness of the damage threatened, as well as the intensity of the encroachment in question, further definitions of risk are distinguished between in order to define the legal boundaries imposed on the actions of the police in the different types of risk. If the harmful event has already occurred, or if its occurrence is highly immanent, or it will occur very soon with a probability bordering on certainty, the risk is current[19]. A major risk applies if damage is threatened to a major legal interest, such as the existence or security of the Federation or of a *Land*, life, health or freedom, major assets, as well as other goods of a comparable importance that are protected by criminal law[20]. These risks may also concur. An urgent risk exists if it is highly probable that a risk will occur to a major legal interest[21]. Other combinations of the definitions of risk, such as current considerable risk, are possible.

Risks generally describe future harm. Risk aversion is then based on the prognosis decision of whether the risk will occur. This decision is to be taken from an ex-ante perspective, typical of the actions of the police and of other risk aversion players.

Also in view of the necessary prognosis decisions, the boundaries between the individual definitions of risk sometimes become blurred in practice. The Federal Administrative Court has for instance developed a formula according to which "lower requirements are to be made of the probability of the damage occurring, the bigger and more consequential the damage is that might take place."[22] This already reveals a trend towards anticipatory risk assessments, enhanced by the relatively new definition of immanent risk. Even if the recognised police risks do not apply, the police can take the measures needed to ascertain the facts of a case, and to prevent the occurrence of a risk to a significant legal interest. An individual's conduct must however give rise to a concrete probability in individual

---

[17] See only Section 2 No. 3(a) BremPolG; section 3 subsection (3) No. 1 SOG M-V; section 2 No. 1 NPOG; section 4 No. 3(a) SächsPVDG.

[18] See only Section 4 No. 3(h) SächsPVDG, section 2 No. 6 NPOG; section 3 subsection (3) (f) SOG LSA.

[19] See only section 2 No. 2 NPOG; section 4 No. 3(b) SächsPVDG; section 9 subsection (1) BWPolG.

[20] See only Section 2 No. 3 NPOG; section 3 subsection (3) No. 3 SOG M-V; section 4 No. 3 (c) SächsPVDG.

[21] See only Section 36 subsection (1) BWPolG; Art. 23 para. 3 BayPAG; section 41 subsection (3) PolG NRW; section 29 subsection (4) SächsPVDG.

[22] BVerwG, NJW 1974, 807 (810), own translation.

cases, or preparatory acts must permit the conclusion – by themselves or together with other specific facts – that attacks of considerable intensity or impact are to be expected in the foreseeable future. State measures may consequently be brought forward in time.

This development is partly so well advanced in everyday police work that criminal offences are anticipated by computer-aided analysis. This particularly involves using a technical analysis of existing data to ascertain places and times when and where criminal offences are highly probable in order to prevent them (known as "predictive policing"). Critics can increasingly see the risk here of encroachments on fundamental rights and discrimination which subsequently prove to be unjustified. This puts the necessary balance of fundamental rights *vis-à-vis* freedom and security to the test.

5. European Law and International Law

Germany is a Member of the European Union. The Union also guarantees to its citizens, and to its Member States, "an area of freedom, security and justice"[23]. It aims to ensure "a high level of security"[24]. The Charter of Fundamental Rights of the European Union guarantees to everyone the explicit "right to liberty and security of person"[25]. Security is always named here in one breath with freedom. European law too does not therefore regulate on a fundamental right to security which always takes priority over other legal interests such as freedom. In any case, the detailed provisions of the law on security are left up to the Member States to a significant degree, and the latter are to transpose them via specific legislation. European law however enjoys priority application *vis-à-vis* national law as part of national European constitutional law.

The European efforts to guarantee the internal security of the Union have been more successful so far than those to protect external security by establishing a joint defence policy. The Treaty on European Union, however, regulates an obligation of assistance in accordance with which an armed attack on one Member State obliges the others to provide all the assistance and support within their power, comparable to NATO's central regulations[26].

Germany is also a member of the NATO, a defensive alliance which seeks to serve peace in the world and resolve international disputes peacefully, in accordance with the United Nations' Charter. A core tool is the mutual defence clause, in accordance with which an attack on one member state is regarded as an attack on all, and all partners in the alliance undertake to provide assistance to the country that has been attacked, and to take the measures which the respective

23 Art. 3 para. 2 TEU; Art. 67 para. 1 TFEU.
24 Art. 67 para. 3 TFEU.
25 Art. 6 CFR.
26 Art. 42 para. 7 TEU.

member state considers necessary[27]. The states have discretion for deciding what measures they take. The NATO alliance obligation is legally weaker in this regard than that of the European Union, which provides that the states are to take all measures within their power. NATO, by contrast, is much more powerful militarily, and more important for the protection of peace, if only because it has the global military might of the USA as a member.

The elementary goal of the United Nations is also to ensure world peace and international security. The 193 Member States are however hardly able to agree together in the event of a risk to world peace and to react within a suitable time. They have therefore conferred "on the Security Council primary responsibility for the maintenance of international peace and security"[28]. The Council is equipped with specific powers to carry out this mandate. The permanent members[29] have a veto when it comes to resolutions beyond procedural matters, on condition that the parties to a dispute abstain when settling disputes[30]. The veto, which is exercised at times by other permanent members of the Security Council in such cases, nonetheless frequently prevents necessary resolutions from being passed[31]. Germany and the European Union therefore also strive to increase their security competences. Germany has a particular commitment towards international law as a whole. In this very sense, German law is to be interpreted as friendly not only towards European law, but also towards international law.

International law strives primarily to ensure world peace, and hence to protect the states from external threats. The term international security shows parallels in this regard towards external security in German law[32]. Terrorism has furthermore come to the fore in recent years in terms of threat awareness, and has been deemed one of the greatest risks to world peace[33]. What is more, violations of territorial borders have also been accompanied by attacks in the digital domain, so that the definition of international law has been expanded to also include the digital perspective[34]. Terrorism and digital attacks are understood in German law as matters of external and internal security, depending on their origin.

---

[27] Art. 5 of the North Atlantic Treaty, explicitly referring to collective self-defence recognised by Art. 51 of the UN Charter.

[28] Art. 24 No. 1 of the UN Charter.

[29] Art. 23 para. 1 of the UN Charter.

[30] Art. 27 No. 3 of the UN Charter.

[31] Cf. Chapter VII of the UN Charter.

[32] On this at 3.

[33] Resolution 1373, adopted at the 4385th meeting of the Security Council on 28 September 2001, p. 1; Resolution 1456 adopted at the 4688th meeting of the Security Council on 20 January 2003, p. 2.

[34] Resolution 65/41 of 8 December 2010; Resolution 73/27 of 5 December 2018; Resolution 79/243 of 24 December 2024.

III. Freedom – The Starting Point Under Constitutional Law

1. Self-Determination of Each Individual – Comprehensive Protection of Freedom

The German legal concept and guarantee of freedom focus on the fundamental rights of the Basic Law. Whilst the constitutions of the Federal *Länder* also guarantee specific freedom rights, they however only play a subordinate role in practice. Their protection is restricted from the outset to the respective Federal *Land*. The Basic Law precedes the constitutions of the *Länder* in the hierarchy of norms, whilst federal law takes precedence over *Land* law (Art. 31 of the Basic Law).

The Basic Law not only starts by designating the dignity and freedom of man, but also guarantees a special breadth of freedom. According to its wording, Art. 2 para. 1 of the Basic Law guarantees the free development of the personality. The rulings of the Federal Constitutional Court have however expanded the protected area to include general freedom of action, according to which "every form of human activity" is protected "without regard for the weight attaching to the activity for personality development"[35]. To name two landmark rulings of the Court, the area protected also includes feeding pigeons in the park[36], or horse-riding on specific paths in the forest[37]. The consequence is that freedom is protected from the outset in a manner which could not be broader.

The Basic Law has thus entered new constitutional territory. The guarantee of freedom and individuality deliberately does not encounter any general restrictions, particularly when it comes to limiting the protected area. The self-projection of man is comprehensively guaranteed. He or she is the only one who knows what constitutes his or her personality and signifies his or her happiness. This happiness may also lie in relatively ordinary actions. Art. 2 para. 1 of the Basic Law unmistakeably and comprehensively orientates the Basic Law towards the freedom of each individual, and hence to a freedom-based society.

The roots of this fundamental right idea branch out broadly and deeply. The freedom of the citizens of the *polis vis-à-vis* a ruler has been positioned at least since *Aristotle*. But for *Aristotle* as well as for *Plato*, the community came before the individual. Everyone had to submit to the good of the *polis*[38]. All in all, ethical and legal stipulations became indistinct in the dense corset of conduct. Ancient Greece did not have a legal culture based on individual freedom. A prerequisite of fundamental right freedom nonetheless already becomes visible in these Greek roots, which Art. 2 para. 1 of the Basic Law also regulates in the boundaries on freedom, in the "rights of others", the "constitutional order", and the "moral law". Freedom takes place in encounters with others, and hence in the community.

---

[35] BVerfGE 80, 137 (152 et seqq.); BVerfGE 6, 32 (36 et seqq.).

[36] BVerfGE 54, 143 (144 et seqq.).

[37] BVerfGE 80, 137 (152 et seqq.).

[38] *Plato*, The Laws [365–348 BC], (weaving), (building); *Aristotle*, Politica [between 329 & 326 BC].

Each community however requires legal and extra-legal rules. Taking a walk entails respecting the usual social manners and the neighbours' fence. The baker complies with the legal hygiene rules, and, when selling, respects the customs of politeness. His or her customers naturally follow the priority principle when queueing. Individual fundamental right protection is demanded, but also a basic order which departs from the individualising perspective, embracing an orientation towards the community and the common good. The community relationship of freedom, and the connection between freedom and the law, were particularly developed by *John Locke* and *Immanuel Kant*[39].

The foundation of man's comprehensive self-projection was laid out by the Greek philosophers, by the development towards the rule of law that was especially supported by *Jean Bodin*[40], and previously in the 15th century by *Pico della Mirandola*. According to *Mirandola*, God created man so that He remained an image-maker of Himself according to His will[41]. Anyone bringing together this central legacy of the Renaissance with the fundamental philosophical realisation of *René Descartes* – "I think, therefore I am."[42] – understands the free individual as his own creator from his knowledge. This concept of self-determination in freedom, the free development of the individual personality – to quote Art. 2 para. 1 of the Basic Law – forms a cornerstone of the modern era and of the Basic Law.

The fundamental rights of the Basic Law protect the positive freedom to carry out acts, and the negative freedom to not carry out acts. In this very sense, the freedom of religion (Art. 4 paras. 1 and 2 of the Basic Law) positively guarantees the option for a religious community, and negatively guarantees the option not to have a faith. The Basic Law thus distinguishes between fundamental rights which apply to all, and fundamental rights for Germans, which according to their wording apply only to Germans within the meaning of Art. 116 para. 1 of the Basic Law. The legal consequences of this distinction are negligible because the corresponding conduct of any person is guaranteed via the general freedom of action. EU nationals are in any case to be treated the same as Germans as a matter of principle, on the basis of the prohibition of discrimination of Art. 18 and Art. 20 AEUV. They therefore enjoy the comprehensive protection of the special fundamental rights for Germans via Art. 2 para. 1 of the Basic Law.

In addition to the written freedom rights of the Basic Law, there are other recognised fundamental rights which the Federal Constitutional Court has developed as part of its line of rulings. These are expressions of existing guarantees such as the general right of personality, and the concomitant rights to know of one's own descent, as well as to informational or sexual self-determination. These fundamental right guarantees are rooted in two explicit fundamental rights, in

---

[39] See at I above.

[40] See at I above.

[41] *Giovanni Pico della Mirandola*, De hominis dignitate [1486], edited and translated by Gerd von der Gönna, 2005, particularly 7 et seqq.

[42] *René Descartes*, Discourse on method [1637], translated by John Veitch, 1913/1989, 35.

the free development of personality (Art. 2 para. 1 of the Basic Law), and in the guarantee of human dignity (Art. 1 para. 1 of the Basic Law)[43]. The case-law has furthermore developed the fundamental right to a guarantee of confidentiality and integrity of information technology systems (the "fundamental IT right")[44]. Even if the German legal system does not follow the *common law* legal tradition, the case-law of the highest courts, and particularly that of the Federal Constitutional Court, has a milestone significance, the impact of which is comparable with this tradition. A new fundamental right developed by the Federal Constitutional Court at least does not require any explicit statutory norming. The Court's rulings are binding on the constitutional bodies of the Federation and of the *Länder*, as well as on all courts and authorities, as if they were laws (section 31 of the Act on the Federal Constitutional Court [BVerfGG]).

The fundamental rights very largely regulate the relationship between the State and man. Only the guarantee of human dignity applies directly between private individuals. German law speaks here of the bipolar relationship between the State and society being supplemented to include a further private aspect. Art. 1 para. 1 of the Basic Law hence develops a "direct third-party effect between private individuals". Purely moral considerations which are not underpinned by the (fundamental) rights are not relevant as a rule in an examination under constitutional law. Fundamental rights as a whole however constitute an objective value system which also contains certain moral ideas. General clauses of non-constitutional law that require interpretation thus need to be interpreted and applied in light of the Basic Law. It is not however possible to derive any direct binding effect of fundamental rights on private individuals from this "direct third-party effect", but only an obligation incumbent on public authorities, and on the courts, to take adequate account of the evaluations of the Basic Law when interpreting the law.

2. Defensive Rights and Protection Obligations

Each freedom right contains at least two dimensions of protection. In the *status negativus*, the fundamental rights act as defensive rights of individuals *vis-à-vis* the State; in the *status positivus*, they give rise to obligations incumbent on the State to provide protection. The defensive right protects individuals against unjustified state encroachments on their fundamental right-protected freedoms.

In order to be able to enjoy any freedoms at all, a basic level of security is however needed, particularly protection against impending violations of major legal interests such as life, physical integrity or property. It is up to the State, within its obligations to protect fundamental rights, to guarantee this protection and to protect people against third-party impairments[45]. The State has a mono-

---

[43] BVerfGE 141, 186 (201 et seqq.); BVerfGE 65, 1 (42 et seqq.).
[44] BVerfGE 120, 274 (303 et seqq.).
[45] See at I and II above.

poly of power. It is only the State which may apply the means of legitimate physical coercion, and thus guarantee the integrity of life, freedom and property against third-party attacks. Public authorities however have broad discretion as to how to comply with the obligations to protect fundamental rights. "The Federal Constitutional Court [only] finds that there has been a violation of an obligation of protection if either no protection precautions have been taken at all, if the measures taken are manifestly unsuitable or completely inadequate to achieve the due aim of protection, or if they fall far short of the goal of protection" (the "*Untermaßverbot*" thus prohibits falling short of protection requirements).[46]

3. The Boundaries on Freedom – Legislation, Judicial Scrutiny

Any encroachment on the fundamental freedom rights requires a foundation in law, and must be justified. The rule-of-law principle of Art. 20 para. 3 of the Basic Law requires in the proviso of the law that any state action that is relevant to fundamental rights must be based on an Act of Parliament. Parliament is the only body of the State which is directly elected. If Parliament resolves on encroachments on fundamental rights in a law, people decide by electing Parliament itself how their freedoms may be restricted. Encroachments on a fundamental right may not be carried out without a statutory basis. The fundamental rights thus emphasise the established link between freedom and the law, between the radical self-projection of man, and the necessary consideration for legal as well as extra-legal rules.

If the scope of protection provided by the general freedom of action is broad, the *Gesetzesvorbehalt* (legal reservation) also becomes expanded, according to an early objection. Public authorities are said to be forced to also legally regulate insignificant acts. The legal reservation is thus said to ultimately lead to over-regulation, and to be detrimental to freedom. This objection ignores, first of all, that it is the public authorities themselves that increase the flood of norms when regulating on minor details. What is more, the scope of Art. 19 para. 1 first sentence of the Basic Law grows along with that of Art. 2 para. 1. Accordingly, laws which are detrimental to fundamental rights must be general in nature, and must not apply to the individual case. The fundamental rights part of the Basic Law starts in terms of human rights by guaranteeing human dignity, and with the general freedom of action. Its conclusion is however the general nature of the law, this old guarantee for free, equal and just legal rules.

According to the recognised, three-tier German fundamental rights dogma, a fundamental freedom right is violated when public authorities – firstly – encroach on the sphere of protection of a fundamental right – secondly – and this encroachment – thirdly – is not constitutionally justified. There is a need to

[46] BVerfGE 157, 30 (114 with further references); own translation.

examine initially whether a fundamental right may be encroached on at all. The guarantee of human dignity, for instance, may never be impaired. No encroachment on Art. 1 para. 1 of the Basic Law can be justified. When it comes to the other fundamental rights, there is a need to discuss under what conditions encroachments are permissible. Firstly, the law enabling the encroachment is examined as to whether it is constitutional. The relevant formal prerequisites of the legislative procedure must be adhered to. Substantively, particularly the principle of proportionality is to be preserved. Furthermore, as has already been mentioned, any act encroaching on a fundamental right must be general, and may not merely apply to single cases (Art. 19 para. 1 first sentence of the Basic Law). The warning function of the principle of naming requires that a fundamental right that may be restricted be designated in the law, stating the Article (Art. 19 para. 1 second sentence of the Basic Law). The essence of a fundamental right may not be altered (Art. 19 para. 2 of the Basic Law). Not only the legal reservation, but also a judicial reserve, applies to specific far-reaching restrictions of freedom, such as detention or search (Art. 104 para. 2 and Art. 13 para. 2 of the Basic Law). The restriction is then generally unconstitutional without a prior court ruling. If the encroachment does not take place directly through a law, but on the basis of a law through a single-case measure, this concrete act of the public powers – an administrative act or a police measure – is additionally examined as to its constitutionality. An encroachment on a freedom right is then only justified if the law and the individual act are constitutional.

The fundamental rights regulate, in separate legal reservations, preconditions under which they may be respectively constitutionally restricted. There are fundamental rights which confirm the general legal reservation. According to their wording, the fundamental rights such as freedom of outdoor assemblies (Art. 8 para. 2 of the Basic Law) may be restricted directly or on the basis of a law. Guarantees with a "qualified legal reservation" such as Art. 11 para. 2 of the Basic Law place additional demands on the restricting law. Expropriation is only permissible for the public good, and may only take place by or on the basis of a law which also determines the nature and extent of compensation (Art. 14 para. 3 second sentence of the Basic Law). There are, finally, fundamental rights which are guaranteed without reservation, such as freedom of religion or academic freedom (Art. 4 para. 1 and para. 2; Art. 5 para. 3 of the Basic Law), which do not entail a written legal reservation. According to the will of the authors of the Basic Law, they provide a higher level of protection. Restrictions are only possible if constitutional interests justify the encroachment. Given the broad general freedom of action and the obligations to protect fundamental rights[47], however, there are many constitutional interests, so that it is virtually impossible to identify a generally higher level of protection. Even with these fundamental rights, a careful

---

[47] At 1 and 2 above.

balance of the constitutional interests is called for in terms of practical concordance[48].

Every law, and every individual measure, must be proportional ("prohibition of disproportionality"). The principle of proportionality is guaranteed if a legitimate goal is pursued, the action is suited to achieve this goal, it is necessary – in other words the mildest action is selected among equally effective ones –, and the encroachment is suitable after a weighing of all the interests affected. A legitimate goal is one which is not explicitly disapproved of by the Constitution. Depending on the fundamental right, and on the severity of the encroachment, only very specific legal interests may be taken as legitimate goals. Fundamental rights that are guaranteed without reservation may only be restricted on the basis of constitutional interests. The legislature has a prerogative of assessment when it comes to the suitability and necessity of the action. It initially assesses whether the goal is promoted, and whether there are equally effective but less incisive measures. It only acts unconstitutionally if it has not selected evidently more suitable or less incisive measures. In terms of suitability, the seriousness of the encroachment is balanced against the magnitude of the goal pursued, and in doing so all colliding constitutional and legal interests affected are weighed. The intensity of the encroachment may not be disproportionate to the goal pursued.

The freedom rights are to be respected by all state players (Art. 1 para. 3 and Art. 20 para. 3 of the Basic Law). The broad general freedom of action, and the further fundamental rights, consequently also have a processual impact. Each party concerned can have the legal boundaries examined by a court. The First Part of the Basic Law, on fundamental rights, starts by guaranteeing human dignity and legally binding all state powers (Art. 1 paras. 1 and 3 of the Basic Law). It ends just as deliberately with the principle of effective legal protection (Art. 19 para. 4 of the Basic Law). Possible violations of freedom are examined by the courts, and ultimately by the Federal Constitutional Court. The judicial power, and particularly the Federal Constitutional Court, have thus become more significant *vis-à-vis* the legislature. This may be criticised from a parliamentary perspective, but every individual has at the same time gained a free right to rational reasoning. The German civil law system does not provide for an explicit "violation" of the case-law, but in reality the courts do not like deviating from their own lines of rulings.

4. Recent Fundamental Rights Discussions

Recent debates on fundamental rights relate to freedom of opinion. It is particularly asked here how far the sphere of protection reaches, and at what point the

---

[48] At II. 1 above.

threshold of criminal liability is overstepped[49]. Data protection and cybersecurity, and with them the right to informational self-determination[50], also play a major role[51]. Above all, since the pandemic-related restrictions, along with health protection, the focus has also been placed on general freedom of action and freedom of assembly[52].

With the climate protection ruling, the Federal Constitutional Court stressed in Germany the concept of generational justice in environmental law[53]. Climate action is regulated in Art. 20a of the Basic Law as a provision on the goals which the State sets itself. The ruling lent it fresh significance as an actionable right, the aspect of intertemporal safeguarding of freedom having the potential to entail major consequences. The legislature is obliged to ensure freedom, including over years and generations. The future perspective is now a part of freedom-based fundamental right protection.

Whilst impairments or losses of freedoms can be described relatively precisely, this does not apply unrestrictedly to arbitrary increases in security. Recent developments pose the fundamental rights question as to the degree to which a large number of in some cases also slight encroachments, and hence a broad impact on fundamental rights, may be constitutionally justified. The struggle against terrorism frequently entails more comprehensive surveillance of many people if rights to information from banks, airlines and telecommunication service-providers, as well as the possibilities with surveillance of the home, are expanded. In the struggle against terrorism, a shift is also noticeable from security measures to the pre-risk period[54]. It is not the risk that is to be prevented, but its very creation. One example of this shift in security measures, and the broad fundamental rights effect, is constituted by the retention of data, in which data from all citizens are to be collected without a concrete reason. The Federal Constitutional Court has addressed questions of powers on prior acts in various rulings[55], has partly rescinded these as unconstitutional, and hence surveyed the relationship between freedom and security more broadly. That having been said, the State may not and must not ignore where citizens (wish to) take up their freedoms in a manner endangering the security and freedom of others and the common good. Security precautions are also to be brought into a practical concordance with freedom.

---

[49] BVerfG (Federal Constitutional Court) of 11 April 2024 – 1 BvR 2290/23 – NJW 2024, 1868; BVerfG of 16 January 2025 – 1 BvR 1182/24 – NJW 2025, 1642.

[50] At 1 with further references.

[51] See at II above.

[52] Recently BVerfG of 1 October 2025 – 1 BvR 2428/20 – NVwZ 2026, 33.

[53] BVerfGE 157, 30.

[54] See at II. 4 above.

[55] BVerfGE 125, 260 on retention of data; BVerfGE 120, 274 on online searches; BVerfGE 120, 378 on automatic vehicle registration recording; BVerfGE 115, 320 on electronic profiling and searches; BVerfGK 10, 330, NVwZ 2007, 688 on video surveillance in the public domain; BVerfGE 113, 348 on preventive telecommunications surveillance.

5. Freedom in European and International Contexts

European law and international law also protect freedom. The Universal Declaration of Human Rights, the International Covenant on Civil and Political Rights, the International Covenant on Economic, Social and Cultural Rights, the European Convention on Human Rights, the EU Charter of Fundamental Rights, the European fundamental freedoms, and other individual guarantees such as the ban on discrimination, apply in Germany[56]. The ECHR and the law of the European Union are ruled on by the ECtHR and the CJEU, respectively. International law, which includes the ECHR, has the status of non-constitutional federal law in the German legal system in accordance with Art. 59 para. 2 of the Basic Law. In de facto terms, a kind of priority relationship is created via the international law-friendly interpretation of the Basic Law, which also includes consideration of the judgments of the ECtHR. European law assumes primacy of application when interpreting German law[57].

Unlike the ECHR and the Charter of Fundamental Rights, the Basic Law does not provide for explicit protection of private life (Art. 7 of the Charter, Art. 8 ECHR). The fundamental right to fair proceedings (Art. 41 and 47 of the Charter, Art. 6 ECHR) exists in German law explicitly only towards the judicature (Art. 103 para. 1 and 19 para. 4 of the Basic Law). On the other hand, German constitutional law has broad general freedom of action in Art. 2 para. 1 of the Basic Law, whilst such a comprehensive freedom exists neither in the ECHR nor in the Charter of the EU. The German Constitution furthermore guarantees strong protection of freedom of religion and freedom of opinion, when weighed against the rights of the individual in an international comparison. Public health is also protected by European law, where it is both an area of competence and a ground for justification for restrictions of specific fundamental freedoms[58].

IV. The Relationship Between Freedom and Security – The Outlook

Freedom and security are frequently compared with one another, but this may only be convincing at first sight if encroachments on freedom serve the purpose of security, or freedoms are unlawfully exercised in order to impair security. Anyone who takes a closer look realises that the comparison does not cover the relationship precisely. Freedom is not possible without security because insecurity paralyses freedom. Long-term, reliable security does not however exist without freedom because the freedom-based powers cannot otherwise develop, and thus act counter to security. The State must guarantee security for the sake of freedom, and vice versa. The State also depends here on man and society to

---

56 At 1 above.

57 Overall BVerfGE 123, 267 (354); BVerfGE 158, 210 (239 et seqq.); at II. 5 above.

58 Art. 4 para. 2(k) TFEU; Art. 45 para. 3 TFEU, Art. 52 para. 1 TFEU.

develop freedoms and ensure internal peace, to also support it at times, and to provide necessary information. All in all, freedom is a precondition for security, and security is a prerequisite for freedom.

It is almost logical that greater freedom does not necessarily mean less security – and vice versa. There can be no absolute security, and no absolute freedom. These goals are also not to be aimed at. "The Basic Law also subjects the pursuance of the goal to create the greatest possible security under the actual circumstances to rule-of-law ties, particularly including the ban on inappropriate encroachments on fundamental rights as rights of aversion of state encroachments"[59]. In accordance with the Basic Law, freedom and security are to be brought into a practical concordance which lends particular consideration to the respective risk and the legal interests in question[60].

Freedom and security are however also core concerns of the European Union. European integration is a godsend for Germany, and one of the legal achievements of the last century. Reconciliation between the countries at the heart of Europe after the Second World War, and the peace built on this rapprochement, enable freedom and serve the elementary state mandate of external security[61]. They formed the necessary foundation for the further development of democracy and the rule of law. The internal market, the Schengen Area, and the Euro, have rendered European integration one of the guarantors of freedoms and prosperity which no country can guarantee by itself. Enlargement to the East in the 1990s through to 2013 has seen further highlights of integration, as this reliably guaranteed to people in the new Member States democratic statehood based on the rule of law in security, freedom and equality. Placing these milestones together in a mosaic provides a picture of the European Union with its own regulation, but especially guaranteeing to people functioning democratic statehood and freedoms. The Union has three sources of strength, namely the European institutions, the states, and above all its people. These sources should not be set off against one another. European centralism and increasing European regulation should not be supported with the unthinking argument that the European institutions must gain ever larger competences and greater influence for uniform law. In fact, the European union of nations should become clearer once again as to its structure, and with this structure the following realisation: If freedom and the states are enhanced, the European Union becomes stronger. But the Union is currently making virtually no use of two of these sources of strength. Statehood and freedom are being neglected.

That having been said, it is not only the degree of regulation that needs to be readjusted. *Thomas Hobbes'*[62] state mandate of security is placed in a new, more elementary intensity today. Russia's war of aggression against Ukraine represents

---

59 BVerfGE 115, 320 (358); own translation.
60 At II above.
61 At II above.
62 At I above.

a caesura in Europe. The security structure which had long been taken for granted was knocked off-balance with this war at the latest. Many NATO member states, the European Union, and especially also Germany, have since been doing more for external security. It also emerges in cybersecurity and digital information for the struggle against terrorism in particular that Germany as well as the European Union rely on other countries, and on the USA in particular. These dependences are to be reduced in the years to come. Germany has consequently upped its security expenditure considerably. The *Bundestag* and the *Bundesrat* amended the Basic Law in 2022, and again in 2025, in order to initially take up new debts of 100 billion Euro, and then unlimited debt if the federal budget's security expenditure exceeds one percent of nominal gross domestic product. These funds, debts which are to be left for the future, are to be used to better equip the *Bundeswehr*, and also spent in other fields of security[63]. There has been a new military service since 1 January 2026. Another pressing political concern is to improve protection of critical infrastructures, also with a view to cybersecurity.

These efforts to become more independent are not however placed into proportion by Germany's fundamental decision to serve peace in the world, and freedom as a member of the European Union and of the community of states. The three visionary fundamental pillars of the Basic Law are unambiguous. The Preamble opts, firstly, in responsibility to God and man, for a unified Europe in a community of states which is obligated to peace in the world. The Constitution is hence about reconciliation right at the beginning, about European integration, peace and, hence, fundamental prerequisites for freedom and security. Art. 1 of the Basic Law expands on this elementary orientation, secondly, in the profoundly humanist and also Christian guarantee of human dignity, as well as of the supranational pledge to respect inalienable human rights. The concrete list of fundamental rights begins finally, thirdly, with dignity, freedom, the human right to the free development of one's personality, and to comprehensive general freedom of action. This far-sighted triad clearly outlines the modern State obligated to man and to the community of states. But the Basic Law does not start with the State, but with man. Each person is his or her own creator, according to his or her ideas. He or she is free as long as he or she does not violate the right of others and the constitutional order.

---

[63] Art. 87a para. 1a and Art. 109 para. 3 fifth sentence of the Basic Law new version.

Artificial Intelligence in Civil Proceedings

Malte Kramme and *Lucas Gerlach*

I. Introduction

Currently, AI-supported tools are not widely used in civil justice. Furthermore, there is no specific legal framework for the use of AI systems in this area. Consequently, the admissibility of such tools is instead governed by general legal standards derived from the Code of Civil Procedure, fundamental rights, the EU AI Act, and data protection law, among other things. Nevertheless, there are working groups within the judiciary, pilot projects and research projects:

In April 2025, the federal and state justice administrations, acting as the E-Justice Council *(E-Justice-Rat)*, established a strategy for the use of AI in the justice system.[1] The strategy's core focus is on coordinating the development of appropriate solutions and providing mutual support for the implementation of AI solutions.[2] The E-Justice Council's AI strategy outlines five overarching objectives for the use of AI in the judiciary and proposes actionable measures to achieve them. These goals include:

- the responsible transformation of administrative processes,
- increased efficiency and effectiveness of administrative processes,
- improved access to justice,
- greater consistency and coherence of administrative processes, and
- increased visibility of the judiciary and promotion of innovation.[3]

A position paper by the working group 'Use of AI and Algorithmic Systems in the Judiciary' for the 74th Annual Conference of the Presidents of the Higher Regional Courts *(Oberlandesgerichte)*, the Court of Appeal *(Kammergericht Berlin)*, the Bavarian Supreme Regional Court *(Bayerisches Oberstes Landesgericht)* and the Federal Court of Justice *(Bundesgerichtshof)* in 2022 explores the potential applications of AI systems within the judiciary, along with their associated legal requirements and limitations.[4] The paper provides an overview of 19 ongoing and

---

[1] E-Justice-Rat, 'Strategie für den Einsatz von Künstlicher Intelligenz in der Justiz. Entwicklung, Einkauf und Einsatz von KI-Systemen in der Justiz koordinieren', 02.04.2025.

[2] E-Justice-Rat (n. 1), 20.

[3] E-Justice-Rat (n. 1), 15.

[4] 'Einsatz von KI und algorithmischen Systemen in der Justiz', Background paper for the 74th Annual Conference of the Presidents of the Higher Regional Courts, the Court of Appeal, the

planned projects for the use of AI in the German judiciary.[5] Those relevant to civil justice fall within the following application areas:
- Metadata processing,
- Automatic tagging and indexing,
- Search systems for legal databases,
- Text comparison, text processing and relation,
- Pattern recognition and assignment of text modules,
- Dialogue systems,
- Text generation and decision-making support,
- Anonymisation, and
- Speech recognition.[6]

New technical solutions are particularly needed to make the justice system more efficient in dealing with mass proceedings. The so-called 'diesel scandal', for example, led to a huge number of similar individual lawsuits against car manufacturers, causing fears of immense overload for the courts.[7] The Higher Regional Court of Stuttgart launched the highly acclaimed OLGA ('*Oberlandesgerichts-Assistent*') project. In collaboration with IBM, they developed an AI-supported multi-tool that can be used to search and pre-sort incoming appeals according to selectable parameters. This is achieved by having the AI semantically evaluate the judgments of the lower courts and the lawyers' pleadings.[8]

The TITAN research project focuses on the efficient and constitutional use of AI in the justice system, with a particular emphasis on large language models (LLMs).[9]

Gold and *Reuß* conducted a comprehensive research project in cooperation with the Lower Saxony Ministry of Justice that addresses the legal and ethical issues surrounding the admissibility of automated decision-making and the use of AI applications that support decision-making.[10] Accompanying the research,

Bavarian Supreme Regional Court, and the Federal Court of Justice from May 23 to 25, 2022, in Rostock, 13.05.2022.

[5] Working group 'Einsatz von KI und algorithmischen Systemen in der Justiz' (n. 4), s. Appendicies.

[6] Working group 'Einsatz von KI und algorithmischen Systemen in der Justiz' (n. 4), s. Appendicies.

[7] *Schmoll/Zitt*, in: Reuß/Windau (eds.), 'Kolloquien im Wintersemester 2021/2022', 2023, 55; *Limperg* NJW 2020, 3011, 3013.

[8] *Spoenle*, in: Reuß/Laß (eds.), 'Kolloquien im Sommersemester 2022 Kolloquien im Wintersemester 2022/2023', 2024.

[9] beck-aktuell, 'KI in der Justiz: Forschungsprojekt will Einsatzmöglichkeiten ausloten', https://rsw.beck.de/aktuell/daily/meldung/detail/ki-einsatz-justiz-forschungsprojekt-unis (22.01.2026).

[10] *Gold/Reuß/Rio Hecklau/Gätjen/J. Kohler/K. Kohler/Kolbe/Thamm/Thomsen*, 'Forschungsprojekt Künstliche Intelligenz und richterliche Entscheidungsfindung'.

an AI tool for mass proceedings (MAKI) was developed and has been used in test courts since 2024.[11]

II. General Overview of AI in Your Jurisdiction

1. Definition of AI

Is there a legally binding definition of AI in your national law? If yes, please provide the definition and its source.

The EU AI Act[12] is the only legislation to contain a definition of AI in the form of the AI system. According to Article 3 Nr. 1 of the AI Act, this is a machine-based system that is designed to operate with varying levels of autonomy and that may exhibit adaptiveness after deployment, and that, for explicit or implicit objectives, infers, from the input it receives, how to generate outputs such as predictions, content, recommendations, or decisions that can influence physical or virtual environments. In any case, according to Recital 12, 'simpler traditional software systems and programming approaches […] based on the rules defined solely by natural persons to automatically execute operations' are not to be covered.[13] Nevertheless, based on the OECD definition,[14] it is sometimes assumed that the introduction of the characteristic 'autonomy' was not intended to narrow the scope.[15]

However, this definition is only binding with regard to the question of whether the EU AI Act applies. It thus regulates the scope of application for a specific product safety law,[16] which would also apply to AI systems and models used in civil justice. However, any civil procedure rules that have yet to be enacted and which would regulate the scope and use of AI would not be bound by this definition.

---

[11] Niedersächsisches Justizministerium (Ministry of Justice of Lower Saxony), https://www.mj.niedersachsen.de/startseite/kunstliche_intelligenz_und_automation_in_der_justiz/kunstliche-intelligenz-und-automation-in-der-justiz-246705.html (10.03.2026).

[12] Regulation (EU) 2024/1689 of the European Parliament and of the Council of 13 June 2024 laying down harmonised rules on artificial intelligence and amending Regulations (EC) No 300/2008, (EU) No 167/2013, (EU) No 168/2013, (EU) 2018/858, (EU) 2018/1139 and (EU) 2019/2144 and Directives 2014/90/EU, (EU) 2016/797 and (EU) 2020/1828 (Artificial Intelligence Act).

[13] Accordingly, Biallaß, for example, assumes that, due to the legislative intention to narrow the definition of an AI system by adding the requirement of 'autonomy', purely rule-based systems should no longer be classified as AI systems within the meaning of the AI Act, see *Biallaß* MMR Zeitschrift für IT-Recht und Recht der Digitalisierung 2024, 646, 647.

[14] OECD, Explanatory memorandum on the updated OECD definition of an AI system, 2024.

[15] *Gold/Reuß et al.* (n. 10), 273; Martini/Wendehorst/*Wendehorst,* 2nd ed. 2026, KI-VO Art. 3 n. 30.

[16] *Borges* CR 2022, 553, 554.

If no legally binding definition exists, is there a commonly accepted definition in academia, legal practice, or other sectors? Please describe how AI is generally understood in your jurisdiction.

There is still no universal definition of AI.[17] The literal translation of artificial intelligence into the German term *'Künstliche Intelligenz'* is even viewed critically by some, who advocate a more nuanced approach to the terminology.[18] In particular, there is no legal definition of how AI should be understood in terms of the requirements for its use in the justice system. At the heart of the discussion is the question mentioned above as to whether mere rule-based algorithms also fall under the term AI.[19] The prevailing view is that they do not:[20] the decisive characteristic of an AI-based programme is machine learning in the sense of independent improvement, which means that only 'digital phenomena' and mere rule-based algorithms are not covered.[21]

Nevertheless, it makes sense to initially include mere rule-based systems under the umbrella term AI, as these are also discussed in the context of automated decision-making.[22] Finally, it is important to differentiate according to the type of AI system and its degree of autonomy, as well as its planned area of application.[23] Sometimes a distinction is made between implicit or self-learning algorithms and explicit or deterministic algorithms, which use an if-then logic.[24]

2. Sector-Specific Definitions

Are there sector-specific definitions of AI adopted by judicial oversight bodies, the Ministry of Justice, or other relevant authorities for the judiciary?

The final report of the federal states' working group 'Legal Tech: Challenges for the Judiciary,' assumes an inconsistent definition of the term AI, but was written before the EU AI Act was introduced. The report distinguishes between strong and weak AI, classifying non-learning rule-based algorithms as weak AI.[25] Official bodies also refer to the definition in the EU AI Act in the context of the use of

[17] *Huber/Giesecke*, in: Ebers/Heinze/Krügel/Steinrötter/Beck (eds.), Künstliche Intelligenz und Robotik: Rechtshandbuch, 2020, 592; *Mielke*, Künstliche Intelligenz in der Justiz, https://legal-tech.de/kuenstliche-intelligenz-in-der-justiz-pilotprojekte/#ki-landschaft (05.02.2026).

[18] *Herberger* NJW 2018, 2825, 2826 et seq.

[19] *Gold/Reuß et al.* (n. 10), 18 et seq.; *Borges* CR 2023, 706, n. 11 et seq.

[20] *Huber/Giesecke* (n. 17), 592; *Funke*, in: Adrian/Kohlhase/Evert/Zwickel (eds.), Digitalisierung von Zivilprozess und Rechtsdurchsetzung, 2022, 235 et seq.

[21] *Huber/Giesecke* (n. 17), 592.

[22] *Gold/Reuß et al.* (n. 10), 33.

[23] *Gold/Reuß et al.* (n. 10), 16 et seq.

[24] *Riehm*, in: Reuß/Windau (eds.), Kolloquien im Wintersemester 2021/2022, 2023, 5.

[25] Working group of the federal states "Legal Tech: Herausforderungen für die Justiz", Abschlussbericht, 10 et seq.

AI in the judiciary. For instance, the E-Justice Council's strategy draws on the EU AI Act's definition of an 'AI system'.[26]

Do other sectors (e. g., finance, healthcare, law enforcement) use distinct definitions of AI? If so, which are the key differences?

The Federal Office for IT Security *(Bundesamt für Sicherheit in der Informationstechnik)* defines artificial intelligence as 'technology and scientific discipline that encompasses several approaches and techniques such as machine learning, machine reasoning and robotics.' According to this definition, AI systems are 'software and hardware systems that use artificial intelligence to act "rationally" in the physical and digital world. Based on perception and analysis of their environment, they act with a certain degree of autonomy to achieve specific goals.'[27] This definition is not only more comprehensive, but also goes significantly further by understanding artificial intelligence more as a field and thus also covering the scientific discipline for researching phenomena that fall under AI.

3. *Strategic Documents on AI and Digitalisation*

Are there official strategic documents (e. g., action plans, government strategies) on the digitalisation of the judiciary that address AI use? Do these documents include concrete timelines for AI implementation? What mechanisms are in place to monitor and evaluate progress toward these goals?

In April 2025, the E-Justice Council — comprising the heads of the federal and state justice administrations and in existence since 2012 — presented a strategy for achieving shared objectives (hereinafter referred to as the E-Justice Council's AI strategy).[28] The document contains seven areas of action, each with different measures:[29]

- Create uniform standards and testing processes in the context of AI in order to generate synergies between the federal government and the states
- Promote flexible use of AI technologies
- Standardise conformity assessment for AI systems
- Identify and implement suitable AI use cases
- Make data usable for AI
- Establish a uniform national AI ecosystem and create a common AI platform
- Strengthen the AI competence of members of the judiciary.

---

[26] E-Justice-Rat (n. 1), 12.

[27] Bundesamt für Sicherheit in der Informationstechnik, Sicherer, robuster und nachvollziehbarer Einsatz von KI, https://www.bsi.bund.de/SharedDocs/Downloads/DE/BSI/KI/Herausforderungen_und_Massnahmen_KI.pdf?__blob=publicationFile&v=6 (05.02.2026).

[28] E-Justice-Rat (n. 1).

[29] E-Justice-Rat (n. 1), 20 et seq.

The implementation of the measures listed is to begin by the end of 2026 at the latest.[30] Monitoring is to be carried out using various indicators (KPIs) to check compliance with defined targets for quantitative (time savings, etc.) and qualitative (e.g. user satisfaction) characteristics.[31]

Prior to this, the final report of the federal states' working group, established in 2017 and entitled 'Legal Tech: Challenges for the Judiciary', had already been presented at the 90th Conference of Ministers of Justice in June 2019.[32]

III. Legal and Regulatory Framework for AI in Civil Justice

1. General Legal Framework

a) Pre-Existing AI Regulations

Before the AI Act, were there legally binding rules on AI use in your jurisdiction? If yes, please describe their scope and key provisions.

The AI Act was the first piece of legislation designed specifically to regulate AI. Prior to its introduction, there were no national laws that explicitly addressed AI. However, legislative initiatives had already been introduced to digitise civil jurisdiction, for example the Act on the Use of Electronic Forms of Communication (BGBl I 2005, No. 18 of 29 March 2005), the Act on the Promotion of Electronic Legal Transactions with the Courts (BGBl I 2013, No. 62 of 16 October 2013)[33] and the Act on the Development and Testing of Online Proceedings in civil justice (BGBl. 2025 I No. 349 of 22 December 2025).

Clearly, AI applications that fall within the scope of these regulations due to their use must be measured against their requirements. However, this does not address the specific challenges posed by AI.

b) Impact of the AI Act

How has the AI Act affected your pre-existing legal framework for AI use in civil justice?

The AI Act, as a special product safety law,[34] sets out the requirements for AI systems and the obligations for operators and providers of AI systems and models. The AI Act pursues a risk-based approach. Whether AI systems used to assist judges are subject to these requirements depends on their specific function:

---

30 E-Justice-Rat (n. 1), 36 et seq.

31 E-Justice-Rat (n. 1), 38.

32 https://www.schleswig-holstein.de/DE/landesregierung/ministerien-behoerden/II/Ministerin/Justizministerkonferenz/Downloads/190605_beschluesse/TOPI_11_Abschlussbericht.pdf?__blob=publicationFile&v=1 (15.1.2026).

33 *Huber/Giesecke* (n. 17), 592 et seq.

34 *Borges* (n. 16) CR 2022, 553, 554.

Article 6 of the AI Act regulates when an AI system is to be classified as high risk. According to Article 6 (2) of the AI Act, all AI systems listed in Annex III to the AI Act are to be classified as high-risk AI systems. According to no. 8a of Annex III, this includes AI systems used by or on behalf of judicial authorities in researching and interpreting facts and the law or to apply the law in concrete cases. This may apply to a wide range of possible AI assistance solutions.[35]

According to Article 6 (3) of the AI Act, AI systems are not considered high-risk under Article 6 (2) in conjunction with Annex III of the AI Act if, among other things, they perform narrow procedural tasks, improve results of a previously completed human activity, or are used only to detect decision-making patterns or deviations without replacing or influencing the human assessment (unverified). Accordingly, mere support systems, such as those used for decision anonymisation and other purely administrative tasks, are not high-risk systems.[36]

German courts must comply with the relevant deployer obligations when using AI systems. Accordingly, courts have to comply with the regulations for deployers of high-risk AI systems if they use AI systems that assist judges in decision making (AI application supporting judges in decision making). This applies all the more for the use of AI systems providing for a fully automated decision making.

If AI systems are used only to facilitate administrative processes, the information and disclosure requirements under Article 50 of the AI Act apply, but only insofar as the AI systems specified therein are concerned.[37] If the judiciary itself (co-)develops AI systems in joint research projects, the provider obligations may also be relevant.[38]

Was the pre-existing framework compatible with the AI Act? If not, which adjustments were required? What are the key differences between the pre-existing regulations and the AI Act?

To date, there are no specific national rules for AI systems, let alone for their use in the justice system. It has therefore not yet been necessary to adapt to the AI Act.

c) *Implementation of the AI Act*

Have legislative or regulatory actions been taken to implement the AI Act in your jurisdiction?

To date (as of January 2026), only a draft bill for a law to implement the AI Act has been presented.[39] Germany has thus missed the deadline specified in Arti-

---

[35] *Biallaß* MMR 2024, 646, 649; *Stürner* GPR 2025, 62, n. 31.

[36] See also recital 61, sentence 4; *Biallaß* MMR 2024, 646, 649; *Stürner* GPR 2025, 62, n. 33.

[37] *Biallaß* MMR 2024, 646, 650.

[38] *Stürner* GPR 2025, 62, n. 30; *Biallaß* MMR 2024, 646, 649.

[39] Draft bill by the Federal Ministry of Digital and Public Administration Draft bill implementing Regulation (EU) 2024/1689 of the European Parliament and of the Council of 13 June

cle 70 (2) of the AI Act, which expired on 2 August 2025, for designating a national notifying authority and a market surveillance authority. The responsible Ministry for Digital and State Modernisation attributes this to the formation of the new government in 2025.[40]

Are there ongoing or planned legislative initiatives related to AI regulation in civil justice?

We are not aware of any such initiatives.

2. AI Governance in the Judiciary

a) Soft-Law Instruments

What soft-law instruments (e.g., guidelines, ethical codes, best practices) apply to AI use in the judiciary? Are these instruments applied in practice? How are they implemented in practice?

The framework for the use of AI in the justice system is provided by the E-Justice Council's AI strategy.[41] The aim is to achieve an uniform assessment of the risks posed by AI systems to be used by the federal states and the federal government, through standardised interpretation practices.[42] In addition, the E-Justice Council's AI strategy is based on existing best practices and strategies, including the European e-Justice Strategy 2024–2028, the Federal Government's AI and data strategies, and the IT Planning Council's strategy for strengthening digital sovereignty in public administration.[43]

Furthermore, the E-Justice Council's AI strategy references the 'Ethics Guidelines for Trustworthy AI' in the EU[44] and the 'Council of Europe Convention on AI'[45] as key reference points for ensuring the trustworthiness of AI systems.[46]

The Federal Office for Information Security *(Bundesamt für Sicherheit in der Informationstechnik, or BSI)* has published several papers on the security and integrity of AI systems. One paper addresses the issue of bias in artificial intelli-

---

2024 laying down harmonised rules on artificial intelligence and amending Regulations (EC) No 300/2008, (EU) No 167/2013, (EU) No 168/2013, (EU) 2018/858, (EU) 2018/1139 and (EU) 2019/2144, as well as Directives 2014/90/EU, (EU) 2016/797 and (EU) 2020/1828 (Regulation on Artificial Intelligence) (Act implementing the AI Regulation).

[40] https://bmds.bund.de/service/gesetzgebungsverfahren/gesetz-zur-durchfuehrung-der-ki-verordnung (13.10.2025).

[41] E-Justice-Rat (n. 1).

[42] E-Justice-Rat (n. 1), 11.

[43] E-Justice-Rat (n. 1), 9.

[44] Ethics guidelines for trustworthy AI, 8.4.2019, https://digital-trategy.ec.europa.eu/en/library/ethics-guidelines-trustworthy-ai (7.12.2025).

[45] CM(2024)52-final – Committee on Artificial Intelligence (CAI) – Council of Europe Framework Convention on Artificial Intelligence and Human Rights, Democracy and the Rule of Law, https://search.coe.int/cm?i=0900001680afb11f (4.12.2025).

[46] E-Justice-Rat (n. 1), 11.

gence and aims to raise awareness of this problem.[47] Another BSI white paper entitled 'Secure, robust and traceable use of AI' presents measures for the security of AI systems.[48]

The Federal Ministry of the Interior and Home Affairs *(Bundesministerium des Inneren und der Heimat)* has also issued guidelines on the use of AI in the federal administration.[49]

b) Data Protection and AI

What measures ensure compliance with data protection regulations (e.g., GDPR[50]) when using AI in the judiciary?

The E-Justice Council's AI strategy states that a data protection impact assessment should be conducted as part of the conformity assessment required under the AI Act.[51] It has not been conclusively clarified whether the individual judge or only their court is the controller within the meaning of the GDPR when an AI system supporting judges in decision-making is used, although there is much to be said for relieving the burden on judges, particularly in light of Article 6 of the ECHR.[52] *Bunes* proposes that the federal states also enshrine this in law.[53] According to the E-Justice Council's AI strategy, the federal and state governments should establish a data governance structure with clearly defined roles and responsibilities with regard to the data processed.[54]

How do national data protection authorities oversee AI use in civil justice?

National data protection authorities only monitor the use of AI by German courts insofar as it is used in administrative matters. Regarding the use of AI systems in the judiciary, Article 74 (8) of the AI Act stipulates that a designated market surveillance authority will be responsible for monitoring.

Specifically: According to § 9 (1) BDSG, the Federal Commissioner for Data Protection *(Bundesdatenschutzbeauftragte)* is responsible for supervising public

---

47 Bundesamt für Sicherheit in der Informationstechnik, Bias in der künstlichen Intelligenz, https://www.bsi.bund.de/SharedDocs/Downloads/DE/BSI/KI/Whitepaper_Bias_KI.pdf?__blob=publicationFile&v=5 (13.10.2025).

48 Bundesamt für Sicherheit in der Informationstechnik (n. 27).

49 Leitlinien für den Einsatz Künstlicher Intelligenz in der Bundesverwaltung, https://www.bmi.bund.de/SharedDocs/downloads/DE/publikationen/themen/moderne-verwaltung/ki/BMI25020-leitlinien-ki-bundesverwaltung.pdf?__blob=publicationFile&v=4 (13.10.2025).

50 Regulation (EU) 2016/679 Of The European Parliament And Of The Council of 27 April 2016 on the protection of natural persons with regard to the processing of personal data and on the free movement of such data, and repealing Directive 95/46/EC (General Data Protection Regulation).

51 E-Justice-Rat (n. 1), 26.

52 *Bunes*, in: Heinze/Steinrötter (eds.), KI und Daten: Digitalregulierung auf dem Höhepunkt?, 2024, 524 et seq.

53 *Bunes* (n. 52), 526.

54 E-Justice-Rat (n. 1), 30.

bodies at the federal level in accordance with data protection law. The respective state commissioners for data protection are responsible for supervising public bodies at state level (see, for example, § 13 HDSIG and § 18 NDSG). The same principle applies to compliance with data protection requirements when using AI systems.[55] However, pursuant to Art. 55 (3) GDPR, the supervisory authorities are not responsible for supervising the processing carried out by courts acting in their judicial capacity.

Supervision is limited to the administrative tasks of the courts that do not fall within the scope of judicial capacity.[56] The provision is intended to protect judicial independence, which is why core judicial activity and judicial decision-making are covered in any case.[57] The ECJ interprets the exception to supervision very broadly: even the disclosure of court files to journalists for reporting purposes is considered part of judicial capacity.[58]

With regard to data protection compliance, judicial activity is therefore subject only to self-regulation by the judiciary.[59] However, no corresponding body has been established within the judiciary in Germany, so that a lack of control can be assumed here.[60] There are many scenarios for AI applications in civil courts that are not subject to external supervision. Any AI applications used to draft proposed judgements, evaluate written pleadings, or otherwise prepare judgements will fall under the exception of Article 55 (3) GDPR. As the ECJ has interpreted the concept of judicial capacity so broadly that it considers even communication measures by the courts to be related to judicial activity and as it believes that external supervision of such measures could jeopardise judicial independence,[61] even AI systems used to anonymise judgments or written pleadings are likely to be subject only to self-regulation by the judiciary. Because anonymisation prepares for publication, it is also part of the courts' communication policy.

According to Article 74 (8), sentence 1 of the AI Act, a special market surveillance authority shall be designated in order to supervise AI systems used in the judicial field (as defined in Annex III No. 8 AI Act), regardless of the designation of the general market surveillance authority under Article 70. In order to fulfil this requirement, the draft bill concerning the enforcement of the AI Act (*Refer-*

---

[55] Position paper of the Konferenz der unabhängigen Datenschutzaufsichtsbehörden des Bundes und der Länder from May 3rd 2024, https://www.datenschutzkonferenz-online.de/media/dskb/20240503_DSK_Positionspapier_Zustaendigkeiten_KI_VO.pdf (03.05.2024), 2.

[56] VG Mainz, ZD 2021, 59.

[57] Paal/Pauly/*Körffer*, 4th ed. 2026, VO (EU) 2016/679 (DSGVO) Art. 55 n. 5 et seqq.; Taeger/Gabel/*Grittmann/Böhm*, 5th ed. 2026, DS-GVO Art. 55 n. 12; Ehmann/Selmayr/*Selmayr*, 3rd Editon 2024, DS-GVO Art. 55 n. 14.

[58] EuGH – C-245/20 (X ua/Autoriteit Persoonsgegevens) (Zuständigkeitsbeschränkung Datenschutzaufsichtsbehörde durch justizielle Tätigkeit) = NJW 2022, 2321.

[59] Paal/Pauly/*Körffer* (n. 57), DS-GVO Art. 55 n. 6.

[60] Paal/Pauly/*Körffer* (n. 57), DS-GVO Art. 55 n. 6; Ehmann/Selmayr/*Selmayr* (n. 57), DS-GVO Art. 55 n. 15.

[61] EuGH, NJW 2022, 2321.

entenentwurf zum Durchsetzungsgesetz der KI-Verordnung) proposes the establishment of an independent AI market surveillance chamber *(Unabhängige KI-Marktüberwachungskammer)* for high-risk AI systems within the meaning of Article 74 (8) sentence 1 AI Act under the umbrella of the Federal Network Agency *(Bundesnetzagentur or BNetzA)*. The BNetzA is also designated as the general market surveillance authority under Article 70 (1) AI Act.[62]

However, it is controversial whether a newly created office fulfils the requirements of Article 74 (8) sentence 1 of the AI Act.[63] Due to their expertise in this area, the supervisory authorities under the GDPR or the Law Enforcement Directive (LED)[64] or another authority designated under the conditions of Art. 41 et seq. LED are also proposed (in Germany: Federal Data Protection Commissioner and State Data Protection Commissioners). Reference is also made to the special expert knowledge of the data protection authorities with regard to matters sensitive to fundamental rights.[65]

However, according to Article 74 (8) sentence 2 of the AI Act, market surveillance activities must not in any way affect the independence of judicial authorities or otherwise influence their actions in the course of their judicial activities. In the context of proportionality, the market surveillance authority must take this prohibition of interference or influence into account in every market surveillance measure.[66]

Have there been any cases of data protection violations linked to AI use in civil proceedings?

We are not aware of any such cases.

---

[62] Draft bill by the Federal Ministry of Digital and Public Administration Draft bill implementing Regulation (EU) 2024/1689 of the European Parliament and of the Council of 13 June 2024 laying down harmonised rules on artificial intelligence and amending Regulations (EC) No 300/2008, (EU) No 167/2013, (EU) No 168/2013, (EU) 2018/858, (EU) 2018/1139 and (EU) 2019/2144, as well as Directives 2014/90/EU, (EU) 2016/797 and (EU) 2020/1828 (Regulation on Artificial Intelligence) (Act implementing the AI Regulation).

[63] In favour of allowing a previously unnamed body to be named: BeckOK KI-Recht/*Djeffal*, 4th ed. 01.11.2025, KI-VO Art. 74 n. 55 et seq.; Martini/Wendehorst/*Hartmann,* 2nd ed. 2026, KI-VO Art. 74 n. 15; In opposition: *Wünschelbaum* MMR 2025, 259, 261.

[64] Directive (EU) 2016/680 of the European Parliament and of the Council of 27 April 2016 on the protection of natural persons with regard to the processing of personal data by competent authorities for the purposes of the prevention, investigation, detection or prosecution of criminal offences or the execution of criminal penalties, and on the free movement of such data, and repealing Council Framework Decision 2008/977/JHA.

[65] *Wünschelbaum* CR 41 (2025), 362, 363; Martini/Wendehorst/*Hartmann,* (n. 63), KI-VO Art. 74 n. 15.

[66] BeckOK KI-Recht/*Djeffal* (n. 63), KI-VO Art. 74 n. 59.

c) Security of AI Systems

What safeguards are in place to ensure the security and integrity of AI systems in civil justice?

The use of AI systems in German courts[67] to date has been limited to purely administrative functions and, at most, supporting judges in their decision-making and preparation. Human control is therefore the key safeguard.

The E-Justice Council's AI strategy also emphasises the central role of humans in decision-making: decision-making authority should always remain under human control.[68] This means that human control is crucial in securing AI systems in civil justice. In addition, non-discriminatory training data must be guaranteed in order to ensure the right to a fair trial (and other rights).[69]

Are there specific national regulations or standards for securing AI tools used in the judiciary?

We are not aware of any specific legal requirements for the security of AI tools used in the judiciary. However, courts that use or wish to use AI systems can adhere to the various soft law instruments issued by national and European authorities. The E-Justice Council's AI strategy is once again central here.[70] The BSI white paper 'Secure, robust and traceable use of AI' explicitly provides for measures to ensure the security of AI systems.[71]

d) Liability for AI-Related Errors

How is liability regulated for errors made by AI systems in the judiciary? Are there special liability frameworks for AI-related mistakes in civil proceedings?

To date, no special liability rules have been created in German law for the use of AI by the judiciary. This issue is also not addressed in the E-Justice Council's AI strategy.[72] Various forms of AI-specific liability have already been explored in anticipation of the adoption of the AI Liability Directive, including strict liability for developers, deployers and users of AI systems.[73] However, this has not yet been introduced into national law either. Therefore, liability for errors caused by AI systems used in the judiciary is governed by existing general liability provisions. These are outlined below. To this end, a fictitious case is used as a basis, in

---

[67] For an overview of 19 pilot projects by 2022, see Working group "Einsatz von KI und algorithmischen Systemen in der Justiz" (n. 3), s. Appendix I.
[68] E-Justice-Rat (n. 1), 4.
[69] *Gold/Reuß et al.* (n. 10), 356; E-Justice-Rat (n. 1), 30.
[70] E-Justice-Rat (n. 1).
[71] Bundesamt für Sicherheit in der Informationstechnik (n. 27).
[72] E-Justice-Rat (n. 1).
[73] *Bomhard/Siglmüller* RDi 2022, 506, 507; *Spindler*, CR 2015, 766, 775.

which the use of an AI system in civil proceedings results in an erroneous judgement, causing financial loss for the affected party.

Claims for damages based on contractual provisions or on the principles of *culpa in contrahendo* are excluded in this case. There is no contractual relationship between the parties to the proceedings and the judiciary or the court. According to the prevailing opinion, the procedural legal relationship *(Prozessrechtsverhältnis)* does not give rise to a legal obligation under § 241 (2) of the German Civil Code (BGB).[74] Therefore, tortious claims are primarily considered, with particular reference to public and state liability *(Amts- und Staatshaftung)* (see below aa).

Furthermore, software constitutes a product according to Article 4 No. 1 of the new European Product Liability Directive[75] (see bb).

Finally, there is a right to compensation for any damage caused by unlawful data processing by an AI system in accordance with Article 82 of the GDPR.

aa) Tort Liability and Official Liability

If AI is used by a judge and a party to the proceedings suffers damage as a result of an error made by this AI, the body in whose service the judge works is liable in accordance with the principles of official and state liability.[76] The employer according to § 3 DRiG is the Federal Republic of Germany for the Federal Courts *(Bundesgerichte)* or the federal states. Liability for judicial misconduct will, in most cases, be excluded by the ruling judge privilege under § 839 (2) sentence 1 BGB, provided that the AI was not only used for administrative tasks.

In the event of misconduct by a public official – in this case, a judge – the public law entity *(Rechtsträger)* is indirectly liable, as the official's liability is transferred to the public law entity in accordance with § 839 (1) sentence 1 German Civil Code *(Bürgerliches Gesetzbuch, or BGB)* and Article 34 of the German constitution *(Grundgesetz)*.[77] A claim under § 839 (1) German Civil Code (in conjunction with Article 34 of the German constitution) requires that a public official culpably ('intentionally or negligently') violates their official duties towards the injured party. A judge's official duties towards the parties to the proceedings arise from the right to justice, and consist of the required acceleration of the proceedings and the decision within a reasonable timeframe.[78] Additionally, as with any civil servant, it is the duty of the judge to exercise their office conscien-

---

[74] Some of the literature takes the opposite view. In any case, the highest court has not yet based any claims for damages on a breach of such duties; for the whole topic see: *Riehm*, BeckOGK BGB, BGB § 280 n. 88 with further references.

[75] Directive (EU) 2024/2853 of the European Parliament and of the Council of 23 October 2024 on liability for defective products and repealing Council Directive 85/374/EEC.

[76] MüKoBGB/*Papier/Shirvani*, 9th ed. 2024, BGB § 839 n. 432; BGH, NVwZ 1992, 298.

[77] *Thomas*, BeckOGK BGB, BGB § 839 n. 19; MüKoBGB/*Papier/Shirvani*, (n. 76), BGB § 839 n. 9.

[78] BGH, NJW 2011, 1072.

tiously and in accordance with the law towards any third party.[79] If a judge uses AI systems and adopts the results as their own when reaching a verdict or justifying a judgement,[80] the judge remains responsible and must carefully review the results.

According to § 839 (1), sentence 2 of the German Civil Code (BGB), official liability is subsidiary, i. e. it only applies if compensation cannot be obtained in any other way.[81] Other compensation options include making claims against third parties, such as the manufacturer of the AI system. However, liability can also be avoided by exercising certain rights, such as contesting or terminating the contract.[82] The claim for public liability is also excluded if possible legal remedies are not exhausted, § 839 (3) BGB.[83] The claim would be excluded if the failure to exercise the legal remedy is culpable.[84]

A particular feature of § 839 (2) BGB is that judges are only liable if a breach of official duty occurs in the judgment of a legal matter and if the breach of duty constitutes a criminal offence *(Spruchrichterprivileg)*. The primary offences to be considered are accepting benefits under § 331 (2) German Criminal Code (StGB), bribery pursuant to § 332 (2) German Criminal Code (StGB) and perversion of justice pursuant to § 339 German Criminal Code (StGB), and, where applicable, insult pursuant to § 185 German Criminal Code (StGB).[85] § 839 (2) German Civil Code (BGB) protects the judicial decision itself in order to ensure legal certainty and legal peace.[86] According to the Federal Court of Justice *(Bundesgerichtshof, or BGH)*, this privilege applies 'to judgement in legal matters' and therefore also to measures intended to 'establish the basis for decisions on the merits'.[87] Judgments that fall under the ruling judge privilege are all 'judgement-representing findings' *(urteilsvertretende Erkenntnisse)* that at least conclude the instance and have potential *res judicata* effect *(der materiellen Rechtskraft fähig)*.[88] If the judge adopts the result of an AI application supporting judges in decision-making by using it in the assessment of the factual or legal situation, the evaluation of court files or the preparation of his written statement, public liability under § 839 (2) BGB is ruled out.[89] According to the above, this applies even in cases where a judge adopts an incorrect output without checking it due to gross negligence.

---

[79] PWW-BGB/*Kramarz*, 20th ed. 2025, BGB § 839 n. 30.

[80] Cf. *Quack*, Automation zivilrechtlicher Entscheidungsfindung, 2025, 202.

[81] MüKoBGB/*Papier/Shirvani*, (Fn. 76), BGB § 839 n. 373; PWW-BGB/*Kramarz*, (n. 79), BGB § 839 n. 40.

[82] MüKoBGB/*Papier/Shirvani*, (Fn. 76), BGB § 839 n. 373.

[83] BGH, NJW 2013, 3237.

[84] PWW-BGB/*Kramarz*, (Fn. 79), BGB § 839 n. 50; BeckOK BGB/*Kümper*, 76th ed. 1.11.2025, BGB § 839 n. 192.

[85] *Thomas*, BeckOGK BGB, BGB § 839 n. 671.

[86] *Thomas*, BeckOGK BGB, BGB § 839 n. 658.

[87] BGH, NJW 1968, 989.

[88] BGH, NJW 2005, 436.

[89] For example: OLGA at OLG Stuttgart: *Spoenle* (n. 8).

However, if AI were to be used to support judicial administration tasks, the privilege of the ruling judge would not apply.[90] However, according to the Federal Court of Justice (BGH), a special liability standard should apply to judges to ensure judicial independence is preserved. Under this standard, a judge's conduct is only considered a breach of duty if it is unreasonable.[91]

In proceedings conducted by judicial officers *(Rechtspfleger)*, the privilege under § 839 (2) BGB does not apply, but the standard of liability is similar to that for judges due to their factual independence, § 9 Judicial Officers Act *(Rechtspflegergesetz, or RPflG)*.[92]

If a fully automated decision-making system issues a legally binding judgement, § 839 (2) German Civil Code (BGB) does not apply. This is because, in such a case, the breach of duty was not committed by a (human) official *(Beamter)* within the meaning of the provision, whose independence would have to be protected.

In addition to claims for public liability according to § 839 (1) German Civil Code (BGB), claims may arise from expropriation-like interference[93] *(enteignungsgleicher Eingriff)* or sacrifice *(Aufopferungsanspruch)*[94]. However, according to the Federal Court of Justice, the ruling judge privilege *(Spruchrichterprivileg)* also precludes such claims.[95]

bb) Product Liability Law (Produkthaftungsgesetz)

Product liability law does not apply to the example case described above. The damage to persons, property or data required under Article 6 of the new Product Liability Directive[96] will generally not be a concern in civil proceedings. Should this nevertheless be the case, the manufacturer of the system may be held liable.

If the judiciary is involved in developing an AI system, it is questionable whether they can be held liable as the manufacturer. Recital 26 suggests that the Directive only addresses economic operators acting in the course of a commercial activity. The term 'commercial activity' is not further defined in the Directive. In any case, the judiciary would be performing a public task when developing an AI system for its own use. This is not comparable to the examples of commercial activity mentioned in Recital 26.

---

90 *Thomas*, BeckOGK BGB, BGB § 839 n. 668.
91 BGH, NJW 2011, 1072; OLG Frankfurt a. M., BeckRS 2013, 9197.
92 *Thomas*, BeckOGK BGB, BGB § 839 n. 669.
93 PWW-BGB/*Kramarz*, (n. 79), BGB § 839 n. 6.
94 PWW-BGB/*Kramarz*, (n. 79), BGB § 839 n. 7.
95 BGH – III ZR 72/65 = NJW 1968, 989; *Thomas* (n. 77), n. 659, 1248.
96 Directive (EU) 2024/2853 of the European Parliament and of the Council of 23 October 2024 on liability for defective products and repealing Council Directive 85/374/EEC.

IV. AI in Practice: Specific Issues in Civil Justice

1. Case Law and Judicial Precedents

a) Existing Case Law

Have courts issued rulings on AI use in civil justice? If yes, please describe key cases and their impact. Have constitutional or supreme courts addressed the compatibility of AI use with fundamental rights?

We were unable to find any court rulings relating to the use of AI in civil justice. Although not all court rulings are published, we assume that, if such a ruling existed, it would still have been published.

There have also been no constitutional rulings yet. This is probably because the use of AI has so far been limited to pilot projects involving administrative or, at most, decision-making support.[97]

Until now, courts have only had to deal with the role of AI in civil proceedings from a different perspective: its use by solicitors.[98] This is difficult to transfer to its use by the courts themselves, as the main issue was the professional diligence standard.[99]

2. AI's Role, Benefits, and Risks

a) Expected Benefits and Functions

What are the anticipated benefits of AI in civil justice? What functions can AI serve in civil litigation (e. g., case management, legal research, decision-making assistance)?

The E-Justice Council's AI strategy cites the following advantages of using AI systems:

- Increased efficiency and effectiveness of the judiciary,
- Improved access to justice, and
- Greater coherence and consistency in civil law jurisprudence.[100]

Efficiency gains can be achieved in terms of time and by reducing complexity, especially in mass proceedings.[101] The need to increase the efficiency[102] and effectiveness of the German judiciary in mass proceedings is often illustrated in

---

[97] See also working group "Einsatz von KI und algorithmischen Systemen in der Justiz" (n. 4), Appendix I et seq.

[98] AG Köln – 312 F 130/25 = IBRRS 2025, 1928; *Schäffer*, Wenn der Richter halluziniert: US-Gerichte erstmals bei KI-Einsatz erwischt, https://rsw.beck.de/aktuell/daily/meldung/detail/richter-nutzt-KI-urteil-halluzination-usa (28.08.2025).

[99] Cf. *Braegelmann* RDi 2025, 214.

[100] E-Justice-Rat (n. 1), 15.

[101] *Gold/Reuß et al.* (n. 10), 4 et seq.

[102] *Stürner* GPR 2025, 62, 69.

Germany using the example of diesel scandal cases.[103] In addition, AI is intended to strengthen access to justice, for example by using chatbots to provide information or explain court proceedings.[104] The use of AI also promises the advantage of more consistent and affordable application of the law.[105]

b) Risks to Fundamental Rights

Which constitutional principles or fundamental rights could be affected by AI use in civil justice (think of e.g. transparency / public justice; directness (immediacy), adversarial proceedings (principle of the party presentation), principle of the equal treatment, independence and impartiality of judges)? How can these risks be mitigated?

aa) Human Dignity, Article 1 (1) German Constitution

According to the case law of the Federal Constitutional Court *(Bundesverfassungsgericht)*, the guarantee of human dignity is infringed when a citizen is 'degraded to a mere object of state power' and his or her status as a subject is called into question, or when state action expresses contempt for the value accorded to him or her as a human being or person.[106] The application of law violates human dignity if it is both objectively and subjectively arbitrary, i.e. if it is objectively unjustifiable and subjectively based on irrelevant motives.[107] This applies regardless of whether the law is applied by a human judge with or without the support of an AI system. If the AI system is unable to safeguard fundamental rights and ensure the proper application of the law independently, this deficit must be compensated for by human control and intervention to prevent arbitrary decisions and ensure that the threshold for violating human dignity is not crossed.

However, some scholars consider fully automated decisions to be incompatible with human dignity, precisely because human judges are not involved. Such systems could only view people as reference objects for data relevant to the decision, rather than perceiving them as human beings. Such systems would therefore only be used if all parties involved in the proceedings had agreed to it voluntarily.[108]

bb) General Principle of Equal Treatment, Article 3 German Constitution

Article 3 (1) of the German constitution (GG) establishes the general principle of equal treatment. Article 3 (1) German constitution (GG) is binding on all state

---

103 *Gold/Reuß et al.* (n. 10), 6 et seq.; *Lerch/Valdini* NJW 2023, 420; *Fries*, Frauke richtet, https://rsw.beck.de/aktuell/daily/magazin/detail/frauke-richtet (last accessed: 12.03.2025).

104 E-Justice-Rat (n. 1), 39.

105 *Bernzen* RDi 2023, 132, 138.

106 BVerfG – 2 BvF 1/69, 2 BvR 629/68, 308/69 = NJW 1971, 275.

107 Dürig/Herzog/Scholz/*Herdegen*, 108th EL August 2025, GG Art. 1 n. 120.

108 *Bernzen* RDi 2023, 132.

authorities, including the judiciary as well as the other state powers.[109] Essentially similar situations must be treated in the same way, and essentially different situations must be treated differently.[110] Civil court decisions can result in cases being judged the same way or differently from previous ones. Such equal or unequal treatment is justified if the decisions fall within the scope of what is permitted by law.[111] The reasons given for decisions provide insight into whether there is a sufficient objective reason for equal or unequal treatment in relation to other situations. Furthermore, the de facto binding effect of Federal Court rulings on lower courts ensures the consistent application of the law.[112]

When self-learning AI systems are used which deliver decisions and reasonings based on probability calculations, there is a risk that the factors that are actually decisive for the decision are non-legal. Upon review, it may become apparent that the decision falls within the bounds of what is legally permissible, and that the reasoning is convincing. However, this is merely a pretext that conceals the true cause of the judgement.[113] This problem arises primarily in AI systems that make decisions themselves, thus replacing the decision of a human judge (*Gold/Reuß et al.* aptly refer to this as 'decision-replacing use')[114].[115]

However, this risk also exists when AI systems are used to support decision-making by human judges: for example, an AI system that searches databases for relevant decisions in preparation for a judgement could select different judgements in similar cases or suppress a potentially decisive judgement. If the court bases its decision on this, it may result in unjustified unequal treatment. The same applies even more so to cases in which AI systems submit decision proposals.[116]

Furthermore, the performance of the system in question is important too. Situations that are unequal may be treated equally, particularly if the AI system is unable to grasp the complexity of the situation being assessed. For example, this may occur when using rule-based (expert) systems if the legally relevant facts cannot be fully reproduced.[117]

It also seems problematic that the AI system itself can discriminate based on the underlying training data.[118] If old judgements used to train an AI system exhibit systematic unequal treatment (without objective reason), e. g. to the detri-

---

[109] BeckOK GG/*Kischel*, 63rd ed. 15.09.2025, GG Art. 3 n. 10; Dürig/Herzog/Scholz/P. *Kirchhof*, 108th EL August 2025, GG Art. 3 Abs. 1 n. 281.

[110] BeckOK GG/*Kischel* (n. 109), GG Art. 3 n. 15 et seq.

[111] Cf. Dürig/Herzog/Scholz/P. *Kirchhof* (Fn. 109), GG Art. 3 Abs. 1 n. 442; BVerfG, NJW 1982, 694, 695.

[112] Dürig/Herzog/Scholz/P. *Kirchhof* (Fn. 109), GG Art. 3 Abs. 1 n. 442.

[113] *Gold/Reuß et al.* (n. 10), 145 et seq.

[114] The terminology originates from the report by *Gold/Reuß et al.* (n. 10), 9.

[115] *Gold/Reuß et al.* (n. 10), 131.

[116] *Gold/Reuß et al.* (n. 10), 109 et seq.

[117] *Gold/Reuß et al.* (n. 10), 106.

[118] *Gold/Reuß et al.* (n. 10), 109.

ment of one gender, and gender is a parameter for the AI system's probability calculations, this discrimination could be adopted.[119] Here, too, the risk of discrimination can arise not only in fully automated decision-making, but also when judges adopt decision proposals made by such AI.

The risks described can at least be reduced by explainable AI. For example, if the AI can show which characteristics it bases a decision or decision proposal on, it is possible to check whether the characteristic is a legally valid consideration.

cc) Judges as Judicial Power and Judicial Independence Pursuant to Article 92, 97 German Constitution and Right to a Lawful Judge Pursuant to Article 101 (1) sentence 2 German Constitution

According to *Article 92* of the German constitution (GG), judicial power is vested in judges. When considering whether this provision precludes the use of AI systems in civil justice, it is important to distinguish between two fundamentally different types of AI system use:

– Of particular concern is an application in which fully automated decision-making takes place, i.e. decisions by human judges would be replaced ('fully automated decision-making'). If Article 92 of the German constitution assigned judicial power to human judges, such use of AI systems would be inadmissible from the outset. This is the prevailing opinion.[120] However, this question is not trivial. The creators of the German constitution certainly did not anticipate the technological development that we are investigating here. *Gold/Reuß et al.* conclude that fully automated decision-making is not ruled out from the outset, but transfer the qualification criteria for judges derived by the Federal Constitutional Court[121] from Article 92 GG to the use of fully automated decision-making: Accordingly, the systems must be factual independent, impartial and competent.[122] These requirements cannot yet be met by information technology systems.[123]

Even if one assumes that Article 92 German constitution does not presuppose human judges from the outset, it seems questionable whether AI systems based on large language models can ever fulfil these requirements. It has already been explained above[124] that such AI systems generate output differently to a human legal scholar applying the methodological requirements of German legal science, i.e. interpretation and subsumption. This means that they lack the characteristic

---

119 *Gold/Reuß et al.* (n. 10), 109.

120 *Bernzen* (n. 105), 134; Working group "Einsatz von KI und algorithmischen Systemen in der Justiz" (n. 4), 6; *Biallaß* in: Ory/Weth, jurisPK-ERV Volume 1, 3rd ed., Chapter 8.1 (01.09.2025), n. 274; BGH – VI ZR 70/62 (Düsseldorf) = NJW 1963, 953; *Enders* JA 2018, 721, 723; *Nink*, Justiz und Algorithmen, 2021, 261 et seq.; *Quack* (n. 80), 250; *Schnabl* SchiedsVZ 2024, 269, 271; *Stürner* (n. 35), 68; *Riehm* (n. 24), 15.

121 BVerfGE 17, 252 (259 et seq.); 21, 139 (146).

122 *Gold/Reuß et al.* (n. 10), 162 et seq.

123 *Wolff*, Algorithmen als Richter, 2022, 121 et seq.; *Gold/Reuß et al.* (n. 10), 174.

124 See IV.2.b).

of professional competence. Against this background, the use of AI systems for fully automated decision-making is conceivable only in a type of preliminary proceedings that could be designed similarly to a order for payment procedure *(Mahnverfahren)*, but not in a separate instance.[125] But even here, it would have to be ensured that the system is developed with the involvement of judges in order to comply with the assignment of judicial functions to the judiciary pursuant to Article 92 German constitution.[126]

– The use of AI systems to support decision-making is less problematic. This is because Article 92 of the German constitution only concerns the assignment of jurisdiction to judges, not the manner in which they perform their duties. Nevertheless, the support must not be so pronounced that the AI system effectively takes over the decision, while the human judge is only formally responsible for the decision.

Article 97 German constitution guarantees the independence of judges. If the term 'judge' in the German constitution is understood to mean only human judges, the complete transfer of decision-making to an information technology system is incompatible with this provision.[127] If this requirement is not imposed, such use may be permissible if it is ensured that there is no risk of irrelevant influence (e.g. by IT service providers or the administration) on evaluative decisions that have already been incorporated into the system during the development process.[128]

The same applies to the use of an AI system in a purely supportive role. Furthermore, the use of an AI system to support decision-making must be voluntary.[129] Because judicial independence is also non-negotiable, judges must not bind themselves, which could occur through "automation bias" or the "default effect".[130] Appropriate measures must therefore be taken to raise awareness in order to ensure compliance.[131]

Article 101 (1) sentence 2 German constitution also establishes the right to a lawful judge. However, this does not fundamentally preclude the use of AI, as long as it is ensured that a judge who uses AI can check and correct its results.[132]

dd) Right to a Fair Hearing

Article 103 (1) German constitution guarantees the right to a fair hearing. This includes the right of a party to the proceedings to be informed of facts relevant to

---

125 For details, see *Gold/Reuß et al.* (n. 10), 175 et seq.

126 *Gold/Reuß et al.* (n. 10), 175 et seq.

127 See the above comments regarding Article 97 for more information on this issue.

128 Cf. *Gold/Reuß et al.* (n. 10), 196; *Wolff* (n. 123), 163 et seq.

129 *Gold/Reuß et al.* (n. 10), 209 et seq.; *Bernzen* (n. 105), 137.

130 *Gold/Reuß et al.* (n. 10), 90 et seq., 202 et seq.

131 *Bernzen* RDi 2023, 132, 137; *Gold/Reuß et al.* (n. 10), 202 et seq.

132 *Gold/Reuß et al.* (n. 10), 223.

the decision[133], the right to express their views,[134] and the right to have those views considered.[135]

Information technology systems are reaching their limits with the current state of technology. In particular, it is difficult to guarantee that these systems themselves will always ensure that statements are adequately assessed. Such systems can therefore only be used to fully automate judicial decisions in cases where the facts relevant to the decision are highly formalised, so that the parties' submissions can be anticipated. In addition, it must be clear that the application of the law has been achieved taking into account the facts of the case. This requires a form of explainable AI. Any use of an AI system in a purely supportive role must be designed in such a way that judges can compensate for weaknesses in the consideration of the facts of the case by intervening themselves.[136]

ee) Judicial Obligation to State Reasons

The judicial obligation to state reasons is based on § 313 (1) No. 6 of the German Code of Civil Procedure (ZPO).[137] It finds its constitutional basis in the requirement for transparency as an expression of the principle of the rule of law under Article 20 (3) German constitution.[138] The obligation to state reasons includes the requirement for reasoning to be clear and comprehensible. It is questionable whether an AI system capable of fully automated decision-making can meet these requirements. While it is true that AI-based text generators are adept at producing such explanations, they do not necessarily reflect the actual considerations that led to the decision. However, the reasoning must reflect the actual considerations that led to the decision. Even a human judge would not fulfil the obligation to provide reasons if they provided reasons that appeared consistent on the surface but were actually guided by different considerations. Nevertheless, it is doubtful that this connection between the decision and the reasoning actually exists in the case of an AI-supported text generator that creates text based on probable word sequences. In any case, the processes leading to the justification must be explainable.

[133] BeckOK GG/*Radtke*, 63rd ed. 15.6.2025, GG Art. 103 n. 8.
[134] BeckOK GG/*Radtke*, 63rd ed. 15.6.2025, GG Art. 103 n. 11.
[135] BeckOK GG/*Radtke*, 63rd ed. 15.6.2025, GG Art. 103 n. 13.
[136] Cf. *Gold/Reuß et al.* (n. 10), 232 et seq.
[137] *Huber/Giesecke* (n. 17), n. 37.
[138] *Gold/Reuß et al.* (n. 10), 137 et seq.

3. Fully Automated Decision-Making

a) Legality of Fully Automated Adjudication

Does your legal system permit fully automated judicial decision-making in any civil cases (i.e., "judge-robots" performing adjudicative functions)? If yes, what preconditions and accountability mechanisms apply? In particular, does the availability of a full (de novo) appellate review before a human judge suffice to allow AI-based adjudication?

There are no legal regulations that permit or prohibit fully automated court decisions in civil proceedings. In the absence of a specific legal or constitutional basis, such decisions must be assessed against the general legal framework for civil court proceedings:

The constitutional requirements were discussed in detail in the explanations to IV.2.b). That said, the admissibility of a fully automated decision that concludes a legal instance depends primarily on whether the term 'judge' in Articles 92 and 97 of the German constitution presupposes a human judge. The answer to this question is inconsistent in legal literature. For the purposes of this discussion, it is assumed that this is the case. In this case, a fully automated court decision would only be conceivable as one element of a procedure in which a review by a human judge could be conducted without significant effort from the parties involved. One possible model for such a procedure is the order for payment procedure *(Mahnverfahren)*, which allows for an objection to be lodged under § 694 ZPO, leading to contentious proceedings being conducted. Therefore, reviewing an automated decision only in an appellate court is insufficient.[139]

Furthermore, some consider fully automated decision-making to be incompatible with the guarantee of human dignity under Article 1 (1) German constitution, unless all parties involved have given their consent.[140]

From a data protection perspective, automated decision-making would still require a legal basis in national legislation for permission under Article 22 (2) lit. b GDPR, which permits such processing for automated court decisions.

It should also be noted that, in addition to their conflict resolution function, civil proceedings, especially in higher courts, have the task of developing the law.[141] Whether this task could be performed by automated systems is debatable. In any case, it should not be performed by automated systems, in order to ensure that assessments concerning human coexistence remain the responsibility of humans. Consequently, the working group of the German Federal States on 'Legal Tech: Challenges for the Judiciary' has concluded that automated decision-making should be prohibited in higher courts.[142]

---

139 Dürig/Herzog/Scholz/*Hillgruber*, GG Art. 92 n. 56.

140 *Bernzen* RDi 2023, 132; *Schnabl* SchiedsVZ 2024, 269.

141 Cf. Dürig/Herzog/Scholz/*Hillgruber*, GG Art. Art. 97 n. 71

142 Working group of the federal states "Legal Tech: Herausforderungen für die Justiz" (n. 25), 65.

b) Appeal Mechanisms for AI-based decisions

Is there a specific appeal mechanism for parties challenging AI-generated decisions? How does this process differ from traditional judicial appeals?

There is currently no such proceeding.

c) Party Autonomy and AI-Based Online Courts

Could parties opt for fully automated online courts in certain cases (e. g., small claims, order for payment proceedings, commercial disputes, family law, court operated public registers)?

To date, the German Code of Civil Proceeding (ZPO) does not provide for a fully automated proceeding in online courts. However, there is already a largely automated order for payment procedure, although this is not powered by AI.[143]

What legal and procedural safeguards would be required?

A potential approach for an AI-based online court could be based on the rules of the order for payment procedure. The order for payment procedure is already seen as a possible scenario for autonomous AI decision-making.[144] The AI-based online court could thus function as a court of first instance. It would even have the advantage over the order for payment procedure of conducting a substantive review.[145] This would allow a title to be obtained quickly and effectively, at least in simple cases with few facts and legal issues.[146] If one party disagrees with the outcome, a transition to the usual jurisdiction could be provided for, which, as in the case of the order for payment procedure, would involve only minimal effort for those seeking justice.[147] The automated issuance of an enforcement order could also be attributed to the debtor's own responsibility.[148]

Are there any mandatory automated online courts?

There are no mandatory automated online courts in Germany.

4. Transparency and Accountability

a) Transparency and Explainability

What transparency requirements apply to AI algorithms used in civil justice?

Constitutional transparency requirements for the use of AI by the judiciary arise from the principle of the rule of law and the principle of democracy, Article 20 (3)

143 Working group "Einsatz von KI und algorithmischen Systemen in der Justiz" (n. 4), 41.
144 Working group "Einsatz von KI und algorithmischen Systemen in der Justiz" (n. 4), 41.
145 *Quack* (n. 80), 251.
146 *Gold/Reuß et al.* (n. 10), 174 et seq.
147 *Quack* (n. 80), 258.
148 *Huber/Giesecke* (n. 17), n. 59.

German constitution. According to this, it is necessary for the judiciary, as a state body, to disclose that AI systems are used in decision-making and to explain the system functions and specific use cases in such a way that this information is publicly accessible.[149]

It is not necessary to publish the source code unless there is a particularly compelling interest in doing so, e. g. because significant doubts have arisen about the trustworthiness of an AI system that has been deployed.[150] These information obligations are derived, on the one hand, from the constitutional requirement for transparency under Article 20 (3) German constitution. On the other hand, they also arise from the right of access under data protection law pursuant to Article 15 (h) of the GDPR, provided that personal data has been processed.[151]

According to Article 50 (4) sub-para. 2 sentence 1 of the AI Act, those who deploy AI systems for text generation or manipulation must disclose the artificial generation or manipulation of the text if it is published in the public interest. According to Art. 50 (4) sub-para. 2, sentence 2 of the AI Act, this obligation does not apply if the AI-generated content has undergone human review or editorial control, and a natural or legal person holds editorial responsibility for its publication. The labelling requirement would thus apply at least to judgements in which an AI system has generated or revised the text or passages thereof. For example, the AI applications Ocos[152] and FRAUKE,[153] or the AI tool for mass proceedings at the Regional Court Kiel *(Landgericht Kiel)*[154] create proposed judgements from preformulated text modules. However, in all examples, the judge retains control over the text and is responsible for combining the text modules into a complete text.

Are there specific requirements for explaining AI-generated decisions?

There are no specific legal regulations for AI-generated decisions. However, an AI-generated decision must be measured in particular against the requirements of the judicial obligation to state reasons. See the comments under IV.2.b) above.

In particular, the reasons for the decision must be sufficiently comprehensible, regardless of whether the AI system only generates decision proposals that must be adopted by the judge or whether it is used autonomously as a decision-making authority.[155] One obstacle here is the lack of explainability in AI systems with a black box effect. An AI system that makes autonomous decisions must then at

---

149 *Gold/Reuß et al.* (n. 10), 147.

150 *Gold/Reuß et al.* (n. 10), 147 et seq.

151 *Gold/Reuß et al.* (n. 10), 148, 321.

152 *Zarychta*, Künstliche Intelligenz soll Richter entlasten, https://www.sueddeutsche.de/muenchen/freising/amtsgericht-erding-kuenstliche-intelligenz-pilotprojekt-bayerisches-justizministerium-entlastung-fluggast-klagen-lux.NGXBwnXkr67ExWzgX1u5to (23.01.2026).

153 Working group "Einsatz von KI und algorithmischen Systemen in der Justiz" (n. 4), Appendix VIII.

154 *Quack* (n. 80), 191.

155 *Gold/Reuß et al.* (n. 10), 358; *Kernchen*, Automatisierung und richterliche Rechtsanwendung, 2025, 224.

least log the decision-making process, present all legal bases and principles leading to the decision[156] and must arrive at the result by means of verifiable reasoning that covers both the facts and the legal circumstances of the individual case.[157]

b) Supervision and Audits

What systems of supervision and control exist for AI tools in courts?

In the absence of a legal framework for the use of AI systems in civil justice, there are currently no specific regulations for systems of supervision and control for AI systems.

Both position paper of the working group 'Use of AI and Algorithmic Systems in the Judiciary' and the E-Justice Council's AI strategy emphasise the need for human oversight,[158] which is to be ensured by control mechanisms.[159]

Pilot projects also provide for control mechanisms:

– With the OLGA tool, which is being tested at the *Oberlandesgericht* (Higher Regional Court) Stuttgart, every AI-supported step remains verifiable through the traceability of the extracted parameters in the evaluated document; the decision remains entirely with the judge.[160]

– For a decision-making assistant tested at the *Landgericht* Kiel, it has also been determined that there is still a high need for adjustment on the part of the presiding judge with regard to the generated decision proposal.[161]

– The Generative Language Model for the Judiciary project aims to develop a judiciary-specific AI language model by and for the judiciary. To this end, certain training methods are planned to take into account embedded information and problematic content, e.g. biased text patterns.[162] In addition, the model is to be tested extensively.

– Tests of AI-based anonymisation tools, e.g. in the LeA project and its follow-up project ALeKs, were evaluated in terms of the true positive rate, i.e. the proportion of data recognised as requiring anonymisation, and the false positive per 100 words, i.e. the number of words or pieces of information that were wrongly

---

156 *Quack* (n. 80), 88.

157 *Gold/Reuß et al.* (n. 10), 150.

158 E-Justice-Rat (n. 1), 4; Working group "Einsatz von KI und algorithmischen Systemen in der Justiz" (n. 4), 41.

159 E-Justice-Rat (n. 1), 4.

160 *Spoenle* (n. 8), 173.

161 *Quack* (n. 80), 191.

162 Bundesministerium der Justiz und für Verbraucherschutz, Generatives Sprachmodell der Justiz (GSJ), https://www.bmjv.de/DE/themen/digitales/digitalisierung_justiz/digitalisierungsinitiative/laendervorhaben/_doc/artikel_vorhaben_06_gsj.html (23.01.2026).

anonymised. The latter rate is also important in order not to distort the content of the anonymised judgements to be published.[163]

Are AI systems required to undergo independent external audits?

According to Annex III No. 8 lit. a AI Act, AI systems used in civil court proceedings are high-risk AI systems if they are to be used as intended to assist in researching and interpreting facts and the law and in applying the law to a concrete set of facts, or if they are to be used in a similar way for alternative dispute resolution. In this case, the systems must undergo a conformity assessment procedure[164] in accordance with Article 43 (2) AI Act (internal control in accordance with Annex VI of the AI Act). The provider of such systems uses the information from the technical documentation to check internally whether the AI system meets the requirements for high-risk AI systems in accordance with Articles 8–15 of the AI Act and also checks whether the quality management system meets the requirements of Art. 17 of the AI Act. The provider may nevertheless decide to involve a notified body in the conformity assessment or to have it carried out by an external audit company.[165] Insofar as the federal and state judicial authorities have the AI systems used for their purposes developed or (co-)develop them themselves, they are subject as providers to the scope of the AI Act pursuant to Art. 2 (1) (a) AI Act[166] and thus to the aforementioned provisions on conformity assessment.

AI systems in civil courts are also subject to market surveillance. According to Article 74 (8) sentence 1 of the AI Act, a separate market surveillance authority is designated for some high-risk AI systems in areas sensitive to fundamental rights and democracy. This applies, among other things, to AI systems used by judicial authorities in accordance with Annex III No. 8 lit. a of the AI Act, insofar as they are high-risk systems in accordance with Article 6 (2) of the AI Act and are not exempted in accordance with Article 6 (3) AI Act. In Germany, according to the draft bill for a law to implement the AI Act (see n. 40), an independent AI market surveillance chamber is to be established at the *Bundesnetzagentur*. According to the draft, the latter will also be designated as the market surveillance authority pursuant to Article 70 of the AI Act. Market surveillance of the judiciary must, in individual cases, comply with Article 74 (8) sentence 2 of the AI Act within the principle of proportionality and must not affect the independence of the judiciary or otherwise interfere judicial activity.[167]

---

[163] *Irskens*, KI in der niedersächsischen Justiz, https://anwaltspraxis-magazin.de/fachbeitraege/elektronischer-rechtsverkehr/2025/02/18/b-ki-in-der-niedersaechsischen-justiz-89/ (23.01.2026).

[164] Unless one of the exceptions in Art. 6 III AI Act applies.

[165] BeckOK KI-Recht/ *Kilian*, KI-VO Art. 43, n. 22.

[166] *Gold/Reuß et al.* (n. 10), 278.

[167] BeckOK KI-Recht/*Djeffal*, KI-VO Art. 74 n. 59.

V. Current or Planned Model of AI in Civil Justice

1. *Existing AI Systems*

Are AI-driven or AI-supported systems currently used (or in the process of deployment, or in the planning and preparatory phase – as the case may be) in civil justice? If yes, please describe their nature, functions and scope. Do the AI systems currently in use or planned for deployment belong to any of the following categories?

- AI performing a narrow administrative or procedural task.
- AI improving the results of a previously completed human activity.
- AI detecting decision-making patterns or deviations but not replacing human assessment without proper human review.
- AI performing preparatory tasks relevant to judicial decision-making, such as:

(i) AI intended to be used by a judicial authority or on their behalf to assist a judicial authority in researching and interpreting facts and the law and in applying the law to a concrete set of facts, or to be used in a similar way in alternative dispute resolution, including in preparing draft (proposals) of judicial decisions and its reasonings

(ii) AI intended to be used by a judicial authority or on its behalf to substitute a judicial authority in researching and interpreting facts and the law and in applying the law to a concrete set of facts, including in rendering judicial decisions and its reasonings

In which types of procedures and courts are they used?

We are aware of the following use cases for AI systems in civil justice:

– The AI system *OLGA* at the OLG Stuttgart is used in mass proceedings relating to diesel cases to automatically summarise similar appeal cases. For example, hearing dates can be automatically scheduled according to cases that have the same parameters. In addition, these parameters can also be automatically inserted as text modules in draft decisions. Every step taken by the AI remains traceable for the judges.[168] OLGA thus performs administrative tasks, but is also used for pattern recognition and does not replace human judgement.

– *Codefy* at the *Landgericht* Frankfurt is also used for structuring and file searches to better manage mass proceedings, which also supports judicial decision-making with text modules and AI review assistants.[169]

– *FRAUKE* is another AI-supported assistance system for judges, designed to help with the preparation of written pleadings by providing text suggestions and text modules.[170]

– *A support tool at the Landgericht Kiel* can recognise metadata from written pleadings in mass proceedings, initially in contribution increase lawsuits brought by private health insurance companies, and, based on a predefined decision-making logic, suggest text modules that the judge has previously created himself.[171]

---

168 *Spoenle* (n. 8).

169 Press release Justizministerium Hessen, https://justizministerium.hessen.de/presse/ki-projekt-codefy-am-landgericht-frankfurt-gestartet (28.08.2025).

170 Working group "Einsatz von KI und algorithmischen Systemen in der Justiz" (Fn. 4), Appendix I et seq.; *Fries* (n. 103).

171 *Quack* (n. 80), 191.

– *Ocos* Solutions GmbH and the Bavarian judiciary have launched a pilot project for mass proceedings, specifically air passenger rights proceedings, at the Erding Magistrates' Court. The AI system extracts metadata from written pleadings and uses text modules to draft a statement of claim, which the judge can then adapt.[172]

– The *FT-CAM* tool developed by the state of Lower Saxony generates a written pleading from text modules, resulting in a digitally performed maintenance calculation in family matters, after the relevant basis for the calculation has been entered.[173]

– *JANO*[174] and the *automated anonymisation project*, which is being supported by FAU Erlangen-Nürnberg, are two examples of AI-supported, automatic anonymisation of judgements.[175]

– *'Generative Language Model for the Judiciary'* is a research project by the North Rhine-Westphalia and Bavarian judiciaries, in which a large language model (LLM) is to be developed specifically for the judiciary.[176]

– *SMART* is a tool for semantic metadata processing. It is designed to enable automated categorisation, document separation and metadata capture for documents that are entered into the e-file.[177]

– *ALeKs* (Anonymisation and Guideline Creation Kit for the Smart Publication of Court Decisions) is a tool for anonymising decisions based on the Automated Anonymisation project of the FAU Erlangen-Nürnberg, which has been supplemented with the functions of automatic guideline creation, keyword indexing and metadata capture. It is being developed and tested by the judicial authorities of Bavaria and Lower Saxony.[178]

– *e2A* is a collection of sub-projects by the state of North Rhine-Westphalia for the integration of AI-based analysis functions into the e-file. The module has various functions: timeline analysis, text comparison, automatic reference to legal norms and content-based file penetration.[179]

– Automation software from *Bryter*: In the project between the state of North Rhine-Westphalia and Bryter GmbH, software was developed that allowed members of the judiciary to 'program' decision trees themselves, even without pro-

---

[172] *Zarychta* (n. 152).

[173] Working group "Einsatz von KI und algorithmischen Systemen in der Justiz" (n. 4), Appendix IX.

[174] https://hessen.de/presse/pressearchiv/baden-wuerttemberg-und-hessen-starten-gemeinsames-ki-projekt.

[175] Working group "Einsatz von KI und algorithmischen Systemen in der Justiz" (n. 4), Appendix I et seq.; s. also https://berliner-gruppe.com/uni-erlangen/ (last accessed: 12.03.2025).

[176] *Sehl* LTO, https://www.lto.de/recht/justiz/j/digitalisierung-justiz-bundestag-haushalt-millionen-sprach-ki-bund-laender-digitalpakt (18.10.2023).

[177] Working group "Einsatz von KI und algorithmischen Systemen in der Justiz" (n. 4), Appendix II.

[178] *Irskens* (n. 163).

[179] Working group "Einsatz von KI und algorithmischen Systemen in der Justiz" (n. 4), Appendix IV.

gramming knowledge, in order to automate procedures and draft applications. Its use is initially limited to non-judicial activities. These include internal judicial administrative procedures, such as part-time applications, but also judicial activities.[180]

– The *S2T speech recognition experiment* is a project from Hamburg aimed at making the drafting of civil proceedings more efficient by means of speech recognition.[181]

The AI systems and projects can be classified into the following categories:

– AI systems with narrow administrative tasks include: speech recognition S2T, SMART, ALeKs, JANO and automatic anonymisation tools.

– AI systems for improving previously completed human activities: text comparison function of e2A.

– AI for recognising decision-making patterns without replacing humans: none to date.

– AI systems for performing preparatory tasks, e. g. drafting pleadings and decision proposals, research, etc.: OLGA, Bryter, e2A, 'Generative Language Model of Justice', FT-CAM, Ocos, LG Kiel support tool, FRAUKE and Codefy.

2. AI in Court Administration

Is AI used for routine administrative tasks (e. g., automatic case assignment, document workflow management, notifications and services, e-filing)?

AI-supported systems are also used in some courts to assist with routine administrative tasks. In addition to its decision-support functions, the OLGA AI system helps with administrative tasks. For instance, by analysing pending cases for similarities, such as identical parameters or plaintiff representatives, the tool facilitates the more efficient scheduling of court days.[182] The SMART tool is used in the courts of Rhineland-Palatinate in service administration, where it automates the tasks of categorisation, document separation and metadata capture for incoming documents in the e-file.[183] The combined projects 'Chatbot for legal application offices' and 'Digital legal action' support the electronic submission of lawsuits and applications.[184]

---

[180] Working group "Einsatz von KI und algorithmischen Systemen in der Justiz" (n. 4), Appendix VI.

[181] Working group "Einsatz von KI und algorithmischen Systemen in der Justiz" (n. 4), Appendix II.

[182] *Spoenle* (n. 8).

[183] Working group "Einsatz von KI und algorithmischen Systemen in der Justiz" (n. 4), Appendix II; Rhineland-Palatinate State Parliament 18th legislative period Printed paper 18/7120: Response of of Ministerium für Arbeit, Soziales, Transformation und Digitalisierung to minor interpellation Printed paper 18/7037: Use of artificial intelligence in ministries and state authorities in Rhineland-Palatinate, 09.08.2023.

[184] Working group "Einsatz von KI und algorithmischen Systemen in der Justiz" (n. 4), Appendix III.

What has been the impact of these AI-driven processes?

OLGA's automated consolidation of proceedings involving the same parties has made court days more effective for the court, the parties involved, and their representatives.[185] The automation of some procedural steps in file processing by SMART has noticeably reduced the workload for service staff, enabling them to perform their core tasks more effectively and with greater focus.[186]

3. *Predictive AI in Case Management*

Are predictive AI systems used for estimating case duration or forecasting court workload and resource allocation?

We are not aware of any German courts that use predictive AI systems for this purpose. In its 2022 position paper, the working group on 'The Use of AI and Algorithmic Systems in the Justice System' concluded that such applications are currently unfeasible.[187] The working group also concludes that, even if feasible, predictive AI systems must not be used to deny legal aid.[188]

4. *AI in Court Registers*

Is AI used in maintaining court registers? If so, in which specific types (e.g., companies registers, land and mortgage registers)?

– The cross-state project 'dabag', led by Bavaria, aims to create a uniform federal database land register, in which some functions, e.g. with regard to support for land register management, are also to be automated.[189]

– For the commercial register, which has been kept electronically for a long time, Background paper by the working group "Use of AI and Algorithmic Systems in the Judiciary" for the 74th Annual Conference of the Presidents of the Higher Regional Courts in 2022 outlines the preliminary examination of facts to be entered as a field of application for AI, which is also considered conceivable for land registry procedures after corresponding comprehensive digitisation (e.g. through the dabag project).[190]

---

185 *Spoenle* (n. 8), 173.

186 Answer of Ministerium für Arbeit, Soziales, Transformation und Digitalisierung (n. 183).

187 Working group "Einsatz von KI und algorithmischen Systemen in der Justiz" (n. 4), 5.

188 Working group "Einsatz von KI und algorithmischen Systemen in der Justiz" (n. 4), 42.

189 Bayerisches Staatsministerium der Justiz, Projekt: dabag, https://www.grundbuch.eu/beschreibung/ (13.10.2025).

190 Working group "Einsatz von KI und algorithmischen Systemen in der Justiz" (n. 4), 28 et seq.

5. Capacity Building, Education and Training

Is AI and its role in the legal profession and civil justice system included in law school curricula and professional training programs? How are future legal professionals being prepared to work with AI-driven systems?

The teaching of AI knowledge and skills lies in the responsibility of the universities. Various programmes offer AI knowledge in law, e. g. as additional certificate courses,[191] or that focus on AI as part of specialised studies, basic seminars[192] or advanced LL.B. or LL.M. courses.[193] Therefore, it remains largely up to individual law faculties to decide whether and to what extent AI skills are integrated into general curricula.

How are judges and court employees trained in AI use?

We have no knowledge of this.

What AI-related knowledge and skills are expected from judicial staff?

The requirement that judges and judicial staff must demonstrate appropriate competence or AI literacy before using AI systems is already set out in Article 4 of the AI Act. The requirements for the level of competence and training that can be derived from this therefore constitute the minimum standard. The federal and state governments intend to develop common training standards in this area.[194]

6. International Cooperation

Is your country involved in international AI projects in the judiciary? How does your jurisdiction share best practices on AI use with international counterparts?

The E-Justice Council's AI strategy calls for 'building partnerships and networks with other EU Member States […] to promote the exchange of best practices and experiences.'[195] Above all, exchanges on compliance with the AI Regulation should take place multilaterally with the EU and other Member States.[196]

---

191 For example the certificate course of study AI and Legal Tech at University Göttingen: https://uni-goettingen.de/de/698161.html (26.08.2025).

192 *Lisiecki/Stürzer*, Einfach mal probieren – Wie das Grundlagenseminar "Künstliche Intelligenz und Recht" das Bewusstsein für KI-Kompetenzen der Studierenden stärken soll, https://www.ml-tech.org/blog/einfach-mal-probieren-wie-das-grundlagenseminar-kuenstliche-intelligenz-und-recht-das-bewusstsein-fuer-ki-kompetenzen-der-studierenden-staerken-soll/ (26.08.2025).

193 *Dötterl* OdW – Ordnung der Wissenschaft 2025, 155, 159.

194 E-Justice-Rat (Fn. 1), 35.

195 E-Justice-Rat (Fn. 1), 22.

196 E-Justice-Rat (Fn. 1), 25.

The AI working group set up by the E-Justice Council is also tasked with monitoring international developments for the purpose of updating the AI strategy.[197]

7. Public Perception and Trust

How do litigants, legal practitioners, and the public perceive AI use in the justice system?

In our view, the expert community is open to the use of AI solutions in the justice system, but this does not translate into unfounded euphoria: the opportunities identified are weighed against the risks outlined here.

Have there been studies measuring public trust in AI-driven legal processes?

Respondents to the 2018 study 'What Germany knows and thinks about algorithms' were asked to choose between two positions that they felt closest to: 'I think it's better when algorithms judge me instead of people. They make objective decisions that are the same for everyone' and 'Algorithms may make objective decisions, but I still feel uncomfortable when computers make decisions about me. I think it's better when humans make such decisions.' 79 % of respondents said they felt uncomfortable with algorithmic decisions.[198] We do not know whether there have been any shifts in this regard over the years. In the past, the public was rather cautious about using digital business models and administrative services. However, this caution is increasingly giving way to the realisation that the digitalisation of many areas of economic and administrative activity is indispensable.

VI. Future Developments and Challenges

1. Assessment of Current Framework

Is the current legal and regulatory framework for AI in civil justice effective?

The current legal framework is characterised by the fact that there are almost no specific legal requirements for the use of AI systems in civil justice.[199] At the same time, the overview provided here shows that the use of AI systems in civil justice is highly sensitive in terms of fundamental rights and affects procedural principles. The use of AI systems in civil justice must therefore be very carefully considered and subject to clear and uniform rules. In our view, legal requirements are

---

197 E-Justice-Rat (n. 1), 6.

198 *Fischer/Petersen/*Bertelsmann Stiftung, Was Deutschland über Algorithmen weiß und denkt, 2018, 25.

199 An exception is the classification of AI systems in the judicial system as high-risk systems under No. 8 (a) of Annex III to the AI Act.

therefore indispensable. As these are currently lacking, the legal framework is inadequate.

Are there gaps or areas of overregulation, underregulation, or misregulation?

There is under-regulation; see the answer to the question above in this regard.

2. Future Outlook

What are your predictions for the future development of AI in civil justice?

We assume that AI systems designed to support decision-making will become widespread in civil justice in the medium term. There are also obvious areas in which AI systems could be used for fully automated decision-making. For example, they could replace the current order for payment procedure. However, this would require a significant improvement in the quality of output from such systems.

What opportunities and risks do you foresee?

The use of AI systems in civil justice offers the opportunity to accelerate proceedings, particularly mass proceedings. If AI systems were used for fully automated decision-making in certain types of online proceedings, it would be possible to enforce the law in a simpler and more cost-effective way. Legal disputes involving relatively small sums could be resolved in court, which would benefit consumers in particular.

However, risks arise when the application of the law by human judges is no longer guaranteed due to the use of AI systems. This could be because the applicable rules of procedure limit them to superficial checks or because judges themselves are less critical in their assessments, trusting in the accuracy of AI results.

When using AI systems in civil justice, two key factors must be kept in mind:

– AI systems based on large language models determine their output, which in the case of the application of law may consist of a decision and its reasoning, not by applying legal methodology, but – to put it simply – by determining probabilities. The judgement generated may no longer be distinguishable from a 'real' (human-written) judgement. However, the loss of the reflection process in the course of genuine application of the law remains.

– Almost every application of the law requires the concretisation of the applicable norms, even with strict adherence to jurisprudential methodology. Therefore, the outcome is to a certain extent dependent on the respective legal practitioner's assessments.[200] Even decisions made by independently deciding AI systems are not free from these assessments, but derive them from the underlying

[200] The only exceptions are the few areas of law that are governed by purely formal criteria, such as the rules on passenger rights in the event of flight cancellations and delays.

training material or from (possibly undisclosed) specifications of their developers.

Both considerations lead to the conclusion that automated decisions should not replace those made by human judges. Appropriate precautions must be taken to ensure this, whether the AI system is used to support decision-making or to make decisions fully automatically. Consequently, there must be a simple option for human intervention in each case if desired by one party. Additionally, it must be ensured that human judges retain the leeway to develop law in all relevant areas of substantive civil law.

VII. Economic and Access to Justice Considerations

1. Costs and Efficiency

How does AI impact the costs and duration of civil proceedings?

The use of AI systems supporting judges in decision-making is expected to be more time-efficient and, in particular, reduce the complexity of procedures.[201] This could also reduce staffing requirements and workloads.[202]

2. AI-Supported E-Services

What AI-supported digital services are available to the public? How do these services facilitate access to justice?

According to the E-Justice Council's AI strategy, the focus should be on improving citizens' access to justice through AI applications. Chatbots are cited as an example.[203] On behalf of the Federal Ministry of Justice and Consumer Protection (BMJV), *Hötter* and *Bäumer* conducted a feasibility study on the development of a chatbot for legal application offices, which was positive overall.[204] Subsequently, also on behalf of the BMJV, the *Boston Consulting Group* developed a concept for the development and use of chatbots in court's clerks offices. This concept proposes the development of a first version of the chatbot as a minimum viable product (MVP) with limited areas of application.[205] According to the con-

---

201 *Gold/Reuß et al.* (n. 10), 4 et seq.

202 Working group "Einsatz von KI und algorithmischen Systemen in der Justiz" (n. 4), 20 et seq.

203 E-Justice-Rat (n. 1), 39.

204 *Hötte*/Bäumer, Machbarkeitsstudie für die Entwicklung eines Chatbots für die maschinengestützte Aufnahme von Anträgen in den Rechtsantragstellen, s. u. https://www.bmjv.de/SharedDocs/Downloads/DE/Fachpublikationen/Chatbot_Rechtsantraege_Machbarkeitsstudie.pdf?__blob=publicationFile&v=4 (05.02.2026); *Hötte/Bäumer/Biallaß/Sommerfeld*, Die Unterstützung der Arbeit auf der Rechtsantragsstelle durch Chatbots, CR 2021, 770.

205 Concept for the development and use of chatbots in legal application offices (Rechtsantragsstellen), Abschlussdokumentation, Mai 2021, s.below. https://www.bmjv.de/SharedDocs/

cept, developers estimate that the use of chatbots within the proposed framework could achieve an average reduction in expenditure of approximately 35 % per department.[206]

A chatbot of this kind is now in use at the Central Payment Office of the North Rhine-Westphalia Justice Department. Developed by the AI lab at the state-owned IT.NRW data centre, it is designed to answer general questions about court costs and payment terms, such as instalments, deferrals, deposits, repayments and security deposits in the context of foreclosure sales.[207] Later, however, the application will also be able to answer questions about specific cases.

The Lower Saxony judiciary uses an AI-supported database in its 'INFOService' information centre. However, this AI application is not yet directly available to the public. It is only used by the service staff to provide consistent information more quickly in direct dialogue. However, it is expressly mentioned that this AI application can serve as the basis for an automated chatbot.[208]

3. *Preventing Digital Exclusion*

What measures ensure equal access to justice in the AI era? How are digitally excluded individuals supported?

If AI-supported online procedures are introduced, the issue of equal access for digitally excluded persons becomes particularly relevant. In civil proceedings before local courts, statements of claim, statements of defence, motions and other declarations can already be added to the court record orally pursuant to § 496 Code of Civil Procedure (ZPO). Therefore, the option to submit oral motions to the court could also be introduced for new proceedings.[209]

For people who are not digitally excluded, an AI-supported chatbot can provide support in the run-up to court proceedings, e.g. by providing information about courts, court proceedings and the provision of information. The E-Justice Council's AI strategy contains corresponding considerations.[210]

Downloads/DE/Fachpublikationen/Chatbot_Rechsantragstelle_Abschlussbericht.pdf?__blob=publicationFile&v=5 (05.02.2026), 3 et seq.

[206] Chatbot concept (n. 205), 4.

[207] Zeit Online, https://www.zeit.de/news/2025-06/17/justiz-setzt-erstmals-chatbot-fuer-antworten-an-buerger-ein, (05.02.2026); Mitteilung auf der Seite der Justiz NRW, https://www.justiz.nrw/mitteilung/2025-06-26 (05.02.2026); Zahlstelle Justiz NRW: https://www.olg-hamm.nrw.de/aufgaben/zentrale-zahlstelle-justiz/index.php. (last accessed: 12.03.2026).

[208] Niedersächsisches Ministerium für Wirtschaft, Arbeit, Verkehr und Digitalisierung, Die Strategie zur Künstlichen Intelligenz, abrufbar unter: https://www.stk.niedersachsen.de/startseite/presseinformationen/landesregierung-stellt-ki-strategie-niedersachsen-vor-211195.html, April 2022, (05.02.2026).

[209] For corresponding proposals, s. *Gold/Reuß et al.* (n. 10), 357; *Stürner* (n. 35), n. 50.

[210] E-Justice-Rat (n. 1), 39.

The right to a fair trial requires that even people without digital skills be given equal access when AI is used for fully automated decision-making, e.g. when online courts are increasingly used. One way of implementing this is through physical legal application centres that provide support with data entry.

Natural Resource Restoration: A Challenge for the Global Sustainable Food System[1]

Kai Purnhagen

I. The State of Natural Resources in Germany

The condition of natural resources in Germany is assessed through a comprehensive and multi-layered system of protected areas, monitoring instruments, and legally binding reporting obligations. Together, these elements provide an overall picture of both the extent of protection and the degree of pressure on ecosystems at national level.

Germany has established an extensive network of protected areas that covers a substantial share of its territory. At present, there are 16 national parks with a combined area of approximately 1,050,000 hectares.[2] Nature reserves account for around 2.7 million hectares[3], while landscape protection areas (numbering almost 8,900) cover roughly 10.1 million hectares.[4] In addition, the Natura 2000 network comprises about 5,200 sites and extends over 15.5 percent of Germany's terrestrial area (around 5.5 million hectares) as well as approximately 45 percent of its marine area.[5] Further layers of protection are provided by 104 nature parks, which together cover about 10.26 million hectares,[6] and 18 biosphere reserves, representing just under two million hectares, or roughly four per cent of the national territory.[7]

---

[1] I am especially indebted to Carmelina Poplutz for research assistance and to Lynn Noufailly and Jan Harrer for editorial assistance. Mistakes are my own. The state of research reflects the field as it stood in 2025.

[2] *Bundesamt für Naturschutz,* Nationalparke, available at: www.bfn.de/nationalparke (20.12.2025).

[3] *Bundesamt für Naturschutz,* Naturschutzgebiete in Deutschland, available at: www.bfn.de/daten-und-fakten/naturschutzgebiete-deutschland (20.12.2025).

[4] *Bundesamt für Naturschutz,* Landschaftsschutzgebiete, available at: www.bfn.de/landschafts schutzgebiete 20.12.2025).

[5] *Bundesamt für Naturschutz,* Natura 2000 Gebiete, available at: www.bfn.de/natura-2000-gebiete (20.12.2025).

[6] *Bundesamt für Naturschutz,* Naturparke in Deutschland und Europa, available at: www.bfn.de/daten-und-fakten/naturparke-deutschland#:~:text=Table_title:%20Fläche%20und%20Anzahl%20der%20Naturparke%20in,in%20Hektar:%2035.758.095%20%7C%20Anzahl:%20104*%20%7C (20.12.2025).

[7] *Bundesministerium für Umwelt, Klimaschutz, Naturschutz und nukleare Sicherheit,* Was sind "Biosphärenreservate" und welche Bedeutung haben sie für den Naturschutz in Deutschland (2024) available at: www.bundesumweltministerium.de/faq/was-sind-biosphaerenreservate-und-welche-bedeutung-haben-sie-fuer-den-naturschutz-in-deutschland (20.12.2025).

These categories of protected areas are not mutually exclusive. On the contrary, they frequently overlap and in some cases are fully congruent. Many nature reserves, for example, are simultaneously designated as Natura 2000 sites, while large parts of nature parks are also classified as landscape protection areas. As a result, the individual figures cannot simply be aggregated to determine the total protected area in Germany; instead, they reflect a dense and interlinked system of spatial protection instruments.[8]

The natural resources on which agriculture depends are subject to scrutiny, especially in rural areas of high ecological significance. Since 2009, the federal government and the Länder have jointly monitored agricultural land with high nature value (HNV). This monitoring focuses on farmland characterised by extensive use, high biodiversity, and the presence of semi-natural elements. According to the most recent assessment, HNV farmland accounted for 13.5 per cent of Germany's agricultural area in 2024, corresponding to approximately 2.6 million hectares.[9] The designation and monitoring of these areas serve as an important indicator of the ecological sustainability of agricultural land use.

With regard to ecosystem degradation and restoration needs, no single consolidated figure currently exists for the proportion of ecosystems requiring restoration. However, binding targets are set at European Union (EU) level. Under the EU Nature Restoration Regulation (EU 2024/1991), Germany is required to implement restoration measures by 2030 on at least 20 per cent of land areas and 20 per cent of marine areas affected by degraded ecosystems. These obligations are to be progressively expanded so that, by 2050, all ecosystems in need of restoration are addressed.

To support these objectives, Germany is further developing its monitoring framework for natural areas and ecosystems. The Federal Agency for Nature Conservation (BfN) is currently establishing a nationwide ecosystem monitoring programme designed to capture changes in biotopes across the entire landscape.[10] This system is intended to complement existing specialised monitoring schemes, such as monitoring under the Habitats Directive[11] and the integrated monitoring of national natural landscapes.[12] Beyond official programmes, volun-

---

[8] *Bundesamt für Naturschutz*, Schutzgebiete, available at: www.bfn.de/schutzgebiete (20.12.2025).

[9] *Bundesamt für Naturschutz*, Monitoring von Landwirtschaftsflächen mit hohem Naturwert, available at: www.bfn.de/monitoring-von-landwirtschaftsflaechen-mit-hohem-naturwert (20.12.2025).

[10] *Bundesamt für Naturschutz*, Ökosystem-Monitoring, available at: www.bfn.de/oekosystem-monitoring (20.12.2025).

[11] *Bundesamt für Naturschutz*, Monitoring FFH-Richtlinie, available at: www.bfn.de/monitoring-ffh-richtlinie (20.12.2025).

[12] *Nationale Naturlandschaften e.V.*, Das integrative Monitoring der Nationalparke und Biosphärenreservate Deutschlands, available at: integratives-monitoring.nationale-naturlandschaften.de (20.12.2025).

tary initiatives also contribute to data collection and public awareness, including citizen-science projects such as "NABU-Naturgucker".[13]

Germany operates a system for assessing the conservation status of natural habitats, which indirectly informs restoration priorities. As part of its reporting obligations under Article 17 of the Habitats Directive 92/43/EEC (Habitats Directive), Germany regularly evaluates the condition of habitat types and species of European importance. The most recent reporting cycle assessed 93 habitat types, 201 individual species, and four species groups. Habitat conservation status is determined on the basis of four parameters: "distribution range", "area", "specific structures and functions", and "future prospects". Each parameter is classified as "favourable", "unfavourable-inadequate", "unfavourable-bad", or, where data are lacking, "unknown".[14]

While this assessment framework provides a robust qualitative basis for identifying habitats in poor or uncertain condition, it does not yet translate into a precise quantitative figure for the total area to be restored by specific target years. Nevertheless, the EU Nature Restoration Regulation establishes clear benchmarks: by 2030, at least 30 percent of degraded habitat types listed in Annex I, giving priority to Natura 2000 sites, must be restored to good condition, with this share rising to 60 percent by 2040 and to 90–100 per cent by 2050. These legally binding targets form the central reference point for future national planning, mapping, and implementation of restoration measures in Germany.

II. Legal Protection of Nature

Germany's system of nature conservation is embedded in a network of international commitments and long-standing national legal traditions. Over recent decades, this framework has evolved into a multilayered regime that combines international conventions, transboundary cooperation, and detailed domestic legislation providing both area-based and object-based protection.

---

13 NABU e.V., available at: www.nabu.de\tiere-und-pflanzen\aktionen-und-projekte\naturgucker\index.html (20.12.2025).

14 *Bundesamt für Naturschutz*, FFH-Bericht 2025, available at: www.bfn.de/ffh-bericht-2025 (20.12.2025).

Table 1: International and National Frameworks of Nature Conservation

International Nature Conservation Conventions	*Ratified*	*Date of Ratification*	*Number of Sites*
Man and the Biosphere Programme[15]	✓	1971	17
UNESCO World Heritage Convention[16]	✓	1976	3
Ramsar convention[17]	✓	25.06.1976	35
Convention on International Trade in Endangered Species of Wild Fauna and Flora (CITES)[18]	✓	20.06.1976	–
Convention on Biological Diversity (CBD)[19]	✓	29.12.1993	–
Convention on the Conservation of Migratory Species of Wild Animals (CMS)[20]	✓	1984	–
Bern Convention[21]	✓	1985	–
OSPAR Convention[22]	✓	25.03.1998	6
Alpine Convention[23]	✓	29.09.1994	–
Aarhus Convention[24]	✓	15.01.2007	–

[15] *Bundesamt für Naturschutz,* UNESCO-Programm "Der Mensch und die Biosphäre" (MAB 1971), available at www.bfn.de/abkommen-richtlinie/unesco-programm-der-mensch-und-die-biosphaere-mab-1971 (12.09.2025).

[16] *Bundesamt für Naturschutz,* Übereinkommen zum Schutz des Natur- und Kulturerbes der Welt (Welterbekonvention der UNESCO, 1972), available at: www.bfn.de/abkommen-richtlinie/uebereinkommen-zum-schutz-des-natur-und-kulturerbes-der-welt-welterbekonvention (12.09.2025).

[17] *Bundesamt für Naturschutz,* Feuchtgebiete internationaler Bedeutung in Deutschland (Ramsar-Gebiete), available at: www.bfn.de/daten-und-fakten/feuchtgebiete-internationaler-bedeutung-deutschland-ramsar-gebiete (12.09.2025).

[18] *Bundesministerium für Umwelt, Klimaschutz, Naturschutz und nukleare Sicherheit,* Washingtoner Artenschutzübereinkommen/CITES (2025), available at: www.bundesumweltministerium.de/themen/artenschutz/internationaler-artenschutz/cites (12.09.2025).

[19] *Bundesministerium für Umwelt, Klimaschutz, Naturschutz und nukleare Sicherheit,* Das Internationale Übereinkommen über die biologische Vielfalt (2025), available at: www.bundesumweltministerium.de/themen/naturschutz/biologische-vielfalt-international/uebereinkommen-ueber-die-biologische-vielfalt (12.09.2025).

[20] *Bundesamt für Naturschutz,* Übereinkommen zur Erhaltung der wandernden wildlebenden Tierarten (Bonner Konvention, CMS, 1979), available at: www.bfn.de/abkommen-richtlinie/uebereinkommen-zur-erhaltung-der-wandernden-wildlebenden-tierarten-bonner (12.09.2025).

[21] *Bundesamt für Naturschutz,* Übereinkommen über die Erhaltung der europäischen wildlebenden Pflanzen und Tiere und ihrer natürlichen Lebensräume (Berner Konvention, 1979), available at: www.bfn.de/abkommen-richtlinie/uebereinkommen-ueber-die-erhaltung-der-europaeischen-wildlebenden-pflanzen-und (12.09.2025).

[22] *Bundesamt für Naturschutz,* Meeresschutzgebiete (OSPAR MPAs), Vertragsstaaten und Konventionsgebiet der OSPAR-Konvention, available at: www.bfn.de/daten-und-fakten/meeresschutzgebiete-ospar-mpas-vertragsstaaten-und-konventionsgebiet-der-ospar; https://www.umweltbundesamt.de/themen/wasser/wasserrecht/meeresschutzrecht#einleitung (12.09.2025).

[23] *Bundesministerium für Umwelt, Klimaschutz, Naturschutz und nukleare Sicherheit,* Alpenkonvention (2023), available at: www.bundesumweltministerium.de/themen/europa/alpenkonvention (24.10.2025).

[24] *Bundesministerium für Umwelt, Klimaschutz, Naturschutz und nukleare Sicherheit,* Die Aarhus-Konvention, (2017), available at: www.bundesumweltministerium.de/themen/umweltinformation/aarhus-konvention (12.09.2025).

At the international level, Germany has ratified the principal global and regional nature conservation conventions and actively participates in their implementation. A prominent example is the UNESCO Man and the Biosphere Programme, under which numerous areas in Germany have been designated as biosphere reserves. Germany is also party to the UNESCO World Heritage Convention, with several natural and mixed natural-cultural sites recognised for their outstanding universal value. In addition, Germany has designated wetlands of international importance under the Ramsar Convention, reflecting the ecological significance of its river systems, lakes, and coastal wetlands.

By contrast, Germany has neither adopted nor proposed any Candidate sites[25] under the Emerald Network, and it does not host any Candidate Emerald sites.[26] Similarly, there are no certified PAN Parks within German territory under the former PAN Parks network.[27] Nevertheless, Germany is closely integrated into broader European ecological connectivity initiatives. Numerous sites contribute to ECONET-type ecological networks that link German regions with neighbouring countries. Examples include the "Network Green Border"[28] and the "Green and Blue Rhine Alliance",[29] both fostering ecological connectivity between North Rhine-Westphalia and the Netherlands. In the Alpine region, Germany participates in the Network of Alpine Protected Areas (ALPARC)[30], while cross-border cooperation between Bavaria and Austria is further strengthened through projects supported by the Interreg programme.[31]

In the agricultural context, areas of high nature value been playing an increasingly important role in linking national conservation objectives with European and international policy agendas. Since 2009, high nature value (HNV) farmland has been systematically identified and monitored in Germany. By 2023, these areas accounted for approximately 13.4 per cent of the country's agricultural

---

[25] *Council of Europe,* Updated list of officially adopted Emerald Network sites (December 2024), (Strasbourg: 2024), available at: rm.coe.int/pa19e-2024-draft-adopted-list-emerald-network-2780-0634-1643-1/1680b27e34 (12.09.2025).

[26] *Council of Europe,* Updated list of officially adopted Emerald Network sites (December 2024), (Strasbourg: 2024), available at: https://rm.coe.int/pa18e-2024-draft-candidate-list-emerald-network-sites-2779-8956-4427-1/1680b27e33 (12.09.2025).

[27] PanParks.org, available at: www.panparks.org (12.09.2025).

[28] *Bundesamt für Naturschutz,* Netzwerk Grüne Grenze – Natur ohne Grenzen zwischen Nordrhein-Westfalen und den Niederlanden, available at: www.bfn.de/projektsteckbriefe/netzwerk-gruene-grenze-natur-ohne-grenzen-zwischen-nordrhein-westfalen-und-den (24.10.2025).

[29] *Gemeinsames INTERREG-Sekretariat bei der Euregio Rhein-Waal,* The Green and Blue Rhine Alliance, available at: interregv.deutschland-nederland.eu/project/the-green-blue-rhine-alliance-2/ (24.10.2025).

[30] alparc.org/de/ (24.10.2025).

[31] *Amt der Oberösterreicherischen Landesregierung,* Interreg Österreich-Bayern, www.interreg-bayaut.net/programm/ (24.10.2025).

land,[32] underscoring their significance not only for biodiversity conservation but also for sustainable land-use practices in rural landscapes.

The domestic legal foundations of nature protection in Germany are rooted in a long tradition that has gradually expanded from the protection of individual natural objects to comprehensive landscape-scale approaches. Central to this framework is the Federal Nature Conservation Act (BNatSchG), which provides for both area-based and object-based forms of protection. Area-based instruments include, among others, national parks (Section 24) and nature reserves (Section 23), which aim to conserve ecosystems, habitats, and natural processes on a larger spatial scale. Complementing these are object-based protection measures, such as the designation of natural monuments (Section 28) and protected landscape features (Section 29), which focus on the conservation of specific natural elements of particular ecological, scientific, or cultural value.

With regard to the protection of landscapes and trees, German law does not establish a single, universal protection regime applicable in all circumstances. Instead, landscape protection is primarily achieved through the designation of protected areas, including national parks, nature reserves, biosphere reserves, and landscape protection areas, each of which imposes varying degrees of restrictions on land use and development. Forests are primarily governed by the Federal Forest Act (BWaldG), which is aimed at safeguarding forest functions as a whole rather than individual trees. Nonetheless, trees benefit from indirect protection through legal requirements relating to tree felling, reforestation, and sustainable forest management.

Additional layers of protection apply to individual tree species and structures. Endangered tree species may be listed on the Red List of threatened species, which serves as an important scientific and policy reference. Moreover, municipalities are expressly empowered under Section 29 of the Federal Nature Conservation Act to adopt local tree protection ordinances. These regulations can impose permit requirements for the removal or pruning of trees and provide for administrative sanctions in the event of violations. Taken together, these instruments illustrate how Germany's nature conservation law combines international obligations with differentiated national and local measures to protect landscapes, habitats, and individual natural features.

---

[32] *Bundesamt für Naturschutz,* Monitoring von Landwirtschaftsflächen mit hohem Naturwert, available at: www.bfn.de/monitoring-von-landwirtschaftsflaechen-mit-hohem-naturwert (12.09.2025).

III. Restoration (Renaturation) of Organic Soils Used for Agricultural Purposes

1. Agricultural Land

Agricultural land in Germany is governed by a differentiated legal framework that combines specific regulatory provisions with functional protection derived from its role in agricultural production. On the one hand, agricultural land is subject to distinct legal rules that depart from general property law. A key example is the Land Transactions Act (GrdstVG), which regulates the sale and transfer of agricultural and forestry land with the objective of safeguarding sustainable agricultural use and preserving an efficient agricultural structure. Through approval requirements and control mechanisms, the Act seeks to prevent speculative land transactions and structural distortions that could undermine agricultural productivity. On the other hand, agricultural land also benefits from certain legal privileges that arise from its productive function. In several areas of public law, most notably nature conservation and spatial planning, agricultural use is afforded preferential treatment or exemptions. For instance, under federal nature conservation law, agricultural activities may be assessed differently from other forms of land use when evaluating interventions in nature and landscape. These privileges, however, are not unconditional; they are typically linked to compliance with environmental standards, sustainable land management practices, and other statutory obligations. Overall, Germany has developed a comprehensive set of legal instruments aimed at managing agricultural land while protecting both its quality and its availability. These instruments operate across multiple fields of law, including land transaction control, planning law, environmental regulation, and agricultural policy.

Table 2: General National Legal Instruments

Legal Instrument	*Level*	*Content/Purpose*	*Relevant Legal Basis/ Programmes*
Federal Nature Conservation Act (BNatSchG)	National	Requirement for official approval for interventions in nature	Sec. 14, 15, 17 BNatSchG
Spatial Planning Act (ROG) and State Planning Acts	National/State	Supra-local spatial planning; designation and protection of priority agricultural areas	Sec. 1, 2 ROG, State Spatial Planning Acts (e.g. Art. 3 BayLPlG)
Fertilizer Regulation (DüV)	National/EU implementation	Regulation of fertilization to avoid nutrient surpluses and groundwater contamination	Sec. 3–6 DüV

Legal Instrument	*Level*	*Content/Purpose*	*Relevant Legal Basis/ Programmes*
EU Environmental law	EU	Protection of natural areas, including in an agricultural context, FFH compatibility assessmentsmanagement requirements in protected areas	Directive 92/43/EEC, Directive 2009/147/ EC
Common Agricultural Policy (CAP)	EU/National	Promotion of sustainable, productive and resource-efficient agriculture, income support	Art. 4–7, 31–70 VO (EU) 2021/2115
Cross-Compliance/ Conditionality	EU/National	Linking direct payments to compliance with environmental, climate, and soil protection standards	Art. 12–15 Regulation (EU) 2021/2115, National implementation: Sec. 1–4 CAP Conditionality Act
Eco-schemes under the CAP (1st pillar)	EU/National	Voluntary environmental measures (e.g. extensive management, permanent grassland conservation) with financial incentives	Art. 31–33 Regulation (EU) 2021/2115, national implementation: CAP Direct Payments Ordinance
Agri-environment-climate measures under the CAP (2nd pillar)	EU/National/State	Voluntary, remunerated measures for biodiversity, soil and water protection	Art. 70 Regulation (EU) 2021/2115, National implementation via State programmes (e.g. KULAP,[33] HALM[34])
Contaminated Sites Management/Soil Remediation	National/State	Remediation of contaminated soils to restore agricultural usability	Sec. 4–9 Federal Soil Protection Act
Joint Task "Improvement of Agricultural Structure and Coastel Protection" (GAK)	National	Financial instrument to promote sustainable agricultural structures, rural development and coastal protection	GAK Act (GAKG); GAK Framework Plan of the Federal Ministry Agriculture, Food and Regional Identity

Legal instruments to prevent land degradation and devastation, such as desertification, salinisation, erosion, and the loss of organic carbon from soil and programmes setting targets for land neutrality by 2030 – 2050 are as follows:

[33] *Bayerisches Staatsministerium für Ernährung, Landwirtschaft, Forsten und Tourismus,* Kulturlandschaftsprogramm (KULAP) – einfach erklärt, available at: www.stmelf.bayern.de/foerderung/agrarpolitik/kulturlandschaftsprogramm-kulap-einfach-erklaert/index.html (24.10.2025).

[34] *Hessisches Ministerium für Landwirtschaft und Umwelt, Weinbau, Forsten, Jagd und Heimat,* HALM 2 Hessisches Agrarumweltprogramm, available at: https://landwirtschaft.hessen.de/landwirtschaft/foerderung/agrarumweltprogramm (24.10.2025).

Table 3: National Legal Instruments to Prevent Land Degradation and Devastation

Legal Instrument	*Legal Basis*	*Addressed Risks*	*Examples of Measures/ Practical Implementation*
Federal Soil Protection Act (BBodSchG)	Sec. 4, 7, 10, 13	Desertification, erosion, salinization, loss of organic carbon from soil (SOC)	– Obligation to use soil-friendly cultivation methods – Restoration obligations for degraded soils
Federal Soil Protection and Contaminated Sites Ordinance (BBodSchV)	Sec. 3–10, 12	Erosion, loss of SOC, Salinization	– Obligation to take precautions against pollutant inputs – Requirements for the introduction or placement of materials on or in the soil
Fertilizer Regulation (DüV)	Sec. 3, 5, 13a	Salinization, loss of SOC	– Fertilization only based on demonstrated plant nutrient demand – Application bans on frozen/snow covered soil
Federal Water Act (WHG)	Sec. 4, 5, 6, 47, 48	Desertification, Salinization	– Limits on groundwater extraction – Maintenance of sustainable water balance
Common Agricultural Policy	Regulation (EU) 2021/2115 Art. 12 et seq.; GAEC 2, 5, 6, 7	Erosion, loss of SOC, Desertification	– No plowing from Dec 1st until Feb 16th – Obligation to cover at least 80 % of arable land with vegetation[35]
EU Water Framework Directive (2000/60/EC)	Art. 4 (implemention: WHG)	Salinization	– Protection of groundwater levels

Germany strives, as a member of the United Nations (UN), to achieve the UN Sustainable Development Goal of Land Degradation Neutrality by 2030 according to UN SDG 15.3.[36] Legal instruments or programmes to improve soil health and water storage, prevent erosion and increase soil biodiversity and carbon sequestration, and prevent greenhouse gas emissions (such as nitrous oxide and

[35] *Ministerium für Ernährung, Ländlichen Raum und Verbraucherschutz Baden-Württemberg,* Erweiterte Konditionalität (2025), available at: https://foerderung.landwirtschaft-bw.de/,Lde/Startseite/Agrarpolitik/Konditionalitaet#:~:text=Dieser%20GLÖZ%2DStandard%20gibt%20vor,und%20Düngemittel%20angewendet%20werden%20dürfen. (30.10.2025).

[36] *Wunder/Kaphengst/Frelih-Larsen et al.*, Implementing SDG target 15.3 on "Land Degradation Neutrality", Umweltbundesamt (pub.) (Dessau-Roßlau: 2018) available at: www.umweltbundesamt.de/sites/default/files/medien/1410/publikationen/2018-02-21_texte_16-2018_land-degration-nutrality_en.pdf (30.10.2025).

methane) or increase their consumption in soil (e.g. through improved drainage, nutrient cycling in the field and soil organic matter) are as follows:

Table 4: National Legal Instruments to Improve Soil and Water

Legal Instrument or Program	*Pursued Effect*
Federal Soil Protection Act (BBodSchG)	Statutory protection of soil against harmful changes and precautionary measures against adverse impacts on the soil
Eco-Schemes of the Common Agricultural Policy[37]	Improvement of soil quality through the cultivation of diverse crops; accumulation of carbon in the soil through extensive farming; avoidance of erosion; improvement of soil life through agroforestry
Alpine Convention[38]	Mutual commitment of the Alpine countries to take measures for the qualitative and quantitative protection of soils in the Alpine region
Agri-environmental and Climate Measures (e.g. AUKM)[39]	Improvement of soil structure, protection of soil from water and wind erosion; reduction of greenhouse gas emissions
Federal Financing Program Water, Soil, Waste (LABO)[40]	Standardization of enforcement in the areas of water, soil, and waste law; promotion of research projects on soil and water protection
EFRE-funded Contaminated Site Remediation[41]	Elimination of existing environmental hazards and reintegration of sites into economic and natural cycles
Federal Humus Program[42]	Improvement of water retention capacity and soil health through funding measures to promote humus-increasing and humus-preserving agriculture

[37] *Bundesministerium für Landwirtschaft, Ernährung und Heimat*, Öko-Regelungen (2025), available at: www.bmleh.de/DE/themen/landwirtschaft/eu-agrarpolitik-und-foerderung/direktzahlung/oeko-regelungen.html (24.10.2025).

[38] *Alpconv.org*, Bodenschutz, available at: www.alpconv.org/de/startseite/themen/bodenschutz/ (24.10.2025).

[39] *Bundesministerium für Landwirtschaft, Ernährung und Heimat*, Agrarumwelt- und Klimamaßnahmen (AUKM), Ökologischer Landbau und Tierschutzmaßnahmen (2019), available at: www.bmleh.de/DE/themen/landwirtschaft/eu-agrarpolitik-und-foerderung/agrarumwelt-und-klimamassnahmen-aukm/agrarumwelt-und-klimamassnahmen-aukm_node.html (30.10.2025).

[40] *Ministerium für Klimaschutz, Landwirtschaft, ländliche Räume und Umwelt Mecklenburg-Vorpommern*, Länderfinanzierungsprogramm, available at: www.labo-deutschland.de/Laenderfinanzierungsprogramm.html (24.10.2025).

[41] *Bayerisches Staatsministerium für Umwelt und Verbraucherschutz*, Flächenrecycling und Altlastensanierung in der EU-Förderperiode 2021–2027, available at: www.stmuv.bayern.de/themen/boden/altlasten/eu_fonds.htm (24.10.2025).

[42] *Fachagentur Nachwachsende Rohstoffe e.V.*, Bundesprogramm Humus, available at: humus.fnr.de/humus/bundesprogramm (15.10.2025).

Legal Instrument or Program	*Pursued Effect*
Natural Climate Protection Action Program (ANK)[43]	Measures for peatland restoration, humus buildup, and increase of natural CO2 sinks

Legal and other instruments for restoring degraded or devastated land and agricultural land and the corresponding responsible for carrying out this task are as follows:

Table 5: National Legal Instruments to Restore Land

Instrument	*Legal Basis*	*Type of Restoration*	*Responsibility*
Federal Soil Protection Act (BBodSchG)	Sec. 4–9	Restoring the functions of the soil; Remediation of contaminated sites	State authorities for soil conservation
Federal Nature Conservation Act (BNatSchG)	Sec. 13–19	Compensation for nature conservation interventions; reservation of soils to ensure their function in the natural balance	Nature conservation authorities
EU Regulation on nature restoration	Regulation (EU) 2024/1991	Restoration of agricultural ecosystems	Federal Ministry fort the Environment, Nature Conservation, Nuclear Safety and Consumer Protection, in cooperation with the State Ministries of the environment
Common Agricultural Policy (CAP)	Regulation (EU) 2021/2115	Restoring soil fertility	Agricultural Ministries of the States
Moor and climate protection programs (e. g. AUKM[44], Action Program for Natural Climate Protection[45])		Restoration of peat, rewetting of peat	Federal Ministry fort the Environment, Nature Conservation, Nuclear Safety and Consumer Protection; Agricultural Ministries of the States

43 *Bundesministerium für Umwelt, Naturschutz, nukleare Sicherheit und Verbraucherschutz* (ed.), Aktionsprogramm Natürlicher Klimaschutz (2023), available at: www.bmuv.de/fileadmin/Daten_BMU/Pools/Broschueren/ank_publikation_bf.pdf (15.10.2025).

44 *Bundesministerium für Landwirtschaft, Ernährung und Heimat*, Agrarumwelt- und Klimamaßnahmen (AUKM), Ökologischer Landbau und Tierschutzmaßnahmen (2019), available at: www.bmleh.de/DE/themen/landwirtschaft/eu-agrarpolitik-und-foerderung/agrarumwelt-und-klimamassnahmen-aukm/agrarumwelt-und-klimamassnahmen-aukm_node.html (30.10.2025).

45 *Bundesministerium für Wirtschaft und Energie*, Förderungen im Rahmen des Aktionsprogramms Natürlicher Klimaschutz (ANK), available at: www.foerderdatenbank.de/FDB/Content/DE/Foerderprogramm/Bund/BMU/ank.html (30.10.2025).

Instrument	*Legal Basis*	*Type of Restoration*	*Responsibility*
EU-LIFE-Programme	Regulation (EU) 2021/783	Restoration of degraded ecosystems, Restoration of soil quality	European Commission; Federal Ministry fort the Environment, Nature Conservation, Nuclear Safety and Consumer Protection

2. Peatlands and Floodplains

Germany has designated 35 wetlands as sites of international importance under the Ramsar Convention. Together, these Ramsar sites cover a total area of approximately 869,265 hectares.[46] Despite this formal recognition, peatlands in Germany continue to be subject to intensive human use. Approximately 75 percent of existing peatland areas are still utilized for agricultural and forestry purposes.[47] From a legal perspective, peatlands are generally not protected as agricultural land. Instead, their regulatory protection primarily derives from nature conservation law rather than water law or agricultural land protection regimes. This fragmented approach reflects the historical perception of peatlands as productive land rather than as ecosystems requiring strict hydrological preservation.

Peat extraction, once widespread, has been substantially reduced and is now limited to a small number of federal states.[48] Where peat extraction occurs, it is subject to authorization requirements under the respective laws of the Länder. Permits are granted on a case-by-case basis, taking into account environmental protection standards and nature conservation objectives. As a result, while economic use of peatlands has not been entirely eliminated, it is increasingly constrained by regulatory instruments aimed at reconciling residual exploitation with broader environmental and climate policy goals.

[46] *Bundesamt für Naturschutz*, Feuchtgebiete internationaler Bedeutung in Deutschland (Ramsar-Gebiete), available at: www.bfn.de/daten-und-fakten/feuchtgebiete-internationaler-bedeutung-deutschland-ramsar-gebiete (17.09.2025).

[47] *Bundesministerium für Umwelt, Klimaschutz, Naturschutz und nukleare Sicherheit und Verbraucherschutz*, Nationale Strategie zur Biologischen Vielfalt 2030 (2024), available at: www.bmuv.de/fileadmin/Daten_BMU/Pools/Broschueren/nationale_moorschutzstrategie_bf.pdf (11.10.2025).

[48] *Bundesministerium für Umwelt, Naturschutz, nukleare Sicherheit und Verbraucherschutz*, Nationale Moorschutzstrategie (2022) 12, available at: www.bmuv.de/fileadmin/Daten_BMU/Pools/Broschueren/nationale_moorschutzstrategie_bf.pdf, 48 (11.10.2025).

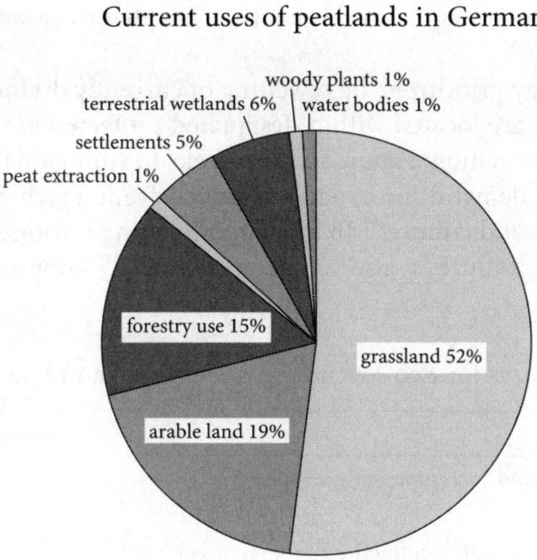

Figure 1, designed by author using data from *Bundesministerium für Umwelt, Naturschutz, nukleare Sicherheit und Verbraucherschutz* (ed.), Nationale Moorschutzstrategie (2022) 12, available at: *https://www.bmuv.de/fileadmin/Daten_BMU/Pools/Broschueren/nationale_moorschutzstrategie_bf.pdf* [last accessed on 11/10/2025].[49]

The national approach to the renaturation and rewetting of agriculturally used peatlands in Germany is primarily structured around the National Peatland Strategy, which establishes a coordinated framework of regulatory, cooperative, and incentive-based measures. Central to this approach is close cooperation between the federal government and the Länder, notably through the Federal–State Target Agreements on Climate Protection through Peatland Protection. This cooperative framework emphasizes regionally adapted solutions developed on a voluntary basis rather than through uniform mandatory requirements.

A key policy objective is to reconcile peatland rewetting with continued land use. Accordingly, agricultural and forestry activities under higher water levels are not categorically excluded but are instead intended to remain possible and to be actively promoted through innovative and sustainable management concepts.[50] These include forms of peatland-compatible use that reduce greenhouse gas emissions while maintaining economic viability. Practical implementation at the regional level is illustrated by programs such as the Bavarian Peatland Farmers'

---

[49] *Bundesministerium für Umwelt, Naturschutz, nukleare Sicherheit und Verbraucherschutz* (ed.), Nationale Moorschutzstrategie (2022) 12, available at: www.bmuv.de/fileadmin/Daten_BMU/Pools/Broschueren/nationale_moorschutzstrategie_bf.pdf, 12 (11.10.2025).

[50] *Bundesministerium für Umwelt, Naturschutz, nukleare Sicherheit und Verbraucherschutz* (ed.), Aktionsprogramm Natürlicher Klimaschutz (2023), available at: www.bundesumweltministerium.de/fileadmin/Daten_BMU/Pools/Broschueren/ank_publikation_bf.pdf#page=12, 14 et seq. (11.10.2025).

Programme, which supports agricultural practices adapted to rewetted peatland conditions (see Table 6).[51]

In parallel, the strategy prioritizes the rewetting of currently drained peatlands, particularly where they are located within designated protected areas.[52] To reinforce these measures, the national approach also seeks to stimulate market-based incentives by fostering demand for products derived from alternative management systems, such as paludiculture.[53] In this way, rewetting is framed not only as an environmental obligation but also as an economically supported land-use transition (see Table 6).

Table 6: National Measures for Eco-Friendly Agricultural Land Use

Measure	*Annual funding rate*
Conversion of agricultural land to permanent grassland	3.300 €/ha
Farming of wet grassland	600 €/ha
Farming of rewetted grassland with a defined water level target	900 €/ha
Cultivation of paludiculture crops	2.200 €/ha

A range of regulatory and incentive-based instruments is employed in Germany to facilitate the conversion of agricultural land to permanent grassland, the transition to extensive grazing or set-aside, and the reduction or reversal of drainage on peatland soils. The primary steering mechanism consists of financial incentives, such as those provided under the Bavarian Peatland Farmers' Programme, which supports peatland-compatible land use. Extensive grazing systems are further encouraged through agri-environmental premium schemes, including Eco-Regulation 4 of the Common Agricultural Policy (CAP) and the Bavarian Cultural Landscape Programme.[54] Although the mandatory set-aside obligation under GAEC 8 was abolished in 2025, farmers may still receive graduated payments under Eco-Regulation 1 of the CAP if they voluntarily designate parts of their arable land as non-productive areas. In addition, the prevention of further peatland drainage is addressed through GAEC 2 of the CAP, which requires offi-

51 *Bayerisches Staatsministerium für Ernährung, Landwirtschaft, Forsten und Tourismus,* Agrarumwelt- und Klimamaßnahmen (AUKM) (2025), available at: www.stmelf.bayern.de/foerderung/foerderung-von-agrarumweltmassnahmen-in-bayern/index.html (11.10.2025).

52 *Bundesministerium für Umwelt, Naturschutz, nukleare Sicherheit und Verbraucherschutz* (ed.), Aktionsprogramm Natürlicher Klimaschutz (2023), available at: www.bundesumweltministerium.de/fileadmin/Daten_BMU/Pools/Broschueren/ank_publikation_bf.pdf#page=12, 14 (11.10.2025).

53 *Bundesministerium für Umwelt, Naturschutz, nukleare Sicherheit und Verbraucherschutz* (ed.), Aktionsprogramm Natürlicher Klimaschutz (2023), available at: www.bundesumweltministerium.de/fileadmin/Daten_BMU/Pools/Broschueren/ank_publikation_bf.pdf#page=12, 15 (11.10.2025).

54 *Bayerisches Staatsministerium für Ernährung, Landwirtschaft, Forsten und Tourismus,* Agrarumwelt- und Klimamaßnahmen (AUKM) (2025), available at: www.stmelf.bayern.de/foerderung/foerderung-von-agrarumweltmassnahmen-in-bayern/index.html (11.10.2025).

cial approval for any deepening, renewal, or expansion of existing drainage systems.[55]

Instruments for restoring river connectivity and the natural functions of floodplains are firmly anchored in water law. River continuity is explicitly mandated under Sections 33 et seqq. of the Federal Water Act (WHG), and is implemented in practice through measures such as the removal of dams and the conversion of weirs or drops into near-natural riverbed structures.[56] Floodplain restoration is primarily pursued through targeted renaturation measures supported by dedicated funding programmes. A prominent example is the federal initiative "Blue Ribbon Germany" (Blaues Band Deutschland), launched jointly by the Federal Ministry of Transport and the Federal Ministry for the Environment. This programme aims to enhance investments in the ecological restoration of federal waterways and their floodplains, with the explicit goal of reconnecting rivers, banks, and floodplain areas. Complementary funding schemes enable associations, municipalities, and other institutions to implement projects aligned with these objectives, including on floodplain land that is not federally owned.[57]

According to expert assessments, these instruments have both restrictive and enabling effects on agricultural production. Floodplain restoration typically results in periodic inundation or sustained waterlogging, which limits conventional soil cultivation practices such as ploughing and reduces the intensity of land use, potentially leading to short-term income losses. At the same time, restored floodplains provide substantial long-term benefits for agriculture. They act as natural flood retention areas, enhance groundwater recharge, reduce drought vulnerability, prevent soil erosion, and function as significant carbon sinks.[58] Moreover, near-natural riparian buffer zones support pollinator habitats,[59] thereby contributing to stable crop yields.[60] Taken together, these ecological functions strengthen the long-term resilience and sustainability of agricultural production systems.

---

55 *Bayerisches Staatsministerium für Ernährung, Landwirtschaft, Forsten und Tourismus*, Erhaltung landwirtschaftlicher Flächen in gutem landwirtschaftlichem und ökologischem Zustand (GLÖZ) (2023), available at: www.stmelf.bayern.de/mam/cms01/agrarpolitik/dateien/info_gloez_20230327.pdf (11.10.2025).

56 *Bayerisches Landesamt für Umwelt*, Durchgängigkeit, available at: www.lfu.bayern.de/wasser/durchgaengigkeit/index.htm (11.10.2025).

57 *Bundesamt für Naturschutz*, Hintergrund, available at: www.bfn.de/hintergrund-bbd (06.11.2025).

58 *Naumann/Müller/Pottgiesser*, Flüssen und Bächen wieder mehr Raum zurückgeben, Umweltbundesamt (ed.) (2025), available at: www.umweltbundesamt.de/sites/default/files/medien/479/publikationen/uba_hgp_fluessen_und_baechen_wieder_mehr_raum_zurueckgeben.pdf, 12 (10.11.2025).

59 *Geschäftsstelle des Sachverständigenrates für Umweltfragen*, Renaturierung: Biodiversität stärken, Flächen zukunftsfähig bewirtschaften (2024), available at: www.bmleh.de/SharedDocs/Downloads/DE/_Ministerium/Beiraete/biodiversitaet/stellungnahme-renaturierung.pdf?__blob=publicationFile&v=2, 19 (10.11.2025).

60 *Geschäftsstelle des Sachverständigenrates für Umweltfragen*, Renaturierung: Biodiversität stärken, Flächen zukunftsfähig bewirtschaften (2024), available at: www.bmleh.de/SharedDocs/

IV. Water Resources for Agriculture

The achievement of a favourable status for water bodies and water-dependent ecosystems remains a significant challenge in Germany. At present, only around 9 percent of surface water bodies reach good ecological status or good ecological potential.[61] Moreover, as of 2021, all surface water bodies were assessed as failing to achieve good chemical status.[62] Groundwater presents a more differentiated picture: while 95.2 percent of groundwater bodies meet good quantitative status,[63] only 67.3 percent achieve good chemical status, leaving nearly one third in poor chemical condition.[64]

In response to these deficits, extensive improvement measures are planned. By 2027, actions addressing flow regulation and hydromorphological alterations are envisaged for approximately 83 percent of surface waters, with a focus on habitat restoration and the re-establishment of longitudinal connectivity. Measures to reduce diffuse pollution, particularly nutrient and pollutant inputs, are planned for 55 percent of surface waters by 2027, with further actions thereafter. For groundwater, 53 percent of water bodies will be subject to measures targeting agricultural nutrient inputs and, to a lesser extent, mining-related pressures. In addition to technical interventions, conceptual measures such as agricultural advisory schemes and research initiatives play a central role in improving both surface and groundwater quality.[65]

With regard to irrigation, German law does not require a permit for irrigation as such, but rather for the abstraction of groundwater. Under Sections 8 and 9(1) No. 5 of the Federal Water Act (WHG), groundwater extraction is subject to

---

Downloads/DE/_Ministerium/Beiraete/biodiversitaet/stellungnahme-renaturierung.pdf?__blob=publicationFile&v=2, 33 (10.11.2025).

[61] *Vökler/Naumann/Arle et al.*, Water Framework Directive – The Status of German Water in 2021. Progress and Challenges, Umweltbundesamt (pub.) (2022), available at: www.umweltbundesamt.de/sites/default/files/medien/1410/publikationen/water-framework-directive-2021_bf.pdf, 53 f. (20.12.2025).

[62] *Vökler/Naumann/Arle et al.*, Water Framework Directive – The Status of German Water in 2021. Progress and Challenges, Umweltbundesamt (pub.) (2022), available at: www.umweltbundesamt.de/sites/default/files/medien/1410/publikationen/water-framework-directive-2021_bf.pdf, 58 f. (20.12.2025).

[63] *Vökler/Naumann/Arle et al.*, Water Framework Directive – The Status of German Water in 2021. Progress and Challenges, Umweltbundesamt (pub.) (2022), available at: www.umweltbundesamt.de/sites/default/files/medien/1410/publikationen/water-framework-directive-2021_bf.pdf, 62 f. (20.12.2025).

[64] *Vökler/Naumann/Arle et al.*, Water Framework Directive – The Status of German Water in 2021. Progress and Challenges, Umweltbundesamt (pub.) (2022), available at: www.umweltbundesamt.de/sites/default/files/medien/1410/publikationen/water-framework-directive-2021_bf.pdf, 64 f. (20.12.2025).

[65] *Vökler/Naumann/Arle et al.*, Water Framework Directive – The Status of German Water in 2021. Progress and Challenges, Umweltbundesamt (pub.) (2022), available at: www.umweltbundesamt.de/sites/default/files/medien/1410/publikationen/water-framework-directive-2021_bf.pdf, 72 ff. (20.12.2025).

authorization.[66] Although Section 46(1) Federal Water Act (WHG) exempts groundwater use for agricultural operations from licensing where no adverse effects on the water balance occur, irrigation through groundwater abstraction is generally considered a significant interference and therefore requires authorization. The concrete requirements vary between the Länder, which are also empowered to levy water abstraction fees. Currently, 13 Länder impose such fees, with differing rates.[67] Bavaria has recently decided to introduce a fee of ten cents per cubic meter of groundwater, subject to an annual exemption threshold, with the first assessment period beginning in the second half of 2026.[68]

The use of treated wastewater in agriculture is governed at EU level by Regulation (EU) 2020/741 on minimum requirements for water reuse, which has applied directly since June 2023. While the Regulation establishes uniform standards across all Member States, adaptations within German law are still required, particularly concerning procedural rules and competent authorities. A draft bill by the Federal Ministry for the Environment therefore proposes the introduction of a dedicated section in the WHG addressing the "treatment, storage, distribution, and reuse of wastewater for agricultural irrigation".[69]

Fertilizers and yield-enhancing substances are regulated through a comprehensive legal framework. The Fertilizer Act (DüngG) and its implementing regulations govern production, marketing, and use. The Fertilizer Regulation (DüMV) sets requirements for placing fertilizers on the market, while the Fertilization Regulation (DüV) defines application standards and constitutes the core instrument for implementing the EU Nitrates Directive. Supplementary provisions, such as the Manure Transport Regulation, ensure traceability of nutrient flows and aim to prevent over-fertilization.[70]

Finally, the monitoring and designation of nitrate-polluted and vulnerable areas are closely aligned with EU law. Under Article 3(2) of the EU Nitrates Directive 91/676/EEC, Member States must designate nitrate-vulnerable zones, an obligation implemented in Germany through Section 13a of the Fertilization Regulation (DüV). Germany is also required to submit a nitrate report to the European Commission every four years, based on data provided by the Länder monitoring networks. This report describes the status and development of water pol-

---

[66] *Martínez*, in: Koch/Hofmann/Reese (eds.), Handbuch Umweltrecht, 6th ed., 2024, 1327.

[67] *Umweltbundesamt*, Übersicht über die Länderregelungen zu Wasserentnahmeentgelten (2022), available at: www.umweltbundesamt.de/sites/default/files/medien/2875/dokumente/tabelle_wasserentnahmeentgelte_laender_stand_sept_2022.pdf (11.10.2025).

[68] *Bayerische Staatskanzlei*, available at: www.bayern.de/wp-content/uploads/2025/07/250729-Ministerrat.pdf (11.10.2025).

[69] *Bundesministerium für Umwelt, Naturschutz, nukleare Sicherheit und Verbraucherschutz*, Entwurf eines Dritten Gesetzes zur Änderung des Wasserhaushaltsgesetzes (2024), available at: www.bundesumweltministerium.de/fileadmin/Daten_BMU/Download_PDF/Glaeserne_Gesetze/20._Lp/whg_3aendg/Entwurf/whg_3aendg_refe_bf.pdf (02.10.2025).

[70] *Umweltbundesamt*, Düngemittel (2025), available at: www.umweltbundesamt.de/themen/landwirtschaft/umweltbelastungen-der-landwirtschaft/duengemittel#rechtliche-regelungen (07.10.2025).

lution in both groundwater and surface waters and includes a map showing the designated vulnerable zones.[71] The nationwide framework for area designation is laid down in the General Administrative Regulation on the Designation of Nitrate-polluted and Eutrophicated Areas (AVV GeA), which harmonizes methodologies across Länder, defines monitoring standards, and enhances legal certainty.[72]

V. Agricultural Ecosystems

Germany has established both a legal framework and comprehensive monitoring systems aimed at assessing and indirectly supporting biodiversity, including butterflies and birds, within agricultural landscapes. Pursuant to Section 6 of the Federal Nature Conservation Act (BNatSchG), the federal government and the Länder are legally obliged to monitor the state and development of nature and landscapes.

In practice, Germany operates extensive monitoring schemes that cover multiple taxonomic groups and habitat types. Bird monitoring is particularly well developed and differentiated according to species groups and ecological contexts. It relies on a combination of standardized volunteer-based surveys, monitoring programmes conducted by the Länder, and systematic seabird counts in the Exclusive Economic Zone carried out by the Federal Agency for Nature Conservation (BfN). Nationwide volunteer monitoring programmes are coordinated by the Federation of German Avifaunists (DDA) and are scientifically evaluated in cooperation with the BfN and the ornithological stations of the Länder.

Comparable monitoring approaches exist for butterflies and other insect groups, providing essential data on population trends and habitat quality. Although these monitoring systems do not themselves constitute regulatory instruments, they play a crucial role in informing agri-environmental policies, conservation measures, and land-use planning. By generating empirical evidence, they enable the federal and state authorities to design, adjust, and evaluate legal and policy measures aimed at halting biodiversity loss and promoting species-rich agricultural landscapes.[73]

---

[71] *Bundesministerium für Umwelt, Klimaschutz, Naturschutz und nukleare Sicherheit*, Nitratberichte (2024), available at: www.bundesumweltministerium.de/download/nitratberichte (07.10.2025).

[72] www.bundesanzeiger.de/pub/publication/soM4ZaXUtP38shNEcKm/content/soM4ZaXUtP38shNEcKm/BAnz%20AT%2016.08.2022%20B2.pdf?inline (07.10.2025).

[73] *Bundesamt für Naturschutz,* Vogelmonitoring, available at: www.bfn.de/vogelmonitoring (30.10.2025).

Table 7: Bird Monitoring Programmes

Bird Monitoring Programme	*Observation Area*	*Method of Observation*
Monitoring of Common Breeding Birds[74]	Nationwide	Volunteer surveys
Monitoring of Rare Breeding Birds[75]	Nationwide	Volunteer surveys
Monitoring of resting Waterfowls[76]	Nationwide	Volunteer surveys
Marine Monitoring of Seabirds	Coastal and marine areas/ Exclusive Economic Zone	Professional surveys
High-Mountain Bird Monitoring[77]	Alpine region	Volunteer surveys
Monitoring of European Raptor and Owl Species (MEROS)[78]	Nationwide	Volunteer surveys
Raptor monitoring Baden-Württemberg[79]	State-wide	Volunteer surveys

Legal measures for bird protection in agricultural areas exist both at the level of national law and at the level of EU law.

Table 8: Legal Basis for Bird Monitoring Programmes

Legal Basis	*Measure*
Sec. 44 (1) No. 3 BNatSchG	Prohibition of removing, damaging, or destroying breeding or resting places of wild animals of specially protected species (includes bird nests and breeding sites)
Sec. 39 (5) BNatSchG	Prohibition of cutting or coppicing hedges, living fences, bushes, or reed beds between March 1 and September 30 (protection of breeding season)
Art. 3 Directive 2009/147/EC (EU Birds Directive)	Obliges member states to maintain and improve habitats for all wild bird species
Art. 5 Birds Directive	Contains core prohibitions (killing, disturbing, destroying nests or eggs) at the EU level
Art. 6 (2) Habitats Directive (92/43/EEC)	Member states must ensure that any planned activity in Natura 2000 sites does not deteriorate protected habitats

74 *Dachverband Deutscher Avifaunisten e.V.*, Monitoring häufiger Brutvögel, available at: www.dda-web.de/monitoring/mhb/programm (02.11.2025).

75 *Dachverband Deutscher Avifaunisten e.V.*, Monitoring häufiger Brutvögel, available at: www.dda-web.de/monitoring/mhb/programm (02.11.2025).

76 *Dachverband Deutscher Avifaunisten e.V.*, Monitoring häufiger Brutvögel, available at: www.dda-web.de/monitoring/mhb/programm (02.11.2025).

77 *Dachverband Deutscher Avifaunisten e.V.*, Alpenvogelmonitoring, available at: www.dda-web.de/monitoring/alpenvogelmonitoring/programm (02.11.2025).

78 *Förderverein für Ökologie und Monitoring von Greifvogel- und Eulenarten e.V.*, available at: www.greifvogelmonitoring.de (20.12.2025).

79 *LUBW Landesanstalt für Umwelt Baden-Württemberg*, Landesweites Greifvogelmonitoring, available at: www.lubw.baden-wuerttemberg.de/natur-und-landschaft/landesweites-greifvo gelmonitoring (02.11.2025).

Legal Basis	*Measure*
Art. 11 EU Nature Restoration Regulation (EU 2024/1991)	Obliges member states to implement restoration measures for nature and biodiversity, including improving bird habitats in agricultural landscapes and protected areas

The butterfly monitoring is carried out in the form of the nationwide Butterfly Monitoring Scheme or within the framework of insect monitoring, although a nationwide program for the latter is still being developed.[80] However, some Länder, such as Baden-Württemberg, have already established state-wide insect monitoring programs.[81]

As legal measures to increase the number of butterflies in agricultural areas, the Insect Diversity Protection Act introduced amendments to the Federal Nature Conservation Act (BNatSchG). For example, since then, nutrient-poor lowland meadows, mountain meadows, species-rich traditional orchards, stone ridges, and dry-stone walls have been legally protected biotopes.

To reverse the decline in pollinator populations by 2030 and establish an upward trend, Germany pursues the protection of pollinator populations through the "Insect Protection Action Program" and the closely linked "National Strategy for Biological Diversity 2030 (NBS 2030)." The action program aims to reverse the decline of insects and improve their living conditions. It covers nine areas of action, including the protection and restoration of insect habitats, reduction of pesticides, enhancement of knowledge through research, and reduction of light pollution.[82] Additionally, the NBS 2030 includes a range of specific insect protection measures. These include new protection projects for endangered insect species, recommendations for insect protection measures in Natura 2000 sites, and the prohibition of insect traps outside enclosed spaces.[83]

80 *Bundesamt für Naturschutz*, Insektenmonitoring, available at: www.bfn.de/insektenmonitoring (02.11.2025).

81 *LUBW Landesanstalt für Umwelt Baden-Württemberg*, Insektenmonitoring, available at: www.lubw.baden-wuerttemberg.de/natur-und-landschaft/insektenmonitoring (02.11.2025).

82 *Bundesministerium für Umwelt, Klimaschutz, Naturschutz und nukleare Sicherheit*, Aktionsprogramm Insektenschutz – Gemeinsam wirksam gegen Insektensterben (2019), available at: www.bmuv.de/fileadmin/Daten_BMU/Pools/Broschueren/aktionsprogramm_insektenschutz_kabinettversion_bf.pdf (07.10.2025).

83 *Bundesministerium für Umwelt, Klimaschutz, Naturschutz und nukleare Sicherheit und Verbraucherschutz*, Nationale Strategie zur Biologischen Vielfalt 2030 (2024), available at: www.bmuv.de/fileadmin/Daten_BMU/Download_PDF/Naturschutz/nbs_2030_1_aktionsplan_bf.pdf, 6 f. (20.12.2025).

Table 9: Programmes to Reverse Pollinator Decline

Programme	*Measures*
Insect Protection Action Programme (API)[84]	– Promote insect habitats and structural diversity in agricultural landscapes – Restore and connect habitats for insects in other landscape areas – Strengthen protected areas as habitats for insects – Reduce the use of pesticides – Reduce input of nutrients and pollutants into soils and waters – Reduce light pollution – Develop, expand, and deepen targeted research on insects – Improve funding for measures against insect decline – Promote public engagement in insect protection measures
National Strategy for Biological Diversity 2030 (NBS 2030)[85]	– Drafting a regulation by 2027 that restricts the use of insect traps outside enclosed spaces – Evaluation of the API by 2027 in order to optimize existing measures or develop new strategies based on the results – Creation of additional protection projects for highly endangered or critically threatened insect species by 2027 – Preparation of recommendations for insect protection measures in Natura 2000 sites by 2027

Nationwide insect monitoring is still in the development stage in Germany; no methodology for the regular monitoring of pollinating insects has yet been implemented. However, a standardized methodological guideline has already been developed, which outlines the basic structure of insect monitoring and contains initial methodological descriptions.[86]

To implement these objectives effectively, Germany has adopted a range of measures. Section 6 of the Federal Nature Conservation Act (BNatSchG) imposes a legal obligation on both the federal government and the Länder to observe and assess the state of nature and landscapes. This duty expressly encompasses systematic monitoring activities and therefore provides the statutory basis for the observation of insect populations, including pollinators. At the EU level, this national monitoring framework is complemented by Article 10 of the EU Regulation on Nature Restoration, which mandates the European Commission to develop and adopt a scientifically sound methodology for monitoring pollinator diversity and population trends. This ensures methodological harmonisation and

[84] *Bundesministerium für Umwelt, Klimaschutz, Naturschutz und nukleare Sicherheit*, Aktionsprogramm Insektenschutz – Gemeinsam wirksam gegen Insektensterben (2019), available at: www.bmuv.de/fileadmin/Daten_BMU/Pools/Broschueren/aktionsprogramm_insektenschutz_kabinettversion_bf.pdf (07.10.2025).

[85] *Bundesministerium für Umwelt, Klimaschutz, Naturschutz und nukleare Sicherheit und Verbraucherschutz,* Nationale Strategie zur Biologischen Vielfalt 2030 (2024), available at: www.bmuv.de/fileadmin/Daten_BMU/Download_PDF/Naturschutz/nbs_2030_1_aktionsplan_bf.pdf, 6 (20.12.2025).

[86] *Bundesamt für Naturschutz*, Insektenmonitoring, available at: www.bfn.de/insektenmonitoring (07.10.2025).

comparability of data across Member States. In parallel, the use of plant protection products is subject to a comprehensive and binding regulatory regime in Germany. On the basis of the Plant Protection Act (PflSchG), its implementing regulations, and directly applicable European legislation, all plant protection products require prior authorization before they may be placed on the market or used. This authorization procedure is carried out by the Federal Office of Consumer Protection and Food Safety (BVL), which assesses products for their safety with regard to human health, animal health, and environmental impacts. Compliance with the applicable requirements is subsequently monitored by the Länder through their competent supervisory authorities. Together, these legal and administrative mechanisms aim to minimize risks associated with plant protection products and to contribute indirectly to the protection of insects and other components of biodiversity in agricultural landscapes.[87]

The use of the neonicotinoids imidacloprid, thiamethoxam, clothianidin, and thiacloprid is prohibited in field applications within the EU and, consequently, in Germany.[88] Only the neonicotinoid acetamiprid is authorised in the EU, and thus in Germany, under certain conditions. The Plant Protection Application Ordinance (PflSchAuwV) envisaged a complete national ban on glyphosate use in Germany from 1 January 2024. However, following the renewed approval of glyphosate by the European Commission, this ban has become incompatible with European law, allowing glyphosate to be authorised EU-wide until 15 December 2033. The ordinance nonetheless provides for numerous restrictions on its use.[89]

To combat invasive alien species, Sec. 40a ff. Federal Nature Conservation Act (BNatSchG), especially Sec. 40a BNatSchG, regulate measures to prevent and control invasive species. These provisions aim to make Regulation (EU) No. 1143/2014 on the prevention and management of the introduction and spread of invasive alien species, the central legal basis for combating invasive alien species operational under German law.

The restoration of ecosystems degraded, damaged, or destroyed by invasive species is carried out primarily in two steps. First, established invasive species are removed to allow site-specific species to re-establish. This is done partly through physical control measures, such as isolating and managing water bodies, for example by installing capture devices to remove invasive species like the

---

[87] *Bundesinstitut für Risikobewertung*, Pflanzenschutzmittel, available at: www.bfr.bund.de/chemikaliensicherheit/pflanzenschutzmittel/ (07.10.2025).

[88] *Europäische Behörde für Lebensmittelsicherheit*, Neonicotinoide: EFSA bewertet Notfallanwendung bei Zuckerrüben im Zeitraum 2020–2021 (2021), available at: www.efsa.europa.eu/de/news/neonicotinoids-efsa-assesses-emergency-uses-sugar-beet-202021 (07.10.2025).

[89] www.bvl.bund.de/SharedDocs/Downloads/07_Untersuchungen/00_Rechtsgrundlagen/01EU/RL_91_414_EWG.pdf;jsessionid=7E04505CBA39AAB9FAF34BECF1EB48E7.internet952?__blob=publicationFile&v=4, https://eur-lex.europa.eu/legal-content/DE/ALL/?uri=CELEX:32018R0113 (07.10.2025).

American bullfrog.[90] In biological control, natural predators, parasites, or viruses of the invasive species are introduced.[91] In the second stage, site-specific species are deliberately reintroduced to help ecosystems recover, for example by promoting shade-providing trees and copses along water edges.[92]

Germany follows its obligations from EU legislation to plant additional trees as part of restoration measures. Article 13 of the EU Nature Restoration Regulation requires all Member States to contribute to the Union's objective of planting at least three billion additional trees by 2030, while giving priority to the use of native tree species.

At the national level, Germany has not established a fixed, legally binding target specifying the exact number of trees to be planted. Instead, implementation is guided by the overarching EU-wide objective, complemented by a broad range of federal and Länder-level programmes, funding schemes, and policy targets that support afforestation and restoration activities. For example, the state forestry authority "Thuringia Forst" aims to plant 1.6 million new seedlings in the Thuringian state forest by spring 2026.[93]

Generally, forests in Germany may only be cleared with the approval of the authority responsible under state law, Sec. 9 Federal Forest Act (BWaldG). This already shows that a large part of legal tree protection in Germany is carried out at the federal level. This protection is complemented by regulation and enforcement through the Länder: In Bavaria, for example, according to Art. 15 Bavarian Forest Act (BayWaldG), clear-cut or following damage-event unstocked forest areas must be reforested within 3 years and illegally cleared properties must be immediately reforested. In addition, many cities and municipalities issue their own tree protection ordinances or statutes.

VI. National Plan for the Restoration of Natural Resources

Due to the entry into force of the EU Regulation on nature restoration on 18 August 2024 Germany has to develop a national restoration plan. Two years after the Regulation enters into force, by 1 September 2026, Germany must submit the

---

[90] *Bundesamt für Naturschutz*, Nordamerikanischer Ochsenfrosch Management und Maßnahmenblatt, available at: https://www.bfn.de/art-19-management (20.12.2025).

[91] *Umweltbundesamt*, Handlungsfeld Biologische Vielfalt (2023), available at: www.umweltbundesamt.de/themen/klima-energie/klimafolgen-anpassung/anpassung-an-den-klimawandel/anpassung-auf-laenderebene/handlungsfeld-biologische-vielfalt/1000 (07.10.2025).

[92] *Nehring/Skowronek.*, Die invasiven gebietsfremden Arten der Unionsliste der Verordnung (EU) Nr. 1143/2014, Bundesamt für Naturschutz (ed.) (2017), available at: https://rp-giessen.hessen.de/sites/rp-giessen.hessen.de/files/2022-02/bfn_skript_471.pdf 46 (12.10.2025).

[93] *Thüringer Ministerium für Umwelt, Energie, Naturschutz und Forsten,* Aufforstung in Thüringer Wäldern: Jährlich über 1,6 Millionen neue Setzlinge (2025), available at: https://umwelt.thueringen.de/aktuelles/listenansicht-zitate/anzeigen-zitat/aufforstung-in-thueringer-waeldern-jaehrlich-ueber-16-millionen-neue-setzlinge (06.11.2025).

draft of its national restoration plan for the period until 2050 to the European Commission for review. Following feedback from the Commission, the final version of the national restoration plan is to be submitted in September 2027.[94] The works on this is pending, and its contents is yet unknown.

VII. Are There Any Specific Food Safety Regulations in Your Country?

In Germany, food safety is ensured through a multi-level legal framework that combines EU law with national legislation and administrative enforcement mechanisms.[95] At the EU level, the cornerstone of food safety regulation is Regulation (EC) No. 178/2002, commonly referred to as the General Food Law (GFL). This regulation establishes the fundamental principles and requirements of EU food law and creates the institutional framework through the establishment of the European Food Safety Authority (EFSA). Article 1(1) GFL defines the overarching objectives of EU food law as ensuring a high level of protection of human health and safeguarding consumers' interests in relation to food. These objectives are given normative effect in Article 14(1) and (2) GFL, which assigns a central role to food safety by providing that food may not be placed on the market if it is unsafe. The GFL specifies the concept of unsafety through a dual normative standard directly linked to its core objectives. Food is considered unsafe where it is, first, injurious to health, thereby reflecting the imperative of human health protection, or, second, unfit for human consumption, corresponding to the protection of consumers' interests. This legal construction demonstrates that food safety under the GFL extends beyond the avoidance of health risks alone and explicitly incorporates broader consumer-related considerations. Accordingly, "food safety" is operationalized through a set of risk-based regulatory standards, including requirements relating to food hygiene, contamination thresholds, traceability obligations, and mechanisms of consumer protection.

At the national level, these requirements are supplemented by the Food and Feed Code (LFGB) (Lebensmittel- und Futtermittelgesetzbuch). The LFGB aims to protect consumers from health risks, deception, and inadequate information. It regulates the production, treatment, marketing, and monitoring of food and feed, and empowers authorities to take preventive and corrective measures, including product recalls and bans, where risks to food safety are identified.

---

[94] *Bundesministerium für Umwelt, Klimaschutz, Naturschutz und nukleare Sicherheit,* Nationaler Wiederherstellungsplan für die Natur in Deutschland (2025), available at: www.bundesumweltministerium.de/themen/naturschutz/wiederherstellung-von-oekosystemen/die-eu-verordnung-zur-wiederherstellung-der-natur/nationaler-wiederherstellungsplan-fuer-die-natur-in-deutschland (02.10.2025).

[95] *Purnhagen,* Einleitung zum Lebensmittelrecht. In: Purnhagen/Schäfer/Horst (eds.): BeckOK Lebensmittelrecht, 2026, para 1 et seqq.

Further legal instruments include the Food Hygiene Regulation, implementing EU hygiene rules (notably Regulations (EC) Nrs. 852/2004 and 853/2004), as well as specific ordinances governing contaminants, residues, novel foods, and food additives. A key structural element of the German system is the division of responsibilities: while the federal level enacts legislation and coordinates risk assessment, enforcement and official food controls are primarily carried out by the Länder through specialized authorities.

German environmental and nature conservation law does not impose restoration obligations that would directly jeopardize food supply. Instead, EU legislation within the framework of restoration-relevant measures in the CAP (such as the rewetting of peatlands, the restoration of floodplains, or the designation of non-productive areas) are relied being upon. In addition, proportionality principles and impact assessments are applied in planning and authorization procedures, ensuring that restoration measures are tailored to local conditions and do not result in disproportionate restrictions on agricultural production. Moreover, restoration policies are increasingly linked to long-term food security objectives by enhancing ecosystem services, such as soil fertility, water retention, and climate resilience, which are essential for the stability of agricultural production under changing environmental conditions.

In Germany forms of agriculture that law and politics define as sustainable are actively promoted through a combination of EU law, national legislation, and funding instruments, with the explicit objective of protecting and restoring natural resources such as soils, water bodies, biodiversity, and the climate. At EU level, the CAP provides the primary legal and financial framework. In Germany, CAP instruments are implemented through the national CAP Strategic Plan pursuant to Regulation (EU) 2021/2115. Eco-schemes and agri-environment-climate measures promote practices associated with organic farming, integrated production, precision farming, and agroecological approaches, including reduced pesticide use, diversified crop rotations, maintenance of permanent grassland, and the creation of non-productive landscape elements. These measures are voluntary and remunerated, thereby encouraging participation while safeguarding farm viability.

Organic farming is specifically supported under both EU and national law. The legal framework is provided by Regulation (EU) 2018/848 on organic production, complemented by funding schemes under the CAP and Länder-level rural development programmes. Germany has further committed, at policy level, to expanding organic farming as part of its sustainability and biodiversity strategies.

Climate-oriented forms of agriculture, such as carbon farming and regenerative practices, are promoted primarily through climate protection instruments. The Federal Climate Change Act (KSG) sets binding sectoral emission targets, including for agriculture, thereby incentivising practices that enhance soil carbon sequestration and reduce greenhouse gas emissions. In addition, peatland rewetting, paludiculture, and climate-friendly soil management are supported through targeted programmes under the National Peatland Strategy.

Precision farming and integrated production are encouraged through advisory services, investment support, and research funding, particularly under rural development law and innovation programmes. Although no single statute comprehensively regulates all sustainable farming concepts, the German legal framework relies on an integrated approach combining environmental law, agricultural subsidies, and climate policy. Taken together, these instruments aim to align agricultural production with the restoration and long-term protection of natural resources while maintaining food security and economic viability.

Innovative Complements and Substitutes for Contracts in German Digital Contract Law[1]

Lena Kunz

I. Preliminary Remarks: A Comprehensive Approach to Digital Contract Law

The questionnaire for this national report relates to (digital) contract law under the banner of commercial law. From a German perspective it is important to underline that in the German legal system contract law is not split off into commercial and non-commercial contract law. In addition, the idea to distinguish between consumer and business contracts was not originally embedded in the German legal system, but it has been absorbed in the German Civil Code (*Bürgerliches Gesetzbuch*, BGB) due to the EU legislation on consumer protection. However, in digital contract law, the distinction between consumers and businesses can be important. Especially automated contracts pose a particular challenge to consumer protection standards. Nonetheless, in the doctrinal discussions about digital contract law, contractual settings are *not* split off according to the role of the contracting parties in the internal market (consumer, businessperson, governmental institution, software agent, employees, employers etc.). This is also reflected in the fact that there is no separate consumer code in German law.

For this reason, the German Civil Code is the main source of rules on contracts, including digital and automated contracts and contracts referring to digital contents or digital services. The rules provided by the BGB are only supplemented by specific regulations laid down in the German Commercial Code (*Handelsgesetzbuch*, HGB). The HGB provides rules on specific contractual settings, i. e., contract types in German legal doctrine (*Vertragstypen*), which only exist in a commercial or business environment (e. g., contract for the carriage of goods by road or by sea; sales contract involving at least one businessperson). Regulations on these specific contractual settings can only be found in the German Commercial Code (*Handelsgesetzbuch*, HGB). Considering, however, the unity of contract law in the German legal system, the issues discussed below are not only specific to commercial law. Thus, my observations to innovative com-

[1] The literature cited hereinafter represents only a selection and is not exhaustive.

plements and substitutes for contracts follow a comprehensive approach to contract law.[2]

Unlike many other legal systems, German private law follows a strict distinction between contractual consent on creating *obligations* (for instance, by concluding a sales contract) and the contractual consensus on producing a transfer of rights (transaction creating a *right in rem* or having proprietary effects). For instance, if A wants to sell an electric car to B, first A and B will conclude a sales contract producing mutual obligations (i.e., obligation to transfer a property right to B and obligation to pay a certain amount of money to A). However, the enforcement of these obligations is only produced by a second contract (and registration when it comes to real estate), i.e., the contract of transaction (*dingliche Einigung*). Even if the contractual consensus on creating mutual obligations is invalid, a transfer of rights can be valid.[3]

Disregarding this distinction in German law, the notion of (smart) contracts used hereinafter covers also (smart) contracts creating, transferring, or assigning rights. This is particularly important for the realm of crypto assets and tokens, including Non-Fungible Tokens (NFTs).[4] Generally speaking, tokens can be regarded as technical manifestations ("shells") of crypto assets. Especially the legal nature of tokens is highly controversial in German (private) law, as tokens can neither be readily qualified as *rights in rem* nor clearly as *rights in persona.*[5] It is therefore much debated how to doctrinally structure the transfer of tokens and potentially associated crypto assets.

---

[2] This national report does not cover the discussion about innovative complements and innovative substitutes for contracts in labor and insurance law (esp. in the field of InsurTech). Furthermore, it will not delve into cross-border implications.

[3] The underlying principles are called *Trennungsprinzip* and *Abstraktionsprinzip*.

[4] The phenomenon of Non-Fungible Tokens (NFTs) leads to many questions, for instance, in German property (and IP) law which I will not delve into below. For, German property law is tailored to rights on things, i.e., physical objects (*res*; *Sache*) and not on rights on other non-physical objects (*Gegenstand*), let alone on tokenized access rights on digital twins or alike.

[5] Unless a token is covered by the *Gesetz über elektronische Wertpapiere* (eWpG), issued on June 3rd, 2021 (BGBl. I 1423). For these tokens, § 4 para. 3, eWpG establishes that an electronic security is considered a *res* within the meaning of § 90 BGB. For all other tokens, it is utmost controversial how to qualify their legal nature and how to doctrinally structure their transfer; for further reading see, e.g., *Omlor*, in: Rieble (copy ed.), Staudinger BGB, rev. ed. 2024, Vorb. §§ 244–248 BGB n. A83 et seqq.; *id.*, Privatrecht der Kryptowerte, NJW 2024, 335, 336–341 (with proposals for amendments to the BGB); *id./Möslein* (eds.), Blockchain und Recht, 2024, especially §§ 2–5; *Thelen*, Kryptowerte in der notariellen Erbrechtspraxis, RNotZ 2023, 425, 428–430.

II. Innovative Complements to Contracts

1. Conceptual Foundations

In German private law (including commercial law), it is *doctrinally* uncommon to distinguish between "innovative complements" and "innovative substitutes" for contracts.[6] However, in digital contract law this distinction does exist. Furthermore, both categories can be found in the German legal landscape from a functional perspective. In *legal* literature, the issues raised in the questionnaire are discussed and captured, for instance, by the headwords of *smart (legal) contracts*[7], *smart devices*, *smart wearables*, *smart contracting*, *automated decision-making*, *digital contract management*, *software agents*, and in a broader sense associated with the rise of *legal tech* (and *legal engineering*) and framed as *digital contract law*. However, the term *contract automatization* (*Vertragsautomatisierung*) seems to be predominant among providers of software solutions in this field, but it seems to be rather uncommon in legal literature.[8]

Regarding these findings, it is not yet possible to spot a clear and settled conceptional and doctrinal framework for neither innovative complements to contracts nor innovative substitutes for contracts. Legal literature concerning both or one of these phenomena is abundant, both reflecting the rapid technological innovations and, at the same time, still searching for a clarified doctrinal framework for the technological development.

2. Typology and Sectoral Application of Complements to Contracts

a) Typology

Complements to contracts may include:
- smart contracts,
- contracting platforms using blockchain-based smart contracting (e.g., *Ethereum*, *OpenSea*),

[6] See, however, the distinction made with regard to smart contracts by *Möslein*, ZHR 183 (2019), 254, 268 et seqq. (stressing the primacy of law); *id.*, Rechtsgeschäftslehre und Smart Contracts, in: Braegelmann/Kaulartz (eds.), Rechtshandbuch Smart Contracts, 2019, 81–98. *Möslein* distinguishes between contract execution instruments (*Instrumente der Vertragsdurchführung*) and functional contract equivalents (*funktionale Vertragsäquivalente*).

[7] Taking a critical stance on the use of this term in law, e.g., *Busche*, in: Säcker et al. (eds.), Münchener Kommentar zum BGB, vol. I, 10th ed., 2025, Vor § 145 BGB n. 38 (calling it a dazzling concept which must not be equated with a contract in a legal sense; for smart contracts only being data records).

[8] Cfr. for the discussion about the concepts of automated contracts and algorithmic contracts in Germany *Wendehorst*, Softwareagenten im vertraglichen Rechtsverkehr, in: Gebauer/Huber (eds.), Künstliche Intelligenz – Zurechnung, Vertrag, Verantwortung – Ergebnisse der 38. Tagung der Gesellschaft für Rechtsvergleichung in Tübingen (Fachgruppe Zivilrecht), 2024, 9, 16.

- any kind of (autonomous or automated) software agents, including the phenomenon of agentic shopping or agentic commerce and robo-advisory services (esp. with neo brokers like Scalable Capital or Trade Republic),[9]
- automated systems for decision-making, embedded, for instance, smart devices (often coupled with IoT-features) like in refrigerators, washing machines, watches, printers, and in car batteries (with remote access by the lessor, see infra for further information on this case),
- rating and review sites, for instance, with AI-based credit checks (credit-scoring-systems) (used by SCHUFA Holding AG and alternative platforms like bonify),
- crowdfunding platforms,
- payment provider services (e.g., PayPal, Klarna, and Wero as embedded systems),
- services for online identification (e.g., BundID, an identification system used at governmental agencies for applications and alike),
- services for digital signatures,
- tools for the conclusion of embedded insurance contracts,
- AI-based workflow programs that are designed to autonomously compose and send e-mails to human beings,[10]
- services for instant messaging (e.g., WhatsApp, Signal, Viber) as means to conclude contracts or to notify of important contractual events.

b) "Smart Contracts" and "Smart Contracting"

"Smart contracts" are regularly defined as self-executing programs (based on algorithms) which are typically (but not necessarily) run on a blockchain system (and in a broader sense on systems based on the *Distributed Ledger Technology*, DLT). Consequently, in legal practice smart contracts are often used as digital components *within* conventional contracts (for instance, in construction contracts – *Bauverträge* – of the real estate industry). By this, these smart contractual components mainly serve the following purposes: automated documentation of contractual obligations (e.g., reaching contractually binding steps of construction within a construction project), automated enforcement of contractual obligations, automated fulfilment of contractual obligations, especially the obligation to pay.

Considering the above, *smart contracts* are conceptionally distinguished from *smart contracting*, i.e., a machine-to-machine contracting (M2M-contracting).[11] M2M-contracting, however, does *not* conceptionally imply that the contracting

[9] The phenomenon of agentic AI, for instance, operating as sales or shopping consultant (agentic shopping) raises issues of pre-contractual liability which will not be explored any further here.

[10] According to general information, such AI-based workflow programs are widely used in the German industry of e-commerce.

[11] See, for instance, *Wendehorst* (fn. 8), 9, 15.

parties are machines. Instead, the contracting parties are still human beings or corporate entities. The discussion in legal academia mainly focuses on how to capture the doctrinal challenges of M2M-contracting.

In legal academia, the phenomenon of *smart contracts* is *not* captured as an independent and legally acknowledged type of contract.[12] In general, smart contracts are neither considered to be smart nor to be contracts. Thus, smart contracts are *not* qualified as contracts in a legal sense. Legal scholars distinguish between the conclusion of a contract in a legal sense and its technical implementation by means of a smart contract.[13] Therefore, smart contracts refer to the level of implementation, but do not constitute a contract in a legal sense. Consequently, the principle "(computer) code as law" is neither acknowledged among German legal scholars nor among legal practitioners in Germany.[14] Instead, contracts concluded in a "smart" way are often regarded as pre-coded agreements concluded in a digital environment.

The issue whether or not the contracting parties have deployed a valid contract is regarded as legally independent from its technological setting as a "smart contract". For, the core element of a valid contract is still consensus among human beings. If this consensus is looser than in a traditional setting (e.g., because two AI agents have declared their "artificial" intent to be legally bound), legal academia draws on the concept of imputation of artificial action (*Zurechnung*) to a human being or a corporate entity.

Currently, the phenomenon of smart contracts or smart contracting is regulated neither by supranational nor by national legislation. Art. 36 EU Data Act (Regulation (EU) 2023/2854) is still exceptional and does not cover smart contracts (or smart contracting) from the angle of contract law. Nonetheless, Art. 36 and Art. 2 n. 39 EU Data Act provide for a (more or less helpful[15]) definition of smart contracts with regard to data sharing agreements and give at least a hint for smart contracts' function within national contract law (cfr. recital 104 in fine of the EU Data Act).

Smart contracts could figure as innovative complements to contracts as well as substitutes of contracts. Considering smart contracts merely as self-executing programs, they can help to keep track, for instance, of the proper fulfilment of contractual payment obligations or any other contractual obligations. In this sense, they can be qualified as mere complements to contracts. In this regard,

---

[12] This might have been different at the outset of the debate about the legal nature of smart contracts.

[13] See, e.g., *Berberich*, in: Wolff et al. (eds.), BeckOK Datenschutzrecht, 54th ed. (online version with date of 11/1/2025), Art. 36 EU Data Act n. 11 providing further references.

[14] See, for instance, *Legner*, Smart Contracts und Finanzdienstleistungen, VuR 2023, 213, 214 et seqq.; *Möslein*, ZHR (fn. 6), 254–293 (stressing the primacy of law while addressing smart contracts as second track for establishing and executing agreements which de facto run parallel to the legal track).

[15] For further discussion, see, e.g., BeckOK Datenschutzrecht/*Berberich* (fn. 13), Art. 36 DA, n. 7 et seqq.

smart contracts are also used as tools for documentation. In addition, smart contracts can even be a powerful tool of contractual enforcement as a case shows which has been judged by the German Federal Supreme Court (*Bundesgerichtshof*, BGH) in 2022 ("Renault-Battery-Case", see infra). In the German debate, smart contracts are largely not classified as contracts in the legal sense.[16] Functionally speaking, smart contracts tend to be qualified as mere complements to contracts using the terminological dichotomy of the questionnaire.

c) Sectoral Application

The finance sector (FinTech), the insurance sector (InsurTech) and the field of e-commerce are likely to be the main areas in which smart contracts and the associated technological infrastructure have great impact on contractual design, execution, and enforcement in Germany (for instance, regarding insurances against flight delays or crop failure). In addition, the pharma-and-life-science industry (e.g. Siemens Healthineers AG) has a high interest in AI tools to comply with regulatory documentation requirements. The relevance for the residential rental market seems to be high when it comes to contract enforcement,[17] but rather unclear regarding the automated conclusion of residential lease contracts.[18]

A specific governmental interest to foster and promote smart contracting seems to exist in the real estate industry and in the energy sector. The Federal Ministry for Economics and Energy (*Bundesministerium für Wirtschaft und Energie*) funded a joint project on BIM[19]contracts underlining the importance of the blockchain technologies in the real estate industry (RE Tech).[20] In addition, the same Ministry is eager to establish a registry for smart contracts (SMC-registry) especially in the energy sector.[21]

---

[16] For an instructive overview see *Borges*, Smart Contracts für Datentransaktionen und der Data Act – Potential und Herausforderungen der automatisierten Bereitstellung von Daten, CR 2024, 425, 429 et seqq. (pointing out that the core question is whether a smart contract being a computer program contains the contractual text written in computer code).

[17] Cfr. the court ruling of BGH regarding a lease contract of a car battery, see infra.

[18] Cfr. *Lindner*, Der programmierte Mietvertrag, NZM 2021, 665–672 (highlighting the relevance of automated residential tenancy agreements in the future).

[19] Building Information Modeling (BIM).

[20] https://www.digitale-technologien.de/DT/Redaktion/DE/Textbausteine/Smarte_Datenwirtschaft_Marginalspalten/Marginalspalten/SDW_BIMcontracts_Infokarte_kopie.pdf?_blob=publicationFile&v=1 (last access: 10/11/25).

[21] The statement of the Government is the following: "Die Bundesregierung startet den Aufbau eines Smart-Contract-Registers in der Energiewirtschaft. Insbesondere in der Energiewirtschaft haben Smart Contracts ein großes Potenzial zur Automatisierung und Effizienzsteigerung. Umso wichtiger ist die Transformation von Vertragsbeziehungen in digitale Sprache bzw. in digitalen Code. Die Bundesregierung hat deshalb jüngst mit der Erarbeitung einer Machbarkeitsstudie zum Aufbau eines SMC-Registers begonnen, das vertragliche Sachverhalte der Energiewirtschaft listet und so die Erfassung und Systematisierung von Smart Contracts ermöglichen soll. Gemeinsam mit der Deutschen Energie-Agentur (dena) und Vertretern aus Wissenschaft, Wirtschaft und Gesellschaft werden wir in einem ersten Schritt einen Austausch dar-

Furthermore, automated contracts are of utmost importance for the private sector of data management (including especially data transactions for multiple use). In addition, the benefits of AI tools are highly valued in compliance management. It is a market driven by private actors, especially suppliers of software solutions, for instance, with regard to the duty of ESG-reporting and of supply chain risk management. Private actors (e. g., Lufthansa Industry Solutions GmbH & Co. KG seated in Norderstedt, Germany; envoria GmbH seated in Munich, Germany; Glacier Carbon Reduction GmbH seated in Vienna, Austria) provide software solutions relying partially on AI tools to support companies in complying with reporting and documentation duties,[22] e. g., pursuant to the *national* Supply Chain Due Diligence Act (*Lieferkettensorgfaltspflichtengesetz*, LkSG; see § 10 LkSG) (see infra).[23]

d) Focus on Automated Contracts

To narrow down the following considerations, it is important to clearly distinguish between three features of the digitalization in contract law. These features are the following.

First, digital contents or digital objects of contracts, i. e., contracts may refer to digital contents, digital services, digital objects, or digitally represented rights. For instance, a contract for streaming services including options to buy or rent movies, e. g., at a platform as offered by Amazon Prime, is a contract referring to digital services. In nearly all occasions, such contracts are concluded at the same time by digital means. (Sales) Contracts on crypto assets technically represented by tokens are another example for contracts on digital objects or digitally represented rights, setting aside the controversial issues, for instance, how to charac-

über führen, welche Sachverhalte in Smart Contracts – unabhängig vom verwendeten Code – überführt werden können. Ziel wird es sein, mit Hilfe der dena eine öffentliche Plattform aufzubauen, die frei zugänglich ist und deren Inhalte permanent gesichtet, bewertet, diskutiert und kommentiert werden. So kann das Register Anwender und Entwickler bei der Ausgestaltung von Smart Contracts unterstützen, da auf ähnliche Anwendungsfälle zurückgegriffen werden kann. Dabei soll das Smart-Contract-Register in der Energiewirtschaft exemplarisch für andere Wirtschaftssektoren stehen und als Basis für die Ausgestaltung und den Aufbau weiterer Register dienen", see: https://www.bundeswirtschaftsministerium.de/Redaktion/DE/Artikel/Digitale-Welt/Blockchain/Textsammlungen/blockchain-strategie-investition-2.html (last access: 12/2/25).

[22] For an overview see, for instance, *Scheffbuch*, KI in der Nachhaltigkeitsberichterstattung, in: Zeitschrift für Bilanzierung, Rechnungswesen und Controlling (BC), 2025 (online version); *Vallant/Drewelies*, Zukunft gestalten: Nachhaltigkeit und KI in der Praxis, IRZ 2025, 427; *Weihe*, Compliance 2024: Was Verantwortliche im Mittelstand wissen müssen, CCZ 2024, 85, 89 et seqq.

[23] The EU Corporate Sustainability Due Diligence Directive (for short, EU Supply Chain Directive) is highly controversial among the German public; conservative (and radical right-wing) forces reject the European attempt on regulation in this field. For further information see, e. g., *Zimmer/Langbein*, Abschaffung des deutschen Lieferkettensorgfaltspflichtengesetzes – europarechtlich zulässig und sinnvoll?, NZA 2025, 1151–1156.

terize tokens and to transfer them.[24] Using the questionnaire's dichotomy, tokens could be qualified as innovative complements to contracts because they can be qualified as digital representatives or technical proxies for the underlying crypto assets.

Second, digital communication, i. e., contracts exclusively *concluded by digital or electronic means* (for instance, distance contracts created by using e-mails or by accessing platform like especially in the field of online shopping). The digital aspect refers to the means of communication, but it still involves at least one human being.

Third, automated contracts without and with autonomous features, i. e., contracts concluded, executed, or enforced by software agents or machines on both sides, i. e., fully automated contracts. Such automated contracts can be based on autonomous declarations or actions of software agents. Typically, such automated contracts are either concluded or enforced by means of the blockchain technology and can be described as smart contracts. Nonetheless, not every smart contract must be founded on autonomous declarations. Smart contracts can be solely automated as well.

In this regard, it is important to note that contracts concluded by a human being at a vending machine (e. g., for food, train tickets) are not a new phenomenon, but often compared with automated contracts without any direct human interaction. I will not tackle the phenomenon of contracts concluded at a vending machine in the following considerations. Instead, I will focus on fully automated contracts not directly involving human beings.

Automated contracts can be either classified as substitutes or as mere supplements to contracts depending on the concrete scenario. In the following consideration, I will set aside contracts concluded via electronic or digital means, even though platforms, e-mails etc. can be qualified as supplements or complements to contracts as well.

3. Interconnection and Interoperability with Contract Law

The digitalization of contract law leads to numerous intersections with areas of law which either did not exist before or were previously more clearly separated from one another. For instance, Consumer Protection Law interacts with Contract Law especially in terms of deployment and termination of contracts. Smart contracting leads to significant challenges to consumer protection standards (see infra). Data Protection Law and AI Law (as laid down in the EU AI Act, Regulation EU 2024/1689) has significant influence on contract drafting. Some German law firms discuss contract drafting strategies under the banner of *AI Contract Law* referring to contracts between providers of AI tools and other companies

---

[24] For extensive considerations see *Omlor/Link*, Kryptowährungen und Token, 2nd ed. 2023, part II (Zivilrecht), chapter 6 (Allgemeines Privatrecht) (online text version), see n. 44, 53, 54.

using these tools within the market. Questions of Intellectual Property Law are related to contract law issues as well (in terms of contract drafting).

Particularly, the regulatory and supervisory response to digital contracts (e.g., in the field of data protection law and AI-related legislation) seems to outrun and to overlap the traditional understandings of contracts being an expression of private autonomous decisions taken by humans on equal footing and due to their free will. The digitalization of (contract) law puts into question the traditional dividing line between private and public law. The impact of regulatory and supervisory rules on contract law (i.e., private law) is an on-going topic among German legal scholars (for instance, regarding supervisory acts like the Markets in Crypto-Assets Regulation – MiCAR).[25] At any rate, the use of smart contracts or smart contracting can both be covered by the freedom of contract guaranteed by the German Constitution. However, the use of the associated technologies poses a risk to the (structurally or personally) weaker contracting party. In my view, it is therefore necessary to take constitutional issues into account to a greater extent than has been the case to date.

To a certain extent, literature on digital contract law is detached from traditional contract law maintaining a life of its own.[26] A few legal scholars propose to establish an independent legal regime for contracts concluded by blockchain technology,[27] disassociating digital from traditional contract law. For good reasons, such approaches are rejected.[28] A similar trend could be observed in the field of trusts and estates in Germany, i.e., the idea to impose the digital estate of the de cujus different rules than the rest of his or her estate. In 2018, the German Supreme Court (*Bundesgerichtshof*) rejected this approach, i.e., the digital estate is part of the de cujus regular estate.

Beyond all these considerations, it is concerning that the majority of the examined literature on private law dealing with the digitalization of contract law takes an uncritical stance toward the threats to democratic systems (and especially to the Rule of Law), particularly with respect to the blockchain technology.[29] Due to the lack of (coherent) governmental regulation in the field of contract law, literature focuses on the doctrinal challenges to capture phenomena like smart contracts, tokens, and the associated technological infrastructure. In addi-

---

[25] Regulation (EU) 2023/1114.

[26] This tendency is also reflected in a significant increase of new chairs specially dedicated to the digitalization of (private) law at German universities. A rising number of these chairs pertains to the group of chairs dedicated to German private law.

[27] E.g., *Borges*, Rechtliche Rahmenbedingungen für autonome Systeme, NJW 2018, 977, 979 (emphasizing the need for new legal approaches for autonomous systems).

[28] Rejected, for instance, by *Busche* in MünchKommBGB/*Busche* (fn. 7), Vor § 145 BGB n. 38; *Möslein*, ZHR (fn. 6), 268 et seqq. (primacy of law); *id.*, Rechtsgeschäftslehre (fn. 6), 81–98.

[29] However, addressing these constitutional aspects *Möslein*, Rechtsgeschäftslehre (fn. 6), 81, 82–87 (considering smart contracts as expressions of contractual freedom in accordance with Art. 2 para. 1 of the German Constitution) and *Omlor*, Demokratische Blockchain-Algorithmen: von "Code is Law" zu "Law is Code"?, JZ 2022, 649–656.

tion, it seems that historically grown legal principles like, for instance, the idea that contracts are based on the free will of the contracting parties, tend to be seen rather as doctrinal obstacles than cornerstones of legal culture. In conclusion, it is important to strengthen an *adequate* interoperability between digital contract law and (European) constitutional law (cfr. Art. 1 para. 1 EU AI Act).[30]

4. Doctrinal and Normative Implications

Generally speaking, legal academia aims at incorporating digital phenomena into the existing contract law as provided in the German Civil Code. Thus, legal scholars seek to use well-known concepts and doctrinal approaches to solve issues raised due to the digitalization of contract law. However, the idea that smart contracts, smart contracting, or any other automated decision-making (with legal relevance) stand alongside the legal system as a second track is not (widely) supported.[31]

Especially the phenomenon of smart contracts challenges the traditional notions of intent and consensus. Furthermore, the irreversible documentation of "intent" within the blockchain collides with the common principle that some errors allow for a contestation of a declarations of intent. In addition, smart contracts go along with the risk of over-enforcement (including self-justice) and a significant threat to consumer protection.[32]

a) The Relevance of Principles and Model Laws on an International and European Level Among German Legal Scholars

International and European (non-governmental) frameworks and model laws like the *Principles of Contract Law in Electronic Commerce* and the *UNCITRAL Model Law on Electronic Commerce* (adopted in 1996 and amended in 1998) are rarely discussed nowadays by German legal academia.

Instead, legal academia focuses on the UNCITRAL paper on *(t)he use of artificial intelligence and automation in contracting* and the *Principles on Blockchain Technology, Smart Contracts and Consumer Protection* issued by the European

---

[30] Cfr. *Hacker/Berz*, Der AI Act der Europäischen Union – Überblick, Kritik und Ausblick, ZRP 2023, 226, 228.

[31] Advocating for specific doctrinal rules for smart contracting, e.g., *Wilhelm*, Smart Contracts im Zivilrecht (Teil II), WM 2020, 1849, 1852 (arguing that the legislator's intervention is inevitable); however, rejecting the idea of independent rules for smart contracting and alike *Busche*, Digitale Kommunikation in der Rechtsgeschäftslehre, in: Joost/Oetker/Paschke (eds.), Selbstverantwortete Freiheit und Recht (Festschrift Franz Jürgen Säcker), 2021, 15, 26.

[32] See, e.g., *Legner* (fn. 14), 213, 216 (putting forward the example that a car insurance company can access a black box in the insured car allowing the receipt of data about the driver's behavior. In the event of a car accident, the car insurer could use the data to automatically adapt the insurance premiums in line with the driver's misconduct). See infra in addition the rental-battery-case decided by the German Supreme Court.

Law Institute (ELI). Both papers have an impact on the doctrinal discussion within the German national contract law, for instance, by adopting the distinction between legal agreements existing off-chain and/or on-chain or both off-and-on-chain (when it comes to smart contracts run on a blockchain).

b) Conclusion of Automated Contracts with Autonomous Elements

Legal academia focuses on the issue how contracts are concluded if the "declarations of intent"[33] are produced by (autonomous) software agents or by automated procedures with autonomous elements (*autonome Willenserklärung*).[34] There are essentially six doctrinal approaches discussed among legal scholars. In most of these approaches, "imputation" figures as doctrinal core concept. The approaches are the following ones:

(1) analogue application of the rules on agency, in analogy to §§ 164 et seqq. BGB;

(2) analogue application of the rules on liability in case of a blanket declaration of intent[35] (*Blanketterklärung*);

(3) imputation according to the principles of the management and the control of risk spheres (*Zurechnung nach den Grundsätzen zur Beherrschbarkeit der Risikosphäre, Risikozurechnung*);

(4) imputation according to the principles of agency in knowledge (*Wissensvertretung*), in analogy to § 166 para. 1 BGB;

(5) generalization of "intent", i.e., it is sufficient if a human being had any intent to be legally bound using AI as a tool for contracting;

(6) recognition of a (partial) electronic legal personality of software agents or other autonomous systems (e-personality).[36]

---

[33] In German contract law, there is no direct equivalent to the doctrine of consideration as known in the common law of contracts, see for a comparative approach *Ostendorf*, Englisches Recht Vertragsgestaltung, 1st ed., 2021, § 3 n. 10–12.

[34] Autonomous declarations of intent are not necessarily combined with smart contracts. Therefore, the issue of autonomous declarations of intent is related to AI but not necessarily to the phenomenon of smart contracts.

[35] A blank declaration of intent is a declaration that does not provide all necessary information to establish a legal bond between the contracting persons. The person issuing a blank declaration intentionally leaves a margin of discretion to a third person to complete the declaration. This completed declaration of intent is attributed to the person issuing the blank declaration drawing on the rules of agency (by means of analogy to §§ 164 et seqq. BGB). Favoring this approach, e.g., *Wilhelm* (fn. 31), 1849, 1852.

[36] Pointing to this direction (with skepticism however), e.g., *Kainer/Förster*, Autonome Systeme im Kontext des Vertragsrechts, ZfPW 2020, 275, 297 et seqq.; *Teubner*, Digitale Rechtssubjekte? – Zum privatrechtlichen Status autonomer Softwareagenten, AcP 218 (2018), 155, 160 et seqq. (esp. 163 et seqq.: pointing at a "new legal status" as possible solution); for skeptical considerations see *Dornis*, Künstliche Intelligenz und Vertragsschluss, AcP 223 (2023), 717, 722 et seqq., 730 et seqq. (emphasizing the need of an AI liability regime based on the principle of trust); *Essers*, Haftungsfragen automatisierter Systeme, 2023, 114–121.

c) Binding Offers in Smart Contracts

Legal scholars discuss what offerings can be qualified as fully binding when deployed on-chain. The issue is whether or not an offering deployed on a blockchain-based smart contract is immediately binding, comparing it to displays in shop windows, in online-shops, or in advertising brochures. In German legal doctrine, for instance, displays in shop windows are not qualified as binding offers but instead as an invitation of the shop owner to make an offer (technically called *invitatio ad offerendum*). Thus, it will be the client who makes a binding offer and the shop owner will be the one who can decide either to accept or to reject it.

Unlike in this scenario, declarations deployed on-chain are automated and automatically trigger further actions (depending on the coding of the smart contract). It is therefore put forward that offerings on-chain are directly binding because the contracting parties are supposedly aware of the automated character and very nature of smart contracts.[37]

d) Erroneous Autonomous Software Agents

A very controversial matter is the question of how to deal with "errors" of autonomous software agents or any other AI tool used when concluding or performing a contract. Two phases are to be distinguished, i. e., errors referring to contractual consent and errors concerning the contractual performance.

A common textbook example is a smart device (e. g., a refrigerator) which orders too much grocery due to a software error of an autonomous software agent. It is an issue whether or not the person who induced a software agent to order grocery can be held liable to pay the full purchase price to the seller or trader. In addition, it is discussed whether or not the trader of the smart device can be liable if the buyer must pay the full price for the grocery. According to the transposed EU Directive on digital contents, a software malfunction can figure as a product defect (non-conformity) leading to contractual liability of the one who sold the smart device (see, esp., §§ 327d et seqq. BGB). In German contract law, contractual liability is not strictly vicarious. However, the entitlement to ask the seller to bring a good into conformity (*Nacherfüllung*), to ask for a proportionate reduction of price (*Minderung*), and to terminate the contract due to lack of contractual conformity (*Rücktritt*) do not require the seller's fault. Generally speaking, the compensation for damages is however fault-based; at the same time, it is combined with the reversal of the burden of proof.

The entitlement to ask for these damages also covers a damage caused by an autonomous but erroneous software agent regarding the buyer's general assets. For instance, if an autonomous software agent of a smart refrigerator orders 100

[37] So, e. g., *Möslein*, Rechtsgeschäftslehre (fn. 6), n. 18.

instead of 10 bottles of milk erroneously and the buyer, who owns the refrigerator, is obliged to pay for 100 bottles of milk, the buyer can ask the seller of the refrigerator for damages (which amount to the total spending for 90 bottles of milk).[38] Principally speaking, the remedy of damages is fault-based. Due to the reversal of the burden of proof, the contractual liability for damages resembles a liability regime based on risk spheres.

A general principle of liability for autonomous software agents, which is put forward by legal academia, is that whoever uses autonomous software agents is also liable for damages caused by these agents. This idea is often associated with § 278 BGB which concerns the debtor's liability for third parties. This provision establishes: "The debtor shall be liable for the fault of his legal representative and of the persons whom he employs to fulfill his obligation to the same extent as for his own fault. […]".[39]

In addition, it is unclear how to handle errors in persona, for instance, in the anonymous or pseudonymous setting of a Decentralized Autonomous Organization (DAO). Blockchain-based smart transactions are not based on trust in the contracting human beings, but on trust in the decentralized technology. In this sense, it seems to be irrelevant who are the real contracting parties, especially considering that parties normally implicitly acknowledge the anonymous or pseudonymous character of the blockchain-based community. For, in a blockchain-based community it is neither necessary nor common to reveal one's identity. Therefore, contracts with the Unknown are generally speaking feasible.[40] However, for parties it may become crucial to know who participates in a DAO at some point (for instance, when suspecting criminals to act within the blockchain-based community).

e) Formal Validity of Declarations of Intent and Contracts

Generally speaking, it is not required to maintain specific formal requirements for a contract being valid in German private law. Exceptions are made, for instance, for real estate transactions and guarantee agreements.

aa) Requirements for Formal Validity of Contracts According to the BGB

Regarding smart contracts, it is uncontroversial that declarations on-chain do *not* comply with the standard of written form pursuant to § 126 BGB (if required by

---

[38] See §§ 327i n. 3, 1st alternative, 280 para. 1, 241 para. 2 BGB. Some may even argue that the damages cover the spendings for 100 bottles of milk.

[39] § 278 (Verantwortlichkeit des Schuldners für Dritte): „Der Schuldner hat ein Verschulden seines gesetzlichen Vertreters und der Personen, deren er sich zur Erfüllung seiner Verbindlichkeit bedient, in gleichem Umfang zu vertreten wie eigenes Verschulden. […]"

[40] See *Möslein*, Rechtsgeschäftslehre (fn. 6), n. 8. For a divergent opinion (with regard to the corporate and contractual character of a DAO) see *Schwintoswki/Klausmann/Kadgien*, Das Verhältnis von Blockchain-Governance und Gesellschaftsrecht, NJOZ 2018, 1401, 1405.

law or by agreement for a certain type of transaction). For, the standard of written form requires a handwritten signature (§ 126 para. 1 BGB).

When it comes to smart contracts, less stringent requirements regarding the form of contracts, especially in § 126a BGB (*Elektronische Form* – electronic form) and in § 126b BGB (*Textform* – written form), are more controversial.[41] These provisions establish:

§ 126a BGB: (1) If the written form required by statute is to be replaced by electronic form, the issuer of the declaration must add his name and affix his qualified electronic signature to the electronic document.

(2) In the case of a contract, the parties must each sign an identical document electronically as described in subsection (1).

§ 126b BGB: If text form is required by statute, a legible declaration naming the person making the declaration must be submitted on a durable medium. A durable medium is any medium that 1. enables the recipient to store or save a declaration on the data carrier that is addressed to them personally in such a way that it is accessible to them for a period of time appropriate to its purpose, and 2. is suitable for reproducing the declaration unchanged.

It seems to be uncontroversial that currently declarations on-chain do not comply with the formal requirement of a qualified electronic signature (as defined in Art. 3 n. 12 eIDAS Regulation[42]) pursuant to § 126a BGB. For, current blockchain-based smart contracting-platforms do not rely upon certified providers of electronic signatures.[43]

bb) Legible Declarations and Recognizability as Formal Standards pursuant to § 126b BGB

As to the requirement of "text form", it is however controversial if declarations on-chain comply with the formal standard set out in § 126b BGB. First, the debate centers on the question of what is meant by "legible declaration" (*lesbare Erklärung*).[44] If "legible" means "readable" in a strict sense, computer code is not embraced, for not being a natural language of contract which can be read and understood by anybody who is able to read. By contrast, in a broader sense "legible" can be interpreted as any text which can be read or deciphered. Such an approach would allow to cover computer code as well and result in formal validity of declarations on-chain (provided that it is required by law or by agreement that a contract must be concluded in text form). Especially in B2C-settings, the require-

---

[41] See, for instance, *Kollmann*, Smart Contracts im bürgerlichen Recht, MMR 2024, 137, 139.

[42] Regulation (EU) No 910/2014 on electronic identification and trust services for electronic transactions in the internal market.

[43] *Möslein*, Rechtsgeschäftslehre (fn. 6), n. 13 points out that future declarations on-chain may comply with these requirements depending on the technological implementations.

[44] See, e.g., *Paulus/Matzke*, Smart Contracts und das BGB – Viel Lärm um nichts?, ZfPW 2018, 431, 457; *Kollmann* (fn. 41), 137, 139.

ments of contractual validity are challenging when business owners and consumers rely upon smart contracting (see infra).

Besides the issue of legibility, controversy unfolds because of the anonymity in blockchain-based networks. For, § 126b (BGB) requires that the person making a declaration (of intent) is "named". Some legal scholars argue that it is sufficient to have a nickname in order to identify the person making a declaration on-chain to meet formal standards.[45]

cc) Contracting via Instant Messaging

Services of instant messaging (e. g., WhatsApp or Signal) have become important means to either conclude contracts or to notify the contracting parties on events of contractual relevance like, for instance, termination of an agreement, receipt of payment, (embedded) links to terms and conditions, or announcements concerning the contractual obligations.

Among courts[46] and among legal scholars[47], two issues are controversial, i. e., first, if such messages (like, for instance, a message on WhatsApp) comply with the formal requirements of *text form* (§ 126b BGB) and, second, at what moment such messages are considered to be received by the opposite party.

Regarding the text form, the issue is raised if an instant message can be preserved on a durable medium. As to the moment of receipt of a declaration (conveyed by a service of instant messaging), courts and legal academia sometimes distinguish whether or not both parties were online at the same time. Others emphasize whether parties have a permanent access to their messages.[48] If this was the case, declarations would be received at the very moment both parties were online. If one party was not online, it can be important whether both parties have previously established a WhatsApp-connection for (pre-contractual) negotiations.[49] At any rate, if a message carries two blue hooks (in WhatsApp) a message is deemed to have been received (according to the Regional Court of Bonn, *Landgericht Bonn*). According to the *Landgericht Bonn*, it is irrelevant in this case whether or not the contracting party has *read* the message.

---

[45] See, e. g., *Möslein*, Rechtsgeschäftslehre (fn. 6), n. 12.

[46] See OLG Frankfurt a. M. of 21 December 2023 – 15 U 211/21, NJW 2024, 1425, 1428 n. 57–63 (using a WhatsApp message to a notice of defects to the contractor regarding to roofing work); for a different approach see OLG München of 11 November 2024 – 19 U 200/24, NJW 2025, 589, 591 n. 52–54 (discussing the legal relevance of emojis in instant messaging); AG Kassel of 15 March 2022 – 410 C 1583/22, BeckRS 2022, 8579 n. 10 (discussing the formal validity of a declaration which was sent via WhatsApp and aimed at terminating a contract).

[47] See, e. g., *Schäfer*, Vereinsrecht: Einladung zur Mitgliederversammlung, NJOZ 2023, 1376, 1378 (with further references).

[48] See, e.g, *Gomille*, in: Gsell et al. (eds.), BeckOGK BGB (online version with date of 1.2.2025), § 130 BGB n. 36.

[49] See LG Bonn of 31 January 2020 – 17 O 323/19, BeckRS 2020, 2835 n. 16, 17, 21.

f) Construction of Declarations of "Artificial" Intent and Contracts Concluded in an Electronic or Digital Environment

Legal scholars do not only discuss how to construe declarations of "artificially created" intent (*KI-Erklärung*), but also how to interpret contract clauses created by an AI tool.[50]

In German contract law, the declarations of intent (*Willenserklärungen*) and the contract, understood as product of mutual consent (based on an offer and an acceptance), are methodologically distinguished when it comes to construction. For, the declarations of intent are qualified as unilateral declarations to conclude a contract, whereas the contract is the product of mutual consent.

Thus, construction is twofold in German contract law, i.e., each and every declaration of intent can be construed analyzing whether or not a party really wanted to give his or her consent (issue of binding effect). However, once mutual consent has been reached, the content of the agreement (contract) itself is subject to interpretation (especially, for determining the mutual duties of the contracting parties).

aa) The Construction of Artificial Intent

Consideration has been given to whether declarations of artificial intent can be construed like terms and conditions of contracts.[51] From there it follows that clauses and declarations created by AI are rather seen as objective declarations (with an objective meaning). From a methodological standpoint, this approach treats artificially created texts (by generative AI) of legal relevance rather like black letter law than a content mutually agreed upon by the contracting parties. By this, artificially created declarations or artificially created terms and conditions of contracts lose their individual or (inter-)subjective meaning.

bb) Computer Code and Contract

Controversy unfolds around programming languages as contract languages in many regards, first, because these unnatural languages are normally only readable by IT experts.

Second, with regard to smart contracts, it is controversial whether or not the computer code represents the content of the contract. If the answer is affirmative, the next issue is how it will be possible and who will be entitled to construe the contract. This issue does not only refer to declarations of intent, but also to any

---

[50] Cfr. *Busche*, Digitale Kommunikation (fn. 31), 15, 25–26.

[51] *Busche* (fn. 31), 15, 26 proposes to construe declarations created by autonomous software agents (in computer code) by its objective meaning (seemingly referring to an expert understanding of computer languages and comparing it to the construction of terms and conditions of contracts); for a more party-related approach see *Möslein*, Rechtsgeschäftslehre (fn. 6), n. 21 in fine, 22–24; *id.*, ZHR (fn. 6), 254, 277 et seqq. (proposing a comprehensive view including the computer code in contract construction).

"smart" proof within the contractual lifecycle (e.g., proof of timely contractual performance; notice of defect). With respect to the proving quality of protocols of automated actions, it is controversial if smart contracts can figure as legally valid instruments or documents to prove certain events of legal relevance.[52]

Most legal scholars distinguish between the contract and its technological implementation via smart contract.[53] Consequently, the agreement between the parties lies in the contract outside the blockchain-based smart contract.[54] It is therefore not necessarily congruent with the smart contract. This leads to the question what happens if the computer code (of a smart contract) does not correspond to the parties' agreement (existing outside the blockchain). In terms of the burden of proof, it is unclear how the principally readable computer code relates to an oral agreement between the parties.[55]

g) Smart Contracts and Consumer Protection

There is considerable controversy as to what extent smart contracts and smart contracting conflict with European consumer law. Academia focuses mainly on the provisions implementing the European Consumer Rights Directive (2011/83/EU), the European Consumer Credit Directive (Directive (EU) 2023/2225), and the European Directive on Distance Marketing of Financial Services (Directive (EU) 2023/2673).[56]

Smart contracts may regularly be qualified as distance contracts (*Fernabsatzvertrag*) and thus be covered by the Consumer Rights Directive if a consumer is involved. For instance, smart household devices (e.g., refrigerators, washing machines, printers) are equipped with software tools to automatically and/or autonomously manage (and pay for) purchases of, e.g., grocery, ink, or washing powder. If a consumer is involved, this consumer may invoke his right of withdrawal (or right to cool-off) for being a contract concluded at distance by means of an online interface (contracts in e-commerce). Thus, smart contracts may typically trigger consumer protection rights, such as the right of withdrawal or cooling-off.[57]

---

52 Affirmative, e.g., *Möslein*, Rechtsgeschäftslehre (fn. 6), n. 11.

53 E.g., with emphasis on the need of consumer protection *Legner* (fn. 14), 213, 214 ("Code is not Law"); *Möslein*, Rechtsgeschäftslehre (fn. 6), 81–98, n. 1 et seqq. For a more skeptical perspective on this issue, for instance, *Borges* (fn. 16), 425, 433 et seqq. (discussing the principle of consistency with regard to Art. 36 DA).

54 However, this is not the general opinion, for a diverging and more integrative approach see, e.g., *Möslein*, Rechtsgeschäftslehre (fn. 6), n. 20–21 and n. 22–24 (*Möslein* points out that users of blockchain-based smart contracts are supposed to have a basic understanding of programming languages).

55 Cfr. *Legner* (fn. 14), 213, 215.

56 About this issue see, e.g., *Legner* (fn. 14), 213 et seqq.

57 See, e.g., *Kollmann* (fn. 41), 137, 139; *Lindner* (fn. 18), 665, 671 et seqq.

In addition, it is controversial how business owners can comply with the consumer protection standards laid down in § 312j BGB,[58] when relying upon blockchain-based smart contracting. According to § 312j para. 3 BGB, business owners shall ensure that consumers when placing their orders explicitly acknowledge that the order implies an obligation to pay.[59] § 312j para. 4 BGB establishes that a contract shall not be valid if a business owner does not comply with consumer-protecting requirements laid down in § 312j para. 3 BGB. Some legal scholars argue that § 312j para. 4 BGB does not establish the invalidity of contract (in detriment of the consumer). Instead, it does not create any obligations in detriment of consumers.[60] By contrast, others argue that a contract is temporarily invalid if entrepreneurs do not strictly comply with the button-requirement laid down in § 312j para. 3 BGB.[61] If consumers use platforms to conclude contracts (and these platforms implement smart contracting technologies), violations of consumer protections standards by the providers of these platforms are typically *imputed* to entrepreneurs pursuant to the liability principles laid down in § 278 BGB.[62]

If a smart household device (e. g., a smart washing machine) orders autonomously a product like washing powder at an online store, consumers are not likely to be aware of each and every ordering (autonomous repeat order). The specific orderings may happen without the consumer's intervention and a concrete awareness of placing an order with an obligation to pay. Sometimes it is suggested to use dash buttons for complying with consumer protection standards.[63] This approach leads to more questions, such as whether or a not a dash button can be seen as a *graphical* button in accordance with § 312j para. 3 sentence 2 BGB.

To protect the consumer's right of withdrawal or cooling-off, it is sometimes proposed to implement *Decentralized Oracle Networks* (DONs)[64] in blockchains for smart contracts.[65] Such DONs could help to implement, for instance, a re-

---

[58] This provision implements Art. 8 para. 2 of the Directive 2011/83/EU.

[59] Cfr. ECJ, judgment of 7 April 2022 – Case 249/21, NJW 2022, 1439.

[60] *Linardatos/Roth-Isigkeit/Rückert*, Recht der Digitalisierung – Fälle und Lösungen, 2025, 125 (n. 20).

[61] See, e. g., *Wendehorst*, in: Säcker et al. (eds.), Münchener Kommentar zum BGB, vol. III, 10th ed., 2025, § 312j BGB n. 34.

[62] For a case study see *Linardatos/Roth-Isigkeit/Rückert* (fn. 60), 119–132, 125 (n. 19).

[63] See, e. g., *Kollmann* (fn. 41), 137, 140 et seqq.

[64] *Oracles* are software interfaces that provide external data (also known as off-chain data) for smart contracts on a blockchain. This is why they are also referred to as middleware. In other words, they are interfaces between a blockchain and the real world. These interfaces allow data outside the blockchain to be included in the automated chain formation (known as blockchain middleware). To preserve the decentralized nature of the blockchain as its core idea (also referred to as the "oracle problem"), it is proposed to implement oracles in the form of Decentralized Oracle Networks (DONs). Practical applications for DONs include the following fields, i. e., feeding asset prices into the financial sector, feeding weather information into the insurance sector, for IoT sensors in supply chains, and for ID verification for public authorities.

[65] *Kollmann* (fn. 41), 137, 139 et seqq.

verse transaction in the blockchain-based smart contracts, i.e., the order, for instance, will be canceled and the associated steps to reverse the transactions will be initiated.[66] Yet others want to introduce a time loop in the computer code of the smart contract. This time loop is supposed to postpone the transaction until the withdrawal period is over.[67] It is considered a violation of consumer protection law if entrepreneurs ask consumers upfront to waive their right of withdrawal.[68] I am not aware of any German (or European) law that forces users of smart contracting tools (in B2C-settings) to implement DONs.[69]

h) The Obligation to Pay and its (Autonomous) Fulfillment by Smart Functions (including E-Money and E-Money-Tokens)

aa) Smart Payment Methods

Within a smart contract setting, the contractual obligation to pay can be fulfilled by an autonomous function. If a smart contract contains programming that triggers a payment in the event of a specific occurrence (e.g., timely delivery of a product), the payment can be executed without any delay and any need for advance payment (or, conversely, without waiting for the money to be received). By this, smart contracts can enhance atomic transactions, i.e., the immediate exchange of goods and services.[70]

Besides, contracts concluded, for instance, in e-commerce are regularly linked to payment service providers, like, for instance, Klarna, PayPal, or Wero. Using the dichotomy of the questionnaire, these services can be qualified as (economically important) innovative complements to contracts, to wit, regardless of its configuration as "smart contracts".

---

[66] *Legner*, Smart Consumer Contracts – Die automatisierte Abwicklung von Verbraucherverträgen, VuR 2021, 10, 14 et seqq.; see for further reference see *Legner* (fn. 14), 213, 217 et seqq. (withdrawal by means of reverse transactions).

[67] See, for instance, *Paulus/Matzke*, Smart Contracts und das BGB – Viel Lärm um nichts?, ZfPW 2018, 431, 461 et seqq.

[68] See, for instance, *Legner* (fn. 14), 213, 217 (with reference to § 312m para. 1 sentence 1 BGB).

[69] The Secretary of Economy has initiated a project about the certification of blockchain-based smart contracts to strengthen the trust in this technology; the certification refers to the congruence between the parties' agreement and the coding of the smart contract; see https://www.bundeswirtschafts-ministerium.de/Redaktion/DE/Artikel/Digitale-Welt/Blockchain/Textsammlungen/blockchain-strategie-investition-2.html (last access: 12/2/25).

[70] Another important development lies in the fulfilment by tokenization which allows atomic transactions as well. For instance, a person rents a car and pays for the rental period. Right after (i.e., an atomic transaction, thus without any delay and without the risk of betrayal due to a performance upfront) the receipt of the digital payment in a smart-contract-setting, the renter of the car will receive the car key as token on his mobile phone. The token is a digital representation of the renter's right to access and to use the rented car. The token is an implementation of the rights and duties of the rental agreement.

bb) Crypto Assets and E-Money as Means of Payment

Under German law, the obligation to pay (*Geldschuld*) cannot be fulfilled by using crypto assets like cryptocurrencies, unless the parties have agreed otherwise.[71] Tokenized cryptocurrencies such as stablecoins, which can be qualified as e-money-tokens (EMTs), are also not suitable as a means of payment in Germany without an agreement between the parties. However, in case of such an agreement, the obligation, for instance, "to pay in BTC" (or "to pay in Tether"), is not unanimously considered to be a *payment obligation*, e.g., within a sales contract.[72] For, cryptocurrencies are not officially recognized as having domestic legal tender status.

According to the directly applicable Markets in Crypto-Assets Regulation (MiCAR),[73] crypto assets are defined as a digital representation of a value or of a right that is able to be transferred and stored electronically using distributed ledger technology or similar technology.[74] In line with European law, crypto assets are to be qualified under §1 para. 11 s. 1 n. 7 *Kreditwesengesetz* (KWG) as mere units of account ("*Rechnungseinheit*"). In accordance with §1 para. 2 s. 3 *Zahlungsdiensteaufsichtsgesetz* (ZAG), crypto assets (like BTC or ETH) are not regarded as e-money.[75]

This is different for transactions executed by payment provider services like PayPal. PayPal issues e-money. According to an EHI[76] study on payment behavior in e-commerce (Online Payment 2025 Study),[77] PayPal is the most widely used payment method for online purchases in Germany.[78] According to EHI

---

[71] For further information on the doctrinal quality of such agreements that provide for a payment method other than cash payment, see, e.g., *Kern*, in: Löwisch (copy ed.), Staudinger BGB, rev. ed. 2026, Vorb. §§362ff. BGB n. 20 et seqq., n. 63 et seqq., n. 77; *Herresthal*, Das Giroverhältnis (part I. A.), in: Drescher et al. (eds.), Münchener Kommentar zum HGB, vol. VI, 5th ed. 2024 (online version), n. 103.

[72] Rejecting such a qualification, e.g., *Schmidt*, in: Säcker et al. (eds.), Münchener Kommentar zum BGB, vol. III., 10th ed. 2025, §362 BGB n. 36; for further reference on this issue see *Looschelders*, in: Gsell et al. (eds.), Beck-Online Großkommentar (online version with date of 10/1/2025), §362 BGB n. 207 (instead doctrinally arguing for an exchange agreement without any obligation to make a payment); *Kerwer*, in: Herberger et al. (eds.), jurisPK-BGB, vol. II, 10th ed. 2023 (online version with date of 4/17/2024), §362 BGB n. 52 (arguing for an exchange agreement when parties argree upon "payment").

[73] Cfr. for the banking system §1 para. 11 s. 4 and s. 5 Kreditwesengesetz (KWG).

[74] Art. 3 para. 1 n. 5 (EU) 2023/1114 in the German text version: "'Kryptowert' eine digitale Darstellung eines Werts oder eines Rechts, der bzw. das unter Verwendung der Distributed-Ledger-Technologie oder einer ähnlichen Technologie elektronisch übertragen und gespeichert werden kann".

[75] For further references see Staudinger/*Kern* (fn. 71), n. 77.

[76] The study was conducted by the EHI Retail Institute GmbH (seated in Cologne, Germany).

[77] https://www.ehi.org/presse/paypal-festigt-spitzenposition/ (last access: 12/16/2025).

[78] Data basis according to the EHI: The "Online Payment 2025" study was conducted between February and April 2025 using an online survey. The panel includes data from 153 retail companies (online pure players and omnichannel retailers in Germany as well as B2C online shops) from various industries and with different turnover sizes, with a total net turnover of € 45.1 billion in 2024.

surveys, 28.5 percent of online purchases were paid for with PayPal in 2024. Based on the findings of the studies, installment purchases (*Ratenkaufverträge*) based on the principle "buy now, pay later" (BNPL), which are offered, for instance, by Klarna (and PayPal as well), are far less common in e-commerce than the use of e-money issued by PayPal.

i) Liability Regimes and the Phenomena of Smart Contract Generators and Smart Contracting

Legal tech companies have gained relevance over the last ten years. Contract generators are one area of application for legal tech. These automatically generated contract components, which can be assembled into a complete contract, are important innovative complements to conventional contract drafting. At the outset these contract generators were (also) designed for non-lawyers. This was viewed with suspicion by the legal services industry. Nowadays, AI tools have great importance for law firms.

Since the rise of AI, the initial contract generators have increasingly been coupled with AI and have turned into AI-powered contract generators. In 2021, the German Federal Supreme Court ruled that a publishing house which offers contract generator (without AI), which is named *Smart Law*, does not offer legal services subject to authorization pursuant to the *Rechtsdienstleistungsgesetz* (RDG) (see §§ 2, 3 RDG).[79] From there it follows that a legal tech service like *Smart Law* does not violate the rules for providing legal services. In addition, the person using contract clauses generated by a smart contract generator is responsible for their selection, assembly, and use. Errors in the AI system (e.g., due to faulty training data) may give rise to product liability on the part of the manufacturer of an AI-powered contract generator.

The forementioned individual court ruling of the BGH certainly benefited the legal tech market, but also left many questions unanswered regarding the general admissibility of legal tech. To my knowledge, there is yet no court ruling that deals with the question to what extent *AI-powered* contract generators can be used without having the prior authorization for offering legal services. It is an open question to what extent contractual clauses created by a black box-AI can trigger the liability of the user of such AI-powered contract generators.[80] Until now, the basic dogmatic assumption has been that it is generally not possible to delegate responsibility when using AI tools. The basic dogmatic principle is that those who use AI must also take responsibility for it. This approach is very based in the core idea expressed in § 278 BGB (see supra).

---

[79] BGH of 9/9/2021 – I ZR 113/20, NJW 2021, 3125.

[80] Regarding *non-contractual* liability, the proposal adapting non-contractual civil liability rules to AI (AI Liability Directive or AILD) was withdrawn by the European Commission in February 2025.

Errors in smart contracting must be distinguished from incorrectly generated contract clauses by smart contract generators. Defects of smart contracts which lead to errors in the process of smart contracting (e.g., the programming triggers a payment, although the product has not been delivered) are the result of wrong programming. This can be classified as product defects. Between the two contracting parties it will be a matter of proof whether a certain event in the real world had taken place (e.g., the delivery of a product). In this sense, users are not held liable because of the flawed programming, but a presumably flawed coding may help the opposing side to overcome a *non liquet* and therefore indirectly trigger the user's liability.[81]

5. Institutional and Regulatory Frameworks

Recent EU legislation provides a significant and highly ramified framework of rules on digital contract law, which have direct impact on German national contract law. First of all, the twin directives (EU) 2019/770 (Digital Content and Digital Services Directive) and (EU) 2019/771 (new Sales of Good Directive) concern mainly contracts on *smart contents* and set up protection standards for consumers.[82] Both directives have been transposed into German private law (see esp. §§ 327a et seqq., 475a to 475c BGB). From a German perspective it is important to note that contracts *on* digital content or digital services are not a new type of contract. The German legislature aimed at integrating the EU regulations into the general rules on contract performance and warranties.

Regarding smart contracts and automated contracts, Art. 36 EU Data Act (DA) is important. The provision highlights the economic importance of automated data transactions based on data sharing agreements and implies the legal relevance of smart contracts (see supra). The EU Data Governance Act (DGA)[83] aims at safeguarding data sovereignty, but the Act does cover smart contracts from the angle of contract law.[84] Nonetheless, data protection law interacts with

---

81 Example: A product or a service was not delivered on time by the contracting party A. However, due to a wrong coding, within the smart contract it is laid down *delivery on time* which triggered a payment of the other contracting party B. If B asks A to return the payment (cancelling the contract at the same time because the timely delivery was essential for the contracting parties), it is the contracting party A who has to prove the timely delivery; for further information on the burden of proof in these scenarios according to German evidence law see *Gaier*, in: Säcker et al. (eds.), Münchener Kommentar zum BGB, vol. III, 10th ed. 2025, § 346 BGB n. 147 (with reference to the principle laid down in § 345 BGB). A situation of a *non liquet* may arise. The registration of a timely delivery within the smart contract (displayed as code) may serve as base for the presumption of delivery on time or at least as an indication or a clue having some probative value as blockchain record.

82 For an exhaustive analysis see *De Franceschi/Schulze* (eds.), Harmonizing Digital Contract Law – The impact of EU Directives 2019/770 and 2019/771 and the regulation of online platforms: a handbook, 2023.

83 Regulation (EU) 2022/868.

84 *Hennemann*, in: Specht-Riemenschneider/Hennemann (eds.), Data Act/Data Governance Act, 2nd ed. 2025, Introduction, 82 et seqq. (n. 140–144).

contract law (e.g., users of IoT[85]-devices have bought these devices due to specific smart functions; for the well-functioning of the IoT-functions it is necessary to have data sharing agreements which are typically deployed between the seller of the IoT-device and a third party and are executed by smart contracts. The terms and conditions of the sales contract between the manufacturer/seller of an IoT-device and the buyer contain typically a privacy policy including consent to data transfer to safeguard the well-functioning of the IoT-features).

The EU AI Act[86] may have an indirect impact on specific contracts by establishing certain duties for providers of AI systems in relation to other entrepreneurs using or incorporating these AI systems in their own AI products. Although the EU AI Act follows a regulatory approach, some duties as established, for instance, in Art. 53 para. 1 lit. b (in conjunction with the annex XII) may directly impact the regime of duties between private contracting parties, regardless of the applicable law pursuant to Rome I Regulation. These "regulatory duties" may be qualified as *ius cogens* for contracting parties (*inter partes effect*).[87] The EU Directive 2023/1114 concerning the Markets in Crypto-Assets Regulation (MiCAR) has no direct relevance for matters of digital contract law. However, its definition of crypto assets in Art. 3 para. 1 n. 5 (in delineation to electronic money) has an impact on the role of crypto assets as means of payment, i.e., the approach to crypto assets decides whether and to what extent monetary debts can be settled with crypto assets (for further discussion see infra).

III. Innovative Substitutes for Contracts

In this subsection, I will focus (again) on smart contracts as presumably the most relevant substitute for contracts, even though this phenomenon has been discussed in the foregoing subsection about innovative complements for contracts.

For, smart contracts can either be qualified as a substitute for a conventional ("analogue") contract or be regarded as a mere complement to contracts (see supra). Most of the legal scholars understand smart contracts as mere instruments for contract execution and not as a functional equivalent to conventional ("analogue") contracts. This approach is often captured by the phrase "Code is not Law".[88] Phenomenologically, smart contracts appear either as smart supplementing "tools" within the contractual lifecycle (e.g., as starter interrupter device,

---

[85] Internet of Things (IoT).

[86] For the current draft proposal to further integrate the EU AI Act into the German national legislation see https://bmds.bund.de/fileadmin/BMDS/Dokumente/Gesetzesvorhaben/CDR_Anlage1-250911_RefE_KIVO-Durchführungsgesetz_Entwurf_barrierefrei.pdf (last access: 10/11/25).

[87] As to the issue of the smart enforcement of a contractual obligation to pay see the ruling of the Bundesgerichtshof (BGH) in October 2022 regarding a smart car battery (BGH of 26 October 2022 – XII ZR 89/21, NJW 2022, 3575). For further details on the court ruling see infra.

[88] For the entire discussion see *Möslein*, Rechtsgeschäftslehre (fn. 6), n. 4–8 (pp. 83–87).

as execution of payment obligations etc.), or they are congruent with the declarations of intent *co-creating* a contractual relationship between human beings. The latter scenario includes isolated M2M-contracting (e.g., a smart refrigerator autonomously orders grocery in collaboration with another smart agent and induces delivery of the order) as well as especially DAOs in the world of decentralized finance. For the scenarios of M2M-contracting and DAOs, it is typical that the computer code (also) contains the contractual obligations and rights of the parties. Especially in this scenario, it is controversial whether computer code can exclusively contain the content of the contract.

1. Conceptual and Legal Foundations

As already explained above, a doctrinal distinction must be made between smart contracts and smart contracting. Smart contracting is based on M2M-contracting, i.e., machine-to-machine contracting. It is important to note that the contracting parties are human beings or corporate entities and not machines (due to a lacking legal personality). Furthermore, the notion of autonomous software agents[89] is important since it is a specific form of M2M-contracting.

2. Typology and Functional Characteristics

When it comes to the typological grouping of substitutes for contracts, the technological phenomenon of smart contracts is examined from various legal perspectives by legal academia. This leads to a typological grouping that takes smart contracts only as a starting point. Automated transaction protocols on a blockchain are considered as a means of proof in court proceedings. In addition, such protocols are open to construction. Declarations of intent are categorized as declarations on-chain and off-chain (see supra as well).

3. Legal Recognition and Challenges

Rulings of German courts on contractual issues related to Artificial Intelligence or to the complete digitalization of contracts are still rare. Most of the rulings refer to patent law, data protection law, and tort law (non-contractual liability for AI).[90]

---

[89] *Wendehorst* emphasizes that smart contracts can be combined with AI tools in such a way that declarations of intent are made on-chain, i.e., by autonomous software agents. However, this combination is not compulsory. Therefore, both technological phenomena must be distinguished producing each different doctrinal challenges; see *Wendehorst* (fn. 8), 9, 15.

[90] For a summary of judgments and rulings on the legal implications of AI see, e.g., *van Hövell* et al., Rechtsprechung zu Künstlicher Intelligenz und deren mögliche Auswirkungen auf die Nutzung von KI-Systemen im Gesundheitswesen, PharmR 2025, 509, 509–513 covering rulings of German courts on patent law, data protection law, copy right, and liability rules.

Nonetheless, two court rulings are particularly interesting. The first of it refers to a fictional simulation of court proceedings and the second ruling (supposedly regarding a smart contract) is a real court ruling of the German Supreme Court in 2022.

a) A Fictional Simulation of Court Proceedings Concerning Smart Contracting

With regard to the enforcement of contracts deployed by smart contracting (M2M-contracting), no court ruling of a German court exists so far (as to my knowledge). However, Georg Borges, a law professor at the University of Saarland in Germany, developed an Industry 4.0 platform in collaboration with legal practitioners, allowing AI agents to autonomously conclude contracts for (fictitious) companies.[91]

In the fictitious case, a company (*Bertel Maschinen GmbH*) (B) had supposedly ordered two ball bearings from another company (*Production Engineering GmbH*) (P), both seated in Germany. The two orders were exclusively placed and executed by autonomous AI agents. On the buyer and vendor side, only AI agents were operating while negotiating pricing and amount. In addition, the AI agents imitated the creation of a smart contract run on a blockchain system.

The parties argued about B's first ordering because B denied having placed this order. With regard to the second order, B put forward that the company had conveyed a timely notification of defect by means of a smart contract. P argued that the notice of defect (*Mängelrüge*) was too late. Besides the issue of the validity of a "machine contract", the court had to deal with the question whether or not a blockchain protocol can serve as a proof of contract and related contractual issues like the timely notification of defect.

Subsequently, these issues were brought before a fictitious court (*Landgericht Südlingen*) and reviewed by real judges in the building of the *Amtsgericht Frankfurt a. M.*[92] One of the most important insights was that the judges considered the completely automated contract as valid, thus legally binding for the (human or human-related) contracting parties (*in casu* two corporate entities). In the course of the fictitious court proceedings, the judges had to construe the contract by reading computer code. For this task, they had to appoint an IT-expert as court expert.

This shows that smart contracting may lead to an outsourcing of some elements of judicial to non-judicial personnel and experts. Considering that the Rule of Law is the backbone of democratic legal systems, this may lead to constitutional challenges in the future (see supra already). Furthermore, the computa-

---

91 The research project is called *Industrie 4.0 Legal Testbed*.

92 See Urteil Landgericht Südlingen, in: Legal Tribune Online, 29 June 2024. For further information see the interview with one of the participating lawyers https://rsw.beck.de/aktuell/daily/magazin/detail/interview-njw-2024-36-simulation-zu-smart-contracts (last access: 10/11/25).

tional language of smart contracts[93] leads to the question to what extent legal engineering should play a role in the education of future lawyers.

b) A Ruling of the Bundesgerichtshof *on Smart Access to Car Batteries According to a Lease Contract (§§ 535 et seqq. BGB)*

In Germany, a case concerning a lease contract of a smart device was brought before courts in 2019, ending at the German Federal Supreme Court in 2022. It is the first case concerning smart devices brought to courts in Germany. In October 2022, the German Federal Supreme Court delivered its ruling.[94] The case was brought to court by a consumer protection association (the procedural setting of a class action is an exception in German procedure law, but in this case admissible pursuant to §§ 1, 3, 4 *Unterlassungsklagengesetz*, UKlaG[95]).

The facts of the case are the following: The plaintiff (here functionally represented by the consumer protection association; the natural person hereinafter referred to as the plaintiff for simplification) had purchased an electric car from a Renault dealer in Germany. In accordance with Renault's marketing strategy, the car's battery had not been sold but leased to the plaintiff. The lease contract came with a general terms and conditions clause that allowed Renault to remotely access the battery (by a starter interrupter device) in order to switch it off in case the lessee was in default of paying the renting fee. Although the published case records do not reveal the technological background of the remote accessibility, it is very likely that the control of receipts of payment and the blocking of the related battery were executed by means of a smart contract.

Subsequently, the lessee could not pay the renting fees for the battery anymore and, after giving notice, Renault remotely turned off the car battery. The lessee who also was the car owner could not use his car anymore. The lessee (plaintiff, represented by the consumer protection association, see supra) sued the lessor (defendant) asking to reactivate the battery, arguing that the general terms and conditions clause is invalid.

The German Federal Supreme Court (BGH) ruled that the clause is invalid. The Court argued that the remote access clause is an unreasonable disadvantage to the lessee as a consumer. For, the clause forces the *lessee* to sue the lessor to reactivate the battery again to use the related car. In the Court's view, such a clause puts upside down the distribution of risk within a lease contract, i. e., instead of the lessor suing the lessee for payment or return of the leased asset,

---

[93] For the language issue cf. Principle 8 (Language) of the ELI Principles on Blockchain Technology, Smart Contracts and Consumer Protection.

[94] BGH of 26 October 2022 – XII ZR 89/21, NJW 2022, 3575.

[95] These special proceedings allow certain consumer protection associations to attack terms and conditions used in consumer contracts. Therefore, courts only check on the legality of these terms and conditions and not on the contract itself. Consequently, the courts did not tackle the issue whether or not smart contracts were an admissible contractual complement.

the lessee must sue the lessor for return of the leased asset. Legal academia describes this situation as *over-enforcement*. This is a common side-effect of smart contracts. From the perspective of the Court, the reverted risk distribution does not correspond to the rules laid down in the rental law of the BGB.[96] Implicitly, the Court qualified the "smart content" of the lease agreement as a mere instrument for contract execution, thus, as a complement to the contract between the parties.

c) The Delegation of Risk Management to AI Tools and/or AI Agents Within the Supply Chain

The *legal* question whether the legal duty of documentation and reporting (along the supply chain) pursuant to the national Supply Chain Due Diligence Act (*Lieferkettensorgfaltspflichtengesetz* – LkSG) can be delegated to an AI tool is rarely discussed (in depth), despite being an important matter in many industrial sectors. According to § 10 LkSG, companies are required to document and report whether, and if so, which human rights and environmental risks or violations of a human rights or environmental obligation the company has identified and how the company deals with them.

If a company does not provide a complete or proper documentation (and report) pursuant to § 10 LkSG, the company *cannot* be held liable for a tort. For, § 10 LkSG is not classified as a protective law pursuant to § 823 para. 2 BGB triggering a liability for torts. The *contractual* liability of the company comes only into play if the company has *contractually* promised the documentation to another company or any other legal subject. In this case, it will not always be easy to quantify the actual damage incurred by the party who has asked for proper and complete documentation and reporting. The enforcement of such contractual claims for damages is only likely to be successful if the parties have agreed on a contractual penalty or on lump-sum damages.[97]

This leads to the following conclusion with regard to the use of AI tools for creating a report: If a company decides to use an AI tool for its report and the report is therefore deficient or incorrect, a sanction in the form of a contractual claim for damages is only possible in exceptional cases. In the event of incorrect or deficient documentation and/or reporting, it is mainly the competent authority which may (and, if necessary, must) intervene instead (see § 14 para. 1 n. 1 LkSG). The imputation of an improper or deficient reporting created by an AI tool can be based on the principle that whoever uses autonomous software agents

96 The court judgment refers to a clause in the general terms and conditions; it does not cover clauses which the parties individually agreed upon (e.g., in a C2C-setting). It is questionable whether the clause is also invalid in this scenario. For, in this setting a clause can only be invalid if it is either illegal (§ 134 BGB) or if it is deemed to be *contra bonos mores* (§ 138 para. 1 BGB) or to the principle of *bona fides* (§ 242 BGB).

97 *Vogel*, in: Johann/Sangi (eds.), Handkommentar zum LkSG, 2023, § 10 LkSG n. 19.

for his own benefit is also liable for damages caused by these agents. In legal academia, this principle is associated with § 278 BGB (see supra).

4. *Comparative and Prospective Analysis*

Finally, it remains to be considered which questions should be explored in greater depth in the future (including from a comparative perspective).

a) *Emergence of a Post-Contractual Legal Order?*

The novel complements to contracts by innovative technology create frictions with conventional doctrinal concepts in contract law. Pheonmena like smart contracts, smart contracting, M2M-contracting, and autonomous software agents conflict to a certain degree with the idea that contracts are based on free will and entirely autonomous decisions of parties who are on equal footing. In addition, the entire field of Artificial Intelligence, crypto assets, and Big Data is approached from a supervisory standpoint on a European level. The legislative steps of the European legislator establish supervisory mechanisms and do not (directly) deal with issues of contract law. Nonetheless, some duties established in European regulations and directives have a direct impact on the contractual relationship (*inter partes* effect). From a continental standpoint, this puts into question the traditional dividing line between private and public law.

However, considering the emergence of terms and conditions as an important contractual tool since the 1970s (including legal control mechanisms), the idea of a post-contractual legal order is not without any parallel in the past. Certainly, recent technological developments carry more weight and suggest that the upheavals in law (and presumably in its methodology) will be far more fundamental than in den 1970s. It would be therefore necessary to analyze how technological upheavals in the past have had an impact on doctrinal concepts of contract law.[98]

Considering the efforts of legal academia to integrate technological innovations in the existing doctrinal framework, we have certainly not yet reached a post-contractual legal system. It is a stretch to speak of a post-contractual legal order *at this stage*. However bearing in mind the constitutional implications of such a possible development, it is of utmost importance to take the constitutional aspects of the technologization and artificialization of contracts into account.

This leads to at least three important fields of potential focus, i. e., (1) the relevance of constitutional law in digital contract law, (2) robo-justice and the role of discretionary notions in statutory law and the algorithmic handling in (civil) proceeding, and (3) the problem of over-enforcement and the Rule of Law.

---

[98] For further reading see esp. *Möslein*, Die digitale Transformation des Vertragsrechts: Ad multos annos, BGB?, JZ 2026, 1–11.

b) Artificial Intent and Artificial Language as Methodological Challenges

The technologization of contracts leads to several methodological questions, e.g. the legal relevance of computer code for construing contract clauses. Computer code as non-natural language is not readable for everybody (literacy problem). If feasible, it will require a translation to a natural language. However, it should also be borne in mind that programming languages can bridge natural language barriers in contracts.

In addition, computer code as a non-natural language may represent artificial as well as natural intent. Legal academia is eager to integrate these new phenomena into traditional doctrinal concepts. Nonetheless, conventional methods to figure out whether two parties have concluded a valid contract (consensus) without any errors assume the free will and the autonomous decision-making of *humans.* The hitherto unclear controllability of autonomously acting machines raises methodological questions in law. For, the gap between free choice (e.g., the free decision to use a smart device) and a machine-driven event caused by a smart device is sometimes significant. It is therefore symptomatic that legal literature frequently refers to the concept of imputation or attribution (*Zurechnung*) in contract law. To impute a fact to a person, it is not necessary that it has actually occurred. Instead, it is sufficient if a judge or another legal authority recognizes this fact as true. Therefore, the methodological bond between "fiction" and "imputation" is close.

The widespread use of the term "imputation" (*Zurechnung*) as a conceptual basis in German legal literature, i.e., to determine the intention to be legally bound and held liable for unlawful "artificial actions", underscores that the fundamental principles of contract law are still important cornerstones in the field of *digital* contract law. However, the concept of *Zurechnung* is metaphorical and blurry. This is particularly evident in digital contract law. If the concept of imputation or attribution (*Zurechnung*) is not analyzed in depth from a doctrinal and methodological perspective, there is a risk that "attribution" will become a mere instrument of judicial discretion lacking clear doctrinal boundaries.

The Phenomenon of Intellectual Monopoly Capitalism

Katharina de la Durantaye and *Arne Radeisen*

I. Introduction

The regulation of intellectual property tells a tale of power shifts. The grant of an intellectual property right (IPR) allocates exclusive power over the use of an intangible object to one or more people. However, that exclusive power is constrained: regulatory interventions, limitations, and exceptions to IP shift power away from the right holder.

Beyond this familiar dynamic lies a second, institutional dimension of control – a tale of who holds the power to allocate and constrain IPRs. Intellectual property law in Germany is not only heavily governed by international treaties such as the Berne Convention.[1] Being a member state of the EU, German IP law is heavily influenced by an additional body of transnational law: law enacted and interpreted by the EU and its courts. Patent law is harmonized by way of regulations[2] and directives[3]. The same is true for trademark law[4] and design law[5]. For our study, then, copyright law is the most fruitful of the various IPRs since the EU does not (yet?) provide for a unitary copyright.[6] However, exploitation rights are almost completely harmonized through 13 directives and two regulations which the EU enacted over the past decades.[7] Indirectly, these directives led to a certain level of harmonization of moral rights, even though personality rights technically

---

[1] Berne Convention for the Protection of Literary and Artistic Works (as amended on September 28, 1979), https://www.wipo.int/wipolex/en/text/283698 (last accessed 12.03.2026).

[2] Key patent acts include the Biotechnology Directive (Directive 98/44/EC) and the IP Enforcement Directive (Directive 2004/48/EC).

[3] The Unitary Patents system is implemented through Regulation (EU) No 1257/2012 and Regulation (EU) No 1260/2012.

[4] Regulation (EU) 2017/1001 establishes a single EU-wide trademark while Directive (EU) 2015/2436 harmonizes national laws on trademarks.

[5] Regulation (EC) No 6/2002 establishes a single EU-wide design right (community design) while Directive (EU) 2024/2823 harmonizes national laws on design protection.

[6] Academics have, on multiple occasions, made proposals to not only harmonize, but unify EU copyright law, cf. only *European Copyright Society*, Letter to Mr Günther Oettinger, Commissioner for Digital Economy and Society, European Commission, on the Unification of Copyright Law (December 2014), https://europeancopyrightsociety.org/wp-content/uploads/2015/12/ecs_letter_to_oettinger_fin-1.pdf (last accessed 12.03.2026).

[7] https://digital-strategy.ec.europa.eu/en/policies/copyright-legislation (last accessed 12.03.2026).

fall outside the competence of the EU.[8] As *Alexander Peukert* aptly stated, "the internationalisation and Europeanisation of IP law has reached a stage where it appears more appropriate to speak of IP law 'in Germany' than of 'German' IP law."[9] While we will do our best to report on the situation in Germany, we might not be doing much reporting on "German" IP law.

To do so, we first (II.) situate German and EU IP within its international context, addressing the role of IP as a puzzle piece for enabling global markets (1.), and the more recent use of IP as an instrument for fostering geopolitical aims (2.). Next (III.), we trace how IP has expanded over the past decades; in this section, we focus on copyright (1.), patents (2.), and trademarks (3.). We then turn to the specific IP regimes in greater depth: copyright (IV.), patents (V.), trademarks (VI.), trade secrets (VII.), design protection (VIII.), and pseudo-IP and functional equivalents to IP (IX.). Throughout these sections, we examine how various aspects of IP, such as the scope of protection, exceptions and limitations, and compulsory licences operate as power-balancing mechanisms that may enclose or open up IP and thus either enable or counteract intellectual monopolies before addressing questions that cut across IP regimes: the overlap between IPRs (X.), the numerus clausus of IPRs (XI.), the abuse of rights (XII.), and questions of enforcement (XIII.). Finally (XIV.), we focus on IP's constitutional dimension.

The report features three recurring themes. First, it demonstrates that German IP is, in fact, largely determined by EU instruments. Second, it illustrates that the development of IP has, over the past decades, resembled an arms race: The legislator strengthened the position of rights holders by expanding exclusive rights, and by introducing new neighboring rights (database, press publishers, OCSSP liability) or regulatory exclusivities outside formal IP (data and market exclusivity, orphan drugs). To counterbalance the costs which these rights create, the legislator strengthened the position of users by introducing exceptions, limitations, or providing for compulsory licences. What is interesting though, is that they rarely reduced the scope of exclusive rights per se. Third, courts – first and foremost the CJEU – have used a fundamental rights analysis, especially in copyright law. They have shifted the balance towards the interests of users, and have taken account of the fact that copyright serves as a master switch for online communication and deliberation, be it political, social, or cultural.

---

8 *de la Durantaye*, in: Gendreau (ed.), Research Handbook on Intellectual Property and Moral Rights, 2023, 152.

9 *Peukert*, Introduction to Intellectual Property Law in Germany, 4 (October 12, 2023 SSRN), https://ssrn.com/abstract=4599740 (last accessed 12.03.2026).

II. Intellectual Property and International Law

1. Globalization

German legal scholars generally regard IPRs as key drivers of the global economy which facilitate trade and open up markets.[10] The national debate is strongly shaped by the EU's trade policy. The European Commission promotes high standards of IP protection; seeking to create legal certainty and an attractive regulatory environment for businesses.[11] As part of this strategy, the EU wants to enhance IP protection in countries of the Global South ("developing countries"), and supports countries that wish to strengthen their IPRs.[12]

Since the second half of the 2000s, however, there is a growing awareness that the expansion of IPRs could lead to a "second enclosure movement" which privatizes knowledge and information that would otherwise be part of the public domain.[13] Proponents emphasize that encoded information and immaterial goods can be digitally reproduced and shared at very low costs, and that IPRs and technical protection measures can lock up knowledge which would otherwise be available to virtually anyone, independently of their geographical location and economic standing.[14] German scholars have written quite a bit on the function of the public domain, and on its importance both for democratic discourse, and for the exercise of human rights; particularly in the field of copyright law.[15] In addition, they have conceptualized license models which tailor information goods to be accessible and shareable,[16] and have highlighted the need for legal rules that are mindful of the social and economic realities within various creative ecosystems.[17] However, there is little critical discourse about the downside which strong IPRs might have for developing countries.[18] One notable ex-

---

[10] Cf. *Ullrich*, GRUR Int. 1984, 89; *Ullrich*, GRUR 2007, 817. For a more contemporary economic analysis of copyright law, cf. *Bisges*, ZUM 2014, 930.

[11] https://trade.ec.europa.eu/access-to-markets/en/content/intellectual-property-rights-and-geographical-indications#:~:text=The%20EU%20supports%20strong%20intellectual,framework%20for%20international%20trade%2C%20including (last accessed 12.03.2026).

[12] Cf. only *European Commission*, Report on the protection and enforcement of intellectual property rights in third countries, 17.05.2023 (SWD(2023) 153 final).

[13] *Boyle*, Law and Contemporary Problems 2003, 33.

[14] Cf. *Kapczynski*, 117 Yale L.J. 804 (2008); *Senftleben*, Reconciling EU Copyright Protection With the Right to Research (November 12, 2025 Verfassungsblog) calls technological protection measures "electronic fences preventing access and use" for research activities, https://verfassungsblog.de/eu-copyright-protection-right-to-research/ (last accessed 12.03.2026).

[15] Cf. only *Peukert*, Die Gemeinfreiheit, 2012; *Stieper*, Rechtfertigung, Rechtsnatur und Disponibilität der Schranken des Urheberrechts, 2009. For a more specific focus on exceptions for research and teaching, cf. only *de la Durantaye*, Bildungs- und Wissenschaftsschranke, 2014.

[16] For the legal construction of goods for the public domain, cf. *Wielsch*, Zugangsregeln, 2008, 211–266.

[17] *Grünberger*, in: Hähnchen (ed.), Eine Methodenlehre oder viele Methoden?, 2020, 79, 90–110; cf. also *Durantaye/Grünberger*, GRUR Int. 2021, 380.

[18] Occasionally, authors do discuss the role which patent law may play in the potential appropriation of traditional knowledge or genetic resources by actors from the Global North to the

ception is the discussions around compulsory licensing for COVID vaccines during the COVID 19 pandemic. Even there, though, scholars mostly cautioned against weakening IP protection; they feared that abolishing or limiting patent protections would not make vaccines more widely available while sending negative signals to future inventors, thereby weakening patent law's function as an incentive for innovation.[19]

2. IP as a Political Tool

a) Geopolitics

Legal systems compete with one another. IPRs are fairly harmonized by international treaties.[20] And yet, IP is one key element which states may use to strategically position themselves. When it comes to the positioning of European countries *vis-à-vis* other regions of the world, especially the U.S. and China, virtually all of these attempts are orchestrated by EU institutions and not by its individual Member States. For quite some time, the EU has used intellectual property to strengthen its position in the global (digital) market. An early example is the database directive[21] from 1996.[22] At the time, the EU wanted to strategically position itself against the U.S.; the hope was that database protection would attract early tech companies.[23]

Today, the EU appears to be pursuing a similar strategy in the hopes of attracting AI companies. A permissive copyright system is viewed as one way of doing so:[24] EU copyright law should allow the use of works for AI training to achieve digital sovereignty and lessen the dependence on U.S. and Chinese companies.[25] To promote AI innovation and protect the European market, the EU has incorporated copyright-related provisions into the AI Act.[26] The EU legislator wanted to circumvent the territoriality principle and de facto extend EU copyright law

---

detriment of communities or societies in the Global South; cf. *Godt*, Eigentum an Information, 2007, 267; *Freischem/Würtenberger*, GRUR 2023, 1602. For a discussion of genetic resources as intellectual property, see *Klünker*, ZGE 2023, 121.

19 *Metzger/Zech*, GRUR 2020, 561, 568–569; *Hilty et al.*, Covid-19 and the Role of Intellectual Property 2021, https://www.ip.mpg.de/fileadmin/ipmpg/content/stellungnahmen/2021_05_25_Position_statement_Covid_IP_waiver.pdf (last accessed 12.03.2026).

20 The most prominent ones are the Berne Convention for the Protection of Literary and Artistic Works (as amended on September 28, 1979) and the Agreement on Trade-Related Aspects of Intellectual Property Rights (TRIPS).

21 Directive (EU) 1996/9. The directive was later amended by Art. 24 of the CDSM Directive (Directive (EU) 2019/790) to lessen the scope of protection.

22 The German transposition is contained in sect. 87a ss. German Copyright Act.

23 Rec. 11 Database Directive: "Whereas there is at present a great imbalance in the level of investment in the database sector both as between the Member States and between the Community and the world's largest database-producing third countries".

24 *de la Durantaye*, IIC 2025, 737.

25 See for example *Hofmann*, ZUM 2024, 166, 172.

26 Regulation (EU) 2024/1689.

beyond the boundaries of the EU by establishing conditions which products must fulfil to enter the EU market.[27] Art. 53(1)(c) EU AI Act obliges providers of general-purpose-AI models "to put in place a policy to comply with Union law on copyright", including opt-outs declared pursuant to Art. 4(3) CDSM Directive.[28]

The EU's Strategy of leveraging IP for its geopolitical advantage is not confined to the digital sphere. It created unitary IP rights to establish an attractive and cost-effective system of protection beyond the Member States' national borders.[29] Its 2012 EU patent package consists of the Unitary Patent Regulation,[30] a language regulation,[31] as well as the Agreement of a Unified Patent Court[32], and seeks to overcome the limitations of protection which are due to the territoriality principle. Similarly, the EU offers a mark with unitary effect throughout the entire EU which cannot be registered for individual Member States (Art. 1 (2) TM Regulation[33]).[34] EU design law provides for the protection of so-called community designs.[35] The EU legislator states: "a more accessible design-protection system adapted to needs of the internal market is essential for Community industries".[36]

When EU Member States use IP to strategically position themselves, they mostly do so to get advantages *vis-à-vis* other Member States of the Union. In patent law and trademark law which are governed by EU regulations with direct and immediate effect in all Member States,[37] there is little wiggle room – the little there is tends to arise primarily from diverging rules of civil procedure rather than from substantive intellectual property. In copyright law, there is more room to manoeuvre. Copyright law is governed by quite a few EU directives. Their transposition allows for Member States to draft rules to distinguish themselves from other Member States. For example, Germany created a new statute to transpose EU rules for the copyright liability of online content sharing service providers (OCSSP) (Art. 17 CDSM Directive[38]). The *Urheberrechts-Diensteanbieter-Gesetz*[39] established much more detailed requirements than the relevant provision in the directive. Germany hoped that the added level of legal certainty would

[27] Cf. *de la Durantaye*, ZUM 2025, 165; *Kuschel*, ZUM 2025, 174.

[28] Cf. *Leistner/Antoine*, GRUR Int. 2025, 1027, 1028; *Peukert*, GRUR Int. 2024, 497.

[29] As to patent law, cf. *Götting*, ZEuP 2014, 349, 350; *Blanke-Roeser*, NJW 2023, 135; *McGuire*, ZEuP 2025, 729, 742–746.

[30] Regulation (EU) No 1257/2012.

[31] Regulation (EU) No 1260/2012.

[32] Agreement on a Unified Patent Court, EC OJ 2013 C 175, 1.

[33] Regulation (EU) 2017/1001.

[34] Cf. *Kochendörfer*, GRUR 2016, 778; *Peukert*, IIC 2016, 60.

[35] Regulation (EC) No 6/2002.

[36] Rec. 8 Community Design Regulation; cf. *Kossak*, GRUR 2025, 206.

[37] Cf. Art. 288 para. 2 TFEU.

[38] Directive (EU) 2019/790.

[39] Act on the Copyright Liability of Online Content Sharing Service Providers. An English language version is available at https://www.gesetze-im-internet.de/englisch_urhdag/ (last accessed 12.03.2026).

attract companies.[40] As the first Member State to implement Art. 17 CDSM Directive, and as the Member State to set very specific obligations for platform operators, Germany hoped to indirectly set the standard for liability of OCSSPs throughout the EU.[41]

b) War and Peace

While IP is not conceptualized as an instrument of warfare, German patent law contains special provisions for inventions for war and defensive purposes (sects. 50–56 PatG):[42] The state may order that inventions which are state secrets remain undisclosed (Sect. 50 PatG), and are listed in a special register (sect. 54 PatG). The inventor may only file for patent protection in other countries if the German government approves (sect. 52 PatG). Since a secrecy order may impede the peaceful exploitation of the invention as well, an unduly affected party may claim economic damages (sect. 55 PatG). The threshold is very high; such damages are virtually never granted.[43]

In addition, throughout the EU, patent law might influence warfare innovations in that protection may be declined for military innovations whose commercial exploitation would be contrary to public order (ordre public) (sect. 2 PatG/ Art. 53 lit. a EPC). The European Patent Office (EPO) considers antipersonnel mines as an obvious example.[44]

Finally, patent law can be used as an instrument for economic sanctions. After the Russian Federation attacked Ukraine, the EU restricted access to the patent system for Russian nationals.[45] Scholars have criticized the decision as being damaging to the patent system.[46]

c) Societal and Political Discourse

To a certain extent, copyright is used as a tool to further societal and political discourse, and to raise resilience against propaganda and misinformation, be they organized by state actors or private individuals. Research institutions, universi-

---

[40] BT-Drs. 19/27426, 42: "Im Interesse der Plattformen definiert der Entwurf möglichst klar, für welche Plattformen die neue Regulierung gilt. Auch die von den Upload-Plattformen zu beachtenden Sorgfaltspflichten werden konkret gefasst." (authors' translation: "In the interest of platform operators, the draft defines as clearly as possible which platforms fall within the scope of the new regulation. It also specifies in concrete terms the due diligence obligations which upload platforms must observe.").

[41] https://legalblogs.wolterskluwer.com/copyright-blog/germany-attempts-to-square-the-circle-in-its-implementation-of-article-17-cdsmd-part-1/#:~:text=national%20implementation%20process,ante (last accessed 12.03.2026).

[42] *Matthews/Ostapenko*, GRUR Int. 2023, 665.

[43] Benkard PatG/*Schäfers/Schacht*, 12th ed. 2023, § 55 Rn. 2; *Breith*, GRUR 2003, 587, 590.

[44] https://www.epo.org/en/legal/guidelines-epc/2025/g_ii_4_1.html (last accessed 12.03.2026).

[45] Art. 1(19) Regulation (EU) 2024/1745 introduced Art. 5s into Regulation (EU) 833/2014.

[46] *Stierle/Khuchua*, ZGE 2025, 169.

ties, public schools and cultural heritage institutions enjoy special privileges under EU Copyright law (Arts. 3, 5, 6, 8–11 CDSM Directive, Art. 5 para. 2 lit. c, para. 3 lit. a InfoSoc Directive[47]); they are producers and guardians of (reliable) information resources. Germany has been at the forefront of this trend: In 2018, the German parliament enacted the *Urheberrechts-Wissensgesellschafts-Gesetz* (UrhWissG) to enable the creation and dissemination of creative content in the knowledge society.

For a while, the general rule, established by the CJEU, was that exceptions and limitations to copyright are to be construed narrowly.[48] Over the past few years, though, the court has begun to conduct a balancing exercise. Increasingly, the CJEU stresses that the rights of rightsholders must be weighed against the right to artistic expression as well as against other communication rights.[49] Similarly, the German Constitutional Court has underlined the importance of human rights such as artistic freedom (*Kunstfreiheit*), and the limits these rights might bring to the rightsholder‘s property (and personality) right.[50]

In some instances, copyright was broadened with the purported aim of ensuring the quality of public discourse. The hotly debated and not very well-received[51] European press publishers' right (Art. 15 CDSM Directive) is – among other things – supposed to ensure that press companies continue to have incentives to engage in free and pluralist journalism in the digital age.[52] The provision's blueprint was the (national) German neighboring right for press publishers (cf. the old version of sect. 87f ss. German Copyright Act).[53]

IP can be understood as a political tool in other areas as well. Strong patents and copyrights may be in conflict with overarching EU sustainability objectives.[54] If IP do set incentives to create and innovate, they lead to inventions and the creation of content which might produce significant negative ecological externalities.[55] For example, patent law grants market exclusivity irrespective of whether the invention is ecologically sustainable. This could, in principle, lead to both overinvestment in non-sustainable technologies, and to underinvestment in sustainable technologies.[56] German scholars are, however, cautious to advocate for changes of patent law since such changes can not diminish the market demand for non-sustainable technologies or increase the market demand for sus-

---

[47] Directive 2001/29/EC.

[48] Cf. for example CJEU, judgment of 16.7.2009 – Case C-5/08 para. 56 (Infopaq).

[49] CJEU, judgment of 29.1.2008 – Case C-275/06 paras. 61–69 (Promusicae); CJEU, judgment of 22.1.2013 – Case C-283/11 paras. 59–60 (Sky Österreich); CJEU, judgment of 27.3.2014 – Case C-314/12 para. 46 (UPC Telekabel Wien); CJEU, judgment of 29.7.2019 – Case C-516/17 para. 56 (Spiegel Online).

[50] BVerfGE 142, 74 (Metall auf Metall).

[51] Cf. only *Ackermann*, ZUM 2019, 375; *Schack*, ZUM 2020, 165.

[52] Rec. 54 CDSM Directive.

[53] See below at III. 1.

[54] *Kraetzig et al.*, GRUR 2025, 802, 807. Cf. also *Kuschel*, ZGE 2025, 135.

[55] Cf. for patent law *Derclaye*, IIC 2009, 249.

[56] Cf. *Hilty/Batista*, GRUR Int. 2023, 821.

tainable technologies.[57] At the same time, patent law seems to be suitable to secure incentives for climate-friendly technologies.[58]

Interestingly, the Recast Design Directive[59] (Art. 19) obliges Member States to implement a repair clause which permits reproductions of parts of complex products for purposes of repair; any existing copyrights remain unaffected.[60] The Design Regulation,[61] too, contains a repair clause for EU designs (Art. 20a). Copyright's exhaustion doctrine permits the use and resale of the copy which was put on the market, but it does not allow for its reproduction;[62] reproducing parts of a product for repair purposes could thus constitute an infringement under copyright, patent, and trademark law.[63] Recently, scholars have begun to argue that the prominent economic perspective on IP should be supplemented by an ecological one, and that a balancing exercises should not be limited to the interests of rightsholders and users but should take collective, societal interests into account as well.[64]

III. Expansion of Intellectual Property and Monopolies

The expansion of IPRs and other exclusive rights has primarily been driven by the EU which, in turn, was sometimes obliged to expansions by international trade agreements such as TRIPS.[65]

1. Copyright Law

The scope of copyright law has materially expanded mostly through case law.[66] Because exploitation rights are unified within the EU, the CJEU was the driving force behind the expansions of the past two decades. The CJEU interpreted both the subject matter, i.e. the term "work", and exclusive rights under copyright law rather broadly. Starting with its decision in *Infopaq*,[67] the Court defined the term

---

[57] Cf. *Hilty/Batista*, GRUR Int. 2023, 821.

[58] *Heinze*, GRUR Int. 2021, 554.

[59] Directive (EU) 2024/2823.

[60] *Kraetzig et al.*, GRUR 2025, 802, 807.

[61] Regulation (EU) 2024/2822.

[62] *Ohly*, GRUR 2025, 1532, 1533.

[63] *Ohly*, GRUR 2025, 1532, 1533.

[64] *Ohly*, GRUR 2025, 1532, 1533. For a copyright example of that practice, cf. CJEU, judgment of 3.9.2014 – Case C-201/13 (Deckmyn). On a more abstract level, cf. *Husovec*, German Law Journal 2019, 840.

[65] On the tendency to expand IP rights, cf. only *Husovec*, German Law Journal 2019, 840, 841–842: "At the same time, legislators almost never revisit obsolete IP regimes, which results in a constant stacking and expansion of intellectual property rights in the legal system."

[66] For an overview, cf. only Dreier/Schulze/*Raue*, UrhG, 8th ed. 2025, § 2 para. 6–19.

[67] CJEU, judgment of 16.7.2009 – Case C-5/08 (Infopaq).

"work" as an "author's own intellectual creation"[68] and held that individual sentences or even parts of sentences of a newspaper article (consisting of only 11 words) can be protected by copyright.[69] Some commentators criticized this threshold for protection as too low.[70] At the same time, the Court developed an autonomous doctrine of communication to the public under Art. 3 InfoSoc Directive to capture internet-typical conduct.[71]

Some of these cases were brought by German courts. One such example is *Pelham/Hütter*,[72] a case which has been pending for roughly 25 years, and which is currently again under review by the CJEU.[73] It was the Federal Supreme Court which initially held that the phonogram producer's right (sec. 85 (1) UrhG[74]) covers even the small sound snippets.[75] The CJEU agreed.[76]

The EU legislature has expanded secondary liability for host providers, thereby expanding the CJEU's jurisprudence.[77] Art. 17 CDSM Directive introduced a special liability scheme for online content-sharing service providers (OCSSPs). Germany implemented the Directive through a new statute (UrhDaG).

What is more, copyright in the broader sense has expanded because it has been supplemented by ancillary or neighboring rights. These rights have often been granted in reaction to technological changes which were perceived as weakening the position of rightsholders. One example for the introduction of a neighboring right required under international law is the legal protection for technical protection measures (TPMs) which was introduced in 2001 through Arts. 6, 7 of the InfoSoc Directive. The protection is in line with Art. 11 WIPO Copyright Treaty: Member States must provide "adequate legal protection against the circumvention of any effective technological measures" (Art. 6 (1) InfoSoc Directive). Germany transposed this obligation in Secs. 95a-96 UrhG. What is important to note: A protection of the technical access layer does not only make the enforcement of exploitation rights more effective, it de facto expands the scope of protection—without access, users cannot engage in uses which would fall under the limitations and exceptions to copyright. And yet, users may not circumvent

68 CJEU, judgment of 22.12.2010 – Case C-393/09 (BSA); CJEU, judgment of 4.10.2011 – Cases C-403/08 and C-429/08 (Football Association Premier League and others); CJEU, judgment of 1.12.2011 – Case C-145/10 (Painer); CJEU, judgment of 13.11.2018 – Case C-310/17 para. 36–37 (Levola Hengelo); CJEU, judgment of 12.9.2019 – Case C-683/17 para. 29 (Cofemel).

69 CJEU, judgment of 16.7.2009 – Case C-5/08 para. 47 (Infopaq).

70 *Metzger*, GRUR 2012, 118, 121.

71 CJEU, judgment of 7.4.2016 – Case C-160/15 (GS Media/Sanoma); cf. *Raue*, EuR 2023, 364, 371–374.

72 CJEU, judgment of 29.7.2019 – Case C-476/17 (Pelham).

73 Cf. Opinion of Advocate General Emiliou delivered on 17 June 2025 – Case C-590/23 CG, YN v Pelham GmbH, SD, UP.

74 Cf. Art. 2 lit. c InfoSoc-Directive.

75 BGH, GRUR 2009, 403 paras. 11, 14 (Metall auf Metall I); BGH, GRUR 2017, 895 para. 18 (Metall auf Metall III); BGH, GRUR 2016, 176 para. 27 (Tauschbörse I).

76 CJEU, judgment of 29.7.2019 – Case C-476/17 para. 39 (Pelham).

77 See only CJEU, judgment of 22.6.2021 – Cases C-682/18 and C-683/18 (Youtube/Cyando).

TPMs for all permitted uses. Sec. 95b UrhG states that circumvention is only permitted for some of the limitations and exceptions contained in secs. 44a ss. UrhG.[78] Notably, circumvention for the production of private copies is only permitted if such copies are on paper or other analogue media; digital copies are not covered (sec. 95b (1) no. 6 lit. a UrhG). Scholars have criticized that legislative decision because it impairs the exercise of communication rights.[79]

However, the EU sometimes introduced new neighboring rights without being required to do so under international law. One very prominent example is the already mentioned database protection under the Database Directive which Germany transposed in sec. 87a-87e UrhG. The sui generis was created in order to induce companies to invest in the generation of data. The scope of protection was later narrowed down a bit by the CJEU, who clarified that the database right does not extend to investment in creating data but that it covers only investment in obtaining, verifying, or presenting data.[80] Another example which we already mentioned is the creation of the press publishers' right (Art. 15 CDSM Directive; sec. 87f-87k UrhG) in 2019. It has been much criticized.[81] Years before, in 2013, the German legislator had created a press publishers' right which allowed publishers exclusive control over the online use of news content. The statute was nullified because Germany failed to notify the EU during the legislative process.[82] Once the national attempt at protection had failed, press publishers lobbied for an EU-wide ancillary right.

2. Patent Law

Much like in copyright law, the subject-matter of patent law has been broadened. Again, this extension is an EU-wide phenomenon. Part of this has been driven by the legislature. For example, the Biotech Directive[83] led to the patentability of inventions relating to biological material (Art. 3); the directive was transposed in sec. 1(2) PatG. While the mere discovery of the components of biological material, such as DNA sequences, does not qualify for protection, the decoding of a gene through a technical process, and the identification of its use may constitute a patentable invention.[84]

---

[78] *Specht-Riemenschneider*, GRUR 2019, 253, 258–259; Dreier/Schulze/*Specht-Riemenschneider/Raue*, UrhG, 8th ed. 2025, § 95b Rn. 12.

[79] Dreier/Schulze/*Specht-Riemenschneider/Raue*, UrhG, 8th ed. 2025, § 95b para. 12; *Ulbricht*, CR 2004, 674; *Holznagel/Brüggemann*, MMR 2003, 767; *Köcher/Kaufmann*, MMR 2005, 753.

[80] CJEU, judgment of 9.11.2004 – Case C-444/02 (Fixtures Marketing I); CJEU, judgment of 9.11.2004 – Case C-338/02 (Fixtures Marketing II); CJEU, judgment of 9.11.2004 – Case C-46/02 (Fixtures Marketing III); CJEU, judgment of 9.11.2004 – Case C-203/02 (British Horseracing).

[81] For a critical analysis, cf. *Ackermann*, ZUM 2019, 375.

[82] CJEU, judgment of 12.9.2019 – Case C-299/17 (VG Media); BT-Drs. 19/27426, 111. Cf. *Heinze*, ZUM 2019, 843; *Stieper*, GRUR 2019, 1264.

[83] Directive 98/44/EC.

[84] Metzger/Zech/*Zech/Ulrich*, SortR, 1st ed. 2016, PatG § 1 para. 19–25.

In addition, thanks to the EU's UPC Agreement[85], inventors may nowadays obtain a European patent with unitary effect in 18 EU Member States and which is enforced by the Unified Patent Court (UPC).

3. Trademark Law

Trademark law follows a similar trend. Since 1996, the EU has had a bifurcated system for trademark protection. Under the trademark regulation, trademark holders may obtain a pan-European right across all Member States[86] which complements national trademark laws. These national laws have been harmonized through the Trademark Directive.[87] In Germany, that harmonization raised the level of protection. Under German trademark law, the party that wanted to register a trademark had to provide a graphic representation of the mark. Nowadays, after a legislative reform[88] and due to CJEU jurisprudence,[89] this is no longer the case. Therefore, various multimedia marks may be protected.[90]

IV. Copyright

1. Protected Subject-Matter

In theory, the term "work" is fully harmonized under EU law.[91] The harmonization was driven by the CJEU, not by the EU legislature. However, much like in other jurisdictions,[92] national courts, practitioners, and scholars are struggling with the term's application.[93] This might be one of the reasons why national courts do, in practice, apply the term differently in different Member States – especially when it comes to useful articles.[94] In its sec. 2 (2), the German Copyright Act states that only personal intellectual creations (*persönliche geistige Schöpfungen*) constitute works under copyright law. Sec. 2 (1) UrhG contains a non-exhaustive list of categories of works; a creation does not have to fall within one of the enumerated categories to receive protection. The category is open.

---

85 Agreement on a Unified Patent Court, EC OJ 2013 C 175,1.

86 For an analysis of its effect, see *Herz/Mejer*, Research Policy 2019, 1841.

87 Directive (EU) 2015/2436.

88 Directive (EU) 2015/2436 replaced Directive 2008/95/EC and explicitly included sound, color, and multimedia marks (cf. Art. 3).

89 CJEU, judgment of 6.5.2003 – Case C-104/01 (Libertel).

90 Fezer/*Fesenmair*, MarkenR, 6th ed. 2025, MarkenG § 8 para. 2.

91 CJEU, judgment of 16.7.2009 – Case C-5/08 paras. 38,39 (Infopaq). The latest judgment is CJEU, judgment of 4.12.2025 – Cases C-580/23 and C-795/23 para. 66 (Mio/konektra).

92 For a critical analysis of the situation in the U.S., cf. only *Tushnet*, UCLA L. REV. 2019, 1216.

93 Cf. *Bently et al.*, IIC 2025, 798.

94 For an overview, cf. only *Sipetas*, IIC 2025, 1392, 1394–1397.

Traditionally, German courts required that four elements be present for a creation to be protected.[95] First, the creation must be personal (*persönlich*), i.e. human. Creations which are directed by animals, or by AI, cannot be protected. Second, the creation must express intellectual content (*geistiger Gehalt*); it may not merely be a creation of craftsmanship or a creation which is from the realm of sports. Third, the creation must be an individual achievement (*individuelle Leistung*) in that it is an expression of its creator's personality. Fourth, the creation must be susceptible to human senses (*wahrnehmbare Form*). The amount of work that goes into the creation, as well as its aesthetic and artistic value are irrelevant.

The CJEU has established that a creation has to meet but two requirements. First, the creation must contain "original subject matter in the sense of being the author's own intellectual creation".[96] Second, "classification as a work is reserved to the elements that are the expression of such creation".[97] The Federal Court of Justice (*Bundesgerichtshof*, BGH) is of the opinion that the first three requirements under German law are basically all contained in the CJEU's first requirement (own intellectual creation) while the CJEU's second requirement equals the fourth requirement under German law.[98]

The determination of whether a creation constitutes a work is especially difficult when it comes to useful articles.[99] The CJEU has held that the creation must "reflect the personality of its author", and that it does so if it is "an expression of his or her free and creative choices".[100] When the realization was solely "dictated by technical considerations, rules or other constraints which leave no room for creative freedom", the creation does not constitute a work. Courts have struggled to apply these rules; both the BGH and its Swedish counterpart asked the CJEU to develop criteria. In its decision, the CJEU clarified that the creative choices must be manifest in the work itself. Alas, the court gives little guidance as to the elements which courts may consider when making that determination.

The court did, however, make one statement which will have to lead to a change of course for German courts. Traditionally, courts who had to decide whether a work was partially reproduced would establish whether the overall impression (*Gesamteindruck*) of an artistic creation was the same as the one which the creation was based upon.[101] According to the CJEU, courts should not compare the overall visual expression of the works in question but should examine whether the part in question expresses the author's own intellectual

---

[95] BGH, GRUR 2014, 175, 176 para. 15 (Geburtstagszug); Schricker/Loewenheim/*Loewenheim/Leistner*, UrhG, 6th ed. 2020, § 2 para. 30–37.

[96] CJEU, judgment of 12.9.2019 – Case C-683/17 para. 29 (Cofemel); CJEU, judgment of 4.12.2025 – Cases C-580/23 and C-795/23 para. 48 (Mio/konektra).

[97] CJEU, judgment of 4.12.2025 – Cases C-580/23 and C-795/23 para. 48 (Mio/konektra).

[98] BGH, ZUM 2025, 343, 346 para. 20 (Birkenstocksandale).

[99] Cf. *de la Durantaye*, ZUM 2025, 747.

[100] CJEU, judgment of 12.9.2019 – Case C-683/17 para. 30–31 (Cofemel).

[101] BGH, GRUR 2022, 899 (Porsche 911).

creation; this could be the case even if what was taken was but a relatively minor part of the work.[102] This part of the ruling received mixed reviews in Germany.[103]

2. Exceptions and Limitations

EU law provides for a limited, exhaustive list of limitations and exceptions to copyright law (Art. 5 InfoSoc Directive, Arts. 3–6 CDSM Directive). The CJEU held that Member States may not expand that list, and may not balance conflicting human rights outside of the boundaries of this exhaustive list.[104] As a consequence, the German legislature had to abolish sec. 24 UrhG which had constituted a general limit to the scope of protection for works which were inspired by earlier works without reproducing any protectable elements in a recognizable way.

An exhaustive list of exceptions provides practitioners with more legal certainty than an open-ended concept such as fair use (sec. 107 U.S.C.). It has its price, though: Innovative uses of works such as those which are made possible by technological developments tend not to be covered by any of the limitations and exceptions which are already in place; when drafting or amending the list, legislatures often have specific use cases in mind. Consequently, companies that want to make use of these new technologies may only do so if they obtain a license—at least until the next round of amendments. Since the legislative process is very slow, the courts would often step in and allow for certain, socially beneficial uses with dubious arguments. For example, the BGH held that every rightsholder who makes content freely available online grants simple consent (*schlichte Einwilligung*) that such content may be used by search engine operators.[105] The court had to find some license-like solution since these uses were not covered by any of the limitations enumerated in Art. 5 InfoSoc Directive.[106] One recent but notable exception to that phenomenon is the limitations for Text and Data Mining (TDM) as contained in Art. 3 and 4 CDSM Directive (sec. 44b UrhG and sec. 60d UrhG): When generative AI hit the market, the EU already had limitations in place which would – under certain conditions – cover the use of protected content for AI training.[107] Art. 3 CDSM Directive was inspired by German law: When enacting the above-mentioned Statute to Align Copyright Law to the Needs of the Knowledge Society, the German legislature introduced a limitation for purposes of TDM into the German Copyright Act (sec. 60d UrhG has entered into force on September 1st 2017).[108]

---

102 CJEU, judgment of 4.12.2025 – Cases C-580/23 and C-795/23 para. 83 (Mio/konektra).

103 *Nordemann*, GRUR 2026, 32, 35 is critical; *Raue*, ZUM 2026, 73, 78–80 is more conciliatory.

104 CJEU, judgment of 29.7.2019 – Case C-476/17 (Pelham).

105 BGH, GRUR 2018, 178 (Vorschaubilder III).

106 Very critical: *Ohly*, GRUR 2018, 178, 187–189.

107 Cf. only *de la Durantaye*, ZUM 2023, 645.

108 The limitation was formally based on Art. 5(3) lit. a InfoSoc Directive; Cf. BT-Drucks. 18/12329, 40.

Until recently, Member States were allowed but not obliged to implement many of the limitations and exceptions listed in Art. 5 InfoSoc-Directive. The CDSM Directive led to a fundamental change in that Member States have to provide for the exceptions and limitations established therein. While we have witnessed an expansion of copyright law in the EU, user rights have been strengthened as well.

What is more: The new mandatory exception for the use of a work to create a pastiche is so broad in scope that it is being discussed whether it constitutes a fair use doctrine of sorts for creative/transformative uses.[109] In Germany, the exception is now contained in sec. 51a UrhG; before the transposition of the CDSM Directive, acts which would now probably be considered a pastiche were justified under the now abolished sec. 24 UrhG. The term "pastiche" is not yet established in German law, and its meaning is ambiguous.[110] It thus comes as no surprise that the BGH jumped at the first opportunity to ask the CJEU to clarify the scope of the limitation.[111]

3. *Open Licenses*

Open licenses instrumentalize exclusive rights to allow uses by an indefinite number of others without the payment of a license fee. The standardization and modular design reduce transaction costs.[112] As such, open licenses are hailed for limiting the emergence of intellectual monopolies. This is true even though rightsholders cannot completely surrender their rights; under German copyright law, a copyright is not transferable (sec. 29 UrhG), authors may only grant exclusive use rights (sec. 31 UrhG). As such, CC0 licenses are being interpreted as a license which surrenders the copyright to the biggest extent possible under German copyright law.[113]

4. *The Public Domain*

The public domain is generally understood as the status of a knowledge resource which is not assigned to any person for exclusive use.[114] The term "public domain" does not appear in the German Copyright Act. While the public domain is considered a legal principle, there is no specific legal doctrine governing it.[115]

---

[109] Cf. only *Kraetzig*, ZUM 2024, 1.

[110] Cf. *Gollnast/Gollnast/Rauh*, GRUR Int. 2025, 132, 142–143.

[111] Request for a preliminary ruling from the Bundesgerichtshof (Germany) lodged on 25 September 2023 – Pelham (C-590/23).

[112] Cf. *Wagner*, MMR 2017, 216, 218; *Jaeger/Metzger*, MMR 2003, 431, 432.

[113] CC-Kommentar/*Petri*, 2025, CC0 para. 4.

[114] *Peukert*, Die Gemeinfreiheit, 2012, 1.

[115] *Peukert*, Die Gemeinfreiheit, 2012.

Even more than open licenses which cannot completely abolish copyright law, the public domain counteracts the emergence of intellectual monopolies. Scholars in other jurisdictions have critically examined whether the construction of the public domain – and the delineation of what it encompasses and what it excludes from copyright protection – reflects gendered norms or structural inequalities between the global North and the global South.[116] Defining traditional knowledge as part of the public domain may enable extraction: knowledge that is deemed "raw material" can be appropriated and re-embedded in works protected under copyright.[117] In Germany, this potentially extractive dimension of the public domain has not been a focus of scholarly debate.[118]

V. Patents

At the time when the TRIPS agreement was concluded, the EU had already enacted the European Patent Convention which provides for virtually all elements which TRIPS requires. No wonder: The EU was one of the main proponents of the TRIPS agreement.[119] The agreement forced many countries of the Global South to adapt their laws, but it mostly cemented the status quo for the major players of the Global North.[120]

The TRIPS Agreement did not force Germany to any overhaul of its patent system. The German Patent Act (PatG) and Art. 52(1) EPC already fulfilled the requirements for patent subject matter and the prohibition of discrimination as laid down in Art. 27(1) TRIPS when the agreement entered into force.[121] The same is true with respect to exceptions and limitations: European patent law (Art. 53a EPC) and German patent law (sec. 2 PatG) already contained the narrowly defined exceptions on grounds of public order or morality which TRIPS allows for (Art. 27(2) TRIPS). Both also already excluded diagnostic, therapeutic, and surgical methods for the treatment of humans or animals, as well as plants and animals (with the exception of microorganisms) from patent protection (Art. 53 EPC; sec. 2a PatG).

The minimum term of protection of 20 years from the filing date (Art. 33 TRIPS) had already been the standard in European (Art. 63(1) EPC) and German (sec. 16 PatG) patent law. Germany had already recognized compulsory licenses

---

[116] Cf. *Craig*, in: Christodoulidis/Dukes/Goldoni (eds.), Research handbook on critical legal theory, 2019, 301.

[117] Cf. *Okediji*, Traditional Knowledge and the Public Domain, CIGI Papers No. 176 (June 2018).

[118] However, German legal scholarship has addressed another potentially extractive effect of IP: that in relation to genetic resources. Cf. *Klünker*, Die Tragödie des Access and Benefit-Sharings, 2024; *Klünker*, ZGE 2023, 121.

[119] Cf. *Devereaux/Lawrence/Watkins*, Case Studies in U.S. Trade Negotiation, 2006, 65.

[120] Cf. *Moerland*, IIC 2017, 760.

[121] Cf. *Klunker*, Harmonisierungsbestrebungen im materiellen Patentrecht, 2010, 19, 35.

(Art. 31, 31bis TRIPS): the option is contained in sec. 24 PatG. Such licences must be granted on a case-by-case basis and for a specific purpose. A prior request for a licence must have been denied, the patent holder must receive adequate remuneration.

1. *Compulsory Licenses*

Compulsory licenses in German patent law do not derive from Union law and predate comparable initiatives by the EU: In the late nineteenth century, the German legislator recognized that compulsory licenses could help restore a balance of power between the patentee and potential users by limiting the exclusivity mediated through intellectual property.[122] Nowadays, compulsory licenses are regulated in sec. 24 PatG; Article 5A Paris Convention and Article 31 TRIPS provide only for a low level of harmonization.

Compulsory licences serve two corrective functions: First, the instrument allows courts to intervene when public interest demands a license. In practice, however, this is not the primary function of sec. 24 PatG; only once did a court only grant such a compulsory license.[123] Second, and more importantly, compulsory licenses can have an indirect corrective effect. The prospect of potentially having to grant a license under sec. 24 PatG influences negotiations between the rightsholder and the party that wishes to use the patent.[124] As such, the mere existence of a compulsory licensing mechanism shifts power, even though that is hard to measure.

EU Member States have different compulsory licensing schemes. During the COVID-19 pandemic, compulsory licensing received added political attention. In 2022, the European Commission launched an initiative on "Compulsory Licensing in the EU".[125] In December 2025, the EU enacted a regulation on compulsory licensing for crisis management.[126] The regime is limited to crises and emergencies.[127]

2. *Standard-Essential Patents*

The CJEU has issued numerous judgments on the licensing of standard-essential patents (SEPs). Since a company which owns a SEP has a dominant market posi-

[122] Benkard/*Kober-Dehm*, PatG, 12th ed. 2023, § 24 para. 1.

[123] BPatG, GRUR 2017, 373 (Isentress I); cf. *Stierle*, GRUR 2024, 419, 420.

[124] *Stierle*, GRUR 2024, 419, 420–421.

[125] European Commission, Call for Evidence for an Impact Assessment – Ares(2022)2413270.

[126] Regulation (EU) 2025/2645.

[127] For a critique of this crisis-centric approach, cf. *Lamping et al.*, Revisiting the Framework for Compulsory Licensing of Patents in the European Union (March 2, 2023). Max Planck Institute for Innovation & Competition Research Paper No. 23–07, https://ssrn.com/abstract=4381959 (last accessed 12.03.2026). For a general analysis of the Compulsory Licensing Regulation, cf. *Huber*, EuZW 2025, 891.

tion,[128] holders of SEPs must conclude licence agreements which are fair, reasonable, and non-discriminatory; the contractual terms must be in accordance with so-called FRAND commitments.[129] If SEP holders breach their FRAND obligations, they may, under certain conditions, not obtain injunctive relief.[130] A key aspect of FRAND licenses, as developed by the CJEU, is the proceduralization of the licensing process. In *Huawei Technologies v ZTE*, the Court developed intricate negotiation requirements.[131] In broad terms, the FRAND procedure follows these steps:[132] first, the patent holder must notify the alleged infringer of the infringement. Subsequently, the user must express their willingness to enter into a licensing agreement. The patent holder must then offer a licence on specific terms, and disclose the method of calculating the licence fee. The alleged infringer must then respond to that offer without delay and in good faith; they must either accept the offer or submit a FRAND-compliant counteroffer. If the parties do not reach an agreement, either one may require that the licence fee be determined by an independent third party.

In Germany, the Federal Court of Justice (BGH) has further refined and rendered more flexible these requirements in *FRAND-Einwand I* and *FRAND-Einwand II (Sisvel/Haier)*.[133] While the *Huawei/ZTE* framework entails five formal steps which have to be taken in consecutive order, the BGH's interpretation of the FRAND requirements under *Sisvel/Haier* is less schematic;[134] according to the court, the parties' behaviour must be assessed holistically: If the alleged infringer does not demonstrate a continuous and unconditional willingness to take a licence, it does not matter whether their initial offer complied with FRAND requirements.[135] While the Court set up relatively strict requirements concerning the implementer's willingness to license, it held that an initial lack of the required willingness can be remedied during a later stage of the negotiations.[136] Only some lower German Courts seem to follow the BGH's path.[137]

---

[128] Cf. *Gajeck/Hegener*, GRUR 2024, 1068.

[129] CJEU, judgment of 16.7.2015 – Case C-170/13 (Huawei Technologies/ZTE).

[130] *Kokoulina*, GRUR Int. 2024, 393; *Denga/Walsh*, JZ 2025, 243.

[131] CJEU, judgment of 16.7.2015 – Case C-170/13 (Huawei Technologies/ZTE).

[132] CJEU, judgment of 16.7.2015 – Case C-170/13 (Huawei Technologies/ZTE); *Coenen*, CR 2025, 353, 354.

[133] BGH, GRUR 2020, 961 (FRAND-Einwand I (Sisvel/Haier)); BGH, GRUR 2021, 585 (FRAND-Einwand II (Sisvel/Haier)).

[134] *Leistner*, GRUR Patent 2025, 163, 166.

[135] BGH, GRUR 2020, 961 para. 94 (FRAND-Einwand I (Sisvel/Haier)).

[136] Cf. *Leistner*, GRUR Patent 2025, 163, 165.

[137] See for an overview of the relevant court cases: *Leistner*, GRUR Patent 2025, 163; *Schumacher/Heusch*, GRUR Patent 2024, 373.

VI. Trademarks

When it comes to competitive market dynamics, sec. 20–26 MarkenG contain limitations to trademark protection. Of particular relevance is sec. 23 MarkenG. It permits the use of names and descriptions when necessary for third parties' economic development. This exception protects not only the interests of the third parties in question but also the public interest in undistorted competition in the market. It is for this reason that uses under sec. 23 MarkenG are considered "privileged".[138]

The lawful use of distinctive signs that belong to other parties' businesses might be embedded in national law. However, they are largely shaped by supranational normative frameworks. Sec. 23 MarkenG is not a national policy choice. With it, the German legislator has implemented Art. 14 (1) Trademark Directive which "seeks to reconcile the fundamental interests of trademark protection with those of free movement of goods and freedom to provide services in the common market".[139] The normative core of the provision is determined by the EU, the national law is but a transposition of that policy choice. In the case of prominent marks, secs. 14 (2) s. 2 no. 3 and 15(3) MarkenG embed a similar balancing requirement as part of the infringement test. Protection requires either unfair advantage or detriment, and is excluded where due cause exists, which functionally restrains the scope of exclusivity.

1. Online Uses of Trademarks

The CJEU plays a central role in delineating the boundaries of lawful online uses. The court does not deem all uses of someone else's trademark as unlawful; the same approach is followed by German courts. One such example is keyword advertising: someone uses a competitor's mark as a search term for to trigger advertisements for their own product or service. In principle, such a use could impair the mark's advertising function. However, the CJEU has held:[140] Since the trademark owner's website appears as a search result as well, the mark's visibility is not negatively affected.[141] Thus, infringement primarily depends on whether the origin function is impaired. The origin function is impaired if the advertisement does not transparently communicate for an objective observer who the originating party of the product is.[142]

---

[138] BGH, GRUR 2019, 165 para. 26 (keine-vorwerk-vertretung); BGH, GRUR 2007, 65 para. 21 (Impuls); BGH, GRUR 2005, 163, 164 (Aluminiumräder); BGH, GRUR 2005, 423, 425 (Staubsaugerfiltertüten).

[139] CJEU, judgment of 10.4.2008 – Case C-102/07 para. 45 (Marca Mode).

[140] CJEU, judgment of 23.3.2010 – Cases C-236/08-C-238/08 para. 93, 95 (Google France); CJEU, judgment of 25.3.2010 – Case C-278/08 para. 33 (Bergspechte).

[141] CJEU, judgment of 23.3.2010 – Cases C-236/08-C-238/08 para. 97 (Google France).

[142] CJEU, judgment of 23.3.2010 – Cases C-236/08-C-238/08 para. 83–90 (Google France); CJEU, judgment of 25.3.2010 – Case C-278/08 para. 35–36 (Bergspechte).

German courts apply the same functional analysis. Keyword advertising is lawful unless the use adversely affects one of the protected functions of the mark, in particular its origin function.[143]

Emerging digital environments, such as the metaverse, raise analogous questions. These issues have sparked academic discussion but have not yet led to case law.[144]

2. De Facto Marks and Renowned Marks

German trademark law knows both de facto and renowned marks, even though the German legislator uses a different terminology. De facto marks are protected, since German trademark law grants protection to signs which are being used and which have acquired recognition within the relevant circles of trade (sec. 4 Nr. 2 MarkenG).[145] Renowned marks are protected under sec. 4 Nr. 3 MarkenG which grants protection to well-known marks in the meaning of Art. 6bis of the Paris Convention for the Protection of Industrial Property.

The German legislature fills a residual space which the EU legislator purposefully left for the Member States; Article 1 Trademark Directive confines harmonisation to individual, guarantee, certification, or collective marks for goods or services that are registered or applied for.[146] The directive's Rec. 11 explicitly allows the Members States "to continue to protect trade marks acquired through use".

3. Confusion and Trademark Distinctiveness

German trademark law traditionally distinguished three categories of confusion: direct confusion, indirect confusion, and confusion in the broader sense (*Verwechslungsgefahr im weiteren Sinn*).[147] Direct confusion or signifier confusion is present when consumers do not detect differences between two marks. Indirect confusion exists when consumers detect differences between marks but assume that the marks stem from the same source because they are similar.[148] Confusion in the broader is present when consumers understand that two marks are different but think that the marks are commercially connected.[149]

---

143 BGH, GRUR 2011, 828 paras. 23–28 (Bananabay II); BGH, GRUR 2013, 290 para. 22 (MOST-Pralinen).

144 *Reinholz*, GRUR-Prax 2023, 585.

145 As to the threshold, cf. *Wagner*, GRUR 2023, 772.

146 Fezer/*Fezer/Glöckner*, MarkenR, 6th ed. 2025, MarkenG § 4 para. 6.

147 BGH, GRUR 2010, 729 (MIXI).

148 BGH, GRUR 2010, 729 para. 39–41 (MIXI); BGH, WRP 2020, 1453 para. 39 (YOOFOOD/YO).

149 BGH, GRUR 2010, 729 para. 43 (MIXI).

EU law has long abandoned these distinctions. The CJEU does not differentiate different categories of confusion; it treats confusion as a unitary concept.[150] It holds that all relevant circumstances of the specific case have to be taken into account in order to assess whether confusion is likely or not.[151] National courts, including German courts, have followed suit.[152]

Trademark law generally grants broader protection to "strong marks":[153] Very strong marks which are especially distinct, are granted preferential treatment, even though the risk of consumer confusion may be more limited than it is for weaker marks.[154]

4. Shape Trademarks

Art. 3 Trademark Directive defines the categories of signs capable of constituting a trademark; a sign must be capable of being represented in the register in a clear and precise manner so that the competent authorities and the public can determine the subject matter of protection.[155] Art. 4(1)(b) Trademark Directive governs the requirement of distinctive character as a ground for refusal.

In the case of shape marks, distinctiveness is assessed by reference to the shape as registered, in relation to the goods concerned and the perception of the average consumer.[156] According to settled CJEU case law, a product shape is inherently distinctive only where it departs significantly from the norms or customs of the sector.[157] Alternatively, distinctiveness may be acquired through use if the relevant public associates the shape with a particular undertaking.[158]

While there is no stricter test for 3D marks, practical difficulties may remain due to the fact that consumers are not in the habit of assuming origin from a products shape.[159]

Accordingly, under German law doctrine, in assessing a shape mark's distinctiveness, courts may only take into account the product's shape as registered, and may not supplement them with extrinsic elements not claimed in the application. If the public recognizes and links the product to a specific undertaking, the distinctive shape might function as an indication of origin.[160]

[150] CJEU, judgment of 12.6.2019 – Case C-705/17 para. 39 (PRV/Hansson).

[151] Since CJEU, judgment of 11.11.1997 – Case C-251/95 para. 22 (Sabel).

[152] See for example BGH, WRP 2020, 1453 para. 19 (YOOFOOD/YO).

[153] *Johnson*, IIC 2024, 185.

[154] *Johnson*, IIC 2024, 185.

[155] Fezer/*Fezer/Bingener*, MarkenR, 6th ed. 2025, MarkenG § 3 para. 4.

[156] CJEU, judgment of 12.2.2004 – Case C-363/99 (Koninklijke KPN Nederland NV/Benelux-Merkenbureau, Postkantoor).

[157] CJEU, judgment of 7.10.2004 – Case C-136/02 P (Mag Instrument Inc v OHIM); CJEU, judgment of 22.6.2006 – Case C-24/05 P (August Storck KG v OHIM).

[158] CJEU, judgment of 18.6.2002 – Case C-299/99 (Koninklijke Philips Electronics NV v Remington Consumer Products Ltd).

[159] *Friedmann*, GRUR Int. 2014, 1195.

[160] BGH, GRUR 2010, 138 para. 34; BGH, GRUR 2008, 510 para. 25.

5. Public Domain Marks

A public domain mark is a sign for which the term of protection under copyright or patent law has expired and which is still protected under trademark law. The BGH stresses that trademark protection is unaffected by a sign's public domain status under copyright or patent law because trademark law serves different purposes than copyright and patent law.[161] According to the Court, the public does not have any elevated interest in the free use of culturally significant works which have fallen in the public domain.[162] However, signs with mere descriptive meaning cannot obtain trademark protection.[163] In addition, the protection of public-domain marks is weakened in that courts often hold that the use of public domain signs is not "trademark use".[164]

VII. Trade Secrets

The legal nature of trade secret protection is ambiguous. In Germany, it was historically governed by unfair competition law as laid down in the *Gesetz gegen den unlauteren Wettbewerb* (UWG), scholars have long emphasized the proximity of trade secret protection to intellectual property:[165] Secrets are immaterial goods of economic value, and they can be subject to contractual agreements ("licenses"). Under certain conditions, trade secrets are protected against third parties.[166]

Today, the protection of trade secrets is shaped by EU law. According to Art. 2(1) Trade Secrets Directive, a trade secret is information that (1) is secret, (2) has commercial value because it is secret, and (3) has been subject to reasonable steps to ensure its secrecy.

Neither the Directive nor its German transposition in the *Geschäftsgeheimnisgesetz* (GeschGehG) clarify the legal nature of trade secrets. On the contrary: The Directive purposefully refrains from allocating exclusive control; the legislature did "not aim to create exclusive rights over know-how or information protected as trade secrets" (Recital 16). Similarly, recitals 1, 2, and 39 distinguish trade secret protection from intellectual property. During the transposition process, the German legislature seems to have been uncertain: In the accompanying document to the GeschGehG, it made contradictory statements, characterizing trade secret

161 Fezer/*Fesenmair*, MarkenR, 6th ed. 2025, MarkenG § 8 para. 364; BGH, GRUR 2012, 618 para. 20 (Medusa).

162 BGH, GRUR 2012, 1044 para. 28 (Neuschwanstein).

163 BPatG, GRUR 2024, 855 para. 25 (Sprung in die Freiheit); BPatG, GRUR 1998, 1021, 1022 (Mona Lisa).

164 BGH, GRUR 2012, 618 para. 17 (Medusa).

165 *Ann*, GRUR 2007, 39, 42; *McGuire*, GRUR 2015, 424, 426; *Ohly*, GRUR 2014, 1, 3.

166 Harte-Bavendamm/Ohly/*Kalbfus/Ohly*, GeschGehG, 2nd ed. 2024, A. para. 26–28.

protection as IP,[167] and stressing that protection of trade secrets does not qualify as IP.[168]

Most scholars (rightly) classify trade secret protection as part of unfair competition law; there are significant differences between trade secret protection and patent law.[169] Whereas patent law confers an exclusive right, the GeschGehG merely protects trade secrets against unfair means of acquisition, use, or disclosure, and expressly refers to "honest commercial practices" (sec. 4(1) sentence 2). Trade secret protection merely protects a pre-existing factual situation; its allocative function is therefore considerably weaker than that of patent law which grants exclusive rights. Both limitations, and remedies are more flexible than those of patents and other IPRs. Classifying trade secret protection as an IPR might lead to an unwarranted expansion of the scope of protection.

VIII. Design Protection

Since 1998, design protection in Germany is governed by the EU Design Directive[170] which Germany implemented in 2004. While design protection under German law (*Geschmacksmusterrecht*) historically followed a "copyright approach", it has since changed into an autonomous regime less concerned with art and cultural expression and more expressive of market-oriented and consumer-facing considerations.[171] In Germany, as in the rest of the EU,[172] design protection is conceived as an IPR.[173]

1. Definition of Design and Scope of Protection

Sec. 1 Nr. 1 DesignG defines a design as the two-dimensional or three-dimensional appearance of the whole or a part of a product, resulting in particular from the features of the lines, contours, colours, shape, surface texture or materials of the product itself or its ornamentation. The appearance can be protected as a registered design if it is sufficiently new and has individual character (sec. 2(1) DesignG). A design is new if no identical design has been disclosed before the filing date (sec. 2(2) DesignG). It has individual character if the overall impression it produces on the informed user differs from the overall impression by any design that has been disclosed before the filing date (sec. 2 (3) DesignG); in asses-

---

[167] BT-Drs. 19/4724, 26.

[168] BT-Drs. 19/4724, 31.

[169] *Berger/Tunze,* ZIP 2020, 52, 56; *Hauck* AfP 2021, 193, 194; Harte-Bavendamm/Ohly/*Kalbfus/Ohly*, 2nd ed. 2024, GeschGehG A. para. 23.

[170] Directive 98/71/EC which was recast by Directive (EU) 2024/2823.

[171] Cf. *Wandtke/Ohst*, GRUR Int. 2005, 91, 92.

[172] Cf. *Kur*, JIPLP 2023, 11.

[173] Jestaedt/Fink/Meiser/*Jestaedt*, DesignG, 7th ed. 2023, Systematik des Designrechts A. para. 20.

sing whether a design has individual character, courts shall take the degree of freedom into account which the designer had while developing the design.[174] The level of freedom which the designer used during the design process determines the breadth of protection.[175]

Design protection lasts for 25 years after registration (sec. 27(2) DesignG). Registration leads to the exclusive right to use the design (sec. 38(1) DesignG).

2. IP Overlap

The CJEU famously states that design and copyright protection "pursue fundamentally different objectives and are subject to distinct rules".[176] Nevertheless, a utilitarian object may fulfil the requirements of protection for both IPRs.[177] German courts, in particular the BGH, interpret the CJEU's case law of the CJEU as largely descriptive, emphasising that overlap *is* the exception.[178] By contrast, some scholars reject this understanding and argue that the CJEU is making a normative claim: design and copyright protection *should* rarely overlap because copyright grants a broader scope of protection.[179] As a result, copyright's originality threshold should be carefully applied when useful articles are at stake.

IX. Pseudo-IP and Functional Equivalents of Intellectual Property

Both German and EU law know forms of exclusivity beyond IP. Like IPRs, these regimes govern immaterial goods and restrict third-party use. They structure access and economic exploitation of information.

1. Information and Data

EU pharmaceutical law provides a paradigmatic example of "regulatory exclusivity"[180] granted alongside intellectual property protection. Art. 10 Directive 2001/83/EG establishes "regulatory data protection" for pre-clinical and clinical trial data – in Germany, it is contained in sec. 24b *Arzneimittelgesetz* (AMG). The protection is supposed to set incentives for innovative developments of pharmaceutical drugs. These "regulatory exclusivities" do not confer a property right;

174 Jestaedt/Fink/Meiser/*Jestaedt*, DesignG, 7th ed. 2023, sec. 2 para. 53.
175 Cf. *Hartwig*, JIPLP 2010, 186; *Hartwig*, JIPLP 2012, 827; *Hartwig*, GRUR Int. 2015, 514.
176 CJEU, judgment of 12.9.2019 – Case C-683/17 para. 50 (Cofemel).
177 Cf. *Kraetzig et al.*, GRUR 2025, 802, 803.
178 Cf. *Kraetzig et al.*, GRUR 2025, 802, 803.
179 Cf. *Kraetzig et al.*, GRUR 2025, 802, 803.
180 Cf. *Valtere*, The Interface between Patents and Regulatory Exclusivities and the View on the New EU Proposals Concerning Patent Compulsory Licensing and Regulatory Exclusivities (October 3, 2023). University of Luxembourg Law Research Paper No. 2023–015, https://ssrn.com/abstract=4591220 (last accessed 12.03.2026); *Gassner*, PharmR 2024, 15.

instead, they establish time-limited barriers to market entry under regulatory law by preventing competitors from relying on the originator's data in the marketing authorisation procedure.[181]

If a pharma company has obtained regulatory data protection, no generic drug manufacturer may rely on those data for their own application for marketing authorization for a period of eight years ("data exclusivity"). Afterwards, manufacturers of generic drugs may file applications based on the data but for two more years, may not market their product ("market exclusivity"). If the originator obtains authorization for another, new indication with significant clinical benefit during the two-years period, market exclusivity may be extended by another year.

Regulatory exclusivity in the pharma sector is not limited to data. Pharma companies that have developed so-called orphan drugs – medication to treat rare diseases which only affect a small part of the population – may obtain ten years of exclusivity according to the Regulation on orphan medicinal products.[182] The EU wants to incentivize the development of these drugs which would otherwise be commercially unattractive.[183] During the ten-year period, no member state may accept another application for marketing authorization, or grant a marketing authorization for similar drug for the same therapeutic indication (Art. 8(1)). Exceptions apply if the orphan drug's holder consents, is not able to sufficiently supply the drug, or if the competing drug has proven superior in clinical trials (Art. 8(3) lit. a-c). The scope of protection for orphan drugs is greater than that of the "regulatory data protection": a company which wishes to market a generic drug may generate its own data to develop a similar drug; competing orphan drugs may not be put on the market.[184]

Just as regulatory exclusivity in the pharma sector is not limited to data, protection of data is not limited to the pharma sector. Competitors may not rely on toxicological, ecotoxicological and environmental studies submitted in support of an application for approval for a defined period without the consent of the original applicant (Art. 59 Regulation (EC) No 1107/2009).

The introduction of regulatory data protection is a deliberate policy intervention by the EU to boost commercial development in the European life science sector. The EU legislator introduced "regulatory data protection" to counteract Europe's shrinking share of global pharmaceutical R&D and an overall innovation crisis in the pharmaceutical industry,[185] and to implement Art. 39(3) TRIPS. Meanwhile, the protection for orphan drugs was inspired by the US Orphan

---

181 *Gassner*, PharmR 2024, 15.

182 Regulation (EC) No 141/2000.

183 Art. 1 Regulation on orphan medicinal products; Cf. *Falck/Slopek/Thiermann*, GRUR 2015, 1050, 1058.

184 *Falck/Slopek/Thiermann*, GRUR 2015, 1050, 1059.

185 *Gassner*, PharmR 2024, 15.

Drug Act.[186] These examples show that EU legislation is influenced by global or third country developments.

2. Non-Legislative Forms of Exclusivity

Exclusivity over immaterial goods cannot only be achieved by way of statutory rights. Companies can hold data in silos under their exclusive control. Data can be encrypted so that only authorized persons can access them;[187] the controller of the storage medium can decide who may access data via ad-hoc downloads, APIs, or data sandboxes. When data are stored on centrally managed servers with encrypted, isolated access, data holders can effectively prevent access by potential users.

In the absence of quantifiable expected returns of investments, companies often do not make their data shareable, and do not open up their silos.[188] They also fear legal risks, especially violations of data protection law, with the entailing liability.[189] Because opening up data creates uncertainty regarding role allocation, governance structures, and viable business models, there is a misalignment between firm centric business models and ecosystem-oriented value creation.[190] Businesses thus use technical measures to protect their data.[191]

3. Interplay Between Intellectual Property and Other Forms of Exclusivity

The Data Act (DA) seeks to align classical IP rights with emerging forms of exclusivity. According to Art. 43 DA, the sui generis database right provided for in Article 7 Database Directive shall not apply when data is obtained from or generated by a connected product or related service.

In principle, the Data Act preserves trade secret protection; however, it shifts the burden of justifying restrictions on data access from the person who wishes to access the data to the data holder (Art. 4(6)-(8); Art. 5(9)-(11)).[192] While the Data Act does not abolish trade secret protection, it thus modifies its procedural architecture in the context of statutory access claims in order to facilitate data flows.

---

186 Cf. *Bourdoncle/Juillard-Condat/Taboulet*, 14 Orphanet J Rare Dis. 1 (2019).

187 OECD, Emerging Privacy Enhancing Technologies: Current Regulatory & Policy Approaches, 2023, 19–22, https://www.oecd.org/en/publications/emerging-privacy-enhancing-technologies_bf121be4-en.html (last accessed 12.03.2026).

188 *Godel/Perkins/von Petersdorff*, Research into the cost considerations of data sharing, 2022, 6.

189 *Williams*, Data Action, 2020, 208–209.

190 *Gessler et al.*, Data in Brief 2025, 1.

191 *Jorzik/Kirchhof/Mueller-Langer*, EJLE 2024, 181, 183.

192 Cf. only *Grützmacher*, CR 2024, 281; *Grapentin*, RDi 2023, 173.

X. IP Overlap

Limitations and exceptions to IP vary across the various IPRs.[193] IP overlap thus potentially comes at great social cost: An act which might be permitted under the exceptions of one regime might not be permitted under one of the other regimes. Holders of multiple IPRs might strategically use all of them to maximize the overall scope of protection. To counter that strategy, scholars have argued that in cases of IP overlap, exceptions and limitations to one IP should have effect for the other IPRs as well.[194]

XI. Numerus Clausus

The German system of intellectual property law is structured by the numerus clausus principle. Exclusive IP rights exist only where they are expressly granted by statute. This principle is grounded in constitutional law (Art. 14 GG) and consistently reflected in the structure of all major IP statutes (UrhG, PatG, MarkenG, DesignG). Private parties cannot create new exclusive rights with an erga omnes effect.

XII. Abuse of Rights

EU competition law – most notably Art. 101, Art. 102 TFEU – can limit the exercise of intellectual property rights.[195] The relationship between IP and competition law is symbiotic: while IP foster dynamic competition, antitrust law safeguards market structures.[196] IPs do not grant immunity against competition scrutiny; instead, competition authorities establish concrete market effects which the exercise of an IPR has in practice.

XIII. Enforcement

The EU Enforcement Directive[197] aims to "ensure a high, equivalent and homogeneous level of protection in the Internal Market"[198]. Germany implemented the

[193] *Kraetzig et al.*, GRUR 2025, 802, 805.

[194] With a special focus on fashion upcycling, cf. *Senftleben*, Fashion Upcycling: The Problem of Overlapping Intellectual Property Rights and How to Solve it, in: Härkönen/Mezei (eds.), Cambridge Handbook on Intellectual Property and Upcycling, 2025 (forthcoming), https://ssrn.com/abstract=5354790 (last accessed 12.03.2026).

[195] Cf. *Jickeli*, FS Schack 2022, 194.

[196] Cf. *Jickeli*, FS Schack 2022, 194.

[197] Directive 2004/48/EC.

[198] Recital 10 Enforcement Directive.

directive in its various IP statutes (secs. 97 UrhG, sec. 139 PatG, sec. 14 MarkenG).[199] Enforcement thus is one other element where EU law fundamentally shapes German IP law.

1. Available Compensatory Remedies

According to sec. 97(2) UrhG, and in implementation of Art. 13 Enforcement Directive, right holders may claim material damages in the form of actual loss, by way of a licence analogy, or by seeking disgorgement of the infringer's profits. They may switch from one method of calculation to another up until the final stage of court proceedings (the so-called threefold calculation of damages). Authors may also claim immaterial damages (sec. 97(2) s. 4 UrhG).

In patent law, the legislature controversially[200] supplemented sec. 139(1) PatG with a proportionality defence, even though the BGH had held that such a defence could be invoked under general civil law (sec. 242 *Bürgerliches Gesetzbuch*).[201] If this defence is successfully invoked, the injured party can claim monetary compensation (sec. 139(1) sentence 4 PatG). A claim of this nature had been foreign to German patent law.[202]

Sec. 139(2) PatG has recently gained attention as well. It is the basis for claiming damages from a person who has culpably infringed a patent. The provision implements Art. 13 Enforcement Directive which provides that the culpable infringer has to pay the right holder damages "appropriate to the actual prejudice suffered by him as a result of the infringement." Unlike the German provision, Art. 13 Enforcement Directive (and Art. 45 TRIPS)[203] explicitly differentiate between infringement and actual damages.[204]

Enforcement can substantially expand the economic effects of IP rights. In a recent case, the German Federal Court decided that when calculating the damages suffered because of an infringement, courts may take into account profits from ancillary transactions – which do not constitute relevant acts of use in themselves – as well as additional damages which occurred after the expiry of the patent.[205] The underlying issue has been extensively debated in the literature.[206] The Court argued that the infringing use of the invention enabled the infringer to enter a market which is why any subsequent profits from entering that market should not remain with the infringing actor.[207] In another case, the

---

[199] Cf. *Heinze*, ZEuP 2009, 282.

[200] Cf. only *Wagner*, GRUR 2022, 294.

[201] BGH, GRUR 2016, 1031 paras. 40–54.

[202] Cf. *Ohly*, GRUR 2022, 303.

[203] Cf. *Hauck*, GRUR 2024, 1761, 1764.

[204] Cf. *Hauck*, GRUR 2024, 1761, 1763.

[205] BGH, GRUR 2024, 273.

[206] *Raue*, GRUR 2022, 603; *Leistner*, GRUR 2022, 609; *Raue*, GRUR 2023, 1491; *Leistner*, GRUR 2023, 1497.

[207] BGH, GRUR 2024, 273, para. 31.

Federal Court found that profits gained outside of the territory of the patent can also be taken into account.[208]

2. Enforcement for the Digital World

Art. 17 CDSM Directive/the UrhDaG not only regulate the material liability of host providers. They also provide for an enforcement procedure. Since host providers are directly liable for unauthorised uploads of protected content by users unless they comply with a set of best effort requirements: even though providers are not under a general monitoring obligation (Art. 17(8)), they have to implement preventive measures against copyright infringing uploads by users which they commonly implement through automated content recognition systems. In addition, providers need to provide for a detailed complaint and redress mechanism which allows users and rightsholders to contest the providers decision – by this, the German legislators tries to thread the needle between over- and underblocking.[209] This procedure effectively shifts enforcement responsibilities to the host providers which need to proactively prevent infringements.[210]

XIV. Intellectual Property and Fundamental Rights

EU law expressly recognizes IP as a fundamental right. Art. 17(2) of the EU Charter of Fundamental Rights declares that "[i]ntellectual property shall be protected".[211] The German Federal Constitution (GG), by contrast, does not explicitly mention IP.

In 1971, the German Constitutional Court famously held that intellectual property constitutes property within the meaning of Art. 14 GG;[212] it covers exploitation rights. Moral or personal rights fall within the scope of the right to personality (Art. 2(1), 1(1) GG), and freedom of artistic expression (Art. 5(3) GG). Property rights are not without boundaries. Art. 14(1) GG establishes that statutory law determines the content and limits of property. Furthermore, Art. 14(2) GG states explicitly that property rights entail a social duty – intellectual property is not only a privilege but also an obligation.[213]

Courts have – over the past decade – more expressly begun to balance competing fundamental rights, especially in copyright law. This is true for the CJEU as

---

[208] BGH, GRUR 2024, 1201.
[209] Cf. *de la Durantaye*, sic! 2022, 594, 596–597.
[210] See for this mechanism only, *Janal*, GRUR 2022, 211, 213–215.
[211] For an in-depth analysis of Art. 17(2) EU Charter with a focus on the functions of IP, cf. *Husovec*, German L.J. 2019, 840.
[212] BVerfGE vol. 31, 229.
[213] Cf. *Peukert*, in: Geiger (ed.), Research Handbook on Human Rights and Intellectual Property, 2016, 132.

well as for national German courts such as the German Constitutional Court. The CJEU held that IP instruments such as the InfoSoc or the Enforcement Directives have to be applied in a manner which strikes a fair balance between IP protection and other fundamental rights such as free expression, privacy, or the freedom to conduct a business.[214] Courts must balance the competing rights within their application of exceptions and limitations to copyright; they may not engage in an extra-statutory balancing exercise.[215] The court is of the opinion that it is the legislature's task to design IP in a way that it takes account of all competing fundamental rights. The court does, however, consider exceptions as rights of users.[216]

The German Constitutional Court ruled that copyright must take account of the freedom of artistic expression (Art. 5(3) GG) of users who engage in artistic, transformative uses. For such uses, exceptions to copyright must be read rather broadly (*kunstspezifische Auslegung*). The case concerned the sampling of a 2-second audio excerpt which the defendant had used without the phonogram producer's permission in another piece of music. The German Constitutional Court held that while the phonogram producer's fundamental right of property was affected, the lower courts had not given proper attention to the sampling artist's freedom of artistic expression under Art. 5(3) GG.[217] When balancing this right with the economic exploitation right of the phonogram producer, courts must consider the size of the economic impact. If the impact is minimal – such as in a very short audio excerpt – users' rights are given preference.[218]

This "constitutionalization"[219] of copyright law has been accompanied by scholarly debate.[220] Some German scholars emphasize that (intellectual) property differs from other fundamental rights in that the protected object only exists because of legislative intervention; other freedoms such as freedom of expression,

---

[214] CJEU, judgment of 29.1.2008 – Case C-275/06 paras. 61–69 (Promusicae); CJEU, judgment of 22.1.2013 – Case C-283/11 paras. 59–60 (Sky Österreich); CJEU, judgment of 27.3.2014 – Case C-314/12 para. 46 (UPC Telekabel Wien); CJEU, judgment of 29.7.2019 – Case C-516/17 para. 56 (Spiegel Online); cf. also *Ohly*, GRUR 2021, 304, 305; *Teunissen*, GRUR Int. 2025, 805, 813–814.

[215] CJEU, judgment of 29.7.2019 – Case C-469/17 paras 57–64 (Funke Medien); CJEU, judgment of 29.7.2019 – Case C-476/17 paras. 59–65 (Pelham).

[216] CJEU, judgment of 29.7.2019 – Case C-469/17 para. 70 (Funke Medien): "However, although Artikel 5 of Directive 2001/29 is expressly entitled 'Exceptions and limitations', it should be noted that those exceptions or limitations do themselves confer rights on the users of works or of other subject matter […]."; cf. also *Goldhammer*, GRUR Int. 2021, 544.

[217] BVerfGE 142, 74 (Metall auf Metall); Cf. also *Mimler*, Queen Mary J. Intell. Prop. 2017, 119.

[218] However, in a later decision the CJEU found the German copyright law to not be compatible with EU law for doctrinal reasons; Cf. *Leistner*, GRUR 2019, 1008.

[219] *Geiger*, IIC 2020, 282.

[220] *Geiger*, IIC 2006, 371; *Drassinower*, J. Corp. L. 991, 998 (2009); *Griffiths*, Europ. L. Rev. 65 (2013); Cf. also *Gervais*, UOLTJ 1 (2008).

privacy, or the freedom to conduct a business can theoretically be exercised independently of legislative creation.[221]

1. Right to Health and Life

Under German constitutional law, humans have a fundamental right to life and bodily integrity under Art. 2(2) GG. This fundamental right has an impact in patent law; Courts may grant compulsory licenses in the public interest. In *Merck v. Shionogi* (2017), the BGH upheld a compulsory license for an HIV drug, finding that the public interest in safeguarding patients' health and access to treatment – protecting their fundamental right of bodily integrity – outweighed the patent holder's property right.[222] The court implicitly interpreted sec. 24 PatG in light of Art. 2(2) GG and Art. 14(1) GG.

2. Right to Education and Access to Knowledge

The German Constitution does not contain an express right to education and access to knowledge. Courts interpret the right to personality (Art. 2(1) GG) and the fact that schools in Germany are supervised by the state (Art. 7(1) GG) such that school children have a right to school education. According to Art. 5(1)1 GG, everyone has the right to information. The German Constitutional Court held that the social obligations of property (Art. 14(2) GG) justifies the promotion of education by limiting the exclusivity of IPRs.[223] The German Copyright Act contains multiple limitations for educational purposes (sec. 60a–60b UrhG). They allow teachers and researchers to use parts of works for knowledge production or teaching. These exceptions originate in the InfoSoc-Directive.[224]

3. Freedom of Scientific Research

Art. 5(3) GG grants freedom of science and research. Copyright reflects this fundamental right in that research products constitute works under sec. 2 UrhG. In addition, the German copyright Act contains multiple limitations and exceptions for research purposes; their purpose is to incentivize scientific discovery. Sec. 60c UrhG contains limitations for scientific research in general, sec. 60d UrhG permits uses for the purposes of scientific text and data mining. Both provisions are based on EU copyright law.[225]

---

221 *Peukert*, in: Geiger (ed.), Research Handbook on Human Rights and Intellectual Property, 2016, 132.

222 BGH, GRUR 2017, 1017.

223 BVerfGE 31, 229.

224 Art. 5(3) lit. a, (4) InfoSoc Directive.

225 Art. 5(3) lit. a InfoSoc Directive; Art. 3 CDSM Directive.

The German Patent Act, too, contains a research exemption (sec. 11 No. 2 PatG), which permits the use of a patented invention for experimental purposes without constituting infringement. Moreover patents may be granted for (non-commercial) scientific inventions. This does not mean, however, that researchers are constitutionally entitled to personally own and exploit such issues under Art. 5(3) GG. In 2002, the German Constitutional Court decided on a case, where a university professor challenged a statute, which eliminated the professor's privilege to personally own the patents of their inventions as part of their university tenure.[226] The court found that Art. 5(3) GG protects the freedom to conduct research and to publish the findings, but does not extend to personal patent ownership. The allocation of exploitation rights concerns commercial interests, which are not protected under Art. 5(3) GG.

[226] BVerfG, NVwZ 2004, 974.

The Future of Work in the Digital Context

Fears and Opportunities from a German Legal Perspective

Judith Brockmann

I. Introduction

AI in German workplaces is expanding. Especially tools like copilots, automation and HR analytics are being used increasingly. However, the adoption and AI-job growth remain uneven.[1] Some studies suggest stagnation, rather than a boom in AI use in employment relations.[2] Surveys show a rising share of companies working on or using AI, the share can be estimated to be higher than 50 %.[3] At the same time, specialised "AI jobs" in online postings have shown stagnation rather than explosive growth through 2024.[4]

Digital literacy must be considered as a challenge in Germany in general, but especially in the labour market. According to the Digital Economy and Society Index (DESI), Germany continues to lag behind the EU average in terms of basic digital skills.[5] A 2022 survey on the continuing education needs of employees in German companies indicates a continuing need to improve digital skills in the German labour market. For example, 55 % reported a need for support in the area

---

[1] KfW, Focus No. 463: Artificial Intelligence, 2024, available at: http://www.kfw.de/PDF/Download-Center/Konzernthemen/Research/PDF-Dokumente-Fokus-Volkswirtschaft/Fokus-englische-Dateien/Fokus-2024-EN/Focus-No.-463-June-2024-AI.pdf, last accessed 14.1.2026.

[2] Bertelsmann Stiftung, KI-Jobs-Deutschland, available at: www.bertelsmann-stiftung.de/fileadmin/files/user_upload/2646__Studie_KI-Jobs-Deutschland.pdf, last accessed 5.2.2026.

[3] Bitkom, Künstliche Intelligenz in Deutschland, available at: www.bitkom.org/sites/main/files/2024-10/241016-bitkom-charts-ki.pdf, last accessed 21.4.2026, 41; KfW, Focus No. 463: Artificial Intelligence, 2024, available at: www.kfw.de/PDF/Download-Center/Konzernthemen/Research/PDF-Dokumente-Fokus-Volkswirtschaft/Fokus-englische-Dateien/Fokus-2024-EN/Focus-No.-463-June-2024-AI.pdf, last accessed 21.4.2026, 1.

[4] Peede/Stops, Artificial intelligence technologies, skills demand and employment: evidence from linked job ads data, IAB-Discussion Paper 15/2024, 5; Bertelsmann Stiftung, KI-Jobs-Deutschland, available at: www.bertelsmann-stiftung.de/fileadmin/files/user_upload/2646Studie_KI-Jobs-Deutschland.pdf, last accessed 5.2.2026, 5.

[5] European Commission, DESI – Compare countries' progress, European Union/Germany, available at: digital-decade-desi.digital-strategy.ec.europa.eu/datasets/desi/charts/compare-countries-progress?indicator=desi_dsk_bab&breakdown=ind_total&unit=pc_ind&country=EU,DE, last accessed 6.3.2026.

of digital technologies.[6] The D21 Digital Index of 2024/25, by contrast, reports the proportion of employees who have participated in formal digital training. While the share was 29 % in 2023, it fell to 27 % in 2024.[7]

This importance of AI varies in different sectors of the labour market. When it comes to blue-collar workers, AI mainly automates routine production tasks. Jobs shift toward higher-skill maintenance and/or operation roles. So far, no significant job losses in specific sectors can be observed, but local displacements occur.[8] White collar workers are highly exposed to the use of AI, many of their activities are now supplemented. Some routine white-collar roles face a substitution risk. Also, hiring and/or wage effects can be observed in places with intensive AI demand.[9] In the creative industries, AI is associated with rapid changes in tasks and productivity gains. For the time being, augmentation appears to dominate; however, pay and market structures are under pressure and disputes over quality and rights may reshape work patterns. Empirical evidence allowing for comprehensive sector-wide quantification remains limited.[10]

Specific regulations governing the use of artificial intelligence in labour law may only be found in the Works Constitution Act concerning information and consultation rights (see VII.1.). Currently no explicit legal regulations governing the use of AI in employment relationships in German individual labour law. However, some general labour law rules[11] are particularly challenged by the use of AI: The prohibition of discrimination under Section 7(1) of the General Act on Equal Treatment (AGG)[12] applies to job application processes in accordance with

---

6 Statista, Weiterbildungsbedarf bei Digitalkompetenzen in Unternehmen, available at: https://www.dihk.de/resource/blob/91516/aac9a26dea81dc7c1bc1e5f28b6105e8/dihk-digitalisierungsumfrage-2022-2023-data.pdf, last accessed 21.4.2026, 8.

7 Initiative D21, D21-Digital-Index 2024/2025, available at: https://initiatived21.de/publikationen/d21-digital-index, last accessed 21.4.2026.

8 ifo Institute, CESifo Working Paper No. 11459, available at: http://www.ifo.de/DocDL/cesifo1_wp11459.pdf, last accessed 14.1.2026, 3–4, 18; *Peede/Stops*, Artificial intelligence technologies, skills demand and employment: evidence from linked job ads data, IAB-Discussion Paper 15/2024, 5.

9 OECD, How Is AI Changing the Way Workers Perform Their Jobs and the Skills They Require?, Report 2024, available at: http://www.oecd.org/content/dam/oecd/en/publications/reports/2024/11/how-is-ai-changing-the-way-workers-perform-their-jobs-and-the-skills-they-require_842aa075/8dc62c72-en.pdf, last accessed 5.2.2026, 3.

10 OECD, How Is AI Changing the Way Workers Perform Their Jobs and the Skills They Require?, Report 2024, available at: www.oecd.org/content/dam/oecd/en/publications/reports/2024/11/how-is-ai-changing-the-way-workers-perform-their-jobs-and-the-skills-they-require_842aa075/8dc62c72-en.pdf, last accessed 5.2.2026, 3; Bertelsmann Stiftung, KI-Jobs-Deutschland, available at: www.bertelsmann-stiftung.de/fileadmin/files/user_upload/2646__Studie_KI-Jobs-Deutschland.pdf, last accessed 5.2.2026, 5.

11 Apart from that, the use of AI may also give rise to questions of trade and business secrets and those concerning IP under the generally applicable laws that will not be treated in the present report, see: *Funke*, in: Müller-Becker/Funke (eds.), Künstliche Intelligenz im Arbeitsverhältnis, Section 1 n. 20.

12 Allgemeines Gleichbehandlungsgesetz in the version of 14 August 2006 (BGBl. I 2006, 1897), as last amended by the Act of 22 December 2023 (BGBl. I 2023, Nr. 414).

Section 2 (1) No. 1 AGG and is also applicable in other areas of the employment relationship in accordance with Section 2 AGG. The use of AI in the work context must also comply with data protection regulations. At EU level, the Regulation (EU) 2016/679 (GDPR) applies. The existing German rule concerning Section 26 (1) of the Federal Data Protection Act (BDSG)[13] was conceived to standardise employee data protection. It has traditionally been interpreted restrictively in order to protect employees' personnel rights.[14] However, in light of the ECJ's ruling in case C-34/21, it can no longer be applied, as it is deemed to be in violation of Article 88 of the GDPR.[15] Furthermore, the use of AI raises questions concerning the division of responsibility between the employer and the employee and liability issues.[16]

Legal issues concerning the use of AI in labour relations are currently widely addressed by legal scholars and legal practitioners, e. g. in specialist journals and handbooks.[17] Legal research on AI and labour law issues, is increasing, more recently, interdisciplinary research also incorporates the legal perspective.[18] Also, a social partnership research project by IBM Germany in collaboration with the trade union *Ver.di* and in cooperation with the BMAS is currently investigating the changes in the world of work brought about using AI.[19]

II. The Use of Algorithmic Management in Employment Relations

1. The Use of Algorithmic Management in Human Resources

a) Recruitment

AI is increasingly used in German working life, particularly in human resources and recruitment. While early survey data from 2019 already indicated significant

[13] Bundesdatenschutzgesetz in the version of 30 June 2017 (BGBl. I 2017, 2097), as last amended by the Act of 6 May 2024 (BGBl. I 2024, Nr. 149).

[14] LAG Berlin-Brandenburg, judgment of 4 June 2020 – 10 Sa 2130/19, n. 62 et seq.

[15] ECJ, judgment of 30 March 2023 – C-34/21.

[16] *Becker/Klengel/Lamertz/Lebro*, Haftung beim Einsatz von KI und die Folgen im Arbeitsverhältnis, NZA 2025, 960.

[17] E. g. Däubler/Klengel (eds.), KI im Betrieb: Handbuch für dei Praxis in Betrieben und Behörden, 2025; *Müller/Becker/Funke*, Künstliche Intelligenz im Arbeitsverhältnis: Rechtshandbuch zum Einsatz von KI im Arbeitsrecht, 2026.

[18] See e. g. *Malorny*, Diskriminierungsschutz als Grenze maschinellen Entscheidens, project "FOR 5906: Rechtliche und gesellschaftliche Folgen maschinellen Entscheidens", available at: gepris.dfg.de/gepris/projekt/574841895, last accessed 6.2.2026; *Bössow/Hensel/Herbig/Jochmann-Döll/Lillemeier/Winter*, Rechtliche Überprüfung und Anpassung des Entgeltgleichheits-Checks (eg-check.de) an die Vorgaben der Entgelttransparenzrichtlinie (RL [EU] 2023/970), available at: www.antidiskriminierungsstelle.de/SharedDocs/forschungsprojekte/DE/Expertise_Rechtl_Pruefg_EG_Check_LFD_Projekt.html, last accessed 6.2.2026.

[19] IBM/Ver.di, Künstliche Intelligenz im Betrieb – Eine Broschüre für die Interessenvertretung, November 2020, available at: cris.maastrichtuniversity.nl/ws/portalfiles/portal/60505914/IBMverdi_KI_Brosch_re_fin_Nov2020.pdf, last accessed 5.2.2026.

interest in AI, its deployment has since expanded and now covers almost all stages of the recruitment process. Core applications include the screening of application documents through people analytics, chatbot-led interviews, and algorithm-supported decision-making.[20]

Algorithmic management plays only a marginal role in the drafting of job descriptions. Existing applications focus primarily on candidate assessment and selection following the definition of job profiles, subject to the GDPR. The most prevalent uses of AI are found on job platforms and within applicant tracking systems, where AI-based tools enable targeted advertising, automated matching, and pre-evaluation of candidates through job advertising optimisation, keyword assignment, and screening based on online profiles.[21] More advanced systems generate "candidate profiles" by analysing job descriptions, historical hiring data, and performance indicators, sometimes via external sourcing tools.[22] By weighting qualifications, experience patterns, or soft skills, these systems may pre-structure an "ideal candidate", giving rise to discrimination risks under the AGG.[23] The last is also true for applications that include AI-based CV screening and the automated administration and scoring of online cognitive or skills tests using machine-learning benchmarks. Video interview tools with automated analysis of tone, wording, or facial expressions are being piloted but are regarded as particularly high-risk due to the processing of biometric data, transparency deficits, and an increased risk of discrimination under the AGG.[24]

---

[20] *Freyler*, Robot-Recruiting, Künstliche Intelligenz und das Antidiskriminierungsrecht, NZA 2020, 284, 285.

[21] *Maasland/Weißmüller*, Blame the Machine? Insights From an Experiment on Algorithm Aversion and Blame Avoidance in Computer-Aided Human Resource Management, Frontiers in Psychology 13 (2022), 12; *Laue*, Leider müssen wir Ihnen mitteilen … Datenschutzgemäße Gestaltung von algorithmischen Systemen im Bewerbungsverfahren, in: Hentschel/Hornung/Jandt (eds.), Mensch – Technik – Umwelt: Verantwortung für eine sozialverträgliche Zukunft, FS Roßnagel (Baden-Baden, 2020), 337 et seq.; *Chugunova/Danilov*, Use of Digital Technologies for HR Management in Germany – Survey Evidence, CESifo Economic Studies 69 (2023), 75; *Feldkamp/Langer/Wies/König*, Justice, Trust, and Moral Judgements When Personnel Selection Is Supported by Algorithms, European Journal of Work and Organizational Psychology 33 (2023), 130–145.

[22] European Parliamentary Research Service, Algorithmic Management: Shaping the Future of Work (EPRS_STU(2025)774670), available at: www.europarl.europa.eu/RegData/etudes/STUD/2025/774670/EPRS_STU(2025)774670_EN.pdf, last accessed 5.2.2026, 37 et seq.; Antidiskriminierungsstelle des Bundes, Diskriminierungsrisiken beim Einsatz von Algorithmen, available at: www.antidiskriminierungsstelle.de/EN/homepage/_documents/download_diskr_risiken_verwendung_von_algorithmen.pdf, last accessed 5.2.2026, 26 et seqq.

[23] Osborne Clarke, Employers Using AI to Recruit Skilled Workers Need to Stay Up to Date in Germany, available at: www.osborneclarke.com/insights/employers-using-ai-recruit-skilled-workers-need-stay-date-germany, last accessed 5.2.2026.

[24] Market Research Future, Germany AI Recruitment Market, available at: www.marketresearchfuture.com/reports/germany-ai-recruitment-market-44592, last accessed 20 January 2026; Osborne Clarke, Employers Using AI to Recruit Skilled Workers Need to Stay Up to Date in Germany, available at: www.osborneclarke.com/insights/employers-using-ai-recruit-skilled-workers-need-stay-date-germany, last accessed 20 January 2026.

HR analytics systems may further generate promotion, talent pool, or development recommendations based on evaluation scores, project histories, and supplementary indicators. Bonus systems, especially in sales and call centres, may calculate variable pay elements via algorithms that combine quantitative metrics (sales, calls, error rates) collected automatically.[25] Algorithmically calculated performance indicators can trigger review procedures, warnings, or, where predefined thresholds are not met, automated reductions in task allocation or temporary suspension of system access, effectively operating as sanctions.[26]

b) *The Use of Algorithmic Management to Organise Work*

Algorithmic task allocation is common in platform work involving German workers (ride-hailing, food delivery, micro-tasking), where apps assign jobs based on location, ratings, and predicted efficiency. In conventional companies (logistics, call centres, retail), 'workforce management' and 'routing' software allocates shifts, routes, or customer contacts according to predefined rules and sometimes predictive analytics.[27] In logistics, warehouse, and manufacturing settings in Germany, digital workflow systems and handheld devices guide workers step by step (pick by voice, pick by light, route optimisation), effectively turning algorithms into operational supervisors. Software can be used to suggest or prescribe processes, speeds or routes and dynamically adjust them based on real-time performance data or process bottlenecks.[28]

c) *The Use of Algorithmic for Various Purposes in the Employment Relationship*

E-learning platforms in Germany deploy recommender algorithms to suggest courses based on job role, past training, and performance scores; in safety-sensitive sectors, completion is tracked and reminders are automated. Some providers use adaptive learning paths where algorithms adjust difficulty and content based on test results or observed behaviour in simulations.[29]

---

[25] *Krzywdzinski/Schneiß/Sperling*, Between Control and Participation: The Politics of Algorithmic Management, New Technology, Work and Employment 2025 (40), 60, 62 et seq.

[26] Eurofound, Regulatory Responses to Algorithmic Management in the EU, available at: www.eurofound.europa.eu/en/publications/all/regulatory-responses-algorithmic-management-eu, last accessed 5.2.2026; *Krzywdzinski/Schneiß/Sperling*, Between Control and Participation: The Politics of Algorithmic Management, New Technology, Work and Employment 2025 (40), 60, 61 et seq.

[27] Eurofound, Regulatory Responses to Algorithmic Management in the EU, available at: www.eurofound.europa.eu/en/publications/all/regulatory-responses-algorithmic-management-eu, last accessed 5.2.2026; *Krzywdzinski/Schneiß/Sperling*, Between Control and Participation: The Politics of Algorithmic Management, New Technology, Work and Employment 2025 (40), 60, 61 et seq.

[28] *Krzywdzinski/Schneiß/Sperling*, Between Control and Participation: The Politics of Algorithmic Management, New Technology, Work and Employment 2025 (40), 60, 65 et seqq.

[29] Eurofound, Regulatory Responses to Algorithmic Management in the EU, available at: www.eurofound.europa.eu/en/publications/all/regulatory-responses-algorithmic-management-eu, last accessed 5.2.2026.

Modern monitoring systems include keystroke or usage logging, time-tracking software, GPS tracking in vehicles or mobile devices, call centre analytics, and productivity dashboards that aggregate performance indicators.[30] Many companies use performance management software that aggregates key performance indicators (sales figures, call handling times, project metrics) into dashboards or ratings. More advanced systems apply predictive analytics to identify 'high' or 'low' performers.[31] Customer ratings, peer feedback, and managerial assessments are increasingly collected via digital platforms and automatically combined into composite scores used for ranking, bonus allocation, or development decisions. In platform-based work, client ratings feed directly into algorithmically processed 'acceptance rates' or 'quality indices', which influence task allocation and may result in restricted platform access.[32]

2. Legal Aspects and Judicial Practice Regarding the Use of Algorithmic Management

In its ruling of 1 December 2020, the Federal Labour Court (see V. 1.) acknowledged, that algorithmic management may be used in labour relationships.[33] However, the modalities of its use were not an issue in the decision, so there is no relevant case law on the question yet.

The use of AI in HR usually constitutes automated processing of personal data and may trigger Art. 22 GDPR and, where sensitive proxies are inferred, Art. 9 GDPR. Where AI systems affect personnel selection or work planning, works councils hold information and co-determination rights pursuant to Section 87 (1) No. 6 and Section 90 BetrVG, as explicitly recognised by the BRMG (see VII.1.).

Art. 22 (1) GDPR, as implemented and interpreted in Germany, grants data subjects the right not to be subject to a decision based solely on automated processing, including profiling, which produces legal effects concerning them or similarly significantly affects them. In legal literature, Article 22 GDPR is sometimes regarded not only as a subjective right, but as a general prohibition, only the narrow exceptions in Art. 22 (2) GDPR apply, which in Germany generally lack a specific labour law basis for automated dismissals.[34] Dismissals clearly have 'legal effects' within the meaning of Art. 22 (1) GDPR, as they terminate the employment relationship and income; without a specific statutory basis allowing

---

[30] *Krzywdzinski/Schneiß/Sperling*, Between Control and Participation: The Politics of Algorithmic Management, New Technology, Work and Employment 2025 (40), 60, 60 et seqq.

[31] Eurofound, Regulatory Responses to Algorithmic Management in the EU, available at: www.eurofound.europa.eu/en/publications/all/regulatory-responses-algorithmic-management-eu, last accessed 5.2.2026.

[32] Eurofound, Regulatory Responses to Algorithmic Management in the EU, available at: www.eurofound.europa.eu/en/publications/all/regulatory-responses-algorithmic-management-eu, last accessed 5.2.2026.

[33] BAG, judgment of 1 December 2020 – 9 AZR 102/20.

[34] *Scholz*, in: Simitis et al. (eds.), DS-GVO, Art. 22 n. 19.

such automation and adequate safeguards, fully automated dismissals are therefore not permitted. German legal commentators give HR examples (e.g. automated dissuasion) to illustrate the breadth of Art. 22 GDPR.[35]

In practice, algorithms may flag "low performers", absenteeism patterns, or restructuring targets, but dismissal decisions in Germany are normally taken by human managers, often with works council involvement under the Employment Protection Act (KSchG)[36] and the BetrVG, precisely to avoid Art. 22 GDPR conflicts. EU wide research on regulatory responses to algorithmic management notes that German law's combination of strong co-determination and data protection rules, together with judicial scrutiny of dismissals, acts as a significant barrier against fully automated firing, even where analytics tools are used to support decision making.[37]

3. Involvement of Social Partners in Adopting an Algorithmic Management System

The German collective labour law system is a dualistic system with two-channel representation of employees' interests. Trade unions and employers' associations or individual employers have the autonomy to negotiate and conclude collective bargaining agreements. This freedom is guaranteed by the constitution (Article 9 (3) GG). Collective bargaining agreements regulate the content, conclusion, and termination of employment contracts. In addition, information and consultation rights are exercised at workplace level by works councils. Their constitution, rights and duties are regulated by the legislator in the BetrVG. Within this legal framework, employers and works councils may conclude works agreements without involving the social partners.

Due to the lack of systematic public registration or publication of collective bargaining agreements and works agreements in Germany, questions about collective labour law sources can only be answered based on empirical studies or research in public sources. In Germany, the first collective bargaining agreement explicitly addressing the use of AI has been concluded in the film and television production sector. Two trade unions, *Ver.di* and the actors' union *Bundesverband Schauspiel e.V.* concluded a collective agreement on the use of generative artificial intelligence ('AI') in film productions in 2025.[38] In practice, collective bargaining

[35] *Martini*, in: Paal et al. (eds.), DSGVO/BSDG, Art. 22 n. 16b.

[36] Kündigungsschutzgesetz in the version of 25 August 1969 (BGBl. I 1969, 1317), as last amended by the Act of 14 June 2021 (BGBl. I 2021, 1762).

[37] Eurofound, Regulatory Responses to Algorithmic Management in the EU, available at: www.eurofound.europa.eu/en/publications/all/regulatory-responses-algorithmic-management-eu, last accessed 5.2.2026; *Krzywdzinski/Schneiß/Sperling*, Between Control and Participation: The Politics of Algorithmic Management, New Technology, Work and Employment 2025 (40), 60, 60 et seqq., 76 et seqq.

[38] Ver.di, press release Tarifverhandlungen zu KI und algorithmischem Management im Dienstleistungssektor, available at: www.verdi.de/presse/pressemitteilungen/++co++62f801ac-e78c-11ef-96b3-adcccb7fc1ea, last accessed 5.2.2026.

agreements on the introduction and use of AI are increasingly negotiated, for example, *Deutsche Telekom's* AI governance framework illustrates collective bargaining agreements operationalize governance through joint risk assessment frameworks and procedural rules.[39] According to trade unionists, issues relating to AI are also the subject of general collective bargaining in various sectors, e.g. regarding training entitlements. In an EU wide sample survey examining collective bargaining on the use of AI in the service sector, Germany scored above average.[40]

III. Specific Issues Regarding the Monitoring of Workers Through Artificial Intelligence

1. The Protection of Employees' Personal Rights

The debates on the use of algorithmic management systems essentially address the question of the permissibility and limits of AI use. When it comes to the question of permissibility of monitoring, a distinction must be made between the individual labour law and the collective law level:

At the individual labour law level, the debate revolves around the question of the extent to which the use of algorithmic management is compatible with the protection of employees' personal rights under Art. 2 (1) in conjunction with Art. 1 (1) of the Basic Law (GG).[41] With regard to data processing, the right to informational self-determination must be observed in particular. This constitutional fundamental right has an indirect effect in labour law in the form of a right of defence against unlawful interference by employers in the personal rights of employees.[42] The protection of personal rights is not unlimited – employee rights are balanced against any legitimate interests of the employer (which are also protected by fundamental rights). Admissibility must be determined by weighing up the respective interests and must comply with the principle of proportionality. At the level of ordinary law, the weighing of interests is reflected, on the one hand, in the limitation of the employer's right to issue instructions to 'reasonable discretion' (Section 106 (1) Trade Regulation Act (GewO)[43]) and the duty of con-

---

39 *Doellgast/Wagner/O'Brady*, Negotiating Limits on Algorithmic Management in Digitalised Services: Cases From Germany and Norway, Transfer: European Review of Labour and Research 28(2) (2022), 106–108.

40 *Brunnerová/Ceccon/Holubová/Kahancová/Lukácová/Medas*, Neue Technologien am Arbeitsplatz. Tarifverhandlungen zu KI und algorithmischem Management im Europäischen Dienstleistungssektor, 2024, 19.

41 Cf. *Wedde*, Automatisierung im Personalmanagement – arbeitsrechtliche Aspekte und Beschäftigtendatenschutz, 2020.

42 *Reichold*, in: Kiel et al. (eds.), Münchener Handbuch zum Arbeitsrecht, vol. 1, 6th ed. 2024, Section 94 n. 4.

43 Gewerbeordnung in the version of 22 February 1999 (BGBl. I 1999, 202), as last amended by the Act of 11 January 2026 (BGBl. I 2026, Nr. 6).

sideration under Section 241 (2) BGB.[44]Anti-discrimination law must also be observed.

The monitoring of employees must comply with the principles of data protection and the GDPR (see II. 2.). According to the case law of the German Federal Labour Court (BAG), monitoring of employees using technical means is permissible in special cases. Total control without concrete evidence is not acceptable. Monitoring is only allowed in special exceptional cases (e. g. criminal offences or serious breaches of contractual obligations), if there is concrete evidence.[45]

At the level of collective labour law, the use of algorithmic management systems triggers co-determination and participation rights under the BetrVG (see VII.1.).

2. *Specific Issues Regarding the Monitoring of Special Categories of Workers*

The monitoring of employees' whereabouts during and outside working hours is carried out in particular regarding 'mobile' workers.[46] It is particularly problematic regarding the protection of the personal rights (see IV. 6.).[47] Regarding teleworkers and remote workers, tensions are addressed concerning the intrusiveness of remote monitoring (screen capture, webcam use, location data) in the home and the difficulty for works councils to effectively audit cloud-based tools supplied by global vendors. Unions stress the need for strict limits and works agreements on what is monitored and for how long.[48]

For platform workers, reputational and rating systems, automatic deactivation, and opaque task-allocation algorithms create de facto performance control and sanctions without clear employment law safeguards. The European Platform Work Directive's[49] transparency and human oversight rules are meant to address these issues, but their effectiveness will depend on German implementation and enforcement.[50]

Concerning both groups, key concerns are linked to a lack of transparency and concern, inter alia, discrimination (e. g. biased algorithms), lack of explainability

---

[44] *Reichold*, in: Kiel et al. (eds.), Münchener Handbuch zum Arbeitsrecht, vol. 1, 6th ed. 2024, Section 55 n. 30.

[45] BAG, decision of 25 April 2017 – 1 ABR 46/15, n. 19 et seq.

[46] *König*, Beschäftigungsdatenschutz, Section 5 n. 81 et seq; *Gola*, Die Ortung externer Beschäftigter – Abwägung zwischen Überwachungsinteresse und schutzwürdigen Arbeitnehmerinteressen, ZD 2012, 308, 308 et seq.

[47] See *Kärcher/Walser*, Vereinbarkeit eines Direktanstellungsgebots in der Paketzustellung mit dem Verfassungs- und Unionsrecht, HIS Working Paper No. 18, 2023, 25 et seq. (concerning parcel delivery services).

[48] INCODING Project, Policy Brief – Germany, available at: ddd.uab.cat/pub/infpro/2024/290691/INCODING_Policy_Brief_Germany_def.pdf, last accessed 5.2.2026.

[49] Directive (EU) 2024/2831 of the European Parliament and of the Council of 23 October 2024 on improving working conditions in platform work (Platform Work Directive), OJ L 2024/2831, 11 Novembre 2024.

[50] Linklaters, EU Platform Work Directive: Council and Parliament Agree on Rules for the Gig Economy, available at: sustainablefutures.linklaters.com/post/102iv87/eu-platform-work-directive-council-and-parliament-agree-on-rules-for-gig-economy, last accessed 5.2.2026.

of scores and rankings, and the difficulty for individual workers to contest algorithmic decisions without collective support from works councils or unions.[51]

Also, monitoring of communications is subject to discussion.[52] The decisive factor in determining the permissibility of monitoring by the employer is whether the employer has permitted the private use of IT communication channels in the workplace. For example, random checks of internet browser history data may be permissible if the purpose of the random checks is to ensure compliance with the ban on private use of company IT communication channels. Regarding the use of keyloggers, the Federal Labour Court emphasised that their use is only permissible in cases of sufficient suspicion of a criminal offence or a serious breach of duty.[53]

3. The Impact of Monitoring Through Artificial Intelligence on the Private Life of Workers

As already mentioned, the use of algorithmic management affects the protection of employees' personal rights under Art. 2 (1) in conjunction with Art. 1 (1) GG.[54] With regard to data processing, the right to informational self-determination must be observed.[55] Monitoring by the employer on a purely conjectural basis is not permitted, nor may the employer use keylogger software without sufficient cause. In this respect, there is a prohibition on use. Case law considers sufficient cause to exist in the event of a concrete suspicion of a criminal offence or a serious breach of duty.[56]

IV. Digital Workers as a Special Category

The term 'digital worker' is rarely used in German. The terms of 'mobile working', 'home office' or 'telework' are more commonly used. Telework is understood in a restrictive sense. In a legal context, the term 'mobile working' is not legally defined nor is the term used as a category in labour law. Employees who work

---

[51] Eurofound, Regulatory Responses to Algorithmic Management in the EU, available at: www.eurofound.europa.eu/en/publications/all/regulatory-responses-algorithmic-management-eu, last accessed 5.2.2026.

[52] *Reichold*, in: Kiel et al. (eds.), Münchener Handbuch zum Arbeitsrecht, vol. 1, 6th ed. 2024, Section 55 n. 33 et seq.; *Petri*, in: Kramer (ed.), IT-Arbeitsrecht, 3rd ed. 2023, n. 79.

[53] BAG, judgment of 27 July 2017 – 2 AZR 681/16, n. 30.

[54] Cf. *Wedde*, Automatisierung im Personalmanagement – arbeitsrechtliche Aspekte und Beschäftigtendatenschutz, Gutachten 2020, https://algorithmwatch.org/de/wp-content/uploads/2020/03/AlgorithmWatch_AutoHR_Gutachten_Arbeitsrecht_Datenschutz_Wedde_2020.pdf.

[55] BVerfG, judgment of 15 December 1983 – 1 BvR 209/83, 269/83, 362/83, 420/83, 440/83, 484/83 (Census judgment – right to informational self-determination).

[56] BAG, judgment of 27 July 2017 – 2 AZR 681/16, n. 30, with reference to Section 26(1) BDSG.

remotely (from home or in a mobile form of work) are therefore to be classified according to the general categories of labour law.[57]

1. The Status of Digital Workers

In general, German labour law recognises the term 'employee' within the meaning of Section 611a BGB. According to Section 611a BGB, an employee is a person who is obliged to perform 'work that is subject to instructions and external control in a relationship of personal dependence'. The personal dependence of the employee primarily results from being subject to instructions and external control.[58] When classifying the legal relationship, Section 611a (1) sentence 5 BGB requires an overall assessment of all circumstances. According to Section 611a (1) sentence 6 BGB, the actual performance of the contract is decisive.

Furthermore, mobile workers may be considered 'employee-like persons', i. e. third category workers. There is no general legal definition of 'employee-like persons' or third category workers in German labour law. However, the legal definition standardised in Section 12a TVG can be used as guidance.[59] In established case law, the BAG defines an 'employee-like person' as a person who, due to a lack of personal dependence, is not an employee within the meaning of Section 611a BGB, but who works on the legal basis of a service contract for work and is therefore self-employed. Characteristics of the group of 'employee-like persons' are their economic dependence and their associated need for social protection comparable to that of an employee.[60]

2. Specific Regulations Applicable to Digital Workers

Specific regulations on digital forms of work are currently only found in relation to telework in a restrictive sense (see section IV. 6).

When it comes to collective labour law, Section 87 (1) No. 14 BetrVG provides for a right of co-determination of the works council regarding the organisation of mobile work performed using information and communication technology. The subject was added to the list of co-determination issues by the BRMG.[61] Regarding mobile work, case law has dealt with issues of co-determination in the workplace. For example, a ruling stated that it violates the right to co-determination in the workplace under Section 87 (1) No. 14 BetrVG if the employer unilaterally

---

[57] Cf. *Picker*, Arbeiten im Homeoffice – Anspruch und Wirklichkeit, NZA 2021, 4, 5.

[58] *Preis*, Section 611a BGB – Potenziale des Arbeitnehmerbegriffs, NZA 2018, 817, 819.

[59] *Röller*, in: Röller (ed.), Küttner Personalbuch, 33rd ed. 2026, Section "Arbeitnehmerähnliche Person", n. 1.

[60] BAG, decisions of 11 April 1997 – 5 AZB 33/96; 30 August 2000 – 5 AZB 12/00; 17 January 2006 – 9 AZR 61/05; and 21 December 2010 – 10 AZB 14/10.

[61] BT-Drs. 271/21 of 1 April 2021, 11.

regulates the scope of mobile working and attendance requirements at the workplace.[62]

In recent years, the introduction of a Mobile Work Act has been under discussion. An initial draft bill was presented by the BMAS in October 2020. The main change was the standardisation of a right to mobile work. It was supposed to be accompanied by further regulations on working time recording, modifications of statutory accident insurance cover, and extension of the right to co-determination in the workplace.[63] As the first draft bill was not adopted, a second, 'leaner' draft was introduced in November 2020, providing only for a right to discussion.[64] However, the legislative process has not been completed, and no corresponding draft bill has been introduced in the current legislative period.

3. Health and Safety of Digital Workers

According to Section 2 (2) No. 1 of the Act on the Implementation of Measures of Occupational Safety and Health to Encourage Improvements in the Safety and Health Protection of Workers at Work (ArbSchG)[65], the provisions of the ArbSchG apply to all employees within the meaning of Section 611a BGB, irrespective of their place of work, as well as to 'employee-like persons' as defined in Section 2 (2) No. 1 ArbSchG. According to the prevailing view, this also applies to the workplaces of remote working employees and employees in mobile forms of work.[66] Accordingly, the employer of remote working employees must comply with all occupational health and safety obligations standardised in the ArbSchG.[67] The general obligations under the ArbSchG are further specified by the Workplace Ordinance (ArbStättV), adopted pursuant to Section 18 ArbSchG.[68] Its rules mainly cover places of work in the company or on a construction site and therefore do not apply to mobile work. Only a limited part of the ArbStättV applies to teleworking workplaces in accordance with the provisions of Section 1 (3) ArbStättV (see IV. 6).

In cases of mobile workers at computer workstations, the Ordinance on Occupational Health Care (ArbMedVV)[69] and thus the examinations offered in

---

[62] LAG Berlin-Brandenburg, decision of 30 January 2024 – 8 TaBV 748/23, n. 62.

[63] *Baeck/Winzer/Schaaf*, Neuere Entwicklungen im Arbeitsrecht, NZG 2021, 14, 16 et seqq.

[64] *Pletke* et al., in: Pletke et al. (eds.), Rechtshandbuch Flexible Arbeit, 2nd ed. 2022, ch. B, n. 1024b et seq.

[65] Arbeitsschutzgesetz in the version of 7 August 1996 (BGBl. I 1996, 1246), as last amended by the Act of 22 December 2025 (BGBl. I 2025, Nr. 369).

[66] W.f.e. *Hidalgo*, Arbeitsschutz im Home Office – ein Lösungsvorschlag, NZA 2019, 1449, 1450.

[67] *Kollmer*, Das Recht der Tele- und Mobilen Arbeit im Lichte des Arbeitsschutzes, NJW 2023, 473, 476.

[68] Arbeitsstättenverordnung in the version of 12 August 2004 (BGBl. I 2004, 2179), as last amended by the Regulation of 27 March 2024 (BGBl. I 2024, Nr. 109).

[69] Verordnung zur arbeitsmedizinischen Vorsorge in the version of 18 December 2008 (BGBl. I 2008, 2768), as last amended by the Regulation of 12 July 2019 (BGBl. I 2019, 1082).

accordance with Section 5 (1) ArbMedVV in conjunction with Annex Part 4 also apply.

There are no specific regulations governing the training of digital employees. In this respect, the general training obligation under Section 12 ArbSchG applies. Accordingly, the employer is obliged to provide its employees with sufficient and appropriate training on safety and health at work during working hours in accordance with Section 12 (1) ArbSchG. In the case of mobile work, the problem of employers' lack of access rights to employees' private rooms is being discussed and a solution is being considered in which the employer has the right to obtain assurance from the employee that the requirements are being correctly implemented.[70]

Concerning occupational accidents, the legislator amended the legal provisions to clarify that employees working remotely at home are also covered by the statutory accident insurance. According to Section 8 SGB VII[71] (1) sentence 3, an 'insured activity' may also fall under the term 'accident at work' if it occurs in the insured person's household or at another location. Case law has clarified that accident insurance cover applies in the home office if the specific task at the time of the accident is intrinsically related to the insured activity and does not primarily serve private purposes.[72] An event in the home office is to be recognised as an accident at work if the specific task being performed at the time of the accident is intrinsically related to the insured activity and does not serve predominantly private purposes.[73] In this sense, it has been established that the insurance does not cover a journey made by the employee within the residential building while working remotely in order to pursue a self-serving activity such as drinking water.[74]

4. Collective Bargaining Agreements and Digital Workers

Whether 'digital employees' can participate in collective bargaining depends on the bargaining power of their association. Since collective agreements pursuant to Section 1 (1) of the Collective Agreements Act (TVG)[75] can in principle only be concluded for the employment relationship, only digital employees with employee status within the meaning of Section 611a BGB can be covered by collective

---

[70] *Kollmer*, Das Recht der Tele- und Mobilen Arbeit im Lichte des Arbeitsschutzes, NJW 2023, 473, 477.

[71] Siebtes Buch Sozialgesetzbuch – Gesetzliche Unfallversicherung (SGB VII) in the version of 7 August 1996 (BGBl. I 1996, 1254), as last amended by the Act of 22 December 2024 (BGBl. I 2025, Nr. 371).

[72] LSG Berlin-Brandenburg, judgment of 9 October 2025 – L 21 U 47/23, n. 42 and 46.

[73] LSG Berlin-Brandenburg, judgment of 9 October 2025 – L 21 U 47/23, n. 42.

[74] BSG, judgment of 5 July 2016 – B 2 U 5/15 R, n. 25.

[75] Tarifvertragsgesetz in the version of 25 August 1969 (BGBl. I 1969, 1323), as last amended by the Act of 20 May 2020 (BGBl. I 2020, 1055).

agreements. Section 12a TVG extends the personal scope of application to include employee-like persons.

Collective bargaining agreements are not registered systematically. This said, an important number of collective bargaining agreements containing stipulations on mobile work can be found.[76] A study conducted in the context of the BMAS platform *Digitale Arbeitswelt* (Digital Working World) found that the regulations and works agreements concluded to date mainly address issues such as technical equipment, working time arrangements, occupational health and safety, working time recording and data security.[77] Representatives of social partners, companies and academia have also identified key points for the effective design and regulation of mobile working in companies. Key factors in the organisation of work include voluntary participation, regular on-site attendance of employees engaged in mobile work, training for employees and managers on specific requirements (particularly health and safety), rules to ensure data protection, provisions on the right to disconnect and, finally, arrangements for working time recording.[78]

5. *The Right to Disconnect*

There are currently no explicit regulations in the German labour law (e. g. working time law or the Federal Leave Act) on a right to disconnect. At the collective law level, German bigger companies are increasingly formulating regulations in the form guidelines or works agreements negotiated with the works council that ensure the right to disconnect of employees outside their regular working hours.[79]

To this date, no clear and established line on the matter can be drawn from case law. Individual assessments can only be gleaned from case-specific decisions. In the case of an employee on sick leave, the BAG clarified that the employee was not required to attend staff meetings at the company.[80] On the other hand, the BAG held that a paramedic must also accept instructions concerning the start of the next shift outside regular working hours on the previous day in order to specify the on-call time assigned in the work schedule. Following the court, receiving the instruction by text message or email does not constitute a significant

[76] E. g. Tarifvertrag über Rahmenbedingungen zum mobilen Arbeiten für die Beschäftigten des Landes Hessen, 15 October 2021; Manteltarifvertrag für das private Versicherungsgewerbe – Mobiles Arbeiten (TV MobA).

[77] Bundesministerium für Arbeit und Soziales, Orts- und zeitflexibles Arbeiten gestalten, brochure a880, available at: www.bmas.de/SharedDocs/Downloads/DE/Publikationen/a880-orts-und-zeitflexibles-arbeiten-gestalten.pdf?__blob=publicationFile&v=2, last accessed 5.2.2026, 11.

[78] Bundesministerium für Arbeit und Soziales, Orts- und zeitflexibles Arbeiten gestalten, brochure a880, available at: www.bmas.de/SharedDocs/Downloads/DE/Publikationen/a880-orts-und-zeitflexibles-arbeiten-gestalten.pdf?__blob=publicationFile&v=2, last accessed 5.2.2026, 22.

[79] E. g. Spiegel Online, Erreichbar nach Dienstschluss: Maßnahmen der Konzerne, available at: www.spiegel.de/karriere/erreichbar-nach-dienstschluss-massnahmen-der-konzerne-a-954029.html, last accessed 5.2.2026.

[80] BAG, judgment of 2 Novembre 2016 – 10 AZR 596/15, n. 11.

restriction of an employee's rest period and was therefore not to be considered working time.[81]

6. The Regulation of Telework

The term 'telework' was legally defined for the first time in Section 2 (7) of the ArbStättV following the amendment of the ArbStättV. According to this rather restrictive definition, telework refers to forms of work in which employees perform at least part of their working hours outside the company using a computer workstation set up by the employer, and where both parties have entered into a corresponding agreement. Section 2 (7) ArbStättV defines teleworking workstations as a type of 'special workplace' and links them to the application of the ArbStättV, although the latter applies only to certain provisions listed in Section 1 (4) ArbStättV. The application of occupational health and safety regulations depends on whether the person is classified as an employee or as an employee-like person.

It should be emphasized, however, that the forms of remote and mobile work currently practised – such as working from home or from another location without a workstation set-up in the employee's home – do not constitute telework in this restrictive sense. However, these forms of remote or mobile work are not regulated by statutory law, but by collective bargaining agreements or works place agreements.[82]

7. The Status of Teleworkers, Remote Workers or Mobile Workers

If persons employed in telework are qualified as employees within the meaning of Section 611a BGB, they fall under the scope of general labour law rules and are subject to full employee protection. Since the employee status is not linked to the place of work but rather to the degree of personal dependence, teleworkers may be classified as employees, depending on their employment situation.

8. The Use of Remote or Mobile Work During the Covid-19 Pandemic

Remote work in a broader sense was increasingly used during the Covid-19 pandemic. However, in many working relationships, e. g. in sectors like production or services, that are performed in person and/or physically, the employee's presence at the workplace is necessary and it is impossible to work remotely. According to the Hans Böckler Foundation, only 17 % of the working population in Germany worked partly, mainly or exclusively remotely from home before the

---

[81] BAG, judgment of 23 August 2023 – 5 AZR 349/22, n. 42, 44.

[82] *Mierich*, Orts- und zeitflexibles Arbeiten – Praxiswissen Betriebsvereinbarungen, 2020, 11 et seq.

Covid-19 pandemic. After the beginning of the pandemic, the share of employees working from home had risen to 44 %. In January 2021, it was still at 38 %.[83] During the Covid pandemic, the SARS-CoV-2 Occupational Safety and Health Regulation (Corona-ArbSchV) came into force on 27 January 2021.[84] According to Section 2 of the Corona-ArbSchV, in the case of office work or comparable activities, employers were obliged to offer their employees the option of carrying out their work in their own premises, provided there were no compelling operational reasons to the contrary. However, this was merely an occupational health and safety obligation. A mandatory right to work from home was not established (neither during nor after the Covid-19 pandemic).

9. *Relevant Judicial Practice Regarding the Use of Telework*

In 2021, the Federal Labour Court held that where an employee had previously worked partly in telework – primarily at a home workplace set up by the employer – and who was subsequently required to work exclusively at the employer's premises, the requirements for co-determination under Section 99 (1) of the BetrVG regarding a relocation of the employee were fulfilled.[85]

Case law has also clarified that the right to issue instructions under the employment contract (Section 106 (1) GewO) does not entitle the employer to assign remote work or telework to their employees.[86]

10. *Advantages and Disadvantages Reported by Teleworkers in Germany*

The opportunities and advantages of teleworking for employees are particularly noticeable in terms of time.[87] These include reduced travel/commuting time for employees, as well as the resulting flexibility in terms of time and the compatibility of work and private life. In addition, there are fewer distractions and interruptions at home, which allows employees to concentrate better on their work. Working from home means that discussions that interrupt the flow of work, among other things, can no longer take place directly and face to face, which increases employees' autonomy and independence in decision-making.

On the other hand, the blurring of the boundaries between private life and work through teleworking is a disadvantage that should not be ignored. Employees took advantage of the opportunity to organise their time freely, but this meant

---

[83] Hans-Böckler-Stiftung, So klappt gute Arbeit im Homeoffice – freiwillig und mit fairen Regeln, available at: www.boeckler.de/de/pressemitteilungen-2675-so-klappt-gute-arbeit-im-homeoffice-freiwillig-und-mit-fairen-regeln-32175.htm, last accessed 5.2.2026.

[84] SARS-CoV-2-Arbeitsschutzverordnung, BAnz AT 22 Januar 2021 V1.

[85] BAG, judgment of 20. October 2021 – 7 ABR 34/20, n. 18.

[86] LAG Berlin-Brandenburg, judgment of 14 November 2028 – 17 Sa 562/18.

[87] Bundesanstalt für Arbeitsschutz und Arbeitsmedizin (BAuA), Telearbeit und Homeoffice, Fokus-Broschüre, available at: www.baua.de/DE/Angebote/Publikationen/Fokus/Telearbeit-Homeoffice.pdf?__blob=publicationFile&v=2, last accessed 6.2.2026, 5 w.f.r.

that they extended their working hours into the evening, generating overtime and living a life of constant availability. This leads to a higher workload and intensity, which can affect the mental and physical health of employees due to the limited free time and the resulting reduction in time for relaxation.[88]

V. Special Categories of Workers: Workers on Digital Platforms

There are no explicit legislative regulations on platform workers in the German legal system. The European Platform Work Directive is to be transposed until 2 December 2026. No draft law has yet been published. Currently, no nationwide, broadly applicable sectoral collective bargaining agreement systematically regulates work on digital platforms in Germany comparable to, for example, the metal or public-sector agreements. Regulation of platform work is therefore a patchwork: general labour and social law norms, forthcoming implementation of the EU Platform Work Directive, enforcement against bogus self-employment, and company-level collective bargaining agreements or works arrangements at individual platforms such as Lieferando, Gorillas/Flink or similar services.

1. The Status of Platform Workers

Due to the heterogeneous legal construction and implementation of platform work, a general legal assessment is hardly possible. What is clear, however, is that platform workers, as natural persons, are holders of rights and obligations. In the German legal system, platform workers can be classified as employees, employee-like or self-employed persons. This will depend on the individual circumstances of every individual situation. Access to labour and social security protection depends on their legal status. Full protection is only granted to employees with an employment contract.

Platform workers have (until now) been predominantly classified as 'self-employed'.[89] In its ruling of 1 December 2020, the BAG[90] ruled for the first time on the legal status of a platform worker and classified the platform worker as an employee. In doing so, the BAG emphasised the actual performance of the contract. The BAG considered the long-term, recurring employment in the form of continuous individual assignments, which lead to a 'combination of individual assignments into a uniform (permanent) employment relationship',[91] to be a con-

---

[88] Bundesanstalt für Arbeitsschutz und Arbeitsmedizin (BAuA), Telearbeit und Homeoffice, Fokus-Broschüre, available at: www.baua.de/DE/Angebote/Publikationen/Fokus/Telearbeit-Homeoffice.pdf?__blob=publicationFile&v=2, last accessed 6.2.2026, 5 w.f.r.

[89] W.f.r. *Oberthür/Chandna-Hoppe*, Handbuch – Mobile Work – Rechtsfragen zu Homeoffice und mobiler Arbeit, 2024, 33.

[90] BAG, judgment of 1 December 2020 – 9 AZR 102/20.

[91] BAG, judgment of 1 December 2020 – 9 AZR 102/20, n. 52.

tractual continuing obligation. The BAG further emphasised that the characteristic subordination and external control of an employment contract can also result from an organisational structure created by the platform operator, in that the employed person can be induced to behave in the desired manner by the constraints associated with it. The external control of the activity would result from the fact that the platform operator in question directs the user behaviour of platform workers by tailoring and combining the assignments in the app. The possibility of receiving more assignments simultaneously at a higher level and thus effectively earning an hourly wage would incentivise platform workers to fulfil assignments on a long-term and continuous basis. The BAG concluded that the actual performance of small orders by the user of an online platform based on an agreement with the operator can be classified as an employment relationship when viewed as a whole.[92]

The ruling was controversially discussed by German legal scholars.[93] Although the ruling has far-reaching implications for the determination of employee status, it cannot be inferred that platform work will generally qualify as an employment relationship in the future. This is because the Court's reasoning is strongly influenced by the specific circumstances of the individual case. In the case at hand, for example, the platform worker was not free to choose the place of work, whereas platform workers are usually free to decide where they work). Legal reforms must be envisaged in order to transpose the provisions of the Platform Labour Directive, in particular the presumption in its Article 5, into German law.[94]

2. *The Use of Work on Digital Platforms During the Covid-19 Pandemic*

The Covid pandemic had varying effects on the platform economy in Germany. A study evaluated findings from ten platform companies in Germany that offered both location-dependent and location-independent services. On the one hand, location-independent platform providers offering micro or macro tasks benefited from the market conditions changed by the pandemic (lockdown, contact restrictions). Delivery service platforms also saw an increase in demand. On the other hand, location-dependent platform services experienced a slump in sales.[95]

3. *Relevant Judicial Practice Regarding the Use of Work on Digital Platforms*

The key decision of the BAG from 2020 on the legal status of platform workers has already been discussed in detail (see VII.1). Another decision by the BAG

---

[92] BAG, judgment of 1 December 2020 – 9 AZR 102/20, n. 45 et seq.

[93] Cf. *Fischels/Sokoll*, Der Arbeitnehmerbegriff – Entwicklungen und Impulse aus der Plattformarbeit, NZA 2024, 656, 660 et seqq.

[94] See *Sagan*, Arbeitnehmerbegriff: Erosion oder Evolution?, NZA 2026, 73.

[95] *Gerber/Wandjo*, Auswirkungen von Covid-19 auf arbeitsvermittelnde Plattformen und Ressourcen der Pandemiebewältigung, Arbeit 32 (2023), 349, 360 et seqq.

from 2021 dealt with the provision of work equipment. A platform-employed (bicycle) delivery driver demanded that his employer provide him with work equipment (bicycle and smartphone). The BAG clarified in this regard that the plaintiff was entitled to the provision of the work equipment essential for the agreed activity under Section 611a (1) BGB in conjunction with the employment contract. The platform as an employer was responsible for providing the work equipment because he organised the work processes and assigned the work to be performed to the employee by virtue of his right to issue instructions pursuant to Section 106 GewO.[96]

4. *Advantages and Disadvantages Reported by Workers on Digital Platforms*

The third Fairwork Report Germany[97] from 2025 analyses working standards in the German platform economy based on the following criteria: fair pay, fair working conditions, fair contracts, fair management processes and fair co-determination. None of the platforms achieved more than four out of a possible 10 points. Only three out of ten platform providers examined were able to demonstrate clear and accessible contracts/terms and conditions. None of the providers were able to demonstrate algorithmic transparency. Instead, there are reports of convoluted employment relationships and employment via subcontractors.[98]

VI. Special Categories of Workers: Workers in Cultural and Creative Industries

Generative AI is putting the creative industry under considerable pressure. It is not yet possible to fully assess the economic impact that the increased use of generative AI will have on the creative sector. What is clear, however, is that the effects are likely to be significant. Initial estimates by GEMA and SACEM (French authors' society) estimate the cumulative total damage to German and French music authors from 2023 to 2028 at approximately EUR 2.7 billion.

These losses are attributed, on the one hand, to increasing competitive pressure and, on the other hand, to the use of copyright-protected works as training data. The survey further revealed that 71 % of the music authors in Germany and France fear that they will no longer be able to secure their livelihoods.[99] In addi-

---

[96] BAG, judgment of 10 Novembre 2021 – 5 AZR 334/21, n. 23.

[97] Fairwork, Fairwork Germany Report 2025, available at: fair.work/wp-content/uploads/sites/17/2025/07/Fairwork-Germany-Report-2025-DE.pdf, last accessed 5.2.2026, 24.

[98] Fairwork, Fairwork Germany Report 2025, available at: fair.work/wp-content/uploads/sites/17/2025/07/Fairwork-Germany-Report-2025-DE.pdf, last accessed 5.2.2026, 24.

[99] GEMA/SACEM/Goldmedia, KI und Musik – Key Facts, available at: www.gema.de/documents/d/guest/gema_sacem_goldmedia_ki-und-musik-key-facts-pdf, last accessed 5.2.2026.

tion to the anticipated economic consequences, the use of AI also raises significant copyright issues.[100]

In February 2025, the trade unions *Ver.di* and the actors' union *Bundesverband Schauspiel e.V.* agreed a collective agreement with the industry association *Produktionsallianz* on the conditions for the use of generative artificial intelligence in film productions. The regulations concern the use of generative AI in relation to acting performances and govern consent and remuneration conditions.[101]

VII. Information and Consultation of Workers Regarding the Use of Artificial Intelligence in the Workplace

1. Information Rights Concerning the Use of Artificial Intelligence in Labour Relations

The Works Constitution Act (BetrVG)[102] as amended by the Works Council Modernisation Act (BRMG),[103] regulates information and consultation rights. It includes explicit rules on the use of AI in employment relationships for the first time. It refers to AI in three respects:

First, AI is mentioned in the context of the general description of the works council's tasks in Section 80 BetrVG. Under Section 80 (3) 1 BetrVG, the works council is entitled to consult experts, where this is necessary for the proper performance of its duties. The provision was expanded to provide that consulting an expert is deemed necessary where questions relating to the use of AI need to be assessed. Second, the information and consultation rights in Section 90 BetrVG include the use of AI. Following Section 90 (1) No. 3 BetrVG, the employer is obliged to inform the works counsel on planned AI use in due delay and provide necessary documents. In addition, under Section 90 (2) 1 BetrVG, the employer must consult the works council on the planned use of AI and its effects on employees, so that the works council's suggestions and concerns can be taken into account. Thirdly, the use of AI in the context of personnel selection for hiring, transfers, reclassifications and dismissals is expressly regulated. For example,

[100] Cf. *de la Durantaye*, Garbage in, garbage out – Die Regulierung generativer KI durch Urheberrecht, ZUM 2023, 645–660. Ver.di, press release Erster Tarifabschluss zum Umgang mit KI in Film- und Fernsehproduktion, available at: www.verdi.de/presse/pressemitteilungen/erster-tarifabschluss-zum-umgang-ki-film-und-fernsehproduktion, last accessed 5.2.2026.

[101] Ver.di, press release Erster Tarifabschluss zum Umgang mit KI in Film- und Fernsehproduktion, available at: www.verdi.de/presse/pressemitteilungen/erster-tarifabschluss-zum-umgang-ki-film-und-fernsehproduktion, last accessed 5.2.2026.

[102] Betriebsverfassungsgesetz in the version of 25 September 2001 (BGBl. I 2001, 2518), as last amended by the Act of 19 July 2024 (BGBl. I 2024, Nr. 248).

[103] Gesetz zur Förderung der Betriebsratswahlen und der Betriebsratsarbeit in einer digitalen Arbeitswelt (Betriebsrätemodernisierungsgesetz), Act of 14 June 2021 (BGBl. I 2021, Nr. 32).

pursuant to Section 95 (2a) BetrVG the consent of the works council is required for personnel selection guidelines developed with the help of AI.

When introducing AI systems that collect personal data, the right of co-determination pursuant to Section 87 (1) No. 6 BetrVG must be observed. Even if AI systems are not expressly named as a regulatory matter, the vast majority of AI systems are technical devices that are objectively suitable for monitoring the performance and behaviour of employees.[104] Any technical equipment that is intended or even merely suitable for monitoring behaviour or performance triggers mandatory co-determination by the works council.[105] Also, voluntary works agreements may be concluded at workplace level. We can confirm, that works agreements on algorithmic management are being concluded, for example, at IBM Central Holding GmbH a 'Group-level works agreement on the introduction and use of artificial intelligence systems' has been adopted, that sets out rules for the internal use of AI within the company.[106]

The provisions of the BetrVG relating to AI essentially involve the works council in the introduction and design of AI systems and thus have a preventive character.[107]

2. Other Rights or Important Legal Aspects

There is a transparency obligation under Art. 13 of Regulation (EU) 2024/1689 for high-risk AI. When collective bargaining agreements or works agreements are negotiated, the issue is one of the important subjects. For example, in practice it is reported, that works agreements on the introduction and use of AI systems often contain information and transparency obligations regarding the functioning and intended use of algorithmic systems.[108]

With the entry into force of the AI Regulation, employers are obliged under Art. 4 of Regulation (EU) 2024/1689 to provide training measures for their employees in the event of AI use, so that they have a sufficient level of AI competence.

---

[104] Following the affirmed case law of the Federal Labour Court, this is decisive for triggering the co-determination right; see BAG, judgment of 23 October 2018 – 1 ABN 36/18, n. 5; see also Section 3.6 for a more detailed analysis.

[105] BAG, judgment of 23 October 2018 – 1 ABN 36/18, n. 5.

[106] WageIndicator, Konzernbetriebsvereinbarung über die Einführung und den Einsatz von Systemen der künstlichen Intelligenz (Artificial Intelligence), available at: https://wageindicator.org/de-de/arbeiten-in-deutschland/tarifvertrag/konzernbetriebsvereinbarung-uber-die-einfuhrung-und-den-einsatz-von-systemen-der-kunstlichen-intelligenz-artificial-intelligence, last accessed 21.4.2026.

[107] This is subject to ongoing debates: The Labour Law Section of the Deutscher Juristentag (Association of German Jurists) will discuss reforms on information and consultation rights in the digital context of work, see *Schubert*, Kooperativ, flexibel, digital – Braucht das Betriebsverfassungsgesetz ein Update?, expert opinion for the Deutscher Juristentag 2026 (forthcoming).

[108] *Doellgast/Wagner/O'Brady*, Negotiating Limits on Algorithmic Management in Digitalised Services: Cases From Germany and Norway, Transfer: European Review of Labour and Research 28(2) (2022), 106–108.

VIII. Advantages of Using Artificial Intelligence in the Workplace

Different possible advantages of using AI in the workplace can be identified. A DEKRA survey conducted by forsa in 2023 shows that 58 % of employees had no significant contact with AI in their professional activities. Only 29 % stated that AI greatly facilitates their professional activities.[109] A survey conducted by Bitkom Research in 2023 asked employees about the advantages and disadvantages of AI in the workplace. The most frequently cited advantage was securing the future viability of companies (50 %). The second most frequently cited advantage was the saving of working time (47 %), followed by the advantage of being able to concentrate on essential tasks using AI (41 %).[110] The deployment of artificial intelligence in working life offers a range of opportunities across occupational safety, inclusion, compliance, training, and work organisation.

In the field of occupational safety and risk management, the first AI-based tools are already available. These systems enable the monitoring and early detection of potential workplace accidents, support early risk analyses, and allow for the generation of individualised instructions, including targeted occupational safety training.[111] AI is also being applied to promote inclusion in the workplace. The BMAS-funded project "KI.ASSIST – Assistance services and artificial intelligence for people with severe disabilities in vocational rehabilitation" examines how AI-supported assistance systems can be used to benefit persons with disabilities with different impairments in the context of vocational rehabilitation.[112]

In human resources, chatbots are increasingly used to simplify communication between employees and HR departments, thereby improving accessibility and efficiency.[113] AI-supported automated equal pay systems are also developed to reduce discrimination.[114] In addition, AI-supported training programmes have been developed in specific regulatory areas, including equal treatment.[115] From a

---

[109] DEKRA, Arbeitssicherheitsreport 2025 – KI am Arbeitsplatz, available at: www.dekra.de/de/arbeitssicherheitsreport-2025-ki-am-arbeitsplatz/, last accessed 5.2.2026, 29.

[110] Statista, Umfrage zu Vorteilen und Nachteilen von KI am Arbeitsplatz, available at: https://de.statista.com/infografik/32054/umfrage-zu-den-vorteilen-und-nachteilen-von-ki-am-arbeitsplatz/, last accessed 21.4.2026.

[111] Cf. WEKA, Künstliche Intelligenz (KI) im Arbeitsschutz, available at: www.weka.de/arbeitsschutz-gefahrstoffe/kuenstliche-intelligenz-ki-im-arbeitsschutz/, last accessed 28 January 2026.

[112] KI-Assist, Ergebnisbroschüre 2022, available at: www.ki-assist.de/fileadmin/ki_assist/Medienkatalog/KI.ASSIST_2022_Ergebnissbroschuere.pdf, last accessed 5.2.2026.

[113] *Garnitz/Schaller*, ChatGPT, Chatbots und mehr – Wie wird künstliche Intelligenz in den HR-Abteilungen von Unternehmen genutzt?, ifo Schnelldienst 76 (2023), 66.

[114] E.g. PDconnect, Equal Pay – Gleichbehandlung effizient umsetzen, available at: pdconnect.de/equal-pay-gleichbehandlung-effizient-umsetzen/, last accessed 5.2.2026.

[115] E.g. lawpilots, AGG-Schulung, available at: https://lawpilots.com/de/schulungen/agg-schulung/?cp=482032164&ag=1145692083723576&msclkid=79db16af1c701b28e7837fd509a9b171&utm_source=bing&utm_medium=cpc&utm_campaign=SEARCH%20%7C%20DACH&utm_term=Antidiskriminierung%20Schulung&utm_content=Search%20%7C%20AGG%20und%20Gleichbehandlung, last accessed 21.4.2026.

compliance perspective, AI-supported tools are being used to assist in the implementation of data protection regulations.[116]

Finally, employees report that the AI-supported reduction and automation of simple tasks enable a more efficient use of working time, thereby allowing greater focus on more complex or value-adding activities.[117]

IX. Possible Risks Caused by the Use of AI in the Workplace

Research highlights risks related to discrimination, surveillance, privacy, and labour market segmentation, but also stress the importance of not overestimating current AI impacts.[118] Discrimination is considered to be an important risk. In a voluntary guideline for the use of AI in the administrative practice of labour and social administration developed by the AI in Labour and Social Administration Network, 'non-discrimination' is listed as one of the fundamental values and highlights the avoidance of bias.[119] Risks of excessive surveillance and an amplification of control have been observed.[120] The challenges of data protection and the protection of personal rights have been stressed in this report. Also, employees report a lack of occupational health and safety and company health promotion measures.[121] Employees state that the boundaries between private life and work are becoming blurred.[122] Waas also points out in detail that the use of AI poses risks to occupational safety. On the one hand, the use of human resource analytics increases the psychological pressure on employees. On the other hand,

---

[116] E.g. Alan, available at: alan.de/?mtm_campaign=alan&mtm_source=microsoft_ads&mtm_medium=cpc&mtm_content=usp_dsgvo&msclkid=b676a75131b6110b1451ce2b26fdabe4, last accessed 5.2.2026.

[117] Bundesanstalt für Arbeitsschutz und Arbeitsmedizin (BAuA), Telearbeit und Homeoffice, Fokus-Broschüre, available at: www.baua.de/DE/Angebote/Publikationen/Fokus/Telearbeit-Homeoffice.pdf?__blob=publicationFile&v=2, last accessed 6.2.2026, w.f.r.

[118] *Hassel/Özkiziltan*, Governing the Work-Related Risks of AI: Implications for the German Government and Trade Unions, Transfer: European Review of Labour and Research 29(1) (2023), 73–76, 85–86.

[119] Bundesministerium für Arbeit und Soziales, Leitlinien zum Einsatz künstlicher Intelligenz in der behördlichen Praxis der Arbeits- und Sozialverwaltung, brochure a862–01, available at: www.bmas.de/SharedDocs/Downloads/DE/Publikationen/a862-01-leitlinien-ki-einsatz-behoerdliche-praxis-arbeits-sozialverwaltung.pdf?__blob=publicationFile&v=2, last accessed 5.2.2026.

[120] *Kärcher/Walser*, Vereinbarkeit eines Direktanstellungsgebots in der Paketzustellung mit dem Verfassungs- und Unionsrecht, HIS Working Paper No. 18 (Frankfurt am Main, 2023), 25 et seq. (concerning parcel delivery services).

[121] Bundesanstalt für Arbeitsschutz und Arbeitsmedizin (BAuA), Telearbeit und Homeoffice, Fokus-Broschüre, available at: www.baua.de/DE/Angebote/Publikationen/Fokus/Telearbeit-Homeoffice.pdf?__blob=publicationFile&v=2, last accessed 6.2.2026, 4 w.f.r.

[122] Bundesanstalt für Arbeitsschutz und Arbeitsmedizin (BAuA), Telearbeit und Homeoffice, Fokus-Broschüre, available at: www.baua.de/DE/Angebote/Publikationen/Fokus/Telearbeit-Homeoffice.pdf?__blob=publicationFile&v=2, last accessed 6.2.2026, 4 w.f.r.

the complex interaction of sensor technology, hardware and software and their connectivity can pose a physical hazard.[123]

Finally, the implementation and use of AI may also lead to trade union rights and employee co-determination being disregarded and curtailed.[124]

Reliable figures on the German labour market concerning the impact of the use of AI are currently still difficult to quantify. The Institute for Employment Research (IAB) has made initial attempts to predict how the German labour market will change by 2040 because of the use of AI. Regarding the absolute number of persons in employment in Germany, the IAB assumes that the use of AI will lead to both job losses and the creation of new jobs. It can be assumed that these opposing developments will ultimately lead to a – rather qualitative – shift in the employment structure.[125] The use of AI can help to make working conditions more flexible and achieve personalisation of tasks.[126]

Increased demand is expected in the areas of AI development, maintenance and optimisation. This is also true for specialists who deal with ethical regulatory issues relating to AI systems. It is also predicted that new occupational fields will emerge in which traditional professions will have to be linked with modern information technologies, such as data scientists in healthcare.[127] On the other hand, a study by the German Institute for Economic Research from 2024 shows that tasks in the areas of typing, graphic design and simple software development are particularly easy to replace with AI.[128]

X. Perspectives on Debates and Public Policies Regarding the Use of Artificial Intelligence in the Workplace

The BMAS addresses issues relating to the handling of AI and takes up topics such as transparency and trustworthiness.[129] In 2025, the Conference of Science Ministers also adopted a position paper entitled 'Artificial intelligence (AI): Key

---

123 *Waas*, Künstliche Intelligenz und Arbeitsrecht, 2022, 178 et seq.

124 Trade unions' digital access rights to companies were discussed and largely ruled out in recent case law, see BAG, judgment of 28 January 2025 – 1 AZR 33/24.

125 IAB, Publikation Nr. 15227157, available at: Zika/Hassemer/Hummel/Krebs/Maier/Mönnig/Schneemann/Weber/Zenk, Künstliche Intelligenz: Potenzielle Effekte für den deutschen Arbeitsmarkt, IAB-Forschungsbericht 23/2025, 9.

126 *Barenkamp*, Wertschöpfung durch KI – Chancen für Unternehmen und Gesellschaft, 1st ed. 2025.

127 *Barenkamp*, Wertschöpfung durch KI – Chancen für Unternehmen und Gesellschaft, 1st ed. 2025.

128 DIW, Generative künstliche Intelligenz reduziert Nachfrage nach Freelance-Arbeit auf Online-Plattformen, DIW Wochenbericht 35/2024, available at: www.diw.de/de/diw_01.c.912148.de/publikationen/wochenberichte/2024_35_1/generative_kuenstliche_intelligenz_reduziert_nachfrage_nach_freelance-arbeit_auf_online-plattformen.html, last accessed 6.2.2026, 542.

129 https://www.denkfabrik-bmas.de/fileadmin/Downloads/Publikationen/barrierefrei_BMAS_DF_Mantel_Algorithmisches_Management.pdf (2026-02-05).

technology for progress and competitiveness in the higher education and science system'.[130] Among other things, the 'Working aid for the practical application of the voluntary AI guidelines in labour and social administration' refers to 'Guidelines for the Design of Trustworthy Artificial Intelligence'. This is an AI test catalogue developed by the Fraunhofer Institute. On the one hand, the catalogue aims to provide AI developers with guidelines for the development and design of trustworthy AI tools. On the other hand, it is intended to support auditors in analysing AI applications for trustworthiness.[131]

German trade unions frame AI governance primarily around worker protection, co-determination and human-centred AI. In September 2024, the German Trade Union Confederation (DGB) published a discussion paper entitled 'For the use of artificial intelligence in the world of work'.[132] The German Trade Union Confederation (DGB) defines three core preconditions for AI use in workplaces: (1) transparency about how AI systems function, (2) employee competencies to assess AI applications, and (3) strong co-determination rights.[133] Central concerns include job displacement, algorithmic surveillance, discrimination risks, and information asymmetries between employers and employees.[134] Works councils demand early involvement in AI implementation processes under Section 87 BetrVG. A key milestone was the BRMG, which explicitly strengthened co-determination rights regarding AI systems.[135] Overall, trade unions advocate binding regulation at EU and national level, transparency, independent certification of high-risk AI systems, and collective bargaining solutions to ensure "good work" in AI-integrated workplaces.

Employer positions are less explicitly documented in the literature but appear mainly within Germany's *social partnership framework*. Employers generally view AI as a tool to enhance competitiveness, productivity and innovation, particu-

---

130 Kultusministerkonferenz, Positionspapier Künstliche Intelligenz, available at: www.kmk.org/fileadmin/Dateien/veroeffentlichungen_beschluesse/2025/2025_01_31-KI-Positionspapier.pdf, last accessed 5.2.2026.

131 Fraunhofer IAIS, KI-Prüfkatalog, available at: www.iais.fraunhofer.de/s/ki-pruefkatalog/index.html#2, last accessed 5.2.2026.

132 Deutscher Gewerkschaftsbund, Regelungsrahmen Künstliche Intelligenz in der Arbeitswelt, discussion paper, available at: www.dgb.de/fileadmin/download_center/Positionen_und_Thesen/241001_DGB-Diskussionspapier_Regelungsrahmen_KI_in_der_Arbeitswelt_oef_fin.pdf, last accessed 5.2.2026.

133 *Krzywdzinski/Gerst/Butollo*, Promoting Human-Centred AI in the Workplace: Trade Unions and Their Strategies for Regulating the Use of AI in Germany, Transfer: European Review of Labour and Research 29(1) (2023), 57–60.

134 *Krzywdzinski/Gerst/Butollo*, Promoting Human-Centred AI in the Workplace: Trade Unions and Their Strategies for Regulating the Use of AI in Germany, Transfer: European Review of Labour and Research 29(1) (2023), 59–61; *Hassel/Özkiziltan*, Governing the Work-Related Risks of AI: Implications for the German Government and Trade Unions, Transfer: European Review of Labour and Research 29(1) (2023), 74–76.

135 *Haipeter/Wannöffel/Daus/Schaffarczik*, Human-Centered AI Through Employee Participation: The Role of Works Councils in Germany, Frontiers in Artificial Intelligence 7 (2024), Article 1272102, 3.

larly in manufacturing and telecommunications.[136] Rather than rejecting regulation outright, German employers tend to favour *collaborative governance through works councils*, reflecting Germany's coordinated market economy model.[137] Company-level agreements (e. g., Deutsche Telekom's AI governance framework) demonstrate willingness to integrate employee participation into AI implementation processes.[138] At the same time, employers emphasize flexibility and innovation capacity, balancing ethical considerations with competitive pressures, especially vis-à-vis the US and China.[139] In short, the employer perspective supports AI adoption for economic modernization while operating largely within Germany's institutionalized co-determination structures.

The use of AI requires a clear legal framework that ensures transparency, fairness and human control. From a labour law perspective, the introduction of minimum standards and protection by statutory provisions seems appropriate. However, Germany's corporatist governance model – characterized by social partnership and institutionalized worker participation – can be considered as a suitable instrument to introduce responsible AI governance.[140]

---

[136] *Molina/Butollo/Mako/Godino/Holtgrewe* et al., It Takes Two to Code: A Comparative Analysis of Collective Bargaining and Artificial Intelligence, Transfer: European Review of Labour and Research 29(1) (2023), 88–90, 94–95; *Haipeter/Wannöffel/Daus/Schaffarczik*, Human-Centered AI Through Employee Participation: The Role of Works Councils in Germany, Frontiers in Artificial Intelligence 7 (2024), Article 1272102, 3.

[137] *Krzywdzinski/Gerst/Butollo*, Promoting Human-Centred AI in the Workplace: Trade Unions and Their Strategies for Regulating the Use of AI in Germany, Transfer: European Review of Labour and Research 29(1) (2023), 62–66.

[138] *Doellgast/Wagner/O'Brady*, Negotiating Limits on Algorithmic Management in Digitalised Services: Cases From Germany and Norway, Transfer: European Review of Labour and Research 28(2) (2022), 106–108.

[139] *Hassel/Özkiziltan*, Governing the Work-Related Risks of AI: Implications for the German Government and Trade Unions, Transfer: European Review of Labour and Research 29(1) (2023), 73–74, 85–86.

[140] *Krzywdzinski/Gerst/Butollo*, Promoting Human-Centred AI in the Workplace: Trade Unions and Their Strategies for Regulating the Use of AI in Germany, Transfer: European Review of Labour and Research 29(1) (2023), 63–68.

Autonomous Ships in German Law

Michael Stöber

I. Introduction

In the wake of digitalisation and the rapid development of artificial intelligence (AI) in recent years, autonomous road vehicles,[1] flying objects[2] and ships – i. e. vehicles controlled partially or completely by AI or other software – have become a focus of interest in legal scholarship in Germany. This article discusses autonomous shipping and the legal issues surrounding it from a German perspective. It primarily deals with the legal situation in maritime shipping. Inland waterway transport, which is largely governed by separate rules in Germany, is only considered in some aspects.[3]

The development of autonomous shipping is still widely in its infancy in Germany. A binding legal framework for the trial or even regular use of autonomous ships does not yet exist, but the Federal Ministry of Transport (*Bundesministerium für Verkehr* – BMV) intends to develop one at national level and also through participation in regulatory projects at international level.[4] With a view to developing a binding legal framework, among other things, the Federal Maritime and Hydrographic Agency (*Bundesamt für Seeschifffahrt und Hydrographie* – BSH), which reports to the BMV, convened a "Round Table on Autonomous Shipping" for the first time in December 2025.[5]

In addition, there are individual research projects for the development and testing of autonomous ships in test fields. For example, the German Aerospace Cèntre (*Deutsches Zentrum für Luft- und Raumfahrt* – DLR), a federal research institution, operates a digital test field on the Spree-Oder waterway and a mar-

---

[1] See, for example, *Stöber/Pieronczyk/Möller*, DAR 2020, 609 et seq.; *Stöber/Möller/Willmer*, NZV 2024, 117 et seq.

[2] See, for example, *Stöber/Anissimov/Willmer*, ZdiW 2022, 186 et seq.

[3] See, for example, *Hoffmann*, LogR 2025, 68 et seq. on the legal admissibility of remote-controlled inland waterway vessels; *Ramming*, RdTW 2024, 242, 243 et seq. on civil liability; *Goebel*, LogR 2024, 127, 128 et seq. on current case law.

[4] See *Paschke/Lutter*, RdTW 2018, 242, 245 et seq. on the parameters for such a legal framework.

[5] For more details, see https://www.deutsche-flagge.de/de/aktuelles/aktuelle-nachrichten/maritime-innovationen (last access: 11 May 2026).

itime test field in the North Sea.[6] Last but not least, there is the "CAPTN Future" cluster, a research network involving the University of Kiel, including the author of this article, alongside other partners from the public sector and industry. Its goal is to develop clean, urban, autonomous water-land mobility chains, which will also include autonomous passenger ferries.[7] However, there are currently no special subsidies or financing initiatives explicitly for research and development in the field of autonomous shipping; rather, financial support is provided on a case-by-case basis from general public funds or subsidy programmes.

The fact that the German federal government and some companies in the shipping industry are supportive and provide selective funding with regard to autonomous shipping demonstrates that the German government and industry see autonomous shipping as an opportunity to create new industries and jobs, as well as to increase the comparatively low number of merchant ships[8] sailing under the German flag.[9]

II. Overview of the Current Legal Framework for Autonomous Shipping in Germany

Special legal regulations for autonomous road vehicles have been in place in Germany for several years. Back in 2017,[10] German lawmakers introduced Sections 1a–1c of the Road Traffic Act (*Straßenverkehrsgesetz* – StVG),[11] which regulate individual aspects of highly automated driving.[12] In 2021, Sections 1d–1l StVG were enacted by the Autonomous Driving Act.[13] With these regulations, Germany became one of the first countries in the world to create a legal framework governing the operation of road vehicles with fully automated driving functions on public roads and specifying the technical requirements for the condition of the vehicles and the obligations of those involved.[14]

---

6 See https://www.dlr.de/de/medien/publikationen/magazine/alle-magazine-webversion/dlr magazin-174/autonom-durchs-wasser (last access: 11 May 2026).

7 For more details, see https://captn.sh/captn-future/ (last access: 11 May 2026).

8 See also X.

9 See https://www.zeit.de/news/2025-02/23/mehr-schiffe-sollen-unter-deutscher-flagge-fah ren (last access: 11 May 2026); generally on the economic advantages of autonomous shipping *Paschke/Lutter*, RdTW 2018, 242, 243 et seq.

10 Through the Eighth Act Amending the Road Traffic Act *(Achtes Gesetz zur Änderung des Straßenverkehrsgesetzes)* of 16 June 2017, Federal Law Gazette (*Bundesgesetzblatt* – BGBl.) I 2017, 1648, which came into force on 21 June 2017.

11 The German laws cited in this article are available – some also in English – at https://www.gesetze-im-internet.de/ (last access: 11 May 2026).

12 See *Stöber/Pieronczyk/Möller*, DAR 2020, 609, 611.

13 *Gesetz zum autonomen Fahren* of 12 July 2021, BGBl. I 2021, 3108, entered into force on 28 July 2021.

14 For more details, see *Stöber/Möller/Willmer*, NZV 2024, 117 et seq.

In contrast, German law does not yet contain any specific legal provisions for autonomous ships in maritime navigation, unlike French law, for example.[15] Currently, there are no concrete legislative plans in Germany to introduce such provisions, nor are there any specific regulations on the testing of autonomous ships. Instead, the approval of autonomous ships for testing in test areas has so far been granted case-by-case on the basis of general administrative and maritime law regulations.[16] Self-regulation or voluntary codes of conduct in the shipping industry have also not yet been established.

However, the efforts of the International Maritime Organisation (IMO) to create internationally binding rules for autonomous shipping are also significant for Germany. Germany is one of the 176 member states of the IMO. As a specialised agency of the UN, the IMO is responsible for developing safety and environmental standards for international shipping.[17]

In 2021, the IMO's Maritime Safety Committee (MSC) presented the preliminary results of a Regulatory Scoping Exercise (RSE) on Maritime Autonomous Surface Ships (MASS),[18] i.e. an investigation of the applicable international shipping agreements to determine whether and under what conditions they permit the operation of autonomous ships and, if necessary, what normative adjustments are required for autonomous ships. The most important of these agreements is the UN Convention on the Law of the Sea (UNCLOS) of 10 December 1982,[19] which was ratified in 1994 by the Federal Republic of Germany, one of a total of 170 contracting states today.[20] In addition, the Brussels Collision Convention (BCC) of 23 September 1910, to which Germany is also a signatory, has to be mentioned.[21] Another international agreement that also applies in Germany is the International Convention for the Safety of Life at Sea (SOLAS), the first version of which was concluded on 20 January 1914 in response to the sinking of the

---

[15] See *Vuattoux-Bock*, Schiffskollision, höhere Gewalt und autonome Schifffahrt, 2023, 25 et seq.

[16] See https://www.deutsche-flagge.de/de/aktuelles/aktuelle-nachrichten/maritime-innovationen (last access: 11 May 2026).

[17] For more information on the IMO, see https://www.imo.org/en (last access: 11 May 2026).

[18] MSC.1/Circ.1638 of 3 June 2021, Outcome of the regulatory Scoping Exercise for the use of Maritime Autonomous Surface Ships (MASS), available at https://www.imo.org/en/mediacentre/hottopics/pages/autonomous-shipping.aspx (last access: 11 May 2026).

[19] Available at https://www.un.org/Depts/los/convention_agreements/texts/unclos/closindx.htm (last access: 11 May 2026).

[20] By Act of 2 September 1994, BGBl. II 1994, 1798.

[21] Convention for the Unification of certain Rules of Law with respect to Collisions between Vessels, available at https://treaties.fcdo.gov.uk/data/Library2/pdf/1913-TS0004.pdf (last access: 11 May 2026); see also Imperial Law Gazette (*Reichsgesetzblatt* – RGBl.) 1913, 49.

Titanic,[22] and which is now in its fifth version from 1974,[23] being constantly updated.[24] Based on the results of the RSE, the IMO intends to develop a binding MASS Code by 2030, i. e. a set of rules governing the operation of autonomous ships.[25]

For inland navigation, which is subject to a separate legal regime in Germany, there are, however, first specific regulations relating to automated ships. Automatic track guidance assistants for inland navigation (TGAINs) have been in use in Germany inland waterway transport for some time. In December 2024, a cargo ship using a TGAIN collided with a lock gate on the Moselle, causing millions of euros worth of damage and interrupting shipping traffic for weeks. In response to this accident, the Federal Waterways and Shipping Directorate-General issued an ordinance[26] which imposes certain control and monitoring obligations on ship operators when using a TGAIN.

Since Germany has largely no specific regulations governing autonomous ships, the general regulations governing maritime and inland waterway vessels also apply to autonomous ships, as these can easily be subsumed under the definition of a ship in the respective regulations.[27] This applies both to international treaties, such as the UNCLOS[28] or the BCC,[29] and to provisions of national law, such as Sections 570 et seq. of the German Commercial Code (*Handelsgesetzbuch* – HGB).[30] Although the current maritime law regulations are primarily tailored to manned ships, they do not prohibit autonomous ships as long as the requirements of the respective regulations are met.[31]

---

[22] Available at https://archive.org/details/textofconvention00inte/page/n5/mode/2up (last access: 11 May 2026).

[23] Available at https://treaties.un.org/doc/Publication/UNTS/Volume%201184/volume-1184-I-18961-English.pdf (last access: 11 May 2026), implemented in Germany by Ordinance of 11 January 1979, BGBl. II 1979, 141.

[24] The consolidated text can be purchased for a fee at https://imo-epublications.org/content/books/9789280117936#overview (last access: 11 May 2026).

[25] For more details, see *Proelß*, in: Chibanguza/Kuß/Steege (eds.), KI-Hdb., 2nd ed. 2026, 2. Teil § 3 R. para. 4 et seq., and https://www.imo.org/en/mediacentre/hottopics/pages/autonomous-shipping.aspx (last access: 11 May 2026).

[26] See Eighth Ordinance on Temporary Deviation from the Inland Waterways Regulations *(Achte Verordnung zur vorübergehenden Abweichung von der Binnenschifffahrtsstraßen-Ordnung)* of 9 October 2025, BGBl. I 2025, No. 237.

[27] See also *Proelß*, in: Chibanguza/Kuß/Steege (eds.), KI-Hdb., 2nd ed. 2026, 2. Teil § 3 R. para. 11 et seq.; for details on the definition of a ship in the UNCLOS, see *Ritt*, Unbemannte Schiffe im Internationalen Seerecht, 2022, 34 et seq.

[28] See *Herkenhoff*, Die Haftung in der unbemannten Schifffahrt, 2020, 30; *Ritt*, Unbemannte Schiffe im Internationalen Seerecht, 2022, 54 et seq.; *Tüngler/tho Pesch*, RdTW 2017, 121, 122.

[29] See *Herkenhoff*, Die Haftung in der unbemannten Schifffahrt, 2020, 133 et seq.

[30] See *Herkenhoff*, Die Haftung in der unbemannten Schifffahrt, 2020, 134.

[31] See in detail *Proelß*, in: Chibanguza/Kuß/Steege (eds.), KI-Hdb., 2nd ed. 2026, 2. Teil § 3 R. para. 13 et seq., 16 et seq.; *Tüngler/tho Pesch*, RdTW 2017, 121, 122 et seq.; with reservations, however, *Herkenhoff*, Die Haftung in der unbemannten Schifffahrt, 2020, 42 et seq.

III. Definition

In the absence of specific legal provisions, there is no legal definition of the term "autonomous ship" in current German law. However, the aforementioned IMO report on the preliminary results of the RSE, which distinguishes between four degrees of automation, provides some guidance:[32]

- Degree 1: Ship with automated processes and decision support. Seafarers are on board to operate and control the ship's systems and functions. Some operations may be automated and temporarily unsupervised, but the seafarers on board are ready to take control.
- Degree 2: Remote-controlled ship with seafarers on board. The ship is controlled and operated from another location. Seafarers are available on board to take control and to operate the systems and functions.
- Degree 3: Remote-controlled ship without seafarers on board: The ship is controlled and operated from another location. There are no seafarers on board.
- Degree 4: Fully autonomous ship: The ship's operating system is capable of making decisions and determining actions by itself.[33]

In the following, the generic term "autonomous ships" is used for ships of all automation degrees, i.e. this term refers not only to fully autonomous ships, which realistically can only be expected in the distant future, but also to ships that continue to operate with a human crew but with partially or fully automated control systems or with remote control or monitoring by a navigator or controller on land.

IV. Cybersecurity and Data Protection for Autonomous Ships

As already mentioned,[34] the SOLAS Convention also applies in Germany. On the basis of Chapter 9 of the SOLAS Convention, the IMO has issued the International Safety Management Code (ISM Code), which is binding on the contracting states and contains provisions on ship safety.[35] In 2017, in view of an emerging increase in cyber attacks on shipping companies and ports,[36] this was supplemen-

---

[32] See MSC.1/Circ.1638 of 3 June 2021 (fn. 18), Annex, 3 et seq.; see also *Proelß*, in: Chibanguza/Kuß/Steege (eds.), KI-Hdb., 2nd ed. 2026, 2. Teil § 3 R. para. 8 et seq.

[33] Criticising the reliance on a human crew and proposing a different categorisation: *Vuattoux-Bock*, Schiffskollision, höhere Gewalt und autonome Schifffahrt, 2023, 12 et seq.

[34] See II.

[35] For general information on the ISM Code, see *Ritt*, Unbemannte Schiffe im Internationalen Seerecht, 2022, 252 et seq.

[36] For more details, see *Ritt*, Unbemannte Schiffe im Internationalen Seerecht, 2022, 252 et seq.

ted by provisions on maritime cyber risk management, which primarily serve to prevent cyber attacks.[37] These rules also apply to autonomous ships.[38]

As far as data protection is concerned, there are no special regulations in Germany specifically for autonomous ships. Rather, the general provisions of the EU's General Data Protection Regulation (GDPR)[39] apply, which, due to their broad material and territorial scope (see Articles 2 and 3 GDPR), also apply to the field of autonomous shipping.[40]

V. EU AI Regulation and Autonomous Shipping

Although EU Member States have not yet produced an internationally competitive AI system, with the US and China having left the EU behind in this respect, this has not prevented the EU from enacting one of the world's first binding sets of rules for AI in the form of the AI Regulation.[41] The comprehensive and complex AI Regulation contains EU-wide rules for the placing on the market, putting into service and use of AI systems, and regulates specific requirements and obligations relating to high-risk AI systems.[42] It means additional bureaucracy and compliance costs for AI companies in the EU, thereby counterproductively weakening their international competitiveness even further.[43]

The broad definition of AI in Article 3(1) of the AI Regulation also covers automated and autonomous assistance and control systems used in ships.[44] Automated and autonomous systems for controlling ships are also likely to be considered high-risk AI systems[45] within the meaning of Article 6(1) in conjunction

---

[37] Current version: MSC-FAL.1/Circ.3/Rev.3 of 4 April 2025, Guidelines on maritime cyber risk management, available at https://www.imo.org/en/ourwork/security/pages/cyber-security.aspx (last access: 11 May 2026); for more details, see *Ritt*, Unbemannte Schiffe im Internationalen Seerecht, 2022, 250 et seq., 255 et seq.

[38] For more details, see *Ritt*, Unbemannte Schiffe im Internationalen Seerecht, 2022, 260 et seq.

[39] Regulation (EU) 2016/679 of 27 April 2016 on the protection of natural persons with regard to the processing of personal data and on the free movement of such data, Official Journal (OJ) L 119 of 4 May 2016, 1.

[40] On autonomous road vehicles, see *Forgó*, in: Oppermann/Buck-Heeb (eds.), Autonomes Fahren, 3rd ed. 2024, Kap. 2.4 para. 22 et seq.

[41] Regulation (EU) 2024/1689 of 13 June 2024 laying down harmonised rules on artificial intelligence, OJ L 2024/1689 of 12 July 2024.

[42] For more details on the content of the AI Regulation, see *Becker/Feuerstack*, KIR 2024, 62 et seq.

[43] See also the warning issued by the Bavarian Minister of State for Digital Affairs *Mehring*, https://www.stmd.bayern.de/mehring-fordert-moratorium-fuer-den-ai-act-europa-darf-sich-nicht-selbst-ausbremsen/ (last access: 19 February 2026).

[44] *Proelß*, in: Chibanguza/Kuß/Steege (eds.), KI-Hdb., 2nd ed. 2026, 2. Teil § 3 R. para. 20; cf. on road vehicles *Bauer/Merkle/Sedlmaier*, KIR 2025, 300, 301 et seq.

[45] See *Bauer/Merkle/Sedlmaier*, KIR 2025, 300, 302 et seq.

with Annex I No. 16 of the AI Regulation and the Marine Equipment Directive.[46] However, due to the exception in Article 2(2) of the AI Regulation, the specific provisions for high-risk AI systems in the AI Regulation itself do not apply, but rather the sector-specific standards of the IMO to be adopted in accordance with Article 8 et seq. AI Regulation, or – in the absence of sufficient IMO standards – the standards to be adopted by the EU Commission itself by means of a delegated act (see Article 105 AI Regulation in conjunction with Article 8 Marine Equipment Directive).[47] It is to be expected that these standards will, in particular, stipulate the effective supervision by a natural person required by Article 14 AI Regulation for high-risk AI systems and take into account the requirements of Article 15 AI Regulation on cyber security.[48]

VI. Registration and Property Law Treatment of Autonomous Ships

Article 94(2)(a) of the UNCLOS obliges each contracting state to maintain a ship register containing the names and details of ships flying its flag. German law provides for the registration of both seagoing ships and inland waterway vessels in separate registers (see Section 3 of the Ship Register Ordinance).[49] There are no special provisions for autonomous ships in this respect either. However, from a registration law perspective, autonomous ships are also subject to the Ship Register Ordinance and can therefore also be entered in the sea or inland waterway ship register.[50]

Ships entered in the maritime or inland waterway register – including autonomous ships, as mentioned above – are subject to a special property law regime in Germany, which is not regulated in the Civil Code (*Bürgerliches Gesetzbuch* – BGB), but in the Ship Rights Act.[51] According to the provisions of the Ship Rights Act, registered ships are largely treated as equivalent to real estate in terms of property law.[52] In particular, according to Sections 15–17 of the Ship Rights Act, the ship register – similar to the land register (Sections 891–893 BGB) – enjoys public credibility and forms the basis for the acquisition in good faith of ownership and other rights to a registered ship.[53]

---

[46] Directive 2014/90/EU of 23 July 2014 on marine equipment, OJ L 257 of 28 August 2014, 146.

[47] S. *Brandt-Steinke*, in: BeckOK KI-Recht, 1 November 2025, Art. 105 KI-VO para. 1 et seq.; cf. for road vehicles *Bauer/Merkle/Sedlmaier*, KIR 2025, 300, 304 et seq.

[48] For more details on the requirements for high-risk AI systems resulting from the AI Regulation, see *Heine*, in: Chibanguza/Kuß/Steege (eds.), KI-Hdb., 2nd ed. 2026, Einl. A. para. 71 et seq.

[49] *Schiffsregisterordnung* in the version published on 26 May 1994, BGBl. I 1994, 1133.

[50] See also *Ritt*, Unbemannte Schiffe im Internationalen Seerecht, 2022, 135.

[51] *Schiffsrechtegesetz* of 15 November 1940, RGBl. I 1940, 1499.

[52] For more details, see *Baur/Stürner*, Sachenrecht, 18th ed. 2009, § 31 para. 1 et seq.

[53] See Federal Court of Justice (*Bundesgerichtshof* – BGH), 25 June 1990 – II ZR 178/89, NJW 1990, 3209, 3210.

VII. Civil Liability for Autonomous Ships

1. General

German law does not contain any liability rules specifically for autonomous ships. In legal literature, some authors, e. g. *Herkenhoff*,[54] *Etzkorn*[55] and *Vuattoux-Bock*,[56] argue in favour of introducing strict liability for ship owners or operators specifically for autonomous ships *de lege ferenda*.[57] However, *de lege lata*, no such special regulations exist to date. Therefore, the liability provisions that apply to ships in general, and regulate fault-based liability, are also applicable to autonomous ships for the time being.[58] This represents a significant difference from the legal situation for road vehicles and aircraft. For road vehicles, Section 7 StVG, and for aircraft, Section 33 of the Air Traffic Act (*Luftverkehrsgesetz* – LuftVG), stipulate strict liability on the part of the owner, which also applies to autonomous vehicles[59] and flying objects.[60] In contrast, liability for damage caused by a ship requires fault on the part of the person responsible for the ship, as will be explained in more detail below.

2. Liability of the Shipowner Under the BCC

Within its scope of application, the aforementioned BCC[61] takes precedence over national liability rules.[62] According to Articles 1 and 12 of the BCC, it applies

- in the event of a collision between maritime ships or between maritime ships and inland waterway vessels,
- with regard to damage caused to the ships or to the property or persons on board,
- regardless of the waters in which the collision took place,

[54] For details, see *Herkenhoff*, Die Haftung in der unbemannten Schifffahrt, 2020, 217 et seq.

[55] *Etzkorn*, Der Schiffszusammenstoß unter Beteiligung autonom fahrender Schiffe, 2022, 350 et seq., 382 et seq.

[56] For more details, see *Vuattoux-Bock*, Schiffskollision, höhere Gewalt und autonome Schifffahrt, 2023, 132 et seq., 147 et seq.

[57] In this sense, see also *Paschke/Lutter*, RdTW 2018, 242, 250 et seq.; generally in favour of strict liability for ships: *Wurmnest*, LogR 2024, 37, 39 et seq.

[58] See *Wurmnest*, LogR 2024, 37, 39; instructive on the historical development of shipping liability law: *Vuattoux-Bock*, Schiffskollision, höhere Gewalt und autonome Schifffahrt, 2023, 28 et seq.

[59] For a detailed discussion of civil liability for autonomous road vehicles, see *Stöber/Pieronczyk/Möller*, DAR 2020, 609 et seq.

[60] In detail on civil liability for autonomous flying objects: *Stöber/Anissimov/Willmer*, ZdiW 2022, 186 et seq.

[61] See II.

[62] *Rabe*, in: Rabe/Bahnsen (eds.), Seehandelsrecht, 5th ed. 2018, Vor § 570 HGB para. 19; *Ramming*, RdTW 2024, 242, 243; see also BGH, 11 March 1976 – II ZR 97/74, BeckRS 1976, 30388043; BGH, 14 July 1980 – II ZR 138/79, BeckRS 1980, 30401516.

- if all the ships involved belong to contracting states,[63] but not all the parties involved belong to the same state as the court dealing with the matter.

However, according to its Article 11, the BCC does not apply to warships or to state ships used exclusively for public service.

According to Article 3 BCC, the obligation to pay compensation generally applies to the ship that caused the collision, whereby, according to Article 5 BCC, the fault of a pilot also gives rise to liability. Although most of the provisions of the BCC refer to the liability of "the ship", it follows from Article 8(2) sentence 2 BCC that the respective shipowner is liable for compensation.[64] Article 3 BCC also refers to the fault of "the ship". However, since fault can only be attributed to persons and not to objects, it must be based on the fault of the shipowner[65] or of a person acting with his consent in connection with the operation of the ship.[66] As expressly stated in Article 5 BCC, this may be a pilot, but also any member of the ship's crew[67] or – in the case of remotely controlled or autonomous ships – also a navigator or controller who is not on board.[68] In the case of pilots, too, it is irrelevant whether they are on board or not.[69] According to the express provision of Article 6 sentence 2 BCC, there is no presumption of fault, so that the respective claimant must prove the fault of the opposing party.[70]

If both ships involved are at fault, both sides are generally liable to each other in accordance with Article 4(1) half-sentence 1 BCC in proportion to their respective share of fault. In accordance with Article 4(3) BCC, the owners of the ships involved are jointly and severally liable for personal injury suffered by third parties. The limitation period is two years from the date of the damaging event, in accordance with Article 7(1) sentence 1 BCC.[71] The BCC does not contain any specific provisions on the content and scope of liability for damages. In this respect, the provisions of the relevant national law apply in addition.[72]

---

[63] See on this requirement BGH, 14 July 1980 – II ZR 138/79, BeckRS 1980, 30401516.

[64] See also *Ramming*, RdTW 2024, 242, 247.

[65] See BGH, 14 July 1980 – II ZR 138/79, BeckRS 1980, 30401516.

[66] Similarly, *Herkenhoff*, Die Haftung in der unbemannten Schifffahrt, 2020, 134; *Vuattoux-Bock*, Schiffskollision, höhere Gewalt und autonome Schifffahrt, 2023, 122.

[67] BGH, 29 March 1973 – II ZR 8/71, BeckRS 1973, 31122987; BGH, 14 July 1980 – II ZR 138/79, BeckRS 1980, 30401516.

[68] See also *Herkenhoff*, Die Haftung in der unbemannten Schifffahrt, 2020, 135 et seq.; dissenting opinion: *Etzkorn*, Der Schiffszusammenstoß unter Beteiligung autonom fahrender Schiffe, 2022, 306 et seq.

[69] Dissenting opinion: *Herkenhoff*, Die Haftung in der unbemannten Schifffahrt, 2020, 140 et seq.

[70] On the burden of proof, see also VII. 5.

[71] BGH, 14 July 1980 – II ZR 138/79, BeckRS 1980, 30401516.

[72] See BGH, 11 March 1976 – II ZR 97/74, BeckRS 1976, 30388043. On the determination of the applicable national law, see also VIII.

3. Liability of the Shipowner Pursuant to Sections 570 et seq. HGB

Outside the scope of the BCC, liability in the event of a ship collision is governed by Sections 570 et seq. HGB, which largely correspond to the provisions of the BCC. It is a non-contractual liability.[73] According to Sections 570 and 573 HGB, in the event of a collision between maritime vessels or between maritime vessels and inland waterway vessels, the shipowner *(Reeder)* of the vessel that caused the collision is liable for the damage caused by the collision to the other vessel and to the persons and property on board the vessels, provided that the shipowner of the ship that caused the accident or a person named in Section 480 HGB is at fault. According to Section 476 HGB, the shipowner is the owner of a ship operated by him for the purpose of maritime commerce. However, Article 7(1)(2) of the Introductory Act to the German Commercial Code (*Einführungsgesetz zum Handelsgesetzbuch* – EGHGB) stipulates that Sections 570 et seq. HGB shall also apply if the ship is not operated for commercial purposes, but is, for example, a private yacht or a research vessel.[74]

Within the scope of Section 570 HGB, the shipowner is also liable for the fault of persons within the meaning of Section 480 HGB, which regulates the so-called adjectival shipowner's liability. Persons within the meaning of Section 480 HGB are all members of the ship's crew (Section 478 HGB) and the pilots working on board,[75] provided that they are acting in the course of their duties. The latter is always the case if the conduct of the person concerned is intrinsically linked to the operation of the ship.[76] While Section 480 HGB otherwise forms a separate basis for claims,[77] in cases of ship collisions covered by Sections 570 et seq. HGB, the provision only applies within the framework of Section 570 HGB to determine the group of persons for whose fault the shipowner is liable under Sections 570 et seq. HGB.

According to Section 478 HGB, the ship's crew consists of the captain, the ship's officers, the seafarers, and all other persons engaged in the operation of the ship, who are employed by the shipowner or ship operator, or who are provided to the shipowner or ship operator by a third party, to perform work in connection with the operation of the ship, and who are subject to the captain's orders. This also includes persons who are not on board but are working ashore in the context of the ship's operation.[78] Accordingly, the shipowner of a remotely

---

[73] *Rabe*, in: Rabe/Bahnsen (eds.), Seehandelsrecht, 5th ed. 2018, Vor § 570 HGB para. 9.

[74] *Rabe*, in: Rabe/Bahnsen (eds.), Seehandelsrecht, 5th ed. 2018, Vor § 570 HGB para. 10; *Steingröver*, in: MünchKomm HGB, 5th ed. 2023, § 570 para. 10.

[75] For more details on the concept of pilot, see *Bahnsen*, in: Rabe/Bahnsen (eds.), Seehandelsrecht, 5th ed. 2018, § 480 HGB para. 23 et seq.

[76] See *Bahnsen*, in: Rabe/Bahnsen (eds.), Seehandelsrecht, 5th ed. 2018, § 480 HGB para. 40.

[77] See *Bahnsen*, in: Rabe/Bahnsen (eds.), Seehandelsrecht, 5th ed. 2018, § 480 HGB para. 3.

[78] See *Bahnsen*, in: Rabe/Bahnsen (eds.), Seehandelsrecht, 5th ed. 2018, § 478 HGB para. 20; *Pötschke*, in: MünchKomm HGB, 5th ed. 2023, § 478 para. 4.

controlled or autonomous ship is also liable for the fault of a navigator or controller working ashore, provided that the other requirements of Section 478 HGB are also met.[79]

According to Section 276(1) sentence 1 BGB, fault is given in the case of intent, but also in the case of negligence within the meaning of Section 276(2) BGB or Section 347(1) HGB.[80] The standard of care is to be determined in accordance with the applicable standards of international or national shipping law.[81] Of particular importance for maritime shipping are the IMO's Collision Prevention Regulations (COLREG)[82] and the provisions on ship safety in the ISM Code mentioned above.[83]

Ships within the meaning of Section 570 HGB are to be equated with floating offshore structures such as drilling rigs, provided and as long as they are moved for the purpose of changing location.[84] If, on the other hand, a ship collides with non-floating structures such as shore facilities, landing stages, fixed drilling platforms, or offshore wind turbines, Sections 570 et seq. HGB do not apply. Liability is then governed by Section 480 HGB and the general tort provisions of Sections 823 et seq. BGB.[85]

If several shipowners are liable for compensation in the event of a collision involving more than one ship, they are generally liable in proportion to their share of fault (Section 571(1) HGB); they are only jointly and severally liable for personal injury to persons on board (Section 571(2) HGB).[86] The limitation period for claims for damages under Sections 570 et seq. HGB is two years from the date of the damaging event (Section 606 No. 2, Section 607(6) HGB).[87] In accordance with the Convention on the Limitation of Liability for Maritime Claims of

---

[79] See also *Herkenhoff*, Die Haftung in der unbemannten Schifffahrt, 2020, 98 et seq.: § 480 HGB analogously; dissenting opinion: *Etzkorn*, Der Schiffszusammenstoß unter Beteiligung autonom fahrender Schiffe, 2022, 105 et seq., 124 et seq.

[80] See also *Herkenhoff*, Die Haftung in der unbemannten Schifffahrt, 2020, 76; *Rabe*, in: Rabe/Bahnsen (eds.), Seehandelsrecht, 5th ed. 2018, § 570 HGB para. 13 et seq.

[81] For more details, see *Rabe*, in: Rabe/Bahnsen (eds.), Seehandelsrecht, 5th ed. 2018, § 570 HGB para. 14 et seq.; see also *Herkenhoff*, Die Haftung in der unbemannten Schifffahrt, 2020, 76.

[82] See Convention on the International Regulations for Preventing Collisions at Sea of 20 October 1972, available at https://treaties.un.org/doc/Publication/UNTS/Volume%201050/volume-1050-I-15824-English.pdf (last access: 11 May 2026), ratified in Germany by Act of 29 June 1976, BGBl. II 1976, 1023.

[83] See *Bahnsen*, in: Rabe/Bahnsen (eds.), Seehandelsrecht, 5th ed. 2018, § 480 HGB para. 54; *Steingröver*, in: MünchKomm HGB, 5th ed. 2023, § 570 para. 22 et seq.

[84] *Herkenhoff*, Die Haftung in der unbemannten Schifffahrt, 2020, 75 et seq.; *Rabe*, in: Rabe/Bahnsen (eds.), Seehandelsrecht, 5th ed. 2018, Vor § 570 HGB para. 11.

[85] *Herkenhoff*, Die Haftung in der unbemannten Schifffahrt, 2020, 76; *Rabe*, in: Rabe/Bahnsen (eds.), Seehandelsrecht, 5th ed. 2018, Vor § 570 HGB para. 11, 14.

[86] For more details, see *Ramming*, RdTW 2024, 242, 245 et seq.

[87] See *Ramming*, RdTW 2024, 242, 243.

19 November 1976[88] and Sections 611 et seq. HGB, the shipowner may limit his liability by contract.[89]

4. Liability Under the General Tort Provisions

In principle, any person who is related to the ship in question and who, through their own culpable conduct, has contributed to a violation of rights or legal interests by the ship, may be liable for damages under the general tort law provision of Section 823(1) BGB.[90] This liability may also apply to the shipowner in particular, for example in the event of a breach of the duty to ensure safety by regularly inspecting and maintaining the autonomous ship and, in particular, its digital components.[91] In the event of a breach of a protective law, such as the provisions of the German Ship Safety Ordinance,[92] liability under Section 823(2) BGB may also be considered.[93]

The shipowner is also liable under Section 831 BGB for violations of rights or legal interests committed unlawfully by a vicarious agent.[94] However, only a person who is subject to instructions can be a vicarious agent.[95] Therefore, the members of the ship's crew employed by the shipowner are particularly likely to be considered vicarious agents. Claims under Sections 823 and 831 BGB are subject to the regular limitation period of three years (Sections 195 et seq. BGB).

Some authors considers that an autonomous vehicle or ship, or the AI controlling it, should also be treated as a vicarious agent, with the result that the shipowner would also be liable for damage caused by a malfunction of the autonomous ship, analogous to Section 831 BGB.[96] However, this view must be rejected. In the event of malfunctions of the autonomous ship, the manufacturer of the control software or of the entire ship may be liable under the Product Liability Act or the rules on producer liability,[97] so that no liability gap and thus no unin-

---

[88] In the version of the Protocol of 2 May 1996, available at https://dgtr.de/wp-content/uploads/1976rev_e.pdf (last access: 11 May 2026), ratified in Germany by Acts of 23 July 1986, BGBl. II 1986, 786, and of 27 June 2000, BGBl. II 2000, 790.

[89] For more details, see *Herkenhoff*, Die Haftung in der unbemannten Schifffahrt, 2020, 78 et seq.

[90] *Etzkorn*, Der Schiffszusammenstoß unter Beteiligung autonom fahrender Schiffe, 2022, 205; *Rabe*, in: Rabe/Bahnsen (eds.), Seehandelsrecht, 5th ed. 2018, § 570 HGB para. 40.

[91] See *Herkenhoff*, Die Haftung in der unbemannten Schifffahrt, 2020, 195 et seq.

[92] *Schiffssicherheitsverordnung* of 18 September 1998, BGBl. I 1998, 3013.

[93] See *Etzkorn*, Der Schiffszusammenstoß unter Beteiligung autonom fahrender Schiffe, 2022, 213 et seq.; *Rabe*, in: Rabe/Bahnsen (eds.), Seehandelsrecht, 5th ed. 2018, § 570 HGB para. 40; also *Herkenhoff*, Die Haftung in der unbemannten Schifffahrt, 2020, 199 et seq., who denies, however, that the provisions of the Ship Safety Ordinance have the character of a protective law.

[94] *Bahnsen*, in: Rabe/Bahnsen (eds.), Seehandelsrecht, 5th ed. 2018, § 480 HGB para. 12 et seq.

[95] See, for example, *Förster*, in: BeckOK BGB, 1 November 2025, § 831 para. 17 et seq.

[96] Affirming liability analogous to § 831 BGB for autonomous systems, for example, *Sommer*, Haftung für autonome Systeme, 2020, 303 et seq.

[97] See VII. 8.

tended regulatory gap can be identified. The shipowner is therefore not liable for malfunctions of the autonomous ship in accordance with Section 831 BGB.[98]

Outside the cases of ship collisions specifically regulated by Sections 570 et seq. HGB, the shipowner is also liable for damage caused by a member of the ship's crew in a manner that gives rise to an obligation to pay damages, pursuant to the so-called adjectival shipowner's liability stipulated in Section 480 HGB. Liability under Section 480 HGB may be considered, for example, if the ship causes damage to shore facilities, landing stages, fixed drilling platforms or offshore wind turbines.[99] AI as such cannot be regarded as a member of the ship's crew based on the considerations already made in relation to Section 831 BGB.[100] However, a navigator or controller working outside the ship can be counted as part of the ship's crew within the meaning of Section 478 HGB under Section 480 HGB.[101]

5. *Questions of Burden of Proof*

All liability cases that may arise in connection with autonomous ships – the provisions of the BCC, Sections 570 et seq. HGB and Section 823 BGB – require fault on the part of the owner or operator of the ship that caused the damage. When using AI to control a ship, the ship owner and operator of the AI system may be at fault in particular if he has failed to select, review, monitor and keep the AI system up to date with the necessary and reasonable care, thereby violating an AI-specific duty to ensure safety.[102]

According to the general rules on the burden of proof in German law, which are based on the so-called *Rosenberg* formula, the burden of proof for the circumstances giving rise to the claim lies with the claimant.[103] In the case of liability under the BCC, Section 570 HGB and Section 823 BGB, the conditions giving rise to liability also include fault, which must therefore be proven by the injured claimant;[104] unlike, for example, Section 831(1) sentence 2 BGB, which regulates liability for vicarious agents, the aforementioned provisions do not provide for a

---

[98] See *Etzkorn*, Der Schiffszusammenstoß unter Beteiligung autonom fahrender Schiffe, 2022, 228 et seq.; *Herkenhoff*, Die Haftung in der unbemannten Schifffahrt, 2020, 192 et seq.; *Vuattoux-Bock*, Schiffskollision, höhere Gewalt und autonome Schifffahrt, 2023, 127 et seq.

[99] See VII. 3.

[100] See also *Herkenhoff*, Die Haftung in der unbemannten Schifffahrt, 2020, 190.

[101] See also *Herkenhoff*, Die Haftung in der unbemannten Schifffahrt, 2020, 98 et seq.: § 480 HGB analogously.

[102] Generally on safety obligations of the operator or user of AI and autonomous systems: *Koch*, VersR 2020, 741, 742 et seq.; *Sommer*, Haftung für autonome Systeme, 2020, 325 et seq.; *Thöne*, Autonome Systeme und deliktische Haftung, 2020, 219 et seq., 270; *Zech*, ZfPW 2019, 198, 210 et seq.

[103] See, for example, BGH, 28 June 2016 – VI ZR 559/14, NJW 2016, 3244, para. 18; *Gottwald*, in: Rosenberg/Schwab/Gottwald, Zivilprozessrecht, 18th ed. 2018, § 116 para. 9.

[104] See *Buck-Heeb/Dieckmann*, in: Oppermann/Buck-Heeb (eds.), Autonomes Fahren, 3rd ed. 2024, Kap. 2.1.1 para. 174 on autonomous road vehicles; *Reusch*, in: Kaulartz/Braegelmann (eds.), Rechtshandbuch Artificial Intelligence und Machine Learning, 2020, Kap. 4.1 para. 297; *Sommer*, Haftung für autonome Systeme, 2020, 364 et seq.

reversal of the burden of proof.[105] Because the circumstances giving rise to fault lie within the sphere of the injuring party, it is often difficult in practice for the injured party to prove fault. This is particularly true if the injuring party has used AI and the damage is attributable to a malfunction of the AI, because the injured party has no insight into the internal working process of the AI and the causes of the malfunction (so-called black box problem).[106]

In view of these difficulties in proving fault, the European Commission presented a proposal for a directive on AI liability[107] in 2022.[108] This was not intended to create a new substantive liability, but rather to make it easier for those harmed by AI systems to enforce their claims in purely procedural terms. On the one hand, this was to be achieved by easing the burden of proof for damages related to AI systems through a rebuttable presumption of causality.[109] In addition, the proposed directive provided that, under certain conditions, the injured party should have the right to disclosure of evidence concerning the respective AI system from those responsible for high-risk AI systems.[110] This right should, of course, be subject to the principle of proportionality; the proportionality test should also take into account the confidentiality interests of those responsible, in particular the interest in protecting trade secrets.[111] In 2025, however, the EU Commission withdrew this proposed directive.[112] Individual elements from the proposal were nevertheless incorporated into the new Product Liability Directive.[113] The latter, of course, only regulates the liability of the manufacturer of products, such as an AI system or an AI component, but not that of its user or operator.

Therefore, the general rules on the burden of proof outlined above continue to apply to the liability of the user or operator of an AI system, such as a control AI for an autonomous ship. In individual cases – such as a proven deviation from nautical standards of conduct or a collision with an anchored ship or fixed installations – *prima facie* evidence may be assumed.[114] Otherwise, however, the injured party bears the full burden of proof for the fault of the ship owner who is, at the same time, the operator of the AI system.

---

105 See on Section 570 HGB *Rabe*, in: Rabe/Bahnsen (eds.), Seehandelsrecht, 5th ed. 2018, § 570 HGB para. 30.

106 See *Fleischmann*, in: Sassenberg/Faber (eds.), Rechtshandbuch Industrie 4.0 und Internet of Things, 3rd ed. 2025, § 11 para. 45.

107 Proposal for a directive on adapting the rules on non-contractual civil liability to artificial intelligence of 28 September 2022, COM (2022) 496 final, available at https://eur-lex.europa.eu/legal-content/EN/TXT/HTML/?uri=CELEX:52022PC0496 (last access: 11 May 2026).

108 See *Eichelberger*, DB 2022, 2783 et seq.; *Staudenmayer*, NJW 2023, 894, 895 et seq.

109 See *Staudenmayer*, NJW 2023, 894, 897 et seq.

110 See *Eichelberger*, DB 2022, 2783, 2784 et seq.; *Staudenmayer*, NJW 2023, 894, 896 et seq.

111 See *Bomhard/Siglmüller*, RDi 2022, 506, 508 et seq.; *Spindler*, CR 2022, 689, 697.

112 See OJ C/2025/5423 of 6 October 2025.

113 See VII. 8. a).

114 For more details, see *Rabe*, in: Rabe/Bahnsen (eds.), Seehandelsrecht, 5th ed. 2018, § 570 HGB para. 31 et seq.

However, with regard to negative facts and, in general, circumstances that lie outside the sphere of the party bearing the burden of proof, but within the sphere of the opposing party, German case law recognises a secondary burden of proof: The opposing party cannot then limit itself to simply disputing the assertion of the party bearing the burden of proof, but must substantiate the circumstances that contradict the assertion; these must then be refuted by the party bearing the burden of proof.[115] Such a secondary burden of proof must also be imposed on the owner of an autonomous ship with regard to its AI-specific safety obligations.[116] In response to the injured party's assertion that the control or assistance system was not properly selected, checked, monitored or updated, the owner of the autonomous ship sued for damages would therefore have to demonstrate, on the basis of his secondary burden of proof,

- that the AI system in question was generally suitable for controlling a vessel of this type and was also error-free *in concreto*;[117]
- when, how and by whom he checked the AI system for functionality before its use;
- and when, how and by whom he monitored and updated the AI system during operation.

To prove the ship owner's fault, the injured party would then have to prove that this statement is not true.

As part of his secondary burden of proof regarding the suitability of the AI system, the shipowner might also have to disclose sensitive details about the AI system that are covered by either his own trade or business secrets or those of the manufacturer of the AI system. In German legal literature, there have been repeated proposals to allow secret evidence proceedings in civil courts to protect trade, business or company secrets,[118] although the proposals differ with regard to the design of such proceedings.[119] In the absence of a statutory provision and in view of the constitutionally guaranteed procedural rights of the other party, however, secret evidence proceedings must be rejected under current German law.[120]

---

115 See, for example, BGH, 17 January 2008 – III ZR 239/06, NJW 2008, 982, para. 16; BGH, 13 June 2012 – I ZR 87/11, NJW 2012, 3774, para. 16 et seq.; BGH, 28 June 2016 – VI ZR 559/14, NJW 2016, 3244, para. 18; BGH, 19 February 2019 – VI ZR 505/17, BGHZ 221, 139, para. 17; see also *Voigt*, in: BeckOGK BGB, 1 November 2025, § 823 para. 471.

116 In relation to AI in general, some authors want to go even further: *Sommer*, Haftung für autonome Systeme, 2020, 383 et seq. advocates for "differentiated rules on the burden of proof" and *Zech*, ZfPW 2019, 198, 211 for a reversal of the burden of proof analogous to Section 831(1) sentence 2 BGB with regard to fault; however, there is no legal basis for this in current law.

117 See also *Reusch*, in: Kaulartz/Braegelmann (eds.), Rechtshandbuch Artificial Intelligence und Machine Learning, 2020, Kap. 4.1 para. 302.

118 See, for example, *Sommer*, Haftung für autonome Systeme, 2020, 388 et seq.

119 For more details, see *Prütting*, in: MünchKomm ZPO, 7th ed. 2025, § 285 para. 11 et seq. with further references.

120 See also *Prütting*, in: MünchKomm ZPO, 7th ed. 2025, § 285 para. 13 et seq.

6. Insurance Obligation

In Germany, the Act on Insurance Certificates in Maritime Shipping,[121] which is based on a EU directive from 2009,[122] stipulates a special insurance obligation for ship owners.[123] This also applies in the case of autonomous ships.[124] According to Section 2(1) sentence 1 of the Act, every owner of a ship with a gross tonnage of at least 300 that either flies the German flag, or calls at or leaves a port in Germany, or calls at or leaves a facility located off the coast within the territorial waters of the Federal Republic of Germany, must maintain insurance or other financial security that meets the requirements of the aforementioned EU Directive in order to cover his liability for maritime claims within the meaning of the Convention on the Limitation of Liability for Maritime Claims.[125] Maritime claims in this sense are, in particular, claims for compensation for personal injury or property damage arising directly from the operation of a ship.[126]

7. Excursus: Liability of the Shipper and the Carrier

In addition to the liability of the shipowner, the shipper of cargo *(Verfrachter)* may also be liable in accordance with the provisions of Sections 498 et seq. HGB, but only in respect of the cargo. Within the scope of application of the Hague Rules,[127] to which Germany is also a signatory, Sections 498 et seq. HGB are modified in accordance with Article 6 EGHGB and thus aligned with the Hague Rules.[128]

According to Section 498(1) HGB, the shipper is liable for damage caused by loss or damage to the goods during the period from acceptance for shipping to delivery. This liability requires fault, but the shipper's fault is presumed.[129] However, the shipper may exonerate himself in accordance with Section 498(2) HGB. Pursuant to Section 499(1) HGB, the shipper is not liable if the loss or damage is due to one of the circumstances listed in this provision – including perils of the

[121] *Seeversicherungsnachweisgesetz* of 4 June 2013, BGBl. I 2013, 1471.

[122] Directive 2009/20/EC of 23 April 2009 on the insurance of shipowners for maritime claims, OJ L 131 of 28 May 2009, 128.

[123] See *Bahnsen*, in: Rabe/Bahnsen (eds.), Seehandelsrecht, 5th ed. 2018, § 480 HGB para. 112 et seq.

[124] For detailed information on insurance law issues specifically relating to autonomous systems, see *Koch*, VersR 2020, 741, 746 et seq.

[125] See VII. 3.

[126] For more details, see *Rabe/Rittmeister*, in: Rabe/Bahnsen (eds.), Seehandelsrecht, 5th ed. 2018, Anh. § 611 HGB para. 4 et seq.

[127] International Convention for the Unification of certain Rules of Law Relating to Bills of Lading of 25 August 1924, available at https://treaties.un.org/doc/publication/unts/volume%2014 12/volume-1412-i-23643-english.pdf (last access: 11 May 2026); see also RGBl. II 1939, 1049.

[128] For more details, see *Herber/Sager*, in: MünchKomm HGB, 5th ed. 2023, Art. 6 EGHGB para. 6 et seq.

[129] *Bahnsen*, in: Rabe/Bahnsen (eds.), Seehandelsrecht, 5th ed. 2018, § 498 HGB para. 8; *Herkenhoff*, Die Haftung in der unbemannten Schifffahrt, 2020, 83.

sea, accidents at sea, acts of war or strikes – unless the damage could have been averted by the diligence of a prudent shipper.[130] According to Section 501 HGB, the shipper is liable for the fault of "his people" and the ship's crew, as well as other persons he employs in the performance of the shipping, to the same extent as for his own fault.[131]

In addition, the carrier of passengers *(Beförderer)* may be liable for personal injury and damage to luggage suffered by his own passengers. This liability is primarily governed (see Section 536(2) sentence 1 HGB) by the EU Athens Regulation[132] in conjunction with the Athens Convention,[133] and otherwise by Sections 536 et seq. HGB.[134] Because the latter largely correspond to the provisions of the Athens Convention,[135] only Sections 536 et seq. HGB are considered here. The carrier is also generally only liable in the event of fault, which is presumed in certain cases (see Section 538(1), Section 539(1) HGB). In the event of personal injury, the carrier may even be liable regardless of fault in accordance with Section 538(2) HGB.[136] The carrier is also liable under Section 540 HGB for the fault of "his people".

The provisions governing the liability of the shipper or carrier also apply to autonomous ships.[137] According to the prevailing opinion, the other persons covered by Sections 501 and 540 HGB, whom the shipper or carrier employs in the performance of the carriage, also include a navigator or controller who remotely controls or monitors the ship from land; the shipper or carrier must therefore also be held responsible for their fault during transport by means of an autonomous ship in accordance with Sections 501 and 540 HGB.[138] The same applies to the fault of a pilot located on land.[139] On the other hand, the software or AI that controls the autonomous ship is not a person within the meaning of Sections 501 and 540 HGB; and in the absence of a comparable constellation, an

---

130 For more details, see *Bahnsen*, in: Rabe/Bahnsen (eds.), Seehandelsrecht, 5th ed. 2018, § 499 HGB para. 20 et seq.

131 See *Bahnsen*, in: Rabe/Bahnsen (eds.), Seehandelsrecht, 5th ed. 2018, § 501 HGB para. 9 et seq.

132 Regulation (EC) 392/2009 of 23 April 2009 on the liability of carriers of passengers by sea in the event of accidents, OJ L 131 of 28 May 2009, 24.

133 Athens Convention relating to the Carriage of Passengers and their Luggage by Sea of 13 December 1974, OJ C 74 E of 20 March 2008, 567.

134 See on the scope of the Athens Regulation and the remaining scope of Sections 536 et seq. HGB *Bahnsen*, in: Rabe/Bahnsen (eds.), Seehandelsrecht, 5th ed. 2018, Vor § 536 HGB para. 14, § 536 HGB para. 18 et seq.

135 See *Bahnsen*, in: Rabe/Bahnsen (eds.), Seehandelsrecht, 5th ed. 2018, Vor § 536 HGB para. 14.

136 See *Bahnsen*, in: Rabe/Bahnsen (eds.), Seehandelsrecht, 5th ed. 2018, § 538 HGB para. 12 et seq.

137 For more details, see *Herkenhoff*, Die Haftung in der unbemannten Schifffahrt, 2020, 144 et seq., 202 et seq.

138 See also *Herkenhoff*, Die Haftung in der unbemannten Schifffahrt, 2020, 163 et seq., who, however, only wants to apply Section 501 HGB to the controller by analogy.

139 See also *Herkenhoff*, Die Haftung in der unbemannten Schifffahrt, 2020, 169 et seq.

analogous application of the provisions must also be rejected. The shipper or carrier is therefore not liable for an error in the software or artificial intelligence controlling the ship pursuant to Sections 501, 540 HGB (analogously).[140]

8. *Liability of the Manufacturer*

a) *Product Liability Under the Product Liability Act*

For damage caused by an autonomous ship, the manufacturer of the ship as a whole, as well as the manufacturer of an individual component of the ship, may also be subject to special product liability, which is a strict liability and thus does not require fault.[141] This may then apply in addition to the fault-based liability of the ship owner or operator. In Germany, product liability has so far been governed by the Product Liability Act (*Produkthaftungsgesetz* – ProdHaftG) of 1989,[142] which is based on the EC Product Liability Directive of 1985 (hereinafter: PLD 1985).[143] In 2024, the EU adopted a revised version of the PLD (hereinafter: PLD 2024).[144] With the revised version, the European legislator also, and above all, wanted to take into account the challenges of digitalisation and create special liability rules for products with digital components, in particular for products with AI systems such as autonomous vehicles.[145]

According to Article 24(1) subpara. 1 sentence 1, the Product Liability Directive 2024 must be implemented by Member States by 9 December 2026. On 19 December 2025, the German Federal Government presented the government draft of an Act to Modernise Product Liability Law.[146] Its core element is a complete revision of the ProdHaftG, adapted to the requirements of the PLD 2024. The following presentation is based on the provisions of the future new ProdHaftG in the version of the government draft (hereinafter: ProdHaftG 2026). Although changes are still possible during the legislative process, no fundamental modifications are to be expected due to the binding requirements of the PLD 2024.

Essentially as before (see Section 1(1) ProdHaftG 1989), the manufacturer will continue to be obliged under Section 1(1) ProdHaftG 2026 to compensate for damage caused to a natural person as a result of a defect in a product that injures their body or health, kills a person or damages or destroys property, unless the

---

[140] Correctly *Herkenhoff*, Die Haftung in der unbemannten Schifffahrt, 2020, 212 et seq.

[141] For details on product liability for autonomous ships under the previous Product Liability Act, see *Lutter*, RdTW 2017, 281 et seq.

[142] *Produkthaftungsgesetz* of 15 December 1989, BGBl. I 1989, 2198.

[143] Directive 85/374/EEC of 25 July 1985, OJ L 210 of 7 August 1985, 29.

[144] Directive (EU) 2024/2853 of 23 October 2024 on liability for defective products, OJ L 2024/2853 of 18 November 2024; for details, see *Brenner*, RDi 2024, 345 et seq.; *Wendehorst*, EuZW 2024, 876 et seq.

[145] See Federal Council document (*Bundesratsdrucksache* – BR-Drucks.) 775/25, 14 et seq.

[146] BR-Drucks. 775/25.

defect is in the product itself, or in an item used exclusively for professional purposes. As under the previous legal situation,[147] property damage caused by a defective autonomous ship will continue to be largely excluded from the scope of the ProdHaftG, because other ships, the goods transported, offshore wind turbines or port facilities are generally items used exclusively for commercial purposes. According to Section 3 sentence 1 ProdHaftG 2026, a manufacturer is primarily someone who develops or manufactures a product himself or has it designed or manufactured.

According to Section 2(1) No. 1 of the ProdHaftG 2026, products continue to be primarily all movable objects. Movable objects in the sense of product liability law are – regardless of the fact that they are partially treated as immovable objects under German civil law – also ships and the individual physical components of which a ship is composed.[148] In autonomous shipping, accidents and damage will often be attributable to errors in the software that controls the ship. Under the PLD 1985 and according to the previous Section 2 ProdHaftG 1989, which explicitly mentioned only movable objects and electricity, it was controversial whether software was to be regarded as a product.[149] Section 2(1) No. 3 ProdHaftG 2026 now expressly clarifies that software – with the exception of free and open source software developed or provided outside of a business activity[150] – is also a product, regardless of the type of provision or use, and in particular regardless of its connection to physical objects.[151] This means that AI systems also fall within the scope of the new product liability law.[152]

In the event that a defective component that has been integrated into or connected to the product by the manufacturer of the product or, with the manufacturer's consent, by a third party causes a defect in the product, Section 4(1) sentence 1 ProdHaftG 2026 stipulates that both the manufacturer of the product and the manufacturer of the component are liable. Section 4(2) ProdHaftG 2026 clarifies that non-physical objects and digital services connected to the product are also components in this sense. The explanatory memorandum to the government draft cites the navigation system of an autonomous vehicle[153] and voice assistants that enable a product to be controlled by means of voice commands

---

[147] See *Herkenhoff*, Die Haftung in der unbemannten Schifffahrt, 2020, 184 et seq.; *Vuattoux-Bock*, Schiffskollision, höhere Gewalt und autonome Schifffahrt, 2023, 130.

[148] See also *Herkenhoff*, Die Haftung in der unbemannten Schifffahrt, 2020, 180 et seq.; *Lutter*, RdTW 2017, 281, 282; *Rebin*, in: BeckOGK ProdHaftG, 1 October 2025, § 2 para. 29; *Vuattoux-Bock*, Schiffskollision, höhere Gewalt und autonome Schifffahrt, 2023, 129; *Wagner*, in MünchKomm BGB, 9th ed. 2024, § 2 ProdHaftG para. 13.

[149] For more details, see *Stöber/Pieronczyk/Möller*, DAR 2020, 609, 612 et seq. with further references.

[150] See *Brenner*, RDi 2024, 345, 346 et seq.

[151] BR-Drucks. 775/25, 24.

[152] S. *Wendehorst*, EuZW 2024, 876, 878.

[153] BR-Drucks. 775/25, 14 et seq.

as examples of connected digital services.[154] Such services are also subject to product liability in the case of autonomous ships.

According to Section 7 sentence 1 of the ProdHaftG 2026, a product is defective if it does not offer the safety required by German law or EU law or that may be expected. Product liability under the ProdHaftG can be triggered by three different types of defects: a manufacturing defect, a design defect or an instruction defect.[155] When assessing defectiveness, all circumstances must be taken into account in accordance with Section 7 sentence 2 ProdHaftG 2026. This provision expressly mentions, among other things, the effects on the product of its ability to continue learning or acquire new functions after being placed on the market or put into service (Section 7 sentence 2 No. 3 ProdHaftG 2026), and the relevant product safety requirements, including safety-related cyber security requirements (Section 7 sentence 2 No. 5 ProdHaftG 2026). In the case of an autonomous ship, it may therefore constitute a defect within the meaning of Section 7 ProdHaftG 2026 if the (adaptive) control AI is programmed in such a way that it learns "in the wrong direction"[156] or if it does not offer sufficient protection against cyber attacks.[157]

According to Section 8(1) ProdHaftG 2026, the decisive moment for assessing defectiveness is generally the point in time at which the product was placed on the market or put into service. Notwithstanding this basic rule – and also the previous legal situation[158] – Section 8(2) ProdHaftG 2026 stipulates that the assessment of defectiveness must be based on the later point in time at which the product left the manufacturer's control if the manufacturer or, with the manufacturer's consent, a third party has carried out a software update or software upgrade after the product was placed on the market or put into service, or is at least in a position to make such updates or upgrades available. Unlike under the ProdHaftG 1989, manufacturers will in future also have a product monitoring obligation in the sense that they must continue to follow developments in science and technology and, if necessary, remedy any faults that become apparent later, provided that they continue to have control over the product.[159] This control is already maintained by the mere fact that the product can be updated.[160] In the case of an autonomous ship, the manufacturer of the updatable control AI will

---

[154] BR-Drucks. 775/25, 26 et seq.

[155] For more details, see *Wagner*, in MünchKomm BGB, 9th ed. 2024, § 1 ProdHaftG para. 35 et seq.; specifically on ships, see *Herkenhoff*, Die Haftung in der unbemannten Schifffahrt, 2020, 182 et seq.

[156] See generally on adaptive AI *Brenner*, RDi 2024, 345, 349.

[157] On autonomous road vehicles, see *v. Bodungen*, in: Chibanguza/Kuß/Steege (eds.), KI-Hdb., 2nd ed. 2026, 2. Teil § 3 I. para. 25 et seq.

[158] See *Wagner*, in MünchKomm BGB, 9th ed. 2024, § 3 ProdHaftG para. 38 et seq.

[159] BR-Drucks. 775/25, 32; *v. Bodungen*, in: Chibanguza/Kuß/Steege (eds.), KI-Hdb., 2nd ed. 2026, 2. Teil § 3 I. para. 30, 33.

[160] See *Brenner*, RDi 2024, 345, 351.

therefore also be liable in future for faulty or inadequate updates to the control software.[161]

Under Section 10(1) ProdHaftG 1989, the manufacturer was liable for personal injury up to a maximum of 85 million euros, based on the total damage suffered by all injured parties combined,[162] if the damage was caused by a product or identical products with the same defect. In the case of property damage, the injured party previously had to bear damages of up to 500 euros themselves under Section 11 of the ProdHaftG 1989. These limits on product liability are completely eliminated under the new ProdHaftG 2026.[163]

Another completely new feature is the provision in Section 19 of the ProdHaftG 2026 on the disclosure of evidence, which is based on Article 9 of the PLD 2024. According to Section 19(1) ProdHaftG 2026, at the request of a plaintiff who has brought an action for compensation for damage caused by a defective product, and has presented facts and evidence that sufficiently support the plausibility of a claim for damages, the court shall order the defendant to disclose relevant evidence in his possession.[164] The disclosure must be limited to what is proportionate; any confidentiality interests must also be taken into account in the proportionality test (Section 19(3) ProdHaftG 2026). If the defendant fails to comply with such an order, the defect in the product is presumed under Section 20(1) No. 1 ProdHaftG 2026.

Claims arising from product liability shall become time-barred pursuant to Section 16 ProdHaftG 2026 three years after the date on which the creditor became aware, or should have become aware, of the defect in the product, the damage and the identity of the debtor. In line with the previous legal situation (Section 14 ProdHaftG 1989), Section 18 ProdHaftG 2026 stipulates that the provisions of the ProdHaftG on the manufacturer's liability for damages cannot be waived to the detriment of the injured party or their legal successors.

b) Producer Liability Under Section 823(1) BGB

As clarified in Article 6(3) PLD 2024, the general national rules on fault-based liability continue to apply alongside the special rules laid down in the Directive. Accordingly, in addition to the new ProdHaftG 2026, the judicial rules on producer liability based on Section 823(1) BGB, which is the general provision on liabi-

[161] See on autonomous road vehicles *v. Bodungen*, in: Chibanguza/Kuß/Steege (eds.), KI-Hdb., 2nd ed. 2026, 2. Teil § 3 I. para. 33.

[162] See *Förster*, in: BeckOK BGB, 1 November 2025, § 10 ProdHaftG para. 6.

[163] BR-Drucks. 775/25, 15.

[164] For more details, see *Wagner*, ZIP 2025, 1243, 1245 et seq.

lity for tort, will continue to apply in Germany in the future. These rules also apply to autonomous ships.[165]

According to the established case law of the German Federal Court of Justice (*Bundesgerichtshof* – BGH), anyone who places a product on the market and thus creates a potential source of danger is subject to manufacturer-specific safety obligations, which require them to take all technically feasible and economically reasonable measures to prevent damage caused by the product.[166] In the event of a culpable breach of such an obligation, the producer is liable for damages in accordance with Section 823(1) BGB. Unlike product liability under the ProdHaftG (see Section 2 ProdHaftG 1989), producer liability has always applied to products of all kinds,[167] including software and, in particular, software for controlling an autonomous ship.[168] In addition, producer liability under Section 823 (1) BGB covers all types of damage, in particular damage to other property used for commercial purposes.[169]

In order to fulfil his safety obligations, the manufacturer must ensure that both the design and manufacture of the product are free from defects.[170] In addition, he must ensure that users are provided with correct instructions for the safe handling of the product.[171] Furthermore, there is an obligation to monitor products that have already been placed on the market.[172] If, in the course of product monitoring, the producer identifies a hazard posed by his product or its interaction with other products, he is obliged to issue a warning or, as a last resort, to recall the product.[173] In contrast to strict product liability under the ProdHaftG, producer liability under Section 823(1) BGB requires fault. However, in order to protect the injured party from the burden of proof they would face if they had to prove circumstances within the sphere of the manufacturer, the BGH assumes a reversal of the burden of proof in favour of the injured party with regard to the manufacturer's fault in cases of manufacturer liability, provided that a defect in

---

[165] See *Etzkorn*, Der Schiffszusammenstoß unter Beteiligung autonom fahrender Schiffe, 2022, 141 et seq.; *Herkenhoff*, Die Haftung in der unbemannten Schifffahrt, 2020, 187 et seq.; cf. on autonomous road vehicles *Stöber/Pieronczyk/Möller*, DAR 2020, 609, 613.

[166] See, for example, BGH, 16 December 2008 – VI ZR 170/07, BGHZ 179, 157, para. 10 et seq.; see also *Förster*, in: BeckOK BGB, 1 November 2025, § 823 para. 677.

[167] *Voigt*, in: BeckOGK BGB, 1 November 2025, § 823 para. 640.

[168] See generally *Lehmann*, NJW 1992, 1721, 1722 et seq.; on autonomous road vehicles, see *v. Bodungen/Hoffmann*, NZV 2016, 503, 507 et seq.; *Stöber/Pieronczyk/Möller*, DAR 2020, 609, 613.

[169] *Förster*, in: BeckOK BGB, 1 November 2025, § 823 para. 686; *Herkenhoff*, Die Haftung in der unbemannten Schifffahrt, 2020, 187.

[170] For more details, see *Wagner*, in: MünchKomm BGB, 9th ed. 2024, § 823 para. 1089 et seq., 1093 et seq. with further references; see also *Stöber/Pieronczyk/Möller*, DAR 2020, 609, 613.

[171] See, for example, BGH, 26 November 1968 – VI ZR 212/66, BGHZ 51, 91, 105; BGH, 9 May 1995 – VI ZR 158/94, BGHZ 129, 353, 358; *Hager*, in: Staudinger, BGB, 2021, § 823 para. F 14 et seq. with further references; *Stöber/Pieronczyk/Möller*, DAR 2020, 609, 613.

[172] See, for example, BGH, 17 March 1981 – VI ZR 286/78, NJW 1981, 1606, 1607 et seq.; *Stöber/Pieronczyk/Möller*, DAR 2020, 609, 613; *Wagner*, VersR 2020, 717, 728.

[173] For more details, see *Förster*, in: BeckOK BGB, 1 November 2025, § 823 para. 735 et seq. with further references; see also *Stöber/Pieronczyk/Möller*, DAR 2020, 609, 613.

the product has been established.[174] This also benefits the injured party in the case of an autonomous ship, provided that they can prove a defect in the control AI.[175]

VIII. Collision Law

In the case of damage resulting from a collision between maritime ships or between maritime ships and inland waterway vessels, where all the ships involved belong to the contracting states and the scope of application of the BCC is open,[176] the provisions of the BCC apply directly, as, according to its Article 1, the BCC applies regardless of the waters in which the collision took place.[177]

Outside the scope of the BCC, liability for damage caused by an autonomous ship is governed by the applicable national law. In Germany, this is primarily determined in accordance with the Rome II Regulation of the EU.[178] Since the cases in question involve non-contractual liability,[179] the law of the state in which the damage occurs applies in accordance with the basic rule of Article 4(1) Rome II Regulation.[180] In the field of shipping, however, this rule only applies if the collision causing the damage occurred in the territorial waters of a state.[181]

German law does not contain any provisions for cases where the collision takes place on the high seas.[182] In such cases, some argue in favour of the *lex fori*,[183] whereas others want to apply the law of the flag state of the damaged ship.[184] However, because these two approaches often lead to random results due to the considerable leeway in the choice of both the court of jurisdiction and the flag

---

174 See, for example, BGH, 2 February 1999 – VI ZR 392/97, NJW 1999, 1028, 1029; see also *Stöber/Pieronczyk/Möller*, DAR 2020, 609, 613; *Wagner*, VersR 2020, 717, 729.

175 See also *Etzkorn*, Der Schiffszusammenstoß unter Beteiligung autonom fahrender Schiffe, 2022, 182 et seq.

176 See also VII. 2.

177 See BGH, 29 March 1973 – II ZR 8/71, BeckRS 1973, 31122987; BGH, 14 July 1980 – II ZR 138/79, BeckRS 1980, 30401516; *Ramming*, RdTW 2024, 242, 243; *Roth/Plett*, RabelsZ 42 (1978), 662, 665 et seq.; *Steingröver*, in: MünchKomm HGB, 5th ed. 2023, Vor § 570 para. 18.

178 Regulation (EC) 864/2007 of 11 July 2007 on the law applicable to non-contractual obligations, OJ L 199 of 31 July 2007, 40.

179 See *Roth/Plett*, RabelsZ 42 (1978), 662, 668.

180 See *Rabe*, in: Rabe/Bahnsen (eds.), Seehandelsrecht, 5th ed. 2018, Vor § 570 HGB para. 24 et seq.

181 See also *Steingröver*, in: MünchKomm HGB, 5th ed. 2023, Vor § 570 para. 11.

182 Criticising this correctly, see *Rabe*, in: Rabe/Bahnsen (eds.), Seehandelsrecht, 5th ed. 2018, Vor § 570 HGB para. 29 et seq.; for a detailed discussion of the treatment under conflict of laws, see *Roth/Plett*, RabelsZ 42 (1978), 662, 681 et seq.

183 See *Roth/Plett*, RabelsZ 42 (1978), 662, 691 et seq.; see also Imperial Supreme Court (*Reichsgericht* – RG), 30 May 1888 – I 96/88, RGZ 21, 136, 137 et seq.

184 See, for example, RG, 12 November 1932 – I 68/32, RGZ 138, 243, 245 et seq. – Casablanca; *Ramming*, RdTW 2024, 242, 244; probably also *Steingröver*, in: MünchKomm HGB, 5th ed. 2023, Vor § 570 para. 27.

state, it is correct to refer to the place from which the damaged ship is regularly operated and with which it has the closest factual and legal connection; this is usually the place where the business entity responsible for the ship is based.[185]

If a claim is made against the manufacturer of the ship or a ship component under product liability law, the special provision of Article 5 of the Rome II Regulation applies. This applies regardless of whether claims are asserted under the Product Liability Act or under general tort law provisions.[186] According to Article 5(1) sentence 1 of the Rome II Regulation, the following shall apply in principle:

- the law of the country in which the injured person had their habitual residence at the time the damage occurred, provided that the product – in the cases at issue here, the autonomous ship as a whole or the steering AI as a component – was placed on the market in that country;
- otherwise, the law of the country in which the product was purchased, if the product was placed on the market in that country;
- or otherwise, the law of the country in which the damage occurred, if the product was placed on the market in that country.

IX. International Jurisdiction

International jurisdiction for civil disputes arising from collisions between maritime vessels or between maritime vessels and inland waterway vessels is governed by the Collision (Civil Jurisdiction) Convention (CCJC) of 10 May 1952,[187] provided that all ships involved are from contracting states to the CCJC (Article 8 (1) CCJC).[188] Within its scope of application, the CCJC takes precedence over the Brussels Ia Regulation of the EU[189] (see Article 71 Brussels Ia Regulation).[190] Like the BCC, the CCJC also applies to autonomous ships. Article 1(1), (2) CCJC stipulates that, subject to a jurisdiction or arbitration agreement (see Article 2 CCJC), an action may, at the plaintiff's discretion, only be brought

---

[185] See, for example, *Rabe*, in: Rabe/Bahnsen (eds.), Seehandelsrecht, 5th ed. 2018, Vor § 570 HGB para. 34 et seq.; ultimately also *Etzkorn*, Der Schiffszusammenstoß unter Beteiligung autonom fahrender Schiffe, 2022, 400 et seq.

[186] See, for example, *Junker*, in: MünchKomm BGB, 9th ed. 2025, Art. 5 Rom II-VO para. 18.

[187] International Convention on certain Rules concerning Civil Jurisdiction in Matters of Collision, Available at https://treaties.un.org/doc/publication/unts/volume%20439/volume-439-i-6331-english.pdf (last access: 11 May 2026), ratified in Germany by Act of 10 October 1957, BGBl. II 1972, 653.

[188] *Steingröver*, in: MünchKomm HGB, 5th ed. 2023, Vor § 570 para. 29.

[189] Regulation (EU) 1215/2012 of 12 December 2012 on jurisdiction and the recognition and enforcement of judgments in civil and commercial matters, OJ L 351 of 20 December 2012, 1.

[190] *Steingröver*, in: MünchKomm HGB, 5th ed. 2023, Vor § 570 para. 29.

- at the court in whose district the defendant – in the cases in question, the owner of the (autonomous) ship that caused the damage – has his habitual residence or a commercial establishment;
- at the court of the place where a seizure has been made of the accused ship or of another ship belonging to the defendant which can be lawfully seized, or where a seizure could have been made and the defendant has provided a guarantee or other security;
- or in the court of the place where the collision occurred, provided that the collision took place in the territory of a port or in internal waters.

In parallel to the BCC, warships or ships belonging to or in the service of the state (see Article 5 CCJC) are also excluded from the mandatory scope of application of the CCJC, as is the situation where all persons involved belong to the same state as the court dealing with the matter (see Article 8(2) sentence 2 CCJC).

Outside the scope of application of the CCJC, international jurisdiction in Germany is governed by the Brussels Ia Regulation. According to Article 4(1) Brussels Ia Regulation, persons domiciled in the territory of a Member State must, in principle, be sued in the courts of that Member State. In the case of companies and legal persons, Article 63(1) Brussels Ia Regulation stipulates that the place of the registered office, central administration or principal place of business shall be deemed to be the place of residence. For actions against the owner of an (autonomous) ship, the courts of the shipowner's country of residence therefore have international jurisdiction. If the collision took place in national territorial waters, the court of the place where the harmful event occurred also has jurisdiction under Article 7 No. 2 Brussels Ia Regulation.[191]

X. Labour Law Aspects

Under German law, the employment and working conditions for the crew of maritime ships are regulated by a special law, the Maritime Labour Act,[192] which is based on the Maritime Labour Convention (MLC) of the International Labour Organization (ILO) of 23 February 2006.[193] According to the flag principle, the German Maritime Labour Act is, in principle, only applicable to merchant ships sailing under the German flag, in accordance with Section 1(1) sentence 1. The German merchant fleet – i.e. merchant ships owned by German legal entities – consists of only around 250 ships flying the German flag and approximately 1,400 ships flying foreign flags.[194] Accordingly, the group of persons subject to the

---

[191] *Steingröver*, in: MünchKomm HGB, 5th ed. 2023, Vor § 570 para. 31 et seq.

[192] *Seearbeitsgesetz* of 20 April 2013, BGBl. I 2013, 868.

[193] Text available at https://www.ilo.org/international-labour-standards/maritime-labour-convention-2006 (last access: 11 May 2026).

[194] See the statistics at https://www.deutsche-flagge.de/de/flagge/handelsflotte (last access: 11 May 2026).

Maritime Labour Act is quite small. The number of seafarers registered in Germany is correspondingly low, amounting to only around 7,000 in 2025.[195]

The Maritime Labour Act does not yet contain any special provisions for the operation of autonomous ships. However, Section 21(1) Maritime Labour Act obliges the shipowner and the captain to ensure that the ship's crew is sufficient in number, qualification and suitability to guarantee safe, efficient and hazard-free ship operation under all operating conditions. It can be inferred from this provision that, at least for reasons of labour law, ships flying the German flag and controlled by AI must also have a sufficient number of persons on board who can take control of the ship in case of need, in particular in the event of AI failure or malfunction.

The fact that ships with autonomous or automated steering will still require a minimum crew for the foreseeable future, combined with the very low number of German seafarers, is likely to be responsible for the fact that, as far as can be seen, there have been no social concerns or resistance from seafarers in Germany to date regarding the possible loss of jobs as a result of the push towards autonomous shipping.

XI. Concluding Remarks

In summary, it can be said that, unlike for autonomous road vehicles, there are currently no specific regulations for autonomous ships in German law. They are therefore subject to the legal provisions that apply to ships in general, although the special features of autonomous ships must be taken into account when applying these provisions. The general legal provisions governing ships in Germany are very strongly rooted in international law; genuinely national regulations are the exception.

The above applies in particular to the area of civil liability for damages caused by an autonomous ship. This is governed by the general liability provisions of international and German law, all of which require fault on the part of the person responsible for the ship. As far as the civil liability of the manufacturer of an autonomous ship or its (digital) components – such as the AI used for control – is concerned, strict liability under the new Product Liability Act applies.

From a conflict of laws perspective, it is striking that German private international law does not provide clear rules on the applicable national law in the event of damage involving ships on the high seas. In contrast, the CCJC and, outside its scope of application, the Brussels Ia Regulation generally allow for a clear determination of the internationally competent national court in legal disputes concerning liability for damage caused by an (autonomous) ship.

[195] See https://www.deutsche-flagge.de/de/aktuelles/nachrichten-archiv/nachrichten-2025/mehr-frauen-an-bord-chancen-auf-see (last access: 19 February 2026).

The Separation of Powers and Constitutional Review[1]

Frank Schorkopf

I. Constitutional Foundation

1. Legal Framework and Historical Development

Since the Basic Law for the Federal Republic of Germany was adopted on 23 May 1949, the separation of powers constitutes a fundamental element of the German constitutional order. "All state authority is derived from the people." states Article 20 (2) sentence 1 of the Basic Law (GG). It is exercised by specific organs of the legislature, the executive and the judiciary (sentence 2), who are also bound by the basic rights (Article 1 (3) GG). This tripartite, institutionalised state power is referred to as the *horizontal separation of powers*.[2]

This aspect is complemented by a strong federalism, which is understood as an element of *vertical separation of powers* (Preamble; Article 20 (1) GG).[3] The federal structure provides for a vertical distribution of powers between the Federal Government and the states (*Länder*), which fulfils the same function of moderating power as the differentiated institutional structure in the horizontal dimension. As guaranteed by Article 28 (1) GG, the states themselves recognise the three branches of government, ensuring horizontal separation of powers at state level.

The Basic Law also contains provisions on the rule of law and legal certainty. Legislation is bound by the constitutional order, executive and judiciary are bound by law and justice (Article 20 (3) GG). In practice and jurisprudence, this is used to derive the principle of the rule of law. Historically, the idea of the separation of powers, is an essential step towards the legal moderation of state power and thus towards the rule of law.[4] Therefore, the separation of powers is regarded in German constitutional law as an expression of the rule of law. Legal certainty, in turn, is an essential component of the rule of law and is also recog-

---

[1] I am grateful to Lena John for the dedicated support in preparing this report.

[2] *Sommermann*, in: Huber/Voßkuhle (eds.), Grundgesetz. Kommentar, 2024, Article 20 para. 208.

[3] *Schwerdtfeger*, in: Kischel/Kube (eds.), Handbuch des Staatsrechts, Vol. 2, 2024, § 36 para. 46.

[4] *Grzeszick*, in: Dürig/Herzog/Scholz (eds.), Grundgesetz. Kommentar, 106th supplementary delivery 2024, Article 20 para. 16.

nised as such by the Federal Constitutional Court (*Bundesverfassungsgericht*).[5] It includes those elements of the principle of the rule of law that relate to the reliability of the law and prevent legal uncertainty.[6]

However, the principle of separation of powers is not a novelty of the Basic Law. Its constitutional history in Germany reaches back to the early 19th century. Based on the classical model of John Locke, refined in the mid-18th century by Montesquieu,[7] the German states have each developed the separation of powers through parliamentary "interlocking powers" (*Gewaltenverschränkung*) between the government and the parliamentary majority, through a strong and independent judiciary, and through pronounced federalism. The dictatorships of the 20th century introduced a deliberate monism of powers (*Gewaltenmonismus*).[8]

In the German Confederation (1815), the separation of powers was organised within the individual states. Early state constitutions, such as those in Bavaria (1818), Baden (1818), Württemberg (1819) and Hanover (1819), established constitutional monarchies with parliaments. Executive power remained with the monarch, to whom ministers were accountable. Judicial independence was recognised, but institutionally only gradually secured. After the revolution of 1848, the Paulskirchen Constitution (1849) drafted a federal, constitutional order with horizontal and vertical separation of powers, fundamental rights and an independent judiciary, which strongly influenced later German constitutions.

Prussia's constitution of 1850 contained a bicameral parliament, but left the executive to the king, not binding the government to the parliamentary majority. The Constitution of the North German Confederation (1867) and the Imperial Constitution of 1871 established a federal system with the *Reichstag* (directly elected) and the *Bundesrath* (representing the governments of the states), creating vertical separation of powers. Horizontally, the Emperor and the *Reich* Chancellor led the government, the Chancellor was accountable to the Emperor, not requiring a parliamentary majority until October 1918. The Imperial Judiciary Acts (*Reichsjustizgesetze* – enacted 1877) and the establishment of the Imperial Court of Justice (*Reichsgericht* – 1879) strengthened the judiciary, although no independent constitutional court existed.

The Weimar Constitution (1919) introduced a parliamentary democracy with fundamental rights, dual legislation consisting of the *Reichstag* and the *Reichsrat*, as well as dual executive legitimacy: a *Reich* Government dependent on parliamentary majorities, and a directly elected *Reich* President with comprehensive

[5] BVerfGE 7, 89 (92 et seqq.); 13, 261 (271); 30, 392 (403); 43, 242 (286); more recently BVerfGE 133, 143 (157 et seqq. para. 40).

[6] *Sachs/von Coelln*, in: Sachs (ed.), Grundgesetz. Kommentar, 2024, Article 20 para. 122; cf. BVerfGE 132, 372 (394 et seqq. para. 62 et seqq.).

[7] BVerfGE 95, 1 (15).

[8] In summary *Heun*, in: Starck (ed.), Staat und Individuum im Kultur- und Rechtsvergleich, 2000, 95–115; *Lauth*, in: Mayer/Weinacht (eds.), Gewaltenteilung, 2021, 191–208.

powers. The judiciary was independent, but the state court did not have the powers of a modern constitutional court.

With the National Socialist takeover in 1933, the separation of powers was effectively abolished. The Enabling Act (*Ermächtigungsgesetz*) authorised the government to legislate without parliamentary control, the states were centralised, the courts were politically instrumentalised, rule of law and constitutional *checks and balances* were suspended.

After the reconstruction of German statehood after 1945, the two German states, the Federal Republic (FRG) and the German Democratic Republic (GDR) differed considerably regarding the separation of powers. In the constitutions of the GDR, legislation, government and jurisdiction were understood as parts of a unified state power, politically led by the single party.[9] Functioning institutions of *checks and balances* did not exist. The first GDR Constitution of 1949 still outwardly displayed elements of a classic system of separation of powers, containing a People's Chamber (*Volkskammer*) and a Chamber of the states (*Länderkammer*), a president, a Council of Ministers and courts. In political practice, however, power was monopolised by the Socialist Unity Party (SED). In 1952, the *Länder* were replaced by districts – a clear step away from vertical separation of powers. In 1960, the State Council (*Staatsrat*) was introduced as the collective head of state and given normative powers. The 1968 Constitution (and its revised version 1974) declared the SED to be the leading force in society, enshrined democratic centralism and defined the People's Chamber as the "supreme organ of state power". Executive bodies were able to issue regulations and orders with the force of law, blurring the line between legislation and government. The judiciary was neither institutionally nor de facto independent.

Building on the previous experiences with centralisation of powers and authoritarian systems, the Federal Republic reorganised state power in 1949, providing horizontal and vertical separation of powers under the Basic Law. A significant qualitative leap is the comprehensive constitutional jurisdiction of the Federal Constitutional Court, which ensures compliance with the Basic Law by all branches of government. Although there have always been points of reference for state jurisdiction in German constitutional history, the Court is a new player in German federalism.[10] In its established case law, the Court states that the purpose of the separation of powers is not to sharply divide the functions of state authority. Rather, the legislative, executive and judicial organs should control and limit each other to moderate state power and to protect the freedom of the individual. The constitutional balance of power must be maintained; no branch of government may be given undue power over the other branches, or may be de-

---

[9] *Brunner*, in: Isensee/Kirchhof (eds.), Handbuch des Staatsrechts, Vol. 1, 2003, § 11 para. 25–27.

[10] *Heun*, in: Heun, Verfassung und Verfassungsgerichtsbarkeit im Vergleich, 2014, 87–99; *Scheuner*, in: Starck (ed.), Bundesverfassungsgericht und Grundgesetz, Vol. 1, 1976, 1–62.

prived of the powers necessary to fulfil its constitutional duties.[11] Therefore, the constitutional organs are obliged to mutual consideration, respect and cooperation in order to jointly fulfil their constitutional responsibility (principle of loyalty between the constitutional organs – *Verfassungsorgantreue*).[12]

2. System of Government

The Federal Republic has a parliamentary system of government,[13] meaning that the Federal Government is dependent on a permanent majority in the parliament – the German *Bundestag* – which elects the Federal Chancellor, selects the ministers from among its members and brings the Federal Government into office. The government relies on the continued confidence of the parliamentary majority, which may elect a new Chancellor at any time.

This system was introduced shortly before the end of the First World War in 1918,[14] and formally established in the Weimar Constitution 1919.[15] Nevertheless, as mentioned, the Weimar system retained a strong presidential component: the directly elected *Reich* President could dissolve the *Reichstag* and exercise extensive executive powers, especially in exceptional political situations. The Basic Law has deliberately reduced presidential authority. The Federal President has primarily representative and integrative functions with only marginal political control, and is no longer directly elected.

In state practice, the executive and legislative branches are typically blurred. Within the parliamentary system of government, they are only formally opposed to each other as institutions; politically, this applies rather to the government majority and the opposition.

---

[11] BVerfGE 3, 225 (247); 7, 183 (188); 9, 268 (279 et seqq.); 22, 106 (111); 34, 52 (59 et seqq.); 95, 1 (15).

[12] Recently BVerfGE 159, 26 (34 et seqq. para. 24) inter alia with reference to BVerfGE 12, 205 (254); 35, 193 (199); 45, 1 (39); 90, 286 (337). Further on the principle of loyalty between the constitutional organs, *Schenke*, Die Verfassungsorgantreue, 1977.

[13] *Meinel*, in: Kischel/Kube (eds.), Handbuch des Staatsrechts, Vol. 3, 2025, § 65, 751–790; *Kersten*, in: Herdegen/Masing/Poscher/Gärditz (eds.), Handbuch des Verfassungsrechts, 2021, § 11, 721–776; *Starck*, in: Akademie der Wissenschaften zu Göttingen (ed.), 70 Jahre Grundgesetz, 2020, 17–40.

[14] Act of 28 October 1918, RGBl. 1918, 1274. The following paragraphs were added to Article 15 of the Constitution: "(3) The *Reich* Chancellor requires the confidence of the *Reichstag* to perform his duties. (4) The *Reich* Chancellor shall be responsible for all acts of political significance undertaken by the Emperor in the exercise of his powers under the *Reich* Constitution. (5) The *Reich* Chancellor and his deputy shall be accountable to the *Bundesrath* and the *Reichstag* for the performance of their duties." [translation by the author].

[15] The Constitution of the German Reich ("Weimar Constitution") of 11 August 1919, RGBl. 1919, 1383.

3. *Constitutional* Checks and Balances

The Basic Law provides a clear framework of control and cooperation mechanisms for the executive and legislative branches. On the recommendation of the Federal President, the *Bundestag* elects the Federal Chancellor by an absolute majority (Article 63 (1) and (2) GG) and supports him with a structural majority over the four-year legislative period. Within the Federal Government, the Chancellor determines and is responsible for the general guidelines of policy (Article 65 sentence 1 GG), while the federal ministers conduct their departments independently and on their own responsibility (sentence 2). The *Bundestag* has budgetary sovereignty (Article 110 GG).

Alongside the *Bundestag*, the *Bundesrat* constitutes the second chamber of the federal parliament, although this representative body of the 16 states does not have the same powers as the *Bundestag*. Even though it must give its constitutive approval to a law, the *Bundesrat* only participates in the majority of legislative procedures, and its vote can be overruled by the *Bundestag*. Still, it enables the states to participate in federal legislation. Nevertheless, German constitutional law considers only the *Bundestag* to be the parliament.

The government can be brought down by a parliamentary vote of no confidence (Article 67 GG) if a successor to the Federal Chancellor is elected by a majority of the members of the *Bundestag* (constructive vote of no confidence). The Federal President must then dismiss the previous Chancellor and recognise the newly elected one; the Federal Government stands or falls with the Chancellor.

In contrast, the possibility to dissolute the *Bundestag* is limited (Article 68 (1) sentence 1 GG). The Federal Chancellor may ask the *Bundestag* to express its confidence in him. If this vote of confidence does not receive a majority, the Federal President *may*, on the recommendation of the Chancellor, dissolve the *Bundestag* and call for new elections. The Federal Chancellor has discretion to propose the dissolution of the *Bundestag* to the Federal President, who has discretion in deciding whether to approve it. If the *Bundestag* is not dissolved, the Basic Law provides for a minority government, which has not yet occurred. Since the 1980s, a de facto right of self-dissolution of the *Bundestag* has been established through state practice, which has been repeatedly declared constitutional by the Federal Constitutional Court. In two cases, the Federal Chancellor did not formally obtain a majority, even though he had the necessary confidence. The vote of confidence had only been called to bring about early elections. The Court did not see a violation of the constitution, as there had been a "politically unstable situation" and the Federal Chancellor had discretion in assessing this.[16]

Judicial power is entrusted to judges (Article 92 GG). The majority of judges are employed by the states, each of which has its own procedure for selecting and

---

16 BVerfGE 62, 1 et seqq.; 114, 121 et seqq. See *Pieper*, ZParl 38 (2007), 287–299.

appointing them. The judges of the highest federal courts – the Federal Court of Justice, the Federal Administrative Court, the Federal Finance Court, the Federal Social Court and the Federal Labour Court – are elected by the Committee for the Election of Judges (*Richterwahlausschuss*) and appointed by the Federal President (Article 95 (2) GG; Judicial Election Act[17]). The committee consists of the 16 State ministers, whose portfolio is concerned (Justice, Labor or Finance), as well as 16 members of the *Bundestag*. It elects the judges by secret ballot and majority vote. The responsible federal minister has no vote but must approve the elected candidate. The appointment of federal judges thus requires intensive cooperation between the executive and legislative branches.

Federal law does not grant the *Bundestag* or the Federal Government direct authority to transfer, retire or dismiss a federal judge. Only the *Bundestag* can apply to the Federal Constitutional Court for such an order if a judge infringes the principles of the Basic Law or the constitutional order of a state (Article 98 (2) GG).

The executive branch has the right to appoint a candidate as a federal judge through the State Ministries of Justice, Labour and Social Affairs or Finance, together with the Committee for the Election of Judges. Nevertheless, the government and the executive branch are prohibited from influencing the manner in which judicial functions are exercised, either through individual instructions or in other ways.[18] This differs for public prosecutors. As civil servants, they must comply with the official instructions of their superiors (§ 146 of the Courts Constitution Act[19]). The Federal Minister of Justice, for example, has the right to issue instructions to all members of the Federal Public Prosecutor's Office. This may be seen as an inadmissible influence of the executive on the judiciary, which, from a European perspective, includes public prosecutors. In 2020, the Grand Chamber of the European Court of Justice refused to recognise German public prosecutors' offices as "enforcing judicial authorities" on the grounds of their dependence on instructions.[20] From a German perspective, this dependence on instructions ensures the democratic legitimacy of executive action and the accountability of the responsible minister. The state is aware of the problem and has issued an administrative regulation stipulating that prosecutors should avoid even the appearance of undue influence by the executive branch on the courts.[21]

---

[17] Judges Election Act (*Richterwahlgesetz*) of 25 August 1950, BGBl. 1950 I, 368, last amended by Regulation of 31 August 2015, BGBl. 2015 I, 1474.

[18] BVerfGE 14, 56 (59).

[19] Courts Constitution Act (*Gerichtsverfassungsgesetz*) of 27 January 1877 in the version published on 9 May 1975 in BGBl. 1975 I, 1077, last amended by the Act of 8 December 2025, BGBl. 2025 I, No. 318.

[20] ECJ (GC), Case C-510/19, Judgment of 24 November 2020, ECLI:EU:C:2020:953 (Openbaar Ministerie).

[21] Instructions on Criminal Procedures and Administrative Fine Procedure (*Richtlinien für das Strafverfahren und das Bußgeldverfahren* – RiStBV) of 28 March 2023, BAnz AT of 19 June 2023 B1, No. 123.

The relationship between the Federal President, the Federal Chancellor and the Federal Government is strictly formalised (Article 64 GG), reflecting the decision in the Basic Law to largely withdraw the President as a political actor. The Federal Chancellor proposes the members of his cabinet to the Federal President, who is generally obliged to appoint them. In very few cases he has refused; this procedure is handled discreetly . In theory, the Federal Chancellor could force the President to follow his personnel proposal by initiating an organ dispute procedure before the Federal Constitutional Court – but this does not happen for reasons of respect for constitutional organs and political considerations. Regarding dismissals, the formal relationship is even stricter. There are no known cases in which the Federal President has not complied with a request from the Federal Chancellor to dismiss a minister. This is also because the Federal Chancellor – unlike the Federal President – is politically responsible for the actions of the cabinet and must justify himself before the *Bundestag*.

Internally, the administration has a strict hierarchy, and, in principle, its internal actions are not subject to judicial review. German civil servants are obliged to follow the official orders of their superiors (§ 62 (1) of the Federal Civil Service Act;[22] § 35 of the Civil Service Status Act[23]). However, if a civil servant has concerns about the legality of an official order, he must immediately raise them to his superior. If the order is upheld, he must contact the next higher superior. If it is further maintained, the civil servant must carry out the instruction and cannot be held criminally responsible. The duty of obedience only ceases to apply if the order is punishable or unlawful – even though the civil servant has acted due reasonable care – or if it violates human dignity. However, it is not possible to challenge an official order before an administrative court.[24]

4. *Larger and More Inclusive Meaning of the Separation of Powers?*

The vertical dimension of separation of powers extends not only to the relationship between the German Federation and the states but also includes a third dimension – municipal self-government. The triad of separation of powers can be found at all three levels, although at the municipal level legal protection is provided by the courts of the states. The decisive criterion for distinguishing between the levels is the distribution of powers, namely the constitutional allocation of responsibility for specific matters. In practice, conflicts repeatedly arise concerning the exact distribution of powers, which are resolved either by the

[22] Federal Civil Service Act (*Bundesbeamtengesetz* – BBG) of 14 July 1953 in the version of 5 February 2009, BGBl. 2009 I, 160, last amended by the Act of 27 February 2025, BGBl. 2025 I, No. 72.

[23] Civil Service Status Act (*Beamtenstatusgesetz* – BeamtStG) of 17 June 2008, BGBl. 2008 I, 1010, last amended by the Act of 20 December 2023, BGBl. 2023 I, No. 389.

[24] See *Grigoleit*, in: Battis (ed.), Bundesbeamtengesetz. Kommentar, 2022, § 63 para. 10.

Federal Constitutional Court or, concerning disputes within a state, by the state constitutional courts.

At all three levels, the principle of separation of powers is strongly influenced by the comprehensive guarantee of legal protection. The Basic Law stipulates that any act of public authority may be challenged before a court (Article 19 (4) GG). There are very few exceptions. Almost every act of the executive can be reviewed, and the review of norms by the Federal Administrative Court and the Federal Constitutional Court also enables to control the legislature in essence.

The parliamentary opposition is not specifically organised as an institution. In 2016, the Federal Constitutional Court ruled that a constitutional "right to organised political opposition" exists, deriving this from the separation of powers, as conveyed by the principle of rule of law. Since a stable majority is essential for a government capable of acting, parliamentary control is not only the responsibility of the parliamentary majority, but in particular of its members and parliamentary groups not supporting the government. "As the parliamentary opposition, they act as the natural opponents of the government and the parliamentary majority supporting it (so-called new or intra-parliamentary dualism […])."[25] Here, too, the difficulty of classifying the *Bundesrat* becomes apparent: A political party may belong to the opposition in the *Bundestag* but nevertheless exert influence in the *Bundesrat* through its participation in a state government. Thus, the concept of opposition cannot be applied to the *Bundesrat*. The opposition is constitutionally protected, primarily through various parliamentary minority rights, for example the right to submit motions for judicial review, the possibility of initiating institutional disputes, and the right to establish a committee of inquiry (Article 44 GG).[26]

As already illustrated, the parliamentary system of government means that the executive has a certain influence on legislation. Most bills originate from the federal ministerial administration. However, it would be a mistake to underestimate the *Bundestag*. Depending on the subject matter, the *Bundestag* introduces internally developed bills, and makes significant changes to draft legislation of the Federal Government. The opposition is able to have bills drafted by state governments in which it participates.[27] These are introduced into federal legislation via the *Bundesrat*.

5. *Evolution in the Jurisprudence of the Constitutional Court*

The case law of the Federal Constitutional Court on the separation of powers has a solid core based on the constitutional-historical concept as it has developed

---

[25] BVerfG, Judgment of 3 May 2016, 2 BvE 4/14, para. 87, https://www.bundesverfassungsgericht.de/SharedDocs/Entscheidungen/EN/2016/05/es20160503_2bve000414en.html [23.12.2025] – BVerfGE 142, 25 (56 para. 87) [German version].

[26] *Ingold*, Das Recht der Opposition, 2015.

[27] *Wrase*, KJ 48 (2015), 314–325.

since John Locke's writings. The separation of powers serves to ensure mutual control of the state organs and thus to moderate state power. These ideas have not changed since the Court began its judicial activity.

However, the Court also opposes a parliamentary system of monism, granting the parliament a privileged position in exercising sovereign power on the basis of its direct democratic legitimacy. According to the Federal Constitutional Court, state decisions should be made as correctly as possible, meaning by the bodies that are best suited to do so in terms of their organisation, composition, function and procedures.[28] This case law is reflected, for example, in the legal concept of the "core area of executive decision-making" (*Kernbereich exekutiver Eigenverantwortung*), which guarantees the Federal Government a constitutionally protected sphere of action into which even parliament cannot intrude,[29] meaning that the parliament should not be able to investigate the executive's sphere of initiative, consultation and action. This core area is not absolutely defined, in state practice, conflicts over the boundaries arise repeatedly. Accordingly, the case law of the Court is developing under the critical scrutiny of legal scholars.[30]

II. Constitutional Review

1. Type of Constitutional Review

The Federal Constitutional Court is a constitutional body and independent court that stands alongside the supreme courts of the federal state, each of which is the last resort in its respective area of jurisdiction (Article 95 GG).

This model was only decided upon very late in the deliberations of the Parliamentary Council. The Constitutional Convention of *Herrenchiemsee*, which prepared the Basic Law, considered two models of how constitutional jurisdiction should be organised: an independent constitutional court, and a unified supreme federal court that would function both as the final court of appeal and the constitutional court. The Parliamentary Council finally decided to introduce an independent constitutional court, which would exist alongside the supreme court (Federal Court of Justice). The reasons for this are not entirely clear. A central consideration was the visible separation of law and politics.[31] Another argument was certainly that an institutionally independent constitutional court may include legal professionals (professors, lawyers, ministerial officials) alongside professional judges. However, the Federal Constitutional Court was not given an

[28] BVerfGE 68, 1 (86); 150, 1 (99 para. 197).

[29] BVerfGE 67, 100 et seqq.

[30] *Starski*, STAAT 62 (2023), 373–418; *Droege*, DVBl. 130 (2015), 937–943; *Cancik*, ZParl 45 (2014), 885–907.

[31] *Schiffer*, Grundlegung der Verfassungsgerichtsbarkeit, 1984, XIV.

independent title in the Basic Law. Instead, it is still listed in Title IX on the judiciary with rather limited constitutional regulation in Articles 93 and 94 GG.

The classification of the Court as part of the judiciary led to an initial dispute with the executive branch immediately after the Court began its work in September 1951. The question was whether the Federal Constitutional Court should be part of the regular judiciary or whether it should be a constitutional organ on equal footing with the other constitutional organs mentioned in the Basic Law. In the first case, the Federal Minister of Justice would have had supervisory authority over the Court and its staff, the Court would not have had its own budgetary autonomy, and communication with other courts and authorities would have had to be conducted through the Federal Minister of Justice. The executive branch would thus have had the opportunity to exert administrative influence over the Court's finances and personnel. This so-called status dispute (*Statusstreit*)[32] ultimately ended in favour of the Federal Constitutional Court. Since the beginning, the Act on the Federal Constitutional Court (*Bundesverfassungsgerichtsgesetz* – BVerfGG)[33] described the Court as "a federal court of justice which is autonomous and independent of all other constitutional organs" (§1 (1) BVerfGG). Although the Court was not included in the Basic Law as a constitutional body until 2024 (Article 93 (1) GG, new version),[34] it had already been regarded as the fifth constitutional body since the mid-1950s. It has its own budget, has authority over its personnel and communicates independently with the authorities, courts and other constitutional organs. As it is a court, the principle of judicial independence applies both to the Court and its members (Article 97 GG).

However, the Court is not included in the hierarchy of specialised courts – it would be wrong to regard it as the highest instance of German federal jurisdiction. This special position is reflected in procedural law in which constitutional complaints are referred to as "extraordinary legal remedies", meaning that they are only admissible if the alleged violation of fundamental rights could not have been remedied in another way.

The status and independence of the Federal Constitutional Court have never been questioned since the Basic Law came into force, nor are there any restrictions on its jurisdiction.

---

[32] *Leibholz*, Der Status des Bundesverfassungsgerichts, 1957; *Laufer*, Verfassungsgerichtsbarkeit und politischer Prozeß, 1968, 254 et seqq. For a detailed account of the early history of the Federal Constitutional Court see *Herchenröder*, Die Selbsterfindung des Bundesverfassungsgerichts (1951–1958), 2026.

[33] Act on the Federal Constitutional Court (*Bundesverfassungsgerichtsgesetz* – BVerfGG) of 12 March 1951 in the version published on 11 August 1993 in BGBl. 1993 I, 1473, last amended by the Act of 22 December 2025, BGBl. 2025 I, No. 349.

[34] Article 93 (1) GG in the version of the Act amending the Basic Law (Articles 93 and 94) of 20 December 2024, BGBl. 2024 I, No. 439, which entered into force on 28 December 2024.

2. Competences

The Basic Law does not conclusively regulate proceedings before the Federal Constitutional Court. It allows for appeals to be lodged with the Court, guarantees the independence of its members and ensures the right to a fair hearing. At the same time, the Basic Law provides that further proceedings may be transferred to the Court by the parliamentary legislature (Article 94 (3) GG). The distribution of powers is therefore not exclusively reserved for the constitution.

As already mentioned, any act of German public authority, meaning laws, actions of constitutional organs, and judgments of the specialised courts, can be challenged (Article 19 (4) GG). Some of the 20 independent types of proceedings are regulated in the Basic Law (Article 94 (1) to (3) GG) and others in the Act on the Federal Constitutional Court (§ 13 BVerfGG). The powers of the Federal Constitutional Court include abstract and concrete judicial review, disputes between federal constitutional bodies, federal-state disputes and constitutional complaints. However, the Court does not have the power to amend the Basic Law.

Constitutional complaints constitute the vast majority of pending proceedings and exist in two forms: against judgments and against laws. In the first case, the Federal Constitutional Court may declare a decision by a specialised court unconstitutional and reverse it. In a successful constitutional complaint against a legal principle, the underlying law is void.

The Basic Law (Article 94 GG), and in more detail the Act on the Federal Constitutional Court (§§ 36 to 97e BVerfGG), contain criteria for the admissibility of the respective proceedings. For reasons of scope, it can only be stated that the access to the Court, the subject matter and the right to file applications and complaints are limited to those bodies and persons who are ultimately affected by the sovereign decision. The Court does not have a free acceptance procedure. Nevertheless, it has created a criterion of admissibility in form of the burden of presentation and substantiation, which enables it to reject applications and complaints as inadmissible. As a rule, applicants or complainants have not presented their complaint to the Federal Constitutional Court in sufficient detail.[35]

Who may appeal to the Court also depends on the relevant type of proceeding. In constitutional complaints, any person who is the addressee of an act of German sovereign authority or who is affected by it in a qualified manner is authorised (Article 94 (1) No. 4a GG; § 90 (1) BVerfGG). In disputes concerning the organisation of the state, the Basic Law specifies the bodies and organs that are entitled to file a complaint (Article 94 (1) No. 1 to 3 GG). For example, in a dispute between constitutional organs, those named in the Basic Law – the Federal Government, the *Bundestag*, the *Bundesrat* and the Federal President – as well as parts of these organs – such as parliamentary groups in the *Bundestag* or its committees – may initiate the proceeding (§ 63 BVerfGG). The federal-state

---

[35] *Schorkopf*, AöR 130 (2005), 465–493; *Lange*, Darlegungs- und Substantiierungspflichten im Verfassungsbeschwerdeverfahren, 2012.

dispute, in which the Federation and one or more states of the Federal Republic are opposed, also concerns the delimitation of competences (Article 94 (1) No. 3 GG). In abstract judicial reviews (Article 94 (1) No. 2 GG), the Federal Government, the governments of the states as well as a quarter of the members of the *Bundestag* are authorised to submit a request, while in a concrete judicial review, a court must submit a constitutional question (Article 100 (1) GG).

The powers of the Federal Constitutional Court in the area of constitutional law have a considerable influence on the separation of powers, for example when the Federal Government and the *Bundestag* are in conflict with each other. Such proceedings concern the issue that one side has violated the constitutional rights or obligations of the other. The Court acts as an arbitrator and draws a binding line between the spheres of the judiciary and the executive. Although there are no direct conflicts between the executive or legislative branches and the judiciary, the Court indirectly addresses this issue by exercising restraint in certain matters, leaving room for assessment and decision-making to both the executive (core area of autonomous executive decision-making) and, albeit to a lesser extent, the legislature, i. e. respecting their autonomy.[36] However, the other constitutional organs repeatedly argue that the Court exercises too much control over their actions, meaning that it interferes too much in their sphere of competence and changes the separation of powers in its favour. These debates can be seen as a concrete negotiation of the boundaries between the three branches of government.

The Court may also be involved in urgent proceedings (§ 32 BVerfGG) and issue far-reaching orders. In addition, it has the option of issuing enforcement orders (§ 35 BVerfGG), meaning that it may take the necessary measures to enforce a decision. The view is taken that these could also be issued *ex officio*.[37] However, there must have already been a previous decision by the Court in pending proceedings.

3. *Effects of Decisions*

Each proceeding before the Federal Constitutional Court concerns a response to the specific question raised. In this respect, an application or complaint is either successful or rejected.

---

36 For the Federal Constitutional Court, *judicial self-restraint* aims to "safeguard the constitutionally guaranteed leeway for the other constitutional organs to freely shape policy", BVerfG, Order of 31 July 1973, 2 BvF 1/73, para. 51, https://www.bundesverfassungsgericht.de/SharedDocs/Entscheidungen/EN/1973/07/rs19730731_2bvf000173en.html [23.12.2025] – BVerfGE 36, 1 (14 et seqq.) [German version]. Criticism that the Federal Constitutional Court had disregarded this principle was also explicitly addressed, cf. BVerfGE 93, 121 (149 et seqq., 151) – dissenting opinion Böckenförde; BVerfGE 125, 260 (364 et seqq., 373) – dissenting opinion Schluckebier.

37 *Burkiczak*, in: Burkiczak/Dollinger/Schorkopf (eds.), Bundesverfassungsgerichtsgesetz, 2022, § 35 para. 32 with reference to BVerfGE 2, 139 (142) (SRP-Verbot/Vollstreckung); 6, 300 (303 et seqq.) (KPD Verbot/Vollstreckung).

The decisions of the Court have far-reaching effects. They are binding "upon the constitutional organs of the Federation and of the *Länder* as well as on all courts and those with public authority" (Article 94 (4) sentence 1 GG; § 31 (1) BVerfGG). Certain decisions of the Court even have the force of law (§ 31 (2) BVerfGG); the legislature, who amended the constitution, incorporated this decision-making effect into the Basic Law in 2024 in order to strengthen the institutional stability of the Federal Constitutional Court.[38]

In constitutional complaint proceedings against judgments, the Court may reverse the previous decision, so that the case is referred back to the competent court (§ 95 (2) BVerfGG). In successful constitutional complaints against legal provisions, the law is to be declared void (§ 95 (3) BVerfGG). The effects of this clear provision have been mitigated in the practice of the Court. For decades, it allowed unconstitutional laws to remain in force in order to give the legislature the opportunity to amend it, primarily when immediate nullity would have had unacceptable consequences. In practice, there are other variants in which the legislature is called upon to take certain measures. In such cases the Federal Constitutional Court often provides guidance in its reasoning as to how the legislature should act.[39] After negative experiences with an inactive parliament, the Court changed its practice to set a deadline for the legislature, after which the law automatically ceases to be in force.[40]

Decisions of the Court are binding in terms of their tenor and the underlying reasons. While the tenor is clearly identifiable at the beginning of a decision, the underlying reasons are more difficult to assess. The observer must ask himself whether a formulation or an argument is necessary to justify the tenor. Naturally, there is room for discretion, and it is not always possible to give a clear answer, partly because the Court tends to make *obiter dicta,* meaning incidental, non-supporting explanations.

Decisions of the Federal Constitutional Court are legally binding once they become final, immediately upon the oral pronouncement or written announcement of the judgment. Only if a decision has the force of law (§ 31 (2) BVerfGG), the operative part must be published in the Federal Law Gazette (*Bundesgesetzblatt* – BGBl.) by the Federal Ministry of Justice. However, publication is not a prerequisite for the decision to take effect.

Decisions of the Court cannot be invalidated by other constitutional bodies or courts. The only way to deprive them of their *future* effect is to amend the constitution itself by a two-thirds majority in the *Bundestag* and the *Bundesrat.* This

---

[38] *Britz,* NJW 78 (2025), 609–613; *Berger,* DVBl. 138 (2023), 973–978.

[39] So-called "appeal decision" (*Appellentscheidung*); for more details see *C. Schröder,* Das Durchsetzungsverfahren des Bundesverfassungsgerichts, 2025, 196 et seqq., 204–206.

[40] This practice is based solely on case law, *Bode,* ZG 36 (2021), 266–289; *Seer,* NJW 49 (1996), 285–290.

has happened in a few cases,[41] – a different constitutional jurisprudence is then normatively prescribed for the future; whether the Court will adhere to this as expected is another question.

4. Procedures for Constitutional Review

The Basic Law does not contain provisions on the allocation of proceedings, which is largely left to the parliamentary legislature and partly to the Court itself. The cases that reach the Federal Constitutional Court are distributed abstractly by the Act on the Federal Constitutional Court (§ 14 (1) to (3) BVerfGG), but in practice, according to a sophisticated proceeding allocation plan. This plan, which is to be decided annually by the two Senates, first distributes the cases to the two Senates and then to one of their eight members (§ 15a (2) BVerfGG; § 20 GO-BVerfG[42]). The law authorises the Plenary of the Court, meaning all 16 members, to deviate from this legal requirement for reasons of equal distribution (§ 14 (4) BVerfGG). In accordance with German court tradition, it is therefore predetermined which judge will deal with a complaint or application. The public proceeding allocation plan specifies both the types of proceedings and the topics as allocation criteria. If a competence is unclear, jurisdiction is determined by the so-called six-member committee (*Sechser-Ausschuss*), in which the President of the Federal Constitutional Court exceptionally has the casting vote (§ 14 (5) BVerfGG).

Originally, the First Senate was supposed to deal with constitutional complaints and the Second Senate with matters relating to the organisation of the state, but it quickly became clear that this distribution was practically dysfunctional because the number of constitutional complaints far exceeded the number of state court proceedings. Therefore, until today, the Second Senate also takes on constitutional complaints to achieve a comparable workload between the panels.

The deliberations of the Senates are secret. Only members of the Court may participate, as stipulated in the rules of procedure of the Federal Constitutional Court, which the Court itself adopts (§ 25 GO-BVerfG).

The majorities required for a decision depend on the type of procedure. For most proceedings, a simple majority is sufficient, meaning five votes in the Senats. In proceedings concerning defensive democracy and impeachment of judges, a successful motion requires a two-thirds majority (§ 15 (4) BVerfGG). If the vote is tied (4 : 4), a constitutional violation cannot be established. In judicial

---

[41] A more recent example is the insertion of Article 91e GG in response to BVerfGE 119, 331 et seqq. Another, even though less clear example, is Article 16a GG, which was added in 1993 with the intention to capture the broad interpretation of Article 16 (2) sentence 2 of the former version of the Basic Law by the administration and the Federal Constitutional Court. For the history of its origins see *Heusch*, in: Epping/Hillgruber (eds.), BeckOK Grundgesetz, 63rd ed. 2025, Article 16a para. 9–13.

[42] Rules of Procedure of the Federal Constitutional Court (*Geschäftsordnung des Bundesverfassungsgerichts* – GO-BVerfG) of 19 November 2014, BGBl. 2015 I, 286.

practice, most decisions concerning constitutional complaints are made by the three-member chambers of the two Senates, which vote unanimously (§ 93d (3) BVerfGG).

Originally, the Act on the Federal Constitutional Court, did not provide for judges to attach separate opinions to a decision. Nevertheless, judges added dissenting opinions, which in one case was also made public.[43] After legal policy debates and majority support by the Plenary of the Court, the legislature amended the procedural law in 1970 to allow separate opinions (§ 30 (2) BVerfGG; § 55 GO-BVerfG).[44] Provided, that he has already expressed his opinion during the deliberations, a judge may make use of this option at his discretion. He can either add a dissenting opinion – if he has a different view on the decision itself – or a concurring opinion – if he agrees with the tenor but not with the underlying reasons.[45] In practice, only about 7 % of Senate decisions include a separate opinion.[46] Nevertheless, some have become well known and even found their way into academic teaching. Regarding the potential impact on the Federal Constitutional Court, the dissenting opinion of Judge Böckenförde in the decision on party donations (*Parteispenden*) is noteworthy. Böckenförde's argumentation was explicitly taken up in a later decision that altered the Court's previous case law,[47] demonstrating that a minority position expressed in a dissenting opinion may develop into the majority during legal discourse. A milder version of the separate opinion is the possibility for the Senate to announce the internal voting result in abstract terms without assigning names to the voting behaviour (§ 30 (2) sentence 2 BVerfGG).

III. Composition of the Federal Constitutional Court

1. *Internal Structure*

The Federal Constitutional Court is a so-called "double" or "twin court" as it consists of two largely autonomous adjucating bodies: the First and Second Senate (Article 93 (2) sentence 1 GG). As already mentioned, both bodies have eight members and exclusive responsibilities. Even if it seems paradoxical, each Senate is "the Federal Constitutional Court".[48]

---

[43] *Geiger*, in: Institut für Staatslehre und Politik e.V. in Mainz (ed.), Der Kampf um den Wehrbeitrag, Vol. 2, 1953, 822 et seqq.; on the proceedings BVerfGE 2, 79 et seqq.

[44] For details, see *Lamprecht*, Richter contra Richter, 1992; most recently *Klatt*, Das Sondervotum beim Bundesverfassungsgericht, 2023.

[45] *Lenz/Hansel*, Bundesverfassungsgerichtsgesetz. NomosHandkommentar, 2024, § 30 para. 23.

[46] *Burkiczak* (n. 41), in: Bundesverfassungsgerichtsgesetz, § 30 para. 48.

[47] BVerfGE 85, 264 (314 et seqq.) with reference to BVerfGE 73, 40 (103 et seqq.) – dissenting opinion Böckenförde; see further *Klatt* (n. 49), 145 et seqq.

[48] BVerfGE 1, 14 (29); 7, 17 (18).

Procedural law provides for a third body: the Plenary, consisting of the 16 members of the Court. In practice, it is mainly entrusted with administrative tasks (§ 1 (2) GO-BVerfG), including the distribution of business between the Senates,[49] and, in rare cases, also has judicial competence. Primarily, the Plenary guarantees the uniformity of case law: If a Senate wishes to deviate from the legal opinion of the other Senate, it must refer the matter to the Plenary (§ 16 BVerfGG), which decides by majority vote.

In the 1950s, the Senates introduced a substructure, which is now referred to as chambers. They consist of three members and were created to reduce the procedural burden in constitutional complaint proceedings (Article 94 (1) No. 4a GG) and concrete judicial review proceedings (Article 100 (1) GG). Each Senate has three to four chambers, so that individual judges sit in several of these subordinate de facto adjudicating bodies. Unlike the Senates and the Plenary, the chambers must decide unanimously.

Members of the Federal Constitutional Court have an independent status that mirrors the status of judges in the specialised courts. Accordingly, the requirements for judges apply with regard to legal training, independence and neutrality. The office of judge at the Court is incompatible with other professional activities, offices or mandates except for university professorship. Law professors at a German university may continue their profession on a part-time basis, albeit to a reduced extent (§ 3 (4) BVerfGG). This possibility was provided for in procedural law in order to promote exchange with legal scholarship and to ensure that constitutional jurisprudence remains intellectually up to date.[50]

The Federal Constitutional Court is supported by its own administration, which comprises around 250 staff members and is headed by the President of the Court, supported in administrative tasks by the Plenary (§ 1 GO-BVerfG). The "judicial clerks", meaning personal research assistants are crucial to the Court's work (§ 13 (1) sentence 1 GO-BVerfG). They prepare the decisions by drafting, and are available to their judge for research and internal consultation. Initially, each judge was assigned one assistant, but with the increasing caseload, this number has risen to four. The members of the Court select their assistants individually. In practice, the staff consists mainly of younger judges from the specialised courts and public prosecutors, and in some cases also of ministry officials and young academics. However, there is no permanent staff – the assistants' positions depend on the judges' terms of office. Although the staff is sometimes referred to as the "Third Senate", this should not lead to the misconception that they have a formal function in the judicial process.[51]

---

[49] *Klein*, in: Benda/Klein, Verfassungsprozessrecht, 2020, § 6 para. 165–166.

[50] *Huber*, Das Bundesverfassungsgericht und die Staatsrechtslehre, 2024, 14 et seqq.

[51] *Maatsch*, DRiZ 89 (2011), 391–392; *Hellmann*, in: van Ooyen/Möllers (eds.), Handbuch Bundesverfassungsgericht im politischen System, Vol. 2, 2025, 887–915. Since 2009, employees have been publishing anthologies on case law at irregular intervals, most recently *Lukosek/A. Schröder*, Linien der Rechtsprechung des Bundesverfassungsgerichts, Vol. 7, 2024.

2. Personnel

The number of members of the Federal Constitutional Court has remained stable since the end of the 1950s, when the judges per Senate were gradually reduced from twelve to eight. The term of office is twelve years, and re-election is not possible (Article 93 (3) sentence 1 GG; § 4 (1) and (2) BVerfGG). This was different in the original version of the Court's constitution. Judges had different terms of office, depending on their previous activities. Previous federal judges were appointed to the Court "for life" until they reached the age limit applicable to professional judges.[52] The other judges were elected for eight years, with the possibility of multiple re-elections, without any age limit. In order to standardise the terms of office and to solve problems of independence and informal campaigning for re-election, the legislature limited the term of office in 1970, introduced an age limit (68 years), abolished re-election and made separate opinions possible.

The formal requirements for the office of judge are briefly outlined in German constitutional law. Women and men who are fully qualified lawyers, and who have reached the age of 40 are eligible for election. Only the Federal President is subject to a minimum age requirement, whereby the Basic Law expresses the expectation that people with a certain amount of life and professional experience should be appointed to the Court.

Of the eight members of a Senate, at least three must be drawn from the ranks of federal judges, meaning from the five highest federal courts. This is intended to ensure judicial professionalism and is certainly also linked to the hope of counteracting excessive politicisation of the Court. From a sociological perspective, it is striking that the other five judgeships are predominantly filled by law professors and, to a lesser extent, by politicians from the federal or state governments; in exceptional cases, a lawyer may also be appointed. In the early decades, the number of ministry officials elected as judges was significantly higher. Since the 1980s, it has been noticeable that the public and the parties entitled to make nominations tried to ensure that candidates are not perceived as overly exposed party politicians. As soon as high-profile politicians stand for election, there is a need for justification, which reflects the desire to avoid politicising the Court.[53] Nevertheless, high-ranking party politicians have repeatedly been elected, including to leadership positions.[54]

There are no quotas for gender or minorities. While in the first decades the Federal Constitutional Court was predominantly staffed by men, the few women

---

[52] In this way, Willi Geiger served for a term of 26 years (1951–1977).

[53] The majority of the members of the Court are members of a political party; this characteristic is not specifically addressed in the selection process.

[54] An overview of the previous activities of members of the Federal Constitutional Court since 1951 can be found in: Burkiczak/Dollinger/Schorkopf (eds.), Bundesverfassungsgerichtsgesetz, 2022, Appendix 5, 1667–1680.

are well-known personalities.[55] Over the past 20 years, appointment practices have changed regarding gender. Federal policy now aims for gender parity, which was achieved at the end of 2025.

The election of judges is always subject to the particular forces of politics and law, democratic legitimacy and quality assurance.[56] The Basic Law first sets the course (Article 94 (1) No. 2 GG) by declaring the Court to be the sole arbitrator for federal conflicts. As a consequence, half of its members are elected by the *Bundesrat*. This substantial participation of the *Länder* ensures their acceptance of decisions. The other half of the judges are elected by the *Bundestag*.

Both the *Bundestag* and the *Bundesrat* must elect candidates by a two-thirds majority. The *Bundesrat* has decided in the Plenary since the Court was established. Until 2015, the responsible electoral body of the *Bundestag* was a 12-member electoral committee, which was formed and appointed by its Plenary. The committee was composed according to the political balance of power between the parliamentary groups. In the course of a debate on the democratic legitimacy of the Court and the transparency of the appointment of judges,[57] this procedure was changed so that the Plenary now votes on the committee's proposal.[58] The committee now only makes a preliminary decision on the candidate to be presented to the Plenary, which then votes without debate. The substantive discussion is still intended to take place in a smaller committee and to be removed from public debate. This allows to focus attention on the preliminary selection of candidates.

Considering the two-thirds majority required for the election and the party political situation at the beginning of the 1950s, the two major parties, the Social Democrats and the Christian Democrats, agreed on the distribution of nomination rights: Both could nominate four judges per Senate. The nomination was linked to the expectation that the other side would accept the candidate. In exceptional cases, it was possible to reject candidates internally. This practice ensured that candidates received the two-thirds majority, as the two major parties together were able to achieve it. This so-called "magic formula" (*Zauberformel*) of a 50:50 political division worked for decades. From the mid-1970s onwards, the two major parties began to cede individual nomination rights to smaller parties, initially from the Christian Democrats to the Liberals and later from the Social Democrats to the Greens. This step was also facilitated by an agreement of the two major parties to nominate a maximum of three candidates who were party

---

[55] See the biographies by *Hansen*, Erna Scheffler (1893–1983), 2020 and *Michl*, Wiltraut Rupp-von Brünneck (1912–1977), 2022.

[56] *Małolepszy*, Die Kriterien und das Verfahren der Richterwahl für die ordentliche Gerichtsbarkeit in Europa im Rechtsvergleich, 2019; *Böckenförde*, Verfassungsfragen der Richterwahl, 1998.

[57] *M. Schröder*, ZG 30 (2015), 150–167; *Wiegand*, RuP 49 (2013), 11–17.

[58] The amendment concerned § 6 of the Act on the Federal Constitutional Court (BVerfGG), see BT-Drs. 18/2737.

members, and one "neutral" candidate.[59] Due to the changing party political constellations and the representation of new parties in the *Bundestag*, the Liberals and the Greens are granted an original right to nominate one member each to one of the Senates since the 2010s. The "magic formula" (4:4) thus changed to a 3:3:1:1 formula.

Who becomes a judge in the Federal Constitutional Court depends crucially on who is proposed as a candidate for election by the committee. The parliamentary groups that are entitled to make proposals select a candidate internally, who is then presented to the other parliamentary groups, insofar as they are required for the qualified majority. The expectation is that the pre-selected person will be accepted, otherwise the rejecting party must expect that its own candidates will not be accepted at a later date.

In 2025, this procedure became a public event. Parts of one parliamentary group refused to vote for the pre-selected candidate. The two-thirds majority could not be achieved, the election was postponed and eventually cancelled. The nominating parliamentary group presented a new candidate, who received the necessary majority. In the meantime, a public debate unfolded about the first candidate, which even continued in public television interviews – a practice that had not been seen before and was not appreciated.[60] This semi-public selection process was a negative example of what the architects of the previous judge selection process had wanted to achieve.

The election procedure for Federal Constitutional Court judges can only be understood by recognising that a debate on the qualifications, character and views of potential candidates should not be conducted in public. Criticism has therefore focused on the fact that the election procedure was transferred from the committee to the Plenary to increase transparency and democratic legitimacy. In this respect, the election procedure may be revised again. However, it should not be overlooked that the problems with the 2025 judicial election were also caused by political shifts in power. In order to systematically exclude unpopular right-wing parties from the election of judges, almost all other parties must cooperate. As a result, smaller parties that have not yet been able to successfully propose a constitutional judge are pushing for the acceptance of "their" candidates as a political price for agreeing to other candidates.

The structural changes in the political landscape of the Federal Republic in 2024 led to important provisions on the election of judges, the organisation of the Federal Constitutional Court and procedural rules being incorporated into the Basic Law. This includes a partial revision of the rules governing the election of judges when either the *Bundestag* or the *Bundesrat* fails to elect a new judge within a period of five months (Article 93 (2) sentence 3 GG; § 7a BVerfGG). In this case, the other electoral body elects the judge instead. The nomination then

[59] *Frank*, in: FS Wolfgang Zeidler, Vol. 1, 1987, 163–173.
[60] *Behnke*, RuP 61 (2025), 345–355.

comes from the Plenary of the Court, which is obliged to submit a list of three candidates to succeed the judge who has left office within two months.[61]

The President and Vice-President of the Court, who sit in different Senates and serve as their chairpersons, are elected alternately by the *Bundestag* and the *Bundesrat* (§ 9 BVerfGG). In this way, the Basic Law once again recognises that the Federal Constitutional Court is the arbitrator of federal conflicts and that the interests of the *Länder* must be institutionally considered.

As the term of office of a judge at the Court ends after twelve years, or upon reaching the age of 68 (§ 4 BVerfGG), candidates older than 56 are effectively no longer eligible for election, as the politicians who select the candidates want to appoint them for the full term.

Furthermore, a judge of the Court can only lose his office if he is permanently incapable to perform his duties or if the Plenary of the Court decides so by a two-thirds majority.[62]

The remuneration of judges of the Court is regulated by a separate law,[63] using the remuneration of ministers of the Federal Government and presidents of the federal supreme courts as benchmarks. A special provision applies to law professors who are allowed to continue their professorship alongside their judicial office (§§ 3 (4) and 101 BVerfGG). Two-thirds of the income from the professorship is offset against the judge's salary, but one-third is paid in addition, so that professor-judges are remunerated significantly better than their fellow judges. Other gainful employments are prohibited for all members of the Court. In the last decade, the Court has adopted a code of conduct that requires the disclosure of non-judicial income, revealing that several judges receive considerable royalties, particularly from publications, and in some cases are also paid for lectures and fees.[64]

IV. Status of Constitutional Judges

1. Prohibitions – Incompatibilities – Conflict of Interest

As already mentioned, the office of judge of the Federal Constitutional Court is incompatible with all other professional activities, offices or mandates. Judges of the highest federal courts or civil servants must cease to exercise their positions in the specialist court and within the authority (§ 101 BVerfGG); the same applies to notaries, while lawyers must suspend their rights arising from their licence

[61] BT-Drs. 21/12977 and the references in n. 34.

[62] See below, Section IV. 2.

[63] Act on the Official Salaries of Members of the Federal Constitutional Court (*Gesetz über das Amtsgehalt der Mitglieder des Bundesverfassungsgerichts*) of 28 February 1964, BGBl. 1964 I, 133, last amended by the Act of 22 December 2023, BGBl. 2023 I, No. 414.

[64] https://www.bundesverfassungsgericht.de/DE/DasBundesverfassungsgericht/Richterinnen Richter/Einkuenfte/Einkuenfte-2023/einkuenfte_2023_node.html [23.12.2025].

during their term of office (§ 104 BVerfGG). The employment relationship of judges and civil servants continues during their term of office at the Court. After its expiry, a federal judge could take up a judicial office at a federal court again, but most judges retire or take up other activities. This issue is solely regulated in the Act on the Federal Constitutional Court and applies independently of individual proceedings. Only professor-judges may hold their professorship as a salaried secondary occupation (§ 3 (4) BVerfGG).

In addition, the Act on the Federal Constitutional Court provides for rules on exclusion and bias that relate to individual proceedings (§§ 18 and 19 BVerfGG). They reflect the usual requirements applying to judges in specialist courts in order to ensure the independence of the judiciary and the impartiality of judges in the interests of fair proceedings.[65] For example, a constitutional judge is *ipso iure* excluded from a case if he was involved in the matter, is or was married to, has another long-term relationship with or is related to one of the parties involved. In contrast, an interest in the outcome of the proceedings is no reason for exclusion – for example because a judge belongs to a political party or has a profession related to the subject matter of the dispute. Additionally, the Act contains two interesting exceptions: It is irrelevant if a judge has previously been involved in the legislative process as a politician, and if he has published or expressed a scientific opinion on the subject matter of the dispute.

The rules on bias correspond to the usual standards of German jurisdiction. A concern is sufficient, meaning a reason that is likely to justify mistrust of a judge's impartiality. This is the case if he is already so determined that he cannot or does not want to detach himself from this determination and is therefore not open to counterarguments.[66] In this situation, the Senate or the chamber decides on the existence of this concern, excluding the rejected judge. A judge may also recuse himself. In both cases a judge from the other Senate is appointed by lot to serve as a substitute in the panel (§ 19 (4) BVerfGG).

2. Liability

Unlike for the Federal President and members of the *Bundestag*, there is no corresponding immunity provision for members of the Federal Constitutional Court in the Basic Law. Accordingly, law enforcement authorities may initiate ordinary criminal investigations against them. In particular, preliminary investigations on suspicion of perversion of justice (§ 339 of the German Criminal Code – StGB[67]), an offence that only judges can commit and which protects the administration of

---

[65] *Klein* (n. 55), in: Verfassungsprozessrecht, § 11 para. 247.

[66] BVerfGE 82, 30 (38); 98, 134 (137); 102, 122 (125); 142, 302 (307 para. 18). There is extensive case law on this subject, see for example *Sauer*, in: BeckOK BVerfGG, 19th ed. 2025, § 19 para. 10–14; *Lechner/Zuck*, Bundesverfassungsgerichtsgesetz. Kommentar, 2019, § 19 para. 5.

[67] German Criminal Code (*Strafgesetzbuch* – StGB) in the version published on 13 November 1998, BGBl. 1998 I, 3322, last amended by the Act of 7 November 2024, BGBl. 2024 I, No. 351.

justice and the confidence in an impartial and non-arbitrary judiciary, may be considered.

Disciplinary law for judges is primarily regulated by the German Judiciary Act (*Deutsches Richtergesetz* – DRiG).[68] However, this Act is only applicable to judges of the Court in a subordinate manner (§69 DRiG), meaning if the Basic Law and the Act on the Federal Constitutional Court do not contain more specific provisions. There is broad agreement that the general disciplinary law for German judges does *not* apply to Court's judges.[69] As a result, they are subject solely to the disciplinary provisions of the Act on the Federal Constitutional Court (§105 BVerfGG; §§49 to 54 GO-BVerfG).[70] These provisions are not disciplinary law in the narrow sense, but consist of the possibility of dismissing a member of the Court. For this to occur, the member must be guilty of a serious breach of duty. Standard examples are a final conviction for a "dishonourable act" – which is worryingly vague[71] – or a sentence of at least six months' imprisonment (§105 (1) No. 2 BVerfGG) – whereby the offence committed is irrelevant.

In dismissal proceedings, the Court must cooperate with the Federal President, who must formally order the dismissal and has discretion in reviewing the case. In this respect, the President also acts as a supervisory authority against abuse. The possibility to initiate dismissal proceedings lies with the Plenary of the Court, but there is no obligation (§105 (1) BVerfGG: "may"). The Plenary's powers also include provisional removal from office, which may be considered if criminal proceedings have been instituted against a judge. Dismissals and removals require a two-thirds majority of the Plenary. In all other respects, the standards for the general impeachment of judges apply (§§58 to 62 BVerfGG).

The possibility of dismissing judges for disciplinary reasons has not played a role in the Court's 75 years of practice.

3. Principle of Independence

The independence of federal constitutional jurisdiction – of the Court itself and its members – is guaranteed, recognised and enforced in the same way as it applies to and is practised by specialised jurisdiction (Article 97 GG).[72] Since

68 German Judiciary Act (*Deutsches Richtergesetz* – DRiG) of 8 September 1961 in the version published on 19 April 1972, BGBl. 1972 I, 713, last amended by the Act of 22 October 2024 published in BGBl. 2024 I, No. 320.

69 *Staats*, Deutsches Richtergesetz, 2019, §69 para. 2.

70 Dismissal proceedings may also be initiated to retire a judge who is permanently unfit for service (§105 (1) No. 1 BVerfGG).

71 Serious insults and defamation (§§185 et seqq. StGB) as well as intentional false criminal complaints (§164 StGB) are possible grounds for this option, but considerable uncertainty remains.

72 The Federal Constitutional Court has expressed itself with remarkable clarity on this point, see BVerfGE 148, 69 (110 et seqq. para. 102): The "political culture in Germany is characterised by a practised and established respect for the independence of the third branch of government and is further safeguarded by non-legally standardised control mechanisms such as public discourse

2024, the status of the Federal Constitutional Court as an independent constitutional body is expressively included in the Basic Law (Article 93 GG).[73]

While the independence of judges does not pose major problems in terms of standards and in practice, the duty of impartiality deserves greater attention. This is due to the proximity of the Court to politics and the difficult distinction between politics and law. It is certainly no coincidence that the Court imposed a Code of Conduct on itself in the 2000s, albeit a non-binding one, aiming to ensure that "the reputation of the Court, the dignity of the office and confidence in its independence, impartiality, neutrality and integrity of the judges are not compromised".[74]

In this context, the extensive case law of the Federal Constitutional Court on bias of its members should be considered. This is particularly evident in a decision from 2021, in which the Court applied a strict standard regarding the political statements of its members. The Court recognised that the judges must and can only assume their new role upon taking office, regardless of previous party political disputes. However, the decision states that the date of taking office is not determined by the formal appointment by the Federal President, but by the date of election. The facts underlying the decision concerned a candidate who had already been elected but had made political statements prior to her appointment, giving rise to concerns about bias.[75] The Court has chosen a strict but correct standard here, showing sensitivity to the fact that the majority of its members is affiliated with political parties and that this could lead to mistrust among citizens with a different political view. The fact that political statements made prior to the election are not relevant is due to the unique nature of the Court, which is to be composed not only of professional judges, but also of prominent lawyers from politics, administration and academia.

A further normative standard is certainly the judicial duty of restraint, which applies generally to judges (§ 39 DRiG) and can be applied to the members of the Court (§ 69 DRiG). However, the main normative burden of ensuring impartiality is borne by the rules on exclusion and bias already explained (§§ 18 and 19 BVerfGG).

---

in associations and the press on the rule of law and the activities of the judiciary." [translation by the author].

[73] See further, *C. Schröder*, DÖV 78 (2025), 96–106.

[74] Code of Conduct for Judges of the Federal Constitutional Court (*Verhaltensleitlinien für Richterinnen und Richter des Bundesverfassungsgerichts*), Section I.1, available at https://www.bundesverfassungsgericht.de/DE/DasBundesverfassungsgericht/RichterinnenRichter/Verhaltensleitlinien/verhaltensleitlinien_node.html [23.12.2025] [translation by the author]. *Lamprecht*, NJW 52 (1999), 2011–2012 cites a negative example that attracted considerable public attention.

[75] BVerfGE 156, 340 (350 et seqq. para. 26 et seqq.).

V. Overall Assessment

In summary, the information presented in this report confirms the initial statement that the separation of powers is a fundamental component of the German constitutional framework. A central element is not only the combination of horizontal and vertical separation of powers, but also the constitutional organisation of the legislative, executive and judicial branches, which are supposed to work independently of each other but are functionally linked in many ways and based on mutual trust, cooperation, and control. A central player in this structure is the Federal Constitutional Court, which – as an independent, extraordinary court and constitutional organ – interprets the provisions of the Basic Law and ensures that the three branches of government comply with the constitution. Ultimately, it is this multi-layered structure of the separation of powers that ensures that the Federal Republic remains a stable, constitutional and democratic system.

Data Protection and Social Media[1]

Moritz Hennemann

I. General Remarks

Germany as well as the European Union (EU) have a long-standing tradition of data protection legislation.

1. General Sources of EU and German Data Protection Law

The primary current source of data protection legislation in Germany is the EU General Data Protection Regulation (GDPR). The GDPR encompasses detailed rules on inter alia general principles (Chapter 2), rights of the data subject (Chapter 3), obligations of controllers and processors (Chapter 4), principles governing the transfer of personal data to third countries or international organisations (Chapter 5), responsibilities, tasks and powers of independent supervisory authorities (Chapter 6) and remedies, liabilities and penalties (Chapter 8). The primary objective of the GDPR is to protect natural persons. Art. 1(1) GDPR stipulates that the regulation "lays down rules relating to the protection of natural persons with regard to the processing of personal data and rules relating to the free movement of personal data". According to Rec. 2 GDPR, the GDPR also intends "to contribute to the accomplishment of an area of freedom, security and justice, an economic union, economic and social progress, the strengthening and the convergence of the economies within the internal market, and to the well-being of individuals".[2]

The GDPR establishes harmonised data protection standards across the EU of which Germany is a member. The GDPR allows partly for national legislation to be introduced. At the German federal level, this role is fulfilled by the Federal Data Protection Act (BDSG). In addition, data protection laws have been enacted at the level of all 16 German federal states (*Länder*). Sector-specific data protec-

[1] The answers to the general rapporteur's questionnaire were pre-drafted by and prepared with the assistance of my Academic Research Assistants Franziska Ruff and Valerius Blumenthal. I very much thank them for their very valuable support. The content and the fields covered (and not covered) of this country report were very much determined and shaped by the questionnaire. For reasons of readability, this report does not follow exactly the order of the questionnaire's questions but does roughly cluster the topics along the section headings of the questionnaire (general and social media, as well as emerging technologies and trends).

[2] Rec. 2 GDPR.

tion provisions can be found in various statutes, inter alia in the Federal Code of Criminal Procedure (StPO), the Federal Criminal Police Office Act (BKAG), and the Federal Police Act (BPolG). Data protection regulation goes as far as church law (KDG and DSG-EKD).

2. Constitutional Framework(s) for EU and German Data Protection Law

Data protection law is inherently intertwined with constitutional law in Europe in general and in Germany in particular.[3] Art. 1(2) GDPR links the GDPR with EU primary law as it underlines that the GDPR "protects fundamental rights and freedoms of natural persons and in particular their right to the protection of personal data". The EU's primary law deals with data protection in the TFEU (Art. 16) and the CFR. Art. 7 and 8 CFR state fundamental rights to respect for private life and protection of personal data. Accordingly and with regard to Art. 8(2) CFR, personal data may only be collected for a specified purpose and on a legitimate basis, regardless of how it is gathered or who has access to it.[4] As a central control mechanism, everyone must be able to access, rectify, and delete data collected about them (cf. also Art. 8(2) CFR).[5] Fundamental rights set out in EU law are directly applicable if they do not require further action by the member state for implementation. Consequently, these rights can also potentially be invoked in front of national courts.[6]

The German Constitution (*Grundgesetz*) does not explicitly contain provisions related to data protection and privacy, but provisions regarding privacy of telecommunications (Art. 10 GG) and the inviolability of the home (Art. 13 GG). Nevertheless, in 1983, the Federal Constitutional Court established the *right to informational self-determination* – as one dimension of the general right of personality – as enshrined in Art. 2(1) GG in conjunction with Art. 1(1) GG.[7] Conceptionally, the *right to informational self-determination* forms the fundament of German (national) data protection law; it has also been very influential on the EU level and its central pillars (and consequences) can be identified throughout the GDPR. In 2008, the Federal Constitutional Court established a further constitutional dimension by establishing a right to the guarantee of confidentiality and integrity of information technology systems.[8]

---

[3] Cf. *Hennemann*, in: Celeste/Heldt/Keller (eds.), Constitutionalising Social Media, 2022, 141.
[4] *Jarass*, Charta der Grundrechte der EU, 2021, Art. 8 n. 6.
[5] *Jarass*, Charta der Grundrechte der EU, 2021, Art. 8 n. 20.
[6] *Vöneky/Weller*, in: Grabitz/Hilf/Nettesheim (eds.), Das Recht der Europäischen Union, 85th ed. 2025, Art. 216 AUEV n. 42.
[7] BVerfGE 65, 1 (42).
[8] BVerfGE 120, 274.

3. General Data Protection Compliance Mechanism

There are several mechanisms in place for ensuring compliance with data protection laws according to EU and German legislation – the starting point always being that controllers have to have a record of processing activities (Art. 30 GDPR).[9] For every (type of) processing of personal data, a legal ground (legal justification) is required (cf. also Art. 8 CFR). Data processing is generally forbidden, if not explicitly allowed by law. One of the enumerated legal grounds of Art. 6(1) and Art. 9 GDPR (partly in conjunction with further EU or national law) must be fulfilled.[10]

Against this background, first and foremost, according to Art. 24(1) sentence 1 GDPR,

> "[t]aking into account the nature, scope, context and purposes of processing as well as the risks of varying likelihood and severity for the rights and freedoms of natural persons, the controller shall implement appropriate technical and organisational measures to ensure and to be able to demonstrate that processing is performed in accordance with [the GDPR]."

An appropriate technical and organisational measure (TOM) might be, for instance, pseudonymisation, Art. 25(1) GDPR. Based on the risk at stake, TOMs should ensure "that, by default, only personal data which are necessary for each specific purpose of the processing are processed" (Art. 25(2) GDPR). The GDPR requires *data protection by design* and *by default.*[11] Furthermore, "where a type of processing, in particular using new technologies, and taking into account the nature, scope, context and purposes of the processing, is likely to result in a high risk to the rights and freedoms of natural persons", the controller has to conduct a data protection impact assessment according to Art. 35 GDPR.[12]

In addition, mandatory reporting duties in case of breaches are established by the GDPR. If a personal data breach occurs, "the controller shall without undue delay and, where feasible, not later than 72 hours after having become aware of it, notify the personal data breach to the supervisory authority competent […], unless the personal data breach is unlikely to result in a risk to the rights and freedoms of natural persons" (Art. 33(1) GDPR). In cases of a likely high risk, "the controller shall [also] communicate the personal data breach to the data subject without undue delay" (Art. 34(1) GDPR).

---

[9] See for details *Füllsack/Kirschke-Biller*, in: Gerecke (ed.), Handbuch Social-Media-Recht, 1st ed. 2023, 289.

[10] See for more details on different legal justification – in the context of social media – sub III.1.

[11] In detail (with regard to social media platforms) *Füllsack/Kirschke-Biller*, in: Gerecke (ed.), Handbuch Social-Media-Recht, 1st ed., 2023, 288.

[12] See for details *Füllsack/Kirschke-Biller*, in: Gerecke (ed.), Handbuch Social-Media-Recht, 1st ed. 2023, 290 et seq.

4. Data Subject's Rights

Data subjects have various rights based in data protection law regarding their personal data.[13] These rights are set out in Chapter III of the GDPR, whereby Art. 12 GDPR stipulates for all rights basis requirements with regard to transparent information, communication, and modalities for the exercise of respective rights – and thereby general procedural rules.[14] Especially and also with regard to Art. 8(2) CFR, transparency of processing is essential. Consequently, Art. 13 and 14 GDPR stipulate information duties depending on whether the personal data has been obtained from the data subject directly or from another source. Art. 15 GDPR establishes the access right of the data subject. It includes inter alia the right to request confirmation of whether and which kind of personal data has been processed.[15]

The right to rectification according to Art. 16 GDPR offers the data subject the possibility to correct and supplement the information collected. Art. 17 GDPR sets out the right to erasure (also known as the "right to be forgotten"), which obliges the controller to delete personal data relating to the data subject in specific circumstances. Respective circumstances encompass inter alia situations in which the processing is unlawful, the legal ground is no longer given, or the data subject is withdrawing her consent. The data subject may also restrict the processing of their data if the reasons listed in Art. 18 GDPR are fulfilled. Furthermore, according to Art. 19 GDPR, any rectifications, erasures, or restrictions relating to the processing of personal data must be communicated to the relevant recipient.

Finally, the right to data portability (Art. 20 GDPR) aims to ensure and to enlarge the control of the data subject with respect for the personal data provided – the data is to be made available in a structured, machine-readable manner to the data subject and/or a named third party. Thereby, Art. 20 GDPR offers the data subject the option to request a transfer from one controller to another. This right is meant to prevent so-called *lock in*-effects – as it shall (at least in theory) reduce/minimise switching costs between controllers.[16] In this regard, it is fair to argue that the right also bears a "competition law"-dimension.[17]

---

[13] See for an introduction (with regard to social media platforms) *Füllsack/Kirschke-Biller*, in: Gerecke (ed.), Handbuch Social-Media-Recht, 1st ed. 2023, 281 et seqq.

[14] Cf. for details *Hennemann*, in: Paal/Pauly, DS-GVO BDSG, 4th ed. 2026, Art. 12 DS-GVO n. 1 et seqq.

[15] Cf. for details *Paal*, in: Paal/Pauly, DS-GVO BDSG, 4th ed. 2026, Art. 15 DS-GVO n. 1 et seqq.

[16] Cf. in detail and with regard to social media *Hennemann*, in: Celeste/Heldt/Keller (eds.), Constitutionalising Social Media, 2022, 143.

[17] In detail, *Hennemann*, PinG 2017, 5; *Paal*, in: Paal/Pauly, DS-GVO BDSG, 4th ed. 2026, Art. 20 DS-GVO n. 4 et seqq.

5. Data Security

The GDPR also addresses aspects of data security – the key norm being Art. 32 GDPR aiming at the highest possible level of processing reliability.[18] Thus, controllers

"shall implement appropriate technical and organisational measures to ensure a level of security appropriate to the risk, including inter alia as appropriate: (a) the pseudonymisation and encryption of personal data; (b) the ability to ensure the ongoing confidentiality, integrity, availability and resilience of processing systems and services; (c) the ability to restore the availability and access to personal data in a timely manner in the event of a physical technical incident [and] (d) a process for regularly testing, assessing and evaluating the effectiveness of technical and organisational measures for ensuring the security of the processing". (Art. 32(1)(a-d) GDPR)

Sector-specific duties have to be adhered to in addition. For example, Sec. 19(4) Telecommunications Digital Services Data Protection Act (TDDDG) stipulates that – insofar as this is technically possible and economically reasonable – providers shall ensure measures to avoid unauthorized access to the technical facilities they use to offer their digital services, including those caused by external attacks.

6. Enforcement

Various civil law, criminal law, and public law options (penalties, fines, and administrative sanctions) exist to ensure compliance with data protection.[19] In practical terms, EU and German data protection regulation relies on a duality of *private* and *public enforcement*.

a) Public Enforcement

According to the GDPR (and national law), controllers are held accountable for violating data protection provisions by supervisory authorities and their enforcement powers. Especially, Art. 83 GDPR offers the options of fines for violations of the GDPR. The amount of the fines depends on various factors, including the nature, severity, and duration of the infringement (Art. 83(2) GDPR) – e.g., violations of Art. 12–22 GDPR (data subject's rights) may lead to fines of up to € 20 million or up to 4 % of the respective company's global annual turnover.

Furthermore, Art. 58 GDPR also grants the competent supervisory authority corrective powers such as warnings, reprimands, and deletion obligations. In addition, fines are possible on the basis of sector-specific (national) law. Sec. 28 TDDDG, for example, provides the option of imposing fines for respective viola-

---

[18] *Martini*, in: Paal/Pauly, DS-GVO BDSG, Art. 32 DS-GVO n. 3.

[19] Cf. in detail *Füllsack/Kirschke-Biller*, in: Gerecke (ed.), Handbuch Social-Media-Recht, 1st ed. 2023, 295 et seqq.

tions of the TDDDG. Further, (public law) sanctions might flow from further EU and national law.[20]

In total, Germany has 18 data protection supervisory authorities (Art. 51(1) GDPR) that are responsible for the public enforcement of data protection law. There is one Federal Commissioner for Data Protection and Freedom of Information (BfDI)[21] and each of the German states also has its own State Commissioner for Data Protection (and Freedom of Information) (LfDI)[22]; Bavaria being the only state with two (one being responsible for data protection with regard to private actors;[23] the other one being responsible for public entities)[24]. The BfDI is responsible for supervising the federal public entities (e. g., the German Federal Ministries); regardless of whether they act as such or operate via public law or publicly controlled undertakings.[25] Furthermore, the BfDI is also responsible for companies that process data of natural or legal persons in the course of telecommunications services, cf. Sec. 29 TDDDG.[26] The LfDIs are responsible for supervising private actors (located in the respective state) as well as the public entities of that very state.[27] Furthermore, additional data protection supervisory authorities exist in specific areas, such as the joint Broadcasting Commissioner for Data Protection.[28]

b) Private Enforcement

According to Art. 82(1) GDPR, "anyone who has suffered material or non-material damage as a result of an infringement of [the GDPR] shall have the right to receive compensation from the controller or processor for the damage suffered".[29] Any controller or processor involved in the data processing who caused the damage is liable, however, with the possibility of exculpation under specific circumstances (Art. 82(2) GDPR). The injured person is guaranteed full compensation for the damage by holding each controller or processor liable for the total

---

20 See sub III.5.d).

21 Sec. 9 BDSG.

22 Sec. 20 LDSG (BW); Art. 15, 18 BayDSG; Sec. 7 BlnDSG; Sec. 14 BbgDSG; Sec. 16 BremDSGVOAG; Sec. 19 HmbDSG; Sec. 8 HDSIG; Sec. 15 DSG M-V; Sec. 18 NDSG; Sec. 25 DSG NRW; Sec. 14 LDSG (RLP); Sec. 16 SDSG; Sec. 15 SächsDSDG; Sec. 22 DSAG LSA; Sec. 17 LDSG (SH); Sec. 3 ThürDSG.

23 Art. 18 (1) BayDSG.

24 Art. 15 (1) BayDSG.

25 Sec. 9 (1) BDSG.

26 Cf. also Sec. 9 (1) BDSG.

27 Sec. 25 LDSG (BW); Art. 15, 18 BayDSG; Sec. 8 BlnDSG; Sec. 18 BbgDSG; Sec. 21 BremDSGVOAG; Sec. 19 HmbDSG; Sec. 13 HDSIG; Sec. 19 DSG M-V; Sec. 22 NDSG; Sec. 26 DSG NRW; Sec. 15 LDSG (RLP); Sec. 16 SDSG; Sec. 14 SächsDSDG; Sec. 22 DSAG LSA; Sec. 17 LDSG (SH); Sec. 4 ThürDSG.

28 Sec. 31j MStV.

29 Art. 82 (1) GDPR.

damage in cases involving multiple controllers or processors (Art. 82(4) GDPR).[30]

If a data protection provision mirrors/equals a contractual duty between the parties, a violation may (also) lead to claims under contract law. Damages can also – under specific circumstances – be obtained under German tort law, especially Sec. 823(1) German Civil Code (BGB), if the breach of data protection law amounts to a violation of the general right of personality[31] or other absolute rights.[32] If criminal offences are committed, tort law claims may also arise (Sec. 823(2) BGB). The GDPR itself does not stipulate any criminal offences, but leaves this option to the member states. The BDSG stipulates criminal sanctions for specific data protection law violations (Sec. 42 and 43 BDSG). It does, for example, impose sanctions (imprisonment or fine) on anyone who trades or processes private personal data without authorisation (Sec. 42(1) and (2) BDSG). Furthermore, breaches of data protection law might go along with additional criminal offences, e.g., spying on data (Sec. 203 German Criminal Code (StGB)), interception of data (Sec. 202b StGB), data modification (Sec. 303a StGB), sabotage (Sec. 303b StGB), and violation of confidentiality (Sec. 203 StGB).

Furthermore, a violation of data protection provisions might also – with further requirements – lead to additional (private) enforcement options under the law of unfair competition (Sec. 3a Unfair Competition Act (UWG)[33]) and competition law (Sec. 33 et seq. Competition Act (GWB))[34].

From a procedural point of view, it is important to highlight that collective interest bodies (e.g., consumer protection associations) might also enforce data protection law within the EU.[35]

---

30 *Gola/Piltz,* in: Gola/Heckmann, DS-GVO, 3rd ed. 2022, DS-GVO Art. 82 n. 7, 8.

31 See sub I.2.

32 *Gola/Piltz,* in Gola/Heckmann, DS-GVO, 3rd ed. 2022, DS-GVO Art. 82 n. 4.

33 Cf. for example LG Düsseldorf, ZD 2024, 410 as well as – with regard to the information duties – *Hennemann*, in: Paal/Pauly, DS-GVO BDSG, 4th ed. 2026, Art. 13 DS-GVO n. 9c and 9f with further references. For detail cf. *Füllsack/Kirschke-Biller*, in: Gerecke (ed.), Handbuch Social-Media-Recht, 1st ed. 2023, 298 et seq.

34 Cf., in particular, CJEU, judgment of 4.7.2023 – Case C-252/21 (Meta Platforms Inc. v Bundeskartellamt), ECLI:EU:C:2023:537, marginal no. 62; BGH, GRUR 2020, 1318; OLG Düsseldorf, GRUR-RS 2019, 18837.

35 Cf. e.g., CJEU, judgment of 11.7.2024 – Case C-757/22 (Meta Platforms Ireland Ltd v Verbraucherzentrale Bundesverband eV), ECLI:EU:C:2024:598; as well as – with further references – *Assion*, NJW 2024, 2590, 2591.

II. General Regulatory Framework for Social Media Platforms

1. Data Protection Regulation

The GDPR does not *specifically* address the collecting and/or other forms of processing of personal data collected through social media platforms[36], but the GDPR regards social media platforms as a prime use case of and for data protection law[37] and applies – taking into consideration the material, territorial, and personal scope (Art. 2 and 3 GDPR) – generally to the processing of personal data by social media platforms.[38, 39] Especially, the processing of personal data by social media platforms in the context of their activities in Germany/targeted at the German market is within the scope of the GDPR.[40] The GDPR legislator was, however, not unaware of social media platforms as such. This awareness is mirrored in Rec. 18 – in the context of the so-called "household exemption" –, where it is said that the GDPR

> "does not apply to the processing of personal data by a natural person in the course of a purely personal or household activity and thus with no connection to a professional or commercial activity. Personal or household activities could include correspondence and the holding of addresses, or *social networking* and online activity undertaken within the context of such activities" (emphasis added).

At the same time, it is underlined that the household exemption does not bar the applicability of the GDPR to the very platforms ("applies to controllers or processors which provide the means for processing personal data for such personal or household activities").[41]

---

[36] *Social media* and *social media platforms* are understood in line with the definition by the EDPB (Guidelines 8/2020 on the targeting of social media users, Version 2.0 (13.4.2021) n. 1, https://www.edpb.europa.eu/system/files/2021-04/edpb_guidelines_082020_on_the_targeting_of_social_media_users_en.pdf (7.1.2026)): "Key characteristics of social media include the ability for individuals to register in order to create "accounts" or "profiles" for themselves, to interact with one another by sharing user-generated or other content and to develop connections and networks with other users.".

[37] See *Hennemann*, in: Celeste/Heldt/Keller (eds.), Constitutionalising Social Media, 2022, 140.

[38] See in detail in this regard *Hennemann*, in: Celeste/Heldt/Keller (eds.), Constitutionalising Social Media, 2022, 139 et seq. as well as specifically with regard to the material, territorial, and personal scope *Füllsack/Kirschke-Biller*, in: Gerecke (ed.), Handbuch Social-Media-Recht, 1st ed. 2023, 235 et seqq.

[39] Beyond the scope of this country report is the even more challenging discussion whether and to what extent EU data protection law does actually *effectively* and *efficiently* regulate social media platforms, see in this regard *Hennemann*, in: Celeste/Heldt/Keller (eds.), Constitutionalising Social Media, 2022, 143 et seqq.

[40] See generally for details – from the perspective of the data protection authorities – EDPB, Guidelines 8/2020 on the targeting of social media users, Version 2.0 (13.4.2021), https://www.edpb.europa.eu/system/files/2021-04/edpb_guidelines_082020_on_the_targeting_of_social_media_users_en.pdf (7.1.2026).

[41] In detail on the household exemption with regard to social media *Füllsack/Kirschke-Biller*, in: Gerecke (ed.), Handbuch Social-Media-Recht, 1st ed. 2023, 236 et seq.

Moreover, the TDDDG is a sector-specific data protection law[42] (also and additionally[43]) governing digital services (and also implementing the E-Privacy-Directive).[44] A provider of digital services is defined as "any natural or legal person who provides their own or third-party digital services, participates in the provision thereof, or facilitates access to the use of their own or third-party digital services"[45] – and includes social media platforms.[46] Sec. 19–26 TDDDG set out inter alia the rules relating to technical and organisational measures in the context of the usage of services, the processing of personal data of minors, the information procedure for basic and traffic-related data, the information procedure for passwords and other access-related data, the recognised consent management services, and end user settings. Of specific interest in the context of social media platforms is Sec. 19(2) TDDDG according to which a digital service has to offer its services with anonymous payment methods and under a pseudonym (if technical feasible and not too burdensome).[47]

To the extent, the activities of social media platforms qualify as journalistic or media activity, further media law provisions come into play. In these cases, social media platforms might also benefit from the so-called "media privileges" (on the basis of Art. 85 GDPR) in federal and state laws (cf., e.g., Sec. 23 MStV, Sec. 12 PresseG BW; Art. 39 BayDSG).[48]

2. Specific Regulation

Specific regulation of social media platforms exists on the EU and on the national level.

a) Digital Services Act

Primarily, social media platforms are specifically regulated by the Digital Services Act (DSA) – the EU's legislative cornerstone in this regard.[49] The DSA encompasses inter alia provisions on the liability of providers of intermediary services (Chapter II), including, for example, online platforms (Art. 3(g)(iii) DSA, Art. 3

---

[42] See also the references to German youth protection law sub III.5.b) and d).

[43] See *v. Lewinski/Rüpke/Eckhardt*, Datenschutzrecht, 3rd ed. 2025, § 18 n. 109.

[44] Cf. for an introduction *v. Lewinski/Rüpke/Eckhardt*, Datenschutzrecht, 3rd ed. 2025, § 18 n. 1 et seqq.

[45] Sec. 2(2) No. 1 TDDDG.

[46] *Füllsack/Kirschke-Biller*, in: Gerecke (ed.), Handbuch Social-Media-Recht, 1st ed. 2023, 241.

[47] Cf. also BGH, NJW 2022, 1314. It is, however, debated whether a respective national provision is in line with EU data protection law, cf. *Gola/Klug*, NJW 2022, 2597, 2599 as well as *Füllsack/Kirschke-Biller*, in: Gerecke (ed.), Handbuch Social-Media-Recht, 1st ed. 2023, 244 et seqq.

[48] Cf. *Pauly*, in: Paal/Pauly, DS-GVO BDSG, 4th ed. 2026 Art. 85 DS-GVO n. 4.

[49] Until recently, the German Network Enforcement Act (NetzDG) stipulated rules for social media platforms and served as a role model for the DSA, cf. *Raue/Heesen*, NJW 2022, 3537, 3541; *Gerdemann/Spindler*, GRUR 2023, 115, 125.

(i) DSA) like social networks[50], as well as due diligence obligations (Chapter III) – and thus sets out "rules for a safe, predictable and trusted online environment that facilitates innovation and in which fundamental rights enshrined in the [CFR], including the principle of consumer protection, are effectively protected".[51]

The *Digitale-Dienste-Gesetz* (DDG) is the German DSA Implementation Act. The DDG came into force in May 2024. "Effective, proportionate and dissuasive" (Art. 52 DSA) sanctions for violations are stipulated by Sec. 33(6) DDG. There is a standardised three-tier penalty system ranging from € 50,000 to € 300,000. According to Sec. 33(7), DDG higher sanctions in certain cases are possible for legal entities, depending on their annual revenue.

Different authorities have been tasked by the DDG to enforce different parts of the DSA (insofar as not a European Commission competence is established by the DSA). Sec. 12(1) DDG stipulates that the German Federal Network Agency (BNetzA) is generally (and primarily) responsible for supervising providers of intermediary services and thereby enforcing the DSA (Art. 49(1) DSA) in Germany. According to Sec. 12(2) DDG, the Federal Agency for the Protection of Children and Young People is responsible for services that mainly address minors. Furthermore, the BfDI is responsible for supervising profiled advertisements using personal data, as set out in Art. 26(3) and in Art. 28(2) and (3) DSA. Hosting service providers are required to address the Federal Criminal Police Office (BKA) when suspecting "that a criminal offence involving a threat to the life or safety of a person or persons has taken place, is taking place or is likely to take place".[52]

The DDG does not only implement requirements set by the DSA, but also includes supplementary legislation in other areas (if not covered by the DSA), replacing the former German Telemedia Act (TMG) and the former NetzDG.[53] The TMG established legal boundaries for electronic information and communication services, including search engines, online shops, and chat rooms. For instance, it required these platforms to have a visible imprint, combat spam, and accept liability for illegal content under certain conditions.[54] The NetzDG mainly contained compliance rules for social media platform providers in the event of specific criminal actions.[55]

---

[50] Rec. 13 DSA.

[51] Art. 1 (1) DSA.

[52] Art. 18 (1) DSA in conjunction with Sec. 13 DDG; *Paschke/Wernicke*, in Taeger/Pohle (eds.), Computerrechts-Handbuch, 40. EL 2025, n. 96.

[53] Federal Law Gazette 2024 I, 149; *Stögmüller*, NJW 2024, 3758.

[54] Cf. *Spindler*, in Spindler/Schmitz (eds.), Telemediengesetz mit Netzdurchführungsgesetz, 2nd ed. 2018, § 1 TMG n. 75 et seqq., § 5 TMG n. 41 et seqq., § 6 TMG n. 30 et seqq., vor §§ 7–10 TMG n. 1 et seqq.

[55] *Liesching*, in Spindler/Schmitz (eds.), Telemediengesetz mit Netzdurchführungsgesetz, 2nd ed. 2018, § 3 NetzDG n. 1 et seqq.

b) Other

Social media platforms are further specifically regulated by German media law. In particular, the Media Law Treaty (MStV) of the German *Länder* defines in Sec. 2 (2) No. 16 MStV "media intermediaries" as "any telemedia that also aggregates, selects and presents journalistic and editorial content from third parties in a generally accessible manner without combining it into a comprehensive offering". This may also include, among other things, social media services[56] and goes along with specific duties (cf. Sec. 91–96 MStV).

Since 2022, the German Civil Code contains specific contract law provisions (Sec. 327 et seqq. BGB) relating to contracts for digital products, which includes the business model of social media platforms (i. e., services in exchange to (a data protection consent to) data (processing)).[57] The provisions were introduced on the basis of the EU directive "on certain aspects concerning contracts for the supply of digital content and digital services"[58].[59] Most importantly, the provisions accept the notion of data as counter-performance (cf. Sec. 327(3) BGB) and explicitly target the contractual consequences of a withdrawal of a data protection consent declaration (cf. Sec. 327q BGB).

Additionally, the EU's Digital Single Market (DSM) Directive via the respective German Implementation Act (Copyright Law Services Act (UrhDaG)) obliges media platforms to monitor uploaded content with regard to copyright infringements – and thereby safeguarding copyright protected works. The monitoring is and can typically be achieved through the use of upload filters (Sec. 7 UrhDaG).

III. Selected Fields Relating To Social Media Platforms

1. Consent and Other Legal Justifications for Processing

Generally, social media platforms require the user's consent in order to process personal data of that very user. According to Art. 6(1)(a) GDPR, social media companies and platforms – as other data controllers – are required to obtain consent before collecting or sharing user data (assuming that the data processing does not fall under one of the other potential legal grounds as spelled out by Art. 6(1)(b)-(f) GDPR and/or Art. 9(2)(b)-(j) GDPR).[60]

Art. 4 No. 11, Art. 6(1)(a), and Art. 7 GDPR set the general standards for a valid consent declaration. According to Art. 4 No. 11 GDPR consent refers to "any

---

[56] VG Schleswig, MMR 2025, 837, 838.

[57] *Metzger*, in Säcker et al. (eds.), Münchener Kommentar zum Bürgerlichen Gesetzbuch, 10th ed., Vol. I, 2025, § 327 BGB n. 8.

[58] Directive (EU) 2019/770.

[59] Federal Law Gazette 2021 I, 2133.

[60] See in detail on the legality of personal data processing by social media platforms, *Füllsack/Kirschke-Biller*, in: Gerecke (ed.), Handbuch Social-Media-Recht, 1st ed. 2023, 255 et seqq.

freely given, specific, informed and unambiguous indication of the data subject's wishes by which he or she, by a statement or by a clear affirmative action, signifies agreement to the processing of personal data relating to him or her". According to Rec. 32:

"[c]onsent should be given by a clear affirmative act establishing a freely given, specific, informed and unambiguous indication of the data subject's agreement to the processing of their personal data"; this can be done verbally, in writing, or electronically. The declaration of consent does not need to be explicit, but must be established by some affirmative action. With regard to special categories of data (Art. 9 GDPR)[61] – to the opposite –, "explicit consent to the processing" is required (Art. 9(2)(a) GDPR).[62]

Furthermore, consent must be freely given.[63] The data subject must have a genuine and free choice.[64] According to Art. 7(4) GDPR,

"[w]hen assessing whether consent is freely given, utmost account shall be taken of whether, inter alia, the performance of a contract, including the provision of a service, is conditional on consent to the processing of personal data that is not necessary for the performance of that contract".

However, the provision establishes (only) an assumption, not an absolute ban of a conditionality of consent declarations. It can be particularly problematic to determine whether a free decision has been made "where there is a clear imbalance of power between the data subject and the controller".[65] According to the CJEU, "the fact that the operator of an online social network holds a dominant position on the market for online social networks" may create a clear imbalance.[66] Nevertheless, this dominant position "does not, as such, preclude the users of such a network from being able validly to consent, within the meaning of [Art. 4(11) GDPR]".[67] Whether or not consent has been freely given, it also and heavily debated in so-called "consent or pay"-scenarios – especially in the context of social media platforms.[68]

---

[61] On Art. 9 GDPR in the context of social media platforms see in detail, *Füllsack/Kirschke-Biller*, in: Gerecke (ed.), Handbuch Social-Media-Recht, 1st ed. 2023, 263 et seqq.

[62] Cf. in this regard also CJEU, judgment of 4.7.2023 – Case C-252/21 (Meta Platforms Inc. v Bundeskartellamt), ECLI:EU:C:2023:537, marginal no. 64 et seqq.

[63] Art. 4 (11) GDPR; Rec. 43 GDPR.

[64] Rec. 42 GDPR.

[65] Rec. 43 GDPR.

[66] CJEU, judgment of 4.7.2023 – Case C-252/21 (Meta Platforms Inc. v Bundeskartellamt), ECLI:EU:C:2023:537, marginal no. 154.

[67] CJEU, judgment of 4.7.2023 – Case C-252/21 (Meta Platforms Inc. v Bundeskartellamt), ECLI:EU:C:2023:537, marginal no. 154.

[68] See for a court decision affirming a valid consent with respect to Meta's consent and pay model, LG Regensburg, GRUR-RS 2024, 11690. In general and in detail – whereas different aspects are highly debatable (cf. *Assion*, NJW 2024, 2590, 2592 et seq.) – EDPB, Opinion 08/2024 on Valid Consent in the Context of Consent or Pay Models Implemented by Large Online Platforms (17.4.2024), https://www.edpb.europa.eu/system/files/2024-04/edpb_opinion_202408_consentorpay_en.pdf (7.1.2026); the opinion was (unsuccessfully due to procedural reasons) challenged by Meta, cf. EGC, order of 29.4.2025 – Case T-319/24 (Meta Platforms Ireland Ltd v

According to Art. 7(3) sentence 1 GDPR, the data subject has always the right to withdraw his or her consent to the processing of their data at any time. The withdrawal of consent shall not affect the lawfulness of processing based on consent before its withdrawal (Art. 7(3) sentence 2 GDPR). Furthermore, the data subject shall be informed of his or her right to withdrawal prior to giving consent (Art. 7(3) sentence 3 GDPR).

It has to be highlighted, however, that the processing of personal by social media platform might – depending on the single case – be justified by one of the other grounds mentioned in Art. 6(1)(b)-(f) GDPR – and therefore not require consent according to Art. 6(1)(a) GDPR. In this regard, it has to be noted that data processing of social media platforms might be based (in parts) on Art. 6 (1)(b), (c), and (f) GDPR. The CJEU holds:

"[Art. 6(1)(b)] GDPR must be interpreted as meaning that the processing of personal data by the operator of an online social network, which entails the collection of data of the users of such a network from other services of the group to which that operator belongs or from visits by those users to third-party websites or apps, the linking of those data with the social network account of those users and the use of those data, can be regarded as necessary for the performance of a contract to which the data subjects are party, within the meaning of that provision, only on condition that the processing is objectively indispensable for a purpose that is integral to the contractual obligation intended for those users, such that the main subject matter of the contract cannot be achieved if that processing does not occur.

[…] [Art. 6(1)(f)] GDPR must be interpreted as meaning that such processing can be regarded as necessary for the purposes of the legitimate interests pursued by the controller or by a third party, within the meaning of that provision, only on condition that the operator has informed the users from whom the data have been collected of a legitimate interest that is pursued by the data processing, that such processing is carried out only in so far as is strictly necessary for the purposes of that legitimate interest and that it is apparent from a balancing of the opposing interests, having regard to all the relevant circumstances, that the interests or fundamental freedoms and rights of those users do not override that legitimate interest of the controller or of a third party.

[…] [Art. 6(1)(c)] GDPR must be interpreted as meaning that the processing of personal data by the operator of an online social network, which entails the collection of data of the users of such a network from other services of the group to which that operator belongs or from visits by those users to third-party websites or apps, the linking of those data with the social network account of those users and the use of those data, is justified, under that provision, where it is actually necessary for compliance with a legal obligation to which the controller is subject, pursuant to a provision of EU law or the law of the Member State concerned, where that legal basis meets an objective of public interest and is proportionate to the legitimate aim pursued and where that processing is carried out only in so far as is strictly necessary."[69]

European Data Protection Board), ECLI:EU:T:2025:435. Furthermore, Meta's consent or pay models was challenged under the DMA, cf. European Commission, Press Release: Commission finds Apple and Meta in breach of the Digital Markets Act (23.4.2025), https://ec.europa.eu/commission/presscorner/detail/en/ip_25_1085 (7.1.2026).

[69] CJEU, judgment of 4.7.2023 – Case C-252/21 (Meta Platforms Inc. v Bundeskartellamt), ECLI:EU:C:2023:537, marginal no. 125, 126, 138.

Furthermore, just recently and heavily discussed in German literature, the Higher Regional Court of Cologne ruled that Meta is allowed to use (personal) user data to train its artificial intelligence (AI) without consent of users as the processing can fall under Art. 6(1)(f) GDPR (Art. 9(1) GDPR was regarded as not being applicable).[70]

2. Options To Control

Both EU and German legislation do require social media platforms to provide users with options to control their account's privacy settings (next to the data subject's rights). If processing is based on consent, such consent can be changed or withdrawn (Art. 7(3) GDPR). Furthermore, according to Art. 21 GDPR, users have the right to object to processing, such as profiling, if processing is based on Art. 6(1)(e) and (f) GDPR.

3. Options Re Profiling

Profiling is generally regulated by the GDPR in different dimensions (e. g., special information duties exist; e. g., Art. 13(2)(f) GDPR) and is defined by Art. 4 No. 4 GDPR as

> "any form of automated processing of personal data consisting of the use of personal data to evaluate certain personal aspects relating to a natural person, in particular to analyse or predict aspects concerning that natural person's performance at work, economic situation, health, personal preferences, interests, reliability, behaviour, location or movements".

If profiling amounts to an automatic decision making, Art. 22 GDPR sets respective regulatory boundaries.

Furthermore, according to the TDDDG, social media platforms (as well as other digital service providers) generally need to give users the option to refuse profiling via cookies or similar tracking technologies. Sec. 25(1) TDDDG states that storing or accessing information on the user's device is only allowed if the user has given prior and informed consent. There are only narrow exceptions according to Sec. 25(2) TDDDG (e. g., if a cookie is strictly necessary for providing a service explicitly requested by the user or to transmit a message over a public network).

The already discussed TDDDG implements the E-Privacy-Directive. According to Art. 5(3) E-Privacy-Directive the use of cookies is only allowed

> "on condition that the subscriber or user concerned is provided with clear and comprehensive information in accordance with Directive 95/46/EC [the predecessor of the GPDR], inter alia about the purposes of the processing, and is offered the right to refuse such processing by the data controller."

---

70 OLG Cologne, NJW 2025, 3156 (3158 et seq.); cf. *Assion*, NJW 2025, 2595, 2596.

The E-Privacy-Directive was implemented in Germany for a long time primarily through the TMG and the German Telecommunications Act (TKG). However, this implementation was found to be incomplete by the CJEU.[71] In particular, the cookie consent requirement (Art. 5(3) E-Privacy-Directive) was not correctly implemented. Subsequently, the E-Privacy-Directive was fully transposed into German law by the Telecommunications Data Protection Act (TTDSG) – recently transformed into the TDDDG.

There are also long-standing and heavily discussed proposals to reform or supplement the E-Privacy-Directive.[72]

4. Retention Periods

Social media platforms are not required by the GDPR to retain data for specific periods to protect user rights. Instead, the principles of storage limitation and data minimisation apply (Art. 5(1)(c) and (e) GDPR). The precise data retention periods depend on the individual contracts as well as the respective consent declarations of the data subjects.

5. Protection of Vulnerable People

a) Elderly People

There is no specific legislation regarding the protection of the elderly's data.

b) Minors

Due to a greater vulnerability and need for protection, there is specific data protection law legislation covering the protection of minors' personal data.[73] The following examples illustrate this approach.

Art. 12(1) GDPR stipulates that any information (e. g., according to Art. 13 and 14 GDPR) must be in a clear and simple language, especially if given to a child. Art. 8 GDPR specifies the requirements for a minor's consent declaration according to Art. 6(1)(a) GDPR ("in relation to the offer of information society services directly to a child"). Any processing of a data relating to a minor under the age of 16 is only legal if there is consent of their parent or guardian (or if member state law provides for a longer threshold than 16 years (but with a set minimum of 13 years)). Sec. 20 TDDDG targets cases where a digital service provider has col-

[71] CJEU, judgment of 1.10.2019 – C-673/17 (Verbraucherzentrale Bundesverband e.V. v Planet49 GmbH), ECLI:EU:C:2019:801.

[72] Cf. https://www.europarl.europa.eu/committees/de/e-privacy-reform/product-details/20170329CDT01341 (7.1.2026) as well as – just recently COM (2025) 837 final (proposal of Art. 88a et seq. GDPR (draft)).

[73] See in detail on data protection law and minors, *Füllsack/Kirschke-Biller*, in: Gerecke (ed.), Handbuch Social-Media-Recht, 1st ed. 2023, 278 et seqq.

lected personal data from minors for the purpose of protecting them, for example through age verification or other technical measures, or has obtained such data in any other way. According to Sec. 20 TDDDG, this data may not be processed for commercial purposes, such as profiling or advertisement tailored to the minor's usage behaviour; no exceptions can be made, meaning that neither consent nor any other legal data processing according Art. 6 GDPR can override the prohibition.[74]

Art. 28 DSA specifically targets the online protection of minors. According to Art. 28(1) DSA, "providers of online platforms accessible to minors shall put in place appropriate and proportionate measures to ensure a high level of privacy, safety, and security of minors, on their service." Furthermore, Art. 28(2) DSA stipulates that respective providers "shall not present advertisements on their interface based on profiling [as defined in Art. 4 No. 4 GDPR] […] using personal data of the recipient of the service when they are aware with reasonable certainty that the recipient of the service is a minor." Furthermore, providers of online platforms are not obliged to "process additional personal data in order to assess whether the recipient of the service is a minor" (Art. 28(3) DSA).

Moreover attention is to be drawn to the Interstate Treaty on the Protection of Human Dignity and Minors in Broadcasting and Telemedia (JMStV) of the German *Länder* – aiming at the creation of a coherent system for the protection of children and teenagers in electronic information and communication media (cf. Sec. 1 JMStV). According to Sec. 2(1) JMStV, the State Treaty applies to telemedia within the meaning of the MStV and thus also to social media.

The German Youth Protection Law (JuSchG) also has a similar protective function. Besides protection in the public (Chapter 2), it also provides for protection of minors in the media (Chapter 3). "Media" within the meaning of the JuSchG encompasses – according to Sec. 1(1a) JuSchG – inter alia digital services. Digital services are understood (Art. 1(3) JuSchG) as digital services according to Sec. 1 (4)(1) DDG in conjunction with Art. 1(1)(b) Directive (EU) 2015/1535 as "any service normally provided for remuneration, at a distance, by electronic means and at the individual request of a recipient of services." In this context, it has been argued that the term "renumeration" must be interpreted broadly (for example covering situations where the service is financed by advertisements or by the sale of data).[75] Consequently, social media platforms are covered by the scope of application.[76] For this reason, the legislative protection also includes protection from media that impairs development, media that is harmful to minors, and

[74] *Schreiber*, in: Geppert/Schütz (eds.), Beck'scher TKG-Kommentar, § 20 TDDDG n. 2 et seqq., 58 et seqq., 62 et seqq.

[75] *Gerdemann*, in: Nomos Handkommentar DDG, 1st ed. 2025, § 1 n. 20.

[76] Cf. *Gerdemann*, in: Nomos Handkommentar DDG, 1st ed. 2025, § 1 n. 20; *Liesching*, in: BeckOK JugendschutzR, 5th ed. 1.6.2025, JuSchG § 1 n. 31d.

protection of the personal integrity of children and young people when using media (Sec. 10a(1–4) JuSchG).[77]

c) *Age Verification*

According to Art. 8(2) GDPR, "[t]he controller shall make reasonable efforts to verify in […] [the] cases [of Art. 8(1) GDPR] that consent is given or authorised by the holder of parental responsibility over the child, taking into consideration available technology."[78] In addition, theoretically on the basis of national youth protection regulation, according to Sec. 2(2) JuSchG, if in doubt, the business must verify the customer's age.

There is no general age requirement for social media use in Germany. Concluding the contract underlying the social media service (platform use contract), however, requires consent of the parents (or another guardian with the power of attorney to act in the name of the child).[79] The validity of the contract is not a question of data protection law, but of national contract law (Art. 8(3) GDPR).[80]

Also, it has to be borne in mind that the data protection consent declaration can only be validly given by the child itself if older than 16 years.[81] However, and also very recently, initiatives are being taken to implement new regulation with regard to age verification in Germany and within the EU.[82]

d) *Sanctions*

Insofar as GDPR provisions are violated and depending on the specific violation, damages and administrative sanctions as well as criminal sanctions according to national law are possible (Art. 82–83 GDPR).[83] For example, in the case of a breach of Art. 8 GDPR, Art. 83(4)(a) GDPR provides for fines of up to € 10 million or, if the offender is a company, up to 2 % of its total worldwide annual turnover in the previous financial year, whichever is higher. These sanctions ap-

---

[77] For the interplay between the DSA and the JuSchG cf. *Liesching*, in: BeckOK JugendschutzR, 5th ed. 1.6.2025, JuSchG § 10a n. 2a.

[78] See for details EDPB, Guidelines 05/2020 on consent under Regulation 2016/679, Version 1.1 (4.5.2020), marginal no. 124 et seqq.; https://www.edpb.europa.eu/sites/default/files/files/file1/edpb_guidelines_202005_consent_en.pdf (7.1.2026); *Füllsack/Kirschke-Biller*, in: Gerecke (ed.), Handbuch Social-Media-Recht, 1st ed. 2023, 279 et seq.

[79] For details see *Füllsack/Kirschke-Biller*, in: Gerecke (ed.), Handbuch Social-Media-Recht, 1st ed. 2023, 280 et seq.

[80] Cf. for details *Füllsack/Kirschke-Biller*, in: Gerecke (ed.), Handbuch Social-Media-Recht, 1st ed. 2023, 280 et seq.

[81] See sub I.6.

[82] Cf. Bayrischer Rundfunk, https://www.br.de/nachrichten/netzwelt/auch-gruenen-chefin-fordert-social-media-verbot-bis-16-jahre,Uw0MPNN (7.1.2026) as well as DIE ZEIT, https://www.zeit.de/politik/deutschland/2025-06/verbot-soziale-medien-bundesjustizministerin-spd-cdu-altersgrenze-forderung (7.1.2026).

[83] See sub I.6.a).

ply to responsible persons or entities who are obliged to take certain actions or implement certain measures.[84]

According to Art. 54 DSA, service recipients have the right to seek compensation for damages if there has been a breach of Art. 28 DSA. Furthermore, the national authorities competent for enforcing the DSA (with special competences regarding Art. 28 DSA, cf. Sec. 12(2) DDG) have additional enforcement options (cf. Sec. 24 et seqq. DDG).

Further administrative fines are possible on the basis of national law. For example, a violation of Sec. 20 TDDDG may lead to a fine of up to € 300,000 (Sec. 28(1) No. 11 and (2) TDDDG). Furthermore, according to the JMStV, supervisory measures pursuant to Sec. 20–22 JMStV can be ordered by the state media authorities, such as obligations to impose restrictions or prohibitions on certain content. In addition, criminal sanctions and fines of up to € 500,000 or up to € 2 million may be imposed in accordance with Sec. 23 and 24 JMStV.[85] Moreover, violations of youth protection law (JuSchG) might lead to criminal and administrative sanctions (Sec. 27–28 JuSchG).

6. *Examples of Public Enforcement*

Different administrative proceedings have been undertaken with regard to social media platforms.

a) General

The following exemplary cases might illustrate the current state in the EU.

As TikTok "failed to specify that the processing included remote access to personal data stored in Singapore and the United States by personnel based in China", the Irish Data Protection Commission (Irish DPC) imposed in May 2025 "administrative fines totalling € 530 million […], consisting of a fine of € 45 million for [the] infringement of [Art.] 13(1)(f) GDPR."[86]

In September 2022, Meta Platforms Ireland Limited received a fine by the Irish DPC of € 405 million for infringements of Art. 5(1)(a), 5(1)(c), 6(1), 12(1), 24, 25(1), 25(2) and 35(1) GDPR.[87]

---

[84] Art. 83(4) GDPR.

[85] For the personal scope see *Schulz/Dreyer*, in: Binder/Vesting (eds.), Beck'scher Kommentar zum Rundfunkrecht, 5th ed. 2024, JMStV § 24 n. 12.

[86] See https://www.dataprotection.ie/en/news-media/latest-news/irish-data-protection-commission-fines-tiktok-eu530-million-and-orders-corrective-measures-following (7.1.2026) as well as *Assion*, NJW 2025, 2595, 2598; the case also concerned an unjustified transfer of data to China.

[87] https://dataprotection.ie/en/news-media/press-releases/data-protection-commission-announces-decision-instagram-inquiry; cf. also Irish DPC, Decision – In the matter of Meta Platforms Ireland Ltd., N-21-4-2 (7.1.2026), https://www.dataprotection.ie/sites/default/files/uploads/2022-12/Final%20Decision_IN-21-4-2_Redacted.pdf

Due to an insufficient legal basis for data processing, which is necessary according to Art. 5 (1)(a) GDPR, Art. 6 (1)(a)(e)(f) GDPR, Art. 13 (1)(c) GDPR, Art. 14 (1)(c) GDPR, the Irish DPC has also imposed a penalty on LinkedIn in the amount of € 310 million.[88]

As Meta Platforms Ireland Limited "did not implement appropriate technical and organisational measures to ensure a level of security appropriate to the risk, including the ability to ensure the ongoing confidentiality of user passwords", the Irish DPC imposed "[a]dministrative fines totalling € 91 million pursuant to Articles 58(2)(i) and 83 GDPR" in September 2024.[89]

b) Germany

Next to several decisions of other member states' authorities (especially by the Irish DPC, which inter alia set a record fine of € 1.2 billion in 2023[90])[91], there are also decisions by German data protection authorities. The following case serves as an example. The Hamburg Data Protection Authority (Hamburg DPA) has fined Facebook Germany GmbH € 51,000 for failing to notify it of the appointment of a data protection officer.[92]

Although there are binding decisions (European Data Protection Board (EDPB)/Irish DPC)) that explicitly sanction social media platforms for inadequate data protection of children,[93] there is no report of a major public ruling by a German national DPA specifically targeting social media platforms' processing of children's data. This is mainly the case because the major social media platforms are generally supervised by the Irish DPC under the one-stop-shop mechanism of the GDPR.[94] The Irish DPC is, for example, the lead authority for TikTok and Facebook.

[88] https://dataprotection.ie/en/news-media/press-releases/irish-data-protection-commission-fines-linkedin-ireland-eu310-million (7.1.2026).

[89] https://www.dataprotection.ie/en/news-media/press-releases/DPC-announces-91-million-fine-of-Meta (7.1.2026).

[90] Irish DPC, Decision – In the matter of Meta Platforms Ireland Limited, IN-20–8–1 (12.5.2023), https://www.edpb.europa.eu/system/files/2023-05/final_for_issue_ov_transfers_decision_12-05-23.pdf (7.1.2026).

[91] Cf. for an overview of decisions by authorities in different member states with regard to social media platforms *Füllsack/Kirschke-Biller*, in: Gerecke (ed.), Handbuch Social-Media-Recht, 1st ed. 2023, 296 with further references.

[92] LfD Hamburg, Tätigkeitsbericht Datenschutz 2019, pp. 105 et seqq.; https://datenschutz archiv.org/fileadmin/Dokumente/2019/28_TB_LfD_Hamburg_2019_oDrsNr_13022020.pdf (7.1.2026).

[93] Binding Decision 2/2023 on the dispute submitted by the Irish SA regarding TikTok Technology Limited (Art. 65 GDPR), https://www.edpb.europa.eu/system/files/2023-09/edpb_bindingdecision_202302_ie_sa_ttl_children_en.pdf (7.1.2026); Irish DPC, Final decision of the Irish Data Protection Commission (1.9.2023), https://www.edpb.europa.eu/system/files/2023-09/final_decision_tiktok_in-21-9-1_-_redacted_8_september_2023.pdf (7.1.2026).

[94] *Nguyen*, in: BeckOK DatenschutzR, 53rd ed. 1.8.2025, DS-GVO Art. 60 n. 1.

Furthermore – but not targeted at a social media company directly –, the BfDI issued in February 2023 a ruling prohibiting the operation of a Facebook page for the federal government, which is run by the Federal Press Office (BPA). In July 2025, the lawsuit filed by the BPA and Meta before the Administrative Court of Cologne was successful, overturning the BfDI's 2023 decision.[95]

In addition, German data protection authorities have published guidelines with regard to social media platforms. Especially, the BfDI has published a guideline on "Using Social Media Legally" which is, however, directed at public bodies and their (potential) data protection law responsibility for social media activities (e.g., a "page" of that very public body on Facebook; focus is on a responsibility *next* to the platform (Art. 26 GDPR)[96]).[97]

7. Examples of Court Proceedings

Next to judgments of the CJEU, various German courts have issued rulings that concern the data processing of social media providers. The following, probably most prominent, data protection law rulings might serve as examples.

In November 2024, the German Federal Court of Justice (BGH) ruled in a case where damages were claimed from Facebook/Meta that a mere (short-term) loss of control over personal data can entitle individuals to GDPR compensation (Art. 82 GDPR).[98] The decision is part of a greater data protection litigation complex regarding the so-called "[Facebook] scraping cases" – having led to proceedings and judgments by many different German courts of all levels.[99] Even after the ruling of the BGH, questions regarding the relevant (and required) loss of control remain open – leading to further divergent judgments by lower courts.[100]

In a separate lawsuit brought by the German Federal Cartel Office (BKartA) against Facebook, the BGH ruled that abusive data-linking and terms and conditions could be challenged under both the GDPR and competition law. This was in line with the BKartA's approach.[101]

---

95 Cologne Administrative Court, judgment of 17.7.2025, 13 K 1419/23.

96 See in general for the difficult determination of a joint controllership together with the platform *Füllsack/Kirschke-Biller*, in: Gerecke (ed.), Handbuch Social-Media-Recht, 1st ed. 2023, 247 et seqq.

97 BfDI, Soziale Netzwerke rechtmäßig nutzen – So geht's – Handreichung zur Nutzung sozialer Netzwerke durch öffentliche Stellen des Bundes (22.8.2025), https://www.bfdi.bund.de/SharedDocs/Downloads/DE/DokumenteBfDI/Dokumente-allg/2025/Handreichung-Social-Media.html (7.1.2026).

98 Federal Court of Justice, judgement of 18.11.2024, VI ZR 10/24.

99 See for details and with further references *Assion*, NJW 2025, 2595, 2597; *Assion*, NJW 2023, 2619, 2623.

100 See for details and with further references *Assion*, NJW 2025, 629, 630 et seq.

101 Federal Court of Justice, resolution of 23.6.2020, KVR 69/19.

The Berlin Regional Court also issued a ruling against Facebook. In this first landmark ruling, the court found that the platform's default settings and contract clauses were unlawful under German consumer and data protection laws.[102]

To the opposite, just recently and heavily discussed in German literature, the Higher Regional Court of Cologne denied a violation of data protection law by Meta with regard to the training of AI. The court had to deal with the question whether Meta is allowed to use (personal) user data to train its AI without the permission of the users. The court affirmed that Meta can legally ground its processing on Art. 6(1)(f) GDPR.[103]

The most significant findings and sanctions relating to the inadequate processing of children's data by platforms originate predominantly from the Irish DPC and the EDPB. German courts, however, regularly rule on civil law and family law disputes.[104] Respective cases often relate to children's photos, parental consent, and image/personality rights – especially if photos are posted on social media platforms.[105]

IV. Emerging Technologies and Trends

1. Fundamental Rights, Artificial Intelligence and Machine Learning, Biometric Data, Targeted Advertising

Overall, Germany has a very high level of protection for human rights against advancing new technologies due to the protection of fundamental rights in its constitution (as well as on the supranational level and via international law commitments).[106] EU and German legislation capture emerging technologies (especially AI and machine learning, biometric data, and targeted advertising) that impact privacy on social media, but a specific regulation has emerged only recently.

The GDPR sets boundaries for targeted advertisement and Art. 9 GDPR explicitly forbids the use of biometric data. Exceptions are only allowed under specific conditions, e.g. labour law obligations, protection of vital interests, or significant public interest.[107] In addition, specific design patterns in social media

---

[102] LG Berlin, judgment of 16.1.2018, 16 O 341/15.

[103] OLG Cologne, NJW 2025, 3156 (3158 et seq.); moreover, the court denied a violation of the DMA, cf. OLG Cologne, NJW 2025, 3156 (3159 et seqq.).

[104] Exemplary: OLG Düsseldorf, decision of 20.7.2021, 1 UF 74/21; OLG Oldenburg, decision of 24.5.2018, 13 W 10/18.

[105] Cf., e.g., Sächsische Datenschutz- und Transparenzbeauftragte, Tätigkeitsbericht Datenschutz 2024, 87 et seq., https://www.datenschutz.sachsen.de/download/taetigkeitsberichte/Taetigkeitsbericht_Datenschutz_2024.pdf (7.1.2026).

[106] See sub I.2.

[107] Art. 9 (2) (a-j), (3), (4) GDPR.

platform interfaces (or their concrete effects) are also subject to GDPR provisions.[108]

The GDPR also covers the data processing in the context of AI – as highlighted by a recent judgment of the Higher Regional Court of Cologne.[109] Furthermore, the recently enacted EU AI Act sets specific guardrails with regard to the use of AI.[110] The AI Act establishes a harmonised regulatory framework for AI within the EU. Although it came into force in August 2024, most obligations relating to high-risk AI systems will not apply until August 2026 – and some will not apply until August 2027.

2. Current Policy Discussions

Several options to update data protection laws relating to social media and emerging technologies are currently discussed – mainly, however, on the EU level. First, there are ongoing discussions regarding a potential EU Digital Fairness Act (DFA).[111] The DFA is an initiative by the European Commission that

> "aims to tackle problematic practices such as: [1] unfair commercial practices related to dark patterns[;] [2] misleading marketing by influencers[;] [3] addictive design of digital products[; as well as] [4] unfair personalisation practices. It also aims to ensure a level playing field for online traders, facilitate enforcement and introduce potential simplification."[112]

Second and most important, the legislative package known as the "Digital Omnibus" proposed by the European Commission in November 2025 aims to update, harmonise, and simplify the EU's digital law framework.[113] The proposals include changes to the GDPR and the AI Act – and also stipulate specific rules on the interplay between AI and data protection (law).

---

[108] See in detail EDPB, Guidelines 03/2022 on Deceptive design patterns in social media platform interfaces: how to recognise and avoid them Version 2.0 (14.2.2023), https://www.edpb.europa.eu/system/files/2023-02/edpb_03-2022_guidelines_on_deceptive_design_patterns_in_social_media_platform_interfaces_v2_en_0.pdf (7.1.2026).

[109] See sub III.1. and III.7.

[110] *Becker/Feuerstack*, KIR 2024, 62.

[111] Cf. https://ec.europa.eu/info/law/better-regulation/have-your-say/initiatives/14622-Digital-Fairness-Act_en (7.1.2026).

[112] https://ec.europa.eu/info/law/better-regulation/have-your-say/initiatives/14622-Digital-Fairness-Act_en (7.1.2026).

[113] Cf. COM(2025) 835 final, 836 final, and 837 final as well as SWD(2025) 836 final.

The Use of Foreign Law by German Courts

Dealing with Administrative Law Matters

Michael Fehling

I. The Circumstances in Which Foreign Law is Used by Judges Dealing with Administrative Law Matters

German administrative courts refer to the law of other countries only occasionally in a few areas of law. This occurs more frequently in relation to preliminary questions of private law but also in relation to preliminary questions of administrative law. Against this background, in order to be able to cover the main manifestations in Germany, I take a broad view of the topic in two respects: By administrative courts, I mean not only general administrative jurisdiction (*allgemeine Verwaltungsgerichtsbarkeit*), but also the tax courts (*Finanzgerichte*) and courts for the law of social benefits (*Sozialgerichte*) as special administrative jurisdictions in which foreign law is more frequently referred to in cross-border matters. Secondly, I also include cases in which it is not administrative law but specifically inheritance, matrimonial, and family law issues under foreign law that are of significance.

When it comes to the frequency of certain constellations and practices, I often have to content myself with plausible assumptions. In Germany, only a fraction of court decisions is published and they cannot be electronically searched comprehensively for relevant cases, which means that I cannot make any statistical statements.

1. Mandatory Use of Foreign Law

a) Examination of Foreign Law Necessary for the Application of National Law

This constellation is by far the most important for our topic.[1]

The following scenarios occur more frequently:

(1) The most relevant cases from administrative jurisdiction are found in *immigration law and the law of political asylum.* Particularly in asylum law, but also in other residence laws for foreigners in Germany, we typically find a strong

[1] *Ohler*, Die Kollisionsordnung des Allgemeinen Verwaltungsrechts, 2005, 49 et seq. – The structure of the contribution follows the questionnaire provided by the general reporter.

international connection. In most cases, however, this is limited to partially foreign circumstances and thus to questions of fact; in a significant number of cases, however, questions of foreign law also become relevant as preliminary questions. A particular legal difficulty arises from the fact that questions of law and questions of fact are strictly separated in German law (including administrative law), but in practice are regularly closely intertwined.[2]

Administrative proceedings often involve preliminary questions of matrimonial or family law, which are questions of private law. A visa for a child to join his parents, for example, depended on a Mongolian custody decision and the applicable law.[3] In the case of a minor refugee, the decisive factor was whether his older brother had custody under Syrian law.[4] In another case, there was a dispute about the validity of an Indian marriage,[5] and in another about a French marriage.[6]

Occasionally, German administrative courts must even refer to foreign criminal law in asylum disputes, for example, together with the Pakistani constitution, in the case of imminent persecution on religious grounds in Pakistan,[7] or in relation to imminent persecution for criminal adultery and extramarital sexual intercourse in Afghanistan.[8]

However, foreign administrative law is also relevant in preliminary questions. In this regard an important group of cases are the so-called "Dublin returnees". For example, the reasonableness of deporting a family seeking asylum to Italy, where they had first set foot on European soil, depended on whether the Italian asylum system guaranteed them the satisfaction of their basic needs for a reasonable period of time.[9] In several similar cases involving potential "Dublin returnees" to Bulgaria, Bulgarian asylum law and its asylum system were decisive factors.[10] Another comparable and particularly well-reasoned case concerned Greece.[11] If, as in the case of Denmark, the country in question is an EU member state that does not participate in the European mutual recognition system for asylum, the asylum system must be examined from a comparative perspective to determine whether it grants a standard of protection comparable to that pro-

[2] See e.g. VG Hamburg of 7.8.2025 – 12 A 5061/25 –, n. 35 et seqq. (juris): risk assessment for an asylum seeker being deported to Greece, where he first entered European territory, depending on what support he could expect under Greek asylum and social welfare law.

[3] BVerwGE 145, 172, n. 13 et seqq. However, this primarily relates to the recognition of the Mongolian court ruling.

[4] BVerwG, EZAR NF 34 Nr. 73, 5.

[5] BVerwGE 143, 369, n. 12 et seqq.

[6] OVG Magdeburg of 6.8.2025 – 2 M 54/15 –, BeckRS 2015, 51147, n. 22 et seqq.

[7] BVerwGE 87, 52, 57.

[8] VG Cottbus of 5.11.2021 – VG 6 K 2518/17.A –, BeckRS 2021, 38305, n. 22.

[9] BVerwGE 184, 151, n. 26 et seqq.

[10] BVerwG of 5.3.2018 – 1 B 155.17 –, BeckRS 2018, 5378, n. 4 et seqq.; see also VGH Mannheim of 27.5.2019 – A 4 S 1329/19 –, EZAR NF 65, Nr. 76, 5 et seq.; with the contrary ruling OVG Lüneburg of 29.1.2028 – 10 L B 82/17 –, BeckRs 2018, 781, n. 32.

[11] Deep examination of Greek law (concerning a person with disabilities who is vulnerable) in VG Hamburg of 7.8.2025 – 12 A 5061/25 –, n. 41 et seqq. (juris).

vided by the relevant EU-Directive.[12] Another group of cases involves administrative court decisions on political asylum or at least the granting of protection status under the Geneva Refugee Convention, whereby preliminary questions to be assessed under foreign law may also be relevant. One example is conscription into military service in Syria under Syrian law and local legal practice.[13] The respective foreign nationality under the foreign law may also be relevant as a preliminary question for the existence of a reason for asylum, for example in connection with the conflict between Ethiopia and Eritrea,[14] family reunification from Syria,[15] or the reasonableness of obtaining identity.[16]

(2) German *nationality and naturalization law* often has close ties to foreign countries, meaning that preliminary questions from foreign law are also relevant here. For example, the Federal Administrative Court dealt with the question whether an applicant for naturalization had lost his Afghan citizenship beforehand.[17] A similar case concerned the loss of Kosovar citizenship.[18]

In another case, it was disputed whether the naturalized citizen had lost his German citizenship by subsequently acquiring Syrian citizenship upon application.[19] A parallel case concerned the issue of naturalization upon application in Armenia.[20]

(3) The *law on compensation for losses* is a historically specific German feature. Germans who fled from what was then territory under Soviet hegemony after World War II, were expelled from there, or moved to Germany later, were able to receive compensation under certain circumstances for lost property or make financial claims. For example, the Federal Administrative Court had to decide as a preliminary question whether a resettler from Poland was entitled to an annual allowance of coal under Polish law,[21] which was admittedly classified as a matter of private law. Another case concerned the confiscation of Jewish property in Hungary under local law, for which compensation was sought.[22]

(4) Foreign law may also be relevant as a preliminary issue in connection with *examinations taken abroad and qualifications acquired there*. However, the equivalence of foreign educational qualifications as a prerequisite for their recognition in Germany is primarily a question of assessing the level of the foreign

---

12 VGH München of 9.1.2024 – 24 B 23.20482 –, n. 31 et seqq. (juris).

13 VGH München of 11.1.2024 – 21 B 19.33072 –, n. 30 et seqq.

14 VG Münster of 30.11.2020 – 9 K 2206/17.A –, BeckRs 2020, 37542, n. 20 et seqq.; see also VG Münster of 22.7.2015 – 9 K 3488/13.A –, BeckRs 2015, 52279; VG Berlin of 28.2.2019 – VG 28 K 247.17 A –, BeckRs 2019, 3736 –, n. 31 et seqq.

15 OVG Lüneburg of 9.12.2002 – 2 L 3490/96 –, BeckRS 2003, 20411, at 1.3.2.1. and 1.3.2.3.

16 BVerwG, EZAR NF 33 Nr. 28, 5.

17 See also BVerwG, NJW 1989, 3107.

18 VG Düsseldorf, ZAR 2024, 355, 356.

19 OVG Münster of 22.8.2018 – 19 B 745/18 –, BeckRs 2018, 19342, n. 5.

20 VG Gießen of 28.1.2026 – 4 K 2129/14.GI –, BeckRs 2016, 43369.

21 BVerwGE 45, 357, 365 et seqq.

22 BVerwG of 29.7.1976 – III C 72.75; VG Bremen of 22.09.1975 – (IV) VI LA 40/74 –, BeckRs 1976, 31267127.

qualification as a matter of fact, not of foreign law. In some cases, however, this is not the case. For example, in a request for recognition of a foreign education as equivalent to the first state law examination in Germany, the preliminary question of the legal structure of Czechoslovakian law studies apparently played a role.[23]

In a slightly different case, the preliminary question regarding university admission in Germany was whether the New Zealand degree allowed access to the university system under local law.[24]

(5) In *data protection law*, which is largely Europeanized but implemented by the member states, foreign law can also be an important preliminary question. Whether "appropriate safeguards" and "effective legal remedies" exist in a third country (such as the US) and whether an administration is therefore entitled to transfer personal data to that country in accordance with Article 46 of the EU General Data Protection Regulation can only be determined by the authority and the supervisory court in accordance with the law of that country.[25] However, I have been unable to find any decisions by German administrative courts on this issue.

(6) Even beyond data protection issues, it seems plausible that foreign law may become relevant in *cross-border police cooperation*. Within the European Union and in the activities of EUROPOL, however, only secondary Union law is likely to be applicable.

(7) *Tax law* now contains a considerable number of provisions whereby the applicability of a provision is linked not only to the treatment of a situation abroad, but also to foreign tax law (so-called "linking rules").

Such preliminary questions of foreign tax law arise particularly frequently in the application of double taxation agreements,[26] but also in constellations in which German tax law refers to taxation abroad.[27]

Even the existence of a child benefit entitlement abroad (in this specific case: in Poland) may potentially influence the taxation of foreigners living in Germany.[28] However, it has not yet been clarified whether a decision on entitlement already issued by a foreign authority would be binding in Germany as a transnational administrative act; in that case the foreign law on which the decision of the local authorities is based would no longer be relevant here.[29]

(8) Finally, there are also cases in *social benefits law* with international implications that raise preliminary questions of foreign law. For example, when granting German basic income support, the question may arise as to whether a foreign

---

23 Not completely clear BVerwG of 30.1.1977 – VIII C 89.76 –, BeckRs 1977, 889, n. 20 et seq.
24 OVG Münster of 22.7.2025 – 19 B 426723 – n. 24 et seqq.
25 *Schmidt-Aßmann*, ZaöRV 78 (2018), 807, 853 et seq.
26 E.g. BFH of 19.12.2007 – I R 46/07 –, BeckRS 2007, 25013149; BFH, IStR 2004, 379, 380.
27 BFH, IStR 2003, 818.
28 See already BFH, SSTRE 2013, 1435, 1437 et seq.
29 BFH, IStR 2014, 30, n. 22 et seqq.

pension is equivalent to it. This depends on the function and structure of the foreign pension and its purpose, which must also be determined by interpretation.[30]

According to a bilateral agreement (in this specific case between Germany and Tunisia), the reimbursement regulations in foreign law may play a role in the reimbursement of costs for emergency treatment following an accident abroad by German health insurance.[31]

The procedural requirement to take foreign law into account in administrative jurisdiction is found in the relevant rules of procedure by reference. Section 173 Administrative Court Procedure Act [*Verwaltungsgerichtsordnung – VwGO*] for the jurisdiction of the general administrative courts [*Allgemeine Verwaltungsgerichtsbarkeit*], Section 76 (1), and Section 155 Financial Court Act [*Finanzgerichtsordnung – FGG*] for the jurisdiction of the financial courts [*Finanzgerichte*], Section 202 Social Court Act – [*Sozialgerichtsgesetz – SGG*] for the jurisdiction of the courts for social claims [*Sozialgerichte*]) to Section 293 of the Code of Civil Procedure (*Zivilprozessordnung – ZPO*).

Section 293 ZPO: Foreign law, customary law; statutes
The law applicable in another state, customary law, and statutes require proof only insofar as they are unknown to the court. When determining these legal norms, the court is not limited to the evidence provided by the parties; it is also authorized to use other sources of information and to order the necessary measures for the purpose of such use.

b) Full or Partial Application of Foreign Law to Resolve a Dispute

aa) Germany's uncodified international public law only regulates when its own law is applicable and, at least in its current form, contains exclusively unilateral conflict-of-law rules. According to these rules, German administrative authorities and the courts that oversee them may only impose legal consequences on the basis of German public law.[32] This is ultimately rooted in the German Basic Law's understanding of democracy and sovereignty. As far as the application of foreign law to the direct decision of a German administrative court proceeding is concerned, one must agree with the otherwise somewhat misleading statement of the Federal Court of Justice that foreign public law is subject to the territorial principle and does not extend beyond the borders of the state in which it was enacted.[33]

This is consistent with the statements made by the Higher Administrative Court of Lueneburg in a cross-border dispute between the Netherlands and Germany concerning a German emission control permit:

The subjective public rights guaranteed to the plaintiff under German law must be granted. Only in this way can the principle of territoriality under international law be upheld. In

[30] LSG Berlin-Brandenburg of 19.3.2015 – L 31 AS 2218/13 –, n. 37 (juris).
[31] BSG, NJOZ 2008, 1114, 1117 et seq.
[32] *Hübner*, Ausländisches Recht vor deutschen Gerichten, 2024, 12 et seq.
[33] BGHZ 31, 367, 370 et seq.

other words, the approval process does not include an examination of whether the project is compatible with the public law of the neighbouring state.[34]

The Federal Administrative Court [*Bundesverwaltungsgericht*] had already ruled similarly in a previous case involving a Dutch neighbour's lawsuit against a nuclear license in Germany, making clear that the possibilities for neighbours to file lawsuits granted under German administrative law also apply to neighbours across the border in other countries.[35]

bb) This means that both complete and partial decisions in German administrative disputes based directly on foreign law are legally impossible; foreign law can only be relevant as a preliminary issue.

cc) In general, the European Regulations Rome I and Rome II do not apply to administrative law matters.[36] This is already indicated by the wording of Article 1 (1) sentence 1 of the Rome I Regulation and also by Article 1(1) sentence 1 of the Rome II Regulation, which refers to 'contractual obligations in civil and commercial matters'. As suggested by Article 1(1) sentence 2, this passage is interpreted negatively by the European Court of Justice, i. e., in contrast to public law. The Rome I Regulation (as well as the Rome II Regulation and the Brussels Ia Regulation) do not apply if the contractual relationship in dispute is related to the exercise and enforcement of sovereign powers (*acta iure imperii*). The reasoning behind this is probably that in such cases, the sovereign authorities of the Member States exercise the power of their state and are bound by their own national laws.[37]

However, the distinction is based on the narrower understanding of public law that generally underlies EU law. According to this, sovereign action does not always occur when an authority or other sovereign entity or an enterprise owned by a sovereign entity acts; in addition, there must be a legal relationship that is characterized by the exercise of powers that go beyond the general rules applicable in relations between private individuals. If sovereign entities act in a non-sovereign or purely fiscal capacity (*acta iure gestionis*), the Rome I Regulation applies without further ado, provided that there are no grounds for exclusion under Art. 1 (2) Rome I Regulation. Typically, however, the ordinary courts have jurisdiction in civil matters, not the administrative courts. This applies, for example, to the assertion of a contractual claim for remuneration for the use of a public parking lot by a company owned by a local authority.[38] the purchase of (office) supplies by a public authority and, more generally, in the awarding of public contracts, but also in the supervision of schoolchildren by a teacher who

---

[34] OVG Lüneburg of 28.7.2003 – 7 ME 262/02 –, BeckRs 2003, 23763, n. 4.

[35] BVerwGE 75, 285, 286 et seqq.

[36] Overview (partially translated here verbatim) by *Paulus*, Art. 1 Rom I-VO in: Budzikiewicz/Weller/Wurmnest (eds.), Beck-Online Großkommentar, Rom I-VO, 1.12.2025, n. 24–26.

[37] ECJ, judgment of 14.10.1976 – Rs. 29/76 –, NJW 1977, 489 (Eurocontrol).

[38] ECJ, judgment of 9.3.2027 – Rs. C-555/15 –, EuZW 2017, 686, n. 35 et seqq. (Pula Parking d.o.o./Tederahn).

may be a civil servant,[39] because, according to Article 34 sentence 3 Basic Law, proceedings for official liability are assigned to the ordinary courts. The collection of tolls for the use of public roads is only apparently an exception, as this concerned cases in which the toll was levied on the basis of a private law contract[40] (contract here understood very broadly as an obligation assumed through voluntary action[41]) and not as a sovereign fee. Ultimately, therefore, the situation remains unchanged: the Rome Regulations play no role for German administrative courts; nor is any indirect influence apparent. Although cases to which the Rome Regulations apply may in rare instances have certain connections to administrative law in the broad sense, in these constellations, which often also concern enforcement issues, the civil courts and not the administrative courts have jurisdiction.

c) Application of Foreign Law Through the Application of Foreign Inspired Supranational Law

aa) In the broadest sense, indirect application of foreign law can be said to occur where EU law provides for the recognition of foreign authorizations and similar instruments. On closer inspection, however, it is not foreign statutory law as such that applies to the German administration and the administrative courts that oversee it. Rather, it is the foreign administrative measure that is recognized as binding both domestically and here. Although the authorization, permit, or similar measure has been issued in another EU country in accordance with local law – which is typically harmonized across the EU – its legality is no longer reviewed domestically in accordance with the law of the country of origin. This principle of mutual recognition is enshrined in various EU secondary legal acts. In German legal doctrine, this is also referred to as transnational administrative acts.[42]

bb) In such cases, there is no spillover effect, i. e. the German administrative courts do not apply the principle or rule of foreign law origin outside of the situations governed by the secondary EU-law.

cc) As already mentioned, the German Administrative Court will not look into the foreign law in greater depth but will normally be content to examine the EU-law. However, harmonized EU law sets out minimum requirements that foreign licenses or similar documents – often limited to formal questions of jurisdiction

---

[39] See ECJ, judgement of 21.04.1993 – Rs. C-172/91 –, NJW 1993, 2091, n. 21 ff. (Sonntag/Weidmann).

[40] ECJ, judgment of 21.9.2021 – Rs. C – 30/21 –, BeckRS 2021, 28872, n. 28 et seqq.; BGH, NJW 2022, 3644, n. 15 et seqq.

[41] *Wiepen/Goebel*, NJW 2022, 3611, n. 3 et seq.

[42] In our context *Ohler*, Die Kollisionsordnung des Allgemeinen Verwaltungsrechts, 2005, 55 et seqq., 156 et seq., 314; short overview e. g. by *Maurer/Waldhoff*, Allgemeines Verwaltungsrecht, 21st ed. 2024, § 9 n. 68 et seq.; for several examples see *Nowak*, in: Terhechte (ed.), Europäisches Rechtsschutz- und Verfahrensrecht, 2nd ed. 2021, § 14 n. 20 et seq.

and procedure – must meet in order to be binding across borders. The German administrative court must, of course, also examine these requirements.

2. The Deliberate Use of Foreign Law

a) Factors and Obstacles to the Use of Comparative Law

aa) German administrative courts – in contrast to the Federal Constitutional Court (*Bundesverfassungsgericht*) – almost never "voluntarily" refer to foreign law in comparative law. At least, I can't find any published decisions on this. Even the very extensive German legal literature, which – unlike in many other countries – is at least partly taken note of and used by the courts, hardly deals with this issue; it focuses entirely on the legal usefulness of comparative law in administrative law scholarship. The dictum of Professor *Häberle* on "comparative law as the fifth method of interpretation"[43] was from the outset more related to constitutional law[44] than to administrative law and does not appear to have influenced the practice of the administrative courts.

The search for precedents plays no role in Germany, which, in contrast to common law countries, focuses entirely on its own statutory law, especially in administrative law and administrative jurisdiction. The discussion about an emerging international (global) administrative law has so far been a topic only for German legal scholars, not for the courts. From a German perspective, making German administrative law more attractive or demonstrating its isolation are purely legal policy considerations that do not concern the (administrative) courts, which are strictly bound by the law (Art. 20 (3) German Constitution [*Grundgesetz* – *GG*]). Where the law (apparently) does not provide a solution for a case, judges must work with general legal principles and constitutional law and, if necessary, substantiate this with classical legal doctrine. The personalities of the judges involved do not make any significant difference in this respect; what is decisive is the German legal doctrine training that they all have in common.

Against this backdrop, German administrative judges can hardly hope to gain any relevant reputation from comparative legal arguments. Of course, it can never be completely ruled out that courts may also pursue political goals using legal interpretation methods; however, if it became apparent that (administrative) judges were using comparative law arguments with this ulterior motive, this would most likely result in a massive loss of reputation and have a negative impact on their own career prospects (appointment to a higher judicial position). However, a criminal law case caused quite a stir around 20 years ago. In an exceptionally detailed ruling, the presiding judge at the regional court [*Landgericht*] had deemed the criminalization of cannabis use to be a violation of fun-

---

[43] *Häberle*, JZ 1989, 913.

[44] *Herdegen*, § 1 in: Herdegen/Masing/Poscher/Gärditz (eds.), Handbuch des Verfassungsrechts, 2021, n. 86 et seqq.; *Voßkuhle/Heitzer*, JuS 2023, 312, 315.

damental rights and had substantiated this, among other things, with comparative legal considerations.[45] Therefore, the regional court referred the relevant criminal provision at the time to the Constitutional Court in a specific review of parliamentary norms (Art. 100 GG). The Federal Constitutional Court subsequently ruled that there had been no violation of the constitution[46] and the regional court had to apply the criminal law. The presiding judge of the regional court at the time was later appointed judge at the Federal Court of Justice; later still, he entered politics and became a member of the Bundestag. It seems reasonable to assume that, in referring the case to the Federal Constitutional Court, the presiding judge of the regional court at the time also intended, as it were, to fuel the legal policy debate on the decriminalisation of cannabis use; legal and political convictions went hand in hand in this respect.

In general, fundamental rights issues are probably the most suitable for comparative legal analysis. This is because the wording is quite open and, in the case of newer conflicts, other methods of interpretation often do not lead to a completely clear result. This is likely to be a major reason for why comparative legal considerations occasionally arise not in the administrative courts but in the Federal Constitutional Court (which comprises of several research assistants for each judge). But even the Federal Constitutional Court does not use the comparative method as an essential part of the reasoning behind the decision but for illustrative purposes only.[47]

In German administrative law, some regulations were originally borrowed from foreign (particularly US) law. This applies in particular to environmental law (namely environmental impact assessments) and economic regulation law (in particular telecommunications law and energy law with non-discriminatory 'third-party access' to network infrastructure). However, this almost always happens through European directives, which must be transposed into national law (cf. Article 288 (3) TFEU). The interpretation then does not refer back to the origins in foreign law, but to the EU directives, on which there is usually already extensive legal literature or even court decisions.

Furthermore, comparative law does not appear to play a significant role in administrative courts either when it comes to demonstrating the compatibility or incompatibility of a legal norm with international law.

bb) There are probably three main reasons why German administrative courts do not refer to foreign law in comparative legal terms. Firstly, the legal dogma of German administrative law, combined with the extremely strict adherence to domestic law and the high density of legislation, leaves little room for other 'crea-

---

45 LG Lübeck, NJW 1992, 1571, 1575.

46 BVerfGE 90, 145 et seqq.

47 Most famous, concerning the freedom of expression, BVerfGE 7, 198, 208 (Lüth): citing the American judge *Cardozo*: 'the matrix, the indispensable condition of nearly every form of freedom'; more recently e.g. BVerfGE 128, 226, 253 (Fraport): refering to the US Supreme Court's "public forum doctrine".

tive' arguments. To put it bluntly, German administrative courts do not have a choice as to which legal principles they apply in resolving a case. Besides, comparative law is not recognised as an independent method of interpretation but can only serve from the outset to further support and substantiate an interpretation obtained by means of classical legal doctrine.

Secondly, the structure of German administrative law with its high degree of differentiation, is relatively far removed not only from common law jurisdictions including the United States but also from other countries of the civil law tradition. This makes comparative law seem of little use when it comes to the relatively narrowly defined individual issues that are usually the subject of administrative court decisions. Functional comparative analysis tends to work better at a very basic, general level.

Thirdly, administrative courts usually lack the time and human resources to carry out a substantial comparison of laws. They also tend to lack experience in this area, as comparative law is not a compulsory subject at university and does not feature in the examinations that are primarily relevant to a career as a judge. Exceptional effort in this regard also seems unattractive if comparative law analysis can ultimately only serve to support a conclusion that has already been reached elsewhere.

Other obstacles may arise, but they play a less important role. Language barriers exist outside of English; however, translation programmes are very powerful today. More important is the often difficult availability of foreign court decisions; even the large US legal databases are usually not available to (lower) German courts. Not everything can be found freely available on the internet, and hardly anything can be found in German legal databases.

On a side note, pride in Germany's long legal tradition and our very formally and logically structured comprehensive statutory law may also play a role in the fact that, at first glance, not too much is expected from looking beyond national borders. Although not as pronounced as in the US, Germany still sees itself primarily as an exporter of its own concept of the rule of law, including in administrative law, rather than as an importer of foreign ideas.

cc) German judges dealing with administrative law certainly make much less frequent use of comparative law than courts dealing with private law matters.

The mandatory application of foreign law pursuant to Section 293 of the Code of Civil Procedure to answer corresponding preliminary legal questions is much more frequently necessary in private commercial law than in administrative law, which is much more closely tied to national particularities. The purely voluntary application of foreign law for the purposes of comparison is not particularly widespread in private law either.

dd) Germany's membership of the European Union or the Council of Europe does not mean that administrative courts refer more frequently to foreign law and foreign court decisions from other Member States. In this respect, German administrative courts are guided almost exclusively by the case law of the European Court of Justice and (less frequently) the European Court of Human Rights. They see the responsibility for the consistent application of harmonised European law lying there. When interpreting EU-law, German administrative courts would also be in breach of Article 267 TFEU in the final instance if they refrained from seeking a preliminary ruling from the European Court of Justice and instead sought to determine the content of Union law themselves by means of comparative law. This is because there could be no question of an *acte claire* in such cases, which alone would make a referral to the Court of Justice unnecessary.[48]

b) Forms and Procedure of Comparative Law

aa) The administrative court alone is fully responsible for interpreting and applying the relevant German law. This also applies if it were to use comparative legal arguments. However, the parties to the proceedings may, of course, present such arguments, but without any claim that the court will take them up.

bb) In German administrative court proceedings, there are no adversarial proceedings in the form familiar from common law jurisdictions. The presiding judge chairs the hearing and asks questions (Section 103 *Verwaltungsgerichtsordnng*) but must also allow the parties to ask questions (Section 104 (2) *Verwaltungsgerichtsordnng*). The administrative court must investigate the relevant facts of its own motion (Section 86 (1) sentence 1 *Verwaltungsgerichtsordnng*) and gather the relevant evidence (Section 96 *Verwaltungsgerichtsordnng*); the court is not bound by the parties' motions (Section 86 (1) sentence 2 VwGO). Official investigation [*Amtsermittlung*] means that the court must, on its own initiative, take everything into account and, if necessary, further clarify anything that 'must be brought to its attention'; the administrative court is only required to consider facts that are not recognisable as significant on its own initiative if they are presented by the parties.[49]

cc) If anything, comparative law arguments by German (not only administrative) courts almost always refer to legal systems with a similar Western tradition of the rule of law. It is no coincidence that my above examples from the Federal Constitutional Court concerned US law.

dd) It is impossible to speak of a 'trend' or a 'model' for comparative law in administrative courts, if only because – as I have pointed out several times – their decisions almost never contain comparative law arguments.

ee) German administrative procedural law does not recognise formal and published preparatory documents (such as those of an *advocate general*, as is the case with the Conseil d'État or the European Court of Justice) in which comparative law could come to light.

---

[48] ECJ, judgement of 06.10.1982 – Rs 283/81 –, Slg. 1982, 3415, n. 13 et seqq. (C.I.L.F.I.T.).

[49] Detailed overview e. g. by *Dawin/Panzer*, § 86 VwGO in: Schoch/Schneider (eds.), Verwaltungsrecht, Kommentar, 2021, n. 61 et seqq., 72 et seqq.

If only because of the secrecy of deliberations, we cannot know anything substantial about informal draft judgements, let alone oral proceedings in court. However, in view of the reasons described above,[50] which make comparative law considerations unattractive for administrative courts, it is hardly to be expected that this will happen to any significant extent.

ff) Accordingly, I cannot cite any examples in which a German administrative court has been subliminally influenced by comparative law.

gg) For the reasons stated above, it is also impossible to say whether German administrative courts explain and interpret foreign law in more detail when voluntarily referring to it.

Even in the Federal Constitutional Court, the rare fact that foreign law is mentioned at all may result from the more or less coincidental knowledge of the judges involved. For example, in the *Fraport* decision,[51] the rapporteur previously (during his time as a law professor) spent time researching in the USA; whether this had any effect remains a matter of speculation. All of this should be transferable to the administrative courts, in the event that decisions with explicit comparative legal considerations can still be found there.

hh) From a legal scholar's perspective, it would certainly be desirable if at least the Federal Administrative Court, would occasionally make explicit comparative legal considerations in order to verify the plausibility of its results obtained through legal dogma or even to draw inspiration from completely new questions that have not yet been dealt with in depth in the literature. Due to extremely limited time and personnel resources (after all, unlike the lower courts, the Federal Administrative Court does have a few research assistants, but far fewer than the Federal Constitutional Court), this is hardly possible without further prolonging the already considerable length of proceedings.

ii) The mandatory recourse to foreign law in preliminary questions has undoubtedly also increased significantly in administrative jurisdiction. This is due to increasing international interdependence (albeit significantly less than in private law) and the much more frequent cross-border relevance of facts in public law as well.

It is conceivable that voluntary comparative legal considerations could indirectly influence administrative court decisions in rare cases, albeit with little impact. This is because comparative law has become much more prevalent in German administrative law scholarship over the past 30 years or so, and legal literature is also being received by the administrative courts (albeit mostly the higher ones). Although these courts rarely refer to legal monographs and major, genuinely jurisprudential articles in law journals, they do refer to legal commentaries, which are extremely influential in Germany. These commentaries are often written by legal scholars, who also incorporate their own (and others') comparative

---

[50] See 2.a).

[51] Fn. 47.

legal findings into them. However, even such a chain of effects in comparative law remains a mere assumption and is likely to be very rare.

II. The Tools Available to Courts Dealing with Administrative Law Issues

1. Procedual Tools

a) Control by All Judges

aa) 'Section 173 VwGO in conjunction with Section 293 ZPO obliges the court in administrative proceedings to investigate foreign law ex officio, making use of all sources of information available to it. In doing so, the principle of maximum approximation to foreign law applies, taking into account the relevant legal practice.'[52] 'However, this presupposes that foreign legal practice provides at least a reasonable concretization or interpretation of the respective legal norms. Legal practice that contradicts the valid legal norms of the respective foreign state is not binding on the German state court [in this specific case: in the context of examining citizenship].'[53] 'The court is fundamentally required to determine foreign law as a whole, as it has developed in the doctrine and case law of the country concerned. This means that the court may further develop foreign law for cases that have not yet been decided by the courts of the country whose law is applicable. The spirit and systemic context of foreign law are decisive in this regard.'[54] 'The wording, structure and meaning and purpose of the standard are particularly relevant for its interpretation. The aforementioned interpretation criteria are not only recognised in the jurisprudence and legal practice of the Federal Republic of Germany, but also (at least in principle) in many other legal systems, both in continental European and Anglo-American law ("common law"), although they are accorded varying degrees of importance in each case.'[55]

bb) According to German private international law, foreign law is only inapplicable if it contradicts the *ordre public*. German constitutional assessments and international fundamental rights guarantees are also used to define the *ordre public*. However, the formative influence of assessments under German law tends to decrease the less the respective case is linked to Germany.[56] Foreign law is therefore not fully integrated into the hierarchy of norms of the German legal system.

---

52 BVerwGE 143, 369, n. 14; instructive example: BVerwGE 87, 52, 59.

53 VG Münster of 30.11.2020 – 9 K 2206/17.A –, BeckRs 2020, 37542, n. 21

54 VG Berlin of 28.2.2019 – VG 28 K 247.17 A –, BeckRs 2019, 3736, n. 32.

55 VG Münster of 30.11.2020 – 9 K 2206/17.A –, BeckRs 2020, 37542, n. 22, VG Münster of 22.7.2015 – 9 K 3488/13.A –, BeckRs 2015, 52279.

56 *Hübner*, Ausländisches Recht vor deutschen Gerichten, 2024, 12 et seq., 54.

The same standards apply when German administrative courts have to refer to foreign private law for preliminary questions.[57] When it comes to foreign administrative law, however, it seems doubtful whether the *ordre public* is sufficient as a barrier to national applicability.[58] In my view, in the particularly sensitive relationship between the state and its citizens, there is much to be said for applying at least the fundamental rights of the Basic Law without restriction as a standard to foreign administrative law as well. As far as can be seen, this question has not yet been clarified, nor has it even been explicitly raised. It is possible that the potential difference between mere *ordre public* and the additional full application of German fundamental rights has not yet become relevant in this respect. In any case, foreign law is indisputably not applicable if it contradicts international human rights guarantees. This has apparently been sufficient so far to resolve problematic cases, especially in asylum law. It is evident in any case that foreign administrative law cannot be decisive if it directly or indirectly legitimizes political persecution.

cc) If foreign law is systematically not applied abroad, this may well be a significant indication that it is not actually recognized as valid. In such cases, it should also not be applied in Germany as preliminary relevant factor.

However, this must be distinguished from mere enforcement deficits in the application of the law. These do not call into question the principle of validity abroad and therefore does not prevent foreign law from being applied in German administrative court proceedings.

dd) In theory, customary law and general principles of foreign administrative law are also applicable as foreign law in preliminary questions for German administrative courts.[59] However, I cannot find any cases relating to this.

ee) Soft law alone does not have legal status within the meaning of Section 293 of the German Code of Civil Procedure and therefore cannot be applied as such by administrative courts. The same applies to legal doctrine. However, both can be used to interpret foreign law and determine foreign application practices.

b) Review by the "Court of Cassation"

The term *court of cassation*, which is not commonly used in German law, here refers to the highest federal courts as courts of last appeal in administrative matters, i.e. the Federal Administrative Court, the Federal Court of Finance (*Bundesfinanzhof*) and the Federal Court for Social Law *(Bundesozialgericht)*.

'In terms of the law of last appeal (*Revisionsrecht*), the determination of foreign law and foreign legal practice in administrative proceedings is not to be classified

---

[57] BVerwGE 145, 153, n. 22; BVerwGE 145, 172, n. 21.

[58] Arguing for the *ordre public*-standard in administrative law, too, *Ohler*, Die Kollisionsordnung des allgemeinen Verwaltungsrechts, 2005, 163 et seq.

[59] Compare BVerwG, EZAR NF 34 Nr. 73, 5.

as legal knowledge but is to be treated as a finding of fact, regardless of any special circumstances.'[60] 'The court of last resort is therefore bound by the findings of the court of appeal on foreign law within certain limits. However, in certain cases, findings of fact may also be introduced into the court of last resort (*Revisionsgericht*) – if necessary, even against the unanimous will of the parties to the proceedings – for example, if the facts are well known or if findings of the court of appeal that are contrary to the case file are replaced by findings that are documented in the case file.'[61] 'The decision of the court of fact as to which foreign legal provisions are to be applied in individual cases in the required interpretation of federal legal norms and how they are to be interpreted is subject to last review (*revisionsgerichtliche Überprüfung*) by the court of appeal only to the extent that it is claimed that the court of the previous instance did not fulfil its duty of investigation or that the result was obtained in violation of other procedural rules.'[62] According to these principles, the court of appeal is not bound by the findings of the lower court regarding the content of foreign law, even if 'they are based on only a cursory overview of the matter at hand.'[63]

2. Material and Intellectual Tools

a) Material Tools

aa) German procedural law does not contain any general guidelines for determining the applicable foreign law. The administrative courts may use any means of investigation they deem appropriate in the specific case.[64] 'The more complex and foreign the applicable law is in comparison to German law, the higher the requirements for the judicial duty of investigation.'[65]

Sometimes judges draw on their own expertise; since the judicial panels of the administrative courts are further specialised, they can occasionally draw on prior knowledge from previous own cases. Judges – or, in federal courts, also their research assistants – also conduct extensive research on the freely accessible internet or in legal databases, insofar as these are accessible to them. Decisions by other German courts in which the same or similar preliminary questions of foreign law were relevant are also cited. Information is also frequently obtained from the Foreign Office or the respective embassy. In very difficult cases, also opinions from legal or other expert institutions play a role. In asylum law in particular,

---

[60] BVerwGE 133, 329, n. 17.

[61] BVerwGE 143, 369, n. 16.

[62] BVerwGE 45, 357, 365; BVerwGE 145, 153, n. 18; BVerwG of 5.3.2018 – 1 B 155.17 –, BeckRS 2018, 5378, n. 4.; similarly, BFH, BeckRS 2007, 25013149.

[63] BFH, DStRE 2013, 1435.

[64] Overview by *Rixen*, § 86 in: Sodan/Ziekow (eds.), Verwaltungsgerichtsordnung, Großkommentar, 2019, n. 22.

[65] OVG Magdeburg of 6.8.2025 – 2 M 54/15 –, BeckRS 2015, 51147, n. 23.

information about the foreign law in action is also obtained from non-governmental organisations[66] involved in refugee aid.

However, if a plaintiff derives a claim from foreign circumstances and the relevant law and asserts it in court, he is subject to an 'increased obligation to provide information and evidence' in tax law (Section 76 (1) sentence 4 *Finanzgerichtsgesetz* in conjunction with Section 90 (2) *Abgabenordnung*). This extended duty to cooperate also covers the non-German area of the European Union.[67]

bb) 'Evidence must be taken to determine the foreign law and the relevant legal practice if the foreign law is unknown to the court, for example because it does not have direct access to it due to language barriers.'[68] The most important evidence here is expert opinions, but also the obtaining of official information, the documentary use of an existing written opinion prepared elsewhere, and written information provided elsewhere.[69] In this respect, the principle of free evaluation of evidence applies (*freie Beweiswürdigung*, Section 108 (1) *Verwaltungsgerichtsordnung*).[70]

In principle, this also applies to summary proceedings for provisional legal protection (*einstweiliger Rechtsschutz*). However, in such cases, obtaining an expert opinion will not normally be considered due to the urgency of the matter. Instead, the burden of cooperation on the parties to the proceedings is intensified to a burden of substantiation.[71] If necessary, the administrative court must make a preliminary decision in summary proceedings after only a summary examination of the foreign legal situation, weighing up the interests of the parties to the proceedings.[72]

cc) Unlike in private law, institutionalised international or regional information systems do not play a particularly important role in administrative law. The Foreign Legal Information Act (*Auslands-Rechtsauskunftsgesetz*), which transposed the European Convention on Information on Foreign Law (London Convention) into German law, does not apply to public law. However, the administrative courts may use the national receiving agency (in Germany, the Federal Ministry of Justice) and the latter, in turn, may use the foreign transmitting agencies for preliminary questions of civil law in the foreign law of other member states of the Council of Europe.[73] The European Judicial Network for the member

[66] *Rixen*, in: Sodan/Ziekow (fn. 64), § 86 n. 21.

[67] BFH, IStR 2014, 30, n. 29.

[68] BVerwG of 5.3.2018 – 1 B 155.17 –, BeckRS 2018, 5378, n. 4.

[69] *Dawin/Panzer*, in: Schoch/Scheider (fn. 49), § 86 VwGO n. 43.

[70] *Dawin/Panzer*, in: Schoch/Scheider (fn. 49), § 86 VwGO n. 33.

[71] *Rixen*, in: Sodan/Ziekow (fn. 64), § 86 n. 23.

[72] *Dawin/Panzer*, in: Schoch/Scheider (fn. 49), § 86 VwGO n. 44a (mentioning the application of German law as a substitute law as an alternative that is also represented).

[73] *Dawin/Panzer*, in: Schoch/Scheider (fn. 49), § 86 VwGO n. 44, 45.

states of the European Union, which is similar to the London Convention, also covers only civil and commercial matters.[74]

Judges occasionally rely on more or less random personal contacts abroad for information on foreign law.

dd) If the parties present detailed and controversial arguments regarding foreign legal practice, the requirements for judicial investigations increase. 'The fact that foreign law may be very complex cannot release the court from this duty of investigation. A decision based on the principles of the burden of proof is not possible in this area; foreign legal principles do not become facts.'[75]

ee) The application of foreign (administrative) law requires not only that it can be found, but also that it can be interpreted in terms of its wording, structure, meaning, and purpose.[76]

If the content of foreign law cannot be determined, German law should be applied as a substitute in private law cases. Insofar, the Federal Administrative Court refers to the fundamental decisions of the Federal Court of Justice.[77] However, this remains highly controversial in legal literature.[78] In the practice of German administrative courts, there appears to be a reluctance to conclude that the relevant foreign law cannot be determined. Instead, the administrative courts seem to be more willing to settle for a low standard of proof with regard to the content of foreign law. German courts are somewhat flexible in this regard because the principle of free evaluation of evidence applies to the determination of judicial conviction without being limited to specific means of evidence.

ff) Even determining the text of foreign law that may be relevant to a decision can be difficult. Although the most important legal texts from other Western industrialised nations can now be easily researched on the internet, this is not the case with more "obscure" subjects and culturally and legally "more foreign" economic powers such as Japan and China, and especially for developing countries.

gg) Translation problems are similar to those described above in relation to determining the legal text. Many widely spoken languages can now be easily translated using freely available translation programmes. However, this is far from being the case for more obscure and, especially, less widely spoken languages.

hh) The increase in information on the internet will undoubtedly make foreign legal texts in their original language easier to find, although this will probably not happen so quickly in all developing countries. To a certain extent, this will also apply to the decisions of the supreme courts. Artificial intelligence could facilitate the evaluation and systematisation of what is available on the Internet. At present,

---

74 *Hübner*, Ausländisches Recht vor deutschen Gerichten, 2024, 257 et seqq.

75 BFH, IStR 2014, n. 27.

76 VG Münster of 30.11.2020 – 9 K 2206/17.A –, BeckRs 2020, 37542, n. 22; VG Münster of 22.7.2015 – 9 K 3488/13.A –, BeckRs 2015, 52279.

77 BVerwGE 143, 369, n. 15; BGHZ 69, 387; BGH, NJW 1982, 1215.

78 *Hübner*, Ausländisches Recht vor deutschen Gerichten, 2024, 352 et seqq.

however, the results found there are still not very reliable, because artificial intelligence tends to "make things up" when there are gaps in its knowledge.

ii) Since practical application is highly significant for the interpretation of foreign law, German administrative courts must also take local court practice into account. Unlike in common law, court rulings do not have independent legal status in the German legal system. They are therefore not applicable foreign law in themselves.

b) Intellectual Tools

aa) In Germany, comparative law plays no significant rule in the training of judges, and is neither part of first nor of the second state examination, which qualifies students for the judiciary and other legal professions.

For the university part of the first examination, in which students can choose one of the elective subjects offered, very few law faculties offer comparative law in administrative law, and then only as a small part of an international elective focus. Only a small minority of students attend a course on comparative law in public law (as opposed to private international law) in this context.

In the legal clerkship that precedes the second state examination, comparative law in administrative law does not feature at all.

bb) I do not know whether training courses in comparative law for administrative judges are even available in – always voluntary – training programmes. If they do exist, they play virtually no noticeable role.

However, some representatives of the highest federal courts meet informally from time to time with colleagues from other European countries. This also serves the purpose of comparative legal exchange, but probably more at a very general and fundamental level. Such meetings take place particularly regularly with colleagues from France, but they also occur occasionally with other European countries.

cc) Traditionally, the study of foreign law has been the domain of private law. However, with the increasing internationalization of administrative law relations, its 'relevance for practice, i.e., its direct significance for authorities and courts in assessing individual legal issues, is now becoming more apparent.'[79]

[79] *Schmidt-Aßmann*, ZaöRV 78, 807, 853; *Schönberger*, § 71 n. 6, in: Bogdandy/Huber (eds.), Handbuch Ius Publicum Europeanum, Bd. 4, 2007.

The State as a Taxpayer

Economic Activity of the State and Related Tax Obligations

Michael Droege

I. Introduction

In recent years, the taxation of the public sector has become increasingly significant within the German tax system.[1] The dynamics of developments in legislation and legal practice, they are primarily determined by Europeanisation and the associated emphasis on competitive neutrality. The taxation of the public sector entails a significant shift in perspective. The concept of the tax state designates the state as the recipient and creditor, thereby imposing taxes on citizens to allocate funds to public authorities for the fulfilment of their responsibilities.[2] In the tax state, self-taxation of the public sector is the big exception to the fundamental tax exemption of the state. Its general self-taxation would not only be a fiscal zero-sum game,[3] but would also counteract the fiscal purpose of taxation.[4]

The state as a taxpayer goes hand in hand with a change of role that leaves the model of the tax state (*Steuerstaat*) far behind. It is the corporate state (*Unternehmerstaat*) that engages in economic activity and becomes a taxpayer for the sake of competitive neutrality (II.). This partial tax liability of the public sector, which relates to economic activity, can be integrated into a constitutional context. Thus, the public sector‘s economic activity triggers a constitutional need for justification. In addition, the taxation objective of competitive neutrality gains constitutional foundations (III.).

On this basis, the outlines of the public sector‘s partial tax liability in corporate tax and VAT law can be traced. While traditionally in both areas the tax liability of the public sector was justified by the maintenance of a business unit of a public law-entity or commercial enterprise (*Betrieb gewerblicher Art*) – and its counterpart, the public authority operation or sovereign enterprise (*Hoheitsbetrieb*),

[1] See: *Droege*, Zur Besteuerung der öffentlichen Hand, 2017; *Hidien/Jürgens*, Die Besteuerung der öffentlichen Hand, 2nd ed. 2023; *Hüttemann*, Die Besteuerung der öffentlichen Hand, 2002; *Musil/Küffner* (eds.), Besteuerung der öffentlichen Hand, 2022. For a general overview of German tax law, see: *Haase/Steierberg*, Tax Law in Germany, 3rd ed. 2024.

[2] Only: *Isensee*, in: FS Ipsen, 1977, 409 et seqq.; see also *Wieland*, in: Herdegen/Masing/Poscher/Gärditz (eds.), Handbuch des Verfassungsrechts, 2025, § 24 n. 10 et seq.

[3] *Hensel*, StuW I 1930, col. 873 ff.

[4] *Hufeld*, in: FS Stober, 2008, 717, 719.

which is exempt from taxation[5] – competition neutrality has led to a functional demarcation of partial tax liability based on the criterion of distortion of competition (IV.). The structural Europeanisation of tax law is contributing to this erosion of the public authority domain (V.). As the conditions for partial tax liability change, so do the role and function of financial administration and tax law protection (VI.). Finally, conclusions are drawn regarding the dogmatic embedding of public sector taxation within overarching regulatory and control contexts (VII.).

II. Public Institutions and Economic Activity

German tax law does not provide a general definition of the tax liability of public institutions. The state as a taxpayer is the entrepreneurial state that fulfils its tasks on the market.[6] Its role as a taxpayer is therefore independent of the forms of action taken by the state and other actors governed by public law.[7] Essentially, the public sector can be defined by reference to the law of administrative organisation. In the context of tax law, the public sector refers primarily to public administrative bodies and to the direct and indirect state administration at the federal, state, and local level.[8] Legal entities under public law, corporations, institutions and, foundations are available to perform public tasks. However, the public sector can also operate public enterprises under private law as wholly-owned companies, i. e. with a qualified majority shareholding, or as mixed-economy companies with private participation in the form of a public-private partnership.[9] From an administrative law perspective, the separation between the sovereign sphere of administration beyond the market and economic activity in the market is fundamental.[10]

As far as economic activity is understood to mean any activity that generally consists of providing goods and services on a market or for the public, as can usually be carried out by private individuals, the public sector has a wide range of forms of action and legal forms at its disposal. There is freedom of choice be-

---

5 Regarding § 4 (5) KStG, see only the administrative opinion in R 4.4 and H 4.4 KStH 2022.

6 On the entrepreneurial state, see only: *Isensee*, in: idem/Kirchhof (eds.), Handbuch des Staatsrechts, 3rd ed. 2007, vol. V, § 122 n. 68 et seqq. with further references.

7 Unlike in VAT law, which is shaped by EU law: *Hüttemann*, JöR 65 (2017), 147, 170.

8 See only: *idem*, in: idem/Jürgens (eds.), Die Besteuerung der öffentlichen Hand, 2nd ed. 2023, § 1 n. 159 et seqq., 167 et seqq., 170 et seqq.

9 *Musil*, in: idem/Küffner, Besteuerung der öffentlichen Hand, 2022, chapter 1, para. 1.3 et seq. and 1.55 et seq.; *Hidien*, in: idem/Jürgens (eds.), Die Besteuerung der öffentlichen Hand, 2nd ed. 2023, § 1, para. 32 et seq.

10 *Musil*, in: idem/Küffner, Besteuerung der öffentlichen Hand, 2022, chapter 1, para. 1.17 et seqq.; *Hidien*, in: idem/Jürgens, Besteuerung der öffentlichen Hand, 2nd ed. 2023, § 1, para. 15 et seqq.

tween operating and managing companies, companies with their own legal personality, and last but not least, forms of organization under private law.[11]

In its economic activities, the public sector is subject to overlapping regulations at the European, constitutional, and administrative law level.[12] In terms of budgetary law, Section 65 (1) No. 1 of the Federal Budget Code (*Bundeshaushaltsordnung*, BHO) makes state participation dependent, inter alia, on a public purpose beyond the commercial purpose in the sense of an "important interest" that cannot be better and more economically achieved by other means.[13] Economic activity as the subject of regulatory administrative law is particularly evident in municipal economic law, where it concerns private-sector companies. The municipal codes of the federal states contain extensive subsidiarity clauses according to which a municipality, regardless of its legal form, may only establish or participate in economic enterprises if, in the case of activities outside the scope of municipal services, the purpose cannot be fulfilled equally and economically well by a private provider.[14] The taxation of the public sector is linked to this economic administrative law and administrative organisational starting point.

However, if the public sector acts in accordance with private law and, as a result of organisational privatisation, uses the legal forms of private company law, it is taxed as a private entity and is therefore subject to corporation tax from the outset in accordance with Section 1 (1) No. 1 of the Corporation Tax Act (*Körperschaftsteuergesetz*, KStG). Public companies in the form of a public limited company (PLCs, "AG") or a limited company (Ltd., "GmbH") are subject to corporation tax by virtue of their legal form, regardless of whether and to what extent the state is involved.[15] They are subject to corporate tax if they operate a business and to VAT within the scope of their business. In this case, tax liability is the rule, as the public sector has relinquished its special rights under public law. Taxation of the public sector in the strict sense refers exclusively to the tax liability of public-law corporations or entities under public law if they are economically active.

Conceptually, two taxation approaches can be distinguished.[16] On the one hand, taxation of the public sector in some types of tax follows the general rules at the level of the facts establishing taxability. For example, the trade tax law does

[11] *Musil*, in: idem/Küffner, Besteuerung der öffentlichen Hand, 2002, chapter 1, para. 1. 77 et seq.

[12] *Hidien*, in: idem/Jürgens (eds.), Die Besteuerung der öffentlichen Hand, 2nd ed. 2023, § 1 para. 52 et seqq., 444 et seqq. See also *Schulte/Kloos*, Handbuch Öffentliches Wirtschaftsrecht, 2016, for a comprehensive overview. On the requirements of Union law for public enterprises and the role of fundamental rights and freedoms of the Union, as well as an overview of Union competition and state aid law, see only: *Musil*, in: idem/Küffner, Besteuerung der öffentlichen Hand, 2nd ed. 2023, chapter 1, para. 1.33 et seqq.

[13] See also: *von Lewinski/Burbat*, in: idem (eds.), Nomos-BR, Kommentar BHO, 1st ed. 2013, BHO § 65 para. 1 et seqq.

[14] For more details, see: *Lange*, Kommunalrecht, 2nd ed. 2019, 884 et seqq.

[15] *Hufeld*, in: FS Stober, 2008, 717 (719).

[16] See also: *Hüttemann*, Die Besteuerung der öffentlichen Hand, 2002, 19 et seqq.

not initially provide any special rules for the taxation of public authorities, so that here too, the sole decisive factor is the existence of a permanent business operation in accordance with Section 2 (1) of the Trade Tax Act (*Gewerbesteuergesetz*, GewStG). Of course, Section 2 (1) sentence 2 GewStG modifies this finding insofar as it declares the aggregation principles of corporation tax law to be applicable, and, according to Section 2 (2) GewStDV, public enterprises are not considered commercial enterprises. In any case, the executive legislator uses the differentiation criteria of corporate tax law in trade tax law.[17] The former wealth tax (Vermögenssteuer, VSt) was also based on trade tax law.[18] According to Section 1 (1) No. 2 lit. g) sentence 1 1 VStG *(Vermögenssteuergesetz)*, all commercial enterprises of legal entities under public law are subject to unlimited wealth tax. Other types of taxes contain exemptions in favour of the public sector. For example, Section 13 (1) No. 15 of the Inheritance Tax Act (*Erbschafts- und Schenkungssteuergesetz*, ErbStG) exempts donations to the federal government, a state or a municipality, or donations that serve their purposes exclusively, from inheritance tax. On the other hand, the tax legislator links the existence of a commercial enterprise to the taxation of the public sector. The legal basis for this in corporation tax law is the maintenance of a commercial enterprise pursuant to Section 1 (1) No. 6 of the Corporation Tax Act (KStG). However, this is increasingly being interpreted from the perspective of the competitive relevance of the activity.[19]

III. Constitutional Determinants of Taxation of the Public Sector

Public sector taxation lies at the intersection of the constitutional models of the *entrepreneurial state* and the *fiscal state*. State involvement in the market may call into question the tax state's overarching neutrality. For this reason, a special regime for the taxation of the public sector is viewed critically by most observers.[20] The design of the partial tax liability of the public sector is increasingly being shifted to the constitutional field, and its guiding principles are understood as constitutional requirements.

The guiding principles of public-sectors taxation – increasing efficiency, securing the federal financial constitution, and, above all, ensuring equal competition –

---

[17] For more details, see: *Westendorf*, in: Musil/Küffner, Besteuerung der öffentlichen Hand, 2022, chapter 7, n. 7.46 et seqq. See in particular on the relationship between Section 4 KStG and Section 2 GewStDV: *Nöcker*, in: Hidien/Jürgens, Besteuerung der öffentlichen Hand, 2nd ed. 2023, section 7 n. 9 et seqq.

[18] This has not been levied since the 1995 assessment period, after the Federal Constitutional Court had previously found violations of the requirements of equal valuation, BVerfGE 93, 121 et seqq., and the federal legislature had not subsequently enacted any new regulations.

[19] *G. Kirchhof*, in: idem/Magen/Korte (eds.), Öffentliches Wettbewerbsrecht, 2014, § 13 n. 12, 60.

[20] On the following, see: *Droege*, Zur Besteuerung der öffentlichen Hand, 2017, 81 et seqq.

already dominated the discourse in the Weimar Republic.[21] In the Weimar debates, the taxation of public enterprises was initially seen as a means of forcing them to adopt "the most rational economic management"[22] and reducing "sloppiness".[23] The requirement for economic efficiency and thriftiness in administration referred to here is now enshrined in constitutional law – for example, as a control standard for external financial control under Article 114 of the German Basic Law (*Grundgesetz*, GG).[24] However, this requirement is an optimisation principle, which is predetermined by the respective objective to be pursued efficiently and is therefore not a hard constitutional standard.[25] Taxation is a poor "instrument for economising the state".[26]

The protection of the financial constitution is also rather ineffective.[27] Naturally, reciprocal taxation or taxing the fulfilment of state tasks by the public sector counteracts the purpose of taxation, namely to finance the performance of state tasks, and removes it from the core area of the concept of taxation in Article 105 GG.[28] If the canon of tax types is exhaustive,[29] then tax-specific limits on taxation by the public sector arise.[30] Especially from a federal perspective, quite a few people advocate a ban on reciprocal taxation of sovereign functions of the federal government and the states.[31] Finally, the financial constitution is understood as a "self-contained framework and procedural code" designed to ensure "clarity and consistency of form"[32]. If the core area of tax-financed sovereign tasks were to be

---

[21] *Droege*, Zur Besteuerung der öffentlichen Hand, 2017, 55 et seqq.

[22] Explanatory memorandum to the draft corporation tax law, Reichstag proceedings, III. legislative period 1924, volume 400, Berlin 1925, Annex 796, p. 8.

[23] *Hensel*, StuW I 1930, col. 873, 880.

[24] On efficiency as a legal principle: *Martini*, Der Markt als Instrument hoheitlicher Verteilungslenkung, 2008, 197 et seqq. with further references.

[25] See, for example, in the context of Article 114 of the Basic Law: *Kube*, in: Maunz/Dürig, GG, Commentary, 72nd edition, 2014, Article 114, n. 104, with further references.

[26] *Hidien*, in: idem/Jürgens (eds.), Die Besteuerung der öffentlichen Hand, 2nd ed. 2023, § 2 para. 220.

[27] See also: *Musil*, in: idem/Küffner, Besteuerung der öffentlichen Hand, 2022, chapter 2, para. 2.62 et seqq.

[28] *Häck*, The Public Sector in Corporation and Turnover Tax Law, 56 et seqq. See also *Hidien*, in: idem/Jürgens (eds.), Die Besteuerung der öffentlichen Hand, 2nd ed. 2023, § 2 n. 276 et seq.; *Storr*, Der Staat als Unternehmer, 2017, 373 et seq.

[29] BVerfG, decision of 13 April 2017, 2 BvL 6/13, NJW 2017, p. 2249 (2251 et seqq. para. 69 et seqq.).

[30] BVerfGE 31, 314 (332 et seq.). See also: *Hidien*, in: idem/Jürgens, Die Besteuerung der öffentlichen Hand, 2nd ed. 2023, § 2 n. 278 et seqq.

[31] *Müller-Werth*, Entwicklung und Grundgedanken der Gegenseitigkeitbesteuerung, 1969, 136. On the state of the discussion with numerous references, see also: *Hidien*, in: idem/Jürgens (eds.), Die Besteuerung der öffentlichen Hand, 2nd ed. 2023, § 2 para. 258 et seqq.

[32] This was precisely the view taken by the Federal Constitutional Court in its unconvincing but still relevant decision on the taxation of broadcasting corporations with regard to the definitive VAT burden on input services provided by the public sector, in which it considered this to be incompatible with the "nature" of VAT as a consumption tax. BVerfGE 105, 185, (193 et seq.). See also: BVerfGE 55, 274 (300 et seq.); BVerfGE 72, 330 (388); BVerfGE 86, 148 (213 et seq.). On this

included in the tax liability, this would result in "additional financial equalisation not provided for in the constitution".[33] This is not very convincing. Fiscal equalisation distributes tax revenue actually generated, rather than the revenue that would be expected under comprehensive taxation.[34]

The most important constitutional basis for public-sector taxation is the competitive neutrality of taxation. This is used in case law as a "mantra"[35] for interpreting tax laws.[36] It is understood as a constitutional requirement addressed to the legislature, which flows from the general principle of equality in Article 3(1) GG in conjunction with the fundamental rights of freedom of occupation and freedom of property (Articles 12 and 14 GG).[37] Tax relief for public enterprises leads to crowding-out effects and constitutes an interference with the constitutionally protected competitive situation, which cannot be justified in the absence of sufficient objective reasons as soon as public enterprises compete with private enterprises.[38] Ultimately, this idea is based on a model in which the state has the right to enter the market and engage in commercial activities for its own economic benefit only in the absence of competition, and thus usually only in the case of market failure. However, this model fails to recognise the openness of competitive neutrality as a constitutional principle.[39]

The principle of competitive neutrality effectively combines competitive equality and competitive freedom, and thus the principles of equality and freedom.[40] The established case law of the Federal Constitutional Court – particularly in the context of value-added tax[41] – refers to the principle of equality as the basis for

subject: *Desens/Hummel*, StuW 2012, 225 et seqq.; *Desens*, in: Schön/Röder (eds.), Future issues in German tax law II, 2014, 1, 18 et seq. with further references.

[33] *Hüttemann*, Taxation of the Public Sector, 2002, 15.

[34] See *Droege*, Zur Besteuerung der öffentlichen Hand, 2017, 106 et seq. for more details; *Wieland*, in: Herdegen/Masing/Poscher/Gärditz (eds.), Handbuch des Verfassungsrechts, 2025, § 24 n. 29 et seq.

[35] *Hidien*, in: idem/Jürgens (eds.), Die Besteuerung der öffentlichen Hand, 2nd ed. 2023, § 2 n. 241, 332 et seqq.

[36] BFH of 20 March 1956 – I 317/55 U, Federal Tax Gazette II 1956, 166, 168; BFH of 14 March 1984 – I R 223/80, Federal Tax Gazette II 1984, 496; BFH of 30 June 1988 – V R 79/84, Federal Tax Gazette II 1988, 910, 911; BFH of 4 December 1991 – I R 74/89, Federal Tax Gazette II 1992, 432, 433; BFH of 23 October 1996 – I R 1–2/94, Federal Tax Gazette II 1997, 139, 142; BFH of 17 February 2010 – I R 2/08, Federal tax Gazette II 2010, 1006; BFH of 7 October 2010 – V R 12/10, Federal Tax Gazette II 2011, 303; BFH of 30 November 2016 – V R 53/15, BFHE 255, 513. See also: Federal Court of Justice of 8 October 2015, I ZR 225/13, MDR 2016, 407; Federal Court of Justice, decision of 16 May 2017, II ZB 7/16, JZ 2017, 894.

[37] On competitive neutrality as a guiding principle of taxation: *Selmer/Schulze/Osterloh*, DÖV 1978, 381, 381 et seqq.; *Lang/Seer*, StuW 1993, 47, 53; *Landwehr*, Betriebe gewerblicher Art von juristischen Personen des öffentlichen Rechts im Körperschaftssteuerrecht, 2000, 103 et seqq.

[38] *Hüttemann*, Die Besteuerung der öffentlichen Hand, 2002, 9.

[39] Rightly so: *Hidien*, in: idem/Jürgens (eds.), Die Besteuerung der öffentlichen Hand, 2nd ed. 2023, § 2 n. 243.

[40] *Englisch*, Wettbewerbsgleichheit im grenzüberschreitenden Handel, 2008, 520 et seqq.

[41] See the so called Schwarzwaldklinik decision: BVerfGE 101, 151 et seqq.

the requirement of equal opportunities in competition.[42] However, a distortion of competition is only unconstitutional if it cannot be justified by a sufficiently weighty reason.[43] It is precisely here that the equality-based source of competition neutrality meets its freedom-based roots in the freedom of occupation and freedom of trade under Article 12 (1) GG.[44] Within the framework of freedom of occupation, the case law of the Federal Constitutional Court establishes the principle of freedom of competition under the premise of a market economy, which is intended to ensure protection against distortion of market conditions through state influence on factors relevant to competition.[45] Freedom of occupation thus ensures participation in competition in accordance with its functional conditions.[46] It protects competition, but not, in principle, from competition itself and rivalry.[47] An intervention is deemed to exist if state measures result in a significant competitive disadvantage.[48] Whether freedom of occupation protects against state competition can be discussed in the context of the principle of the tax state. The "principle of tax priority"[49] elevates the market economy as a form of economic organisation to the "prerequisite of the tax state".[50] The strict separation of state and economy is a defining feature.[51] This limits the state's own economic activity to an exceptional role.[52] The logic of the tax state corresponds to financing the common good through participation in the profits of private economic actors and not through direct profits from state participation in the market.[53] However, the tax constitution does not respond to the self-financing of the public sector with restrictions on market access,[54] but with the requirement of competitive neutrality as a rule of market conduct.[55]

---

[42] BVerfGE 21, 12 (27 et seq.); BVerfGE 27, 375 (386); BVerfGE 36, 321 (334); BVerfGE 43, 58 (72); BVerfGE 101, 132 (139); BVerfGE 101, 151 (155 et seq.).

[43] BVerfGE 21, 12 (27 et seq.).

[44] *Droege*, Gemeinnützigkeit im offenen Steuerstaat, 2010, 416 et seqq.; *Englisch*, Wettbewerbsgleichheit im grenzüberschreitenden Handel, 2008, 524 et seqq.

[45] BVerfGE 105, 252 (268); BVerfGE 106, 275 (298). Already: BVerfGE 32, 311 (317); BVerfGE 46, 120 (137); BVerfGE 86, 28 (37).

[46] BVerfGE 105, 252 (268); BVerfGE 106, 275 (298). See also: *Wissmann*, in: Herdegen/Masing/Poscher/Gärditz (eds.), Handbuch des Verfassungsrechts, 2025, § 23, para. 86 et seq.

[47] BVerfGE 7, 377 (408); BVerfGE 11, 168 (188 et seq.); BVerfGE 93, 362 (370); BVerfGE 97, 12 (31); *Englisch*, Wettbewerbsgleichheit im grenzüberschreitenden Handel, 2008, 522.

[48] *Englisch*, Wettbewerbsgleichheit im grenzüberschreitenden Handel, 2008, 523; with reference to: BVerfGE 82, 209 (223 et seq.); BVerfGE 86, 28 (37).

[49] *K. Vogel*, in: idem/Kirchhof (eds.), Handbuch des Staatsrechts II, 3rd ed., 2004, § 30, para. 70; similarly: *Drüen*, StuW 2008, 154, 154.

[50] *Isensee*, in: idem/Kirchhof (eds.), Handbuch des Staatsrechts V, 3rd ed., 2007, § 122, para. 70.

[51] *Isensee*, in: idem/Kirchhof (eds.), Handbuch des Staatsrechts V, 3rd ed., 2007, § 122, para. 72 et seq.

[52] *Kube*, in: Kischel/idem (eds.), Handbuch des Staatsrechts II, 4th ed., 2024, § 42, para. 104.

[53] On this point: *Ehlers*, Verwaltung in Privatrechtsform, 1984, 88 et seqq.; *G. Kirchhof*, in: idem/Magen/Korte (eds.), Öffentliches Wettbewerbsrecht, 2014, § 13, para. 1.

[54] *Storr*, Der Staat als Unternehmer, 2001, 100 et seqq.

[55] See also: *Droege*, Zur Besteuerung der öffentlichen Hand, 2018, 160 et seqq.

Nevertheless, the economic activities of the public sector are not an anomaly that needs to be overcome in the economic constitution of the Basic Law. Above all, the economic activities of local authorities are an element of public services and thus of the guarantee of local self-government under Article 28 (2) GG.[56] The tax legislator can therefore justify any tax-induced competitive advantages of municipal enterprises on the basis of municipal self-government as an intervention in the competitive neutrality of taxation.[57]

The strict interpretation of competitive neutrality, which denies any justification for tax exemptions for public enterprises, also contradicts the economic neutrality of the constitution.[58] The Basic Law does not prescribe a particular economic system, but leaves the shaping of the economic and social order to the political process and the democratic responsibility of the legislature. This openness of the Basic Law is also supported by EU law, which gives Member States extensive freedom in determining the boundaries between the private and public sectors (Article 345 TFEU).[59] There is no "priority for private provision of services" under EU law.[60]

Competitive neutrality is therefore not an immutable outcome of a fundamental rights-based assessment, but rather serves the initial reference point for such an evaluation. It constitutes an open principle that permits for legislative intervention when supported by sufficient public interest considerations. Economic activity by the public sector is not a foreign concept in constitutional law. On the contrary, it remains bound to the public interest of the state. For the public sector, profit-making is not an end in itself, but serves to finance public tasks. The limits of the partial tax liability of the public sector are open under constitutional law. The neutral economic and financial constitution of the Basic Law gives the legislature freedom of design.

---

[56] *Cronauge*, Kommunale Unternehmen, 6th ed., 2016, 127 para. 118; *Lange*, Kommunalrecht, 2nd ed., 2019, 884, para. 65.

[57] *Droege*, Zur Besteuerung der öffentlichen Hand, 2017, 93 with further references.

[58] Fundamental: BVerfGE 4, 7 (17); 7, 377 (400); 50, 290 (337). See also: *R. Schmidt*, in: Isensee/Kirchhof (eds.), Handbuch des Staatsrechts IV, 3rd ed. 2006, § 92, para. 24 et seqq.; *Wollenschläger*, in: idem/R. Schmidt (eds.), Kompendium Öffentliches Wirtschaftsrecht, 6th ed., 2024, § 2, para. 3 et seqq.; *idem*, in: G. Kirchhof/Magen/Korte (eds.), Öffentliches Wettbewerbsrecht, 2014, § 6, para. 56.

[59] On the economic constitution of Union law, see: *Hatje*, in: v. Bogdandy/Bast (eds.), Europäisches Verfasungsrecht, 2009, 801 (809 et seqq.); *Wollenschläger*, in: idem/R. Schmidt (eds.), Kompendium Öffentliches Wirtschaftsrecht, 2024, § 1, para. 3 et seqq.

[60] *Wernicke*, in: Grabitz/Hilf/Nettesheim, Das Recht der Europäischen Union, Kommentar, 61st ed. April 2017, Art. 345, para. 5.

IV. Taxation and Its Peculiarities in Relation to the Economic Activities of the Public Sector

1. Corporate Income Tax Law

In corporate income tax law, commercial operations are the decisive limiting factor for partial tax liability on the part of the public sector.[61] The legal basis for this in corporation tax law is the maintenance of a commercial operation in accordance with Section 1 (1) No. 6 of the Corporation Tax Act (KStG).[62] This is defined in more detail in Section 4 KStG. According to this, it must be a sustainable economic activity aimed at generating income outside of agriculture and forestry, which also stands out economically within the overall activities of the legal entity.[63] According to Section 4 (1) sentence 2 KStG, the intention to make a profit and participation in general economic transactions are dispensable – in a surprising departure from the established type of commercial income for income tax purposes.[64] According to Section 4 (5) KStG, the public authority operation or sovereign enterprises, i.e. enterprises that primarily serve the exercise of public authority, are not commercial enterprises.[65]

The tax exemption of the public sector outside its commercial enterprises is thus already derived from Section 4 (1) sentence 1 KStG.[66] Section 4 (5) KStG concerns so-called mixed enterprises and is significant in this respect in that it is intended to ensure a distinction in cases where institutions of legal entities under public law only partially serve the exercise of public authority and otherwise serve economic activities.[67]

According to Section 4 (3) KStG, commercial enterprises necessarily include utilities supplying water, gas, electricity and heat, as well as port and transport companies.[68] This legal definition of a commercial enterprise enriches adminis-

[61] On the following, see also: *Droege*, Zur Besteuerung der öffentlichen Hand, 2017, 29 et seqq. and *Hinder*, in: Musil/Küffner (eds.), Besteuerung der öffentlichen Hand, 2022, chapter 4, para. 4.14 et seqq.; *Hidien*, in: idem/Jürgens (eds.), Besteuerung der öffentlichen Hand, 2nd ed. 2023, § 4, para. 85 et seqq.

[62] On the opinion and distinction made by the tax authorities: R 4.1 and H 4.1 KStH 2022 on BgA pursuant to Section 4 (1) KStG.

[63] For more details: *Hinder*, in: Musil/Küffner (eds.), Besteuerung der öffentlichen Hand, 2022, chapter 4, para. 4.33; *Hidien*, in: idem/Jürgens (eds.), Besteuerung der öffentlichen Hand, 2nd ed. 2023, § 4, para. 157 et seqq.

[64] *Hidien*, in: idem/Jürgens (eds.), Besteuerung der öffentlichen Hand, 2nd ed. 2023, § 4 para. 254 et seqq.

[65] BFH of 8 July 1971, V R 1/68, BStBl. II 1972, p. 70 et seqq.; *Meier/Semelka*, in: Herrmann/Heuer/Raupach (eds.), EStG/KStG, 319. Lfg., 7/2023, § 4 KStG para. 20.

[66] *Hüttemann*, Besteuerung der öffentlichen Hand, 2002, 75 et seq. with further references.

[67] *Meier/Semelka*, in: Herrmann/Heuer/Raupach (eds.), EStG/KStG, 319. Lfg., 7/2023, § 4 KStG para. 70; *Hinder*, in: Musil/Küffner (eds.), Besteuerung der öffentlichen Hand, 2022, chapter 4 para. 4.105 et seqq.

[68] For more details, see: *Hinder*, in: Musil/Küffner (eds.), Besteuerung der öffentlichen Hand, 2022, Chapter 4, para. 4.66 et seqq.

trative practice with a quantitative materiality threshold by considering an annual turnover exceeding EUR 130,000 to be indicative of the "economically independent entity" required here in the factual characteristic of the institution.[69] Quantitatively, it also determines and indicates the legal criterion of economic prominence if an annual turnover of EUR 45,000 is sustainably exceeded.[70]

Income tax law also uses commercial operations as a reference point for capital gains taxation. According to Section 20 (1) No. 10 lit. a Income Tax Act (*Einkommenssteuergesetz*, EStG), payments from a commercial operation with its own legal personality that is not exempt from corporation tax lead to income from capital assets that is subject to income tax. Section 10 (1) No. 10 lit. b EStG extends this type of income to profit transfers from a legally dependent commercial enterprise to the respective supporting body.[71]

A distinctive feature of public sector taxation is the linking of tax liability to the individual and separated commercial enterprise. The wording of Section 1 (1) No. 6 of the Corporation Tax Act (KStG) declares "commercial enterprises of legal entities under public law" to be subject to unlimited tax liability, thus suggesting that they are liable for tax.[72] Income tax is thus decoupled from the principle of personality[73] and the role of the legal entity under public law as an administrative body and the entity to which tax rights and obligations are assigned. The Federal Finance Court (*Bundesfinanzhof*, BFH) rightly opposed this half a century ago. The Federal Finance Court has taken the view that it is not the individual commercial enterprise, but the legal entity under public law that is to be regarded as the taxable entity and "as the entity to which Section1 (1) No. 6 KStG applies for each individual commercial enterprise".[74]

However, case law does not consistently apply this allocation of the commercial enterprise to its supporting body; instead it treats the commercial enterprise as independent for the purpose of determining the tax base. For example, the Federal Finance Court considers the commercial enterprise to be partially independent persuant to Section 1 (1) No. 6 KStG and treats it as an independent profit determination unit.[75] The supporting body is only to be treated as a tax entity "for each of its commercial enterprises"[76]. However, the income for each

---

[69] Guideline 4.1 (4) sentence 2 KStR 2022; *Meier/Semelka*, in: Herrmann/Heuer/Raupach (eds.), EStG/KStG, 319. Lfg., 7/2023, § 4 para. 22.

[70] Guideline 4.1 (5) sentence 1 KStR 2022; *Meier/Semelka*, in: Herrmann/Heuer/Raupach (eds.), EStG/KStG, 319. Lfg., 7/2023, § 4 para. 46.

[71] *Hüttemann*, Besteuerung der öffentlichen Hand, 2002, 20.

[72] Still: BFH of 15 September 1961 – VI 228/60 U, Federal Tax Gazette III 1961, 552, 553.

[73] Fundamental: *Palm*, Person im Ertragssteuerrecht, 2013.

[74] BFH of 13 March 1974 – I R 7/71, Federal Tax Gazette II 1974, p. 391 (393). On this point: *Droege*, Gemeinnützigkeit im offenen Steuerstaat, 2010, 271 et seq.

[75] *Märtens*, in: Gosch (ed.), KStG, 4th ed. 2020, § 4, para. 23 et seq.; *Wallenhorst*, in: idem/Halaczinsky (eds.), Die Besteuerung gemeinnütziger und öffentlich-rechtlicher Körperschaften, 2017, chapter H para. 2 et seqq.

[76] BFH of 11 February 1997 – I R 161/94, BFH/NV 1997, 625 (625 with further references) and already BFH of 13 March 1974 – I R 7/71, Federal Tax Gazette II 1974, 391 et seq.

commercial operation is to be determined separately, "as if the commercial operation were an independent tax entity in the legal form of a corporation and the supporting body were its sole shareholder"[77]. Accordingly, the offsetting of profits and losses between commercial operations is generally excluded. The commercial enterprise, "which was initially denied the status of a taxable entity, is therefore treated at the level of legal consequences as a fictitiously independent 'virtual corporation'".[78]

This atomization of the tax subjectivity of public corporations and the independence of commercial operations is not only inconsistent.[79] It also discriminates against public law entities compared to other corporations that are subject to corporate tax.[80]

Above all, they lead to compensation strategies that are questionable from a tax perspective in the form of a complex area of exceptions to the offsetting of profits and losses. This refers to the legal regulation of cross-subsidisation or interconnection (*Querverbund*) in the form of Sections 4 (6), 8 (7) to (9) and 15 (4) and (5) KStG.[81] The rationale behind cross-subsidisation and tax cross-connection is to overcome the determination of profits for public corporations based on individual commercial operations in accordance with Section 1 (6) KStG.[82] Via the references in Sections 8 (7) to (9), 15 sentence 1 nos. 4 and 5 KStG, the principles set out in Section 4 (6) KStG apply accordingly to the consolidation of public enterprises within the framework of a corporation and in a tax group. Section 4 (6) KStG now allows the consolidation of commercial enterprises in the case of the catalogue enterprises listed in Section 4 (3) KStG, if they are of a similar nature and if, based on the overall picture of the actual circumstances, there is objectively a close mutual technical and economic interdependence of some significance between them. The tax authorities have specified these regulations in

---

77 BFH of 3 February 1993 – I R 61/91, Federal Tax Gazette II 1993, 459, 460; BFH of 9 July 2003 – I R 48/02 Federal Tax Gazette II 2004, 425 et seqq. However, see also on profit reduction through special use fees paid to the supporting body: BFH, decision of 6 November 2007, I R 72/06, Federal Tax Gazette II 2009, 246 et seqq. On profit determination in BgA, see also: *Schleiter*, Der kommunale Querverbund im System des deutschen Ertragssteuerrechts, 2014, 60 et seqq.

78 See also: *Damas*, DStZ 2005, 866, 867: "Fictitious independence"; *Wallenhorst*, in: idem/Halaczinsky (eds.), Die Besteuerung gemeinnütziger und öffentlich-rechtlicher Körperschaften, 2017, chapter H, para. 62 et seqq.

79 *Wenk/Stein*, FR 1999, 573 (576): "contrary to the system".

80 *Seer/Wendt*, DStR 2001, 825, 834 et seq. For a review of the dispute, see: *Siegel*, Der Begriff des "Betriebs gewerblicher Art" im Körperschafts- und Umsatzsteuerrecht, 1999, 51 et seqq.

81 Act of 19 December 2008, Federal Law Gazette 2008 I, 2794, 2794; See also: Draft bill of the Federal Government, BT-Drs. 16/1089; Recommendation for a decision and report of the Finance Committee, BT-Drs. 16/11055, 16/11108. For details, see only: *Hinder*, in: Musil/Küffner (eds.), Besteuerung der öffentlichen Hand, 2022, chapter 4, para. 4.116 et seqq.; *Jürgens/Menebröcker*, in: Hidien/Jürgens (eds.), Die Besteuerung der öffentlichen Hand, 2nd ed. 2023, § 5 para. 213 et seqq.

82 BFH of 11 February 1997 – I R 161/94 – BFH/NV 1997, 625 with further references, and already BFH of 13 March 1974 – I R 7/71, Federal Tax Gazette 1974 II, 391.

relation to questions of so-called chain consolidation,[83] i. e. consolidation with consolidated commercial enterprises, but also in an artificial manner in relation to the concept of a utility company within the meaning of Section 4 (3) KStG.[84] By waiving the material criteria of similarity and close mutual technical and economic interdependence for the consolidation of the businesses listed in Section 4 (3) KStG, the legislator privileges these loss-making areas of municipal public services. In terms of regulation, there are clear parallels with the withdrawal of the regulatory claim of municipal commercial law through the fiction of non-commercial activities for catalogued activities in the field of municipal services, which is widespread in municipal law.[85]

The regulation of cross-subsidisation takes on the character of a non-application law primarily because, according to Section 8 (7) KStG, the maintenance of permanent loss-making operations should not lead to a hidden distribution of profits.[86] First, the legislator grants tax recognition for losses from permanently loss-making commercial operations. According to Section 8 (1) sentence 2 KStG, neither participation in general business transactions nor the intent to make a profit is required to generate income. The new regulation then excludes the legal consequences of a hidden profit distribution in deviation from Section 8 (3) KStG. The exclusion of legal consequences in Section 8 (7) KStG applies to permanent loss-making operations as defined in the sentence 2 of that section. According to this, a permanent loss-making enterprise exists if an economic activity is maintained for reasons of traffic, environmental, social, cultural, educational or health policy without cost-covering remuneration.[87] According to the clarification of the Federal Ministry of Finance, the determination of a permanent loss is based on the fact that a positive or balanced result or a total taxable profit is not to be expected on the basis of a forecast according to the circumstances of the respective assessment period.[88]

The preferential treatment of permanent losses applies not only to the determination of profits in commercial enterprises, but also in municipal enterprises and tax units. In the case of proprietary companies, however, Section 8 (7) sentence 1 No. 2 KStG requires that the majority of voting rights be held directly or indirectly by legal entities under public law and that the permanent losses be

---

83 *Bracksiek*, FR 2009, 15, 16; *Hüttemann*, DB 2009, 2629, 2630.

84 BMF of 12 November 2009, IV C 7 – S 2706/08/10004, Federal Tax Gazette 2009 I, 1303 margin note 9 et seq., 64 et seq. For detailed case studies, see: *Jürgens/Menebröcker*, in: Hidien/Jürgens (eds.), Die Besteuerung der öffentlichen Hand, 2nd ed. 2023, § 5 para. 314 et seqq., 364 et seqq.

85 For example, § 107 (2) GO NW. See also: *Cronauge*, Kommunale Unternehmen, 2016, 138 et seq. margin note 404.

86 In detail: *Hinder*, in: Musil/Küffner (eds.), Besteuerung der öffentlichen Hand, 2022, Chapter 4, para. 4.236 et seqq.; *Jürgens*, in: Hidien/idem (eds.), Die Besteuerung der öffentlichen Hand, 2nd ed. 2023, § 5 para. 662 et seqq.

87 *Meier*, FR 2010, 168.

88 BMF of 12 November 2009, IV C 7 – S 2706/08/10004, Federal Tax Gazette 2009 I, 1303, n. 36.

demonstrably borne exclusively by these entities.[89] In order to prevent the limitations of the privilege of permanent loss-making enterprises from being circumvented or extended by joint determination of profits, section 8(8) KStG provides for restrictions on the use of losses in combined enterprises. In the case of a merger of different business activities, permanent losses are generally frozen for the duration of the merger. In the case of corporations in which joint determination of profits is the norm in their various fields of activity, the legislator simulates this isolated determination of the total amount of income by means of the highly complex divisional accounting pursuant to Section 8 (9) KStG.

Finally, this brief overview of the basic structures of public sector income taxation would be incomplete if it focused solely on the issues of personal tax liability of the public sector and thus on the sphere of taxability. This is because the public sector benefits from a wide range of factual tax exemptions in individual tax laws, which translate the public interest of its activities into tax terms. This refers to the tax-exempt status of the public sector across tax types. Tax-exempt entities, as defined in Sections 51 et seq. of the German Fiscal Code (*Abgabenordnung*, AO), enjoy numerous tax exemptions. In terms of income tax, they are exempt from corporation tax pursuant to Section 5 (1) No. 9 KStG and from trade tax pursuant to Section 3 (1) No. 6 GewStG. A corresponding exemption was granted by Section 3 (1) No. 12 Wealth Tax Act (*Vermögensteuergesetz*, VStG) for the wealth tax last levied in the 1995 assessment period, and is granted by Section 3 (1) No. 3b Property Tax Act (*Grundsteuergestz*, GrStG) for property tax. Donations to non-profit organisations are also exempt from gift and inheritance tax pursuant to Section 13 (1) No. 16b, 17 Inheritance and Gift Tax Act (ErbStG).[90] The public sector can, in principle, enjoy non-profit status. Provided that they meet the formal requirements of their articles of incorporation, commercial enterprises have the option of obtaining non-profit status if their governing body decides to adopt articles of incorporation that meet the requirements of Section 60 AO.[91] The tax exemption of the sovereign domain and the traditional factual parallel between Section 4 (1) KStG and Section 64 German Fiscal Code mean that non-profit law is important in the area of economic activity of the public sector and thus its commercial enterprises.[92] The non-profit status of the public sector is determined – and its significance is exhausted – in the concept of special-purpose operations or ancillary business pursuant to Sections 65 et seq. AO and their tax exemption.[93]

---

[89] *Westermann/Prechtl*, KStZ 2010, 149, 150 et seq.

[90] *Meincke/Hannes/Holtz*, in: idem (eds)., ErbStG, 19th ed. 2025, § 13 n. 71; *Jülicher*, in: Troll/Gebel/idem/Gottschalk (eds.), ErbStG, 86. Lfg. 3/2024, § 13 n. 187.

[91] See *Mehren*, in: Schauhoff/Kirchhain (eds.), Handbuch der Gemeinnützigkeit, 4th ed. 2023, § 5 n. 16 on formal compliance with the articles of association.

[92] *Mehren*, in: Schauhoff/Kirchhain (eds.), Handbuch der Gemeinnützigkeit, 4th ed. 2023, § 5 n. 10 et seqq.

[93] *Hüttemann*, in: idem (ed.), Gemeinnützigkeitsrecht und Spendenrecht, 6th ed. 2025, chapter 2 para. 2.90.

The distinction made there between the promotion of the common good and the protection of competitive neutrality culminates in the competition clause of Section 65 No. 3 AO, according to which economic business operations may not compete with non-privileged businesses of the same or a similar type to a greater extent than is unavoidable in fulfilling the tax-privileged purposes, but which is interpreted restrictively by case law in transfer of what were originally VAT assessments.[94] In the field of non-profit law, too, the case law of the Federal Fiscal Court finally implements the shift towards a functional determination of the limits of partial tax liability, which is so characteristic for the tax treatment of the public sector in general.[95]

2. Value Added Tax Law

In the past, commercial operations were also the central concept,[96] which, in VAT law, marked the partial tax liability of the public sector in line with income tax law:[97] Section 2 (3) Value Added Tax Act (*Umsatzsteuergesetz*, UStG) (old version)[98] linked commercial activity – and thus the entrepreneurial status of the public sector – to the maintenance of a commercial operation.

However, the consistency with corporate income tax law traditionally established in VAT law by linking it to commercial operations was in contradiction with the VAT System Directive, which was recognised early on[99] but was surprisingly accepted for a long time.[100] EU law also initially requires that the public sector engage in economic activity within the meaning of Article 9 of the VAT Directive.[101] Following on from this, Article 13 of the VAT Directive distinguishes be-

---

[94] For example, BFH of 17 February 2010 – I R 2/08, Federal Tax Gazette 2010 II, 1006; BFH of 7 October 2010 – V R 12/10, Federal Tax Gazette 2011 II, 303; of 30 November 2016 – V R 53/15, Federal Tax Gazette 2017 II. See also BGH of 8 October 2015 – I ZR 225/13, NJOZ 2016, 1618; of 16 May 2017 – II ZB 7/16, BGHZ 215, 69; BFH of 18 August 2022 – V R 9/19, Federal Tax Gazette 2023 II, 298; of 21 April 2022 – V R 26/20, Federal Tax Gazette 2022 II, 599.

[95] For example: BFH of 18 August 2011 – V R 64/09, HFR 2012, 784; BFH of 24 September 2014 – V R 11/14, BFH/NV 2015, 528 et seqq.

[96] *Hidien*, in: FS Schmidt-Jortzig, 2011, 483, 490.

[97] *Reimer*, in: Seer (ed.), Umsatzsteuer im Europäischen Binnenmarkt, DStJG 32 (2009), 325, 336 et seqq.

[98] Repealed by Art. 12 No. 2 of the Tax Amendment Act 2015, Federal Law Gazette 2015 I, 1843. See also: Recommendation and report of the Finance Committee on the draft bill of the Federal Government, BT-Drs. 18/4902, BT-Drs. 18/6094, 91 et seq. and BMF of 16 December 2016, III C 2 – S 7107/16/10001, Federal Tax Gazette 2016 I, 1451.

[99] BRH, Bericht nach § 99 BHO zur umsatzsteuerlichen Behandlung der öffentlichen Hand – Vorschläge für eine EG-konforme Besteuerung juristischer Personen des öffentlichen Rechts, BT-Drs. 15/4081.

[100] See *Heidner*, in: Musil/Küffner (eds.), Besteuerung der öffentlichen Hand, 2022, chapter 5, para. 5.42

[101] Council Directive 2006/112/EC on the common system of value added tax, of 28 November 2006, EC OJ 2006 L 347, 1, corr. EU OJ 2007 L 335, 60, as amended on 27 June 2016. See the requirements for self-employment arising from Article 9 of the VAT Directive: ECJ, judgment v.

tween different spheres depending on whether public law institutions carry out activities that are incumbent upon them within the framework of public authority.[102] Similar to the provision in Section 4 (3) KStG, this does not apply to the activities listed in Annex 1 to the VAT Directive, in particular, in a municipal context, the supply of water, gas, electricity, and thermal energy under point 1. Under Article 13 (2) of the VAT Directive, Member States may also designate activities in the area of optional VAT exemptions as being carried out in the exercise of public authority. However, due to the exception in Article 13 (1) sentence 2 of the VAT Directive, activities that are the responsibility of public law institutions within the scope of public authority are assigned to the commercial sphere if their tax exemption would lead to "significant distortions of competition".[103]

The ECJ defines the term "exercise of public authority" entirely within the competition paradigm, not according to the subject matter of an activity, but rather based on the legal framework of the activity.[104] The resulting shifts in boundaries can be understood using the example of asset management, which is generally harmless in terms of income tax.[105] Here, the ECJ not only clarified that the question of whether an activity qualifies as a sovereign activity and whether this leads to major distortions of competition is not determined by the effects on the specific local market, but that it must be answered in relation to the activity as such.[106] In the Salix case, the Court also ruled that the letting of land is, in principle, a commercial activity carried out by public law institutions.[107]

As a result of these developments, the Federal Court of Finance has largely removed the concept of commercial activities from its use in income tax law, based on the competition criterion of Article 13 of the VAT Directive,[108] and ultimately rendered Section 2 (3) of the UStG (old version) "de facto invalid".[109] The most far-reaching intervention was the extension of the public sector's entrepreneurial sphere to forms of municipal cooperation in the form of so-called

29.9.2015 – Case C-276/14, MwStR 2015, 926; see also: ECJ, judgment v. 12.10.2016 – Case C-340/15, MwStR 2016, 905; BFH of 15 December 2016 – V R 44/15, BFH/NV 2017, 707.

102 On the individual criteria: *Küffner*, in: Musil/idem (eds.), Besteuerung der öffentlichen Hand, 2022, chapter 3, para. 3.60 et seqq.

103 *Beinert/Kostic*, in: Hoppe/Uechtritz/Reck (eds.) Handbuch Kommunale Unternehmen, 3rd ed. 2012, § 11 para. 161 et seqq.

104 *Reimer*, in: Seer (ed.), Umsatzsteuer im Europäischen Binnenmarkt, DStJG 32 (2009), 325, 339 et seq. with further references.

105 See: *Hidien*, in: idem/Jürgens (eds.), Die Besteuerung der öffentlichen Hand, 2nd ed. 2023, § 4 para. 430 et seqq.

106 ECJ, judgment v. 16.9.2009 – Case C-288/07 (Isle of Wight), ECR 2008, I-7203.

107 ECJ, judgment v. 4.6.2009 – Case C-102/08 (Salix), ECR 2009, I-4631.

108 For example: BFH of 20 August 2009 – V R 70/05, Federal Tax Gazette 2017 II, 825 et seqq.; BFH of 20 August 2009 – V R 30/06, Federal Tax Gazette 2010 II, 863 ff.; BFH of 17 March 2010 – XI R 17/08, Federal Tax Gazette 2017 II, 828 et seqq.; BFH of 15 April 2010 – V R 10/09, Federal Tax Gazette 2017 II, 863; BFH of 10 November 2011 – V R 41/10, Federal Tax Gazette 2017 II, 869 et seqq. On the application of case law under § 2b UStG n.F.: BMF of 27 July 2017, II C 2 – S7106/0:002, Federal Tax Gazette 2017 I, 1239.

109 *Heidner*, UR 2016, 45.

municipal assistance services.[110] The legislator sought to satisfy the need for normative adjustment to the VAT treatment of the public sector, which was fuelled both by the judiciary and by EU law, with the new regulation of Section 2b UStG.[111]

According to the basic provisions of Section 2b (1) sentence 1 UStG, legal entities under public law are not considered entrepreneurs as they perform activities that fall within the scope of public authority, even if they levy customs duties, fees, contributions or other charges in connection with these activities. The provision thus expressly refers only to activities within the scope of public authority, so that the entrepreneurial status of legal persons under public law outside this scope is governed by the general criteria of Section 2 (1) UStG. Section 2b (1) sentence 1 UStG also applies to the activities listed in Section 2b (4) UStG, which are in any case to be classified as business activities. According to Section 2b (1) sentence 2 UStG, however, the exclusion of the entrepreneurial status in the public sector does not apply if the treatment as a non-entrepreneur would lead to significant distortions of competition. In this respect, the federal legislator has not only adopted the central concepts but also the regulatory technique of directive law. However, it has also defined the concept of significant distortion of competition in more detail. According to Section 2b (2) UStG, "in particular" no significant distortion of competition is to be assumed if the turnover of a legal entity under public law from similar activities is not expected to exceed EUR 17,500 per calendar year (No. 1) or if comparable services provided under private law without the right of waiver (Section 9 UStG) are tax-exempt (No. 2). While the latter case is intended to prevent competitive disadvantages for the public sector and thus maintain a level playing field[112] the residual threshold consideration is alien to Article 13 of the VAT Directive.[113]

Section 2b of the UStG denies the existence of a significant distortion of competition, in particular in the case of certain activities carried out for another legal entity under public law. The legislator's aim is to maintain the VAT exemption in the area of administrative cooperation.[114] According to Section 2b (3) sentence 1 UStG, there is no significant distortion of competition if a service is provided to another legal entity under public law if, on the basis of statutory provisions, the services may only be provided by legal entities under public law (No. 1) or if the

[110] BFH of 10 November 2011 – V R 41/10, Federal Tax Gazette 2017 II, 869 et seqq.

[111] Art. 12 of the Tax Amendment Act 2015 of 2 November 2015, Federal Law Gazette 2015 I, 1834. See also: *Menebröcker*, in: Hidien/Jürgens (eds.), Die Besteuerung der Öffentlichen Hand, 2nd ed. 2023, § 9 para. 372 et seqq. See also: Recommendation for a decision and report of the Finance Committee on the Federal Government's draft bill, BT-Drs. 18/4902, BT-Drs. 18/6094, 91.

[112] Recommendation for a decision and report of the Finance Committee on the Federal Government's draft bill, BT-Drs. 18/4902, BT-Drs. 18/6094, p. 91.

[113] See also: *Hidien*, in: idem/Jürgens (eds.), Die Besteuerung der öffentlichen Hand, 2nd ed. 2023, § 4 para. 1216 et seqq.

[114] Recommendation for a decision and report of the Finance Committee on the draft bill of the Federal Government, BT-Drs. 18/4902, BT-Drs. 18/6094, 91 et seq.

cooperation is determined by common specific public interests (No. 2). The latter shall be the case in accordance with Section 2b (3), No. 2 sentence 2 lit. a-d UStG, this should regularly be the case if the services are based on long-term public law agreements, serve to maintain public infrastructure and perform a public task incumbent on all parties involved, are provided exclusively against reimbursement of costs, and the service provider essentially provides similar services to other legal entities under public law.

The new regulation not only requires considerable adaptation, but also leaves considerable room for interpretation, especially because it refers to undefined legal concepts, such as the specific public interest, in the contours of the quantitative element of distortion of competition.[115] It is therefore not surprising that the tax authorities immediately tried to limit the new regulation through executive standard setting.[116]

A few comments on the specific requirements: First, Section 2b UStG requires a legal entity under public law. The norm establishes a causal link between entrepreneurial status and the constitution as a legal entity under public law.[117] This includes, in particular, local authorities, religious communities under public law, and other entities that have their own legal personality under public law. However, Article 13 of the VAT Directive does not refer to legal personality, but rather to the existence of a "body governed by public law". In its autonomous interpretation of the criterion of "public law", the ECJ has focused on the integration of an institution into the organisation of public administration and the associated powers of control[118] and has thus also classified an institution in the legal form of a private law public limited company as a public institution.[119] However, the ECJ does not consider the transfer of tasks alone to be sufficient for this purpose.[120] This means that Section 2b UStG is in principle also open to municipal companies under private law. However, in addition to the transfer of tasks by way of a mandate,[121] in such cases of organisational privatisation, according to case law[122] and the tax authorities,[123] sufficient integration into the

---

[115] For criticism of this, see: *Baldauf*, DStZ 2016, 355, 369: "unclear legal terms"; *Müller*, UR 2017, 8, 17.

[116] BMF of 16 December 2016, III C 2 – S 7107/16/10001, Federal Tax Gazette 2016 I, 1431.

[117] *Treiber*, in: Sölch/Ringleb (eds.), UStG, 97. Lfg. 3/2023, § 2b n. 32.

[118] ECJ, judgment v. 29.10.2015 – C-174/14 (Saudaçor), n. 56; ECJ, judgment v. 21.5.2008 – C-456/07 (Mihal), n. 18.

[119] ECJ, judgment v. 29.10.2015 – C-174/14 (Saudaçor), n. 61.

[120] ECJ, judgment v. 22.2.2018 – C-182/17 (Ntp. Nagyszénás (NTN)), MwStR 2018, 348 w n *Sterzinger*.

[121] Section 2b.1 (2) UStAE in conjunction with BMF letter of 18 September 2019, Federal Tax Gazette I 2019, 921 = MwStR 2019, 881.

[122] BFH of 21 March 2018 – XI B 113/17, BeckRS 2018, 9899.

[123] No. 2b.1 (2) UStAE in conjunction with BMF letter dated 18 September 2019, Federal Tax Gazette I 2019, 921 = MwStR 2019, 881.

public administration is required, accompanied by control instruments similar to those of a fiscal unity.[124]

Second, Section 2b of the UStG, with reference to Section 2 (1) of the UStG, requires that a legal entity under public law that engages in business activities must do so on a commercial basis in the sense of a sustainable activity aimed at generating income.[125] An economic activity within the meaning of Article 9 of the VAT Directive is understood to be an independent, sustainable activity aimed at generating income which stands out within the overall activities of a legal person governed by public law.[126] This is lacking in the case of a complete disproportion between performance and (only symbolic) remuneration.[127] In this case, there is not only a lack of remuneration for services rendered, but also a lack of economic activity justifying subjective tax liability. The other limits of taxability resulting from Section 2 (1) of the UStG, such as the exclusion of so-called ancillary transactions due to a lack of sustainability, also remain unchanged.[128]

Third, Section 2b of the UStG requires that the activity in question is assigned to the public sector. According to both EU law and the opinion of the legislator, it is not the material qualification of the activity that is decisive here. Rather, only those activities in which the legal entity under public law acts within the framework of a special regulation under public law are considered to be activities incumbent upon a legal entity under public law within the framework of public authority.[129] The traditional area of sovereign activity, which was characterised by the peculiarities and reservations of the public sector,[130] is being replaced by the special legal regime peculiar to and reserved for the public sector. An activity does not constitute an exercise of public authority if a legal entity under public law provides services on the basis of private law and thus under the same legal conditions as private economic operators.[131]

---

[124] Section 2b.1 (2) UStAE in conjunction with BMF letter dated 18 September 2019, Federal Tax Gazette I 2019, 921 = MwStR 2019, 881.

[125] BMF letter dated 16 December 2016, Federal Tax Gazette I 2016, 1451 n. 4 = DStR 2017, 40; *Bunjes,* in: idem/Korn (eds.), UStG, 24th ed. 2025, § 2b n. 5, 11 mVwa, § 2 n. 7; *Stadie*, in: Rau/Dürrwächter (eds.), Kommentar zum Umsatzsteuergesetz, 198. Lfg., 3/2022, § 2b UstG n. 339 et seqq.

[126] See BMF letter dated 16 December 2016, Federal Tax Gazette I 2016, 1451 n. 4 = DStR 2017, 40; see also BFHE 256, 557 = DStR 2017, 656; *Ehrke-Rabel*, in: Weitemeyer/Schauhoff/Achatz (eds.), Umsatzsteuerrecht für den Nonprofitsektor, 2019, n. 6.15 et seqq.

[127] ECJ, judgment v. 12.5.2016 – Case 520/14 (Gemeente Borsele), ECLI:EU:C:2016:334.

[128] See BMF letter 16 December 2016, Federal Tax Gazette I 2016, 1451 n. 19 et seqq. = DStR 2017, 40; section 2b.1 (9) UStAE.

[129] For justification, see ECJ, judgment v. 17.10.1989 – Case 231/87, Case 129/88 (Ufficio distrettuale delle imposte dirette di Fiorenzuola d'Arda), ECR 1989, 3233.

[130] For example, RFH, judgment v. 9.7.1937 – V D 1/37, RStBl. 1937, 1306, 1307; 2.7.1938 – GrS D 5/38, RStBl. 1938, 743.

[131] BMF letter dated 16 December 2016, Federal Tax Gazette I 2016, 1451 n. 6 = DStR 2017, 40; see also: Recommendation for a decision and report of the Finance Committee on the draft bill of the Federal Government, BT-Drs. 18/4902, BT-Drs. 18/6094, 91.

Fourth, the classification of activities as public authority activities results in their non-taxability for VAT purposes only if they do not cause significant distortions of competition. In contrast to the traditional distinction between public and private activities, this means that, in principle, the entire sphere of activity of legal entities under public law is subject to competition restrictions and taxation. The tax authorities have rightly pointed out that what matters is the market relevance of a legal entity's activity.[132] The assessment should be made irrespective of whether or not the institutions concerned are exposed to competition at the local market level, except in exceptional cases where private operators do not have access to the local market.[133] If there are no specific purchase and purchase obligations for services of the same type in a geographically defined area, potential competition cannot be excluded in principle.[134]

Market relevance should primarily be determined based on the type of service provided. Two services are similar and in competition if, from the average consumer‘s perspective, they satisfy the same needs.[135] Differences in the legal framework of the services are generally irrelevant, unless the differences in the legal framework of the services result in a distinction from the consumer's point of view in terms of satisfying his own needs or in restrictions on market access for a private entrepreneur.[136] In adaptation of the case law of the ECJ,[137] the Federal Ministry of Finance also points out that it is also potential competition that is harmful in this respect, provided that there is a real and not merely hypothetical possibility for private economic operators to enter the relevant market.[138] This is particularly true if and to the extent that there are spatially limited management regimes with corresponding purchase obligations.[139] Public monopolies, therefore, also hinder potential competition.[140]

---

[132] BMF letter dated 16 December 2016, Federal Tax Gazette I 2016, 1451 n. 23 et seqq. = DStR 2017, 40.

[133] BMF letter dated 16 December 2016, Federal Tax Gazette I 2016, 1451 n. 24 et seqq. = DStR 2017, 40. See also ECJ, judgment v. 16.9.2008 – Case 288/07 (Isle of Wight), ECR 2008, I-7203. See also: *Hüttemann*, UR 2017, 129, 132.

[134] See also the example of cremation: BMF letter dated 16 December 2016, Federal Tax Gazette I 2016, 1451 n. 28 = DStR 2017, 40; BFH of 5 October 2006 – VII R 24/03, Federal Tax Gazette II 2007, 243 = DStR 2006, 2310. Most recently on this subject, ECJ, judgment v. 19.1.2017 – Case 344/15 (National Roads Authority), ECLI:EU:C:2017:28.

[135] BMF letter 16 December 2016, Federal Tax Gazette I 2016, 1451 n. 24 = DStR 2017, 40.

[136] BMF letter dated 16 December 2016, Federal Tax Gazette I 2016, 1451 n. 26 = DStR 2017, 40.

[137] ECJ, judgment v. 16.9.2008 – Case 288/07 (Isle of Wight), ECR 2008, I-7203.

[138] BMF letter 16 December 2016, Federal Tax Gazette I 2016, 1451 n. 24 = DStR 2017, 40.

[139] BMF letter dated 16 December 2016, Federal Tax Gazette I 2016, 1451 n. 28 = DStR 2017, 40. See also a corresponding ruling by the Federal Fiscal Court (BFH) dated 5 October 2006 – VII R 24/03, Federal Tax Gazette II 2007, 243 = DStR 2006, 2310.

[140] ECJ, judgment v. 16.9.2008 – Case 288/07 (Isle of Wight), ECR 2008, I-7203; 13.12.2007 – Case 408/06 (Götz), ECR 2007 I-11295. See also ECJ, judgment v. 19.1.2017 – Case 344/15 (National Roads Authority), ECLI:EU:C:2017:28.

The legislator has also quantitatively defined the scope of VAT liability with regard to the criterion of significant distortion of competition.[141] According to Section 2b (2) No. 1 UStG, there is no distortion of competition if the turnover generated by a legal entity under public law from similar activities is not expected to exceed € 17,500 in a calendar year.[142] The ECJ interprets a greater distortion of competition to mean that such disortion must exeed merely "insignificant" levels.[143] Finally, a major distortion of competition is excluded if corresponding services provided by a private individual without the right of option are tax-exempt pursuant to Section 2b (2) No. 2 UStG.[144] The legislator makes use of the possibility offered by Art. 13 (2) of the VAT Directive.[145] However, this involves designating an otherwise tax-exempt activity as the exercise of public authority, so that the competitive exclusion is likely to exceed the scope of regulation available to Member States.[146]

While tax exemption is always desirable for the state as a taxpayer in corporate tax law, this is not the case in VAT law. There are two sides to non-taxability. For the public sector, however, the exclusion of entrepreneurial status under Section 2b UStG can backfire because it is linked to the exclusion of input tax deduction under Section 15 UStG.[147] Input tax deduction is inextricably linked to entrepreneurial status. If Section 2b UStG applies, input tax deduction is therefore excluded. Particularly in the case of high investment costs and an excess of input turnover, the definitive VAT burden on input turnover can be extremely disadvantageous from an economic point of view.[148] Ultimately, the only way to structure the business position to obtain input tax deduction is to deliberately fail to meet the criteria for exclusion of distortion of competition, for example by deliberately failing to meet the cost recovery principle in administrative cooperation pursuant to Section 2b (3) UStG.

The alteration in the taxation of public sector turnover imposes high requirements on the administration. The extent of the conceptual change in partial tax

---

141 Section 2b (2) (1) UStG. BMF letter dated 16 December 2016, Federal Tax Gazette I 2016, 1451 n. 33 et seq. = DStR 2017, 40. See *Müller*, UR 2017, 11.

142 *Menebröcker*, in: Hidien/Jürgens (eds.), Besteuerung der öffentlichen Hand, 2nd ed. 2023, section 9 n. 518 et seqq.

143 ECJ, judgment v. 16.9.2008 – Case 288/07 (Isle of Wight), ECR 2008, I-7203; *Wiesch*, Die umsatzsteuerliche Behandlung der öffentlichen Hand, 2016, 228.

144 For more details, see *Bunjes*, in: idem/Korn, UStG, 24th ed. 2025, § 2b n. 36–42.

145 Recommendation for a decision and report of the Finance Committee on the draft law of the Federal Government, BT-Drs. 18/4902, BT-Drs. 18/6094, 91; BMF letter dated 16 December 2016, Federal Tax Gazette I 2016, 1451 n. 38 et seqq. = DStR 2017, 40.

146 *Heidner*, UR 2016, 45 (49); dissenting opinion: *Menebröcker*, in: Hidien/Jürgens (eds.), Besteuerung öffentlichen Hand, 2nd ed. 2023, § 9 n. 524.

147 For details: BMF dated 12 June 2024 – III C 2 – S 7300/22/10001 :001, Federal Tax Gazette 2024 I p. 1041. As well as comprehensive coverage in the literature: *Sterzinger*, in: Hidien/Jürgens (eds.), Besteuerung der öffentlichen Hand, 2nd ed. 2023, § 9 n. 666 et seqq.; *Küffner*, in: idem/Musil (eds.), Besteuerung der öffentlichen Hand, 2022, chapter 3 n. 3.160 et seqq.

148 *Desens*, in: Schön/Röder (eds.), Zukunftsfragen des deutschen Steuerrechts II, 2014, 1 et seqq.

liability is particularly evident in VAT law in the form of extensive, cushioning transition periods. Even a decade after its entry into force, Section 2b UStG is rarely applicable: the transitional law of Section 27 (22), (22a) UStG means that Section 2 (3) UStG may still apply to turnover generated until 1 January 2025. The previously applicable Section 2 (3) UStG was repealed on 1 January 2016 by the 2015 Tax Amendment Act of 2 November 2015[149] and replaced by Section 2b UStG, but according to Section 27 (22) sentence 1 UStG in the 2016 calendar year to transactions carried out after 31 December 2015 and before 1 January 2017. According to Section 27 (22) sentence 2 UStG, Section 2b UStG is to be applied for the first time to transactions carried out after 31 December 2016. However, according to Section 22 (22) sentence 3 UStG, legal entities under public law could opt for the application of the old law for all services performed until 1 January 2021 by means of a declaration revocable for the future until 31 December 2016. Section 27 (22a) UStG, which was added in 2020, initially extended the transitional arrangement until 31 December 2022,[150] then until 31 December 2024[151] and finally[152] until 1 January 2027.[153]

V. Structural Europeanisation of Public Sector Taxation

The structural Europeanisation of tax law has led to the dominance of competitive neutrality, which has noticeably shifted the boundaries of the state's partial tax liability and eroded the sovereign domain exempt from taxation.[154] Driven by European legislation and the jurisprudence of the European Court of Justice, this process began with harmonised VAT legislation, but has since spread to income taxation.[155]

In this context, the role of national tax jurisdiction must be viewed critically: the scope for implementation by member states provided for in European law is shrinking in German tax law, as the principle of competitive neutrality is often treated as absolute in case law. The principle of competitive neutrality is becoming the rule, and the sparse reasoning behind some ECJ decisions is becoming the credo of the Federal Finance Court's adapting jurisprudence.[156] The sacraments

149 Federal Law Gazette 2015 I, 1834.

150 Federal Law Gazette 2020 I, 1385.

151 Federal Law Gazette 2022 I, 2294.

152 JStG 2024 of 2 December 2024 (Federal Law Gazette I 24, No. 387).

153 *Menebröcker*, in: Hidien/Jürgens (eds.), Besteuerung der öffentlichen Hand, 2nd ed. 2023, § 9 n. 378 et seqq.; *Heuermann*, in: Sölch/Ringleb (eds.), UstG, 105. EL., 10/2025, § 27 n. 76–81.

154 *Droege*, Zur Besteuerung der öffentlichen Hand, 2017, 111 et seqq.

155 For details on the following, see: *Droege*, Zur Besteuerung der öffentlichen Hand, 2017, 111 et seqq.

156 Examples: BFH of 20 August 2009, V R 70/5, Federal Tax Gazette II 2017, p. 825; BFH of 20 August 2009, V R 30/06, Federal Tax Gazette II 2010, p. 863 et seq.; BFH of 17 March 2010, XI R 17/08, Federal Tax Gazette II 2017, 828 et seq.; BFH of 15 April 2010, V R 10/09, Federal Tax

of competitive neutrality presented in EU law serve as instruments that are all too readily taken up in the face of overly hesitant tax legislators. The supremacy of EU law encompasses the interpretative jurisdiction of the European Court of Justice and frees German tax jurisdiction from its binding effect on law and legislation,[157] as exemplified by the competition-oriented interpretation of commercial transactions. Even in the non-harmonised area of direct taxation, the sovereignty reservations of the Member States are effectively overcome by case law. The collapse of traditional tax boundaries and their judicial interpretation can hardly be repaired by national legislators; their role is often merely reactive. This is demonstrated by the attempt to base the partial VAT liability under Section 2b of the German VAT Act not only on a basis consistent with EU law, but also on a basis compatible with the interpretation of case law.

The strong focus on competitive relevance – derived from the VAT System Directive[158] and, in particular, the ECJ case law on Article 13 of the VAT System Directive[159] – obscures the fact that EU primary law does leave Member States some leeway to shape state participation in the market and the public interest. Within the internal market, competition and competitive neutrality constitute "institutional Union objectives and values enshrined in legal principles", which also must be harmonised with other Union values and objectives.[160] Primary law recognises not only competition but also services of general economic interest (SGEI).[161] The fact that the principle of neutrality in VAT law is merely a principle of interpretation and not a rule of primary law is often overlooked in its national transposition into income tax law.

In the area of direct taxation, positive integration is replaced by the safeguarding of competition in state aid law (Art. 107 et seq. TFEU).[162] This leads to an ambivalent development: on the one hand, it stimulates the development of tax law, but on the other hand, concerns about notification procedures for existing benefits (old aid) lead to a "petrification" of the status quo, as can be seen in the case of municipal cross-subsidies.[163] Central to the distinction is the concept of

Gazette II 2017, 863 et seq.; BFH of 10 November 2011, V R 41/10, Federal Tax Gazette II 2017, 869; BFH of 1 December 2011, V R 1/11, Federal Tax Gazette II 2017, p. 834.

[157] *Droege*, Zur Besteuerung der öffentlichen Hand, 2017, 112 et seqq.

[158] Advocate General Kokott, Opinion of 8 June 2017 – Case 246/16 (Enzo Di Maura v Agenzia delle Entrate – Direzione Provinciale di Siracusa), juris, para. 40.

[159] ECJ, judgment v. 13.3.2014 – Case 204/13, 592 (595 para. 43) (Malburg).

[160] *Hidien*, in: idem/Jürgens (eds.), Die Besteuerung der öffentlichen Hand, 2nd ed. 2023, § 2 para. 405. See also: *Behrens*, Europäisches Marktöffnungs- und Wettbewerbsrecht, § 3 para. 14 et seq.

[161] *M. Schulte/Kloos/Apel*, in: M. Schulte/Kloos (eds), Handbuch Öffentliches Wirtschaftsrecht, 2016, § 1 para. 18. On public welfare tasks in EU law, see only: *Behrens*, Europäisches Marktöffnungs- und Wettbewerbsrecht, 2017, § 39 n. 1483 with numerous references.

[162] See, for example: ECJ, judgment v. 8.9.2011 – Case C-78/08 et al. (Paint Graphos), ECR 2011, I-7611 para. 49 with references to established case law. From the literature see also: *Koschyk*, Steuervergünstigungen als Beihilfen, 1999, 146 et seqq.

[163] *Droege*, Zur Besteuerung der öffentlichen Hand, 2017, 114 et seqq.

aid, which presupposes an economic activity; sovereign tasks are excluded. However, as long as the state acts as an undertaking, the state aid regime applies unless there is an exception for SGEIs (Art. 106 (2) TFEU). The tax privileges granted to services of general interest often fail to meet the requirements of state aid law since tax laws can hardly meet the strict requirements of the "Altmark" ruling,[164] because they are abstract, general rules that do not allow for precise cost control in individual cases. The discussion on cross-subsidisation under Section 4 (6) et seq. KStG and on profit allocation illustrates the problem under state aid law. The preferential treatment of activities that generate permanent losses deviates from the tax system, as losses would normally be irrelevant for tax purposes if there is no intention to make a profit (or if there is a hidden distribution of profits). However, applying of the arm's length principle and the model of the conscientious manager to municipal activities is problematic, as this model originates from the profit-oriented private sector and does not take into account the specificities of municipal services of general interest. In order to circumvent the prohibition on implementation (Art. 108 (3) TFEU), cross-subsidisation must be classified as "existing aid" (old aid).[165] Tax exemptions in non-profit law for commercial businesses that serve as special-purpose entities for the realisation of non-profit purposes are also suspected of constituting aid, as they offer selective advantages in competition.[166]

In summary, a look at Europeanisation reveals an insufficient adaptation of the primary legal balance between competition and the common good in German case law. EU law offers potential for better justifying the legitimacy of tax incentives for non-profit actors, which has remained untapped to date. At the same time, state aid law acts as a mirror that ruthlessly exposes the inconsistencies in the German tax system.[167]

---

164 ECJ, judgment v. 24.7.2003 – Case 280/00 (Altmark Trans), ECR 2003, I-7747, para. 89 et seqq. See also: *Bartosch*, EU-Beihilfenrecht, Kommentar, 4th ed. 2025, Art. 107(1) TFEU, para. 62 et seqq.; *Behrens*, Europäisches Marktöffnungs- und Wettbewerbsrecht, 2017, § 42 para. 1559; *Egger/Hoffer*, in: Birnstiel/Bungenberg/Heinrich (eds.), Europäisches Beihilfenrecht, 2013, Art. 107 (3) TFEU para. 1947 et seq.; *Wollenschläger*, in: G. Kirchhof/Korte/Magen (eds.), Öffentliches Wettbewerbsrecht, 2014, § 6 para. 50.

165 *Droege*, Zur Besteuerung der öffentlichen Hand, 2017, 129 et seqq. for the extremely multifaceted debate.

166 A current example is provided by the recent referral decision of the Federal Finance Court to the ECJ on the aid assessment of the tax-law non-profit status of service corporations: BFH of 22 May 2025, V R 22/23, ECLI:DE:BFH:2025:VE.220525.VR22.23.0. On the role of state aid law in non-profit law: *Droege*, in: Winheller/Geibel/Jachmann-Michel (eds.), Gesamtes Gemeinnützigkeitsrecht, 3rd ed. 2025, Chapter 18, para. 13 et seqq.; ibid., § 65 AO, para. 12 et seq.

167 For more details, see: *Droege*, Zur Besteuerung der öffentlichen Hand, 2017, 138 et seqq.

VI. Tax Administration and Fiscal Jurisdiction

The partial tax liability of the public sector poses challenges for tax administration, tax procedural law and, above all, effective legal protection by the tax courts.[168] The tax administration largely takes into account the specificities of the taxation of the public sector. This is evident in the executive interpretation of the standards in the letters from the Federal Ministry of Finance. The tax authorities have taken a differentiated and detailed position on the requirements for combining commercial operations and offsetting profits across groups in the context of income tax,[169] and on the contours of partial tax liability in the context of VAT.[170] Sector-specific characteristics, such as in higher education[171] or the taxation of cemeteries,[172] are taken into account. The scope for interpretation has frequently been utilised to the benefit of the public sector. However, the tax authorities also play a corrective role when the legislator exceeds the limits set by EU law. An example is the privileged treatment of public assistance services in Section 2b (3) UStG.[173]

In addition to setting general standards, the tax authorities also contribute to reducing complexity and ensuring legal certainty in individual cases under tax procedural law. Uncertainty in the tax base definition can be reduced for the future by requesting binding information. According to Section 89 (2) of the German Fiscal Code (AO), tax offices and the Federal Central Tax Office may, upon request, provide binding information on the tax assessment of precisely defined, not yet realised circumstances if there is a particular interest in this regarding the significant tax implications. However, binding information is strictly limited to circumstances that have not yet materialized[174] and is not sui-

[168] See also: *Baum*, in Musil/Küffner (eds.), Besteuerung der öffentlichen Hand, 2022, chapter 8, para. 8, 32 et seqq.

[169] BMF, letter dated 12 November 2009, letter concerning questions of application of the provisions in the Annual Tax Act 2009 on the taxation of commercial operations and proprietary companies of legal entities under public law, I 2009, 1303; BMF, letter dated 6 July 2021, Disproportionate loss allocation for own companies with several public-law entities as shareholders within the meaning of section 8 (7) KStG, Federal Tax Gazette 2021 I, 914; BMF, letter dated 15 December 2021, Leasing by the public sector, Federal Tax Gazette 2021 I, 2483.

[170] See only: BMF, letter dated 16 December 2016, Sales taxation of public sector services; questions regarding the application of section 2b UStG, Federal Tax Gazette 2016 I, 1451; BMF, letter dated 12 June 2024, Input tax deduction for legal entities under public law engaged in commercial activities, Federal Tax Gazette 2024 I, 1041; BMF, letter dated 18 September 2019, on legal entities under private law within the scope of Section 2b UStG, Federal Tax Gazette 2019 I, 921.

[171] BMF, letter dated 26 November 2020, questions regarding the application of Section 2b UStG to universities, DStR 2021, 292.

[172] BMF, letter dated 23 November 2020, questions regarding the application of Section 2b UStG in connection with cemeteries and funeral services, Federal Tax Gazette 2020 I, 1335.

[173] See: BMF, letter dated 14 November 2019, Separate examination of possible major distortions of competition in section 2b (3) no. 2, Federal Tax Gazette 2019 I, 1140.

[174] Nos. 3.5.2, 3.5.3 on Section 89 AEAO 2022.

table for legal uncertainties resulting from mere changes in the law that arise in realised circumstances.[175] Nevertheless, it can play an important role in public sector restructuring.[176]

Legal protection in tax matters also follows the general rules for the public sector in the bilateral tax liability relationship between taxpayers and the tax authorities.[177] Out-of-court legal protection is granted in appeal proceedings (Sections 347 et seq. AO), which, following the administrative appeal procedure, serve both the self-monitoring of the tax authorities and as preliminary proceedings to tax court proceedings.[178] The judicial legal protection system of the Fiscal Procedure Code (FGO) largely corresponds to general administrative court legal protection in terms of the types of actions it covers.[179]

After all, this has special features in the role of the state as a taxpayer: the partial tax liability of the public sector transforms the fundamentally "bipolar"[180] tax relationship, with the inclusion of the non-privileged competitor, into a multidimensional administrative legal relationship, because and insofar as norm-related third-party protection is mediated.[181] Established case law has opened the way for non-privileged competitors to bring competitor actions.[182] The Federal Finance Court has also opened up the possibility of individual legal protection in competitive relationships with commercial enterprises of legal entities under public law.[183] The third-party protection effect is based here on the correspond-

---

175 See *Wernsmann*, in: Hübschmann/Hepp/Spitaler (eds.), AO/FGO, Kommentar, 273. Lfg., 4/2023, § 89 AO n. 278.

176 On binding information as a means of tax compliance in this sense, see only: *Talaska*, in: Streck/Mack/Schwedhelm (eds.), Tax Compliance, 3rd ed. 2019 n 1.15.

177 See only: *Baum*, in Musil/Küffner (eds.), Besteuerung der öffentlichen Hand, 2022, chapter 8 n. 8.500 et seqq.

178 For general information on legal protection in tax matters and on appeal proceedings, see *Tappe*, in: Hübschmann/Hepp/Spitaler (eds.), AO/FGO, Kommentar, 280. Lfg., 6/2024, § 347 AO n. 8 et seqq.; *Seer*, in: Tipke/Kruse (eds.), Kommentar zur AO und FGO, 164. Lfg., 2/2021, § 347 n. 1 et seqq.

179 See *Tappe*, in: Hübschmann/Hepp/Spitaler (eds.), AO/FGO, Kommentar, 287. Lfg., 7/2025, § 347 n. 12 et seqq.; *Seer*, in: Tipke/Kruse (eds.), Kommentar zur AO und FGO, 164. Lfg., 2/2021, § 347 n. 15 et seqq.

180 *Enders*, Die Konkurrentenklage im Steuerrecht, 1993, 28.

181 The following can also be found in *Droege*, in: Winheller/Geibel/Jachmann-Michel (eds.), Gesamtes Gemeinnützigkeitsrecht, § 65 n. 25 et seqq. using the example of § 65 AO. See also: *Droege*, Zur Besteuerung der öffentlichen Hand, 2017, 143 et seqq.

182 Fundamental BFH of 15 October 1997 – I R 10/92, Federal Tax Gazette II 1998, 63 = DStRE 1998, 110. See also BFH of 8 July 2004 – VII R 24/03, Federal Tax Gazette II 2004, 1034 = DStR 2004, 1829; 18 September 2007 – I R 30/06, Federal Tax Gazette II 2009, 126 = DStR 2008, 290; 5 October 2006 – VII R 24/03, Federal Tax Gazette II 2007, 243 = DStR 2006, 2310. For inadmissible but nevertheless considered competitor lawsuits outside of non-profit law, see, for example, BFH of 18 September 1984 – VII R 50–51/82, Federal Tax Gazette II 1985, 12 = NVwZ 1985, 375; BFH of 13 October 1987 – VII B 96/87, Federal Tax Gazette II 1988, 67 = BeckRS 1987, 22008247. For competitor lawsuits in the literature, see *Enders*, Die Konkurrentenklage im Steuerrecht, 1993; *van Lishaut*, Die Konkurrentenklage im Steuerrecht, 1993.

183 BFH of 5 October 2006 – VII R 24/03 Federal Tax Gazette II 2007, 243 = DStR 2006, 2310.

ing third-party protection content of European secondary law.[184] The ECJ already considered Art. 4 (5) subpara. 2 of the 6th VAT System Directive[185] as being committed to the principle of tax neutrality at,[186] and considered the provision to be directly applicable.[187] The same applies today to Art. 13 of the VAT Directive and to the third-party protection content of Section 2b UStG.[188]

The derivation of the right to sue requires recognition of the subjective legal position of a third party not involved in the tax relationship. In this respect, the Federal Finance Court expressly refers to the case law on competitor lawsuits under economic administrative law[189] and uses the categories of the protective norm theory[190] to decide whether subjective rights can be derived from simple legal norms.[191] Both the principle of competitive neutrality expressed in the wording and teleology of the norms governing the tax exemption of special-purpose enterprises in Section 65 AO and the partial tax liability of the public sector in Section 2b UStG show that the norms do not serve only fiscal interests and thus the general public, but also "the protection of [....] competing and non-tax-privileged enterprises".[192] For a third-party protective effect, it is sufficient that the group of protected persons is "normatively sufficiently clearly distinguished from the general public, i.e. that the rights holders can be individualised".[193] Here, the substantive legal criteria of the specific competitive relationship find their procedural counterpart.[194]

---

184 For details, see *Englisch*, StuW 2008, 43 (53 et seqq.); *Wernsmann*, Die Verwaltung 2003, 67 (96 et seqq.).

185 Directive 77/388/EEC, OJ 1977 L 145, 1 et seqq. See now Article 13 (1) subparagraph 2 of the VAT Directive of 28 November 2006, OJ 2006 L 347, 1, corr. OJ 2017 L 336, 60.

186 ECJ, judgment v. 8.6.2006 – Case 430/04 (Feuerbestattungsverein Halle), ECR 2006, I-4999 = DStR 2006, 1082 para. 24. The Federal Fiscal Court (BFH) felt obliged to assess the existence of a claim for information against the tax authorities in advance and to prepare a competitor's action for submission, BFH of 8 July 2004 – VII R 24/03, Federal Tax Gazette II 2004, 1034 = DStR 2004, 1829.

187 ECJ, judgment v. 8.6.2006 – C-430/04 (Feuerbestattungsverein Halle), ECR 2006, I-4999 = DStR 2006, 1082 para. 31. On the direct effect of Article 4 (5) of Directive 77/388/EEC, see also ECJ, judgment v. 17.10.1989 – Case 231/87, Case 129/88 (Ufficio distrettuale delle imposte dirette di Fiorenzuola d'Arda), ECR 1989, I-3233 = EuZW 1991, 120 para. 31, 33.

188 *Stadie*, in: Rau/Dürrwächter (eds.), Kommentar zum Umsatzsteuergesetz, 198. Lfg., 3/2022, § 2b UStG para. 27.

189 BFH of 15 October 1997 – Federal Tax Gazette II 1998, 63, expressly refers, inter alia, to BVerwGE 30, 191 (197 et seq.); 60, 154; 65, 167 (171) and 66, 307.

190 On this point, see *Münch*, in: Hübschmann/Hepp/Spitaler, AO/FGO, Kommentar, 286. Lfg., 5/2025, § 40 FGO n. 219 et seqq.

191 BFH of 15 October 1997 – I R 10/92, Federal Tax Gazette II 1998, 63, 65 = DStRE 1998, 110 uVwa BVerfG 9 January 1991 – 1 BvR 207/87, BVerfGE 83, 182 (194) = NJW 1991, 1878 – Pensioners' privilege.

192 BFH of 15 October 1997 – I R 10/92, Federal Tax Gazette II 1998, 63 (67) = DStRE 1998, 110.

193 BFH of 15 October 1997 – I R 10/92, Federal Tax Gazette II 1998, 63 (67) = DStRE 1998, 110.

194 Jurisprudence places high demands on substantiation of the right to sue BFH of 15 October 1997 – I R 10/92, Federal Tax Gazette II 1998, 63, 68 = DStRE 1998, 110. See also *Münch*, in: Hübschmann/Hepp/Spitaler, AO/FGO, Kommentar, 286. Lfg., 5/2025, § 40 FGO n. 224 et seqq. More generous: BFH of 18 August 2022 – V R 49/19, Federal Tax Gazette II 2023, 298 = DStRE

In practice, however, competitor litigation poses significant challenges with respect to the competitor's tax secrecy.[195] Typically, competitor lawsuits are staged. Effective judicial protection against competition is preceded by a claim for information against the tax authorities by the non-beneficiary competitor.[196] The Federal Fiscal Court (BFH) directly cites the principle of the rule of law in conjunction with the fundamental right to freedom of occupation under Article 12 (1) GG and the fundamental right to legal proceedings under Article 19 (4) GG as the legal basis for the right to information.[197] The tax authorities agree with this.[198]

VII. Conclusion

In summary, there are three findings and conclusions for a dogmatic embedding of public sector taxation in overarching control contexts that are compatible with transnational discourse.

First, Europeanisation has led to the dominance of competitive neutrality, which has noticeably shifted the boundaries of the state's partial tax liability and eroded the sovereign domain exempt from taxation. The change in the determinants of partial tax liability leads to changes in the functions of tax administration and tax protection. The procedural dimension is becoming more important, as private competitors can now challenge tax privileges granted to the public sector. In all this, the strong focus on competition relevance obscures the fact that primary EU law leaves Member States considerable leeway to shape state participation in the market and the commitment to the common good. The central task for the future is to readjust the balance between competitive neutrality and the commitment to the common good in state activity.

Second, the demarcation of the public sector's sphere of partial tax liability requires not only a tax doctrine open to the international context, but also attention to corresponding sphere boundaries in neighbouring areas of law. Examples include insolvency law and competition law. The commercial issue is structurally equivalent to the tax issue of competitor litigation.[199] The demarcation of the

---

2023, 274. See also BFH of 17 November 2022 – V R 12/20, Federal Tax Gazette 2023, 367 = DStRE 2023, 278 n. 18.

[195] *Münch*, in: Hübschmann/Hepp/Spitaler, AO/FGO, Kommentar, 286. Lfg., 5/2025, § 40 FGO n. 220, 236, 238 et seqq.

[196] See also *Münch*, in: Hübschmann/Hepp/Spitaler, AO/FGO, Kommentar, 286. Lfg., 5/2025, § 40 FGO § 40 n. 238.

[197] BFH of 5 October 2006 – VII R 24/03, Federal Tax Gazette II 2007, 243 = DStR 2006, 2310.

[198] AEAO on § 30 No. 4.6 p. 1: "Requests for information on the taxation of third parties in the application of third-party protection standards (including §§ 64 to 68 AO and § 2 (3) UStG) are generally admissible for the preparation of a competitor lawsuit"; cf. BFH of 5 October 2006 – VII R 24/03, Federal Tax Gazette II 2007, 243 = DStR 2006, 2310.

[199] *Hidien*, in: idem/Jürgens (eds.), Besteuerung der öffentlichen Hand, 2nd ed. 2023, § 2 n. 116 et seqq.

sovereign domain can also be found in the partial insolvency of the public sector and in the protection from enforcement (Sections 11, 12 Insolvency Code (*Insolvenzverordnung*, InsO), Section 882a Code of Civil Procedure (*Zivilprozessordnung*, ZPO)).[200] The VAT privilege for administrative cooperation in Section 2b (3) No. 2 UStG refers to criteria originally derived from public procurement law.[201] In fact, it is obvious to compare the limits of competition in the regulation of the demand power of the public sector with the limits of competition in the regulation of its taxation.[202]

Third, tax doctrine must respond to this "overlap" of legal fields and develop appropriate reception competencies.[203] Particularly in the field of public taxation, which is determined not by fiscal interests but by competitive neutrality, it is important to consider public economic administrative law and tax law together from a regulatory perspective. It is time to embrace tax law as a field of special administrative law.[204] A comparative legal perspective on the role of the state as a taxpayer is a concern not only of comparative tax law, but also of comparative administrative law.

[200] *Lewinski*, Öffentlichrechtliche Insolvenz und Staatsbankrott, 2011.

[201] On "interstate" agreements: Art. 12 Directive 2014/24/EU. See only: ECJ, judgment v. 9.6.2009 – Case 480/06 (Commission v Germany), ECR 2009, I-4747. See also: ECJ, judgment v. 19.12.2012 – Case 159/11 (Lecce), NVwZ 2013, 710, 711 para. 34 et seq.; ECJ, judgment v. 13.6.2013 – Case 386/11 (Piepenbrock), NVwZ 2013, 931.

[202] On the purposes of public procurement law: *Burgi*, Vergaberecht, 4th ed. 2025, § 2 para. 30 et seq., § 6 para. 1 et seq.

[203] *Droege*, Eigenheiten der Steuerrechtswissenschaft, 2016, 94.

[204] *Droege*, in: idem/Seiler (eds.), Eigenständigkeit des Steuerrechts, 2019, 127 et seqq.; idem, Zur Besteuerung der öffentlichen Hand, 2017, 161 et seqq.

Sexual Offences in German Criminal Law

The Current State of the Law and Some Unresolved Questions

Bettina Weisser

I. Introduction

German criminal law on sexual offences has come a long way: A first shift of paradigms in this field of the law was introduced in the wake of the 1960s' sexual revolution, when in 1973 the general approach of protecting morality and public decency[1] through sexual offences was replaced by the new goal of protecting the sexual self-determination of individuals.[2] Since then, violations of individual rights are at the heart of sexual offences. However, it took the legislator until 1994 to fully[3] decriminalize homosexual acts among consenting adults after the German reunification.[4] It was not before 1997, that the legislator formulated sexual assault in a gender-neutral way and extended the criminalization of rape to marital rape.[5] Until 2016, under German criminal law, non-consensual sexual acts were only punishable if they were committed by overcoming the victim's resistance through the use of force or threats of force, or by exploiting the victim's vulnerable situation.[6] In 2016, however, sexual offences underwent a comprehensive reform, which, among other things, replaced this coercion-based concept of sexual assault (including rape) with a consent-based model.[7] Apart from that, the legislator introduced two new offences in § 184i PC (sexual harassment) and § 184j PC (offences committed out of groups). And most recent, a new offence

[1] The heading of Section 13 of the Penal Code previously read 'Offences against Public Decency' (*Verbrechen und Vergehen wider die Sittlichkeit*). Today, this heading is replaced by 'Offences against Sexual Self-Determination' (*Straftaten gegen die sexuelle Selbstbestimmung*).

[2] 4. Gesetz zur Reform des Strafrechts v. 23.11.1973, BGBl. I, 1725. Cp. also *Weigend*, in: Weigend/Hoven (eds.), Consent and Sexual Offenses (2022), 183; for a description of the historical emergence of the term cp. *Stoff, Schmincke*, and *Valentiner*, in: Burghardt/Schmidt/Steinl (eds.), Sexuelle Selbstbestimmung jenseits des Körperlichen (2024), 15 et seqq.; 31 et seqq.; 45 et seqq.

[3] In 1969 and 1973, the former criminal blanket ban of homosexual acts among adults had already been limited to men who (consensually) interacted with men under the age of 18.

[4] 29. StrÄndG (1994), BGBl. I, 1168.

[5] 33. StrÄndG (1.7.1997), BGBl. I, 1607; BGH NStZ 2020, 662, n. 18.

[6] The scenario of the perpetrator exploiting the victim's vulnerable situation was introduced in 1997, 33. StrÄndG (1.7.1997), BGBl. I, 1607.

[7] 50. StrÄndG of 4.11.2016 (BGBl. I 2460), entry into force on 10.11.2016. Amended by 57. StrÄndG of 3.3.2020 with a minor change in § 184i (1) PC.

came into force that does not entail physical assault, but is limited to image-based sexual abuse, known as "upskirting" and/or "downblousing". The offence criminalizes the unauthorized taking of photographs or other images of the genitals, buttocks, female breast or of underwear which is covering those body parts of another person – provided that the body parts are protected from view (§184k PC).[8] Finally, in order to combat sexual violence against children, §184l PC was introduced in 2021: The provision criminalizes the putting into circulation, procurement and possession of childlike sex dolls[9] and is based on the legislator's assumption that the use of such items lowers the threshold for possible perpetrators to commit sexual violence against children.

Further lacunae in the protection of sexual autonomy through the criminal law are currently under discussion: Since sexual harassment requires physical contact under German criminal law,[10] the need to criminalize phenomena such as catcalling, revenge porn, or other non-physical violations of an individual's sexual self-determination is being considered.[11]

II. The System of Sexual Offences Under German Criminal Law

Sexual offences protect the right of individuals to sexual self-determination, which is an expression of the right to free development of personality (Art. 2 (1) of the Basic Law (GG)). The autonomy and self-determination of individuals are enshrined in human dignity (Art. 1 (1) GG).[12] Sexual self-determination is defined as the right to autonomously decide whether, when, with whom and under which circumstances a person engages in sexual activities.[13] The right has a positive and a negative dimension – the sexual offences of section 13 of the PC

---

[8] §184k PC: Violation of intimate body parts by taking photographs or otherwise distribute such body images, introduced by 59. StrÄndG zur Verbesserung des Persönlichkeitsschutzes bei Bildaufnahmen (9.10.2020), BGBl. I, 2021, 2075, entry into force on 1.1.2021.

[9] Gesetz zur Bekämpfung sexualisierter Gewalt gegen Kinder (16.6.2021), BGBl. I, 2021, 1810 (1812), entry into force on 1.7.2021.

[10] *Hörnle*, in: Hörnle (ed.) Sexual Assault (2023), 141 (153).

[11] See for an overview of the current discussion the contributions collected in: Burghardt/Schmidt/Steinl (eds.), Sexuelle Selbstbestimmung jenseits des Körperlichen (2024); in particular *Burghardt*, 131 (139 et seq.) on the one hand, and *Weigend*, (146 et seq.) on the other; furthermore *Greif*, Strafbarkeit von bildbasierten sexualisierten Belästigungen. Eine phänomenologische und strafrechtsdogmatische Betrachtung des sog. Image-based sexual abuse (2023), passim; for differing views on catcalling cp. *Goede/Greven/Bartsch*, in: Burghardt/Schmidt/Steinl (eds.), Sexuelle Selbstbestimmung jenseits des Körperlichen (2024), 113; *Metz*, NJW 2025, 3463; *Pörner*, ZRP 2025, 56; *K. Weißer*, ZPR 2024, 240; for revenge porn cp. *Kretschmer*, JA 2022, 41.

[12] *Eisele*, in: Tübinger Kommentar StGB, 31st ed. 2025 ('TK-StGB (2025)'), Vor §§174 et seqq. n. 1, with further references.

[13] OLG Hamm NStZ-RR 2022, 276; *Eisele*, TK-StGB (2025), §177 n. 6; *Noltenius*, in: Systematischer Kommentar StGB, 10th ed. 2024 ('SK-StGB (2024)'), §177 n. 8; *Vavra*, ZIS 2018, 611 (612); for a critical view on this concept see *Corrêa Camargo*, ZStW 2022, 351.

concern the *negative* component of sexual self-determination,[14] protecting the individual from unwanted interferences by others.

The sexual offences regulated in section 13 of the PC can be categorized as follows: The general offence of sexual assault, including numerous qualifications and sentencing guidelines, is stipulated in § 177 PC. Sexual acts through *physical* contact that remain below the threshold of sexual assault pursuant to § 177 PC are punishable as sexual harassment under § 184i PC.

Child and youth abuse offences (§§ 174, 176–176e, 180, 182, 184g PC[15]) are not only aimed at protecting the integrity and sexual self-determination of children and adolescents, but also at ensuring their undisturbed sexual development.[16] The aforementioned criminal prohibition on sex dolls with a childlike appearance under § 184l PC serves the same purpose. Further cases of abuse cover sexual assaults within legally defined power and dependency relationships, stipulated in §§ 174a, 174b, 174c PC.[17]

The commercial exploitation of prostitutes and pimping are punishable under §§ 180a PC and 181a PC. The practice and use of prostitution is generally legal, but § 184f PC criminalizes prostitution in restricted areas, and § 184g PC covers prostitution endangering minors.

To a certain extent, the criminal law also protects individuals against being confronted with manifestations of sexuality in the form of pornography in §§ 184–184c PC and § 184e PC (including child and youth pornography as well as violent sexual acts and sexual acts with animals), exhibitionist acts performed by a man, § 183 PC, and sexually connotated public nuisance, § 183a PC.

Finally, § 184j PC criminalizes "offences committed out of groups".[18] The provision is hard to understand: Its actus reus consists of the perpetrator belonging

---

[14] *Eisele*, TK-StGB (2025), Vor §§ 174 et seqq. n. 2; *Hörnle*, ZStW 127 (2015), 851 (859); *Valentiner*, in: Burghardt/Schmidt/Steinl (eds.), Sexuelle Selbstbestimmung jenseits des Körperlichen (2024), 45 (56 et seq.); *Vavra*, ZIS 2018, 611 (612); cp. also *Wiedmer*, Die Strafbarkeit sexueller Übergriffe (2024), 68.

[15] § 174 PC: sexual abuse of children under the care, custody or authority of the perpetrator in contexts of education, training, guardianship or family relations. § 176 PC: Sexual abuse of children, in § 176a PC without physical contact, aggravated cases of sexual abuse of children: § 176c PC, in § 176d PC abuse of children resulting in their death. The preparation of child abuse is criminalized in § 176b PC, while § 176e PC covers the general distribution or possession of instructions for child abuse.

[16] This is particularly true for § 180 PC: The provision criminalizes the encouragement of sexual acts by persons under the age of 16, either by arranging sexual encounters or by providing opportunities for such acts. The provision does not apply to parents or other legal guardians, unless they violate their duty of care.

[17] The provisions criminalize sexual abuse of prisoners, persons in custody, vulnerable individuals in institutions as well as sexual abuse by exploiting an official position or a counselling, treatment, or care relationship.

[18] § 184j PC: Offences committed out of groups
Whoever promotes an offence by participating in a group of persons who exert pressure on another person to commit an offence against that person incurs a penalty of imprisonment for a term not exceeding two years or a fine where an offence under § 177 or § 184i PC is committed

to a group of people who coerce a third person with the aim to commit a sexual offence against that person. If such an offence occurs, the group member is punishable irrespective of any individual contribution to the commission of said sexual offence. The offence description is highly questionable in light of the rule of law, considering the requirements of legal certainty and personal blameworthiness as indispensable conditions for any individual criminal liability. While the offence still awaits any practical significance,[19] it has certainly incited significant dismay in scholarly circles,[20] primarily due to its highly questionable linguistic as well as legal construction.

III. Rape Within the System of Sexual Offences in Section 13

The Penal Code does not entail a specific standalone offence of rape. Instead, rape forms part of the overall offence of sexual assault in § 177 PC[21] and is stipu-

---

by one of the participants of the group and the offence is not subject to a more severe penalty under other provisions.
Official translation of the Penal Code, provided by *Michael Bohlander/Ute Reusch*, accessible at https://www.gesetze-im-internet.de/englisch_stgb/englisch_stgb.html#p1876 (last access 20.2. 2026).

[19] The provision was introduced after the incidents on New Year's Eve 2015/16 in Cologne (and other cities), when a large number of women was sexually assaulted by groups of men in front of the Cathedral. The events led to public outrage and a rather ill-considered, hasty reaction of the legislature, cp. *Eisele*, TK-StGB (2025), § 184j n. 1, with further references.

[20] *Bezjak*, KJ 2016, 557 (569 et seq.); *Deckers*, StV 2017, 410; *Kuchinke*, ZJS 2022, 494; *Reuer*, NJOZ 2024, 609; *Renzikowski*, NJW 2016, 3553.

[21] § 177: Sexual assault; sexual coercion; rape
(1) Whoever, against a person's discernible will, performs sexual acts on that person or has that person perform sexual acts on them, or causes that person to perform or acquiesce to sexual acts being performed on or by a third person incurs a penalty of imprisonment for a term of between six months and five years.
(2) Whoever performs sexual acts on another person or has that person perform sexual acts, or causes that person to perform or acquiesce to sexual acts being performed on or by a third person incurs the same penalty if
1. the offender exploits the fact that the person is not able to form or express a contrary will,
2. the offender exploits the fact that the person is significantly impaired in respect of the ability to form or express a will due to said person's physical or mental condition, unless the offender has obtained the consent of that person,
3. the offender exploits an element of surprise,
4. the offender exploits a situation in which the victim is threatened with serious harm in case of offering resistance or
5. the offender has coerced the person to perform or acquiesce to the sexual acts by threatening serious harm.
(3) The attempt is punishable.
(4) The penalty is imprisonment for a term of at least one year if the inability to form or express a will is due to the victim's illness or disability.
(5) The penalty is imprisonment for a term of at least one year if the offender
1. uses force against the victim,
2. threatens the victim with a present danger to life or limb or

lated as one of the particularly serious cases of sexual assault described in subsec. 6 of said offence. In addition to the above-mentioned shift from a coercion-based to a consent-based model of sexual coercion, § 177 PC was restructured in 2016 and expanded to include offences that were not previously covered.[22] The reform of § 177 PC resulted in a lengthy, extremely complex provision with a considerable number of inconsistencies.

1. The Basic Offence: actus reus *of Sexual Assault under § 177 (1) PC*

Within the intricate regulatory framework set out in § 177 PC, sexual assault under subsec. (1) constitutes the overarching basic description of any sexual assault:

---

3. exploits a situation in which the victim is unprotected and at the mercy of the offender's influence.
(6) In especially serious cases, the penalty is imprisonment for a term of at least two years. An especially serious case typically occurs where
1. the offender has sexual intercourse with the victim or has the victim have sexual intercourse or commits such similar sexual acts on the victim or has the victim commit them on them which are particularly degrading for the victim, especially if they involve penetration of the body (rape), or
2. the offence is committed jointly by more than one person.
(7) The penalty is imprisonment for a term of at least three years if the offender
1. carries a weapon or other dangerous implement,
2. otherwise carries an instrument or other means for the purpose of preventing or overcoming the resistance of another person by force or threat of force or
3. places the victim at risk of serious damage to health.
(8) The penalty is imprisonment for a term of at least five years if
1. the offender uses a weapon or other dangerous implement during the commission of the offence or
2. the offender
a) seriously physically abuses the victim during the offence or
b) by committing the offence places the victim in danger of death.
(9) In less serious cases under subsections (1) and (2), the penalty is imprisonment for a term of between three months and three years, in less serious cases under subsections (4) and (5) imprisonment for a term of between six months and 10 years, and in less serious cases under subsections (7) and (8) imprisonment for a term of between one year and 10 years.

[22] Sec. 177 in its former version read: Sexual coercion, rape
(1) Who coerces another person
1. by means of violence,
2. by threat of imminent danger to life or limb, or
3. by exploiting a situation in which the victim is unprotected and at the mercy of the offender, to tolerate sexual acts by the offender or a third person or to engage in sexual activity with the offender or a third person, will be punished with imprisonment of not less than one year.
(2) In particularly serious cases the punishment shall be imprisonment for not less than two years. A particularly serious case typically occurs if
1. the offender performs sexual intercourse with the victim or performs similar sexual acts on the victim or makes the victim perform such acts on him that degrade the victim, particularly if they entail penetration of the body (rape), or
2. the offense is committed jointly by more than one person

§ 177 (1) PC: Whoever, against a person's discernible will, performs sexual acts on that person or has that person perform sexual acts on them, or causes that person to perform or acquiesce to sexual acts being performed on or by a third person incurs a penalty of imprisonment for a term of between six months and five years.

Sexual assault requires the perpetrator or the victim (!) to perform a sexual act against the victim's recognisable will. The offence also extends to the (unwanted) performance or toleration of sexual acts on or by a third person by or on the victim, and, finally, to the performance of sexual acts by the victim on themselves (*hands-off constellation*).

a) Sexual Acts

As a general rule, a sexual act must have an objectively sexual connotation and must be of a certain significance in order to be punishable (§ 184h no. 1 PC).[23] Socially accepted behaviour such as hugging or kissing someone on the cheek as a greeting is excluded from the scope of the offence because it lacks the necessary sexual character.[24] Furthermore, acts below a trivial threshold are excluded, for instance a brief touch on the naked thigh,[25] a brief hug while the person is partly naked,[26] or light caressing of the body over clothing.[27] In cases where there is some ambiguity, the assessment of significance is contingent on the particular circumstances of each individual case and must be evaluated in terms of both quality and quantity. However, the delineation of these boundaries remains ambiguous. It is evident that it does not provide any clear guidelines, but rather opens the door to an assessment on a case-by-case basis, considering the specific circumstances surrounding the case.[28] For instance, it was considered of minimal significance that the perpetrator had forced a 'short French kiss' on a 15-year-old girl without any other physical contact.[29] A seemingly absurd element of the court's reasoning for this was that a French kiss would not have been anything unfamiliar to the 15-year-old girl.[30] However, this should not be decisive in determining whether the girl's sexual integrity was violated. Sexual acts will generally not be 'unfamiliar' to those affected. The decisive factor for their criminal

---

[23] Section 184h: Definitions: Within the meaning of this statute,
1. 'sexual acts' are only those which are of some relevance to the protected legal interest in question, […]"
See for an extensive debate on the Concept of an "Act of a Sexual Nature" in German Criminal Law, *Corrêa Camargo/Renzikowski*, German Law Journal 2021, 753 et seqq.

[24] *Noltenius*, SK-StGB (2024), § 184i n. 5. This view is criticized by *Corrêa Camargo/Renzikowski*, German Law Journal 2021, 753 (758).

[25] BGH NStZ 2001, 370.

[26] BGH NStZ-RR 2017, 43 (44).

[27] BGH NStZ 2013, 708.

[28] See for a general discussion of the "act of a sexual nature" *Corrêa Camargo/Renzikowski*, German Law Journal 2021, 753, 756 et seq.

[29] BGH NStZ-RR 2010, 45.

[30] BGH NStZ-RR 2010, 45 (46).

relevance is not the fact that the victim might not have engaged in sexual activity of the kind before, but the question of whether the act entailed a significant violation of her sexual integrity. If physical contact is established with a victim, but the level of severity as defined by § 177 (1) PC is not reached, the conduct may still be classified as sexual harassment under § 184i PC.[31]

b) Against the Victim's Discernible Opposing Will: 'No Means No'

The essential feature of any sexual assault is the perpetrator disregarding the victim's recognizable opposing will. Subsec. (1) of § 177 PC incorporates the so-called no-means-no approach obligating the victim to clearly express their opposing will to make his or her rejection of sexual advances discernible. It is not necessary for coercive measures to be used to overcome the victim's rejection. However, it is imperative that the victim's opposing will is clearly discernible. The benchmark for this is not the perpetrator's subjective perception[32], but the assessment of an objective observer.[33] The determination of recognisability is thus made from an external perspective, involving an objective ex-post assessment of the victim's conduct. Thus, the focus of the legal analysis of the incident shifts from the perpetrator's conduct to the victim's reaction[34] – it does not suffice that the perpetrator overstepped the victim's boundaries. He must have done so against the victim's recognizable will. Hence, the victim is obligated to clearly communicate this opposing will,[35] which need not be done verbally, but can also be implied in gestures or any other non-verbal act, for example crying, turning away, pushing the perpetrator away etc.[36]

The shift of the legal assessment is also reflected in judicial practice: Following the no-means-no approach, the court's assessment will focus on whether the victim made it sufficiently clear that the perpetrator's advances were unwanted.

---

[31] § 184i PC: Sexual harassment
(1) Whoever touches another person in a sexual manner, and thereby harasses that person, incurs a penalty of imprisonment for a term not exceeding two years or a fine, unless the offence is subject to a more severe penalty under other provisions of this Division.
(2) In especially serious cases, the penalty is imprisonment for a term of between three months and five years. An especially serious case typically occurs where the offence is committed jointly by more than one person.
(3) The offence is prosecuted only upon request, unless the prosecuting authority deems there to be a special public interest in prosecution which calls for ex officio intervention.

[32] The perpetrator's subjective perspective is of course decisive in determining mens rea, see III.2.

[33] BT-Drs. 18/9097, 22; BGH NStZ-RR 2022, 211 (213); *Eisele*, TK-StGB (2025), § 177 n. 19c; *Hörnle*, in: Hörnle (ed.) Sexual Assault (2023), 141 (148) 'hypothetical third person'.

[34] *Torenz*, German Law Journal 2021, 718 (724); *Weigend*, in: Hoven/Weigend (eds.), Consent and Sexual Offenses (2022), 183 (190).

[35] *Eisele*, TK-StGB (2025), § 177 n. 19c; *Hörnle*, in: Hörnle (ed.) Sexual Assault (2023), 141 (146); *Wolters*, in: Bublitz et al. (eds.), FS Merkel (2020), 951 (955).

[36] *Eisele*, TK-StGB (2025), § 177 n. 19c; *Hörnle*, German Law Journal 2017, 1309 (1320); *Weigend*, in: Hoven/Weigend (eds.), Consent and Sexual Offenses (2022), 183 (189).

If the victim's conduct remains ambiguous, such that no clear communication of rejection is apparent from the perspective of an objective observer, the no-means-no approach concludes that sexual assault is ruled out.

In cases where the victim's behaviour would appear ambiguous to a hypothetical third party, but the perpetrator knew the victim well and was therefore able to correctly interpret the victim's response as "no", because, for example, they knew from experience that a certain behaviour on the part of the victim meant clear rejection, the perpetrator's special knowledge (*Sonderwissen*) is taken into account as part of the 'objective perspective'. Provided that the perpetrator's special knowledge relates to an externally apparent element of the victim's behaviour, the victim's opposing will is considered sufficiently recognizable in such cases.[37]

c) The underlying rationale of the no-means-no concept

The legal regulation is based on the assumption that it is not unfair to expect the victim to clearly signal their rejection of sexual acts to the perpetrator.[38] The main argument for the victim's obligation to communicate clearly is that ambiguities should not be to the detriment of the perpetrator, because a conviction as a sex offender would have massive consequences for them.[39] Others add that even the mere allegation of a sexual offence, even before a possible conviction, can have devastating consequences for the perpetrator's reputation.[40]

To describe the consequences of this approach quite bluntly: Under § 177 (1) PC, for the absence of sexual assault, the addressed person's consent with a sexual act is *not* required, it is perfectly sufficient that he or she did not manage to communicate their opposing will clearly enough[41] and therefore, from an objective ex-post perspective, the refusal was not recognizable. However, even if the victim's opposing will *was* expressed in a sufficiently discernible way, it is still possible for the perpetrator to contend that they did not realize this and therefore did not have the required intent to violate the victim's rights (see *III. 2.*).[42]

---

37 *Eisele*, TK-StGB (2025), § 177 n. 19c; *May*, JR 2010, 130 (136 et seq.).

38 BT-Drs. 18/9097, p. 22 et seq.; *Hörnle*, in: Hörnle (ed.) Sexual Assault (2023), 141 (146);

39 *Hörnle*, in: Hörnle (ed.) Sexual Assault (2023), 141 (146: 'It does not seem too heavy a burden on complainants to communicate 'no', while for the other person it is a harsh consequence to be convicted as a criminal offender'); *Hörnle*, German Law Journal 2017, 1309 (1320): '[…] potentially life-destroying criminal conviction as a sex offender is too strong a response to the failure to deal appropriately with ambiguity.' The latter argument, however, is not entirely convincing since in cases of factual errors, the perpetrator lacks the necessary intent for sexual assault.

40 *Frommel/Buchholz*, NK 2018, 368 (382); *Hörnle*, NStZ 2019, 439.

41 *Weigend*, in Hoven/Weigend (eds.) Consent and Sexual Offenses (2022) 183 (190 "a lack of protest […] equals consent").

42 *Weigend*, in Hoven/Weigend (eds.) Consent and Sexual Offenses (2022) 183 (190 "doubtful whether the court will later accept the defendant's claim of a bona fide mistake of fact"); differing *Hörnle*, in: Hörnle (ed.) Sexual Assault (2023), 141 (158: 'traditionally offender-friendly approach' of German courts).

2. Mens rea *of Sexual Assault*

The subjective element of sexual offences is twofold: The actor must not only intentionally carry the sexual act out but must also have intent regarding the victim's discernible opposing will. Intent presupposes at least *dolus eventualis*, meaning that the offender at least accepts that the sexual act takes place against the recognizable opposing will.[43] As a result, even if the victim's opposing will *is* objectively recognizable, it is possible to argue that the perpetrator did not *subjectively* recognize this and therefore did not act intentionally. In judicial practice, this objection is raised very frequently – it is then up to the trial court to assess the credibility of such claims.[44] If the court cannot dispel any remaining doubts about the perpetrator's intent, the principle *in dubio pro reo* applies and a conviction is ruled out. Since in cases of sexual offences, only the victim is usually available as a witness and statements typically contradict each other, this outcome is not unlikely to occur. Some legal literature complains that judicial practice is overly 'perpetrator-friendly', especially when it comes to recognizing errors of fact with regard to the victim's contrary will.[45] Against this background, it is not far-fetched to conclude that this is one of the reasons why victims of sexual offences often shy away from initiating criminal proceedings by reporting the offence (see *VII.*).

3. Sexual Assault and Sexual Coercion in Cases Where the Victim is Unable to Communicate or Cannot Reasonably Be Expected to Do So, § 177 (2) PC

Subsec. (2) of § 177 PC concerns cases in which the victim is either unable or cannot legally be expected to communicate their opposing will, due to certain circumstances. Alternatively, the victim is, due to his or her general or situational condition, unable to form an opposing will.[46]

§ 177 (2) PC: Whoever performs sexual acts on another person or has that person perform sexual acts, or causes that person to perform or acquiesce to sexual acts being performed on or by a third person incurs the same penalty if

1. the offender exploits the fact that the person is not able to form or express a contrary will,

---

[43] BGH NStZ-RR 2022, 211 (213). For an explanation of the concept of *dolus eventualis* under German criminal law see *Hörnle*, in: Hörnle (ed.) Sexual Assault (2023), 141 (149).

[44] In BGH NStZ-RR 2022, 211 (213), the victim had clearly communicated her opposing will which the perpetrator ignored and carried on with sexual intercourse. Because the victim did not physically resist the intercourse, the perpetrator claimed he had assumed her consent. The BGH found this claim not convincing and expressly stated that mere passivity did not suffice after the victim had clearly communicated her opposition.

[45] *Hörnle*, in: Hörnle (ed.) Sexual Assault (2023), 141 (158); Deutscher Juristinnenbund (German women's law association), Policy Paper st 24/40 (18.11.2024), p. 3.

[46] *Hörnle*, in: Hörnle (ed.) Sexual Assault (2023), 141 (147: "Opting for 'no means no' requires laws with additional versions of sexual assault").

2. the offender exploits the fact that the person is significantly impaired in respect of the ability to form or express a will due to said person's physical or mental condition, unless the offender has obtained the consent of that person,
3. the offender exploits an element of surprise,
4. the offender exploits a situation in which the victim is threatened with serious harm in case of offering resistance or
5. the offender has coerced the person to perform or acquiesce to the sexual acts by threatening serious harm.

Situations in which the victim is unable to express their objection include, for example, unconsciousness or intoxication (no. 1). Furthermore, a state of tonic immobility caused by the shock of being sexually assaulted falls under § 177 (2) no. 1 PC (see also *V. 3.*). § 177 (2) no. 3 PC covers cases in which the victim's inability to form or express their opposing will is caused by the offender's sexual act taking them by surprise.

Furthermore, the law does not expect the victim to express their opposing will in cases of sexual coercion, that is, if the perpetrator bends the victim's opposing will by threatening serious harm, either expressly or conclusively (§ 177 (2) no. 5 PC[47]) or if the assault takes place within a general climate of violence, for example within a violent relationship, § 177 (2) no. 4 PC. In such a climate of violence, the perpetrator does not even need to actively repeat a specific threat of violence, because the victim is aware that violence will be the result of their resisting the perpetrator's sexual activity.

§ 177 (2) no. 2 PC constitutes an exception to the general no-means-no approach to sexual assault in § 177 PC: If the perpetrator exploits the fact that the victim is 'significantly impaired in respect of the ability to form or express a will due to said person's physical or mental condition', he commits a punishable sexual assault, 'unless the offender has obtained the consent of that person'. Accordingly, if the impaired victim communicated affirmative consent, sexual acts are not punishable.

The victim's impairment can either be situational – for example due to intoxication[48] – or depending on the victim's condition – for example due to a significant cognitive impairment or another mental condition that prevents them from expressing their will in a legally binding way.[49] As a rule, such a situation would result in the person concerned being completely excluded from consensual sexual acts due to their disability or situational impairment. To avoid this, the law permits sexual acts if the less impaired partner first obtains the active and explicit consent of the other person. In such cases, the law follows the concept of affirma-

[47] *Hörnle*, Sexual Assault (2023), 141 (150): "The serious harm must be the consequence of having refused sex – employee's rejection of sexual demands would result in dismissal"; (157): "massive and long-lasting social and economic consequences of separation ([…] family breadwinner, deportation […]) can constitute a serious threat" pursuant to § 177 (2) no. 5 PC.

[48] Vgl. BT-Drs. 18/9097 S. 24; *Eisele,* TK-StGB (2025) § 177 n. 33.

[49] Vgl. BT-Drs. 18/9097 S. 24; *Eisele,* TK-StGB (2025) § 177 n. 35.

tive consent, which is already implied in the de facto consent of the impaired person. This is the only case in which the German criminal law accounts for the yes-means-yes approach.

4. Actus reus *of Aggravated Cases of Sexual Assault and/or Sexual Coercion*

Subsec. (4), (5), (7), and (8) of § 177 PC stipulate specific qualified cases of sexual assault that carry significantly higher penalties. The qualifying factors consist of

- 77 (4): the victim being ill or disabled;[50]
- 77 (5):[51] the use of force,[52] threatening imminent danger to bodily integrity or life, or exploitation of the victim's vulnerable situation;
- 77 (7):[53] carrying weapons or other dangerous items, or causing risk of serious harm for the victim; and
- 77 (8):[54] the use of weapons or other dangerous items, serious bodily assault, or causing a risk of death for the victim.

One of the inconsistencies of § 177 PC is that these aggravated cases are based on sexual assault pursuant to § 177 (1) PC, which does *not* require an element of coercion. However, the use of force or threats amounts to sexual coercion, which is covered by the offence description of § 177 (2) no. 4 and no. 5 PC. Accordingly, in cases of § 177 (5), (8) PC[55] the perpetrator's conduct will also amount to sexual coercion pursuant to § 177 (2) no. 4 or no. 5 PC. The difference between a 'basic' sexual assault pursuant to § 177 (2) no. 4 and 5 PC and aggravated cases pursuant to § 177 (5) and (8) PC is that in basic cases under § 177 (2) no. 4 and 5 PC, serious

---

[50] § 177 (4) PC: The penalty is imprisonment for a term of at least one year if the inability to form or express a will is due to the victim's illness or disability.

[51] § 177 (5) PC: The penalty is imprisonment for a term of at least one year if the offender
1. uses force against the victim,
2. threatens the victim with a present danger to life or limb or
3. exploits a situation in which the victim is unprotected and at the mercy of the offender's influence.

[52] The offence does not require that the perpetrator uses violence to overcome the victim's opposition, it is also sufficient if the violence is used in order to enhance the pleasure he gains from the act, BT-Drs. 18/9097, p. 27; *Winkler*, GA 2025, 614 (622).

[53] § 177 (7) PC: The penalty is imprisonment for a term of at least three years if the offender
1. carries a weapon or other dangerous implement,
2. otherwise carries an instrument or other means for the purpose of preventing or overcoming the resistance of another person by force or threat of force or
3. places the victim at risk of serious damage to health.

[54] § 177 (8) PC: The penalty is imprisonment for a term of at least five years if
1. the offender uses a weapon or other dangerous implement during the commission of the offence or
2. the offender
a) seriously physically abuses the victim during the offence or
b) by committing the offence places the victim in danger of death.

[55] The same will be true in many cases of § 177 (7) PC if the perpetrator carries dangerous items.

danger is only threatened, whereas pursuant to §177 (5) and (8) PC, force is actually used or there is a threat of imminent danger to life or limb.

This is different with §177 (7) no. 1 PC, which entails the simple "carrying" of dangerous implements or weapons. 'Carrying' does not require more than simply having the dangerous object within reach at some point in time during the commission of the offence. Therefore, if a sexual assault is committed, for example, by one partner of a cohabiting couple in their kitchen and there is a knife block within his reach, this would suffice to fulfil an aggravated case of sexual assault under §177 (7) no. 1 PC (no less than three years of imprisonment). This is true even if the perpetrator neither used nor considered using any coercive means. Against this backdrop, some authors argue that §177 (7) PC can only apply if the perpetrator at least contemplates the use of the dangerous instrument should the victim resist the sexual act.[56] Although this restrictive approach seems convincing, it is not entirely commensurable with the fact that the carrying of an object with such intent is already covered by §177 (7) no. 2 PC which would therefore be superfluous if the restriction of §177 (7) no. 1 PC were accepted.

The law's inconsistency in this regard could have been avoided, had the legislator restricted the aggravated cases of §177 (7) and (8) PC to cases of sexual coercion pursuant to §177 (2) no. 4, 5, (5) PC. In general, it would have helped to reduce the complexity of the provision, had the legislator decided to create separate provisions for sexual assault and sexual coercion instead of squeezing the different offences into one provision that is further complicated by adding numerous qualifications and sentencing provisions.

Another critique targets the qualifying circumstance of §177 (4) PC, which builds on §177 (2) no. 1 PC, regarding the exploitation of a victim who is unable to form or to express their opposing will. The offence is aggravated and carries a penalty of at least one year imprisonment only if the victim's condition stems from an illness or a disability. Thus, it does not apply if the victim's condition emerged at the time the offence was committed due to substance abuse, i. e., intoxication through alcohol or drugs. This differentiating approach still bears traces of victim blaming – the 'good' victim cannot help not being able to clearly communicate their opposition due to their disability. Victims who are under the influence, on the other hand, do not seem to deserve the same level of legal protection – this carries the underlying notion that they were partly to blame for the sexual assault they suffered.[57]

---

[56] *Heger,* in: Lackner/Kühl/Heger-StGB, 31st ed. 2025, §177 n. 25; *Renzikowski,* in: Münchener Kommentar StGB, 5th ed. 2025 (‚MK-StGB (2025)'), §177 n. 167; *Eisele,* TK-StGB (2025), §177 n. 112.

[57] Cp. Deutscher Juristinnenbund, Policy Paper st 24/40 (18.11.2024), p. 7.

5. Rape: A Particularly Serious case of Sexual Assault or Sexual Coercion, §177 (6) PC

§177 (6) PC entails two particularly serious cases of sexual assault or sexual coercion under §177 (1) or (2) PC:

(6) In especially serious cases, the penalty is imprisonment for a term of at least two years. An especially serious case typically occurs where
1. the offender has sexual intercourse with the victim or has the victim have sexual intercourse or commits such similar sexual acts on the victim or has the victim commit them on them which are particularly degrading for the victim, especially if they involve penetration of the body (*rape*), or
2. the offence is committed jointly by more than one person.

While §177 (6) no. 2 PC relates to the joint commission of a basic offence by more than one person, rape constitutes a particularly serious case of sexual assault pursuant to §177 (6) no. 1 PC. Since rape builds on sexual assault, the offence does not necessarily presuppose any coercive element.[58] Because of this lack of a coercive element, the current rape definition is criticized as too broad and beyond the common perception of rape as physically forced intercourse.[59]

Since the offence description's entry into force in 2016, rape comes into play if one of the sexual acts described in §177 (6) PC is performed despite the victim's clearly expressed rejection. The legal definition of rape provided in §177 (6) no. 1 PC covers sexual intercourse – meaning the penetration of the vagina by a penis[60] – and extends to similar sexual acts that are equally degrading to the victim and must be performed either by the perpetrator, a third person, or the victim themselves. A humiliating effect similar to vaginal penetration by a penis occurs if the specific nature or manner of the sexual act degrades the victim to a mere object of sexual arbitrariness, disregarding their human dignity.[61] According to this very general description of rape, the offence includes not only penetration with the penis in cases of vaginal, anal or oral intercourse,[62] but also the insertion of other body parts (such as a finger[63]) or objects into the victim's natural body orifices.[64] Rape also encompasses the insertion of bodily fluids without additional

---

[58] BT-Drs. 18/9097, p. 28.

[59] *Hörnle*, in: Leipziger Kommentar StGB, 13th ed. 2023 ('LK-StGB (2023)'), §177 n. 227; *Löffelmann*, StV 2017, 413 (416); *Renzikowski*, NJW 2016, 3553 (3556).

[60] BT-Drs. 18/9097, p. 28.

[61] *Eisele*, TK-StGB (2025), §177 n. 100 et seqq.; *Noltenius*, SK-StGB (2024), §177 n. 90; *Renzikowski*, MK-StGB (2025), §177 n. 158.

[62] BGH NStZ 2000, 27 (28); BGH NStZ-RR 2003, 325, (326); BGH NStZ-RR 2009, 238; *Renzikowski,* MK-StGB (2025) §177 n. 159.

[63] In judicial practice, the vaginal or anal penetration with fingers is typically classified as rape, BGH NStZ 2000, 254 (255); BGH NStZ 2001, 369; BGH NStZ 2001, 598; BGH NStZ 2004, 440.

[64] BGH NJW 2000, 672; BGH NStZ-RR 2009, 238; *Renzikowski,* MK-StGB (2025), §177 n. 159.

penetration – such as ejaculating into the victim's mouth.[65] Furthermore, rape includes the defined sexual acts performed by the victim on themselves – such as self-penetration (with an object).[66] Rape can also consist of the victim acquiescing to a third person committing such acts on them or to having intercourse with an animal.[67] The particular humiliation of the victim as a result of the act must be justified in each individual case.

The classification of rape as a particularly serious case amounts to a 'specified sentencing rule' (*benannte Strafzumessungsregel*). As a result, in the cases described by law, the specified increased penalty (here: a sentence of between two and fifteen years) is generally applied. At the same time, however, it is also possible to classify the regulatory effect as inappropriate in individual cases due to special circumstances and therefore not to impose the higher penalty. This is discussed, for example, in connection with rape in cases of stealthing[68] (see also *V. 2.*). Since in these cases, the victim had consented to protected sexual intercourse, there is a debate as to whether the unprotected sexual intercourse that took place instead – which was not desired by the victim – is less humiliating than in a normal case of rape.[69] If this were the case, the regulatory effect of § 177 (2) PC could be waived despite penetration having taken place, and the increased penalty range would not apply.

A hardly convincing consequence of the legislator's decision to regulate rape as a particularly serious case of sexual assault is that a distinction must be made between the standard examples of sexual assault and sexual coercion in § 177 (2) PC and the aforementioned aggravating circumstances in § 177 (4), (5), (7), (8) PC, and § 178 PC (see *III.4.*). If the factual requirements of one of those aggravating circumstances are met, the higher penalty range applies not only "as a rule" (as it would with the particularly serious cases constituting rape), but is mandatory when the elements of § 177 (4), (5), (7), (8) PC, or § 178 PC are fulfilled. It is impossible to disprove the commission of the aggravated offence once the qualifying circumstances have been established, hence there is no need for a separate examination of whether the offence is particularly serious in individual cases. It does not seem logical that, of all kinds of sexual assault, the legislator has defined only rape by way of a 'specified sentencing rule' and not as a mandatory description of an aggravated case, since rape is commonly understood as the most severe case of sexual assault.[70] That, however, is not entirely reflected in the very broad

---

[65] BGHSt 53, 118 (120); BGH NStZ 2009, 262; *Eisele*, TK-StGB (2025), § 177 n. 102.

[66] BGH NStZ-RR 2020, 276 (277).

[67] *Hörnle*, NStZ 2017, 13 (19).

[68] Stealthing means that the perpetrator secretly does not use or gets rid of a condom, even though the victim expected them to use a condom and only agreed to sexual intercourse under this condition.

[69] For a restriction of § 177 (6) PC in these cases *Hoffmann*, NStZ 2019, 16 (18); similar *Hörnle*, LK-StGB (2023), § 177 n. 233; *Hoven*, NStZ 2020, 578 (581).

[70] The fact that rape is regulated as a qualifying circumstance (not a specified sentencing rule) if the victim is a child, § 176c (1) Nr. 2a PC, adds further inconsistency to this rape concept.

regulation of rape the legislator chose to stipulate in § 177 (6) PC, covering the wide range of conduct that has been described. Against this backdrop, it is not an exaggeration to state that the whole legal concept of rape as it is laid down in § 177 (6) PC is considerably flawed.

IV. Sentencing Factors Regarding Rape

The minimum sentence for rape pursuant to § 177 (6) PC is two years of imprisonment – however, the regulation of rape as a "particularly serious case of sexual assault" allows for a rejection of rape in cases that are exceptional[71] and, therefore, do not reach the level of a 'particularly serious case' (see *III.5.*). Yet, if, in addition to committing rape, the perpetrator committed one of the qualifying circumstances under § 177 (7), (8), 178 PC, the increase of the sentence is mandatory. The minimum sentence for § 177 (7) PC[72] is three years of imprisonment. If the requirements of one of the qualifying factors of § 177 (8) PC[73] are met, the minimum sentence rises to five years of imprisonment. If the death of the victim is recklessly caused (but not intended), the sentence is imprisonment of ten years up to life imprisonment, § 178 PC. However, if the perpetrator recognized the risk that the death of the victim might result from his actions and he willingly accepted that risk for the sake of the wanted sexual acts, the offence can amount to murder to obtain sexual gratification under § 211 PC. In this case, life imprisonment is mandatory. Foreign citizens can be expelled from Germany depending on the severity of the sentence.[74]

---

[71] Furthermore, even if rape is asserted and, therefore, the higher sentence of at least two years of imprisonment applies, the court can, due to the regulation as a "particularly serious case", still decide to suspend the sentence on probation, cp. *Eisele*, TK-StGB (2025), § 177 n. 151.

[72] Qualifying factors under § 177 (7) PC are the carrying of a weapon or other dangerous objects, or carrying any other instrument or object with him with the intent to use it during the offence, or causing a risk of severe bodily harm for the victim.

[73] That is the use of a weapon or dangerous object, or inflicting severe bodily harm on the victim or causing the risk of death for the victim.

[74] OVG Magdeburg, NVwZ-RR 2025, 157: The state has a particularly strong interest in deporting a foreign national who has been convicted of sexual assault and sentenced to at least one year's imprisonment, § 54 (1) no. 1 lit. c) *Aufenthaltsgesetz*. Subject to a case-by-case assessment, this interest can outweigh the foreign national's interest in staying in Germany. Since the minimum sentence for rape is imprisonment for at least two years, the initial threshold of a strong interest in expulsion will usually be met.

V. Shortcomings of the German No-Means-No Concept of Sexual Assault and Rape

Since German law considers rape a special case of sexual assault and defines rape in an overly broad manner,[75] the shortcomings of the no-means-no approach cannot be identified specifically for cases of rape but must be linked to the concept of sexual assault in general. In cases of sexual coercion, the problems associated with the no-means-no concept do not arise, as the perpetrator uses coercive means to prevent or overcome the victim's resistance. Therefore, the question of a recognizable opposing will does not come up here. However, there are a considerable number of other cases of sexual assault and rape without the use of coercion, that are difficult to grasp following the German no-means-no approach, and lead to multiple factual and legal problems.

1. Active Participation of the Victim

Two – closely related – factual situations are particularly problematic: firstly, the legal assessment of the active participation of the victim and, even more so, secondly, cases in which the victim's active participation is limited to performing sexual acts on themselves. Both scenarios are particularly difficult to legally assess if the rape does not involve sexual coercion but is based on sexual assault pursuant to § 177 (1) PC. Since sexual assault can be committed by the simple performance of sexual acts against the recognizable will of the victim, it is difficult to explain how the victim can actively participate in sexual acts against their own recognizable will if the perpetrator has not used coercive means. In other words: If the victim actively participated despite the absence of any coercive element, how can his or her actions be considered against their will?[76] Some authors reject this possibility altogether[77] – if that were right, active participation could only amount to a sexual offence, if at least some element of coercion on the part of the offender was at play.

A widely discussed example illustrating this problem was the so-called "chief physician case":[78] The perpetrator – chief physician in a hospital – had asked the victim – one of the physician assistants – to perform oral sex on him. After the victim had rejected this several times, she finally gave in and took his penis into her mouth for one or two seconds. She did so because she wanted to avoid future complications at work, while at the same time she wanted to end the situation

[75] *Hörnle*, LK-StGB (2023), § 177 n. 227; *Renzikowski*, MK-StGB (2025), § 177 n. 155.

[76] *Hörnle*, in: Hörnle (ed.) Sexual Assault (2023), 141 (155).

[77] *Noltenius*, SK-StGB (2024), § 177 n. 15; *Weigend*, in: Hoven/Weigend (eds.), Consent and Sexual Offenses (2022), 183 (193: "barring exceptional circumstances, an unforced sexual activity […] should not be regarded as involuntarily"); *Wolters*, in: Bublitz et al. (eds.), FS Merkel (2020), 951 (968).

[78] "Chief physician case" of Bamberg, BGH NStZ 2019, 717 (n. 18 et seq.).

and get rid of him. The Federal Court of Justice (*Bundesgerichtshof*, 'BGH') overturned the defendant's conviction for sexual assault because the reasoning of the lower court did not sufficiently explain how the victim's opposing will would have been apparent, even though the defendant did not use coercive means and the victim had actively performed the sexual act – which, given the circumstances, she could simply have refrained from.

Some authors agree with the BGH's assessment and contend it to be logically impossible that where the victim's active participation was not coerced, her conduct would still contravene her – clearly communicated – discernible opposing will.[79] Others argue that an autonomous decision to engage in sexual acts cannot realistically be established in a hierarchical relationship like the one between a chief physician and one of his medical assistants.[80]

The case highlights the difficulties of the German no-means-no solution in conjunction with the overly broad definition of rape: Is an underlying power structure[81] sufficient to make the victim's unwillingness clear, even though she actively performs the unwanted sexual act? And if so, how could the defendant's claim that he believed the victim had changed her mind and given up her opposing will be assessed?

The same difficulty arises in so-called *hands-off constellations* of rape: The offence description of rape extends to acts committed by the victim against themselves and does not require the presence of the perpetrator or even his perception of the victim's sexual act.[82] As long as the basic requirement of the victim acting against their recognizable will is met, the perpetrator can commit rape even if they are completely absent from the scene of the crime. In a case decided by the BGH in 2020, the perpetrator – by using multiple fake online personalities – made the victim believe that only by performing sexual acts on herself, recording them on video and providing the recording to the perpetrator afterwards could she spare another (in fact, inexistent) woman from being forced into prostitution by an (also inexistent) third party over whom the perpetrator claimed he had no influence.[83] The victim clearly expressed her opposing will, but finally agreed to

---

[79] *Fischer*, NStZ 2019, 580 (582); *Noltenius*, SK-StGB (2024), § 177 n. 15; *Renzikowski*, MK-StGB (2025), § 177 n. 56 et seq.

[80] *Hörnle*, in: Hörnle (ed.) Sexual Assault (2023), 141, 156 ("it is possible to actively do something against one's will, in the absence of the offender's coercive acts"); *Hörnle*, NStZ 2019, 439 (440) states that the victim's change of will might have been rational, but had not been self-determined; *Vavra*, Die Strafbarkeit nicht-einvernehmlicher sexueller Handlungen zwischen erwachsenen Personen (2020), 177 et seq.; *Winkler*, GA 2025, 614 (625 et seq., 632) argues that in such cases § 177 (6) PC should not be applied.

[81] The existence of §§ 174–174c PC, which criminalize the sexual abuse of persons in care, prisoners, sick or vulnerable institutionalised persons, as well as the punishability of sexual abuse exploiting counselling, treatment or care relationships, clearly shows that German criminal law generally considers such power structures to be relevant in sexual offences.

[82] BGH NStZ-RR 2020, 276; *Eisele*, TK-StGB (2025), § 177 n. 15.

[83] The prevailing view in Germany is that this amounts to a mere warning which does not suffice to establish coercion, since the perpetrator does not pretend to have any influence on the

perform the demanded acts in order to prevent the third party from inflicting harm to the (fictitious) woman. The BGH upheld the perpetrator's conviction of rape, based on the assumption that no coercive element is needed for rape, while self-pernetration falls into the scope of the offence and the victim's opposing will was clearly communicated.[84] The decision earned criticism for not sufficiently explaining how the victim's opposing will could still be present while she consciously sacrificed herself in the interest of the other woman she believed she would save by performing the sexual act.[85] Additionally, the court was criticized for not providing sufficient reasons for the comparable humiliating nature of self-penetration,[86] as the particularly degrading effect of rape is typically associated with an unwanted penetration performed by another.

The complexity of the case in question is exacerbated by the deceptive element in the perpetrator's conduct: Had the victim not believed that she could save the woman – who did not actually exist – by performing the requested actions, she would not have done so. However, the legal relevance of deception is also unclear when it comes to assessing the victim's conflicting will under § 177 (1) and (6) PC.

2. Rape by Deception?

If the perpetrator has deceived the victim and the victim's consent is based on this deception, the question arises as to what extent the deception makes the victim's consent legally invalid. In such cases, a distinction can be made based on the reference point of the victim's error: if the misconception relates to the sexual act itself, consent may be lacking and a conflicting intention may be considered. However, if the error caused by deception relates to circumstances beyond the sexual act itself, e. g., to the characteristics or motives of the partner, to the expectation of a lasting relationship or remuneration, this may be irrelevant to the so-called 'natural or factual' will with regard to the sexual act, and an opposing will may be ruled out in this respect. This distinction can be justified by the fact that coping with 'every-day life risks' of misjudging a partner or a certain situation cannot be the task of the criminal law on sexual offences. However, some authors reject this view as too narrow and consider any error that is decisive for the victim's consent to be legally relevant, provided that the perpetrator is aware of the misconception and the fact that the victim would not have consented if

---

occurrence of the harm, see *Küper*, GA 2006, 439 (441); *Wolters*, SK-StGB (2024), § 240 n. 21. Others criticize this interpretation of coercion as too narrow since the coercive effect on the victim is the same – despite the perpetrator's claim to have no influence on the occurrence of the harm, see for example *Wagner*, NStZ 2021, 592 (595).

[84] BGH NStZ-RR 2020, 276.

[85] *Wagner*, NStZ 2021, 592 (594).

[86] *Wagner*, NStZ 2021, 592 (595); *Winkler*, GA 2025, 614 (624 et seq., 632).

they had known the truth.[87] According to this view, the lack (or presence) of so-called 'dealbreakers' (which were clearly communicated) makes sexual assault conceivable – even if the 'deal-breaking' factors are motivated by discriminatory prejudices etc.[88] However, the clearly prevailing view in scholarly debate as well as in judicial practice rejects this position and holds that errors caused by deception are irrelevant as long as they do not relate to the sexual act itself.[89] The error must therefore relate directly to the quality of the sexual actions, entailing the necessary relevance to the victim's sexual self-determination.

A prominent example of rape by deception is discussed in the context of *stealthing*: If the perpetrator pretends to use a condom and then secretly removes it or does not use one from the outset, sexual assault has occurred if it is clear that the victim's consent related solely to protected intercourse.[90] The legal reasoning for this is that protected versus unprotected intercourse constitute different sexual acts. If the victim's consent referred to a specifically defined sexual act that did not actually take place, but instead another act took place, then there was no consent with regard to the latter. If the victim had also clearly specified their consent in advance only to a specific act, then the opposing will regarding the act that was actually performed was also unambiguously recognizable. On this basis, stealthing is classified as sexual assault under § 177 (1) PC.[91] A separate question is whether the specific sentencing rule for rape under § 177 (6) PC should apply in this situation (see *III. 5.*).[92] This would require the victim to have been particularly humiliated by the penetration – which is not immediately apparent if the penetration itself was consensual but was not carried out in the agreed manner. Therefore, some authors do not consider the act to be particu-

---

[87] *Vavra*, ZIS 2018, 611 (613); *Vavra*, Die Strafbarkeit nicht-einvernehmlicher sexueller Handlungen zwischen erwachsenen Personen (2020), 422; similar *Pschorr*, StraFo 2021, 279 (284 et seq.).

[88] *Vavra* ZIS 2018, 611 (617); for a critique of this view see *Hoven/Weigend*, KriPoZ 2018, 156 (160); *Wiedmer*, Die Strafbarkeit sexueller Übergriffe (2024), 114.

[89] *Denzel/Kramer da Fonseca Calixto*, KriPoZ 2019, 347 (353); *Eisele*, TK-StGB (2025), § 177 n. 19; *Keßler*, Sexuelle Täuschungen, 2022, 271; *Renzikowski*, MK-StGB (2025), Vorb. § 174 n. 11; *Schneider*, ZJS 2023, 360 (364); *Wolters*, in: Festschrift Merkel (2020), 951 (964); dissenting *Franzke*, BRJ 2019, 114 (120), who argues that it is impossible to distinguish misconceptions concerning the sexual act itself from misconceptions concerning other surrounding circumstances.

[90] This view is criticized as too narrow by the Deutscher Juristinnenbund, Policy Paper st 24/40 (18.11.2024), p. 6. They argue that the more the use of a condom is taken for granted, the less need the victim will feel to explicitly address this as a condition for sexual acts. As a result, the scope of § 177 (1) PC will be restricted in relationships where the use of a condom is generally taken for granted.

[91] BGH NStZ 2023, 229; BayObLG NStZ-RR 2022, 43; OLG Schleswig, NStZ 2021, 619 (621); *Heger/Huthmann*, JR 2023, 509 (511); *Hoven* NStZ 2023, 230 et seq.; *Pschorr*, StraFo 2021, 279 (284 et seq.); *Wiedmer*, Die Strafbarkeit sexueller Übergriffe (2024), 122 et seqq.; *Wolters*, in: Festschrift Merkel (2020), 951 (965); dissenting *Denzel/Kramer da Fonseca Calixto*, KriPoZ 2019, 347 (353 et seq.): sexual self-determination not affected; similar *Franzke*, BRJ 2019, 114 (119 et seq.).

[92] Cp. *Bauer* KriPoZ 2023, 96; *Denzel/Kramer da Fonseca Calixto*, KriPoZ 2019, 347 (351).

larly humiliating in such cases. According to this view, stealthing amounts to sexual assault under § 177 (1) PC, but does not deserve to be sentenced as rape within the meaning of § 177 (1), (6) PC.[93] Others assume that, since the victim did not consent to unprotected intercourse, there is no convincing reason to reject § 177 (6) PC.[94] As a result, the penalty would be a minimum of two years imprisonment pursuant to § 177 (6) PC, even in the absence of any coercive element. However, this is not a specific consequence of stealthing cases but a result of rape no longer presupposing a coercive element since the 2016 law reform.

The principles governing cases of stealthing could also be applied to other situations in which it was clearly communicated that only certain sexual acts were desired – while others were not.[95] Examples would include, in addition to consent limited to protected intercourse, consent limited to unprotected intercourse or certain forms of intercourse, or cases in which intercourse is to be terminated before ejaculation.[96] The motivation is irrelevant for all these limitations of consent – these are dispositions regarding sexual integrity that must be accepted. If sexual acts exceed the clearly recognizable limits of consent, they are unlawful in this respect and are subject to the communicated refusal, meaning that they fulfil the elements of the offence under § 177 (1) PC.

A borderline case is one in which the perpetrator conceals the sexual nature of the act – to which the victim consents – for example, by performing a sexual act under the pretence of a medical examination. Some legal literature suggests that consent given on a completely different basis must also be invalid in this case, and that sexual assault must therefore be affirmed.[97] This could be justified by the fact that in such cases, the sexual nature of the act is concealed – which relates to the act itself and could therefore invalidate the consent. This would be conceivable, for example, if a doctor pretends that a certain act is for diagnostic purposes only. One could then argue that the victim's consent relates exclusively to a medical examination and thus not to the sexual nature of the act performed. However, this classification is not clear-cut – because, unlike in the stealthing constellation,

---

[93] *Bauer* KriPoZ 2023, 96; *Hoven* NStZ 2023, 229 (231); *Denzel/Kramer da Fonseca Calixto*, KriPoZ 2019, 347 (351); *Wiedmer*, Die Strafbarkeit sexueller Übergriffe (2024), 128 et seqq.

[94] Cp. BayObLG NStZ-RR 2022, 43; *Eisele*, TK-StGB (2025) § 177 n. 100; *Keßler*, StraFo 2023, 173 (175); *Makepeace*, KriPoZ 2021, 10 (14); *Schneider*, ZJS 2023, 360 (369); *Vavra*, Die Strafbarkeit nicht-einvernehmlicher sexueller Handlungen zwischen erwachsenen Personen (2020), 424.

[95] *Heger/Huthmann*, JR 2023, 509 (512) *Pschorr*, StraFo 2021, 279 (285).

[96] OLG Hamm, NStZ-RR 2022, 276; *Eisele*, TK-StGB (2025), § 177 n. 19a.

[97] *Weigend*, in: Hoven/Weigend (eds.) Consent and Sexual Offenses (2022), 183 (192) contends the same were to be applied if the perpetrator deceived the victim about his identity (see also *Wiedmer*, Die Strafbarkeit sexueller Übergriffe (2024), 116). However, this is doubtful as long as the consent of the person concerned is specific to the partner with whom the act is performed. Errors regarding certain identity-determining factors of this person can then no longer be classified as relevant to the effectiveness of factual consent. *Weigend* suggests a distinction: Sexual assault would not apply if the perpetrator simply presented himself under a false name, but would be limited to cases where the perpetrator made the victim believe he was another person familiar to the victim.

the physical act as such is in principle covered by the victim's consent. One could therefore also argue that this case is solely about the perpetrator's motivation for the act and not about the act itself. On this basis, the victim's consent would then be affirmed and a sexual assault against the recognizable opposing will of the victim would be rejected. However, this conclusion is not convincing as the victim's disposition over their sexual integrity was not recognizable as such to the victim – in this respect, sexual self-determination is indeed affected and sexual assault should be affirmed.

3. *Recognizability of the Victim's Opposing Will in Cases of Tonic Immobility*

Another problem in assessing the recognizability of the victim's opposing will arises in cases of tonic immobility: Empirical evidence shows that victims of sexual assault often fall into a neurological state of shock that makes it impossible for them to communicate.[98] In German law, this situation would be covered by § 177 (2) no. 1 PC. Given the frequency of this reaction as determined in the study mentioned,[99] convictions under § 177 (2) no. 1 PC relating to such cases should be commonplace in current judicial practice. However, this has not been the case so far. It seems reasonable to assume that in cases of tonic immobility, the purely passive behaviour of the victim is interpreted as a lack of recognizable opposition on the part of the victim, so that sexual assault is rejected on these grounds alone. In practical terms, however, § 177 (2) no. 1 PC additionally requires that the perpetrator exploits the victim's state of shock to carry out the sexual act. This is usually contradicted by the fact that tonic immobility is an incontrollable neurological condition that can neither be directed by the perpetrator nor by the victim themselves. Accordingly, it can hardly be assumed that the perpetrator aimed at inducing a state of tonic immobility. Related to this is the perpetrator's further obvious claim that he not only did not take advantage of the state of shock, but also did not recognize that the victim's passivity was due to shock. All these uncertainties in the legal assessment of such constellations make it understandable that, at least so far, there are hardly any known cases in which a court has applied § 177 (2) no. 1 PC due to the victim's state of tonic immobility at the time of the offence.

---

[98] *Möller/Söndergaard/Helström*, Acta Obstetricia et Gynecologica Scandinavica 96 (2017), 932 et seqq.

[99] *Möller/Söndergaard/Helström*, Acta Obstetricia et Gynecologica Scandinavica 96 (2017), 932: 'Tonic immobility at the time of the assault was assessed in 298 women who had visited the emergency clinic for raped women within one month of a sexual assault. After 6 months, 189 women were assessed regarding the development of posttraumatic stress disorder and depression. Of the 298 women, 70 % reported significant tonic immobility and 48 % reported extreme tonic immobility during the assault. Tonic immobility was associated with the development of post-traumatic stress disorder […] and severe depression […] at 6 months.'

VI. The German Version of No-Means-No from the Perspective of International Law

Against the backdrop of all these shortcomings of the German no-means-no concept, it is doubtful and controversial whether the law is in line with the current 'state of the art' represented in the international human rights discourse. Even so, the 2016 reform's departure from the coercion-based model is consistent with the case law of the European Court of Human Rights, which in its landmark decision *M.C. v. Bulgaria* stated that it was

"persuaded that any rigid approach to the prosecution of sexual offences, such as requiring proof of physical resistance in all circumstances, risks leaving certain types of rape unpunished and thus jeopardising the effective protection of the individual's sexual autonomy. In accordance with contemporary standards and trends in that area, the member states' positive obligations under Articles 3 and 8 of the Convention must be seen as requiring the penalisation and effective prosecution of any non-consensual sexual act, including in the absence of physical resistance by the victim."[100]

This requirement is met by the provision of § 177 PC, which is no longer linked to an element of coercion. However, it is nevertheless questionable and contentious in legal literature, whether the German criminal law can be interpreted as being in line with the requirements of the European Council's Istanbul Convention (IC).[101] In fact, it was one of the legislator's goals to adapt the German criminal law on sexual offences to the requirements of the Convention, in particular to

Article 36 Istanbul Convention – Sexual violence, including rape

1 Parties shall take the necessary legislative or other measures to ensure that the following intentional conducts are criminalised:

a. engaging in non-consensual vaginal, anal or oral penetration of a sexual nature of the body of another person with any bodily part or object;

b. engaging in other non-consensual acts of a sexual nature with a person;

c. causing another person to engage in non-consensual acts of a sexual nature with a third person.

2 Consent must be given voluntarily as the result of the person's free will assessed in the context of the surrounding circumstances. […]

The Convention requires the Member States to criminalize non-consensual sexual acts and requires the victim's autonomous consent in Art. 36 (2) IC. Nevertheless, some authors argue that the German solution is in line with the Convention, since explanatory note to Art. 36 of the Convention grants the Member States a broad margin of appreciation,[102] that they do not consider exceeded by

---

[100] M.C. v. Bulgaria, App. no. 39272/98 (4.12.2003), para 153.

[101] Council of Europe Convention on preventing and combating violence against women and domestic violence, 11.5.2011, CETS 210. Germany acceded the Convention on May 11, 2011, and ratified it on October 12, 2017; the Convention entered into force in Germany on February 1, 2018 (BGBl. II, 2017, 1026).

[102] Explanatory note 193 to the Convention reads:

the German regulations.[103] Others criticize the German solution as falling short of the Convention's requirements.[104]

The national report on Germany[105] delivered by GREVIO[106] stated that § 177 (1) PC does not fully comply with the standard of criminalization of all non-consensual sexual acts as required by Art. 36 IC, notably the requirement that consent must be given voluntarily. The report criticizes that German law does not cover cases in which the victim remains passive while it does not consent to the sexual acts performed. Art. 36 IC requires the criminalization of such cases. Additionally, the report notes that the victim's obligation to communicate their opposing will shifts the focus of criminal investigations from the perpetrator's conduct to the victim's reaction – which leaves room for gender stereotypes and rape myths[107] in interpreting the victim's conduct from the perspective of an "objective spectator".[108] Furthermore, the report explicitly points to the phenomenon of tonic immobility and considers the German solution unconvincing in that regard.[109] However, the overall recommendation of GREVIO limits itself to

> "encourage the German authorities to monitor and further evaluate the implementation of the new sexual offences legislation, in particular Article 177 of the German Criminal Code, with a view to further aligning its definition of consent with that set out in Article 36, paragraph 2, of the Istanbul Convention."[110]

Despite this rather mild criticism, a small group of authors still take the view that Art. 36 IC calls for an affirmative consent model.[111] Their recommendation is to extend the only-yes-means-yes concept of sexual assault from its exceptional application in cases of a victim unable to communicate (§ 177 (2) no. 2 PC) to all cases of sexual assault.[112] However, there are only very few voices in the German discussion in favour of a general definition of sexual assault along the lines of a

---

193. In implementing this provision, Parties to the Convention are required to provide for criminal legislation which encompasses the notion of lack of freely given consent to any of the sexual acts listed in lit. a to lit. c. It is, however, left to the Parties to decide on the specific wording of the legislation and the factors that they consider to preclude freely given consent.

[103] See *Eisele*, TK-StGB (2025), § 177 n. 11, with further references.

[104] Deutscher Juristinnenbund, Policy Paper st 24/40 (18.11.2024), p. 11; *Kempe*, Lückenhaftigkeit und Reform des deutschen Sexualstrafrechts vor dem Hintergrund der Istanbul-Konvention, 2018, 224 et seq., 230.

[105] GREVIO/Inf(2022)21 Germany.

[106] Group of Experts on Action against Violence against Women and Domestic Violence (GREVIO) – members of GREVIO are elected by the State parties for terms of four years.

[107] For further explanation see *Steinl*, ZStW 2021, 819 (833 et seq.).

[108] See also Deutscher Juristinnenbund, Policy Paper st 24/40 (18.11.2024), p. 8.

[109] GREVIO/Inf(2022)21 Germany, para. 252.

[110] GREVIO/Inf(2022)21 Germany, para. 253.

[111] Deutscher Juristinnenbund, Policy Paper st 24/40 (18.11.2024), p. 1; *Kempe*, Lückenhaftigkeit und Reform des deutschen Sexualstrafrechts vor dem Hintergrund der Istanbul-Konvention, 2018, 224 et seq.; *Torenz*, German Law Journal 2021, 718 (721).

[112] Deutscher Juristinnenbund, Policy Paper st 24/40 (18.11.2024), p. 1; *Herning/Illgner*, ZPR 2016, 77 (80).

yes-means-yes concept.[113] Most authors reject this approach as inappropriate[114] and even during the debate around the reform in 2016, almost nobody advocated for such a concept.[115]

VII. Law Enforcement and Procedural Aspects

A study commissioned by the Federal Criminal Police Office and published on February 10, 2026, has revealed that only three per cent of women who are victims of sexual assault actually report it.[116] Although it is impossible to pinpoint the exact reasons why each individual victim is reluctant to report the crime, it is not pure speculation to assume that one of the reasons for the low number of reports lies in the numerous consequences that reporting a sexual offence has for the victim: When law enforcement agencies become aware of a suspected sexual offence, they are obliged to initiate a criminal investigation (principle of legality, pursuant to § 152 (2), § 163 Code of Criminal Procedure (CCP)). Hence, once a victim has reported a sexual offence, the whole matter is out of his or her hands and criminal proceedings are inevitable. Linked to this are multiple burdens for the victim who is typically the only witness. For example, the obligation to testify (§ 48 (1) 2 CPP) multiple times during the course of the proceedings, including a public witness statement in a courtroom, and being confronted with the perpetrator. Ultimately, due to the concept of the German no-means-no model, the witness will feel the need to convince the court that a 'no' has been communicated clearly. In some cases, courts seem to extend their inquiry not only to the facts and circumstances of the alleged offence, but also to the victim's former sexual experiences and conduct.[117] Although the CCP explicitly limits the court's

[113] Deutscher Juristinnenbund, Policy Paper st 24/40 (18.11.2024), p. 9; *Herning/Illgner*, ZPR 2016, 77 (80). Interestingly, in an interview in Ocotber 2025, the German Minister of Justice, Stefanie Hubig, advocated for a yes-means-yes approach for young people in order to better protect them against sexual assault, further changes were 'to be discussed'; https://www.bmjv.de/SharedDocs/Interviews/DE/2025/1024_TAZ_Min.html (last access 20.2.2026).

[114] Cp. *Hörnle* in: Hörnle (ed.), Sexual Assault; Law Reform in a Comparative Perspective (2023), 141 (145); for a critique of both the yes-means-yes and the no-means-no concept, see *Torenz*, German Law Journal 2021, 718 (724 et seqq., offering no solution to the problem).

[115] See for an exception *Herning/Illgner*, ZRP 2016, 77 (80), arguing from the perspective of social sciences.

[116] 'Ergebnisse der Dunkelfeldstudie "Lebenssituation, Sicherheit und Belastung im Alltag", Gewalterfahrungen innerhalb und außerhalb von Partnerschaften', p. 15; accessible at https://www.bka.de/DE/UnsereAufgaben/Forschung/ForschungsprojekteUndErgebnisse/Dunkelfeldforschung/LeSuBiA/Ergebnisse_Publikationen/ergebnisse_node.html (last access 20.2.2026).

[117] BGHSt 45, 164 states that in case of sexual offences, it is usually necessary to assess the victim's 'sexual knowledge and experience' ("Geht es aber um […] Sexualdelikte […], ist regelmäßig die Einschätzung seiner sexual-bezogenen Kenntnisse und Erfahrungen notwendig."). In the same vein LG Landshut, judgement of 7.10.2021, 1 KLs 401 Js 585–13, n. 275 '*ausführliche Sexualanamnese*'; and Saarländisches OLG, judgment of 23.11.2017, 4 U 26/15, n. 114. This contravenes Art. 54 Istanbul Convention (CETS 210), see also para. 278 of the explanatory report:

authority to inquire about the victim's personal (and intimate former) life to questions indispensable for the purpose of finding out the truth about the incident reported,[118] it is mainly up to the court's discretion to decide which information is indispensable for the investigation. Accordingly, the duty to testify brings about the risk of psychologically adding to traumatized victims' stress and in some cases even the risk of re-traumatization.[119] In order to reduce these risks, § 406g CCP stipulates that victims can avail themselves of psychological support during criminal proceedings, especially if the victim is particularly vulnerable and has to deliver a witness statement in court.

Another highly problematic aspect of criminal proceedings in sexual offence cases is that some lawyers apparently still believe that victims should refrain from seeking psychotherapeutic support during ongoing criminal proceedings because law enforcement authorities might suspect the victim's memory would be impaired by therapeutic measures. Recent case law clearly rejects this view, as the BGH explained in a Court order of September 2025:

> "The Senate does not understand why [...] it should be advisable to wait until the main hearing before starting therapy. The fact that a victim of sexual abuse undergoes therapy to alleviate the mental pain and suffering caused by the offence does not detract from the credibility of their statements".[120]

Nevertheless, victims are often advised to wait until after the criminal proceedings have been concluded before undergoing psychotherapy.[121] This is in stark contrast to the fact that victims of sexual assault, including rape, are entitled to psychotherapeutic intervention provided by outpatient trauma clinics for an impending mental health disorder that was (likely to be) caused by a traumatic event (§§ 32, 33 *Sozialgesetzbuch* XIV). However, as long as psychotherapy is considered a potential source of memory changes in legal practice,[122] victims are

---

'Article 54 entails the obligation for Parties to take the necessary legislative or other measures to ensure that evidence relating to the sexual history and sexual conduct of the victim shall be permitted or considered only when it is relevant and necessary. [...] Where judges admit previous sexual history evidence, it should only be presented in a way that does not lead to secondary victimisation. Victims should have access to legal recourse without suffering additional trauma because of their sexual history and conduct.'

[118] Section 68a CCP: Limitation of right to ask questions to protect privacy
(1) Questions concerning facts which may dishonour the witness [...] or which concern their personal sphere of life are, as a rule, to be asked only if they cannot be dispensed with.
(2) Questions concerning circumstances justifying the witness's credibility in the case at hand, in particular concerning his or her relationship with the accused or the aggrieved person, are to be asked insofar as this is necessary.

[119] Cp. *Vavra*, Die Strafbarkeit nicht-einvernehmlicher sexueller Handlungen zwischen erwachsenen Personen (2020), p. 106.

[120] BGH 5 StR 394/25, Decision of 9.9.2025, accessible at https://www.bundesgerichtshof.de/SiteGlobals/Forms/Suche/EntscheidungssucheBGH_Formular.html (last access 20.2.2026).

[121] *Bublitz*, Gesundheit oder Glaubhaftigkeit? Auswege aus dem traumatherapeutischen Dilemma. Ethik in der Medizin 2000, 32 (65 et seqq.).

[122] See for example *Hohoff* (a judge at the BGH), stating in NStZ 2020, 387 (388), that holding back therapy from children who were victims of sexual abuse was predetermined by the objective

locked in a so-called trauma-therapeutic dilemma: It may seem that in order to care for their mental health and obtain therapeutic support, they jeopardize the credibility of their testimony – at least in the eyes of the judiciary.

A good solution for this dilemma – beyond advisable trainings for professionals participating in such legal proceedings – would be to offer the opportunity to anonymously testify and document the verbal statement for future criminal proceedings when the victim is mentally stabilized by psychotherapeutic support. The German legal system already provides for a 'confidential collection of *physical* evidence'[123] (e.g. DNA, documentation of injuries), i.e. physical injuries are documented within the public health care system and then stored until the victim has received medical and psychological help. This ensures that the (anonymous) victim can postpone the decision whether to report the crime until they feel strong enough to face the following criminal proceedings. For verbal statements – often the central evidence in sexual offences – there is currently no comparable option. This gap became even more apparent with the shift of § 177 (1) PC from the coercion-based to the consent-based concept in 2016. Since then, in many cases of sexual assault, there will be no physical evidence as the offence no longer requires the use of coercive means. As a result, the importance of the victim's testimony has increased significantly. Although procedural law provides for the documentation of an early witness statement before a judge,[124] including the possibility of sparing the victim multiple statements during the proceedings,[125] this opportunity is offered on a case-by-case basis and not as a rule victims could rely upon. A future strengthening of victims' rights in that regard would certainly add to a more efficient prosecution of sexual offences.

VIII. Conclusions

Although the debate about the basic concept of sexual offences in Germany has quieted down, there is still much to be done: the number of reports is alarmingly low; a recent study by the Federal Criminal Police Office estimates the reporting

---

of every criminal proceeding to establish the truth. In her view, postponing therapy serves this goal by ensuring that spontaneous and authentic statements of the children can be obtained.

[123] §§ 27 (1) no. 6, sentence 4, 132k Social Code Book V – Statutory health insurance.

[124] § 58a Code of Criminal Procedure: Video and audio recording of examination
(1) A video and audio recording may be made of the examination of a witness. […] The examination must, following an evaluation of the relevant circumstances, be recorded and conducted as a judicial examination if the interests meriting protection of persons who have been aggrieved by offences against sexual self-determination (sections 174 to 184j of the Criminal Code) can thus be better safeguarded and the witness consented, prior to the examination, to the video and audio recording being made.

[125] § 255a (2) 1 CCP: In proceedings relating to offences against sexual self-determination […] the examination of a witness […] may be substituted by the showing of an audio-visual recording of his or her previous judicial examination …

rate for sexual assaults against women at 3.0 %.[126] This shows that victims have little confidence in the German justice system's ability to respond to sexual offences adequately. The reasons for this can be found at both the substantive and procedural levels.

In substantive criminal law, the eclectic and poorly structured current state of sexual criminal law does not help efficient prosecution. In particular, the legal definition of rape is anything but precise and far removed from the understanding of rape that is prevalent among the population. However, this broad definition of rape does not lead to greater and therefore better protection against violations of sexual self-determination, but rather complicates the work of law enforcement agencies and the judiciary. Legal certainty suffers when the legal boundaries of rape are not clearly defined by law and therefore need to be specified by judicial practice.

Yet the main reason for the dysfunctionality of German criminal law on sexual offences lies in the difficulty of proving the core element of the basic offence of sexual assault: the victim's opposing will as well as the perpetrator's intent relating to it. The necessity of this proof is based on the assumption entailed in § 177 (1) PC that, as a general rule, sexual acts are permitted. Accordingly, a sexual act can only amount to a criminal offence if the victim clearly communicates their opposing will.[127] The requirement that a victim must clearly express their refusal of intrusions into their personal sphere of rights, *before* such intrusions occur, in order for the actus reus of a criminal offence to be fulfilled, is unique among the offences against individual rights in the PC. Nevertheless, this is considered appropriate because the criminal relevance of a sexual act cannot be based solely on the thoughts of the person concerned, but must also be reflected in the outside world.[128] But this is not a convincing argument. From the outside, the intrusive nature of a (physical) sexual act is no more difficult to identify than that of, say, trespassing. Sexual acts are regularly recognizable as intrusions into the intimate sphere of the person concerned. Why the act as such is nevertheless considered to only amount to the actus reus of sexual assault if the victim's opposition was discernible, requires justification. Some argue that classifying sexual acts as principally capable to bring about the actus reus of sexual assault paints an outdated

[126] 'Ergebnisse der Dunkelfeldstudie "Lebenssituation, Sicherheit und Belastung im Alltag", Gewalterfahrungen innerhalb und außerhalb von Partnerschaften', p. 10, 76.

[127] Unless there is a valid reason for the impossibility or unreasonableness of communication by the victim pursuant to § 177 (2) PC.

[128] Cp. the legislator's explanation for the amendment of § 177 (1) PC in 2016, BT-Drs. 18/9097, p. 23, stating that the 'victim's mere inner reservation is not decisive. Cases in which the victim's motives are ambivalent are also not covered by the provision. This is because the victim can be expected to clearly express their opposing will at the time of the act' ('*Der bloße innere Vorbehalt des Opfers ist jedoch nicht maßgeblich. Auch werden Fälle, bei denen die Motivlage des Opfers ambivalent ist, nicht von der Vorschrift erfasst. Denn es ist dem Opfer zuzumuten, dem entgegenstehenden Willen zum Tatzeitpunkt eindeutig Ausdruck zu verleihen*').

picture of sexuality.[129] Yet, this is only correct insofar as consensual sexual interaction between consenting individuals lacks any unilateral intrusion into the intimate sphere of another person and therefore any criminal relevance. As a result, even from an outside perspective, there is no assault but simply a consensual interaction in the intimate sphere. Criminal law has no role to play here.

However, the situation changes fundamentally if the sexual act is performed unilaterally – and simply encounters passivity on the part of the other person. In this case, according to German law, the intrusion into the other person's sphere would only constitute sexual assault if they communicated their rejection beyond their mere passivity. The same applies in cases of 'ambivalent' behaviour – typically situations in which there is initially consensual interaction, but then one of the partners refrains from further interaction. Some authors consider it unfair to require the active partner to ascertain whether consent still exists, even though the victim could easily communicate their refusal.[130] Overlooked is the fact that it would be just as easy for the active person to simply stop their actions in order to avoid any allegation of sexual assault. In any case, the distribution of communication obligations by the criminal law regarding sexual offences runs counter to the usual distribution of risks between persons who interfere in other people's legal spheres and those whose legal spheres are interfered with: In principle, anyone who crosses such a threshold is obliged to obtain the consent of the person affected. However, this legal ground rule is turned on its head when it comes to the intimate legal interest of sexual integrity. Here, the victim is obliged to defend themselves against the attack through communication *before* the violation of the integrity boundary is even classified as a criminal offence. For comparison: in cases of trespassing, no one would think of classifying the unilateral intrusion into another person's property as a criminal offence only on the condition that they had clearly expressed their objection. On the contrary: entering someone else's premises is only permissible if it is covered by the consent of the person concerned. It would be completely inappropriate to protect domestic privacy better than sexual privacy. Therefore, in both cases, permission to cross the boundary of integrity – in accordance with the Istanbul Convention[131] – should be a prerequisite for the criminal irrelevance of the conduct in question. Adequate protection of sexual self-determination therefore requires that crossing the boundary of integrity is only irrelevant under criminal law if it is covered by the consent of the person concerned – which is regularly the case if they actively participate in sexual acts.[132] If this is not the case, however, a unilateral assault is at issue and the question of consent arises. In situations where the victim calmly

---

[129] *Hoven*, NK 2018, 392 (395); *Hoven/Weigend*, JZ 2017, 182 (186); similar *Frommel*, NK 2018, 368 (371), stating that, from a criminal law perspective, sexual acts were neutral.

[130] *Hörnle*, in: Hörnle (ed.) Sexual Assault (2023), 141 (146); *Hoven*, NK 2018, 392 (395).

[131] Art. 36 (2) Istanbul Convention: Consent must be given voluntarily as the result of the person's free will assessed in the context of the surrounding circumstances.

[132] For exceptions see above *V. 1.*

assesses their situation and concludes that any resistance would be futile, a purely passive reaction to sexual acts may be a rational course of action – although it does not entail consent. The victim may hope that this will allow them to get through the assault as quickly as possible and without serious injury. However, the law considers this victim's opposition to the sexual act insufficiently recognizable – and thus relieves the perpetrator of the obligation to ensure that his intrusion into the victim's intimacy is not unwanted. This also implies a subtle message to those affected that by not sufficiently fulfilling their communication obligations they bear at least partial responsibility for the violation of their own rights.

On the procedural level, this rather unfair distribution of obligations leads to enormous stress for victims of sexual offences. In many cases, they will be the only witness in a situation where one person's word stands against another's. The focus of the legal proceedings will then not be on the question of how the accused concluded that the victim consented to the intrusion into their privacy. Instead, the judiciary will focus primarily on the question of the extent to which the victim communicated their opposing will sufficiently clearly. This may give victims the impression that the subject of legal consideration is less the punishability of the perpetrator's conduct and more the adequacy of their refusal of this conduct – a direct consequence of the legislative decision not to base sexual assault (in the absence of coercion) on the perpetrator's act alone, but to link it to the additional requirement of the victim's properly clear communication.

All this shows that while the German legislature did well to extend the scope of sexual offences in 2016 to include offences beyond the use of coercion, the legal framework of the German consent model offers only a half-hearted solution. Nevertheless, it is unlikely that German lawmakers will fundamentally reform the complex issue of sexual offences again in the near future or even switch to a yes-means-yes model.

Yet, there is in fact no doubt that action is needed in view of the low reporting rates. The first step should be to adapt procedural law to the substantive legal changes: The legislative waiver of an element of coercion in sexual assault increases the importance of witness testimony regarding the course of events. Accordingly, anonymous testimony in preparation of future criminal proceedings should be possible in order to enable victims to seek psychotherapeutic assistance without having to worry about the credibility of later statements. An increase in the number of reports seems achievable, if victims were able to work on their mental stabilization after traumatic events before they decide about the initiation of criminal proceedings, if necessary, with further psychosocial support.

Furthermore, training for law enforcement agencies and the judiciary remains essential to ensure that victims who are witnesses are treated with sensitivity, given the imbalance in the substantive criminal law. This should also counteract the influence of rape myths, which are still very much alive. An effective criminal justice system that can adequately deal with sexual offences depends not only on appropriate legislative framework, but also relies heavily on the comprehensive expertise, knowledge, and sensitivity of those who apply the law. The creation of special departments within the judiciary to prosecute sexual offences would be a first step – this would allow the necessary expertise to be concentrated with regard to the implications of criminal proceedings involving traumatized victim witnesses.

Above all, the top priority should be the prevention of sexual offences through comprehensive measures. The message of education and awareness-raising campaigns throughout society must be that the responsibility for encroaching on the intimate sphere of others lies with those who cross the boundaries of others' integrity.

Participation of Non-Judges in the Administration of Criminal Justice in Germany

Also: Criminal Adjudication Under Pressure

Anna Helena Albrecht

I. Introduction

When the Code of Criminal Procedure (CCP) – a compromise between liberal aspirations and conservative persistence – and the Courts Constitution Act (CCA) came into force in 1877,[1] the adjudication of criminal cases was entrusted to the courts. Decisions were to be rendered by professional judges and, in some courts, by lay judges, who sat either on joint panels with the professional judges or as part of a jury. Judicial independence was established by statute. The public prosecutor's authority was confined to deciding, at the conclusion of the preliminary investigation, whether to bring charges or apply for a penalty order, provided there was sufficient suspicion, or to discontinue the proceedings should such suspidion be lacking.

Over the past 150 years, however, much has changed, while other aspects have come to be viewed in a new light. In many instances, these developments can be attributed to increasing pressure on courts and judges.

II. Lay Judges in German Criminal Proceedings

The starting point for this consideration shall be the institution of lay judges. While some see them as an 'indispensable part of the criminal justice system'[2], voices calling for the abolition of lay judges have grown louder. They describe them as 'anachronistic ornaments of mistrust'[3], consider the reasons for their introduction to be outdated,[4] see them as a useless and burdensome nuisance,

[1] For an overview of the legislative history of the Reichs CCP with further references see *Koch*, ZIS 2009, 542 et seqq.; https://www.zis-online.com/dat/artikel/2009_10_365.pdf. (all websites were last accessed on 12 January 2026).

[2] *Jung*, in: FS 150 Jahre Landgericht Saarbrücken, 1985, 317, 331. Unless otherwise indicated, all English translations are by the author.

[3] *Gerson*, https://www.lto.de/recht/justiz/j/schoeffen-strafsachen-justiz-strafverfahren-strafrecht-ehrenamt.

[4] *Kühne*, in: Löwe-Rosenberg, StPO, Einl. Abschn. J, n. 30.

particularly in economic criminal proceedings,[5] or as a gateway for prejudice and extremist tendencies[6]. This warrants a brief examination of the historical foundations of lay participation, as well as of its current structure and legal status.

1. Historical Development of Lay Participation in German Criminal Procedure

The (re)introduction of lay judges into criminal proceedings in Germany was part of the 19th-century reform movement.[7] Rooted in the literature, the movement sought to abolish the absolutist inquisitorial process, from which, in its final form, in most of the German states any participation by lay judges had been eliminated;[8] and it instigated its transformation into the so-called reformed inquisitorial process, which still prevails in current German law.

The demands of the reform movement were directed, among other things, against the personal union of investigative and adjudicative authority, against the broad discretionary powers of the inquisitor – and thus the relative powerlessness of the accused – and against the reliance on written material, which may have been biased and was obtained in secret preliminary proceedings beyond public scrutiny.[9] The participation of lay citizens in the administration of justice was intended to curb the power of professional judges, who were suspected of being loyal to and influenced by the rulers.[10]

The demand for lay participation ultimately led to its introduction into the criminal justice systems in the individual German states during the 19th century, albeit in different forms: In some states, jury trials were established, in which decision-making responsibilities were divided between jurors (*Geschworene*) and professional judges; in other states, mixed panels of professional judges and honorary lay judges (*Schöffen*) were created to decide jointly on questions of guilt and sentencing.[11]

The Reich Court Constitution Act 1877, as a uniform codification for the entire German Empire, combined both models as a compromise: Courts with joint panels of *Schöffen* and professional judges were tasked with deciding minor crimes, while in jury courts (*Schwurgericht*), twelve jurors sat periodically with three professional judges and were responsible for determining guilt in serious

[5] https://www.lto.de/recht/nachrichten/n/jumiko-antrag-mecklenburg-vorpommern-wirtschaftsstrafverfahren-ohne-schoeffen; *Volk*, in: FS Dünnebier, 1982, 381.

[6] *Gerson* (fn. 3).

[7] For the earlier history of lay judges' participation, see, for example *Andoor*, Laien in der Strafrechtsprechung, 2013, 23 et seqq.; *Löhr*, Zur Mitwirkung der Laienrichter im Strafprozess, 2008, 11 et seqq.

[8] *Benz*, Zur Rolle der Laienrichter im Strafprozeß, 1982, 44; *Löhr* (fn. 7), 47 with further references.

[9] See inter alia *Schmidt*, Einführung in die Geschichte der deutschen Strafrechtspflege, §§ 284 et seqq.

[10] See, for example (albeit critically) *Feuerbach*, Betrachtungen über das Geschwornen-Gericht, 1813, 27 et seqq.; *Kern*, Geschichte des Gerichtsverfassungsrechts, 1954, 59.

[11] *Benz* (fn. 8), 47 et seqq.; *N. Lieber*, Schöffengericht und Trial by Jury, 2010, 159 et seqq.

crimes. Adjudicating moderately serious offences, high treason, treason, and appeals was reserved for professional judges.[12]

Shortly after its introduction, and even more so after the First World War, proposals emerged to abolish or reform the jury court, initially on substantive grounds.[13] Ultimately, however, economic considerations during the economically strained years of the Weimar Republic period led to the abolition of juries and their replacement by another form of lay judges' court, in which professional judges and six *Schöffen* (albeit still termed *Geschworene*) continued to decide together on a periodic basis, while criminal divisions at the *Landgericht* were supplemented with two *Schöffen*.[14]

The National Socialists initially saw lay participation as a means to implant their ethno-nationalist ideology in criminal justice and therefore extended it to the highest courts to ensure that 'healthy popular sentiment' ('*gesundes Volksempfinden*') prevailed.[15] With the outbreak of the war, however, all lay participation was abolished,[16] which could be expected in light of the democracy-affirming origins of lay participation.[17]

After the Second World War, these changes were repealed, restoring the situation as it had been after 1924. In 1974, large lay courts became permanently sitting tribunals, and the number of lay judges reduced from six to two.[18] The stated reasons were simplification and procedural expediency, and, given the independence of professional judges, it was considered unnecessary for *Schöffen* to have the power to outvote their professional counterparts.[19]

2. Current Legal Framework Governing Lay Participation in German Criminal Procedure

This is the legal situation that we still find today: *Schöffen* decide jointly with professional judges not only, but most importantly on questions of guilt and sentencing, thus render judgments together with professional judges 'in the name of the people'.

---

[12] CCA 1877, Sections 25 et seqq., 73 et seqq., 79 et seqq.

[13] *Kern* (fn. 10), 158 et seqq.; *N. Lieber* (fn. 11), 171 et seqq.

[14] Verordnung über die Gerichtsverfassung und Strafrechtspflege of 4 Januar 1924, Sections 11, 12; for further details see *N. Lieber* (fn. 11), 175 et seqq.; *Linkenheil*, Laienbeteiligung an der Strafjustiz, 114 et seqq.

[15] For further details see *N. Lieber* (fn. 11), 178 et seq.

[16] Verfügung über Maßnahmen auf dem Gebot der Gerichtsverfassung und der Rechtspflege vom 1. September 1939.

[17] *Linkenheil* (fn. 14), 123; *Rüping*, JR 1974, 269, 271 with further references.

[18] Erstes Gesetz zur Strafverfahrensreform, Federal Law Gazette 1974 I, 3393 et seqq.

[19] BT-Drs. 7/55,153 et seq.

a) Jurisdiction of Schöffen *in Criminal Courts*

The composition and jurisdiction of judicial panels involving lay participation in Germany may be summarized as follows: Local courts (*Amtsgerichte*), regional courts (*Landgerichte*), and higher regional courts (*Oberlandesgerichte*) adjudicate criminal cases as courts of both fact and law, whereas the Federal Court of Justice (*Bundesgerichtshof*) sits solely as a court of error on points of law.

The *Amtsgericht* has jurisdiction over cases where the expected custodial sentence does not exceed four years, provided that preventive detention is not under consideration and the case lacks 'particular significance' (Section 24 CCA). Minor offenses are decided by a single professional judge (*Strafrichter*, Section 25 CCA). More serious offenses fall to the lay judges' court (*Schöffengericht*, Section 28 CCA), which is composed of one professional judge and two lay judges (*Schöffen*). In complex proceedings, an extended *erweitertes Schöffengericht* – comprising two professional and two lay judges – is convened (Section 29(2) CCA).

Cases exceeding these jurisdictional thresholds are heard by the *Landgericht*, unless they fall within the original jurisdiction of the *Oberlandesgericht*, such as offenses against national security or parliamentary bribery (Section 120 CCA). First-instance cases are adjudicated by the Grand Criminal Division (*Große Strafkammer*), which generally sits with three professional and two lay judges (Section 76(1)–(2) CCA); however, for the main hearing, the number of professional judges may be reduced to two. By contrast, for the *Schwurgericht* – which has jurisdiction over a specific catalog of particularly serious offenses – the full bench of three professional judges and two lay judges remains mandatory (Sections 74 (2), 76(2) CCA)

Appeals against *Amtsgericht* judgments, which entail a de novo review of both facts and law, are heard by the Small Criminal Division (*Kleine Strafkammer*) of the *Landgericht*. This division is composed of one professional judge – or two if the appeal originates from an *erweitertes Schöffengericht* – and two *Schöffen* (Section 76(1) CCA). By contrast, appeals on points of law (Revision) and proceedings before the *Oberlandesgerichte* are, as a rule, decided by professional judges only (Sections 116, 122 CCA).

b) Legal Status of Schöffen

Schöffen are honorary judges (Section 31(1) CCA). They are appointed for a fixed term of five years (Section 42 CCA) and are assigned to a specific court panel rather than to an individual case. For the duration of their tenure, they form an integral part of the court and thus constitute the 'legally assigned judge' (*gesetzlicher Richter*, Art. 101(1) sentence 2 Basic Law, BL). In contrast to jurors in many other legal systems, there is no case-specific voir dire or similar selection mechanism; like professional judges, *Schöffen* may only be disqualified for bias, either by operation of law or upon motion, pursuant to Sections 22 et seq. and 31 of the CCP.

Their participation is limited to the main hearing, including deliberations and voting on the verdict.[20] Under Section 30(1) CCA, they generally exercise judicial office in full and with the same voting rights as professional judges. They also participate in procedural decisions made during the main hearing that do not directly relate to the final judgment, such as rulings on adjournments, trials in absentia, or the exclusion of the public. Accordingly, judgments rendered with the participation of *Schöffen* are subject to the standard appellate remedies.

How *Schöffen* acquire the necessary legal knowledge is not specified by law, nor does the law require any pre-service training. Instead, the Instructions on Criminal Procedure and Administrative Fines Procedure[21] contain only a rather brief provision (No. 126(1)), according to which professional judges are tasked with assisting *Schöffen* in fulfilling their duties, in particular by explaining formalities and technical terms that they do not understand. Consequently, the presiding judge bears the responsibility of imparting the requisite knowledge of substantive and procedural law during deliberations. Beyond this, optional introductory and continuing education is available through adult education centers (*Volkshochschulen*) or lay judge associations.[22] There are differing views in both jurisprudence and academia as to whether *Schöffen* should be granted the same access to case files as professional judges.[23]

Statutory rules on panel composition and voting grant *Schöffen* a blocking minority regarding decisions adverse to the defendant on both guilt and sentencing; professional judges thus require the concurrence of at least one lay judge to convict. In the *Schöffengericht* (*Amtsgericht*) and the *Kleine Strafkammer* (*Landgericht*), the lay judges may even outvote the single professional judge. While panel decisions under Section 196(1) CCA generally require an absolute majority – with the presiding judge holding the casting vote in the event of a tie (e. g., in the *Erweitertes Schöffengericht* or *Große Strafkammer*, Section 196(3) CCA) – Section 263(1) CCP[24] mandates a qualified two-thirds majority for any decision concerning guilt or legal consequences. To safeguard their independence and prevent influence,[25] Section 197 CCA dictates that *Schöffen* cast their votes before the professional judges.

---

[20] CCA, Sections 30, 76(1) sentence 2.

[21] These are internal administrative guidelines governing the conduct of criminal and administrative fines proceedings by the investigative authorities.

[22] E. g. https://www.volkshochschule.de/kurswelt/gesellschaft_politik_umwelt/schoefinnenwahl.php; https://schoeffen-nrw.de/startseite/veranstaltungshinweise.html

[23] For an overview of the discussion, see *N. Lieber* (fn. 11), 269 et seqq.; *Degener*, in: SK-stop, vol. IX, § 30 n. 6 et seqq., both with further references.

[24] English translation of the CCP provided by the Ministry of Justice and Consumer Protection, available at https://www.gesetze-im-internet.de/englisch_stpo/englisch_stpo.html#p2017

[25] *Tschentscher*, Demokratische Legitimation der dritten Gewalt, 165; MüKoStPO/*Kulhanek* GVG § 197 n. 1, with further references.

De jure, *Schöffen* bear the same responsibilities and exert the same influence on judicial outcomes as their professional counterparts. In practice, this may differ, not least because *Schöffen*, like professional judges, must apply the law, but are dependent upon the professional judges with whom they sit to acquire case-specific legal expertise. Nevertheless, given their equal legal standing, they are functionally equivalent to professional judges and, as such, enjoy the full protections afforded by the principle of judicial independence.[26]

c) In Particular: Judicial Independence

Judicial independence is a core feature of the status of judges under German law. It can be divided into the professional and personal independence of judges.

Professional independence is guaranteed by Article 97(1) of the BL.[27] This principle is reiterated in Section 1 CCA and in Section 25 German Judiciary Act (GJA)[28] for professional judges, as well as in Section 44(1), first sentence, GJA for honorary judges. Professional independence ensures that judges can exercise their judicial decision-making freely and without external influence.[29] It extends not only to the application of the law but also to the preparation of decisions and other actions directly related to the determination of the law.[30] Accordingly, judges may not receive instructions and must be shielded from any avoidable influence; this largely precludes civil, criminal, or disciplinary liability for judicial decisions.[31] With regard to criminal law, it only finds its limits in the criminal offense of perversion of justice pursuant to Section 339 German Criminal Code,[32] which is interpreted very restrictively in practice. This provision is considered to have a preclusive effect meaning that a judge can generally only be prosecuted for other offenses committed in connection with a judicial decision if the conduct simultaneously constitutes a perversion of justice.[33] Civil liability only arises for criminal offenses under to Section 839 (2) German Civil Code, which is signifi-

---

[26] *Wysk*, in: Stern/Sodan/Möstl, StaatsR, vol. II, § 51 n. 35.

[27] English translation of the BL provided by the Ministry of Justice and Consumer Protection, Protection available at https://www.gesetze-im-internet.de/englisch_gg/

[28] English translation of the GJA provided by the Ministry of Justice and Consumer Protection, available at https://www.gesetze-im-internet.de/englisch_drig/

[29] BVerfGE 148, 60, 90 et seq.

[30] *Payandeh*, in: Bonner Kommentar, 221. Lfg. 2023, Art. 97 n. 133 with further references.

[31] *Classen*, in: Huber/Voßkuhle (ed.), GG, 8th ed. 2024, Art. 97 n. 17; *Payandeh*, in: Bonner Kommentar, 221. Lfg. 2023, Art. 97 n. 133; *Wolff*, in: Hömig/Wolff/Kluth (ed.), GG, 14th ed. 2025, Art. 97 n. 4.

[32] CC, Section 339 – Judicial perversion of justice. Judges, other public officials or arbitrators who, in the course of conducting or deciding a legal matter, bend the law for the benefit or to the detriment of a party incur a penalty of imprisonment for a term of between one year and five years.

[33] BVerfG, NJW 2020, 675, 678; BGHSt 10, 294, 298; 364 et seq.; BGH NStZ 2013, 655, 657 n. 22; *Uebele*, in: MüKoStGB § 339 n. 71; critical *Stein*, in: SK-StGB, § 339 n. 6 ff., both with further references.

cantly more restrictive than the liability of other civil servants.[34] According to Section 26(1) GJA, judges are subject to supervisory oversight only insofar as their independence is not compromised. However, formal immunity is not explicitly provided for in the law.

Personal independence is intended as a safeguard to ensure professional independence.[35] It protects judges from adverse consequences of their decisions relating to their office or status.[36] This is regulated in Article 97(2) sentence 1 BL only with regard to professional judges. The Federal Constitutional Court, however, has consistently emphasized that the personal independence of non-professional judges is likewise guaranteed to a degree sufficient to secure their professional independence. On the constitutional level, this is considered to be enshrined in Article 33(5) of the BL, in which the personal independence of honorary judges is understood 'as a principle characteristic of the official status of judges within the meaning of Article 33(5) BL'.[37] From this, the Court derives that honorary judges too can only be dismissed against their will before the end of their term of office under the conditions specified by law and only by virtue of a judicial decision.[38] At the level of ordinary law it is laid down in Section 44(3) GJA.

Thus the appointment of *Schöffen* may be terminated by judicial decision under Sections 44(2) and 44b GJA if circumstances arise or become known that would have constituted an obstacle to the appointment. According to Section 51 CCA, she shall be removed from office by judicial decision if found guilty of a gross breach of official duties.

Institutional independence of the judiciary as a whole is, in contrast, not explicitly guaranteed in German law; the BL establishes the principle of separation of powers, but at the same time provides for their interlinking.[39] This will already become apparent in connection with the appointment of *Schöffen* at municipal level, and will be explored in greater depth in connection with the appointment of professional judges.

d) Procedure for the Selection of Schöffen

The statutory requirements for appointment as *Schöffe* are set out in Section 44a of the GJA and Sections 31 et seq. of the CCA. No specific professional qualifica-

[34] *Payandeh*, in: Bonner Kommentar, 21. Lfg. 2023, Art. 97 n. 173, with further references.

[35] BVerfGE 14, 56, 69; BVerfGE 139, 64, 122; BVerfGE 148, 69, 94; *Payandeh*, in: Bonner Kommentar, 221. Lfg. 2023, Art. 97 n. 241.

[36] BVerfGE 148, 69, 94; *Wittreck*, Gutachten, G. 27, et seqq with further references.

[37] BVerfGE 12, 81, 88; BVerfGE14, 34, 70; BVerfGE14 42, 206, 209 et seq.; *Payandeh*, in: Bonner Kommentar, 204. Aktualisierung 2020, Art. 92 n. 305; *Schulze-Fielitz*, in: Dreier, GG-Kommentar, vol. 3, 3rd ed. 2018, n. 60; *Sodan*, in: HdB-StaatsR, vol. V, 3rd ed. 2007, § 113 n. 73.

[38] BVerfGE 14, 56, 70; BVerfGE 27, 312, 322; *Schulze-Fielitz*, in: Dreier, GG-Kommentar, vol. 3, 3rd ed. 2018, n. 60.

[39] *Wittreck*, Gutachten, G15, G 32 et seqq.; differentiating *Payandeh*, in: Bonner Kommentar, 21. Lfg. 2023, Art. 97 n. 245 et seq.; on the link between judicial independence and the separation of powers, including permissible connections, see also BVerfGE 148, 69, 88.

tion is required, but candidates must hold German citizenship (Section 31, second sentence, CCA) and are ineligible if they lack the capacity to hold public office by judicial decision, have been sentenced to more than six months' imprisonment for an intentional offence, or are subject to pending criminal investigations that may result in such loss of capacity (Section 32 CCA).

Under Sections 44a GJA and 33 CCA, appointment should also be declined if a candidate inter alia has violated fundamental principles of humanity or the constitutional state, does not meet the statutory age requirements, or cannot freely dispose of her assets. Section 34 CCA further excludes certain public offices and professions from appointment, either because of their constitutional significance (e.g., the Federal President or members of federal or Land governments) or to prevent doubts as to judicial independence and impartiality, particularly regarding judges, public prosecutors, police officers, and prison staff.

According to Section 36 CCA, municipalities must compile a proposal list of candidates every five years, containing twice the number of persons required to fill *Schöffe* positions and taking appropriate account of gender, age, profession, and social status. Selection is typically based on random sampling from the population register, voluntary applications, or nominations by third parties such as associations, churches, trade unions, and political parties. Inclusion on the list requires approval by a two-thirds majority of the municipal council members present, but at least one half of the statutory number of council members (Section 36(2) CCA); objections may be raised where mandatory or discretionary exclusion grounds under Sections 32 to 34 CCA apply (Section 37 CCA).

A separately convened selection committee, chaired by a local court judge and composed of an administrative official appointed by the state government and seven trusted laypersons, decides on objections by simple majority and selects principal and substitute *Schöffen* by a two-thirds majority (Sections 40–42 CCA).

3. *Debate on the Abolition of Lay Participation in German Criminal Procedure*

The reintroduction of lay judges aimed to curb administrative arbitrariness through popular participation in the judiciary.[40] And unlike public scrutiny, the oversight provided by *Schöffen* extends into the judges' consultation room.[41]

In the modern era of a democratic *Rechtsstaat*, where judicial independence is constitutionally entrenched, some scholars argue this purpose to be obsolete.[42] It is also questioned whether *Schöffen* are truly capable of doing so: normatively,

---

[40] See also *Eser*, in: Kroeschell/Cordes (eds.), Vom nationalen zum transnationalen Recht, 1995, 161, 163, with further references.

[41] See above fn. 10; critical *Kühne*, ZRP 1985, 237 et seq.; *Volk*, in: FS Dünnebier, 378 et seq.

[42] *Jescheck*, in: FG Schultz, 229 (238); *Kühne* in: Löwe-Rosenberg, StPO, n. 30; *Volk*, in: FS Dünnebier, 1982, 373, 378; *Gerson* (fn. 3); see also *Degener*, SK-StPO § 28 n. 6; doubtful *H. Lieber*, https://www.lto.de/recht/meinung/m/schoeffen-wichtig-nicht-abschaffen-kommentar-reformen-justiz-strafrecht-ehrenamt

since the jury was abolished and the jurisdiction of the *Schöffengericht* was curtailed,[43] but above all factually, given the complexity of the law and of the process of its application.[44] As mentioned, this skepticism is especially acute in white-collar criminal proceedings with particularly complex and comprehensive issues, not only from a legal, but also from an economic perspective. Since *Schöffen* are thus heavily reliant on the explanations provided by professional judges, it appears doubtful whether they can simultaneously function as an effective counterbalance.[45] Empirical data, however, presents a nuanced picture: while over 80 % of *Schöffen* in a survey admitted to relying on professional assessments, 90 % reported having sufficient opportunity to voice their views, and 70 % believed they genuinely influence the verdict.[46] Some scholars, on the other hand, caution that the influence of *Schöffen* could permit 'emotional considerations of equity' to prevail over the correct and consistent application of the law.[47]

Nonetheless, the participation of lay persons – also in light of their election – continues to be understood as an element of representative democracy in the administration of justice. In this context, *Schöffen* are attributed a twofold intermediary role: unlike lay judges in other branches of the judiciary, they are not selected on the basis of their specialist or professional knowledge, which they could contribute to the decision-making process.[48] However, particularly in view of the social homogeneity of professional judges[49] they could bring the general views of the population into the administration of justice and, on the other hand, communicate the course of proceedings back to the general public. As such, they are seen as an important factor contributing to the trust in and the acceptance of criminal justice and its decisions.[50] Critics, however, contend that the selection

---

[43] *Degener*, in: SK-StPO GVG, § 28 n. 6; *Satzger*, JURA 2011, 518, 520; *Volk*, in: FS Dünnebier, 378 et seqq.

[44] *Gerson*, KriPoZ 2017, 104, 108; id. (n. 3); *Volk*, in: FS Dünnebier, 373, 384 et seqq.; *Kühne*, in: Löwe-Rosenberg, StPO, Einl. Abschn. J, n. 29; with similar arguments already *Feuerbach* (fn. 10), 169.

[45] *Kühne*, ZRP 1985, 237, 238; *Gerson*, Kripoz 2017, 104, 108; *Zwiehoff*, in: Marutschke (ed.), Laienrichter in Japan, Deutschland und Europa, 32, 37 et seqq.; see also already *Feuerbach* (fn. 10), 190 et seqq.; in agreement *Duttge*, JR 2006, 358, 359 et seqq.

[46] *Iberl/Kinzig*, Die Rolle der Schöffen bei Absprachen im Strafprozess, 2023, 57 et seqq.

[47] *Kühne*, in: Löwe-Rosenberg, StPO, Einl. Abschn. J, n. 29; ZRP 1985, 237, 238; see also *Volk*, in: FS Dünnebier, 373, 376; *Duttge*, JR 2006, 358, 361 et seqq.; contra: *Eser* (fn. 40), 161, 180.

[48] This is e. g. the case with honorary judges at the commercial chambers at the regional court who are to be appointed on the qualified recommendation of the chambers of industry and commerce and must have certain relevant expertise, cf. CCA, Sections 105, 108, 109.

[49] On this point *Baer*, Rechtssoziologie, 6th ed. 2025, § 5 n. 14 et seqq., with further references.

[50] *Eser* (fn. 40), 161, 180 et seq.; *Kern* (fn. 10) 115; *Fischer/Kudlich*, Handbuch des Strafrechts § 14 n. 52; BT-Drs. 15/3191, 2; *Rieß*, in: FS Schäfer, 1980, 155, 217 et seq.; *K. Schäfer*, in: LR, StPO, vol. 1, 24th ed. 1988, Einl. Kap. 15 n. 8; *Schreiber*, in: FS Welzel, 1974, 941, 952; *Huber*, JuS 2009, 406; *Wassermann*, Bürgerbeteiligung, 15; *Kühne*, in: Löwe-Rosenberg, StPO, Einl. Abschn. J, n. 30: at least an attempt to bring justice closer to their citizens; *Staats*, in: Nomos-BR/Staats DRiG §§ 44 – 45 a n. 2: Representatives of the population.

process fails to achieve true demographic representativeness and that the assumed 'multiplier effect' on public perception remains empirically unproven.[51]

Others identify the merits of lay participation in its internal procedural impact, paradoxically rooted not in the *Schöffen's* expertise, but in their lack of prior knowledge regarding both the case and the law. Unlike professional judges, lay judges in practice have little to no access to the investigative files. Consequently, they must form their convictions exclusively on the evidence presented during the oral and immediate main hearing; they are thus regarded as 'guarantors of the principles of orality and immediacy'.[52] Furthermore, the duty of professional judges to explain legal concepts forces them to render their reasoning comprehensible to laypersons.[53] In this sense, lay participation might serve as a mechanism to ensure the plausibility and reality of judicial decisions.[54]

Recent developments have further fuelled the debate on abolishing the *Schöffen* system, and this is related to political pressure. In the last few years, right-wing populist to extreme right-wing parties have sought use the selection procedure to have their supporters elected to the office of *Schöffe*.[55] This has sparked concerns that this will lead to ideologically biased individuals being appointed to the bench, distorting the application of the law and compromising the neutrality and resilience of the criminal justice system against party political influence.[56] As a result, there is currently a bill to legislate the constitutional duty of lay judges to uphold the constitution.[57]

These concerns are countered by the fact that both the nomination for the electoral roll and the final election to the office require – as noted above – a two-thirds majority within the respective electoral bodies, which serves as a safeguard to ensure a broad democratic consensus.[58] Furthermore, some argue that the independence of professional judges is itself not absolute; unlike *Schöffen*, professional judges may be susceptible to institutional pressures, such as internal

---

51 *Duttge*, JR 2006, 362 with reference to *Machura*, Fairneß und Legitimität, 2001, 272 et seqq., 298 and *Rennig*, Die Entscheidungsfindung durch Schöffen und Berufsrichter in rechtlicher und psychologischer Sicht, 1993, 516; *Kühne*, ZRP 1985, 237, 238 f.; *Volk*, in: FS Dünnebier, 373, 374, 378.

52 *Börner*, ZStW 122, 2010, 190; in a similar direction *Baumann* et al., AE-StPO, Reform der Hauptverhandlung, 1985, 65 et seq.; *Eschelbach*, in: FS Neuhaus, 2025, 539, 544; critical *Rüping*, JR 1974, 269, 271.

53 *H. Lieber* (fn. 42); *Kühne*, ZRP 1985, 237, 238; *Vultejus*, ZRP 2004, 63.

54 *Benz* (fn. 8), 210 et seq.; *Eser* (fn. 40),161, 178 et seq.; *Rüping*, JR 1976, 269, 273; *Wassermann*, Bürgerbeteiligung, 17; doubting *Jescheck*, in: FG Hans Schultz, 1977, 229, 242 et seq.; contra *Volk*, in: FS Dünnebier, 373, 387.

55 *Müller*, Rechte Richter, 2nd ed., 243 et seqq.

56 *Gerson*, https://www.lto.de/recht/justiz/j/schoeffen-strafsachen-justiz-strafverfahren-straf recht-ehrenamt

57 Legislative papers, BT-Drs. 20/8761, https://www.bundestag.de/dokumente/textarchiv/20 24/kw03-pa-recht-richtergesetz-985014, including expert opinions; for a critical analysis see *Grossmann*, GA 2025, 271 et seqq.

58 *H. Lieber* (fn. 42).

collegiality and professional career advancement, whereas lay judges remain outside these hierarchical structures.[59]

III. Independence of Professional Judges

This provides an impetus to examine whether the independence of professional judges is more robustly secured, or whether political influence remains a cause for concern in this regard as well. As previously noted, the substantive independence of all judges – including professional ones – is enshrined in Article 97(1) of the Basic Law (BL), while paragraph (2) guarantees their personal independence.

In international rule-of-law rankings, Germany is consistently highly rated, currently holding sixth place in the World Justice Project's Rule of Law Index, both overall and specifically within criminal justice.[60] According to the 2025 EU Rule of Law Report, 72 % of the general population and 70 % of companies perceive judicial independence as 'fairly or very good'. However, the report also highlights a notable eight-percentage-point decline in public perception since 2021.[61] This trend aligns with intensifying domestic discourse among legal experts regarding the practical realization of judicial independence. Central to this debate, and forming the focus of the following remarks, are the deliberations of the 73rd German Jurists' Conference (*Deutscher Juristentag*, DJT)[62] and the 'Justice Project' (*Justiz-Projekt*) spearheaded by the academic platform *Verfassungsblog*.[63]

In 2022, the 73rd *Deutscher Juristentag* (DJT) addressed the question: 'Are reforms to safeguard judicial independence during the appointment process recommended?'. The deliberations were informed by Wittreck's extensive expert opinion, which provides a comprehensive review of the current standing in both case law and legal scholarship. The report identifies several potential gateways for external influence – and thus threats to judicial independence – including judicial appointments and promotions, performance evaluations, supervisory oversight, and disciplinary measures, but also more subtle decisions, such as the allo-

---

[59] *H. Lieber* (fn. 42).

[60] https://worldjusticeproject.org/rule-of-law-index/global/2025/Germany/

[61] https://commission.europa.eu/document/download/88f3fdf4-5c1e-4ac1-a45e-47af7f93f45f_en?filename=9_1_63941_coun_chap_germany_en.pdf

[62] The German Jurists' Conference is a meeting held every few years where lawyers, judges, and legal scholars in Germany discuss current legal issues and make recommendations for legislation and judicial practice.

[63] Verfassungsblog is an academic platform where experts discuss and analyze constitutional law, politics, and human rights. The Justice Project is a research project running since early 2025 that examines how vulnerable the independent and impartial judiciary in Germany is to authoritarian and populist strategies. The final report, which is referenced below as *Zillesen/Brandau/Laude*, Das Justizprojekt, https://verfassungsblog.de/wp-content/uploads/2025/12/ZillessenBrandauLaude_DasJustizProjekt_2025.pdf

cation of resources,[64] as well as threats to personal independence through dismissal and involuntary transfer.[65] Due to space constraints, the following analysis focuses – drawing a parallel to the selection of lay judges – on appointments to the *Amtsgerichte* and *Landgerichte*.[66]

Pursuant to Sections 5 and 9(3) GJA, judges must be qualified to hold judicial office, necessitating the completion of law studies and the first state examination, followed by a period of compulsory legal training and a second state examination. Additionally, Section 9 GJA stipulates that candidates must hold German citizenship, provide a guarantee of their commitment to the free democratic basic order within the meaning of the Basic Law, and possess the requisite social skills. Furthermore, as judges are public officials, their appointment is governed by the principle of merit-based selection under Article 33(2) BL.[67]

The appointment of judges to the aforementioned courts falls within the competence of the sixteen federal states, where different procedures have developed. The selection process usually consists of a personal interview; in some federal states, an assessment centre is also used to determine the personal and professional qualities of the candidates. The authority for the initial appointment of professional judges generally rests with the executive branch – most often the respective Minister of Justice – though this power may be delegated, for instance, to higher courts. Furthermore, approximately half of the federal states have exercised the option under Article 98(4) BL to mandate that judges be chosen jointly by the Minister of Justice and a judicial selection committee (*Richterwahlausschuss*), at least for lifetime appointments.[68] Depending on state law, these committees are composed of a majority of state parliament members, judges, and, in some instances, lawyers.[69] Even in cases of purely ministerial selection, however, a relevant judicial influence is assumed,[70] also due to the formal involvement of judicial representative bodies in several federal states.[71]

The involvement of non-judicial bodies is not inherently viewed as a threat to judicial independence or a violation of the separation of powers. Instead, it is conceptualized as a mechanism for channeling democratic legitimacy to the judicial branch – a practice considered compatible with the standards set by the ECtHR and the CJEU.[72] The institution of judicial selection committees is also

[64] *Wittreck*, Verhandlungen des 73. Deutschen Juristentages, vol. 1: Gutachten/Teil G, 2020, G18 et seqq. with further references.

[65] *Wittreck*, Gutachten, G27 et seqq. with further references.

[66] With regard to the remaining avenues of influence see *Wittreck*, Gutachten, G47 et seqq.; *Zillesen/Brandau/Laude*, Das Justizprojekt, 175 et seqq.

[67] See e.g. *Brosius-Gersdorf*, in: Dreier GG Art. 33 n. 85 with further references.

[68] *Wittreck*, Gutachten, G37 et seqq.; *Tschentschner* 340 et seqq.; *Zillesen/Brandau/Laude*, Das Justizprojekt, 155 et seqq. with references to the respective federal state provisions.

[69] *Zillesen/Brandau/Laude*, Das Justizprojekt, 156 et seq.; *Wittreck*, Gutachten, G96 et seqq.

[70] *Wittreck*, Gutachten, G39.

[71] *Zillesen/Brandau/Laude*, Das Justizprojekt, 154 et seqq., table 2 and 3.

[72] *Payandeh*, in: Bonner Kommentar, 221. Lfg. 2023, Art. 97 paras 139 ff., 146 with further references.

credited with contributing to the democratic legitimacy of the judiciary, increasing acceptance of ministerial appointment decisions, and bolstering judicial independence.[73] Historically, the constitutional option to establish such committees was included in the Basic Law (BL) as a safeguard; following the experiences of the Weimar Republic and the National Socialist era, the involvement of elected bodies was seen as a means to ensure the 'democratic reliability' of the bench.[74] However, already at that time, it was criticised for precisely the opposite reason: opponents raised concerns that such committees might diffuse political accountability compared to direct ministerial appointments and could inadvertently invite partisan interests to influence judicial selection.[75]

According to *Wittreck*, these concerns were well-founded, particularly as parliamentary members often hold a clear majority within selection committees and would perceive judicial vacancies as 'political leverage' in broader negotiations. Furthermore, the judicial members of these committees might be influenced by a candidate's affiliation with one of the major judges' associations, which are frequently perceived as being aligned with specific political camps. Consequently, both factors risked compromising the merit-based selection of judges by allowing partisan or institutional interests to take precedence over professional qualifications.[76]

Recent developments have heightened concerns that judicial selection committees could be instrumentalized for purposes contrary to their constitutional mandate. A stark illustration is the obstruction of the committee's reconstitution in Thuringia. Under Article 89(2) of the Thuringian Constitution, lifetime judicial appointments require the committee's consent. Two-thirds of its members are elected by the state parliament with a two-thirds majority and each parliamentary group must be represented by at least one person. Since gaining representation in the Thuringian state parliament, the AfD has employed two strategies to prevent the committee from being properly reconstituted: first, it did not nominate anyone for election to the committee, and later it only did so in exchange for political concessions from the other parties. After securing more than one-third of the parliamentary seats in the last state election, it used its blocking minority to prevent a new election of the judicial selection committee.

This demonstrates that the composition of the judicial selection committee can be leveraged for political purposes. Finally, there is a risk that the elections held by the selection committee itself could be politicised, for instance by electing only ideologically compliant candidates to judicial office. As a result, the selection of

[73] *Scholz/Hillgruber,* in: Dürig/Herzog GG Art. 98 n. 3; *Morgenthaler/Münkler*, in: BeckOK GG Art. 98 n. 19 with further references.

[74] *Selbert* in: Der Parlamentarische Rat 1948–1949. Akten und Protokolle, vol. 14, 2009, 726; see further, *Wittreck*, in: Rechtskonflikte, FS Dreier, 489, 491 et seqq., 494.

[75] *Dehler/Seebohm* in: Der Parlamentarische Rat 1948–1949. Akten und Protokolle, vol. 14, 2009, 721, 723.

[76] *Wittreck*, Gutachten, G42 et seq.; id., FS Dreier, 497 et seqq. with further references.

judges may become increasingly politicised, and doubts about the political independence of the courts may arise or intensify.[77] Moreover, it provides anti-democratic parties with the opportunity to appoint judges who hold anti-democratic tendencies.[78] While some federal states mitigate this risk through a two-thirds majority requirement within the committee, others rely on a simple majority, leaving them more vulnerable to partisan influence.[79]

In federal states without a judicial selection committee, in which judges are appointed solely by ministerial decision, the risks lie elsewhere: the party controlling the Ministry of Justice could exploit this mechanism to fill judicial positions based on political considerations, unhindered by any veto from a judicial selection committee.[80]

The assessments of judicial independence discussed above suggest that, despite such potential channels for influence, the integrity of the judiciary and public confidence in its impartiality have remained largely intact. This resilience is attributable, at least in part, to a prevailing culture of cross-party cooperation and a long-standing adherence to established political conventions regarding judicial appointments. However, as political and societal polarization intensifies, the future stability of this institutional framework – and its ability to withstand strategic departures from these norms – remains an open and critical question.

IV. Resorts to Non-Judicial Decision-Making

Currently, the primary challenge facing both professional and lay judges is arguably not political pressure, but the mounting burden of temporal constraints. Some observers attribute the increasing duration of criminal proceedings to the rigid structural requirements of the main hearing. Adherence to the principles of orality and immediacy necessitates that witnesses be re-examined in court and all documentary evidence be read into the record – though scholars note that these foundational principles have already undergone significant systemic erosion.[81] Others identify the true or additional drivers of prolonged proceedings – both in the investigative and trial phases – as the burgeoning complexity of the law and the factual circumstances involved, particularly in white-collar criminal law, alongside the exponential growth in digital evidentiary data.[82]

---

77 *Wittreck*, in: FS Dreier, 503 et seq.; *Zillesen/Brandau/Laude*, Das Justizprojekt, 159 et seqq.

78 Whereby it should be added that Thuringian law offers particularly wide scope in this regard, *Wittreck*, in: FS Dreier, S. 501; *Zillesen/Brandau/Laude*, Das Justizprojekt, 160.

79 *Zillesen/Brandau/Laude*, Das Justizprojekt, 156 et seq. Table 4.

80 *Wittreck*, in: FS Dreier, 501 et seq.; *Zillesen/Brandau/Laude*, Das Justizprojekt, 160.

81 *Deiters*, Verhandlungen des 73. Deutschen Juristentages, vol. 1: Gutachten/Teil C, C28 ff., with further references.

82 See e. g. Federal Court of Justice Judge *Mosbacher*, NStZ 1/2026, Editorial; the Chairperson of the German Judges' Association *Rebehn*, Strafjustiz am Limit, available at https://www.drb.de/

As the history of lay participation illustrates, demands for greater expediency and procedural efficiency have persisted for over a century. These pressures have led not only to a restriction of lay involvement but also to a curtailment of judicial decision-making in criminal adjudication more generally. Regardless of the underlying causes for the strain on law enforcement and the courts, these constraints create incentives to resort to pragmatic mechanisms that shorten the duration of criminal proceedings.

1. Alternatives to Indictment

In law, this is reflected, inter alia, in the introduction as well as subsequent expansions of provisions relating to the principle of opportunity which allow the public prosecutor to refrain from initiating court proceedings. The same legislation that abolished jury participation also introduced Sections 153 and 153a of the CCP, again with the aim of reducing the judiciary's workload and expediting criminal proceedings.[83] These provisions authorize the discontinuance of proceedings for petty offenses based on the insignificance of guilt (Section 153 CCP) or subject to conditions and instructions, such as monetary payments. In 1993 the legislature extended the scope of Section 153a CCP from the category of minor offenses to include moderately serious offenses.[84]

The scope of the penal order procedure (*Strafbefehlsverfahren*) has likewise been considerably broadened, further marginalizing the main hearing and the participation of lay judges. While the maximum custodial sentence imposable by penal order was limited to six weeks in 1877, it now permits sentences of up to one year, provided the accused is represented by counsel and the sentence is suspended on probation (Section 407(2) CCP). Current legislative debates even contemplate a further expansion of this threshold to custodial sentences of up to two years.[85] Although the order is formally issued by a judge, the public prosecutor's office exerts a dominant influence in practice; the prosecutor's application must already specify the legal assessment and the proposed sanction, while the court's role is limited to either issuing the order, rejecting the application or scheduling a main hearing (Sections 407 (1), 408 CCP). Consequently, the prosecutor's preliminary evaluation often de facto predetermines the judicial outcome.

In practice, the percentage of cases in which the public prosecutor's office brings charges instead of opting for a discontinuation on grounds of opportunity or for a request for a penalty order has been steadily declining for years. While in

---

newsroom/presse-mediencenter/nachrichten-auf-einen-blick/nachricht/news/strafjustiz-am-limit.

[83] Verordnung über die Gerichtsverfassung und Strafrechtspflege vom 4. Januar 1924, sections 23, 24.

[84] Gesetz zur Entlastung der Rechtspflege (Federal Law Gazette I, 50), Art. 2 nos. 2, 3.

[85] See inter alia the 2022 resolution of the Conference of Ministers of Justice, available at https://www.justiz.nrw/sites/default/files/imported/files/2022-11/TOP-II_7--Erweiterung-Strafbe fehlsverfahren.pdf

2004 charges were brought in almost 12 percent of all cases, by 2024 this figure had fallen to just over 6 percent.[86] The figures on court case resolution practices paint a similarly clear picture: in 2004, local and regional courts disposed of 904,693 cases, 433,391 of which, or almost 48 %, were decided by judgment. In 2024, the number of cases disposed of was 557,552, of which 209,976, or just under 38 %, were decided by judgement. From a statistical perspective, proceedings in which judges decide in accordance with the original concept of criminal proceedings based on public hearings are therefore the exception and even becoming increasingly rare.[87]

2. Negotiated Agreements

Where a main hearing remains unavoidable, judicial practice frequently resorts to consensual procedural elements to streamline proceedings. Such negotiations had been employed in German criminal practice for decades prior to their formal codification in Section 257c CCP, following a series of landmark rulings by the *Bundesgerichtshof* aimed at curbing procedural excesses.[88]

Under Section 257c CCP, the scope of a negotiated agreement is limited to the legal consequences subject to judgment, certain procedural measures, and the defendant's procedural conduct, primarily a confession. Conversely, the determination of guilt and the legal classification of the offense are expressly excluded from the negotiation process. The court initiates the procedure by outlining the potential terms of the agreement, frequently specifying a sentencing frame with defined upper and lower limits. The agreement attains legal validity only upon formal acceptance by both the defendant and the Public Prosecutor's Office. However, the court maintains the right to withdraw from the agreement if material legal or factual circumstances were overlooked, or if subsequent evidence renders the agreed sentencing range disproportionate to the defendant's guilt. Should an agreement be invalidated, any confession made in reliance upon it becomes inadmissible as evidence.

The primary incentive for such an agreement lies in the fact that, according to prevailing practice, a confession substantially diminishes the necessity for extensive further evidence.[89] In the German criminal justice system, a confession is

---

[86] See the respective public prosecutor's office statistics on cases disposed of, available at https://www.destatis.de/DE/Themen/Staat/Justiz-Rechtspflege/Publikationen/_publikationen-innen-gerichte-straf-anwaltschaft.html

[87] See the respective criminal court's statistics on cases disposed of, available at https://www.destatis.de/DE/Themen/Staat/Justiz-Rechtspflege/Publikationen/_publikationen-innen-gerichte-straf-anwaltschaft.html

[88] For an analysis of negotiated settlements in German criminal law and the legislative history of Section 257c StPO, cf. *Stuckenberg*, in: Löwe-Rosenberg, StPO, vol. 6/2, 26th ed. 2013, § 257c n. 1 et seqq.; *Velten*, in: SK-stop, vol. 4, 6th ed. 2026, § 257c n. 1 et seqq.

[89] For an overview of the discussion, see *Velten*, in: SK-stop, vol. 4, 6th ed. 2026, § 257c n. 35 et seqq.

conceptualized solely as a means of establishing the truth rather than a formal procedural act, such as a 'guilty plea' in common law jurisdictions. Consequently, it does not absolve the court of its duty of ex officio investigation under Section 244(2) CCP (see also Section 257c(1) sentence 2 CCP). Given that the prospect of a negotiated agreement may exert undue pressure or create incentives for false confessions, the court is required to corroborate the confession through independent evidence.[90] Nevertheless, in practice, a confession facilitates a significant contraction of the evidentiary phase – an outcome particularly coveted in the context of complex white-collar criminal proceedings.[91]

An empirical study indicates that courts and participants of the proceedings frequently continue to engage in informal agreements that operate outside the statutory framework of Section 257c CCP.[92] Furthermore, both penal orders and the discontinuation of proceedings under Section 153a CCP are often the products of prior negotiations.[93] The exact prevalence of such consensual arrangements remains difficult to quantify, as even formal agreements under Section 257c CCP are not systematically recorded in official judicial statistics.

From a formalistic perspective, decision-making authority remains vested in the judiciary: the court is directly involved in both formal and informal agreements, issues penal orders, and may decide on the discontinuation of proceedings subject to conditions and instructions pursuant to Section 153a(2) CCP. Where the Public Prosecutor's Office decides to discontinue proceedings under Section 153a(1) CCP, judicial consent is required for all but the most minor offenses. Thus, the court theoretically retains a veto power over the outcomes negotiated between the prosecution and the defense.

In practice, however, the substantive details of an agreement are often prenegotiated between the prosecution and defense counsel, effectively predetermining the judicial decision. The law seeks to ensure at least some degree of transparency in such preliminary negotiations by imposing documentation requirements. With respect to Section 257c CCP, the statute explicitly mandates that these preliminary discussions be documented in accordance with Sections 202a, 243(4)2, and 273(1a) CCP. Outside of such formal agreements, the obligation to document preliminary discussions arises from Section 160b CCP.

With the legal or even merely de facto shift of decision-making power to the Public Prosecutor's Office, this authority remains in the hands of fully qualified lawyers. However, the German Public Prosecutor's Offices are part of the execu-

---

[90] BVerfGE 133, 168, 209 f. n. 70 ff.; see also *Eschelbach*, in: BeckOK-StPO, 57th ed. as of 01.10.2025, § 257c n. 13, 31; *Stuckenberg*, in: L/R, StPO, vol. 7, 27th ed. 2025, § 257c n. 47, with further references.

[91] See BVerfGE 133, 168, 171 n. 3; *Jahn/Müller*, NJW 2009, 2625, 2631.

[92] *Altenhain/Jahn/Kinzig*, Die Praxis der Verständigung im Strafprozess, 2020, 530; *Iberl/Kinzig* (fn. 47), 78, 169.

[93] *Jahn*, in: MüKo-StPO, vol. 2, 2nd ed. 2024, § 160b n. 19; *Wegner*, in: S/S/W, StPO, 6th ed. 2025, § 160b n. 8.

tive branch and, as such, are subject to instructions from the Federal Ministry of Justice or the respective state's Ministry of Justice pursuant to Section 147 CCA. While this authority is rarely exercised in practice – notably, the Minister of Justice in Mecklenburg-Western Pomerania recently issued a decree formally waiving this right[94] – its mere existence carries significant legal implications. The Court of Justice of the European Union (CJEU) has formally ruled that German public prosecutors do not constitute a 'judicial authority' within the meaning of the European Arrest Warrant framework, citing a lack of institutional independence from the executive.[95] Even so, legislative proposals to abolish ministerial oversight of prosecutorial authorities have so far not prevailed; proponents argue that such oversight ensures political accountability and democratic control over prosecutorial conduct.[96]

Empirical research further indicates that *Schöffen* are often excluded from preliminary deliberations concerning negotiated agreements[97] and they do not partake in decisions concerning the termination of proceedings outside of the main hearing. Accordingly, mechanisms of consensual case resolution serve to further curtail the influence exercised by lay judges.

3. Integration of Artificial Intelligence?

As a key tool for expediating and processes, AI is now finding its way into everyday life. Nevertheless, the transfer of criminal judicial decision-making power to AI is currently neither a reality nor subject to serious discussion. Articles 92 and 97 of the BL stipulates that justice may only be administered by independent judges, i. e. humans.[98] This is also the position taken by the Federal and State Ministers of Justice[99] and also in the judiciary, according to which, the denial of a human judge constitutes a removal from the jurisdiction of his *gesetzlicher Richter* and thus also a violation of Article 101 BL.[100] Against this constitutional

---

[94] https://www.regierung-mv.de/Aktuell/?id=216834.

[95] ECJ, Judgment of 17 June 2019 – joined Cases C-508/18 and C-82/19 (Minister for Justice and Equality v OG and PI).

[96] *Brocke*, in: MüKo-StPO, vol. 4, 2nd ed. 2025, §146 GVG n. 27, with an overview of the reform efforts and further references.

[97] *Iberl/Kinzig* (fn. 47), 83 et seqq.

[98] *Bernzen*, RDi 2023, 132, 134; *Ebers*, Stichwortkommentar Legal Tech, KI n. 56 et seqq.; *Dötterl*, NJW 2025, 3409 et seqq.; *Hartmann*, LTZ 2024, 93; *v. Münch/Kunig/Kau*, GG, Art. 97 n. 71; *Martini/Nink*, Strafjustiz ex machina, in: Bertelsmann Stiftung (ed.), Automatisch erlaubt? 2020, 47 et seqq.; *Poseck*, LTZ 2023, 73, 74, all with further references.

[99] Gemeinsame Erklärung zum Einsatz von Künstlicher Intelligenz in der Justiz, 2, available at https://justiz.de/laender-bund-europa/bund_laender/Gemeinsame-Erklaerung-zum-Einsatz-KI/Gemeinsame-Erklaerung-zum-Einsatz-von-KI.pdf

[100] Einsatz von KI und algorithmischen Systemen in der Justiz, Grundlagenpapier zur 74. Jahrestagung der Präsidentinnen und Präsidenten der Oberlandesgerichte, des Kammergerichts, des Bayerischen Obersten Landesgerichts und des Bundesgerichtshofs, 6 et seq., available at https://www.justiz.bayern.de/media/images/behoerden-und-gerichte/oberlandesgerichte/nuernberg/einsatz_von_ki_und_algorithmischen_systemen_in_der_justiz.pdf.

backdrop, the assignment of the judicial mandate to human actors remains universally accepted. German jurisprudence does not seriously contest this principle,[101] nor do any current legislative initiatives exist that would permit the delegation of final decision-making authority to non-human systems.

V. Conclusion

The past 150 years of both the legal and practical evolution of criminal procedure have been fundamentally shaped by the demands of procedural efficiency. They fostered pragmatic mechanisms and, in the process, gradually diminished formal procedural safeguards including the classical ideal of independent judicial decision-making.

Today, this strain is compounded by emerging political pressures on the judiciary and the criminal justice system. The more the system relies on procedural discretion and informal settlements to maintain functionality, the more vulnerable it becomes to instrumentalization. Consequently, legislators, legal practitioners, and scholars alike are called upon to critically reassess where the primary threats to the rule of law truly reside.

---

[101] See the references in fn. 98.

Germany's Commitment to the Rule of Law

Andreas von Arnauld

I. The Rule of Law in Germany

1. Rechtsstaatlichkeit *in the German Constitutional Order*

In the German constitutional tradition, the rule of law is wedded to the concept of statehood as such.[1] The *Rechtsstaat* denotes a state based on the rule of law as its defining element. This concept was born around 1800 in the context of developing constitutional guarantees for a rising civic society and economy against the executive power of the monarchy.[2] Later, around 1900, it became a central argument in the debate about the introduction of an independent administrative judiciary, moulded after the French example.[3] In today's German constitutional order under the *Grundgesetz* (GG, 'Basic Law'), *'Rechtsstaatlichkeit'* is considered one of the structural constitutional elements, alongside democracy, republicanism, federalism, and the welfare state. Following the pre-1949 tradition, interrupted by National-Socialism (NS), this has been generally acknowledged since the foundation of the Federal Republic of Germany, notwithstanding the curious fact that, different from the other structural principles mentioned and solemnly proclaimed in Article 20(1) GG, the federation is nowhere explicitly proclaimed as a *'Rechtsstaat'* in the text of the Basic Law.

Instead, we find elements of *Rechtsstaatlichkeit*, such as legality, access to (administrative) justice and basic rights; the term *'Rechtsstaat'* or *'rechtsstaatlich'*, however, is only mentioned in connection with polities beyond the federal level: Since 1949 already, according to Article 28(1) cl 1 GG, the constitutional order on the state (*Länder*) level has to conform to the 'principles of a republican, democratic and social state governed by the rule of law within the meaning of this Basic Law.' Since this clause is meant to guarantee a basic constitutional homogeneity between the federal and the state levels, it at least mirrors that the federal constitutional order erected by the *Grundgesetz* conceives of itself as *'rechtsstaatlich'*. Other express references to the rule of law concern the extradition of German

---

[1] In a comparative perspective, Andreas von Arnauld, 'Rechtsstaat' in Otto Depenheuer and Christoph Grabenwarter (eds.), Verfassungstheorie (Mohr Siebeck 2010), 703, marginal numbers (mn.) 12 et seqq.

[2] Katharina Sobota, *Das Prinzip Rechtsstaat: Verfassungs- und verwaltungsrechtliche Aspekte* (Mohr Siebeck 1997) 266 et seqq; von Arnauld (n. 1) mn. 6.

[3] Sobota (n. 2) 338 et seqq.

nationals to other EU member states and international criminal courts, Article 16 (2) GG, and the commitment to European integration, Article 23(1) GG.

Without expressly mentioning the term *'Rechtsstaat'*, a core constitutional guarantee of the rule of law is generally considered to be contained in Article 20 (3) GG:[4] 'The legislature shall be bound by the constitutional order, the executive and the judiciary by law and justice.' Together with the other structural principles of the *Grundgesetz*, this guarantee is shielded in substance against constitutional amendments.[5] According to Article 79(3) GG, '[a]mendments to this Basic Law affecting […] the principles laid down in Articles 1 and 20 shall be inadmissible.'

Apart from those references, there is no formal legal definition of what the rule of law entails. *Rechtsstaatlichkeit* is a concept whose content is defined by legal discourse and its participants. A certain conceptual fuzziness has even given rise to doubts about the existence of a coherent principle.[6] Traditionally, two concepts of *Rechtsstaat* are being contrasted, one formal, centred on legality and accountability of public power as well as access to courts, one substantive ('material'), centred on the 'idea of justice', with respect for human rights as its most important element.[7] While during the Second Empire (1871–1918) the formal understanding was the most widely shared among lawyers, and during the Weimar period (1919–1933) different positions as to the rule of law were at the heart of the *'Methodenstreit'* among constitutional lawyers,[8] after the atrocities of NS, it has been uncontested that, under the Basic Law, the concept of *Rechtsstaat* comprises both dimensions, the formal and the substantive one.[9]

The omnipresence of an almost all-encompassing concept in Germany's legal discourse can best be illustrated by reference to the 1997 monograph by Katharina Gräfin von Schlieffen, *née* Sobota, who identified more than 140 *topoi* connected in legal discourse with the concept of *Rechtsstaatlichkeit*, clustered around certain key elements:[10] supremacy of the constitution and constitutional jurisdic-

[4] Karl Peter Sommermann, 'Artikel 20 GG' in Peter M. Huber and Andreas Voßkuhle (eds.), *Grundgesetz* (8th ed., CH Beck 2024) mn. 227, with further references.

[5] Only to the extent that elements of the rule of law are contained in Article 20 GG: Brun-Otto Bryde, 'Artikel 79 GG' in Ingo von Münch and Philip Kunig (eds.) *Grundgesetz-Kommentar* (8th ed., CH Beck 2025) mn. 55 et seqq; Karl-Eberhard Hain, 'Artikel 79 GG' in Huber and Voßkuhle (n. 4) mn. 88 et seqq.

[6] Philip Kunig, *Das Rechtsstaatsprinzip: Überlegungen zu seiner Bedeutung für das Verfassungsrecht der Bundesrepublik Deutschland* (Mohr Siebeck 1986) 457 et seqq., 481 et seqq. Against this, Sobota (n. 2) 399 et seqq; von Arnauld (n. 1) mn. 2 et seqq.

[7] Markus Kotzur, 'Artikel 20 GG' in von Münch and Kunig (n. 5) mn. 140 et seqq; Sommermann (n. 4) mn. 229 et seqq.

[8] On this, Manfred Friedrich, 'Der Methoden- und Richtungsstreit: Zur Grundlagendiskussion der Weimarer Staatsrechtslehre' (1977) 102 Archiv des öffentlichen Rechts, 161; David Dyzenhaus, *Legality and Legitimacy: Carl Schmitt, Hans Kelsen and Hermann Heller in Weimar* (Clarendon Press 1997).

[9] von Arnauld (n. 1) mn. 10; Christian von Coelln, 'Artikel 20 GG' in Michael Sachs (ed.), *Grundgesetz* (10th ed., CH Beck 2024) mn. 74, both with further references.

[10] Sobota (n. 2) 27 et seqq., 253 et seqq., 471 et seqq. Her 25 key elements have been slightly condensed here.

tion; liberty, equality before the law, and fundamental rights; separation of powers; legality; justice; legislative reserve; clarity of norms; clarity of competence; transparency of state action; functional organisation of public authority; fair administrative procedure; legal certainty; access to justice and judicial protection against public authority; state liability; proportionality.

2. Selected Elements of the Rule of Law in the German Constitutional Order

a) Legality

The principle of legality is enshrined in Article 20(3) GG, with two notable additions in reaction to historic experiences: Firstly, the 'constitutional order' is expressly binding also for the legislator, a point of contention in legal doctrine under the Weimar Constitution of 1919. The Federal Constitutional Court (*Bundesverfassungsgericht*, BVerfG) has the power (and jurisdictional monopoly) to invalidate norms violating the Basic Law and has done so numerous times over the decades, where an interpretation in accordance with the Constitution is impossible. To avoid the consequences of declaring a norm void *ab initio*, the Court has developed a nuanced toolbox. Often, it will declare a provision merely unconstitutional, in order to give time for a new regulation. Thus, in a recent decision on surveillance and remote searches of smartphones and similar devices, the Court declared the provision on source surveillance partially void due to infringement of fundamental rights, while the provision on remote searches, which lacked an express citation of the respective fundamental right, in contravention of Article 19(1) cl 2 GG, was only declared unconstitutional but applicable until amended.[11]

Secondly, Article 20(3) GG binds the executive and judiciary to 'law and justice' ('*Gesetz und Recht*'). This was specifically included in reaction to inherently unjust, especially racially discriminating laws from the NS period[12] which, according to a seminal 1946 article by the legal philosopher Gustav Radbruch, should be deemed as 'non-law' and therefore not binding upon the executive and the judiciary ('Radbruch formula').[13] Arguably, the only point of application so far has been the conviction of members of the GDR Defence Council and border guards involved in the killing of East Germans who had attempted to escape to West Germany during the time of separation. Here, the BVerfG determined that the official sanctioning of these killings could not be relied on as a

[11] ECLI:DE:BVerfG:2025:rs20250624.1bvr018023 (BVerfG NJW 2025, 3424) *Trojaner II*.

[12] Bernd Grzeszick, 'Artikel 20 GG' in Günter Dürig, Roman Herzog, and Rupert Scholz (eds.), *Grundgesetz* (CH Beck, R 108, August 2025) mn. 63 et seqq; Birgit Hoffmann, *Das Verhältnis von Gesetz und Recht* (Duncker&Humblot 2003) 51 et seqq. See also ECLI:DE:BVerfG:1973:rs19730214.1bvr011265 (BVerfGE 34, 269 [286 et seq.] *Soraya*); Differently, Sommermann (n. 4) mn. 265 et seqq.

[13] Gustav Radbruch, Gesetzliches Unrecht und übergesetzliches Recht, [1946] *Süddeutsche Juristenzeitung* 105.

legal justification. By 'seriously disregarding the human rights generally recognised in the international community [...] the holder of state power committed extreme state injustice, which can only be maintained as long as the state power responsible for it actually exists.'[14] The application of the 'Radbruch formula' here was certainly due to the unique historic moment, with the GDR having ceased to exist. It is an open question whether executive and judicial institutions would as willingly set aside formally valid parliamentary legislation if dark times were to return. Experiences from the Nazi period have shown that *Gleichschaltung* is, mostly, a process of self-assimilation. Thus, the reference to 'justice' in Article 20(3) GG has been fittingly called primarily a 'moral appeal to the legislator.'[15]

Concerning legality in everyday practice, there is an added complexity in Germany through federalism on four levels: EU, national, *Länder*, and municipalities – which are guaranteed 'the right to regulate all local affairs on their own responsibility within the limits prescribed by the laws' in Article 28(2) cl 1 GG. As far as they are binding, all these regulations are considered as 'law' in the sense of Article 20(3) GG.[16] Due to the dualist stance of Basic Law and BVerfG, however, Article 20(3) GG primarily covers national legislation. International law is only included if it has been adopted into the German legal order (see II.1. for details). EU law, finally, is only covered by Article 20(3) GG insofar as it is directly applicable.[17]

In general, abiding by the law (and by rather bureaucratic internal regulations, especially) is ingrained in German administrative culture. Therefore, the COVID-19 pandemic proved a hard case. Measures taken were (apart from questions of human rights proportionality) dubious as to the distribution of competences between federation and *Länder* and between governments and parliaments.[18] Furthermore, government regulations and executive measures ordering shutdowns and lock-downs were initially based on a law which only provided for individual quarantines and similar measures.[19] With some delay – due to the unprecedented situation and lack of scientific certainty –, however, governments, legislators and courts in Germany managed to steer the anti-COVID-19 policies

[14] ECLI:DE:BVerfG:1996:rs19961024.2bvr185194 (BVerfGE 95, 96 [133] *Mauerschützen*); The European Court of Human Rights found no violation of Article 7(1) ECHR in these cases: *Streletz, Kessler and Krenz v Germany* App nos 35532/97, 34044/96 and 44801/98 (ECtHR, 22 March 2001).

[15] Grzeszick (n. 12) mn. 70.

[16] Grzeszick (n. 12) mn. 60 et seqq; von Coelln (n. 9) mn. 107. Differently, Sommermann (n. 4) mn. 264 (only parliamentary statutes; other sources of law should be considered as 'Recht').

[17] Grzeszick (n. 12) mn. 60; von Coelln (n. 9) mn. 107.

[18] Jens Kersten and Stephan Rixen, *Der Verfassungsstaat in der Corona-Krise* (3rd ed., CH Beck 2022) 322 et seqq.

[19] Uwe Volkmann, 'Heraus aus dem Verordnungsregime: Die erheblichen Grundrechtseingriffe der Corona-Krise bedürfen endlich einer tragfähigen Rechtsgrundlage' [2020] Neue Juristische Wochenschrift (NJW) 3153.

back into the normal constitutional framework.[20] Unlike several other European states, Germany did not declare an emergency under Article 15 ECHR.

A more troubling concern is that, in the futile attempt to win over voters from the right-wing populist – and at least in large part right-wing extremist[21] – AfD, the Federal Government seems to have embarked on a policy of 'law and order' that at times seems to put order above the law. This is especially notable in the area of migration:[22] comprehensive border controls hardly reconcilable with EU law,[23] an illegal policy of a general refusal of refugees at the German borders,[24] detention pending deportation without a court order,[25] deportation programmes looking at figures and symbolic policy rather than at the situation on the ground,[26] large-scale revocation of admission commitments for Afghans under special threat of persecution by the Taliban, mostly local staff that had supported the German military before their withdrawal from Afghanistan 2021.[27] A troubling disregard of the law and legal procedure can also be observed in other areas. Here, the case of Maja T., a German Antifa activist whose surrender was requested under a European arrest warrant by Hungary for physical assaults on a Neonazi convention in Budapest, is especially noteworthy. After the activist's submission that detention conditions for non-binary persons in Hungary would violate their human dignity had been rejected without closer investigation by the

---

[20] Kersten and Rixen (n. 18) 74 et seqq.

[21] On the status of the AfD's classification as 'right-wing extremist' by the Federal Office for the Protection of the Constitution, Sarah Steffen and Jan D. Walter, 'Fact check: Germany's AfD no longer 'right-wing extremist'?' (*Deutsche Welle*, 10 May 2025) www.dw.com/en/german-afd-party-right-wing-extremist-label-fact-check/a-72495162. All websites cited here were last accessed on 23 January 2026.

[22] For the official announcement of 'Germany's new migration policy' by the Ministry of the Interior in 2025, see www.bmi.bund.de/SharedDocs/schwerpunkte/EN/migration-dobrindt_EN/migration-dobrindt-schwerpunkt.html

[23] Jannik Luhm, 'Deutschlands Grenzüberschreitung' (*Verfassungsblog*, 18 September 2024) https://verfassungsblog.de/warum-die-wiedereinfuhrung-der-grenzkontrollen-gegen-europa recht-verstost/

[24] ECLI:DE:VGBE:2025:0602.6L191.25.00 (VG Berlin NJW 2025, 2045); see Maximilian Pichl, 'Zurückweisungen vor Gericht' (*Verfassungsblog*, 3 June 2025) https://verfassungsblog.de/zuruckweisungen-gericht-migration-asyl/

[25] In violation of the Basic Law, see ECLI:DE:BVerfG:2025:rk20250804.2bvr032922 (BVerfG NJW 2026, 153).

[26] Michelle Lynn Kahn, 'Germany's plans to deport Syrian refugees echoes 1980s effort to repatriate Turkish guest workers' (*The Conversation*, 10 December 2025), https://theconversation.com/germanys-plan-to-deport-syrian-refugees-echoes-1980s-effort-to-repatriate-turkish-guest-workers-271475

[27] In a recent case, the BVerfG saw no violation of a binding commitment but only obliged the Federal authorities to decide on the claimants' visa applications: ECLI:DE:BVerfG:2025:rk20251204.2bvr151125. Critical discussion by Christian Rath, 'Freibrief zum Wortbruch' (*Legal Tribune Online*, 4 December 2025) www.lto.de/recht/hintergruende/h/bundesverfassungsgericht-zu-afghanischem-richter. On 18 January 2026, the Taliban raided a 'safe house' for Afghans from the German resettlement programme. The inhabitants had recently been forced to leave Pakistan after having outstayed their welcome there while waiting in vain for their visa for Germany: www.tagesschau.de/ausland/asien/razzia-safehouse-afghanistan-100.html

Berlin *Kammergericht*, they were flown off to Austria for further deportation in a cloak-and-dagger operation while a request for an injunction was pending before the BVerfG. The BVerfG's order to bring her back to Germany was disregarded by the German authorities. In its final decision, the BVerfG found a violation of Article 4 CFR.[28] A further point of concern are pre-emptive bans and police crack-downs on pro-Palestinian protests during the war in Gaza. In February 2025, a podium discussion with the UN Special Rapporteur on the Occupied Palestinian Territories, Francesca Albanese, at Free University Berlin was cancelled after public pressure from the Berlin government; a private *ersatz* event could only be held with a heavy police presence and under close scrutiny by state authorities.[29] In a joint statement of October 2025, six UN Independent Experts and Special Rapporteurs expressed to be 'alarmed by the persistent pattern of police violence and apparent suppression of Palestine solidarity activism by Germany.'[30] While such cases of disrespect for the law may not yet be widespread and the courts are still defending the rule of law, it is troubling that the 'culture of legality' seems to be eroding in some parts of politics, administration, and the broader population, as well.

b) Legal Certainty

Legal certainty is acknowledged as an implicit constitutional principle derived from the *Rechtsstaat* principle.[31] It is permeating the whole German legal order, giving rise to practices, legislation and constitutional arguments to guarantee law's accessibility, stability, and foreseeability.[32] Though having been received as a constitutional principle since several decades, it has not caused a complete constitutionalisation of the legal order and practice *sub specie* legal certainty.[33]

---

[28] ECLI:DE:BVerfG:2025:rk20250124.2bvr110324 (BVerfG NJW 2025, 955); on the case and its context, see Tanja Podolski, 'Auslieferung nach Ungarn war rechtswidrig' (*Legal Tribune Online*, 6 February 2025) www.lto.de/recht/nachrichten/n/bverfg-2bvr110324-maja-t-auslieferung-ungarn-rechtswidrig

[29] Ben Knight, 'Germany: Second talk by top UN official cancelled' (*Deutsche Welle*, 19 February 2025) www.dw.com/en/germany-anger-over-cancelled-talks-by-un-special-rapporteur-for-palestinian-territories/a-71662122

[30] See press statement, UN experts urge Germany to halt criminalisation and police violence against Palestinian solidarity activism (16 October 2025) www.ohchr.org/en/press-releases/2025/10/un-experts-urge-germany-halt-criminalisation-and-police-violence-against

[31] Well established in the case law, cf only ECLI:DE:BVerfG:2002:ls20020220.1bvl001997 (BVerfGE 105, 48 [57]); ECLI:DE:BVerfG:2012:rs20120620.2bvr104811 (BVerfGE 131, 268 [309 f.]) *vorbehaltene Sicherungsverwahrung*.

[32] Andreas von Arnauld, *Rechtssicherheit. Perspektivische Annäherungen an eine* idée directrice *des Rechts* (Mohr Siebeck 2006) 104 et seqq. (*Erkennbarkeit*, *Verlässlichkeit*, *Vorhersehbarkeit*).

[33] von Arnauld (n. 32) 661 et seqq.

aa) Law's Accessibility

Questions of law's accessibility circle around its proclamation, form, and complexity. These questions are partly regulated on constitutional, partly on statutory level, e.g. in Article 82 GG for federal statutes (promulgation in the Federal Law Gazette), in Sections 35 ff. Administrative Procedure Act for administrative decisions. Of constitutional relevance is the requirement for laws to be sufficiently specific and clear. According to a recent ruling of the BVerfG, specificity and clarity are two aspects of the same postulate. Thus, an almost overly detailed regulation of the Federal Elections Act 2020 was upheld even though it was hardly comprehensible for an average reader.[34] The Senate's majority argued that the Act primarily addresses specialists. Three dissenting judges treated clarity of the law as a separate postulate and stressed that election laws that cannot be understood by the voters might be specific but not clear enough. A violation of the clarity of norms, however, was found by the Court in another recent case concerning the rules on data transfer by the Federal Office for the Protection of the Constitution. Here, the legislator had determined a list of crimes covered by those rules by reference to norms that deal with completely unrelated issues, namely a list of criminal offences in an Act regulating the jurisdiction of federal courts.[35]

Concerning specificity, the BVerfG demands an act of parliament as basis for all important decisions, especially interferences with freedom and property, and demands a heightened degree of detailing the more important an issue is. Therefore, in 2002 it declared void Section 43a(1) Criminal Code (*Strafgesetzbuch*, StGB) as a rule without a yardstick:[36]

> 'If the law refers to this provision, the court may, in addition to a life sentence or a prison sentence of more than two years, order the payment of a sum of money limited by the value of the offender's assets (financial penalty).'

Concerning consistency of the law, the BVerfG also derives from the rule of law a principle that the legal order should be free of inner contradictions, not always easy to realise over four levels of federalism. In a recent case concerning a tax on disposable packaging by the city of Tübingen the Court held that the exercise of legislative competences with regard to taxes designed to create incentives is only permissible if this does not lead to contradictions with the substantive law governing that same area. As it found that the tax did not run counter to the overall concept or individual provisions of applicable federal waste legislation the local regulation passed the test.[37]

---

34 ECLI:DE:BVerfG:2021:fs20210720.2bvf000121 (BVerfGE 159, 40) *Wahlrechtsreform 2020*.

35 ECLI:DE:BVerfG:2022:rs20220928.1bvr235413 (BVerfGE 163, 43) *BVerfSchG – Übermittlungsbefugnisse*.

36 ECLI:DE:BVerfG:2002:rs20020320.2bvr079495 (BVerfGE 105, 135) *Vermögensstrafe*.

37 ECLI:DE:BVerfG:2024:rs20241127.1bvr172623 (BVerfGE 171, 1) *Tübinger Verpackungssteuer*.

bb) Law's Stability

The finality of court decisions and administrative acts are regulated in the laws of judicial procedure and the administrative procedure acts of the federation and the *Länder*.[38] A resumption of proceedings is only possible under strictly limited conditions. This is especially important in the case of criminal law, where Article 103(3) GG expressly guarantees the principle *ne bis in idem* as an individual right. In a recent judgment, the BVerfG stressed that this fundamental right does not merely prohibit multiple punishment, but also multiple prosecution, protecting both convicted and acquitted persons equally.[39] By stressing that Article 103 (3) GG gives priority to legal certainty over substantive justice it voided an amendment to Section 362 No 5 Criminal Procedures Act (*Strafprozessordnung*, StPO) that had introduced the possibility to retry a person, once acquitted, on the basis of new facts or evidence – in the case that triggered the legislation, a DNA analysis that had not been technically feasible at the time the acquittal became final.

Law's stability is intimately connected also with questions of intertemporality. The Basic Law contains an explicit prohibition of retroactive penal legislation in Article 103(2) GG. This, however, only relates to the elements of a crime and criminal sanctions, neither to statutes of limitations or to 'measures of custody or reformation,' such as psychiatric hospitalization. For this reason, the BVerfG found the *nulla poena* principle inapplicable in the case of retrospective extensions of preventive detention of former prisoners beyond the maximum period permissible at the time of offence.[40] When the European Court of Human Rights (ECtHR) found a violation of Article 7(1) ECHR – as it saw little difference in practice between imprisonment and preventive detention[41] –, the BVerfG still denied a violation of Article 103(2) GG, but agreed that the less strict standards derived from the rule of law in cases of retrospective legislation had been violated.[42]

With this, the Court could build on its own jurisprudence on retroactive and retrospective legislation. Retroactive laws are only permissible under strictly limited conditions, usually if the law was unclear or new legislation had already been 'visibly' introduced into parliament. These exceptions serve to eliminate incentives to circumvent the law or to knowingly make use of legal loopholes. In this line of reasoning, the BVerfG recently confirmed a retroactive recovery of illegal tax gains ('Cum Ex') which it saw justified by overriding public interest consid-

[38] von Arnauld (n. 32) 277 et seqq.

[39] ECLI:DE:BVerfG:2023:rs20231031.2bvr090022 (BVerfGE 166, 359) *Wiederaufnahme StPO*.

[40] ECLI:DE:BVerfG:2004:rs20040210.2bvr083402 (BVerfGE 109, 190) *Nachträgliche Sicherungsverwahrung*.

[41] *Haidn v. Germany* App no 6587/04 (ECtHR, 13 January 2011).

[42] ECLI:DE:BVerfG:2011:rs20110504.2bvr236509 (BVerfGE 128, 326 [391 et seqq.]) *EGMR Sicherungsverwahrung*.

erations, namely justice and the inviolability of the legal system.[43] Here, the taint of criminal origin precluded legitimate expectations.

This protection of legitimate expectations (*Vertrauensschutz*) plays a seminal role in German law. It does not only give procedural but also substantive protection against retrospective laws and has a great impact on legislation. Transitional and hardship provisions are regularly included in German laws and regulations, whenever new rules are introduced. In practice, the BVerfG considers legitimate expectations in the context of the specific fundamental right concerned, as an aspect of proportionality review. A good example is a recent decision concerning an amendment of the Offshore Wind Energy Act that changed the system of allotting sites for offshore wind parks in the German Exclusive Economic Zone.[44] This frustrated expectations of investors that had, at their own expense, conducted planning and site investigations in the area previously allotted to them. Since no installations had yet been built and concrete business perspectives were still too distant, the Court denied here any legitimate property-based (Article 14 GG) and business-based (Article 12 GG) expectations, but found a violation of a *Vertrauensschutz* principle which it directly based on the rule of law in connection with Article 2(1) GG (general freedom) for investments made in the run-up to the commencement of an activity, such as the costs for the site investigations.

cc) Law's Foreseeability

Law is foreseeable when new legal acts remain in the paths paved by previous acts.[45] Therefore, it is important that the administrative courts acknowledge self-imposed restrictions of the administration (see c) below), binding it, as a matter of principle, to its previous practice. For the judiciary, judicial independence (see e) below) runs counter the idea of binding precedents. In the everyday practice of German courts, however, an orientation on precedents, especially those of higher and federal courts, helps to foresee the chances in a potential court case.[46]

c) Prohibition of Arbitrariness

The prohibition of arbitrariness is not explicitly mentioned in the Basic Law, but is generally seen as the minimum guarantee enshrined in Article 3(1) GG, equality before the law. That administrative discretion knows limits is a fundamental element of German administrative law; administrative courts are regularly screening executive decisions for an error in or a misuse of discretion.[47] Going

---

[43] ECLI:DE:BVerfG:2021:ls20210210.2bvl000819 (BVerfGE 156, 354) *Vermögensabschöpfung*.

[44] ECLI:DE:BVerfG:2020:rs20200630.1bvr167917 (BVerfGE 155, 238) *WindSeeG*.

[45] von Arnauld (n. 32) 391 et seqq.

[46] von Arnauld (n. 32) 472 et seqq; Michael Reinhardt, *Konsistente Jurisdiktion: Grundlegung einer verfassungsrechtlichen Theorie der rechtsgestaltenden Rechtsprechung* (Mohr Siebeck 2020).

[47] Michael Sachs, '§ 40 VwVfG' in Paul Stelkens, Heinz-Joachim Bonk, and Michael Sachs (eds.), *Verwaltungsverfahrensgesetz* (10th ed., CH Beck 2023), mn. 53 et seq.

beyond the mere protection against arbitrariness, equality before the law demands that citizens are treated equally and thus serves as the legal basis for self-imposed restrictions by and on the administration,[48] especially through constant practice and (arguably) administrative regulations. This, however, does not apply to a practice that contravenes the law. That there is 'no equality in illegality' ('*keine Gleichheit im Unrecht*') underlines the precedence of the principle of legality in case of a conflict.

For reason of judicial independence much less stringent standards derive from Article 3(1) GG for the application of the laws by courts. In practice, 'outliers' are usually eliminated by appeal proceedings before higher courts. As its function is to apply and protect only the constitution and not the principle of legality as such, outside fundamental rights protection (where there is full judicial scrutiny under a proportionality standard) the BVerfG only exercises restrained control of court decisions, limited to an arbitrariness standard. According to the Court's constant jurisprudence an application of the law by a court is arbitrary, 'if an obviously relevant provision is disregarded, the content of a provision is grossly misunderstood or otherwise applied in a manner that is no longer comprehensible.'[49]

d) Access to Justice

In the German federal system, the judiciary lies mainly with the *Länder*. Next to the ordinary jurisdiction (civil and criminal) there are specialised courts: administrative, finance, labour, and social courts. The respective federal courts – Federal Court of Justice (BGH, civil and criminal), Federal Administrative Court (BVerwG), Federal Finance Court (BFH), Federal Labour Court (BAG), and Federal Social Court (BSG) – predominantly serve as supreme courts with the task to guarantee a uniform interpretation and application of federal laws and regulations. Outside these stages of appeal stand the BVerfG and the constitutional courts of the *Länder*.

Access to justice is explicitly guaranteed in Article 19(4) GG in the context of holding the executive power accountable. Read together with Section 40(1) Code of Administrative Court Procedure (*Verwaltungsgerichtsordnung*, VwGO), this provision guarantees access to administrative courts and – for mostly historic reasons – to civil courts in matters of state liability. The right to access to justice in civil matters is based on the rule of law principle.[50] Direct legal protection against legislative acts is not provided; they can, however, be challenged indirectly via a referral by a court that has to apply a statute that it deems as unconstitutional or – within one year after entry into force – by a constitutional complaint to the BVerfG by persons directly affected by them. There is no constitu-

[48] von Arnauld (n. 32) 423 et seqq.
[49] ECLI:DE:BVerfG:2016:rk20160719.2bvr047008 (BVerfG NJW 2016, 3153).
[50] Peter M. Huber, 'Artikel 19 GG' in Huber and Voßkuhle (n. 4) mn. 410 et seqq.

tional right to legal protection against court decisions; the Basic Law does not guarantee a right to a second (and further) instance;[51] in practice, the laws and institutions in Germany in most cases offer at least the possibility for one further instance of appeal. If conditions are met, a case can go through up to three instances and then be even brought before the BVerfG.

According to the BVerfG, access to justice implies that legal protection must also be effective. This includes accessible and timely legal protection; no excessively long proceedings; comprehensive examination of the facts and legal situation (this is different in summary proceedings);[52] binding and enforceable decisions.[53] This applies wherever the laws grant access to a court, regardless of whether Art. 19(4) GG requires such access or not.

e) Independence of the Judiciary

aa) (S)Election of judges

On the basis of Article 95(2) GG and the Judge Election Act (*Richterwahlgesetz*, RiWG), professional judges for the federal supreme courts are elected by a committee consisting of one minister or senator for each of the 16 *Länder* and an equal number of members elected by the *Bundestag* who have to be 'experienced in legal matters,' Sect. 4(1) RiWG. Nominations can only be submitted by Committee members or the competent federal minister. Based on a professional documentation and a written comment on each of the candidates by the Presiding Council of the court at which the judge is to serve, the Committee will decide by secret ballot with a majority of the votes cast. According to Section 13 RiWG, the competent federal minister has to agree with the result. This procedure has been criticised for its lack of transparency and the role of the executive in the nomination, election and confirmation procedure. It opens up the procedure for party politics. Moreover, apart from a commenting role, there is no involvement of professional judges.[54]

While becoming a judge at one of the federal courts is a decisive step in a longer judicial career, being appointed to the judiciary of one of the *Länder* is something quite different. In Germany, the position as judge is a career occupation. In fact, the 'qualification to hold judicial office' (*'Befähigung zum Richteramt'*) is the central training objective for the second state examination, which is

---

[51] Ibid mn. 485.

[52] ECLI:DE:BVerfG:2016:rk20160914.1bvr133513 (BVerfG NVwZ 2017, 149): no objections against summary examination in preliminary judicial protection; however, with imminent infringement of right, the required intensity of examination increases.

[53] Huber (n. 50) mn. 504 et seqq., 516 et seqq.

[54] Maximilian Amos, 'Neue Richter bekommt das Land – aber wie transparent?' (*Legal Tribune Online*, 5 July 2018) www.lto.de/recht/nachrichten/n/bundesrichter-wahl-bgh-bverwg-bag-bsg-bfh-verfahren-kritik-intransparent

required for all traditional legal professions, including advocacy. Regarding the appointment of judges in and by the *Länder*, Article 98(4) GG stipulates: 'The states may determine that the appointment of judges in the states shall be decided jointly by the state ministers of justice and a judicial selection committee.' Nine of the sixteen *Länder* have judicial selection committees, though with different competences.[55] Otherwise, the appointment of judges rests with the minister of justice of the respective state. Usually, the election committees are set up by parliament and include, next to members of the state parliament, professional judges and members of the advocacy.

The election of judges of the BVerfG follows yet another procedure. According to Article 93 GG, the Court consists of two Senates with eight judges each. Half of the members of each Senate are elected by the *Bundestag* and half by the *Bundesrat* with a two-thirds majority. The judges are elected for twelve years (or until they reach the age of sixty-eight), with no re-election possible. According to Section 2(3) BVerfGG, three judges of each Senate have to be elected from among the judges of the supreme federal courts. As a general rule, only judges who have served for at least three years at one of the supreme federal courts shall be elected. All candidates have to possess the 'qualification to hold judicial office' (some *Länder* constitutional courts also allow for non-lawyers to be elected).

Those positions to be filled in by the *Bundestag* were, until 2015, subject to election by a committee mirroring its political composition. Since then, the candidates selected by the committee have to be confirmed in parliament by plenary vote. While this was intended to raise the democratic legitimacy of the court, it also opened the procedure for further politicization.[56] For a long time already, the right to nominate candidates has been divided between the major political parties, most recently according to the formula 3:3:1:1 (3 for CDU/CSU and SPD each, 1 each for Greens and FDP). While this practice raises legitimate doubts, the required two-thirds majority has until now prevented the nomination of candidates with a too pronounced political profile and agenda. With the further fragmentation of the political landscape and the rise of the AfD, this consensus procedure is under pressure, though.[57]

---

[55] On the compatibility of the election process in the *Land* of Hesse with judicial independence, see ECJ, Case C-272/19 *VQ v Land Hessen* ECLI:EU:C:2020:535, paras 51 et seqq.

[56] On the 2025 causa Brosius-Gersdorf and its implications, see Klaus Ferdinand Gärditz, 'Parlamentskultur und Bundesverfassungsrichterwahl' (*Verfassungsblog* 15 July 2025) https://verfassungsblog.de/bundesverfassungsrichterwahl-frauke-brosius-gersdorf-wahlverfahren/

[57] Joschka Buchholz/Markus Sehl, 'Eine geheime Kandidatin und die Zukunft der Verfassungsrichterwahl' (*Legal Tribune Online*, 27 August 2025), www.lto.de/recht/nachrichten/n/bverfg-verfassungsrichter-wahl-brosius-gersdorf-barley-miersch-grimm-papier-luebbe-wolet seqq.

bb) Judicial Independence

Article 97 GG stipulates that judges shall be independent and subject only to the law. They are appointed on a permanent basis – judges on probation have to be appointed judges for life after five years, Section 12(2) German Judiciary Act (*Deutsches Richtergesetz*, DRiG) – and are protected against any removal or transfer against their will. Supervision of judges must not compromise their independence and can be challenged before special service courts (Sections 26, 77 ff. DRiG). It must not be used as a means of exerting influence on specific judicial decisions.[58]

While the procedure for an impeachment for infringement of the constitution in Article 98(2) GG (as well as similar procedures on the *Länder* level) has not been put to practice so far, two recent cases of removal from office made use of another avenue.[59] In the case of a judge from Saxony, Jens Maier, a prominent and outspoken member of the right-wing extremist so-called *'Flügel'* ('Wing') of the AfD, his enforced early retirement was based on Section 31 DRiG, which allows such measures if 'facts unconnected with their judicial occupation make a measure of this kind imperative in order to avoid grave prejudice to the administration of justice'. In his case, the BGH, sitting as the Federal Service Court, confirmed that Maier no longer guaranteed 'that he will uphold the free democratic basic order within the meaning of the Basic Law at all times' and that his public appearances gave 'the impression that, for political reasons, he will base his future conduct in office on his personal assessment and no longer solely on the principles of factual accuracy, adherence to the law, justice, objectivity and the common good.'[60] The same provision was used in 2023 in proceedings against a Berlin judge, Birgit Malsack-Winkemann, another AfD politician, who had been actively involved in a secret conspiracy aimed at carrying out a violent coup d'état. While proceedings were still pending, in this high-profile case that attracted a lot of publicity, the Service Court saw a very high probability that disciplinary proceedings under Section 31 would lead to her removal from office and ordered her temporary suspension and a 50 % income cut.[61]

Another limit to the independence of judges is erected by Section 339 StGB, penalising 'perversion of justice.' This provision is interpreted restrictively by the BGH, though. The breach of law must constitute a fundamental violation of the

---

58 BVerfG, 2 BvR 147/70, BVerfGE 38, 139 (151 et seq.); ECLI:DE:BVerwG:2021:150421U2C13.20.0 (BVerwGE 172, 187) mn. 16.

59 Mehrdad Payandeh and Parissa Rahimian, 'Die Richteranklage zwischen wehrhafter Demokratie und richterlicher Unabhängigkeit' [2023] *Juristische Schulung (JuS)* 1108; critical, Classen, 'Artikel 98 GG' in Huber and Voßkuhle (n. 4) mn. 19; Other grounds for retirement against their will are unfitness for service (Section 34 DRiG, only on the strength of a final judicial decision) and termination of service in the case of qualified criminal convictions (Section 24 DRiG).

60 ECLI:DE:BGH:2023:051023URIZ.R.1.23.0 (BGH NVwZ 2023, 1932).

61 ECLI:DE:VGBE:2023:0315.DG1.23.00 (Richterdienstgericht Berlin).

administration of justice, and has to include a conscious and serious deviation from the law.[62] As a result, a violation of applicable norms only falls under Section 339 StGB if the conduct can be assessed as an attack on fundamental principles of law or on the legal system as a whole, and the judge is not guided by a desire for formal or substantive justice.[63]

That the judiciary in Germany is administered by the ministries of justice has occasionally been raised as a concern with regard to judicial independence. Decisions about administrative staff, premises and facilities, communications and IT infrastructure as well as data protection are ultimately taken by the respective ministries. They also are competent for the appraisal of judges and for prescribing the external and internal organisation of the courts or tribunals (excluding the assigning of cases). While some of these administrative dependencies might seem problematic, the procedural safeguards to protect judicial independence make it unlikely that they can be abused. Loading more administrative tasks onto courts whose capacities are already at the limit due to extraordinary case loads does not seem the best alternative, either.[64]

cc) Right to One's Lawful Judge

The rights to one's lawful judge, Article 101(1) cl 2 GG requires prior determination of competences. This is realised by statutes establishing jurisdiction concerning the branches of the judiciary, the competent local courts, and the respective courts of first and last instances. Within the courts, the case allocation plans are drafted by the courts' presidents and must not be changed in a manner that allows to assign a given case to a specific judge or formation of judges (cf also Article 101(1) cl 1, prohibiting 'special courts' as *lex specialis*[65]). Article 101(1) cl 2 GG also conveys a subjective right to impartiality and independence of the court in a given case and protects against arbitrary application of rules on recusal, paving the way for a constitutional complaint before the BVerfG.[66] 'Lawful judge' within the meaning of Article 101(1) GG is also the ECJ, turning the guarantee into a tool for enforcing a preliminary ruling to the ECJ via a constitutional complaint.

---

[62] BGH, 2 StR 479/13, NJW 2014, 1192 (1193); 1 StR 330/86, BGHSt 34, 146 (149); 4 StR 23/94, BGHSt 40, 272 (283).

[63] Markus Bange, '§ 339 StGB' in Bernd von Heintschel-Heinegg (ed), *BeckOK StGB* (67th ed., CH Beck 1 November 2025) mn. 12.

[64] For an in-depth defense of the existing system, see Fabian Wittreck, *Die Verwaltung der Dritten Gewalt* (Mohr Siebeck 2006).

[65] On these, cf BVerfG, 1 BvR 335/51, BVerfGE 3, 213 (223).

[66] ECLI:DE:BVerfG:2020:rk20200930.1bvr049519 (BVerfG NJW 2021, 1156); ECLI:DE:BVerfG:2021:rk20210701.2bvr089020 (BVerfG NVwZ 2021, 1220).

dd) Fair Trial

Article 103(1) GG guarantees fair hearing before courts. This implies the right to be heard, to have one's submission considered, and to be informed.[67] Inherent limitations are based on the expediency of proceedings. In case of a lack of hearing, the omission must have influenced the decision to violate the right to be heard; subsequent hearing is possible. Apart from Article 103(1) GG, the Basic Law does not expressly list fair trial rules. These are predominantly enshrined in the statutes regulating the respective court procedures, but can also be based on the rule of law principle in Article 20(3) GG interpreted in the light of Art. 6 ECHR.[68]

f) Separation of Powers

The separation of powers finds its basis in Article 20(2) cl 2 GG and is generally understood as an essential element of the rule of law.[69] Apart from the independence of the judiciary, however, the principle is not strictly adhered to. The German constitutional order is rather characterised by '*Gewaltenverschränkung*' ('intertwining of powers') in a parliamentary democracy, with close interlinkages between government and parliament. Thus, Chancellor and Federal Ministers are mostly recruited from the ranks of members of parliament; other Members of the *Bundestag* are given portfolios as Parliamentary State Secretaries; it is in the ministries that most bills are drafted. In practice, there is close political coordination and alignment between the government and those factions of parliament that support the government.

aa) Creation of Government

Different from the Weimar Constitution of 1919, where the President selected the Chancellor, the Federal Chancellor is elected by the *Bundestag*, Article 63 GG.[70] The *Bundestag* can only overturn the Government by electing a new Chancellor by the vote of a majority of its Members; in this case, the Federal President is obliged to dismiss the Chancellor and to appoint the person elected, Article 67(1) GG. In return, the Federal President is only allowed to dissolve the *Bundestag* in two cases. Both relate to an instability of government due to a lack of parliamentary support: if a Chancellor is elected (after several rounds of elections) only with a relative majority, Article 63(4) GG; and if a motion of the Federal Chan-

[67] BVerfG, 1 BvR 986/91, BVerfGE 86, 133 (144).

[68] BVerfG, 2 BvR 589/79, BVerfGE 74, 358 (370) *Unschuldsvermutung*.

[69] Differentiating, Christoph Möllers, *Gewaltengliederung. Legitimation und Dogmatik im nationalen und übernationalen Rechtsvergleich* (Mohr Siebeck 2005): combination of rule of law and democracy principles.

[70] This also applies to the *Länder* level. In some *Länder*, also ministers are elected by State parliament, eg Article 34(2) Verf HA: confirmation of the Senate by the *Bürgerschaft*.

cellor for a vote of confidence is not supported by the majority of the Members of the *Bundestag*, Article 68 GG.

bb) Control of Government

The control of the federal government by requests for information (right of interpellation) is exercised on the basis of the Rules of Procedure of the *Bundestag* (GOBT), Sections 27(2), 100 et seqq. However, the BVerfG bases these rights on the free mandate guaranteed to every Member of the *Bundestag* by Article 38(1) cl 2 GG. The Federal Government is obliged to give substantial answers and can only refer to confidentiality if it specifies the grounds and the application of a special confidentiality procedure is not feasible.[71] While in general, the right of interpellation lies with every Member of the *Bundestag*, under the conditions of a parliamentary democracy it is the opposition that exercises control in practice. Thus, while parliamentary committees of inquiry are established by the *Bundestag* with a majority vote, on the motion of one quarter of its Members it is obliged to take the respective vote and is also bound to respect the minority's determination of the investigative mandate. Furthermore, minority motions must not be blocked by the majority also within the committee itself.[72] The right to parliamentary inquiry ends at the 'core area of executive responsibility,' which precludes the *Bundestag* from investigating the decision-making process within the government.[73] Since all courts and administrative authorities are required to provide legal and administrative assistance to the committee, Article 44(3) GG, noncompliance must have a basis in the constitution.[74] The same quorum, 25 % of the Members of the *Bundestag*, is needed to call upon the BVerfG for assessing the constitutionality of any federal or *Länder* legislation, Article 94(1) No 2 GG.

cc) Legislative Reserve

Though not expressly mentioned, the legislative reserve (*'Gesetzesvorbehalt'*) is often also based on Article 20(3) GG.[75] This principle prescribes that (1) a formal law is required as basis for interferences with freedom and property and for any other important decision, and that (2) the more important an issue is, the more the legislator must regulate itself, thus limiting executive discretion.[76] Especially

---

[71] ECLI:DE:BVerfG:2009:es20090701.2bve000506 (BVerfGE 124, 161) *Überwachung von Abgeordneten*; ECLI:DE:BVerfG:2017:es20171107.2bve000211 (BVerfGE 147, 50) *Parlamentarisches Auskunftsrecht.*

[72] For details, see the 2001 Statute on Parliamentary Committees of Inquiry (PUAG) that draws on previous judgments of the BVerfG.

[73] BVerfG, 2 BvE 11/83, 2 BvE 15/83, BVerfGE 67, 100 (139) *Flick-Untersuchungsausschuss.*

[74] ECLI:DE:BVerfG:2016:es20161013.2bve000215 (BVerfGE 143, 101) *NSA-Untersuchungsausschuss.*

[75] See Grzeszick (n. 12) mn. 75 et seqq.

[76] BVerfG, 2 BvL 8/77, BVerfGE 49, 89 (126 et seq.) *Kalkar I*; ECLI:DE:BVerfG:1999:fs19990706.2bvf000390 (BVerfGE 101, 1 [34]) *Hennenhaltung.*

in the field of covert surveillance measures, the BVerfG has over the last years detailed numerous requirements that have to be met by the legislator.[77] Different from the 1919 Weimar Constitution, the Federal President or the Federal Government cannot issue decrees without authorisation by the Bundestag. Article 80(1) GG only allows to issue statutory instruments if the Federal Government or a *Land* government has been expressly authorised by a law that specifies content, purpose and scope of the authority conferred.

dd) Federal Constitutional Court

A special place in the system of checks and balances under the Basic Law is occupied by the BVerfG. Established in 1951, it has played a pivotal role in shaping the legal order of the Federal Republic of Germany. In general, the Court is held in high esteem, among the general public as among the legal community. Criticism is mostly confined to specific judgments, such as the *Kruzifix* order of 1995[78] or the 2020 *PSPP* judgment declaring the European Central Bank's Public Sector Purchase Programme and the ECJ judgment confirming it as acts *ultra vires*[79]. There has also been more general criticism of the Court for a judicial interventionism encroaching upon the competences of other institutions and powers.[80] Epithets like 'superior court of appeal' ('*Superrevisionsinstanz*') and 'substitute legislator' ('*Ersatzgesetzgeber*') criticise the BVerfG's interventions into the realms of the regular courts and of the legislator, respectively.[81] It has to be noted, however, that these interventions practically always were and are part of the BVerfG's extensive fundamental rights jurisprudence.

Recently, the focus has been not so much on shielding other institutions from the BVerfG's influence, though, but rather on how to protect the Court. With a surge of right-wing populism also in Germany, the aim was to counter possible attempts to curtail the Court's powers or to stack it with judges partial to the ruling party, as it happened in Hungary and Poland. This resulted in September 2024 in an amended Article 93 (formerly Article 94) GG which in its first paragraph states that the BVerfG 'shall be a federal court of justice which is autonomous and independent of all other constitutional organs.' The main aspect of the

---

77 See only ECLI:DE:BVerfG:2022:rs20220426.1bvr161917 (BVerfGE 162, 1) *Bayerisches VerfSchG*.

78 ECLI:DE:BVerfG:1995:rs19950516.1bvr108791 (BVerfGE 93, 1) *Kruzifix*. On this highly contested order, see Gary S. Schaal, 'Der "Kruzifix-Beschluss" und seine Folgen' in Robert Chr. van Ooyen and Martin Möllers (eds.), *Das Bundesverfassungsgericht im politischen System* (VS Verlag für Sozialwissenschaften 2006) 175.

79 ECLI:DE:BVerfG:2020:rs20200505.2bvr085915 (BVerfGE 154, 17) *PSPP*; Critical assessment in [2020] Europäische Zeitschrift für Wirtschaftsrecht (EuZW), issue 12.

80 Matthias Jestaedt, Oliver Lepsius, Christoph Möllers, and Christoph Schönberger, *Das entgrenzte Gericht. Eine kritische Bilanz nach sechzig Jahren Bundesverfassungsgericht* (Suhrkamp 2011).

81 On these common tropes, see only Helmut Simon, 'Das Bundesverfassungsgericht – Ersatzgesetzgeber und Superrevisionsinstanz?' [1996] Neue Justiz 169.

amendment, however, is that the number of judges, their term of office, age limits and the number of Senates are now enshrined in the Basic Law, thus requiring a two-thirds majority to be amended. A new Section 7a BVerfGG – itself subject to a possible future amendment by a simple majority, however – introduces the possibility that, in the case of a blockade of either *Bundestag* or *Bundesrat*, the Plenary of the BVerfG shall propose candidates and that, eventually, the other electoral organ may exercise the right to elect a candidate.

g) Accountability of Public Power

aa) Control of the Executive

Apart from the parliamentary control of government on the federal and *Länder* level (see f) bb) above), accountability of public power is secured predominantly by means of judicial control and courts of auditors.[82] With the historic exception of financial state liability for which civil courts are competent, judicial control of executive action (or inaction) lies with administrative courts. In general, they conduct a full judicial review, especially where individual rights are in play. Only in certain areas where special expertise is involved extended discretionary powers of the executive are respected.[83] Section 114(2) VwGO allows to submit additional reasons for an administrative act during court proceedings, in particular if the authority wishes to amend its discretionary decision. The reasons submitted subsequently must have already existed in substance at the time of the original decision, must not significantly alter the content of the decision, and must not impair the legal defence of the person concerned.[84] The courts of auditors are independent state financial control authorities on the level of the Federation (Federal Court of Auditors, *Bundesrechnungshof*) and the *Länder* that examine the legality, regularity, efficiency and economy of public budgetary and economic management in order to monitor taxpayers' money and identify waste. They advise, reprimand abuses, and make recommendations but have no authority to issue instructions; instead, they report to parliament.

bb) State Liability

Concerning state liability, the German legal order possesses a plethora of rules and claims, both customary and statutory, which have grown from different sources over centuries and, if not based completely on case law, are very much

---

[82] Walter Krebs, *Kontrolle in staatlichen Entscheidungsprozessen. Ein Beitrag zur rechtlichen Analyse von gerichtlichen, parlamentarischen und Rechnungshof-Kontrollen* (CF Müller 1984).

[83] Isabel Schübel-Pfister, '§ 114 VwGO' in Erich Eyermann (ed), *VwGO* (16th ed., CH Beck 2022) mn. 59 et seqq.

[84] Ibid mn. 84 et seqq.

shaped by jurisprudence.[85] Though it is difficult to describe them as a system, some guidance can be drawn from constitutional law. In certain cases, the Basic Law explicitly demands financial compensation (especially in the case of the right to private property, Article 14 GG). Furthermore, the principle of the rule of law demands that a violation of a right shall be prevented, and, if this is not possible, redressed or compensated.[86] With regard to the substantive rules, there are two types of claims: Claims based on *'Amtshaftung'* (government liability for tortious acts of its agents) and claims based on *'Aufopferung'* (sacrificial encroachment).[87] These claims have developed over the last centuries mainly independently from each other and form the basis of all other claims in the law of public authority liability. Claims for damages face both substantive and procedural restrictions. Most important are the priority of primary remedies and the respective subsidiarity of secondary ones.[88] This means that the individual is not free in the choice of remedies. Inasmuch as someone was able to prevent harm by challenging an act of state violating their rights, they are not able to claim damages later.

h) Respect for Human Rights and Non-Discrimination

aa) Inviolability of Human Dignity

Reacting to the then recent experiences of Nazi dictatorship and the Holocaust, the Basic Law's First Part is dedicated to fundamental rights (which, in the Weimar Constitution of 1919, previously had been relegated to Articles 109 et seqq.). Article 1 GG proclaims the inviolability of human dignity (para 1), acknowledges 'inviolable and inalienable human rights as the basis of every community, of peace and of justice in the world' (para 2), and orders that the 'following basic rights shall bind the legislature, the executive and the judiciary as directly applicable law' (para 3). Article 79(3) GG declares inadmissible any amendment to the Basic Law affecting 'the principles laid down in Articles 1 and 20.' The specific fundamental rights provisions are subject to amendment and even (in theory, at least) deletion. However, the commitment to human dignity and human rights in Article 1(1) and (2) GG ensures that fundamental aspects of physical and mental integrity, of personal identity, of equality, self-determination and humane living conditions can withstand – at least within the doctrinal construction of the

---

[85] For a detailed overview, see Andreas von Arnauld, 'Damages for the Infringement of Human Rights in Germany' in Ewa Bagińska (ed), *Damages for Violations of Human Rights* (Springer 2016) 101.

[86] Steffen Detterbeck, Kay Windthorst, and Hans-Dieter Sproll, *Staatshaftungsrecht* (CH Beck 1999) 83; Marten Breuer, *Staatshaftung für judikatives Unrecht* (Mohr Siebeck 2011) 113; sceptical as to the precise content of the rule of law principle in this regard Bernd Grzeszick, *Rechte und Ansprüche* (Mohr Siebeck 2002) 130.

[87] Grzeszick (n. 86) 10 et seqq; Detterbeck, Windthorst, and Sproll (n. 86) 8 et seqq.

[88] Cf BVerfG, 1 BvL 77/78, BVerfGE 58, 300 *Nassauskiesung*; See also, BGH, III ZR 309/96, BGHZ 138, 247 (251).

Grundgesetz – potential attempts to turn Germany into an 'illiberal democracy' by amending the Basic Law.[89]

bb) System of Rights Protection

The German legal order has, under the Basic Law of 1949, experienced an unprecedented process of constitutionalisation. This is mainly due to the influence of its fundamental or 'basic' rights.[90] Since its establishment in 1951, the BVerfG has made it its mission to develop and enforce the fundamental rights enshrined in the Basic Law through often extensive and dynamic interpretation. Going beyond merely preventing interference, constitutional jurisprudence has formulated positive state obligations to protect, most recently – in the context of climate change – also including future generations,[91] and has expanded the protection of fundamental rights through organisation and procedure.[92] According to the BVerfG, the fundamental rights embody an 'objective value system'[93] reflecting a fundamental constitutional decision for all areas of law. Mediated by general clauses and open legal terms in statutory law and in contracts, these have an impact also on private legal relationships. Where private individuals control places and forums of 'general communication,' or where they have particular social power, fundamental rights can acquire a binding effect comparable to that of the state.[94]

Different from the constitutions of some German states which guarantee also economic, social and cultural rights,[95] the Basic Law's catalogue is limited to classic civil and political rights and has not been formally expanded since 1949.[96] Exten-

---

89 Cf ECLI:DE:BVerfG:1996:rs19960514.2bvr193893 (BVerfGE 94, 49 [102 et seq.]) *Sichere Drittstaaten*.

90 See only Hans D. Jarass, 'Die Konstitutionalisierung des Rechts, insb. durch Grundrechte' in Fabian Wittreck (ed.), *60 Jahre Grundgesetz: Verfassung mit Zukunft?* (Nomos 2010) 47 et seqq.

91 ECLI:DE:BVerfG:2021:rs20210324.1bvr265618 (BVerfGE 157, 30 [111 et seqq.]) *Klimaschutz*.

92 Eg, to protect the freedom of science, BVerfG, 1 BvR 424/71, 1 BvR 325/72, BVerfGE 35, 79 (114 et seqq.).

93 BVerfG, 1 BvR 400/51, BVerfGE 7, 198 (205) *Lüth*.

94 ECLI:DE:BVerfG:2011:rs20110222.1bvr069906 (BVerfGE 128, 226) *Fraport*: departure hall of an airport; ECLI:DE:BVerfG:2015:qs20150720.1bvq002515 (BVerfGE 139, 378) *Flashmob Passau*: public square in private ownership; ECLI:DE:BVerfG:2018:rs20180411.1bvr308009 (BVerfGE 148, 267) *Stadionverbot*: prohibition of access to a football stadium.

95 Bavaria (right to adequate housing), Berlin (rights to work and to education), Brandenburg (right to education), Bremen (rights to work and to adequate housing), Hesse (right to work and to fair working conditions), Mecklenburg-Vorpommern (right to education), Lower Saxony (rights to education, to work, to adequate housing), Northrhine-Westphalia (rights to education and to work), Saarland (rights to education and to work), Saxony (right to a dignified existence), Saxony-Anhalt (right to education), Schleswig-Holstein (protection and support for people in need of care, access to basic digital services), Thuringia (right to a shelter). Minority rights as group rights are recognised in the constitutions of Brandenburg (Article 25), Saxony (Article 6) and Schleswig-Holstein (Article 6).

96 An exception is the introduction of Article 3(3) cl 2 GG prohibiting discrimination of persons with disabilities.

sions, however, have been realised by way of interpretation. From Article 1(1) GG in conjunction with the welfare state principle, Article 20(1) GG, e. g., the BVerfG has derived a right to a minimum standard of living.[97] By interpreting Article 2(1) GG (free development of personality) as a guarantee of general freedom of conduct,[98] the state is subject to a comprehensive duty to justify any interference with personal freedom, even where specific guarantees are lacking. The rights catalogue has also been updated and expanded by deriving 'new' fundamental rights, in particular through the general right of personality based on Article 2(1) in conjunction with Article 1(1) GG,[99] from which, in turn, the right to informational self-determination[100] and, most recently, the fundamental right to the integrity of IT systems[101] have been derived. By extending the obligation to justify interferences from classic state interventions to indirect and *de facto* interferences – for example, through state information[102] or "nudging"[103] – new forms of state action have also been covered by the system of fundamental rights protection.

Judicial review of state interference with fundamental rights in Germany is based on an elaborate proportionality test.[104] This demands that the objective of the interference is (1) lawful in itself and (2) that it can be furthered by the means employed; furthermore, (3) the means must be necessary, i. e., the least intrusive one that equally furthers the objective, and (4) adequate (or proportionate *sensu strictu*). This last step of the assessment usually includes a complex balancing of all interests in play and is mostly responsible for criticism that marks the BVerfG for being overly intrusive with respect to the legislator or the regular courts.[105]

Protection of fundamental rights through the BVerfG is guaranteed via three procedures. To review the constitutionality of laws, the BVerfG may be called upon by the Federal Government, a state government or a quarter of the members of the Bundestag (Article 94 (1) No. 2 GG), or by courts that consider a norm to be unconstitutional in a pending case (Article 100(1) GG). However, by far the

[97] ECLI:DE:BVerfG:2010:ls20100209.1bvl000109 (BVerfGE 125, 175 [222 et seqq.]) *Hartz IV*.

[98] BVerfG, 1 BvR 253/56, BVerfGE 6, 32 (36 et seqq.) *Elfes*; 1 BvR 921/85, BVerfGE 80, 137 (152 et seqq.) *Reiten im Walde*.

[99] BVerfG, 1 BvR 112/65, BVerfGE 34, 269 (280 et seqq.) *Soraya*, subscribing to the jurisprudence of the BGH.

[100] BVerfG, 1 BvR 209/83, BVerfGE 65, 1 (41 et seqq.) *Volkszählung*.

[101] ECLI:DE:BVerfG:2008:rs20080227.1bvr037007 (BVerfGE 120, 274 [306 et seqq.]) *Online-durchsuchung*; ECLI:DE:BVerfG:2025:rs20250624.1bvr018023 (BVerfG NJW 2025, 3424) *Trojaner II*.

[102] ECLI:DE:BVerfG:2018:fs20180321.1bvf000113 (BVerfGE 148, 40 [50 et seqq.]) *Lebensmittel-pranger*.

[103] Eg, in the context of measures against the COVID-19 pandemic, ECLI:DE:BVerfG:2021:rs20211119.1bvr078121 (BVerfGE 159, 223 [331 et seqq.]) *Bundesnotbremse I*; ECLI:DE:BVerfG:2022:rs20220427.1bvr264921 (BVerfGE 161, 299 [345 et seqq.]) *Impfnachweis COVID-19*.

[104] In a comparative perspective, Andreas von Arnauld, 'Theorie und Methode des Grundrechtsschutzes in Europa: am Beispiel des Grundsatzes der Verhältnismäßigkeit' [2008] *Europarecht – Beiheft 1*, 41.

[105] In this vein, Bernhard Schlink, *Abwägung im Verfassungsrecht* (Duncker & Humblot 1976).

most important procedure is the constitutional complaint, which 'may be filed by any person alleging that one of his basic rights or one of his rights under paragraph (4) of Article 20 or under Article 33, 38, 101, 103 or 104 GG has been infringed by public authority' (Article 94(1) No 4a GG). Here, not only statutes, but also other acts of public authority – in practice mainly decisions by courts of last instance – can be challenged. It is not necessary to employ a solicitor. Moreover, it is possible to apply for a preliminary injunction according to Section 32 BVerfGG, 'if this is urgently required to avert severe disadvantage' for the claimant.

Constitutional complaints account for over 95% of the cases before the BVerfG, with around 5,000–6,000 new applications per year.[106] In order to protect the Court from an excessive workload, constitutional complaints are subject to admission for decision and can be rejected if they have neither general constitutional significance nor are they appropriate to enforce the basic rights of the claimant (Section 93a BVerfGG). While constitutional issues which have not yet been fully determined have to be decided by the Senate, Chambers of three judges will deal with the bulk of applications without an oral hearing. If refusing to admit the constitutional complaint for decision the Chamber does not have to state reasons (cf Sections 93b-93d BVerfGG). In practice, though, these decisions mostly are accompanied by some brief reasoning.

The most important limitation for constitutional complaints is the obligation to exhaust all available judicial remedies before lodging it. This does not only include formally available legal recourse to other courts (cf Section 90(2) BVerfGG), but also other ways to obtain a judicial review indirectly, when this is possible without jeopardising the rights in question or running a risk to be penalised.[107] The BVerfG stresses the principle that the constitutional complaint is an extraordinary and thus subsidiary means to protect and enforce one's basic rights. Thus, the everyday task of judicial human rights protection falls on the regular courts. By consequence, every German court is applying the Basic Law's fundamental rights be it directly or indirectly, via an interpretation in their light, on an almost daily basis. Constitutional complaint procedures also exist on the state level in most of Germany's 16 *Länder*, though far less frequently employed than the procedure on federal level. Whenever the constitutional court of a *Land* reviews a case which involves the application of federal law, the BVerfG demands that this court has to interpret the rights in the constitution of the *Land* in the same manner as the BVerfG interprets the respective right in the Basic Law in

[106] Cf statistics for the years 1951 to 2020: Bundesverfassungsgericht, *Jahresstatistik 2020*, 1, 7, available via www.bundesverfassungsgericht.de/DE/Mediathek/Jahresberichte/Jahresstatistiken/2020/gb2020/Gesamtstatistik-2020.pdf

[107] See only, BVerfG, 1 BvF 1/76, BVerfGE 43, 291 (387) *Numerus clausus*; 1 BvR 602/78, BVerfGE 60, 360 (372); 1 BvR 1509/83, BVerfGE 74, 69 (74 et seq.).

order to guarantee the uniform application of federal statutes throughout Germany.[108]

cc) Non-Discrimination

Issues of non-discrimination are addressed in Article 3 GG. According to Article 3(3) cl 1 GG, '[n]o person shall be favoured or disfavoured because of sex, parentage, race, language, homeland and origin, faith or religious or political opinions.' In light of a 2017 decision of the BVerfG, 'sex' here has to be interpreted as including, next to male and female, also divers/non-binary.[109] While there has been growing concern about racial profiling by police forces,[110] the problem has only occasionally been taken to court so far.[111] Since Article 3(3) cl 1 GG only prohibits differentiating 'because of' the criteria listed, it is limited to a prohibition of direct discrimination. Article 3(2) cl 1 GG ('Men and women shall have equal rights'), however, also covers indirect discrimination, while its cl 2 obliges the State to 'promote the actual implementation of equal rights for women and men and take steps to eliminate existing disadvantages.' This serves as the legal basis for preferential treatment of women, especially in the fields of employment and access to public service.[112] Article 3(3) cl 2 GG, according to which '[n]o person shall be disfavoured because of disability', also affords protection against indirect discrimination. It has recently been interpreted by the BVerfG also as a source of positive state obligations which, in situations of particular vulnerability, 'may culminate in a specific duty to take protective action. This includes situations where persons are subject to targeted exclusion that must be regarded as an attack on human dignity, where disadvantaging on the basis of disability entails risks for high-ranking fundamental rights interests, or in situations of structural inequality.'[113]

Overall, non-discrimination is markedly less developed than are the fundamental freedoms in German constitutional law. Firstly, the grounds for discrimination in Article 3(3) GG have not been expanded since 1949, with the exception of the inclusion of persons with disabilities in 1994. Thus, discriminations because of sexual orientation, age or infirmity, e.g., have to be measured against the less stringent standard of Article 3(1) (equality before the law, see c) above) by default. Secondly, non-discrimination remains conceptually underdeveloped, by

---

108 ECLI:DE:BVerfG:1997:ns19971015.2bvn000195 (BVerfGE 96, 345 [364 et seqq.]) *Landesverfassungsgerichte*.

109 Cf ECLI:DE:BVerfG:2017:rs20171010.1bvr201916 (BVerfGE 147, 1) *Geschlechtsidentität*.

110 UN Human Rights Committee, CCPR/C/DEU/CO/7 (30 November 2021) mn. 12 et seq.

111 See, eg, ECLI:DE:OVGRLP:2016:0421.7A11108.14.0A (OVG Koblenz NJW 2016, 2820), finding a violation of Article 3(3) GG.

112 Sigrid Boysen, 'Artikel 3 GG' in von Münch and Kunig (n. 5) mn. 164 et seqq.

113 ECLI:DE:BVerfG:2021:rs20211216.1bvr154120 (BVerfGE 160, 79) *Triage I*, headnote 2; The case concerned access to life-sustaining medical resources in intensive care during the COVID-19 pandemic.

being mostly limited to direct discrimination and by showing little awareness of intersectionality issues. While EU law has had some influence on German law in this respect,[114] the same criticism has also been levelled against the General Act on Equal Treatment (*Allgemeines Gleichbehandlungsgesetz*, AGG) of 2006, with which the German legislator implemented the EU's anti-discrimination directives. Several UN human rights treaty bodies have called for an expansion of discrimination categories and the inclusion of indirect and multidimensional forms of discrimination, for expanding the scope of application to, *inter alia*, encompass also public authorities, to remove exceptions and to improve enforceability.[115]

i) Pluralism and Participation

aa) Pluralism of Opinions

Pluralism of opinions is mainly guaranteed by fundamental rights. Of central importance are here the freedoms of expression and to receive information (Article 5(1) cl 1 GG), the freedoms of mass media (Article 5(1) cl 2 GG), the freedom of arts and science (Article 5(3) GG) and the freedom of assembly (Article 8 GG). Special protection is awarded to institutions relevant for safeguarding this plurality.

While the press in Germany has been dominated from the outset by private publishers, competing with each other on the "marketplace of opinions", broadcasting had for decades been organised exclusively by a limited number of public broadcasters. For this reason, the BVerfG has imposed "internal pluralism" on broadcasters, i.e. they must ensure plurality of opinion within their programme;[116] this is reflected in the composition of their advisory bodies, which must include representatives of various social groups and avoid the decisive influence of certain political orientations or social groups.[117] Since public broadcasters have to be independent from the state (*'Gebot der Staatsferne'*), the BVerfG decided that no more than one third of the members of their advisory

---

[114] Mostly by means of secondary legislation, but potentially in future also through Article 21 (1) CFR, where applicable. For discrimination on grounds of age cf (before entry into force of Treaty of Lisbon) ECJ, Case C-144/04 *Mangold v Helm* ECLI:EU:C:2005:709, paras 74 et seq.; Case C-555/07 *Kücüdevici v Swedex* ECLI:EU:C:2010:21, mn. 23 et seqq.

[115] Magdalena Otto, 'Das Antidiskriminierungsrecht in der Kritik internationaler Menschenrechtsgremien: Empfehlungen der UN-Fachausschüsse zur Reform des Allgemeinen Gleichbehandlungsgesetzes (AGG)' (*Deutsches Institut für Menschenrechte: Information Nr. 49*, June 2024) www.institut-fuer-menschenrechte.de/fileadmin/Redaktion/Publikationen/Information/Information_Das_Antidiskriminierungsrecht_in_der_Kritik_internationaler_Menschenrechtsgremien.pdf

[116] BVerfG, 2 BvG 1/60, 2 BvG 2/60, BVerfGE 12, 205 (261 et seqq.) *Deutschland-Fernsehen GmbH*.

[117] ECLI:DE:BVerfG:2014:fs20140325.1bvf000111 (BVerfGE 136, 9 [30 et seqq.]) *ZDF-Aufsichtsgremien*.

bodies may be affiliated with the state, and that these members may not have a decisive influence on the selection of the other members.[118]

Those principles continue to apply to public broadcasters even under the conditions of the "dual broadcasting system," which was introduced in 1984 with the licensing of private broadcasters, closely accompanied by the broadcasting jurisprudence of the BVerfG. According to that case law, private broadcasting financed by advertising poses the risk that content is narrowed based on market considerations. Therefore, the continued existence of fees-funded public service broadcasting is a prerequisite for maintaining the dual broadcasting system. In this system, public broadcasters are responsible for providing 'basic service' ('*Grundversorgung*').[119] Their programme must reach the entire population, be comprehensively varied, and ensure diversity of opinion. Private broadcasters, on the other hand, may offer pay-TV and special-interest channels. Regarding plurality, Section 51(1) of the Interstate Media Treaty (*Medienstaatsvertrag*) only requires them to respect the 'moral, religious and ideological convictions of others.'

This Interstate Media Treaty of 2020, between the federal and state governments, for the first time also covers 'media intermediaries' (news aggregators, search engines, social networks, etc), media platforms (telemedia services that bundle existing services into a diverse offering) with their user interfaces, as well as video-sharing services (such as YouTube). These are required to exercise journalistic diligence (if they offer such services) and to indicate their client in the case of advertising of a political, ideological or religious nature (Sections 19, 22). Media platforms and user interfaces are required by Section 84(3) to present their entire broadcasting offering at the first level of selection and to make public service programmes and such private programmes 'that make a particular contribution to the diversity of opinion and offerings in the federal territory' easy to find.

Concerning universities, the legislature is under an obligation to regulate institutions and procedures to avoid any structural threats to the freedom of teaching and research. From this follows, *inter alia*, a system of self-administration that must ensure that in decisions concerning teaching and research, academic staff members possess the majority of votes in governing bodies of universities.[120] The legislator is barred from regulating matters which essentially fall into the core areas of academic freedom, such as the granting of PhD titles.[121]

---

118 Ibid 33 et seqq.

119 BVerfG, 1 BvF 1/84, BVerfGE 73, 118 (157 et seqq.) *Niedersächsisches Rundfunkgesetz.*

120 ECLI:DE:BVerfG:2014:rs20140624.1bvr321707 (BVerfGE 136, 338 [363]) *Niedersächsisches HSG*; ECLI:DE:BVerfG:2025:rs20250930.1bvr114119 *Thüringer HSG*, mn. 81 et seqq.

121 ECLI: ECLI:DE:VERFGBE:2004:1101.210.03.0A (VerfGH Berlin Wissenschaftsrecht 2005, 67).

bb) Civil Society and Political Pluralism

Central for the work of civil society organisations is Article 9(1) GG which guarantees the freedom of association to all Germans (for non-Germans, the right follows from the general freedom in Article 2(1) GG). According to Article 9(2) GG, '[a]ssociations whose aims or activities contravene the criminal laws or that are directed against the constitutional order or the concept of international understanding shall be prohibited.' Since the scope of Article 9 GG is not limited to non-profit associations but also includes business organisations, there also have been cases in which media companies were prohibited on the basis of Article 9(2) GG. This is accepted by the judiciary if the prohibition is not based solely on the content of publications or broadcasts but also on the broader activities of the company.[122] Furthermore, the prohibition has to be proportionate. Recently, the BVerwG found that the prohibition of a company publishing a far right-wing magazine was disproportionate, in that only a part of the articles published violated human dignity and other fundamental tenets of the Basic Law.[123]

Political pluralism in Germany is mostly guaranteed by political parties which, according to Article 21(1) cl 1 GG, 'shall participate in the formation of the political will of the people.' Formally private associations, they have certain constitutional privileges and can challenge acts or omissions by constitutional bodies, especially the Federal Government, before the BVerfG under Article 94(1) No 1 GG. This is especially important to enforce their right to equal treatment and, eg, against derogatory remarks by government members.[124] Article 21(1) GG further stipulates that parties may be freely established, but that their internal organisation must conform to democratic principles; furthermore, they must publicly account for their assets and for the sources and use of their funds. Concerning the financing of parties, direct state support must not exceed self-financing; also, there must be limits to private donations in order to preserve 'civic equality'.[125] Under Article 21(2) GG, parties that, 'by reason of their aims or the behaviour of their adherents, seek to undermine or abolish the free democratic basic order or to endanger the existence of the Federal Republic of Germany shall be unconstitutional.' The decision is taken by the BVerfG, Article 21(4) GG, on application by the Federal Government, *Bundesrat* or *Bundestag*. Thus far, only two parties have been prohibited, in the early years of the Federal Republic of Germany.[126] An attempt to prohibit of the right-wing extremist NPD failed in 2017 because

[122] ECLI:DE:BVerwG:2020:290120U6A1.19.0 (BVerwGE 167, 293) *linksunten-indymedia*. Cf in general, ECLI:DE:BVerfG:2018:rs20180713.1bvr147412 (BVerfGE 149, 160 [190 f.]) *Vereinsverbote*.

[123] ECLI:DE:BVerwG:2025:240625U6A4.24.0 (BVerwG NJW 2025, 3650) *COMPACT-Verbot*.

[124] ECLI:DE:BVerfG:2014:es20141216.2bve000214 (BVerfGE 138, 102) *'Spinner'*; ECLI:DE:BVerfG:2018:es20180227.2bve000116 (BVerfGE 148, 11) *'Rote Karte für die AfD'*; ECLI:DE:BVerfG:2020:es20200609.2bve000119 (BVerfGE 154, 320) *Seehofer-Interview*; ECLI:DE:BVerfG:2022:es20220615.2bve000420 (BVerfGE 162, 207) *Thüringen-Wahl 2020*.

[125] BVerfG, 2 BvE 2/89, BVerfGE 85, 264, 290 (315 et seqq.) *Parteienfinanzierung II*.

[126] BVerfG, 1 BvB 1/51, BVerfGE 2, 1 *SRP*; 1 BvB 2/51, BVerfGE 5, 85 *KPD*.

(mainly due to the rise of the AfD) the party had lost support and no longer seemed a real threat to the constitutional order.[127] On the basis of Article 21(3) GG, newly introduced in 2017, following a hint by the BVerfG, the Party was, however, excluded from state financing.[128]

cc) Direct Participation of the People in Public Power

In general, Article 20(2) cl 2 GG determines that state authority 'shall be exercised by the people through elections and other vote.' Plebiscites, though, exist in practice only in the *Länder* and on local level. Here, different types are legally established and frequently used: popular initiatives (forcing parliament to address a topic); public petitions (forcing to hold a referendum); popular votes (binding decisions on the submission of a popular initiative or petition); referenda (binding votes on a government bill). On federal level, the Basic Law only provides for referenda in the case of a reorganisation of the federal territory (Articles 28, 118, 118a GG) and, arguably, in the case of a replacement of the Basic Law by another Constitution (Article 146 GG). Given the inevitable conflicts with parliamentary legislation,[129] the introduction of plebiscites as a means of popular legislation on federal level would need an amendment of the Basic Law.[130] However, there has been the occasional experiment with citizens' councils in special policy areas, where citizens selected at random advise the legislative bodies, even going so far as to co-draft legislative initiatives.[131]

Direct participation of the people in the administration is made possible by Article 33(2) GG, according to which '[e]very German shall be equally eligible for any public office according to his aptitude, qualifications and professional achievements.' Furthermore, in all *Länder*, there are elected bodies on the local level (district assemblies, city parliaments, etc) which, functionally, fulfil administrative duties.[132] Apart from this, participation in local self-administration can take various forms, especially consultative bodies on certain issues (e.g. youth, traffic, etc) or local areas (city district advisory boards, etc), as well as online fora. Other means are the participation in bodies of functional self-administration, e.g. water management associations.[133] In the judiciary, lay judges are widely employed in criminal proceedings in Germany, see Sections 28 ff. Courts Constitution Act (*Gerichtsverfassungsgesetz*, GVG).

---

[127] ECLI:DE:BVerfG:2017:bs20170117.2bvb000113 (BVerfGE 144, 20 [224 et seqq.]) *NPD II*.

[128] Confirmed by ECLI:DE:BVerfG:2024:bs20240123.2bvb000119 (BVerfGE 168, 193) *Finanzierungsausschluss*.

[129] Cf, on the experiences in the State of Hamburg, Andreas von Arnauld, '"Refolution" an der Elbe: Hamburgs neue direkte Demokratie – die Verfassungsänderungen der Jahre 2008 und 2009 im Kontext' (2009) 1 *Jahrbuch für direkte Demokratie* 90.

[130] Kotzur (n. 7) mn. 124; Sommermann (n. 4) mn. 162.

[131] Kotzur (n. 7) mn. 124a, with further references.

[132] Cf BVerfG, 1 BvB 1/51, BVerfGE 2, 1 (76) *SRP*; 2 BvF 3/56, BVerfGE 6, 104 (115 et seq.).

[133] See ECLI:DE:BVerfG:2002:ls20021205.2bvl000598 (BVerfGE 107, 59) *Lippeverband*.

j) Transparency of Decision-Making

Though generally scoring well in the established corruption indexes, Germany has not a long-standing tradition when it comes to the transparency of decision-making.

aa) Legislation

The legislative drafting process is mostly opaque, especially in the most frequent case, namely bills drafted within the government. Here, no systematic information about external advice and opinion is provided.[134] In some cases, drafting has even been outsourced to specialised law firms.[135] Once introduced into the *Bundestag*, a higher level of transparency is guaranteed. According to Rule 76(2) GOBT, bills must – and motions may – be accompanied by a short explanatory memorandum. Plenary sessions of the Bundestag are open to the public; the public can only be excluded on the basis of a two-thirds majority, Article 42(1) GG. However, the main drafting process is entrusted to the specialised committees. Their meetings are not open to the public, if the committee does not decide otherwise, Rule 69(1) GOBT.

In 2022, a federal statute (*Lobbyregistergesetz*, LobbyRG) introduced a 'lobby register,' replacing an 'open list of registered associations and their representatives' that had been kept by the President of the Bundestag since 1972. This list had been incomprehensive as registration was voluntary. Section 2 LobbyRG introduces a mandatory registration, while Section 3 obliges to publish information on the content and scope of activities. After initial criticism, significantly stricter rules were introduced in 2024, demanding information on the specific bills and other projects of interest, financial information on the origin and use of funds, as well as information on the identity of clients for whom the representation of interests is carried out. The definition of 'lobbying' in Section 1(3) is broad and includes non-profit organisations as well as profit-oriented lobby groups, as long as they maintain 'any contact […] for the purpose of directly or indirectly influencing the decision-making process of the organs, committees, members, factions or groups of the German Bundestag or for the purpose of directly or indirectly influencing the decision-making process of the Federal Government.' However, while lobbying activities in and around Parliament are relatively well documented now, the 'executive footprint' is still lacking. Since June 2024, officials in Federal Ministries are required to disclose the influence of lobbyists on legislative drafts according to Section 43(1) No 13 of the Joint Rules of Procedure

---

[134] Cf answer of the Federal Government to an interpellation by the parliamentary faction 'Die Linke': Deutscher Bundestag, Drucksache 19/31646 (20 July 2021), 3: no obligation, but voluntary commitment to aim for more transparency in this regard.

[135] Julian Krüper, 'Lawfirm – legibus solutus? Legitimität und Rationalität des inneren Gesetzgebungsverfahrens und das ‚Outsourcing' von Gesetzentwürfen' [2010] Juristen-Zeitung 655 et seqq.

of Federal Ministries (*Gemeinsame Geschäftsordnung*, GGO). However, this does not encompass meetings in person with lobbyists and only relates to input that contributed to a 'significant extent' or led to changes of 'core aspects' of the draft, providing for a wide discretion. Criticism is also voiced against blanket exemptions for certain groups, such as employee and employer associations and against often vague and incomplete reporting.[136]

Laws and statutory instruments are formally promulgated in the Federal Law Gazette (Article 82 GG) which is published in print and online.

bb) Government and Administration

Decision-making processes within the government *tel quel* are usually not disclosed and even shielded against parliamentary control ('core area of executive responsibility', see above). Concerning the administration, the federal Freedom of Information Act (*Informationsfreiheitsgesetz*, IFG) of 2006 allows everyone to request official information from the authorities, 'official information' being defined in Section 2 as 'every record serving official purposes, irrespective of the mode of storage,' but excluding 'drafts and notes which are not intended to form part of a file.' Sections 3 to 6 contain wide-ranging exceptions for the protection of special public interests, against obstruction of ongoing proceedings, of personal data as well as intellectual property, and of business or trade secrets. Similar laws were enacted around the same time in most *Länder*, some of these also including the local administration. A new generation of transparency laws was spearheaded by Hamburg which in 2012 promulgated the first Transparency Act, obliging the administration to proactively publish the relevant information. Other states have followed this example, with varying degrees of transparency according to the specific drafting of the statutes.[137] Next to this, Environmental Information Acts serve to implement the respective EU legislation[138], itself fulfilling obligations under the 1998 Aarhus Convention on Access to Information, Public Participation in Decision-making and Access to Justice in Environmental Matters.

The press laws of the *Länder* provide for specific rights of the press and media to information 'that serves to fulfil their public functions' (in the wording of Section 4(1) Hamburg Press Act). Since press regulation falls within the exclusive legislative competence of the states, no such law exists for the federal authorities.

---

[136] Karsten Mause and Andreas Polk, 'Lobbyregulierung in Deutschland: eine kritische Bestandsaufnahme' (2024) 71 Zeitschrift für Politik 310 et seqq; European Commission, 2024 Rule of Law Report, Country Chapter on the rule of law situation in Germany, SWD(2024) 805 final (24 July 2024) 17.

[137] Comparative assessment by Arne Semsrott/Mehr Demokratie e.V., *Transparenzranking 2021* (Berlin 2021) https://transparenzranking.de/static/files/ifg-ranking.pdf

[138] Directive 2003/4/EC of the European Parliament and of the Council of 28 January 2003 on public access to environmental information and repealing Council Directive 90/313/EEC [2003] OJ L 41/26.

Here, the BVerwG held that the freedom of the press (Article 5(1) cl 2 GG) confers a direct right to information from federal authorities in the absence of more specific legislation.[139]

cc) Judiciary

Apart from the special case of the BVerfG whose chamber formations deal with the bulk of constitutional complaints without an oral hearing (see above), Section 169(1) GVG determines that '[h]earings before the adjudicating court, including the pronouncement of judgments and rulings, are public,' with exceptions being made in family matters and in non-contentious matters, in order to protect the parties to the proceedings and for security and other reasons (cf Section 172 GVG). Audio and television or radio recordings are only admissible to a very limited extent. There is no constitutional obligation to further permit television and radio broadcasts.[140] Deliberations and votings are conducted *in camera*, with all participants obliged to observe secrecy (Section 193 GVG). According to Section 173, '[t]he pronouncement of the judgment as well as the final decision in matrimonial matters and family dispute matters must in any case be public.' This, however, only applies as far as an oral hearing was held.[141]

On a general level, the BVerwG has held that the publication of court decisions is a constitutional duty of every court, based on the principles of rule of law and democracy. This applies to all decisions in which the public has or may have an interest (subject to anonymization). While courts may leave the publication to private initiatives of interested parties, they have a duty of neutrality and must not privilege some publishers over others.[142] Today, while judgments and orders by the federal courts and the highest *Länder* courts are usually published online (and, in a selection, in printed official collections and widely via private publishers and data bases), there is still a lack of publications of court decisions in Germany in general. According to a recent study, only 1% of all decisions are published, posing serious problems with view to public accountability as well as transmission of knowledge and digitalisation of the law.[143]

---

139 ECLI:DE:BVerwG:2016:160316U6C65.14.0 (BVerwGE 154, 222).

140 ECLI:DE:BVerfG:2001:rs20010124.1bvr262395 (BVerfGE 103, 44) *ntv*.

141 Steffen Pabst, '§173 GVG' in Wolfgang Krüger and Thomas Rauscher (eds.), *Münchner Kommentar zur Zivilprozessordnung* (Vol. 3, 6th ed., CH Beck 2022), GVG §173 mn. 2.

142 ECLI:DE:BVerwG:1997:260297U6C3.96.0 (BVerwGE 104, 105).

143 Hanjo Hamann, 'Der blinde Fleck der deutschen Rechtswissenschaft: Zur digitalen Verfügbarkeit instanzgerichtlicher Rechtsprechung' [2021] Juristen-Zeitung 656 et seqq., with dataset: 'Präjudizienpublizität der ordentlichen Gerichte in Deutschland 1971–2019' https://intrechtdok.de/receive/mir_mods_00010572

3. *External Scrutiny and Accountability of the Rule of Law in Germany*

Lacking a recent domestic situation or crisis threatening the rule of law, there has not yet been any international surveillance mechanism which has been created or activated specifically with respect to Germany. There are, however, general mechanisms in place within the institutional contexts of the EU, the Council of Europe (COE), and the UNO.

a) EU Mechanisms

aa) Rule of Law Report: General Assessment

The most pertinent mechanism within the EU context is the annual Rule of Law Report, introduced by the European Commission in 2020 as part of the European Rule of Law Mechanism. It rests on four pillars: the justice system, the anti-corruption framework, media pluralism and other institutional issues related to checks and balances. Apart from a synthesis on the state of the rule of law in the EU itself, it contains country chapters addressing challenges and achievements and recommending measures to improve the situation. The Report is drafted in close collaboration with national authorities and builds on written submissions as well as country visits, in which delegates from the Commission and other member states or enlargement countries ('country visits country') meet with national authorities, independent bodies and stakeholders, especially civil society organisations. The drafting of the reports is supported by the network of national contact points on the rule of law, the member for Germany being the Ministry of Foreign Affairs. Prior to the adoption of the Report, national authorities are given the opportunity to provide factual updates to their country chapter.

In all four pillars of the report, Germany generally consistently has received good scores so far. There is solid trust in the independence of its judiciary among the population and companies (more than 70 rate it as 'fairly or very good'), quality and efficiency of the judicial system are overall high.[144] Germany has a functioning anti-corruption framework in place and operation, even though it dropped from a 5th place among EU Member States and a 9th place worldwide in 2020 to an 8th place (EU) and a 15th place (world) in the Transparency International Corruption Perception Index.[145] The work of the *Länder* media authorities and of the self-regulation of the press, good transparency of media ownership, and a legally secured independence of public service broadcasters provide for a

---

[144] SWD(2020) 304 final (30 September 2020) 2 et seq.; SWD(2021) 706 final (20 July 2021) 2; SWD(2022) 505 final (13 July 2022) 3 et seq.; SWD(2023) 805 final (5 July 2023) 3 et seq.; SWD (2024) 805 final (24 July 2024) 3 et seq.; SWD(2025) 905 final (8 July 2025) 3.

[145] SWD(2020) 304 final (30 September 2020) 5; SWD(2025) 905 final (8 July 2025) 7.

healthy media pluralism.[146] The general institutional setup to guarantee a working system of checks and balances is up to the task.[147] However, where the Commission has identified issues and made recommendations, Germany has been slow – at best – to address them.

bb) Justice System

With view to the judiciary, longer-term challenges concern recruitment and digitalisation. While the Commission has noted some progress in the latter case, with extra funding by the Federation and the *Länder*, but variable implementation,[148] the upcoming wave of retirements among judges and prosecutors call for improving the attractiveness of the job. Repeated admonitions by the European Commission to raise the salaries and bring them in line with European standards on resources and remuneration for the justice system have brought little progress.[149] It remains to be seen if referrals made by administrative courts in Thuringia and Schleswig-Holstein to the BVerfG in late 2025 will prove a game-changer.[150]

An issue regarding the independence of judicial institutions has been on the table since the first report of 2020. In a 2019 preliminary ruling, the ECJ found that Germany's public prosecutors were not legally entitled to issue European Arrest Warrants, as they do not qualify as 'issuing judicial authority,' within the meaning of Article 6(1) of Council Framework Decision on the European Arrest Warrant.[151] The reason is that in Germany, prosecutors traditionally are part of the executive. Therefore, they are subordinate to the respective *Land* or federal Ministry of Justice and may be obliged to follow instructions in individual cases (see Sections 146 and 147 GVG). Recommendations by the European Commission to strengthen the independence of public prosecutors against potential political interference have not yet led to any result.[152] A draft bill by the Federal

[146] SWD(2020) 304 final (30 September 2020) 8 et seqq; SWD(2023) 805 final (5 July 2023) 21 et seqq; SWD(2024) 805 final (24 July 2024) 21 et seqq; SWD(2025) 905 final (8 July 2025) 13 et seqq.

[147] SWD(2020) 304 final (30 September 2020) 10 et seqq.

[148] SWD(2020) 304 final (30 September 2020) 4; SWD(2023) 805 final (5 July 2023) 7 et seqq; SWD(2024) 805 final (24 July 2024) 8 et seqq; SWD(2025) 905 final (8 July 2025) 5.

[149] SWD(2020) 304 final (30 September 2020) 4; SWD(2021) 706 final (20 July 2021) 4 et seq.; SWD(2022) 505 final (13 July 2022) 3, 6 et seq.; SWD(2023) 805 final (5 July 2023) 2, 5 et seqq; SWD(2024) 805 final (24 July 2024) 2, 7 et seq.; SWD(2025) 905 final (8 July 2025) 2, 4 et seq.

[150] See N.N., 'Richterbesoldung in Thüringen verfassungswidrig niedrig?' (*Legal Tribune Online*, 6 November 2025) www.lto.de/recht/justiz/j/vg-meiningen-bverfg-vorlage-richterbesoldung-verfassungswidrig-niedrig and N.N., 'Jetzt muss Karlsruhe ran: Richterbesoldung in Schleswig-Holstein verfassungswidrig?' (*beck-aktuell*, 11 November 2025) https://rsw.beck.de/aktuell/daily/meldung/detail/vg-schleswig-bverfg-landesbesoldung-verfassungswidrig

[151] ECJ, Cases C-508/18, C-82/19 *OG (Parquet de Lübeck)* ECLI:C:2019:456.

[152] SWD(2020) 304 final (30 September 2020) 3; SWD(2021) 706 final (20 July 2021) 3; SWD (2022) 505 final (13 July 2022) 4 et seq.; SWD(2023) 805 final (5 July 2023) 4; SWD(2024) 805 final (24 July 2024) 5 et seq.

Ministry of Justice of September 2025 proposes to turn the court competent for issuing the national arrest warrant into the issuing authority under the Framework Directive, on application by the prosecutor's office.[153] While this might elegantly solve the problem with European arrest warrants, it does not address fears of a potential abuse of the subordinate role of the prosecution if political forces take power in one of the German *Länder* that aim to abuse institutions for their own purposes. This danger has also been criticised by the UN Human Rights Council which recommended that Germany 'should consider introducing legal reforms to ensure the independence of prosecutors from the executive branch of the Government, both in law and in practice, therefore reinforcing judicial independence.'[154]

cc) Anti-Corruption Framework

Another concern that has remained unheeded relates to the introduction of a meaningful executive 'footprint' to allow for the monitoring and tracing of all interest representatives who seek to influence and contribute to specific legislative texts. While the provisions of the LobbyRG and the GGO have been amended (see 2. j) aa)), the European Commission still agrees with anti-corruption stakeholders that more should be done.[155] With view to the 'revolving door' issue of high ranking public officials who take up employment in the private sector, some progress was acknowledged after a 2024 amendment to the Federal Civil Service Act extended 'cooling-off' periods and introduced new reporting obligations.[156] Another issue that was resolved concerns the protection of whistleblowers. Here, the new Whistleblower Protection Act of 2023 even went beyond the requirements of the EU Whistleblower Directive.[157] Yet unresolved issues are the monitoring of secondary activities of members of Parliament[158] and asset disclosure rules for members of the Federal Government.[159]

dd) Media Pluralism

With regard to media pluralism, the Commission voiced growing concern about increasing harassment of journalists through physical attacks, online threats,

---

[153] See Section 173 Act on International Mutual Assistance in Criminal Matters (Gesetz über die internationale Rechtshilfe in Strafsachen, IRG), draft bill (*Referentenentwurf*), www.bmjv.de/SharedDocs/Gesetzgebungsverfahren/DE/2025_IRG_Reform.html?nn=110518

[154] UN Human Rights Committee, CCPR/C/DEU/CO/7 (30 November 2021), mn. 40 et seq.

[155] SWD(2023) 805 final (5 July 2023) 2, 16; SWD(2024) 805 final (24 July 2024) 2, 17; SWD (2025) 905 final (8 July 2025) 2, 9 et seq.

[156] SWD(2025) 905 final (8 July 2025) 2, 9 et seq.

[157] SWD(2024) 805 final (24 July 2024) 20 et seq.; For the previous comments and recommendations, see SWD(2020) 304 final (30 September 2020) 8; SWD(2021) 706 final (20 July 2021) 3; SWD(2022) 505 final (13 July 2022) 7 et seqq.

[158] SWD(2023) 805 final (5 July 2023) 17 et seq.; SWD(2024) 805 final (24 July 2024) 18 et seq.

[159] SWD(2023) 805 final (5 July 2023) 18 et seq.; SWD(2024) 805 final (24 July 2024) 19.

privacy invasions, and SLAPP strategies, but also noted that German authorities attempt to counter these developments.[160]

ee) Other Institutional Issues

The Commission continues to remind Germany that a legal basis for a right to information of the press as regards federal authorities is needed. Though the BVerwG has in principle based such a right on the freedom of the press (see 2. j) bb), a more specific regulation should be drafted that takes into account European standards on access to documents.[161]

After a 2019 BFH ruling concerning the criteria for civil society organisations to benefit from tax privileges for non-profit associations with a public benefit purpose,[162] the Commission has repeatedly noted challenges to the operation of these organisations in practice. It recommended Germany to adapt its laws, taking into account European standards on funding for civil society organisations.[163]

Recently, the Commission also criticised growing restrictions of civic space, Germany's Civicus rating having been downgraded from 'open' to 'narrowed' in December 2023.[164] This is mainly due to restrictions on protests, connected with climate change protests and demonstrations against Israel's war in Gaza. As examples, the 2024 Report notes pre-emptive blanket bans on protests, pre-emptive detention against protestors, and, in one case, the targeting of an organisation engaged in acts of civil disobedience (*'Letzte Generation'*) by suspecting them of forming or supporting a criminal organisation. Also, certain techniques used by the police are critically mentioned in this context.

b) Council of Europe Mechanisms

While the Venice Commission for Democracy through Law has only once commented on a piece of German legislation so far,[165] within the broader institutional framework of the Council of Europe it is mostly the ECtHR which provides practical oversight over matters relevant for the rule of law with respect to Ger-

---

[160] SWD(2020) 304 final (30 September 2020) 8 et seqq; SWD(2021) 706 final (20 July 2021) 13 et seqq; SWD(2022) 505 final (13 July 2022) 19 et seq.; SWD(2023) 805 final (5 July 2023) 24 et seq.; SWD(2024) 805 final (24 July 2024) 24 et seq.

[161] SWD(2022) 505 final (13 July 2022) 3; SWD(2023) 805 final (5 July 2023) 2, 23 et seq.; SWD(2024) 805 final, 24.7.2024, 2, 23 et seq.

[162] ECLI:DE:BFH:2019:U.100119.VR60.17.0 (BFHE 263, 290).

[163] SWD(2020) 304 final (30 September 2020) 12; SWD(2021) 706 final (20 July 2021) 17 et seq.; SWD(2022) 505 final (13 July 2022) 3, 24 et seq.; SWD(2023) 805 final (5 July 2023) 2, 27 et seq.; SWD(2024) 805 final (24 July 2024) 2, 28 et seq.; SWD(2025) 905 final (8 July 2025) 2, 18.

[164] SWD(2024) 805 final (24 July 2024) 29.

[165] See Joint opinion of the Venice Commission and OSCE/ODIHR on the amendments of the German Federal Election Act and their compliance with Council of Europe standards, CDL-AD(2023)020 (12 June 2023), criticising a 2023 amendment for lack of a broad cross-party support, but without criticism in substance.

many. Going by population, Germany is among the States with the least number of applications allocated to a judicial formation of the ECtHR,[166] with an overall quota of 0.23 % of the cases pending before the Court in 2024.[167]

One of the most protracted issues which also triggered the only pilot judgment against Germany so far, identifying a structural problem,[168] concerned excessive length of court proceedings in violation of Article 6(1) ECHR. The federal legislator reacted in 2011 by introducing a new objection to delay (*Verzögerungsrüge*), with a subsequent compensation claim to be lodged at the Court of Appeal (Sections 198 ff. GVG, and, by reference, Section 173 cl 2 VwGO), thus ending a decades-long conflict with the ECtHR.[169] Another major criticism concerned the system of preventive detention of former prisoners in which the Court found several violations of Articles 5(1) and 7(1) ECHR.[170] After a thorough reform of that system the problem seems to be solved at last, detention now being subject to additional conditions, having a primarily preventive effect and, unlike punishment, its duration being based solely on the behaviour of the detainee.[171] Occasionally, also preventive police detention in the context of major events has come under the ECtHR's scrutiny,[172] while it continues to be a problem in case of recent climate protests.[173] An issue that has not been fully resolved yet is how to deal with the incitement of crimes by undercover police agents. While the ECtHR has repeatedly found that in such cases, Article 6(1) ECHR demands that criminal proceedings be discontinued and that evidence should be inadmissible,[174] some of the BGH Senates still want to allow proceedings to continue and only to take account of the provocation of the crime by state agents when determining the sentence.[175]

---

166 In 2024, there were 0.05 cases per 10,000 inhabitants from Germany, while the average (without Russia) stood at 0.38 cases. Together with Ireland and the UK, Germany has been consistently among the three Convention States with the least cases per inhabitant, see ECtHR, *Analysis of Statistics 2024* (January 2025) www.echr.coe.int/documents/d/echr/stats-analysis-2024-eng, 15.

167 See ibid 13.

168 *Rumpf v Germany* App no 46344/06 (ECtHR, 2 September 2010) mn. 64 et seqq.

169 *Taron v Germany* App no 53126/07 (ECtHR, 29 May 2012) mn. 37 et seqq.

170 *M. v Germany* App no 19359/04 (ECtHR, 17 December 2009) (retroactive extension of time-limit); *Haidn v Germany* App no 6587/04 (ECtHR, 13 January 2011) (subsequent and reserved order of detention); *H. W. v Germany* App no 17167/11 (ECtHR, 19 September 2013) (continued prevention without medical control).

171 Cf *Bergmann v Germany* App no 23279/14 (ECtHR, 7 January 2016), mn. 103 et seqq., 151 et seqq.

172 *Schwabe and M. G. v Germany* App no 8080/08 and 8577/08 (ECtHR, 1 December 2011): G8 summit.

173 ECLI:DE:VGGE:2022:0810.17K4838.20.00 (VG Gelsenkirchen), with reference to Article 5(1) ECHR. On the conditions in general, see ECLI:DE:BVerfG:2016:rk20160418.2bvr183312 (BVerfG NJW 2016, 2800).

174 *Furcht v Germany* App no 54648/09 (ECtHR, 23 October 2014); *Akbay and Others v Germany* App no 40495/15, 40913/15, and 37273/15 (ECtHR, 15 October 2020).

175 Accepting this practice, ECLI:DE:BVerfG:2014:rk20141218.2bvr020914 (BVerfG NJW 2015, 1083). In this vein, ECLI:DE:BGH:2018:040718U5STR650.17.0 (Fifth Senate); Following the

Germany has deficits in implementing ECtHR judgments, as has been pointed out by the European Commission in the Rule of Law Reports,[176] though slight progress can be noted. From 13 leading judgments pending implementation on 1 January 2022, the number decreased to 7 as of 16 June 2025, the implementation rate increased from 63 % to 71 %. The average time that judgments are pending is between 3 to 4 years, with some judgments pending implementation for up to 7 years.

c) UN Mechanisms

Of the ten UN human rights conventions, Germany has ratified all but the Migrant Workers Convention, including their optional protocols. Thus, it is under a general obligation to submit periodic reports to the respective UN treaty bodies and has submitted to individual complaint procedures under the Conventions against Torture (CAT), on Civil and Political Rights (CCPR), on the Elimination of Discrimination against Women (CEDAW), against Enforced Disappearances (CED), on the Elimination of Racial Discrimination (CERD), on Economic, Social and Cultural Rights (CESCR), on the Rights of the Child (CRC), and the Rights of Persons with Disabilities (CRPD). It has accepted inquiry procedures under CAT, CED, CEDAW, CESCR, CRC, CRPD and the Interstate communication procedure under Article 32 CED. As a member of the Human Rights Council, Germany is also subject to its Universal Periodic Review procedure, the last report having been presented in 2023.[177]

Apart from criticising *Länder* legislation on banning headscarves and religious coverings for teachers and civil servants[178] and the lack of implementation of children's rights in the German legal order,[179] the Human Rights Committee, especially, has voiced concern about recent reports on police violence and a lack of effective investigations in such cases,[180] and has also expressed concerns about an increase of hate speech, including verbal attacks, and online hatred, but also of violent attacks, and recommended to ensure 'that all hate crimes are thoroughly investigated, that perpetrators are prosecuted and punished and that victims are provided with effective remedies.'[181]

ECtHR, BGH, 2 StR 97/14, BGHSt 60, 276 (Second Senate); ECLI:DE:BGH:2021:161221U1 STR197.21.0 (BGH NStZ 2023, 243) (First Senate).

[176] SWD(2022) 505 final (13 July 2022) 23; SWD(2023) 805 final (5 July 2023) 26; SWD(2024) 805 final (24 July 2024) 26 et seq.; SWD(2025) 505 final (8 July 2022) 17 et seq.

[177] See UN Human Rights Council, Report of the Working Group on the Universal Periodic Review: Germany, A/HRC/55/10 (22 December 2023).

[178] UN Committee on the Elimination of Discrimination against Women, CEDAW/C/DEU/CO/9 (31 May 2023), para 44(a); UN Human Rights Committee, CCPR/C/DEU/CO/7 (30 November 2021), mn. 44 et seq.

[179] UN Committee on the Rights of the Child, CRC/C/DEU/CO/5–6 (23 September 2022), mn. 6, 15 et seqq., 20 et seqq., 30 et seqq., 41 et seqq.

[180] UN Human Rights Committee, CCPR/C/DEU/CO/7 (30 November 2021), mn. 26 et seq.

[181] UN Human Rights Committee, CCPR/C/DEU/CO/7 (30 November 2021), mn. 10, 11(d).

II. Germany's Contribution to an International Rule of Law

1. Effectuating International Law within the Domestic Legal System

a) International Treaties and Custom in the German Legal Order

To underline the rejection of the law and policies of the NS era, the Basic Law was deliberately drafted in 1949 for an "open constitutional state" (*offener Verfassungsstaat*),[182] '[i]nspired by the determination to promote world peace as an equal partner in a united Europe' (Preamble).[183] According to Article 25 GG, '[t]he general rules of international law shall be an integral part of federal law. They shall take precedence over the laws and directly create rights and duties for the inhabitants of the federal territory.' While the clause on the rights and duties is inspired by events immediately preceding the drafting of the Basic Law – the Nuremberg Trials and the Universal Declaration of Human Rights –, Article 25 GG not only refers to customary human rights, humanitarian law, and international criminal law, but to international custom and general principles of law in the meaning of Article 38(1) lit b and lit c ICJ Statute in general.[184] Thus, while formally ranking below the Basic Law itself, customary international law and general principles take precedence over federal statutes and, as part of federal law, over the law of the *Länder*, cf Article 31 GG. If the existence of such a general rule of international law is in doubt in a case before a German court, the court has to stay the proceedings and request a decision by the BVerfG, Article 100(2) GG.

The 'automatic' adoption of these 'general rules of international law' into the German legal order in Article 25 GG could lead to the conclusion of a monist stance towards the relationship between international and domestic law. This, however, is not reflected in the jurisprudence of the BVerfG, which maintains that the Basic Law adopts a dualist conception of the relationship between national and international law and does not formally grant precedence to interna-

---

182 On this concept, Klaus Vogel, *Die Verfassungsentscheidung des Grundgesetzes für eine internationale Zusammenarbeit: ein Diskussionsbeitrag zu einer Frage der Staatstheorie sowie des geltenden deutschen Staatsrechts* (Mohr 1964); Stephan Hobe, *Der offene Verfassungsstaat zwischen Souveränität und Interdependenz: eine Studie zur Wandlung des Staatsbegriffs der deutschsprachigen Staatslehre im Kontext internationaler institutionalisierter Kooperation* (Duncker & Humblot 1998).

183 For a contextualisation, see Christian Tomuschat, 'The Concept of International Law: The German Perspective' in Peter Hilpold (ed) *European International Law Traditions* (Springer 2021) 19 (28 et seq.).

184 On Article 25, see Tomuschat (n. 183) 29 et seqq; see also, more generally, Rüdiger Wolfrum, Holger Hestermeyer, and Silja Vöneky, 'The reception of international law in the German legal order: An introduction' in Erika de Wet, Holger Hestermeyer, and Rüdiger Wolfrum (eds.) *The Implementation of International Law in Germany and South Africa* (Pretoria University Law Press 2015), 2 et seqq; Andreas von Arnauld, 'Germany', in Anne van Aaken, Pierre d'Argent, Lauri Mälksoo, and Johann Justus Vasel (eds.), *The Oxford Handbook of International Law in Europe* (OUP 2025) 587 (589 et seqq.).

tional law.[185] Therefore, treaties which are binding on Germany internationally only become part of the German legal order when they are adopted by a domestic regulation. Article 59(2) stipulates in this regard: 'Treaties that regulate the political relations of the Federation or relate to subjects of federal legislation shall require the consent or participation, in the form of a federal law, of the bodies responsible in such a case for the enactment of federal law.' While the term 'political relations' had been understood rather restrictively in the early years of the Basic Law,[186] most of the important international treaties concluded by Germany – in the fields of human rights and humanitarian law, in environmental and economic matters and many more – have entered the German legal order by way of consenting federal legislation. As such, they rank on the same level as federal statutes.

That this opens up the possibility to 'override' treaty obligations by way of counter-legislation, has been expressly acknowledged by the BVerfG in a 2015 decision.[187] The main reason behind this is that the *Bundestag* can only assent to the ratification of a treaty concluded by the Government, whereas the suspension or renunciation of a treaty lies solely with the Government. However, such a 'treaty override' has to be explicit. So there is no implicit repeal, but rather a general assumption that parliament does not intend to legislate against Germany's international obligations; furthermore, the Court made an exception for human rights treaties with their quasi-constitutional status (see below).

As a general rule, an international treaty ranks on the same level as the law or statutory instrument that adopts it into the domestic legal order. If no such adoption has taken place, the respective treaty is without binding force within Germany. Thus, in theory, international obligations could be ignored by German authorities if they have not become part of German law or if they are in conflict with rules and principles of a higher normative rank domestically.

b) 'Moderate Dualism' through Völkerrechtsfreundlichkeit

The BVerfG, however, seeks to avoid such harsh consequences. In a holistic interpretation of the Basic Law, it has proclaimed a constitutional principle of *Völkerrechtsfreundlichkeit* ('openness towards international law')[188] which helps to overcome problems of direct applicability and hierarchy of norms. Therefore, a treaty that has not become part of the German legal order – such as the 1972 UNESCO

---

[185] ECLI:DE:BVerfG:2004:rs20041014.2bvr148104 (BVerfGE 111, 307 [318]) *Görgülü*, with further references.

[186] BVerfG, 2 BvE 2/51, BVerfGE 1, 372 (380 et seqq.) *Deutsch-Französisches Wirtschaftsabkommen.*

[187] ECLI:DE:BVerfG:2015:ls20151215.2bvl000112 (BVerfGE 141, 1, 26, head notes nos 3–5) *Treaty override.*

[188] In more depth, Mehrdad Payandeh 'Völkerrechtsfreundlichkeit als Verfassungsprinzip – Ein Beitrag des Grundgesetzes zur Einheit von Völkerrecht und nationalem Recht' (2009) 57 Jahrbuch des öffentlichen Rechts der Gegenwart 465.

World Heritage Convention – nevertheless has to be taken into account when making decisions relevant to such a treaty.[189] Furthermore, the constitutional duty to interpret domestic law in conformity with international law allows to align the whole body of national law to Germany's international legal obligations.[190] Thus, the underlying constitutional concept is usually termed as 'moderate dualism' (*gemäßigter Dualismus*).[191]

This alignment by interpretation is especially marked with view to human rights treaties, most importantly the ECHR.[192] Formally ranking as a simple federal statute, the Convention has been constitutionalised by the BVerfG in three steps: (1) It has *de facto* precedence over other federal statutes due to the (in theory: rebuttable) presumption that the legislator did not intend to deviate from the obligations under the ECHR. (2) Based on Articles 1(2) and 59(2) GG, its guarantees have to be taken into account when interpreting the respective provisions of the Basic Law, especially its fundamental rights. (3) The same applies to judgments of the ECtHR which are only to be disregarded where the inherent limits of interpretation are reached, or if they should be incompatible with fundamental tenets of the Basic Law.[193] The latter rule is based on a 'factual orientation and guidance function' of ECtHR decisions and includes not only judgments binding upon Germany but also judgments against other Convention States where applicable.[194] Occasionally, the BVerfG has also taken non-binding international human rights standards into account, if only as indicating a violation of Basic Law guarantees if these have been disregarded.[195]

c) Limits to 'Friendliness'

The concept of the "open constitutional state" as developed by the BVerfG is ambivalent, though, since it is hinged on the idea of sovereign statehood. Accord-

---

189 OVG Sachsen DÖV 2007, 564; ECLI:DE:BVerfG:2007:rk20070529.2bvr069507 (BVerfG NVwZ 2007, 1176) *Waldschlösschenbrücke*, mn. 10, 34 et seq.

190 Cf only, ECLI:DE:BVerfG:2004:rs20041014.2bvr148104 (BVerfGE 111, 307 [316 et seqq.]) *Görgülü*.

191 Andreas von Arnauld, *Völkerrecht* (5th ed., CF Müller 2023) mn. 524 et seqq.

192 On cases involving other human rights treaties, see ECLI:DE:BVerfG:2019:cs20190129.2bvc006214 (BVerfGE 151, 1 [26 et seqq.]) *Wahlrechtsausschluss*; ECLI:DE:BVerfG:2021:rs20211216.1bvr154120 (BVerfGE 160, 79 [115 et seqq.]) *Triage I*, both applying the UN Convention on the Rights of Persons with Disabilities.

193 ECLI:DE:BVerfG:2004:rs20041014.2bvr148104 (BVerfGE 111, 307 [315 et seqq.]) *Görgülü*.

194 ECLI:DE:BVerfG:2011:rs20110504.2bvr236509 (BVerfGE 128, 326 [368 f.]) *EGMR Sicherungsverwahrung*; In such a case, it is necessary to contextualise the respective judgments to establish inhowfar they are applicable also to the problem at hand under German law: ECLI:DE:BVerfG:2018:rs20180612.2bvr173812 (BVerfGE 148, 296 [354]) *Streikverbot für Beamte*.

195 ECLI:DE:BVerfG:2006:rs20060531.2bvr167304 (BVerfGE 116, 69 [90 f.]) *Jugendstrafvollzug*; on this, see Katharina Reiling 'Die Anwendung des Grundsatzes der Völkerrechtsfreundlichkeit auf rechtsunverbindliche internationale Standards' (2018) 78 Zeitschrift für ausländisches öffentliches Recht und Völkerrecht/Heidelberg Journal of International Law (ZaöRV/HJIL) 311.

ing to the Court, '[t]he openness to international law of the Basic Law is […] the expression of an understanding of sovereignty which is not only not in conflict with an integration into international and supranational contexts and their further development, but actively presumes and expects them. Against this background, even the "last word" of the German constitution is not opposed to an international and European dialogue of courts, but is the normative basis for this.'[196] Thus, sovereignty serves both as the basis for and as limitation to international and European integration.

In recent years, the BVerfG has been involved in battles over "last words".[197] With the ECtHR, the battle was mainly fought over balancing privacy rights of celebrities with the freedom of the press.[198] More openly confrontational has been the relationship with the ECJ. In May 2020, the BVerfG for the first time declared an EU legal act as *ultra vires* and attested the ECJ's judgment on this matter to be 'not comprehensible' and 'arbitrary from an objective perspective.'[199] While, in general, acknowledging the principles of supremacy and direct effect of EU law as part and parcel of an EU membership, in its 2009 judgment on the compatibility of the ratification of the Treaty of Lisbon with the Basic Law the BVerfG made it especially clear that it views the EU Treaties as nothing more than international treaties,[200] thus challenging the ECJ's claim of a legal order *sui generis*.[201]

Even though individual decisions and arguments can be justly criticised, it is more than just parochial instinct or vanity that moves the BVerfG. Mainly, it is the concern that growing competences on the side of the EU are out of synch with democratic legitimacy and human rights protection. While the Second Senate's take on pluri-level democracy does have a parochial tinge, its insistence on an effective protection of fundamental rights in the 'Solange I' judgment of 1974,[202] has pushed the ECJ to develop its fundamental rights jurisprudence. And with the 'Solange II' reversal in 1986,[203] it accepted the ECJ's precedence in principle, while reserving a right to apply the Basic Law when reviewing acts of German public authorities implementing EU law, as far as these acts are not fully determined by Union law.[204] After a phase of some irritation, the First Senate has consolidated the framework of cooperation with the ECJ in 2019 in two decisions

---

196 ECLI:DE:BVerfG:2011:rs20110504.2bvr236509 (BVerfGE 128, 326 [369]) *EGMR Sicherungsverwahrung*.

197 Tomuschat (n. 183) 45.

198 ECLI:DE:BVerfG:1999:rs19991215.1bvr065396 (BVerfGE 101, 361) *Caroline von Monaco II*; *von Hannover v Germany* App no 59320/00 (ECtHR, 24 June 2004).

199 ECLI:DE:BVerfG:2020:rs20200505.2bvr085915 (BVerfGE 154, 17) *PSPP*, headnote 2.

200 ECLI:DE:BVerfG:2009:es20090630.2bve000208 (BVerfGE 123, 267) *Lissabon*.

201 Cf ECJ, Case 6/64 *Costa v ENEL* [1964] ECR 585, ECLI:EU:C:1964:66.

202 BVerfG, 2 BvL 52/71, BVerfGE 37, 271 *Solange I*.

203 BVerfG, 2 BvR 197/83, BVerfGE 73, 339 *Solange II*.

204 ECLI:DE:BVerfG:2010:rs20100302.1bvr025608 (BVerfGE 125, 260 [306 f.]) *Vorratsdatenspeicherung*.

on the 'right to be forgotten:'[205] While in matters fully determined by EU law, the BVerfG will apply only the EU's CFR (and eventually refer to the ECJ for decisions on interpretation), in matters not fully determined by EU law it will continue to apply the Basic Law – if it is not established in a given case that either the EU legislator deliberately referred to a harmonised fundamental rights standard or the CFR should provide a higher level of protection than the Basic Law.

d) International Law in German Court Practice

Since about twenty or so years, the BVerfG, in particular, has upheld a constitutional obligation of the regular courts to take into account the relevant international rules and standards and to use them as a guidance for interpreting German laws and the Basic Law, even where they might not be applicable *sensu strictu*. Through this, international law has become more and more important for the practice of German courts.[206] For a long time, whether international law was being applied depended on a number of factors, 'inter alia on specialization, express reference or on a more or less aleatory "awareness by contact".'[207] While German judges can still not be considered true "internationalists", through the guidance by the BVerfG, especially, as well as through the inclusion of international legal obligations in commentaries on German laws and statutes, which seems now to be the standard (to a greater or lesser degree, depending on the editors), the situation is markedly better. The practical importance that international law in general, and the ECHR in particular, have for the everyday legal practice makes it all the more regrettable that the German law school syllabus (defined centrally by the ministers of justice of the Federation and the *Länder*) is still all-too introvert.[208] No specific training on international law and its relevance for the everyday practice of law exists in Germany.

Another, more recent, encounter with international law has been provoked by instances of strategic public interest litigation. Prominent examples are claims brought against the government or private companies in the context of climate

---

205 ECLI:DE:BVerfG:2019:rs20191106.1bvr001613 (BVerfGE 152, 152) *Recht auf Vergessen I*; ECLI:DE:BVerfG:2019:rs20191106.1bvr027617 (BVerfGE 152, 216) *Recht auf Vergessen II*.

206 A query in the 'International Law' section of the jurisprudence database *juris*, adjusted for decisions of international or foreign courts, yields the following numbers of hits: 1950–59: 34; 1960–69: 128; 1970–79: 265; 1980–89: 362; after reunification (which was accompanied by a rise in the number of courts): 1990–99: 631; 2000–10: 900; 2010–19: 2004; 2020–25: 1049.

207 Andreas von Arnauld 'Public International Law and the Role of Federal Courts in Germany' in Christian Tomuschat and Joe Verhoven (eds.), *Les pratiques comparées du droit international en France et en Allemagne* (Pedone 2011), 12 (24).

208 For a critical assessment, see Wissenschaftsrat ([German] Council of Science and Humanities), *Prospects of Legal Scholarship in Germany: Current Situation, Analyses, Recommendations* (2012), English translation www.wissenschaftsrat.de/download/archiv/2558- 12_ engl.pdf.

change,[209] claims concerning the export of arms and military material to Israel during the Gaza war,[210] or challenging the US drone war in Yemen by going against the use of a German Air Base.[211] Such claims have been made possible in substance by judgments, especially from the BVerfG, confirming extraterritorial fundamental rights obligations of the German State, including positive obligations.[212] Procedurally, however, court proceedings in Germany are party-driven and serve to effectuate individual rights. Thus, NGOs cannot bring claims in their own name,[213] nor can they serve as *amicus curiae*, as the institute is unknown to German law. Instead, they offer their services for potential claimants in model cases, mostly *pro bono*, and are often involved in the 'casting' of the claimants themselves. The most active of these NGOs in Germany so far has been the European Center for Constitutional and Human Rights (ECCHR), based in Berlin.

As the recent cases of arms exports and the Federal Government's obligations with regard to the US drone programme show, there are limits to judicial oversight when it comes to matters of foreign policy. BVerfG and BVerwG generally apply a restricted standard of judicial review here. Though there is no political questions doctrine, the review standard is defined by recourse to executive discretion and margins of appreciation.[214] Not fully convincingly,[215] the BVerfG accords some leeway to the Federal Government also in the interpretation of international law and the assessment of the legality of their own and their partner nation's actions: Their legal view 'must be carefully considered insofar as that legal view proves to be tenable.'[216] Full judicial review, however, is conducted with view to external operations of executive organs below the "political" level.[217]

[209] ECLI:DE:BVerfG:2021:rs20210324.1bvr265618 (BVerfGE 157, 30) *Klimaschutz*; ECLI:DE:OVGBEBB:2024:0516.11A22.21.00 (OVG Berlin-Brandenburg); ECLI:DE:OLGHAM:2025:0528.5U15 (OLG Hamm NJW 2025, 2171).

[210] ECLI:DE:VGBE:2024:0610.4L44.24.00; ECLI:DE:VGBE:2025:1112.4K45.24.00 (both, VG Berlin); on this, see Moritz Rhades, 'Von Waffen wissen müssen' (*Verfassungsblog*, 20 June 2024) https://verfassungsblog.de/waffenexporte-gericht-israel/

[211] ECLI:DE:OVGNRW:2019:0319.4A1361.15.00 (OVG Nordrhein-Westfalen, NJW 1919, 1898); ECLI:DE:BVerwG:2020:251120U6C7.19.0 (BVerwGE 170, 345); ECLI:DE:BVerfG:2025:rs20250715.2bvr050821 (BVerfG, NJW 2025, 3560) *Drohneneinsatz Ramstein*.

[212] See, eg ECLI:DE:BVerfG:2020:rs20200519.1bvr283517 (BVerfGE 154, 152) on extraterritorial surveillance of telecommunication.

[213] With the exception of recognised nature conservation associations under Section 64 Federal Natural Protection Act (*Bundesnaturschutzgesetz*, BNatSchG), as introduced in implementation of EU directives.

[214] Cf, eg, ECLI:DE:BVerwG:2020:251120U6C7.19.0 (BVerwGE 170, 345), headnotes 3 et seq.

[215] Critical for valid reasons, Sebastian Runschke, *Außenpolitik und Völkerrecht. Zum internationalisierten Rechtsschutzauftrag deutscher Gerichte* (Springer 2024).

[216] ECLI:DE:BVerfG:2025:rs20250715.2bvr050821 (BVerfG, NJW 2025, 3560), headnote 2 lit. e.

[217] ECLI:DE:BVerfG:2020:rs20200519.1bvr283517 (BVerfGE 154, 152): extraterritorial bulk surveillance programme; BVerfG, 18 November 2020, ECLI:DE:BVerfG:2020:rk20201118.2bvr047717 (BVerfG NJW 2021, 2108) *Kunduz*: actions of German armed forces abroad.

e) Enforcing International and Foreign Decisions in Germany

The general rule that judgments by international courts which are binding upon Germany must be respected and implemented within the domestic legal order has, at least in principle, never been in dispute.[218] However, the means of implementation have been less clear for considerable time. With view to judgments of the ECtHR, a new Section 359 No 6 StPO was introduced in 1998, according to which the reopening of proceedings concluded by a final judgment is admissible for the convicted person's benefit, 'if the European Court of Human Rights has held that there has been a violation of the European Convention on the Protection of Human Rights and Fundamental Freedoms or of its Protocols and the judgment was based on that violation.' Similarly, since 2006, according to Section 580 No 8 Code of Civil Procedure (*Zivilprozessordnung*, ZPO) an action for retrial of the case may be brought under the same conditions in civil cases. By explicit reference, this also applies in proceedings before labour courts (Section 79 ArbGG), fiscal courts (Section 134 FGO), and social courts (Section 179(1) SGG), as well as in general administrative court proceedings (Section 153(1) VwGO).

Foreign judgments from non-EU countries[219] have to undergo a two-step procedure before German courts to ensure their enforcement: recognition (Sections 328 ff. ZPO, here incompatibility with Germany's *ordre public* might be argued) and enforcement (Sections 722 ff. ZPO); for foreign arbitral awards similar rules apply according to Section 1061 ZPO in connection with the 1958 United Nations Convention on the Recognition and Enforcement of Foreign Arbitral Awards (New York Convention). For arbitral awards under the ICSID Agreement, the 1969 Act on the Convention of 18 March 1965 on the Settlement of Investment Disputes between States and Nationals of Other States prescribes an abbreviated procedure in which, especially, *ordre public* objections are precluded.

Concerning cooperation in criminal matters – independently whether such cooperation is treaty-based or conducted *ad hoc* –, the Act on International Mutual Assistance in Criminal Matters (*Gesetz über die internationale Rechtshilfe in Strafsachen*, IRG) is comprehensively dealing with questions of extradition, enforcement of foreign judgments, and other forms of mutual assistance. Especially due to adaptations to newer developments concerning the European Arrest Warrant it is under general review at the moment.[220]

The implementation of decisions by international organisations, finally, is constitutionally based on Article 24 GG. This allows for the integration into the international society of states by accession to international organisations (para

[218] Cf ECLI:DE:BVerfG:2004:rs20041014.2bvr148104 (BVerfGE 111, 307 [319 et seqq., 323 et seqq.]) *Görgülü*.

[219] For judgments from other EU Member States, the Regulation (EU) No 1215/2012 of 12 December 2012 on jurisdiction and the recognition and enforcement of judgments [2012] OJ L351/1 applies.

[220] See draft bill (*Referentenentwurf*) (n. 153).

1) and to join alliances of collective security (para 2). On the basis of Article 24(2), the Federal Republic joined NATO (1950), and UNO (1973), on the basis of Article 24(1), among many others, the Council of Europe (1950). Article 24(1) also formed the constitutional basis for the European integration. Its unprecedented dynamic, however, made more specific rules necessary which were introduced in the wake of the Maastricht Treaty in 1993 in a revised Article 23 GG.[221] Based on either Article 23 or 24 GG (in connection with the law consenting to the respective constituent treaty under Article 59(2) GG), binding decisions by international and supranational organisations to which Germany is a member will be implemented via the competent authorities – e. g., in the case of financial sanctions, through the Federal Financial Supervisory Authority. In theory, the implementation of any such decision could be challenged before German courts if it arguably violates individual rights. With a working cooperation framework between BVerfG and ECJ in place with regard to the protection of fundamental rights and the ECJ's jurisprudence on UN sanctions since *Kadi* now firmly established, there are hardly any practical instances of "judicial disobedience" today. Where Germany tends to be rather slow, however, is in implementing EU directives.

2. Germany's Positions on Selected Issues of an International Rule of Law

a) Championing Multilateralism and the Rule of Law

For a long time, Germany has taken pride in being a champion of multilateralism and international law.[222] Germany is a member to some 120 international organisations, among them UNO, EU, COE, OECD, NATO, WTO, and has ratified innumerable international treaties.[223] It has also submitted to extensive external monitoring. Apart from the ECJ (as an EU Member State), the ECtHR, and virtually every UN human rights body, Germany has opted, under Part XV UNCLOS, for the jurisdiction of the International Tribunal for the Law of the Sea, residing in Hamburg, Germany. Furthermore, it has been a champion and sponsor of the International Criminal Court since the early drafting stages of the Rome Statute.[224] To make the crimes in the Statute punishable offences under German law, the federal legislator enacted a Code of Crimes against International Law (*Völkerstrafgesetzbuch*). Regarding the ICJ, Germany submitted generally to its jurisdiction under Article 36(2) ICJ Statute in 2008. The declaration at this point was limited only – apart from the usual clauses on non-retroactivity and

---

[221] For details, Tomuschat (n. 183) 39 et seqq.

[222] For further detail, see von Arnauld (n. 184) 593 et seqq.

[223] The Foreign Office keeps no record of the number of treaties: Deutscher Bundestag, Wissenschaftliche Dienste, *Sachstand: Ratifikation völkerrechtlicher Verträge*, WD 2 – 3000 – 062/15 (27 March 2015) 4.

[224] Cf www.auswaertiges-amt.de/en/aussenpolitik/themen/internatrecht/hintergrund-node

reciprocity – by excluding matters concerning the deployment of Germany's armed forces abroad and the use of its territory for military purposes by others. By commitment and performance, Germany thus can boast a good track record in upholding the international rule of law. For decades, practically all Federal Governments, irrespective of the party coalition in power, have consistently turned to international law as a determining factor for German foreign policy.

Germany has also been active for a long time in promoting the rule of law internationally. Germany has contributed to post-conflict peacebuilding in Kosovo, Bosnia, and Afghanistan, especially. Its contributions involved significant support for security sector reform, governance, economic development, and institution-building. Mostly, this was achieved in the context of international missions (like KFOR/EULEX), but also through bilateral aid. In July 2019, the Federal Government for the first time published an official strategy on promoting the rule of law in the fields of crisis prevention, conflict resolution and peacebuilding.[225] It commits to a dialogue-centred and context-sensitive promotion of the rule of law by assisting states in building and improving structures and procedures of state institutions, supporting legal reforms, strengthening the judicial system and its independence, binding the administration to the law, and supporting political participation and constructive relations between the state and society on the one hand;[226] on the other, it aims at strengthening international jurisdictions, including especially the ICC, and at supporting of the formulation of rules and standards on the global as well as on the regional level.[227]

Germany's foreign policy choices have often been guided by a value-oriented understanding of international law in which human rights and democracy play an important role.

b) Military Engagement

Germany so far has only once participated in a military humanitarian intervention, namely in the 1999 NATO mission in Kosovo. This was preceded by a controversial debate within the then coalition government of SPD and Greens, and especially within the Green Party of Foreign Minister Joschka Fischer. Though lacking a mandate from the UN Security Council, the operation was deemed necessary as Germany had received reports about alleged genocidal military strategies on the side of Serbia.[228] After the terrorist attacks of September 11, 2001,

---

225 Strategy of the Federal Government for promoting the rule of law in the fields of crisis prevention, conflict resolution and peacebuilding, https://peacelab.blog/uploads/Rechtsstaatsfo%CC%88rderung-EN-WEB.pdf

226 Ibid 20 et seqq.

227 Ibid 24 et seqq.

228 Notwithstanding widespread violations of humanitarian law, these reports later proved unreliable, cf UK House of Commons, Session 1999–2000, Select Committee on Foreign Affairs Fourth Report, mn. 93 et seqq.

Germany gave political support to the USA as its close ally, but did not join the military operations against Afghanistan. Only after the defeat of the Taliban, Germany got engaged: through good offices for the constitution-making process, and by sending German armed forces for the UN-backed ISAF mandate. The most extensive engagement of German armed forces abroad yet, ISAF was replaced from 2015 to 2021 by the mission 'Resolute Support,' where Germany contributed mostly through training of and advice to Afghan officers and institutions. Given a widespread opinion among the German population that the 2003 invasion of Iraq by a "coalition of the willing" under US and UK leadership was illegal, the German Federal Government refused to participate in the war. In fact, Chancellor Gerhard Schröder had campaigned for re-election in 2002 with the promise that Germany would not contribute to a military operation without a UN mandate.[229] However, as a close ally of the USA, Germany indirectly supported the war efforts by, inter alia, substituting for US personnel in guarding US military bases and establishments in Germany, or by military cooperation on a technical and on intelligence level.[230] While its critical stance was clear, the Federal Government also refrained from explicitly calling the invasion illegal.[231]

When, in February 2011, the UN Security Council authorised the use of military force for the protection of civilians in the civil war in Libya with its Resolution 1973 (2011), taking up the concept of a 'responsibility to protect' (R2P), Germany as a non-permanent member of the Council, to the surprise of many, abstained in the vote. This hints at a cautious position of Germany to the R2P which has been treated as a principle 'in the making' rather than part of the international *lex lata*.[232] While supportive of the idea of sovereignty as responsibility and the cooperative aspects of the concept, Germany has been reluctant to embrace its more interventionist elements and is tying the concept to the multilateral framework of the 2005 World Summit Outcome.[233]

More ambivalent was Germany's position in the context of the civil war in Syria, however. Here, Germany participated in the Western coalition fighting the so-called 'Islamic State' in Syria (ISIS). Rather than subscribing to the problematic standard of 'unwilling or unable'[234] promoted by the USA, Germany pre-

---

229 See N.N., 'A German View of the Iraq War' (*Voice of America*, 12 December 2003) www.voanews.com/a/a-13-a-2003-12-12-33-1-67593822/289336.html

230 On the ambiguous position of the German government at the time, see Matthias Herdegen and Thilo Rensmann, 'Is There a Specific German Approach to the Prohibition of the Use of Force?' (2007) 50 German Yearbook of International Law (GYIL) 349 (372 et seq.).

231 Tomuschat (n. 183) 48, with further references.

232 Sarah Brockmeier, 'The future of Germany's support to the Responsibility to Protect' in Doutje Lettinga and Lars van Troost (eds.), *Shifting Power and Human Rights Diplomacy: Germany* (Amnesty International Netherlands 2016), 73 (74 et seqq.).

233 See Statement of Germany in the UN General Assembly Debate, 'Responsibility to Protect and the Prevention of Genocide, War Crimes, Ethnic Cleansing and Crimes Against Humanity' (30 June 2023), https://new-york-un.diplo.de/un-en/2604620-2604620

234 For a thorough critique, see Dire Tladi, 'The Nonconsenting Innocent State: The Problem with Bethlehem's Principle' (2013) 107 American Journal of International Law 570; Paulina Stars-

ferred to base its contribution on a combination of two half-convincing arguments: collective self-defence for France, and the ambiguous[235] Security Council Resolution 2249 (2015).[236] After the defeat of ISIS, German troops remained deployed on Syrian territory until April 2022, arguably to fight underground networks working towards a return of ISIS to power in parts of Syria.[237] Concerning the US- and UK-led airstrikes against Syria after the use of chemical weapons in 2017 and 2018, the Federal Government in office at the time called these 'understandable' and 'necessary and appropriate,'[238] thus deliberately eschewing the language of international law, given the at best shaky legal basis for these strikes.[239]

While Germany's position on question of the *jus ad bellum* might not always have lived up to its professed creed, it takes its own obligations under the *jus in bello* serious. As German soldiers are usually rarely directly involved in combat, an incident in Kunduz (Afghanistan) on 4 September 2009 had caused quite a stir. Here, a German commander on the ground had ordered the dropping of bombs on two petroleum tankers hijacked by the Taliban, resulting in the deaths of an indeterminable number of people.[240] The incident triggered a flood of criminal, civil and administrative court cases in Germany which, in the end, absolved the responsible officers from any legal responsibility. In a judgment of 16 February 2021, the ECtHR found that Germany had fulfilled all positive obligations under Article 2 ECHR to investigate the case.[241]

c) Recognition of States and Governments

In perfect conformity with international law, Germany has never recognised the Turkish Republic of Northern Cyprus nor any of the proto-states created by Rus-

---

ki, 'Right to Self-Defense, Attribution and the Non-State Actor – Birth of the "Unable or Unwilling" Standard?' (2015) 75 ZaöRV/HJIL 455; Olivier Corten, 'The "Unwilling or Unable" Test: Has it Been, and Could it be, Accepted?' (2016) 29 Leiden Journal of International Law 777.

[235] See Dapo Akande and Marko Milanovic, 'The Constructive Ambiguity of the Security Council's ISIS Resolution' (*EJIL:Talk!*, 21 November 2015) www.ejiltalk.org/the-constructive-ambiguity-of-the-security-councils-isis-resolution/

[236] For a critique, see von Arnauld (n. 191) mn. 1135; Mehrdad Payandeh and Heiko Sauer, 'Die Beteiligung der Bundeswehr am Antiterroreinsatz in Syrien: Völker- und Verfassungsrechtliche Rahmenbedingungen' [2016] Zeitschrift für Rechtspolitik 34.

[237] Cf Stefan Talmon, 'German Government on foreign troop presence in Syria' (*German Practice in International Law (GPIL)*, 17 February 2020) https://gpil.jura.uni-bonn.de/2020/02/german-government-on-foreign-troop-presence-in-syria/

[238] For a critical discussion, see Helmut Philipp Aust and Mehrdad Payandeh, 'German Practice with regard to the Use of Force in Syria' (2019) 61 GYIL 451.

[239] See Marko Milanovic, 'The Clearly Illegal US Missile Strike in Syria' (*EJIL:Talk!*, 7 April 2017) www.ejiltalk.org/the-clearly-illegal-us-missile-strike-in-syria/; 'The Syria Strikes: Still Clearly Illegal' (*EJIL:Talk!*, 15 April 2018) www.ejiltalk.org/the-syria-strikes-still-clearly-illegal/

[240] On this incident, see Emma J. Marchant, 'Insufficient Knowledge in Kunduz: The Precautionary Principle and International Humanitarian Law' (2020) *25* Journal of Conflict and Security Law *53*.

[241] *Hanan v Germany* App no 4871/16 (ECtHR, 16 February 2021).

sia in her 'near abroad' (Abkhazia, South Ossetia, Transnistria, Donezk, Luhansk, etc). Under the impression of bloodshed in the civil wars on the West Balkan, it was, however, in the 1990s among the first states to recognise the independence of Slovenia and Croatia, and in 2008 the independence of Kosovo. That Germany still doubts that Palestine is a state under international law is most certainly motivated by the special relationship with Israel (see e) below).

Where two opposing factions claim to be the government of another State, Germany tends to favour legitimacy over legality, if the 'legitimate' contender (from the German perspective) is powerful enough to challenge the incumbent. Thus, Germany was fast in recognising the 'Majdan' government in Ukraine in 2014 and recognised Juan Gaidó as President *ad interim* of Venezuela when there seemed to be a realistic chance for him to win the fight against Nicolás Maduro in early 2019.[242] In the case of Syria, Germany treated Bashar al-Assad as Syrian President until his overthrow in December 2024, but recognised the combined forces of the opposition as 'legitimate representatives of the Syrian people' in 2012.[243] These cases are exceptional since, in general, Germany has no established practice of recognising governments. Usually, the Federal Government will deal with the effective government without express recognition or de-recognition and address questions of legitimacy by criticising human rights violations, election fraud, etc.

d) Sanctioning Serious Breaches of International Law

Germany for a long time already has actively participated in sanctions addressing serious breaches of international law, most notably as an EU (and before that: EEC) Member State. Thus, it was already engaged in the suspension of the Association Agreement with Greece (1969) and the suspension of the Lomé I Convention with Uganda (1977), the Central African Republic (1979), and Liberia (1980), in reaction to military coups d'état and ensuing human rights violations.[244] During the Kosovo conflict in 1998 and 1999, especially, it took part in the EU's asset freeze, investment ban and flight ban against the Federal Republic of Yugoslavia in 1999.[245] Since 2014, finally it has implemented the several packages of sanctions reacting to the Russian aggression against Ukraine.[246] While, in general, Ger-

---

[242] See Wissenschaftliche Dienste des Deutschen Bundestages, Rechtsfragen zur Anerkennung des Interimspräsidenten in Venezuela, WD 2–3000–017/19 (15 February 2019).

[243] Pierre Thielbörger, 'Die Anerkennung oppositioneller Gruppen in den Fällen Libyen (2011) und Syrien (2012)' [2013] Humanitäres Völkerrecht – Informationsschriften 34; Isabelle Haßfurther, 'Transforming the "International Unsociety": Towards Eutopia by Menas of International Recognition of Peoples' Representatives' (2017) 60 GYIL 451.

[244] Martin Dawidowicz, *Third-Party Countermeasures in International Law* (OUP 2017), 118 f., 121 et seqq., 124 et seqq., 127.

[245] Ibid 185 et seqq.

[246] For an up-to-date overview, see www.consilium.europa.eu/en/policies/sanctions-against-russia/

many plays by the rules in keeping with the EU scheme, after the invasion of Ukraine on 24 February 2022, Germany was slow in suspending its controversial Nord Stream 2 pipeline project with Russia[247] and somewhat reluctant to broaden the scope of the cut-off of Russian financial institutions from the SWIFT payment system by the EU, at least in the early stages of the conflict.

e) Exceptions to the Rule: National Interests and Special Relations

The last example already shows that there are some exceptions to the rule (and, thus, to the rule of law) which can be explained by national interests, primarily economic, and special relations.[248] The traditionally close links with the USA have been put under heavy strain by the open disdain for international law, multilateralism, and NATO partnership shown by the second Trump Administration. While Chancellor Friedrich Merz and Foreign Minister Johann Wadephul called the invasion of Venezuela and the arrest and kidnapping of President Maduro in January 2026 'legally complex', with 'various things that we need to take into account', more principled opposition has been shown in countering US plans to invade and annex Greenland as a part of another NATO partner, Denmark.[249]

While in the case of the USA, some caution might be attributed to attempts not to irritate the unpredictable and ill-tempered ruler in the White House, it is Germany's special relations with Israel that are capable of ruining Germany's reputation and self-conception of a champion of the international rule of law. Already in 2008, then-Chancellor Angela Merkel, in a speech before the Knesset, called Israel's security a 'reason of state' (*Staatsräson*) for Germany; fifteen years later, after the horrific Hamas attack on Israel of 7 October 2023, then-Chancellor Olaf Scholz repeated these words and added that: 'There is only one place for Germany to stand now: next to Israel.' His Foreign Minister, Annalena Baerbock, promised 'unconditional solidarity' with Israel.[250]

Even when it became evident that Israel went far beyond any conceivable limits of self-defence under international law, Germany was hesitant in criticising Israel and even announced to intervene under Article 63 ICJ Statute on Israel's side in the proceedings instituted by South Africa.[251] The Press Spokesperson of the Federal Government declared on this occasion: 'We know that different countries

247 Bjorn Gens, 'Germany's Russia policy and geo-economics: Nord Stream 2, sanctions and the question of EU leadership towards Russia' (2019) 5 Global Affairs 315.

248 In more detail, von Arnauld (n. 184) 596 et seqq.

249 Jörg Luyken, 'Silence on Venezuela – a wise strategy?' (*The German Review*, 7 January 2026) www.thegermanreview.de/p/silence-on-venezuela-a-wise-strategy

250 Zafer Meşe, 'What's behind Germany's Unconditional Support for Israel?' (*Politics Today*, 19 February 2024) https://politicstoday.org/whats-behind-germanys-unconditional-support-for-israel/

251 Federal Government, Press Release No. 10 (12 January 2024) www.bundesregierung.de/breg-de/service/archiv-bundesregierung/erklaerung-der-bundesregierung-zur-verhandlung-am-internationalen-gerichtshof-2252842

have different views on Israel's operation in the Gaza Strip. However, the German government firmly and unequivocally rejects the accusation of genocide now being brought against Israel before the International Court of Justice. This accusation is completely unfounded.' While such an intervention has not taken place so far, the fact that Germany in the case of Israel argues a narrow construction of the UN Genocide Convention, is in flagrant contradiction with its intervention (jointly with Canada, Denmark, France, the Netherlands and the United Kingdom) of 15 November 2023 in the proceedings between The Gambia and Myanmar concerning the fate of the Rohingya.[252] To be fair, the last Federal Government (the 'traffic light' coalition of SPD, Greens, and FDP) was usually anxious to emphasise that international law, especially international humanitarian law had to be respected and that they trusted in Israel's adherence to democratic values and the rule of law.[253] Blind trust, however, in the face of unpunished atrocities and of a rhetoric that even the ICJ interpreted as a possible incitement of genocide, seems genuinely misplaced.

The same line of argument was pursued by Germany in an *amicus curiae* brief to the ICC commenting on the Office of the Prosecutor's request for arrest warrants against, inter alia, Israeli Prime Minister Benjamin Netanyahu and then-Minister of Defence, Yoav Gallant.[254] Here, Germany argued inadmissibility under Article 17(1) ICC Statute (complementarity), pointing to Israel's independent judiciary and commitment to the rule of law in general. Since Article 17(1) is only triggered if the case is already being investigated or prosecuted by a State which has jurisdiction, and no such investigations against Netanyahu and Gallant were in sight, Germany submitted that 'Israel is subject to an ongoing armed attack and faces serious threats from additional actors', thus it 'should be given an appropriate and genuine opportunity to put its accountability mechanisms into action before the Prosecutor may request warrants for arrest under Article 58 of the Statute.' This, however, would generally bar such requests for war crimes and other crimes in ongoing armed conflicts, if not reduced to a '*lex* Israel.'

When the arrest warrants were finally released in November 2024, they met with open criticism by some oppositional politicians, while the Federal Government reacted evasively with abstract musings and referring to complex legal questions,[255] different from the arrest warrant against Vladimir Putin that had

---

[252] ICJ, Application of the Convention on the Prevention and Punishment of the Crime of Genocide (The Gambia v. Myanmar: 11 States intervening). Text of the intervention: www.icj-cij.org/case/178/intervention

[253] Torsten Benner, '"Reason of state": Germany's support for Israel and its limits' (*Agenda Pública*, 11 December 2023) https://agendapublica.es/noticia/18962/reason-of-state-germany-support-for-israel-and-its-limits

[254] Federal Republic of Germany, Observations Pursuant to Rule 103(1) of the Rules of Procedure and Evidence, ICC-01/18-307 (6 August 2024).

[255] See video: Jung & Naiv, 22 November 2024 – Sehenswerte Regierungspressekonferenz BPK (*YouTube*, 22 November 2024) www.youtube.com/watch?v=NRl3X5nN4R4; Erklärungen

been openly and explicitly welcomed in March 2023.[256] An open rejection of the Court's authority, however, came from (at this point still: future) Chancellor Friedrich Merz who, on the evening of his election victory of 23 February 2025, declared that he had invited Prime Minister Netanyahu to Germany in a telephone call and had promised him to find means and ways not to arrest him.[257] Since such 'means and ways' are hard to find if national legislation implementing Germany's obligations under the ICC Statute is to be observed and public prosecutors not advised to act against the law,[258] the plans were silently shelved.

A lack of understanding of and for the international rule of law on the side of the new German Chancellor was also evident in his reaction to Israel's air raids against Iran, targeting its nuclear programme and assassinating scientists on 13 June 2025.[259] In an interview with a TV journalist, Merz commented that '[T]his is dirty work that Israel is doing for all of us,' taking up a term ('*Drecksarbeit*') suggested by the journalist. He continued: 'I can only say, [I have] the greatest respect for the fact that the Israeli army had the courage to do this, that the Israeli state leadership had the courage to do this.'[260] Fortunately, on the occasion of his inaugural visit to Israel, Merz himself found the courage, next to emphasising that 'Germany stands by Israel's side in deep friendship,' to mention the plight of the Palestinian civilian population in Gaza, cautiously criticise Israel's settlement policy in the West Bank, and refer to a two-state solution.[261]

There seem to be two major reasons why Nicaragua took Germany before the ICJ when it instituted proceedings on 1 March 2024 for support of Israel's war in Gaza. The first is, that both, Germany and Nicaragua, have recognised the Court's jurisdiction under Article 36(2) ICJ Statute. This, however, is also the case with other supporters of Israel, such as Canada or the United Kingdom. Another reason, most probably, is that Germany has presented itself as a staunch ally of Israel, irrespective of the ongoing atrocities in Gaza and everyday state-tolerated vio-

---

des Auswärtigen Amts in der Regierungspressekonferenz vom 04.04.2025 www.auswaertiges-amt.de/de/newsroom/regierungspressekonferenz-2711834

256 Malcolm Jorgensen, 'A "Democratic Exception" to ICC Jurisdiction: The Law and Politics of Double Standards' (*Verfassungsblog*, 6 December 2024), https://verfassungsblog.de/exception-to-icc-jurisdiction/

257 See N.N., 'Merz says he will find a way for Netanyahu to visit Germany without being arrested' (*Reuters*, 24 February 2025) www.reuters.com/world/europe/election-winner-merz-invites-netanyahu-germany-says-israelis-office-2025-02-24/

258 Kai Ambos, 'Rechtsbruch mit Ansage' (*Verfassungsblog*, 25 February 2025) https://verfassungsblog.de/rechtsbruch-netanjahu-merz-festnahme-haftbefehl-rechtswidrig/

259 On the illegality of these attacks and the subsequent bombing of three nuclear facilities by the USA, see Marko Milanovic, 'The Illegal Israeli-American Use of Force Against Iran: A Follow-Up' (*EJIL:Talk!*, 23 June 2025) www.ejiltalk.org/the-illegal-israeli-american-use-of-force-against-iran-a-follow-up/

260 James Angelos and Nette Nöstlinger, 'Merz's 'dirty work'' (*Politico*, 20 June 2025), www.politico.eu/newsletter/berlin-bulletin/merzs-dirty-work/

261 Federal Chancellor, Press Release (8 December 2025) www.bundeskanzler.de/bk-en/news/support-israel-2228294

lence against Palestinians in the West Bank.[262] In its decision of 30 April 2024 the ICJ rejected the request for provisional measures, stating that 'at present,'[263] circumstances did not require their indication given that Germany possesses a robust legal framework on the export of weapons and other military equipment, and that Germany had hardly exported any war weapons to Israel.[264] After having partially suspended all weapons deliveries to Israel because of high civilian casualties in Gaza in August 2025, the ban has been lifted by the Federal Government again in November 2025 before Chancellor Merz' inaugural visit to Israel.[265]

Already on 21 October 2025, Foreign Minister Wadephul had submitted a new declaration under Article 36(2) ICJ Statute with additional procedural restrictions.[266] Though not far-reaching in substance, this further adds to the impression that the new German government, especially its CDU and CSU members, are less committed to the international legal order than their predecessors. German foreign policy today seems out of step with a decade-long tradition of standing by the international rule of law. Previous actions, like Kosovo, had still an exceptional character and the responsible actors tried to argue legally. More and more, the language of international law is either absent ('understandable,' '*Drecksarbeit*') or the German Government resorts to double standards. Such a policy is seriously jeopardising the credibility of Germany's advocacy for an international rule of law.[267] It is time to reconsider.[268]

---

[262] On the latter, see Moritz Rhades, 'Settler Violence Through the Lens of State Responsibility' (*Völkerrechtsblog*, 24 April 2024) https://voelkerrechtsblog.org/de/settler-violence-through-the-lens-of-state-responsibility/

[263] On this phrase and its previous occurrence in the ICJ's jurisprudence, see Carla Fischer, Gundula Maxwill, and Rota Shima, 'Provisional Middle Ground? The ICJ's Practice of Not Indicating Provisional Measures under 'the circumstances, as they now present themselves to the Court' (2025) 68 *GYIL* (forthcoming).

[264] ICJ, Alleged Breaches of Certain International Obligations in respect of the Occupied Palestinian Territory (Nicaragua v. Germany), order of 30 April 2024, ICJ Reports 2024, 560, paras. 17 et seqq. For an assessment of that decision, Stefan Talmon, 'The International Court of Justice Severely Limits Germany's Ability to Transfer Arms to Israel' (*GPIL*, 2 May 2024) https://gpil.jura.uni-bonn.de/2024/05/why-the-provisional-measures-order-in-nicaragua-v-germany-severely-limits-germanys-ability-to-transfer-arms-to-israel/

[265] Alex Berry, 'Germany to lift partial weapons embargo on Israel' (*Deutsche Welle*, 17 November 2025), www.dw.com/en/germany-to-lift-partial-weapons-embargo-on-israel-amid-gaza-ceasefire/a-74773312

[266] See https://www.icj-cij.org/declarations/de

[267] Marcus Schneider and Jannis Grimm, 'Germany's fall from grace' (*IPS Journal*, 5 June 2024) www.ips-journal.eu/topics/foreign-and-security-policy/germanys-fall-from-grace-7536/

[268] See 'Respect for International Law: A Declaration by German Speaking International Law Scholars' (*Verfassungsblog*, 20 March 2025) https://verfassungsblog.de/declaration-respect-for-international-law/

III. The Future for the Rule of Law: A Cautionary Outlook

In the 20th century, Germany was responsible for an unprecedented level of barbarism and lawlessness. The Federal Republic of Germany seized the opportunity for rebirth after the Second World War. Despite some continuity in personnel, with the help of the constitutional framework of the Basic Law and the guiding case law of the BVerfG, it has succeeded in building and developing a state for which the rule of law has become the core of its identity, both internally and externally. The fixation on the law is so characteristic of the Federal Republic that complaints about an excess of laws and court proceedings have repeatedly led to a search for deregulation and alternative forms of dispute resolution. Stable institutions, an independent judiciary, a culture of legality, low levels of corruption, and a preference for legal regulation in its foreign relations, preferably in a multilateral context – this is how the Federal Republic sees itself and how it is often viewed from outside.

A good eighty years after the end of the Second World War, the rule of law and democracy are under pressure worldwide. Demagogues in all parts of the world are dividing society by inciting hatred against those who are supposedly to blame for everything, above all "migrants" who threaten "us". In this culture war, it is not the 'Normative State' that helps against the supposed existential threats, but only the 'Prerogative State',[269] tough crackdowns instead of legally ordered and fair procedures.

This development has not left Germany unscathed. Racism and xenophobia, hatred and incitement, intimidation of journalists who report differently from what the algorithm feeds us via social media are creating a social climate that promotes the erosion of the rule of law. However, the response to this must not be a light version of the 'Prerogative State' in which the rights of migrants and demonstrators have to give way (according to what are probably the most important warnings from the European Commission and UN bodies). The 'monsters', the 'negative emotions of billions of individuals – fear, *Angst*, hatred, and vengeance – fomented and instrumentalised by socio-pathic leaders,'[270] cannot be appeased in this way. They will demand a strong man who embodies authority in an authoritarian manner and who is also prepared to take decisive action externally: my country first.

Given its historical experiences, Germany should remain firmly committed to the rule of law and counteract its erosion, internally and externally. By further

---

[269] Cf Ernst Fraenkel, *The Dual State. A Contribution to the Theory of Dictatorship* (OUP 1941).

[270] Anne Peters, 'International Law and its Scholarship in the Time of Monsters' *Max Planck Institute for Comparative Public Law & International Law (MPIL) Research Paper* No 2025–05 (6 May 2025), 12.

strengthening constitutional and democratic institutions[271] and – joining forces with like-minded states – an international order in which international law is developed into a law of genuine and equal cooperation, including with states in the Global South, regardless of the fact that a few powerful states believe they can profit from violence, threats and lawlessness for short-term gains. The rule of law is too important to be abandoned lightly.

[271] Friedrich Zillessen, Anna-Mira Brandau, and Lennart Laude (eds.), *Das Justiz-Projekt. Verwundbarkeit und Resilienz der dritten Gewalt* (Verfassungsbooks 2025).

The Application of the *Lex Fori*

Developments in Practice and Foundations in Theory

Felix M. Wilke

I. Introduction

The *lex fori* as an issue seems to have surfaced at irregular intervals in the German academic private international law context, often in *Festschriften*, occasionally in monographs.[1] In contemporary German textbooks, treatises, and commentaries, it is hard to see a strong conceptual interest in the *lex fori*.[2] One reason for this might be that it has become increasingly difficult to discuss it from a single conceptual point of view. As is well-known, EU private international law (mainly found in regulations) now covers significant parts of (German) conflict of laws. This affects the role of the *lex fori*. It appears under different auspices depending on the source of conflict-of-laws rules.

In a purely autonomous national system of conflict of laws, the conflict-of-laws rules and the rules of the *lex fori* (whether substantive or procedural) share the same origin. Whatever the exact source – legislation, case law, custom… –, the source for both is domestic. To think about the relevance of the *lex fori* rests on the simple dichotomy between the own and the foreign.

For EU conflict-of-laws rules, the notion of the *lex fori* evokes a different set of issues. A unified system of conflict of laws corresponds to a relative, fragmented system of applicable law (with the exception of some areas of substantive law harmonised by the EU). There is no single *lex fori*, but there is the *lex* of each forum. Public policy clauses and rules on overriding mandatory provisions may

---

[1] See *Wengler*, in: FS Rheinstein (1969), 299; *Ehrenzweig*, in: FS Wengler (1973), vol. II, 251; *Heldrich*, in: FS Ferid, 1978, 209; *A. K. Arnold*, *Lex fori* als versteckte Anknüpfung, 2009; Staudinger/*F. Sturm/G. Sturm* (2012), Einleitung zum IPR n. 213 et seq.; less pronounced in the new edition Staudinger/*Looschelders* (2024) Einleitung IPR n. 222 et seq.; *Fogt*, in: FS Schack, 2022, 406; with an expressly or markedly (or at least tendentially) procedural emphasis *Niederländer*, RabelsZ 20 (1955), 1; *Grunsky*, ZZP 89 (1976), 241; *H. Roth*, in: FS Stree/Wessels (1993), 1045; *Jaeckel*, Die Reichweite der *lex fori* im internationalen Zivilprozeßrecht (1995); *Kronke*, ZZPInt 20 (2015), 399; *Brinkmann*, ZZP 129 (2016), 461.

[2] See e.g. *Junker*, Internationales Privatrecht, 6th ed. 2024: no pertinent entry in the register (but some references to the homeward trend, see *infra* II. before 1.) and § 5 n. 34 (concerning the potential conflict-of-laws interest in applying the *lex fori*); only in passing *Gössl/Kienle*, Grundkurs IPR/IZVR, 2025, § 1 n. 30; but see (from two decades ago) *Kropholler*, Internationales Privatrecht, 6th ed. 2006, § 7 (42 et seq.).

serve to illustrate the ensuing issues. They undergo a change in nature when "moving up" to the level of EU law. The German public policy clause *mandates* the non-application of foreign law due to a contravention of fundamental German values;[3] the unwritten[4] German rule for domestic overriding mandatory provisions is that the general conflict-of-laws rules apply without prejudice for the former (meaning that they *will* be applied[5]). The corresponding EU rules, however, essentially only provide *gateways* for the application of the public policy and overriding mandatory provisions of each Member State. Art. 21 Rome I, for example, *allows* the application of the law designated by the Regulation to be refused if certain conditions are met. Art. 9(2) Rome I reflects a principle of self-restraint with respect to overriding mandatory provisions of the respective forum, provided the provisions meet the requirements of Art. 9(1) Rome I. Whether a national court will make use of this leeway technically is a question for the law of the respective Member State.

The issues outlined in the preceding paragraph arise for all Member States of the EU. For a country report specifically concerned with Germany, a focus on genuine issues of German law seems more adequate, even where they do not differ substantially from EU law. The following remarks therefore, for the most part, leave EU law to one side. They concentrate on those areas of private international law that the EU has not (yet) harmonised, with a large part of the relevant conflict-of-laws rules enshrined in the Introductory Act to the Civil Code (*Einführungsgesetz zum Bürgerlichen Gesetzbuche: EGBGB*[6]) and many relevant rules of procedure found in the Code of Civil Procedure (*Zivilprozessordnung*: *ZPO*). The structure of this report largely follows the questionnaire submitted to all national rapporteurs even in the few instances where it arguably deviates from what German readers might consider as the conventional ordering of the subject matter.

II. Conflict of Laws

"*Heimwärtsstreben*"[7] – literally "striving homeward", sometimes translated as the "homeward trend"[8] – refers to the inclination of courts in particular to find ways

---

[3] *Infra* II. 9.

[4] The former Art. 34 EGBGB on overriding mandatory provisions in the context of contractual obligations was abolished in light of Rome I.

[5] See only *Gössl/Kienle* (fn. 2), § 13 n. 186; *Kropholler*, IPR (fn. 2) § 52 IX 1 (499). How could it be any different? The legislator has created an *overriding* mandatory provision to *override* the otherwise applicable conflict-of-laws rules.

[6] For a concise English overview of why there is no separate German Private International Law Act or Code, see *Wilke*, A Conceptual Analysis of European Private International Law, 2019, 58–60.

[7] To the best of my knowledge coined by *Nußbaum*, Deutsches Internationales Privatrecht, 1932, § 56 II (384).

[8] Recently *Willems*, ERPL 2025, 667.

to apply[9] the *lex fori*. Depending on the perspective, the court in question has never actually left the *lex fori* and thus simply cannot strive home*ward*; rather, it merely *stays* at home. Accordingly, the homeward trend is sometimes also described as a "remain-at-home" trend.[10] Most German private international law scholars tend to regard this phenomenon with suspicion, although they sometimes express an understanding for such judicial practice. The underlying attitude may be summarised as: "Better to apply one's own law correctly than to risk applying a foreign law incorrectly."[11] The application of the *lex fori* as such is not regarded as a legitimate component of conflicts justice. At the same time, the *parties* may have an interest in the simpler ascertainment of the applicable law and there may likewise be a *public* interest in swifter and more predictable decisions.[12]

1. Characterisation

Already the German Imperial Court held that a German court must proceed from German-law considerations when classifying legal patterns.[13] This has also been the position of the German Federal Supreme Court at least since the 1950s.[14] The Court has also expressly been recognising that the German judge must ascertain the provisions of foreign law – particularly where they contain a legal concept unknown to German law – in light of their meaning and purpose, assess their significance from the standpoint of the foreign legal system, and compare them with institutions of the German legal order.[15] Hence, German courts are not to stick too rigidly with German substantive law. The overarching considerations concern the function of the concept under foreign law according to the *lex fori*.[16] This (not any more particularly) "modern" approach thus is often known as "functional characterisation".[17] It is widely practiced.[18] The *lex fori* – including binding rules of EU law – also decides about the characterisation of a dispute as belonging to civil or to public law[19] (relevant for the allocation of the dispute to the ordinary or administrative courts). A strict *lex fori*-approach would not only

---

[9] In the context of uniform law, the "homeward trend" is supposed to mean *interpreting* uniform law by recourse to domestic law, see in particular *Ferrari*, Unif. L. Rev. 2017, 244 (249 et seq).; *Cross*, Ohio State L. J. 68 (2007), 133; *Honnold*, Documentary history of the uniform law for international sales, 1989, 1.

[10] *Coester-Waltjen*, Internationales Beweisrecht, 1983, n. 137.

[11] *Kegel/Schurig*, Internationales Privatrecht, 9th ed. 2004, § 2 II 3 d (145).

[12] Ibid., § 2 II 3 d (143).

[13] RGZ 138 [1932], 243 (245).

[14] BGHZ 29, 137 = NJW 1959, 717 (718).

[15] Ibid.; for a more recent example see BGHZ 210, 59 = NJW 2016, 2322 (n. 36–39).

[16] Staudinger/*Looschelders*, 2024, Einl. IPR, n. 1091.

[17] Ibid.; MüKoBGB/*von Hein*, 9th ed. 2024, Einl. IPR n. 121; *Gössl/Kienle* (fn. 2), § 13 n. 85; *Junker*, IPR (fn. 2), § 7 n. 28; *Kropholler*, IPR (fn. 2), § 17 (126–130).

[18] Staudinger/*Looschelders*, 2024, Einl. IPR n. 1096–1098, provides numerous references.

[19] BGH, NJW 2022, 3644 (n. 15); BGH, NJW-RR 2006, 198 (199).

not work for legal concepts unknown to German law; if German courts then dismissed actions with the argument that it is impossible to determine the law applicable to the claim, they would violate the right of access to justice.[20]

The functional approach (even) applies to the *lex fori* itself in the sense that the position of a legal rule in the civil code is not necessarily decisive for its characterisation. For example, § 566 BGB is found deep in the part of the second book of the German Civil Code that deals with contractual obligations. It states that obligations concerning a residential lease persist the transfer of the respective property to a new owner. ("A sale does not extinguish a lease", as the official title of the provision misleadingly reads.) A right under contract law thus (partially) assumes an *erga omnes* effect typical for property rights. For this reason, § 566 BGB is characterised as pertaining to rights *in rem* as opposed to concerning contractual obligations.[21]

2. Incidental (Preliminary[22]) Questions

German statutory law does not contain a rule on incidental questions in conflict of laws. The idea that one simply might apply the *lex fori* to them – as hypothesised by the questionnaire – seems to appear entirely far-fetched to German scholars. They apparently deem this approach too trivial even to mention.[23] Indeed, some do not even bring up the (arguably slightly less far-fetched, but equally doctrinally unacceptable) option of applying the *lex causae*.[24]

The debate focuses on only two possibilities: Whether to apply the conflict-of-laws rules of the forum or whether to apply the conflict-of-laws rules of the *lex causae*. The prevailing general rule, subject only to few exceptions, is the former alternative, the so-called "independent" solution.[25] Indeed, since the general – and generally accepted – rule is to apply the forum's conflict-of-laws rules, what requires justification is the decision *not* to apply the German ones rather than the decision to apply them.

3. Precedence of a German Nationality: Preference for the lex fori

Where conflict-of-laws rules use nationality as the connecting factor, German law will apply if the relevant person is a German national. This is even true for people

[20] *Junker*, IPR (fn. 2), § 7 n. 18.

[21] MüKoBGB/*Wendehorst*, 9th ed. 2025, Art. 43 EGBGB n. 63 with further references.

[22] For my preference for the designation as "incidental" rather than "preliminary" see *Wilke*, A Conceptual Analysis (fn. 6), 121 et seq.

[23] See the works referred to in the following two footnotes in which it does not appear.

[24] *Gössl/Kienle* (fn. 2), § 13 n. 107 et seq.; expressly discarding this approach e.g. *Junker*, IPR (fn. 2), § 10 n. 4 et seq.; MüKoBGB/*von Hein* (fn. 17), Einl. IPR n. 163.

[25] MüKoBGB/*von Hein* (fn. 17), Einl. IPR n. 184; *Gössl/Kienle* (fn. 2), § 13 n. 116; *Junker*, IPR (fn. 2), § 10 n. 17 et seq.; BGH, NJW 1981, 1900 (1901) (for a marriage as an incidental question in a succession case).

with more than one nationality: Just like quite a few other EU Member States,[26] Germany always gives preference to the German nationality of a multi-national, Art. 5(1) cl. 2 EGBGB. By contrast, for multiple nationalities in general, pursuant to Art. 5(1) cl. 1 EGBGB the effective nationality is decisive.

The preference for the German nationality among more than one had already been expressed by the German Imperial Court.[27] But towards the end of the 1970s, the German Federal Supreme Court concluded that a foreign nationality should be given preference if the person had substantially a closer connection to the other country than to Germany.[28] Less a than decade later, the legislator returned to the former solution with Art. 5(1) EGBGB as it stands until today.[29] The main reasons for this change were legal clarity and practicability;[30] the legislator also referred to its consideration for civil registrars (*Standesbeamte*).[31] In other words, the legislator emphasised the benefit for judges and registrars to be able to avoid any analysis of which nationality is effective and to apply the *lex fori*. In much more recent times, the German Federal Supreme Court relied on the latter aspect when interpreting Art. 8(c) Rome III in conjunction with Art. 17(2) EGBGB.[32]

In its decision before the reform, the German Federal Supreme Court had not denied these potential advantages. Yet it had – quite correctly – pointed out that the preference even for an ineffective German nationality cannot be squared with the notion that a main reason for using nationality as a connecting factor is its indication of a strong connection between a person and a legal system.[33] Accordingly, German private international scholars have been almost unanimously critical of Art. 5(1) cl. 2 EGBGB.[34] They have denounced it as a "just about unfathomable step backwards",[35] as a "calamity",[36] as a triumph of the "simple [the connotation 'simplistic' suggests itself] reinforcement of the *lex fori* over conflicts justice".[37] What is more, the advantage of practicability is less clear-cut than it appears at first sight. It may not just be that a person with an ineffective German nationality will be taken by complete surprise if German law applies to their case.

[26] See the references provided in *Wilke*, A Conceptual Analysis (fn. 6), 207 (n. 1379).

[27] With further references RGZ 150 [1936], 374, 382; among others, the Bavarian Highest Regional Court still applied the rule in the times of the Federal Republic of Germany, BayObLGZ 1964, 385 (388).

[28] BGHZ 75, 32 = NJW 1979, 1776 (1778).

[29] In the 1986 Act to Reform Private International Law, Federal Law Gazette 1986 I, 1142.

[30] BT-Drucks. 10/504, 40.

[31] BT-Drucks. 10/504, 41.

[32] *Infra* IV. 2.b).

[33] BGHZ 75, 32 = NJW 1979, 1776 (1778).

[34] In addition to the references in the following footnotes, just see MüKoBGB/*von Hein* (fn. 17), Art. 5 EGBGB n. 70.

[35] *Von Bar*, JZ 1984, 126.

[36] *Kegel/Schurig* (fn. 11), § 13 II 5 (456).

[37] *Von Bar/Mankowski*, Internationales Privatrecht I, 2nd ed. 2003, § 7 n. 119.

The judicial task can also be complicated.[38] This is because the person will likely have based their conduct on a different law (namely another – the effective – *lex patriae*), implying the need for corrective measures to avoid disappointing the person's expectations completely. By contrast, one likely would be able to apply the law of the person's effective nationality without such legal contortions.

Most observers recognise, however, that the critique is one of policy, and that the law must be applied as written even in extreme cases such as that of a person with multiple nationalities who has never set foot in Germany.[39] The critique assumes a legal nature, though, where the effective nationality is that of another EU Member State. A majority of commentators agrees that the application of Art. 5(1) cl. 2 EGBGB then would violate Art. 18 TFEU.[40] The German Federal Supreme Court at least is aware of these concerns, but has thus far not seen a need to refer the issue to the CJEU.[41] Then again, as a matter of German constitutional law, it has essentially been accepted for decades that the *Grundgesetz* (*GG*) neither requires[42] nor precludes[43] (a rule like) Art. 5(1) cl. 2 EGBGB.

4. Choice of Law

a) Mandatory Nature of Conflict-of-Laws Rules

Some authors, with varying nuances, have argued that the parties should (almost) never be denied a choice of the *lex fori*.[44] It is, however, settled law that German conflict-of-laws rules, whether statutory or unwritten, are mandatory.[45] Courts must apply them *ex officio*. It is of no import whether either party invokes the

---

38 See MüKoBGB/*von Hein* (fn. 17), Art. 5 EGBGB n. 70.

39 MüKoBGB/*von Hein* (fn. 17), Art. 5 EGBGB n. 72; *Kegel/Schurig* (fn. 11), § 13 II 5 (456); against an unwritten exception also the Higher Regional Court Hamm: OLG Hamm, NJW-RR 1993, 1352 (1354); the Higher Regional Court Saarbrücken seems ever so slightly more open to the idea: OLG Saarbrücken NJW 2016, 1185 (n. 8); but see *von Bar/Mankowski* (fn. 37), § 7 n. 119.

40 See MüKoBGB/*von Hein* (fn. 17), Art. 5 EGBGB n. 71; HK-BGB/*Dörner*, 12th ed. 2024, Art. 5 EGBGB n. 4; *Junker*, IPR (fn. 2), § 6 n. 29; *Heiderhoff*, JZ 2021, 260 (262); *Wilke*, A Conceptual Analysis (fn. 6), 209–212.

41 With further references to its case law BGHZ 226, 365 = JZ 2021, 254 (257).

42 See MüKoBGB/*von Hein* (fn. 17), Art. 5 EGBGB n. 70; *Mansel*, NJW 1986, 625; but see *Scholz/Pitschas*, NJW 1984, 2721 (with a focus on the relationship to the German Democratic Republic).

43 MüKoBGB/*von Hein* (fn. 17), Art. 5 EGBGB n. 70 (with fn. 322); but see *von Bar/Mankowski* (fn. 37), § 7 n. 119.

44 E.g. *Maultzsch*, JPIL 2016, 466 (479 et seq.); *G. Wagner*, ZEuP 1999, 6; the notion of a "facultative system of conflict of laws" is particularly associated with the name of *Flessner*, see, *inter alia*, his contribution in RabelsZ 34 (1970), 547, and (for EU conflict of laws) in: LA for Walter Pintens, 2012, 593.

45 Also for the following BGH, NJW-RR 2023, 1599 (n. 26); BGH, NZG 2016, 1187 (n. 10) with further references.

application of foreign law. Most commentators share this position as well.[46] In the course of the 1986 reform of German conflict of laws, the legislator expressly dismissed alternative approaches.[47]

For arbitral tribunals with a seat in Germany, by contrast, the general German (or EU) conflict-of-laws rules are not applicable.[48] According to § 1051(1) ZPO, the parties can choose the applicable law. In the absence of choice, pursuant to § 1051(2) ZPO, the tribunal must apply the law most closely connected to the case.

b) Implied Choice of German Law

At least until decades ago, German courts had been rather liberal in their assumption of an implied choice of German law in proceedings before them.[49] In this context, the Federal Supreme Court once even disregarded a contractual choice of Austrian law. It did so – admittedly among other reasons – because the claimant had chosen to bring proceedings in Germany, although its own general terms and conditions contained an asymmetric jurisdiction clause designating an Austrian forum while allowing it to sue elsewhere.[50] More than fifteen years ago, the Federal Supreme Court arguably tightened the conditions, even though only underlining the almost self-evident requirement of a mutual dispositive intention ("*Gestaltungswillen*").[51]

Nowadays, it is doubtful that German judges often assume an implied choice of German law[52] (even more so with the intention to avoid the application of foreign law). Rather, they will draw the parties' attention to the applicability of foreign law where they seem to be pleading on the basis of German law.[53] If the parties then continue to plead in a way that is geared towards German law, one can assume an implied choice of German law.[54]

c) Mandatory Rules as a Limit for Choice of Law

Modern German conflict of laws affords a relatively wide scope to choose the applicable law. For example, spouses may choose the law applicable to their ma-

---

[46] MüKoBGB/*von Hein* (fn. 17), Einl. IPR n. 318; Staudinger/*Looschelders,* 2024, Einl. IPR n. 135; *M. Stürner*, in: FS Stürner, vol. 2, 2013, 1071 (1081); *Kropholler*, IPR (fn. 2), § 7 II 2 (45 et seq.); particularly for EU private international law *Wilke*, A Conceptual Analysis (fn. 6), 97–102.

[47] BT-Drucks. 10/504, 26.

[48] Prevailing opinion, see only MüKoBGB/*von Hein* (fn. 17), Einl. IPR n. 320; Musielak/Voit/*Voit,* ZPO, 22nd ed. 2025, § 1051 n. 6 et seq.

[49] See, e. g., the copious references provided by *G. Wagner*, ZEuP 1996, 6 (in fn. 2); for references from the 19th century, see *Nußbaum* (fn. 7), § 16 I (97).

[50] BGH, NJW-RR 1986, 456 (457); critically (concerning the judgment as well as the general practice of implied choice of law agreements) *Schack*, IPRax 1986, 272.

[51] BGH, NJW 2009, 1205 (1206).

[52] *M. Stürner/Krauß*, Ausländisches Recht in deutschen Zivilverfahren, 2018, 88.

[53] Ibid.

[54] *Junker*, IPR (fn. 2), § 15 n. 13 (for Rome I).

trimonial surname (Art. 10(2) EGBGB); they can choose the law applicable to the effects of marriage (Art. 14(1) EGBGB) – to the extent that they are not covered by Regulation (EU) 2016/1103; for non-contractual obligations beyond Rome II, the parties can choose the applicable law after the event giving rise to the obligation (Art. 42 cl. 1 EGBGB); the principal can choose the law applicable to voluntary representation (Art. 8(1) cl. 1 EGBGB). In the two former instances, the choice is limited to certain laws to which the spouses have a certain connection, anyway; in the latter two, there is no such restriction.

In particular with regard to Art. 42 EGBGB, scholars have raised the question of a choice of law in the absence of a cross-border element. As German conflict-of-laws rules are to apply only in cases "with a connection to a foreign State" (Art. 3 EGBGB) and due to Art. 14(2) Rome II, there seems to be consensus that, without such an element, there cannot be a genuine choice of law.[55] In other words, the (simple) mandatory rules of the *lex fori* cannot be derogated from in this situation. One would think that the same argument, perhaps enriched by a reference to Art. 3(3) Rome I, should apply to voluntary representation pursuant to Art. 8(1) EGBGB.[56] (Although Art. 3(3) Rome I itself, as EU law, lies beyond the scope of this contribution, it would be remiss to mention a much-noted judgment of the German Federal Supreme Court from November 2023. The Court ruled that the case of a lease – drafted in the language of the chosen foreign law – of an apartment located in Germany by a foreign legal entity with its habitual residence abroad did not involve sufficiently significant cross-border elements.[57])

It is notoriously difficult to determine in the abstract which cross-border elements suffice for a connection to a foreign State and which do not.[58] Most observers assume that, in general (beyond the specific issue of party autonomy) and in spite of the wording of Art. 3 EGBGB, (German) private international law (in theory) does not require any cross-border element.[59]

[55] MüKoBGB/*Junker*, 9th ed. 2025, Art. 42 EGBGB n. 27; MüKoBGB/*von Hein* (fn. 17), Art. 3 EGBGB n. 11; BeckOGK/*Fornasier*, 01.10.2025, Art. 42 EGBGB n. 7.

[56] See MüKoBGB/*von Hein* (fn. 17), Art. 3 EGBGB n. 11.

[57] BGH, NJW-RR 2024, 140; see *Thiede*, EuZW 2024, 472 (473); *Reibetanz*, IPRax 2024, 374 (377) – both commentators noting a homeward trend here. For a slightly earlier discussion of Art. 3(3) Rome I see e.g. *Thorn/Thon*, in: FS Kronke, 2020, 569.

[58] See MüKoBGB/*von Hein* (fn. 17), Art. 3 EGBGB n. 9 et seq.; BeckOGK/*Fervers*, 01.07.2021, Art. 3 EGBGB n. 56 et seq.

[59] See BeckOK BGB/*Lorenz*, 1.11.2025, Art. 3 EGBGB n. 2; MüKoBGB/*von Hein* (fn. 17), Art. 3 EGBGB n. 12; *Wilke*, A Conceptual Analysis (fn. 6), 103 et seq.; *Kegel/Schurig* (fn. 11), § 1 III (6 et seq.); *Kropholler* IPR (fn. 2), § 1 IV (7).

5. *Determination of the Contents of Foreign Law*

a) Foreign Law in the German Courts

Foreign law is understood as *law* in German law.[60] As an important consequence for proceedings conducted in default of the defendant, the courts may not assume that the claimant's assertions regarding the content of foreign law are correct[61] – as they do to the extent that factual assertions are concerned.[62] If, however, the court does not (by lucky coincidence) know the applicable foreign law, it is necessary to take evidence as if a *fact* was concerned (see § 293 cl. 1 ZPO).[63] While § 293 ZPO as a whole is not entirely clear in this regard, German courts since the Imperial Court have held that the applicable foreign law must be established *ex officio*.[64] Accordingly, there is no technical burden of proof on either party in respect of foreign law.[65]

Pursuant to § 293 cl. 2 ZPO, the courts have discretion as to how[66] to ascertain foreign law. This means, first, that they are not limited by the usual "strict" five means of evidence for the establishment of facts. If a judge possesses sufficient language skills and has access to pertinent sources, she can do her own research (as she would have to do for the *lex fori*).[67] Second, the courts can require the parties to contribute to the process. If a party has access to sources of foreign law but does not elaborate sufficiently on it in spite of a judicial request, the courts are permitted to assume that these sources would not change their assessment.[68] The details are less clear than the frequently rather broad assertions to this effect would suggest.[69] In practice, courts will often request an expert's[70] opinion on foreign law.[71] In doing so, they rely on one of the "strict" forms of evidence, after all, which means that the formal rules for expert evidence in general apply. In particular, when one of the parties requests the oral examination of the expert, the court must summon that person (§§ 402, 397(1) ZPO).[72] The divergent view

---

[60] BGH, NJW 2013, 3656 (n. 19).

[61] MüKoZPO/*Prütting*, 7th ed. 2025, § 293 ZPO n. 55; there is, however, isolated judicial authority to the contrary: OLG München, NJW 1976, 489.

[62] § 331(1) ZPO.

[63] In general, one can only take evidence of (disputed) *facts*, § 359 No. 1 ZPO.

[64] RGZ 126 [1929], 196 (202); BGH, NJW 1962, 961 (962); also e.g. *Nußbaum* (fn. 7), § 16 I (96).

[65] BGH, NJW 1961, 410; but see the next paragraph on the parties' potential obligations to contribute.

[66] Not: as to *whether* to apply foreign law, *supra* 4.a).

[67] Stein/Jonas/*Thole*, ZPO, 23rd ed. 2018, § 293 n. 39 et seq.

[68] BGH, NJW 1976, 1581 (1583).

[69] MüKoZPO/*Prütting* (fn. 61), § 293 ZPO n. 52 et seq.

[70] Usually academics from the Hamburg Max-Planck-Institute or pertinent university institutes.

[71] *Junker*, IPR (fn. 2), § 11 n. 8; MüKoZPO/*Prütting* (fn. 61), § 293 ZPO n. 29 et seq.; see e.g. BGH, NJW 1991, 1418.

[72] BGH, NJW 1994, 2959 (2960).

according to which the courts have more leeway even in this situation because the strict rules only concern ("actual") facts does not seem to have many followers.[73]

The question of whether the court has complied with the procedural requirements for ascertaining foreign law can be raised and reviewed on appeal. It is worth noting this as the German Federal Supreme Court takes a different view as to appealing errors in the application of foreign law.[74]

b) Failure to Ascertain the Applicable Law

The "failure" to ascertain the applicable law designates a situation in which it either is indeed impossible to establish the content of foreign law with sufficient certainty or in which that content can be established only at disproportionate cost and with substantial delay to the proceedings.[75] This situation should not be assumed prematurely. The German Federal Supreme Court flatly stated once that the fact that an expert opinion will cost several times the amount in dispute is not, by itself, a sufficient reason to forgo obtaining it.[76] Another time, however, it did assert that it is impossible to ascertain the content of the applicable foreign law if the German judge is unable to assess with sufficient certainty an issue that is disputed under foreign law and has not yet been decided in the respective foreign jurisdiction's case law.[77] German scholars have taken issue with this seemingly lenient standard, pointing out that a German judge nevertheless could decide the issue for the case at issue, based on any available sources and even if scholars of the foreign legal system disagree as to the outcome.[78]

How to deal with a failure to ascertain the applicable law has been subject to dispute. To be sure, it has been accepted for a long time that the German courts cannot simply refuse to decide the case and cannot simply decide against the party relying on the applicable law.[79] The first option runs afoul of the right of access to justice;[80] the second would amount to a ruling rendered on burden-of-proof grounds with respect to foreign law alien to German law.[81] But there is disagreement which law should be used primarily to decide the case in lieu of the law that should have governed. In the leading decision on the issue, the German Federal Supreme Court held in 1977 that, generally, the *lex fori* should be

---

[73] *Schack*, Internationales Zivilverfahrensrecht, 9th ed. 2025, n. 766.

[74] *Infra* d).

[75] See BGH, NJW 1978, 496 (497 et seq.).

[76] BGH, NJW 2014, 1244 (n. 24).

[77] BGH, MDR 1982, 566; also see BGH, NJW 1978, 496 (498) (if, according to academic contributions, the legal issue at hand has not been settled yet).

[78] MüKoBGB/*von Hein* (fn. 17), Einl. IPR n. 329; *Kropholler*, IPR (fn. 2), § 31 I 2 (213).

[79] The latter seems to have been suggested mainly at end of the 19th and at the beginning of the 20th century; this is also what the lower court in the case of BGH, MDR 1982, 566, seems to have done.

[80] *Junker*, IPR (fn. 2), § 11 n. 11.

[81] BGH, MDR 1982, 566.

applied as the most practicable solution.[82] If, however, the application of the *lex fori* seems highly unsatisfactory in a given case, it might be justified to apply a kindred law.[83] Many scholars have criticized this approach as establishing a wrong rule/exception relation. They argue that it should be the other way around: A kindred law should be applied as a rule, and only if this step fails (as well), the *lex fori* should govern.[84] One should not too readily submit to the siren call of the *lex fori* and ignore the conflict-of-laws rule determining the application of foreign law.[85] The application of a law closely related to the one that cannot be ascertained respects the domestic conflict-of-laws rule to the greatest degree possible.[86] It is said to correspond better to the goal of applying the law with the closest connection to the case.[87] In more recent times, however, support for the Federal Supreme Court's stance seems to be growing.[88] It has been pointed out that the *lex fori* usually is not without a *certain* connection to the case or the parties, in particular where jurisdiction is not (only) based on the defendant's domicile.[89] By contrast, the Supreme Court seems to have indicated that a tenuous connection to the *lex fori* would be an instance where its application could or would be deemed "highly unsatisfactory",[90] thus triggering the exception to the rule.

c) Interim Proceedings

The determination of the applicable foreign law in interim proceedings is a matter of debate in Germany. There is consensus that the nature of proceedings does not fundamentally alter the court's duty to ascertain and apply the applicable law *ex officio*. In other words, and in particular, it is not permissible to apply the *lex fori* automatically[91] in interim proceedings. Even where the content of foreign law cannot readily be established with certainty, to decide based on the *lex fori* would *indubitably* be incorrect.[92] But there is some (potential) disagreement as to the

---

[82] BGH, NJW 1978, 496 (498).

[83] Ibid.

[84] MüKoBGB/*von Hein* (fn. 17), Einl. IPR n. 330; Staudinger/*Looschelders*, 2024, Einl. IPR n. 232; *Kegel/Schurig* (fn. 11), § 15 V 2 (512 et seq.).

[85] See *Schack*, IZVR (fn. 73), n. 771.

[86] See *Kropholler*, IPR (fn. 2), § 31 III 2a (217).

[87] *Junker*, IPR (fn. 2), § 11 n. 15.

[88] *Gössl*, in: Peters/Hobe/Kieninger (eds.), Koloniale Kontinuitäten im Internationalen Recht, 2024, 45 (65 et seq., 71); *Duden*, IPRax 2023, 49 (53 et seq.).

[89] *Duden*, IPRax 2023, 49 (54 et seq.); see also the perspective that *Kropholler*, IPR (fn. 2), § 31 III 1 (216), assumed: *if* there is a strong connection to Germany, the harm to conflicts justice done by applying the *lex fori* is not indefensible.

[90] BGH, NJW 1978, 496 (498): emphasizing the connections to Germany in the given case as a justification for applying the *lex fori*.

[91] The old Art. 24(3) EGBGB, in force until December 31, 2022, however, expressly mandated the application of the *lex fori* for protective measures in the field of care and support relationships.

[92] See Stein/Jonas/*Thole* (fn. 67), § 293 n. 64. If the *outcome* is also wrong – a claim would exist under the *lex fori*, but not under the applicable foreign law –, the petitioner would be liable

details. According to one view, the court's duty is limited by the time available; if foreign law cannot be ascertained within this timeframe, the consequences described in the preceding paragraphs concerning a failure to ascertain the applicable law arise.[93] This approach thus can rather quickly lead to the *lex fori*, after all. Others argue that, if the foreign law cannot be determined with sufficient certainty, the courts should proceed on the basis of a *prima facie* assessment of the application. If the foreign law appears likely to support the applicant's claim, the court may grant interim relief, although many add that this can only happen after balancing the interests of applicant and respondent, given the significantly reduced likelihood of correctness of the decision.[94]

d) Errors in the Application of Foreign Law

As foreign law is "law"[95] and, under § 545(1) ZPO, a *Revision* (appeal on points of law) may be brought solely in the event of an error of "law", a natural reading of this provision would suggest that the German Federal Supreme Court must review the application of foreign law. This reading is reinforced by a comparison with the predecessor provision of § 545(1) ZPO, which was in force until 31 August 2008. Appeals on points of law were previously permissible only in cases involving breaches of federal law or provisions whose territorial scope extended beyond the district of a Higher Regional Court. While it was hard to reconcile foreign law with the old requirements, the reform removed any such hurdle. To be sure, the German Federal Supreme Court cannot authoritatively determine the content of the law of the country concerned, but it can provide legal certainty for all cases before German courts in which that law must be applied. Arguably, therefore, appellate review of the application of foreign law is also consistent with the purpose of the appeals provisions. In light of these considerations, many scholars support this reading.[96]

Only a few years after the reform, however, the German Federal Supreme Court took the opposite position, which other commentators support.[97] While

---

to the respondent for damages incurred because of the enforcement of the interim decision (§ 945 ZPO).

[93] For this view (potentially) Musielak/Voit/*Röß*, ZPO, 22nd ed. 2025, § 293 n. 12.

[94] MüKoBGB/*von Hein* (fn. 17), Einl. IPR n. 327; Stein/Jonas/*Thole* (fn. 67), § 293 n. 64; OLG Frankfurt a. M., GRUR-RR 2020, 493 n. 42.

[95] *Supra* 5.a).

[96] *Hess/Hübner*, NJW 2009, 3132; *Hau*, IPRax 2014, 397; *Riehm*, JZ 2014, 73; MüKoZPO/*Prütting* (fn. 61), § 293 ZPO n. 68; Stein/Jonas/*Thole* (fn. 67), § 293 n. 82; MüKoBGB/*von Hein* (fn. 17), Einl. IPR n. 336; at least from a policy perspective *R. Magnus*, LMK 2013, 352015; for a reform already, *inter alia*, *Mäsch*, EuZW 2004, 321.

[97] See e. g. MüKoZPO/*Krüger*, 7th ed. 2025, § 545 n. 11; Musielak/Voit/*Ball*, 22nd ed. 2025, § 545 n. 7; Stein/Jonas/*Jacobs*, 23rd ed. 2018, § 545 n. 21 (but calling for a reform, n. 23); *H. Roth*, NJW 2014, 1224; Staudinger/*Looschelders*, 2024, Einl. IPR n. 1296, does not express a particular opinion.

conceding that the wording of § 545(1) ZPO could cover foreign law,[98] it referred to § 560 ZPO,[99] noted that the issue of foreign law had not come up during the reform of § 545 ZPO,[100] and submitted that, as a German court, it could never definitively resolve questions of foreign law.[101] Lower courts would therefore not be able to rely on the Supreme Court's decision in the future, but would have to verify the current state of foreign law afresh in each case. The German Federal Labour Court, which had initially reached a different conclusion based on the (equally broad) provision in the Labour Courts Act,[102] has since aligned itself with this position.[103] One caveat remains: The Supreme Court recently affirmed the traditional exception for foreign *conflict-of-laws* rules, insofar as the (non-) application of *German* law depends on their correct interpretation.[104] This means that instances of remission and those instances of transmission in which one law ultimately refers to German law are subject to an appeal on points of law.[105]

The issue appears to be settled for practical purposes. One might leave it at that. This state of the law, however, remains unsatisfactory in light of the case law on appeals on points of law in the context of § 293 ZPO. Technically speaking, there is nothing wrong with the view that compliance with the requirements for ascertaining foreign law under § 293 ZPO[106] must be subject to appellate review. The provision is *German* law. As a consequence, the Supreme Court itself ascertains, interprets, and applies foreign law where the lower court has failed to do so.[107] It will also take foreign law into account when assessing whether the lower court has insufficiently ascertained it.[108] Yet in practical terms, lawyers often will not find it too difficult to argue that an error in the application of foreign law was based on an error in ascertaining it.[109] Whether the Supreme Court *actually* will review the application of foreign law therefore often comes down to semantics.

98 BGH, NJW 2013, 3656 (n. 19).

99 Setting forth that the appeals court is bound by the lower court's decision concerning the content of law *not* subject to appeals – a provision that arguably would be irrelevant if § 545(1) ZPO covered foreign law.

100 BGH, NJW 2013, 3656 (n. 20).

101 Ibid. (n. 21).

102 BAG, MDR 1975, 874 (abandoning its previously held position to the contrary).

103 BAG, NZA 2021, 225 (n. 76, thus re-assuming the previously held position); critically *Mankowski*, RIW 2020, 709 (710).

104 BGH, WM 2024, 1618 (n. 16); BGH, NJW 1958, 750.

105 *Junker*, IPR (fn. 2), § 11 n. 25.

106 *Supra* 5.a).

107 E.g. BGH, NJW 2010, 1070 (1072), applying Latvian law based on an unofficial English translation.

108 With further references BGH, NJW-RR 2017, 313 (n. 66).

109 *R. Magnus*, LMK 2013, 352015: "The court must have made a mistake in ascertaining the foreign law, otherwise it would have applied it correctly."

6. Fraus Legis/*Evasion of the Law*

By and large, the *fraus legis* issue is a non-starter in Germany. It has often been noted that the entire concept (even beyond private international law) is slippery: Where the law successfully combats an *attempted* evasion, there has been no *actual* evasion; and where the law does not object to the attempt and thus the desired effect is achieved in accordance with the law, one can hardly speak of "evasion".[110] While authors do not outright ignore evasion of the law in German conflict of laws,[111] they often quickly either refer to other legal systems[112] or state that German conflict of laws, in principle, will not object to parties consciously creating the factual circumstances leading to the application of a certain law.[113] The respective sections in even the most comprehensive commentaries are *relatively* short.[114]

There is no special provision on evasion of the law in German conflict of laws. Commentators point out that modern private international law contains specific tools to prevent fraudulent behaviour (e.g. limits for choice of law or connecting factors that are hard to manipulate to begin with).[115] *A contrario*, where the law affords the parties a degree of latitude in structuring their relationship, one can hardly call their actions "evasion of the law". The public policy clause[116] cannot be utilised to combat instances of perceived *fraus legis*.[117] It would, in any case, not be of any use where the issue is the evasion of *foreign* law for the benefit of the *lex fori*.[118] Incidentally, this demonstrates that *fraus legis* is not a concept confined to the homeward-trend debate.

Along these lines, the German Federal Supreme Court decided a case in which a German-Syrian couple, with two people personally unknown to them acting as their representatives on site, married in the Mexican State of Baja California Sur. It held that a), pursuant Art. 11(1) and (3) EGBGB, the marriage was formally valid under the applicable State law and b) that this result does not violate German public policy.[119] (Had the marriage been concluded in Germany, then the special provision of Art. 13(4) EGBGB would have mandated the observance of

---

110 With further references *Wilke*, A Conceptual Analysis (fn. 6), 172.

111 But see *Junker*, IPR (fn. 2), where at least I was not able to spot a discussion of the issue.

112 *Kropholler*, IPR (fn. 2), § 23 before I (156): "especially in the Roman legal family".

113 *Gössl/Kienle* (fn. 2), § 13 n. 185.

114 Staudinger/*Looschelders*, 2024, Einl. IPR, n. 1210–1217; MüKoBGB/*von Hein* (fn. 17), Einl. IPR n. 303–306.

115 Staudinger/*Looschelders*, 2024, Einl. IPR, n. 1213; MüKoBGB/*von Hein* (fn. 17), Einl. IPR n. 304.

116 *Infra* 9.

117 *Gössl/Kienle* (fn. 2), § 13 n. 185; MüKoBGB/*von Hein* (fn. 17), Einl. IPR n. 303 (also with references for the mostly historical opposite position); the German Federal Supreme Court seems to have considered applying the German public policy clause in a case even in the 2010s, but quickly denied its requirements, BGH, NJW 2015, 623, n. 26.

118 *Kropholler*, IPR (fn. 2), § 23 II 2 (160); the application of the *lex fori* is not subject to the German public policy clause, *infra* 9.a).

119 BGH, IPRax 2022, 634 (635 et seq.); on this decision see, e.g., *C. Mayer*, IPRax 2022, 593.

German formal requirements.) In particular, the Court explained that the German legislator had willingly accepted the formal validity of marriages concluded in accordance with foreign formal requirements.[120] This must be seen against the background that Art. 11 EGBGB, the general rule on formal validity, used to cover all kinds of legal acts. But now, since the conflict of laws of contractual obligations has come to be governed by Rome I instead of the EGBGB, marriages concluded abroad form a core area of its application. The German Federal Supreme Court did mention *fraus legis* in passing when dealing with Art. 3(3) Rome I in 2023. It noted that this provision does *not* require the intent to evade a certain law (fraudulently).[121] As far as ascertainable, the Supreme Court only seems to have used the term "fraudulöse Anknüpfung" ("fraudulent connection") only once, more than 40 years ago.[122] The respective judgment is one of the few instances, however, in which it held that one should ignore the law that would be applicable due to fraudulent behaviour.

Most observers seem to agree that even for potentially remaining (extreme) cases in which it would indeed be warranted to combat evasive behaviour of the parties, one can do so without any particular conflict-of-laws provision. The problem simply can be framed as an instance of the general problem of (not) applying a statutory provision to a case ostensibly covered by its wording, but not by its purpose – and extending the effect of another statutory provision (the one whose application the parties tried to avoid) to a case not covered by its wording.[123]

The topic of evasion of law seems more prevalent as a matter of substantive (private) law in Germany. One of the most recent statements is that of a Higher Regional Court: If the chosen contractual design frustrates the purpose of a statutory provision, this constitutes a ground for invalidity under § 134 of the Civil Code[124] (violation of statutory prohibitions).[125] It referred to a judgment of the German Federal Supreme Court on what is now § 476(4) of the Civil Code safeguarding the mandatory nature of many provisions of consumer sales law against contractual circumventions.[126] This is beyond the scope of this contribution.

120 BGH, IPRax 2022, 634 (636 et seq.).

121 BGH, NJW-RR 2024, 140 (n. 45); this is the same case as mentioned *supra* 4.c).

122 BGH, NJW 1981, 522 (524).

123 See Staudinger/*Looschelders*, 2024, Einl. IPR n. 1216; MüKoBGB/*von Hein* (fn. 17), Einl. IPR n. 305; *Kropholler*, IPR (fn. 2), § 23 II 3 (160 et seq.); *Kegel/Schurig* (fn. 11), § 14 IV (482 et seq.).

124 Another basis could be § 138 of the Civil Code (violation of good morals), touched on by BGH, NJW 2016, 2652 (n. 29).

125 OLG Hamm, Judgment of February 9, 2023, I-18 U 125/22.

126 BGH, NJW-RR 2006, 1066 (n. 13), with further references on case law on evasion of law.

7. Renvoi

German conflict of laws, whether statutory or judge-made,[127] admits all types of *renvoi* as a rule. Exclusion of *renvoi* forms the exception. This follows from the wording of Art. 4(1) cl. 1 EGBGB which mandates that the conflict-of-laws rules of the foreign law referred to "also"[128] must be applied, "unless" this would be contrary to the purpose of the reference. This rule/exception relation was also clearly envisioned in the legislative process.[129] The legislator justified this stance *inter alia* with the "significantly more frequent" application of the *lex fori* (in case of remission).[130]

Obvious exceptions to the general rule are found in Art. 4(2) cl. 1 EGBGB (for instances where German conflict of laws expressly refers to "substantive provisions") and Art. 4(2) cl. 2 EGBGB (instances where the parties chose the applicable law[131]). The "purpose clause" has been subject to much debate. Most would agree that to admit *renvoi* would be contrary to the purpose behind the determination of the applicable law by way of an escape clause.[132] For the purposes of this contribution, it seems worthwhile to underscore that this part of Art. 4 EGBGB only pertains to German conflict-of-laws rules. As Art. 4 EGBGB does not contain any restrictions in this regard, the application of foreign conflict-of-laws rules generally includes the *respective* rules on *renvoi*,[133] whatever they may be. The position that the first remission to a foreign law already determined to apply in a series of transmissions should be decisive (regardless of that law's rules for

[127] Art. 4 EGBGB applies to judge-made conflict-of-laws rules as well, e.g. in the field of international company law: See BGH, NJW 2004, 3706 (3707) for the German approach of the "real seat".

[128] This addition is misleading because conflict-of-laws rules determine the application *either* of foreign conflict-of-laws rules *or* of substantive law.

[129] See BT-Drucks. 10/504, 38 (original draft: general admission of *renvoi*); BT-Drucks. 10/5632, 39 (Legal Affairs Committee of the German Bundestag: introduction of the "unless" part but designation of the admission of *renvoi* as the rule).

[130] BT-Drucks. 10/504, 38.

[131] The effects of Art. 4(2) cl. 2 EGBGB are not entirely clear, however: This provision contains a prohibition of a choice of conflict of laws which, taken literally, would mean that any such (unequivocal) choice by the parties would be void; thus, the applicable law would have to be determined under conflict-of-laws provisions applicable in the absence of choice. For this position see, with further references, BeckOGK/*Prinz von Sachsen Gessaphe*, 01.08.2025, Art. 4 EGBGB n. 160. Others seem to read the provision more in the sense of giving a certain meaning to a choice by the parties, meaning that any choice of law clause would have to be read to refer to substantive law exclusively. This would only constitute an exclusion of *renvoi*. For this position apparently MüKoBGB/*von Hein* (fn. 17), Art. 4 EGBGB n. 34; BeckOK/*Lorenz* (fn. 59), Art. 4 EGBGB n. 16; *Junker*, IPR (fn. 2), § 8 n. 27; likely also BGH, NJW-RR 2022, 361 (n. 22). The legislator spoke of a "general limitation of choice of law" (BT-Drucks. 10/504, 39) – which arguably could mean both.

[132] See only MüKoBGB/*von Hein* (fn. 17), Art. 4 EGBGB n. 43; *Junker*, IPR (fn. 2), § 8 n. 26; for a divergent view HK-BGB/*Dörner* (fn. 40), Art. 4 EGBGB n. 10.

[133] See already BT-Drucks. 10/504, 38.

this situation), has, however, gained traction in German conflict of laws scholarship.[134]

Connected with this issue is another one implicating the *lex fori*. If "the" foreign law[135] refers back to German law, German substantive law will be applied (Art. 4(1) cl. 2 EGBGB). In cases where the foreign law excludes *renvoi* when referring to German law, this result theoretically already follows from the application of the foreign rules on *renvoi* that was just mentioned. Where, however, foreign law admits *renvoi*, Art. 4(1) cl. 2 EGBGB is necessary in order to arrive at the application of the *lex fori*. This prevents any similar foreign conflict-of-laws rule from operating in favour of *that* State's *lex fori*. In practical terms, Art. 4(1) cl. 2 EGBGB simplifies the judicial task in two respects. First, the court does not have to establish whether foreign conflict of laws admits or excludes *renvoi* to the extent that it refers to German law. Second, the court can apply the *lex fori* to the merits.

Finally, another concept of German(-Austrian)[136] private international law has clear *lex fori* implications: the notion of the "hidden" or "hypothetical" *renvoi*.[137] This concerns a situation in which German conflict-of-laws rules determine the application of a foreign law that does not expressly determine which law should apply – because the courts of the respective State always apply their own law if they have jurisdiction. From the German perspective, this *modus operandi* could be understood as *containing* the implicit conflict-of-laws rule that foreign courts with jurisdiction should apply *their lex fori*.[138] Many would add the requirement that German courts must have jurisdiction under the foreign rules of jurisdiction as applied to Germany.[139] As can easily be imagined, the idea to "find" an omnilateral[140] conflict-of-laws rule in a foreign jurisdictional rule (containing, if at all, a unilateral conflict-of-laws rule) has also attracted sharp criticism.[141] The position that the respective foreign substantive law should apply in such a situation

---

[134] See only MüKoBGB/*von Hein* (fn. 17), Art. 4 EGBGB n. 113 with further references.

[135] This seems to pertain only to the foreign law determined by German conflict of laws directly, but no one seems to doubt that it also applies to an instance where it is a third, fourth, etc. foreign law, after cases of *trans*mission, that determines the application of German law. Indeed, the German legislator took this view: BT-Drucks. 10/504, 38.

[136] Recently *Verschraegen*, IPRax 2026, 2.

[137] Both terms can mean different things (see e.g. MüKoBGB/*von Hein* (fn. 17), Art. 4 EGBGB n. 57; *Kegel/Schurig* (fn. 11), § 10 VI (409 et seq.)); it does not seem necessary for present purposes to go into detail here.

[138] *Junker*, IPR (fn. 2), § 8 n. 43.

[139] E.g. MüKoBGB/*von Hein* (fn. 17), Art. 4 EGBGB n. 56/64; HK-BGB/*Dörner* (fn. 40), Art. 4 EGBGB n. 16.

[140] For my preference for this term over "multilateral" and "bilateral" see *Wilke*, A Conceptual Analysis (fn. 6), 4.

[141] *Verschraegen*, IPRax 2026, 2 (6 et seq.); BeckOGK/*Prinz von Sachsen Gessaphe* (fn. 131), Art. 4 EGBGB n. 133 et seq.

has been gaining traction.[142] Recently, authors also stopped dealing with the topic as it has lost much of its practical relevance.[143]

8. Adaptation

German case law[144] and authors[145] do contemplate modifications of the applicable foreign law to make it consistent with the requirements of the forum's legal system. The issue rarely appears exclusively framed as one of the *lex fori* but is considered a "general" issue of private international law.[146] In particular, the need for modifications can also arise in the context of the interplay of more than one applicable *foreign* law. Furthermore, modifications of the applicable foreign law, i.e. modifications of substantive law, are not the only viable and, in principle, accepted approach to tackle inconsistencies. The notion of adaptation within the area of conflict of laws– typically: by re-characterising an issue[147] – also exists.

Finally, it is worth mentioning Art. 47 EGBGB as an example of *statutory* law dealing with potential inconsistencies of foreign law with the German *lex fori.* It concerns names acquired under foreign law that, after a *conflit mobile*, are now governed by German law. The person concerned herself can make certain changes to the name. To be clear: This is no case of adaptation in the strict sense, but rather the legislative attempt to avoid the issue by giving the person concerned different options of how to proceed.[148]

9. Public Policy

Probably every conflict-of-laws system in the world – at least unless one exclusively unilaterally determined the application of the *lex fori* – contains a public policy reservation.[149] In the EU at least, the respective public policy reservations (whether domestic or in EU regulations) share many features.[150] Hence, Art. 6 cl. 1 EGBGB will look very familiar to most readers: "A legal provision of another state shall not be applied if its application would lead to a result that is manifestly incompatible with fundamental principles of German law." This wording quite

---

142 *Verschraegen*, IPRax 2026, 2 (8); BeckOGK/*Prinz von Sachsen Gessaphe* (fn. 131), Art. 4 EGBGB n. 138 et seq.; *Mansel/Kronenberg*, in: FS 25 Jahre Deutsches Notarinstitut, 2018, 809 (812 et seq.).

143 *Junker*, IPR (fn. 2), § 8 n. 44 (referring to the 3rd edition of his book).

144 See e.g. the German Federal Supreme Court's textbook-like exposition in BGH, NJW 2014, 1383 (n. 19).

145 *Gössl/Kienle* (fn. 2), § 13 n. 193 et seq.; *Junker*, IPR (fn. 2), § 11 n. 26 et seq.; *Kropholler*, IPR (fn. 2), § 34 (234 et seq.).

146 See also *Wilke*, A Conceptual Analysis (fn. 6), 271 et seq.

147 See MüKoBGB/*von Hein* (fn. 17), Einl. IPR n. 274, on the discussion whether it is permissible to proceed in this manner.

148 See MüKoBGB/*Gössl*, 9th ed. 2024, Art. 47 EGBGB n. 3.

149 See *Symeonides*, Codifying Choice of Law, 2014, 156 et seq.

150 *Wilke*, A Conceptual Analysis (fn. 6), 257 et seq.

clearly expresses the negative function of public policy in contemporary German private international law:[151] it is but a safety valve for emergencies,[152] a "lifeline".[153] Public policy and the *lex fori* intersect in at least three respects.

a) "Avoiding" Public Policy

Where the conflict-of-laws analysis has determined that German law applies (whether based on sound policy or due to a problematic homeward trend), no public policy review can take place.[154] Only foreign law is (and indeed can be) subject to the public policy clauses. This is another way in which the application of the *lex fori* simplifies the judicial task. There is no room for the additional analytical step of making sure there is no public policy violation *every* time[155] that a court applies foreign law. If a German judge considers federal *German* substantive law to contravene (even) the constitution, she is typically[156] not allowed simply to disregard it. Rather, the question must be referred to the German Federal Constitutional Court under Art. 100(1) GG.

b) The Determination of Public Policy

Under Art. 6 cl. 1 EGBGB, the fundamental principles of *German* law constitute the pertinent yardstick. The second clause of Art. 6 EGBGB singles out ("in particular") the incompatibility of the result with "*the* fundamental rights".[157] Read in conjunction with the first clause, the definite article points to the *German* fundamental rights under the GG. The legislative materials support this reading.[158] Their explanation for using the phrase "in particular" is twofold: For one, it is supposed to indicate that public policy is about more than just compliance with "the" fundamental rights. The drafters added that, for another, "fundamental rights" do not only stem from German federal or state law, but also from international conventions. To put it differently, the words "in particular" are also supposed to make sure that human rights conventions are not excluded from the purview of Art. 6 EGBGB. This clarification would be rather unnecessary if

---

151 On that function see only *Junker*, IPR (fn. 2), § 12 n. 3–7.

152 *Kropholler*, IPR (fn. 2), § 36 II 3 (246).

153 *Wurmnest*, in: Leible (ed.), General Principles of European Private International Law, 2016, § 14.01 (305).

154 BeckOGK/*M. Stürner*, 01.08.2025, Art. 6 EGBGB n. 74; *Henrich*, IPRax 2022, 37 (38).

155 This is why I have classified public policy as a formally general issue in the strict sense, *Wilke*, A Conceptual Analysis (fn. 6), 256.

156 For the sake of completeness, it must be mentioned that these constraints only apply to post-constitutional law. As the German Federal Constitutional Court decided at a very early stage on, the ordinary German courts have retained the power to set aside pre-constitutional law, see BVerfGE 2, 124 = NJW 1953, 49.

157 Emphasis added.

158 See BT-Drucks. 10/504, 44.

"the fundamental rights" already covered all fundamental rights (applicable for a German judge).

Admittedly, if fundamental rights in international conventions are covered as well, anyway, it appears somewhat pointless for Art. 6 cl. 2 EGBGB exclusively to focus on German fundamental rights. It must be considered as a declaratory provision against the background of the 1971 "Spaniard" order of the German Federal Constitutional Court,[159] holding for the first time that the German fundamental rights are binding on the German legislator even if the legislation at issue "only" concerns conflict-of-laws rules (and not substantive law).[160] What is more, Art. 6 cl. 2 EGBGB also could give the incorrect impression that a result violating German fundamental rights in a hypothetical (purely) internal situation automatically is a public policy violation in a cross-border case.[161] Rather, one would have to assess whether the pertinent fundamental right itself perhaps applies less stringently in the latter situation – and how exactly.[162] All in all, one wonders whether Art. 6 cl. 2 EGBGB should not be abolished. That Art. 6 EGBGB serves as the (or at least one) "point of entry" of German fundamental rights had been accepted even previously.[163]

The initial statement that the principles of German law make up the yardstick against which to measure the result requires further refinement. First, the standard that the Federal Supreme Court and the lower courts repeatedly apply is as follows: There is a violation of public policy only where the result of applying the foreign law would so strongly contradict the fundamental principles of the German rules and the notions of justice embodied in them that it would be regarded as intolerable according to domestic standards.[164] Second, these "domestic" standards must not be misunderstood as restricted to "purely" German law. The relevance of fundamental rights other than those of the German constitution was already mentioned. More generally, the Federal Supreme Court has stated that public policy is not immutable but constitutes an expression of the fundamental values of the domestic and, increasingly, the European legal community, is subject to changes in those values, and follows them, albeit at times with a certain

[159] See MüKoBGB/*von Hein* (fn. 17), Art. 6 EGBGB n. 146.

[160] BVerfGE 31, 58 = NJW 1971, 1509 (1510 et seq.).

[161] Warning against this misunderstanding BeckOK/*Lorenz* (fn. 59), Art. 6 EGBGB n. 15. One could argue, however, that the wording "*incompatible* with fundamental rights" deliberately avoids the term "violation", see *Junker*, IPR (fn. 2), §12 n. 25. Then again, this subtle difference can be missed easily.

[162] See already BVerfGE 31, 58 = NJW 1971, 1509 (1511 et seq.); also e.g. BGHZ 120, 29 = JZ 1993, 208 (209).

[163] See e.g. BGH, NJW 1973, 417 (419); the German Federal Constitutional Court had suggested as much, see BVerfGE 31, 58 = NJW 1971, 1509.

[164] See BGH, EuZW 2023, 240 (n. 18); BGH, NJW 2022, 3644 (n. 25); also BGHZ 123, 278 = NJW 1993, 3269 (3270) (in the context of recognition, with many references from older cases); also e.g. OLG Stuttgart, Order of 23.9.2025, 17 UF 73/25, juris (n. 54).

temporal delay.[165] Hence, a violation of fundamental principles of EU law, e. g. the Fundamental Freedoms of the TFEU, can constitute a violation of German public policy.[166]

Theoretically, even another state's public policy can be relevant for German courts. To be sure, the view that it cannot be observed as a rule still is a widely held in Germany.[167] Already due to its negative function,[168] Art. 6 EGBGB cannot serve as a basis to enforce foreign public policy.[169] Yet, typically in the same breath, several commentators add that the answer is less clear-cut where German conflict-of-laws rules admit *renvoi* (as, again,[170] is the general stance of German conflict of laws, see Art. 4(1) EGBGB).[171] The idea is that then it should not matter to German courts why and how the applicable[172] foreign conflict-of-laws rules lead to a certain result, whether through its regular conflict-of-laws rules or the public policy clause.[173] Where German conflict-of-laws rules call for the application of foreign conflict of laws in the interest of international harmony of decisions, it would be nonsensical to apply the foreign conflict-of-laws rules only partially.[174] The goal of international harmony of decisions would be severely hampered if one ignored foreign public policy in the circumstances just described.[175] The result reached by the German court – that is: after applying German conflict-of-laws rules, foreign conflict-of-laws rules, the foreign applicable law and the public policy of the State whose conflict-of-laws rules determined the ultimately applicable law – must not violate German public policy.[176]

[165] BGHZ 169, 240 = JZ 2007, 738 (740); see also, e. g., *Wurmnest* (fn. 153), § 14.03 B (315 et seq.).

[166] BeckOK/*Lorenz* (fn. 59), Art. 6 EGBGB n. 15; in depth on the relevance of primary and secondary EU law MüKoBGB/*von Hein* (fn. 17), Art. 6 EGBGB n. 176–184; for the ECHR as well as EU freedoms e. g. *Helms*, IPRax 2017, 153 (156 et seq.).

[167] MüKoBGB/*von Hein* (fn. 17), Art. 6 EGBGB n. 83; *Junker*, IPR (fn. 2), § 12 n. 44; but see *Bruening*, Die Beachtlichkeit des fremden ordre public, 1997; this book seems to have caused *Kegel/Schurig* (fn. 11), § 16 VII (540), to reconsider the issue.

[168] *Supra* 9. (before a)).

[169] *Kubis*, RabelsZ 64 (2000), 797 (803). *Bruening*, Die Beachtlichkeit des fremden ordre public, 1997, 296, expressly suggested to read Art. 6 EGBGB as an omnilateral conflict-of-laws rule.

[170] *Supra* 7.

[171] MüKoBGB/*von Hein* (fn. 17), Art. 6 EGBGB n. 86; BeckOGK/*M. Stürner* (fn. 154), Art. 6 EGBGB n. 147; *Junker*, IPR (fn. 2), § 12 n. 44; *Kegel/Schurig* (fn. 11), § 16 VII (540); *Kropholler*, IPR (fn. 2), § 36 VII (258).

[172] The public policy clause of a state whose conflict-of-laws rules are not applicable (not even after a further *renvoi*) is always irrelevant, BeckOGK/*M. Stürner* (fn. 154), Art. 6 EGBGB n. 148.

[173] *Kropholler*, IPR (fn. 2), § 36 VII (258).

[174] Ibid.

[175] *Gebauer*, in: FS Jayme, 2004, 223 (238); but see BeckOK/*Lorenz* (fn. 59), Art. 6 EGBGB n. 19.

[176] BeckOGK/*M. Stürner* (fn. 154), Art. 6 EGBGB n. 151 and 153; MüKoBGB/*von Hein* (fn. 17), Art. 6 EGBGB n. 90; *Junker*, IPR (fn. 2), § 12 n. 45; some merely state that foreign public policy (itself) could be incompatible with German public policy, e. g. *Kegel/Schurig* (fn. 11), § 16 VII (540). But perhaps this merely is a shorthand formulation for the more nuanced approach.

c) *Consequences of a Public Policy Violation*

The only[177] explicit legal consequence of Art. 6 cl. 1 EGBGB is the non-application of the respective rule of foreign law. *A contrario*, all other rules of the *lex causae* – i.e. those that do not violate German public policy – within the scope of the reference must still be applied.[178] This can create gaps. If, for example, the *lack* of a rule on the respective issue under the applicable law runs afoul of German public policy, only the application of *some* rule will remedy the violation. Most German courts, scholars and the legislator proceed on the basis of a principle of minimal encroachment upon the *lex causae*[179] or a principle of maximally "sparing" the *lex causae*.[180] Accordingly, the application of the *lex fori* is not the primary solution. Rather, the courts should rely on the *lex causae* as much as possible and use the *lex fori* only as the fallback option.[181] Unlike for the case of a failure to ascertain the applicable law,[182] courts and (most) scholars[183] agree with this approach.

III. International Civil Procedure

1. *The* Lex Fori (Processualis) *Rule*

As a longstanding fundamental rule in Germany, matters of procedure are governed solely by the procedural law of the court seised.[184] The rule is not expressly laid down in written law, but some provisions of the Civil Procedure Code (ZPO) seem to rest on it.[185] But at least since *Grunsky's* seminal contribution in the 1970s,[186] the question is marked by a lack of certainty.[187]

---

177 *Spickhoff*, Der ordre public im internationalen Privatrecht, 1989, 103.

178 See BGHZ 234, 166 = IPRax 2023, 316 (320) (pertaining to Art. 35 Succession Regulation); *Spickhoff*, (fn. 177), 105; BT-Drucks. 10/504, 43 et seq.

179 *Spickhoff* (fn. 177), 105 (with further references).

180 MüKoBGB/*von Hein* (fn. 17), Art. 6 EGBGB n. 230; BT-Drucks. 10/504, 44.

181 BGHZ 234, 166 = IPRax 2023, 316 (320) – pertaining to Art. 35 Succession Regulation, but referring to decisions under the EGBGB, i.e. BGHZ 169, 240 = JZ 2007, 738 (741); BGHZ 120, 29 = JZ 1993, 208 (210).

182 *Supra* 5.b).

183 MüKoBGB/*von Hein* (fn. 17), Art. 6 EGBGB n. 230; Staudinger/*Voltz*, 2013, Art. 6 EGBGB n. 212; *Junker*, IPR (fn. 2), §12 n. 36; *Gössl/Kienle* (fn. 2), §13 n. 177; *Kropholler*, IPR (fn. 2), §36 V (255); but see *von Bar/Mankowski* (fn. 37), §7 n. 285.

184 BGH, WM 2024, 1618 (n. 9); Stein/*Althammer*, 24th ed. 2024, Einleitung n. 325.

185 E.g. §369 ZPO: If the taking of evidence by a foreign authority complies with the laws applicable by the (German) trial court, no objection may be raised on the ground that it is deficient under the foreign law.

186 *Grunsky*, ZZP 89 (1976), 241.

187 *Kronke* even called the effect of the contribution "the Grunskian Turn": ZZPInt 20 (2015), 399 (400).

a) Rationale

In Germany, there seems to always have been scepticism of using public policy as a rationale for the *lex fori* rule.[188] Indeed, it would be incompatible with the today widely accepted negative function of public policy to assign it such a (strong) positive role. If one wanted to rely on the protection of core values of the forum in a positive, "offensive" way, the pertinent concept in private international law would be the one of overriding mandatory provisions.[189] This line of thought implicating governmental interests provides a segue to one of the supposed main reasons behind the rule: the nature of civil procedural law as public law.[190]

This nature itself is often heavily qualified. There are strong reservations, even warnings against using this character as a basis for interpreting or applying civil procedure law.[191] Similar reservations have been made against making inferences from it for the question at issue. The idea is that, while civil procedure law may "technically" be public law, the state does not primarily appear in a commanding or demanding role in civil proceedings, but assumes a more restrained, almost observing role, only providing a forum for a private dispute.[192] Such a statement itself runs the risk of being criticized as too broad to be able to make inferences from it. That said, in the version most recently propagated by *Brinkmann*, the approach expressly and plausibly contains the acknowledgment of *parts* of civil procedure being very close to "core" public law.[193]

For present purposes, this point does not have to prove decisive, anyway. Even if civil procedure law were the purest of pure public law,[194] the *lex fori* rule would not automatically arise from it. To be sure, it seems ingrained in many people's minds that German – or, indeed, all – public law has but one conflict-of-laws rule, i. e. that the applicable law will be court's (or agency's) own law. While there had always been detractors,[195] this notion came under heavy attack in particular at the beginning of the 21st century, both from public and private international scholars.[196] They demonstrate that, far from being a theoretical necessity, the notion is also contradicted by actual scenarios in which a German body applies foreign

---

188 See, in particular, *Coester-Waltjen* (fn. 10), n. 103–109.

189 *Wilke*, A Conceptual Analysis (fn. 6), 141–143.

190 For this as the main reason *Junker*, Internationales Zivilverfahrensrecht, 6th ed. 2023, § 21 n. 2.

191 E. g. Stein/*Althammer* (fn. 184), Einleitung n. 118.

192 *Brinkmann*, ZZP 129 (2016), 461, 466; *Coester-Waltjen* (fn. 10), n. 122.

193 *Brinkmann*, ZZP 129 (2016), 461, 467.

194 As is suggested when adjudication is sometimes called a direct expression of sovereign authority, *von Bar/Mankowski* (fn. 37), § 5 n. 77.

195 Between 1910 and 1930 already, *Neumeyer* published his "Internationales Verwaltungsrecht" in four volumes.

196 *Hemler*, Die Methodik der "Eingriffsnorm" im modernen Kollisionsrecht, 2019, 61–74 and passim; *Menzel*, Internationales Öffentliches Recht, 2011; *Kment*, Grenzüberschreitendes Verwaltungshandeln, 2010; *Ohler*, Die Kollisionsordnung des Allgemeinen Verwaltungsrechts, 2005.

public law. Germany's Federal Administrative Court mentioned the potential applicability of foreign public law in passing in the 1960s already.[197]

Against this background, the current consensus – albeit itself not without its critics[198] and/or proposals of more nuanced versions[199] – bases the *lex fori* rule on the notions of practicality and efficiency.[200] It can hardly be denied that court organisation and the rules of procedure should be aligned with one another so far as possible.[201] The difference to the application of foreign substantive law as expressed by *Kegel/Schurig*: To *apply* foreign law is a different animal than to *comply* with it.[202] Compliance would lead to a serious complication of proceedings. "Subtle debates as to the law applicable to each individual procedural step would run counter to the objective of affording the parties effective legal protection."[203]

b) (Potential) Exceptions

Although the *lex fori* rule often appears in absolute, unrestricted terms, it is generally agreed that there can be exceptions to it.[204] What those exceptions are and how far they reach – that is a different question subject to controversy.

The German Federal Supreme Court held in 2024 that, "by way of exception to this fundamental rule [i.e. the *lex fori* rule]", the question of the power of disposition over the right in dispute, which precedes and underlies the capacity to conduct proceedings, is governed by the *lex causae*.[205] It is up for debate whether this actually constitutes an exception. One might also ask the other way around why the (German) conflict-of-laws rules on the power of disposition over a right should *not* apply where the issue arises as an incidental question in civil procedure law. Does the *lex fori* rule really say that, in principle, even incidental questions of substantive law are governed by German procedural law unless one can make room for an exception – or are they outside of the rule, anyway? Ten years earlier, when deciding along the same lines about *voluntary* procedural standing, the German Federal Supreme Court had been less explicit about the relationship between the *lex fori* rule and the application of the potentially foreign *lex causae* applicable for incidental questions of substantive law.[206] Arguably, the *lex causae*

---

197 BVerwGE 18, 26 (29).

198 *Schack*, IZVR (fn. 73), n. 49; *von Bar/Mankowski* (fn. 37), § 5 n. 78.

199 E.g. *Geimer*, Internationales Zivilprozessrecht, 9th ed. 2024, n. 333 et seq.

200 Stein/Althammer (fn. 184), Einleitung n. 325 and 327; *Kropholler*, IPR (fn. 2), § 56 IV 5 (596); *G. Wagner*, Prozeßverträge, 1998, 355–357; with nuances, *Jaeckel* (fn. 1), 47–49.

201 *Linke/Hau*, Internationales Zivilverfahrensrecht, 9th ed. 2024, n. 2.10.

202 *Kegel/Schurig* (fn. 11), § 22 III (1055).

203 Stein/*Althammer* (fn. 184), Einleitung n. 325.

204 *Linke/Hau* (fn. 201), n. 2.10; *Junker*, IZVR (fn. 190), § 21 n. 3.

205 BGH, WM 2024, 1618 (n. 10).

206 BGH, IBRRS 2014, 0081 (n. 34).

should always apply where German procedural rules give rise to an incidental question of substantive law.[207]

With regard to the capacity to be a party to legal proceedings, the conceptual picture is clearer. According to § 50 ZPO, this special capacity follows directly from a party's *legal* capacity. It would seem to follow that the latter must be determined according to the law applicable to legal capacity, as determined by German conflict of laws, i. e. Art. 7(1) EGBGB.[208] (Unlike as shown in the preceding paragraph, such a treatment of an incidental question does not seem to be regarded as an exception from the *lex fori* rule, by the way;[209] it rather appears to be its confirmation.) But despite some confusion even within the Supreme Court itself,[210] the prevailing approach is much simpler: One should determine whether someone has the capacity to be a party to German legal proceedings by looking at the respective *procedural* capacity under their personal law (instead of by looking at their *legal* capacity under substantive law).[211] This is an omnilateral procedural conflict-of-laws rule and, as such, a clear exception to the *lex fori* rule. To be sure, some commentators accept the *lex fori* approach as an alternative prong.[212] As this view only adds layers instead of negating the existence of the unwritten rule, however, it does not challenge the isolated consensus regarding the existence of the exception.

The ZPO does contain a rule on foreigner's capacity to *conduct* legal proceedings. According to § 55 ZPO, a foreigner who does *not* have procedural capacity under his own law is regarded as having such capacity if he is endowed with it under the law of the forum. As it only enshrines an *alternative* conflict-of-laws rule (determining the application of the *lex fori*),[213] the rule does not expressly say how the capacity to conduct legal proceedings should be determined in the first place. Some assume the *lex fori* rule to apply. This means applying §§ 51, 52 ZPO which make the capacity dependent upon the capacity to conclude contracts under substantive law. Hence, one would need to determine the applicable law to that question according to German conflict of laws, i. e. Art. 7(2) EGBGB.[214] But the prevailing view assumes another (unwritten) exception to the *lex fori* rule

207 See *Kern*, LMK 2024, 816842.

208 The approach indeed taken by the Higher Regional Court of Berlin: KG NJW 2014, 2737.

209 *Junker*, IZVR (fn. 190), § 21 n. 11 (stating that this would be the *result* of the *lex fori* rule); similarly Stein/*Jacoby*, ZPO, 24th ed. 2024, § 50 n. 48.

210 See BGH, GRUR 2023, 1561, 1562 (n. 12: one must determine a company's *legal* capacity under its home law! – n. 13: the company has lost its capacity *to be party to legal proceedings* under its home law!).

211 Stein/*Jacoby* (fn. 209), § 50 n. 48; *Junker*, IZVR (fn. 190), § 21 n. 12; BGH, NJW 1999, 1871.

212 Among several prongs, see MüKoZPO/*Hau*, 7th ed. 2025, § 50 n. 63; Michalski/Heidinger/Leible/Schmidt/*Leible*, GmbHG, 4th ed. 2023, vol. 1 Int. GesR n. 130; *Brinkmann*, ZZP 129 (2016), 461 (488).

213 It is doubtful that § 55 ZPO itself is an exception to the *lex fori* rule, see *von Bar/Mankowski* (fn. 37), § 5 n. 82 (no actual *application* of foreign law).

214 BGH, JZ 1956, 535.

here, one at least foreshadowed by § 55 ZPO ("[not…] under his own law").[215] In an approach that structurally corresponds to that taken concerning the issue of the capacity to be a party to proceedings, one is supposed to look at a person's capacity to conduct legal proceedings under the law of their nationality.[216] Both approaches used to lead to the same results as the capacity to conclude contracts was governed by the law of a person's nationality as well (Art. 7 EGBGB in the version in force between 1986 and 2022). However, as the revised Art. 7(2) EGBGB employs habitual residence as its connecting factor, the outcome now may depend on which approach one adopts. At least for this reason, the ZPO should be reformed here (as the Federal Ministry of Justice and Consumer Protection has recognised by now).[217]

c) Characterisation

It is once more, in principle, the *lex fori* that determines whether an issue is characterized as procedural (leading to the application of the *lex fori* rule) or substantive (leading to the application of conflict of laws).[218]

2. Jurisdiction, Parallel Proceedings, Enforcement

a) Jurisdiction

In principle, the autonomous German law of civil procedure does not mention international grounds of jurisdiction. To determine whether German courts have international jurisdiction, the general idea is to apply the ZPO[219] rules concerning venue (local jurisdiction); they thus have a double function.[220] Due to their original function of allocating competence among courts *within* Germany, grounds of exclusive jurisdiction generally have not been designed with the purpose of protecting the forum's interest in a "proper" interpretation of its law.

Nor is not obvious that the nature of jurisdiction would necessarily stay the same when extending a rule on venue to the international plane. In other words, exclusive jurisdiction of one court within Germany does not inescapably entail that German courts must be considered to have exclusive jurisdiction vis-à-vis

[215] *Hau*, IPRax 2024, 125 (126).

[216] MüKoZPO/*Hau* (fn. 212), § 55 n. 1; *Junker*, IZVR (fn. 190), § 21 n. 13.

[217] *Hau*, IPRax 2024, 125 (126 and 128 with a proposal *de lege ferenda*); under the draft bill for a reform of German arbitration law (*infra* fn. 275), § 55 ZPO uses habitual residence as the connecting factor.

[218] *Junker*, IZVR (fn. 190), § 21 n. 4.

[219] For express rules on international jurisdiction beyond the ZPO see § 98 FamFG et seq. (Act on Procedure in Family Matters and Maters of Non-Contentious Jurisdiction). International jurisdiction of the German courts for enforcement proceedings presupposes that enforcement is sought against assets located within Germany, BGH, IPRax 2007, 128 (129).

[220] *Schack*, IZVR (fn. 73), n. 288; *Junker*, IZVR (fn. 190), § 18 n. 7; BGH, NJW 1985, 2090.

the courts of other States. While the absence of such an automatism appears to be widely accepted, there is less agreement as to which is the rule and which constitutes the exception.[221] More than a century ago, the German Imperial Court considered jurisdiction concerning rights (mostly) *in rem* in immovable property (§ 24 ZPO) to be internationally exclusive, reasoning that German sovereignty would not allow foreign judges to make decisions in respect of such property within German borders.[222] This seems excessive. In particular, a foreign decision about who the owner of a property located in Germany is does not – indeed: cannot – have any impact on German territory as such.[223] Finally, it seems worth mentioning that exclusivity generally only operates as between courts. Arbitration agreements are not invalid merely because they concern matters falling within the exclusive jurisdiction of German courts.[224] This realisation calls into question the strength of the alleged State interests underlying rules of exclusive jurisdiction. Surely, if they were compelling, they should also prevail where one is not concerned with a choice between courts but between courts and arbitral tribunals?

b) Parallel Proceedings

Where parallel proceedings in another State are not subject to Art. 29 et seq. Brussels I*bis*,[225] to a multilateral convention like the CMR or to a bilateral convention,[226] German statutory law is silent. If the foreign court was seised earlier in respect of the same dispute ("*Streitgegenstand*"), the courts – since the time[227] of the Imperial Court[228] – consider such proceedings to bar subsequent proceedings in Germany just like earlier proceedings in one German court would bar parallel proceedings in all other German courts under § 261(3) No. 1 ZPO.[229] The *lex fori* governs the assessment of whether the disputes are identical.[230]

---

221 For a parallel treatment as the rule *Schack*, IZVR (fn. 73), n. 248; *Kropholler*, Handbuch des IZVR I, 1982, Ch. III §1 n. 153 et seq.; against almost any governmental interest justifying exclusive international jurisdiction *Geimer* (fn. 199), n. 878 et seq.

222 RGZ 102 [1921], 251 (253).

223 *J. Schröder*, Internationale Zuständigkeit, 1971, 367.

224 BGH, NJW 1996, 1753 (1754).

225 Including Art. 33 et seq. Brussels I*bis* on certain situations involving third States.

226 There is a 1977 agreement between Germany and Israel about the recognition and enforcement of judicial decisions in civil and commercial matters.

227 See *Gebauer*, in: FS Schack, 2022, 585 (586 et seq.) for a recent account of the developments in German law.

228 RGZ 49 [1901], 340 (344).

229 E.g. BGH, NJW 2019, 2935 (n. 24); NJW-RR 2008, 1169 (n. 17 et seq.); BGH, NJW 2001, 524 (525).

230 *Schack*, IZVR (fn. 73), n. 894; OLG München, NJW 2014, 1893.

Many observers assume that, doctrinally, this way of dealing with foreign parallel proceedings amounts to applying § 261(3) No. 1 ZPO by analogy.[231] Quite recently, *Gebauer* touched on the idea that the issue actually might be understood in terms of substitution.[232] This would fit the case law well since, as far as I can see, the courts have not analysed the requirements of an analogy *lege artis*. The German Federal Supreme Court, e.g., at least on one occasion seems to have applied § 261(3) No. 1 ZPO simply "directly".[233] If the provision were indeed being applied by analogy, its consequence would seem to have to follow: unlike under Article 29(1) Brussels I*bis*, the German court second seised would not merely stay the proceedings but would have to decline jurisdiction. This, in fact, appears to be the position of the German Federal Supreme Court.[234] Many scholars reject this rather categorical approach and instead favour a stay of proceedings (by applying § 148 ZPO by analogy),[235] a view the Supreme Court itself had once espoused for certain cases.[236]

In any event, however, foreign proceedings will have an effect[237] only if a decision rendered in them (likely) would be recognised in Germany.[238] Such a requirement is not found in § 261 ZPO, which comes as no surprise, as, originally, the provision only concerns parallel proceedings within Germany. At least nowadays, not many authors seem to bother to explain where this prerequisite derives from in cross-border situations. One can argue that the bar of § 261(3) No. 1 ZPO (generally) presupposes that the claimant can achieve her procedural objectives in the other proceedings, a condition that is not fulfilled where the resulting decision would not be recognised in Germany.[239] Furthermore, it would be paradoxical if parallel foreign proceedings could have more impact in Germany than the resulting decision.[240] Accordingly, determining the relevance of foreign parallel proceedings requires an analysis of the German rules of recognition, as laid down e.g. in conventions or in § 328 ZPO.[241] German public policy (§ 328(1) No. 4 ZPO) often will not be relevant at this stage because and to the extent that

---

[231] *Linke/Hau* (fn. 201), n. 7.27; MüKoZPO/*Becker-Eberhard*, 7th ed. 2025, § 261 n. 73; Stein/*H. Roth*, ZPO, 24th ed. 2024, § 261 n. 54; but see *Gebauer*, in: FS Schack (fn. 227), 585 (595), for a new alternative approach: applying the pertinent provisions of Brussels I*bis* by analogy.

[232] *Gebauer*, in: FS Schack (fn. 227), 585 (587).

[233] BGH, NJW 2001, 524 (525).

[234] BGH, NJW 2001, 524 (525).

[235] *Schack*, IZVR (fn. 73), n. 910; *Linke/Hau* (fn. 201), n. 7.27; but see Stein/*H. Roth*, ZPO, 24th ed. 2024, § 261 n. 70.

[236] BGH, NJW 1986, 2195 (2196).

[237] For the older view that foreign proceedings could not have an effect, see the references provided by Stein/*H. Roth*, ZPO, 24th ed. 2024, § 261 n. 55 (with fn. 232).

[238] BGH, NJW 2019, 2935 (n. 24); NJW-RR 2008, 1169 (n. 17 et seq.); BGH, NJW 2001, 524 (525); RGZ 49 [1901], 340 (344 et seq.).

[239] *Schack*, IZVR (fn. 73), n. 896.

[240] This was the (brief) reasoning of the Imperial Court, RGZ 49 [1901], 340 (344 et seq.).

[241] *Schack*, IZVR (fn. 73), n. 897; Stein/*H. Roth* (fn. 237), § 261 n. 62 et seq.; *Linke/Hau* (fn. 201), n. 7.27.

its violation by the foreign decision will not yet be apparent. Easier cases for the necessary prognosis are international jurisdiction of the foreign courts according to the *German* rules of jurisdiction (§ 328(1) No. 1 ZPO), proper and timely service on the defendant (§ 328(1) No. 2 ZPO), and the question of reciprocity (§ 328(1) No. 5 ZPO).[242]

c) Enforcement

The *lex fori* governs the conduct of enforcement proceedings in Germany.[243] Where foreign judgments can and must be enforced without an *exequatur* (in particular: within the scope of Brussels I*bis*), the foreign decision itself is enforced – but according to (in principle: autonomous) German rules.[244] This is what is laid down in Art. 41(1) cl. 1 Brussels I*bis*. There are some instances in German law of special rules for such foreign decisions. Notable in this context is the new § 929(2) cl. 2 ZPO (in force since January 1, 2022). For a foreign interim protective measure enforceable without *exequatur*, the general one-month time limit for enforcement (§ 929(2) cl. 1 ZPO)[245] is extended to two months, giving the creditor more time to enforce the measure in this particular cross-border setting.[246]

In all other cases, the German *exequatur* decision is enforced. What else but the German rules could apply?[247] The CJEU confirmed this for Brussels I: The procedural rules of the Member State in which enforcement is sought are to apply to "the phase of enforcement in the strict sense", without any requirement to apply any provisions of the national legislation of the Member State of origin.[248] There is, however, the familiar EU-law caveat that the procedural rules in which enforcement is sought must not be liable to undermine the effectiveness of the European rules on recognition and enforcement.[249]

IV. The *Forum/Ius* Alignment

There are three ways to conceptualise the alignment of *forum* and *ius*.[250] First, one can keep conflict of laws and jurisdiction as separate areas of law but align

---

[242] *Schack*, IZVR (fn. 73), n. 897; Stein/*H. Roth* (fn. 237), § 261 n. 63 et seq.

[243] *Schack*, IZVR (fn. 73), n. 1133.

[244] *Geimer* (fn. 199), n. 3240.

[245] It used to be applicable to interim measures from other Member States in the Brussels I context. This was the object of the CJEU's ruling in Case C-379/19, to be discussed in the following paragraph.

[246] BT-Drucks. 19/27636, 34.

[247] For the application of German law e.g. *Geimer* (fn. 199), n. 3155; BGH, IHR 2019, 128 (129) – but see, conceptually critically, *Rentsch*, IPRax 2020, 337 (341); BGH, NJW-RR 2009, 279 (n. 9).

[248] CJEU [Case C-379/19], IPRax 2020, 363 (n. 32 et seq.).

[249] CJEU [Case C-379/19], IPRax 2020, 363 (n. 44).

[250] See *J. Schröder* (fn. 223), 504 et seq.

the connecting factors (to the extent possible under each system's own policy). Second, one can make the applicable law dependent upon jurisdiction. Third, the other way around, one can make jurisdiction dependent upon the applicable law.

1. Alignment of Connecting Factors

The first approach appears in EU conflict of laws. It heavily relies on the connecting factor of habitual residence. Habitual residence often aligns with domicile. Hence, where jurisdiction depends on a party's domicile (e.g. Art. 4 Brussels I*bis*) and the applicable law on the same party's habitual residence, the competent court will apply its own law. The choice of habitual residence over nationality as a connecting factor in conflict of laws thus generally facilitates the alignment of *forum* and *ius*.[251] Yet in Germany in recent years, jurisdictional concerns only played a minor role, if any,[252] when the German legislator changed some connecting factors under German conflict of laws from nationality to habitual residence: for the capacity to contract, Art. 7(2) EGBGB, for care and support relationships,[253] Art. 24(1) EGBGB, and for a person's name, Art. 10(1) EGBGB.

2. Ius *Following the* Forum

a) In Divorce Cases

The second approach appears in Art. 8(d) Rome III. As there will only be jurisdiction under Brussels II*ter* if there is at least some connection to the forum, there will also always be a connection somewhat relevant for conflict of laws. It is far from obvious, however, that it will be a "close" connection in the sense of Recital 21 Rome III. For Germany, pursuant to Art. 17(2) EGBGB, large parts of Rome III are even applicable outside its scope, i.e. for private divorces. But Art. 17(2) No. 4 EGBGB excludes Art. 8(d) Rome III from this extension. This, however, is no expression of disagreement with this type of alignment of *forum* and *ius*, but simply due to the fact that there is no *forum* – and thus no *lex fori* – in the case of a private divorce.[254]

---

[251] E.g. *Dutta*, IPRax 2017, 139 (143).

[252] For the new Art. 10(1) EGBGB (changed by the law of June 11, 2024), see BT-Drucks. 20/10997, 41 et seq.: integration as the main aspect; for the new Art. 7(2) EGBGBG and Art. 24(1) EGBGB (both changed by the law of May 4, 2021), see BT-Drucks. 19/24445, 126: the international trend as the main aspect – but also 318: promotion of legal certainty (scil. for other people in Germany) and facilitation of legal dealings.

[253] I.e. guardianship, custodianship, and caretaking arrangements.

[254] See BT-Drucks. 19/4852, 38.

b) Alignment as an Argument

Why align *forum* and *ius* in the first place? To improve the quality, efficiency, and speed of the judicial process. This thought is not only relevant for legislators. It was also one of the reasons for the German Federal Supreme Court to apply the precedence of the German nationality pursuant to Art. 5(1) cl. 2 EGBGB[255] in the context of Art. 8(c) Rome III (where applicable due to Art. 17(2) EGBGB[256]).[257] Since the CJEU has held that even a shared ineffective nationality supports the application of Art. 3(1)(b) Brussels II*bis* (now: Art. 3(b) Brussels II*ter*),[258] the precedence of the German nationality at least leads to the application of the *lex fori*.

3. Forum *Following* Ius: *The Example of the new Commercial Court Dresden*

With effect from November 1, 2025, amendments to the Ordinance of the Saxon State Ministry of Justice and for Democracy, European Affairs and Gender Equality (Saxon Judicial Administration Ordinance: *Sächsische Justizorganisationsverordnung, SächsJOrgVO*),[259] established a commercial court as a division of the Higher Regional Court Dresden, officially called the "Commercial Court Dresden" (§ 7(1) SächsJOrgVO). Under § 119b of the federal Courts Organization Act (*Gerichtsverfassungsgesetz, GVG*), the German states can set up one or more divisions ("senates") of a Higher Regional Court as a commercial court. They have jurisdiction in certain areas over disputes with an amount in controversy of EUR 500,000 or more. Several states already have made use of this option; among others, there now are commercial courts in Berlin, Frankfurt, Hamburg and Munich. The new Commercial Court Dresden stands out, however. For one, Saxony has not determined that proceedings can be conducted in the English language.[260] For another, pursuant to § 7(2) cl. 1 SächsJOrgVO, the Court only has jurisdiction over disputes "which are to be judged according to German law". In other words, jurisdiction depends on the applicability of German law.

It is unclear what prompted the Saxon Ministry of Justice to adopt this regulatory approach. German scholars widely frown upon the idea of such a combination of jurisdiction and conflict of laws.[261] The main reason is that jurisdiction

---

255 *Supra* II. 3.

256 *Supra* a).

257 See BGHZ 226, 365 = JZ 2021, 254 (259).

258 See CJEU [Case C-168/08], IPRax 2010, 66 (70 et seq.), for a shared nationality of a Member State; for the extension to the shared nationality of a third state see *Hau*, IPrax 2010, 50 (52 et seq.).

259 The changes were brought about by the 15th ordinance of the Saxon State Ministry of Justice changing the Saxon Judicial Administration Ordinance of October 1, 2025.

260 Pursuant to § 184a (1) GVG, Saxony would have had (and still has) the power to do so.

261 MüKoZPO/*Patzina*/*Windau*, 7th ed. 2025, § 12 n. 63; Stein/*H. Roth*, ZPO, 24th ed. 2024, Vorbemerkungen vor § 12 ZPO, n. 42; *Schack*, IZVR (fn. 73), n. 267; *Kropholler*, Handbuch IZVR I (fn. 221), Ch. III n. 115.

must be predictable. Requiring a conflict of laws analysis as a precondition for determining jurisdiction is difficult to reconcile with that objective. Some cross-border element is particularly likely to exist in large commercial disputes. It seems that the necessity to apply foreign law even to only a small part of the dispute would exclude the jurisdiction of the Commercial Court Dresden.

It should be noted that this example is no "classic" instance of *forum legis*. § 7(2) cl. 1 SächsJOrgVO is confined to (and, for reasons of legislative competence, must be confined to) the special jurisdiction of the Commercial Court Dresden as a division of the Higher Regional Court. If it turns out that a commercial dispute originally brought before the Commercial Court would involve the application of foreign law, this does not, in itself, negate the international jurisdiction of the German courts.

V. Equality between the *Lex Fori* and Foreign Law

German law does not merely tolerate the application of foreign substantive law but positively mandates it.[262] This amounts to a recognition of foreign law as equal to the *lex fori*.[263] The general equality between foreign and domestic law is also inherent in the "Savignian" approach to start the analysis with a set of facts and ask which law applies to it.[264] As a rule, therefore, the content of foreign law does not matter – unless, of course, its application violates German public policy.[265] Nor do the purported governmental interests behind (domestic and foreign law) play a role in the conflict-of-laws process. The method of governmental interest analysis has mostly been viewed critically, at least as regards its potential application in Germany or continental Europe.[266] In the course of the private international law reform in the 1980s, the German legislator explicitly declined to incorporate this concept.[267] It is a different matter that there has been an ongoing discussion about the "neutral" or "political" nature of conflict-of-laws rules.[268]

The conflict-of-laws rules in the original EGBGB 1900 mostly had a unilateral character. It fell to the courts to construct them as omnilateral[269] rules.[270] Today,

---

[262] *Supra* as to the mandatory nature of conflict-of-laws rules.

[263] BeckOGK/*Fervers* (fn. 58), Art. 3 EGBGB n. 8.

[264] See *Kropholler*, IPR (fn. 2), § 3 I (16).

[265] *Supra* 9.

[266] See *Kropholler*, IPR (fn. 2), § 11 IV 2 (90 et seq.) and 6 (93 et seq.); *Kegel/Schurig* (fn. 11), § 6 V (323) (potentially rather pejoratively).

[267] BT-Drucks. 10/504, 26.

[268] See e.g. *Hornung*, Internationales Privatrecht zwischen Wertneutralität und Politik, 2021; Heindler/Melcher (eds.), Die Achtung des Fremden, 2024; *M. Stürner*, in: FS Herbert Kronke, 2020, 557; Gebauer/Huber (eds.), Politisches Kollisionsrecht, 2021.

[269] *Supra* fn. 140.

[270] See e.g. MüKoBGB/*von Hein* (fn. 17), Einl. IPR n. 22 et seq./90.

the rules – what's left of them in light of the pertinent EU rules – are predominantly omnilateral. Some unilateral rules still exist, and some were introduced more recently. Whether provisions such as Art. 10(3) cl. 1 No. 2 EGBGB[271] and the new Art. 15 EGBGB[272] can and/or should be "omnilateralised" is subject to some discussion.[273] As far as can be ascertained, a majority view opposes this move, and there is no case law to this effect.

VI. Arbitration

At the outset, it is important to note that Germany appeared poised to modernise the rules for arbitration when the government introduced a respective bill in 2024.[274] Only a few months later, however, the German government collapsed; general elections were held in February 2025. Owing to the rule of parliamentary discontinuity, whereby unfinished legislative business does not carry over to a new parliament, the reform process stalled. In January 2026, it restarted with a departmental draft bill.[275]

1. Seat of Arbitration

The seat of arbitration is relevant for the jurisdiction of German courts. If it is in Germany, its precise location determines which Higher Regional Court has local jurisdiction pursuant to § 1062(1) ZPO for the matters enumerated therein. These concern the formation of the arbitral tribunal, determinations as to whether arbitral proceedings are admissible or inadmissible, the enforcement, annulment and variation of interim measures ordered by the tribunal, as well as the setting aside and recognition for enforcement of arbitral awards. If the seat is abroad, the German higher regional courts have jurisdiction pursuant to § 1062(2) ZPO over most[276] of these issues, with venue depending on e. g. the respondent's domicile. If all else fails, the Higher Regional Court Berlin (the "Kammergericht") has jurisdiction in these cases. If there is no seat yet, German courts have jurisdiction

---

[271] The option to choose *German* law for a child's family name if one parent is habitually resident in *Germany*.

[272] Application of a provision of the *German* Civil Code on mutual representation as between spouses in matters of health care carried out in *Germany*.

[273] See, with further references, MüKoBGB/*von Hein* (fn. 17), Einl. IPR n. 91; as to Art. 15 EGBGB e.g. MüKoBGB/*Lipp*, 9th ed. 2024, Art. 15 EGBGB n. 6; BeckOK BGB/*Mörsdorf*, 01.11.2024, Art. 15 EGBGB n. 3; both authors oppose an omnilateral understanding.

[274] BT-Drucks. 20/13257; on this draft, see only (with further references) *Kiehl/Gebhard*, SchiedsVZ 2024, 173; *Armbrüster*, ZRP 2024, 66.

[275] Available at https://www.bmjv.de/SharedDocs/Gesetzgebungsverfahren/DE/2026_Modernisierung_Schiedsverfahrensrecht.htmlxQß (last access: April 29, 2026); for an early assessment and a comparison with the previous draft, see *Risse/Oehm*, BB 2026, 579.

[276] Exceptions: Formation of the tribunal and the positive decision of a tribunal about the admissibility of arbitration.

under § 1025(3) ZPO for measures supporting the formation of the tribunal, provided that one of the parties has its domicile or habitual residence in Germany. It is, however, doubtful to apply § 1025(3) ZPO where the parties have not (yet) determined a precise seat of arbitration but did agree that it should be in a country other than Germany.[277] Finally, for support concerning the taking of evidence, jurisdiction always lies with the local courts, specifically with the local court in whose district the measure is to be carried out (§ 1062(4) ZPO). This rule applies irrespective of whether the seat of arbitration is in Germany or abroad (or, indeed, whether it has not yet been determined).[278]

2. Subject-Matter Arbitrability

The general German rule on subject-matter arbitrability is found in § 1030(1) ZPO. Every claim of a pecuniary matter (*"vermögensrechtliche Streitigkeit"*) can be subject of an arbitration agreement; arbitration agreements concerning non-pecuniary matters have legal effect to the extent that the party could settle a dispute about the subject matter. Exceptions to these rules pertain to disputes relating to the existence of a tenancy of residential premises in Germany (§ 1030(2) ZPO) and (potentially) certain matters of patent law.[279] The question of subject-matter arbitrability is a question for the *lex fori*, whether or not the seat of arbitration is in Germany.[280] (Domestic awards will be set aside if there is no subject-matter arbitrability under German law, see § 1059(2) No. 2(a) ZPO.)

3. Procedure

The fundamental framework for arbitral proceedings in Germany is laid down in § 1042 ZPO. The parties cannot choose the applicable procedural rules in the sense of being able to escape from this framework; any choice only has a substantive[281] effect[282] (like an incorporation by reference, see Recital 13 Rome I). This approach can be seen as a safeguard for fundamental procedural guarantees, namely for equality of arms, the right to be heard, and the right to represented by

[277] More than 20 years ago, the Highest Regional Court in Bavaria did apply the provision to such a case (BayObLG SchiedsVZ 2004, 316 [317]); observers have been critical, see *G. Wagner*, SchiedsVZ 2004, 317 (318); Stein/Jonas/*Schlosser*, ZPO, 23rd ed. 2014, § 1062 n. 12.

[278] Musielak/Voit/*Voit* (fn. 48), § 1062 n. 8; BeckOK ZPO/*Wilske*/*Markert*, 01.03.2026, § 1062 n. 8.

[279] On the ongoing discussion see, with further references, recently *Heinze*, GRUR 2025, 963; also e.g. *Schack*, IZVR (fn. 73), n. 1414; Musielak/Voit/*Voit* (fn. 48), § 1030 n. 3; MüKoZPO/*Münch*, 6th ed. 2022, § 1030 n. 34.

[280] *Schack*, IZVR (fn. 73), n. 1416; MüKoZPO/*Münch* (fn. 279), § 1030 n. 22 et seq.; Stein/Jonas/*Schlosser* (fn. 277), § 1030 n. 30.

[281] As paradoxical as this might sound for *procedural* rules.

[282] *Schack*, IZVR (fn. 73), n. 1470.

a lawyer. None of these guarantees may be derogated from (§ 1042(1) and (2) ZPO).

Subject to these guarantees and to a number of other mandatory procedural rules, the parties are free, pursuant to § 1042(3) ZPO, to agree on the conduct of the proceedings or to refer to institutional rules. Whether, and/or to what extent, a reference to institutional rules that themselves emphasise the tribunal's discretionary powers entails a derogation from the non-mandatory elements of the *lex loci arbitri* does not seem to have been conclusively settled yet.[283] The issue is delicate as, under § 1042(4) cl. 1 ZPO, the *lex loci arbitri* itself grants the tribunal procedural discretion only to the extent that the parties have not made an agreement/a reference and that the ZPO does not provide applicable rules (*including* its non-mandatory provisions). An expansive reading of institutional discretion would risk hollowing out the residual regulatory function of the *lex loci arbitri*, while an overly restrictive approach would unduly limit party autonomy and the practical operation of institutional arbitration.

4. Public Policy

The potential impact of public policy depends on the nature of the arbitral award. A violation of public policy constitutes one of the grounds on which a German court may set aside a *domestic* arbitral award (§ 1059(2) No. 2(b) ZPO) and refuse to declare it enforceable (§ 1060(2) cl. 1 ZPO, referring to § 1059(2) ZPO). With respect to the recognition and enforcement of *foreign* arbitral awards, § 1061(1) cl. 1 ZPO refers to the New York Convention, irrespective of whether they originate in a Contracting State; this includes its Art. V(2)(b) on public policy as a ground for refusing recognition and enforcement.

a) "Interne" *or* "International" – *or Neither?*

While there appears to be consensus that there is no point in distinguishing an *ordre public interne* from an *ordre public international* in the realm of German conflict of laws, the German Federal Supreme Court has on occasion added the adjective "*international*" to "*ordre public*" in the context of the recognition of judicial decisions and arbitral awards.[284] Thus, for example, it has stated that foreign decisions should not be assessed by reference to national public policy standards (Art. 6 EGBGB), but rather under the supposedly less stringent standard of the *ordre public international.*[285] Doctrinally, this is misleading. First, no "international" standard of public policy is at play here, but – as usual – the

[283] For a derogation from the non-mandatory rules Stein/Jonas/*Schlosser* (fn. 277), § 1040 n. 3.

[284] Concerning an arbitral award quite recently BGH, WM 2025, 896 (n. 64).

[285] BGH, NJW-RR 2018, 1473 (n. 15); BGHZ 203, 350 = NJW 2015, 479; BGHZ 138, 331 (n. 28) = NJW 1998, 2358 (with further references).

relevant benchmark is the *lex fori*, German law. Second, the wording of the public policy clauses for recognition of foreign decisions in § 328(1) No. 4 ZPO and § 109(1) No. 4 FamFG contains the same elements as Art. 6 EGBGB, namely that (only) the result of the recognition/application matters, that it must be contrary to fundamental principles of German law, and that the incompatibility must be manifest. (§ 1059(2)(b) ZPO does not mention the latter two requirements; the Supreme Court has held, however, that the different phrasing does not entail a substantive difference.[286]) As the requirements of Art. 6 EGBGB are relatively strict to begin with (and, in particular, it does *not* simply cover all mandatory rules of German law), the distinction has no practical effect.[287]

One way to explain the Supreme Court's approach is to assume a certain inattentiveness in dragging along boilerplate language. A more charitable explanation is to attribute a practical, admonitory function to this choice of words: reminding the lower courts that German law is recognition-friendly.[288] Others understand it as a reference (albeit not ideally phrased) to an *effet atténué* of public policy in the field of recognition.[289] This reflects the typically smaller impact of a recognition decision than the actual application of foreign law. Finally, one should mention that there is also (recent) case law in which the Court itself does not add "*international*" even where the lower court, as quoted by the Supreme Court, *has* used this term.[290] Additionally, already more than a decade ago, the Court characterised the difference between the two notions of public policy as "at most marginal".[291]

b) Content, in Particular: Procedural Public Policy

Not least in light of the above, commentators often assume that the standards for a public policy review of arbitral awards are the same as for foreign decisions.[292] They encompass both substantive and procedural elements.[293] The latter requires that there has been such deviation from the fundamental principles of German procedural law that the decision cannot be regarded as having been rendered in an orderly procedure governed by the rule of law.[294] As regards the right to be

---

286 BGH, NJW 2014, 1597 (n. 7 et seq.); BGH, NJW 2009, 1215 (n. 5).

287 See MüKoZPO/*Adolphsen*, 6th ed. 2022, Art. 5 UNÜ n. 69.

288 BeckOGK/*M. Stürner* (fn. 154), Art. 6 EGBGB n. 172.

289 MüKoBGB/*von Hein* (fn. 17), Art. 6 EGBGB n. 111 et seq.; to this effect also Stein/Jonas/*Schlosser* (fn. 277), Anh. zu § 1061 n. 317.

290 E. g. BGH, SchiedsVZ 2025, 146.

291 BGH, NJW 2009, 1215 (n. 5); but a few years later, the old distinction was back: BGH, NJOZ 2017, 802 (n. 21). One can note, however, that these decisions originated with different bodies within the Supreme Court (the third Senate and the first Senate, respectively).

292 In particular Stein/Jonas/*Schlosser* (fn. 277), Anh. zu § 1061 n. 326 (to which the author refers in his comments on § 1059: n. 50); MüKoZPO/*Münch* (fn. 279), § 1059 n. 43 (expressly noting the parallels); Musielak/Voit/*Voit* (fn. 48), § 1059 n. 25.

293 Musielak/Voit/*Voit* (fn. 48), § 1059 n. 25; MüKoZPO/*Münch* (fn. 279), § 1059 n. 48 et seq.

294 Paradigmatically OLG Köln, SchiedsVZ 2005, 163 (165).

heard (constitutionally[295] protected pursuant to Art. 103(1) GG), for example, the Higher Regional Court Cologne has held that arbitral tribunals must, in principle, adhere to the same standards as (German) courts, meaning that parties must not only be able to make their statements, but that the tribunal must take note of them and take them into account.[296] Equality of arms (constitutionally[297] protected by Art. 3(1), 20(1) GG) is another element of procedural public policy,[298] as is the tribunal's neutrality.[299] The German procedural rules relevant for courts (or rather their core principles) serve as guidelines, but particularities of arbitration must be taken into account.[300]

In comments made *obiter* that nevertheless attracted considerable attraction, the Higher Regional Court Frankfurt a. M. pondered in 2020 that the publication of a dissenting opinion in domestic arbitration proceedings would constitute a violation of procedural public policy.[301] On appeal, the German Federal Supreme Court expressly left the question open.[302] The issue must be seen against the backdrop of the confidentiality of judicial deliberations in Germany. Commentators are divided.[303]

Recently, the Bavarian Highest Regional Court, applying § 1061(1) ZPO with Art. V(2)(b) New York Convention by analogy, seems to have argued that recognition of an arbitral would fail on public policy grounds if there is no valid arbitration agreement.[304] The German Federal Supreme Court did not agree. It noted that there is no gap in the law here requiring the application of public policy (by analogy); in the case of an existing arbitral award, the question of a valid arbitration agreement simply is covered by Art. V(1)(a) New York Convention.[305]

c) Recognition of Foreign Judgments in Arbitration-Related Matters

Exequatur sur exequatur ne vaut – this has been the line of Germany's Highest Courts with regard to foreign decisions[306] as well as arbitral awards.[307] This is

---

[295] For arbitration in Germany also see § 1042(1) cl. 2 ZPO and *supra* 3.

[296] OLG Köln, SchiedsVZ 2005, 163 (165).

[297] For arbitration in Germany also see § 1042(1) cl. 1 ZPO and *supra* 3.

[298] BGH, SchiedsVZ 2021, 46.

[299] BGH, NJW 1969, 750.

[300] For the examination of witnesses see BGH, SchiedsVZ 2021, 46 (n. 20 et seq.).

[301] OLG Frankfurt, BeckRS 2020, 4606 (n. 206).

[302] BGH, BeckRS 2020, 39395 (n. 41).

[303] See e.g. *Schack*, IZVR (fn. 73), n. 1508; *Sessler/Ruß*, SchiedsVZ 2020, 201; *Bickmann/P. K. Wagner*, GWR 2020, 295; *Bartels*, SchiedsVZ 2014, 133; *Wilske*, in: FS Schütze II, 2015, 729.

[304] BayObLG, SchiedsVZ 2025, 41 (n. 43 et seq.).

[305] BGH, WM 2025, 896 (n. 32 et seq.); approvingly *van der Beck*, ZIP 2025, 1917; *Barth*, LMK 2025, 815781; but see MüKoZPO/*Adolphsen* (fn. 268), Art. 5 UNÜ n. 72 (*both* public policy *and* Art. V(1)(a)).

[306] BGH, NJW 2009, 2826 (2827).

[307] See already RGZ 5 [1881], 397 (400); RGZ 30 [1892], 368 (369 et seq.).

because a foreign exequatur decision has no effect that could be recognised.[308] Most observers assume that this also applies to decisions entered in the terms of an arbitral award from other EU Member States, due to Art. 1(2)(d) Brussels I-*bis*.[309] In a 1984 judgment, the German Federal Supreme Court had ruled differently for a foreign (third State) "merger" decision[310] but returned to the former position 25 years later.[311] Commentators mostly agree.[312]

Rather recently, the German Federal Supreme Court expressly held that a foreign decision (in the country of the seat of arbitration) refusing[313] to set aside an arbitral award cannot be recognised in Germany.[314] By contrast, in exequatur proceedings concerning domestic arbitral awards, the *res iudicata* effect of a decision refusing to set aside the award precludes reliance on all reasons of denying enforceability that the earlier decision covers (§1060(2) cl. 2 ZPO). The effects, if any, of a decision by the courts of the country of the seat of arbitration that sets aside an award discussion are a highly contentious issue among scholars.[315] The Higher Regional Court Munich once held that a foreign award set aside in the country of origin cannot have any domestic effects and, thus, cannot be declared enforceable in Germany.[316] The German Federal Supreme Court declined to address the issue on appeal.[317] Under Art. IX(1) of the European Convention on International Commercial Arbitration (to which Germany is a Contracting State[318]), the setting aside in a Contracting State of an arbitral award constitutes a reason for the refusal of recognition or enforcement only in the four cases listed; this is a limitation of Art. V(1)(e) New York Convention. Finally, a current subject of debate among German authors – and, one would expect, among authors in all other Member States as well – are the implications of the CJEU decision in "London Steam-Ship Owner's Mutual Insurance Association", according to which

[308] *Schack*, IZVR (fn. 73), n. 1537; Rauscher/*Mankowski*, EuZPR/EuIPR, 5th ed. 2021, Art. 1 Brüssel Ia-VO n. 217.

[309] Stein/Jonas/*Thole*, ZPO, 23rd ed. 2022, Art. 1 EuGVVO n. 65; Rauscher/*Mankowski* (fn. 308), Art. 1 Brüssel Ia-VO n. 216 et seq.; also see CJEU [case C-700/20], IPRax 2023, 280 (n. 47).

[310] BGH, MDR 1984, 933; essentially confirmed two months later, BGH, NJW 1984, 2763.

[311] BGH, NJW 2009, 2826 (2827 et seq.).

[312] Musielak/Voit/*Voit* (fn. 48), §1061 n. 6; MüKoZPO/*Gottwald*, 7th ed. 2025, §328 n. 64; MüKoZPO/*Münch* (fn. 279), §1061 n. 35 et seq.; *Schack*, IZVR (fn. 73), n. 1538; *Geimer*, IPRax 2010, 346; *Plaßmeier*, SchiedsVZ 2010, 82; but see *Borges*, LMK 2010, 308128; Stein/Jonas/*Schlosser* (fn. 277), §1061 n. 8 et seq.

[313] In cases where the award is indeed set aside, Art. V(1)(e) New York Convention applies; but the Convention does not contain provisions on the reverse case at issue here.

[314] BGH, SchiedsVZ 2023, 228 (with references to the different views found in German scholarship); but see *Steinbrück*, IPRax 2024, 366.

[315] *Schack*, IZVR (fn. 73), n. 1569.

[316] OLG München, SchiedsVZ 2012, 339.

[317] BGH, SchiedsVZ 2013, 229.

[318] Federal Law Gazette 1964 II, 425.

judgments confirming arbitral awards can, under certain conditions, have an effect pursuant to Art. 45(1) Brussels I*bis*.[319]

VII. Conclusion

At first sight, the issues discussed in this contribution appear too disparate to admit of a single overarching conclusion. Yet they allow a recurring structural dynamic to be expressed with some clarity. Across the different doctrinal contexts examined, German law maintains a formal and often actual commitment to the equality of foreign and domestic law and to a neutrality-oriented conflict-of-laws methodology. At the same time, the *lex fori* repeatedly reasserts itself at structurally sensitive points. Courts and legislators alike at various points resort to forum-based reference points. Such moves are rarely framed as principled departures from neutrality; instead, they are – or are presented as – technical necessities, pragmatic choices in the face of complexity where foreign law plays a role, and safeguards of fundamental values of German law. The resulting pattern neither reflects a systematic privileging of the forum's law nor a categorical resistance to its application. Rather, it suggests a legal system that accords the *lex fori* a stabilising role without elevating it to a dominant principle.

[319] CJEU [case C-700/20], IPRax 2023, 280 (n. 48 et seq.); discussion by, e.g., *Pika*, IPRax 2023, 238; *Solomon*, ZEuP 2023, 683.

The Aspiration of Self-Sufficiency of International Contracts and the Challenge of Their Uniform Interpretation in the Resolution of Commercial Disputes

Ben Köhler

I. Introduction

Many, if not most, international contractual disputes turn, in one way or another, on the interpretation of the contract or of specific contract terms. This is hardly surprising: the contract specifies the rights and duties of the parties but, like all other statements, contracts cannot be understood without interpretation. Parties thus cannot altogether escape the issue of potentially diverging interpretations and resulting disputes on the existence or extent of contractual rights and duties. The inherent risk of diverging interpretations is amplified in international contracts. This is not just a function of possibly different legal and cultural backgrounds of parties, negotiators and counsel involved in international transactions or the potential need for the translations of documents. It is also a consequence of potentially very different approaches to contract interpretation, depending on where the dispute is heard and which law governs the interpretation of the contract. For instance, the outcome of a dispute may very well turn on the question of whether the law governing contract interpretation allows adjudicators to consider the negotiations between the parties rather than restricting their analysis to the "four corners" of the contract documents.

Parties to international contracts will try to mitigate the risks associated with uncertainty as to the interpretation of their contract. They can try to do this in very different ways: They may set out very detailed definitions of terms in their contract in order to avoid ambiguity. However, this may be expensive and will, in some cases, increase rather than reduce complexity. A common indirect measure is the attempt to control who interprets the contract, for instance via the insertion of a choice-of-forum or an arbitration clause. This choice of the forum or of arbitration will in most cases be coupled with a choice-of-law clause. There are also more direct ways of restricting the courts' leeway in contract interpretation: parties may themselves include stipulations on how their contract is to be interpreted or expressly exclude certain methods of or materials for interpretation. Finally, parties may include or refer to standard contract clauses which have been interpreted in numerous decisions or awards, thereby reducing the potential for surprises in the interpretation.

Parties will often combine these different elements, thus making contract interpretation the result of a complex interaction of international procedural law, conflict-of-laws, domestic substantive law and international contract practice. The present report is based on the questionnaire which touches upon questions from all these different layers of law implicated in the interpretation of international commercial contracts. It begins with a brief recapitulation of the private international law framework from a German perspective (II.), before presenting the legal framework for contract interpretation under German domestic law (III.). The report will then analyse the interpretation of specific clauses on contract interpretation and supplementation from a German legal point of view (IV.), prior to addressing a selection of the most common classes of substantive clauses in international transactions (V.). It ends with a brief conclusion (VI.).

II. The Conflict-of-Laws Rules on the Interpretation and Supplementation of Contracts

The questionnaire requires the reports to answer the questions of contract interpretation against the backdrop of four different settings of dispute resolution and choice-of-law assumptions. It is therefore necessary to set out first how these different settings and choice-of-law issues influence the exercise of contract interpretation and supplementation before German state courts and arbitral tribunals with their seat in Germany. The questionnaire specifies four choice-of-law scenarios: the express choice of the domestic law of the *lex fori* (1.), the express choice of a state law other than the *lex fori* or the background law (2.), the express choice of a set of non-state rules on contracts (3.), and the absence of an (express) choice-of-law clause (4.).

1. Express Choice-of-Law Clause in Favour of Domestic lex fori

The first setting is characterized by the express choice of the domestic law of the forum, i.e. German law, as *lex causae*. For the purposes of the reports, the national reporters have been asked to assume that the parties have excluded the application of the CISG pursuant to Art. 6 CISG. German state courts would thus revert to the conflict-of-laws rules in the Rome I-Regulation, more specifically Art. 3 (1) Rome I-Regulation which allows for the choice of the governing law.[1]

[1] Given the focus on international commercial transactions in this report, the limitations in Art. 3 (3), Art. 6 (2) Rome I-Regulation are deemed to be inapplicable. For some international contracts, the Rome I-Regulation may be inapplicable due to the exclusions in Art. 1 (2) Rome I-Regulation.

Art. 12 (1) (a) Rome I-Regulation expressly affirms that the law applicable to the contract also governs its interpretation. The choice of the domestic law of the forum would thus extend to the interpretation of contracts as well as their potential supplementation.[2] If, despite the express choice of the domestic law of the forum, the contract is drafted against the backdrop of another jurisdiction, this does not change the general application of the German rules for contract interpretation via Art. 3 (1), 12 (1) (a) Rome I-Regulation.[3] Under the German rules on interpretation, terminology taken from other legal systems will, as a general matter, be interpreted in accordance with its original meaning as it is understood in the legal systems of origin.[4] The adoption of foreign terminology despite the express choice of German domestic law thus does not change the applicable law but will in many cases influence the outcome of the exercise of contract interpretation.[5]

If the dispute is heard by an arbitral tribunal, the relevant conflict rules are not to be found in the Rome I-Regulation, which does not bind arbitral tribunals.[6] If the seat of arbitration is in Germany, the applicable conflict rule is Section 1051 of the German Code of Civil Procedure (*Zivilprozessordnung, ZPO*), a provision based on Art. 28 of the UNCITRAL Model Law.[7] If the contract contains an express choice-of-law clause, the arbitrators will apply the substantive law chosen by the parties.

2. Express Choice-of-Law Clause in Favour of a State Law Other than lex fori *or the Background Law*

The second setting concerns the express choice of the law of a state other than the forum or the background law. German courts will again revert to Art. 3 (1), 12 (1) (a) Rome I-Regulation. The issues of contract interpretation and supplementation will hence be governed by the chosen law. The same is true for arbitral tribunals, pursuant to Section 1051 (1) ZPO. The adjudicators will need to estab-

---

[2] *Ferrari*, in: Ferrari/Kieninger/Mankowski et al. (eds.), Internationales Vertragsrecht, Rome I, Art. 12 n. 8; *Kleinschmidt*, in: MünchKomm-BGB, 9th ed. 2025, Art. 12 n. 22; *Spickhoff*, in: BeckOK BGB, 76th ed. 1.5.2025, Art. 12 n. 4.

[3] For details, see below sub. II.2.e); *Kleinschmidt*, in: MünchKomm-BGB, 9th ed. 2025, Art. 12 n. 15; *Matthias Weller*, in: BeckOGK BGB, Rom I-VO, 1.9.2025, Art. 12 n. 23.

[4] For details, see below sub. II.2.e); *Kleinschmidt*, in: MünchKomm-BGB, 9th ed. 2025, Art. 12 n. 22.

[5] For details and illustrations, see below sub. II.2.e); *Kleinschmidt*, in: MünchKomm-BGB, 9th ed. 2025, Art. 12 n. 15; *Matthias Weller*, in: BeckOGK BGB, Rom I-VO, 1.9.2025, Art. 12 n. 23.

[6] This is the prevailing view in German doctrine; see, with further references, *Martiny*, in: MünchKomm-BGB, 9th ed. 2025, Vor Art. 1 Rom I-VO n. 106, with further references; *Wilske/Markert*, in: Vorwerk/Wolf, BeckOK ZPO, 58th ed. 1.9.2025, § 1051 n. 4; for a nuanced position, see *Münch*, in: MünchKomm-ZPO, 6th ed. 2022, § 1051 n. 10.

[7] *Münch*, in: MünchKomm-ZPO, 6th ed. 2022, § 1051 n. 6; *Wilske/Markert*, in: Vorwerk/Wolf, BeckOK ZPO, 58th ed. 1.9.2025, § 1051 n. 1.

lish the rules of the chosen law on contract interpretation[8] and determine, for instance, to which extent these rules allow them to consider the origin of the terminology adopted by the parties.

3. Express Choice of Non-State Rules

In the third scenario, the parties have not chosen the law of a state but a non-state set of rules, such as the UNIDROIT Principles of International Commercial Contracts (UPICC).[9] It is generally acknowledged that the choice of non-state rules like the UPICC does not amount to the choice of a governing law under Art. 3 (1) Rome I-Regulation.[10] Absent a choice of state law under Art. 3 (1) Rome I-Regulation, the law governing the interpretation of the contract will be determined pursuant to Art. 4 Rome I-Regulation which, as a general rule, refers to the law of the habitual residence of the party required to effect the characteristic performance. This does, however, not mean that the choice of the UPICC is deprived of all legal effect.[11] Rather, it is a question to be settled by the applicable law whether and to which extent it allows the parties to modify the rules of contract interpretation. As far as the applicable law allows for such modifications, the choice of UPICC can be interpreted as a contractual modification of the rules on interpretation and supplementation of contracts.[12] If German contract law is applicable to the contract pursuant to Art. 4, 12 (1) (a) Rome I-Regulation, this type of modification is permitted as the rules on contract interpretation can be subject to contractual modifications.[13]

The situation is different for arbitral tribunals: Pursuant to Section 1051 (1) ZPO, the tribunal will apply the rules of law chosen by the parties. The term "rules of law" (*Rechtsvorschriften*) is understood to include sets of non-state rules such as the UPICC or the Principles of European Contract Law (PECL).[14] In

---

[8] BGH NJW 1987, 591; BGH NJW-RR 1990, 248 n. 11; *Hausmann*, in: Staudinger-BGB, 2021, Rom I-VO, Art. 12 n. 32.

[9] UNIDROIT Principles of International Commercial Contracts, 4th edition, 2016, www.unidroit.org/instruments/commercial-contracts/unidroit-principles-2016/ (07.01.2026).

[10] *Ulrich Magnus*, in: Staudinger-BGB, 2021, Rom I-VO, Art. 3 n. 40; *Martiny*, in: MünchKomm-BGB, 9th ed. 2025, Rom I-VO, Art. 3 n. 29 et seqq., with further references; *Spickhoff*, in: BeckOK BGB, 76th ed. 1.5.2025, Rom I-VO, Art. 3 n. 7; *Wendland*, in: BeckOGK BGB, 1.3.2025, Rom I-VO, Art. 3 n. 75.

[11] *Martiny*, in: MünchKomm-BGB, 9th ed. 2025, Rom I-VO, Art. 3 n. 34; *Ulrich Magnus*, in: Staudinger-BGB, 2021, Rom I-VO, Art. 3 n. 40.

[12] In the German terminology, this type of clause is called *materiell-rechtliche Verweisung* which is distinguished from a proper choice of the governing law (*kollisionsrechtliche Verweisung*).

[13] See below sub. IV.

[14] *Saenger*, ZPO, 10th ed. 2023, § 1051 n. 4; *Schlosser*, in: Stein/Jonas, Zivilprozessordnung, 23th ed. 2014, § 1051 n. 23; *Wilske/Markert*, in: Vorwerk/Wolf, BeckOK ZPO, 58th ed. 1.9.2025, § 1051 n. 4.

these cases, the UPICC are applied as the governing law and not merely as contractual clauses.

4. *Absence of (Express) Choice-of-Law Clause*

In the absence of an express choice-of-law clause, German courts would inquire whether there is an implicit choice of the governing law under Art. 3 (1) Rome I-Regulation. Pursuant to this provision, courts should conclude that the parties have chosen the governing law if such choice "is clearly demonstrated by the terms of the contract or the circumstances of the case". The criteria for the establishment of implicit choices of the governing law follow from Art. 3 (1) Rome I-Regulation itself and are hence to be developed by way of autonomous interpretation of the regulation.[15]

Within the context of international commercial transactions, a first indication can be the language of the transactions. As a general rule, the language of the document is a weak indicator which needs to be supplemented by other, more meaningful indications.[16] This is especially true if the contractual documents are drafted in English which will be used in many transactions by default rather than by choice.[17] Courts will therefore be reluctant to consider the use of English as indicative of an implicit choice of a particular jurisdiction, even if one of the parties has its place of business in a jurisdiction where English is the official language.[18] An implicit choice of law can however be justified if the contract clearly refers to legal terms or concepts from a particular jurisdiction.[19] In these circumstances, German courts might conclude that the background law, which has influenced or has been referred to in the provisions of the contract, was in fact implicitly chosen by the parties.[20] If such choice is found, the court would apply the background law to the interpretation of the contract, pursuant to Art. 12 (1) (a) Rome I-Regulation.

If the court does not find an implicit choice of law, the applicable law will be determined according to Art. 4 Rome I-Regulation. If the applicable law is a law other than the background law, it depends on the *lex causae* to what extent the background law can be considered to establish the meaning of specific terms

[15] *Spickhoff*, in: BeckOK BGB, 76th ed. 1.5.2025, Rom I-VO, Art. 3 n. 21.

[16] BAG NZA 2017, 502 n. 43; *Ulrich Magnus*, in: Staudinger-BGB, 2021, Rom I-VO, Art. 3 n. 98; *Wendland*, in: BeckOGK BGB, 1.3.2025, Rom I-VO, Art. 3 n. 174.

[17] *Kleinschmidt*, in: MünchKomm-BGB, 9th ed. 2025, Art. 12 n. 33.

[18] See, e.g., BGHZ 19, 110 (112); BGH NJW-RR 1992, 423 (424); OLG Nürnberg BeckRS 2021, 7538 n. 94; *Kleinschmidt*, in: MünchKomm-BGB, 9th ed. 2025, Art. 12 n. 33.

[19] *Ulrich Magnus*, in: Staudinger-BGB, 2021, Rom I-VO, Art. 3 n. 90 et seqq.; *Martiny*, in: MünchKomm-BGB, 9th ed. 2025, Rom I-VO, Art. 3 n. 59 et seqq.; *Spickhoff*, in: BeckOK BGB, 76th ed. 1.5.2025, Rom I-VO, Art. 3 n. 25; *Wendland*, in: BeckOGK BGB, 1.3.2025, Rom I-VO, Art. 3 n. 164.

[20] For the relevance of references to specific jurisdictions for the implicit choice of law, see, e.g., BGH NJW 2011, 2809 n. 47; BGH NJW-RR 2000, 1002 (1004); BGH NJW-RR 1996, 1034.

derived from its legal context. The situation is similar for arbitral tribunals. They will, under Section 1051 (1) ZPO, also inquire whether the parties have implicitly chosen the governing law.[21] Absent such choice, they will apply the law most closely connected to the substance of the dispute.[22]

III. Contractual Interpretation and Gap-Filling Rules

After a brief overview of the legal framework for interpretation and supplementation of the contract (1.), the report describes the relevant rules for contract interpretation (2.) and contract supplementation (3.).

1. The Legal Framework of Interpretation and Supplementation of Contracts

Unlike other codifications or international sets of principles,[23] the German Civil Code (*Bürgerliches Gesetzbuch*, BGB) does not contain a detailed set of rules on the interpretation and supplementation of contracts. This is a consequence of the BGB's focus on the concept of declaration of will (*Willenserklärung*).[24] Courts thus resort to different rules which are spread out within the BGB and, if applicable, the Commercial Code (*Handelsgesetzbuch*, HGB). Apart from special rules in international instruments, such as Article 8 of the CISG,[25] neither the BGB nor the HGB distinguish between domestic and international contracts for the purpose of contract interpretation.

The main rules for contract interpretation are to be found in Sections 133 and 157 BGB. Section 133 BGB deals with the interpretation of declarations of will (*Willenserklärungen*), while Section 157 BGB seems to address the interpretation of contracts. Despite the seeming distinction between declarations of will and contracts, it is universally acknowledged that the two provisions need to be read together.[26] The principles of interpretation that follow from Sections 133, 157 BGB govern not only the interpretation of contracts but also the interpretation of other juridical acts like notifications of termination of contract.[27] Some special rules on the interpretation of standard terms can be found in the provisions on standard

---

[21] *Münch*, in: MünchKomm-ZPO, 6th ed. 2022, § 1051 n. 16.

[22] See Section 1051 (2) ZPO.

[23] See, e.g., UPICC, Chapter 4 – Interpretation; Art. 1188 et seqq. French Code civil.

[24] *Vogenauer*, Interpretation of Contracts, in: Max-EuP 2012, https://max-eup2012.mpipriv.de/index.php/Interpretation_of_Contracts (18.01.2026).

[25] Art. 8 CISG was excluded from the scope of the questionnaire. It is therefore not addressed in this report.

[26] BGH NJW 1956, 1475; *Busche*, in: MünchKomm-BGB, 10th ed. 2025, § 133 n. 19, 20; *Mansel*, in: Jauernig, BGB, 19th ed. 2023, § 133 n. 7; *Riesenhuber*, in: Soergel, BGB, 14th ed. 2023, § 133 n. 4.

[27] *Mansel*, in: Jauernig, BGB, 19th ed. 2023, § 133 n. 7.

terms, for example the interpretation contra proferentem in Section 305c (2) BGB.[28]

The BGB does not expressly address the issue of contract supplementation. It is, however, universally accepted that courts may supplement contracts in certain circumstances (*ergänzende Vertragsauslegung*).[29] Courts cite Section 157 BGB in conjunction with Section 242 BGB (good faith) as a legal basis for the supplementation of contracts.[30]

2. Contract Interpretation

a) The Primacy of the Common Intention of the Parties over Objective Criteria

Pursuant to Section 133 BGB, the interpretation of a declaration of will needs to establish the true intention of the party. Section 157 BGB stipulates that contracts should be interpreted as required by good faith and customary practice. The Federal Court of Justice has concluded, in its long-standing case law, that a joint reading of these provisions leads to the primacy of a common true intention of the parties over the literal or objective meaning of the contractual stipulations or other criteria.[31] If possible, courts therefore need to establish the true intent of the parties at the time of the conclusion of the contract. If the common understanding of the parties diverges from the objective meaning of the words used in the contract, the former understanding prevails over the latter.[32] This doctrine is known by the latin adage of *falsa demonstratio non nocet.*[33] The principle is also applicable if the contract is subject to a form requirement and the document contains the objectively wrong language,[34] unless the parties deliberately chose the objectively wrong language to disguise the actual terms of the contract.[35] The

---

[28] See below, II.2.g).

[29] See, e.g., *Busche*, in: MünchKomm-BGB, 10th ed. 2025, § 157 n. 26; *Riesenhuber*, in: Soergel, BGB, 14th ed. 2023, § 157 n. 2: supplementation is necessary but should not be labeled supplementation by interpretation.

[30] BGH NJW 1953, 937; BGH NJW 1980, 1681 (§ 242 BGB); BGH NJW 2006, 54 n. 24 et seqq.

[31] Settled case law, see, e.g., BGH NJW 1984, 721; BGH NJW 1989, 526 (527); BGH NJW-RR 2018, 906 n. 36; BGH BeckRS 2019, 27039 n. 20; BGH NJW 2023, 2942 n. 18; *Riesenhuber*, in: Soergel, BGB, 14th ed. 2023, § 133 n. 25; *Singer*, in: Staudinger-BGB, 2021, § 133 n. 6, with further references.

[32] See the famous Haakjöringsköd-case: RGZ 99, 147; settled case law, see, e.g, BGH NJW 2008, 1658 n. 12; BGH BeckRS 2019, 27039 n. 20; *Singer*, in: Staudinger-BGB, 2021, § 133 n. 13, with further references.

[33] BGH NJW 2008, 1658 n. 12; *Singer*, in: Staudinger-BGB, 2021, § 133 n. 13, with further references.

[34] Settled case law, see, e.g., BGH NJW 1969, 131 (132); BGH NJW 1983, 1610; BGH NJW 2008, 1658 n. 13; BGH NJW 2023, 2942 n. 18.

[35] Settled case law, see, e.g., BGHZ 74, 116 n. 18; *Singer*, in: Staudinger-BGB, 2021, § 133 n. 36, with further references.

Federal Court of Justice has also extended the application of the principle to the interpretation of standard terms.[36]

b) The Primacy of the Objective Understanding over the Inexistence of the Contract

While the common subjective intention of the parties trumps the literal meaning of the contract, it will rarely be successfully established in practice. Courts will then engage in an objective interpretation from the perspective of an objective third party in the position of the recipient of the declaration (*objektiver Empfängerhorizont*). If the parties attach different meanings to the contract terms, courts will use this objective analysis to determine the content of the contract.[37] If this interpretation of the declarations of the parties leads to a convergent meaning, the contract is considered concluded and is, in principle, valid and enforceable.[38] However, under certain circumstances, a party who has misunderstood the meaning of its declaration, can avoid the contract pursuant to Section 119 (1) BGB.[39] If the objective interpretation does not lead to a convergent understanding of the basic and essential features of the contract, the adjudicator will consider the contract to be inexistent (*versteckter Totaldissens*).[40] If the misunderstanding only concerns a specific point without extending to the essential features of the contract, Section 155 BGB contains a presumption of valid conclusion of the contract irrespective of the misunderstanding.

c) The Criteria of the Objective Interpretation

If there is no common subjective understanding of the parties, courts need to interpret the contract from the perspective of an objective third party in the position of the recipient of the relevant declarations. Adjudicators will thus need to construct the understanding of an objective third party.[41] It is settled case law that the objective meaning is to be determined by how, in light of customary practice and good faith, an objective third party in the position of the recipient would have understood the declaration (*Empfängerhorizont*).[42] In order to deter-

[36] BGHZ 113, 251 n. 37; BGH NJW 1983, 2638; *Singer*, in: Staudinger-BGB, 2021, § 133 n. 14, with further references.

[37] See, e.g., BGH NJW 1993, 1798; *Bork*, in: Staudinger-BGB, 2025, § 155 n. 5.

[38] BGH NJW 1961, 1668 (1669); BGH NJW 1993, 1798 (1799); *Bork*, in: Staudinger-BGB, 2025, § 155 n. 6.

[39] BGH NJW 1961, 1668 (1669); *Bork*, in: Staudinger-BGB, 2025, § 155 n. 6.

[40] BGH NJW-RR 2000, 158 (1659); BGH NJW-RR 2006, 1139 (1141); *Busche*, in: Münch-Komm-BGB, 10th ed. 2025, § 154 n. 3; *Bork*, in: Staudinger-BGB, 2025, § 155 n. 13; *Möslein*, in: BeckOGK BGB, 1.2.2018, § 155 n. 11.

[41] *Arnold*, in: Erman BGB, 17th ed. 2023, § 133 n. 19; *Wendtland*, in: BeckOK BGB, 76th ed. 1.11.2025, § 133 n. 27.

[42] Settled case law, see, e.g., BGH ZIP 2021, 245 n.19; BGH NJW 2010, 2422 n. 33, with further references.

mine this understanding, courts look to the wording of the declaration or the relevant clause, the totality of the behavior of the parties as well as the respective interests of the parties at the time of conclusion of the contract.[43] The recipient is held to a standard diligence which can be reasonably expected under the circumstances.[44] The expected degree of diligence may vary depending on the person of the recipient. In international business transactions, it will be the average level of diligence of a person involved in the relevant branch of trade or business community.[45] The Federal Court of Justice has developed special criteria for the interpretation of standard terms.[46] Standard terms are to be interpreted objectively from the perspective and in light of the interests of an honest party which corresponds to the average client in the relevant field of business.[47] The interpretation needs to rely on a generalised, typical understanding of the clause, without recourse to circumstances which are known only to particular parties.[48]

d) The Admissible Material for the Interpretation of Contracts

The precise wording of the contract is the starting point for the exercise of contract interpretation.[49] However, it is settled case law that courts are not limited to the contract documents to establish the meaning of a contract term.[50] They are invited to consider the totality of the behavior of the parties, as far as it is relevant for the interpretation of the contract.[51] The Federal Court of Justice has repeatedly held that even a seemingly clear and unambiguous formulation in the contract does not exclude a recourse to the context of the transaction.[52] The question of whether a contract clause is unambiguous can, according to the Court, only be answered by interpretation of the clause in light of all relevant materials and

[43] Settled case law, see, e.g., BGH NJW 2018, 146 n. 30; BGH RNotZ 2019, 204 n. 19; BGH GRUR 2021, 721 n. 19; *Mansel*, in: Jauernig, BGB, 19th ed. 2023, § 133 n. 9.

[44] Settled case law, see, e.g., BGH NJW 2007, 2110 n. 19; BGH NJW 2008, 2702 n. 30; *Riesenhuber*, in: Soergel, BGB, 14th ed. 2023, § 133 n. 52; *Wendtland*, in: BeckOK BGB, 76th ed. 1.11.2025, § 133 n. 27.

[45] *Singer*, in: Staudinger-BGB, 2021, § 133 n. 19.

[46] See, e.g., BGH NJW 2005, 1183 (1184); BGH NJW 2011, 1342 (1344); BGH NJW 2014, 2269 n. 25; BGH NJW 2020, 399 n. 34; see, with details and further references: *Busche*, in: MünchKomm-BGB, 10th ed. 2025, § 133 n. 25; *Riesenhuber*, in: Soergel, BGB, 14th ed. 2023, § 133 n. 111.

[47] See, e.g., BGH NJW 2005, 1183 (1184); BGH NJW 2011, 1342 (1344); BGH NJW 2020, 399 n. 34; *Busche*, in: MünchKomm-BGB, 10th ed. 2025, § 133 n. 25, with details and further references.

[48] BGH NJW 2014, 2269 n. 25; *Busche*, in: MünchKomm-BGB, 10th ed. 2025, § 133 n. 25, with details and further references.

[49] BGH NJW-RR 1993, 945 (946); BGH RNotZ 2019, 204 n. 19; *Riesenhuber*, in: Soergel, BGB, 14th ed. 2023, § 133 n. 61; *Wendtland*, in: BeckOK BGB, 76th ed. 1.11.2025, § 133 n. 23.

[50] See, e.g., BGH NJW-RR 1993, 945 (946); BGH ZIP 2021, 245 n. 19; BGH NJW-RR 2021, 872 n. 10; *Wendtland*, in: BeckOK BGB, 76th ed. 1.11.2025, § 133 n. 25.

[51] See, e.g., BGH ZIP 2021, 245 n. 19.

[52] See, e.g., BGH NJW 1975, 536; BGH NJW 2002, 1260 (1261); BGH NJW-RR 2018, 906 n. 36; BGH NJW-RR 2021, 872 n. 10.

circumstances.[53] This context includes the negotiations of the parties,[54] the genesis of the particular contract term,[55] prior dealings between the parties as well as the purpose of the transaction.[56]

Under German law, there is thus no concept akin to the four corners rule or the parol evidence rule that would restrict the relevant material for interpretation to the contractual documents. Extrinsic material is admissible to establish the meaning of a contract term.[57] However, this does not mean that the written instrument does not enjoy a certain priority over other circumstances: it is settled case law that a written contractual instrument is presumed to be complete and to correctly reflect the agreement of the parties.[58] If a party thus relies on a meaning that is materially different from a literal meaning of the written instrument, it needs to establish and prove the facts it relies on to justify this understanding.[59]

e) Interpretation of Clauses Inspired by Foreign Law

The words used in the declaration or in the contract documents are the starting point for the interpretation of contracts under German law.[60] For the purposes of the interpretation of international contracts, it is noteworthy that courts will try to establish the understanding that is common within the relevant branch of trade or business community.[61] The situation is slightly more complex if legal terminology from other jurisdictions is used. If German law is applicable to the interpretation of the contract, either because the parties have chosen German law or because it is the objectively applicable law, German rules on interpretation govern the interpretation of the contract.[62] The application of German law, however, does not mean that the legal terms within the contract need to be construed in accordance with the relevant meaning in the German legal context.[63] Rather, courts will, in application of Sections 133, 157 BGB, consider the meaning that is associated with the terms in another jurisdiction if they are indeed inspired by

[53] BGH NJW 2002, 1260 (1261); see also *Riesenhuber*, in: Soergel, BGB, 14th ed. 2023, § 133 n. 31.

[54] BGH NJW 1975, 536; BGH NJW 2003, 2235 (2236).

[55] BGH NJW 2003, 2235 (2236).

[56] BGH NJW 1975, 536; BGH NJW 2003, 2235 (2236); BGH NJW 2010, 2422 n. 33.

[57] BGH NJW-RR 1993, 945 (946); *Busche*, in: MünchKomm-BGB, 10th ed. 2025, § 133 n. 63.

[58] BGH NJW 2002, 3164; BGH DNotZ 2017, 48 n. 6.

[59] BGH NJW 2002, 3164; BGH DNotZ 2017, 48 n. 6.

[60] BGH RNotZ 2019, 204 n. 19; *Arnold*, in: Erman BGB, 17th ed. 2023, § 133 n. 24; *Riesenhuber*, in: Soergel, BGB, 14th ed. 2023, § 133 n. 61.

[61] See, e.g., BGH NJW-RR 2007, 1470 n. 11; BGH NJW-RR 1994, 1108; *Singer*, in: Staudinger-BGB, 2021, § 133 n. 45.

[62] Art. 12 (1) (a) Rome I-Regulation; see above sub. II.1.

[63] BGH NJW-RR 1992, 423 (425); OLG Hamburg GRUR Int 1990, 388 (389); *Martiny*, in: Reithmann/Martiny, Internationales Vertragsrecht, 9th ed. 2022, n. 3.115; *Kling*, Sprachrisiken im Privatrecht, 2008, 383 et seq.; *Triebel/Balthasar*, NJW 2004, 2189 (2192).

this jurisdiction of origin.[64] They will, however, need to research carefully whether the parties adopted the terminology – and hence the understanding – of a particular jurisdiction. It is equally possible that they used the terms as generic legal terms without any specific connection to a particular jurisdiction or understood the foreign terminology in accordance with its meaning in the domestic context.[65] In some contexts, parties may simply conclude the contract in English because the standard template only exists in English or third parties need to be able to understand the contract.[66] One factor in this determination can be whether the negotiators of the contract come from or are at least familiar with the legal system at issue.[67]

In the leading case on the issue, the Federal Court of Justice has held that, in principle, an indemnity clause, that was developed against the backdrop of English law, needs to be interpreted as it would be in the context of English law, even if German law governs the interpretation of the contract.[68] However, it then went on to conclude that the parties, who both were German business persons, understood the clause according to its meaning in the German legal context. The court reasons that the validity of the clause was dubious under English law and that the parties also used the clause in other German contracts.[69]

The analysis can lead to different results for different clauses within the same contract.[70] For example, the *Reichsgericht* held that the English annex to an insurance contract concluded by two German public companies was to be interpreted according to the English understanding while the rest of the contract, which was written in German, needed to be construed in accordance with its domestic meaning.[71]

---

[64] BGH NJW-RR 1992, 423; RGZ 39, 65 (68); *Kleinschmidt*, in: MünchKomm-BGB, 9th ed. 2025, Rom I-VO, Art. 12 n. 25; *Triebel/Balthasar*, NJW 2004, 2189 (2192).

[65] BGH NJW-RR 1992, 423 (425); RGZ 19, 33 (46); *Kleinschmidt*, in: MünchKomm-BGB, 9th ed. 2025, Rom I-VO, Art. 12 n. 25; see also *Triebel/Balthasar*, NJW 2004, 2189 (2194); see also BGH NJW 1990, 2257 (2258).

[66] For M&A contracts, see *Korch*, Unternehmenskaufverträge, 2024, 168; see also RGZ 11, 100 (104).

[67] OLG Hamburg GRUR Int 1990, 388 (389); *Martiny*, in: Reithmann/Martiny, Internationales Vertragsrecht, 9th ed. 2022, n. 3.115; *Triebel/Balthasar*, NJW 2004, 2189 (2195); see also in this direction: OLG Nürnberg BeckRS 2021, 7538 n. 95.

[68] BGH NJW-RR 1992, 423 (425); accord: *Armbrüster*, NJW 2011, 812 (817); *Martiny*, in: Reithmann/Martiny, Internationales Vertragsrecht, 9th ed. 2022, n. 3.114; for a criticism of this starting point, see *Triebel/Balthasar*, NJW 2004, 2189 (2193).

[69] BGH NJW-RR 1992, 423 (425).

[70] *Korch*, Unternehmenskaufverträge, 2024, 173.

[71] Reichsgericht 7 November 1928, I 159/28, RGZ 122, 233 (235); on this decision, see also *Korch*, Unternehmenskaufverträge, 2024, 173.

f) The Role of Customary Business Practices and Trade Usages

Section 157 BGB expressly refers to customary practice for the interpretation of contracts. A special provision for commercial transactions can be found in Section 346 HGB, pursuant to which relevant trade usages are to be taken into account among commercial parties. These provisions mainly inform the interpretation of the contract but can also help to fill gaps within the contract.[72] For instance, the Federal Court of Justice has held that an arbitration agreement can be derived from the trade usage, even if the contract does not contain an arbitration clause.[73] According to the court, the parties would have needed to expressly exclude arbitration in their contract, if they had wished to deviate from the usage.[74] However, due to a subsequent modification of the ZPO, the conclusion of an arbitration agreement by trade usage is no longer possible.[75] There is a trade usage in terms of Section 346 HGB if there is a widely accepted and firmly established, uniform practice within the relevant business community or branch of trade.[76] This can include international trade usages in particular industries.[77]

g) Special Maxims for Contract Interpretation

In cases of ambiguity of contract clauses, special maxims of interpretation may help courts and tribunals to choose one meaning over another. The most notable of these maxims is the principle of *contra proferentem*. The BGB explicitly refers to *contra proferentem* in the context of the rules on standard terms. Pursuant to Section 305c (2) BGB, in cases of ambiguous clauses, courts should choose the meaning which is less favourable to the party who supplied the terms. The maxim is not limited to consumer contracts but will also apply in business-to-business transactions.[78] There is less clarity as to whether contra proferentem can also be applied in the interpretation of individually negotiated contract clauses.[79] According to the prevailing view, the mere fact that a party drafted a particular clause does not per se justify its interpretation *contra proferentem*.[80] German

[72] BGH NJW 1993, 1798.

[73] BGH NJW 1993, 1798.

[74] BGH NJW 1993, 1798.

[75] BGH NJW-RR 2017, 1531 n. 21; but see also OLG Bremen BeckRS 2010, 4308 n. 22: inclusion of contractual documents that contained an arbitration clause via trade usage.

[76] BGH NJW 1994, 659 (660); BGH NJW 2001, 2464 (2465); BGH NJW 2018, 1957 n. 30; *Lehmann-Richter*, in: BeckOK HGB, 49th ed. 1.10.2025, § 346 n. 5; *Leyens*, in: Hopt, HGB, 45th ed. 2026, § 346 n. 1.

[77] *Lehmann-Richter*, in: BeckOK HGB, 49th ed. 1.10.2025, § 346 n. 14; *Pamp*, in: Oetker, Handelsgesetzbuch, 8th ed. 2024, § 346 n. 23.

[78] BGH NJW-RR 1988, 113 (114); BGH NJW-RR 2002, 1027 (1029); *Fornasier*, in: MünchKomm-BGB, 10th ed. 2025, § 305c n. 29.

[79] *Busche*, in: MünchKomm-BGB, 10th ed. 2025, § 157 n. 8.

[80] *Busche*, in: MünchKomm-BGB, 10th ed. 2025, § 157 n. 8.

courts seem to additionally require that the drafting party used its superior bargaining position to impose the clause on the other party.[81]

Another rule to resolve conflicts between different contract clauses can be found in Section 305b BGB, pursuant to which the individually negotiated clauses enjoy primacy over conflicting clauses within standard terms. The doctrinal foundations of the provision remain disputed. Some authors consider the rule to be a mandatory maxim of contract interpretation,[82] while others consider it to be a priority rule.[83] The Federal Court of Justice has repeatedly held that the provision is a validity rule.[84] At least for the Federal Court of Justice, the priority of individually negotiated terms does not constitute a question of interpretation: standard terms which are in conflict with individually negotiated clauses are considered invalid.[85] The rule is not limited to business-to-consumer contracts but also applies to business-to-business transactions.[86]

h) Relationship between Interpretation and Validity

The interpretation of the contract precedes the question of its material validity.[87] The contract is thus interpreted to reveal the common intention of the parties before its material validity can be assessed. In cases of doubt, courts tend to assume that the parties intended to conclude a lawful contract.[88] There is, however, only room for this assumption if the contract or the clause is ambiguous.[89]

If the interpretation of the contract leads, completely or in part, to a result which is illegal or against common decency, the contract or the particular clause would, in principle, be void.[90] Before holding the contract or the clause invalid, courts can reinterpret the contract under Section 140 of the BGB. Despite the term reinterpretation (*Umdeutung*), this is – strictly speaking – not part of the interpretation of contract.[91] Under Section 140 BGB, courts need to consider whether the parties could have concluded essentially the same transaction by other lawful means and would have done so if they had been aware of the illeg-

---

81 *Busche*, in: MünchKomm-BGB, 10th ed. 2025, § 157 n. 8; *Singer*, in: Staudinger-BGB, 2021, § 133 n. 53.

82 *Lehmann-Richter*, in: BeckOGK BGB, 1.12.2025, § 305b n. 3, with further references; *Schulte-Nölke*, in: HK-BGB, 12th ed. 2024, § 305b n. 1.

83 *Fornasier*, in: MünchKomm-BGB, 10th ed. 2025, § 305b n. 1; *Looschelders*, in: Erman BGB, 17th ed. 2023, § 305b n. 1; *Mäsch*, in: Staudinger-BGB, 2025, § 305b n. 17, with further references.

84 BGH NJW 2007, 2036 n. 22; BGH NJW-RR 1990, 613 (614).

85 BGH NJW 2007, 2036 n. 22; BGH NJW-RR 1990, 613.

86 BGH NJW 2007, 2036 n. 22; BGH NJW-RR 1990, 613; *Fornasier*, in: MünchKomm-BGB, 10th ed. 2025, § 305c n. 6.

87 *Busche*, in: MünchKomm-BGB, 10th ed. 2025, § 140 n. 3.

88 BGH NJW 2003, 819; *Möslein*, in: MünchKomm-BGB, 10th ed. 2025, § 133 n. 80.

89 BGH NJW 2017, 1660 n. 22.

90 See Sections 134, 138 BGB.

91 BGH NJW 1956, 297; *Beurskens*, in: BeckOGK BGB, 1.11.2025, § 140 n. 9.

ality of the contract.[92] The substitute transaction does not need to be identical to the invalid transaction as long as it achieves essentially the same economic end.[93] However, the Federal Court of Justice has repeatedly held that the substitute transaction cannot surpass the invalid transaction in its requirements and effects.[94]

A reinterpretation is only admissible, if courts can establish the hypothetical will of the parties at the time of the conclusion of the contract.[95] There is tendency to presume this hypothetical will of the parties to conclude the lawful version of their contract, if they can essentially achieve the intended results by lawful means.[96] For instance, if the parties agreed on an exclusion of liability and this exclusion is invalid, a higher regional court has held that the exclusion of liability can be reinterpreted as a clause prohibiting the assignment of damages claims.[97] Parties are, of course, free to address the issue of reinterpretation in their contract. They can expressly provide for reinterpretation in cases of invalidity or exclude or restrict a potential reinterpretation under Section 140 BGB.[98]

3. *Contract Supplementation*

a) The Doctrinal Foundations of Contract Supplementation

Under German law, it is generally acknowledged that courts can, in principle, supplement contracts if they are found to contain gaps.[99] There is less clarity regarding the doctrinal foundations of contract supplementation: courts and some authors consider the supplementation of contract to still form part of the interpretation of the contract *largo sensu*, as the German term for supplementation (*ergänzende Vertragsauslegung*) would suggest.[100] Other authors understand supplementation to constitute a special form of judicial law-making grounded in good faith (Section 242 BGB).[101]

92 BGH NJW 1980, 2350.

93 BGH NJW 1977, 1233 (1234); *Beurskens*, in: BeckOGK BGB, 1.11.2025, § 140 n. 53; *Busche*, in: MünchKomm-BGB, 10th ed. 2025, § 140 n. 16.

94 BGH NJW 2011, 2713; BGH NJW 1994, 1785 (1787); BGH NJW 1956, 1198; *Busche*, in: MünchKomm-BGB, 10th ed. 2025, § 140 n. 17.

95 BGH NJW 1994, 1785; *Beurskens*, in: BeckOGK BGB, 1.11.2025, § 140 n. 61; *Wendtland*, in: BeckOK BGB, 76th ed. 1.11.2025, § 140 n. 13.

96 BGH NJW 1956, 297.

97 OLG Bremen OLGZ 1966, 136.

98 *Busche*, in: MünchKomm-BGB, 10th ed. 2025, § 140 n. 6.

99 *Mansel*, in: Jauernig, BGB, 19th ed. 2023, § 157 n. 2; *Roth*, in: Staudinger-BGB, 2025, § 157 n. 4, with further references.

100 BGHZ 9, 273 n. 7, 8; *Roth*, in: Staudinger-BGB, 2025, § 157 n. 4.

101 *Busche*, in: MünchKomm-BGB, 10th ed. 2025, § 157 n. 28, with further references.

b) The Requirements of Contract Supplementation

Courts will only resort to contract supplementation if they find that the contract contains gaps. The yardstick for the analysis is whether, in light of the purpose of the contract and the structure of the transaction, one would expect the contract to contain a clause which is in fact missing.[102] Courts will therefore, in a first step, interpret the contract to establish its content before, if need be, resorting to supplementation.[103]

There is some disagreement on the relationship of contract supplementation and statutory default rules.[104] Courts tend to resort primarily to statutory default rules in order to fill gaps within contracts. The Federal Court of Justice has repeatedly held that there is generally no need to supplement the contract if statutory default rules address the issue left open by the contract.[105] It has allowed for exceptions to the primacy of gap-filling by statutory default rules in certain areas, most notably in the context of company law.[106] Other authors distinguish between contracts which conform to one of the statutory types of contracts and other atypical contracts: While the application of statutory default rules is preferable for the former category, courts should be more favorable to supplement contracts falling into the latter group.[107] This relationship between statutory default rules and supplementation may be of particular relevance for the interpretation of complex international contracts. If the contract is governed by German substantive law, but is drafted against the backdrop of another legal system or tradition, German default rules may be unsuitable to supplement the transaction.[108] The Federal Court of Justice does not seem to consider international contracts as exempt from the general primacy of statutory default rules over contract supplementation. However, in international contracts, courts may be more likely to conclude that the parties would not have wished for the application of domestic statutory default rules.[109]

---

[102] BGH NJW 2015, 955 n. 27; BGHZ 77, 301 n. 15; *Mansel*, in: Jauernig, BGB, 19th ed. 2023, § 157 n. 2; *Roth*, in: Staudinger-BGB, 2025, § 157 n. 4, with further references.

[103] *Roth*, in: Staudinger-BGB, 2025, § 157 n. 4.

[104] For further references and exceptions to the general rule, see *Roth*, in: Staudinger-BGB, 2025, § 157 n. 23.

[105] BGH NZM 2015, 211 n. 70; BGH NJW 2012, 844 n. 24, with further references.

[106] Settled case law, see, e.g., BGH NJW 1979, 1705 (1706); BGH NJW 1985, 192 (193); BGH NJW 1993, 3193 (3194); *Busche*, in: MünchKomm-BGB, 10th ed. 2025, § 157 n. 46; for a critique, see, e.g., *Riesenhuber*, in: Soergel, BGB, 14th ed. 2023, § 157 n. 23, with further references.

[107] *Busche*, in: MünchKomm-BGB, 10th ed. 2025, § 157 n. 45; *Mansel*, in: Jauernig, BGB, 19th ed. 2023, § 157 n. 3.

[108] For standardised contracts, see *Korch*, Innovation und Standardisierung in der Vertragsgestaltung, AcP 224, 554 (571 et seqq.).

[109] See, for instance, BGH NJW-RR 1990, 817.

c) The Criteria for Developing the Supplemented Terms

If courts identify a gap in the contract which ought to be filled by contract supplementation, they will supplement the term on which honest parties would have agreed upon if they had been aware of the gap.[110] The yardstick for supplementation is thus the hypothetical will of the parties.[111] Adjudicators therefore need to look at the purpose of the transaction and the respective interests of the parties to find a suitable solution for the individual transaction.[112] Courts are thus not free to choose any solution they deem appropriate.[113] The supplementation finds its limits in the autonomy of the parties: supplementation therefore cannot contradict the actual contracts terms or force upon the parties a term that they consciously omitted from the contract.[114] Additionally, the Federal Court of Justice has repeatedly held that courts cannot engage in contract supplementation if the choice among several solutions is not supported by the hypothetical will of the parties.[115]

d) The Role of Good Faith in the Supplementation of Contracts

As the reference to "honest" (*redlich*) parties would suggest, courts regularly invoke the principle of good faith to justify the supplementation of a term.[116] The concept of good faith in this context is, however, not used to introduce general considerations of ethical or socially desirable behaviour. Rather, courts invoke it to find solutions that are fair and balanced in light of the interests of both parties.[117] In many cases, the reasonable solution can be taken from established practices in the relevant industry or branch of trade.[118] Absent any contrary indications, the reference to good faith can, for example, lead to the equal apportionment of a risk that the parties did not envisage at the time of conclusion of the contract.[119]

---

[110] Settled case law, see, e.g., BGH NJW 2002, 2310 (2311); BGH NJW 2013, 2820 n. 16; BGH NJW 2019, 2298 n. 61.

[111] Settled case law, see, e.g., BGH NJW 2002, 2310 (2311); BGH NJW 2019, 2298 n. 61; BGH NJW 2020, 337 n. 28; *Busche*, in: MünchKomm-BGB, 10th ed. 2025, § 157 n. 47, 48; for a critique of the reference to the hypothetical will of the parties: *Riesenhuber*, in: Soergel, BGB, 14th ed. 2023, § 157 n. 26, with further references.

[112] BGH NJW 2019, 2298 n. 61; *Busche*, in: MünchKomm-BGB, 10th ed. 2025, § 157 n. 47.

[113] BGH NJW 2009, 1962 n. 36; BGH NJW 1999, 711 (712).

[114] BGH NJW 2002, 2310 (2311); *Busche*, in: MünchKomm-BGB, 10th ed. 2025, § 157 n. 55; *Riesenhuber*, in: Soergel, BGB, 14th ed. 2023, § 157 n. 29.

[115] BGH NJW 2009, 1962 n. 36; BGH NJW 1999, 711 (712).

[116] Settled case law, see, e.g., BGH NJW 2004, 2449; BGH NJW 2019, 2298 n. 61.

[117] See, e.g., BGH NJW 1994, 3287; BGH NJW 2019, 2298 n. 61.

[118] See for the relevance of trade usages, above sub. III.2.f).

[119] BGH NJW 2000, 894.

IV. Interpretation and Application of the Parties' Agreed Terms on the Interpretation and Supplementation

Parties may choose to take matters of interpretation into their own hands. They can do so by including a general clause on the applicable rules of contract interpretation into their contract (1.) or by providing contractual clauses for specific aspects of contract interpretation and modification (2.).

1. Contract Interpretation Rules and Party Autonomy

a) Contract Interpretation Rules as Statutory Default Rules

There is little discussion on the question of whether and to what extent the parties can modify or replace the interpretation rules laid down in Sections 133, 157 BGB.[120] According to the prevailing doctrinal view, clauses modifying or replacing the interpretation rules are possible if German law is the *lex causae*.[121] It is indeed hard to think of any reasons why parties should not be able to modify or replace the rules on interpretation of their contract.[122] Although there is little case law on the overall replacement of interpretation rules, the principle of party autonomy in contract law mandates that parties can provide rules for the interpretation of their contract, as long as they do not deviate from mandatory provisions.[123] Parties can thus, in principle, also stipulate their own rules of contract interpretation and thereby replace or modify the otherwise applicable Sections 133, 157 BGB.[124] For instance, they may agree on a literal understanding of the contracts terms and exclude references to good faith or to precontractual negotiations or documents.[125]

---

[120] *Möslein*, in: BeckOGK BGB, 1.10.2020, § 133 n. 12.

[121] *Czarnecki*, Vertragsauslegung und Vertragsverhandlungen, 2016, 210; *Kähler*, Begriff und Rechtfertigung abdingbaren Rechts, 2012, 73; *Möslein*, in: BeckOGK BGB, 1.10.2020, § 133 n. 12; *Riesenhuber*, in: Soergel, BGB, 14th ed. 2023, § 133 n. 14; for a template of such a clause under German law, see *Walz*, Beck'sches Formularbuch Zivil-, Wirtschafts- und Unternehmensrecht, 6th ed. 2026, A.II.10.

[122] *Czarnecki*, Vertragsauslegung und Vertragsverhandlungen, 2016, 211; *Möslein*, in: BeckOGK BGB, 1.10.2020, § 133 n. 12.

[123] *Möslein*, in: BeckOGK BGB, 1.10.2020, § 133 n. 12; *Kähler*, Begriff und Rechtfertigung abdingbaren Rechts, 2012, 72 et seqq.; *Riesenhuber*, in: Soergel, BGB, 14th ed. 2023, § 133 n. 14.

[124] *Möslein*, in: BeckOGK BGB, 1.10.2020, § 133 n. 12; *Riesenhuber*, in: Soergel, BGB, 14th ed. 2023, § 133 n. 14, 15.

[125] *Kähler*, Begriff und Rechtfertigung abdingbaren Rechts, 2012, 73; *Riesenhuber*, in: Soergel, BGB, 14th ed. 2023, § 133 n. 14, 15.

b) Choice of the Law Applicable to Contract Interpretation

In principle, parties to international contracts are free to choose the applicable law for their contract.[126] This choice also extends to the rules on interpretation and supplementation.[127] The choice of law can also be limited to the rules on interpretation and supplementation: Art. 3 (1) Rome I-Regulation expressly specifies that parties may choose the law applicable to only a part of the contract. Construction clauses, which stipulate that the contract is to be interpreted or construed in accordance with a particular law, will often be interpreted as the choice of law for the entire contract.[128] This interpretation should be adopted unless the parties expressly specify that the choice should only extend to the interpretation rules and select the law of another jurisdiction for other matters.[129]

If the parties have chosen the law of another jurisdiction as governing law for their contract, German courts will apply the foreign rules on contract interpretation and supplementation.[130] The domestic rules of contract interpretation and supplementation neither constitute overriding mandatory provisions under Art. 9 (1) Rome I-Regulation nor do they, as a general matter, allow courts to deny the application of foreign law based on the public policy exception in Art. 21 Rome I-Regulation. Of course, the application of the foreign rules on interpretation could, in extreme cases, lead to outcomes that violate German public policy under Art. 21 Rome I-Regulation.[131]

c) Choice of Self-Sufficient Interpretation Without Reference to National Law?

Party autonomy, in principle, also allows parties to stipulate that the contract is self-sufficient in the sense that the otherwise applicable rules of contract interpretation should not be applied and that the contract is to be interpreted and supplemented exclusively in accordance with the text of the contract and the principles on which it is based. It is important to note, however, that, at least before state courts, this clause would not have the effect of liberating the contract from an applicable national law altogether, as parties cannot comprehensively exclude the application of state law under Art. 3 (1) Rome I-Regulation.[132] The clause could therefore only exclude the application of non-mandatory rules of the objectively applicable contract law. At least under German law, the interpretation

---

[126] Art. 3 (1) Rome I-Regulation; see above sub. II.1.

[127] Art. 12 (1) (a) Rome I-Regulation; see above II.1.

[128] *Ulrich Magnus*, in: Staudinger-BGB, 2021, Rom I-VO, Art. 3 n. 89; *Kleinschmidt*, in: MünchKomm-BGB, 9th ed. 2025, Art. 12 n. 15; *Spickhoff*, in: BeckOK BGB, 76th ed. 1.5.2025, Rom I-VO, Art. 3 n. 25; *Wendland*, in: BeckOGK BGB, 1.3.2025, Rom I-VO, Art. 3 n. 160.1.

[129] *Kleinschmidt*, in: MünchKomm-BGB, 9th ed. 2025, Art. 12 n. 15.

[130] See above, sub. II.2.; BGH NJW 1987, 591; BGH NJW-RR 1990, 248 n. 11.

[131] In the context of an application to set-aside an arbitral award, see BGH NJW 2025, 896 n. 42.

[132] *Ulrich Magnus*, in: Staudinger-BGB, 2021, Rom I-VO, Art. 3 n. 55.

rules in Sections 133, 157 BGB should be considered as non-mandatory default rules.[133] However, it still seems unclear how this clause would operate in practice if courts are faced with the task of interpreting the contract. It seems plausible that they would focus on a literal and systematic interpretation of the contract documents as far as possible or refer to international principles such as the UP-ICC.

2. Selected Clauses on Contract Interpretation and Modification

a) Interpretation in Good Faith

The parties may, under German law, include a clause to the effect that the contract is to be interpreted in good faith or in a fair and equitable manner. It is, however, difficult to see how such a clause would change the standard for interpretation. Under the German default rules on interpretation, the requirements of good faith form part of the objective interpretation.[134]

b) Inclusion or Exclusion of Trade Usages and Established Practices

If both parties are commercial entities and form part of the relevant branch of trade, trade usages are incorporated into the contract by law, pursuant to Section 346 HGB.[135] It will nevertheless in many cases be reasonable for the parties to expressly agree on the inclusion of certain trade usages,[136] e. g. to avoid misunderstandings or disputes as to the existence or scope of the particular usage. If the usage is not applicable as such, parties can, of course, include a reference to the usage into their contract. Conversely, parties may exclude the application of trade usages which would otherwise be applicable.[137] The clause excluding the trade usage can be contained in standard terms.[138] The Federal Court of Justice requires that a party expressly rejects the application before or at the time of conclusion of the contract[139] or that the interpretation of the contract necessarily implies an exclusion of the trade usage.[140] Parties would, thus, be well advised to

---

133 See above, sub. III.1.a).

134 See above, sub. III.2.c); *Riesenhuber*, in: Soergel, BGB, 14th ed. 2023, § 133 n. 51 et seqq.

135 See above, sub. III.2.f).

136 *Lehmann-Richter*, in: BeckOK BGB, 48th ed. 1.10.2025, § 346 n. 6.

137 *Maultzsch*, in: MünchKomm-HGB, 6th ed. 2025, § 346 n. 26, *Pamp*, in: Oetker, Handelsgesetzbuch, 8th ed. 2024, § 346 n. 3.

138 *Fest*, in: Ebenroth/Boujong, Handelsgesetzbuch, 5th ed. 2024, § 346 n. 188; *Maultzsch*, in: MünchKomm-HGB, 6th ed. 2025, § 346 n. 26; *Pamp*, in: Oetker, Handelsgesetzbuch, 8th ed. 2024, § 346 n. 3.

139 BGH NJW 1966, 502; BGH 2 May 1984, VIII ZR 38/83 – juris, n. 28; *Maultzsch*, in: MünchKomm-HGB, 6th ed. 2025, § 346 n. 26; but see *Fest*, in: Ebenroth/Boujong, Handelsgesetzbuch, 5th ed. 2024, § 346 n. 188: express rejection by one party not always sufficient.

140 BGH 2 May 1984, VIII ZR 38/83 – juris, n. 28; *Fest*, in: Ebenroth/Boujong, Handelsgesetzbuch, 5th ed. 2024, § 346 n. 188; *Maultzsch*, in: MünchKomm-HGB, 6th ed. 2025, § 346 n. 26.

exclude the trade usage expressly, as it might otherwise be deemed incorporated into their contract under Section 346 HGB.[141]

Customary or established practices, which are not proper trade usages, will not be incorporated into the contract under Section 346 HGB.[142] They may however inform the objective interpretation of the contract under Sections 133, 157 BGB.[143] If parties wish to elevate the practices to contractual rights or duties, they need to include the practice into contract, either expressly or implicitly.[144] Conversely, they may also exclude them from the interpretation of the contract.

c) Exclusion or Restriction of Supplementation of Contract

It is generally acknowledged that the contract cannot be supplemented or reinterpreted if this contradicts the will of the parties.[145] The parties can thus agree in their contract that no supplementation or reinterpretation ought to be carried out. They may also specify criteria for the supplementation in their contract. The purpose of the supplementation is to fill the gaps in accordance with the parties' intentions and their regulatory plan, as laid down in the contract. The criteria chosen by the parties will thus bind the court in the exercise of supplementation, provided that their application does not lead to illegal or otherwise invalid outcomes. For instance, the parties could stipulate that potential gaps in the contract are to be filled by recourse to the UPICC or the PECL. While the reference to soft law instruments cannot constitute a proper choice of law in terms of Art. 3 (1) Rome I-Regulation, parties may very well incorporate them into their contract or refer to them as a contractual gap-filling tool.

d) Entire Agreement Clauses

If an international contract is finalized and executed in writing, there is a presumption that the contractual documents contain the full agreement of the parties and correctly reflect their contractual rights and duties (*Vermutung der Vollständigkeit und Richtigkeit der Urkunde*).[146] The presumption can be rebutted.

---

[141] *Maultzsch*, in: MünchKomm-HGB, 6th ed. 2025, § 346 n. 26.

[142] *Fest*, in: Ebenroth/Boujong, HGB, 5th ed. 2024, § 346 n. 29.

[143] *Fest*, in: Ebenroth/Boujong, HGB, 5th ed. 2024, § 346 n. 29; *Maultzsch*, in: MünchKomm-HGB, 6th ed. 2025, § 346 n. 2.

[144] *Fest*, in: Ebenroth/Boujong, HGB, 5th ed. 2024, § 346 n. 29.

[145] BGH NJW 2002, 2310 (2311); *Busche*, in: MünchKomm-BGB, 10th ed. 2025, § 157 n. 55; *Riesenhuber*, in: Soergel, BGB, 14th ed. 2023, § 157 n. 29, 30; *Roth*, in: Staudinger-BGB, 2025, § 157 n. 38; *Wendtland*, in: BeckOK BGB, 76th ed. 1.11.2025, § 157 n. 43; for reinterpretation, see BGH NJW 1971, 420.

[146] BGH NJW 2002, 3164; *Einsele*, in: MünchKomm-BGB, 10th ed. 2025, § 125 n. 40, with further references.

The party challenging the presumption would then need to establish the facts which show that the documents are incomplete or incorrect.[147]

Many contracts contain clauses according to which the contractual documents fully embody the agreement of the parties which cannot be contradicted or supplemented by reference to prior statements or agreements (so-called "merger clause", "integration clause", "entire agreement clause" or *Vollständigkeitsklausel*).[148] These clauses are not uncommon in German contract practice.[149] They are considered valid in principle, even if introduced via standard terms.[150] Courts generally interpret these clauses to have the same effect as the presumption of completeness and validity.[151] According to the Federal Court of Justice, the clause thus does not preclude a party from rebutting the presumption and establishing the prior agreement.[152]

It is a different question whether these types of clauses also restrict the relevant material for the interpretation of the contractual document.[153] If one accepts that parties can modify the regime for contract interpretation,[154] it is a matter of interpretation of the clause whether it should be read to exclude recourse to extrinsic material or not. The prevailing view in German practice seems to be that the entire agreement or merger clauses should, in principle, not be understood to affect the admissible material for the interpretation of the contract terms.[155]

e) Exclusion of Oral Modifications

Clauses that exclude oral modifications of contracts are common in German contract practice.[156] The effects of such clauses depend on whether the clause is individually negotiated or introduced via standard terms.

---

147 BGH NJW 2002, 3164 (3165); BGH NJW 1999, 1702 (1703); *Einsele*, in: MünchKomm-BGB, 10th ed. 2025, § 125 n. 40.

148 For a detailed discussion, see *Olaf Meyer*, RabelsZ 2008, 562.

149 See, e.g., BGH NJW-RR 2021, 872 n. 13; for templates of this type of clause, see, e.g., *Schlingmann*, in: BeckOF IntHandelsR, 1.9.2025, Form, 1.3.2 Anm. 1.

150 *Czarnecki*, Vertragsauslegung und Vertragsverhandlungen, 2016, 208 et seq.; *Olaf Meyer*, RabelsZ 2008, 562 (589).

151 BGH NJW 2000, 207 (208); BGH NJW-RR 2021, 872 n. 13; for a detailed discussion, see *Olaf Meyer*, RabelsZ 2008, 562 (587 et seqq.).

152 BGH NJW 2000, 207 (208); BGH NJW-RR 2000, 273 (275).

153 *Korch*, Unternehmenskaufverträge, 2024, 202 et seq.; *Olaf Meyer*, RabelsZ 2008, 562 (591); see, for Art. 8 CISG, *Schmidt-Kessel*, in: Schlechtriem/Schwenzer/Schroeter, UN-Kaufrecht, 8th ed. 2025, Art. 8 n. 35b.

154 *Contra*, in the context of entire agreement clauses, *Krümmel*, in: Röhricht/Graf v. Westphalen/Haas/Mock/Wöstmann, HGB, 2023, Internationales Vertragsrecht, n. 40a; *Krümmel*, IWRZ 2018, 207 (212); for a detailed discussion, see *Olaf Meyer*, RabelsZ 2008, 562 (592).

155 *Bischoff*, ZVglRWiss 103 (2004), 190 (211); *Korch*, Unternehmenskaufverträge, 2024, 203, with further references; *Olaf Meyer*, RabelsZ 2008, 562 (592); *Vogenauer* Auslegung von Verträgen, HWB-EuP 2009, 2 d); but see, in the context of Art. 8 CISG, *Schmidt-Kessel*, in: Schlechtriem/Schwenzer/Schroeter, UN-Kaufrecht, 8th ed. 2025, Art. 8 n. 35b, citing international law case law which predominnatly excludes references to extrinsic material in case of a merger clause.

156 *Hertel*, in: Staudinger-BGB, 2023, § 127 n. 56.

With respect to individually negotiated clauses, there is no doubt that parties can agree that modifications of the contract can only be carried out in writing.[157] This so-called "simple" no-oral-modification clause (*einfache Schriftformklausel*) will, however, most likely not have the desired effect before German courts: the Federal Court of Justice has repeatedly held that subsequent oral modifications include the implicit agreement to waive the no-oral-modification clause.[158] Subsequent oral modifications thus prevail over the no-oral-modification clause.[159] German contract practice has responded to this line of case law by inserting so-called "double" no-oral-modification clauses (*doppelte Schriftformklausel*). This type of clause not only requires modifications of the contract to be carried out in writing but specifies that the no-oral-modification clause itself can only be modified in writing.[160] The Federal Court of Justice has held that, in contracts involving commercial parties, this type of clause cannot be modified by oral agreements.[161] As a consequence, subsequent oral agreements have no effect on the contract.[162] Most courts tend to extend the primacy of "double" no-oral-modification clauses over subsequent oral agreements to contracts which are not concluded by commercial parties.[163]

If no-oral-modification clauses are contained in standard terms, courts will disregard the clause if the parties subsequently amend the contract orally.[164] As individually negotiated terms, the oral agreements prevail over standards terms pursuant to Section 305b BGB.[165] In a recent decision, the Federal Court of Justice has affirmed this line of case law for "double" no-oral-modification clauses contained in standard terms.[166]

---

157 *Hertel*, in: Staudinger-BGB, 2023, § 127 n. 56 et seqq., with further references.

158 Settled case law, see, e.g., BGH NJW 1962, 1908; BGHZ 66, 378 n. 46; BGHZ 71, 162 n. 17; *Hecht*, in: BeckOGK BGB, 1.10.2025, § 125 n. 116; *Mansel*, in: Jauernig BGB, 19th ed. 2023, § 125 n. 11.

159 BGHZ 71, 162 n. 17; BGH 26 November 1964, VII ZR 111/63, NJW 1965, 293; *Arnold*, in: Erman BGB, 17th ed. 2023, § 125 n. 26; *Hertel*, in: Staudinger-BGB, 2023, § 127 n. 59 et seqq., with further references.

160 *Hecht*, in: BeckOGK BGB, 1.10.2025, § 125 n. 116; *Hertel*, in: Staudinger-BGB, 2023, § 127 n. 62 et seqq.

161 BGH NJW 1976, 1395.

162 BGH ZUM 2010, 431 n. 21; BGH NJW 1976, 1395; OLG Munich NZG 2025, 1282 n. 37.

163 BAGE 106, 345 n. 37; BAGE 126, 364 n. 18; KG NZM 2005, 908 n. 22; *Hertel*, in: Staudinger-BGB, 2023, § 127 n. 63 et seqq., with further references.

164 BGH NJW 2017, 1017 n. 16 et seqq.; *Schmidt*, in: Graf von Westphalen/Thüsing/Pamp, Vertragsrecht und AGB-Klauselwerke, 52. EL Oktober 2025, n. 99; *Zschieschack*, in: BeckOGK BGB, 1.12.2025, § 307 n. 34.

165 BGH NJW 2017, 1017 n. 16 et seqq.; *Fornasier*, in: MünchKomm-BGB, 10th ed. 2025, § 305b n. 16.

166 BGH NJW 2017, 1017 n. 16 et seqq.

f) Multiple Language Clauses

There are various reasons why parties may decide to draft separate contract documents in different languages. In this case, parties are well advised to include a clause which deals with the relationship between the two versions.[167] One option is to declare one version as the authentic instrument which is binding upon the parties. The other versions will then not be binding and simply serve as a translation for information purposes.[168] Parties may also stipulate that both versions are binding. In these cases, parties will often specify a priority rule.[169] In principle, these clauses are valid under German law. However, there may be some limits to their effectiveness if they are introduced via standard terms. For instance, an individually negotiated term in one language prevails over standard terms in another language irrespective of a potential priority rule in the standard terms.[170] If both parties try to impose priority of their respective languages via standard terms which are irreconcilable, the contract will be considered to be concluded without the irreconcilable priority clauses.[171] If the contract does not stipulate a priority rule, courts will have to apply the common rules on contract interpretation to determine which understanding reflects the common intention of the parties. In cases of doubt, the language used in the negotiations can be presumed to reflect the bargain of the parties more correctly than other languages.[172]

V. Interpretation and Application of Selected Contract Clauses

There are many types of clauses which are common in international commercial transactions. The questionnaire has provided a selection of such typical clauses which the report will address in the order of the questionnaire.

1. Self-Sufficiency Clause

Parties may try to isolate their contract from national rules on interpretation by including a self-sufficiency clause according to which the contract shall be interpreted independently from a national legal system and be governed by general

---

[167] *Martiny*, in: Reithmann/Martiny, Internationales Vertragsrecht, 9th ed. 2022, n. 1.176.

[168] For this type of clause, see *Walz*, Beck'sches Formularbuch Zivil-, Wirtschafts- und Unternehmensrecht, 6th ed. 2026, A.II.2 Anm. 2.

[169] For this type of clause, see *Schlingmann*, in: BeckOF IntHandelsR, 1.9.2025, Form, 1.3.1 Anm. 1; *Walz*, Beck'sches Formularbuch Zivil-, Wirtschafts- und Unternehmensrecht, 6th ed. 2026, A.II.2 Anm. 4.

[170] Section 305b BGB; for details, see above (sub. III.2.g).

[171] For further details on this knock-out-rule (*Restgültigkeitstheorie*), see *Maultzsch*, in: MünchKomm-HGB, 6th ed. 2025, Vor § 343 n. 45.

[172] In the context of the CISG, see *Schroeter*, in: Schlechtriem/Schwenzer/Schroeter, CISG, 8th ed. 2025, Art. 14 n. 158.

principles of commercial contract practice. As discussed above, such a clause will not be considered a choice of the governing law under Art. 3 (1) Rome I-Regulation which only allows for the choice of state law. The clause can, however, function as a modification or replacement of the default rules on interpretation of the governing law. In principle, there seems to be no reason why such a clause should not be valid under German law. Courts would then need to interpret the reference to international commercial contract practice. Absent specific standard practices in particular branches of trade, it seems plausible to assume that courts would look for guidance in the UPICC or PECL.

2. Good Faith and Fair Dealing Clause

Good faith and fair dealing clauses are meant to oblige the parties to perform the contract in good faith. There is no doubt that these clauses are valid under German law. However, if German law is the *lex causae*, the clause will hardly have any additional legal effects, as the performance of the contract in good faith is expressly foreseen in Section 242 BGB. Section 157 BGB also specifies that the contract is to be interpreted with reference to good faith.[173] In most cases, good faith and fair dealing clauses will merely reflect the role of good faith under German contract law.

3. Best Efforts Clause

The term "best efforts" does not have a functional equivalent in German legal terminology.[174] The term is, however, sometimes used in contracts which are governed by German law, most notably in M&A contracts.[175] There does not seem to be a settled case law on how to interpret the term "best efforts" in contracts governed by German law. There are different doctrinal approaches on the meaning of best-efforts-clauses in the German legal context: Some authors conclude that, while the interpretation of the specific clause needs to be informed by the circumstances of each case, the best efforts clause will in many cases simply reflect the obligations of a party under the German default rules, most notably to perform the contract in good faith.[176] Another interpretation understands the reference to best efforts as a means to qualify the obligations of the parties which may, in certain cases, change the character of the transaction.[177] Other authors

---

173 See above III.2.c).

174 For so-called "*Bemühensklauseln*" (efforts clauses), see *Graf von Westphalen*, NZM 2022, 1.

175 *Hoenig/Sprado*, NZG 2014, 688; *Ulrich*, GmbHR 2011, R198; see also, e.g., OLG Frankfurt BeckRS 2011, 26867; for templates involving "best" or "reasonable" efforts clauses, see, e.g., *Meyer-Sparenberg*, in: BeckFormB BHW, 15th ed. 2026, Form. III. A. 19.

176 See *Maier-Reimer*, NJW 2010 2545 (2547).

177 *Von Bary*, ZIP 2021, 1902 (1908); see also OLG Nürnberg BeckRS 2021, 7538 n. 116, arguing that the obligor could have qualified its obligations by including a reasonable efforts clause.

point to the case of law of the Federal Court of Justice, according to which clauses inspired by foreign law should be interpreted in accordance with the understanding in their jurisdiction of origin.[178] They argue that best efforts clauses should hence be read in light of the US-American contract practice.[179] This approach may be justified in particular circumstances but would require a clear connection to a particular jurisdiction, given that the term is not interpreted in a consistent manner across common law jurisdictions.[180] Given that there is little to no clarity as to how best effort clauses should be interpreted from the perspective of German law, courts should, in the absence of a clear connection to a specific jurisdiction, turn to the internationally accepted definition in Art. 5.1.4 (2) UPICC which requires a party to undertake measure which "would be made by a reasonable party of the same kind in the same circumstances."[181]

4. General Trade Standard Clause

Clauses, by which parties agree that the performance needs to comply with general trade standards or with the general state of the art, are common in international contract practice. These clauses do not present any particular problems under German law. In most cases, they will simply reflect the statutory default rules. For instance, in a sales contract, the seller is expected to deliver goods that conform to the generally expected technological state of the art of the industry in question.[182] If sellers are obliged to deliver goods of a certain class, they must deliver goods of an average kind and quality within the class.[183] These provisions are, of course, not mandatory.[184] Parties may contractually elevate the standards for performance, e.g. by requiring observance of the highest market standards.[185] Conversely, they may also lower the standard for performance, e.g. by including so-called *tel quel* clauses.[186] Tel quel clauses are interpreted as allowing for the delivery of goods conforming to the lowest quality standards of the class.[187]

---

178 *Hoenig/Sprado*, NZG 2014, 688 (691).

179 *Hoenig/Sprado*, NZG 2014, 688 (691); *Wied*, RIW 2013, 768 (772).

180 *Von Bary*, ZIP 2021, 1902 (1908); for an overview, see *Beardwood*, CRi 2021, 45.

181 See Art. 5.1.4. (2) UPICC.

182 BGH NJW 2009, 2056 (2057); *Maultzsch*, in: MünchKomm-BGB, 9th ed. 2024, § 434 n. 56.

183 See, § 360 HGB and § 243 (1) BGB.

184 *Martens*, in: MünchKomm-HGB, 6th ed. 2025, § 360 n. 17; *Moussa*, in: BeckOK HGB, 49th ed. 1.10.2025, § 360 n. 7.

185 For sales contracts, see *Maultzsch*, in: MünchKomm-BGB, 9th ed. 2024, § 434 n. 45, 56.

186 See, e.g., *Fest*, in: Ebenroth/Boujong, HGB, 5th ed. 2024, § 346 n. 369.

187 BGH NJW 1954, 385; *Martens*, in: MünchKomm-HGB, 6th ed. 2025, § 360 n. 19; *Maultzsch*, in: Oetker, HGB, 8th ed. 2024, § 360 n. 11; *Moussa*, in: BeckOK HGB, 49th ed. 1.10.2025, § 360 n. 8.

5. Subject to Contract Clause

Subject to contract clauses are common in German contract practice.[188] In the German terminology, they are usually called "*freibleibend*" or "*ohne obligo*".[189] Despite their frequent inclusion, these clauses do not have a fixed meaning and are thus to be interpreted in light of the circumstances and the context of the specific transaction.[190] Courts will often understand this term as indicating that the document is an invitation to issue an offer (*invitatio ad offerendum*).[191] If the recipient of the invitation then issues an offer based on the same terms, the offeree needs to object if it does not wish to enter into the contract. Absent such objection, courts may consider the contract to be concluded, as the offeror could reasonably understand the silence of the offeree as an acceptance.[192] Depending on the circumstances and the exact wording of the clause, courts have also interpreted the term "*freibleibend*" as a freely revocable offer to conclude the contract.[193] For a contract in which the parties used the term "subject to contract" in English, the Higher Regional Tribunal Frankfurt concluded that the clause was to be read as a clear indication that parties did not wish to enter into a binding agreement.[194]

6. Validity and Replacement Clauses

a) Validity Clauses

By the inclusion of a validity clause, the parties confirm that they consider the contract valid and binding. They will in many cases also add that the contract should remain valid if any of the contractual provisions are found to be invalid. Such clauses, which are known as "*salvatorische Klauseln*" or "*Erhaltungsklauseln*", are very common in German contract practice. Courts generally consider them valid, including if they are introduced via standard terms.[195] They operate as a contractual reversal of the statutory default presumption contained in Sec-

---

188 For templates, see, e.g., *Piltz*, in: BeckOF IntHandelsR, 1.9.2025, Form. 2.1.4.1.; *Piltz*, in: BeckOF IntHandelsR, 1.9.2025, Form. 2.1.3.1.

189 *Bork*, in: Staudinger-BGB, 2025, § 145 n. 26; *Leyens*, in: Hopt, HGB, 45th ed. 2026, § 346 n. 40.

190 *Busche*, in: MünchKomm-BGB, 10th ed. 2025, § 145 n. 7; *Maultzsch*, in: MünchKomm-HGB, 6th ed. 2025, § 346 n. 86.

191 BGH NJW 1996, 919 (920); see also obiter BGH NJW 1958, 1628 (1629); *Armbrüster*, in: Erman BGB, 17th ed. 2023, § 145 n. 17; *Leyens*, in: Hopt, HGB, 45th ed. 2026, § 346 n. 40.

192 BGH NJW 1996, 919; see also RGZ 102, 227 (230); *Bork*, in: Staudinger-BGB, 2025, § 145 n. 30.

193 BGH NJW 1984, 1885, holding that the term "*freibleibend entsprechend unserer Verfügbarkeit*" constitutes an offer; see also *Bork*, in: Staudinger-BGB, 2025, § 145 n. 31, arguing that, in cases of doubt, courts should interpret the clause as a freely revocable offer.

194 OLG Frankfurt 9 July 1998, 3 U 61/97, – juris.

195 See, e.g., BGHZ 233, 54 n. 50; *Bonin*, in: BeckOGK BGB, 1.10.2025, § 306 n. 72; *Roth*, in: Staudinger-BGB, 2025, § 139 n. 22.

tion 139 BGB, pursuant to which, in case of its partial invalidity, the entire contract is deemed invalid unless it can be assumed that the parties would have concluded the contract without the invalid part.[196] Despite the inclusion of a validity clause, courts may determine that the entire contract is void if the invalid part concerns the essential parts of the contract or if the parties would not have concluded the contract without the invalid part.[197] The validity clause thus does not have an absolute effect. Rather, it operates as a presumption for the validity of the remaining part of the contract in case of its partial invalidity.[198] If a party maintains that the entire contract should be considered void irrespective of the validity clause, it will bear the burden of proof.[199]

b) Replacement Clauses

In contract practice, validity clauses are often combined with replacement clauses (*Ersetzungsklauseln*).[200] Pursuant to these clauses, the invalid part of the contract is to be replaced by another provision. This supplemented provision can be specified in the contract. The parties can also agree that they will renegotiate replacement terms in good faith if a clause is found invalid.[201] Replacement clauses are considered valid if they are individually negotiated.[202] If the clauses are contained in standard terms, courts will in most cases invalidate them for lack of transparency or for circumvention of the provisions on the review and invalidation of standard terms.[203] If standard terms combine a validity clause with a supplementation clause, the Federal Court of Justice has held that the invalidity of the supplementation clause does not extend to the validity clause which remains enforceable.[204]

7. Representation and Warranty Clause

Representation and warranty clauses, which are commonplace in contracts inspired by common law jurisdictions, are difficult to fit within the context of Ger-

---

[196] *Busche*, in: MünchKomm-BGB, 10th ed. 2025, § 139 n. 13; *Roth*, in: Staudinger-BGB, 2025, § 139 n. 22.

[197] *Roth*, in: Staudinger-BGB, 2025, § 139 n. 22.

[198] BGH NJW 2005, 2225; *Roth*, in: Staudinger-BGB, 2025, § 139 n. 22.

[199] BGHZ 233, 54 n. 50; BGH NJW 2005, 2225; *Roth*, in: Staudinger-BGB, 2025, § 139 n. 22.

[200] See, e. g., BGH NJW 2005, 2225.

[201] See, e. g., BGH NJW 2016, 401 n. 26; BGH NJW 2002, 894 (895); OLG Düsseldorf BeckRS 2025, 12177 n. 26.

[202] *Bonin*, in: BeckOGK BGB, 1.10.2025, § 306 n. 76; *Busche*, in: MünchKomm-BGB, 10th ed. 2025, § 139 n. 13.

[203] Settled case law, see, e. g., BGH NJW 2016, 401 n. 26; BGH NZG 2016, 31 n. 19; BGH NJW 2015, 1952 n. 45; BGH NJW 2002, 894 (895); *Bonin*, in: BeckOGK BGB, 1.10.2025, § 306 n. 73 et seq., with further references.

[204] BGH NJW 2005, 2225.

man law.[205] They are nevertheless often included in specific types of contracts governed by German law,[206] for instance certain finance contracts[207] or M&A contracts.[208] The exact operation of these clauses will very much depend on the type of contract and the circumstances of the particular case. As a general matter, courts will interpret the representation and warranties clauses in accordance with the meaning in the jurisdiction of origin, if they are inspired by the law and contract practice of particular jurisdiction.[209] However, the interaction between the clause on the one hand and the statutory default rules on the other remains difficult and will largely depend on the context. Generally, most courts and authors understand the clauses to institute a strict liability regime.[210] If a party represents and warrants, without qualification, that all information provided to the other party is true, courts and arbitral tribunals will most likely hold the party liable if the information turns out to be objectively false, irrespective of whether the party knew or could have known of the incorrectness.[211] This tendency has been widely criticized in legal doctrine.[212] In these cases, the interpretation will largely be a function of the precise wording of the clause in light of the context and the purpose of the transaction.[213]

8. Termination Clauses in Long-Term Contracts

Provisions on termination are an important part of many long-term contracts. Termination clauses can provide for termination for cause as well as termination for convenience. The validity and the construction of these clauses will in many

---

[205] *Krümmel*, in: Röhricht/Graf von Westphalen/Haas/Mock/Wöstmann, HGB, 6th ed. 2023, Internationales Vertragsrecht, n. 33; *Ostendorf*, in: Ostendorf, Internationale Wirtschaftsverträge, 3rd ed. 2023, § 16 n. 50; see also *Triebel/Vogenauer*, Englisch als Vertragssprache, 2018, n. 618.

[206] See, e. g., OLG Nürnberg BeckRS 2021, 7538 n. 95, 103 et seqq.

[207] For certain types of underwriting agreements, see *Diekmann*, in: Habersack/Mülbert/Schlitt, Unternehmensfinanzierung am Kapitalmarkt, 5th ed. 2025, § 30 n. 30.65 et seqq.

[208] *Rosengarten/Burmeister/Klein*, M&A, 3rd ed., 2020, J. V. 5.; for templates, see, e. g., *Stummel*, in: Stummel, Standardvertragsmuster, 6th ed. 2021, Form. V. 2.

[209] See above sub. II.2.

[210] For underwriting agreements: *Diekmann*, in: Habersack/Mülbert/Schlitt, Unternehmensfinanzierung am Kapitalmarkt, 5th ed. 2025, § 30 n. 30.65 et seqq.; see generally *Krümmel*, in: Röhricht/Graf von Westphalen/Haas/Mock/Wöstmann, HGB, 6th ed. 2023, Internationales Vertragsrecht, n. 35; see also OLG Frankfurt NZG 2016, 435 n. 67 et seqq.: "*harte Bilanzgarantie*"; left open in a decision on a sponsorship agreement: OLG Nürnberg BeckRS 2021, 7538 n. 131 et seqq.

[211] OLG Frankfurt NZG 2016, 435 paras. 67 et seqq.; OLG Munich BeckRS 2011, 7200; for a report of an arbitral award, see *Pickrahn*, in: Elsing/Pickrahn/Pörnbacher/Wagner, M&A-Streitigkeiten vor DIS-Schiedsgerichten: Praxishandbuch, 2022, B.V. 1, no. 63; for a detailed discussion in the M&A context, see *Korch*, Unternehmenskaufverträge, 2024, 265 et seqq.

[212] See *Korch*, Unternehmenskaufverträge, 266 et seqq., with a detailed discussion and further references.

[213] *Pickrahn*, in: Elsing/Pickrahn/Pörnbacher/Wagner, M&A-Streitigkeiten vor DIS-Schiedsgerichten: Praxishandbuch, 2022, B.V. 1, n. 327.

cases depend on the type of contract and the circumstances of the case. A few general points on the termination of long-term contracts can be made.

a) Clauses on Termination for Cause and Termination for Convenience

The general statutory default rule on termination of long-term contracts for compelling reason can be found in Section 314 BGB. Courts consider the core of this general right to terminate long-term contracts for compelling reason to be mandatory.[214] Parties may thus not altogether exclude termination for cause in their contract.[215] They may, however, define and reasonably restrict the compelling reasons for termination, e. g. by specifying the types of breaches that permit termination.[216] If the clause restricts the right to terminate for compelling reason, courts will have to consider whether the restriction is excessive.[217] For instance, courts will most likely accept a clause pursuant to which termination for cause requires a material breach of contract which is not cured in a particular period of time.[218]

Contractual specifications of compelling reasons will still be subject to interpretation. For instance, the Federal Court of Justice has held that a clause, providing for a right to terminate a commercial agency agreement in case of the breach of a non-competition clause, is open to interpretation.[219] The Federal Court of Justice considered the clause to still require the court to balance the interests of the parties in case of breach of the non-competition clause.[220] It held that breaches that are so minor that they cannot lead to a breakdown of trust between the company and commercial agent should not be considered compelling reasons in terms of the clause.[221]

Parties may also include a right to terminate for convenience.[222] This clause should specify the applicable notice period. Depending on the applicable law and the type of contract, the autonomy of the parties in this respect may be limited by mandatory provisions that protect one of the parties.[223]

---

214 See BGH BeckRS 1973, 31125503; *Gaier*, in: MünchKomm-BGB, 10th ed. 2025, § 314 n. 7; *Lorenz*, in: BeckOK BGB, 76th ed. 1.11.2025, § 314 n. 28; for clauses unduly restricting termination for compelling reasons in standard terms, see BGH NJW 1986, 3134.

215 See *Ostendorf*, in: Ostendorf (ed.), Internationale Wirtschaftsverträge, 3rd ed. 2023, § 16 n. 47.

216 BGH NJW-RR 1988, 1381 (1382); *Ostendorf*, in: Ostendorf, Internationale Wirtschaftsverträge, 3rd ed. 2023, § 16 n. 47.

217 *Ostendorf*, in: Ostendorf (ed.), Internationale Wirtschaftsverträge, 3rd ed. 2023, § 16 n. 47.

218 See for a similar clause for exchange contracts, *Ostendorf*, in: Ostendorf (ed.), Internationale Wirtschaftsverträge, 3rd ed. 2023, § 16 n. 56.

219 BGH NJW 2011, 608 n. 20.

220 BGH NJW 2011, 608 n. 22 et seqq.

221 BGH NJW 2011, 608 n. 22.

222 *Ostendorf*, in: Ostendorf (ed.), Internationale Wirtschaftsverträge, 3rd ed. 2023, § 16 n. 62.

223 *Ostendorf*, in: Ostendorf (ed.), Internationale Wirtschaftsverträge, 3rd ed. 2023, § 16 n. 63.

b) Clauses on Termination in Case of Insolvency

The legal status of clauses that allow for termination in case of insolvency of the other party has been controversial for quite some time[224] and will depend on the specific context of the transaction and the circumstances of the case. In a recent decision, the Federal Court of Justice has discussed the validity of such clauses in detail, concluding that they are invalid if they lead to a circumvention of insolvency law.[225] This will be the case if the terminating party is a creditor of a monetary debt.[226] The clause may be valid if it protects legitimate interests of the parties.[227] The situation gets more complex for international contracts if the applicable contract law is different from the applicable insolvency law.[228] Courts will then need to characterize the issue of the validity of the termination clause to determine whether it is governed by the *lex fori concursus* or the *lex contractus*.[229] In a case involving German contract law and French insolvency law, the Higher Regional Court of Karlsruhe has applied German contract law to uphold the termination clause which would have been invalidated by French insolvency law.[230] This decision has been widely criticized in legal doctrine.[231] The prevailing opinion under Art. 7 (2) (e) of the European Insolvency Regulation, however, considers the *lex fori concursus* to govern the issue.[232]

c) Consequences of Termination

If the contract is terminated, the parties may wish to specify the consequences of termination.[233] The clause will typically address the fate of the obligations of the parties before and after termination of the contract as well as its potential effect on other rights and remedies. For instance, a clause obliging the parties to perform their obligations until the termination takes effect would be in line with the statutory default rules on long-term contracts under German law.[234] Similarly, a clarification that the termination does not affect the availability of other reme-

224 See, with further references on the discussion, BGH NJW 2023, 603.
225 BGH NJW 2023, 603.
226 BGH NJW 2023, 603.
227 BGH NJW 2023, 603.
228 For an overview of the problem, see *J. F. Hoffmann*, in: MünchKomm-InsO, 5th ed. 2025, § 119 paras. 55, 56.
229 *Ostendorf*, in: Ostendorf (ed.), Internationale Wirtschaftsverträge, 3rd ed. 2023, § 16 n. 10.
230 OLG Karlsruhe NJW 2012, 3106.
231 *Damann/Lehmkuhl*, NJW 2012, 3069; *Ostendorf*, in: Ostendorf (ed.), Internationale Wirtschaftsverträge, 3rd ed. 2023, § 16 n. 10.
232 See *Brinkmann*, in: K. Schmidt (ed.), Insolvenzordnung, 20th ed. 2023, EuInsVO, Art. 7 n. 27; *Mock*, in: BeckOK Insolvenzrecht, 41st ed. 1.11.2025, EUInsVO Art. 7 n. 37; *Reinhart*, in: MünchKomm-InsO, 4th ed. 2021, EuInsVO, Art. 7 n. 30.
233 *Ostendorf*, in: Ostendorf (ed.), Internationale Wirtschaftsverträge, 3rd ed. 2023, § 16 n. 69 et seqq.
234 *Gaier*, in: MünchKomm-BGB, 10th ed. 2025, § 314 n. 62; *Martens*, in: BeckOGK BGB, 1.12.2025, § 314 n. 80.

dies, such as damages claims, would reflect the default position of German contract law.[235]

9. Indemnification Clauses

Indemnity clauses are a common feature of international commercial contracts.[236] Despite their prevalence in international contracts, the term "indemnity" does not have a precise equivalent in German legal terminology and can be a source of considerable confusion in the German legal context.[237] Under the indemnities or indemnification clause, a party is obliged to indemnify the other parties from all claims, expenses and other losses arising from a breach of the agreement or other conduct specified in the clause. The indemnity clause thus institutes a claim against the indemnifying party to hold harmless the other party of certain specified categories of claims (*Freistellungsanspruch*).[238] Whether the clause only encompasses third party claims or also covers claims of the beneficiary of the clause, is a matter of interpretation.[239] Indemnity clauses are common in very different kinds of contracts which makes general statements on their interpretation and application difficult. Much will depend on the wording of the clause as well as the type and context of the transaction.[240] Subject to these qualifications, a few general points can be made.

In principle, parties are free to include indemnity clauses into their contract.[241] The clauses are typically interpreted to contain an independent claim which is directed at the extinction of the third party claim.[242] Absent any indication to the contrary, German courts understand indemnity clauses to also encompass the defense against unfounded claims.[243] According to the Federal Court of Justice, the inclusion of claims which prove to be unfounded is one of the essential features of the clause. The clause will thus be read to include these types of claims unless the wording or the specific interests of the parties mandate the restriction

---

[235] See the clarification in § 314 (4) BGB; *Martens*, in: BeckOGK BGB, 1.12.2025, § 314 n. 85 et seqq., with details and further references.

[236] *Ostendorf*, in: Ostendorf, Internationale Wirtschaftsverträge, 3rd ed. 2023, § 7 n. 1.

[237] *Triebel/Vogenauer*, Englisch als Vertragssprache, 2018, n. 618; also see *Ostendorf*, in: Ostendorf (ed.), Internationale Wirtschaftsverträge, 3rd ed. 2023, § 7 n. 1.

[238] *Ostendorf*, in: Ostendorf (ed.), Internationale Wirtschaftsverträge, 3rd ed. 2023, § 7 n. 2 et seqq.

[239] *Ostendorf*, in: Ostendorf (ed.), Internationale Wirtschaftsverträge, 3rd ed. 2023, § 7 n. 3.

[240] With examples, see *Ostendorf*, in: Ostendorf (ed.), Internationale Wirtschaftsverträge, 3rd ed. 2023, § 7 n. 44 et seqq.

[241] *Schütt*, NJW 2016, 980.

[242] *Ostendorf*, in: Ostendorf (ed.), Internationale Wirtschaftsverträge, 3rd ed. 2023, § 7 paras. 12, 13.

[243] BGH NJW 2011, 2719 n. 51; BGH NJW-RR 2011, 479 n. 12; BGH NJW 1970, 1594; *Ostendorf*, in: Ostendorf (ed.), Internationale Wirtschaftsverträge, 3rd ed. 2023, § 7 n. 16.

to justified claims.[244] There seems to be some uncertainty as to which measures the indemnifying party needs to undertake to defend the other party against third party claims.[245]

The use of indemnity clauses via standard terms is subject to the general provisions on the review of standard terms in Section 307 BGB.[246] Courts regularly consider indemnities clauses in standard terms invalid if they lead to a strict liability[247] or include unfounded third-party claims.[248] The indemnities clauses also need to conform to the transparency requirement under Section 307 (1) BGB: in a recent decision, the Federal Court of Justice has confirmed the invalidation of an indemnities clause in a sale of a limited partnership share for lack of transparency as the level of economic exposure following from the clause was unclear.[249]

10. Force Majeure and Hardship Clauses

Force majeure and hardship clauses are common in international commercial transactions.[250] In principle, force majeure and hardship are two separate concepts. They may, however, touch upon similar issues, are sometimes addressed within the same clause and may overlap or interact.[251]

a) Force Majeure Clauses

Force majeure clauses deal with the consequences of circumstances or events that prevent or impede a party from performing its contractual obligations.[252] The clauses typically define the requirements for exemption of specific performance and damages claims in case of non-performance as well as further legal effects of the events on the obligations of the parties. For instance, force majeure clauses may include a catalogue of events that are presumed to constitute force majeure

244 BGH NJW-RR 2011, 479 n. 13.

245 *Ostendorf*, in: Ostendorf (ed.), Internationale Wirtschaftsverträge, 3rd ed. 2023, § 7 n. 17.

246 See, e. g., LG München I 20 May 2025, 1 HK O 15370/20, 1 HKO 15370/20 – juris, n. 463; *Ostendorf*, in: Ostendorf (ed.), Internationale Wirtschaftsverträge, 3rd ed. 2023, § 7 n. 26.

247 See OLG Koblenz ZUM-RD 2005, 393; *Ostendorf*, in: Ostendorf (ed.), Internationale Wirtschaftsverträge, 3rd ed. 2023, § 7 n. 27.

248 *Ostendorf*, in: Ostendorf (ed.), Internationale Wirtschaftsverträge, 3rd ed. 2023, § 7 n. 27.

249 BGH BB 2019, 1296 n. 12 et seqq.

250 See, e. g., the ICC Force Majeure and Hardship Clause, March 2020, https://iccwbo.org/wp-content/uploads/sites/3/2020/03/icc-forcemajeure-hardship-clauses-march2020.pdf (16.01.2026).

251 See *Grün/Ostendorf*, in: Ostendorf (ed.), Internationale Wirtschaftsverträge, 3rd ed. 2023, § 10 n. 5; *Vogenauer*, IWRZ 2021, 57 (58).

252 For a model force majeure clause, see ICC Force Majeure and Hardship Clause, March 2020, https://iccwbo.org/wp-content/uploads/sites/3/2020/03/icc-forcemajeure-hardship-clauses-march2020.pdf (16.01.2026).

events[253] or they may specify a notification requirement and consequences of a failure to notify.[254] The concept of force majeure, which is known in some but not all jurisdictions, has become an internationally recognized, transnational concept.[255] The reasons for and the consequences of including a force majeure clause may, however, very much depend on the otherwise applicable contract law. In a contract governed by English law, the role of the force majeure clause will be to define and, in many cases, extend the grounds for exemption from liability for damages which would otherwise be governed by the, in many respects stricter, doctrine of frustration.[256]

The German provisions on non-performance of contractual obligations do not refer to the concept of force majeure.[257] Under German contract law, the obligee can be exempt from damages claims if they prove that neither they nor the persons they reverted to in the performance of their contractual duties acted negligently.[258] A force majeure event will, by definition, exclude the obligee's negligence. The exemption for absence of fault thus covers force majeure events but also extends to other events, provided that the obligee was not negligent. In this legal context, the inclusion of a force majeure clause may be understood as a restriction of grounds for exemption and lead, in essence, to a strict liability regime.[259] If courts were to retain this interpretation, the obligee would lose their route to exemption by proving that there was no negligence. Exemption would require the proof of a force majeure event. Depending on the circumstances, courts may however also conclude that the clause should not restrict other, potentially wider legal grounds for exemption.[260] The parties are therefore well advised to expressly address the relationship of the clause to the statutory default rules on exemption for non-performance.[261]

Despite the unclear fit with German rules on non-performance of contracts, force majeure clauses can be found in many contracts governed by German

[253] ICC Force Majeure and Hardship Clause, March 2020; *Grün/Ostendorf*, in: Ostendorf (ed.), Internationale Wirtschaftsverträge, 3rd ed. 2023, § 10 n. 40.

[254] ICC Force Majeure and Hardship Clause, March 2020, https://iccwbo.org/wp-content/uploads/sites/3/2020/03/icc-forcemajeure-hardship-clauses-march2020.pdf (16.01.2026); see also *Grün/Ostendorf*, in: Ostendorf (ed.), Internationale Wirtschaftsverträge, 3rd ed. 2023, § 10 n. 40.

[255] See, e. g., Art. 7.1.7 UPICC; see also Art. 8:108 PECL and Art. 79 CISG, which do not employ the label force majeure but embody the same principle.

[256] *Grün/Ostendorf*, in: Ostendorf, Internationale Wirtschaftsverträge, 3rd ed. 2023, § 10 n. 29; *Triebel/Vogenauer*, Englisch als Vertragssprache, n. 611.

[257] The German equivalent term "*höhere Gewalt*" plays a minor role in other contexts; see, e. g., Sections 206, 701 (3) BGB as well as former Section 651j BGB.

[258] See Section 280 (1) BGB.

[259] *Lejeune*, ITRB 2009, 189 (191); *Triebel/Vogenauer*, Englisch als Vertragssprache, n. 611.

[260] See *Grün/Ostendorf*, in: Ostendorf (ed.), Internationale Wirtschaftsverträge, 3rd ed. 2023, § 10 n. 52, who argue that this reading should be the default assumption.

[261] *Grün/Ostendorf*, in: Ostendorf (ed.), Internationale Wirtschaftsverträge, 3rd ed. 2023, § 10 n. 52; *Vogenauer*, IWRZ 2021, 147 (153).

law.[262] They are considered valid in principle,[263] even if they are introduced via standard terms.[264] Depending on the exact formulation, the clauses may be interpreted very differently: Courts may, for instance, understand the clause to refer to the case law of the Federal Court of Justice on the concept of *höhere Gewalt* in other contexts.[265]

b) Hardship Clauses

Hardship clauses address the consequences of unforeseen events that fundamentally change the contractual equilibrium. The BGB contains a provision addressing unforeseen changes of circumstances which formed the basis of the transaction in Section 313 BGB. If there is indeed such a change, Section 313 BGB provides for a claim for adaptation or, if adaptation is not possible, termination of the contract.[266] This provision is a manifestation of the principle of good faith and is therefore mandatory in its core.[267] Parties may, however, contractually modify and define the requirements and consequences of a change of circumstances, for instance by providing for a special procedure for contract adaptation or excluding adaptation in favour of termination.[268]

Despite the statutory default rule in Section 313 BGB, hardship clauses (or: *Wirtschaftsklauseln*) are not uncommon in German contract practice.[269] These clauses are generally considered valid and enjoy priority over the default rule in section 313 BGB.[270] If the clauses are contained in standard terms, their scope of application may be limited by the priority of individually negotiated terms pursuant to Section 305b BGB: In the case of a long-term energy supply contract, the Federal Court of Justice has declined to apply a *Wirtschaftsklausel* to a fixed price agreement which the parties had negotiated for months.[271] The Court held that, by carefully negotiating the fixed price agreement with a three year term, each party had assumed the risk that the price would develop to their disfavour.[272]

---

[262] See, e.g., BGH NJW 1995, 1959; for a template combining the choice of German law and an exemption for force majeure events, see, e.g., *Metzlaff/Schulzweida*, in: Osterrieth (ed.), Formularkommentar Lizenzverträge, 5th ed. 2026, Art. 20.

[263] See, e.g., RGZ 92, 87.

[264] *Vogenauer*, IWRZ 2021, 209 (210); *contra Graf von Westphalen*, ZVertriebsR 2020, 275 (280).

[265] For this question, see, e.g., *Graf von Westphalen*, ZVertriebsR 2020, 275; for the notion of *höhere Gewalt*, see, e.g., BGH NJW 2017, 2677 n. 8; BGH NJW 1987, 1938 (1939).

[266] For the priority of adaptation over termination, see, e.g., BGH NJW 2012, 373 n. 25; *Lorenz*, in: BeckOK BGB, 76th ed. 1.11.2025, § 313 n. 83, with further references.

[267] See *Martens*, in: BeckOGK BGB, 1.12.2025, § 313 n. 47.

[268] See *Martens*, in: BeckOGK BGB, 1.12.2025, § 313 n. 48.

[269] See, e.g., BGH NJW 2013, 2745; see *Maultzsch*, in: MünchKomm-HGB, 6th ed. 2025, § 346 n. 62.

[270] See, e.g., BGH NJW 2013, 2745 n. 16.

[271] BGH NJW 2013, 2745.

[272] BGH NJW 2013, 2745 n. 18.

This individually negotiated assumption of risk, so the Court reasons, takes priority over the hardship clause in the standard terms.[273] This case is illustrative as to how German courts approach hardship clauses: They will first interpret the contract to discern whether a party has contractually assumed a particular risk.[274] If the court finds that a party has contractually assumed a risk, recourse to the hardship clause is considered precluded.[275]

VI. Conclusion

Self-sufficiency of international contracts can be an aspiration, but not a reality. Adjudicators will always need to apply certain rules in order to properly interpret and understand the contract, if the parties themselves cannot agree on the meaning of contract terms. The report has shown that, as general matter, these rules are designed to help revealing the common intention of the parties and are thus an expression of respect for party autonomy. However, as always, the devil is in the details. For instance, the criteria for the interpretation of contracts which are drafted against the backdrop of another legal system or which are based on standard forms inspired by contract practice from another jurisdiction still seem somewhat uncertain. Also, party autonomy is curtailed in the context of standard terms: the review of standard terms in commercial transactions may, from an international perspective perhaps surprisingly often, lead to the invalidity of specific clauses. Parties are therefore well-advised to research carefully how their choice-of-forum, arbitration or choice-of-law clauses will affect the interpretation of their contract.

---

[273] BGH NJW 2013, 2745.

[274] See, e.g., OLG Munich EnWZ 2020, 21 n. 209; OLG Hamm BeckRS 2013, 20587; LG Stuttgart BeckRS 2016, 129038.

[275] BGH NJW 2013, 2745.

Arbitration and the International Commercial Courts

Meik Thöne

I. Introduction

The (potential) significance of a business location is closely linked to the ability to enforce laws and subjective rights effectively. This holds particularly true in times of global supply chains and international trade, which often give rise to legal disputes between companies from different countries. Since legal certainty, procedural efficiency, and cost predictability are of paramount importance in this context, the lack of modern and attractive procedural options leads to cross-border commercial disputes being conducted in other jurisdictions or within private arbitration.[1] As this can result in disadvantages for domestic companies and the domestic judicial system, the German legislature (also taking into account the significant decline in the number of cases filed with the civil courts[2]) has recognized the need to revise the applicable law in order to strengthen Germany as a center of business and justice.[3]

An essential step in this direction is the establishment of commercial courts. They are intended to serve as a fast, efficient, and attractive judicial instrument that is tailored to the needs of economy, allows judges to acquire specialist knowledge,[4] and fosters the development of law in the field of commercial civil law.[5] The focus is on providing the parties with special tools – largely based on elements that have proven successful in arbitration and are accepted beyond the individual national legal systems[6] – to adequately resolve their (international

---

[1] Bundestag Publication (BT-Drs.) 20/8649, 1 (competition with foreign courts and arbitration tribunals; see in this regard *Vogenauer*, European Review of Private Law 21 (2013), 13 vs. *Wagner*, Rechtsstandort Deutschland im Wettbewerb (2017)).

[2] Cf. Final Report: Research into the causes of the decline in the number of cases brought before civil courts, 52, published by the Federal Ministry of Justice, https://www.bmjv.de/SharedDocs/Downloads/DE/Fachinformationen/Abschlussbericht_Eingangszahlen_Zivilgerichte.html (May 4, 2026).

[3] Bundestag Publication (BT-Drs.) 20/8649, 1, 16 et seqq.; see additionally *Koch*, MDR 2024, 1015 n. 3; *Rühl*, ZfPW 2024, 397, 410; *Wagner*, ZEuP 2025, 221.

[4] Cf. Final Report (fn. 2), 343 n. 22; see for a broader view *Antonopoulou*, Journal of Int Dispute Settlement 14 (2023), 328, 330 et seqq.

[5] Bundestag Publication (BT-Drs.) 20/8649, 1, 16 et seqq.

[6] Interestingly arbitration is said to continuously lose its flexibility, cf. *Rühl*, in: Häcker/Ungerer (eds.), Default Rules in Private Law (2025), 225.

commercial) disputes.[7] These include the possibility of choosing English as the language of the proceedings, the parties' ability to customize the (formal) course of the proceedings, the preparation of a verbatim transcript of the hearing or the taking of evidence, and the unrestricted access to appeal before the Federal Court of Justice (*BGH*).[8]

II. Genesis

The idea of a German commercial court has its origins in the 2000s.[9] Since that time various legislative initiatives have sought, to varying extents, to establish the necessary framework for the introduction of commercial courts in Germany – but without success.[10] Despite these failed attempts to change existing procedural law, or perhaps precisely because of them, some federal states have attempted to promote the idea of commercial courts on the basis of the law applicable at that time. The federal state of Baden-Württemberg, e. g., introduced commercial courts (as specialized chambers of regional courts [*Landgerichte*]) in 2020, which offered case management conferences, hearings lasting several consecutive days and the possibility to (largely) use English as language of the proceedings.[11]

The actual breakthrough (in the sense of a statutory recognition of commercial courts) can be can be attributed to a legislative initiative in August 2023[12] which resulted in the Judicial Location Strengthening Act (*Justizstandort-Stärkungsgesetz*)[13] that covers three structurally independent but substantively linked areas of regulation: (1) Establishment of the legal framework for the introduction of commercial courts (Section 119b of the Courts Constitution Act [*Gerichtsverfassungsgesetz*; hereafter referred to as GVG], Sections 610–614 of the German Code of Civil Procedure [*Zivilprozessordnung*, hereafter referred to as ZPO]): The federal law gives the individual federal states the option of establishing commercial courts (alone or jointly with other federal states), stipulates that commercial courts are not intended to be separate and independent courts or institutions but rather constitute specific parts within (existing) higher regional courts (*Oberlandesgerichte*), and regulates the proceedings before them. Beyond that, the fed-

---

[7] *Rühl*, ZfPW 2024, 397, 410; *Wolff*, NJW 2025, 1081 n. 1.

[8] See in more detail sub IV, V.

[9] *Dalitz*, Gerichtswettbewerb und Gerichtssprache, 2025, 203; *Wolff*, SchiedsVZ 2023, 209; *Wagner* (fn. 1), 212 et seqq., 216 et seqq.

[10] Cf. Bundestag Publication (BT-Drs.) 17/2163; Bundestag Publication (BT-Drs.) 18/1287; Bundestag Publication (BT-Drs.) 19/1717; Bundestag Publication (BT-Drs.) 19/30745; Bundestag Publication (BT-Drs.) 20/1549.

[11] *Diekmann*, NJW 2021, 605 n. 4 et seqq.; *Raeschke-Kessler*, SchiedsVZ 2023, 158, 162. See additionally *Dalitz*, ZRP 2017, 248 (English-language hearings before the Frankfurt Regional Court).

[12] See *Raeschke-Kessler*, SchiedsVZ 2023, 158, 162.

[13] Federal Law Gazette 2024 I, 302, 1.

eral states are granted a high degree of freedom in deciding whether and to what extent they are willing to use the instruments provided. This avoids an inflationary creation of structures for which there is no need,[14] but, at the same time, creates a (partially) heterogeneous judicial landscape.[15] At this point in time, nine federal states have made use of the option to establish commercial courts;[16] the (rather theoretical) opportunity to establish a unified commercial court remained unused.[17] – Having said this, a brief distinction is to be made. Commercial courts should not be confused with commercial chambers; the latter are special chambers within regional courts (cf. Section 184a(1)(1) No. 1 GVG) to which some, but not all, of the rules concerning commercial courts apply (it is, e. g., not possible to agree on their jurisdiction in order to directly choose them as adjudicating body; but see Sections 612 and 613 ZPO).[18]

(2) Admissibility of English as the language of proceedings (Sections 184a, 184b GVG and Sections 606–609 ZPO):[19] The possibility of conducting proceedings in English is considered an essential, albeit not sufficient, prerequisite for Germany's international recognition as an adequate legal location. However, bringing a case before a commercial court does not necessarily mean that the proceedings will be conducted in English. Rather, the basic rule (German as language of the proceedings, cf. Section 184 GVG) applies unless and to the extent that the parties agree otherwise (see sub IV. 4).

(3) Strengthening confidentiality through the protection of trade secrets (Section 273a ZPO): Proceedings before the commercial court are not confidential by nature (cf. Section 169 GVG), but civil courts have been given the option of protecting specific trade secrets (by classifying them as confidential; see sub IV. 5).

As already emphasized, the main reason for these amendments and in particular the introduction of commercial courts is to increase the attractiveness of the German judicial system for commercial law proceedings involving high amounts in dispute.[20] The background to this is, on the one hand, the right to justice and, in this respect, the desire to enable the parties to effectively enforce their rights instead of referring them to other legal mechanisms and systems. On the other hand, the introduction of commercial courts is intended to counteract the decline in the number of cases before the civil courts[21] and to strengthen the develop-

---

14 *Wolff*, SchiedsVZ 2023, 209, 211; *Wagner*, ZEuP 2025, 221, 224.

15 See, e. g., sub III and more detailed BeckOGK GVG/*Melin*, 25.11.2025, Section 119b GVG n. 244 et seqq.

16 Bavaria, Baden-Württemberg, Berlin, Bremen, Hamburg, Hessen, Lower Saxony, North Rhine-Westphalia, Saxony.

17 Cf. *Rühl*, ZfPW 2024, 397, 410 and *Wagner*, ZEuP 2025, 221, 225 (constitutional amendment necessary).

18 See in this respect *Wagner*, ZEuP 2025, 221, 226; this article, however, focuses on commercial courts.

19 See as to whether public access is adequately granted in English-language proceedings, Bundestag Publication (BT-Drs.) 20/8649, 29.

20 *McGuire/Andjic*, ZZP 138 (2025), 139, 140.

21 Cf. *Raeschke-Kessler*, SchiedsVZ 2023, 158, 158 et seqq.; *Rühl*, ZfPW 2024, 397, 410.

ment of law (as a migration of cases to arbitration[22] leads to legal stagnancy and loopholes in certain fields of law[23] [e.g. company acquisitions and takeovers]).[24] The prospect of court fees (and increased tax revenues due to additional legal advice provided by domestic lawyers) may also have been relevant. In addition to this, pilot projects that were conducted in the run-up to the legislation have shown that many judges are interested in hearing and deciding high-quality and legally challenging cases rather than being limited to recurring run-of-the-mill cases, so that introducing commercial courts may also serve as an instrument to attract particularly qualified young talent.[25]

If the aim is to increase the attractiveness of a judicial system, it makes sense to take inspiration from other dispute resolution mechanisms that already enjoy broad support and to consult those who deal with the relevant issues on a daily basis (either because they apply the law or study it in an academic context). Hence, it is not suprising that the legislative work has been profoundly influenced by the development and structure of international commercial arbitration as its elements have proven successful and are understood to reflect an international consensus on dispute resolution,[26] and that the legislative process was accompanied by various experts ([active and retired] judges, academics and other stakeholders) who were invited by the parliamentary groups to submit their opinions on the draft law to the Legal Affairs Committee of the German Bundestag.[27] Whether or not the introduction of commercial courts will ultimately be successful and the legislative expectations will be met cannot be reliably assessed at this point in time. While legislature assumed a caseload of twenty-one lawsuits per year,[28] only one decision has been handed down so far (and only a few cases concerning sales law, insurance law, private construction law, and a post-M&A dispute are pending).[29] In any case, the reactions to the change in the law (espe-

---

[22] The number of proceedings administrated by the German Arbitration Institute (*DIS*) has increased from 48 in 1998 to 191 in 2023 and 158 in 2024 respectively (https://www.disarb.org/en/about-us/our-work-in-numbers, May 4, 2026); but see *McGuire/Andjic*, ZZP 138 (2025), 139, 164 et seqq.

[23] *McGuire/Andjic*, ZZP 138 (2025), 139, 140; *Raeschke-Kessler*, SchiedsVZ 2023, 158, 158 et seqq.

[24] Bundestag Publication (BT-Drs.) 20/8649, 1, 16 et seqq.

[25] Cf. *Wagner*, ZEuP 2025, 221, 222.

[26] See Bundestag Publication (BT-Drs.) 20/8649, 1; BeckOGK ZPO/*Melin*, 15. 11. 2025, Section 612 ZPO n. 6 et seqq. and Section 613 ZPO n. 3; *Wagner*, ZEuP 2025, 221, 225.

[27] Cf. https://www.bundestag.de/presse/hib/kurzmeldungen-983004; https://www.bundestag.de/dokumente/textarchiv/2023/kw09-pa-recht-commercial-courts-934778; Bundesrat Publication (BR-Drs.), 374/23, 15 with https://www.rechtsstandort-hamburg.de/uploads/media/Mindestanforderungen.pdf (each on May 4, 2026).

[28] Bundestag Publication (BT-Drs.) 20/8649, 22; see for a critical view *Burianski/Fleckenstein*, ZRP 2023, 162; *McGuire/Andjic*, ZZP 138 (2025), 139, 143; more lenient *Wagner*, ZEuP 2025, 221, 227 et seqq. The (former) Stuttgart Commercial Court recorded more than 60 cases/year, cf. *Raeschke-Kessler*, SchiedsVZ 2023, 158, 162.

[29] Cf. https://www.justiz.nrw.de/presse/2025-04-24 (May 4, 2026).

cially in academia) have been predominantly positive[30] (even though some of the "innovations" could also have been implemented under the old law [e.g., structuring of proceedings]).

III. Jurisdiction

Commercial courts do not have general or automatic jurisdiction. Their power to decide on the merits rather depends on three distinct conditions: the amount in dispute, the subject matter, and the existence of a corresponding party agreement. First, the jurisdiction of commercial courts is limited to disputes involving sums exceeding 500,000 EUR (Section 119b(1)(1) GVG).[31] This restriction is due to the fact that the commercial courts are intended to specialize in (major) commercial disputes with sufficient resources guaranteed for individual cases. Even though it has to be acknowledged that a fixed threshold is not a suitable mechanism for separating complex from less complex procedures (since legal disputes involving large sums of money do not necessarily raise difficult legal issues and are not always more demanding than legal disputes involving small sums of money), experience shows that proceedings are conducted differently and more intensively when large amounts are at stake (and in this way making the proceedings more complex and time-consuming).[32] Against this background, the (initial)[33] limitation appears appropriate in order to avoid a flood of proceedings that would prevent the court from working efficiently. The remaining problem of uncertainty for the parties at the time of the agreement (will the threshold be reached in future proceedings?)[34] may possibly be mitigated by a supplementary choice of a suitable regional court (with a commercial chamber) and English as the language of the proceedings (in cases where the value in dispute threshold is not reached).[35]

Secondly, the jurisdiction of a commercial court is limited in terms of content (Section 119b(1)(1) GVG). It only covers certain types of disputes:[36] legal disputes between entrepreneurs (with the exception of those relating to industrial prop-

---

[30] *McGuire/Andjic*, ZZP 138 (2025), 139, 164, 168; *Klink*, IPRax 2024, 127, 133; *Koch*, MDR 2024, 1015 n. 32; *Waclawik*, NJW 2025, 3457 n. 36; *Wagner*, ZEuP 2025, 221, 226; *Wolff*, SchiedsVZ 2023, 209, 211.

[31] Cf. Bundestag Publication (BT-Drs.) 20/11466, 25; *Koch*, MDR 2024, 1015 n. 11; *Wagner*, ZEuP 2025, 221, 226; with a critical comment *Rühl*, ZfPW 2024, 397, 415 et seqq.; see with regard to earlier drafts (threshold of 1,000,000/2,000,000 EUR) Bundestag Publication (BT-Drs.) 20/8649, 2, 19 (risk of too few cases).

[32] *Wagner*, ZEuP 2025, 221, 226.

[33] See Bundestag Publication (BT-Drs.) 20/8649, 24 (evaluation after five years).

[34] Cf. *Rühl*, ZfPW 2024, 397, 415; *Koch*, MDR 2024, 1015 n. 11; see with regard to a subsequent increase in the amount in dispute, either by extension of the demand for relief or by counterclaim, Section 611(2) ZPO (referral to commercial court if agreed or consented).

[35] *Klink*, IPRax 2024, 349, 353; *McGuire/Andjic*, ZZP 138 (2025), 139, 144.

[36] Cf. BeckOGK GVG/*Melin* (fn. 15), Section 119b GVG n. 57 et seqq.

erty rights, copyright, and claims under the Unfair Competition Act (UWG)[37];[38] No. 1), disputes arising from or in connection with the acquisition of a company or shares in a company (No. 2), and disputes between a company and members of its management or supervisory board (with the exception of disputes concerning defects in resolutions; No. 3 in connection with Section 119b(1)(4) GVG).[39] Disputes before the commercial courts will therefore generally involve entrepreneurs; consumers within the meaning of Section 14 of the German Civil Code (*Bürgerliches Gesetzbuch*; hereafter referred to as BGB) can only (exceptionally) gain access to the commercial courts under the circumstances described in No. 2 and 3.[40]

However, this is no conclusive enumeration since the law allows for deviations from the (above outlined) general rule. Pursuant to Section 119(b)(1)(2) and (3) GVG, the federal states may both narrow the courts' jurisdiction to specific areas and extend the courts' jurisdiction to subject matters that fall within the exclusive jurisdiction of a regional court or another exclusive jurisdiction.[41] In the interests of specialized and effective administration of justice, the federal states enjoy great flexibility and are not bound by the list in Section 119b(1)(1) GVG,[42] but may limit the commercial courts they have established to the clarification of specific legal issues (or assign these to different commercial courts) or include (specific) additional legal issues that appear appropriate within the jurisdiction of their commercial courts.[43]

As a result, the individual federal states have taken different paths.[44] Only the commercial courts in Lower Saxony and Hamburg were granted the "full jurisdiction" under Section 119b(1)(1) GVG;[45] apart from that, a mosaic of competences emerged (that is particularly characterized by a restriction of the broad rule of Section 119b(1)(1) No. 1 GVG): e.g., the jurisdiction of the Stuttgart Commercial Court (Baden-Württemberg) is confined to company law disputes and

[37] This covers a wide range of legal disputes, including those relating to patents, utility models, (EU) trademarks and designs as well as claims for removal, injunctive relief, and damages under the Unfair Competition Act (UWG), cf. Bundestag Publication (BT-Drs.) 20/8649, 24 et seqq.

[38] This exclusion is due to the existing specialization of the competent chambers of the regional courts, cf. Bundestag Publication (BT-Drs.) 20/8649, 24 et seqq.; *McGuire/Andjic*, ZZP 138 (2025), 139, 142; and for a critical view *Waclawik*, NJW 2025, 3457 n. 29.

[39] See for a critical view on Section 119b(1)(4) GVG *Waclawik*, NJW 2025, 3457 n. 24 (exclusion goes beyond its purpose).

[40] Bundestag Publication (BT-Drs.) 20/8649, 25 and 20/11466, 25 referring to BGHZ 165, 43 = NJW 2006, 431; this may apply to shareholders who are classified as entrepreneurs by case law and in cases of corporate liability lawsuits.

[41] E. g., cases that are to be decided by the Chamber for Commercial Matters at the Regional Court (*Kammer für Handelssachen am Landgericht*) and Sections 24, 29a ZPO respectively.

[42] See *Waclawik*, NJW 2025, 3457 n. 11 (Section 119b(1) GVG provides only initial guidance).

[43] Bundestag Publication (BT-Drs.) 20/8649, 25.

[44] BeckOGK GVG/*Melin* (fn. 15), Section 119b GVG n. 243 et seqq.

[45] Section 1(1) Niedersächsische Commercial-Court-Verordnung (Lower Saxony); Section 1 (1) Commercial-Court-Verordnung (Hamburg).

disputes arising out of acquisitions of (at least) three percent of the shares in a company;[46] the Munich Commercial Court (Bavaria) has jurisdiction over supply chain disputes between entrepreneurs;[47] the jurisdiction of the Düsseldorf Commercial Court (North Rhine-Westphalia) comprises disputes between entrepreneurs arising from insurance contracts (particularly D&O insurance contracts), construction and architect contracts, and company law disputes;[48] the Frankfurt am Main Commercial Court (Hessen) has jurisdiction over specific commercial disputes, such as actions against a merchant, actions arising from the legal relationship of a commercial company and claims arising from the acquisition of a commercial business (disputes arising from capital investment matters are explicitly excluded);[49] the Dresden Commercial Court (Saxony) has jurisdiction over disputes between business people arising from real estate rental and lease agreements, banking transactions subject to the banking act, and disputes in the field of corporate law (the noteworthy Saxonian peculiarities are that jurisdiction depends on the application of German law and that the language of proceedings has to be German).[50] This system (of basic rules, limitations and extensions) may seem complicated and might make it difficult to determine the correct forum, but it is accepted in order to avoid the establishment of unnecessary courts. However, it has to be noted that the fact that the commercial court's competence to try a case is (mainly) based on a decision made by the federal states and not on generally binding and uniform national law entails a considerable risk: e. g., a reevaluation and amendment of the jurisdiction of the commercial court by the federal states may result in an agreement subsequently becoming ineffective.[51] Therefore, the parties should make provisions not only for the event that the threshold value is not reached, but also for the event that the chosen court can no longer serve as a forum.

One additional point: Despite the obvious structural similarity (or convergence) between the two types of proceedings, there is currently no explicit connection between commercial courts and arbitration.[52] However, a draft law (Act on the Modernization of Arbitration Law [*Gesetz zur Modernisierung des Schiedsverfahrensrechts*]) that has not yet been finalized provides for the transfer of certain tasks to commercial courts (cf. Sections 1062(5)(2) and 1063a of the draft);[53] these include, in particular, the appointment and rejection of arbitrators, deci-

[46] Section 7(2) Zuständigkeitsverordnung Justiz (Baden-Württemberg).

[47] Section 1a(2) Gerichtliche Zuständigkeitsverordnung Justiz (Bavaria).

[48] Section 1(2) Commercial-Court- und Commercial-Chambers-Verordnung (North Rhine-Westphalia).

[49] Section 9a(1) Justizzuständigkeitsverordnung (Hessen).

[50] Section 7(2) Sächsische Justizorganisationsverordnung (Saxony).

[51] See, e. g., the change in jurisdiction in Hessen brought by Article 1 No. 1c of the amending ordinance of December 12, 2025, GVBl. 2025, No. 98 (exclusion of disputes concerning the award of public contracts, concessions, or framework agreements).

[52] *Dalitz* (fn. 9), 260 et seqq.

[53] See https://www.bmjv.de/SharedDocs/Gesetzgebungsverfahren/DE/2026_Modernisierung_Schiedsverfahrensrecht.html (April 19, 2026).

sions on the admissibility or inadmissibility of arbitration proceedings, and the annulment, recognition and enforcement of arbitral awards.[54]

Thirdly, there must be a party agreement conferring jurisdiction on a commercial court (Section 119b(2) GVG).[55] This may be express or implied and does not require a specific form (e. g., an agreement by phone or email is sufficient; similar to Section 38(1) ZPO [general rule on jurisdiction agreements]).[56] The requirements are therefore not overly demanding, but the opt-in mechanism[57] still seems justified as proceedings before the commercial court involve higher costs and a shortening of the appeal process (see sub IV. 3, V; additionally, it may strengthen the acceptance of the court).[58]

In the event of a valid agreement, the parties confer binding local, subject matter, and functional jurisdiction to the commercial court. Unless the parties have agreed otherwise, the established jurisdiction is exclusive (cf. Section 119b (2)(2) GVG and similar Article 25(1)(2) of the Regulation (EU) 1215/2012 [Brussels Ibis]). Section 119b(2) GVG is *lex specialis* and takes precedence over the general requirements of Sections 38 and 40 ZPO.[59] If the party agreement relates to international jurisdiction as well (e. g., cross-border cases) provisions in international agreements and legal acts of the European Union must be taken into account (cf. Section 119b(7) GVG); in case of an agreement conferring jurisdiction to a German commercial court, it therefore has to satisfy the requirements of the relevant international law rule or Article 25 of the Regulation (EU) 1215/2012 (Brussels Ibis).[60]

If the parties have not agreed (or have failed to agree) to conduct the proceedings before the commercial court, the agreement can be replaced by an uncontested admission to a claim brought before the commercial court (cf. Section 119b (2)(3) GVG). – To complete the picture, a final remark as to the jurisdiction of commercial courts is necessary. Pursuant to Section 119b(4) GVG, the federal states are authorized to assign to the commercial court the decision of appeals and complaints against such decisions of the regional courts which are based on a dispute relating to the areas of jurisdiction of the commercial court (this will regularly, but not necessarily, be a decision of a commercial chamber); the amount in dispute and the existence of a corresponding agreement are irrelevant in this case.[61]

---

[54] See in this regard *Wagner*, ZEuP 2025, 221, 230.

[55] BeckOGK GVG/*Melin* (fn. 15), Section 119b GVG n. 142 et seqq.; *McGuire/Andjic*, ZZP 138 (2025), 139, 144.

[56] Bundestag Publication (BT-Drs.) 20/8649, 26; BeckOGK GVG/*Melin* (fn. 15), Section 119b GVG n. 142 et seqq., 159, 167; *Rühl*, ZfPW 2024, 397, 411 et seqq.

[57] Cf. *Antonopoulou*, Journal of Int Dispute Settlement 14 (2023), 328, 335 (opt-in mechanism as general principle).

[58] *Wolff*, NJW 2025, 1081 n. 28 and SchiedsVZ 2023, 209, 214.

[59] *Rühl*, ZfPW 2024, 397, 412; *McGuire/Andjic*, ZZP 138 (2025), 139, 144.

[60] Cf. *Klink*, IPRax 2024, 349, 354; *Rühl*, ZfPW 2024, 397, 413.

[61] Bundestag Publication (BT-Drs.) 20/8649, 26.

IV. Procedure

In proceedings before the commercial courts the provisions governing ordinary proceedings (i. e., those before the regional courts) apply with the exception of the rules concerning the judge sitting alone (*Einzelrichter*) so that it is always the entire senate that has to decide (cf. Section 610(1) ZPO in contrast to Sections 348 et seqq., 526 ZPO [availability of full judicial expertise]). In addition to this, Section 610(2) ZPO with Sections 612–614 ZPO (proceedings before the commercial court) and Sections 606–609 ZPO (English language proceedings) contain special provisions that shape the character of commercial court proceedings.

First, the claimant has to apply for the proceedings to be conducted in the first instance before the commercial court and to indicate the corresponding agreement in the statement of claim (Section 610(2) ZPO; see also Sections 96, 98 GVG). In this respect, however, it should suffice if the written submission is addressed to the commercial court (or a comparable indication of the intention to institute proceedings before the commercial court becomes visible).[62] The requirement to present the agreement on the conduct of proceedings before the commercial court serves only an organizational function,[63] so that a failure does not render the action inadmissible.[64] In the absence of such an agreement, the claimant may nevertheless request the case to be heard before the commercial court in the statement of claim as the court's jurisdiction can be established subsequently either by the defendant's consent or his failure to object to the court's jurisdiction (cf. Section 119b(2)(3) GVG [proceedings before commercial court], and Section 611(1)(1) ZPO [proceedings before regional court; referral to the commercial court only with consent of the parties[65]]); if this is not the case, the court must decline jurisdiction and dismiss the action, or refer the dispute to the competent court upon claimant's request (cf. Section 281(1)(1) ZPO).[66]

Furthermore, Section 612 ZPO provides for an organizational hearing to reach agreements with the parties on the course of the proceedings (see in more detail below, sub IV. 1), Section 613 ZPO stipulates the possibility of producing a verbatim transcript of the hearing and the taking of evidence (cf., e. g., Article 29(2) DIS Arbitration Rules; see in more detail below, sub IV. 2), Section 614 ZPO allows for unrestricted appeals against judgments of the commercial court to the

[62] Musielak/Voit/*Wolff*, ZPO, 22nd Ed. 2025, Section 610 n. 5.

[63] This requirement was added in order to avoid uncertainty concerning the court's jurisdiction, Bundestag Publication (BT-Drs.) 20/8649, 36 et seqq.; see addititionally Article 4(3)(e) ICC Arbitration Rules and Article 5.2(vi) DIS Arbitration Rules.

[64] BeckOGK ZPO/*Melin* (fn. 26), Section 610 n. 32; Musielak/Voit/*Wolff* (fn. 62), Section 610 n. 6.

[65] This may also be expressed tacitly, cf. Section 119b(2)(1) GVG. The same applies to cases in which a subsequent increase in the amount in dispute establishes the jurisdiction of the commercial court, cf. Section 611(2) ZPO.

[66] Cf. Bundestag Publication (BT-Drs.) 20/8649, 36 et seqq.; BeckOGK GVG/*Melin* (fn. 15), Section 119b GVG n. 223 et seqq., 232.

BGH (see in more detail below, sub IV. 3 and V), and Sections 606–609 ZPO regulate the use of the English language in German courts (see in more detail below, sub IV. 5).

1. Organizational Hearing

The most significant feature of the proceedings before the commercial court is – in addition to the implementation of English as the language of proceedings – the introduction of the organizational meeting in Section 612 ZPO.[67] It was inspired by the case management conference which has become common practice in commercial arbitration (cf., e.g., Article 27 DIS Arbitration Rules, Article 24 ICC Arbitration Rules),[68] and deviates from the (German) historical understanding of judicial duty to direct the course of the proceedings (cf. Sections 136, 139, 272 ZPO). Although German civil procedure law recognizes the possibility to structure the proceedings and separate certain issues in dispute through (judicial and unilateral) procedural management measures, this option (which is at the discretion of the judge) has rarely been used in practice.[69]

Section 612 ZPO now stipulates the mandatory nature of the organizational meeting which serves to systematize and separate the facts and points of contention and to reach agreements on a procedural timetable with the parties (in contrast to a judicial order[70] and with the expectation that delays caused by requests to reschedule appointments may be avoided).[71] Exceptions can only be made for practical or organizational reasons, e.g., the dispute is limited to a legal issue (so that there are no facts that have to be structured);[72] time constraints or difficult journeys cannot justify a failure to comply since the meeting can also take place as a telephone or video conference (cf. Section 128a ZPO).[73]

Holding an organizational meeting and reaching the respective agreements as soon as possible[74] enables the parties to focus their arguments on the relevant points of dispute and ensures a thorough examination of the crucial facts by the commercial court (as the only fact-finding instance).[75] Having stressed the rele-

---

67 *McGuire/Andjic*, ZZP 138 (2025), 139, 149.

68 Cf. Bundestag Publication (BT-Drs.) 20/8649, 37; *Riehm*, ZIP 2023, 1561, 1564.

69 The exception to this may be the chambers that have already been implemented as commercial courts at the Stuttgart Regional Court in 2019 as they already offered a case management within the given legal framework, cf. fn. 11.

70 Of course, the parties cannot be forced to come to an agreement. If no consensus can be reached on a procedural timetable, the court will issue unilateral procedural orders (cf. Sections 136, 139 ZPO).

71 Bundestag Publication (BT-Drs.) 20/8649, 37; *Wolff*, NJW 2025, 1081 n. 22.

72 Bundestag Publication (BT-Drs.) 20/8649, 37.

73 Bundestag Publication (BT-Drs.) 20/8649, 37.

74 Cf. BeckOGK ZPO/*Melin* (fn. 26), Section 612 n. 3, 27 et seqq.; *Wolff*, NJW 2025, 1081 n. 23 (directly after statement of defence has been submitted).

75 Cf. BeckOGK ZPO/*Melin* (fn. 26), Section 612 n. 41 et seqq.; BeckOK ZPO/*Bodendiek*, 58th Ed. 01.09.2025, Section 612 n. 9.

vance of Section 612 ZPO (and the resulting increased influence of the parties on the proceedings), it should be clarified that it primarily serves to ensure effective proceedings and does not grant unlimited (procedural) party autonomy. This is expressed in Section 612 sentence 2 ZPO, which refers to Sections 224, 296 and 356 ZPO and, in this way, makes clear that the extension of (agreed) deadlines is permissible under certain conditions only, specifically if there is an objective reason for doing so, that the failure to adhere to certain deadlines may (in the absence of sufficient excuse) result in the rejection of submissions, and that the commercial court may disregard evidence after the expiration of a certain period (for producing evidence) if its use would delay the proceedings.[76] Moreover, the scope of application of the provision is limited to formal aspects of the proceedings (such as the number of rounds of written submissions, deadlines for written submissions, date or dates for the oral hearing [possibly blocked for several days in a row], timing of the judgment [cf. also Section 310(1)(2) ZPO], separation of individual issues (and assignment to individual dates), need, availability and order of examination of [expert] witnesses, need for interpreters and use of video examinations, need for the preparation of a transcript; if necessary, the language of the proceedings [in particular with view to the opportunities given by Section 184a(3)(2) GVG]). Thus, Section 612 ZPO cannot be used as a (specific) basis for substantive changes to the applicable procedural law (see in contrast Section 1042(3) ZPO concerning arbitral proceedings [the parties are free to establish rules for the procedure]) – rather, the general rules apply in this respect (cf., e.g., Sections 128(2), 139, 284(1)(2–3) ZPO).[77]

2. Verbatim Transcript

Section 613 provides for the possibility of obtaining a verbatim transcript of the hearing and the taking of evidence and, thus, adopts another standard practice in arbitral proceedings (cf., e.g., Article 29(2) DIS Arbitration Rules).[78] In the event of a unanimous[79] request by the parties, a verbatim transcript of the hearing must be prepared, unless there are factual reasons preventing this.[80] The minutes may be taken by court staff;[81] according to Section 613(2)(1) ZPO it is also possible

---

[76] Bundestag Publication (BT-Drs.) 20/8649, 37 et seqq.; BeckOK ZPO/*Bodendiek* (fn. 75), Section 612 n. 12–14.

[77] Musielak/Voit/*Wolff* (fn. 62), Section 612 n. 7; BeckOK ZPO/*Bodendiek* (fn. 75), Section 612 n. 7 et seqq.; for a comprehensive overview, see *Thöne*, Grenzen verfahrensrechtlicher Gestaltung, 2025, and *Maultzsch/Klingbeil*, in: Schmidt-Kessel (ed.), German National Reports on the 21st International Congress of Comparative Law, 2022, 257.

[78] BeckOK ZPO/*Bodendiek* (fn. 75), Section 613 n. 1; *Wolff*, SchiedsVZ 2023, 209, 216.

[79] Critical as to the fact that an application of one party is not regarded sufficient *Wolff*, NJW 2025, 1081 n. 24 (better: leaving decision to the discretion of the court when the parties disagree).

[80] E.g., sudden illness of the person who should take the minutes and unavailibility of a substitute, Bundestag Publication (BT-Drs.) 20/8649, 38.

[81] Bundestag Publication (BT-Drs.) 20/8649, 38.

that one or more suitable non-court recorders may be called in to prepare the transcript (an AI supported transcription is not admissible[82]).

The verbatim transcript must be readable by the parties during the hearing, unless they jointly waive this right (cf. Section 613(1)(2) ZPO).[83] This option is intended to facilitate dialogue between the parties and consultation with persons also affected by the legal dispute who are outside, or far away from the courtroom.[84]

3. Stages of Appeal

The commercial court is (as part of a higher regional court) the court of first instance. Section 614 ZPO allows for a review by the BGH (*Revision*), but waives the requirement of leave to appeal (cf. Section 614 sentence 2[85] and see on the contrary Section 543 ZPO). Thus, the parties are offered proceedings in a "flattened" court system;[86] by agreeing to the jurisdiction of the commercial court, they waive the first instance (the commercial court as only fact-finding instance) but are guaranteed access to the third instance (contrary to arbitration which typically dispenses with a second instance).[87]

This may be seen as a conflict between the different purposes of the law which, on the one hand, aims to enforce the parties' rights as quickly and cost-effectively as possible and, on the other hand, is intended to strengthen the (further) development of the law (do economic actors actually want to develop the law, or will their expectations ultimately be disappointed?).[88] However, the criticism that may be expressed in this regard must be put into perspective, as the parties have the option to waive the right to appeal.[89] If they want to avoid extended proceedings (including the possibility to rectify judicial mistakes), they are free to exclude this option (e. g., when agreeing on the jurisdiction of the commercial court).

---

[82] BeckOGK ZPO/*Melin* (fn. 26), Section 613 n. 21; *Rühl*, ZfPW 2024, 397, 420; *Wolff*, SchiedsVZ 2023, 209, 216; see on the contrary *Koch*, MDR 2024, 1015 n. 29 and *McGuire/Andjic*, ZZP 138 (2025), 139, 149.

[83] BeckOK ZPO/*Bodendiek* (fn. 75), Section 613 n. 6; *Wolff*, NJW 2025, 1081 n. 26.

[84] Bundestag Publication (BT-Drs.) 20/8649, 38.

[85] See additionally Section 119b(4) GVG (commercial court as court of appeal).

[86] Bundestag Publication (BT-Drs.) 20/8649, 17.

[87] *Wagner*, ZEuP 2025, 221, 225.

[88] Cf. *McGuire/Andjic*, ZZP 138 (2025), 139, 150 (applicability of the ordinary rules preferrable [Section 543 ZPO]); *Wolff*, NJW 2025, 1081 n. 28 and SchiedsVZ 2023, 209, 216; *Koch*, MDR 2024, 1015 n. 26; *Reichert/Groh*, NZG 2023, 1007, 1009.

[89] MüKoZPO/*Rimmelspacher*, 7th Ed. 2025, Section 515 n. 35; *Rädler*, SchiedsVZ 2025, 228, 230.

4. Language

Section 184a(1) GVG sets out the admissibility of English as language used in court[90] and, thereby, harmonizes the language of proceedings and the language of contracts (in order to avoid expensive translations).[91] As an exception to the general rule of Section 184 GVG, this requires a corresponding decision by the parties, which may be made explicitly or implicitly (cf. Section 184a(3)(1) GVG [including acceptance by non-objection]) and is not subject to any formal requirements (e.g., an agreement by email is sufficient).[92] Such an agreement therefore constitutes a prerequisite for the use of the English language, but does not necessarily establish its exclusive admissibility. It still may be permissible to submit to the court in German, provided that the appropriate consent has been given by the opposing party, so that it is (theoretically) possible to switch languages flexibly (cf. Sections 184a(3)(2) [including absence of immediate objection] and 184a(5) GVG).[93]

In addition to Section 184a GVG, Sections 606–609 ZPO apply and form the English-language proceedings. According to these, the statement of claim (*Klageschrift*) must be written in English, request that the (following) proceedings be conducted in English and (if this is the case) state that the parties have agreed to this (Section 606 ZPO).[94] This rule does not appear to be particularly well designed; a submission in English will generally suffice to express the will to conduct the proceedings in English, so that an additional request seems dispensable.[95] If the claimant has complied with these requirements, the hearing as well as the taking of evidence will be held and the judgment will be delivered in English. By choosing English, the proceedings can therefore be conducted completely in English without the necessity to call in interpreters and to translate documents (cf. Section 184a(3)(1) GVG and to the contrary Section 185 GVG and Section 142 (3) ZPO).[96] However, at the request of one of the parties, the judgment must be translated into German, Section 608(1) ZPO (the same applies to enforceable

[90] Section 184a(1) GVG is an opening clause that allows the federal states to introduce English as language of the proceedings before the commercial chambers and commercial courts (see already above sub II).

[91] *Wolff*, NJW 2025, 1081 n. 29; *McGuire/Andjic*, ZZP 138 (2025), 139, 146.

[92] Bundestag Publication (BT-Drs.) 20/8649, 29.

[93] See *McGuire/Andjic*, ZZP 138 (2025), 139, 147 (flexibility and efficiency gains) and *Rädler*, SchiedsVZ 2025, 228, 231 proposing to agree (in advance) that written submissions must be submitted in both German and English.

[94] Conversely, it is also possible to conduct proceedings before a commercial court in German.

[95] Cf. *Rühl*, ZfPW 2024, 397, 405. – The mere institution of proceedings before a commercial court is not sufficient, the parties have to (more or less) actively choose English as language of the proceedings.

[96] If a party submits a document in German, the court may, upon request, order the provision of a translation into English, Section 184a(3)(1) No. 3 GVG.

settlements, Section 608(2) ZPO);[97] in this case and if the publication of this decision is intended, both language versions must be published together, Section 608(3) ZPO.

While the possibility of conducting international proceedings in English is undoubtedly welcome, a few aspects of the legal framework appear (at least) problematic. First, the tension between the possibility to conduct proceedings in English and the right to a public hearing is not addressed by the legislature (but see Section 608(3) ZPO).[98] The same applies to the hearing of a witness who does not speak English; conducting the hearing in English with calling in an interpreter would seem artificial (and would certainly be no efficient solution – instead, proceeding in German appears clearly preferable in such a case, cf. Section 184a(3)(2) GVG, supplemented by Section 185(2) GVG if appropriate).[99] Secondly, there is no guarantee that the proceedings will be conducted in English throughout all instances as this issue is at the discretion of the respective senate of the BGH on appeal stage (cf. Section 184b(1)(1) No. 3 GVG – choice of language only in the first instance [before the higher regional court]). This may render render the idea of a fast, and cost-effective procedure absurd and make the option of taking legal action before a commercial court unattractive.[100]

5. *Confidentiality*

In addition to those specific provisions concerning commercial courts, attention should be drawn to the generally applicable Section 273a ZPO which has also been newly incorporated into the law. According to this provision, the court may, at the request of one of the parties, classify information that is part of the subject of the dispute as confidential, if it may constitute a trade secret pursuant to Section 2 No. 1 of the Trade Secrets Protection Act (*Gesetz zum Schutz von Geschäftsgeheimnissen*). Since confidentiality is considered an essential feature and a substantial advantage of arbitration (see on the contrary the right to a public hearing pursuant to Section 169 GVG and Article 6(1) of the European Charter of Human Rights), this provision might close (or at least narrow) the gap between arbitration and litigation.[101]

---

[97] Caution is advised when transferring translation tasks to AI applications without further consideration (see in this regard *McGuire/Andjic*, ZZP 138 [2025], 139, 146 [applications can translate easily and efficiently using artificial intelligence]). Although the ZPO does not set out any explicit requirements regarding the quality of a translation, it has to meet the requirements of the enforcement proceedings and must not undermine their effectiveness.

[98] See BeckOGK GVG/*Melin* (fn. 15), Section 184a n. 12 et seqq.

[99] Cf. *McGuire/Andjic*, ZZP 138 (2025), 139, 145; *Wolff*, SchiedsVZ 2023, 209, 220.

[100] See BeckOGK GVG/*Melin* (fn. 15), Section 184b n. 2; *Wolff*, NJW 2025, 1081 n. 35 and *Koch*, MDR 2024, 1015 n. 25 adding that proceedings before the BGH require the appointment of a specifically admitted lawyer (cf. Sections 162 et seqq. Federal Lawyers' Act [*BRAO*]); more optimistic *Rädler* SchiedsVZ 2025, 228, 231 et seqq.

[101] Parties are no longer forced to decide whether to lose their trade secret or the case, cf. Bundestag Publication (BT-Drs.) 20/8649, 32.

However, Section 273a ZPO serves only to protect specific trade secrets, not to seal off the entire proceedings.[102] It is, thus, not possible to completely exclude the public.[103] But it is, at the same time, important to distinguish between non-public and confidential,[104] and in this respect a comparison depends very much on the specific circumstances of the arbitration proceedings (the specific agreement or the chosen arbitration rules are the decisive object of comparison),[105] whereas litigation provides for coercive measures (i.e., fines and arrest) and prohibitions on use.[106] Hence, German civil procedure law may now offer similarly effective tools to prevent certain information from becoming public knowledge.

6. *Third Parties*

Another feature that should be mentioned, particularly in order to distinguish commercial court proceedings from arbitration proceedings, can be found in Section 184a(4) GVG and Section 607 ZPO. These provisions apply if a third party is to be involved in (pending) English language proceedings (e.g., third-party notice pursuant to Sections 72–74 ZPO[107]) who does not understand English.[108] In accordance with the fundamental requirement of consent to English-language proceedings, the third party is given the opportunity to object to the service of an English language document that is intended to effect his involvement (within two weeks, cf. Section 607(1) ZPO). In this case, the service, however, may be effected by providing the third party with a German translation;[109] if the purpose of service is to ensure that deadlines are met, particularly to suspend the limitation period, service is deemed effective upon the initial service if the translation is provided to the third party within two weeks of the respective court request (cf. Section 607(3) ZPO). If the third party has been involved in the legal dispute, he may, pursuant to Section 184a(4) GVG, request the assistance of an interpreter and the translation of English documents. This complements Section 607 ZPO and ensures effective legal protection;[110] despite this, third parties may be involved in proceedings before the commercial courts whether they want to be or not.

---

102 *Riehm*, ZIP 2023, 1561, 1569 et seqq.; *Wolff*, SchiedsVZ 2023, 209, 222.

103 See Section 608(3)(2) ZPO (partial translation to guarantee confidentiality).

104 Cf. *McGuire/Andjic*, ZZP 138 (2025), 139, 156 et seqq.

105 Cf. *Münch*, ZZPInt 20 (2015), 431; *McGuire*, ZZPInt 24 (2019), 385.

106 See also the comparison made by *McGuire/Andjic*, ZZP 138 (2025), 139, 157.

107 The involvement of a new or further defendant (i.e., a party to the proceedings) does not fall within the scope of the provision, cf. BeckOGK ZPO/*Melin* (fn. 26), Section 607 n. 5, in contrast to *Koch*, MDR 2024, 1015 n. 21.

108 Similar to Article 12 of the Regulation (EU) 2020/1784 (Service Regulation); cf. ECJ, Judgment of May 8, 2008 – Case C-14/07 (Weiss/IHK Berlin), n. 80 et seqq.

109 The party requesting the involvement has to bear the costs of the translation irrespective of the outcome of the proceedings, cf. Section 607(4) ZPO.

110 Cf. *McGuire/Andjic*, ZZP 138 (2025), 139, 146; *Wolff*, SchiedsVZ 2023, 209, 220.

7. Arbitralization of Litigation?

The approach of adopting successful and recognized elements of international arbitration law in the context of commercial court proceedings has certainly blurred the distinction between litigation and arbitration ("arbitralization of courts"),[111] but numerous differences remain. First and foremost, the following still applies: Proceedings before commercial courts remain state proceedings, and are therefore embedded in the national civil procedure law. Consequently, they lack the flexibility that characterizes arbitration proceedings, but they do provide effective means of coercion and can exercise sovereign authority even against the will of the persons (to be) involved.

In state proceedings constitutional obligations apply directly and without any qualifications,[112] and (other) procedural requirements, such as the strict rules on the taking of evidence (*Strengbeweisverfahren*) and the principle of parties' responsibility for gathering evidence (*Beibringungsgrundsatz*)[113] must be complied with. Hence, it is not possible to (completely) reshape proceedings by way of agreement (see by contrast Section 1042(3) ZPO).[114] Even though Section 612 ZPO strengthens the influence of the parties on the course of proceedings and sets out that formal case management is no longer exclusively a matter for the court, it does not grant any procedural powers which would enable the parties to affect the legally prescribed nature of the proceedings or redraw the boundaries of what is permissible. Thus, the parties are not allowed to replace the applicable rules on evidence taking; they may, e.g., limit the taking of evidence to certain types of evidence[115] (see additionally Section 284(1)(2) ZPO), but are not able to introduce new modes of taking evidence (e.g., no agreement on the applicability of IBA Rules[116]). They cannot freely choose the place of the hearing (cf. Sections 219, 128a ZPO vs. Section 1043 ZPO), nor can they specify any language as the language of proceedings (cf. Sections 184, 184a GVG vs. Section 1045 ZPO). Moreover, they may not select one or more specific judges as Article 101(1)(2) of the German Basic Law (*Grundgesetz*, hereafter referred to as GG) provides that the judge hearing a case must be determined in advance on the basis of abstract legal rules (*gesetzlicher Richter*). Furthermore, the possibility to choose the applicable substantive law is limited to state law and is subject to certain restrictions (cf. Article 3 Regulation (EC) 593/2008 [Rome I][117] vs. Section 1051 ZPO [choice of provisions; decision ex aequo et bono]); in this respect, it is of particular im-

---

111 *Antonopoulou*, Journal of Int Dispute Settlement 14 (2023), 328; *Bookman*, Vanderbilt Law Rev 72 (2019), 1119 and Virginia Journal of Int Law 61 (2021), 161.

112 But see BVerfG NJW 2022, 2677 with a comment by *Thöne*, NJW 2022, 2650.

113 See on the contrary MüKoZPO/*Münch*, 6th Ed. 2022, Section 1042 ZPO n. 149, 150, 155.

114 Cf. *Thöne* (fn. 77) and in the context of arbitration MüKoZPO/*Münch* (fn. 113), pre-section 1025 n. 114.

115 Cf. BGH NJW-RR 2019, 719 n. 19.

116 BeckOK ZPO/*Bodendiek* (fn. 75), Section 612 n. 8 (with further references).

117 See additionally Art. 3(3–4), 6(2), 7(3), 8(1), 9 Regulation (EC) 593/2008 (Rome I).

portance that the parties may render the law governing standard terms and conditions inapplicable for companies in arbitration proceedings[118] (including purely domestic proceedings, provided that public order is not affected).[119]

With regard to confidentiality, it is to be noted that trade secrets now enjoy better protection in state courts (see above, V. 5); however, confidentiality cannot be agreed upon, but is subject to court orders and the scope of Section 273a ZPO. In addition to this, the enforcement of a state judgment may be more cumbersome than enforcing an arbitral award (in particular if enforcement is based on bilateral international agreements and non-harmonized national enforcement rules in contrast to the New York Convention on the Recognition and Enforcement of Foreign Arbitral Awards; but see Articles 36, 39 of the Regulation 1215/2012 [Brussels Ibis]).

However, commercial courts may offer services and safeguards an arbitral tribunal may not be able to provide. Since arbitration is primarily based on contract[120] and requires an arbitral tribunal to be constituted, it has difficulties in resolving multi-party proceedings, involving third parties in the legal dispute,[121] or ensuring immediate and comprehensive[122] legal protection. Furthermore, an important argument that may prompt the parties to bring their dispute before the commercial court could be the anticipated costs. In this respect, the principle of "costs follow the event" applies in civil proceedings, meaning that the losing party must bear the costs of the legal dispute and, in particular, reimburse the costs incurred by the opposing party, insofar as these were necessary for the appropriate pursuit or defense of legal rights (Section 91(1) ZPO);[123] if a party prevails in part the costs are to be shared proportionately (Section 92 ZPO). These rules significantly reduce the cost risk compared to arbitration proceedings in two ways: first, in arbitration a more flexible standard applies to the allocation of costs (cf. Section 1057(1)(2) ZPO [arbitral tribunal decides at its discretion]),[124] and secondly, (opposing) attorneys' fees exceeding the fees payable under the Lawyers' Fees Act (*Rechtsanwaltsvergütungsgesetz*) are also reimbursed.[125] As to the court fees, proceedings before the commercial court are likely to be less expensive

---

[118] The German law on standard terms and conditions has been identified as a factor that could discourage economic parties from selecting German substantive law and bringing their cases before German civil courts, cf. *Flockermann/Deuring*, NJW 2024, 879 n. 15 et seqq.; *Groh*, GmbHR 2025, 561 n. 12 et seqq.

[119] *Pfeiffer*, NJW 2012, 1169; *Flockermann/Deuring*, NJW 2024, 879 n. 15 et seqq.

[120] *Born*, International Commercial Arbitration, 3rd Ed. 2021, 280 et seqq. with fn. 145 ("creature of contract").

[121] Cf. *Flockermann/von Möllendorf*, GmbHR 2025, 1, 2; *Walden/Gramsch*, RIW 2025, 701, 705; *McGuire/Andjic*, ZZP 138 (2025), 139, 160 et seqq.

[122] Regarding the arbitral need for state assistance, e.g. when witnesses refuse to cooperate, MüKoZPO/*Münch* (fn. 113), pre-section 1025 n. 17 and Section 1050 n. 1, 4 et seqq.

[123] With regard to the limiting effect of the statutory fee under the Lawyers' Fees Act (*Rechtsanwaltsvergütungsgesetz*), MüKoZPO/*Schulz*, 7th Ed. 2025, Section 91 ZPO n. 71.

[124] But see BGH NJW 2012, 1811 n. 9 (likely to follow Sections 91 et seqq. ZPO).

[125] MüKoZPO/*Münch* (fn. 113), Section 1057 n. 32–34.

than arbitral proceedings, as a rough overview (including the appeal stage in civil proceedings[126]) shows:

Table 1

Currency: EUR	500,000			5 million		
	1st instance	2nd instance	total	1st instance	2nd instance	total
Commercial Court	16,552	20,690	37,242	92,152	115,190	207,342
DIS Arbitration[127]	46,585	–	46,585	177,185	–	177,185
ICC Arbitration[128]	88,709	–	88,709	275,733	–	275,733

V. Appeals

Judgments of the commercial court are subject to appeal which may be lodged with the BGH and do not require (separate) leave to appeal if the commercial court acts as the court of first instance (Section 614 ZPO). This leads to a reduction in the number of instances (from three to two; see above sub IV. 3) and makes it easier to appeal to the BGH;[129] but apart from that, the usual appeal procedure applies (supplemented only by Section 609 ZPO regarding the notice of appeal).[130]

Accordingly, the following applies: If the appellant wishes to continue proceedings before the BGH in English, a corresponding application has to be submitted and the appeal has to be filed in English. In case the application is rejected (this is at the discretion of the competent senate within the BGH[131] but is likely to happen before the grounds for appeal are to be submitted pursuant to Section 551 ZPO[132]), the appeal must be resubmitted in German at the request of the court, Section 609(2) ZPO.[133] Regardless of the language of the proceedings, the court of appeal examines whether the decision of the commercial court is based on a

[126] But notice that, despite the absence of a genuine appellate body, additional costs may arise in arbitration if setting-aside and enforcement proceedings are initiated, *McGuire/Andjic*, ZZP 138 (2025), 139, 160.

[127] See https://www.disarb.org/en/tools-for-dis-proceedings/cost-calculator (May 4, 2026); costs do not include VAT, cf. Sections 6.1, 6.3 of the Schedule of Costs DIS Rules.

[128] See https://iccwbo.org/dispute-resolution/dispute-resolution-services/arbitration/costs-and-payment/costs-calculator (May 4, 2026) (amounts in dispute equivalent to EUR).

[129] Cf. *Koch*, MDR 2024, 1015 n. 15 (objectives: compensation for the loss of the first instance; development of law).

[130] Regarding the resulting contradictions cf. BeckOGK ZPO/*Melin* (fn. 26), Section 614 n. 13 et seqq.

[131] Cf. Section 184b(1)(1) No. 3 GVG; *Rühl*, ZfPW 2024, 397, 402.

[132] BeckOK ZPO/*Bodendiek* (fn. 75), Section 609 n. 4.

[133] If no such application is made, the appeal is to be filed in German (irrespective of the fact that the preceding proceedings have been conducted in English); the opposing party cannot

violation of law (i. e., a legal norm has not been applied, or has not been applied properly, cf. Sections 545, 546 ZPO). A review is therefore only carried out from a legal, not a factual,[134] perspective, and is limited to determining whether the contested decision is legally flawed (i. e., incorrect not merely unreasonable).[135] If the appeal is justified the contested judgment is to be reversed (Section 562(1) ZPO). As a rule, the case is to be referred (back) to the commercial court for a new hearing and a new decision (which is to be based on the legal assessment of the BGH, cf. Section 563(1, 2) ZPO). However, if the matter is already ready for decision, i. e., no further clarification of the facts is required, the BGH has to decide on the matter itself (cf. Section 563(3) ZPO).

VI. Efficiency

Whether the legislative goal of making court proceedings more effective[136] can be achieved by introducing commercial courts in Germany cannot be assessed at this stage. This is partly due to the lack of a suitable benchmark as higher regional courts usually do not act as courts of first instance in civil matters,[137] meaning that there is no statistical empirical data available in this regard. If, instead, the regional courts are taken as a basis for comparison – the duration of standard civil proceedings in the first instance is 17.5 months (2024)[138] – an assessment must take into account that only one case before the commercial courts has been concluded to date (taking approximately four months from the filing of the action to the judgment).[139] Against this background, one might assume, albeit only with the utmost caution, that the special features of proceedings before the commercial court have the potential to make proceedings more efficient and faster than those conducted under the ordinarly rules. Ultimately, however, we will have to wait and see whether they can actually have a greater impact.

---

force the appeal proceedings to be conducted in English. The use of the wrong language renders the appeal inadmissible, BeckOGK ZPO/*Melin* (fn. 26), Section 609 n. 8, 14.

[134] The determination of facts may also be carried out in a procedurally incorrect manner (and constitute a ground for appeal).

[135] Cf. *Rosenberg/Schwab/Gottwald*, Zivilprozessrecht, 18th Ed. 2018, § 143 and Section 545(2) ZPO.

[136] With regard to "efficiency" *Grohmann*, Internationalisierung der Handelsgerichtsbarkeit, 2022, 369 et seqq.

[137] See for exceptions Section 118 GVG (exemplary proceedings in capital market disputes) and Section 3 Consumer Rights Enforcement Act (*Verbraucherrechtedurchsetzungsgesetz*) (collective actions).

[138] Federal Statistical Office, Statistical Report – Civil Courts – 2024, https://www.destatis.de/DE/Themen/Staat/Justiz-Rechtspflege/Publikationen/Downloads-Gerichte/statistischer-bericht-zivilgerichte-2100210247005.html?templateQueryString=Zivilgerichte (May 4, 2026).

[139] https://www.commercial-court.hamburg/bundesweit-erstes-commercial-court-urteil-verkuendet-1123910 (May 4, 2026).

VII. Judges

A significant difference between arbitral tribunals and commercial courts is that the latter do not need to be specifically constituted (to decide a dispute) but exist permanently (with judges and administration[140]). The judges of the commercial courts are judges of the higher regional court (into which the commercial court is integrated). Sitting as a judge of the commercial court thus requires that the conditions of the German Judiciary Act (*Deutsches Richtergesetz*; hereafter referred to as DRiG) are met. Accordingly, judges must be German citizens within the meaning of Article 116 GG and be qualified to hold judicial office (a qualification that is usually obtained by passing two state law examinations, cf. Sections 5 (1), 9 DRiG). Beyond these general requirements, judges do not join the higher regional court directly (i.e., at the beginning of their careers), but only become judge at the higher regional court after a corresponding promotion (based on extensive experience and proved performance in the judiciary).[141] The specific selection of judges (which judge of the higer regional court serves as judge of the senate that forms the commercial court?) is governed by the schedule of responsibilities (*Geschäftsverteilungsplan*) drawn up by the court's presiding committee (cf. Section 21e(1) GVG [independent composition of the adjudicating bodies; the parties' right to choose is limited to the selection of the commercial court and does not extend to specific judges]).

Judges are state officials and are not paid according to the number or financial value of the cases they hear, but receive a fixed salary. Working at the commercial court is part of the regular duties of a judge at the higher regional court and is a full-time job. However, this does not mean that individual judges cannot be members of another senate of the same higher regional court and thus, in addition to their work for the commercial court (or the corresponding senate), also work in other areas. Additionally, they may act as arbitrators provided that specific (strict)[142] conditions are fulfilled (cf. Section 40(1)(1) DRiG [appointment jointly by the parties or an independent body and approval by authority considering any prior or future judicial involvement with the arbitral matter]). In this case, they are legally excluded from exercising judicial office pursuant to Section 41 No. 6 ZPO if they were previously involved in the issuance of the contested decision.[143]

---

140 In particular, court registries (*Geschäftsstellen*) and registry clerks (*Urkundsbeamte der Geschäftsstelle*).

141 Cf. e.g., Section 5(5) Judiciary Act of Lower Saxony (*Niedersächsisches Richtergesetz*) (necessity of trial and evaluation) and additionally BeckOGK GVG/*Melin* (fn. 15), Section 119b n. 47.1.

142 Cf. *Raeschke-Kessler*, SchiedsVZ 2023, 158, 159 (judges are pratically barred from acting as arbitrators).

143 The judges of the commercial courts are not subject to any regulations concerning ethical behavior or conflict of interest beyond those applicable to judges in general, cf. Section 42(2) ZPO (recusal for fear of bias).

Energy Transition: German Regulation of New Sources of Energy[1]

Sabine Schlacke

I. Introduction

The energy transition is inseparably linked to the transformation of the energy system towards climate neutrality through the use of renewable energy sources. As the European Union (EU) member state with the strongest industry in terms of gross domestic product, the Federal Republic of Germany faces particular challenges due to its phase-out of nuclear energy and the planned phase-out of coal-fired power generation by 2038. According to a recently published study by the Agora Energiewende think tank, the expansion of renewable energies in Germany increased in 2025, with greenhouse gas emissions falling in the industrial sector but rising in the building and transport sectors.[2]

This article provides an overview of the German legal framework for the energy transition. It is not an easy task to organise and systematise this framework, and it is hardly possible to paint a complete picture given the diversity and multifaceted nature of the legal and sub-legal regulations. In order to identify the cornerstones of the German energy transition, the term 'energy transition' is first defined (II.). This article then outlines the EU legal background that must be taken into account by Germany (III.). The main components of the German legal framework for the energy transition, presented in (IV.), are the constitutional foundations (IV. 1.), climate protection legislation (IV. 2.) and energy industry legislation relating to the energy transition (IV. 3.). This is followed by a presentation of the regulations in the core sectors of the energy transition (V.): the electricity sector (EEG, V. 1.), the building-/heating sector (V. 2.) and the transport-/fuel sector (V. 3.). Regulations for area-based control of renewable energy expansion (VI.), comments on legal protection (VII.) and a summary assessment with an outlook (VIII.) conclude the article.

---

[1] I would like to thank research assistants Tim Heidler and Eva Linde for their valuable support in preparing this article.

[2] Agora Energiewende (2026): Die Energiewende in Deutschland – Stand der Dinge 2025. Rückblick auf die wesentlichen Entwicklungen sowie Ausblick auf 2026. Available under https://www.agora-energiewende.de/fileadmin/Projekte/2025/2025-28_DE_JAW25/A-EW_391_Die_Energiewende_in_Deutschland_Stand_der_Dinge_2025_WEB.pdf. (12.03.2026).

II. Energy Transition – a German and European Perspective

1. The Term 'Energy Transition'

The term 'energy transition' is ambiguous and has not been conclusively defined. In the German context, the phase-out of nuclear energy following the Fukushima incident in Japan (2011) and the associated legislative package were referred to as the 'energy transition' by the responsible Federal Ministry of Economics.[3] Compared to other European countries, Germany's phase-out of nuclear energy is an exceptional case and a U-turn in energy policy.[4] Subsequently, however, the Federal Government and legal scholars used the term 'energy transition' in a broader sense to refer to the phase-out of fossil fuels in the entire energy sector.[5] The term is used in several provisions of the Federal Energy Industry Act (EnWG).[6] At the state level, Berlin and Schleswig-Holstein have enacted state laws explicitly on the 'energy transition' and climate protection.[7] Policy advisory research projects – such as the Kopernikus project Ariadne[8] – also understand this to mean decarbonisation of the energy sector. The German Advisory Council on the Environment (SRU) uses this term to refer to an energy supply based on 100 % renewable energies in the electricity sector.[9] There is currently no legal definition of the term 'energy transition' in German law.

The EU also has a broad understanding of the term 'energy transition': numerous recitals in recent secondary legislation on energy and climate protection refer to a 'clean energy transition', without defining this in greater detail. From the context, it can be concluded that this refers to a transition of the energy sector

[3] Cf. Federal Government, 'Energiewende', available at https://www.bundesregierung.de/statisch/jb11-12/Webs/Breg/DE/Themen/Jahresbericht_2011_2012/03_Energie/1_Energiewende/_node.html (9.1.2026); the same classification is adopted by *Danner/Kühling*, in: Theobald/Kühling, Energierecht, introductory n. 32 et seqq. (122nd update 2023); *Säcker*, in: Säcker (ed.), Berliner Kommentar, 4th ed. 2019, ch. 1 A., n. 37 et seq.; an 'Energiewende' already beginning before 2011 is noted by *Kahl/Bews*, JZ 2015, 232 et seq.

[4] *Schlacke/Kröger*, in: Heimbach-Steins (ed.), Jahrbuch für christliche Sozialwissenschaften, vol. 56, 2015, 37 et seqq.

[5] See, for example, *Grzeszick*, Rückwirkung und Vertrauensschutz im Recht der Energiewende, 2018, 1; *Unnerstall*, in: Pritzsche/Vacha (eds.), Energierecht, 2nd ed. 2024, § 2 n. 10 et seqq.; *Säcker* (fn. 3) ch. 1 A. n. 3.

[6] Sections 23d, 53b, 118, 119 EnWG.

[7] Gesetz über die Energiewende, den Klimaschutz und die Anpassung an die Folgen des Klimawandels Schleswig-Holstein, GVOBl. 2017, 124; Berliner Klimaschutz- und Energiewendegesetz, GVBl. 2016, 122.

[8] It seeks to develop a 'guiding thread' through the Energiewende; cf. https://ariadneprojekt.de/ (9.1.2026).

[9] Cf. German Advisory Council on the Environment (SRU), 'Thesen zur Zukunft der Kohle', available at https://www.umweltrat.de/SharedDocs/Downloads/DE/05_Kommentare/2012_2016/2015_06_KzU_14_10_Thesen_Zukunft_Kohle.html (9.1.2026).

towards renewable energies.[10] The reduction of greenhouse gases and the transition to climate neutrality are to be understood as part of an energy transition. Some recitals additionally specify that the energy transition is to be fair[11] or clean[12], i.e. without generating CO_2 emissions."

Overall, it can be concluded that neither German federal and state law nor EU law clearly or even bindingly define the term 'energy transition': consequently, energy transition is not yet a legal term.[13] In this article, energy transition is understood as a partial contribution to achieving climate neutrality by replacing fossil fuels with renewable energy sources in the energy sector.

2. Energy Transition as a Key Contribution to Achieving Climate Neutrality

In order to implement the Paris Agreement (PA)[14] target of keeping the global average temperature well below 2°C above pre-industrial levels or limiting it to 1.5°C,[15] the EU and Germany have established a legally binding framework of climate protection targets and corresponding measures to reduce emissions.[16] The EU is fulfilling its obligations under international law through the targets enshrined in the EU Climate Law (Regulation (EU) 2021/1119)[17] of a 55% reduction in greenhouse gas emissions by 2030 and climate neutrality[18] by 2050. Germany is implementing the PA through a 2030 GHG reduction target of 65% and a net greenhouse gas neutrality target by 2045, as enshrined in the Federal Cli-

10 Regulation (EU) 2021/1119 (European Climate Law), recital 22 ('Carbon sinks play an essential role in the transition to climate neutrality in the Union'); recital 25 ('transition to climate neutrality'), recital 34 ('energy transition').

11 Regulation (EU) 2021/1119 (European Climate Law), recital 2: 'The European Green Deal also aims to protect, conserve and enhance the Union's natural capital, and protect the health and well-being of citizens from environment-related risks and impacts. At the same time, this transition must be just and inclusive, leaving no one behind.'; Regulation (EU) 2018/1999, recital 19: 'A socially acceptable and just transition to a sustainable low-carbon economy requires changes in investment behaviour'; Directive (EU) 2023/2413 (Renewable Energy Directive, as amended), recital 1: 'The Union's climate neutrality objective requires a just energy transition which leaves no territory or citizen behind'.

12 Directive (EU) 2023/2413, recitals 51, 78; Regulation (EU) 2024/1735 (Net-Zero Industry Act), recitals 1, 3.

13 *Franzius*, Jura 2025, 1082, already speaks of an 'energy transition law' (Energiewenderecht).

14 BGBl. II 2016, 1082.

15 Art. 2(1)(a) PA; see, inter alia, *Falkner*, International Affairs 2016, 1107; *Bodansky*, American Journal of International Law 2016, 288.

16 See already *Schlacke*, EnWZ 2020, 355; and *Schlacke*, NVwZ 2022, 905.

17 OJ L 243/1; for the EU Climate Law, see *Schlacke/Köster/Wentzien/Thierjung*, Oxford Open Energy 2022, 1.

18 The KSG does not refer to climate neutrality, but rather to net greenhouse gas neutrality as the balance between anthropogenic emissions of greenhouse gases from sources and the removal of such gases by sinks, see section 2 no. 9. Since 2025, climate neutrality has also been enshrined in Article 143h GG, a financial constitutional provision, without further specification, see *Heidler*, ZUR 2025, 397 et seqq.

mate Change Act.[19, 20] In addition to sectors such as industry, transport, buildings, and land use, it is the energy industry that has to undergo the most fundamental transformation to undergo in order to achieve net-zero emissions: according to the Intergovernmental Panel on Climate Change (IPCC), the energy supply sector accounts for the largest share of global GHG emissions.[21] This also applies at the EU level: in 2022, the energy supply sector accounted for almost a third of total European emissions.[22] Likewise, in Germany, the energy industry has been one of the most emission-intensive sectors in 2023, accounting for a third of total emissions.[23]

Achieving European and German climate protection targets requires a fundamental transformation towards decarbonisation of energy production and energy supply. Due to the provisions of the EU treaties, the EU leaves it to the member states to achieve climate protection targets and determine the energy mix.[24] In Germany, due to the legally stipulated phase-out of coal-fired power generation by 2038[25] and the equally legally stipulated phase-out of nuclear energy,[26] renewable energy sources must replace these energy sources, which still account for a large proportion of primary energy.[27] Germany is also aligning its entire climate, energy, and economic policy with the 1.5°C climate protection path to which the European Union has committed itself under the PA.[28]

In order to achieve this transformation of the energy system towards decarbonisation and the 1.5°C climate protection path, the German legal framework has been significantly amended in recent years (see IV.). The European legal framework for the energy transition (see III.) had to be and continues to be taken into account in this context.

---

19 BGBl. I 2019, 2513, as last amended by Act of July 15, 2024, BGBl. I 2024, 235.

20 Art. 2(1), Art. 4(1) Regulation (EU) 2021/1119; Section 3(1), (2) sentence 1 KSG.

21 IPCC, Climate Change 2014: Mitigation of Climate Change, Contribution of Working Group III to the Fifth Assessment Report of the Intergovernmental Panel on Climate Change, 2014, 516.

22 Cf. https://www.europarl.europa.eu/topics/de/article/20180301STO98928/treibhausgasemissionen-nach-landern-und-sektoren-infografik (9.1.2026).

23 Federal Government, Klimaschutzprogramm 2030 der Bundesregierung zur Umsetzung des Klimaschutzplans 2050, 2019, 31, available at https://www.bmleh.de/SharedDocs/Downloads/DE/_Landwirtschaft/Klimaschutz/Klimaschutzprogramm2030.html (9.1.2026); cf. https://www.umweltbundesamt.de/daten/energie/energiebedingte-emissionen#entwicklung-der-energiebedingten-treibhausgas-emissionen (9.1.2026).

24 Art. 194(2) subpara. 2 AEUV; on EU competences see also *Gärditz*, RdE 2018, 457, 459 et seqq.; *Schlacke*, in: Schlacke/Wagner (eds.), Klimarecht, 2026, § 2 n. 36 et seqq.

25 Section 4(1) Kohleverstromungsbeendigungsgesetz (KVBG).

26 Section 7 AtG.

27 Cf. https://www.umweltbundesamt.de/daten/energie/primaerenergieverbrauch#definition-und-einflussfaktoren (9.1.2026).

28 BT-Drs. 20/1630, S. 1.

III. European Legal Framework for the Energy Transition

Energy and thus, the energy transition is a matter regulated by the Union (1.), in which it has limited powers (2.).

1. Energy as a Regulatory Issue for the EU

EU law recognises energy as a subject of regulation: in primary EU law, Article 4(2)(i) of the Treaty on the Functioning of the EU (TFEU)[29] mentions but does not define the term 'energy' as a policy area in which competence is shared between the EU and the Member States. According to Article 194(1) TFEU, EU energy policy pursues the objectives of ensuring the functioning of the energy market, guaranteeing security of energy supply, promoting energy efficiency and energy savings, developing new and renewable energy sources, and promoting the interconnection of energy networks. No definition is provided there either. Only the extensive secondary legislation on energy[30] contains such a definition: According to Article 2(1) of the Energy Efficiency Directive in conjunction with Article 2(d) of Regulation (EC) No 1099/2008[31], energy includes all forms of energy products, fuels, heat, energy from renewable sources, electricity, or energy in any other form.

2. Legislative Powers of the EU

While the addition of Article 191(1), indent 4, at the end of the TFEU ('Combating climate change') by the Treaty of Lisbon in 2009 did not entail any change or extension of the EU's legislative competence in the field of environmental policy, the then newly inserted Title XXI 'Energy' has taken on central importance for the EU's legislative competence: Article 194 TFEU supplements and renews the EU's primary legal bases of competence with a specific legislative power in the field of energy policy.[32] Although the terms 'energy' and 'energy policy' are not defined in primary law, the objectives enshrined in Article 194(1) TFEU (see above III.1.) permit a broad understanding that encompasses all stages and areas of the energy market: The concept of security of energy supply includes solidarity-based access to energy sources and energy production (Article 194(1)(b) TFEU);[33] the interconnection of energy networks (Article 194(1)(d) TFEU) in-

---

[29] Treaty on the Functioning of the European Union (TFEU), OJ C 326/47 of 26.10.2012.

[30] Overview in *Winkler/Baumgart/Ackermann*, Europäisches Energierecht, 2nd ed. 2024, ch. 5 n. 6 et seqq.; ch. 6 n. 6 et seqq.; ch. 7 n. 6 et seqq.

[31] Directive (EU) 2023/1791 of September 13, 2023 on energy efficiency and amending Regulation (EU) 2023/955 (recast), OJ L 231.

[32] *Nettesheim*, JZ 2010, 19, 20; on division of competences see *Kreuter-Kirchhof*, in: FS Büdenbender, 2018, 129, 150 et seqq.

[33] *Calliess*, in: Calliess/Ruffert (eds.), EUV/AEUV, 6th ed. 2022, Art. 194 TFEU n. 13.

cludes the transmission and distribution of energy; energy efficiency aims to achieve greater returns from unavoidable energy expenditure;[34] energy saving means 'avoiding unnecessary consumption of energy';[35] the development of new energy sources and renewable energies also includes, at a minimum, research.[36] The targets are embedded in the three principles of European energy policy: 'spirit of solidarity', 'realisation or functioning of the internal market' and 'need to preserve and improve the environment'.[37]

According to paragraph 1(c), the climate protection approach of Article 194 TFEU consists, in promoting energy efficiency and energy savings as well as the development of new and renewable energy sources. Since the end of 2009, environmental energy law measures aimed at energy efficiency, energy saving or renewable energies have been based on Article 194 TFEU and no longer on Article 192 TFEU (Environment): Thus, Article 194 TFEU was used as the sole legal basis for the Energy Efficiency Directive adopted in 2012[38] and for the Directive on the energy performance of buildings[39], although energy efficiency-related legal acts had previously been based on the environmental policy competence title (Articles 174 and 175 EC Treaty, now Articles 191 and 192 TFEU). Article 194(1)(c) TFEU has developed into a more specific basis for authorising environmental and energy legislation than Articles 192 and 191 TFEU.

The objectives of Article 194(1)(a), (b) and (d) TFEU that are not related to environmental or climate protection are nevertheless subject to environmental protection influences. The requirements of environmental protection must be taken into account in the definition and implementation of Union policies and measures, in particular to promote sustainable development in accordance with the horizontal clause in Article 11 TFEU, including in the areas of securing the energy market, security of supply and interconnection of networks.[40]

Environmental energy legislation measures, as an expression of an integrated climate protection and energy policy, regularly combine three key objectives: firstly, sustainable climate protection and environmental compatibility; secondly, competitiveness; and thirdly, energy supply security.[41] Climate protection, com-

---

[34] *Ehricke/Hackländer*, ZEuS 2008, 579, 588 et seqq.

[35] *Ehricke/Hackländer*, ZEuS 2008, 579, 590.

[36] In this sense cf. *Nettesheim*, JZ 2010, 19, 20; on the targets in detail *Ehricke/Hackländer*, ZEuS 2008, 579, 586 et seqq.

[37] On the requirements in detail *Ehricke/Hackländer*, ZEuS 2008, 579, 585, 592 et seqq.; *Papenkort/Wellershoff*, RdE 2010, 77, 78etseq.

[38] Directive 2012/27/EU of October 25, 2012 on energy efficiency, OJ L 315/1 of October 25, 2012; now Directive (EU) 2023/1791 of September 13, 2023 on energy efficiency (recast), OJ L 231 of September 20, 2023.

[39] Directive 2010/31/EU of May 19, 2010 on the energy performance of buildings, OJ L 153 of June 18, 2010, 13.

[40] *Calliess*, in: Calliess/Ruffert (eds.), EUV/AEUV, 6th ed. 2022, AEUV Art. 194 n. 8.

[41] Cf. *Kahl*, in: Schulze-Fielitz/Müller (eds.), Europäisches Klimaschutzrecht, 2009, 21, 23; *Kahl*, EuR 2009, 601 et seq.; on overlaps with 'Umweltenergierecht' see *Schlacke*, Umweltrecht, 9th ed. 2023, § 16 n. 67.

petitiveness, and security of energy supply are each areas of action for the EU with their own objectives and tasks, but they are increasingly being linked together in individual legal acts in the form of a triangle of objectives.[42]

More serious disparities between the EU's legislative competence in energy policy and environmental policy arise with regard to Member States' measures to strengthen protection. While Article 193 TFEU allows Member States to maintain or adopt stricter environmental protection despite secondary EU law measures – (known as enhanced protection) –, provided that these are notified and comply with primary law, Article 194 TFEU does not allow for so-called unilateral national action.[43]

IV. German Legal Framework for the Energy Transition

The German legal framework for the energy transition is primarily found in constitutional law (1.). The relevant federal regulations governing the energy transition are not codified in a single piece of legislation. Instead, there are numerous regulations which are dispersed across several federal laws. At the core of these regulations stand the climate protection legislation (2.) and energy industry legislation relating to the energy transition (3.).[44]

1. Constitutional Principles

a) Climate Protection as a National Objective

The constitutional obligation to protect the climate is enshrined in Article 20a of the German Basic Law (*Grundgesetz*, GG) as a responsibility of the state.[45] This national objective encompasses the protection of natural resources, i.e. the protection of the environment in a broad sense,[46] which also includes climate protec-

---

[42] *Papenkort/Wellershoff*, RdE 2010, 77, 78; cf. *Kahl*, EuR 2009, 601 et seq., with further references.

[43] Applying Art. 193 TFEU to matters falling under Art. 194 TFEU would contradict the systematics (Title XX Environment) and the wording (reference to Art. 192 TFEU) of Art. 193 TFEU; if stronger protection within Art. 194 TFEU had been intended, a cross-reference would have sufficed, but is absent; see also *Heselhaus*, in: Pechstein/Nowak/Häde (eds.), Frankfurter Kommentar, 2nd ed. 2023, AEUV Art. 193 n. 23.

[44] For an overview of fundamental case law and legislation in energy and climate protection law from 2021 to 2025 – Climate protection and energy security law see *Schlacke/Ludwigs*, NVwZ 2025, 1228 et seqq.

[45] *Peters*, in: Fellenberg/Guckelberger (eds.) KSG, 2022, §1 n. 27; *Calliess*, in: Dürig/Herzog/Scholz (eds.) GG, 108th ed. 2025, Art. 20a n. 40; *Schlacke* (fn. 41) §4 n. 6 et seqq.

[46] See, inter alia, *Jarass*, in: Jarass/Pieroth (eds.), GG, 18th ed. 2024, Art. 20a n. 3 with further references.

tion.[47] The content of this state mandate for climate protection is essentially determined by scientific findings, above all the concept of planetary boundaries,[48] which 'describes the limits of the carrying capacity of ecological systems'[49]. These limits are determined in a first step by identifying so-called tipping points, i. e. certain threshold values which, once exceeded, will cause the Earth's existing functions to change in a non-linear, possibly even abrupt manner, according to scientific forecasts.[50] As a result irreversible negative environmental damage, some of which would even threaten humanity.[51] Applying a certain safety margin to these critical thresholds, a safe operating space for human activity is then defined in a second step. However, its determination is based on climate science findings, so that no concrete measures or requirements for the international community or individual states follow from it.[52]

Article 20a GG contains a judicially enforceable mandate for all state authorities to prevent any (further) exceedance of the scientifically defined ecological carrying capacity by means of a long-term, coherent and legally binding protection concept.[53] Close cooperation between politics and science in the field of climate protection law is a prerequisite for fulfilling this constitutional obligation: While the 'red lines' are drawn by the natural sciences, in particular earth system and climate sciences, it is the task of politics and jurisprudence to discuss, evaluate, and implement them legally.[54]

For decades, the climate protection dimension of Article 20a GG had little relevance in judicial practice. In case law – particularly that of the Federal Constitutional Court (BVerfG) – Article 20a GG only took on a prominent role with the climate protection ruling of 24 March 2021[55].[56] The BVerfG has attributed a benchmark significance to the planetary boundaries in climate protection – in the form of the 1.5°C and 2°C targets, enshrined in the PA (Article 2(1)(a)) – by linking this requirement to Article 20a GG. This benchmark is significant for all exercise of state authority.[57]

---

[47] BVerfG, judgment of November 5, 2014 – 1 BvF 3/11 et al., BVerfGE 137, 350, n. 47; BVerfG, order of March 24, 2021 – 1 BvR 2656/18 et al., BVerfGE 157, 30, n. 198; BVerfG, order of March 13, 2022 – 1 BvR 1187/17 et al., BVerfGE 161, 63, n. 104.

[48] *Rockström/Steffen/Noone* et al., Nature 2009, vol. 472 (474 et seq.); updated by *Richardson/Rockström* et al., Science 2015, vol. 347, 1259855.

[49] Dürig/Herzog/Scholz/*Calliess,* GG, Art. 20a n. 41.

[50] On tipping points and their legal implications see *Wolf/Wunderling,* KlimR 2022, 216.

[51] Cf., e. g., SRU, Sondergutachten, 2019, n. 70 et seqq.

[52] Dürig/Herzog/Scholz/*Calliess,* GG Art. 20a n. 44.

[53] Dürig/Herzog/Scholz/*Calliess,* GG Art. 20a n. 44; cf. also *Schlacke,* in: FS Ramsauer, 2023, 33 (33 et seqq.).

[54] Dürig/Herzog/Scholz/*Calliess,* GG Art. 20a n. 45 et seqq.

[55] BVerfG, order of March 24, 2021 – 1 BvR 2656/18 et al., BVerfGE 157, 30 – Climate Protection. An English version is available at https://www.bundesverfassungsgericht.de/SharedDocs/Entscheidungen/EN/2021/03/rs20210324_1bvr265618en.html (9.1.2026).

[56] Mentioned only in BVerfG, order of August 5, 2020 – 2 BvR 1985/19, 2 BvR 1986/19, n. 48 – 'Containern'.

[57] BVerfG, order of March 24, 2021 – 1 BvR 2656/18 et al., BVerfGE 157, 30, n. 211.

In addition, Articles 20(3), 25 and 59 GG and Article 23 GG indirectly give rise to fundamental rights requirements for climate protection, at least insofar as these require Germany to implement its obligations under international and EU law. This is also emphasised by the Federal Constitutional Court in its climate protection ruling, in which the Court refers to the legislature's commitment to these very international and EU law requirements in Section 1 (3) of the Federal Climate Change Act[58] (*Bundes-Klimaschutzgesetz*, KSG). The state must cooperate with other states to develop joint and global solutions for climate protection, including measures for the energy transition.[59]

b) No Fundamental Right to Climate Protection, Intertemporal Guarantee of Freedom

The Federal Constitutional Court's climate protection ruling of 24 March 2021 may have broken new ground[60] in terms of fundamental rights doctrine, but it did not create a new fundamental right to climate protection.[61] Nevertheless, by linking fundamental freedoms to the national objective of environmental protection (Article 20a GG), the Federal Constitutional Court has conferred a new dimension of protection on fundamental rights in the form of an intertemporal guarantee of freedom. The state is obliged to take a cross-generational, 'intertemporal' perspective when safeguarding freedoms, because fundamental rights can, when viewed in a temporal dimension, develop into defensive rights: If it is almost certain that climate change will require significantly more intensive interventions in the future – including emission reductions – and the state nevertheless continues to adopt only low-intensity measures, these measures already constitute an intervention into future freedoms today, i. e. in the present, due to their lack of current severity and the negative consequences that can therefore be expected for future generations. The principle of proportionality demands that the state exercise particular care to ensure that one generation does not use up a significant portion of the CO_2 budget due to a comparatively mild reduction burden, thereby de facto imposing a radical reduction burden on subsequent generations, which carries the risk of serious restrictions on freedom.[62] In interpreting restrictions on the guarantee of freedom, the court thus attaches importance to the factor of 'time' that has not previously been recognised, at least not to

---

[58] Official translation of the Federal Ministry of the Environment, Climate Action, Nature Conservation and Nuclear Safety: available at https://www.bundesumweltministerium.de/en/law/federal-climate-change-act (9.1.2026).

[59] BVerfG, order of March 24, 2021 – 1 BvR 2656/18 et al., BVerfGE 157, 30, n. 210.

[60] *Calliess*, ZUR 2021, 355 (356); *Schlacke*, NVwZ 2021, 912 (912).

[61] *Fellenberg*, NVwZ 2022, 913 (915); *Polzin*, DÖV 2021, 1089 (1092 et seq.); *Uechtritz/Ruttloff*, NVwZ 2022, 9 (15); *Schlacke* (Fn. 53), 33 (37).

[62] *Schlegel*, NJW 2021, 2782 (2787 et seq.); *Winter*, ZUR 2022, 215 (216); *Janda*, ZRP 2021, 149 (149 et seqq.); *Schlacke*, NVwZ 2021, 912 (916 et seqq.).

this extent. This decision was made in recognition of the previous dogmatic limits of fundamental rights protection obligations.[63] In terms of the negative dimension of fundamental freedoms, the decision ultimately establishes an earlier intervention threshold.[64]

The implication of this case law is a new task for the legislative, executive, and judicial branches: all three branches of government must examine whether the freedoms of individuals are sufficiently protected across time and generations.[65] The resulting legislative mandate is directed not only at the federal government, but also at the states, and affects local authorities in the context of their self-government tasks (Article 28(2) GG).[66]

However, a prerequisite for the existence of such an intertemporal obligation to safeguard freedom is that there are clear, scientifically based means of quantification and causalities between specific government (in)action and the negative effects in the future. This is almost never the case in situations outside the realm of anthropogenic climate change, meaning that the ruling and its dogma can hardly be applied to other environmental areas (such as biodiversity protection).[67] Furthermore, the availability of judicial review of state action requires a transition from scientific facts to applicable law, i. e. the legalisation of limit values in the form of a temperature target (1.5 to 2°C target) and a long-term target (greenhouse gas neutrality or climate neutrality). In practical conditions, it is necessary to be able to express the impact of greenhouse gases on climate change in terms of a budget. Without such budgeting, there are no intertemporal obligations to safeguard freedom at any level of the federal state.

The benchmark for assessing whether fundamental rights are being infringed in this sense is the national greenhouse gas budget, compliance with which is considered to make it still possible to fall short of the Paris temperature targets. The interim targets established in the Climate Change Act (KSG) are, or should be, merely a legislative derivation of this overall benchmark. In this respect, the law, or the action of the legislator, must be assessed against the previously established scientifically defined budget. However, the omission of individual current measures by the legislature – such as not imposing a speed limit on motorways – cannot yet be judicially reviewed. It has not been possible to demonstrate that, at the relevant time of assessment today, it is foreseeable with sufficient certainty that the omission of a specific individual measure will inevitably lead to dispro-

---

63 *Winter,* ZUR 2022, 215 (217); *Koch/Hofmann/Resse,* in: HdB UmweltR/*Schwerdtfeger,* § 4 n. 22; *Franzius,* KlimR 2022, 102 (103); *Schlacke,* NVwZ 2021, 912 (914).

64 *V. Weschpfennig,* ZfL 2023, 304 (307 et seq.), rightly draws a comparison to the planning authority's pre-assessment duty regarding the expropriation effect of a plan-approval decision.

65 *Thalhammer/Breidenbach,* ZRP 2023, 183 (184); *Schlacke* (fn. 53), 43 et seqq.; *Schlacke,* NVwZ 2022, 905 (911).

66 BVerfG, order of March 24, 2021 – 1 BvR 2656/18 et al., BVerfGE 157, 30, n. 149.

67 *Wahnschaffe/Lücke,* DÖV 2021, 1099 (1109); *Uechtritz/Ruttloff,* NVwZ 2022, 9 (14); *Fellenberg,* NVwZ 2022, 913 (916 et seq.); *Schlacke* (fn. 53), 38.

portionate state restrictions on fundamental freedoms in the future.[68] A constitutional complaint is only possible with regard to the totality of permitted emissions, 'because it is only these, and not specific actions or omissions on the part of the state, that could disproportionately shift the burden of reduction to the future.' Even a failure to take measures in individual sectors, such as the transport sector, whose targets are exceeded due to insufficiently ambitious action, could only be effectively challenged if the failure to act would inevitably result in the climate protection targets not being achieved.[69]

c) Legislative and Executive Powers in the Federal German State

According to Article 70(1) of the Basic Law, the *Länder* have the legislative power in principle, unless the Basic Law confers legislative powers on the Federation.[70] The Basic Law does not establish a specific title of competence for the subject of energy transition. Regulations that focus on the energy transition through energy industry and climate protection measures are primarily based on the concurrent legislative competence for the economy (Article 74(1)(no 11) GG) and air pollution control (Article 74(1)(no 24) GG). Therefore, both the federal government and the states can, in principle, take legislative action. However, if the federal government has enacted laws that exhaustively regulate a matter, the states are prohibited from legislating in that same field. Federal regulations therefore dominate in the areas of energy policy and climate change law. An exception to this are opening clauses, which allow the federal government to grant the states the right to legislate, as has been done in the area of climate protection.[71] In some areas of administrative law related to the energy transition, the federal government is precluded from regulating by law due to the division of powers. These include monument protection and municipal law.

According to Article 83 GG, the enforcement of laws, including federal laws, is normally the responsibility of the Länder. Therefore, the state administrations regularly apply the federal energy regulations and implement them locally. However, consistent enforcement across 16 federal states is not always guaranteed.

2. Climate Protection Legislation

Climate protection is a cross-cutting task that requires specialist measures such as the reduction of greenhouse gases in the energy, building and transport sectors.[72] In this respect, many specialist laws contain climate protection-oriented objec-

---

[68] Cf. BVerfGE 157, 30, n. 70 et seq., 92; BVerfG, order of January 18, 2022 – 1 BvR 1565/21 et al., NJW 2022, 844, headnote 1, n. 12.

[69] BVerfG, order of December 15, 2022 – 1 BvR 2146/22, ZUR 2023, 234, 234 et seq.

[70] On fundamental-rights issues of the Energiewende see *Eichberger*, RdE 2018, 453 et seqq.

[71] For climate legislation, Section 14(1) KSG provides an opening clause.

[72] Early on already *Gärditz*, JuS 2008, 324.

tives and instruments, such as the Building Code (BauGB).[73] Such specialist legal regulations are not included in the narrower climate protection legislation discussed below. Rather, this article only discusses laws that formulate cross-sectoral climate protection targets, in particular for the reduction of greenhouse gases,[74] and also contain cross-sectoral instruments for achieving these targets.

a) Federal Level: Federal Climate Change Act

At the federal level, the Climate Change Act (KSG) of 2019, which has been amended twice to date, enshrines these climate protection targets.[75] In a comprehensive manner and without quantification, Section 1 of the KSG requires compliance with European targets and international commitments, in particular the above-mentioned target of the Paris Agreement (limitation to 2°C or 1.5°C).

In addition to the 2030 target (65 % GHG reduction compared to 1990),[76] the 2040 target (88 % GHG reduction compared to 1990)[77] and the 2045 target (greenhouse gas neutrality)[78], the law outlines the path to achieving climate neutrality for the period up to 2030 and for the years 2031 to 2040 by enshrining annual emission reduction targets in law.[79] For the years 2041 to 2045, the legislator is obliged to submit a legislative proposal for the remaining reduction targets until 2045 by 2032 at the latest.[80]

Since 2024, the KSG has furthermore included staggered targets for natural sinks that emit greenhouse gases due to land use, land use changes and forestry.[81] However, there are still no legal targets for technical sinks: Section 3b KSG provides for a regulatory authorisation in favour of the Federal Government to determine these for the years 2035, 2040 and 2045. Overall, the KSG establishes a large number of different climate protection targets that are intended to contribute to the success of the energy transition.[82]

---

[73] Sections 1(5) sentence 2, 1a(5) sentence 1, 5, 9 BauGB.

[74] Under Section 2 no. 1 KSG, greenhouse gases are carbon dioxide (CO_2), methane (CH_4), nitrous oxide (N_2O), sulphur hexafluoride (SF_6), nitrogen trifluoride (NF_3), as well as partially fluorinated hydrocarbons (HFCs) and perfluorinated hydrocarbons (PFCs).

[75] Art. 1 First Act Amending the KSG (Act of August 18, 2021), BGBl. I 2021, 3905; Art. 1 Second Amending Act (Act of July 15, 2024), BGBl. I 2024, 235; see also *Wiedmann*, NVwZ 2024, 876.

[76] Section 3(1) no. 1 KSG.

[77] Section 3(1) no. 2 KSG.

[78] Section 3(2) sentence 1 KSG.

[79] Section 4(1) sentences 3 and 4 KSG in conjunction with Annexes 2 and 3 KSG.

[80] Section 4(1) sentence 7 KSG.

[81] Section 3a(1) sentence 3 KSG: The average of the annual emissions balances of the respective target year and the three preceding calendar years for the land use, land-use change and forestry sector shall be improved as follows: 1. to at least minus 25 million tonnes of carbon dioxide equivalent by 2030, 2. to at least minus 35 million tonnes of carbon dioxide equivalent by 2040, 3. to at least minus 40 million tonnes of carbon dioxide equivalent by 2045.

[82] For an overview of the instruments of the German Climate Change Law see *Schlacke*, in: Krönke/Wolff, Verwaltung der Klimakrise – Die Vermessung des Klimaverwaltungsrechts, Die Verwaltung, Beiheft 13, 2025, 73 et seqq.

b) State Level: Länder Climate Protection Laws

The majority of the *Länder*[83] in the Federal Republic of Germany have their own state climate protection laws in which they establish state-specific climate protection aims. This is constitutionally possible due to an opening clause in Section 14 KSG. In addition to interim goals for reducing emissions, the state laws also include targets for climate and greenhouse gas neutrality, with the target corridor between 2040 and 2050 varying between the states.[84]

c) Binding Effect

The climate protection goals of the Federal Climate Change Act are binding on the federal government. However, they are not binding on private individuals. Nor are they directly binding on the federal states. Non-compliance does not result in legal sanctions, but at most in a loss of political prestige and in public pressure to comply with the targets. However, due to the requirement to take them into account under Section 13(1) of the Climate Change Act, the climate protection targets are indirectly legally binding on other public bodies:[85] Accordingly, public authorities, i. e. primarily government agencies, are obliged to take the climate protection targets of the KSG into account within the framework of their legal scope for action and decision-making (in particular when weighing competing interests and in discretionary decisions). Since the implementation of federal law is the responsibility of the federal states (Art. 83 GG), the state authorities are also indirectly bound by these targets. Taking into account does not mean that the climate protection goals are mandatory or take precedence over other considerations, but rather that they must be included in the assessment (which may encompass questions of interpretation, the weighing of competing interests, or discretionary decision).[86]

The climate protection targets of the federal states are also binding for the respective state government. Here, too, the state climate protection laws do not provide for sanctions in the event of non-achievement. The federal states may set

---

[83] By now, 12 of 16 Länder have adopted climate protection statutes: Baden-Württemberg (KlimaG BW); Bavaria (BayKlimaG); Berlin (EWG Bln); Bremen (BremKEG); Hamburg (HmbKliSchG); Hesse (HKlimaG); Lower Saxony (NKlimaG); North Rhine-Westphalia (KSG NRW); Rhineland-Palatinate (LKSG RP); Saarland (SKSG); Schleswig-Holstein (EWKG SH); Thuringia (ThürKlimaG); references by *Schlacke/Heidler*, in: Schlacke/Wagner (eds.), Klimarecht, 2026, § 4 n. 51 et seqq.

[84] Cf. the overviews in *Schlacke/Thierjung*, in: Kreuter-Kirchhof/Schlacke (eds.), Klimaschutzrecht, 2025, KSG, introductory n. 172a; *Schlacke/Heidler* (fn. 83), § 4 n. 51 et seqq.

[85] For an in-depth discussion of Section 13 KSG see *Kling*, Klimaverträglichkeitsprüfung vor Gericht, 2023, 144 et seqq.

[86] *Müller/Schlacke*, in: Kahl/Ludwigs (eds.), Handbuch des Verwaltungsrechts VII, 2025, § 207 n. 58 et seq.; on the increasing weight of the requirement as the remaining budget is depleted see *Guckelberger*, KlimR 2022, 294, 297; *Siegel*, DÖV 2023, 329, 333.

more ambitious state climate protection targets than the federal government.[87] Furthermore, consideration requirements in the state climate protection laws accompany the provision of Section 13(1) KSG. However, there are differences between the individual requirements in the state laws, particularly with regard to the scope of application, the subject matter to be considered and the weigh accorded to climate protection concerns.[88]

3. Energy Industry Legislation Relating to the Energy Transition

The Energy Industry Act (EnWG)[89] is the core law governing the energy industry. It regulates competition in network access, between different networks and around networks. It also contains specifications for fill level requirements for gas storage facilities,[90] for ensuring security of supply, for energy deliveries to end consumers[91] and for licensing requirements for energy lines.[92]

a) Objectives of the EnWG

The central challenges of the energy transition are expressed in the energy industry law objectives set out in Section 1(1) EnWG: The purpose of regulatory policy-making in the field of energy supply is to ensure a secure, affordable, consumer-friendly, efficient, environmentally friendly and greenhouse gas-neutral grid-based supply of electricity, gas and hydrogen to the general public, which is increasingly based on renewable energies. According to Section 1(2) sentence 2 no. 2 EnWG, regulation to achieve the objectives set out in Section 1(1) EnWG takes particular account of the generation and use of electricity from renewable energies and hydrogen. In this context, regulation means ensuring competition in network access, between different networks and around networks.[93] A more recent element of this purpose of the EnWG is the greenhouse gas neutrality of energy supply, which was added in 2022;[94] the explicit mention of hydrogen as an additional form of energy alongside gas and electricity is also a novelty in this regard.[95]

---

[87] *Siegel*, in: Fellenberg/Guckelberger (eds.), KSG, 2022, § 14 n. 15.

[88] Cf. *Schlacke/Thierjung*, in: Kreuter-Kirchhof/Schlacke (eds.), Klimaschutzrecht, 2025, KSG, Introduction n. 172a; *Schlacke/Heidler* (fn. 83), § 4 n. 104 et seqq.

[89] Energiewirtschaftsgesetz of July 7, 2005 (BGBl. I 2005, 1970, 3621), as last amended by Act of December 8, 2025 (BGBl. I 2025, 317).

[90] See § 35b EnWG (storage level requirements): 80 % by 1st October, 90 % by 1st November, 30 % by 1 February (each as a percentage of the working gas volume).

[91] §§ 36 et seqq. EnWG.

[92] §§ 43 et seqq. EnWG; as a rule, construction, operation, and modification of installations require plan approval (Planfeststellung).

[93] *Kment*, in: Kment (ed.), EnWG, 3rd ed. 2023, § 1 n. 12.

[94] Introduced by Art. 1 of the Act of July 19, 2022, BGBl. I 2022, 1214.

[95] Inserted by Art. 1 of the Act implementing EU requirements and regulating dedicated hydrogen networks in energy law of July 16, 2021, BGBl. I 2021, 3026.

The most immediate technical challenge is to ensure a secure, grid-based energy supply. The regulation under the Energy Industry Act (EnWG) serves to ensure effective and undistorted competition in the supply of electricity and gas and to safeguard the long-term, efficient and reliable operation of energy supply networks (Section 1(2) sentence 1 EnWG).[96] Security of electricity supply requires that electricity generation and consumption are balanced at all times, as electricity cannot be stored. This simple fact is particularly relevant in light of the planned expansion of renewable energies, which are supply-dependent, meaning that they generate electricity depending on weather conditions. Accordingly, feed-in to the grid is also limited and unpredictable. In the interests of security of supply, the expansion of renewable generation units therefore requires solutions that enable to balance power fluctuations in the electricity grid. An additional essential component for the system integration of renewable energies is the provision of high-performance electricity storage facilities (see below IV. 3.b)).[97]

Furthermore, Section 1a EnWG sets out the principles of the electricity market. According to Section 1a(3) EnWG, particular emphasis should be placed on making supply and demand more flexible. This principle aims to remove barriers to flexibility and to efficiently link the heating and transport sectors with the electricity sector. Competition between efficient and flexible generation plants, electricity storage facilities and loads, the efficient coupling of the heating and transport sectors with the electricity sector, and the integration of the charging infrastructure for electric vehicles into the electricity supply system are intended to reduce the costs of energy supply, enable the transformation to an environmentally friendly, reliable, affordable and secure energy supply system.

According to Section 1a(4) EnWG, electricity supply networks should be expanded in line with demand, taking into account the expansion of electricity generation from renewable energies, security of supply and economic efficiency. There is a certain tension between the principle of minimising the costs of energy supply and, at the same time, promoting the expansion of renewable energies and ensuring an efficient and secure electricity supply.[98] Paragraph 4 addresses grid expansion so that grid operators do not need to expand for the 'last kilowatt hour' but can, for example, curtail renewable energy plants.[99]

As principles, the provisions are not directly enforceable, but primarily serve to specify the application of the other provisions of the EnWG.[100]

---

[96] On the legislative history of the EEG in detail EEG *Prall/Ewer*, in: Koch/Hofmann/Reese (eds.), Handbuch Umweltrecht, 5th ed. 2024, § 9 n. 115 et seqq.

[97] *Kopplow*, in: Pritzsche/Vacha (fn. 3), § 7 n. 2.

[98] BT-Drs. 18/7317, S. 77.

[99] *Hellermann/Hermes*, in: Bourwieg/Hellermann/Hermes (eds.), EnWG, 4th ed. 2023, § 1a n. 7.

[100] *Kment*, in: Kment (ed.), EnWG, 3rd ed. 2024, § 1a n. 2.

b) Grid Expansion

Essentially, the Energy Industry Act regulates the planning and approval of electricity grids (Sections 43 et seq EnWG). With the expansion of renewable energies, the structure of energy generation has increasingly shifted from centralised to decentralised, and the amount of volatile feed-in is rising. One challenge of the energy transition is therefore the grid integration of renewable energies while maintaining the overall stability of the electricity grid. In particular, the increasing expansion of wind farms requires massive line expansion measures to avoid bottlenecks at the transmission grid level.[101] In order to simplify and accelerate the planning and approval procedures for power lines, the legislator first enacted legislative measures for extra-high voltage lines in 2009 through the Energy Line Expansion Act (EnLAG).[102] Following the decision to phase out nuclear energy and in order to transport offshore wind power from the north to the high-consumption centres in southern Germany,[103] the federal legislature created a three-stage planning and approval system for priority transmission grid projects in 2011, consisting of demand planning, federal technical planning and plan approval.[104] Based on the development of a scenario framework and a network development plan by the four transmission system operators, the Federal Network Agency (‘*Bundesnetzagentur*’)[105] establishes a federal requirements plan containing cross-border extra-high voltage transmission network projects, which is enacted into law.[106] Based on this, the Transmission Grid Expansion Acceleration Act (NABEG)[107] regulates the federal technical planning for the determination of the route corridor,[108] which is intended to relieve the subsequent planning approval procedure for individual projects.[109] The Federal Network Agency, as the competent higher federal authority, is entrusted with the planning and ap-

---

[101] Monopolkommission, n. 46. The Dena Grid Study II estimates the grid expansion requirement at 3,600 km.

[102] Energieleitungsausbaugesetz of August 21, 2009 (BGBl. I, 2870), which was amended by Article 5 of the Act of March 7, 2011 (BGBl. I, 338).

[103] See also the challenges of energy infrastructure law in the context of the energy transition *Franzius*, EnWZ 2022, 302.

[104] Gesetz zur Neuregelung energiewirtschaftlicher Vorschriften of July 26, 2011 (BGBl. I, 1554).

[105] See the independence of the Federal Network Agency required under EU law (ECJ, EC-718/18, ECLI:EU:C:2021:662, EuZW 2021, 893) and its implementation in German law *Markus*, NVwZ 2025, 1146 et seqq.

[106] Annex to Section 1 Abs. 1) Bundesbedarfsplangesetz (BBPlG) v. Juli 23, 2013 (BGBl. I, 2543; 2014 I S. 148, 271), last amended by Article 1 of the Act of July 16, 2024 (BGBl. 2024 I Nr. 239).

[107] Gesetz zur Beschleunigung des Netzausbaus Elektrizitätsnetze v. 28.7.2011 (BGBl. I, 1634 und 1690), last amended by Article 3 of the Act of December 22, 2025, BGBI. I 351; see also *Appel*, EnWZ 2021, 435; *Sangenstedt*, EnWZ 2022, 103.

[108] §§ 4 et seqq. NABEG.

[109] Cf. *Franzius*, JuS 2018, 28, 31 et seq.; *Holznagel*, ZUR 2020, 515.

proval of transmission grids, so that grid expansion, which was previously the responsibility of the federal states, become partly a matter of the Federation.

Despite having created these legal foundations (EnLAG, EnWG, NABEG), the results regarding the expansion of the transmission grid up to 2019 were sobering: Of the approximately 1,800 km total length of the EnLAG projects, only about 850 km were realised,[110] and of the 5,900 km total length of the transmission grid projects, only about 600 km were approved and about 300 km were constructed.[111] Further adjustments to energy industry legislation, greater flexibility and acceleration of the planning and approval process for transmission grid expansion followed,[112] in particular with the aim of improving the integration of the three planning levels mentioned above.[113] These measures have had an effect: by the end of 2025, 4,660 km of lines had been approved or were already under construction.[114] In 2024, the number of approved route kilometres was five times as high as in 2021.[115]

V. Regulations Governing the Core Sectors of the Energy Transition

Regulations governing the core sectors (electricity, buildings/heat, transport/fuels) of the energy transition are the Renewable Energy Sources Act (EEG),[116] which includes the promotion of renewable energies in the electricity sector (1.), the Building Energy Act (GEG) and the Heat Planning Act for the heating sector (2.), and several regulations on the use of renewable energies in the fuel sector (3.).

1. Electricity Sector: Renewable Energy Sources Act (EEG)

The core law governing renewable energies – also known as 'environmental energy law'[117] – is the Renewable Energy Sources Act 2023 (EEG 2023), which regulates the promotion and expansion of renewable energies. It exists in a tension between competition law and climate protection law. It can be classified as a sub-area of energy industry law, with one of its central support instruments being

---

110 *Bundesnetzagentur*, Monitoring des Stromnetzausbaus: Erstes Quartal 2019, 25 available under https://data.bundesnetzagentur.de/Bundesnetzagentur/SharedDocs/Mediathek/Monitoringberichte/monitoringbericht_energie2019.pdf (9.1.2026).

111 *Bundesnetzagentur* (fn. 110).

112 Gesetz zur Beschleunigung des Energieleitungsausbaus of May 13, 2019, BGBl. I, 706; dazu *Leidinger*, NVwZ 2020, 1377.

113 BT-Drs. 19/7375, S. 1 et seq.; BT-Drs. 20/3497, 24, BGBl. I 2022, 37; vgl. *Eding*, Bundesfachplanung nach §§ 4 et seqq. NABEG, 2016; *Appel*, EnWZ 2021, 435; *Sangenstedt*, EnWZ 2022, 103.

114 Agora Energiewende (fn. 1), 58.

115 Cf. https://www.bundeswirtschaftsministerium.de/Redaktion/DE/Downloads/M-O/netzausbau-schreitet-voran.pdf?__blob=publicationFile&v=23 (12.1.2025).

116 The recent legal developments outline in general *Scholtka/Keller-Herder*, NJW 2025, 874; *Frenz*, RdE 2025, 67; especially on jurisprudence *Ludwigs*, NVwZ 2025, 1146.

117 Cf. *Kahl*, JuS 2010, 599.

an individual right to connection to and access to the electricity grid. At the same time, it may also be regarded as part of as climate protection law, as it aims to achieve the most sustainable, low-greenhouse-gas energy production possible by replacing fossil fuel-based electricity supply with renewable energy sources.[118] In addition to combating ever-worsening climate change, the EEG also aims to maintain and restore energy security and to achieve greater independence from foreign energy imports.

a) Legal Facts

In 2024, renewable energies accounted for 54 % of gross electricity consumption,[119] but their share of total German final energy consumption is only 22.5 % due to stagnating figures in the heating and transport sectors.[120] Biomass and biofuels (48 %) represent the largest share of renewable energies; followed by wind (27 %), hydropower (4 %) and photovoltaics (15 %).[121] The market share of green electricity is rising steadily and now accounts for around 25 %.[122] The use of renewable energies has considerable potential beyond climate protection purposes, which is to be exploited intensively through expansion in the coming decade: In addition to the advantages of using renewables for labour market and industrial policy,[123] the enormous benefits in terms of (supply) security[124] and affordability[125] have now become particularly apparent as a result of Russia's war of aggression against Ukraine in violation of international law since February

---

[118] On internal ecological conflicts see *Gärditz*, DVBl. 2010, 214; *Anger/Gerhold*, ZfBR-Beil. 2012, 90.

[119] Cf. Umweltbundesamt, available at https://www.umweltbundesamt.de/indikator-anteil-erneuerbare-am#die-wichtigsten-fakten (9.1.2026).

[120] Cf. Umweltbundesamt, 'Umweltindikatoren: Indikator Erneuerbare Energien', available at https://www.umweltbundesamt.de/daten/umweltindikatoren/indikator-erneuerbare-energien#die-wichtigsten-fakten (9.1.2026).

[121] Cf. Umweltbundesamt, 'Erneuerbare Energien in Zahlen', available at https://www.umweltbundesamt.de/themen/klima-energie/erneuerbare-energien/erneuerbare-energien-in-zahlen#ueberblick-beitrag-erneuerbare (9.1.2026).

[122] Cf. Umweltbundesamt, 'Ökostrom', available at https://www.umweltbundesamt.de/umwelttipps-fuer-den-alltag/haushalt-wohnen/oekostrom#-2 (9.1.2026).

[123] *Becker/Lutz*, GWS Research Report 2021/01, 2021, 920 et seqq., available under https://papers.gws-os.com/gws-researchreport21-1.pdf (9.1.2026).

[124] On renewables expansion as a core element of German security policy see *Schirwon/Kornhuber/Vinke*, Energie- und Klimapolitik im Kontext von Russlands Krieg: Nachhaltige Ansätze zur Lösung globaler Krisen. Statement, 2022, 5 et seq., available under https://www.ssoar.info/ssoar/bitstream/handle/document/80044/ssoar-2022-schirwon_et_al-Energie-_und_Klimapolitik_im_Kontext.pdf?sequence=1&isAllowed=y&lnkname=ssoar-2022-schirwon_et_al-Energie-_und_Klimapolitik_im_Kontext.pdf (9.1.2026).

[125] For the expansion of renewable energies as a 'lever to limit electricity price increases', see *Sachverständigenrat zur Begutachtung der gesamtwirtschaftlichen Entwicklung*, Energiekrise solidarisch bewältigen, neue Realität gestalten. Annual Report 2022/23, 2022, n. 337, available under: https://www.sachverstaendigenrat-wirtschaft.de/fileadmin/dateiablage/gutachten/jg202223/JG202223_Gesamtausgabe.pdf (9.1.2026).

2022 and the subsequent sharp rise in energy costs. A further advantage is the aspect of supply independence.

b) Origin and Development of the EEG

In the electricity sector, legal regulation in the form of the promotion of renewable energies was implemented early on. The Electricity Feed-in Act of 7 December 1990[126] was the predecessor to the Renewable Energy Sources Act (EEG), which came into force on 1st April 2000 and is regarded internationally as exemplary.[127] The Act has undergone comprehensive amendments in recent years and is now in force in the form of the EEG 2023.[128]

The Electricity Feed-in Act (StrEG)[129], which came into force on 1 January 1991, followed the model of the existing antitrust remuneration claim of private producers of surplus electricity,[130] usually from renewable energies, against sovereign grid operators.[131] The basic concept of the StrEG, which comprised only five paragraphs, consisted of a purchase obligation (Section 2 StrEG) and a remuneration claim (Section 3 StrEG) for the feed-in of renewable electricity vis-à-vis the energy supply company. The level of remuneration was no longer based on the economic value of the feed-in – as had been the case under antitrust law – but on the environmental policy objective of conserving resources and protecting the climate, which was pursued through the use of renewable energies.[132] The remuneration for electricity from hydropower, landfill and sewage gas, as well as from products or biological residues and waste materials from agriculture and forestry, amounted to at least 75 % of the average revenue per kilowatt hour from the sale of electricity by electricity companies to end consumers, and at least 90 % for electricity from solar and wind power.[133] Until the enactment of its successor, the Renewable Energy Sources Act (EEG) in 2000, the StrEG underwent two amendments, which essentially extended its scope to include energy production from biomass.[134]

The EEG 2000[135] extended the right of renewable energy plant operators to have their electricity purchased and remunerated by electricity suppliers by granting them the right to connect to the grid. Moreover, legally defined remu-

---

[126] BGBl. I 1990, 2633.

[127] IRENA, REmap 2030, 2015, 1 et seq.

[128] See *Harsch/Schäfer*, KlimR 2022, 334; *Frenz*, EnWZ 2024, 339.

[129] See n. 126; on the legislative history in detail see *Prall/Ewer*, in: Koch/Hofmann/Reese (fn. 96), § 9 n. 115 et seqq.

[130] §§ 26(2), 103(5) sentence 2 GWB (old version, 1980); on the amendment BGBl. I 1980, 458.

[131] For a detailed account *Altrock/Oschmann*, in: Altrock/Oschmann/Theobald (eds.), EEG, 4th ed. 2013, Introduction n. 5 et seqq.

[132] BT-Drs. 11/7816, 3.

[133] Section 3(1) sentence 1 and (2) StrEG.

[134] *Altrock/Oschmann*, in: Altrock/Oschmann/Theobald (eds.), EEG, 4th ed. 2013, Introduction n. 13 et seqq.

[135] BGBl. I 2000, 305.

neration levels for electricity feed-in from various types of renewable energy plants were established for a period of 20 years.[136] As a result, the share of renewable energies in the electricity sector grew from 4.6% (1994) to 10% (2004), with wind energy accounting for the largest share.[137]

The Renewable Energy Sources Act (EEG), which underwent its last significant amendment on 1 January 2023 (EEG 2023),[138] is considered the most effective support instrument to date in terms of achieving the expansion targets for renewable energies in the electricity sector.[139]

c) *Targets of the EEG 2023*

The EEG 2023 pursues several intertwined and overlapping objectives: The overarching objective of the EEG, particularly in the interest of climate and environmental protection, is to transform the electricity sector into a sustainable and greenhouse gas-neutral electricity supply based entirely on renewable energies (Section 1(1) EEG). This objective is not legally binding and is set for 2035.[140]

To this end, the share of electricity generated from renewable energies in gross electricity consumption in the territory of the Federal Republic of Germany, including the German exclusive economic zone (federal territory), is now to be increased to at least 80% in 2030 (Section 1(2) EEG).

At the same time, in light of the objectives of Section 1 of the Energy Supply Act (energy supply security, efficiency, consumer friendliness, environmental compatibility, affordability), the expansion of renewable energies required to achieve the objective set out in paragraph 2 must be carried out in a steady, cost-efficient, environmentally compatible and grid-compatible manner (Section 1(3) EEG). Furthermore, following the coal phase-out, greenhouse gas neutrality in Germany's electricity supply is to be achieved (Section 1a(1) EEG).

The extent to which the individual technologies (especially wind, solar and biomass) are to contribute to these targets is determined by the expansion pathways set out in Section 4 EEG, which have been significantly increased in light of the enormous increase in ambition in Section 1(2) EEG. Solar power plants (400 gigawatts in 2040) and wind power plants (160 gigawatts in 2040) are to continue to account for the largest share (Section 4(1) No. 1, 3 EEG). To this end, the expansion of renewable energies is to be promoted by a variety of accel-

---

136 Section 9(1) EEG 2000.

137 Cf. https://www.umweltbundesamt.de/themen/klima-energie/erneuerbare-energien/erneuerbare-energien-in-zahlen#uberblick (9.1.2026).

138 BGBl. I 2022, 1237.

139 On the regulation of renewable electricity generation under German and EU law see *Oschmann/Sösemann*, ZUR 2007, 1; on the UK quota system cf. *Laube/Toke*, ZNER 2006, 132.

140 BT-Drs. 20/1630, 1.

eration measures.[141] Once again, the importance of targets – as in the case of climate protection – for the success of the energy transition is evident.

d) The EEG as a Financial Support Instrument

The core of the EEG 2023 remains the obligation for grid operators to connect, purchase, distribute, transmit and remunerate electricity from renewable energies (and, conversely, a corresponding entitlement of plant operators vis-à-vis the grid operator).[142]

The original support mechanism, which obliged grid operators to purchase electricity from renewable energies in return for a fixed feed-in tariff for a period of 20 years, now only applies in exceptional cases for very small plants (Section 19 (1) No. 2 EEG).[143] Since 2014, the direct marketing has been the legally desired practice in order to integrate renewable energy generation into the electricity market, which until then had been largely detached from market mechanisms.[144] Direct marketing refers to the sale of electricity from renewable energies to third parties, unless the electricity is consumed in the immediate vicinity of the plant and is not transmitted through a grid.[145] In addition, a market premium[146] was introduced alongside the feed-in tariff and currently remains the predominant support model.[147] The market premium compensates for the difference between the average market price for electricity and a legally defined support value. Thus, it aims to make renewable electricity more competitive.[148]

In 2017, the legislator converted price-based subsidies for certain renewable energy plants – in particular wind power and solar power plants – into volume-based subsidies. Operators can now only benefit from EEG subsidies if they have successfully participated in a tender process and offered a corresponding subsidy amount: although this instrument is a direct subvention, the subsidy amount is determined in competitive auctions.[149]

To refinance the costs incurred by grid operators, the EEG provided for a multi-stage remuneration and financing mechanism that balanced out the regional differences in financial burdens, particularly those associated with fixed

[141] On this in comprehensive fashion *Schlacke/Wentzien/Römling*, NVwZ 2022, 1577.

[142] Section 8(1) EEG stipulates the priority of electricity generated from renewable energy sources.

[143] *Stangl*, in: Baumann/Gabler/Günther (eds.), EEG, 2020, § 21 n. 3.

[144] *Prall/Ewer*, in: Koch/Hofmann/Reese (fn. 96), Section 9, n. 125.

[145] Section 3 no. 16 EEG 2023.

[146] Section 19(1) no. 1 in conjunction with § 20 EEG, see *Kahles/Nysten*, EnWZ 2019, 147, 150 et seqq.

[147] *Wiemer*, in: BeckOK EEG, 2025, § 19 n. 23.

[148] *Hermeier*, in: Säcker (fn. 3), EEG § 20 n. 5 et seqq.

[149] See *Baumann/Strauß*, in: Baumann/Gabler/Günther, § 28 n. 1 et seqq.; *Haucap* et al., Strommarktdesign 2030. Die Förderung der erneuerbaren Energien wirksam und effizient gestalten, 2022.

feed-in tariffs, by distributing them evenly across all electricity supply companies (known as the EEG surcharge). The compensation was structured as a legal obligation at all levels (energy suppliers, transmission as well as distrubution system operators and end consumers).[150] This support mechanism did not constitute direct or indirect state aid within the meaning of Article 107 TFEU, as the European Court of Justice correctly ruled in 2019.[151] This system of financing the promotion of electricity generation from renewable energies was removed from the EEG in 2022 and transferred to the Energy Financing Act (EnFG)[152]. The so-called EEG surcharge was abolished.[153] It has been replaced by a compensation claim by the transmission system operators against the Federal Republic of Germany (Section 6(1) sentence 1 EnFG), which, however, can also be reversed if the grid operators' balance sheet is positive (Section 6(1) sentence 2 EnFG).

e) The EEG as a Substantive Legal Instrument for Accelerating Expansion

Although financial support for the expansion of renewable energies has proven to be very effective, the expansion of wind energy and photovoltaics in Germany stalled at the end of the last decade. The energy transition, and in particular the expansion of wind and ground-mounted solar energy systems, is an extremely 'space-intensive' undertaking that competes with other land uses such as agriculture, housing development, defence, nature conservation and monument protection. The resulting conflicts of use and collisions with other interests are to be resolved nationwide in favour of the expansion of renewable energies by means of Section 2 EEG[154], which was added in 2022.[155]

---

[150] Regulation of June 17, 2009 on the further development of the nationwide EEG compensation mechanism (AusglMechV), BGBl. I 2009, 2101, last amended by Article 2 of the Act of August 17, 2012, BGBl. I 2012, 1754; cf. on the system and further development of the compensation mechanism *Altrock/Eder*, ZNER 2009, 128; *Oschmann*, NJW 2009, 264, *Kachel*, ZUR 2012, 32; *Fricke*, 28 et seqq.

[151] ECJ, judgment of March 28, 2019 – Case C-405/16 P (Federal Republic of Germany v European Commission); see *Kahles/Nysten*, EnWZ 2019, 147, 151 et seq.

[152] Act on the financing of the energy transition in the electricity sector through payments by the Federal Government and the levying of surcharges (Energiefinanzierungsgesetz – EnFG) of July 20, 2022, BGBl. I 1237, last amended by Article 25 of the Act of December 18, 2025, BGBl. I, 347.

[153] See also *Franzius*, Jura 2025, 1082, 1089.

[154] Act on immediate measures for the accelerated expansion of renewable energies and further measures in the electricity sector (Gesetz zu Sofortmaßnahmen für einen beschleunigten Ausbau der erneuerbaren Energien und weiteren Maßnahmen im Stromsektor) of July 20, 2022, BGBl. I 1237, last amended by Article 2 Act of December 19, 2022, BGBl. I 2479. On the history and genesis of Section 2 pf the EEG cf. *Attendorn*, NVwZ 2022, 1586 (1586); *Appel/Pfeuffer*, DVBl 2024, 537 (537 et seqq.).

[155] BT-Drs. 20/1630, 1.

Section 2 EEG contains a balancing directive.[156] The construction and operation of renewable energy plants and associated ancillary facilities are considered to be in the overriding public interest and to serve public health and safety (sentence 1). In addition, until electricity generation in Germany is virtually greenhouse gas-neutral, renewable energies are to be given priority when balancing protected interests (sentence 2). With the help of this balancing directive[157] in sentence 1 and the presumption of a relative weighting priority in favour of the construction of renewable energy plants in sentence 2, approval procedures for the expansion of such plants and infrastructure are to be accelerated by means of provisions at the substantive law level.[158] Although this priority in weighing up interests can be refuted in individual cases – i. e. renewable energy plants do not always have absolute priority –, it imposes a high burden of justification and reasoning on the competent authority for any deviation.[159]

This is intended to give renewable energy projects a 'high degree of enforceability'[160] in individual cases within the framework of official weighing and discretionary decisions. Exceptions to habitat protection (Section 34(3)(1) BNatSchG) or species protection (Section 45(7)(1)(5) BNatSchG) are thus made considerably easier, or, so to speak, preset by law.[161] Its counterpart in EU law, which was introduced a year later, can be found in Article 16f of the Renewable Energy Directive. The technology-neutral provision of Section 2(1) EEG has also been enshrined in law for offshore wind turbines and offshore connections (Section 1(3) WindSeeG), storage facilities (Section 11c EnWG) and the expansion of the electricity grid.[162]

f) The EEG as an Instrument for Promoting a Green Hydrogen Economy

In the future, hydrogen is set to play a key role in the decarbonisation of the energy system, particularly in areas where the direct electrification of individual economic sectors is not possible. Section 1(1) of the Energy Industry Act (EnWG) (see above IV. 3.) also mentions a greenhouse gas-neutral, grid-based supply of

---

[156] *Schlacke/Wentzien/Römling*, NVwZ 2022, 1577, 1578; regarding acceleration through prioritisation *Eh*, IR 2022, 279 and 302; also *Appel/Pfeuffer*, DVBl. 2024, 537.

[157] See the effect of Section 2 EEG on discretionary decisions in connection with an extension of the deadline pursuant to Section 18(1) BImSchG Higher Administrative Court Schleswig, decision of May 3, 2023 – Case 5 MR 1/23, NVwZ 2023, 1185 (1187), see *Lingemann*, NVwZ 2023, 1634 (1635).

[158] *Schlacke/Wentzien/Römling*, NVwZ 2022, 1577, 1578; *Stäsche*, EnWZ 2022, 435, 442.

[159] *Müller/Schlacke*, in: Kahl/Ludwigs, HVwR VII, 2025, § 207 n. 61.

[160] *Appel*, in: BerlKommEnergieR NABEG, § 1 n. 16.

[161] See on the observance of section 2 EEG within the balancing of conflicting interests (visually obtrusive effect of a wind turbine) OVG NRW, order of January 24, 2024 – 7 D 59/23. AK, juris n. 68; on section 2 EEG in approval procedures under monument protection law OVG Sachsen-Anhalt, order of March 7, 2024 – 2 M 70/23, juris n. 46 et seqq.

[162] See also Section 1(2) sentence 1 NABEG, Section 1(2) sentence 3 EnLAG and Section 1(1) sentence 2 BBPlG.

hydrogen to the general public – in addition to the supply of gas and electricity – as a goal of the energy industry. The first steps towards establishing a climate-neutral hydrogen economy were taken with the introduction of subsidies for hydrogen-based electricity storage (Sections 28f, 39o EEG) and generation, provided that the electricity is created from so-called green hydrogen (Sections 28g, 39p EEG). Green hydrogen is hydrogen that is produced electrochemically in accordance with a regulation by consuming electricity from renewable energies, whereby the hydrogen can also be stocked chemically or physically for storage or transport in other energy carriers (Section 3 No. 27a EEG). In October 2025, the German government passed the draft of a Hydrogen Acceleration Act to speed up the development of a hydrogen economy.

2. Buildings/Heating Sector

In addition to the electricity sector, the heating sector is the second sector that is legally central to the decarbonisation of the energy sector (see a)).[163] The Building Energy Act (GEG), which is flanked by the Heat Planning Act (WPG), is decisive for the heating sector (see b)).

a) Legal Facts

For years, heating has consistently accounted for more than half of the total energy consumption.[164] At the same time, just over 80 % of heating continues to be based on fossil fuels:[165] In particular, residential buildings are still predominantly heated using fossil gas and oil.[166] However, the use of heat pumps is on the rise thanks to a variety of legal and financial measures. For example, two-thirds of new buildings constructed in 2024 will now be heated using a heat pump.[167]

At almost 65 %, solid biomass accounted for the largest share of renewable energy used to meet heating demand in 2024, whereas solar thermal energy, geothermal energy and environmental heat represented only around 16 %.[168] Renewable energies currently account for around 20 % of district heating,[169] which

---

[163] *Winkler/Zeccola/Tejkl*, EnWZ 2022, 339 et seq.

[164] Cf. https://www.umweltbundesamt.de/daten/energie/energieverbrauch-fuer-fossile-erneuerbare-waerme (9.1.2026).

[165] Cf. https://www.umweltbundesamt.de/daten/energie/energieverbrauch-fuer-fossile-erneuerbare-waerme (9.1.2026).

[166] Agora Energiewende, Die Energiewende in Deutschland: Stand der Dinge 2022, 68, available under: https://static.agora-energiewende.de/fileadmin/Projekte/2022/2022-10_DE_JAW2022/A-EW_283_JAW2022_WEB.pdf (9.1.2026).

[167] Cf. https://www.destatis.de/DE/Presse/Pressemitteilungen/2025/06/PD25_N031_31_51.html (9.1.2026).

[168] Cf. https://www.umweltbundesamt.de/daten/energie/energieverbrauch-fuer-fossile-erneuerbare-waerme (9.1.2026).

[169] Cf. https://www.unendlich-viel-energie.de/mediathek/grafiken/fernwaermeerzeugung-nach-energietraegern-in-deutschland-2024 (9.1.2026).

offers the major advantage of being able to integrate different renewable energy sources and supply a large number of customers simultaneously.[170]

However, unlike electricity, heat cannot be transported using a large-scale network of pipes and cables, due to primarily economic and technical reasons: In order to keep the end product, i. e. heat, usable suppliers must maintain a largely constant temperature, which makes transport over long distances uneconomical.[171] At the same time, the existing supply structure in the heating sector is predominantly municipal. In the future, heating networks are to take over a significantly larger share, which is why their expansion is being promoted through legal policy.[172]

b) Legal Requirements

In order to advance the so-called heat transition, the German legislator is increasingly focusing on the building sector.[173] The core law in the heating sector is the Building Energy Act (GEG), which entered into force on 1st November 2020.[174] It combines various previously scattered regulations governing heat into a new law,[175] while simultaneously repealing the old laws, and implements the requirements of the EU Buildings Directive[176] for newly constructed buildings.[177]

According to Section 1(1) sentence 1 GEG, the purpose of the Act is to contribute to national climate protection targets, i. e. the targets set out in the Federal Climate Change Act (see above IV. 2.a)).

In addition to the requirements for promoting the generation of heat or cold from renewable energies and energy efficiency measures (Sections 89 et seq. GEG), the GEG contains numerous requirements and prohibitions for building and property owners regarding the construction of new (Sections 10 et seq. GEG) and existing buildings (Sections 46 et seq. GEG): Among other things, it obliges that a heating system may only be installed or set up for commissioning in a building if at least 65 % of the heat provided by the system is generated from renewable sources (Section 10(2) No. 3 in conjunction with Section 71 GEG). However, the law includes a regulation on achieving minimum thermal insulation (Section 11 GEG) and a ban on the operation of certain fossil fuel boilers from 2045 onwards (Section 72(4) GEG). These obligations are limited by the

---

170 *Jacobshagen/Kaspers/Maiworm*, ZUR 2022, 523.

171 *Winkler/Zeccola/Tejkl*, EnWZ 2022, 339 et seq.

172 *Jacobshagen/Kaspers/Maiworm*, ZUR 2022, 523.

173 *Kahl*, EnWZ 2023, 433 (433), describes 2023 as the year of the heat transition.

174 Cf. BT-Drs. 19/16716, 106.

175 Cf. BT-Drs. 19/16716, 1; see on the essential contents and the developement process also *Schütte/Winkler*, ZUR 2020, 180; *Kaßler*, ZWE 2020, 58; on the contents of the amendment to the GEG presented on the basis of the draft law see *Reeh/Schäfer-Stradowsky*, KlimR 2022, 240.

176 Directive 2010/31/EU of May 19, 2010 on the energy performance of buildings, ABlEU L 153/13, lastly amendended by Reg. (EU) 2018/1999 of December 11, 2018, ABlEU L 328/1.

177 Cf. BT-Drs. 19/16716, 1.

comprehensive principle of economic efficiency pursuant to Section 5 GEG.[178] Sections 79 et seq. GEG contain regulations on energy performance certificates for buildings. They aim to make the energy requirements or energy consumption of a flat or building a factor in purchase, rental or lease decisions, so that more efficient properties indirectly increase in value and their owners are given incentives to carry out energy-efficient renovations. According to Section 10 GEG, the buildings covered (cf. Section 2(1) GEG) must generally be constructed as nearly zero-energy buildings. In addition, mandatory energy consulting has been introduced (Section 48(3) GEG).

The GEG is flanked by the Heat Planning Act (WPG),[179] which came into force on 1 January 2024. It contains the legal framework for accelerating the decarbonisation of grid-based heat supply[180] and aims to achieve climate neutrality in heating networks by 2045 (Sections 1(1) and 31(1) WPG).[181] The central instrument for achieving this goal is the obligation imposed on the federal states to carry out heat planning (Section 4(1) WPG), which ultimately has to be implemented by the municipalities (Section 6(1) WPG). In addition to this obligation on local authorities to introduce comprehensive municipal heat planning, the Act contains a second pillar of requirements for heat network operators to gradually decarbonise heat networks, including specific target values for the share of renewable energies in new and existing heat networks[182].[183] To this end, heat network operators must draw up heat network expansion and heat decarbonisation roadmaps in accordance with Section 32 WPG.

The provisions of the GEG are supplemented by those of the Carbon Dioxide Cost Allocation Act (CO2KostAufG).[184] It aims to replace the existing principle of tenancy law, according to which the tenant bears the heating costs and thus, among other things, the additional CO2 costs resulting from emissions trading, with a polluter-oriented allocation of costs between both parties. This is intended to create an incentive for landlords to renovate buildings. In this respect, the Act supports the price signal of emissions trading. The effects of the second emissions trading system for the building and transport sectors (EU ETS II), which will begin on 1 January 2027, remain to be seen.[185]

---

[178] *Hofmann*, in: Knauff (ed.), GEG, 2nd ed.2024, § 5 n. 2; more detail see *Halbig/Antoni*, EnWZ 2018, 259.

[179] Act of December 20, 2023, BGBl. 2023 I (Nr. 394); overview in *Werthmüller/Reith*, IR 2024, 60; *Schnittker/Fründ*, NVwZ 2024, 289.

[180] *Radimeczky-Krekel/Hentschel/von Schack*, ZUR 2024, 269.

[181] For an overview of the legal requirements of the heat planning see *Wagner*, in: Schlacke/Wagner (eds.), Klimarecht, 2026, § 6 n. 470 et seqq.

[182] Sections 29(1) number 1 and 2, 30(1) WPG.

[183] In detail see *Radimeczky-Krekel/Hentschel/von Schack*, ZUR 2024, 269 (272 et seq.).

[184] Act of December 5, 2022, BGBl. I, 2154, see *Ahlers/Burbach*, IR 2023, 2.

[185] See *Kreuter-Kirchhof*, in: Kreuter-Kirchhof/Schlacke, Klimaschutzrecht, 2025, EU-Emissionshandel n. 114 et seqq.

3. *Transport/Fuel Sector*

The third energy sector, the fuel sector, which is relevant to the transport branch, differs significantly from the electricity and heating sectors. The differences are not only in terms of market structure and players (mineral oil producers and suppliers, transport operators). Unlike electricity and heating, fuels are not transported and distributed via a supply network and the choice of renewable energies that can be used is more limited (only biomass in the form of biofuels). According to the Renewable Energy Directive, the target is to achieve a 14 % share of renewable energies in the transport sector by 2030 (Art. 25(1) EE-RL). This achievement is at risk due to the virtual stagnation of the share of renewable energies in final energy consumption, which stood at 7.3 % in 2024.[186]

After initially only receiving tax breaks for biofuels under the Energy Tax Act (EnergieStG)[187], the share of renewable energies in fuel consumption has been increased in recent years through various legislative and executive measures.[188] However, it remains unlikely that the targets set out in the Renewable Energy Directive will be achieved. The provisions of Sections 37a et seq. of the Federal Immission Control Act (BImSchG) are particularly noteworthy.[189] According to Section 37a(4) BImSchG, distributors must ensure that the greenhouse gas emissions of the fossil petrol and diesel fuels they place on the market, plus the greenhouse gas emissions of the compliance options they use, are reduced by a specified percentage compared to a reference value. From the calendar year 2030 onwards, this percentage is to be 25 %. In contrast to the heating sector, this does not impose any obligations on end consumers. For climate protection reasons, since 2015 the reference point for the quota obligation has no longer been the energy content of the fuels, but rather their relative greenhouse gas reduction potential in accordance with Section 37a(4) BImSchG.[190]

VI. Spatially-Based Control of the Expansion of Renewable Energies[191]

The expansion of renewable energies and thus the energy transition has stalled in Germany in recent years, mainly due to conflicting land use claims. German legislators have recently attempted to establish land use targets (1.) for the expansion of onshore wind energy and to prioritise (2.) and privilege (3.) renewable

---

186 Cf. https://www.umweltbundesamt.de/daten/energie/erneuerbare-energie-im-verkehr#erneuerbare-energien-im-verkehr (9.1.2026).

187 EnergieStG of July 15, 2006, BGBl. I, 1534; as last amended by Article 6 of Act of December 22, 2025, BGBl. I Nr. 341.

188 In detail see *Schlacke*, Umweltrecht, 9th ed. 2023, § 16 n. 75 et seqq.

189 Also see *Jarass*, BImSchG, 15th ed. 2024, § 37a n. 1 et seqq.

190 For a detailed account *Probst*, ZUR 2015, 393.

191 This section is closely based on *Schlacke/Plate*, ZUR 2024, 323 (324 et seqq.).

energy uses in order to manage land use competition and land shortages in favour of the energy transition.

1. Land Use Targets for Onshore Wind Energy

Area-related statutory targets have been set specifically for the expansion of renewable energy plants. Section 4 of the Renewable Energy Sources Act (EEG) mandates performance increases for onshore and offshore wind turbines as well as solar and biomass plants (see above V. 1.c)). Although these increases in output can also be achieved technologically, the Thünen Institute estimates that a total of approximately 116,000 hectares of new land will be required by 2030 for the expansion of renewable energies.[192]

The Wind Energy Area Requirement Act (WindBG)[193] does not aim to increase the capacity of wind turbines, but rather to directly promote the expansion of wind energy through area targets. It can already be qualified as a role model for the acceleration of the wind energy explansion on shore.[194] The aim is to double the area designated for wind energy in 2022.[195] To this end, the Act sets a total expansion target of 2 % of the federal territory in accordance with Section 3(1) WindBG in conjunction with Annex 1, which is to be achieved by the individual federal states through state-specific area contribution values for onshore wind energy.[196] The Act therefore starts at the legal planning level, which precedes the project-related approval decision for wind turbines. The federal states generally fulfil their specific area contribution value by designating priority areas for wind energy in regional spatial plans. The municipalities, in turn, specify the region plans by means of urban land-use planning. This legally determined massive expansion of land designation in favour of wind energy use is supported by provisions such as Section 6 WindBG, according to which neither an environmental impact assessment nor a species protection assessment needs to be carried out at project level if a strategic environmental assessment has been carried out at planning level.[197] In addition, expansion will be promoted in the future by the designation of so-called acceleration areas.[198]

---

[192] *Osterburg* et al., Flächennutzung und Flächennutzungsansprüche Thünen Working Paper 224, 2023, 68 table 14, available under https://literatur.thuenen.de/digbib_extern/dn067046.pdf (9.1.2026).

[193] Act of July 20, 2022, BGBl. I 2022, 1353.

[194] *Schlacke/Plate/Thierjung*, NVwZ 2025, 441.

[195] BT-Drs. 20/2355, 1.

[196] Cf. *Kment*, NVwZ 2022, 1153 (1154); Cf. BT-Drs. 20/2355, 2; *Schmidt-Eichstaedt*, ZfBR 2023, 10 (10); *Groneberg*, Enk-Aktuell 2023, 010136.

[197] More detail in *Schlacke/Thierjung*, DVBl. 2023, 635 (637 et seqq.); *Rieger*, NVwZ 2023, 1042 (1043).

[198] Art. 15c RL (EU) 2018/2001; see *Teßmer*, in: BeckOK KlimR, 2024, WindBG § 6a n. 1 et seqq.

2. Prioritisations

In addition to setting binding area-based targets, legislators have recently been making greater use of prioritisation, an instrument already used in the expansion of the electricity grid, in order to accelerate the expansion of renewable energies and the infrastructure required for this.[199] Prioritisation means assigning specific concerns or projects a predominant or even overriding public interest and/or qualifying them as serving public safety. This gives such concerns and projects a legally established relative priority in the context of official weighing and discretionary decisions made under sector-specific laws.[200] Particularly noteworthy is the aforementioned Section 2 of the EEG (see above V. 1.e)). However, it is problematic if – as intended – almost all infrastructure facilities are given this type of prioritisation, as is now provided for in the draft Infrastructure Future Act, as this negates the effect of the uniqueness of paramount importance.[201]

3. Privileges

In addition to prioritisation, the legislator is constantly expanding the catalogue of projects privileged under urban development planning law in rural areas (Section 35 BauGB) in favour of renewable energy projects, such as wind energy (No. 5), biomass (No. 6), solar energy, including on roof and exterior wall surfaces, along motorways and railways (No. 8), and solar installations at certain businesses (No. 9). Such projects are generally permissible under urban development planning law in rural areas, i. e. roughly speaking in unpopulated areas, provided that they do not conflict with public interests and that adequate development is ensured.[202] The legislator thus gives these privileged projects greater enforceability with regard to their implementation in rural areas, which are generally to be kept free of development.

VII. Legal Protection: Climate Lawsuits, Individual Lawsuits and Environmental Appeals

Since there are no specific requirements for climate lawsuits in Germany, 'Climate lawsuit' is not a legal term. It serves as a collective concept for proceedings related to climate change or climate protection. These lawsuits often pursue not

[199] Cf. Section 1(2) sentence 1 NABEG, section 1(2) sentence 3 EnLAG and section 1(1) sentence 2 BBPlG.

[200] Although the explanatory memorandum to the law only speaks of 'balancing', cf. BT-Drs. 20/1630, 159. It is also likely to cover other facts that are designed with official scope and interpretation, such as discretionary decisions or undefined legal terms.

[201] BR-Drs. 780/25.

[202] *Baars*, NVwZ 2023, 1857 (1857).

only specific procedural goals, but also aim to communicate the subject matter of the dispute in a media-effective manner.[203] A distinction can be made between vertical lawsuits brought by private individuals against the state and horizontal lawsuits between private individuals; in most cases, the defendant is a company that emits greenhouse gases. In the vertical dimension, this may involve challenging climate-related official licensing, award or subsidy decisions, or the obligation to tighten climate protection targets, increase regulatory intervention, refrain from climate-damaging activities or disclose information, etc.[204] Between private individuals, it may involve compensation for climate change-related damage or the cessation of climate-damaging advertising[205] or other behaviour.

In Germany, lawsuits against private individuals are heard by the ordinary courts (civil matters, see 1.).[206] Lawsuits against the state are primarily dealt with by the administrative and constitutional courts. Access to legal protection concerning disputes under public law is governed by the Code of Administrative Court Procedure (VwGO) and the Environmental Appeals Act (UmwRG) (see 2.).[207]

1. Horizontal Climate Actions: Civil Legal Protection

The best-known horizontal German climate litigation is the civil proceedings brought by Peruvian plaintiff Lliuya against RWE AG.[208] The plaintiff saw his property in Peru under acute threat from flooding caused by climate change-induced rising water levels in a lagoon above the property. In 2025, the Higher Regional Court of Hamm recognised the merits of a civil claim[209] against RWE AG for contribution to the costs of appropriate measures to protect Lliuya's property from the anticipated consequences of climate change in the amount of its global share of emissions. This share undisputedly amounted to 0.47 %. The distance between the property and the source of emissions is irrelevant in this case. With regard to causality and attribution of climate change-related damage, the court entered dogmatic uncharted territory.[210] Nevertheless, the court dismissed the action because it denied the factual requirement of a concrete risk of flooding within the meaning of Section 1004(1) sentence 2 of the German Civil Code

---

203 *Fellenberg*, NVwZ 2022, 913 (913).

204 *Fellenberg*, NVwZ 2022, 913 (914); *Heymann*, IR 2022, 60 (60).

205 *Viniol*, GRUR-Prax 2023, 289; *Wasner*, GRUR-Prax 2023, 588; *Schlacke*, Sustainability and Consumer Protection Law in Germany, in: Schlacke, Sustainability and Consumer Protection Law in Brazil, China, Germany and Indonesia, 2022, p. 43.

206 Section 40(2) VwGO.

207 Section 13 Gerichtsverfassungsgesetz (GVG).

208 *Heymann*, IR 2022, 60 (62); *Fellenberg*, NVwZ 2022, 913 (920).

209 Sections 1004(1) sentence 2, 1011 and Sections 677 et seqq., Section 812 BGB.

210 Alternative view *Kieninger*, EuZW 2025, 849 (851 et seqq.).

(BGB) with a one per cent probability of occurrence within a period of 30 years.[211]

2. Vertical Climate Lawsuits: Administrative Legal Protection

Access to judicial administrative law protection in Germany requires that a plaintiff can assert a violation of their own substantive right – known as an action by an injured party.[212]

a) Individual Plaintiffs

In principle, individual plaintiffs, i. e. natural or legal persons under private or public law, such as municipalities, can take legal action and challenge renewable energy plant permits if their property rights may be infringed by the permit.[213] While these lawsuits hinder the energy transition.[214]

Lawsuits calling for more climate protection, i. e. ambitious contributions to the energy transition, are also admissible. In exceptional cases, individuals can lodge a constitutional complaint with the Federal Constitutional Court if they are able to substantiate a violation of fundamental rights in the form of a future, disproportionate restriction of freedom due to a currently insufficient greenhouse gas reduction burden (see above IV. 1.). Individuals cannot currently demand specific individual measures,[215] nor can they request the enactment of state climate protection laws.[216] In this respect, the Federal Constitutional Court only reprimands gross errors of discretion on the part of the legislature but does not decide on the exact dimensioning and distribution of the reduction burden.[217] This order is an expression of the separation of powers.

b) Association Plaintiffs

Environmental associations cannot take legal action against the state to call for increased climate protection and the implementation of the energy transition across the board; they are not entitled to bring a constitutional association lawsuit. However, they can bring climate protection-related issues before the courts if

[211] OLG Hamm, order of May 28, 2025– 5 U 15/17, ZUR 2025, 494 (501, n. 354(a)).

[212] Section 42(2) half-sentence 2 VwGO.

[213] See *Steinkemper*, in: Schlacke/Wagner (eds.), Klimarecht, 2026, § 14 n. 4 et seqq.

[214] *Schlacke/Römling*, in: Aarhus-Handbuch – Information, Beteiligung und Rechtsschutz in Umweltangelegenheiten, 2019, n. 1 et seqq.

[215] BVerfG, order of December 15, 2022– 1 BvR 2146/22, ZUR 2023, 234 (235).

[216] BVerfG, order of January 18, 2022– 1 BvR 1565/21 a.o., NJW 2022, 844 n. 9.

[217] *Winter*, ZUR 2022, 215 (216).

a law specifically grants them the right to sue.[218] In the environmental sector, such supra-individual legal standing exists for officially recognised environmental associations[219] in accordance with Section 2(1) of the Environmental Appeals Act (UmwRG). It contains an exhaustive list of subjects of legal action (Section 1(1) UmwRG). With regard to the energy transition, environmental associations, like individual plaintiffs, can challenge permits for renewable energy plants if, for example, they complain about deficiencies in an environmental impact assessment. However, environmental associations can also demand that the targets and measures of the climate protection programme[220] which are to be drawn up by the federal government, be tightened. A successful lawsuit brought by an environmental association to tighten the immediate programme under the Climate Change Act showed that the exhaustive list of subjects of legal action under the UmwRG is contrary to EU law because it is incomplete.[221] The current draft amendment to the UmwRG, which provides for a considerable expansion of the scope of application,[222] will not remedy this situation in a manner that complies with EU law.

VIII. Summary and Outlook: Trends and Developments in Energy Transition Law

The German energy transition, understood as the transformation of the energy system towards 100 % renewable energies with the aim of achieving climate neutrality by 2045 while simultaneously phasing out nuclear energy and coal-fired power generation, is unique compared to other populous industrialised nations in and outside Europe.

So far, it has been successful in achieving the legally enshrined targets in the electricity sector. The Renewable Energy Sources Act, which now not only provides for financial support and market integration of renewable energies but also gives them priority over other concerns (such as nature conservation and monument protection) in substantive law, is largely responsible for this success. This prioritisation acts as a right-of-way rule in controlling the expansion of onshore wind and photovoltaic installations and resolves land use conflicts. However, the expansion of energy transmission lines is proving more difficult, although it has

218 An overview of the so called meta-individual legal remedies in Germany, which includes environmental appeals is provided by *Schlacke*, § 102 Überindividuelle Rechtsbehelfe, in: Kahl/Ludwigs (eds.), Handbuch des Verwaltungsrechts, vol. 4, 2022, 385.

219 Recognition is granted in accordance by Section 3 UmwRG.

220 See Section 9 KSG.

221 OVG Berlin-Brandenburg, order of November 30, 2023 – 11 A 1/23, ZUR 2024, 300, see the note by *Schlacke*, NVwZ 2024, 564 et seqq.

222 Cf. https://www.bundesumweltministerium.de/gesetz/referentenentwurf-eines-gesetzes-zur-aenderung-des-umwelt-rechtsbehelfsgesetzes-und-weiterer-umweltrechtlicher-vorschriften-2025 (9.1.2026).

recently received a boost from further legal flexibilisation and acceleration measures. The building and transport sectors do not have a comparable track record, which on one hand is due to inconsistent funding instruments and, on the other hand, to a lack of core legislation. Finally, these sectors probably also face the strongest resistance from the population.[223]

Concerning access to justice, lawsuits by individuals and associations can hinder or promote energy transition projects. Climate lawsuits, which are primarily intended to generate media attention, are rare in Germany. Instead, administrative and civil courts focus on the application of the law. There is no evidence of case law exceeding the limits set by legislation. This situation is unlikely to change in the foreseeable future.

---

223 *Pritzsche/Vacha* (fn. 5), § 1 n. 31.

Artificial Intelligence in German Legal Education

Philipp Hacker

I. Introduction

German legal education stands at a crossroads where centuries-old traditions meet accelerating technological transformation. The country's distinctive two-examination system, which has produced generations of 'unified jurists' through rather rigorous doctrinal training, now faces fundamental questions about how artificial intelligence and digital tools will reshape legal practice and pedagogy. While Germany has been slower than some jurisdictions to embrace educational technology, COVID-19 accelerated digitization, and the 2024 EU AI Act has forced systematic reconsideration of how technology integrates into legal training. Against this background, this report provides an analysis of the traditional model, ongoing digital transformation, regulatory adaptations, and broader implications for the law's role in German society.

The integration of artificial intelligence into legal education has become a pressing concern for law faculties globally. Germany is no exception here. The digital transformation of legal education in general and the use of AI in particular present both opportunities for enhancing teaching quality and critical challenges regarding academic integrity, critical inquiry, examination practices, and professional preparation. As *Möslein* and *Hartmann* rightly observe, the question is no longer whether AI can be integrated into the daily work of lawyers, but only how its use can be sensible, responsible, and legally secure.[1]

The practical relevance of AI in the legal profession is beyond dispute. More than two-thirds of legal departments and law firms now use generative AI at least once a week.[2] This widespread adoption creates an urgent need to prepare law students for an AI-mediated professional environment.[3] The Legal Tech Monitor

---

1 *Möslein/Hartmann*, Künstliche Intelligenz in rechtswissenschaftlichem Studium und juristischer Praxis, JURA 2025, 1271, 1273; see also *Dötterl*, Der Elefant im Raum – Generative künstliche Intelligenz und die Zukunft der juristischen Ausbildung, OdW 2025, 155; *Bauermeister/Grünberger/Pesch*, Hamburger Protokoll: KI-Edition, 2026.

2 *Wolters Kluwer*, Future Ready Lawyer Studie (2024), www.wolterskluwer.com/de-de/know/future-ready-lawyer-2024 (17.12.2025).

3 *Möller-Klapperich*, Künstliche Intelligenz (KI) in der (universitären) juristischen Ausbildung, NJ 2025, 529, 530.

2025 reveals that over 80 % of German legal tech providers integrate AI into their business models, primarily for document analysis and generation.[4]

Against this background, the remainder of the report is structured as follows. Section 1 provides an overview of the traditional model of German legal education. Section 2 details descriptively the integration of digital technologies, including AI tools, in legal education and practice in Germany. The following Section 3 provides a critical evaluation of the use of AI in legally dictation, based on available theoretical discussions and empirical evidence. Section 4 offers an overview of legislative and regulatory developments dealing with AI in education. Based on this overview, Section 5 makes ten specific policy and institutional suggestions for dealing with AI in legal education, ranging from obvious proposals, such as strengthening critical AI literacy, to novel types of examination, and culminating in the proposal of a "mixed strategy" between AI exposure and renunciation in different classes. Section 6 provides perspectives on the law's societal role vis-à-vis the digital transformation, and Section 7 concludes.

II. The Traditional Model of German Legal Education

1. Legal University Education

a) The Einheitsjurist *and the Two-Examination Pathway*

German legal education operates on the foundational principle of the *Einheitsjurist* (unified jurist)[5] – the idea that all legal professionals, whether destined for the bench, the bar, or public administration, should receive identical foundational training. This distinguishes Germany from common-law jurisdictions where legal education follows separate tracks for barristers and solicitors or permits greater early specialization.

The pathway to becoming a fully qualified jurist requires successfully passing two state examinations: the First State Examination and the Second State Examination, with an intervening period of practical training. The first examination, formally known as the *Erste Juristische Prüfung* since 2003 reforms, comprises two components: a university-administered specialization portion accounting for 30 % of the final grade, and a state-administered compulsory subjects examination accounting for 70 %. Students face five to eight written examinations depending on their *Bundesland* (state), each lasting five hours, followed by oral

[4] *Legal Tech Verband*, Legal Tech Monitor (2025), www.legaltechverband.de/en/aktivitaeten/legal-tech-monitor-2025-a-market-in-transition/ (17.12.2025).

[5] *Korioth*, Legal Education in Germany Today, 24 Wis. Int'l LJ (2006), 85, 86; see this instructive article for more details on many of the other idiosyncrasies of German legal education.

examinations. The failure rate is notoriously high: approximately 25–30 % fail the First State Examination.[6]

University study preceding the first examination typically spans nine to ten semesters (4.5–5 years). The curriculum divides into the *Grundstudium* (foundation studies) covering introductory civil, criminal, and public law during the first two to three semesters; the *Hauptstudium* (main studies) exploring advanced doctrinal areas through semester six; and the *Schwerpunktbereich* (specialization phase) where students choose from areas such as corporate law, international law, or criminal law. The final two to three semesters are typically dedicated to intensive examination preparation.

b) Traditional Pedagogical Methods

German legal pedagogy traditionally centers on the *Vorlesung* (lecture): large-format sessions of 100–500+ students where professors present doctrinal content systematically. Lectures are supplemented by *Arbeitsgemeinschaften* (working groups), small-group tutorials of 15–30 students led by research assistants or advanced students.

The cornerstone of German legal methodology is the *Gutachtenstil* (expert opinion style), a prescribed analytical structure distinguishing German legal training from approaches elsewhere. The method follows four steps: the *Obersatz* (major premise/hypothesis) formulates the legal question using conditional phrasing; the *Definition* states the abstract legal requirements derived from statute, case law, and doctrine; the *Subsumtion* (subsumption) applies the facts to each element of the definition; and the *Ergebnis* (conclusion) confirms or denies the hypothesis.

c) Assessment and Grading

German legal education employs a distinctive 18-point grading scale: 16–18 points represents *sehr gut* (very good), 13–15 *gut* (good), 10–12 *vollbefriedigend* (fully satisfactory), 7–9 *befriedigend* (satisfactory), 4–6 *ausreichend* (sufficient/passing), 1–3 *mangelhaft* (poor), and 0 *ungenuegend* (insufficient). Grades of 16+ are almost never awarded; the average examination score hovers around 6 points. The threshold for *Prädikatsexamen* is 9 points. This implies that German legal education has, in contrast to other subjects, successfully avoided grade inflation so far.

---

[6] *Federal Office of Justice*, Ausbildungsstatistik, Übersicht über die Ergebnisse der Ersten Juristischen Prüfung im Jahre 2023 (neues Recht) (as at 11.6.2025) (pass rate of 72.5 %); see also *Redaktion Beck-aktuell*, Statistik 2021: Hälfte der erfolgreichen Jura-Prüflinge in Berlin erreicht Prädikat (Beck aktuell, 31. 7. 2023), https://rsw.beck.de/aktuell/daily/meldung/detail/statistik-der-juristischen-pruefungen-2021 (6.1.2026).

This demanding system creates intense pressure and has spawned a parallel industry of *Repetitorien*: private examination preparation courses. Many students attend commercial providers like Alpmann Schmidt, Hemmer, or Jura Intensiv, paying 2,000–4,000+ EUR for comprehensive courses. To counter this tendency, many universities now offer free *Universitätsrepetitorien* (UniRep programs).

d) Financing of Law Schools

German legal education operates predominantly through publicly funded universities. Since 2014, undergraduate study at public universities has been generally tuition-free throughout Germany. Students pay only modest semester fees of 100–350 EUR covering student services, public transport tickets, and administrative costs.

Three prominent private alternatives exist: Bucerius Law School in Hamburg, founded in 2000 as Germany's first private law school; EBS Law School in Wiesbaden; and the BSP Business & Law School in Berlin.

2. Professional Legal Education

a) The Referendariat*: Practical Training*

After first examination, aspiring jurists enter the *Referendariat*, a two-year period of compulsory practical training that reflects Germany's tradition of state-supervised professional formation. *Referendare* hold the status of civil servants on probation (*Beamte auf Widerruf*) and receive a very modest monthly salary from the state. The training rotates through mandatory *Stationen* (stages): three to four months at civil courts; a similar period in criminal courts or with public prosecutors, and then with administrative authorities; and several months at law firms. A final elective station permits placements at international organizations, foreign law firms, or in-house legal departments.

The second state examination (*Assessorexamen*) follows the *Referendariat* and emphasizes procedural law and practical legal drafting more heavily than the first examination. Pass rates are considerably higher, typically 85–90 %,[7] which reflects both the practical preparation and the self-selection of candidates who have already demonstrated competence by passing the First State Examination.

b) Pathways to Professional Roles

Completion of both examinations qualifies individuals for all regulated legal professions. To become a *Rechtsanwalt* (attorney), graduates apply for bar admission through their regional professional organization. No further exam or training is

[7] *Federal Office of Justice*, Ausbildungsstatistik, Übersicht über die Ergebnisse der Zweiten Juristischen Staatsprüfung im Jahre 2023 (neues Recht) (as at 11.6.2025).

required. Appointment as a *Richter* (judge) or *Staatsanwalt* (prosecutor) requires competitive grades – typically a *Prädikatsexamen* (distinction) – and proceeds through justice ministry selection. The *Notar* (civil-law notary) position is the most competitive and requires exceptional grades and/or extensive additional experience. Only approximately 30 % of candidates achieve *Prädikatsexamen* status (9+ points on the 18-point scale) in the first examination, and around 20 % in the second.[8]

c) Regulatory Framework

The *Deutsches Richtergesetz* (German Judges Act, DRiG) provides the federal framework for legal education. Section 5 establishes that qualification for judicial office requires both state examinations. Section 5a specifies core subjects (civil law, criminal law, public law, procedural law), and requires coverage of European law, legal methodology, and the philosophical and historical foundations of law. Notably, it mandates engagement with National Socialist and Communist injustice, a reflection of Germany's past and particular historical consciousness.

Because education is a state (*Länder*) competency, each of Germany's sixteen federal states enacts its own *Juristenausbildungsgesetz* (legal education law). The judicial examination offices, typically attached to Higher Regional Courts, administer the state examinations. The *Wissenschaftsrat* (German Council of Science and Humanities) provides advisory recommendations on legal education. Its influential 2012 report on the perspectives of legal study and academia in Germany noted that the limits of studyability had been reached due to curriculum expansion and called for strengthening foundational subjects while increasing interdisciplinarity.[9]

3. Digitization of Primary Legal Sources

Germany has achieved substantial digitization of primary legal materials, though commercial databases dominate comprehensive access. The Federal Ministry of Justice operates a dedicated legal domain, gesetze-im-internet.de, in partnership with juris GmbH, which provides free access to virtually all current consolidated federal laws and ordinances updated daily. English translations of over 100 major statutes are available. For case law, rechtsprechung-im-internet.de and other specific websites of individual courts offer a large amount of decisions from the highest federal courts, but also lower courts.

---

[8] *Steudle*, Prädikatsexamen: Die Noten im Jura-Studium (Beck Stellenmarkt, August 2025), www.beck-stellenmarkt.de/ratgeber/karriere/studium-berufsstart-weiterbildung/noten-im-jura-studium (6.1.2026).

[9] *German Science and Humanities Council*, Perspektiven der Rechtswissenschaft in Deutschland – Situation, Analysen, Empfehlungen (Dr S. 25 58–12, 9.11.2012), 7, 57.

However, comprehensive and easily searchable access to historical legislation, lower court decisions, and scholarly commentary requires commercial subscriptions. juris GmbH, partially government-owned, serves as the principal database provider for German courts and governmental authorities. beck-online, operated by leading legal publisher C.H. Beck, provides access to statutes, court decisions, and major commentaries. Beck recently launched Beck-Noxtua, an AI-enabled legal workspace combining database content with large language models trained for legal tasks (see also below, German Legal AI Tools).

III. Integration of Digital Technologies

1. Digital Infrastructure in Legal Education

a) Pre-COVID Digital Infrastructure

Before March 2020, German higher education's digital infrastructure was notably underdeveloped. A 2019 study found that only 1.7 % of German universities rated their teaching digitalization as 'well advanced.'[10] Germany ranked last in the CEPS Index of Readiness for Digital Lifelong Learning in Europe.[11] Research by Olaf Zawacki-Richter at the University of Oldenburg revealed that only 15.4 % of students had participated in a fully online course by 2018, and only 20.9 % had experienced blended learning.[12] This is not a concerning result per se, as some subjects – such as legal doctrine – may well benefit from in-person classes and pedagogy. But it does show that e-learning did not play a major role, and acceptance was actually declining before COVID: lecture recordings fell from rank 12 in student preferences in 2012 to rank 43 in 2018.[13]

The predominant learning management systems were ILIAS (developed at the University of Cologne in 1998) and Moodle, used primarily as document repositories rather than interactive teaching platforms.[14] Notable early Legal Tech initiatives included Bucerius Law School's Legal Tech Summer Program launched in 2018, and public lectures at various universities.[15]

---

10 *Gilch* et al., Digitalisierung der Hochschulen – Ergebnisse einer Schwerpunktstudie für die Expertenkommission Forschung und Innovation (Hannover: HIS-Institut für Hochschulentwicklung, 2019), 30.

11 *Beblavý* et al., Index of Readiness for Digital Lifelong Learning: Changing How Europeans Upgrade Their Skills (CEPS Final Report, 2019), www.ceps.eu/wp-content/uploads/2019/11/Index-of-Readiness-for-Digital-Lifelong-Learning.pdf (6.1.2026).

12 *Zawacki-Richter*, The current state and impact of Covid-19 on digital higher education in Germany, 3.1 Hum Behav Emerg Technol (2021), 218, 224.

13 *Zawacki-Richter*, 3.1 Hum Behav Emerg Technol (2021), 218, 223.

14 *Schochow/Steger*, State of digital education options in the areas of medical terminology and the history, theory and ethics of medicine, 32.2 GMS Zeitschrift für Medizinische Ausbildung (2015), 1, 3.

15 *Fries*, Legal Tech an meiner Uni? (Legal Tech Blog, 24.10.2018), https://legal-tech.blog/legal-tech-an-meiner-uni (6.1.2026).

b) COVID-19 Transformation

The pandemic forced radical acceleration. By peak lockdown, 85 % of European universities had shifted to distance learning.[16] German universities implemented 'Emergency Remote Teaching' within weeks, with platforms such as Zoom, Microsoft Teams, and the open-source BigBlueButton rapidly deployed.

German law faculties faced distinctive challenges: infrastructure gaps left many institutions unprepared for video conferencing at scale,[17] faculty digital literacy varied enormously, and the traditional emphasis on handwritten essay examinations proved particularly difficult to adapt.

Post-pandemic preference surveys at the University of Oldenburg found: 19 % of students wanted fully online teaching, 42 % preferred hybrid formats, and 39 % wanted to return to classroom instruction – a result which suggests lasting demand for digital options even as in-person teaching resumed.[18]

c) E-Examen: A Structural Innovation

The introduction of E-Examen (electronic state examinations) represents German legal education's most consequential structural change. Saxony-Anhalt pioneered electronic second state examinations in 2019 – before the pandemic. The rollout has accelerated dramatically: Saxony followed suit in 2021 and other states as well, such as Berlin/Brandenburg in December 2023, and Bavaria and North Rhine-Westphalia in 2024.

Adoption rates demonstrate overwhelming student preference for electronic format: 99 % of Berlin/Brandenburg *Referendare* chose E-Examen in January 2024, and 97 % in North Rhine-Westphalia.[19] Handwritten options remain available, electronic examination is voluntary.

In December 2024, the University of Bielefeld conducted a landmark pilot: the first fully digitalized law examination (but not for a state exam). Students used LexMea digital law books with personal annotations, and submissions were corrected by two different AI systems. This was characterized as a 'milestone in digital transformation of German legal education.'[20]

---

[16] *Zawacki-Richter*, 3.1 Hum Behav Emerg Technol (2021), 218, 218.

[17] *Skulmowski/Rey*, COVID-19 as an accelerator for digitalization at a German university: Establishing hybrid campuses in times of crisis, 2.3 Hum Behav Emerg Technol (2020), 212.

[18] *Zawacki-Richter*, 3.1 Hum Behav Emerg Technol (2021), 218, 219.

[19] *Schopf*, E-Examen: Staatsprüfung 2.0 oder Digitalisierung auf Deutsch? (Beck-aktuell, 22.3.2025), https://rsw.beck.de/aktuell/daily/meldung/detail/e-examen-staatspruefung-erstes-zweites-examen-laender-berlin-nrw (6.1.2026).

[20] *Harenberg*, Die erste komplett digitalisierte Juraklausur Deutschlands (LTO, 18.12.2024), www.lto.de/karriere/jura-studium/stories/detail/klausur-digitalisierung-jurastudium-pilot-online-gesetzbuch (6.1.2026).

d) Current Hybrid Teaching Models

Post-COVID, German law faculties have institutionalized hybrid approaches. LMU Munich uses Moodle as its primary platform with materials available digitally alongside primarily in-person lectures. My own European University Viadrina combines Moodle with Panopto video management and maintains an e-learning cooperation with WWU Münster through unirep-online.de, an exam preparation network that also includes the Universities of Bielefeld, Bochum, and the *FernUniversität* in Hagen.[21]

The latter remains Germany's only state distance-learning university and offers the full legal education program through digital formats with limited in-person requirements.

2. German Legal AI Tools

a) AI Tools for General Legal Use

Germany has developed distinctive legal AI tools that emphasize GDPR compliance and European data sovereignty.[22] Beck-Noxtua, branded as 'Europe's first sovereign Legal AI,' represents a partnership between publisher C.H. Beck and Berlin-based AI company Noxtua. Features include deep legal research, document review with matrix analyses, and contract drafting with change tracking. The platform is hosted on European servers (IONOS, Open Telekom Cloud) with certifications that include BSI C5, ISO 42001, 9001, and 27001 – a reflection of German emphasis on data protection and security.

Libra.ai offers a German-developed 'Legal AI Workspace' that integrates multiple AI models (GPT-4o, Mistral, Llama) in a GDPR-compliant environment with ISO 27001 certification. They recently partnered with the large legal publisher Wolters Kluwer for access to further legal materials. BRYTER AI provides AI Agents for law firms with hosting in Germany.[23]

b) AI Tools for Legal Education

German institutions have developed specialized AI tools for legal education.

aa) OneTutor

lmu.onetutor (OneTutor), originally developed by TUM students and deployed at LMU Munich's Law Faculty beginning Summer Semester 2025, represents a sig-

---

[21] *LTO-Karriere*, Jurastudium an der Universität Frankfurt (Oder) (undated), www.lto.de/karriere/jura-studium/unis/frankfurt-oder (6.1.2026).

[22] *Schillmöller*, Besser als ChatGPT? Diese fünf KI-Chatbots für Kanzleien sollten Sie kennen (Legal-Tech, 8.4.2025), https://legal-tech.de/fuenf-ki-chatbots-fuer-kanzleien/ (6.1.2026).

[23] See https://bryter.com/press-releases/bryter-partners-with-soldan/ (9.1.2026).

nificant educational innovation. The platform offers AI-generated quizzes curated by instructors and a RAG-based chatbot that accesses course-specific materials.[24] The goal is to offer students an alternative to general-purpose large language models, which can produce hallucinations, in the hope that the RAG-based system hallucinates less.[25] Winter 2024/25 pilot statistics were promising: 3,000 students, 100,000 quiz participations, and 50,000 chat messages.[26] The system is now deployed at over 30 German and Austrian universities across disciplines.[27] The project has spun off into a startup and is being studied through the 'AIffectiveness in Education' research project that spans five Bavarian universities.[28]

bb) LegalWriter

Another notable example is LegalWriter, a system developed at the University of Kassel as part of the Komp-HI project.[29] LegalWriter is a writing support system based on natural language processing and machine learning. It helps students learn the *Gutachtenstil* – the formal style of legal argumentation that is central to German legal education.

The system works by analyzing student submissions and marks which sentences conform to the *Gutachtenstil*. It identifies the structural components of legal argumentation, such as the *Obersatz* (definition), the *Subsumtion* (application), and the *Konklusion* (conclusion).[30] The system was trained on 413 case solutions from the general part of the German Civil Code (BGB) and uses a BERT-Transformer model to identify and classify the structure of legal examinations.[31] LegalWriter was first deployed at the University of Hamburg during the winter semester 2022/23 as part of a voluntary exam preparation course.[32]

---

24 *Bavarian Academy of Sciences and Humanities*, Effektiver studieren mit KI: Bayerische Hochschulen erproben Lernerfolg von Künstlicher Intelligenz im Hörsaal, Press Release (17.3.2025), https://badw.de/en/die-akademie/presse/pressemitteilungen/pm-einzelartikel/detail/effektiver-studieren-mit-ki-bayerische-hochschulen-erproben-lernerfolg-von-kuenstlicher-intelligenz-im-hoersaal.html (6.1.2026).

25 See *Ludwig-Maximilians-University Munich*, lmu.onetutor ai-enhanced learning (LMU, 17.3.2025), www.jura.lmu.de/de/aktuelles/newsuebersicht/news/lmu.onetutor-ai-enhanced-learning.html (17.12.2025).

26 *Schäffer*, LMU München setzt KI-Tutor für das Jurastudium ein (JURios, 8.5.2025), https://jurios.de/2025/05/08/lmu-muenchen-setzt-ki-tutor-fuer-das-jurastudium-ein/ (6.1.2026).

27 *Rinner*, Successful study with AI, TUM Press Release (8.10.2025), www.tum.de/en/news-and-events/all-news/press-releases/details/successful-study-with-ai accessed (6.1.2026).

28 *Bavarian Academy of Sciences and Humanities* (n. 23).

29 *Weber* et al., Intelligente Unterstützung beim Erlernen des Gutachtenstils im rechtswissenschaftlichen Studium, 11(4) ZDRW (2024), 336, 337.

30 *Weber* et al., 11(4) ZDRW (2024), 336, 339.

31 *Weber* et al., 11(4) ZDRW (2024), 336, 338.

32 *Weber* et al., 11(4) ZDRW (2024), 336, 341.

cc) Other Institutional Tools

The HTW Berlin provides all students and staff with data-privacy-compliant access to GPT-4o through a tool called ChatKI. Users log in with university credentials, and no personal data is transmitted to OpenAI.[33]

The University of Bayreuth launched ExamSim in winter 2024/25 – an AI-powered oral examination simulator.[34] At FAU Erlangen-Nürnberg, pilots in 2023/24 used ChatGPT to correct practice examinations in cooperation with the University of Passau's DeepWrite project.[35]

c) Pilot Projects and Research Initiatives

The University of Bielefeld launched a pilot project in 2025 that allows law students in family law to use AI-supported research tools for their seminar papers. The AI tool operates exclusively with verified content from the juris legal database and provides transparent source references. Students must adapt their declaration of independent work to document their responsible use of the technology.[36] The University of Saarbrücken has established the '*Juristisches KI-Projekt Saarbrücken*' (JIPS), which investigates the potential of generative language models for legal studies. Initial results indicate that AI makes many errors and often produces only mediocre substantive content, but can already be useful for formal tasks such as checking formatting requirements or finding legal references.[37] In a remarkable project, Christoph Engel and Johannes Kruse from the Max Planck Institute for Collective Goods have designed and trained an LLM-based system that competently drafted an entire legal commentary on freedom of assembly in the European Convention on Human Rights. According to their independent evaluation, the result is on par with its best human written competitor, the guide drafted by the Court itself.[38]

---

[33] See *HTW-Berlin University of Applied Sciences*, ChatKI – ChatGPT an der HTW Berlin (HTW, undated), www.htw-berlin.de/lehre/lehre-gestalten/ki-in-lehre-und-pruefungen/chatki (17.12.2025).

[34] *Schäffer*, ExamSim: Der KI-gestützte Prüfungssimulator an der Uni Bayreuth (JURios, 19.3.2025), https://jurios.de/2025/03/19/examsim-der-ki-gestuetzte-pruefungssimulator-an-der-uni-bayreuth/ (6.1.2026).

[35] *Friedrich-Alexander-University*, Chat-GPT korrigiert an der FAU juristische Probeklausuren, Press Release (15 October 2023), www.jura.rw.fau.de/chat-gpt-korrigiert-an-der-fau-juristische-probeklausuren/ (6.1.2026).

[36] See *Janowski*, Jura-Studierende schreiben als Erste Hausarbeit mit KI (Universität Bielefeld, 07.5.2025), https://aktuell.uni-bielefeld.de/2025/05/07/jura-studierende-schreiben-als-erste-hausarbeiten-mit-ki/ (17.12.2025).

[37] See *Saarland University*, Was bringen KI-Tools im Jurastudium? Juristisches KI-Projekt Saarbrücken stellt Ergebnisse vor (Saarland University 23.9.2025), www.uni-saarland.de/intern/news/jips-ki-tools-39664.html (17.12.2025).

[38] *Engel/Kruse*, Professor GPT. Having a Large Language Model Write a Commentary on Freedom of Assembly, Working Paper, 2024.

3. Institutional Guidelines, Policies and Specific Courses

a) Institutional Guidelines for AI Use

Several German universities have developed guidelines for the use of AI. The University of Tübingen's guidelines emphasize three core principles: critical-reflective use, transparency, and responsibility in the sense of good scientific practice.[39] The University of Regensburg permits general use of AI tools, subject to the requirement that AI-supported sections be clearly marked.[40] European University Viadrina has a similar policy.[41] In contrast, the Universities of Cologne and Münster prohibit the use of AI tools for the production of seminar papers.[42]

Free University Berlin offers KI.AssistßATßFU, a central access point for generative AI hosted on European infrastructures, which is supposed to ensure equitable, legally compliant access for all university members.[43] Heidelberg University established a university-wide framework recognizing AI's transformative potential while encouraging thoughtful, ethical, and legally compliant integration into scholarly endeavors. Students must submit declarations of independence and disclosure for all coursework, which specify AI tool use for text, images, videos, music, and any AI-created elements.[44]

b) Legal Tech Programs at German Universities

German universities have responded to the digitalization of law by establishing specialized programs that integrate AI and technology into legal education. The University of Würzburg offers an LL.M. in Digitalization & Law, which provides knowledge in IT law, legal tech, AI, computer science, and data protection law.[45] The University of Passau pioneered the Bachelor Legal Tech program in 2020, which represents one of the few German universities that offer undergraduate

---

39 See *University of Tübingen*, Guidelines for using generative AI tools (University of Tübingen, undated), www.internetofus.eu/uni-tuebingen.de/en/research/support/good-scientific-practice/guidelines-on-generative-ai/index.html (17.12.2025).

40 See *University of Regensburg*, Studium und Lehre Rechtswissenschaften (University of Regensburg, 25.11.2025), www.uni-regensburg.de/rechtswissenschaft/fakultaet/studium/index.html (17.12.2025).

41 See https://www.europa-uni.de/de/universitaet/profil/ki-viadrina/ki-richtlinie/index.html (9.1.2026).

42 *Möller-Klapperich*, NJ 2025, 529, 530.

43 See *Free University of Berlin*, Guidelines for the Use of AI-Based Systems and Tools in Teaching and Learning (FU, October 2025), www.ki.fu-berlin.de/_dokumente/Guidelines-for-the-Use-of-AI-Based-Systems-and-Tools-in-Teaching-and-Learning.pdf (17.12.2025).

44 See *University of Heidelberg*, Guidelines on the Use of AI in Teaching and Learning at Heidelberg University (University of Heidelberg, undated), https://backend.heiskills.uni-heidelberg.de/de/dokumente/ai-guideline-en/download (17.12.2025).

45 See *University of Würzburg*, LL.M. Digitalization & Law, www.jura.uni-wuerzburg.de/en/studium/postgraduales-studium/aufbau-und-masterstudiengaenge/llm-digitalization-law/ (17.12.2025).

degrees in this field.[46] Bucerius Law School's summer program in AI, Legal Technology, and Operations is an intensive, three-week course designed for students and young professionals to explore the future of the legal services market through classes and a final hackathon.[47]

The Munich Intellectual Property Law Center (MIPLC) has incorporated AI Law and Policy as a key curriculum area within its one-year intensive LL.M. program, alongside Data Economy Law and Digital Competition Law.[48] The University of Osnabrück offers a Master of European Technology Law, which targets graduates from law or informatics backgrounds.[49]

Legal tech programs at German universities have expanded significantly in recent years, typically combining traditional legal education with courses in computer science, data science and digital governance to prepare graduates for technology-driven legal practice. Institutions such as the University of Passau, University of Osnabrück and the University of Regensburg offer dedicated Legal Tech or Legal Informatics degrees that cover IT law, data protection, artificial intelligence and practical skills for designing and managing digital legal services in law firms, companies and public authorities. These programs are generally interdisciplinary, often open to both law graduates and technically trained professionals, and aim to train roles like legal engineers and technology-oriented lawyers who can bridge doctrinal analysis with automation, algorithmic tools and innovation in legal service delivery.

At European University Viadrina, legal tech is integrated into the broader digitalization agenda rather than offered as a stand-alone track, with the Master of Digital Entrepreneurship (MoDE) at the European New School of Digital Studies playing a central role by embedding law alongside economics, social science and computer science in project-based work on digital transformation.[50] Within MoDE, where I teach, students work in interdisciplinary teams on practice-oriented projects that address regulatory, entrepreneurial and technical aspects of digital innovation, which naturally includes issues of AI and platform regulation, data governance and algorithmic decision-making.

c) Specialized Courses and Lecture Series

Beyond degree programs, several German universities have introduced dedicated courses on AI in legal education. The University of Bayreuth offers an online lecture series on generative AI in legal training. This series addresses topics such

[46] See *University of Passau*, LL.B Legal Tech, www.uni-passau.de/en/llb-legal-tech (17.12.2025).

[47] See *Bucerius Law School*, AI, Legal Technology and Operations, www.law-school.de/international/education/bucerius-summer-programs/legal-technology-and-operations (18.12.2025).

[48] See Munich Intellectual Property Law Center, www.miplc.de (17.12.2025).

[49] See University of Osnabrück, www.uni-osnabrueck.de/fb10/en/fachbereich/institute/elsi/master-of-european-technology-law (17.12.2025).

[50] European New School of Digital Studies, https://europeannewschool.eu/ (20.3.2026).

as the use of AI for exam simulations and the preparation of seminar papers (*Hausarbeiten*).[51] Bucerius Law School takes a different approach through its AI Legal Club, which forms part of the school's executive education program. Participants complete an online course to prepare for the age of artificial intelligence.[52]

d) Generative AI Policies at German Universities

The *Hochschulrektorenkonferenz* (HRK, German Rectors' Conference), which represents 272 member institutions and 90 % of German students, has articulated key positions on AI. President Walter Rosenthal emphasized that universities must ensure GDPR-compliant AI use, prohibit personal data in AI prompts, require disclosure of AI use in seminar papers and research applications, and 'rethink exams' with a focus on knowledge application rather than mere recall.[53]

The *Hochschulforum Digitalisierung* (HFD) has developed a competency framework for AI use with seven recommendations. These include the identification of AI as a strategic institutional priority, promotion of general AI understanding, fostering of source criticism, and creation of spaces for interdisciplinary exchange.[54]

Academic integrity remains a central concern. There is clear consensus that presenting AI-generated text as one's own work constitutes plagiarism. However, AI detection tools remain unreliable, and this has prompted shifts toward oral examinations, competency-based assessment, and mandatory AI disclosure requirements.

e) European University Viadrina Policy on AI-Assisted Writing Tools

European University Viadrina has developed a detailed policy on the use of AI-assisted writing tools in examinations (adopted April 2025). The policy supports responsible, reflective, and transparent use of AI tools such as Large Language Models and systems like ChatGPT. It distinguishes them from tools that provide only language corrections (e. g., Grammarly, ProWritingAid), which are not covered.

---

51 See *University of Bayreuth*, Generative KI in der juristischen Ausbildung, www.jura.uni-bayreuth.de/de/studium/ki-im-studium/index.html (17.12.2025).

52 See *Bucerius Law School*, AI Legal Club, www.law-school.de/executive-education/im-fokus/ai-legal-club (17.12.2025).

53 *Schmermund*, Hochschulen müssen sichtbarer werden (Forschung und Lehre, 6.11.2023), www.forschung-und-lehre.de/management/hochschulen-muessen-sichtbarer-werden-6019 (6.1.2026).

54 *Filipovic* et al., Künstliche Intelligenz: Grundlagen für das Handeln in der Hochschullehre – Ergebnisse der Arbeitsgruppe 'Künstliche Intelligenz: Essenzielle Kompetenzen an Hochschulen' (Hochschulforum Digitalisierung, Arbeitspapier Nr. 86, 2025), 30 et seqq.

The policy establishes labeling obligations for text creation. If text passages are generated by AI and adopted verbatim by the student, they must be treated as direct quotes. They should be enclosed in quotation marks and properly cited in a footnote that indicates the AI tool used, the input prompt, and the date of generation. By contrast, if a student rewrites a text generated by AI, the passage does not require quotation marks but must be linguistically indicated as indirectly adopted. The footnote should specify the AI tool used, the input prompt, and the date of generation. The student should also indicate whether the text was adopted as-is or significantly altered.

For text editing and correction, other rules apply. If AI tools are used to rewrite or paraphrase text written by another person (e. g., QuillBot), the original author, source, AI tool, input prompt, and date must be cited. Texts translated with AI tools (e. g., DeepL) must include the original author, source, the AI translation tool used, and the date. If AI-generated content is only used for personal understanding and not directly or indirectly included in the examination, it does not need to be cited.

For long text pieces such as the MA thesis, students must submit a declaration that affirms that all AI-assisted writing tools used in the creation of the examination have been properly labeled and documented. The declaration should confirm that the work was independently written and only the indicated sources and tools were used. When assessed, an examination will be rated as insufficient if it merely consists of assembled AI-generated text passages.

f) MOOCs and Digital-Centered Legal Education

German law offerings on international platforms like Coursera and edX remain limited due to the specificity of German legal content. Domestic platforms dominate. The *Virtuelle Hochschule Bayern* (vhb) offers three program types: CLASSIC vhb (credit-bearing courses free for consortium students), OPEN vhb (free courses for everyone), and SMART vhb (shorter learning units). Law courses include International Criminal Law (LMU), administrative law, criminal law preparation, and comprehensive civil law offerings from University of Würzburg.

The unirep-online.de network connects WWU Muenster, University of Bielefeld, Ruhr-University Bochum, European University Viadrina, and *FernUniversität* in Hagen with exam preparation resources, and this includes a database of 500+ original examination cases and self-test modules.

IV. Evaluation of Legal AI Practices

1. Empirical Evidence from Classroom Experiments

The empirical literature on AI in legal education is growing but remains fragmented. A two-year classroom experiment conducted by Thibault Schrepel at the Vrije Universiteit Amsterdam provides instructive evidence.[55] The experiment divided students into three groups: one barred from using ChatGPT, one exposed to it without instruction, and one that received structured training in prompting and critical evaluation.

The results reveal several important findings. First, AI had almost no measurable effect on factual recall. Multiple-choice test scores were essentially flat across all groups, with performance gaps of only 0.12 to 0.21 points.[56] Second, structured AI training produced clear gains in open-ended exams and legal writing tasks. In 2024, the trained group scored 7.65 on the take-home exam, compared to 6.67 for the group without AI access.[57] By 2025, these differences narrowed as students became more familiar with AI tools on their own, but the trend remained: the trained group consistently outperformed others.[58] Third, and perhaps most importantly, the group without access to ChatGPT consistently finished last across both years. This finding suggests that prohibiting AI may have undesirable consequences as those who comply with this rule may be structurally disadvantaged concerning graded course outcomes vis-à-vis those who break the rule in unnoticed ways – a valid concern given the difficulty of detecting AI-generated writing faithfully.[59]

2. Evaluation of the LegalWriter System

These results mirror the outcomes of another study. The LegalWriter system was evaluated empirically at the University of Hamburg. The course was divided into two groups: a control group that worked without technical aids, and a treatment group that used the system.[60] The results showed positive effects on both *Gutachtenstil* adherence and overall exam grades. Students who trained with LegalWriter demonstrated better application of the formal argumentation style and achieved higher scores on their practice exams.

---

55 *Schrepel*, Generative AI in Legal Education: A Two-Year Experiment with ChatGPT, Law Innov Technol (forthcoming, 2026), 36 et seqq.

56 *Schrepel*, Law Innov Technol (forthcoming, 2026), 42 et seqq.

57 *Schrepel*, Law Innov Technol (forthcoming, 2026), 44.

58 *Schrepel*, Law Innov Technol (forthcoming, 2026), 45.

59 *de Melo*, Detecting AI-generated Content: Challenges and Opportunities, in: Hacker et al. (eds), The Oxford Handbook of the Foundations and Regulation of Generative AI, 2025, https://doi.org/10.1093/oxfordhb/9780198940272.013.0008 (6.1.2026).

60 *Weber* et al., 11(4) ZDRW (2024), 336, 341.

The system offers several advantages over traditional instruction, according to the authors. It provides immediate feedback, which allows students to correct errors and improve their writing in real time. The guidance is directly constructive, meaning students can implement suggestions at once rather than waiting for instructor comments. The system is available independent of location, time, and instructor availability, which is particularly valuable for students who cannot attend office hours or who prefer to study at unconventional times.[61]

3. Generic LLM Performance in Legal Tasks

This assessment is different for generic LLMs. Studies show that such large language models currently continue to struggle with specific tasks in the legal domain. In legal writing tasks, ChatGPT performs worse than average law students on assessments of substantive legal reasoning.[62] LLMs often fail to accurately summarize court decisions, as they miss relevant arguments or mischaracterize the holdings.[63] In the legal domain, Magesh and others (2025) evaluated, in the first preregistered empirical setting, several commercial AI legal research tools that claim to eliminate hallucinations through retrieval-augmented generation (RAG). The authors tested LexisNexis's Lexis+ AI, Thomson Reuters's Ask Practical Law AI, Westlaw's AI-Assisted Research, and GPT-4 with over 200 legal queries. The study revealed that the marketing claims of major legal research providers are overstated: hallucination rates ranged from 17% to 33% for the proprietary RAG-based tools. The authors identified several recurring failure modes, which included naive retrieval, inapplicable authority, sycophancy, and basic reasoning errors such as misunderstanding case holdings and failing to distinguish between legal actors.[64] These limitations highlight the importance of teaching students to verify AI outputs and to use the technology as a starting point rather than a final product.

The risk of hallucinations is particularly acute in legal contexts. German courts have already addressed cases where lawyers submitted fabricated citations generated by AI tools. The *AG* Cologne stated that lawyers must refrain from such practices because they hinder the finding of law, mislead uninformed readers, and damage the reputation of the rule of law.[65] The *LG* Frankfurt similarly noted

---

[61] *Weber* et al., 11(4) ZDRW (2024), 336, 341 et seq.

[62] *Choi* et al., ChatGPT Goes to Law School, 71 Journal of Legal Education (2023), 387, 391.

[63] *Deroy/Ghosh/Ghosh*, How Ready are Pre-trained Abstractive Models and LLMs for Legal Case Judgement Summarization?, Proceedings of the Third International Workshop on Artificial Intelligence and Intelligent Assistance for Legal Professionals in the Digital Workplace (2023), 8, 11.

[64] *Magesh* et al., Hallucination-Free? Assessing the Reliability of Leading AI Legal Research Tools, 22(2) J Empir Leg Stud (2025), 216.

[65] AG Köln, KIR 2025, 341 n. 24.

that it should be among the basic duties of lawyers not to invent legal citations or to adopt unverified text sources proposed by chatbots.[66]

4. *Cognitive Offloading and Critical Thinking*

While the use of AI tools may improve the grades of students in specific areas in the short-term, empirical research highlights the long-term problem of cognitive offloading. When students rely heavily on AI tools, their engagement in deep reflective thinking decreases.[67] Studies have found that younger users who frequently relied on AI had measurably lower critical thinking scores than those who did not use such tools regularly.[68] This finding raises concerns about whether allowing or encouraging AI use might handicap students' intellectual growth. Ultimately, the challenge is to manage the degree of offloading so that it supports learning rather than undermining it.

5. *Academic Integrity and Plagiarism*

Academic integrity presents a significant challenge. By 2024, approximately 92 % of UK undergraduates reported using AI tools for assessments.[69] Similar usage rates have been reported at Harvard.[70] Law professors grading exam answers have failed to recognize answers written entirely by ChatGPT. In one study, ten AI-generated answers were mixed with real student exam papers without the graders' knowledge; none of the graders suspected those answers were machine-produced.[71]

Traditional plagiarism detection tools typically rely on matching text to known sources, but AI generates new text that often evades such detection.[72] AI-output detectors exist, but they have high error rates and can mislabel original work as AI, which raises due process issues.[73] These findings suggest that relying solely on an honor system and punitive approaches may be insufficient; proactive pedagogical strategies are needed.

---

[66] LG Frankfurt/Main, NJW 2025, 3174 n. 3.

[67] *Gerlich*, AI Tools in Society: Impacts on Cognitive Offloading and the Future of Critical Thinking, 15 Societies (2025), 6.

[68] *Gerlich*, 15 Societies (2025), 6; *Schrepel*, Law Innov Technol (forthcoming, 2026), 25.

[69] *Freeman*, Student Generative AI Survey 2025 (HEPI Policy Note 61, 26.2.2025), www.hepi.ac.uk/reports/student-generative-ai-survey-2025/ (6.1.2026).

[70] *Hirabayashi* et al., Harvard Undergraduate Survey on Generative AI (2024), https://arxiv.org/abs/2406.00833 (6.1.2026).

[71] *Alimardani*, Generative artificial intelligence vs. law students: an empirical study on criminal law exam performance, 16 Law Innov Tech (2024), 777, 819.

[72] *Schrepel*, Law Innov Technol (forthcoming, 2026), 21.

[73] *Schrepel*, Law Innov Technol (forthcoming, 2026), 22.

6. The Challenge of Long-Form Assignments

The emergence of generative AI compels academia to reconsider not only day-to-day assessments but also the role of long-form assignments, such as master theses in European curricula (see also below in the policy proposals, "Redesign Assessments"). Traditionally, the thesis has been valued as a culminating exercise. Students are expected to synthesize the literature, formulate a research question, and sustain an argument in written form. Its distinctive virtue lay in forcing students to undergo a prolonged process of research and writing, an exercise in intellectual endurance that shorter memos prepared during the year cannot replicate.[74]

AI undercuts this rationale. By scaling writing in minutes, tools such as large language models, and especially the new 'deep research' functions, strip away the pedagogical value of long-form engagement that once justified the thesis. With sufficient prompting, current models produce literature reviews that meet accepted standards of coherence. As detection is unreliable, the thesis increasingly loses its function as a test of individual mastery.[75]

V. Legislative and Regulatory Adaptations

1. The Legislative Framework

a) German Legislation Governing AI in Education

Germany lacks dedicated federal legislation that specifically governs AI use in education. The regulatory framework instead relies on horizontally applicable regulations: the DSGVO/GDPR[76] governs all personal data processing in educational contexts, and this includes AI-based systems; it is supplemented by the *Bundesdatenschutzgesetz* (BDSG).[77] Higher education laws (*Hochschulgesetze*) are enacted at the state level, and most have not yet been specifically updated to address AI tools.

According to academic analysis, fundamental questions remain legally unsettled: whether unmarked use of AI writing tools like ChatGPT in academic papers constitutes academic dishonesty under existing regulations, and whether examination regulations require modification.[78] The *Datenschutzkonferenz* (DSK,

---

[74] *Schrepel*, Law Innov Technol (forthcoming, 2026), 32 et seqq.

[75] *Schrepel*, Law Innov Technol (forthcoming, 2026), 33.

[76] Regulation (EU) 2016/679 of the European Parliament and of the Council of 27 April 2016 on the protection of natural persons with regard to the processing of personal data and on the free movement of such data (General Data Protection Regulation), OJ L 119, 4.5.2016, 1.

[77] Bundesdatenschutzgesetz in the version of 30.6.2017 (BGBl. I S. 2097), das zuletzt durch Artikel 7 des Gesetzes vom 23.6.2021 (BGBl. I S. 1858) geändert worden ist = Federal Data Protection Act of 30.6.2017 (Federal Law Gazette I p. 2097), as last amended by Article 10 of the Act of 23.6.2021 (Federal Law Gazette I, p. 1858; 2022 I p. 1045).

[78] *Zielinski*, ChatGPT in German Examination Law, 12 International Journal of Academic Research and Reflection (2024), 10.

conference of German data protection authorities) published guidance in May 2024 ('Orientierungshilfe Künstliche Intelligenz und Datenschutz') that provides data protection principles applicable to educational AI use.[79]

b) EU AI Act: Classification of Educational AI as High-Risk

The EU AI Act[80] represents the world's first comprehensive AI regulatory framework with direct applicability in Germany. The implementation timeline proceeds in stages: February 2, 2025 marks the date when prohibited AI practices take effect and AI literacy requirements applied;[81] August 2, 2025 is when General Purpose AI model obligations started;[82] August 2, 2026 is when most high-risk AI system requirements become fully applicable, even though this deadline is currently under negotiation in the AI Omnibus package;[83] and August 2, 2027 marks the deferred and currently also discussed application deadline for certain high-risk AI in regulated products.[84]

Under Annex III, Section 3 (Education and vocational training), the following are classified as high-risk AI systems: AI that determines access or admission to educational institutions; AI that evaluates learning outcomes (this includes AI that steers learning processes); AI that assesses appropriate education levels; and AI that monitors and detects prohibited behavior during tests (proctoring).[85] Recital 56 explicitly states that 'AI systems used in education or vocational training [...] should be considered high-risk, since they may determine the educational and professional course of a person's life.'[86]

---

[79] *Data Protection Conference*, Orientierungshilfe der Konferenz der unabhängigen Datenschutzaufsichtsbehörden des Bundes und der Länder: Künstliche Intelligenz und Datenschutz, Version 1.0, 6.5.2024.

[80] Regulation (EU) 2024/1689 of the European Parliament and of the Council of 13.6.2024 laying down harmonised rules on artificial intelligence and amending Regulations (EC) No 300/2008, (EU) No 167/2013, (EU) No 168/2013, (EU) 2018/858, (EU) 2018/1139 and (EU) 2019/2144 and Directives 2014/90/EU, (EU) 2016/797 and (EU) 2020/1828 (Artificial Intelligence Act), OJ L 2024/1689, 12.7.2024.

[81] Regulation (EU) 2024/1689 of the European Parliament and of the Council [2024] OJ L2024/1689, Arts. 113(a), Art. 4 AI Act.

[82] Regulation (EU) 2024/1689 of the European Parliament and of the Council 2024] OJ L2024/1689, Art. 113(b).

[83] Regulation (EU) 2024/1689 of the European Parliament and of the Council 2024] OJ L2024/1689, Art. 113; see also *Hacker/Kilian/Costas*, "Simplifying" European AI Regulation. An Evidence-based Study (Bertelsmann, 2025), https://www.bertelsmann-stiftung.de/en/publications/publication/did/simplifying-european-ai-regulation-an-evidence-based-study (9.3.2026).

[84] Regulation (EU) 2024/1689 of the European Parliament and of the Council 2024] OJ L2024/1689, Art. 113(c).

[85] Regulation (EU) 2024/1689 of the European Parliament and of the Council 2024] OJ L2024/1689, Art. 6(2) in conjunction with Annex III, Section 3(a)-(d).

[86] Regulation (EU) 2024/1689 of the European Parliament and of the Council 2024] OJ L2024/1689, Recital 56.

Additionally, emotion recognition in educational institutions has been prohibited as of February 2025 (except for medical or safety reasons).[87] Universities that use AI for admissions, grading, or learning assessment are considered 'deployers' under Article 3(4).[88] Compliance requirements include risk management systems, data governance, technical documentation, transparency, human oversight, adequate performance, post-market surveillance, and registration in a dedicated EU database.[89]

c) German AI Act Implementation: the KIMIG

The *KI-Marktüberwachungs- und Innovationsförderungsgesetz* (KI-MIG), building on an earlier draft (KIMÜG) from late 2024 that aimed to designate national enforcement authorities for the AI Act, was delayed by the February 2025 federal elections.[90] The Federal Ministry for Digital Affairs and Government Modernisation (BMDS) now bears responsibility for the German implementation. The new coalition government has reaffirmed commitment to 'low bureaucracy, innovation-friendly' AI Act implementation.[91] In February 2024, the Federal Ministry of Justice (BMJ) also emphasized this, and characterized the AI Act as product regulation rather than research regulation – a signal of intent to avoid excessive compliance burdens on universities and research institutions.[92]

---

[87] Regulation (EU) 2024/1689 of the European Parliament and of the Council 2024] OJ L2024/1689, Art. 5(1)(f).

[88] Regulation (EU) 2024/1689 of the European Parliament and of the Council 2024] OJ L2024/1689, Art. 3(4).

[89] *Ehlers*, AI Act: This applies to AI in universities and research (KPMG Law, 20.3.2025), https://kpmg-law.de/en/ai-act-this-applies-to-ai-in-universities-and-research (6.1.2026).

[90] *Federal Ministry for Digital Transformation and Government Modernisation*, Entwurf eines Gesetzes zur Durchführung der Verordnung (EU) 2024/1689 des Europäischen Parlaments und des Rates vom 13.6.2024 zur Festlegung harmonisierter Vorschriften für künstliche Intelligenz KI-Marktüberwachungs- und Innovationsförderungsgesetz – KI-MIG) (Referentenentwurf, 12.09.2025), https://bmds.bund.de/service/gesetzgebungsverfahren/gesetz-zur-durchfuehrung-der-ki-verordnung (5.1.2026); *Federal Ministry for Digital Transformation and Government Modernisation*, KI-Aufsicht: Start für Konsultationen zum Gesetzentwurf (12.09.2025, Pressemitteilung 11/2025), https://bmds.bund.de/aktuelles/pressemitteilungen/detail/ki-aufsicht-start-fuer-konsultationen-zum-gesetzentwurf (5.1.2026).

[91] Koalitionsvertrag zwischen CDU, CSU und SPD, 21. Legislaturperiode, April 2025, 70.

[92] *Federal Ministry of Justice*, Positionspapier: Innovationsfreundliche und praxistaugliche Umsetzung der KI-Verordnung, Februar 2024, 2.

2. Lawyerly and Professional Guidelines

a) BRAK Guidelines: Professional Ethics for AI Use

The *Bundesrechtsanwaltskammer* (BRAK, Federal Chamber of Lawyers) published comprehensive guidance on AI use in December 2024 (*Hinweise zum Einsatz von künstlicher Intelligenz*).[93]

Core principles derive from existing professional obligations. Section 43 BRAO (Federal Lawyers Act) requires '*gewissenhafte Berufsausübung*' (conscientious professional practice) – AI serves for support only, not replacement.[94] Section 613 BGB (Civil Code) mandates personal responsibility: lawyers must conduct independent review and final control of all AI outputs.[95] There is currently no obligation to use AI, though Section 5 BORA (Rules of Professional Practice, office requirements) may require AI and Legal Tech in mass proceedings contexts.[96]

Attorney-client privilege under Section 43a(2) BRAO creates additional specific constraints.[97] Confidential client information must remain protected when AI is used. BRAK recommends 'abstract' prompts and anonymization of uploaded documents.[98] AI use does not trigger Section 203 StGB (criminal breach of confidentiality) penalties if properly managed through contractual and technical safeguards.[99]

IT-outsourcing rules under Section 43e BRAO govern relationships with AI providers.[100] Providers may access confidential information only if necessary, and the need-to-know principle applies strictly.[101] Providers must be contractually bound to confidentiality with acknowledgment of criminal law consequences. BRAK expresses preference for EU/German server locations and notes that OpenAI was not EU-US Data Privacy Framework certified as of December 2024 – a fact which requires extra measures for US-based tools.[102]

b) Positions of the German Lawyers' Association

The *Deutscher Anwaltverein* (DAV, German Lawyers' Association) issued its AI Working Group's July 2025 initiative statement, which affirms that AI use is permitted under strict observance of professional ethics, data protection, copyright,

---

93 *Remmertz*, Hinweise zum Einsatz von künstlicher Intelligenz, BRAK-Mitt. (2024).
94 Section 43 BRAO.
95 Section 613 BGB.
96 *Remmertz* (n. 93), 2.33; Section 5 BRAO.
97 Section 43a(2) BRAO.
98 *Remmertz* (n. 93), 3.1, 3.
99 Section 203 StGB; *Remmertz* (n. 93), 3.
100 Section 43e BRAO.
101 *Remmertz* (n. 93), 3.2, 3.
102 *Remmertz* (n. 93), 3.3, 4.

and trade secret protections.[103] Mandatory independent verification of AI outputs is required. External AI and cloud providers may be used without client consent if necessary and if they are contractually bound under Section 43e BRAO. There is no general anonymization duty when properly contracted service providers are used – free public tools, however, require complete anonymization before any confidential information is input.[104]

Earlier DAV positions include Position Paper 57/2021, which supported the risk-based approach of the then-proposed AI Act while criticizing the narrow AI definition. DAV advocated for five risk levels rather than binary high/non-high risk classification, called for prohibition of fully automated judicial decisions, and supported biometric surveillance bans.[105] In 2025, DAV partnered with BRYTER to provide its approximately 60,000 member lawyers access to the BEAMON AI platform.[106]

c) European Professional Guidelines

The Council of Bars and Law Societies of Europe (CCBE) and the European Lawyers Foundation jointly published the 'Guide on the use of Artificial-Intelligence-based tools by lawyers and law firms in the EU' in 2022, which emerged from the AI4Lawyers Project (2020–2022).[107] The CCBE also contributed to the 'European Ethical Charter on the Use of AI in Judicial Systems'[108] by the European Commission for the Efficiency of Justice (CEPEJ) and published 'CCBE Considerations on the Legal Aspects of Artificial Intelligence.'[109] Key concerns include independence when AI tools may interfere with lawyer autonomy, and warnings about large clients potentially pressuring smaller firms regarding AI adoption. The European Bars Federation (FBE) published 'European Lawyers in the Era of ChatGPT' (2023), which the BRAK (*Bundesrechtsanwaltskammer*) recommends as supplementary guidance.[110]

---

[103] *German Bar Association*, Initiativ-Stellungnahme zum Einsatz von KI in der Anwaltschaft, DAV-SN Nr. 32/2025, July 2025.

[104] *Ibid.*, 11.

[105] *German Bar Association*, Stellungnahme zum Vorschlag der EU-Kommission für eine Verordnung zur Festlegung harmonisierter Vorschriften für künstliche Intelligenz, DAV-SN Nr. 57/2021, November 2021.

[106] *German Bar Association*, Neuer DAV-Kooperationspartner: BRYTER bringt KI in die Kanzleien, DAV-Depesche 27(2025)7/25, 11.7.2025.

[107] *Council of Bars and Law Societies of Europe/European Lawyers Foundation*, Guide on the use of Artificial Intelligence-based tools by lawyers and law firms in the EU (31.3.2022).

[108] *Council of Europe*, European Ethical Charter on the use of Artificial Intelligence in Judicial Systems and their environment, CEPEJ (2018)14, (4.12.2018).

[109] *CCBE*, CCBE Considerations on the Legal Aspects of Artificial Intelligence, (2020) CCBE.

[110] *Federation des Barreaux d'Europe*, European Lawyers in the Era of ChatGPT: Guidelines on how lawyers should take advantage of the opportunities offered by large language models and generative AI (FBE Report, June 2023): Guidelines on how lawyers should take advantage of the opportunities offered by large language models and generative AIFBE Report June.

3. Judicial Perspectives and AI Strategy

The June 2025 *Bund-Länder-Digitalgipfel* (federal-state digital summit) produced a joint declaration that adopted a *KI-Strategie* (AI Strategy) for the German judiciary.[111] Core principles emphasize that human decision-making must remain paramount: that technology only serves to support, not to replace human judiciaries.

Current AI pilot projects in German courts include: *OLGA* (*OLG* Stuttgart) for AI-assisted analysis of diesel scandal appeals[112]; FraUKE (*AG* Frankfurt) for adjudicating mass proceedings, like flight passenger rights Codefy for document structuring in complex cases (*LG* Frankfurt)[113]; AKIRA (Baden-Wuerttemberg) as an AI assistant for social courts developed with Aleph Alpha[114]; JANO for AI anonymization of judgments (Baden-Wuerttemberg/Hessen)[115]; ALeKS (Bavaria/Niedersachsen) for AI anonymization and headnote creation[116]; and GSJ (*Generatives Sprachmodell der Justiz*) as a Bavaria/NRW joint project with TU Munich and Cologne University[117].

The 200 million EUR *Digitalisierungsinitiative für die Justiz* (2023–2026) supports a central AI platform for shared solutions across jurisdictions. Goals include an increase in court decision publication rates from the current level below 3 %.[118] AI systems 'intended to assist a judicial authority in researching and inter-

---

[111] *The Federal and State Ministers of Justice*, Gemeinsame Erklärung zum Einsatz von Künstlicher Intelligenz in der Justiz, Sechster Bund-Länder-Digitalgipfel, (Juni 2025); *E-Justice-Rat*, Strategie für den Einsatz von Künstlicher Intelligenz in der Justiz, Version 1.0 (April 2025).

[112] *Spoenle*, Künstliche Intelligenz im Einsatz bei Dieselverfahren, DRiZ 2023, 68.

[113] *Hessian Ministry of Justice*, KI-Projekt Codefy am Landgericht Frankfurt gestartet (Hessian Ministry of Justice, 2023), https://justizministerium.hessen.de/presse/pressearchiv/ki-projekt-codefy-am-landgericht-frankfurt-gestartet (5.1.2026).

[114] *Ministry of Justice Baden-Württemberg*, Assistenzprogramm zur Aktenstrukturierung in der Justiz gestartet (Ministry of Justice Baden-Württemberg, 2024), https://www.baden-wuerttemberg.de/de/service/presse/pressemitteilung/pid/assistenzprogramm-zur-aktenstrukturierung-in-der-justiz-gestartet (5.1.2026).

[115] *Hessian Ministry of Justice*, Hessen und Baden-Württemberg setzen KI-Tool JANO künftig in der Justiz ein (Hessian Ministry of Justice, 2025), https://justizministerium.hessen.de/presse/hessen-und-baden-wuerttemberg-setzen-ki-tool-jano-kuenftig-in-der-justiz-ein (5.1.2026).

[116] *Lower Saxony Ministry of Justice*, Künstliche Intelligenz und Automation in der Justiz (Lower Saxony Ministry of Justice, 2023), www.mj.niedersachsen.de/startseite/kunstliche_intelligenz_und_automation_in_der_justiz/kunstliche-intelligenz-und-automation-in-der-justiz-246705.html (5.1.2026).

[117] *Bavarian State Chancellery*, Künstliche Intelligenz im Einsatz für die Justiz: Start für gemeinsames Forschungsprojekt von Bayern und NRW – Generatives Sprachmodell soll Richterinnen und Richter entlasten (Bavarian State Chancellery, 2024), www.bayern.de/kuenstliche-intelligenz-im-einsatz-fuer-die-justiz-start-fuer-gemeinsames-forschungsprojekt-von-bayern-und-nrw-generatives-sprachmodell-soll-richterinnen-und-richter-entlasten-wissenschaftliche (5.1.2026).

[118] *Federal Ministry of Justice and Consumer Protection*, Gerichtsentscheidungen durch KI leichter veröffentlichen (Federal Ministry of Justice and Consumer Protection, 2023), www.bmjv.de/DE/themen/digitales/digitalisierung_justiz/digitalisierungsinitiative/laendervorhaben/_doc/artikel_vorhaben_14_ALeKS.html (5.1.2026).

preting facts and the law' are classified as high-risk under Annex III Nr. 8a of the AI Act – though this applies to judicial authorities, not to lawyers who use AI for case preparation.[119]

The *34. EDV-Gerichtstag* (September 2025, Saarbrücken) convened under the theme 'Next Generation Law – Von AI bis ZPO digital,' and addressed effective civil law enforcement, access to justice, Legal Tech, AI's transformation of work, and media regulation modernization.[120]

Finally, in a rare case involving potential rights for an AI system, the BGH DABUS Decision (June 11, 2024, X ZB 5/22) confirmed that only natural persons can be inventors under German patent law – AI systems cannot be named as inventors.[121]

VI. Policy and Institutional Recommendations

The observations in the preceding sections lead to ten policy and institutional recommendations, which culminate in the suggestion of a 'mixed strategy' approach: it combines AI-free foundational courses where students master core legal research, analysis, and writing skills with dedicated AI-enhanced courses that teach responsible use of AI tools and systematic verification techniques to address the hallucination problem.

1. Maintain Pedagogical Freedom

The first credo in legal education should be pedagogical freedom, within the constraints of the mixed strategy pursued by the institution as a whole. Calls for centralized and uniform rules that dictate what individual members of the teaching body may or may not do should be resisted. Such approaches run contrary to the ethos of intellectual independence that sustains higher education. Professors should be encouraged to experiment with different ways of integrating AI into the classroom without fear of restrictive guidelines.[122] Pedagogy thrives on ownership, not prescription, so professors must remain free to experiment. Overall, the institution only needs to ensure that, between the different formats chosen by different teachers, the mixed strategy remains active and in place. This may, in some cases, require specific rules on the use or prohibition of AI for certain professors who teach core classes in the mixed strategy approach.

---

119 Art. 6(2) in conjunction with Annex III, Section 8(a) AI Act.

120 *74. Deutscher Juristentag*, Thesenpapier: Next Generation Law – Von AI bis ZPO digital, September 2024, DGVB; Neuer Schwung für die Justizdigitalisierung – Der 34. EDV-Gerichtstag setzt die Agenda (DGVB, 2025), https://dgvb.de/neuer-schwung-fuer-die-justizdigitalisierung-der-34-edv-gerichtstag-setzt-die-agenda (5.1.2026).

121 BGH 11.6.2024 – X ZB 5/22, GRUR 2024, 1182.

122 *Schrepel*, Law Innov Technol (forthcoming, 2026), 49.

2. Invest in Faculty Training

Many instructors currently feel ill-equipped to provide AI instruction themselves.[123] Effective teaching with technology requires technological knowledge, pedagogical knowledge, and content knowledge.[124] This is known as the TPACK model (Technological Pedagogical Content Knowledge).[125] Law professors need support in all three areas to teach effectively with AI: understanding the AI tools, knowing how to teach with them, and integrating them appropriately into the legal subject matter. Institutional efforts should include formal workshops, continuing legal education modules, peer-to-peer faculty exchanges, and partnerships with industry experts. Wherever possible, open-source and locally hosted tools should be used for reasons of data protection and data sovereignty.[126]

3. Develop AI Literacy as a Core Competence

AI literacy should be treated as a core lawyering skill, akin to legal writing or statutory interpretation.[127] The competencies that need to be taught can be organized according to the 'AI Literacy Heptagon,' which conceptualizes AI literacy as a set of seven interrelated competencies spanning technical, legal, ethical, and societal dimensions. Within the context of legal education, the needed competencies include the ability to critically evaluate AI outputs, to verify sources and citations, to understand the limitations and risks of AI tools, to use AI in compliance with professional responsibility rules, and to document the use of AI in legal work products.[128]

The competencies required for AI use in legal practice can be divided into three leve: basic competencies (*Basiskompetenzen*), application competencies (*Anwendungskompetenzen*), and development competencies (*Entwicklungskompetenzen*).[129] Basic competencies include understanding the relationship between prompts and output quality, as well as the legal risks associated with AI use, such as copyright infringement, data protection violations, and professional responsibility issues. These basic competencies should be part of university education from the beginning of legal studies. The other competences can be added at later stages.

---

[123] *Schrepel*, Law Innov Technol (forthcoming, 2026), 50.

[124] *Bliss*, A conversation with John Bliss on the benefits and risks of generative AI for lawyers, Harvard Law School, Center on the Legal Profession (14.2.2024).

[125] *Rodríguez Moreno/Agreda Montoro/Ortiz Colon*, Changes in teacher training within the TPACK model framework, 11 Sustainability (2019), 1870.

[126] See also *Zenner* et al., The European Way, Report, 2025.

[127] *Schrepel*, Law Innov Technol (forthcoming, 2026), 50–51.

[128] *Hackl/Müller/Sailer*, The AI Literacy Heptagon: A Structured Approach to AI Literacy in Higher Education (arXiv preprint arXiv:2509.18900, 2025), https://arxiv.org/pdf/2509.18900 (6.1.2026).

[129] *Möller-Klapperich*, NJ 2025, 529, 531.

4. Redesign Assessments

Notably, traditional assessment formats require reconsideration. If an AI can produce a passing answer on a law school exam, traditional assessments may no longer effectively distinguish students' knowledge.[130] A group of German law professors recently proposed a differentiated framework for legal assessments in 2030.[131] Their core premise is that legal education should test skills that correspond to a modern legal work environment – skills that current examination formats no longer adequately capture. They suggest three layers of increasingly digitally meditated examinations, and revised rules for take-home exams.

A first and rather straightforward response is to preserve examinations without AI access. The ability to critically evaluate AI-generated content presupposes that students have first acquired legal knowledge and methodological competence on their own. Situations will persist – in oral arguments, client consultations, or scholarly debate – where lawyers must recall knowledge without technological assistance. For this reason, conventional written exams without access to databases or AI tools remain necessary. This corresponds to the AI-free zones in the mixed strategy.

A second, additional response according to the authors is to introduce 'hybrid exams' with limited digital tools. Similar to examinations in the German second state exam that allow access to legal commentaries, universities could permit access to a restricted set of online legal databases without large language models. Students would face numerous standard legal problems and demonstrate their ability to quickly identify and correctly analyze issues. The expectation of performance rises because students no longer need to memorize schemas and definitions.

The third response is to create 'AI exams' with full digital access. Students would have access to all available digital tools – legal databases, large language models, and other AI applications – to produce a legal opinion under supervision within a limited time (for example, five hours). The assigned fact patterns would contain significantly more and more demanding legal problems. The evaluation would assess both the capacity to handle complex legal questions and the competent, critical use of the permitted digital tools. Students could be required to include linked source references, as they would in a research paper.

For take-home assignments such as term papers, AI use will become practically impossible to prohibit.[132] Rather than abolish these formats, they can be transformed into 'AI-assisted papers.' AI tools would be permitted for text generation, but students would remain responsible for verifying sources and following the principles of good scholarly practice. When the AI fabricates citations or

---

[130] *Schrepel*, Law Innov Technol (forthcoming, 2026), 29 et seqq.

[131] *Fries* et al., Juristisches Prüfen 2030 (Verfassungsblog, 23.9.2025), https://verfassungsblog.de/juristisches-prufen-2030/ (6.1.2026); see also *Dötterl*, OdW 2025, 155, 164 et seq.

[132] *Ibid.*

plagiarizes, the student bears responsibility. The difficulty of the assignment and the expected quality of the work must rise accordingly. Topic-based papers that raise entirely new questions – such as an analysis of a recent judgment with little existing commentary – are particularly well-suited to this approach.

Such AI-assisted papers should, where feasible, be supplemented by rigorous oral examinations. This combination allows instructors to verify whether students have engaged with the material in depth and can answer follow-up questions spontaneously. The oral component might be weighted more heavily, or a single combined grade might be awarded.

Next to this proposed framework, Schrepel suggests an alternative to the traditional master thesis as a 'Master Dossier.' Rather than evaluate students solely on a final written product, this model would assess how students process legal knowledge in a world with AI. On top of the quality of the argument, the dossier would evaluate how students prompt, verify, and refine AI outputs, how ethically they deploy the technology, and how they demonstrate professional judgment in the identification of errors and limitations. Students would be required to submit a personal reflection that documents their journey with AI use over the course of the program.[133]

5. *Establish Clear Policies*

Universities should set clear policies and honor code rules around AI usage, paired with education on those policies. As Schrepel suggests, policies should state plainly when an assignment requires exclusive human authorship. For other evaluations, instructors may allow AI use but require full disclosure, such as mandating that students append the raw AI output and cite any AI-generated language.[134] Transparency should also apply to privacy, copyright, and other legal constraints. Students should be informed about the privacy implications of any AI tools they are required to use,[135] as well as potential copyright implications.

6. *Document and Share Best Practices*

Law schools have prioritized classroom trials over sustained investment in faculty development, experimentation, and evaluation. Hence, new projects are needed, but they require consistent documentation and rigorous assessment. The objective is to create an extensive, practice-oriented repository of instructional strategies. To extract meaningful insight from this worldwide effort, institutions need a standardized framework for recording methods and performance indicators that

---

133 *Schrepel*, Law Innov Technol (forthcoming, 2026), 54.

134 *Schrepel*, Law Innov Technol (forthcoming, 2026), 31.

135 *Balan*, Examining the ethical and sustainability challenges of legal education's AI revolution, 31(3) Int J Legal Prof (2024), 330.

support comparison and shared learning across schools.[136] German law faculties should share their experiences through publications, conferences, and inter-institutional networks.

7. Invest in Infrastructure and Resources

The use of AI does not come without cost. Open-source tools may, among other advantages, lower upfront costs. Beyond this, however, universities also need to invest in the required technical infrastructure for training and deploying AI in legal education. This includes campus-wide reliable high-speed internet, classroom technology supporting hybrid and online instruction, and learning management systems that integrate effectively with AI tools. As the *Wissenschaftsrat* emphasizes, technical systems and applications should be as simple and user-friendly as possible, accessible to all faculty and students, designed with low barriers, and supported by adequate training and assistance.[137]

Shared infrastructure across institutions can increase efficiency and reduce costs. State-level initiatives should develop common platforms for legal education technology, AI tool licenses negotiated collectively, and shared repositories of teaching materials. The *Wissenschaftsrat* recommends that federal and state governments build a cross-state infrastructure for Open Educational Resources (OER), and that they link existing collections and repositories through a meta-search engine to improve findability and accessibility of educational materials nationally.[138]

8. Harmonize Regulatory Frameworks

Germany requires clear, consistent legal frameworks governing AI use in higher education. Data protection frameworks require clarification. The AI Act classifies AI-supported assessment and selection procedures in education as 'high-risk' systems subject to comprehensive compliance requirements. Universities must understand precisely what obligations this imposes: documentation requirements, risk assessment procedures, human oversight mechanisms, and transparency standards.

The examination legal framework (*Prüfungsrecht*) also requires modernization, as current regulations were not designed for AI and create ambiguities about what constitutes independent work, permissible assistance, and academic misconduct.[139]

---

[136] *Schrepel*, Law Innov Technol (forthcoming, 2026), 51.

[137] *German Sciences and Humanities Council*, Empfehlungen zur Digitalisierung in Lehre und Studium (2022), 10.

[138] *German Sciences and Humanities Council* (n. 137), 12.

[139] *Schwartmann/Kurth/Köhler*, Der Einsatz von KI an Hochschulen–eine rechtliche Betrachtung, 3 Ordnung der Wissenschaft (2024), 163.

9. Expand Professional Training

Legal professionals already in practice require accessible continuing education on AI competencies. Judges and prosecutors also require specialized training. The judiciary's unique position requiring both technological competence and independence demands careful attention to training design. Whether AI can fulfill functions in the judiciary efficiently while strengthening basic rights, democracy, and the rule of law depends significantly on acceptance by members of the judiciary, which in turn depends on understanding and trust.[140]

10. Adopt a 'Mixed Strategy' for AI Integration

Overall, institutions should pursue a mixed strategy that combines AI-free learning environments with dedicated AI-enabled instruction. This dual approach recognizes that students must first master foundational legal skills before they can use AI tools responsibly and effectively.

Certain courses should be designated as AI-free zones. In these classes, students learn the core techniques of legal research, analysis, thinking, and writing without technological assistance. The rationale is straightforward: students who have never conducted legal research manually cannot evaluate whether an AI tool has retrieved the correct sources. Students who have never constructed a legal argument from scratch cannot assess whether an AI-generated argument is logically sound. The traditional *Gutachtenstil*, case briefing, statutory interpretation, and doctrinal synthesis require deliberate practice that AI shortcuts would undermine. These foundational courses – typically in the early semesters – should emphasize slow, careful work that builds the cognitive patterns necessary for expert legal reasoning.

Other courses should be dedicated to AI-enhanced learning. In these classes, instructors guide students through best practices for AI use, with a particular focus on the hallucination problem. Research demonstrates that this problem is severe. Chelli and others (2024) found that when ChatGPT and Google Bard were asked to retrieve scientific references for systematic reviews, hallucination rates – the proportion of fabricated or non-existent references – ranged from 28.6 % (GPT-4) to 91.4 % (Bard).[141] Even real papers were often retrieved with incorrect metadata or applied to inappropriate contexts. In the legal domain, Magesh and others (2025) noted high hallucination rates even among specific legal tools.[142]

---

140 *University of Freiburg*, Artificial Intelligence in the Judiciary (19.2.2025), https://uni-freiburg.de/en/artificial-intelligence-in-the-judiciary/ (17.12.2025).

141 *Chelli* et al., Hallucination Rates and Reference Accuracy of ChatGPT and Bard for Systematic Reviews: Comparative Analysis, 26(1) J Med Internet Res (2024), e53164.

142 *Magesh* et al., 22(2) J Empir Leg Stud (2025), 216.

These findings have direct pedagogical implications. AI-enabled courses should incorporate exercises that expose students to these failure modes. One effective approach is to present students with AI-generated legal analysis and require them to identify errors – a form of critical evaluation that reinforces substantive knowledge while building AI literacy. Students should learn systematic verification techniques: checking every citation against primary sources, confirming that quoted language actually appears in the cited document, verifying that cases remain good law, and assessing whether cited authorities are jurisdictionally appropriate. Assessment criteria in these courses should reward students who identify AI errors rather than accept outputs uncritically.

The sequencing matters. Students should complete AI-free foundational courses before progressing to AI-enhanced instruction. A student who has never struggled to find the relevant statute or to articulate why one case controls over another will lack the judgment necessary to evaluate AI outputs. The mixed strategy thus serves both pedagogical and professional goals: it produces graduates who possess genuine legal competence and who can deploy AI tools without becoming dependent on systems that remain, for the time being, unreliable.

VII. Perspectives on Digital Technologies and Law's Societal Role

1. *The 'Code is Law' Thesis in German Legal Scholarship*

Lawrence Lessig's seminal 'Code is Law' thesis has been extensively discussed in German legal scholarship, though with critical nuances that reflect the country's distinctive regulatory tradition.[143] German scholars like Wilhelm Steinmüller had developed related concepts of technological variability, dynamics and (over)complexity that influence regulatory outcomes before Lessig's work.[144] Austrian-trained Viktor Mayer-Schönberger offered fundamental discussions of Lessig's theorization of the technology-society relationship.[145]

German engagement with 'Code is Law' has focused particularly on platform regulation. Germany pioneered the *Netzwerkdurchsetzungsgesetz* (NetzDG, 2017), which requires social networks to remove illegal content within 24 hours – this represents Germany's attempt to reassert state sovereignty over algorithmic platform governance.[146] This law served as a model for the EU's Digital Services

143 *Lessig*, Code and Other Laws of Cyberspace, 1999; *id.*, Code: Version 2.0, 2006.

144 *Steinmüller*, Informationstechnologie und Gesellschaft: Einführung in die Angewandte Informatik, 1993, 134–153 and 385–388.

145 *Mayer-Schönberger*, The Shape of Governance: Analyzing the World of Internet Regulation, Virginia Journal of International Law 43 (2003), 605 et seqq.

146 Netzwerkdurchsetzungsgesetz (NetzDG), BGBl. I 2017, 3352.

Act.[147] The subsequent *Digitale-Dienste-Gesetz* (DDG) implements the DSA while maintaining strong platform oversight.[148]

2. Access to Justice and Legal Technology

Professor Giesela Rühl has documented how legal tech companies are addressing Germany's access-to-justice gap.[149] German local courts have lost approximately 60 % of their cases since the early 2000s – many lower-value claims simply go unenforced or move to other venues.[150] Legal tech companies, including *Flightright* (air passenger rights)[151] and *wenigermiete.de* (rent law),[152] have entered the market since approximately 2015 and use contingency fees and digital accessibility to reach consumers who would otherwise not pursue claims. They fill the gaps left by a court system viewed as unattractive by many consumers of claimants of small claims.

The Legal Tech Act of 2021 (*Gesetz zur Förderung verbrauchergerechter Angebote im Rechtsdienstleistungsmarkt*) attempted to balance regulation between traditional attorneys and legal tech debt collection services.[153] As Rühl observes, the focus has been on digital transformation of analog processes rather than reimagining legal services – a situation which suggests potential for more fundamental reform, for example concerning the admission of financial investors, the funding of litigation, and the use of contingency fees, but also the use of digital technology throughout the whole pipeline of court proceedings.[154] In my view, this may, for example, include feedback from approved chatbots to parties, especially those without legal counsel, monitored in novel ways by judges and, potentially, by new techno-legal counsels at the courts.

3. The Future of the German Legal Profession

In this impending transformation, new professional roles are emerging: legal data analysts, legal operations managers, AI compliance specialists, and legal engineers. The TUM Legal AI Use Case Radar 2025 documents current applications in document analysis and generation, legal research automation, contract review,

---

[147] Regulation (EU) 2022/2065 of 19.10.2022 on a Single Market for Digital Services (Digital Services Act), OJ L 277, 27.10.2022, 1.

[148] Digitale-Dienste-Gesetz (DDG) of 6.5.2024, BGBl. I 2024 Nr. 149.

[149] *Rühl*, Legal Tech Companies and Access to Justice in Germany, in: Freeman Engstrom/ Freeman Engstrom (eds.), Rethinking the Lawyer's Monopoly: Access to Justice and the Future of Legal Services, 2025, 300 et seqq.

[150] *Rühl* (n. 148), in: Rethinking the Lawyer's Monopoly, 300 et seq.

[151] See https://www.flightright.de (17.12.2025).

[152] See https://www.wenigermiete.de (17.12.2025).

[153] Gesetz zur Förderung verbrauchergerechter Angebote im Rechtsdienstleistungsmarkt vom 10. August 2021, BGBl. I 2021, 3415.

[154] *Rühl* (n. 148), in: Rethinking the Lawyer's Monopoly, 314 et seq.

and compliance monitoring.[155] However, limitations remain significant – *MIT Technology Review* rightly notes that while 47.8 % of attorneys at large US law firms use AI,[156] 'LLMs are still far from thinking like lawyers' – models struggle with novel questions, have difficulty synthesizing scattered sources, and frequently hallucinate case citations.[157]

VIII. Conclusion

German law faculties are responding to the rise of AI with a variety of initiatives. However, most law students still complete their education with minimal systematic exposure to technologies that increasingly shape legal practice. The basic law degree program (*Staatsexamen*) does not introduce prospective lawyers to AI and legal tech systematically, which forces students to seek additional courses if interested.

The empirical evidence suggests that structured AI training may improve student performance on complex analytical tasks. However, in the longer run, significant reliance on AI tools may undermine critical thinking and deprive students of core competences they need to build and foster. Yet, prohibiting AI may leave students at a disadvantage and, given imperfect enforcement, punish those actually adhering to the rule.

The regulatory landscape remains in flux, with the EU AI Act's creation of new compliance obligations while professional bodies like BRAK and DAV develop guidance that emphasizes human oversight and ethical constraints. The German judiciary's explicit commitment to 'support, not replacement' articulates a consensus that AI tools should enhance rather than substitute for human legal judgment.

The path forward requires a balance between innovation and caution. Hence, I suggest a "mixed strategy." Institutions should designate early-semester courses as AI-free zones to build foundational legal competencies, while later courses should integrate AI instruction with a focus on identifying hallucinations and verifying outputs. Within this mixed strategy, law schools should maintain pedagogical freedom, invest in faculty training, develop AI literacy as a core competence, redesign assessments for the AI era, establish clear policies, document and share best practices, invest in infrastructure, harmonize regulatory frameworks,

---

155 *TUM*, Legal AI Use Case Radar 2025, https://legal-ai-radar.de/ (6.1.2026).

156 *Calaguas*, 2024 Artificial Intelligence TechReport (2025), https://www.americanbar.org/groups/law_practice/resources/tech-report/2024/2024-artificial-intelligence-techreport/ (23.12.2025).

157 *Kim*, AI Might Not Be Coming for Lawyers' Jobs Anytime Soon, MIT Technology Review, 15.12.2025, https://www.technologyreview.com/2025/12/15/1129181/ai-might-not-be-coming-for-lawyers-jobs-anytime-soon/ (23.12.2025); see also above, *Magesh* et al., 22(2) J Empir Leg Stud (2025), 216.

and expand professional training opportunities. The challenge for German legal education is to produce jurists capable of operating in both registers: masters of the sophisticated doctrinal reasoning who also understand how algorithms shape the legal landscape they will navigate.

The question is no longer whether AI will transform legal education, but how. German and international law faculties that invest in thoughtful integration of AI – for both students and faculty – will be better positioned to prepare the next generation of lawyers for an AI-enabled legal profession. Success requires commitment from multiple actors: universities must prioritize digital transformation and provide necessary resources; faculty must engage with pedagogical innovation and develop new competencies; students must take responsibility for their learning in technology-augmented environments; federal and state governments must provide funding, create appropriate legal frameworks, and modernize examination systems; and professional associations must ensure practicing lawyers maintain current, adequate, and critical competencies.

Property Law Issues in International Investment Arbitration

A German Perspective

Robert Magnus and *Christian Reichelt*

I. Introduction

With 113 bilateral investment treaties (BITs) in force, Germany remains one of the frontrunners in terms of BITs.[1] In view of the current government's coalition agreement, which states: "We aim to conclude further trade and investment agreements" it is unlikely that this will change.[2]

Germany is currently home to 87 investors who are suing host countries under BITs.[3] At the same time, Germany is being sued as a host country by Azienda Elettrica Ticinese for phasing out coal and by Mainstream Renewable Power Ltd. for regulations in the wind energy sector.[4] This raises a general and specific need for discussion with regard to a legal position that is frequently asserted in investment disputes: ownership. Questions arise as to how far-reaching the concept of ownership is in BITs, how far-reaching this ownership is protected by expropriation provisions, and what the consequences of unlawful expropriation are. The latter question has implications beyond investment arbitration proceedings. Even in a domestic private law dispute based, for example, on an action for restitution or damages, the question of ownership may at any time arise. Accordingly, it may be necessary to clarify as a preliminary question whether a foreign expropriation, including its substantive legal effects, is to be recognized in German court proceedings. Traditionally, the so-called International Expropriation Law (IEL) deals with these questions. It answers, for example, the question whether or not a foreign act of expropriation is recognized by the local courts. It applies, in general, when states have not specifically regulated the recognition and enforcement

---

1 Federal Ministry for Economic Affairs and Energy, at: https://www.bundeswirtschaftsministerium.de/Navigation/DE/Service/Investitionsschutzvertraege/investitionsschutzvertraege.html (last accessed on September 12, 2025).

2 Responsibility for Germany – Coalition Agreement between the CDU, CSU, and SPD, 2025, p. 9, at: https://www.cdu.de/app/uploads/2025/04/KoaV-2025-Gesamt-final-0424.pdf (last accessed on March 12, 2026).

3 https://investmentpolicy.unctad.org/investment-dispute-settlement (last accessed on September 12, 2025).

4 Azienda Elettrica Ticinese v. Germany, ICSID Case No. ARB/23/47; Mainstream Renewable Power Ltd. and others v. Germany, ICSID Case No. ARB/21/26.

of sovereign acts. For the present work, the IEL is therefore used to compare the results with and without an existing BIT. But that is not all, because the comparison should not be limited to questions of recognition, but should also include the scope of protection by the BITs. To this end, a comparison with German investment protection rules is attempted.

To highlight the relevance of the questions just raised, it should be briefly noted that, according to the European Court of Justice (ECJ), the dispute settlement mechanism in Intra-EU-BITs, i. e., those concluded between two EU member states, is contrary to EU law.[5] The decisive factor for the ECJ was that European law provides for an autonomous system of legal protection, in particular the possibility of a referral to the ECJ under Article 267 TFEU. However, since arbitral tribunals are, in principle, not allowed to refer questions to the ECJ, the dispute settlement mechanism in BITs (investor-state arbitration proceedings) violates the European legal and judicial system. After all, without the involvement of the ECJ in European legal issues, it cannot be ensured that EU law is applied correctly.[6] As a consequence of this judgment, 23 EU member states have signed a termination agreement under which existing Intra-EU-BITs are to be dissolved.[7] In this context, national courts are not only competent to review arbitral awards under a limited scope, which includes, for example, an public policy review (cf. Section 1059 II German Code of Civil Procedure). According to Article 7 of the agreement, the member states involved are even obliged to ensure that in a dispute before state courts the arbitral award is set aside, not recognized, or at least not enforced.[8] Article 10 I, II of the termination agreement provides a certain substitute for the ineffectiveness of a concluded arbitration agreement. According to this article, access to national courts should be made possible. However, since the terminated BIT is not to be regarded as part of the applicable law in these proceedings pursuant to Art. 10 III of the termination agreement, EU investors are in fact no longer protected by the BIT. Instead, the national and European law applies. However, Non-EU investors continue to be protected by BITs concluded

[5] ECJ, judgment of March 6, 2018 – C-284/16, Achmea; ECJ, judgment of September 2, 2021 – C-741/19, Kom- stroy; see *Voit*, in: Musielak/Voit, ZPO, 22nd ed. 2025, § 1029 n. 10; *Kläger*, comment on ECJ, judgment of March 6, 2018 – C-284/16, SchiedsVZ 2018, 186, 191 et seqq.; *Gundel*, comment on ECJ, judgment of March 6, 2018 – C- 284/16, NVwZ 2018, 723, 727 et seqq.; *Kuplewatzky*, comment on the ECJ judgment of September 2, 2021 – C- 741/19, EuZW 2021, 945, 950 et seqq.; cf. on the handling of ECJ case law by arbitral tribunals, Strabag SE v. Germany, ICSID Case No. ARB/19/29, Award, December 18, 2024, para. 162 et seqq.

[6] ECJ, judgment of March 6, 2018 – C-284/16 para. 33 et seqq., Achmea.

[7] Art. 2 of the Agreement for the termination of Bilateral Investment Treaties between the Member States of the European Union, May 29, 2020.

[8] Art. 7 of the Agreement for the termination of Bilateral Investment Treaties between the Member States of the European Union, May 29, 2020; see also BGH, SchiedsVZ 2023, 289, 297; *Kuplewatzky*, comment on the ECJ ruling of September 2, 2021, EuZW 2021, 945, 952; *Schwalb/Weiler*, comment on the ECJ ruling of September 2, 2021, SchiedsVZ 2022, 34, 40.

by their home countries and Germany.[9] As a result investors from EU and Non-EU countries are, according to German and European law, at the moment protected by quite different regimes.[10]

II. The Concepts of Ownership and Investment

1. Overlapping of the Concept of Ownership with the Concept of Investment

The first issue addressed in this essay is of a conceptual nature. It arises from the comparison of the terms "investment" and "property". When viewed from the perspective of German constitutional law, these terms reveal significant differences from the approach taken in international investment law. For example, the German Federal Constitutional Court defines the concept of property under Article 14 section 1 of the German Constitution (GG) as "all property rights assigned to the entitled party by the legal system in such a way that the latter may exercise the associated powers for his or her own private benefit at his or her own discretion".[11] This definition is the reason why investments are not directly protected by Article 14 section 1 GG, as they are simply regarded as expenses and not as a "right" in the aforementioned sense. It is therefore always necessary for the investment to be linked to a legal position capable of ownership in accordance with Art. 14 section 1 GG.[12] In other words, Article 14 section 1 GG only protects what has been acquired and not the acquisition itself. It is therefore directed towards the past. Future acquisitions are primarily guaranteed by Article 12 section 1 GG.[13] However, the protection of legal positions under Article 12 I GG is very limited and significantly less elaborated than under Art. 14 section 1 GG.[14] Due to the concept of property in Article 14 section 1 GG investments in Germany are primarily preserved by the general principle of protection of legitimate expecta-

---

[9] It should be noted, however, that since the Treaty of Lisbon, EU member states have been prohibited from concluding BITs independently, as foreign direct investment falls within the competence of the EU (Art. 3 I lit. e TFEU). However, existing BITs remain in force until a corresponding BIT between the EU and the other contracting state has been brought into force, Art. 3 Regulation No. 1219/2012 of the European Parliament and of the Council of December 12, 2012, establishing transitional arrangements for bilateral investment protection agreements between Member States and third countries (known as the "Grandfathering Regulation"), OJ No. L 351/40.

[10] See, for example, *Germelmann*, EuZW 2008, 596, on aspects of investment protection under EU law.

[11] BVerfG, NJW 2005, 879, 880; BVerfG, NJW 2006, 1191, 1193; BVerfG, NVwZ 2012, 1463, 1464.

[12] BVerfG, NJW 2017, 217, 232; BVerfG, NVwZ-RR 2021, 177 n. 88.

[13] See BGH, NJW 1996, 2422, 2423; BVerfG, NJW 1997, 2871, 2873; *Papier/Shirvani*, in: Dürig/Herzog/Scholz, GG, 108th ed. 2025, Art. 14 n. 160, n. 353; *Jarass*, in: Jarass/Pieroth, GG, 18th ed. 2024, Art. 12 n. 4.

[14] BVerfG, NJW 2017, 217 390 et seq.; BVerfG, NVwZ-RR 2021, 177 f. n. 110.

tions.[15] Once again, this protection is quite weak as citizens trust in the continuation of a legal situation is generally not worthy of protection if changes in the law – as is often the case in investment law – were foreseeable.[16] There is also only limited investment protection under state liability law, as many state liability claims require the existence of a legal position protected by Article 14 section 1 GG and are therefore not applicable for investments in future business opportunities. Other claims require a distinguished individual hardship (in German: *Sonderopfer*) or are not applicable to acts of the legislation at all.[17]

German investment protection treaties offer a different approach. As is well known, these treaties are not primarily concerned with protecting property, but rather with protecting investments. Although ownership of movable, immovable, tangible, or intangible assets is listed as an example of protected assets in many BITs, this list is not exclusive and additional assets are included in the definition of investment, that would not fulfill the criteria of ownership under Art. 14 section 1 GG. This shows that the intended protection is wider and stronger influenced by economic criteria than by purely legal concepts. Therefore, it is not surprising that Article 1 of the German Model Treaty provides that a change of the form in which assets are invested (e.g., real estate is sold and the money invested in shares) does not affect their status as a protected investment. Arbitral tribunals in investment law cases, therefore, apply a concept of an investment that differs considerably from the German concept of ownership. This is also reflected by Article 25 Section 1 of the ICSID Convention, that requires for the jurisdiction of the arbitral tribunals only that a "legal dispute arising directly out of an investment" is concerned. The concept of an investment is defined by arbitral tribunals by recourse to the so-called Salini criteria, according to which an investment is characterized by the following criteria: a monetary contribution by the investor, a project of a certain duration, the burden of economic risks, an expected regular profit from the project, and a contribution to the development of the host-country.[18] Although it should be noted that the exact definition of these criteria and their function is controversial,[19] their importance for the practice of investment arbitration is unanimously acknowledged. This is illustrated for example by the

[15] The general principle of protection of legitimate expectations is derived from the principle of the rule of law and thus from Art. 20 GG, see *Grzeszick*, in: Dürig/Herzog/Scholz, GG, 108th ed. 2025, Art. 20 Section VII n. 1 et seqq., 70 et seqq.; BVerfG, NVwZ-RR 2021, 177, 122 et seqq.; *Schill*, ZaöRV 2018, 33, p. 46 et seqq.

[16] See BVerfG, NVwZ 2004, 463, 467; *Grzeszick*, in: Dürig/Herzog/Scholz, GG, 108th ed. 2025, Art. 20 n. 71.

[17] *Maurer/Waldhoff*, Allgemeines Verwaltungsrecht, § 26 n. 52 et seqq., § 28 n. 12 et seqq.

[18] Salini Costruttori S.S.A. and Italstrade S.S.A. v. Kingdom of Morocco, ICSID Case No. ARB/00/4, Decisions on Jurisdiction, July 23, 2001, para. 52 et seqq.; Bayindir Insaat Turizm Ticaret VE Sanayi A.S. v. Islamic Republic of Pakistan, ICSID Case No. ARB/03/29, Decisions on Jurisdiction, November 14, 2005, para. 130 et seqq.; *Schill*, ZaöRV 2012, 261, 284 et seqq.

[19] See *Dolzer/Kriebaum/Schreuer*, Principles of International Investment Law, 2022, p. 91 et seqq.

fact that newer BITs often state that the protection of an investment does not depend only on the ownership of certain assets, but on the influence that the investor has on the assets and on the Salini criteria (e.g., Art. 8.1 CETA).

One difference between the approaches described is particularly evident in relation to concessions given to investors in accordance with public law. From a German constitutional law perspective, a concession for the construction and operation of nuclear or wind power plants is itself not protected property.[20] This leads to the surprising conclusion that only investments made in relation to an already constructed plant are effectively protected from governmental regulations. The expenses incurred prior to the obtaining of a concession, which thus form the basis for the subsequent property, are not effectively protected. In BITs, on the other hand, concessions given to investors in accordance with public law are also part of a protected investments (e.g., Art. 1 No. 1 lit. f German Model Treaty). From an economic perspective, this is not surprising since the obtaining of a concession is often a necessary regulatory and transitional stage and, thus, forms the basis for the assets that will be created in the future. As a result, the legal concept of ownership is in BITs therefore replaced by the economic concept of investment. As a consequence the question, whether or not a certain position is protected property in accordance with German constitutional law, is considerably less important, if a BIT is applicable.

2. Residual Significance of the Concept of Ownership in Relation to the Obligation to Pay Compensation?

At a secondary level, i.e., when considering whether a compensation for an expropriation can be claimed, a distinction must be made between different types of expropriations typically mentioned in BITs. For a so-called direct expropriation the assets concerned must be regarded as property owned by the investor, since a direct expropriation within the meaning of a BIT is defined by the fact that the investor has been formally deprived of his legal ownership.[21] As the BITs themselves do not define, whether or not and under which conditions a factual position qualifies as property of the investor, a recourse to the applicable substantive property law is necessary. With regard to the legal concept of direct expropriation, there is a necessary link between the ownership of the investor on an asset on the one hand and the possibility to claim compensation for its loss under a BIT on the other.

If, by contrast, indirect expropriation is brought forward in accordance with a BIT such a link does not exist. But still the concept of ownership could potentially provide some guidance as to when a compensation can be claimed. However, the

---

[20] BVerfG, NJW 2017, 217, 232; BVerfG, NVwZ-RR 2021, 177 para. 88.

[21] Rockhopper v. Italian Republic, ICSID Case No. ARB/17/14, Award, July 14, 2017, para. 190 et seqq.; *Akporiaye*, RIPE 2024, vol. 31, No. 2, 728, 730.

practice of arbitral tribunals in investment law cases rather shows a different picture. The tribunals base their decisions concerning indirect expropriations primarily on economic criteria like whether or not a measure leads to a "substantial deprivation of the value, use or enjoyment of an asset" in view of the "the intensity and duration of the economic deprivation suffered by the investor".[22] Still they are not using clearly defined legal concepts for the allocation of goods but are rather referring to the economic effects of the disputed measures.[23] In line with this approach, newer BITs also use the criteria mentioned above, when defining whether a measure qualifies as an "indirect expropriation".[24] From a German perspective, Article 14 section 2 GG, which states that property entails obligations and that its use should also serve the public good, would apply. The German concept of property is not absolute, as it clearly incorporates restrictions on the right to use the property. Therefore, restrictions concerning only the use of assets in the ownership of the investor would, in general, not be classified as expropriation simply because they are permissible by law as can be seen in Art. 14 section 2 GG. In BITs on the other hand, not the narrow concept of property but the wider term of investment is protected. As a consequence, the question of indirect expropriation is based primarily on the economic consequences a certain measure has for the investor. In claims concerning indirect expropriation, the concept of property therefore has no fundamental role to play. Instead, it is replaced by a concept protecting frustrated investments from a rather economic point of view.

The same applies to measures that have the same effect as expropriation. In most cases arbitral tribunals do not make a strict distinction between indirect expropriation and measures having the same effect as an indirect expropriation.[25] A plausible reason for such a distinction would be to consider only assets that can be owned as directly and indirectly expropriable while assets that cannot be owned could be exposed only to measures equivalent to expropriation. However, this would require the arbitral tribunals to first examine whether or not assets are property under the applicable national property law, which is for the above mentioned reasons not current practice. Instead, these measures are often discussed together with direct expropriation under the broadly interpreted term "expropriation".[26] The result is a very broad concept of expropriation, which, in the absence of different legal consequences, does not give rise to any clear distinc-

---

[22] Telenor Mobile Communications A.S. v. The Republic of Hungary, ICSID Case No. ARB/04/15, Award, September 13, 2006, para. 65; Phillip Morris v. Republic of Uruguay, ICSID Case No. ARB/10/7, Award, July 8, 2016, para. 192.

[23] *Dolzer/Kriebaum/Schreuer*, Principles of International Investment Law, 2022, p. 163.

[24] See *Krajewski*, Model Investment Protection Agreement with Investor-State Arbitration for Industrialized Countries, Taking into Account the USA, p. 14 et seqq.

[25] LG&E v. Argentine Republic, ICSID Case No. ARB/02/1, Decision on Liability, October 3, 2006, para. 187 et seqq.

[26] See Art. 4 II 1 of the BIT between Germany and China.

tion.[27] Such a broad concept of expropriation once again leads to legal classifications being overridden by economic consequences. If compensation were only considered as a result of direct expropriation, then (according to the German concept of property) only the applicable property law would be relevant. This would link investment protection to national property protection and ultimately make it dependent solely on the applicable national property law regime.[28] This would never do justice to an economic and international perspective. Although direct expropriation, indirect expropriation and measures equivalent to expropriation are in international investment law disputes formally understood as separate categories, they are often not clearly distinguished, due to the fact that the distinction has no direct impact on the claim for compensation.

From a practical point of view, the distinction, however, has some relevance for the burden of proof: While direct expropriation is usually relatively easy to prove, demonstrating indirect expropriation or a comparable measure in relation to other assets is sometimes extremely difficult. For example, the question of whether a wind turbine owned by a foreign investor is now owned by the host country can be proven by easily accessible evidence such as the ownership status in a corresponding register. The situation is different if "only" an "expropriation-like measure" or "indirect expropriation" is being examined.[29] In this case, the question of expropriation cannot be answered by a printout from a register, but only by a recourse to the economic criteria mentioned above.

3. Consequence: Disadvantageous Position for Domestic Investors

The rather worrying consequence of these considerations is that foreign investors are – compared with domestic investors – in a very favorable position. As an example, it should be noted that, according to the Federal Constitutional Court, the 13th amendment to the Atomic Energy Act in Germany did not, for the most part, violate Article 14 section 1 GG as it concerned the licensing of nuclear power plants. Due to the relevant definition of property, the granted licenses to build a nuclear power plant were already excluded from the scope of protection under Article 14 section 1 GG. In addition, although the scope of protection of Article 14 section 1 GG was considered to apply to the nuclear plants themselves, the Federal Constitutional Court defined the concept of expropriation very narrowly.

---

[27] *Kindler*, in: MüKo, BGB, vol. 13, 9th ed. 2025, International Commercial Law, n. 972.

[28] This refers to economies that reject the concept of property altogether or place it in a very strict social context.

[29] See Marvin Feldman v. Mexico, ICSID Case No. ARB/99/1, Award, December 16, 2002, para. 100: "Recognizing direct expropriation is relatively easy: governmental authorities take over a mine or factory, depriving the investor of all meaningful benefits of ownership and control. However, it is much less clear when governmental action that interferes with broadly-defined property rights – an 'investment' under NAFTA, Article 1139 – crosses the line from valid regulation to a compensable taking, and it is fair to say that no one has come up with a fully satisfactory means of drawing this line."

According to its opinion, an expropriation requires not only a deprivation of property rights, but also a sovereign acquisition of goods.[30] As a consequence, the legislative act was qualified as defining in conformity with the constitution the content and limits of ownership and, thus, in general no compensation was awarded.[31] On the other hand, it was very likely that the investment arbitration tribunal in the case Vattenfall v. Germany would have affirmed an indirect expropriation within the meaning of the Energy Charter Treaty and would have awarded a compensation.[32] Since this proceeding was terminated by a settlement, the possible outcome remains unclear. Nevertheless, it is certain that the threat of an arbitral award in its favor enabled Vattenfall to negotiate settlement terms, obliging the Federal Republic of Germany to pay around € 1.43 billion to them as a compensation for electricity that could no longer be produced and sold on the German market. This clearly illustrates, that comparable investors who did not have the opportunity to bring a claim before an arbitral tribunal in accordance with a BIT and could not by this means exert pressure on the host state have a clearly higher risk of frustrated investments.[33]

III. The Question of Recognition

If we consider the legal consequences of expropriation in addition to the obligation to pay compensation, we recognize another property law problem, namely the effect of expropriation on private law. Anyone who has been expropriated can no longer be regarded as the owner of the asset in question. The sovereign act of expropriation thus has an influence on the property situation under private law and the issue of expropriation may also become relevant in proceedings before national courts. This could, for example, be the case, if the buyer of a receivable under a factoring agreement claims damages against the investor as the seller of the receivable for not transferring the receivable on time (Artt. 453 section 1, 433 of the German Civil Code [BGB]). It is also possible that a movable object that is subject to expropriation is transferred to the home country and then destroyed by a third party.[34] In both cases, the national courts cannot avoid the question of whether the investor still has ownership rights or whether these rights have been lost as a result of the expropriation.[35] It is also possible that the investor has insured its investment project at a domestic insurance company and is now in

---

30 BVerfG, NJW 2017, 217 para. 243.

31 BVerfG, NJW 2017, 217 para. 267 et seqq.

32 Vattenfall vs. Germany, ICSID Case No. ARB/12/12.

33 See also *Krajewski*, Vattenfall, the German nuclear phase-out and international investment law, 2013, available at: https://www.rph1.rw.fau.de/files/2016/02/vattenfall-.pdf. (last accessed on March 12, 2026).

34 See *Deren*, Internationales Enteignungsrecht, p. 45.

35 *Wendehorst*, in: MüKo, BGB, vol. 13, 9th ed. 2025, Annex Art. 46 EGBGB, n. 1, 4.

dispute with the insurance company over the existence of an insured event. Article 10 section 5 of the German Model Treaty (GMT) provides that a contracting state cannot invoke the fact that the investor has received compensation under insurance law. Therefore, the BIT and the arbitration proceedings may have a relevant impact also on insurance disputes.

1. Relevance Regardless of the Form of Expropriation

Only in the rather rare cases of direct expropriation the owner's legal position is formally revoked.[36] In all other cases, i. e., in the event of an indirect expropriation or a measure equivalent to expropriation, the investor remains the formal owner. Terminologically it is also possible to consider a private law effect in these cases as well, especially if a BIT does not distinguish between different kinds of expropriations but merges them all under the same broad term. However, by such an approach the BIT would probably only intend to harmonize the obligation to pay compensation. It would not intend to abandon the distinction between different forms of expropriation also with respect to effects they have in private law. Nevertheless, indirect expropriation and measures equivalent to expropriation themselves can also have an impact on proceedings before national courts. For example, there are cases in which certain factual requirements of national liability standards can be justified or rejected because of an indirect expropriation or a measure equivalent to expropriation. Coming back to the above mentioned example, the investor who has promised to assign a receivable could argue that the host state has enacted a new regulation according to which the promised receivable is already time-barred or of a strictly personal nature and can therefore no longer be assigned. Under German law, it would, hence, be doubtful if the seller of the receivable could be held responsible for his lack to assign it to the buyer.[37] It is also possible that expropriation, regardless of its exact form, has been included in a contract as a reason for termination. The question whether or not the expropriation is recognized therefore also arises in corresponding termination proceedings.

2. The Principle of Territoriality in International Expropriation Law

The principle of territoriality plays a fundamental role in International Expropriation Law (IEL) as the rule of thumb for recognizing foreign expropriations. The IEL is applied by German Courts, when no BITs or similar agreements have been concluded with the foreign state. The existence and applicability of the principle of territoriality is widely recognized. Its justification is based on princi-

36 *Dolzer/Kriebaum/Schreuer*, Principles of International Investment Law, 2022, p. 153.

37 Under German law, a contractual claim for damages requires that the debtor is not responsible for the breach of duty, Sections 280 I 2, 276 I BGB and Section 286 IV BGB.

ples of public policy. On the one hand, the decision of a local court not to recognize a foreign expropriation would, in general, not help the parties and have no practical effect, when the assets are located in the foreign state. It only leads to legal uncertainty concerning the legal status of the assets in different countries. On the other hand, the decision not to recognize a foreign expropriation might cause tensions on a diplomatic level and provoke retaliatory measures by the foreign state.[38] The rule of thumb in IEL therefore states that expropriations affecting assets located in the territory of the expropriating state must be recognized. This also means that expropriations affecting assets not located in the territory of the expropriating state are, in general, not recognized.[39] The principle of territoriality, thus, allows a clear distinction in accordance with criteria, that are, in general, easy to establish and to prove when physically existing goods are in dispute. However, when intangible goods, such as receivables, copyrights or digital content are at stake the principle of territoriality functions less sufficient.[40] For example, the location of a receivable or the location of decentralized digital information cannot be physically traced. For these goods the principle of territoriality has therefore to be extended and modified. Depending on the dominant view in the academia the location of a receivable is, for example, either determined by the applicable law of obligations, or by the place where the debt is due, or by the creditor's place of residence, or at every place where an enforcement into the assets of the debtor is possible.[41] This clearly illustrates the difficulties the principle of territoriality encounters, when it is applied to intangible assets.

3. The Recognition rule in BITs

a) Territoriality Principle or Contractual Recognition Rule?

With regard to BITs some particularities have to be considered. BITs, in general, provide that all investments of capital made by an investor in the territory of the host state are protected. Therefore, assets "*in the territory of the host state*" may only be expropriated under specifically mentioned conditions (e.g., Art. 1 section 1 German Model Treaty). Moreover, it should be noted that disputes between an investor and a contracting state are settled by a binding arbitral award that cannot be challenged by any legal remedies other than those provided for in the

---

[38] See BVerfG, NJW 1991, 1597, 1600; for details, see *Deren*, Internationales Enteignungsrecht, p. 108 et seqq.

[39] BVerfG, NJW 1991, 1597, 1599 et seq.; *Zimmermann*, in: BeckOGK, as of 01.02.2026, Art. 43 EGBGB, n. 206.

[40] On the dispute over the concept of the matter under Art. 43 EGBGB, see *Wendehorst*, in: MüKo, BGB, vol. 13, 9th ed. 2025, Art. 43 EGBGB, n. 11 et seqq.; *Mansel*, in: Staudinger, BGB, 2015, Art. 43 EGBGB, n. 2 et seqq. On the problematic applicability to claims and digital content, see *Wendehorst*, in: MüKo, BGB, vol. 13, 9th ed. 2025, Art. 43 EGBGB, n. 32, 38.

[41] *Wendehorst*, in: MüKo, BGB, vol. 13, 9th ed. 2025, Annex Art. 46 EGBGB, n. 42 et seqq.; *Mansel*, in: Staudinger, 2015, Annex I to Art. 43–46 EGBGB, n. 34 et seqq.; *Deren*, Internationales Enteignungsrecht, p. 229.

relevant arbitration rules (e.g., Art. 10 section 3 GMT). From these provisions follows a different picture. The location of the assets, which is the decisive criterion for the principle of territoriality, is in investment law disputes under a BIT only the starting point. The BIT and its offered protection is only applicable when the affected assets are located in a contracting state. However, expropriation by the foreign host state is not per se recognized, but only if they fulfill the conditions negotiated and laid down in the BIT. The question whether or not an expropriation by a foreign state is recognized is, thus, less dominated by public policy and more of a contractual nature.[42]

b) Recognition After a Decision by an Arbitral Tribunal

If an arbitral tribunal has already ruled on the expropriation issue and determined that the expropriation was lawful, the obligation to recognize the award follows from the need to ensure that the contractually agreed dispute resolution mechanism is effective.[43] If national courts would then refuse to recognize the effect of the expropriation in private law cases, the investor would find itself in a contradictory situation. On the one hand, the arbitral tribunal has approved that the host state has legitimately deprived him of his property, but on the other hand, he could be liable as the owner of the property before the national courts. This is clearly not the legal situation or an effect intended by the parties of the BIT. Therefore, the national courts are bound to recognize also the effects a valid expropriation has in private law.

But are the national courts competent to decide for themselves whether or not an expropriation by the foreign host state fulfills the conditions laid down in the BIT and is therefore valid? Or are they bound by the decision of the arbitral tribunal, even when they would not concur with its legal point of view? It must be conceded that the contracting parties would, in general, not commit themselves to recognize expropriations that clearly violate the requirements of the treaty. However, an obligation to recognize only expropriations, that according to the view of the national courts comply with the requirements of the BIT is also problematic. The question of expropriation is often unclear and politically influenced. It can and will often be answered differently by different courts and tribunals. Giving the national courts the final say in this question would, therefore, jeopardize the legal certainty and the common understanding the BIT is trying to achieve. Moreover, in these politically sensitive disputes a neutral and impartial forum, such as an arbitral tribunal, gives the award a special legitimacy. Eventually, even arbitral awards can be annulled by national courts in accordance with the national arbitration law, for example via the public policy reservation. This

---

42 *Deren*, Internationales Enteignungsrecht, p. 49.
43 *Deren*, Internationales Enteignungsrecht, p. 49.

means that the obligation to recognize the private law effects of the expropriation could be suspended in the case of an obviously incorrect arbitral award.

c) Recognition Without or Before an Arbitral Award is Issued

If an investment arbitration tribunal has not yet ruled on the expropriation issue, it is possible to consider returning to the principle of territoriality. After all, the treaty-autonomous recognition rule could be reduced to the fact that the BIT provides for a special dispute resolution mechanism. If this has not (yet) been initiated, the general recognition rule in the form of the principle of territoriality could apply. However, it should be noted that arbitration proceedings can also be initiated after national court proceedings have been instituted. In this case, the national proceedings must be suspended until an arbitral award has been rendered, so that the question of recognition must be answered in accordance with the principles just outlined.

If, on the other hand, suspension is not an option, because the investor is, for example, reluctant to bear the costs of investment arbitration proceedings, it must be clarified how the national courts should proceed. There are, in principle, two possible ways of handling this situation. First, the national courts are not allowed to review the question whether or not the expropriation complies with the requirements of the BIT. Hence, they would – similar to the approach of the principle of territoriality – in general have to assume that the sovereign acts of the host state are lawful and comply with the BIT.[44] This presumption would then give rise to an obligation to also recognize the private law effects of the expropriation. This approach is, on the one hand, based on the expectation that the contracting states will, in general, respect the requirements they negotiated themselves. On the other hand, it emphasizes that the specific dispute resolution mechanism agreed upon, that means the binding decisions by a neutral forum in the form of an arbitral tribunal, is a key element of the BIT and can and should under no circumstances be substituted by similar competences for the national courts.

The second approach would be to simply allow such a review of the requirements by the national courts as long as arbitration proceedings have not (yet) been initiated. From a practical point of view, it is not very convincing to simply assume that an expropriation complies with the BIT, even if there is strong and available evidence proving the contrary. Furthermore, dispute resolution through investment arbitration in BITs should only serve to extend legal protection before a neutral court. There is no obligation to settle disputes before an arbitral tribunal. The binding effect of the arbitral award or the risk of conflicting decisions can therefore only supersede the review powers of national courts if such arbitration proceedings are actually initiated. Moreover, the expectations of the contracting parties are probably better reflected, when the legality of sovereign acts

---

[44] *Deren*, Internationales Enteignungsrecht, p. 47 et seq.

is truly reviewed and not merely assumed. The German legislator seems to share this point of view, since Art. 4 section 2 s. 5 GMT states, that "the legality of any such expropriation […] must be subject to review by due process of law". This wording could be understood as a reference also to the legal review by the national courts, if arbitration is not available or initiated. According to this convincing point of view, national courts have, in general, the authority to review the compliance of sovereign acts of foreign states with the respective requirements of the BIT. This authority is simply suspended at the moment an arbitration proceeding is initiated.

4. Summary

With regard to the question of recognizing the effects an expropriation has on private law, BITs paint a very clear picture: If arbitration proceedings are taking place or have already taken place, the legality of the measure is determined by the tribunals. This also includes the effects the act has on private law. If it is sufficiently clear that arbitration proceedings will not be initiated (in the near future), national courts must decide for themselves on the legality of the measure and thus also on the resulting consequences. Compared with the traditional approach under the IEL and the principle of territoriality, BITs in fact offer a relatively well-functioning form of protection for investments in foreign countries even against expropriations of the host state. Here, the recognition of a foreign expropriation is always linked to the judicially reviewed substantive legal protection standards laid down in the BIT and does not only depend on the location of an asset. However, the result is for cases concerning only EU member states, that are as a consequence of the judgements of the ECJ[45] no longer available for the specific protection standard of a BIT, less dramatic than it seems. In this situation, investors do not fall back on the principle of territoriality, since for them actually the high protection standards of the EU law apply (e.g., Art. 63 TFEU, Art. 1 of the First Additional Protocol to the ECHR).

IV. Public Policy as a Limit to Recognition

1. Public Policy in International Expropriation Law

According to German understanding, the principle of territoriality is limited by a public policy exception. Accordingly, the recognition of the private law effects of a foreign expropriation must be refused if it contradicts fundamental principles of the national law.[46] However, a sufficient connection to the domestic forum is necessary, which is established, for example, by the German nationality of the

---

[45] See page 3.
[46] *Wendehorst*, in: MüKo, BGB, vol. 13, 9th ed. 2025, Annex Art. 46 EGBGB, n. 25.

expropriated party or by the transfer of the property or its fruits to Germany.[47] Public policy is discussed primarily in relation to expropriations without any compensation.[48] This is likely due to the fact that, according to the German understanding, public policy is particularly relevant when the recognition of the act would be in conflict with fundamental rights, in particular with the obligation to provide compensation under Article 14 section 3 sentence 1 GG (see also Article 6 sentence 2 Introductory Act to the German Civil Code [EGBGB]). However, there are also doubts as to whether the lack of compensation under public policy per se leads to an incompatibility with fundamental principles of German law.[49] Rather, an overall assessment of the circumstances must be made, which must also take into account the question who would benefit from the recognition.[50] The necessity of an overall assessment of all circumstances of the case is also confirmed by the case law, that illustrates that judgements often do not clearly distinguish, whether the recognition fails due to the lack of compensation or due to further (legal or factual) consequences of the expropriation[51] or whether the principle of territoriality excludes the recognition due to the fact that the assets are strongly linked to the domestic forum.[52]

2. *Public Policy and the Principle of Territoriality in BITs*

BITs typically do not comment on public policy exception. There are two reasons for this. First, they generally do not explicitly address the recognition of the private law effect of an expropriation. Therefore, they also do not answer the question, when an exception should be made from this effect. Second, BITs establish themselves the essential legal requirements for permissible expropriations. These requirements largely coincide with the requirements under national law that could justify an application of the of public policy exception. For example, both the German Model Treaty and Article 14 section 1 GG state that an expropriation is only permissible for the public good and in return for a compensation. Therefore, the prominent cases of expropriation without compensation in IEL are hardly imaginable in international investment law. Nevertheless, the public pol-

---

[47] BGH, NJW 1988, 2173, 2174; *Mansel*, in: Staudinger, BGB, 2015, Annex I to Art. 43–46, n. 63 et seqq.; *Wendehorst*, in: MüKo, BGB, vol. 13, 9th ed. 2025, Annex Art. 46 EGBGB, n. 58.

[48] BGH, NJW 1988, 2173, 2175; *Wendehorst*, in: MüKo, BGB, vol. 13, 9th ed. 2025, Annex Art. 46 EGBGB, n. 58; *Mansel*, in: Staudinger, BGB, 2015, Annex I to Art. 43–46, n. 60. See also BVerfG, NJW 1991, 1597, 1600, although it is not clear here whether the court does not want to include the lack of compensation for expropriation under public policy or whether it simply does not see a sufficient domestic connection in this.

[49] BVerfG, NJW 1991, 1597, 1600.

[50] *Mansel*, in: Staudinger, BGB, 2015, Annex I to Art. 43–46, n. 60 et seqq.

[51] See BGH, NJW 1963, 1541, 1542; BVerfG, NJW 1991, 1597, 1600; BGH, NJW 1988, 2173, 2175.

[52] After all, it is possible that the connection to the domestic forum precludes the assumption of a location in the expropriating state. This means that recognition is not covered by the principle of territoriality and there is no need to resort to the public policy exception.

icy exception should also apply to investment protection treaties. The reason for this is that it cannot be ruled out that the legality of an expropriation will be decided in the expropriating state (Article 4 section 2 sentence 5 GMT). If minimum procedural standards are not met in this regard, there is an interest in refusing the recognition of the respective award or judgement in exceptional cases.[53] This is especially relevant if the expropriating state does not agree to arbitration and is therefore bound solely by decisions of the national courts.

An application of public policy exception could also be considered, when an arbitral tribunal awards compensation for a lawful expropriation that negatively affects concessions that were given to the investor for the operation of nuclear or wind power plants in accordance with public law. As explained above, these concessions would – according to the German doctrine – not constitute property and would, thus, not be protected by the German Constitution. Therefore, it could be claimed that the arbitral award violates Article 14 section 1 GG and the public policy exception should be applied (cf. Article 6 sentence 2 EGBGB). However, such an understanding would disregard the nature of the public policy exception as a means of last resort for extreme and exceptional circumstances. It can not be applied only because the national concept of property protection differs from the rules established within a bilateral investment protection treaty. With its signature to the bilateral treaty Germany has accepted the different approach these treaties provide by the concept of an investment as well as the different requirements and consequences of an expropriation. Discrepancies with arbitral award that are based on these different concepts and requirements are a logical and necessary consequence. They can only be avoided by a termination of the respective BIT but not by a recourse to the public policy exception.

To sum up, even though investors are also protected by the public policy exception when a BIT applies, the BITs themselves, in general, provide for a high standard of protection that makes the need for a recourse to the public policy exception even more exceptional.

V. Conclusion

BITs establish an independent substantive standard for the protection of assets. Compared with the German constitutional law, the range of protected legal positions is considerably wider. And also, the method to decide whether or not a certain position is legally protected is based on quite different criteria. This results in unequal treatment of investors who can base their claims on a BIT and those that – due to their country of origin – can not. At the level of recognition this inequality continues. Investors who are not protected by a BIT must – due to

---

[53] See *Lorenz*, in: BeckOK, BGB, 77th ed. 2026, Art. 6 EGBGB, n. 14, on the exceptional nature of public policy.

the prevailing principle of territoriality – effectively accept expropriations without compensation, when they concern assets that are located in the expropriating state. In rare cases and after an extensive consideration of all relevant factors an application of the public policy exception might as a last resort be possible. Investors protected by a BIT, on the other hand, can also rely on solid substantive protection by the requirements for the legality of an expropriation laid down in the BIT. The BITs, in general, also include rules concerning the judicial review and establishing a dispute resolution by neutral arbitral tribunals. The parties, thus, do not have to bring their claims to the courts of the state, where the expropriation took place, which (statistically) increases their chances for a fair and eventually successful proceeding. However, the termination of Intra-EU BITs does, in general, not expose EU investors to these disadvantages, since they are still protected by the EU legal standards and the legal remedies foreseen in EU law. For Non-EU investors, however, the disadvantages described above remain. In Germany in particular, the large number of BITs that have come into force and the German government's efforts to conclude further investment protection agreements suggest that these differences will gradually disappear.

Arts and Law: The Challenge of Contemporary Art to Private Law

Hannes Wais

I. Copyright and the Berne Convention

Is your country of investigation a party to the Berne Convention? If so, since when? What sources of national law govern the rights of artists (a general copyright law, several laws, Sections in a Civil Code)?

Germany signed the Berne Convention on September 9, 1886. It was ratified on September 5, 1887. The date of its entry into force is December 5, 1887. The rights of artists with respect to their works are governed by a general copyright law (*Gesetz über Urheberrecht und verwandte Schutzrechte* [UrhG]). In some cases, general provisions of the German Civil Code (*Bürgerliches Gesetzbuch* [BGB]) may also apply, e.g. the general rule of tort liability in § 823 (1) BGB[1] or unjust enrichment in § 812 (1) BGB[2]. Where the fundamental rights of artistic freedom and the general personality right are concerned, provisions of the Basic Law (*Grundgesetz* [GG]) may have an indirect bearing on a case between privates, too. In some cases, the protection provided by copyright law and competition law or design law may overlap.[3]

II. Aesthetic Neutrality

As is well known, more than a century ago, Justice Oliver Holmes stated: "It would be a dangerous undertaking for judges, who are trained only to the law, to constitute themselves final judges of the worth of pictorial illustrations, outside of the narrowest and most obvious limits". Similarly, according to Article 112-1 of the French Intellectual Property Code, the principle of aesthetic neutrality inspires judicial activity. Are these principles equally expressed in your national law and in judgments? Could you provide some examples (case law) where a discrepancy between the statement of principle and the practice of its implementation is highlighted?

§ 2 (1) UrhG states that "protected works of literature, science, and art include, in particular […]". The list that follows contains different kinds of works. There is

1 *Schack*, Urheber- und Urhebervertragsrecht, 10th ed. 2021, n. 902.
2 *Schack*, Urheber- und Urhebervertragsrecht, 10th ed. 2021, n. 905.
3 *Schack*, Urheber- und Urhebervertragsrecht, 10th ed. 2021, n. 80 et seq.

no express requirement with regard to the aesthetic appeal of the works. Pursuant to § 2 (2) UrhG only "personal intellectual creations" qualify as works within the meaning of this act. It is generally accepted that the assessment of whether a work is a personal intellectual creation pursuant to § 2 (2) UrhG, shall be made objectively and independently of the judge's personal attitude toward certain forms of artistic expression.[4] Pursuant to the case-law of the German Federal Court of Justice, a certain degree of originality is necessary for copyright protection to be granted.[5] The question of what degree of originality is sufficient is determined by the opinion of those who are reasonably familiar with literary and artistic matters.[6] With regard to furniture, the court held that "whether something is a work of art depends [...] on whether the content [...] is sufficient to qualify as art according to prevailing views on art".[7] The law is hence not entirely neutral with regard to the question of what is art "worthy of protection" and what is not.[8] Some authors have expressed their concern about this caselaw.[9] There are some parallels between this question and the constitutional question of the scope of freedom of art as granted by article 5 (3) GG.[10]

III. The Author – the Fact of Creation

How does your national legislation implement Article 6bis of the Berne Convention?

Article 6bis of the Berne Convention is implemented primarily by § 14 UrhG.[11] Pursuant to this provision, the author has the right to prohibit any distortion or other impairment of his work that may be prejudicial to his legitimate intellectual or personal interests in the work. Besides the general provision of § 14 UrhG, several more provisions exist that have a narrower and more specific scope. § 39 UrhG is aimed at the holder of a right to (commercially) exploit a certain protected work. According to this provision, the holder of an exploitation right may not modify the work, its title, or the author's designation, unless otherwise agreed, but exceptions may apply if the author cannot refuse consent according to the principle of good faith. § 62 UrhG extends the scope of § 39 UrhG to the cases of legally permitted exploitation of a protected work – albeit with some

---

4 Wandtke/Bullinger/*Bullinger*, Urheberrecht, 6th ed. 2022, § 2 n. 5; Fromm/Nordemann/*A. Nordemann*, Urheberrecht 13th ed. 2024, § 2 n. 16

5 BGH v. 19.11.1971 – I ZR 31/70 (GRUR 1972, 143, 144); BGH v. 30.05.1958 – I ZR 21/57 (GRUR 1958, 562, 563).

6 BGH v. 19.11.1971 – I ZR 31/70 (GRUR 1972, 143, 144); BGH v. 30.05.1958 – I ZR 21/57 (GRUR 1958, 562, 563).

7 BGH v 10.12.1986 – I ZR 15/85 (GRUR 1987, 903, 904).

8 *Schack*, Urheber- und Urhebervertragsrecht, 10th ed. 2021, n. 198.

9 Möhring/Nicolini/*Ahlberg*, Urheberrecht, 4th ed. 2018, § 2 n. 158; Dreier/Schulze/*Schulze*, Urheberrechtsgesetz, 8th ed. 2025, § 2 n. 32.

10 BeckOK UrhR/*Rauer/Bibi*, 48th ed. 01.12.2025, UrhG § 2 n. 18.

11 Dreier/Schulze/*Specht-Riemenschneider*, 8th ed. 2025, UrhG § 14 n. 3.

modifications that apply to specific categories of works. § 93 UrhG contains a specific rule for works of film which is narrower than the general rule in § 14 UrhG.

IV. Author and Copyright Register

Is there a need for registration of the work to activate the protection of copyright?

Protection of copyright does not require registration under German law.[12]

V. Condition of Copyright Protection – Creativity

What is the standard definition of "creativity" in your country's copyright law, as well as in the practice of its judicial implementation?

Pursuant to § 2 (2) UrhG, only a "personal intellectual creation" can be protected by copyright. The term "intellectual creation" refers to intellectual work of a human being.[13] The work must reach a certain higher level of creativity.[14] According to settled case law of the German Federal Court of Justice, a "personal intellectual creation" is a creation of individual character whose aesthetic content has reached such a level that, in the opinion of persons receptive to art and reasonably familiar with artistic views, it can be described as an "artistic" achievement.[15] Importantly, the required degree of creativity may vary depending on the type of work.[16]

VI. Condition of Copyright Protection – Originality

1. The Concept of Originality

What is the standard definition of "originality" in your country's copyright law, as well as in the practice of its judicial implementation?

Under German law, the work must be an "individual" creation, i. e. the result of a creative act reflecting the personality of the author.[17] Whether or not the requirement of individuality is synonymous with the requirement of originality is a matter of definition. If originality of a work simply means "one's own work" (in

12 *Schack*, Urheber- und Urhebervertragsrecht, 10th ed. 2021, n. 263.

13 Dreier/Schulze/*Raue*, 8th ed. 2025, UrhG § 2 n. 21; BeckOK UrhR/*Rauer/Bibi*, 48th ed. 01.12.2025, UrhG § 2 n. 47.

14 Wandtke/Bullinger/*Bullinger*, Urheberrecht, 6th ed. 2022, § 2 n 23.

15 BGH v. 9.11.2023 – I ZR 203/22 (GRUR 2024, 386 n. 25).

16 Wandtke/Bullinger/*Bullinger*, Urheberrecht, 6th ed. 2022, § 2 n 25.

17 *Schack*, Urheber- und Urhebervertragsrecht, 10th ed. 2021, n. 194.

contrast to an imitation or copy), individuality is in fact a stricter requirement.[18] Individuality requires that there is some room for the author's personality to unfold.[19] There need not be a particularly high level of individuality. For example, a collection of court decisions was held to satisfy the requirement of individuality.[20] Everyday works that are delivered as a matter of routine are not considered to be individual works.[21]

2. *Influence of EU Law*

Has the European Union notion of originality changed the jurisprudence of your country with regard to the definition of Author?

Pursuant to §7 UrhG, the person who created a work is the author of that work. There is a close connection between §7 UrhG and §2 (2) UrhG, pursuant to which only personal intellectual creations can be considered works in the legal sense. Accordingly, only a person that created a work within the meaning of §2 (2) UrhG is an author under §7 UrhG. It follows that the European Union notion of originality may have changed German jurisprudence concerning the definition of author provided that it has changed the definition of works within the meaning of §2 (2) UrhG. Whether this is the case is at the center of an ongoing discussion.[22] Pursuant to the German Federal Court of Justice, however, the definition of "works" within the meaning of §2 UrhG does not differ from autonomous concept of EU law as regards its substance.[23] Whether this assumption holds true for every element of the national concept of "works" is not yet entirely clear. It could be argued that the EU definition does not entail the requirement of a specific level of creativity of the work and therefore is less strict.[24]

VII. The Notion of a Work of Art – Fixation

1. *No Requirement Under German Law*

To ensure the legal protection of works of art, the Berne Convention mentions a requirement to fix the shape (Art. 2.2), although it does so in non-binding terms. It provides that

[18] *Schack*, Urheber- und Urhebervertragsrecht, 10th ed. 2021, n. 196.

[19] BGH v. 12.03.1987 – I ZR 71/85 (GRUR 1987, 704, 706)

[20] *Schack*, Urheber- und Urhebervertragsrecht, 10th ed. 2021, n. 198; OLG Frankfurt/M v. 10.01.1985 – 6 U 30/84 (GRUR 1986, 242); OLG Düsseldorf v. 16. 04. 1996 – 20 U 68–95 (NJW-RR 1998, 116, 117).

[21] Dreier/Schulze/*Raue*, 8th ed. 2025, UrhG §2 n. 33; *Schack*, Urheber- und Urhebervertragsrecht, 10th ed. 2021, n. 198.

[22] Dreier/Schulze/*Raue*, 8th ed. 2025, UrhG §2 n. 5; BeckOK UrhR/*Rauer/Bibi*, 48. ed. 01.12.2025, UrhG §2 n. 36 et seq.

[23] BGH v. 15.12.2022 – I ZR 173/21 – n. 14 (GRUR 2023, 571); BGH v. 7.4.2022 – I ZR 222/20 – n. 29 (GRUR 2022, 899).

[24] Wandtke/Bullinger/*Bullinger*, Urheberrecht, 6th ed. 2022, §2 n. 14.

"It shall, however, be a matter for legislation in the countries of the Union to prescribe that works in general or any specified categories of works shall not be protected unless they have been fixed in some material form". This vague requirement is intended to allow parties to the Convention to determine whether they wish to impose a requirement that the work be fixed in a tangible format, that it has not been fixed at all, or that it meets other standards in between. Is there in your legislation a legal, judicial, or doctrinal notion of fixation? In light of the above, please describe how your national legal system has implemented Article 2.2 of the Berne Convention. In particular, it is interesting to understand how the Idea-Expression dichotomy is structured (with or without fixation?).

German copyright law does not require a fixation of the work. This is evidenced by § 2 (1) no. 1 UrhG which refers to "verbal works such as written works and speeches". Hence, even unrecorded free speech can be protected.[25] With the entry-into-force of the UrhG, also the fixation requirement regarding pantomimic and choreographic works that had previously existed was removed.[26] Generally speaking, the transient nature of a work does not preclude its protection under the UrhG. However, an indirect requirement of fixation may result from the fact that a work must be perceptible[27] (with human senses). For this reason, it is argued that e. g. scientific-technical presentations require some sort of fixation.[28]

2. *Requirement of Perceptibility*

If the criterion of fixation is excluded, how has case law analyzed the notion of the "form of expression" of the work? Has it evolved in relation to certain contemporary forms of expression? If the criterion of fixation is excluded, how have doctrine and case law analyzed the notion of "form of expression" of the work? Has it evolved in relation to certain contemporary forms of expression?

A work can only be protected by copyright if it is perceptible with human senses.[29] This requirement corresponds to the notion of "expression" under the Berne Convention. There is no express notion of perceptibility under German copyright law. Rather, this requirement is considered an element of the notion of "personal intellectual creation" under § 2 (2) UrhG. A work is a creation within the meaning of § 2 (2) UrhG if the author has expressed it in such a way that it is perceptible to other people.[30] Ideas that exist only in the author's mind cannot be protected by copyright.[31]

---

25 *Schack*, Urheber- und Urhebervertragsrecht, 10th ed. 2021, n. 207, 262.
26 *Schack*, Urheber- und Urhebervertragsrecht, 10th ed. 2021, n. 262.
27 Wandtke/Bullinger/*Bullinger*, 6th ed. 2022, UrhG § 2 n. 19.
28 *Schack*, Urheber- und Urhebervertragsrecht, 10th ed. 2021, n. 192, 262.
29 BGH v. 09.05.1985 – I ZR 52/83 (GRUR 1985, 1041, 1046).
30 Wandtke/Bullinger/*Bullinger*, 6th ed. 2022, UrhG § 2 n. 19.
31 Wandtke/Bullinger/*Bullinger*, 6th ed. 2022, UrhG § 2 n. 19.

VIII. Numerus Clausus

1. The List Contained in § 2 I UrhG

Is the list of mediums in your law imperative or enumerative?

The first paragraph of § 2 UrhG reads "Protected works of literature, science, and art include, in particular […]". The provision lists seven different mediums: verbal works, musical works, pantomime works, works of fine art, photographic works, cinematographic works, and representations of a scientific or technical nature, such as drawings, plans, maps, sketches, tables, and plastic representations. The initial mentioning of "literature, science, and art" is generally considered to have no actual relevance; the terms must be given a very broad meaning and are viewed as a reminiscence to the traditional framework of copyright[32] rather than an actual limitation of its scope[33]. The list of works is not conclusive either as is evidenced by the word "in particular".[34] The listed mediums are intended as examples.[35]

2. Openness of the Provision

The Berne Convention does not explicitly include in its classification types of works of art such as performances, ready-mades, hybrids, appropriations, land-art, video art or works placed on other new media. To your knowledge, is this omission corrected by the law, or by its judicial implementation?

As the list of works in § 2 (1) UrhG is not conclusive, the fact that a certain type of works does not fall within any of the categories does not preclude it from being protected by copyright. New types of works are protected if they qualify as a personal intellectual creation within the meaning of § 2 (2) UrhG.[36] Copyright thus also protects newly emerging forms of artistic expression or integrated forms of work such as multimedia works that contain elements of various conventional types of work.[37] Due to the use of image sequences as a means of representation, video art often falls within the notion of film works in § 2 (1) no. 6 UrhG.[38]

---

32 Dreier/Schulze/*Schulze/Raue*, 8th ed. 2025, UrhG § 1 n. 2.
33 *Schack*, Urheber- und Urhebervertragsrecht, 10th ed. 2021, n. 184
34 Dreier/Schulze/*Raue*, 8th ed. 2025, UrhG § 2 n. 102.
35 BeckOK UrhR/*Rauer/Bibi*, 48th ed. 01.12.2025, UrhG § 2 n. 170.
36 *Schack*, Urheber- und Urhebervertragsrecht, 10th ed. 2021, n. 256.
37 Wandtke/Bullinger/*Bullinger*, Urheberrecht, 6th ed. 2022, § 2 n. 4; Schricker/Loewenheim/*Loewenheim/Leistner*, Urheberrecht 6th ed. 2020, § 2 n. 26.
38 Dreier/Schulze/*Raue*, 8th ed. 2025, UrhG § 2 n. 192.

IX. Video Art

Traditionally, copyright law does not cover video art products; Can you identify other ways to protect video art within your national legal system?

Under German copyright law, a work of video art is protected if it entails a personal intellectual creation under § 2 (2) UrhG. In some cases, involving the use of the work by a competitor, competition law may also provide protection. It should be noted, however, that the unauthorized use of a work is not per se a violation of competition law.[39] Competition law comes into play only if the work has a certain market relevance and the unauthorized use is unfair ("*unlauter*" in German).[40] This may be the case, in particular, where the competitor makes use of an exact copy to pursue legitimate purposes, while these purposes can be achieved also without such direct imitation.[41] In some cases, it might also be possible to register video art as a protected design under the German Design Act (*Designgesetz*), although there is some uncertainty regarding the question whether the term "design" actually includes motion pictures. The EU-Directive on the legal protection of designs (2024/2823) will remove this uncertainty as its article 2 specifically provides that "design" may also refer to "the movement, transition or any other sort of animation of those features" of a product.

X. Creations that Cannot Be Protected

What types of creations remain definitively excluded from copyright protection in your country?

Food flavors and fragrances cannot be protected by copyright.[42]

XI. Permanence of the Work Over Time

1. Ephemeral Works

Does your national legislation regulate the case of ephemeral works? Or of the specificity of the site as an essential component of the work? In a civil law situation, some courts (in France, for example) have relaxed the formal requirement and accepted in their interpretation the relevance of aspects external to the form/expression dichotomy, such as context, to recognize the protection of installations, of readymade. Do you see an evolution like the one in France driven by case law within your legal system?

---

[39] Wandtke/Bullinger/*Bullinger*, 6th ed. 2022, UrhG § 2 n. 160.

[40] Wandtke/Bullinger/*Bullinger*, 6th ed. 2022, UrhG § 2 n. 161.

[41] *Schack*, Urheber- und Urhebervertragsrecht, 10th ed. 2021, n. 43.

[42] *Schack*, Urheber- und Urhebervertragsrecht, 10th ed. 2021, n. 244; ECJ, 13.11.2018 – C-310/17 (Gerechtshof Arnhem-Leeuwarden), n. 44.

It is assumed that the mere presentation of an already existing object does not meet the requirement of a personal intellectual creation under § 2(2) UrhG and therefore is not protected by copyright law.[43] However, there are some voices that propose taking into consideration also the creation of a specific context that may be sufficient for a work to enjoy copyright protection.[44]

2. The Requirement of Manifestation

Permanence in time is a traditional feature of the visual arts; this characteristic does not consider expressions such as performances, or installations that need to be reactivated. Contemporary artists are demanding recognition in the law and judicial protection of the ephemeral. How is this issue addressed in your legal system? What value is recognized to the documentation (such as photos, video-recording)?

Under German copyright law, a permanent fixation is not required, but there must be some sort of manifestation, i. e. the work must be objectively perceptible to other people at a specific point in time.[45] Hence, even improvisations and happenings can have the character of a work.[46] The purpose of the requirement of manifestation is to exclude abstract intellectual communication in the form of methods, concepts, rules, or systems, from copyright protection.[47]

XII. Site-Specific Works

Does your national legislation take into account or exclude the relevance of the specificity of the location as an essential component of the work?

Courts have not yet adopted the view shared by some authors that the creation of the context – which may involve the selection of a certain location – could provide a sufficient element of human creation. The ideas of *Kummer* pertaining to the presentation as such have been rejected by the courts.[48]

XIII. Design

As a rule, industrial designs are only protected by law if they have "artistic value". Within European Union law, the definition of the latter is left to the interpretation of experts and courts. Is this situation common to your legal system?

---

[43] Dreier/Schulze/*Raue*, 8th ed. 2025, UrhG § 2 n. 24; Wandtke/Bullinger/*Bullinger*, 6th ed. 2022, UrhG § 2 n. 15.

[44] BeckOK UrhR/*Rauer/Bibi*, 48th ed. 01.12.2025, UrhG § 2 n. 50.

[45] BGH v. 27.02.1962, ZR 118/60 (GRUR 1962, 470, 472); BGH v. 09.05.1985, ZR 52/83 (GRUR 1985, 1041, 1046).

[46] BeckOK UrhR/*Rauer/Bibi*, 48th ed. 01.12.2025, UrhG § 2 n. 115.

[47] BeckOK UrhR/*Rauer/Bibi*, 48th ed. 01.12.2025, UrhG § 2 n. 116.

[48] OLG Hamburg v. 29.11.2001 – 3 U 288/00 (GRUR-RR 2002, 217, 218).

The situation is common. For example, in a decision regarding furniture designed by Le Corbusier, the German Federal Court[49] stressed that the armchairs in question may be protected by copyright only if, regardless of the intended use, they qualify as art according to prevailing views. The assessment may also consider the circumstances at the time the work was created and the attention it received in professional circles and among the general public. The presentation of the LC2 armchair in art museums and art exhibitions may also provide information as to its artistic value. If the expertise of the trial judge and the submissions of the parties do not provide a sufficient basis for valuation, obtaining an expert opinion may be considered.

XIV. Works in the Future – Open Works

Works in progress, 'open' works of art, works left for public participation and, in the digital sphere, user-generated content, are protected. Depending on your investigative legal system, please explain whether: – the situation described is still relevant; – the situation described has been explicitly modified by law or modified by case law. An explicit reference to case law would be much appreciated.

The law makes reference to "drafts" only with regard to works of "fine arts" in § 2 (1) no. 4 UrhG, but it is accepted that work in progress is generally protected by copyright law if it meets the requirement of a personal intellectual creation under § 2 (2) UrhG.[50] The same requirements apply to user-generated content.[51]

XV. Copyright – Moral Rights

The national implementation of moral rights is a major case of diversity in the legal protection of artists. Would you describe your legal system as being closer to generous protection or rather limited protection?

The author's moral rights have a constitutional underpinning. Moral rights of the author are a specific form of his general personality right.[52] They are derived from the protection of human dignity (article 1 GG) and personal freedom (article 2 (1) GG).[53] The purpose of moral rights of the author is the protection of the author's moral interests associated with his works, whereas copyright is intended

---

49 BGH v. 10.12.1986 – I ZR 15/85 (NJW 1986, 2678).

50 BGH v. 23.6.2005 – I ZR 227/02 (GRUR 2005, 854, 856); BGH v. 09.05.1985 – I ZR 52/83 (NJW 1986, 192, 196); Schricker/Loewenheim/*Loewenheim/Leistner*, 6th ed. 2020, UrhG § 2 n. 49; Wandtke/Bullinger/*Bullinger*, 6th ed. 2022, UrhG § 2 n. 41.

51 *Reinemann/Remmertz*, Urheberrechte an User-generated Content, ZUM 2012, 216, 218.

52 BGH v. 05.03.1971 – I ZR 94/69 (GRUR 1971, 525, 526).

53 BGH v. 05.03.1971 – I ZR 94/69 (GRUR 1971, 525, 526).

to protect his economic interests.[54] Some authors argue that moral rights also serve economic purposes.[55] The fact that the author's moral rights are closely related to the author's general personality right suggests that, in this regard, the German legal system is one of generous protection. The legislator has also passed specific legislation concerning the moral rights of the author, in particular the right to publish his work (§ 12 UrhG), to be acknowledged as the author (§ 13 UrhG) and to object to any alteration or mutilation of his work that may harm his legitimate interests in his work (§ 14 UrhG).

XVI. Paternity

Another situation of diversity affects the power to acknowledge authorship on the work; national legal systems are different because of a heterogeneous identification of moral rights, and the different recognition of the transferability of those rights by will. Could you describe who has the right to declare the authorship of a work of art, and whether the case law has faithfully followed the text of the law? Could you describe who is the holder, according to the law, of the right to protect the authorship of a work of art, whether there is a statute of limitations for this action, and whether the case law has faithfully followed the text of the law?

Pursuant to § 7 UrhG, the natural person who created the work through personal intellectual effort is regarded the author within the meaning of § 2 (2) UrhG. It follows that legal entities or partnerships can never be authors, as they do not engage in intellectual activity themselves.[56] Since § 7 UrhG is a mandatory provision that cannot be deviated from, it is not for the author to decide whether his work is protected by copyright or not, nor whether someone else will become the author of the work. Pursuant to §§ 28, 29 UrhG, the copyright associated with authorship may be transferred onto another person only by means of inheritance and acts related to inheritance.

It follows from § 13 UrhG that the author of the work has a right to be acknowledged as the author of his work. There is no right to *declare* authorship because copyright exists by virtue of the law as it does not require anything else than a personal intellectual creation within the meaning of § 2 (2) UrhG.

§ 97 (1) UrhG provides certain rights to protect the authorship to the author or the person who, by way of inheritance or inheritance-related act, has become his successor.[57] The claimant may request that the violation of the author's right stops and that he be compensated for the damage caused by that violation. The author may also provide a third person with the authority to litigate, but the third person

[54] BeckOK UrhR/*Götting*, 48th ed. 01.12.2025, UrhG § 12 n. 1; Schricker/Loewenheim/*Peukert*, 6th ed. 2020, UrhG § 12 n. 1.

[55] Wandtke/Bullinger/*Bullinger*, 6th ed. 2022, UrhG vor § 12 n. 1.

[56] Wandtke/Bullinger/*Thum*, 6th ed. 2022, UrhG § 7 n. 1.

[57] Wandtke/Bullinger/*v. Wolff/Bullinger*, 6th ed. 2022, UrhG § 97 n. 7.

must show that he has a legitimate interest in bringing the proceedings on behalf of the author.[58] This includes cases in which the author has granted the third person with a right to use, provided that this right is negatively affected by the violation, too.[59] Pursuant to § 102 UrhG this right is subject to statutes of limitation; in most cases the limitation period is three years.[60]

XVII. Collaborations

The insistence on the conceptual aspect of the artwork can lead to a difficult legal identification of the contributors (executors, collaborators). Had the jurisprudence in your country to confront this question? If so, what criteria have been applied?

The question of authorship in cases of collaboration is dealt with by § 7 UrhG. Generally speaking, persons who have collectively created a work will be considered co-authors if it is impossible to discern the individual contributions (which must each amount to a personal intellectual work within the meaning of § 2 (2) UrhG), or if – for other reasons – the individual works cannot be separated.[61] If co-authorship is established, the collective work may only be exploited or otherwise made use of by the group of co-authors as a whole.[62] Inseparability under § 7 UrhG may also be assumed if an individual part of the collaborative work, albeit discernable and separable in a factual sense, cannot exist on its own but would require to be integrated into another object.[63] For example, drawings in a book that illustrate the story are inseparable.[64] Persons who have contributed work that is in every way separable, on the other hand, qualify as authors already by virtue of their work alone and are protected by copyright law. At the other end of the spectrum are those contributions that do not on their own meet the requirement of personal intellectual work. They are irrelevant also in the context of co-authorship.[65] In short, with regards to collaborations, a twofold test is applied: The first and most important question is whether a specific contribution is a work on its own, the second question is whether the work is separable so that the copyright can be made use of separately, without conflicting with the copyrights of others.

58 Schricker/Loewenheim/*Leistner*, 6th ed. 2020, UrhG § 97 n. 49.
59 BGH v. 27.02.1961 – I ZR 127/59 (GRUR 1961, 635, 636).
60 Wandtke/Bullinger/*Bohne*, 6th ed. 2022, UrhG § 102 n. 1.
61 Wandtke/Bullinger/*Thum*, 6th ed. 2022, UrhG § 8 n. 26.
62 Schricker/Loewenheim/*Loewenheim/Peifer*, 6th ed. 2020, UrhG § 8 n. 14.
63 BeckOK UrhR/*Rauer/Bibi*, 48th ed. 01.12.2025, UrhG § 8 n. 19.
64 LG München I v. 23.01.2009 – 21 O 13662/07 (BeckRS 2009, 04738).
65 BGH v. 7.4.2022 – I ZR 222/20 – n. 90 (GRUR 2022, 899).

XVIII. Integrity of the Work and Deliberate Deterioration

Certain choices made by some contemporary artists about the quality and type of materials used in the making of the artwork, combined with the artist's desire not to preserve the work, can lead to early deterioration of the work; if this were the case, a tension could arise between the moral rights of the author and, on the other hand, the interests of collectors or the conservation duties of curators. How would this conflict be regulated in your legal system? What is the role of good faith in relation to a possible duty of the author to provide all the necessary information? Could you identify in the case case-law whether the judge has decided for the repair or restoration of a work?

Pursuant to § 14 UrhG, the author has a right to prohibit any distortion or other impairment of his work that is likely to be prejudicial to his legitimate intellectual or personal interests in the work. The notion of "distortion or other impairments" includes interventions that change the character of the work.[66] If the deterioration process is part of the author's personal intellectual creation, the prevention of the deterioration or the removal of its material consequences will change the character of the work.[67] However, the author only has a right to prohibit such an intervention if his interests outweigh those of the owner.[68] As a general principle, the law protects the interest of the owner to freely decide what to do with his property.[69] Whether the author's interests prevail will depend on the specific case. If a work is publicly displayed, his interests are more likely to outweigh the property interests of the owner than in cases where the work is locked away from the public[70] – in particular, if the work in question is one of minor relevance with respect to the author's oeuvre as a whole.[71] If the deterioration process or its effects are not part of artist's creation, on the other hand, the owner's interest in saving the work from its decay are more likely to prevail.

XIX. Destruction

Does the owner of the work have the right to destroy it in your legal system?

In a case concerning the removal of an art installation in a museum, the German Federal Court of Justice[72] held that the destruction of a protected work by its owner may be prohibited under § 14 UrhG if the destruction of a work will gravely affect legitimate intellectual or personal interests of the author relating to the work's continuous impact on its environment. These interests are protected also under

[66] Wandtke/Bullinger/*Bullinger*, 6th ed. 2022, UrhG § 14 n. 3
[67] Wandtke/Bullinger/*Bullinger*, 6th ed. 2022, UrhG § 14 n. 44.
[68] BeckOK UrhR/*Götting*, 48th ed. 01.12.2025, UrhG § 14 n. 21; Wandtke/Bullinger/*Bullinger*, 6th ed. 2022, UrhG § 14 n. 10.
[69] Wandtke/Bullinger/*Bullinger*, 6th ed. 2022, UrhG § 14 n. 14.
[70] Wandtke/Bullinger/*Bullinger*, 6th ed. 2022, UrhG § 14 n. 20.
[71] Dreier/Schulze/*Specht-Riemenschneider*, 8th ed. 2025, UrhG § 14 n. 25.
[72] BGH v. 21.2.2019 – I ZR 98/17 – n. 28 et seq. (GRUR 2019, 609).

article 5 (3) GG. However, the court stressed that on the constitutional level, as per article 14 GG, also the owner's interests relating to his property are protected. This conflict must be resolved by balancing the protected interests of both parties. Regarding the author's interests, relevant questions include whether the work is a one-off, whether it has general and personal significance, whether a high level of creativity is displayed, and whether the work serves a particular use-purpose or is purpose-free. With regards to the owner's interest, it is particularly important whether the work can be removed from other property of the owner without being destroyed. Where no such removal is possible, the owner's interests usually prevail.

XX. Restauration

Does the owner have a duty in your legal system to restore the work of art?

Under German law, the owner does not have a duty to restore a protected work, unless the author and the owner have contractually agreed on such a duty.[73]

XXI. Denial

1. Case Law

The practice of denying the work of art has been adopted by conceptual artists as a defense against unauthorized uses that do not conform to the artist's indications by collectors, museums, and intermediaries: do you have any case law on this subject?

In 2006, the district court of Munich[74] had to decide a case concerning the cover of a paper calendar on which the name of the claimant was mentioned. The claimant was the author of the cover illustration, but the mentioning of his name on the cover created the impression that the claimant was the author of the entire calendar. The court held that pursuant to § 13 UrhG, the claimant had a right not to be mentioned as the author of his work. The court issued a cease-and-desist order against the publisher of the calendar based on the violation of the author's moral rights.

2. The Act of Denial Is Also Proposed as a Work of Art in Itself

Under what conditions can an author legally refuse to refer to his or her work personally? And what is the effect of the withdrawal on the rights of interested buyers or third parties?

§ 13 UrhG provides the author with the right to be mentioned as the author of his work. Uncertainty surrounds the question of whether this right – which forms part of the author's moral right – also includes the right *not* to be mentioned as

[73] *Schack*, Kunst und Recht, 4th ed. 2024, n. 483.
[74] LG München I v. 8.06.2006 – O 17592/04 (ZUM 2006, 664, 665).

the author of his own work. There are voices in the literature that argue that § 42 UrhG expressly deals with the author's right to distance himself from previous work only with regard to exploitation rights and that granting the author a general right not to be mentioned as an author would circumvent the rather narrow scope of § 42 UrhG.[75] It is also argued that in cases where the author has sold the work, a withdrawal of authorship would pose a violation of the property rights of the (new) owner.[76] Others seem to accept a general right of the author not to be mentioned exists under § 13 (1) UrhG, stressing that such a right is particularly important where ownership has changed, since in these cases the author does not have the right to destroy his work due to the property interests of the owner.[77] However, it is also argued that the interests of the author must be balanced against the interests of the owner pertaining to the cost and effort of implementing that request (for example if the removal of the author's name is very difficult).[78] Provided that a right not to be mentioned as the author exists, a follow-up question concerns the legal consequences of the exercise of said right in contractual relationships. If authorship is withdrawn only after the buyer took possession of the work, it is difficult to argue that the work has a defect in the legal sense, since this would require that the defect existed already at the time of the delivery (§ 434 (1) BGB). In cases in which the seller is also the author, withdrawal of authorship may be construed as a violation of the seller's obligation to be considerate of the buyer's interests (§ 241 (2) BGB). Ultimately, this depends on the contractual agreement between the parties.

XXII. Censorship and Freedom of Expression

Contemporary art often challenges political and social norms, leading to legal battles over whether museums or other institutions should remove works deemed insulting. Do you have any case law on this subject?

In 2013, the district court of Berlin[79] had to decide a case involving an exhibition of street photography on larger-than-life posters which depicted a randomly chosen woman on a street in Berlin. The woman was completely unknown to the public and had not consented to the photographs, nor had she agreed on the exhibition. The exhibition was organized by a non-profit foundation. After the exhibition, the foundation issued a cease-and-desist declaration at the woman's request. The woman later sued the foundation on various grounds, but only her claim for compensation of the legal costs pertaining to the cease-and-desist declaration was successful. In this regard the court held that while the woman was

75 Schricker/Loewenheim/*Peukert*, 6th ed. 2020, UrhG § 13 n. 19.
76 *Schack*, Kunst und Recht, 4th ed. 2024, n. 258.
77 Dreier/Schulze/*Specht-Riemenschneider*, 8th ed. 2025, UrhG § 13 n. 32.
78 Dreier/Schulze/*Specht-Riemenschneider*, 8th ed. 2025, UrhG § 13 n. 32.
79 LG Berlin v. 03.06.2014 – 27 O 56/14 (ZUM 2014, 729, 732).

on a public street, she was clearly engaged in a purely private activity with no public relevance. It would significantly restrict the personality rights of a person, if they were unable to move freely in public streets because of the risk of being photographed on private occasions and without a right to object. The woman was presented on a larger-than-life poster for several weeks, stripped of anonymity. She felt embarrassed because it might have seemed to others that she had made herself available for the photograph in return for remuneration. Her personality rights therefore prevailed over artistic freedom.

In 2022, the Federal Court of Justice[80] had to decide a case involving a sandstone relief from the 13th century, originally intended as an insult to Jews. This case is only loosely connected to the posed question because – as per the legal reasoning – it does not involve artistic freedom. It is argued, however, an analysis of a conflict with artistic freedom would not have seemed far-fetched.[81] The relief depicts Jewish children feeding from the teats of a sow, and a rabbi lifting the sow's tail and staring at the sow's anus. The relief is attached to the outer walls of a church. Below the relief is memorial which commemorates the Jewish victims of the Holocaust. There is also an explanation of the historical background of the relief. The claimant, a member of the Jewish community in Germany, requested that the local parish remove the relief. The court dismissed the claim, arguing that, while the relief as such clearly violated the personality rights of Jewish people, the addition of the memorial and the explanatory note were sufficient to divest the relief of its derogatory nature.

XXIII. Unlawful Work

As a rule of contract law, contracts must have a lawful purpose; is this general rule in any way modified in the case where the illegality concerns a work of art?

A work that falls within the notion of work under § 2 UrhG is protected by copyright irrespective of its lawful or unlawful nature. However, the unlawfulness may preclude certain rights of use.

XXIV. Property Law & Public Space Interventions

1. Conflict of Property Rights and Copyright

Murals and graffiti (e.g., Banksy's works) challenge traditional property law, as building owners claim rights over artwork they did not commission. Legal battles have emerged over whether artists or property owners control such works. Could you provide a description of the situation in the legal system that is the subject of your analysis?

---

80 BGH v. 14.6.2022 – VI ZR 172/20 (NJW 2022, 2406).
81 *Gostomzyk*, Anm. zu BGH VI ZR 172/20, NJW 2022, 2410.

In a case regarding the sale of fragments of the Berlin Wall, the Federal Court of Justice[82] held that generally, when art is created unlawfully against the will of the owner whose property is affected, property rights prevail over artistic freedom. The fact that the unlawfulness of a work does not preclude copyright protection does not imply that the owner is required to accept violations of his property rights. He is free to destroy the work in question, despite the existing copyright. Regarding the right of commercial use of the work, the court held that the owner cannot generally infer from his property such a right. This is because, unlike its destruction, the use of a work by the owner does not eliminate the interference with his property. However, the court made an exception with respect to the commercial use associated with the sale of property. Where the property is intended to be tradeable, the fact that it was unlawfully used as a canvas for art does not deprive the owner of his right to sell his property, as such deprivation would be fundamentally incompatible with the very essence of property. The views expressed in this decision have found support in literature, too.[83]

2. Case Law

Cases like the destruction of 5Pointz graffiti in New York raise legal questions about artists' rights when property owners erase or alter artworks, testing laws like the U.S. Visual Artists Rights Act (VARA). Could you identify in the case law whether the judge has decided for the protection of a street artwork?

In the above decision regarding the sale of fragments of the Berlin Wall, the German Federal Court of Justice[84] held that authors of graffiti works on the Berlin wall had to be compensated for the sale of wall fragments on which their works were visible. The court argued that the Berlin Wall was never intended to be an object of trade. Hence, the copyright of the authors would not interfere with the property rights of the owner in the same way as they would, had the Berlin Wall been a tradable item from the start. It is this particularity of the case which, in the eyes of the court, justifies a greater emphasis on the interests of the authors of the unlawful works – to the detriment of the owner.

XXV. Contract and Certificate of Authenticity

1. Advantages

Contracts and certificates have acquired a particular interest in contemporary art. What do you think is the role played by contracts and certificates and in the production of works of

[82] BGH v. 23.02.1995 – I ZR 68/93 (GRUR 1995, 673, 675).
[83] *Schack*, Kunst und Recht, 4th ed. 2024, n. 197.
[84] BGH v. 23.02.1995 – I ZR 68/93 (GRUR 1995, 673, 675).

art? Do you find, in particular, contract law useful for the recognition of creative freedom and for the respect of the artist's intention?

Contracts and certificates may prove particularly useful with regard to cases in which the notion of originality is unclear, in particular in the case of photography and film and digital art, and generally in the context of limited editions. In these cases, authors can contractually agree not to exceed the quoted number of the limitation, providing prospective buyers with a certain sense of security. Reducing the uncertainty relating to limited editions may in turn make the sale more profitable for the artists.

2. Irrelevance of Certificates for the Question of Ownership

In their effort to reduce materiality and focus on the idea, some visual artists have used certificates, to make the transfer of the artwork viable. How does your legal system react to the loss of the certificate? Does the said disappearance imply the loss of the work?

Pursuant to § 929 I 1 BGB, the transfer of ownership of a work of art requires an agreement between the parties and the delivery of the work. § 929 I 1 is a mandatory provision. Since the parties are not free to implement additional legal requirements for the transfer to be effective, the issuance of a certificate is irrelevant for the effectiveness of said transfer. The certificate is equally irrelevant if the work is exclusively immaterial: An immaterial work is neither a thing nor a right, thus it cannot be the subject of ownership, and it cannot be transferred to another person. Hence, if an artist issued a certificate to accompany his immaterial work, property rights would only ever pertain to the certificate as a thing, but ownership of the certificate would not imply ownership of the immaterial work. Since the owner of the certificate does not own the immaterial work, the loss of the certificate would have no relevance either.

XXVI. Conceptual and Ephemeral Art and Property Rights

Some works by conceptual artists may be devoid of materiality, but nevertheless objectively identifiable. Is there an attempt in your legal system on the part of jurists to distinguish between the materiality and the objectification of a good? What is the legal value of the means of documentation?

It appears that there is no such discussion. There is, however, a discussion to the related question of whether the law recognizes ownership of NFTs.[85]

---

[85] *Infra*, XXX.

When artists are focused on the idea, rather than the product, their work may encounter some difficulties in being recognized by private law; in particular, property law is not in a position to regulate events of ephemeral entities without any objectivity. Would it be possible, in your jurisdiction, to determine that a conceptual artist should be qualified – rather than a seller of objects that he or she has decided not to do – as a supplier of intellectual work, or a service provider?

Under German law, a contract on the delivery of an art performance would be conceivable as a service contract within the meaning of § 611 BGB if the artist simply owed an activity. It would be categorized as a contract to produce a work within the meaning of § 631 BGB if the artist owed a certain success to be achieved by the performance.

XXVII. Photography

Almost everywhere in the world, art photography receives weak legal protection; several experts call for an update in legal regulation. Could you provide a description of the situation in the legal system that is the subject of your analysis? Does your legal system make some distinction between taking pictures and printing? How is the determination of the serial number regulated?

Photography is protected by copyright pursuant to § 2 (1) no. 5 UrhG provided that it is a personal intellectual creation within the meaning of § 2 (2) UrhG. It is necessary for the photograph to have an individual design, i.e., to contain an artistic statement that goes beyond a simple depiction.[86] Such personal intellectual creation includes, for example, the choice of image detail, the distribution of light and shadow, and subsequent editing.[87] Photographs that do not meet the requirements of personal intellectual creation in § 2 (2) UrhG are protected by § 72 (1) UrhG. A key difference is that pursuant to § 72 (3) UrhG such photographs are protected only over a period of 50 years.

A necessary requirement of the notion of "works of photography" is that it must be the result of light or another kind of radiation hitting a radiation-sensitive background.[88] The copyright protects the visual perceivability of the photo motif.[89] From the outset, one may argue that every edition of the photograph is an original. Regarding works of fine arts, however, § 6 UrhG distinguishes "originals" and "copies". Whether this differentiation is authoritative also with respect to works of photography is unclear. Some authors assume that works of photography can have multiple originals provided that the number of copies is limited and each copy has been authorized by the artist and/or the seller.[90] Exceedance of

---

86 *Schack*, Kunst und Recht, 4th ed. 2024, n. 895.
87 *Schack*, Kunst und Recht, 4th ed. 2024, n. 895.
88 BGH v. 20.12.2018 – I ZR 104/17 n. 23 (GRUR 2019, 284).
89 BeckOK UrhR/*Rauer/Bibi*, 48th ed. 01.12.2025, UrhG § 2 n. 383.
90 *Michl*, Die limitierte Auflage (2017), p. 155.

the limitation number by the artist may result in contractual liability of the artist.[91]

XXVIII. Privacy and Data Protection

1. Conflicts

Surveillance Art and Biometric Data: artists like Trevor Paglen and Ai Weiwei use surveillance footage and biometric data to critique power structures, often clashing with privacy laws such as the EU's GDPR. How would your legal system react to these practices?

These questions touch upon various problems regarding the scope of article 85 of the General Data Protection Regulation of the EU (GDPR) and the interplay of that regulation and national law. For various reasons that need not be addressed here, it is unclear whether the issue would fall under article 6 (1) (f) GDPR or under §§ 22, 23 of the German Copyright Act relating to Fine Arts and Photography (KUG).[92] However, according to the German Federal Court of Justice, there is no need to decide this question as both the European and the German provision require the same weighing of conflicting interests of data protection and artistic freedom.[93] Thus, whether or not artwork that uses surveillance footage and biometric data is compatible with the EU provisions on data protection will ultimately depend on the severity of the interference with personality rights.

2. Balancing the Conflicting Interests

Deepfake and AI-Generated Images: Some artists use AI to create hyper-realistic images or videos, leading to legal concerns about consent, defamation, and identity rights. Could you provide a description of the situation in the legal system that is the subject of your analysis?

Pictures which are created with the help of AI and are intended to appear as authentic images of a real person are caught by § 22 (1) KUG, pursuant to which "portraits" may only be distributed or publicly displayed with the consent of the person depicted. Pursuant to settled case law, an image is considered a portrait of the person depicted if it is intended and able to present a person to the viewer in their lifelike and unique external appearance.[94] With regards to AI-generated images that (from the viewpoint of the AI-user) only coincidentally resemble a real person, the question arises whether these images are also caught by § 22 (1) KUG, since there is no intentional presentation of a real person. Some authors assume that if the resemblance of the person depicted to another is only coincidental, § 22 (1) KUG is not applicable, unless there are other intentional refer-

---

[91] *Michl*, Die limitierte Auflage (2017), p. 223 et seq., 265 et seq.
[92] BGH v. 24.2.2022 – I ZR 2/21 – n. 32 (GRUR 2022, 665).
[93] BGH v. 24.2.2022 – I ZR 2/21 – n. 32 (GRUR 2022, 665).
[94] BGH v. 09.06.1965 – Ib ZR 126/63 (GRUR 1966, 102, 103).

ences.[95] This is supported by the argument that the personality right of the person depicted shall not be affected by the personality right of the person he or she coincidentally appears to be.[96] In other words: Whether the image of the person actually depicted may or may not be publicly displayed should depend solely on his or her consent and not on the consent of someone with a close resemblance. Arguably however, the situation is different in AI-generated images, when the person depicted is purely fictious. Moreover, the person coincidentally depicted by AI might also base his claim directly on a violation of his general personality right derived from article 1 and article 2 (1) GG.

XXIX. Artificial Intelligence

Technological advances have "enabled" machines to create works that are recognized by the art world as having artistic relevance; these artificially generated sculptures or images have been collected and sold in the art markets. What is, in your legal system of investigation, the approach of copyright to these products?

Output of generative AI can be protected by copyright only if a human has sufficient control over the creative elements of the work – results produced autonomously by AI are precluded from copyright protection.[97] There is a general consensus that, generally speaking, neither a person who has programmed an AI system nor a person who has trained said system has such control.[98] They cannot be regarded authors in the legal sense.

XXX. NFTs

In the field of digital art, NFTs have become a reliable method of archiving information and certifying a title deed. Does your legal system recognize a legal status to NFTs?

An NFT is not considered a thing under German law because it lacks materiality.[99] No property rights or other absolute rights attach to an NFT.[100] Some authors call for a reform of the existing laws in order to afford NFTs the protec-

95 Schricker/Loewenheim/*Götting*, 6th ed. 2020, KUG § 22 n. 21;

96 Dreier/Schulze/*Specht-Riemenschneider*, 8th ed. 2025, KUG § 22 n. 3.

97 Dreier/Schulze/*Raue*, 8th ed. 2025, UrhG § 2 n. 25; BeckOK UrhR/*Rauer/Bibi*, 48th ed. 01.12.2025, UrhG § 2 n. 53.

98 *Gomille*, Kreative künstliche Intelligenz und das Urheberrecht, JZ 2019, 969 (972f.); *Wagner*, KI-generierter Content: Ein Boost für den Public Domain oder Quell neuer Urheberrechtswerke?, MMR 2023, 811 (812); Dreier/Schulze/*Raue*, 8th ed. 2025, UrhG § 2 n. 25.

99 OLG Frankfurt a. M. v. 19.4.2023 – 13 U 82/22 – n. 30 (BKR 2023, 460); BeckOK BGB/*Fritzsche*, 76th ed. 01.11.2025, BGB § 90 n. 29.

100 *Rauer/Bibi*, Non-fungible Tokens – Was können sie wirklich?, ZUM 2022, 20, 25; BeckOK BGB/*Fritzsche*, 76th ed. 01.11.2025, BGB § 90 n. 29.

tion of an absolute right.[101] Nor is an NFT protected by copyright. This is because the code which it consists of usually will not meet the requirement of a personal intellectual creation under § 2 (2) UrhG.[102]

XXXI. Art Law

To your knowledge, is "Art Law" the subject of university courses? Are you familiar with legal journals dedicated to the subject in a specialized way?

At some universities, students can choose courses on Art Law. There is a law journal called "*Kunst und Recht*" (KUR) dedicated specifically to the subject.

XXXII. Conclusion

To conclude this analysis, could you assess the "state of the art" in the scientific debate on the tensions and challenges posed to private law by contemporary art? Are legal scholars inclined to recommend reforms or amendments to the law?

It seems that German copyright law is not faced with overwhelming challenges or tensions with regard to contemporary art. This is mainly due to the broadness of the notion of work in § 2 UrhG and, in particular, the fact that copyright protection does not require fixation. It is for these reasons that most modern categories of works are protected by copyright. One deficit might be the lack of protection of so-called readymades. If confronted with such a case, courts would be well-advised to accept that the setting of a presentation and, generally, the choice of its context may involve a highly creative element. Other issues regarding the conflict of artistic freedom and personality rights are at the center of an ongoing discussion but are not issues specifically pertaining to contemporary art. In addition, there is a degree of uncertainty that surrounds the question of the effects of EU harmonization of national copyright law but again this is not an issue that arises solely in the context of contemporary art.

---

101 *Guntermann*, Non Fungible Token als Herausforderung für das Sachenrecht, RDi 2022, 200, 208.

102 *Rauer/Bibi*, Non-fungible Tokens – Was können sie wirklich?, ZUM 2022, 20, 25.

Contributors

Anna H. Albrecht (Doctorate Münster 2011; second monograph 2020) is Professor for criminal law, criminal procedure, media criminal law and comparative criminal law at the university of Potsdam. She is a board member of the German Association of Comparative Law.

Andreas von Arnauld (Doctorate Hamburg 1998; Habilitation Berlin 2005) is Professor for Public, Public International and EU Law, University of Kiel. He is Director of the Walther Schücking Institute for International Law, University of Kiel.

Judith Brockmann (Maîtrise en Droit Paris 2002; Doctorate Hamburg 2010) is Professor for Economic, Social and Labour Law at Kassel University.

Katharina de la Durantaye (Doctorate Berlin 2003; LL.M. Yale 2005; Habilitation Berlin 2019) is Professor of Private Law and Law of the Digital Transformation at Humboldt-Universität zu Berlin. Her research focuses on IP, especially on copyright law, and on the regulation of the digital economy, including platform and AI regulation. She is a board member of the German Association of Comparative Law.

Michael Droege (Doctorate Bielefeld 2003; Habilitation Frankfurt am Main 2009) is Professor of public law, administrative law, constitutional law on religion, ecclesiastical law, and tax law at Eberhard Karls University in Tübingen. He is also the director of the Institute for Financial and Tax Law there.

Michael Fehling (Doctorate Freiburg 1993; LL.M. Berkeley 1996; Habilitation Freiburg 2000) is Professor of Public Law and Comparative Law at Bucerius Law School in Hamburg since 2001. In 2023, Fehling was elected a member of the Academy of Sciences in Hamburg. Since 2014, he is Academic director of the Energy Law Initiative (as of 2022: "Center for Interdisciplinary Research on Energy, Climate and Sustainability" – CECS) at Bucerius Law School.

Lucas Gerlach is a doctoral student working at Professor Malte Kramme's Chair of Civil Law and IT Law at Leibniz University Hannover.

Philipp Hacker (LL.M. Yale 2014; Doctorate 2016; Habilitation Berlin 2020) is Professor for the Law and Ethics of the Digital Society at the Faculty of Law and at the European New School of Digital Studies, European University Viadrina Frankfurt (Oder).

Moritz Hennemann (Doctorate Freiburg 2011; M. Jur. Oxford 2011; Habilitation Freiburg 2019) is Professor for Civil Law with Information Law, Media Law, Internet Law and Director of the Institute of Media and Information Law at the University of Freiburg. Moritz Hennemann serves as Judge (part-time) at the Higher Regional Court of Karlsruhe (10th Civil Division).

Gregor Kirchhof (Doctorate Bonn 2005; Habilitation Bonn 2009) is Professor for Public Law, Financial Law and Tax Law at the University of Augsburg, where he is also the Director of the Institute for Business and Tax Law. After obtaining a Master of Laws in the

London Law Program at the University of Notre Dame (USA) he was a Fellow at the "Forschungskolleg normative Gesellschaftsgrundlagen" research facility in Bonn.

Ben Köhler (LL.M. Harvard 2019; Doctorate Saarbrücken 2020) is Junior Professor for Private Law, EU Private Law and Private International Law at the University of Bayreuth. He is a Fellow of the European Law Institute.

Malte Kramme (Doctorate Bayreuth 2013; Habilitation Bayreuth 2020) is Professor for Civil Law and IT Law at the Institute for Legal Informatics at Leibniz University Hannover.

Lena Kunz (Doctorate Heidelberg 2011; LL.M. UChicago 2014; Habilitation Heidelberg 2025) is Professor for Civil Law, German and European Legal History, Private International Law and Comparative Law at the University of Kiel.

Robert Magnus (Doctorate Freiburg 2009; Habilitation Heidelberg 2017) is Professor for Private Law and German and International Civil Procedure at the University of Bayreuth.

Kai Purnhagen (LL.M. Wisconsin-Madison 2007; M.J.I Gießen 2009; PhD Firenze 2011) is Professor for Food Law at the University of Bayreuth.

Arne Radeisen (LL.M. Amsterdam 2020) is a doctoral candidate and research assistant at Prof. Dr. Katharina de la Durantaye's Chair for Private Law and the Law of Digital Transformation, Humboldt-Universität zu Berlin.

Caroline Sophie Rapatz (MPhil. Cambridge 2006; Doctorate Würzburg 2015; Junior Professorship Würzburg 2016–2022; Habilitation Würzburg 2022) is Professor of Civil Law, European and International Private and Procedural Law and Comparative Law at Christian-Albrechts-Universität zu Kiel. She is a board member of the German Association of Comparative Law.

Christian Reichelt is Research Assistant at the Chair for Private Law and German and International Civil Procedure at the University of Bayreuth.

Sabine Schlacke (Doctorate Bremen 1997; Habilitation Rostock 2007) is Professor of Public Law, specialising in Administrative and Environmental Law, University of Greifswald. She is Director of the Institute of Energy, Environmental and Maritime Law, University of Greifswald.

Mareike Schmidt (LL.M. Tsinghua 2008; Doctorate Basel 2012; Junior Professorship Hamburg 2016–2023) heads the Max Planck Research Group 'Transformations in Private Law: Culture, Climate, and Technology' in the Department 'Law & Anthropology' at the Max Planck Institute for Social Anthropology in Halle (Saale) and is Professor at the University of Hamburg.

Frank Schorkopf (Doctorate Hamburg 1999; Habilitation Bonn 2007) is Professor for Public Law and European Law at the University of Göttingen since 2009 and full Member of the Göttingen Academy of Sciences and Humanities.

Michael Stöber (Doctorate Marburg 2005; Habilitation Marburg 2011) is Professor for Civil Law, German and International Tax, Commercial and Business Law and Civil Procedure Law as well as Director of the Institute of Business and Tax Law at the University of Kiel. He is co-founder and President of the German-Colombian Lawyers' Association and has already carried out two research projects on legal issues relating to autonomous vehicles funded by Federal Ministries.

Meik Thöne (M.Jur. Oxford 2013; Doctorate Göttingen 2015; Habilitation Göttingen 2024; Junior Professorship 2018–2024 Potsdam) is Professor for Private Law and Civil Procedure including the aspects of European Law at the University of Potsdam.

Hannes Wais (Doctorate Heidelberg 2013; LL.M. Cambridge 2015; Habilitation Heidelberg 2021) is Professor for Private Law, European Private and Procedural Law and Comparative Law at EBS University Oestrich-Winkel.

Bettina Weisser (Doctorate Konstanz 1995; Habilitation Cologne 2010) is Professor for Criminal Law and Criminal Procedure at the University of Cologne, where she serves as Director of the Institute for Comparative Criminal Law. She is an ordinary member of the European Academy of Sciences and Arts (Class V), an associate member of the International Academy of Comparative Law, and a member of the board of the German Association of Comparative Law.

Felix M. Wilke (LL.M. Michigan 2013; Doctorate Bayreuth 2017; Habilitation Bayreuth 2025) is Professor for Civil Law, Civil Procedure, Private International Law and International Civil Procedure at EBS Universität für Wirtschaft und Recht, Oestrich-Winkel.

Rechtsvergleichung und Rechtsvereinheitlichung

Edited by the
Gesellschaft für Rechtsvergleichung e.V.,

represented by
general secretary Martin Schmidt-Kessel

Comparative Law and Unification of Law is a new series which deals with changes in comparative law. Comparative law has become a function of the unification of law as well to a larger extent than it used to be, in particular the unification of law in a European setting.

ISSN: 1861-5449
Suggested citation: RuR

All published volumes at *www.mohrsiebeck.com/rur*

Mohr Siebeck
www.mohrsiebeck.com